# Sapling Plus

Pre-class Tutorials

Introduce new topics in a more manageable, less intimidating way, to help students better retain what they've learned for class time.

Everything You Need in a Single Learning Path

SaplingPlus is the first system to support students and instructors at every step, from the first point of contact with new content to demonstrating mastery of concepts and skills. It is simply the best support for Principles of Economics.

Classroom Activities

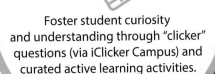

Foster student curiosity and understanding through "clicker" questions (via iClicker Campus) and curated active learning activities.

Test Bank

Multiple-choice and short-answer questions to help instructors assess students' comprehension, interpretation, and ability to synthesize.

Developing Understanding

LearningCurve Quizzes identify knowledge gaps and then nudge each student to fill those gaps through an enhanced e-Book, videos, and interactives.

Assessment

Homework Assignments—with an intuitive approach to graphing—offer multi-part questions and targeted feedback.

For more information on SaplingPlus, visit www.macmillanlearning.com.

MACROECONOMICS

MACROECONOMICS

Fifth Edition

Paul Krugman
Graduate Center of the City University of New York

Robin Wells

worth publishers
Macmillan Learning
New York

Vice President, Program Management: **Charles Linsmeier**
Director of Content and Assessment: **Shani Fisher**
Executive Program Manager: **Simon Glick**
Marketing Manager: **Andrew Zierman**
Marketing Assistant: **Morgan Ratner**
Executive Development Editor: **Sharon Balbos**
Assessment Manager: **Kristyn Brown**
Assessment Editor: **Joshua Hill**
Consultant: **Ryan Herzog**
Director of Media Editorial: **Noel Hohnstine**
Media Editor: **Emily Schmid**
Editorial Assistant: **Courtney Lindwall**
Director, Content Management Enhancement: **Tracey Kuehn**
Managing Editor: **Lisa Kinne**
Project Editor: **Martha Emry**
Director of Design, Content Management: **Diana Blume**
Interior Design: **Blake Logan**
Cover Design: **Lyndall Culbertson and Blake Logan**
Illustrations: **codeMantra, Network Graphics**
Illustration Coordinator: **Janice Donnola**
Photo Editor: **Cecilia Varas**
Photo Researcher: **Elyse Rieder**
Senior Workflow Project Supervisor: **Susan Wein**
Production Supervisor: **Lawrence Guerra**
Media Project Manager: **Andrew Vaccaro**
Supplements and Media Project Editors: **Jodi Isman and Lisa Kinne**
Composition: **codeMantra**
Printing and Binding: **LSC Communications**

ISBN-13: 978-1-319-09875-9
ISBN-10: 1-319-09875-4

Library of Congress Control Number: 2017944025

Printed in the United States of America
Second printing

Worth Publishers
One New York Plaza
Suite 4500
New York, NY 10004-1562
www.macmillanlearning.com

PAUL KRUGMAN, recipient of the 2008 Nobel Memorial Prize in Economic Sciences, is a faculty member of the Graduate Center of the City University of New York, associated with the Luxembourg Income Study, which tracks and analyzes income inequality around the world. Prior to that, he taught at Princeton University for 14 years. He received his BA from Yale and his PhD from MIT. Before Princeton, he taught at Yale, Stanford, and MIT. He also spent a year on the staff of the Council of Economic Advisers in 1982–1983. His research has included pathbreaking work on international trade, economic geography, and currency crises. In 1991, Krugman received the American Economic Association's John Bates Clark medal. In addition to his teaching and academic research, Krugman writes extensively for nontechnical audiences. He is a regular op-ed columnist for the *New York Times*. His best-selling trade books include *End This Depression Now!*, *The Return of Depression Economics and the Crisis of 2008*, a history of recent economic troubles and their implications for economic policy, and *The Conscience of a Liberal*, a study of the political economy of economic inequality and its relationship with political polarization from the Gilded Age to the present. His earlier books, *Peddling Prosperity* and *The Age of Diminished Expectations*, have become modern classics.

Ligaya Franklin

ROBIN WELLS was a Lecturer and Researcher in Economics at Princeton University. She received her BA from the University of Chicago and her PhD from the University of California at Berkeley; she then did postdoctoral work at MIT. She has taught at the University of Michigan, the University of Southampton (United Kingdom), Stanford, and MIT.

Vision and Story of *Macroeconomics*

This is a book about economics as the study of what people do and how they interact, a study very much informed by real-world experience. These words, this spirit, have served as a guiding principle for us in every edition.

While we were driven to write this book by many small ideas about particular aspects of economics, we also had one big idea: an economics textbook should be built around narratives, many of them pulled from real life, and it should never lose sight of the fact that economics is, in the end, a set of stories about what people do.

Many of the stories economists tell take the form of models—for whatever else they are, economic models are stories about how the world works. But we believe that student understanding of and appreciation for models are greatly enhanced if they are presented, as much as possible, in the context of stories about the real world that both illustrate economic concepts and touch on the concerns we all face living in a world shaped by economic forces.

You'll find a rich array of stories in every chapter, in the chapter openers, Economics in Actions, For Inquiring Minds, Global Comparisons, and Business Cases. As always, we include many new stories and update others. We also integrate an international perspective throughout, more extensively than ever before. It starts with a new introduction and an opening story on China's Pearl River Delta that sets the stage for new attention to China's ascendance in the global economy. An overview of the types of narrative-based features in the text is on p. x.

We also include pedagogical features that reinforce learning. For example, each major section ends with three related elements devised with the student in mind: (1) the Economics in Actions: a real-world application to help students achieve a fuller understanding of concepts they just read about; (2) a Quick Review of key ideas in list form; and (3) Check Your Understanding self-test questions with answers at the back of the book. Our thought-provoking end-of-chapter problems are another strong feature. The Work It Out feature appears in all end-of-chapter problem sets, offering students online tutorials that guide them step-by-step through solving key problems. With the Fifth Edition, a new feature, Discovering Data exercises, offers students the opportunity to use interactive graphs to analyze interesting economic questions. An overview of the text's tools for learning is on p. xi.

Students also benefit from the impressive set of online resources that are linked to specific chapter content. These include several exciting new digital features as well as adaptive quizzing, tutorials, interactive activities, graphing questions, and data-analysis questions. All have been devised with the goal of supporting instructor teaching and student learning in principles of economics courses.

We hope your experience with this text is a good one. Thank you for introducing it into your classroom.

Paul Krugman   Robin Wells

Engaging Students in the Study of Macroeconomics

We are committed to the belief that students learn best from a complete textbook program built around narratives, steeped in real life and current events, with a strong emphasis on global matters and with proven technology that supports student success.

Narrative Approach

This is a textbook built around narratives and stories, many pulled from real life. In every chapter, stories are used to teach core concepts and motivate learning. We believe that the best way to introduce concepts and reinforce them is through memorable, real-world stories; students simply relate more easily to them.

Global Focus

This book is unrivaled in the attention paid to global matters. We have thoroughly integrated an international perspective into the text, in the numerous applications, cases, and stories and, of course, in the data-based Global Comparison feature.

Technology That Builds Success

Macroeconomics is not just a textbook. It has evolved to become a complete program with interactive features designed and built to extend the goals of the text. This program encourages even stronger student engagement, mastery of the material, and success in the course.

> **interactive activity** Look for this Interactive Activity icon throughout the text to find materials that are enhanced by our online tools.

What's New in the Fifth Edition?

Technology that offers the best value and price. Because students' needs are changing, our most powerful learning option is now our most affordable. SaplingPlus is a new digital solution that combines LearningCurve with an integrated e-Book, robust homework, improved graphing, and fully digital end-of-chapter problems including Work It Outs. And if print is important, a package with a loose-leaf copy of the text is only a few dollars more.

Discovering Data exercises help students interpret, analyze, share, and report on data. Students develop data literacy by completing these new interactive exercises, step-by-step problems that have students use up-to-the-minute FRED data.

Current events framed by the world's best communicators of economics. No other text stays as fresh as this one. The authors—who have explained economics to millions through trade books and newspaper columns—offer a new online feature, News Analysis, that pairs journalistic takes on pressing issues with questions based on Bloom's taxonomy. This complements the text's unparalleled coverage of current topics: sustainability, the economic impact of technology, pressing policy debates, and much more.

A richer commitment to broadening students' understanding of the global economy. With unparalleled insight and clarity, the authors use their hallmark narrative approach to take students outside of the classroom and into our global world, starting in the Introduction with a new opening story on the economic transformation in China's Pearl River Delta. The global focus is carried throughout in chapter openers, Economics in Action, Business Cases, and Global Comparisons. There is now more on the ascendance of China's economy, along with real-world stories about the economies of Europe, Bangladesh, and Japan, among many others.

Engaging Students with a Narrative Approach

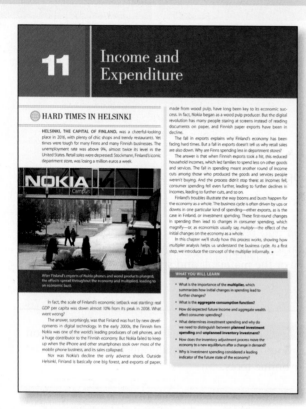

11 Income and Expenditure

HARD TIMES IN HELSINKI

ECONOMICS >> in Action
An Economic Breakthrough in Bangladesh

Western news media rarely mention Bangladesh: it's not a political hot spot, it doesn't have oil, and it's overshadowed by its immense neighbor, India. Yet it is home to more than 160 million people—and although it is still very poor, it is nonetheless one of the greatest economic success stories of the past generation.

As recently as the 1980s, real GDP per capita in Bangladesh—which achieved independence from Pakistan in 1971, after a brutal war—was barely higher than it had been in 1950, when the country was so poor that it literally lived on the edge of starvation. In the early 1990s, however, the nation began a process of political and economic reform, making the transition from military rule to democracy, freeing up markets, and achieving monetary and fiscal stability. And growth took off, most notably with the rise of Bangladesh as a major exporter of clothing to Western markets. Real GDP per capita grew at over 3% per year, from the late 1980s through 2010, doubling over the twenty-year period from 1990 to 2010.

By 2015 real GDP per capita was almost 2½ times what it had been in 1990. Other measures also showed dramatic improvements in the quality of life: life expectancy rose by a dozen years, child mortality fell by 70 percent, school enrollment rose sharply, especially for girls.

Make no mistake, Bangladesh is still incredibly poor by American standards. Wages are very low although rising, while working conditions are often terrible and dangerous—a point highlighted in 2013, when a factory complex collapsed, killing more than a thousand workers. But compared with its own past,

Although Bangladesh remains a very poor country, a high growth rate has improved living standards over the last 25 years.

GLOBAL COMPARISON THE BIG MONEYS

Americans tend to think of the dollar as the world's leading currency—and it does remain the currency most likely to be accepted in payment around the globe. But there are other important currencies, too. One simple measure of a currency's importance is the value of the quantity of that currency in circulation. This figure shows the value, in billions of dollars, of the quantity of four major currencies in circulation as of April 2017. The euro, used by a group of countries whose combined economies are roughly comparable in size to America's, is used almost as often as the dollar. China, with its rapidly growing economy, has a currency (the yuan) that isn't far behind the euro. And Japan's yen isn't far behind the big three, despite its much smaller economy, largely because the Japanese make much more use of cash, as opposed to checks, credit cards, or debit cards, than either Europeans or Americans.

Currency in circulation, April 2017 (billions of US$): United States $1,540; Euro area $1,206; China $993; Japan $863.

Data from: Federal Reserve Bank of St. Louis; European Central Bank; Bank of Japan; The People's Bank of China.

BUSINESS CASE Parking Your Money at PayPal

Officially, PayPal, the electronic funds-transfer firm—which is also the owner of Venmo, a mobile-phone payment service that has become extremely popular—isn't considered a bank. Instead, regulators consider it a *money transmitter*, an entity that sends your money someplace rather than holding it and keeping it safe.

However, as users accumulate substantial sums in their PayPal accounts, that distinction has started to look questionable. Venmo users, in particular, often seem willing to let incoming payments sit in their accounts until the funds are spent. As a result, PayPal's accounts were estimated to total more than $13 billion in 2016. If those billions were considered bank deposits, PayPal would be considered among the 50 largest banks in the United States.

At first glance, leaving significant sums in PayPal accounts seems counterintuitive for two reasons. First, these accounts aren't protected by federal deposit insurance. Second, they pay no interest. But upon closer examination, this behavior makes good economic sense. People will typically hold only a tiny fraction of their wealth in their PayPal account, thereby making the lack of federal deposit insurance an acceptable risk. And interest rates on bank accounts are so low at the time of this writing (around 0.03% in Spring 2017) that losing that interest is a reasonable price to pay to avoid the hassle of moving funds back and forth between a bank account and a PayPal or Venmo account. The result is that many people are behaving like one user quoted by the *Wall Street Journal*, who now waits a while before transferring funds out of her Venmo account to her regular bank account: "I'm starting to intentionally keep my money in there a bit longer."

But will PayPal/Venmo or something like it begin to make major inroads into traditional banking? Some analysts think so. Others suggest, however, that conventional banks will find ways to make mobile payments easier, and that rising interest rates will lure customers back to conventional bank deposits. Time will tell.

QUESTIONS FOR THOUGHT

1. PayPal accounts aren't counted as part of the money supply. Should they be? Why or why not?

2. In 2010, only around 25% of mobile phones in the United States were smartphones. In 2017, that number increased to more than 80%. How does this situation play into the PayPal story, and how does it fit into the broader pattern of monetary history?

3. How might future actions by the Federal Open Market Committee affect the future of PayPal and similar services?

- To engage students, every chapter begins with a compelling story. **What You Will Learn** questions help students focus on key concepts in the chapter.

- So students can immediately see economic concepts applied in the real world, **Economics in Action** applications appear throughout chapters.

- To provide students with an international perspective, the **Global Comparison** feature uses data and graphs to illustrate why countries reach different economic outcomes.

- So students can see key economic principles applied to real-life business situations, each chapter concludes with a **Business Case.**

Engaging Students
with Effective Tools for Learning

ECONOMICS >> in Action
China Pegs the Yuan

In the early years of the twenty-first century, China provided a striking example of the lengths to which countries sometimes go to maintain a fixed exchange rate.

In the first act of this story, China acted to keep its currency down. The country's spectacular success as an exporter had produced a rising surplus on current account, and private investors became increasingly eager to shift funds into China, to invest in its growing domestic economy.

These capital flows were somewhat limited by foreign exchange controls—but kept coming in anyway. As a result of the current account surplus and private capital inflows, China found itself in the position described by panel (b) of Figure 18-7: at the target exchange rate, the demand for yuan exceeded the supply. Yet the Chinese government was determined to keep the exchange rate fixed at a value below its equilibrium level.

To keep the rate fixed, China had to engage in large-scale exchange market intervention, selling yuan, buying up other countries' currencies (mainly U.S. dollars) on the foreign exchange market, and adding them to its reserves. Indeed, between early 2009 and early 2014 China added $2 trillion to its foreign exchange reserves, which by mid-2014 had risen to a remarkable $4 trillion, roughly 40% of GDP. Not surprisingly, China's exchange rate policy led to some friction with its trading partners, who felt that it had the effect of subsidizing Chinese exports.

But then came the second act of the story. After 2012 China's current account surplus declined, partly reflecting rising wages and the rise of new competitors like Vietnam and Bangladesh. Also, China's economic growth, while still fast, slowed, and investors grew nervous about a possible financial or political crisis. So capital inflows turned into capital outflows: the 2015 outflow was estimated at an amazing $1 trillion, the great majority of it going to the United States.

In the absence of government intervention, this capital flight might well have caused a sharp decline in the yuan. But the Chinese government was reluctant to see its currency fall as it had once been to see it rise. So China began using its reserves of foreign currency to buy large quantities of yuan. And by early 2017 reserves had fallen from $4 trillion to less than $3 trillion.

China provides a striking example of the lengths to which countries sometimes go to maintain a fixed exchange rate.

>> Quick Review

- Countries choose different **exchange rate regimes.** The two main regimes are **fixed exchange rates** and **floating exchange rates.**

- Exchange rates can be fixed through **exchange market intervention**, using **foreign exchange reserves.** Countries can also use domestic policies to shift supply and demand in the foreign exchange market (usually monetary policy), or they can impose **foreign exchange controls.**

- Choosing an exchange rate regime poses a dilemma. Stable exchange rates are good for business. But holding large foreign exchange reserves is costly, using domestic policy to fix the exchange rate makes it hard to pursue other objectives, and foreign exchange controls distort incentives.

>> Check Your Understanding 18-3
Solutions appear at back of book.

1. Draw a diagram, similar to Figure 18-7, representing the foreign exchange situation of China when it kept the exchange rate fixed. Express the exchange rate as U.S. dollars per yuan. Then show with a diagram how each of the following policy changes will eliminate the disequilibrium in the market.
   a. China no longer fixes its exchange rate and allows it to float freely.
   b. Placing restrictions on foreigners who want to invest in China
   c. Removing restrictions on Chinese who want to invest abroad
   d. Imposing taxes on Chinese exports, such as shipments of clothing, that are causing a political backlash in the importing countries

---

PITFALLS

DEMAND VERSUS QUANTITY DEMANDED

When economists say "an increase in demand," they mean a rightward shift of the demand curve, and when they say "a decrease in demand," they mean a leftward shift of the demand curve—that is, when they're being careful.

In ordinary speech most people, including professional economists, use the word *demand* casually. For example, an economist might say "the demand for air travel has doubled over the past 15 years, partly because of falling airfares" when he or she really means that the *quantity demanded* has doubled.

It's OK to be a bit sloppy in ordinary conversation. But when you're doing economic analysis, it's important to make the distinction between changes in the quantity demanded, which involve movements along a demand curve, and shifts of the demand curve (see Figure 3-3 for an illustration). Sometimes students end up writing something like this: "If demand increases, the price will go up, but that will lead to a fall in demand, which pushes the price down . . ." and then go around in circles.

If you make a clear distinction between changes in *demand*, which mean shifts of the demand curve, and changes in *quantity demanded*, which means movement along the demand curve, you can avoid a lot of confusion.

---

3. Access the Discovering Data exercise for Chapter 16 online to answer the following questions.
   a. How much did the monetary base change in the last year?
   b. How did the change in the monetary base help in the government's efforts to finance its deficit?
   c. Why is it important for the central bank to be independent of government policy makers?

- To reinforce learning, sections within chapters conclude with three tools: an application of key concepts in the **Economics in Action;** a **Quick Review** of key concepts; and a comprehension check with **Check Your Understanding** questions. Solutions for these questions appear at the back of the book.

- **Pitfalls** teach students to identify and avoid common misconceptions about economic concepts.

- End-of-chapter **Work It Out** skill-building problems provide interactive step-by-step help with solving select problems from the textbook.

- **Discovering Data** exercises offer students the opportunity to use interactive graphs to analyze interesting economic questions.

WORK IT OUT Interactive step-by-step help with solving this problem can be found online.

15. There is only one labor market in Profunctia. All workers have the same skills, and all firms hire workers with these skills. Use the accompanying diagram, which shows the supply of and demand for labor, to answer the following questions. Illustrate each answer with a diagram.

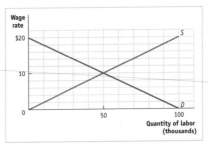

a. What is the equilibrium wage rate in Profunctia? At this wage rate, what are the level of employment, the size of the labor force, and the unemployment rate?
b. If the government of Profunctia sets a minimum wage equal to $12, what will be the level of employment, the size of the labor force, and the unemployment rate?
c. If unions bargain with the firms in Profunctia and set a wage rate equal to $14, what will be the level of employment, the size of the labor force, and the unemployment rate?
d. If the concern for retaining workers and encouraging high-quality work leads firms to set a wage rate equal to $16, what will be the level of employment, the size of the labor force, and the unemployment rate?

Engaging Students with Technology

The technology for this new edition has been developed to spark student engagement and improve outcomes while offering instructors flexible, high-quality, research-based tools for teaching this course.

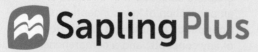

NEW! SaplingPlus combines powerful multimedia resources with an integrated e-Book and the robust problem library of Sapling Learning, creating an extraordinary new learning resource for students. Online homework helps students get better grades with targeted instructional feedback tailored to the individual. And it saves instructors time preparing for and managing a course by providing personalized support from a PhD or Master's level colleague trained in Sapling's system.

NEW! Pre-Lecture Tutorials foster basic understanding of core economic concepts before students ever set foot in class. Developed by two pioneers in active-learning methods—Eric Chiang, Florida Atlantic University, and José Vazquez, University of Illinois at Urbana–Champaign—this resource is part of the SaplingPlus learning path. Students watch Pre-Lecture videos and complete Bridge Question assessments that prepare them to engage in class. Instructors receive data about student comprehension that can inform their lecture preparation.

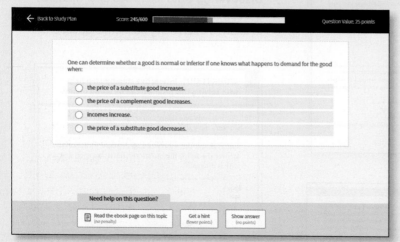

<< LearningCurve Adaptive Quizzing

Embraced by students and instructors alike, this incredibly popular and effective adaptive quizzing engine offers individualized question sets and feedback tailored to each student based on correct and incorrect responses. Questions are hyperlinked to relevant e-Book sections, encouraging students to read and use the resources at hand to enrich their understanding.

NEW! Graphing Questions >>

Powered by improved graphing, multi-step questions paired with helpful feedback guide students through the process of problem solving. Students are asked to demonstrate their understanding by simply clicking, dragging, and dropping a line to a predetermined location. The graphs have been designed so that students' entire focus is on moving the correct curve in the correct direction, virtually eliminating grading issues for instructors.

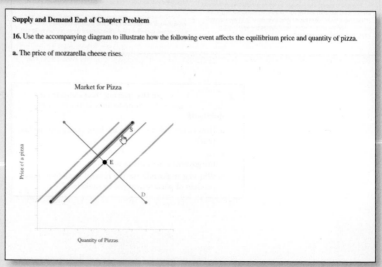

Work It Out >>

These skill-building activities pair sample end-of-chapter problems with targeted feedback and video explanations to help students solve problems step-by-step. This approach allows students to work independently, tests their comprehension of concepts, and prepares them for class and exams.

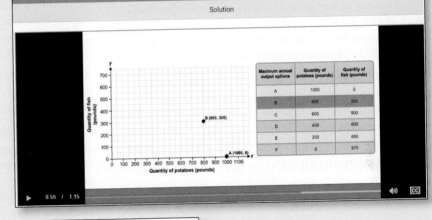

Trade-Offs and Trade Work It Out: Question 1 of 4

Atlantis is a small, isolated island in the South Atlantic. The inhabitants grow potatoes and catch fish. The accompanying table shows the maximum annual output combinations of potatoes and fish that can be produced. Obviously, given their limited resources and available technology, as they use more of their resources for potato production, there are fewer resources available for catching fish.

Using the data in the table, place the points in the accompanying graph to depict Atlantis's production possibilities frontier.

Solution

Maximum annual output options	Quantity of potatoes (pounds)	Quantity of fish (pounds)
A	1000	0
B	800	300
C	600	500
D	400	600
E	200	650
F	0	675

0:55 / 1:15

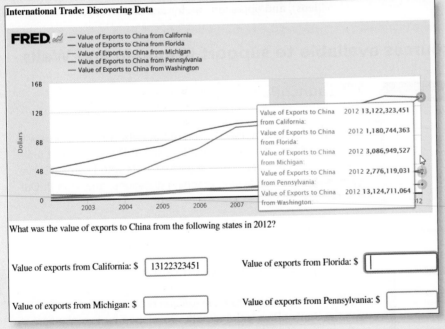

International Trade: Discovering Data

FRED

— Value of Exports to China from California
— Value of Exports to China from Florida
— Value of Exports to China from Michigan
— Value of Exports to China from Pennsylvania
— Value of Exports to China from Washington

Value of Exports to China from California:	2012 13,122,323,451
Value of Exports to China from Florida:	2012 1,180,744,363
Value of Exports to China from Michigan:	2012 3,086,949,527
Value of Exports to China from Pennsylvania:	2012 2,776,119,031
Value of Exports to China from Washington:	2012 13,124,711,064

What was the value of exports to China from the following states in 2012?

Value of exports from California: $ 13122323451

Value of exports from Florida: $

Value of exports from Michigan: $

Value of exports from Pennsylvania: $

<< **NEW! Discovering Data Exercises** help students interpret and analyze data by completing interactive, stepped-out exercises that use up-to-the-minute FRED data. These exercises help students develop data literacy and synthesizing skills, encourage economic analysis based on recent trends, and build an understanding of the broader economy.

Powerful Support for Instructors

FOR ASSESSMENT

Test Bank Fully revised for the Fifth Edition, the Test Bank, authored by Syon Bhanot, Swarthmore College, and Kevin Beckwith, Salem State University, contains multiple-choice and short-answer questions to help instructors assess students' comprehension, interpretation, and ability to synthesize.

End-of-Chapter and Work It Out Questions The in-text end-of-chapter problems have been converted to a multiple-choice format accompanied by answer-specific feedback. **Work It Out** activities walk students through each step of solving an end-of-chapter problem using choice specific feedback and video explanations for each step.

Homework Assignments Each chapter concludes with homework of various question types, including graphing questions featuring our updated graphing player, providing instructors with a curated set of multiple-choice and graphing questions that are easily assigned for graded assessment.

Practice Quizzes Designed to be used as a study tool for students, Practice Quizzes allow for multiple attempts as students familiarize themselves with chapter content.

ADDITIONAL RESOURCES

A Gradebook This useful resource offers clear feedback to students and instructors on individual assignments and on performance in the course.

LMS integration Included so that online homework is easily integrated into a school's learning management system and that an instructor's Gradebook and roster are always in sync.

Instructor's Resource Manual Authored by Tori Knight, Carson-Newman University, this manual offers instructors teaching materials and tips to enhance the classroom experience, along with chapter objectives, outlines, and other ideas.

Solutions Manual Prepared by the authors of the text, this manual offers detailed solutions to all of the text's end-of-chapter problems and the Business Case questions.

Interactive Presentation Slides These brief, interactive, and visually interesting slides, authored by Solina Lindahl, California Polytechnic State University, San Luis Obispo, are designed to hold students' attention in class with graphics and animations demonstrating key concepts, real-world examples, hyperlinks to relevant outside sources (including videos), and opportunities for active learning.

Additional technology resources available to support Krugman and Wells

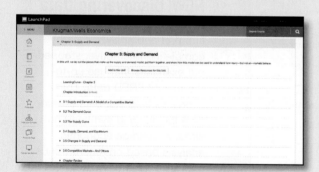

LaunchPad
macmillan learning

For longtime users, a new version of **LaunchPad** is available with this Fifth Edition. It includes an interactive e-Book, pre-built units offering instructors ready-made assignments with LearningCurve quizzes, graded homework, graphing questions, and Work It Out skill-building activities.

FlipItEcon FlipItEcon.com

FlipItEcon is available as a standalone resource or integrated with the SaplingPlus learning path. Developed by two pioneers in active-learning methods—Eric Chiang, Florida Atlantic University, and José Vazquez, University of Illinois at Urbana–Champaign—FlipIt gets students actively involved in learning economics in a fresh way. Students watch Pre-Lectures and complete Bridge Question assessments before class, helping them prepare for class so they can be engaged. FlipIt also gives instructors data about student comprehension that can inform their lecture preparation.

WHAT'S NEW IN THIS EDITION?

There are 33 new opening stories, Business Cases, and Economics in Action applications in this edition—nearly a third of these stories are new, ensuring that the Fifth Edition is truly current and relevant. Many other stories have been updated and refreshed.

Ryan Pyle/Getty Images

9 New Opening Stories

A Day in the Megacity
Big City, Not So Bright Ideas
Liftoff
Paying for a Hidden Empire
Hard Times in Helsinki
Different Generations, Different Policies
Spending Our Way Out of a Recession
Not So Funny Money
Old Books and New Ideas

Bjoern Wylezich/Shutterstock

8 New Business Cases

How Priceline Revolutionized the Travel Industry
Uber Gives Riders a Lesson in Supply and Demand
Why Taxi Medallion Lenders Are Feeling Like Roadkill
TaskRabbit
Raising the Bar(code)
Toyota Makes Its Move
Parking Your Money at PayPal
Dining and Dollars in Buenos Aires

Smileus/Shutterstock

16 New Economics in Action Applications

The Fundamental Law of Traffic Congestion
Economists: What Are They Good For?
Why Price Controls in Venezuela Proved Useless
Solar Disputes
An Economic Breakthrough in Bangladesh
The Rise, Fall, and Return of the Productivity Paradox
What's the Matter with Italy?
To Shale and Back
Sticky Wages in the Great Recession
A Tale of Two Stimuli
Trying to Balance Budgets in a Recession
Reducing Implicit Liabilities
Financial Regulation After the 2008 Crisis
Up the Down Staircase
Japan's Escape Attempt
Strong Dollar Woes

Acknowledgments

Our deep appreciation and heartfelt thanks go out to **Ryan Herzog,** Gonzaga University, for his hard work and extensive contributions during every stage of this revision. Ryan's creativity and insights helped us make this Fifth Edition possible. And special thanks to our three accuracy checkers of page proofs, to whom we are most grateful: Barbara Alexander, Babson College, Dixie Dalton, Southside Virginia Community College, and Thomas Dunn.

We must also thank the many people at Worth Publishers for their work on this edition: Chuck Linsmeier, Shani Fisher, Simon Glick, Sharon Balbos, Lukia Kliossis, Courtney Lindwall, Emily Schmid, Lindsay Neff, Kristyn Brown, and Joshua Hill in editorial. We thank Andrew Zierman, Tom Digiano, Tom Acox, and Travis Long for their enthusiastic and tireless advocacy of this book. Many thanks to the incredible production, design, photo, and media teams: Tracey Kuehn, Lisa Kinne, Susan Wein, Martha Emry, Blake Logan, Deb Heimann, Cecilia Varas, Elyse Rieder, Chris Efstratiou, Andrew Vaccaro, and Daniel Comstock.

Our deep appreciation and heartfelt thanks to the following reviewers, whose input helped us shape this Fifth Edition.

Seemi Ahmad, *Dutchess Community College*
Barbara Alexander, *Babson College*
Osbourne Allen, *Miami Dade College*
Gabriel Azarlian, *California State University, Northridge*
David Barber, *Quinnipiac University*
Sandra Barone, *Gonzaga University*
Klaus Becker, *Texas Tech University*
Doris Bennett, *Jacksonville State University*
Syon Bhanot, *Swarthmore College*
Stacey Brook, *University of Iowa*
Kevin Brown, *Asbury University*
Basanta Chaudhuri, *Rutgers University*
Greg Colson, *University of Georgia*
Patrick Crowley, *Texas A&M University, Corpus Christi*
Dixie Dalton, *Southside Virginia Community College*
Joseph Dipoli, *Salem State University*
Thomas Dunn
Mohammadmahdi Farsiabi, *Wayne State University*
Irene Foster, *George Washington University*
John Gahagan, *Shoreline Community College*
Jason Gurtovoy, *Cerritos College*
Ian Haberman, *Hunter College*
Ryan Herzog, *Gonzaga University*
Grover Howard, *Shoreline Community College*
Mervin Jebaraj, *University of Arkansas*
Dennis Kaufman, *University of Wisconsin, Parkside*
Noreen Lephardt, *Marquette University*
An Li, *Keene State College*

Ross Mohr, *Chapman University*
Soloman Namala, *Cerritos College*
Alexandre Olbrecht, *Ramapo College of New Jersey*
Ram Orzach, *Oakland University*
Jennifer Pakula, *Cerritos College*
Tove Rasmussen, *Southern Maine Community College*
Jason Reed, *Wayne State University*
Jack Reynolds, *Navarro College*
Tim Reynolds, *Alvin Community College*
Luis Rosero, *Framingham State*
Elizabeth Sawyer-Kelly, *University of Wisconsin, Madison*
Jake Schild, *Indiana University*
Aschale Siyoum, *Catholic University of America*
Mark Sniderman, *Case Western Reserve University*
Ralph Sonenshine, *American University*
James Sterns, *Oregon State University*
Henry Terrell, *George Washington University*
Jill Trask, *Tarrant County College—Southeast*
Magda Tsaneva, *Clark University*
Phillip Tussing, *Alvin Community College*
Nathaniel Udall, *Alvin Community College*
Sujata Verma, *Notre Dame de Namur University*
Aimee Vlachos-Bullard, *Southern Maine Community College*
Xiao Wang, *University of North Dakota*
Michael Williams, *Prairie View A&M University*
Kelvin Wont, *University of Minnesota*
Hyun Woong Park, *Allegheny College*
Kristen Zaborski, *The State College of Florida*

We are indebted to the following reviewers, class testers, focus group participants, and other consultants for their suggestions and advice on previous editions.

Carlos Aguilar, *El Paso Community College*
Seemi Ahmad, *Dutchess Community College*
Terence Alexander, *Iowa State University*
Innocentus Alhamis, *Southern New Hampshire University*

Morris Altman, *University of Saskatchewan*
Farhad Ameen, *State University of New York, Westchester Community College*
Giuliana Campanelli Andreopoulos, *William Patterson University*
Becca Arnold, *San Diego Mesa College*

Dean Baim, *Pepperdine University*
Jeremy Baker, *Owens Community College*
Christopher P. Ball, *Quinnipiac University*
David Barber, *Quinnipiac College*
Jim Barbour, *Elon University*
Janis Barry-Figuero, *Fordham University at Lincoln Center*
Sue Bartlett, *University of South Florida*
Hamid Bastin, *Shippensburg University*
Scott Beaulier, *Mercer University*
Richard Beil, *Auburn University*
David Bernotas, *University of Georgia*
Joydeep Bhattacharya, *Iowa State University*
Marc Bilodeau, *Indiana University and Purdue University, Indianapolis*
Kelly Blanchard, *Purdue University*
Joanne Blankenship, *State Fair Community College*
Emma Bojinova, *Canisius College*
Michael Bonnal, *University of Tennessee, Chattanooga*
Milicia Bookman, *Saint Joseph's University*
Ralph Bradburd, *Williams College*
Mark Brandly, *Ferris State University*
Anne Bresnock, *California State Polytechnic University, Pomona*
Douglas M. Brown, *Georgetown University*
Joseph Calhoun, *Florida State University*
Colleen Callahan, *American University*
Charles Campbell, *Mississippi State University*
Douglas Campbell, *University of Memphis*
Randall Campbell, *Mississippi State University*
Kevin Carlson, *University of Massachusetts, Boston*
Joel Carton, *Florida International University*
Andrew Cassey, *Washington State University*
Shirley Cassing, *University of Pittsburgh*
Semih Cekin, *Texas Tech University*
Sewin Chan, *New York University*
Mitchell M. Charkiewicz, *Central Connecticut State University*
Joni S. Charles, *Texas State University, San Marcos*
Adhip Chaudhuri, *Georgetown University*
Sanjukta Chaudhuri, *University of Wisconsin, Eau Claire*
Eric Chiang, *Florida Atlantic University*
Hayley H. Chouinard, *Washington State University*
Abdur Chowdhury, *Marquette University*
Kenny Christianson, *Binghamton University*
Lisa Citron, *Cascadia Community College*
Timothy Classen, *Loyola University Chicago*
Maryanne Clifford, *Eastern Connecticut State University*
Steven L. Cobb, *University of North Texas*
Barbara Z. Connolly, *Westchester Community College*
Stephen Conroy, *University of San Diego*
Thomas E. Cooper, *Georgetown University*
Cesar Corredor, *Texas A&M University and University of Texas, Tyler*

Chad Cotti, *University of Wisconsin, Oshkosh*
Jim F. Couch, *University of Northern Alabama*
Attila Cseh, *Valdosta State University*
Maria DaCosta, *University of Wisconsin, Eau Claire*
Daniel Daly, *Regis University*
H. Evren Damar, *Pacific Lutheran University*
James P. D'Angelo, *University of Cincinnati*
Antony Davies, *Duquesne University*
Greg Delemeester, *Marietta College*
Sean D'Evelyn, *Loyola Marymount University*
Ronald Dieter, *Iowa State University*
Patrick Dolenc, *Keene State College*
Christine Doyle-Burke, *Framingham State College*
Ding Du, *South Dakota State University*
Jerry Dunn, *Southwestern Oklahoma State University*
Robert R. Dunn, *Washington and Jefferson College*
Christina Edmundson, *North Idaho College*
Hossein Eftekari, *University of Wisconsin, River Falls*
Ann Eike, *University of Kentucky*
Harold Elder, *University of Alabama*
Tisha L. N. Emerson, *Baylor University*
Hadi Salehi Esfahani, *University of Illinois*
Mark Evans, *California State University, Bakersfield*
William Feipel, *Illinois Central College*
Rudy Fichtenbaum, *Wright State University*
David W. Findlay, *Colby College*
Mary Flannery, *University of California, Santa Cruz*
Sherman Folland, *Oakland University*
Cynthia Foreman, *Clark College*
Robert Francis, *Shoreline Community College*
Amanda Freeman, *Kansas State University*
Shelby Frost, *Georgia State University*
Frank Gallant, *George Fox University*
Robert Gazzale, *Williams College*
Bruce Gervais, *California State University, Sacramento*
Satyajit Ghosh, *University of Scranton*
Stuart Glosser, *University of Wisconsin, Whitewater*
Robert Godby, *University of Wyoming*
Fidel Gonzalez, *Sam Houston State University*
Julie Gonzalez, *University of California, Santa Cruz*
Michael G. Goode, *Central Piedmont Community College*
Douglas E. Goodman, *University of Puget Sound*
Marvin Gordon, *University of Illinois at Chicago*
Kathryn Graddy, *Brandeis University*
Alan Gummerson, *Florida International University*
Eran Guse, *West Virginia University*
Alan Day Haight, *State University of New York, Cortland*
Mehdi Haririan, *Bloomsburg University*
Robert Harris, *Indiana University and Purdue University, Indianapolis*
Hadley Hartman, *Santa Fe College*
Clyde A. Haulman, *College of William and Mary*
Richard R. Hawkins, *University of West Florida*
Mickey A. Hepner, *University of Central Oklahoma*
Ryan Herzog, *Gonzaga University*
Michael Hilmer, *San Diego State University*

Tia Hilmer, *San Diego State University*
Jane Himarios, *University of Texas, Arlington*
Jim Holcomb, *University of Texas, El Paso*
Don Holley, *Boise State University*
Alexander Holmes, *University of Oklahoma*
Julie Holzner, *Los Angeles City College*
Robert N. Horn, *James Madison University*
Scott Houser, *Colorado School of Mines*
Steven Husted, *University of Pittsburgh*
Hiro Ito, *Portland State University*
Ali Jalili, *New England College*
Mike Javanmard, *Rio Hondo Community College*
Jonatan Jelen, *The City College of New York*
Carl Jensen, *Seton Hall University*
Robert T. Jerome, *James Madison University*
Donn Johnson, *Quinnipiac University*
Shirley Johnson-Lans, *Vassar College*
David Kalist, *Shippensburg University*
Lillian Kamal, *Northwestern University*
Roger T. Kaufman, *Smith College*
Elizabeth Sawyer Kelly, *University of Wisconsin, Madison*
Herb Kessel, *St. Michael's College*
Farida Khan, *University of Wisconsin, Parkside*
Ara Khanjian, *Ventura College*
Rehim Kilic, *Georgia Institute of Technology*
Grace Kim, *University of Michigan, Dearborn*
Miles Kimball, *University of Michigan*
Michael Kimmitt, *University of Hawaii, Manoa*
Robert Kling, *Colorado State University*
Colin Knapp, *University of Florida*
Janet Koscianski, *Shippensburg University*
Sherrie Kossoudji, *University of Michigan*
Stephan Kroll, *Colorado State University*
Charles Kroncke, *College of Mount Saint Joseph*
Reuben Kyle, *Middle Tennessee State University (retired)*
Katherine Lande-Schmeiser, *University of Minnesota, Twin Cities*
Vicky Langston, *Columbus State University*
Richard B. Le, *Cosumnes River College*
Yu-Feng Lee, *New Mexico State University*
David Lehr, *Longwood College*
Mary Jane Lenon, *Providence College*
Mary H. Lesser, *Iona College*
Liaoliao Li, *Kutztown University*
Solina Lindahl, *California Polytechnic Institute, San Luis Obispo*
Haiyong Liu, *East Carolina University*
Jane S. Lopus, *California State University, East Bay*
Fernando Lozano, *Claremont McKenna College*
María José Luengo-Prado, *Northeastern University*
Volodymyr Lugovskyy, *Indiana University*
Rotua Lumbantobing, *North Carolina State University*
Ed Lyell, *Adams State College*
Martin Ma, *Washington State University*
John Marangos, *Colorado State University*

Stephen Marks, *Claremont McKenna College*
Ralph D. May, *Southwestern Oklahoma State University*
Mark E. McBride, *Miami University (Ohio)*
Wayne McCaffery, *University of Wisconsin, Madison*
Larry McRae, *Appalachian State University*
Mary Ruth J. McRae, *Appalachian State University*
Ellen E. Meade, *American University*
Meghan Millea, *Mississippi State University*
Ashley Miller, *Mount Holyoke College*
Norman C. Miller, *Miami University (Ohio)*
Michael Mogavero, *University of Notre Dame*
Khan A. Mohabbat, *Northern Illinois University*
Myra L. Moore, *University of Georgia*
Jay Morris, *Champlain College in Burlington*
Akira Motomura, *Stonehill College*
Gary Murphy, *Case Western Reserve University*
Kevin J. Murphy, *Oakland University*
Robert Murphy, *Boston College*
Ranganath Murthy, *Bucknell University*
Anna Musatti, *Columbia University*
Christopher Mushrush, *Illinois State University*
Anthony Myatt, *University of New Brunswick, Canada*
Steven Nafziger, *Williams College*
Kathryn Nantz, *Fairfield University*
ABM Nasir, *North Carolina Central University*
Gerardo Nebbia, *El Camino College*
Pattabiraman Neelakantan, *East Stroudsburg University*
Randy A. Nelson, *Colby College*
Charles Newton, *Houston Community College*
Daniel X. Nguyen, *Purdue University*
Pamela Nickless, *University of North Carolina, Asheville*
Dmitri Nizovtsev, *Washburn University*
Nick Noble, *Miami University (Ohio)*
Gerald Nyambane, *Davenport University*
Fola Odebunmi, *Cypress College*
Thomas A. Odegaard, *Baylor University*
Constantin Oglobin, *Georgia Southern University*
Charles C. Okeke, *College of Southern Nevada*
Terry Olson, *Truman State University*
Una Okonkwo Osili, *Indiana University and Purdue University, Indianapolis*
Maxwell Oteng, *University of California, Davis*
Tomi Ovaska, *Youngstown State University*
P. Marcelo Oviedo, *Iowa State University*
Jeff Owen, *Gustavus Adolphus College*
Orgul Demet Ozturk, *University of South Carolina*
James Palmieri, *Simpson College*
Walter G. Park, *American University*
Elliott Parker, *University of Nevada, Reno*
Tim Payne, *Shoreline College*
Sonia Pereira, *Barnard College, Columbia University*
Michael Perelman, *California State University, Chico*
Nathan Perry, *Utah State University*
Brian Peterson, *Central College*
Dean Peterson, *Seattle University*
Ken Peterson, *Furman University*

David Pieper, *City College of San Francisco*
Paul Pieper, *University of Illinois at Chicago*
Dennis L. Placone, *Clemson University*
Michael Polcen, *Northern Virginia Community College*
Linnea Polgreen, *University of Iowa*
Raymond A. Polchow, *Zane State College*
Eileen Rabach, *Santa Monica College*
Matthew Rafferty, *Quinnipiac University*
Jaishankar Raman, *Valparaiso University*
Margaret Ray, *Mary Washington College*
Arthur Raymond, *Muhlenberg College*
Helen Roberts, *University of Illinois at Chicago*
Greg Rose, *Sacramento City College*
Jeffrey Rubin, *Rutgers University, New Brunswick*
Rose M. Rubin, *University of Memphis*
Lynda Rush, *California State Polytechnic University, Pomona*
Matt Rutledge, *Boston College*
Michael Ryan, *Western Michigan University*
Martin Sabo, *Community College of Denver*
Sara Saderion, *Houston Community College*
Djavad Salehi-Isfahani, *Virginia Tech*
Mikael Sandberg, *University of Florida*
Michael Sattinger, *University at Albany*
Duncan Sattler, *Wilbur Wright College*
Lucie Schmidt, *Williams College*
Jesse A. Schwartz, *Kennesaw State University*
Chad Settle, *University of Tulsa*
Steve Shapiro, *University of North Florida*
Robert L. Shoffner III, *Central Piedmont Community College*
Joseph Sicilian, *University of Kansas*
Zamira Simkins, *University of Wisconsin, Superior*
Judy Smrha, *Baker University*
John Solow, *University of Iowa*
John Somers, *Portland Community College*

Ralph Sonenshine, *American University*
Stephen Stageberg, *University of Mary Washington*
Monty Stanford, *DeVry University*
Rebecca Stein, *University of Pennsylvania*
William K. Tabb, *Queens College, City University of New York (retired)*
Sarinda Taengnoi, *University of Wisconsin, Oshkosh*
Daniel Talley, *Dakota State University*
Kerry Tan, *Loyola University, Maryland*
Henry Terrell, *University of Maryland*
Rebecca Achée Thornton, *University of Houston*
Michael Toma, *Armstrong Atlantic State University*
Julianne Treme, *University of North Carolina at Wilmington*
Brian Trinque, *University of Texas, Austin*
Boone A. Turchi, *University of North Carolina, Chapel Hill*
Nora Underwood, *University of Central Florida*
J. S. Uppal, *State University of New York, Albany*
John Vahaly, *University of Louisville*
Lee Van Scyoc, *University of Wisconsin, Oshkosh*
Jose J. Vazquez-Cognet, *University of Illinois, Urbana–Champaign*
Daniel Vazzana, *Georgetown College*
Roger H. von Haefen, *North Carolina State University*
Andreas Waldkirch, *Colby College*
Christopher Waller, *University of Notre Dame*
Gregory Wassall, *Northeastern University*
Robert Whaples, *Wake Forest University*
Thomas White, *Assumption College*
Jennifer P. Wissink, *Cornell University*
Mark Witte, *Northwestern University*
Kristen M. Wolfe, *St. Johns River Community College*
Larry Wolfenbarger, *Macon State College*
Louise B. Wolitz, *University of Texas, Austin*
Jadrian Wooten, *Pennsylvania State University*
Gavin Wright, *Stanford University*
Bill Yang, *Georgia Southern University*
Jason Zimmerman, *South Dakota State University*

Organization of This Book

To help plan your course, we've listed what we consider to be core and optional chapters, with descriptions about the coverage in each.

Optional

Introduction: An Engine for Growth and Discovery
Initiates students into the study of economics using China's Pearl River Delta as the motivating story. Includes basic terms and explains the difference between microeconomics and macroeconomics.

Core

1. First Principles
Outlines 12 principles underlying the study of economics: principles of individual choice, interaction between individuals, and economy-wide interaction.

2. Economic Models: Trade-offs and Trade
Employs two economic models—the production possibilities frontier and comparative advantage—as an introduction to gains from trade and international comparisons. Also introduces the circular-flow diagram.

Optional

2 Appendix: Graphs in Economics
A comprehensive review of graphing and math skills for students who would find this background helpful.

Core

3. Supply and Demand
Covers the essentials of supply, demand, market equilibrium, surplus, and shortage.

4. Price Controls and Quotas: Meddling with Markets
Covers market interventions and their consequences: price and quantity controls, inefficiency, and deadweight loss.

Optional

5. International Trade
An examination of comparative advantage, tariffs and quotas, the politics of trade protection and international trade agreements, and the controversy over imports from low-wage countries. With new coverage of hyperglobalization, the EU and Brexit, outsourcing, and reshoring.

5 Appendix: Consumer and Producer Surplus
Introduces students to market efficiency, the ways markets fail, the role of prices as signals, and property rights.

Core

6. Macroeconomics: The Big Picture
Introduces the big ideas of macroeconomics with an overview of recessions and expansions, employment and unemployment, long-run growth, inflation versus deflation, and international economics.

7. GDP and the CPI: Tracking the Macroeconomy
Explains how the numbers macroeconomists use are calculated and why, including the basics of national income accounting and price indexes. Sets the stage for upcoming chapters with a newly simplified presentation of the expanded circular-flow diagram.

8. Unemployment and Inflation
Covers the measurement of unemployment, emphasizing that continual job creation and destruction are features of modern economies. Examines the problems inflation poses for policy makers and the economy.

9. Long-Run Economic Growth
Emphasizes an international perspective—economic growth is about the world as a whole—and explains why some countries have been more successful than others, with an updated section on sustainability.

10. Savings, Investment Spending, and the Financial System
An introduction to financial markets and institutions, loanable funds and the determination of interest rates. Includes coverage of present value.

Contents

PART 8 The International Economy

Chapter 18
International Macroeconomics / 531

Photo Credits

Front Cover

Credits are listed left to right.

First Row: Fireman, Kris Timken/AGE Fotostock

Second Row: Commuter train, tovovan/Shutterstock; Fruit stand, Richard A McMillin/Shutterstock

Third Row: Cows, Stockbyte/Photodisc; Business woman giving presentation, Tinpixels/Getty Images; Solar panels, iurii/Shutterstock

Fourth Row: Gas prices, Nickolay Stanev/Shutterstock; Depression era man holding sign, akg-images/The Image Works; Wall Street sign, Thinkstock

Fifth Row: Woman looking in microscope, Tetra Images/AGE Fotostock; Money exchange rates, Bankoo/Shutterstock; Shopping for a mobile phone, Juice Images/AGE Fotostock

Sixth Row: Busy Asian street, Tom Bonaventure/Getty Images; Construction workers, mikeledray/Shutterstock; Cargo ship, EvrenKalinbacak/Shutterstock

Seventh Row: Baby having heartbeat checked, Darren Brode/Shutterstock; Powerlines, Brand X Pictures; Smoking coal power plant, iStockphoto/Thinkstock; Lightbulbs, fStop Images GmbH/Alamy

Eighth Row: Workers examining boxes, Jupiterimages/Getty Images; Infrastructure repair, Nightman1965/Shutterstock; Currency, Lucia Pitter/Shutterstock

Back Cover

First Row: Filing taxes, PTstock/Shutterstock

Second Row (left to right): Cargo containers, rodho/Shutterstock; Printing money, matthiashaas/Thinkstock; Coral reef and fish, John_Walker/Shutterstock

Third Row: Waiter, Steven Miric/Getty Images; Cupcakes, Tobias Titz/AGE Fotostock; Shopper deciding, Noel Hendrickson/Getty Images; Graduates, Prasit Rodphan/Shutterstock

Fourth Row: Flags, yui/Shutterstock; Cars in lot, Matushchak Anton/Shutterstock; Robotic arm for packing, wellphoto/Shutterstock

Fifth Row: Traffic, Artens/Shutterstock; Shopping in city street, Peathegee Inc/AGE Fotostock; Fracking rig, CSP_LonnyGarris/AGE Fotostock; Concert, Wittybear/Shutterstock

Sixth Row: Sushi, Ipatov/Shutterstock; Stacks of wood, Fedor Selivanov/Shutterstock; Soybean farm, Fotokostic/Shutterstock; Credit cards, Olleg/Shutterstock; Diamonds, The Adventurer/Shutterstock

Introduction: An Engine for Growth and Discovery

A DAY IN THE MEGACITY

LONDON, NEW YORK, AND TOKYO have something in common: they are megacities—huge metropolitan complexes that contain tens of millions of people and are spread over immense tracts of land. While most people are familiar with these megacities, not everyone knows about the biggest of them all: the vast urban complex known as China's Pearl River Delta (the PRD).

Thirty years ago China was very poor with a backward economy. Now it produces sophisticated goods for the world, allowing it to deliver relatively comfortable incomes to many of its people.

Roughly the same size as the state of Delaware, the PRD is home to more than 40 million people. Driving across the PRD (as one of the authors has done), with its endless succession of factories, office buildings, and apartment towers, is an unforgettable—and very long—experience.

What are all those people doing? A significant percentage of them are engaged in producing goods for world markets, especially, but by no means only, electronic components: just about every smartphone, tablet, and computer contains components produced in the PRD. But the megacity's residents are consumers as well as producers. While the wage of an average worker in the PRD is relatively low by U.S. standards, overall wages and income are high enough to support a vast retail sector, ranging from mom-and-pop local stores to shops selling expensive luxury goods.

But not so long ago, neither the PRD nor the economic dynamism it embodies was visible. As recently as 1980, 800 million people in China subsisted on less than $1.50 a day. The average Chinese citizen more or less had enough to eat and a roof over his or her head, but not much more than that. In fact, the standard of living wasn't much higher than it had been centuries earlier. And from 1959 to 1961, in what is now known as "The Great Leap Backward," the Chinese government got the economy so wrong that millions of Chinese died from man-made famine.

However, in the years since 1980, Chinese incomes have soared more than tenfold in real terms as the poverty rate (percentage of population subsisting on less than $1.90 a day) has fallen from 88% in 1981 to 1.9% in 2013. The rise of the PRD is one chapter of an incredible success story in which hundreds of millions of Chinese have been lifted out of abject poverty over the past few decades. Never in human history have so many seen so much progress.

Although this is a remarkable story, it is not entirely unprecedented. From 1840 to 1910, British workers also experienced a marked rise in their standard of living. And this success was repeated soon afterward in the United States, setting the stage for the high levels of prosperity we now enjoy. Commenting on how English workers were lifted out of poverty, the great economist Alfred Marshall made an observation that is equally relevant for Chinese workers today: "The hope that poverty and ignorance may gradually be extinguished, derives indeed much support from the steady progress of the working classes during the nineteenth century."

These unprecedented sets of events have touched our lives today in a dizzying number of ways. You are using smartphones, tablets, and laptops that are manufactured in the PRD as you pursue a first-rate education in the United States, one of the richest countries in the world.

What can economics say about all of this? Quite a lot, it turns out. What you will learn from this book is how these momentous changes, which lifted hundreds of millions of people out of poverty, are related to a simple, but very important, set of questions involving economics. Among these questions are:

- How does our economic system work? That is, how does it manage to deliver the goods?

- When and why does our economic system sometimes go astray, leading people into counterproductive behavior?

- Why are there ups and downs in the economy? That is, why does the economy sometimes have a bad year?

- Why is the long run mainly a story of ups rather than downs? That is, why has China, like Great Britain and the United States, become much richer over time?

Let's take a look at these questions and offer a brief preview of what you will learn in this book. ●

‖ The Invisible Hand

The massive industrial and consumer complex that is today's Pearl River Delta is a quite new creation. As recently as 1980 much of the region was an economic backwater; the nucleus, Shenzhen, was then a small and very poor fishing village. How did this backwater turn into the electronics workshop of the world, making it a dynamic creator of wealth?

To achieve the level of prosperity we have in America, a level the average resident of the PRD can only now begin to aspire to, you need a well-functioning system for coordinating productive activities—the activities that create the goods and services people want and get them to the people who want them. That kind of system is what we mean when we talk about the **economy.** And **economics** is the social science that studies the production, distribution, and consumption of goods and services.

An economy succeeds to the extent that it, literally, delivers the goods. And as we've discussed, over the past 30 years the Chinese economy has achieved a spectacular increase in the amount of goods it delivers both to its own citizens and to the rest of the world.

So China's economy must be doing something right, and we might want to compliment the people in charge. But guess what? There isn't anyone in charge—not anymore.

In the 1970s, before the PRD began its incredible rise, China was a *command economy* in which decisions about what factories would produce and what goods would be delivered to households were made by government officials. But experience shows that command economies don't work very well. Producers in command economies like China before 1980 or the Soviet Union before 1991 routinely found themselves unable to produce because they did not have crucial raw materials, or if they succeeded in producing, they found nobody wanted their products. Consumers were often unable to find necessities like toilet paper or milk. Command economies are infamous for long lines at shops. And as we mentioned, from 1959 to 1961, the Chinese government got its command economy terribly wrong, inflicting enormous hardship and causing millions of unnecessary deaths.

In 1978 the Chinese government finally admitted that its economic model wasn't working, and began a remarkable transformation into a **market economy,** one in which production and consumption are the result of decentralized decisions by many firms and individuals. The United States has a market economy. And in today's China there is no central authority telling people what to produce or where to ship it. Each individual producer makes what he or she thinks will be most profitable; each consumer buys what he or she chooses. It's important to realize, however, that the Chinese government intervenes in markets much more than the U.S. government does; in particular, while China's government rarely tells producers what to produce, it often tells banks how much to lend and to whom.

If you had never seen a market economy in action, you might imagine that it would be chaotic. After all, nobody is in charge. But market economies are able to coordinate even highly complex activities and reliably provide consumers with the goods and services they want. Indeed, people quite casually trust their lives to the market system: residents of any major city would starve in days if the unplanned yet somehow orderly actions of thousands of businesses did not deliver a steady supply of food. Surprisingly, the unplanned "chaos" of a market economy turns out to be far more orderly than the planning of a command economy. And that's why almost every country in the world—North Korea and Cuba are the only exceptions—has become a market economy.

In 1776, in a famous passage in his book *The Wealth of Nations*, the pioneering Scottish economist Adam Smith wrote about how individuals, in pursuing their own interests, often end up serving the interests of society as a whole. Of a businessman whose pursuit of profit makes the nation wealthier, Smith wrote: "[H]e intends only his own gain, and he is in this, as in many other cases, led by an invisible hand to promote an end which was no part of his intention."

An **economy** is a system for coordinating society's productive activities.

Economics is the social science that studies the production, distribution, and consumption of goods and services.

A **market economy** is an economy in which decisions about production and consumption are made by individual producers and consumers.

Ever since, economists have used the term **invisible hand** to refer to the way a market economy manages to harness the power of self-interest for the good of society.

The study of how individuals make decisions and how these decisions interact is called **microeconomics.** One of the key themes in microeconomics is the validity of Adam Smith's insight: individuals pursuing their own interests often do promote the interests of society as a whole.

So the answer to our first question—"How does our economic system manage to deliver the goods?"—is that we rely on the virtues of a market economy and the power of the invisible hand.

But the invisible hand isn't always our friend. It's also important to understand when and why the individual pursuit of self-interest can lead to counterproductive behavior.

The **invisible hand** refers to the way in which the individual pursuit of self-interest can lead to good results for society as a whole.

Microeconomics is the branch of economics that studies how people make decisions and how these decisions interact.

When the individual pursuit of self-interest leads to bad results for society as a whole, there is **market failure.**

A **recession** is a downturn in the economy.

My Benefit, Your Cost

In most ways, life in the PRD is immensely better than it was in 1980. Two things have, however, gotten much worse: traffic congestion and air quality. At rush hour, the average speed on the PRD's roads is only around 12 miles an hour and the air is seriously unhealthy much of the year.

Why do these problems represent failures of the invisible hand? Consider the case of traffic congestion.

When traffic is congested, each driver is imposing a cost on all the other drivers on the road—he is literally getting in their way (and they are getting in his way). This cost can be substantial: one estimate found that someone driving a car into lower Manhattan on a weekday causes more than three hours of delays to other drivers, and around $160 in monetary losses. Yet when deciding whether or not to drive, commuters have no incentive to take the costs they impose on others into account.

Traffic congestion is a familiar example of a much broader problem: **market failure,** which happens when the individual pursuit of one's own interest, instead of promoting the interests of society as a whole, actually makes society worse off. Another important example of market failure is air pollution, which is all too visible, literally, in the PRD. Water pollution and the overexploitation of natural resources such as fish and forests reflect the same problem.

The environmental costs of self-interested behavior can sometimes be huge. And as the world becomes more crowded and the environmental footprint of human activity continues to grow, issues like climate change and ocean acidification will become increasingly important.

The good news, as you will learn if you study microeconomics, is that economic analysis can be used to diagnose cases of market failure. And often, economic analysis can also be used to devise solutions for the problem.

Good Times, Bad Times

China has become an enormous economic powerhouse in the last 30 years. (And, depending upon the data source used, China and the United States vie for top place among the world's economies.) One somewhat ironic consequence of China's rise is that people around the world get nervous at any signs of trouble in Chinese industry, because it's such a big source of demand for raw materials. And in 2016, there was a lot to be nervous about. Official data said that the Chinese economy was still strong, but many independent observers looked at indicators like electricity consumption and saw them as evidence that a sharp slowdown was in progress.

Such troubled periods are a regular feature of modern economies. The fact is that the economy does not always run smoothly: it experiences fluctuations, a series of ups and downs. By middle age, a typical American will have experienced three or four downs, known as **recessions.** The U.S. economy experienced serious recessions beginning in 1973, 1981, 1990, 2001, and 2007. During a severe recession, millions of workers may be laid off.

ECONOMICS 101

"Remember, an economic boom is usually followed by an economic kaboom."

© Dave Carpenter/Cartoonstock

Like market failure, recessions are a fact of life; but also like market failure, they are a problem for which economic analysis offers some solutions. Recessions are one of the main concerns of the branch of economics known as **macroeconomics,** which is concerned with the overall ups and downs of the economy. If you study macroeconomics, you will learn how economists explain recessions and how government policies can be used to minimize the damage from economic fluctuations.

Despite the occasional recession, however, over the long run the stories of all major economies contain many more ups than downs. And that long-run ascent is the subject of our final question.

Onward and Upward

The overall standard of living of the average resident of the PRD, while immensely higher than it was in 1980, is still pretty low by American standards. But then, America wasn't always as rich as it is today. Indeed, at the beginning of the twentieth century, most Americans lived under conditions that we would now think of as extreme poverty. Only 10% of homes had flush toilets, only 8% had central heating, only 2% had electricity, and almost nobody had a car, let alone a washing machine or air conditioning. But over the course of the following century America achieved a remarkable rise in living standards that ultimately led to the great wealth that we see around us today.

Such comparisons are a stark reminder of how much lives around the world have been changed by **economic growth,** the increasing ability of the economy to produce goods and services. Why does the economy grow over time? And why does economic growth occur faster in some places and times than in others? These are key questions for economics, because economic growth is a good thing, as the residents of the PRD can attest, and most of us want more of it.

However, it is important for economic growth to take place without irreparable damage to the environment. What we need is *sustainable long-run economic growth*, which is economic growth over time that balances protection of the environment with improved living standards for current and future generations. Today, the goal of balancing the production of goods and services with the health of the environment is an increasingly pressing concern, and economic analysis has a key role to play, particularly in the analysis of market failure.

An Engine for Discovery

We hope we have convinced you that what the great economist Alfred Marshall called the "ordinary business of life," the economic actions and transactions that go on every day not just in the PRD but around the world, is really quite extraordinary, if you stop to think about it, and that it can lead us to ask some very interesting and important questions.

In this book, we will describe the answers economists have given to these questions. But this book, like economics as a whole, isn't a list of answers: it's an introduction to a discipline, a way to address questions like those we asked earlier. Or as Alfred Marshall put it: "Economics . . . is not a body of concrete truth, but an engine for the discovery of concrete truth."

So let's turn the key and start the ignition.

Macroeconomics is the branch of economics that is concerned with overall ups and downs in the economy.

Economic growth is the growing ability of the economy to produce goods and services.

1 First Principles

🌐 COMMON GROUND

THERE WAS A TIME when most of the world's college students were located in wealthy Western nations. Today, however, the number of college students in developing countries like China and India is rapidly overtaking the number in the United States and Western Europe. In fact, China already has more students enrolled in college than the United States does.

One must choose.

And what are these students studying? A variety of subjects, of course. But regardless of the region of the world, a lot of students will be studying economics.

You might wonder, however, whether the economics being taught at, say, Shanghai University or the University of Mumbai bears much resemblance to the economics being taught in U.S. colleges. After all, there are big differences between nations in levels of income, political institutions, and the problems they face. Doesn't this mean that the economics in these countries is different, too?

The answer is, yes and no. "Yes," because different circumstances and history affect what both students and practitioners need to know. That's why there are international editions of this textbook. Canada, for example, is different enough from the United States to warrant its own edition with explanations about Canadian economic issues and institutions.

The answer is also "no" because much of the material covered in basic economics is the same wherever you are around the world. The reason for this is that all economics is based on a set of common principles that apply to many different issues, regardless of the particular setting.

Some of these principles involve *individual choice*—for economics is, first of all, about the choices that individuals make. Do you save your money and take the bus or do you buy a car? Do you keep your old phone or upgrade to a new one? These decisions involve *making a choice* from among a limited number of alternatives—limited because no one can have everything that he or she wants. Every question in economics at its most basic level involves individuals making choices.

But to understand how an economy works, you need to understand more than how individuals make choices. None of us are like Robinson Crusoe, living alone on an island. Every person must make decisions in an environment that is shaped by the decisions of others. So in this chapter we will learn about four principles of economics that guide the choices made by individuals.

Indeed, in a modern economy even the simplest decisions you make—say, what to have for breakfast—are shaped by the decisions of thousands of other people, from the banana grower in Costa Rica who decided to grow the fruit you eat to the farmer in Iowa who provided the corn in your cornflakes.

Because each of us in a market economy depends on so many others—and they, in turn, depend on us—our choices interact. So although all economics at a basic level is about individual choice, in order to understand how market economies behave we must also understand *economic interaction*—how my choices affect your choices, and vice versa. To that end, in this chapter you will study the five principles that govern how individual choices interact in the economy.

Many important economic interactions can be understood by looking at the markets for individual goods, like the market for corn. However, when we consider the economy as a whole, we see that it is composed of an enormous number of markets for individuals goods. Viewed from this angle, it is also apparent that these markets interact. As a result, the larger economy experiences ups and downs. In order to understand economy-wide interactions, in this chapter we will study the three principles that underlie their behavior.

These twelves principles—four principles of individual choice, five principles of interaction of individual choices, and three principles of economy-wide interactions—are the basis of all economic analysis. They also form the common ground of economics; they apply just as much in Shanghai or Mumbai, as they do in Omaha or Atlanta. ●

WHAT YOU WILL LEARN

- What four principles guide the choices made by individuals?
- What five principles govern how individual choices interact?
- What three principles illustrate economy-wide interactions?

Principles That Underlie Individual Choice: The Core of Economics

Every economic issue involves, at its most basic level, **individual choice**—decisions by an individual about what to do and what not to do. In fact, you might say that it isn't economics if it isn't about choice.

Take Walmart or Amazon.com. There are thousands of different products available, and it is extremely unlikely that you—or anyone else—could afford to buy everything you might want to have. And anyway, there's only so much space in your dorm room or apartment. So will you buy another bookcase or a mini-refrigerator? Given limitations on your budget and your living space, you must choose which products to buy and which to leave on the shelf.

The fact that those products are on the shelf in the first place involves choice—the store manager chose to put them there, and the manufacturers of the products chose to produce them. All economic activities involve individual choice.

Four economic principles underlie the economics of individual choice, as shown in Table 1-1. We'll now examine each of these principles.

Principle #1: Choices Are Necessary Because Resources Are Scarce

You can't always get what you want. Everyone would like to have a beautiful house in a great location, a new car or two, and a nice vacation in a fancy hotel. But even in a rich country like the United States, not many families can afford all that. So they must make choices—whether to go to Disney World this year or buy a better car, whether to make do with a small backyard or accept a longer commute in order to live where land is cheaper.

Limited income isn't the only thing that keeps people from having everything they want. Time is also in limited supply: there are only 24 hours in a day. Choosing to spend time on one activity means choosing not to spend time on a different activity—studying for an exam means forgoing a night spent watching a movie. Indeed, many people faced with the limited number of hours in the day are willing to trade money for time. For example, convenience stores normally charge higher prices than a regular supermarket. But they fulfill a valuable role by catering to time-pressed customers who would rather pay more than travel farther to the supermarket.

This leads us to our first principle of individual choice:

> *People must make choices because resources are scarce.*

A **resource** is anything that can be used to produce something else. Lists of the economy's resources usually begin with land, labor (the time of workers), capital (machinery, buildings, and other man-made productive assets), and human capital (the educational achievements and skills of workers). A resource is **scarce** when there's not enough of the resource available to satisfy all the ways a society wants to use it.

There are many scarce resources. These include natural resources that come from the physical environment, such as minerals, lumber, and petroleum. There is also a limited quantity of human resources, such as labor, skill, and intelligence. And in a growing world economy with a rapidly increasing human population, even clean air and water have become scarce resources.

Just as individuals must make choices, the scarcity of resources means that society as a whole must make choices. One way a society in a market economy makes choices is by allowing them to emerge as the result of many individual choices. For example, Americans as a group have only so many hours in a week: how many of those hours will they spend going to supermarkets to get lower prices, rather than saving time by shopping at convenience stores? The answer is

---

TABLE 1-1 The Principles of Individual Choice

1. People must make choices because resources are scarce.

2. The opportunity cost of an item—what you must give up in order to get it—is its true cost.

3. "How much" decisions require making trade-offs at the margin: comparing the costs and benefits of doing a little bit more of an activity versus doing a little bit less.

4. People usually respond to incentives, exploiting opportunities to make themselves better off.

Individual choice is the decision by an individual of what to do, which necessarily involves a decision of what not to do.

A **resource** is anything that can be used to produce something else.

Resources are **scarce**—not enough of the resources are available to satisfy all the various ways a society wants to use them.

the sum of individual decisions: each of the millions of individuals in the economy makes a choice about where to shop, and the overall choice is simply the sum of those individual decisions.

But for various reasons, there are some decisions that a society decides are best not left to individual choice. Take the case of cod fishing. By 1992, excessive fishing by individual fisherman had left the stocks of cod in the North Atlantic close to extinction. The Canadian government intervened to limit the amount harvested by fishermen; as a result, by 2016 cod stocks were on their way to recovery.

Principle #2: The True Cost of Something Is Its Opportunity Cost

It is the last term before you graduate, and your class schedule allows you to take only one elective. There are two, however, that you would really like to take: Intro to Web Design and History of Jazz.

Suppose you decide to take the History of Jazz course. What's the cost of that decision? It is the fact that you can't take the web design class, your next best alternative choice. Economists call that kind of cost—what you must give up in order to get an item you want—the **opportunity cost** of that item. This leads us to our second principle of individual choice:

> *The opportunity cost of an item—what you must give up in order to get it—is its true cost.*

So the opportunity cost of taking the History of Jazz class is the benefit you would have derived from the Intro to Web Design class.

The concept of opportunity cost is crucial to understanding individual choice because, in the end, all costs are opportunity costs. That's because every choice you make means forgoing some other alternative.

Sometimes critics claim that economists are concerned only with costs and benefits that can be measured in dollars and cents. But that is not true. Much economic analysis involves cases like our elective course example, where it costs no extra tuition to take one elective course—that is, there is no direct monetary cost. Nonetheless, the elective you choose has an opportunity cost—the other desirable elective course that you must forgo because your limited time permits taking only one. More specifically, the opportunity cost of a choice is what you forgo by not choosing your next best alternative.

You might think that opportunity cost is an add-on—that is, something *additional* to the monetary cost of an item. Suppose that an elective class costs additional tuition of $750; now there is a monetary cost to taking History of Jazz. Is the opportunity cost of taking that course something separate from that monetary cost?

Well, consider two cases. First, suppose that taking Intro to Web Design also costs $750. In this case, you would have to spend that $750 no matter which class you take. So what you give up to take the History of Jazz class is still the web design class, period—you would have to spend that $750 either way. But suppose there isn't any fee for the web design class. In that case, what you give up to take the jazz class is the benefit from the web design class *plus* the benefit you could have gained from spending the $750 on other things.

Either way, the real cost of taking your preferred class is what you must give up to get it. As you expand the set of decisions that underlie each choice—whether to take an elective or not, whether to finish this term or not, whether to drop out or not—you'll realize that all costs are ultimately opportunity costs.

Sometimes the money you have to pay for something is a good indication of its opportunity cost. But many times it is not.

One very important example of how poorly monetary cost can indicate opportunity cost is the cost of attending college. Tuition and housing are major monetary expenses for most students; but even if these things were free, attending

Resources are scarce.

The real cost of an item is its **opportunity cost:** what you must give up in order to get it.

Mark Zuckerberg understood the concept of opportunity cost.

college would still be an expensive proposition because most college students, if they were not in college, would have a job. That is, by going to college, students *forgo* the income they could have earned if they had worked instead. This means that the opportunity cost of attending college is what you pay for tuition and housing plus the forgone income you would have earned in a job.

It's easy to see that the opportunity cost of going to college is especially high for people who could be earning a lot during what would otherwise have been their college years. That is why star athletes like LeBron James and entrepreneurs like Mark Zuckerberg, founder of Facebook, often skip or drop out of college.

Principle #3: "How Much" Is a Decision at the Margin

Some important decisions involve an "either–or" choice—for example, you decide either to go to college or to begin working; you decide either to take economics or to take something else. But other important decisions involve "how much" choices—for example, if you are taking both economics and chemistry this semester, you must decide how much time to spend studying for each. When it comes to understanding "how much" decisions, economics has an important insight to offer: "how much" is a decision made at the margin.

Suppose you are taking both economics and chemistry. And suppose you are a pre-med student, so your grade in chemistry matters more to you than your grade in economics. Does that therefore imply that you should spend *all* your study time on chemistry and wing it on the economics exam? Probably not; even if you think your chemistry grade is more important, you should put some effort into studying economics.

Spending more time studying chemistry involves a benefit (a higher expected grade in that course) and a cost (you could have spent that time doing something else, such as studying to get a higher grade in economics). That is, your decision involves a **trade-off**—a comparison of costs and benefits.

How do you decide this kind of "how much" question? The typical answer is that you make the decision a bit at a time, by asking how you should spend the next hour. Say both exams are on the same day, and the night before you spend time reviewing your notes for both courses. At 6:00 P.M., you decide that it's a good idea to spend at least an hour on each course. At 8:00 P.M., you decide you'd better spend another hour on each course. At 10:00 P.M., you are getting tired and figure you have one more hour to study before bed—chemistry or economics? If you are pre-med, it's likely to be chemistry; if you are a business major, it's likely to be economics.

Note how you've made the decision to allocate your time: at each point the question is whether or not to spend *one more hour* on either course. And in deciding whether to spend another hour studying for chemistry, you weigh the costs (an hour forgone of studying for economics or an hour forgone of sleeping) versus the benefits (a likely increase in your chemistry grade). As long as the benefit of studying chemistry for one more hour outweighs the cost, you should choose to study for that additional hour.

Decisions of this type—whether to do a bit more or a bit less of an activity, like what to do with your next hour, your next dollar, and so on—are **marginal decisions.** This brings us to our third principle of individual choice:

> *"How much" decisions require making trade-offs at the margin: comparing the costs and benefits of doing a little bit more of an activity versus doing a little bit less.*

You make a **trade-off** when you compare the costs with the benefits of doing something. Decisions about whether to do a bit more or a bit less of an activity are **marginal decisions.** The study of such decisions is known as **marginal analysis.**

The study of such decisions is known as **marginal analysis.** Many of the questions that we face in real life involve marginal analysis: How many minutes should I exercise? How many workers should I hire? What is an acceptable rate of negative side effects from a new medicine? Marginal analysis plays a central role in economics because it is the key to deciding "how much" of an activity to do.

Principle #4: People Usually Respond to Incentives, Exploiting Opportunities to Make Themselves Better Off

An **incentive** is anything that offers rewards to people to change their behavior.

One day, while listening to the financial news, the authors heard a great tip about how to park cheaply in Manhattan. Garages in the Wall Street area charge as much as $30 per day. But according to this news report, some people had found a better way: instead of parking in a garage, they had their oil changed at the Manhattan Jiffy Lube for $19.95—and they keep your car all day!

It's a great story, but unfortunately it turned out not to be true—in fact, there is no Jiffy Lube in Manhattan. But if there were, you can be sure there would be a lot of oil changes there. Why? Because when people are offered opportunities to make themselves better off, they normally take them—and if they could find a way to park their car all day for $19.95 rather than $30, they would.

In this example economists say that people are responding to an **incentive**—an opportunity to make themselves better off. We can now state our fourth principle of individual choice:

> *People usually respond to incentives, exploiting opportunities to make themselves better off.*

When you try to predict how individuals will behave in an economic situation, it is a very good bet that they will respond to incentives—that is, exploit opportunities to make themselves better off. Furthermore, individuals will *continue* to exploit these opportunities until they have been fully exhausted. If there really were a Manhattan Jiffy Lube and an oil change really were a cheap way to park your car, we can safely predict that before long the waiting list for oil changes would be weeks, if not months.

In fact, the principle that people will exploit opportunities to make themselves better off is the basis of *all* predictions by economists about individual behavior.

If the earnings of those who get MBAs soar while the earnings of those who get law degrees decline, expect more students to go to business school and fewer to go to law school. If the price of gasoline rises and stays high for an extended period of time, expect people to buy smaller cars with higher gas mileage—making themselves better off by driving more fuel-efficient cars.

FOR INQUIRING MINDS   Using Incentives to Break the Cycle of Poverty

For Dinalva Pereira de Moura and her family, the Brazilian antipoverty program Bolsa Familia (Family Grant) has significantly improved their quality of life. The program currently reaches over 12 million Brazilian families, with the poorest families receiving around $35 monthly per child, and moderately poor families receiving $13 to $15 monthly per child. According to Mrs. de Moura, "The Bolsa Familia helps me buy food. My children know that when we receive the money they will have more to eat, and that makes them happier. And they don't skip school, because they know the money depends upon their going."

Bolsa Familia wasn't designed to just make everyday life more bearable for poor families; rather, it was primarily intended to break the cycle of poverty that keeps the poor trapped generation after generation.

To do that, researchers understand that poor families need to invest in their children. And to motivate families to undertake those investments, researchers employed incentives—making rewards conditional on results. So the fact that the de Moura children "don't skip school because they know the money depends upon their going" lies at the heart of the success of the program.

Bolsa Familia is an example of what is generally known as a *conditional cash transfer* program or CCT: families are given cash stipends conditional on achieving various benchmarks such as having their children vaccinated, taking them for annual health checkups, and maintaining satisfactory school attendance. Researchers have found that Bolsa Familia has accounted for a significant increase in school attendance and positive health indicators, and a significant reduction in income inequality in Brazil.

While principally found in Latin America (where the first CCT program began in 1997 in Mexico), CCT programs are now spreading throughout the world. In Bangladesh, Pakistan, and Turkey, CCT programs have reduced the gap between boys' school attendance and girls' school attendance. And in New York City, a CCT program increased families' use of preventive medical care as well as school attendance and completion rates.

Before the advent of CCT programs, the cycle of poverty across generations within families had seemed unbreakable, with some even arguing that the poor no longer responded to incentives. Yet CCT programs have proved that the poor do indeed respond to well-designed incentives and that there is hope for breaking poverty's grip.

One last point: economists tend to be skeptical of any attempt to change behavior that *doesn't* change incentives. For example, a plan that calls on manufacturers to reduce pollution voluntarily probably won't be effective. In contrast, a plan that gives them a financial reward to reduce pollution is a lot more likely to succeed because it has changed their incentives.

So are we ready to do economics? Not yet—because most of the interesting things that happen in the economy are the result not merely of individual choices but of the way in which individual choices interact.

ECONOMICS >> *in Action*
Boy or Girl? It Depends on the Cost

In China, the cost of having a baby girl compared to a baby boy has fallen due to changes in the economy and in government policy.

One fact about China is indisputable: it has lots of people. As of 2016, the estimated Chinese population is over 1,405,000,000. That's right: over *one billion four hundred five million* people. And trends in Chinese demographics have shifted over time the cost of having a child; in particular, the cost of having a boy or a girl.

In the 1970s, China was a very, very poor country with an already large and growing population. Concerned that it would be unable to adequately provide and care for such a large number of people, the Chinese government introduced the one-child policy in 1978. It restricted most couples to only one child and imposed penalties on those that defied the mandate. By 2016 the average number of children per Chinese woman had fallen to 1.6, from more than 5 in the 1970s.

But the one-child policy has an unfortunate unintended consequence. Until recently China was an overwhelmingly rural country. In the countryside, because of the physical demands of farming, sons are strongly preferred over daughters. In addition, tradition dictated that it was sons, not daughters, who took care of elderly parents. The effect of the one-child policy was to greatly increase the perceived cost to a Chinese family of a female child. As a result, while some were given up for adoption abroad, many Chinese females simply "disappeared" during the first year of life, victims of neglect and mistreatment.

In fact, in 1990 Nobel-prize-winning Indian-born economist Amartya Sen calculated that there were 100 million "missing women" in Asia due to the perceived higher cost of female children, with estimates rising to 160 million.

Recent events, however, have shifted the relative costs of a boy versus a girl toward a greater balance. Because China is quickly urbanizing, boys are no longer prized in order to do manual labor. So the gender imbalance between Chinese boys and girls peaked in 1995 and has fallen toward the biologically natural ratio since then. And in 2015 the Chinese government officially ended the one-child policy.

Yet the consequences will endure for many more years. There are now estimated to be over 30 million *excess men* in China—the number of men in excess of the number of women who will reach adulthood by 2020. There have also been reports of Chinese villages full of lonely men. Not surprisingly, websites have popped up advising couples on how to have a girl rather than a boy.

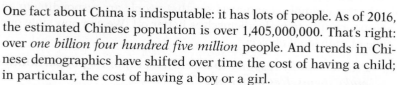

ED JONES/Getty Images

>> *Check Your Understanding* 1-1
Solutions appear at back of book.

1. Explain how each of the following illustrates one of the four principles of individual choice.
   a. You are on your third trip to a restaurant's all-you-can-eat dessert buffet and are feeling very full. Although it would cost you no additional money, you forgo a slice of coconut cream pie but have a slice of chocolate cake.

b. Even if there were more resources in the world, there would still be scarcity.

c. Different teaching assistants teach several Economics 101 tutorials. Those taught by the teaching assistants with the best reputations fill up quickly, with spaces left unfilled in the ones taught by assistants with poor reputations.

d. To decide how many hours per week to exercise, you compare the health benefits of one more hour of exercise to the effect on your grades of one fewer hour spent studying.

2. You make $45,000 per year at your current job with Whiz Kids Consultants. You are considering a job offer from Brainiacs, Inc., that will pay you $50,000 per year. Which of the following are elements of the opportunity cost of accepting the new job at Brainiacs, Inc.?

a. The increased time spent commuting to your new job

b. The $45,000 salary from your old job

c. The more spacious office at your new job

Interaction: How Economies Work

An economy is a system for coordinating the productive activities of many people. In a market economy like we live in, coordination takes place without any coordinator: each individual makes his or her own choices.

Yet those choices are by no means independent of one another: each individual's opportunities, and hence choices, depend to a large extent on the choices made by other people. So to understand how a market economy behaves, we have to examine this **interaction** in which my choices affect your choices, and vice versa.

When studying economic interaction, we quickly learn that the end result of individual choices may be quite different from what any one individual intends. For example, over the past century farmers in the United States have eagerly adopted new farming techniques and crop strains that have reduced their costs and increased their yields. Clearly, it's in the interest of each farmer to keep up with the latest farming techniques.

But the end result of each farmer trying to increase his or her own income has actually been to drive many farmers out of business. Because American farmers have been so successful at producing larger yields, agricultural prices have steadily fallen. These falling prices have reduced the incomes of many farmers, and as a result fewer people find farming worth doing. That is, an individual farmer who plants a better variety of corn is better off; but when many farmers plant a better variety of corn, the result may be to make farmers as a group worse off.

A farmer who plants a new, more productive corn variety doesn't just grow more corn. Such a farmer also affects the market for corn through the increased yields attained, with consequences that will be felt by other farmers, consumers, and beyond.

Just as there are four economic principles that underlie individual choice, there are five principles underlying the economics of interaction. These principles are summarized in Table 1-2 and we will now examine each of them more closely.

Principle #5: There Are Gains from Trade

Why do the choices I make interact with the choices you make? A family could try to take care of all its own needs—growing its own food, sewing its own clothing, providing itself with entertainment, writing its own economics textbooks. But trying to live that way would be very hard.

The key to a much better standard of living for everyone is **trade,** in which people divide tasks among themselves and each person provides a good or service that other people want in return for different goods and services that he or she wants.

The reason we have an economy, not many self-sufficient individuals, is that there are **gains from trade:** by dividing tasks and trading, two people

Interaction of choices—my choices affect your choices, and vice versa—is a feature of most economic situations. The results of this interaction are often quite different from what the individuals intend.

In a market economy, individuals engage in **trade:** they provide goods and services to others and receive goods and services in return.

There are **gains from trade:** people can get more of what they want through trade than they could if they tried to be self-sufficient. This increase in output is due to **specialization:** each person specializes in the task that he or she is good at performing.

TABLE 1-2 The Principles of the Interaction of Individual Choices

5. There are gains from trade.

6. Because people respond to incentives, markets move toward equilibrium.

7. Resources should be used as efficiently as possible to achieve society's goals.

8. Because people usually exploit gains from trade, markets usually lead to efficiency.

9. When markets don't achieve efficiency, government intervention can improve society's welfare.

"I hunt and she gathers—otherwise, we couldn't make ends meet."

(or 6 billion people) can each get more of what they want than they could get by being self-sufficient. This leads us to our fifth principle:

There are gains from trade.

Gains from trade arise from this division of tasks, which economists call **specialization**—a situation in which different people each engage in a different task, specializing in those tasks that they are good at performing. The advantages of specialization, and the resulting gains from trade, were the starting point for Adam Smith's 1776 book *The Wealth of Nations*, which many regard as the beginning of economics as a discipline.

Smith's book begins with a description of an eighteenth-century pin factory where, rather than each of the 10 workers making a pin from start to finish, each worker specialized in one of the many steps in pin-making:

> One man draws out the wire, another straights it, a third cuts it, a fourth points it, a fifth grinds it at the top for receiving the head; to make the head requires two or three distinct operations; to put it on, is a particular business, to whiten the pins is another; it is even a trade by itself to put them into the paper; and the important business of making a pin is, in this manner, divided into about eighteen distinct operations. . . . Those ten persons, therefore, could make among them upwards of forty-eight thousand pins in a day. But if they had all wrought separately and independently, and without any of them having been educated to this particular business, they certainly could not each of them have made twenty, perhaps not one pin a day. . . .

The same principle applies when we look at how people divide tasks among themselves and trade in an economy. *The economy, as a whole, can produce more when each person specializes in a task and trades with others.*

The benefits of specialization are the reason a person typically chooses only one career. It takes many years of study and experience to become a doctor or to become a commercial airline pilot. Many doctors might well have had the potential to become excellent pilots, and vice versa; but it is very unlikely that anyone who decided to pursue both careers would be as good a pilot or as good a doctor as someone who decided at the beginning to specialize in that field. So it is to everyone's advantage that individuals specialize in their career choices.

Markets are what allow a doctor and a pilot to specialize in their own fields. Because markets for commercial flights and for doctors' services exist, a doctor is assured that she can find a flight and a pilot is assured that he can find a doctor. As long as individuals know that they can find the goods and services they want in the market, they are willing to forgo self-sufficiency and to specialize. But what assures people that markets will deliver what they want? The answer to that question leads us to our second principle of how individual choices interact.

Principle #6: Markets Move Toward Equilibrium

It's a busy afternoon at the supermarket; there are long lines at the checkout counters. Then one of the previously closed cash registers opens. What happens? The first thing, of course, is a rush to that register. After a couple of minutes, however, things will have settled down; shoppers will have rearranged themselves so that the line at the newly opened register is about the same length as the lines at all the other registers.

How do we know that? We know from our fourth principle that people will exploit opportunities to make themselves better off. This means that people will rush to the newly opened register in order to save time standing in line. And things will settle down when shoppers can no longer improve their position by switching lines—that is, when the opportunities to make themselves better off have all been exploited.

A story about supermarket checkout lines may seem to have little to do with how individual choices interact, but in fact it illustrates an important principle. A situation in which individuals cannot make themselves better off by doing something different—the situation in which all the checkout lines are the same length—is what economists call an **equilibrium.** An economic situation is in equilibrium when no individual would be better off doing something different.

Recall the story about the mythical Jiffy Lube, where it was supposedly cheaper to leave your car for an oil change than to pay for parking. If the opportunity had really existed and people were still paying $30 to park in garages, the situation would *not* have been an equilibrium. And that should have been a giveaway that the story couldn't be true. In reality, people would have seized an opportunity to park cheaply, just as they seize opportunities to save time at the checkout line. And in so doing they would have eliminated the opportunity! Either it would have become very hard to get an appointment for an oil change or the price of a lube job would have increased to the point that it was no longer an attractive option (unless you really needed an oil change). This brings us to our sixth principle:

> *Because people respond to incentives, markets move toward equilibrium.*

As we will see, markets usually reach equilibrium via changes in prices, which rise or fall until no opportunities for individuals to make themselves better off remain.

The concept of equilibrium is extremely helpful in understanding economic interactions because it provides a way of cutting through the sometimes complex details of those interactions. To understand what happens when a new line is opened at a supermarket, you don't need to worry about exactly how shoppers rearrange themselves, who moves ahead of whom, which register just opened, and so on. What you need to know is that any time there is a change, the situation will move to an equilibrium.

The fact that markets move toward equilibrium is why we can depend on them to work in a predictable way. In fact, we can trust markets to supply us with the essentials of life. For example, people who live in big cities can be sure that the supermarket shelves will always be fully stocked. Why? Because if some merchants who distribute food *didn't* make deliveries, a big profit opportunity would be created for any merchant who did—and there would be a rush to supply food, just like the rush to a newly opened cash register.

So the market ensures that food will always be available for city dwellers. And, returning to our fifth principle, this allows city dwellers to be city dwellers—to specialize in doing city jobs rather than living on farms and growing their own food.

A market economy, as we have seen, allows people to achieve gains from trade. But how do we know how well such an economy is doing? The next principle gives us a standard to use in evaluating an economy's performance.

Witness equilibrium in action on the checkout line.

Principle #7: Resources Should Be Used Efficiently to Achieve Society's Goals

Suppose you are taking a course in which the classroom is too small for the number of students—many people are forced to stand or sit on the floor—despite the fact that large, empty classrooms are available nearby. You would say, correctly, that this is no way to run a college. Economists would call this an *inefficient* use of resources. But if an inefficient use of resources is undesirable, just what does it mean to use resources *efficiently*?

An economic situation is in **equilibrium** when no individual would be better off doing something different.

Construction Photography/Corbis

Sometimes equity trumps efficiency.

You might imagine that the efficient use of resources has something to do with money, maybe that it is measured in dollars-and-cents terms. But in economics, as in life, money is only a means to other ends. The measure that economists really care about is not money but people's happiness or welfare. Economists say that *an economy's resources are used efficiently when they are used in a way that has fully exploited all opportunities to make everyone better off.* To put it another way, an economy is **efficient** if it takes all opportunities to make some people better off without making other people worse off.

In our classroom example, there clearly was a way to make everyone better off—moving the class to a larger room would make people in the class better off without hurting anyone else in the college. Assigning the course to the smaller classroom was an inefficient use of the college's resources, whereas assigning the course to the larger classroom would have been an efficient use of the college's resources.

When an economy is efficient, it is producing the maximum gains from trade possible given the resources available. Why? Because there is no way to rearrange how resources are used so that everyone can be made better off. When an economy is efficient, one person can be made better off by rearranging how resources are used *only* by making someone else worse off.

In our classroom example, if all larger classrooms were already occupied, the college would have been run in an efficient way: your class could be made better off by moving to a larger classroom only by making people in the larger classroom worse off by making them move to a smaller classroom.

We can now state our seventh principle:

> **Resources should be used as efficiently as possible to achieve society's goals.**

Should policy makers always strive to achieve economic efficiency? Well, not quite, because efficiency is only a means to achieving society's goals. Sometimes efficiency may conflict with a goal that society has deemed worthwhile to achieve. For example, in most societies, people also care about issues of fairness, or **equity.** And there is typically a trade-off between equity and efficiency: policies that promote equity often come at a cost of decreased efficiency in the economy, and vice versa.

To see this, consider the case of disabled-designated parking spaces in public parking lots. Many people have difficulty walking due to age or disability, so it seems only fair to assign closer parking spaces specifically for their use. You may have noticed, however, that a certain amount of inefficiency is involved. To make sure that there is always a parking space available should a disabled person want one, there are typically more such spaces available than there are disabled people who want one. As a result, desirable parking spaces are unused. (And the temptation for nondisabled people to use them is so great that we must be dissuaded by fear of getting a ticket.)

So, short of hiring parking valets to allocate spaces, there is a conflict between *equity*, making life "fairer" for disabled people, and *efficiency*, making sure that all opportunities to make people better off have been fully exploited by never letting close-in parking spaces go unused.

Exactly how far policy makers should go in promoting equity over efficiency is a difficult question that goes to the heart of the political process. As such, it is not a question that economists can answer. What is important for economists, however, is always to seek to use the economy's resources as efficiently as possible in the pursuit of society's goals, whatever those goals may be.

An economy is **efficient** if it takes all opportunities to make some people better off without making other people worse off.

Equity means that everyone gets his or her fair share. Since people can disagree about what's "fair," equity isn't as well defined a concept as efficiency.

Principle #8: Markets Usually Lead to Efficiency

No branch of the U.S. government is entrusted with ensuring the general economic efficiency of our market economy—we don't have agents tasked with checking that brain surgeons aren't plowing fields or that Minnesota farmers aren't trying to grow oranges. The government doesn't need to enforce the efficient use of resources, because in most cases the invisible hand does the job.

The incentives built into a market economy ensure that resources are usually put to good use and that opportunities to make people better off are not wasted. If a college were known for its habit of crowding students into small classrooms while large classrooms went unused, it would soon find its enrollment dropping, putting the jobs of its administrators at risk. The "market" for college students would respond in a way that induced administrators to run the college efficiently.

A detailed explanation of why markets are usually very good at making sure that resources are used well will have to wait until we have studied how markets actually work. But the most basic reason is that in a market economy, in which individuals are free to choose what to consume and what to produce, people normally take opportunities for mutual gain—that is, gains from trade.

If there is a way in which some people can be made better off, people will usually be able to take advantage of that opportunity. And that is exactly what defines efficiency: all the opportunities to make some people better off without making other people worse off have been exploited. This gives rise to our eighth principle:

> **Because people usually exploit gains from trade, markets usually lead to efficiency.**

However, there are exceptions to this principle that markets are generally efficient. In cases of *market failure*, the individual pursuit of self-interest found in markets makes society worse off—that is, the market outcome is inefficient. And, as we will see in examining the next principle, when markets fail, government intervention can help. But short of instances of market failure, the general rule is that markets are a remarkably good way of organizing an economy.

Principle #9: When Markets Don't Achieve Efficiency, Government Intervention Can Improve Society's Welfare

Let's recall from the Introduction the nature of the market failure caused by traffic congestion—a commuter driving to work has no incentive to take into account the cost that his or her action inflicts on other drivers in the form of increased traffic congestion.

There are several possible remedies to this situation; examples include charging road tolls, subsidizing the cost of public transportation, and taxing sales of gasoline to individual drivers. All these remedies work by changing the incentives of would-be drivers, motivating them to drive less and use alternative transportation. But they also share another feature: each relies on government intervention in the market. This brings us to our ninth principle:

> **When markets don't achieve efficiency, government intervention can improve society's welfare.**

That is, when markets go wrong, an appropriately designed government policy can sometimes move society closer to an efficient outcome by changing how society's resources are used.

An important part of your education in economics is learning to identify not just when markets work but also when they don't work, and to judge what government policies are appropriate in each situation.

ECONOMICS >> *in Action*
The Fundamental Law of Traffic Congestion

Driving through the middle of Boston used to be a nightmarish experience. The Central Artery—the stretch of Interstate 93 that goes through the heart of the city—was a continuous traffic jam from early morning into evening. What could be done? Boston's answer was the Big Dig, a huge project that involved putting 3½ miles of highway underground, adding a new tunnel to Logan Airport, and building a new bridge over the Charles River.

In building more roads, planners failed to understand the equilibrium outcome: congestion was not reduced because more people chose to drive.

The Big Dig took much longer—15 years—and cost far more—over $20 billion—than anyone had predicted. Still, once it was completed in 2007, the effect was striking: traffic in central Boston flowed much faster than before. This was a big win for commuters, right?

Well, maybe not. A 2008 study by the *Boston Globe* found that while traffic congestion inside Boston was much reduced, traffic had gotten much worse on roads leading into Boston, so that typical commute times probably hadn't decreased much if at all. The explanation, the paper suggested, was that reduced congestion along the Central Artery induced more people to drive into the city, creating congestion in other places, and that this process continued until the overall driving time was back to its original level.

It's a plausible story, because similar results have been seen in many places. Researchers call it the "fundamental law of traffic congestion": if a city builds more roads, this induces more driving, and this increase in traffic continues until a new equilibrium is reached, with commuting times more or less back where they started. And it really does seem to be a law: a statistical analysis published in 2011 found that a 10% increase in the mileage of interstate highways within a metropolitan area leads to a 10.3% increase in the number of vehicle-miles driven, as more trucks take to the roads and commuters move farther out from the city center.

By the way, expanding public transit also has little effect on traffic congestion, for the same reason: any increase in traffic speed simply induces more driving, which pushes commute times back up.

The fundamental law of traffic congestion is a discouraging result for urban planners trying to make commuters' lives easier. It is, however, a good illustration of the importance of thinking about equilibrium.

>> Quick Review

• Most economic situations involve the **interaction** of choices, sometimes with unintended results. In a market economy, interaction occurs via **trade** between individuals.

• Individuals trade because there are **gains from trade**, which arise from **specialization**. Markets usually move toward **equilibrium** because people exploit gains from trade.

• To achieve society's goals, the use of resources should be **efficient**. But **equity**, as well as efficiency, may be desirable in an economy. There is often a trade-off between equity and efficiency.

• Except for certain well-defined exceptions, markets are normally efficient. When markets fail to achieve efficiency, government intervention can improve society's welfare.

>> Check Your Understanding 1-2

Solutions appear at back of book.

1. Explain how each of the following illustrates one of the five principles of interaction.
   a. Using Amazon any student who wants to sell a used textbook for at least $30 is able to sell it to someone who is willing to pay $30.
   b. At a college tutoring co-op, students can arrange to provide tutoring in subjects they are good in (like economics) in return for receiving tutoring in subjects they are poor in (like philosophy).
   c. The local municipality imposes a law that requires bars and nightclubs near residential areas to keep their noise levels below a certain threshold.
   d. To provide better care for low-income patients, the local municipality has decided to close some underutilized neighborhood clinics and shift funds to the main hospital.
   e. On Amazon books of a given title with approximately the same level of wear and tear sell for about the same price.

2. Which of the following describes an equilibrium situation? Which does not? Explain your answer.
   a. The restaurants across the street from the university dining hall serve better-tasting and cheaper meals than those served at the university dining hall. The vast majority of students continue to eat at the dining hall.
   b. You currently take the subway to work. Although taking the bus is cheaper, the ride takes longer. So you are willing to pay the higher subway fare in order to save time.

Economy-Wide Interactions

The economy as a whole has its ups and downs. For example, in 2007 the U.S. economy entered a severe recession in which millions of people lost their jobs, while those who remained employed saw their wages stagnate. It took 7 years—until May 2014—for the number of Americans employed to return to its pre-recession level. However, as of 2016 wages had still not recovered to their pre-recession levels.

To understand recessions and recoveries, we need to understand economy-wide interactions, and understanding the big picture of the economy requires three more economic principles, which are summarized in Table 1-3.

Principle #10: One Person's Spending Is Another Person's Income

Between 2005 and 2011, home construction in America plunged more than 60% because builders found it increasingly hard to make sales. At first the damage was mainly limited to the construction industry. But over time the slump spread into just about every part of the economy, with consumer spending falling across the board.

But why should a fall in home construction mean empty stores in the shopping malls? After all, malls are places where families, not builders, do their shopping.

The answer is that lower spending on construction led to lower incomes throughout the economy; people who had been employed either directly in construction, producing goods and services builders need (like roofing shingles), or in producing goods and services new homeowners need (like new furniture), either lost their jobs or were forced to take pay cuts. And as incomes fell, so did spending by consumers. This example illustrates our tenth principle:

> *One person's spending is another person's income.*

In a market economy, people make a living selling things—including their labor—to other people. If some group in the economy decides, for whatever reason, to spend more, the income of other groups will rise. If some group decides to spend less, the income of other groups will fall.

Because one person's spending is another person's income, a chain reaction of changes in spending behavior tends to have repercussions that spread through the economy. For example, a fall in consumer spending at shopping malls leads to reduced family incomes; families respond by reducing consumer spending; this leads to another round of income cuts; and so on. These repercussions play an important role in our understanding of recessions and recoveries.

Principle #11: Overall Spending Sometimes Gets Out of Line with the Economy's Productive Capacity

Macroeconomics emerged as a separate branch of economics in the 1930s, when a collapse of consumer and business spending, a crisis in the banking industry, and other factors led to a plunge in overall spending. This plunge in spending, in turn, led to a period of very high unemployment known as the Great Depression.

The lesson economists learned from the troubles of the 1930s is that overall spending—the amount of goods and services that consumers and businesses want to buy—sometimes doesn't match the amount of goods and services the economy is capable of producing. In the 1930s, spending fell far short of what was needed to keep American workers employed, and the result was a severe economic slump. In fact, shortfalls in spending are responsible for most, though not all, recessions.

It's also possible for overall spending to be too high. In that case, the economy experiences *inflation*, a rise in prices throughout the economy. This rise in prices occurs because when the amount that people want to buy outstrips the supply,

TABLE 1-3 The Principles of Economy-Wide Interactions
10. One person's spending is another person's income.
11. Overall spending sometimes gets out of line with the economy's productive capacity.
12. Government policies can change spending.

producers can raise their prices and still find willing customers. Taking account of both shortfalls in spending and excesses in spending brings us to our eleventh principle:

> *Overall spending sometimes gets out of line with the economy's productive capacity.*

Principle #12: Government Policies Can Change Spending

Overall spending sometimes gets out of line with the economy's productive capacity. But can anything be done about that? Yes—which leads to our last principle:

> *Government policies can change spending.*

In fact, government policies can dramatically affect spending.

For one thing, the government itself does a lot of spending on everything from military equipment to health care—and it can choose to do more or less. The government can also vary how much it collects from the public in taxes, which in turn affects how much income consumers and businesses have left to spend. And the government's control of the quantity of money in circulation gives it another powerful tool with which to affect total spending. Government spending, taxes, and control of money are the tools of *macroeconomic policy*.

Modern governments deploy these macroeconomic policy tools in an effort to manage overall spending in the economy, trying to steer it between the perils of recession and inflation. These efforts aren't always successful—recessions still happen, and so do periods of inflation. But it's widely believed that aggressive efforts to sustain spending in 2008 and 2009 helped prevent the financial crisis of 2008 from turning into a full-blown depression.

ECONOMICS >> *in Action*
Adventures in Babysitting

The website, myarmyonesource.com, which offers advice to army families, suggested that parents join a babysitting cooperative—an arrangement that is common in many walks of life. In a babysitting cooperative, a number of parents exchange babysitting services rather than hire someone to babysit. But how do these organizations make sure that all members do their fair share of the work?

As myarmyonesource.com explained, "Instead of money, most co-ops exchange tickets or points. When you need a sitter, you call a friend on the list, and you pay them with tickets. You earn tickets by babysitting other children within the co-op." In other words, a babysitting co-op is a miniature economy in which people buy and sell babysitting services. And it happens to be a type of economy that can have macroeconomic problems.

A famous article titled "Monetary Theory and the Great Capitol Hill Babysitting Co-Op Crisis" described the troubles of a babysitting cooperative that issued too few tickets. Bear in mind that, on average, people in a babysitting co-op want to have a reserve of tickets stashed away in case they need to go out several times before they can replenish their stash by doing some more babysitting.

In this case, because there weren't that many tickets out there to begin with, most parents were eager to add to their reserves by babysitting but reluctant to run them down by going out. But one parent's decision to go out was another's chance to babysit, so it became difficult to earn tickets. Knowing this, parents became even more reluctant to use their reserves except on special occasions.

As participants in a babysitting co-op soon discovered, fewer nights out made everyone worse off.

kevinsan/Getty Images

In short, the co-op had fallen into a recession. Recessions in the larger, non-babysitting economy are a bit more complicated than this, but the troubles of the Capitol Hill babysitting co-op demonstrate two of our three principles of economy-wide interactions. One person's spending is another person's income: opportunities to babysit arose only to the extent that other people went out.

An economy can also suffer from too little spending: when not enough people were willing to go out, everyone was frustrated by the lack of babysitting opportunities.

And what about government policies to change spending? Actually, the Capitol Hill co-op did that, too. Eventually, it solved its problem by handing out more tickets, and with increased reserves, people were willing to go out more.

>> Check Your Understanding 1-3

Solutions appear at back of book.

1. Explain how each of the following illustrates one of the three principles of economy-wide interactions.
   a. The White House urged Congress to pass a package of temporary spending increases and tax cuts in early 2009, a time when employment was plunging and unemployment soaring.
   b. With oil prices plummeting, Canadian and U.S. oil companies have been forced to shut down their productive wells. In cities throughout North Dakota, Wyoming, Taxes, and Alaska, restaurants and other consumer businesses are failing.
   c. In the mid-2000s, Spain, which was experiencing a big housing boom, also had the highest inflation rate in Europe.

>> Quick Review

• In a market economy, one person's spending is another person's income. As a result, changes in spending behavior have repercussions that spread through the economy.

• Overall spending sometimes gets out of line with the economy's capacity to produce goods and services. When spending is too low, the result is a recession. When spending is too high, it causes inflation.

• Modern governments use macroeconomic policy tools to affect the overall level of spending in an effort to steer the economy between recession and inflation.

How Priceline Revolutionized the Travel Industry

If you owned shares of the Priceline Group, the online provider of travel-related reservations and search services, in fall 2015, you would have been one happy camper. That is when its price per share hit an all time high of over $1,400, resulting in a company valuation of over $73 billion dollars.

Even more remarkable is the fact that in 2002, the company was in such deep trouble that many doubted it would survive. From 1999 to 2002, Priceline lost 95% of its value, going from a company valuation of $9 billion to a paltry $425 million. What went so right, then so terribly wrong, and then so incredibly right again at Priceline?

When the company (originally Priceline.com) was formed in 1998, investors were immediately impressed by how it revolutionized the travel industry. Its success lay in its ability to spot exploitable opportunities for itself and its customers. The company understood that when a plane departs with empty seats or a hotel has empty beds, there is a cost—the revenue that would have been earned if the seat or bed were filled. Priceline's innovation was to bring airlines and hotels with unsold capacity together with travelers.

It works this way: customers specify the price they are willing to pay for a given trip or hotel, and then Priceline presents them with a list of options from airlines or hotels that are willing to accept that price. Typically, price declines as the trip date nears. Although some travelers like the security of booking their trips well in advance and are willing to pay for that, others are quite happy to wait until the last minute, and risk not getting their first choice flight or hotel in order to benefit from a lower price.

Priceline, then, found a way to make everyone better off—including itself, since it charged a small fee for each trade it facilitated.

Yet, in 2002 the company was at risk of going under. After the terrorist attacks of September 11, 2001, many Americans simply stopped flying. As the economy went into a deep slump, airplanes sat empty on the tarmac and the airlines lost billions of dollars. Several major airlines spiraled toward bankruptcy, and Priceline was losing several million dollars a year.

In order to avert a meltdown of the airline industry, Congress passed a $15 billion aid package that was critical in stabilizing the industry. It was the seed of Priceline's turnaround. The company managed to survive and eventually thrive.

Quick on its feet when it saw its market challenged by newcomers Expedia and Orbitz, it responded aggressively by moving more of its business toward hotel bookings and into Europe, where the online travel industry was still quite small. Its network was particularly valuable in the European hotel market, composed of many more small hotels compared to the U.S. market, which is dominated by nationwide chains. The efforts paid off, and by 2003 Priceline was turning a profit. From 2005 to 2014, Priceline.com expanded by acquiring the travel websites Booking.com, KAYAK, agoda.com, rentalcars.com, and OpenTable, transforming itself into the Priceline Group, with revenue of $10 billion in 2016.

QUESTION FOR THOUGHT

1. Explain how each of the twelve principles of economics is illustrated in this case.

SUMMARY

1. All economic analysis is based on a set of basic principles that apply to three levels of economic activity. First, we study how individuals make choices; second, we study how these choices interact; and third, we study how the economy functions overall.

2. Everyone has to make choices about what to do and what *not* to do. **Individual choice** is the basis of economics—if it doesn't involve choice, it isn't economics.

3. The reason choices must be made is that **resources—** anything that can be used to produce something else—are **scarce.** Individuals are limited in their choices by money and time; economies are limited by their supplies of human and natural resources.

4. Because you must choose among limited alternatives, the true cost of anything is what you must give up to get it—all costs are **opportunity costs.**

5. Many economic decisions involve questions not of "whether" but of "how much"—how much to spend on some good, how much to produce, and so on. Such decisions must be made by performing a **trade-off** *at the margin*—by comparing the costs and benefits of doing a bit more or a bit less. Decisions of this type are called **marginal decisions,** and the study of them, **marginal analysis,** plays a central role in economics.

6. The study of how people *should* make decisions is also a good way to understand actual behavior. Individuals usually respond to **incentives—**exploiting opportunities to make themselves better off.

7. The next level of economic analysis is the study of **interaction—**how my choices depend on your choices, and vice versa. When individuals interact, the end result may be different from what anyone intends.

8. Individuals interact because there are **gains from trade:** by engaging in the **trade** of goods and services with one another, the members of an economy can all be made better off. **Specialization—**each person specializes in the task he or she is good at—is the source of gains from trade.

9. Because individuals usually respond to incentives, markets normally move toward **equilibrium—**a situation in which no individual can make himself or herself better off by taking a different action.

10. An economy is **efficient** if all opportunities to make some people better off without making other people worse off are taken. Resources should be used as efficiently as possible to achieve society's goals. But efficiency is not the sole way to evaluate an economy: **equity,** or fairness, is also desirable, and there is often a trade-off between equity and efficiency.

11. Markets usually lead to efficiency, with some well-defined exceptions.

12. When markets fail and do not achieve efficiency, government intervention can improve society's welfare.

13. Because people in a market economy earn income by selling things, including their own labor, one person's spending is another person's income. As a result, changes in spending behavior can spread throughout the economy.

14. Overall spending in the economy can get out of line with the economy's productive capacity. Spending below the economy's productive capacity leads to a recession; spending in excess of the economy's productive capacity leads to inflation.

15. Governments have the ability to strongly affect overall spending, an ability they use in an effort to steer the economy between recession and inflation.

KEY TERMS

Individual choice, p. 6
Resource, p. 6
Scarce, p. 6
Opportunity cost, p. 7
Trade-off, p. 8

Marginal decisions, p. 8
Marginal analysis, p. 8
Incentive, p. 9
Interaction, p. 11
Trade, p. 11

Gains from trade, p. 11
Specialization, p. 11
Equilibrium, p. 13
Efficient, p. 14
Equity, p. 14

PROBLEMS

interactive activity

1. In each of the following situations, identify which of the twelve principles is at work.

   a. You choose to purchase your textbooks online through Chegg rather than paying a higher price for the same books through your college bookstore.

   b. On your spring break trip, your budget is limited to $35 a day.

   c. Craigslist allows departing students to sell items such as used books, appliances, and furniture rather than give them away as they formerly did.

   d. After a hurricane did extensive damage to homes on the island of St. Crispin, homeowners wanted to purchase many more building materials and hire many more workers than were available on the island. As a result, prices for goods and services rose dramatically across the board.

   e. You buy a used textbook from your roommate. Your roommate uses the money to buy songs from iTunes.

   f. You decide how many cups of coffee to have when studying the night before an exam by considering how much more work you can do by having another cup versus how jittery it will make you feel.

   g. There is limited lab space available to do the project required in Chemistry 101. The lab supervisor assigns lab time to each student based on when that student is able to come.

   h. You realize that you can graduate a semester early by forgoing a semester of study abroad.

   i. At the student center, there is a bulletin board on which people advertise used items for sale, such as bicycles. Once you have adjusted for differences in quality, all the bikes sell for about the same price.

   j. You are better at performing lab experiments, and your lab partner is better at writing lab reports. So the two of you agree that you will do all the experiments and she will write up all the reports.

   k. State governments mandate that it is illegal to drive without passing a driving exam.

   l. Your parents' after-tax income has increased because of a tax cut passed by Congress. They therefore increase your allowance, which you spend on a spring break vacation.

2. Describe some of the opportunity costs when you decide to do the following.

   a. Attend college instead of taking a job

   b. Watch a movie instead of studying for an exam

   c. Ride the bus instead of driving your car

3. Liza needs to buy a textbook for the next economics class. The price at the college bookstore is $65. One website offers it for $55, and another site, for $57. All prices include sales tax. The accompanying table indicates the typical shipping and handling charges for the textbook ordered online.

Shipping method	Delivery time	Charge
Standard shipping	3–7 days	$3.99
Second-day air	2 business days	8.98
Next-day air	1 business day	13.98

   a. What is the opportunity cost of buying online instead of at the bookstore? Note that if you buy the book online, you must wait to get it.

   b. Show the relevant choices for this student. What determines which of these options the student will choose?

4. Use the concept of opportunity cost to explain the following.

   a. More people choose to get graduate degrees when the job market is poor.

   b. More people choose to do their own home repairs when the economy is slow and hourly wages are down.

   c. There are more parks in suburban than in urban areas.

   d. Convenience stores, which have higher prices than supermarkets, cater to busy people.

   e. Fewer students enroll in classes that meet before 10:00 A.M.

5. For the following examples, state how you would use the principle of marginal analysis to make a decision.

   a. Deciding how many days to wait before doing your laundry

   b. Deciding how much time to spend researching before writing your term paper

   c. Deciding how many bags of chips to eat

   d. Deciding how many class lectures to skip

6. This morning you made the following individual choices: you bought a bagel and coffee at the local café, you drove to school in your car during rush hour, and you typed your course notes for your roommate because she was texting in class—in return for which she will do your laundry for a month. For each of these actions, describe how your individual choices interacted with the individual choices made by others. Were other people left better off or worse off by your choices in each case?

7. The Hatfield family lives on the east side of the Hatatoochie River, and the McCoy family lives on the west side. Each family's diet consists of fried chicken and corn-on-the-cob, and each is self-sufficient,

raising their own chickens and growing their own corn. Explain the conditions under which each of the following would be true.

a. The two families are made better off when the Hatfields specialize in raising chickens, the McCoys specialize in growing corn, and the two families trade.

b. The two families are made better off when the McCoys specialize in raising chickens, the Hatfields specialize in growing corn, and the two families trade.

8. Which of the following situations describes an equilibrium? Which does not? If the situation does not describe an equilibrium, what would an equilibrium look like?

a. Many people regularly commute from the suburbs to downtown Pleasantville. Due to traffic congestion, the trip takes 30 minutes via highway but only 15 minutes via side streets.

b. At the intersection of Main and Broadway are two gas stations. One station charges $3.00 per gallon for regular gas and the other charges $2.85 per gallon. Customers can get service immediately at the first station but must wait in a long line at the second.

c. Every student enrolled in Economics 101 must also attend a weekly tutorial. This year there are two sections offered: section A and section B, which meet at the same time in adjoining classrooms and are taught by equally competent instructors. Section A is overcrowded, with people sitting on the floor and often unable to see what is written on the board at the front of the room. Section B has many empty seats.

9. For each of the following, explain whether you think the situation is efficient or not. If it is not efficient, why not? What actions would make it efficient?

a. Electricity is included in the rent at your dorm. Some residents in your dorm leave lights, computers, and appliances on when they are not in their rooms.

b. Although they cost the same amount to prepare, the cafeteria in your dorm consistently provides too many dishes that diners don't like, such as tofu casserole, and too few dishes that diners do like, such as roast turkey with dressing.

c. The enrollment for a particular course exceeds the spaces available. Some students who need to take this course to complete their major are unable to get a space even though others who are taking it as an elective do get a space.

10. Discuss the efficiency and equity implications of each of the following. How would you go about balancing the concerns of equity and efficiency in these areas?

a. The government pays the full tuition for every college student to study whatever subject he or she wishes.

b. When people lose their jobs, the government provides unemployment benefits until they find new ones.

11. Governments often adopt certain policies in order to promote desired behavior among their citizens. For each of the following policies, determine what the incentive is and what behavior the government wishes to promote. In each case, why do you think that the government might wish to change people's behavior, rather than allow their actions to be solely determined by individual choice?

a. A tax of $5 per pack is imposed on cigarettes.

b. The government pays parents $100 when their child is vaccinated for measles.

c. The government pays college students to tutor children from low-income families.

d. The government imposes a tax on the amount of air pollution that a company discharges.

12. In each of the following situations, explain how government intervention could improve society's welfare by changing people's incentives. In what sense is the market going wrong?

a. Pollution from auto emissions has reached unhealthy levels.

b. Everyone in Woodville would be better off if streetlights were installed in the town. But no individual resident is willing to pay for installation of a streetlight in front of his or her house because it is impossible to recoup the cost by charging other residents for the benefit they receive from it.

13. Tim Geithner, a former U.S. Treasury Secretary, has said, "The recession that began in late 2007 was extraordinarily severe. But the actions we took at its height to stimulate the economy helped arrest the free fall, preventing an even deeper collapse and putting the economy on the road to recovery." Which two of the three principles of economy-wide interaction are at work in this statement?

14. A sharp downturn in the U.S. housing market in August 2007 reduced the income of many who worked in the home construction industry. A *Wall Street Journal* news article reported that Walmart's wire-transfer business was likely to suffer because many construction workers are Hispanics who regularly send part of their wages back to relatives in their home countries via Walmart. With this information, use one of the principles of economy-wide interaction to trace a chain of links that explains how reduced spending for U.S. home purchases is likely to affect the performance of the Mexican economy.

15. In October 2015, Hurricane Joaquin caused massive destruction to North and South Carolina, New York, and Florida. Catastrophic flooding occurred, with hundreds of people requiring rescue, 25 killed, and estimated damage of $12 billion. Even those who weren't directly affected by the destruction were hurt because businesses failed or contracted and jobs dried up. Using one of the principles of economy-wide interaction, explain how government intervention can help in this situation.

16. During the Great Depression, food was left to rot in the fields or fields that had once been actively cultivated were left fallow. Use one of the principles of economy-wide interaction to explain why.

Economic Models: Trade-offs and Trade

FROM KITTY HAWK TO DREAMLINER

BOEING'S 787 DREAMLINER was the result of an aerodynamic revolution—a super-efficient airplane designed to cut airline operating costs and the first to use superlight composite materials.

To ensure that the Dreamliner was sufficiently lightweight and aerodynamic, it underwent over 15,000 hours of wind tunnel tests, resulting in subtle design changes that improved its performance, making it

The Wright brothers' model made modern airplanes, including the Dreamliner, possible.

more fuel efficient and less pollutant emitting than existing passenger jets. In fact, some budget airlines such as Norwegian Air (Europe's third largest budget airline) have been offering transatlantic flights at half the price of their rivals, expecting that the super fuel-efficient Dreamliner will shrink fuel costs enough to make their discount strategy profitable.

The first flight of the Dreamliner was a spectacular advance from the 1903 maiden voyage of the Wright Flyer, the first successful powered airplane, in Kitty Hawk, North Carolina. Yet the Boeing engineers—and all aeronautic engineers—owe an enormous debt to the Wright Flyer's inventors, Wilbur and Orville Wright.

What made the Wrights truly visionary was their invention of the wind tunnel, an apparatus that let them experiment with many different designs for wings and control surfaces. Doing experiments with a miniature airplane, inside a wind tunnel the size of a shipping crate, gave the Wright brothers the knowledge that would make heavier-than-air flight possible.

Neither a miniature airplane inside a packing crate nor a miniature model of the Dreamliner inside Boeing's state-of-the-art Transonic Wind Tunnel is the same thing as an actual aircraft in flight. But it is a very useful *model* of a flying plane—a simplified representation of the real thing that can be used to answer crucial questions, such as how much lift a given wing shape will generate at a given airspeed.

Needless to say, testing an airplane design in a wind tunnel is cheaper and safer than building a full-scale version and hoping it will fly. More generally, models play a crucial role in almost all scientific research—economics very much included.

In fact, you could say that economic theory consists mainly of a collection of models, a series of simplified representations of economic reality that allow us to understand a variety of economic issues.

In this chapter, we'll look at two economic models that are crucially important in their own right and illustrate why such models are so useful. We'll conclude with a look at how economists actually use models in their work. ●

WHAT YOU WILL LEARN

- What are economic **models** and why are they so important to economists?
- How do three simple models—the **production possibility frontier, comparative advantage,** and the **circular-flow diagram**—help us understand how modern economies work?
- Why is an understanding of the difference between **positive economics** and **normative economics** important for the real-world application of economic principles?
- Why do economists sometimes disagree?

A **model** is a simplified representation of a real situation that is used to better understand real-life situations.

The **other things equal assumption** means that all other relevant factors remain unchanged.

Models in Economics: Some Important Examples

A **model** is any simplified representation of reality that is used to better understand real-life situations. But how do we create a simplified representation of an economic situation?

One possibility—an economist's equivalent of a wind tunnel—is to find or create a real but simplified economy. Take, for example, an economist who wants to know how an increase in the government-mandated minimum wage would affect the U.S. economy. It would be impossible to do an experiment that involved raising the minimum wage across the country and seeing what happens. Instead, the economist will observe the effects of a smaller economy that is raising its minimum wage (like the city of Seattle did in 2015) and then extrapolate those results to the larger U.S. economy.

Another possibility is to simulate the workings of the economy on a computer. For example, when changes in tax law are proposed, government officials use *tax models*—large mathematical computer programs—to assess how the proposed changes would affect different types of people.

Models are important because their simplicity allows economists to focus on the effects of only one change at a time. That is, they allow us to hold everything else constant and study how one change affects the overall economic outcome.

So an important assumption when building economic models is the **other things equal assumption,** which means that all other relevant factors remain unchanged.

But you can't always find or create a small-scale version of the whole economy, and a computer program is only as good as the data it uses. (Programmers have a saying: "garbage in, garbage out.") For many purposes, the most effective form of economic modeling is the construction of "thought experiments": simplified, hypothetical versions of real-life situations.

In Chapter 1 we illustrated the concept of equilibrium with the example of how customers at a supermarket would rearrange themselves when a new cash register opens. Though we didn't say it, this was an example of a simple model—an imaginary supermarket, in which many details were ignored. (What were customers buying? Never mind.) This simple model can be used to answer a "what if" question: what if another cash register were opened?

FOR INQUIRING MINDS   The Model That Ate the Economy

A model is just a model, right? So how much damage can it do? Economists probably would have answered that question quite differently before the financial meltdown of 2008–2009 than after it. For it was an economic model—a bad economic model, it turns out—that played a significant role in the origins of that severe financial crisis.

The model that is the title for this box originated in finance theory, the branch of economics that seeks to understand what assets like stocks and bonds are worth. Financial theorists often get hired (at very high salaries, mind you) to devise complex mathematical models to help investment companies decide what assets to buy and sell and at what price. Searching for a new

product to sell to investors, Wall Street investment companies created a complex asset whose value was tied to the overall market for American homes. Known as an MBS (for "mortgage-backed security"), the complexity of the asset made it devilishly hard for financial theorists to agree on how it should be priced.

But in 2000, a Wall Street financial theorist announced that he had solved the problem by adopting a huge mathematical simplification, thereby creating a model of how an MBS should be priced. Financial firms loved the model because it opened up a hugely profitable market for them in the selling of billions of dollars in MBSs to investors, and generated billions in profits for themselves. However, some

financial experts warned that the simple model used to price MBSs was just plain wrong. The warnings fell on deaf ears—no doubt because financial firms were making so much money.

In 2008–2009, the problems critics had warned about exploded in catastrophic fashion. Over the previous decade, American home prices had risen to unsustainable heights, and as home prices fell to earth, MBSs fell sharply in value. When investors around the world realized the extent of their losses, the global economy ground to an abrupt halt. People lost their homes, companies went bankrupt, and unemployment surged. It wasn't until five years later, in 2014, that employment in the United States returned to prerecession levels.

As the cash register story showed, it is often possible to describe and analyze a useful economic model in plain English. However, because much of economics involves changes in quantities—in the price of a product, the number of units produced, or the number of workers employed in its production—economists often find that using some mathematics helps clarify an issue. In particular, a numerical example, a simple equation, or—especially—a graph can be key to understanding an economic concept.

Whatever form it takes, a good economic model can be a tremendous aid to understanding. The best way to grasp this point is to consider some simple but important economic models and what they tell us.

- First, we will look at the *production possibility frontier,* a model that helps economists think about the trade-offs every economy faces.
- We then turn to *comparative advantage,* a model that clarifies the principle of gains from trade—trade both between individuals and between countries.
- We will also examine the *circular-flow diagram,* a schematic representation that helps us understand how flows of money, goods, and services are channeled through the economy.

In discussing these models, we make considerable use of graphs to represent mathematical relationships. Graphs play an important role throughout this book. If you are already familiar with how graphs are used, you can skip the appendix to this chapter, which provides a brief introduction to the use of graphs in economics. If not, this would be a good time to turn to it.

Trade-offs: The Production Possibility Frontier

The first principle of economics we introduced is that resources are scarce and that, as a result, any economy—whether it's an isolated group of a few dozen hunter-gatherers or the 6 billion people making up the twenty-first-century global economy—faces trade-offs. No matter how lightweight the Boeing Dreamliner is, no matter how efficient Boeing's assembly line, producing Dreamliners means using resources that therefore can't be used to produce something else.

To think about the trade-offs that face any economy, economists often use the model known as the **production possibility frontier.** The idea behind this model is to improve our understanding of trade-offs by considering a simplified economy that produces only two goods. This simplification enables us to show the trade-off graphically.

Suppose, for a moment, that the United States was a one-company economy, with Boeing its sole employer and aircraft its only product. But there would still be a choice of what kinds of aircraft to produce—say, Dreamliners versus small commuter jets. Figure 2-1 shows a hypothetical production possibility frontier representing the trade-off this one-company economy would face. The frontier—the line in the diagram—shows the maximum quantity of small jets that Boeing can produce per year *given* the quantity of Dreamliners it produces per year, and vice versa. That is, it answers questions of the form, "What is the maximum quantity of small jets that Boeing can produce in a year if it also produces 9 (or 15, or 30) Dreamliners that year?"

There is a crucial distinction between points *inside* or *on* the production possibility frontier (the shaded area) and *outside* the frontier. If a production point lies inside or on the frontier—like point *C*, at which Boeing produces 20 small jets and 9 Dreamliners in a year—it is feasible. After all, the frontier tells us that if Boeing produces 20 small jets, it could also produce a maximum of 15 Dreamliners that year, so it could certainly make 9 Dreamliners.

However, a production point that lies outside the frontier—such as the hypothetical production point *D*, where Boeing produces 40 small jets and

The **production possibility frontier** illustrates the trade-offs facing an economy that produces only two goods. It shows the maximum quantity of one good that can be produced for any given quantity produced of the other.

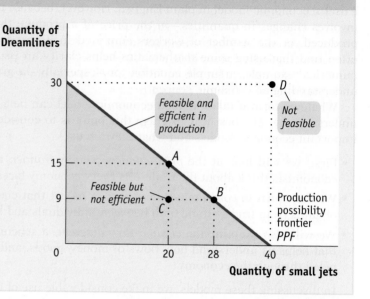

FIGURE 2-1 The Production Possibility Frontier

The production possibility frontier illustrates the trade-offs Boeing faces in producing Dreamliners and small jets. It shows the maximum quantity of one good that can be produced given the quantity of the other good produced. Here, the maximum quantity of Dreamliners manufactured per year depends on the quantity of small jets manufactured that year, and vice versa. Boeing's feasible production is shown by the area *inside* or *on* the curve. Production at point C is feasible but not efficient. Points A and B are feasible and efficient in production, but point D is not feasible.

30 Dreamliners—isn't feasible. Boeing can produce 40 small jets and no Dreamliners, *or* it can produce 30 Dreamliners and no small jets, but it can't do both.

In Figure 2-1 the production possibility frontier intersects the horizontal axis at 40 small jets. This means that if Boeing dedicated all its production capacity to making small jets, it could produce 40 small jets per year but could produce no Dreamliners. The production possibility frontier intersects the vertical axis at 30 Dreamliners. This means that if Boeing dedicated all its production capacity to making Dreamliners, it could produce 30 Dreamliners per year but no small jets.

The figure also shows less extreme trade-offs. For example, if Boeing's managers decide to make 20 small jets this year, they can produce at most 15 Dreamliners; this production choice is illustrated by point A. And if Boeing's managers decide to produce 28 small jets, they can make at most 9 Dreamliners, as shown by point B.

Thinking in terms of a production possibility frontier simplifies the complexities of reality. The real-world U.S. economy produces millions of different goods. Even Boeing can produce more than two different types of planes. Yet it's important to realize that even in its simplicity, this stripped-down model gives us important insights about the real world.

By simplifying reality, the production possibility frontier helps us understand some aspects of the real economy better than we could without the model: efficiency, opportunity cost, and economic growth.

Efficiency First of all, the production possibility frontier is a good way to illustrate the general economic concept of *efficiency*. Recall from Chapter 1 that an economy is efficient if there are no missed opportunities—there is no way to make some people better off without making other people worse off.

One key element of efficiency is that there are no missed opportunities in production—there is no way to produce more of one good without producing less of other goods. As long as Boeing operates on its production possibility frontier, its production is efficient. At point A, 15 Dreamliners are the maximum quantity feasible given that Boeing has also committed to producing 20 small jets; at point B, 9 Dreamliners are the maximum number that can be made given the choice to produce 28 small jets; and so on.

But suppose for some reason that Boeing was operating at point C, making 20 small jets and 9 Dreamliners. In this case, it would not be operating efficiently and would therefore be *inefficient*: it could be producing more of both planes.

Although we have used an example of the production choices of a one-firm, two-good economy to illustrate efficiency and inefficiency, these concepts also carry over to the real economy, which contains many firms and produces many goods. If the economy as a whole could not produce more of any one good without producing less of something else—that is, if it is on its production possibility frontier—then we say that the economy is *efficient in production*.

If, however, the economy could produce more of some things without producing less of others—which typically means that it could produce more of everything—then it is inefficient in production. For example, an economy in which large numbers of workers are involuntarily unemployed is clearly inefficient in production. And that's a bad thing, because the economy could be producing more useful goods and services.

Although the production possibility frontier helps clarify what it means for an economy to be efficient in production, it's important to understand that efficiency in production is only *part* of what's required for the economy as a whole to be efficient. Efficiency also requires that the economy allocate its resources so that consumers are as well off as possible. If an economy does this, we say that it is *efficient in allocation*.

To see why efficiency in allocation is as important as efficiency in production, notice that points *A* and *B* in Figure 2-1 both represent situations in which the economy is efficient in production, because in each case it can't produce more of one good without producing less of the other. But these two situations may not be equally desirable from society's point of view. Suppose that society prefers to have more small jets and fewer Dreamliners than at point *A*; say, it prefers to have 28 small jets and 9 Dreamliners, corresponding to point *B*. In this case, point *A* is inefficient in allocation from the point of view of the economy as a whole because it would rather have Boeing produce at point *B* instead of point *A*.

This example shows that efficiency for the economy as a whole requires *both* efficiency in production and efficiency in allocation: to be efficient, an economy must produce as much of each good as it can given the production of other goods, and it must also produce the mix of goods that people want to consume. And it must also deliver those goods to the right people: an economy that gives small jets to international airlines and Dreamliners to commuter airlines serving small rural airports is inefficient, too.

In the real world, command economies, such as the former Soviet Union, are notorious for inefficiency in allocation. For example, it was common for consumers to find stores well stocked with items few people wanted but lacking such basics as soap and toilet paper.

Opportunity Cost The production possibility frontier is also useful as a reminder of the fundamental point that the true cost of any good isn't the money it costs to buy, but what must be given up in order to get that good—the *opportunity cost*. If, for example, Boeing decides to change its production from point *A* to point *B*, it will produce 8 more small jets but 6 fewer Dreamliners. So the opportunity cost of 8 small jets is 6 Dreamliners—the 6 Dreamliners that must be forgone in order to produce 8 more small jets. This means that each small jet has an opportunity cost of $6/8 = 3/4$ of a Dreamliner.

Is the opportunity cost of an extra small jet in terms of Dreamliners always the same, no matter how many small jets and Dreamliners are currently produced? In the example illustrated by Figure 2-1, the answer is yes. If Boeing increases its production of small jets from 28 to 40, the number of Dreamliners it produces falls from 9 to zero. So Boeing's opportunity cost per additional small jet is $9/12 = 3/4$ of a Dreamliner, the same as it was when Boeing went from 20 small jets produced to 28.

However, the fact that in this example the opportunity cost of a small jet in terms of a Dreamliner is always the same is a result of an assumption we've made, an assumption that's reflected in how Figure 2-1 is drawn. Specifically, whenever we assume that the opportunity cost of an additional unit of a good doesn't change regardless of the output mix, the production possibility frontier is a straight line.

Moreover, as you might have already guessed, the slope of a straight-line production possibility frontier is equal to the opportunity cost—specifically, the opportunity cost for the good measured on the horizontal axis in terms of the good measured on the vertical axis. In Figure 2-1, the production possibility frontier has a *constant slope* of −³/₄, implying that Boeing faces a *constant opportunity cost* for 1 small jet equal to ³/₄ of a Dreamliner. (A review of how to calculate the slope of a straight line is found in this chapter's appendix.) This is the simplest case, but the production possibility frontier model can also be used to examine situations in which opportunity costs change as the mix of output changes.

Figure 2-2 illustrates a different assumption, a case in which Boeing faces *increasing opportunity cost*. Here, the more small jets it produces, the more costly it is to produce yet another small jet in terms of forgone production of a Dreamliner. And the same holds true in reverse: the more Dreamliners Boeing produces, the more costly it is to produce yet another Dreamliner in terms of forgone production of small jets. For example, to go from producing zero small jets to producing 20, Boeing has to forgo producing 5 Dreamliners. That is, the opportunity cost of those 20 small jets is 5 Dreamliners. But to increase its production of small jets to 40—that is, to produce an additional 20 small jets—it must forgo producing 25 more Dreamliners, a much higher opportunity cost. As you can see in Figure 2-2, when opportunity costs are increasing rather than constant, the production possibility frontier is a bowed-out curve rather than a straight line.

Although it's often useful to work with the simple assumption that the production possibility frontier is a straight line, economists believe that in reality opportunity costs are typically increasing. When only a small amount of a good is produced, the opportunity cost of producing that good is relatively low because the economy needs to use only those resources that are especially well suited for its production.

For example, if an economy grows only a small amount of corn, that corn can be grown in places where the soil and climate are perfect for corn-growing but less suitable for growing anything else, like wheat. So growing that corn involves

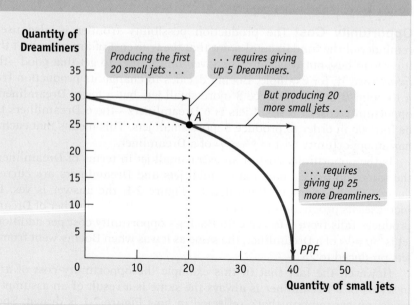

FIGURE 2-2 Increasing Opportunity Cost

The bowed-out shape of the production possibility frontier reflects increasing opportunity cost. In this example, to produce the first 20 small jets, Boeing must forgo producing 5 Dreamliners. But to produce an additional 20 small jets, Boeing must forgo manufacturing 25 more Dreamliners.

giving up only a small amount of potential wheat output. Once the economy grows a lot of corn, however, land that is well suited for wheat but isn't so great for corn must be used to produce corn anyway. As a result, the additional corn production involves sacrificing considerably more wheat production. In other words, as more of a good is produced, its opportunity cost typically rises because well-suited inputs are used up and less adaptable inputs must be used instead.

Economic Growth Finally, the production possibility frontier helps us understand what it means to talk about *economic growth*. In the Introduction, we defined the concept of economic growth as *the growing ability of the economy to produce goods and services.* As we saw, economic growth is one of the fundamental features of the real economy. But are we really justified in saying that the economy has grown over time? After all, although the U.S. economy produces more of many things than it did a century ago, it produces less of other things—for example, horse-drawn carriages. Production of many goods, in other words, is actually down. So how can we say for sure that the economy as a whole has grown?

The answer is illustrated in Figure 2-3, where we have drawn two hypothetical production possibility frontiers for the economy. In them we have assumed once again that everyone in the economy works for Boeing and, consequently, the economy produces only two goods, Dreamliners and small jets. Notice how the two curves are nested, with the one labeled "Original *PPF*" lying completely inside the one labeled "New *PPF*." Now we can see graphically what we mean by economic growth of the economy: economic growth means an *expansion of the economy's production possibilities;* that is, the economy *can* produce more of everything.

For example, if the economy initially produces at point *A* (25 Dreamliners and 20 small jets), economic growth means that the economy could move to point *E* (30 Dreamliners and 25 small jets). *E* lies outside the original frontier; so in the production possibility frontier model, growth is shown as an outward shift of the frontier.

What can lead the production possibility frontier to shift outward? There are basically two sources of economic growth. One is an increase in the economy's **factors of production,** the resources used to produce goods and services. Economists usually use the term *factor of production* to refer to a resource that is not used up in production. For example, in traditional airplane manufacture workers used riveting machines to connect metal sheets when constructing a plane's

Factors of production are resources used to produce goods and services.

FIGURE 2-3 Economic Growth

Economic growth results in an *outward shift* of the production possibility frontier because production possibilities are expanded. The economy can now produce more of everything. For example, if production is initially at point *A* (25 Dreamliners and 20 small jets), economic growth means that the economy could move to point *E* (30 Dreamliners and 25 small jets).

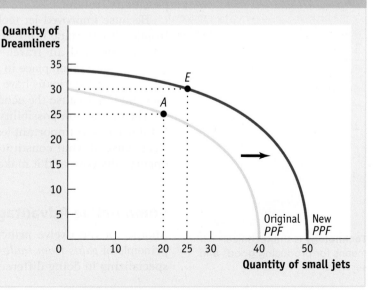

The four factors of production: land, labor, physical capital, and human capital.

fuselage; the workers and the riveters are factors of production, but the rivets and the sheet metal are not. Once a fuselage is made, a worker and riveter can be used to make another fuselage, but the sheet metal and rivets used to make one fuselage cannot be used to make another.

Broadly speaking, the main factors of production are the resources land, labor, physical capital, and human capital. Land is a resource supplied by nature; labor is the economy's pool of workers; physical capital refers to created resources such as machines and buildings; and human capital refers to the educational achievements and skills of the labor force, which enhance its productivity. Of course, each of these is really a category rather than a single factor: land in North Dakota is quite different from land in Florida.

To see how adding to an economy's factors of production leads to economic growth, suppose that Boeing builds another construction hangar that allows it to increase the number of planes—small jets or Dreamliners or both—it can produce in a year. The new construction hangar is a factor of production, a resource Boeing can use to increase its yearly output. We can't say how many more planes of each type Boeing will produce; that's a management decision that will depend on, among other things, customer demand. But we can say that Boeing's production possibility frontier has shifted outward because it can now produce more small jets without reducing the number of Dreamliners it makes, or it can make more Dreamliners without reducing the number of small jets produced.

The other source of economic growth is progress in **technology,** the technical means for the production of goods and services. Composite materials had been used in some parts of aircraft before the Boeing Dreamliner was developed. But Boeing engineers realized that there were large additional advantages to building a whole plane out of composites. The plane would be lighter, stronger, and have better aerodynamics than a plane built in the traditional way. It would therefore have longer range, be able to carry more people, and use less fuel, in addition to being able to maintain higher cabin pressure. So in a real sense Boeing's innovation—a whole plane built out of composites—was a way to do more with any given amount of resources, pushing out the production possibility frontier.

Because improved jet technology has pushed out the production possibility frontier, it has made it possible for the economy to produce more of everything, not just jets and air travel. Over the past 30 years, the biggest technological advances have taken place in information technology, not in construction or food services. Yet Americans have chosen to buy bigger houses and eat out more than they used to because the economy's growth has made it possible to do so.

The production possibility frontier is a very simplified model of an economy. Yet it teaches us important lessons about real-life economies. It gives us our first clear sense of what constitutes economic efficiency, it illustrates the concept of opportunity cost, and it makes clear what economic growth is all about.

Comparative Advantage and Gains from Trade

Technology is the technical means for producing goods and services.

Another of the twelve principles of economics described in Chapter 1 is the principle of *gains from trade*—the mutual gains that individuals can achieve by specializing in doing different things and trading with one another. Our second illustration of an economic model is a particularly useful model of gains from trade—trade based on *comparative advantage*.

One of the most important insights in all of economics is that there are gains from trade—that it makes sense to produce the things you're especially good at producing and to buy from other people the things you aren't as good at producing. This would be true even if you could produce everything for yourself: even if a brilliant brain surgeon *could* repair her own dripping faucet, it's probably a better idea for her to call in a professional plumber.

How can we model the gains from trade? Let's stay with our aircraft example and once again imagine that the United States is a one-company economy where everyone works for Boeing, producing airplanes. Let's now assume, however, that the United States has the ability to trade with Brazil—another one-company economy where everyone works for the Brazilian aircraft company Embraer, which is, in the real world, a successful producer of small commuter jets. (If you fly from one major U.S. city to another, your plane is likely to be a Boeing, but if you fly into a small city, the odds are good that your plane will be an Embraer.)

In our example, the only two goods produced are large jets and small jets. Both countries could produce both kinds of jets. But as we'll see in a moment, they can gain by producing different things and trading with each other. For the purposes of this example, let's return to the simpler case of straight-line production possibility frontiers. America's production possibilities are represented by the production possibility frontier in panel (a) of Figure 2-4, which is similar to the production possibility frontier in Figure 2-1. According to this diagram, the United States can produce 40 small jets if it makes no large jets and can manufacture 30 large jets if it produces no small jets. Recall that this means that the slope of the U.S. production possibility frontier is $-\frac{3}{4}$: its opportunity cost of 1 small jet is $\frac{3}{4}$ of a large jet.

Panel (b) of Figure 2-4 shows Brazil's production possibilities. Like the United States, Brazil's production possibility frontier is a straight line, implying

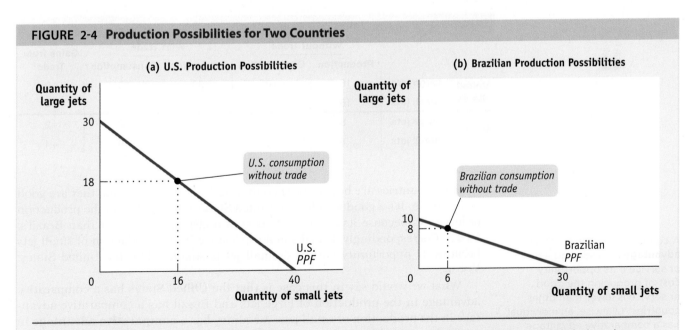

FIGURE 2-4 Production Possibilities for Two Countries

(a) U.S. Production Possibilities

(b) Brazilian Production Possibilities

Here, both the United States and Brazil have a constant opportunity cost of small jets, illustrated by a straight-line production possibility frontier. For the United States, each small jet has an opportunity cost of ¾ of a large jet. Brazil has an opportunity cost of a small jet equal to ⅓ of a large jet.

TABLE 2-1 U.S. and Brazilian Opportunity Costs of Small Jets and Large Jets

	U.S. Opportunity Cost	Brazilian Opportunity Cost
1 small jet	$3/4$ large jet $>$	$1/3$ large jet
1 large jet	$4/3$ small jets $<$	3 small jets

a constant opportunity cost of a small jet in terms of large jets. Brazil's production possibility frontier has a constant slope of $-1/3$. Brazil can't produce as much of anything as the United States can: at most it can produce 30 small jets or 10 large jets. But it is relatively better at manufacturing small jets than the United States; whereas the United States sacrifices $3/4$ of a large jet per small jet produced, for Brazil the opportunity cost of a small jet is only $1/3$ of a large jet. Table 2-1 summarizes the two countries' opportunity costs of small jets and large jets.

Now, the United States and Brazil could each choose to make their own large and small jets, not trading any airplanes and consuming only what each produced within its own country. (A country "consumes" an airplane when it is owned by a domestic resident.) Let's suppose that the two countries start out this way and make the consumption choices shown in Figure 2-4: in the absence of trade, the United States produces and consumes 16 small jets and 18 large jets per year, while Brazil produces and consumes 6 small jets and 8 large jets per year.

But is this the best the two countries can do? No, it isn't. Given that the two producers—and therefore the two countries—have different opportunity costs, the United States and Brazil can strike a deal that makes both of them better off.

Table 2-2 shows how such a deal works: the United States specializes in the production of large jets, manufacturing 30 per year, and sells 10 to Brazil. Meanwhile, Brazil specializes in the production of small jets, producing 30 per year, and sells 20 to the United States. The result is shown in Figure 2-5. The United States now consumes more of both small jets and large jets than before: instead of 16 small jets and 18 large jets, it now consumes 20 small jets and 20 large jets. Brazil also consumes more, going from 6 small jets and 8 large jets to 10 small jets and 10 large jets. As Table 2-2 also shows, both the United States and Brazil reap gains from trade, consuming more of both types of plane than they would have without trade.

TABLE 2-2 How the United States and Brazil Gain from Trade

		Without Trade		With Trade		Gains from Trade
		Production	Consumption	Production	Consumption	
United States	**Large jets**	18	18	30	20	+2
	Small jets	16	16	0	20	+4
Brazil	**Large jets**	8	8	0	10	+2
	Small jets	6	6	30	10	+4

A country has a **comparative advantage** in producing a good or service if its opportunity cost of producing the good or service is lower than other countries'. Likewise, an individual has a comparative advantage in producing a good or service if his or her opportunity cost of producing the good or service is lower than for other people.

Both countries are better off when they each specialize in what they are good at and trade. It's a good idea for the United States to specialize in the production of large jets because its opportunity cost of a large jet is smaller than Brazil's: $4/3 < 3$. Correspondingly, Brazil should specialize in the production of small jets because its opportunity cost of a small jet is smaller than the United States: $1/3 < 3/4$.

What we would say in this case is that the United States has a comparative advantage in the production of large jets and Brazil has a comparative advantage in the production of small jets. A country has a **comparative advantage** in producing something if the opportunity cost of that production is lower for that country than for other countries. The same concept applies to firms and people: a firm or an individual has a comparative advantage in producing something if its, his, or her opportunity cost of production is lower than for others.

FIGURE 2-5   Comparative Advantage and Gains from Trade

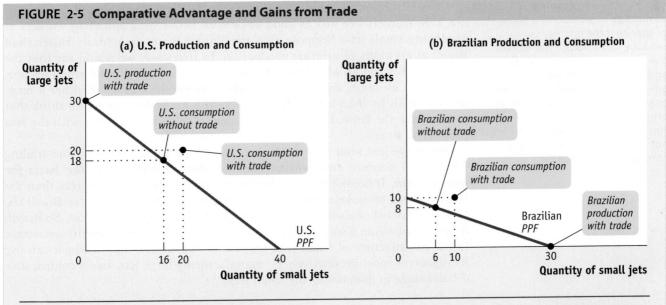

By specializing and trading, the United States and Brazil can produce and consume more of both large jets and small jets. The United States specializes in manufacturing large jets, its comparative advantage, and Brazil—which has an *absolute* disadvantage in both goods but a *comparative* advantage in small jets—specializes in manufacturing small jets. With trade, both countries can consume more of both goods than either could without trade.

One point of clarification before we proceed further. You may have wondered why the United States traded 10 large jets to Brazil in return for 20 small jets. Why not some other deal, like trading 10 large jets for 12 small jets? The answer to that question has two parts. First, there may indeed be other trades that the United States and Brazil might agree to. Second, there are some deals that we can safely rule out—one like 10 large jets for 10 small jets.

To understand why, reexamine Table 2-1 and consider the United States first. Without trading with Brazil, the U.S. opportunity cost of a small jet is ³⁄₄ of a large jet. So it's clear that the United States will not accept any trade that requires it to give up more than ³⁄₄ of a large jet for a small jet. Trading 10 large jets in return for 12 small jets would require the United States to pay an opportunity cost of ¹⁰⁄₁₂ = ⁵⁄₆ of a large jet for a small jet. Because ⁵⁄₆ is greater than ³⁄₄, this is a deal that the United States would reject. Similarly, Brazil won't accept a trade that gives it less than ¹⁄₃ of a large jet for a small jet.

The point to remember is that the United States and Brazil will be willing to trade only if the "price" of the good each country obtains in the trade is less than its own opportunity cost of producing the good domestically. Moreover, this is a general statement that is true whenever two parties—countries, firms, or individuals—trade voluntarily.

While our story clearly simplifies reality, it teaches us some very important lessons that apply to the real economy, too.

First, the model provides a clear illustration of the gains from trade: through specialization and trade, both countries produce more and consume more than if they were self-sufficient.

Second, the model demonstrates a very important point that is often overlooked in real-world arguments: each country has a comparative advantage in producing something. This applies to firms and people as well: *everyone has a comparative advantage in something, and everyone has a comparative disadvantage in something.*

A country has an **absolute advantage** in producing a good or service if the country can produce more output per worker than other countries. Likewise, an individual has an absolute advantage in producing a good or service if he or she is better at producing it than other people. Having an absolute advantage is not the same thing as having a comparative advantage.

Crucially, in our example it doesn't matter if, as is probably the case in real life, U.S. workers are just as good as or even better than Brazilian workers at producing small jets. Suppose that the United States is actually better than Brazil at all kinds of aircraft production. In that case, we would say that the United States has an **absolute advantage** in both large-jet and small-jet production: in an hour, an American worker can produce more of either a large jet or a small jet than a Brazilian worker. You might be tempted to think that in that case the United States has nothing to gain from trading with the less productive Brazil.

But we've just seen that the United States can indeed benefit from trading with Brazil because *comparative, not absolute, advantage is the basis for mutual gain.* It doesn't matter whether it takes Brazil more resources than the United States to make a small jet; what matters for trade is that for Brazil the opportunity cost of a small jet is lower than the U.S. opportunity cost. So Brazil, despite its absolute disadvantage, even in small jets, has a comparative advantage in the manufacture of small jets. Meanwhile the United States, which can use its resources most productively by manufacturing large jets, has a comparative *dis*advantage in manufacturing small jets.

Comparative Advantage and International Trade, in Reality

Look at the label on a manufactured good sold in the United States, and there's a good chance you will find that it was produced in some other country—in China, or Japan, or even in Canada. On the other side, many U.S. industries sell a large fraction of their output overseas. This is particularly true of agriculture, high technology, and entertainment.

Should all this international exchange of goods and services be celebrated, or is it cause for concern? Politicians and the public often question the desirability of international trade, arguing that the nation should produce goods for itself rather than buying them from foreigners. Industries around the world demand protection from foreign competition: Japanese farmers want to keep out American rice, American steelworkers want to keep out European steel. And these demands are often supported by public opinion.

Economists, however, have a very positive view of international trade. Why? Because they view it in terms of comparative advantage. As we learned from our example of U.S. large jets and Brazilian small jets, international trade benefits both countries. Each country can consume more than if it doesn't trade and remains self-sufficient. Moreover, these mutual gains don't depend on each country being better than other countries at producing one kind of good. Even if one country has, say, higher output per worker in both industries—that is, even if one country has an absolute advantage in both industries—there are still gains from trade. The following Global Comparison illustrates just this point.

PITFALLS 🌐

MISUNDERSTANDING COMPARATIVE ADVANTAGE

Students do it, pundits do it, and politicians do it all the time: they confuse *comparative advantage* with *absolute advantage*. For example, back in the 1980s, when the U.S. economy seemed to be lagging behind that of Japan, one often heard commentators warn that if we didn't improve our productivity, we would soon have no comparative advantage in anything.

What those commentators meant was that we would have no *absolute advantage* in anything—that there might come a time when the Japanese were better at everything than we were. (It didn't turn out that way, but that's another story.) And they had the idea that in that case we would no longer be able to benefit from trade with Japan.

But just as Brazil, in our example, was able to benefit from trade with the United States (and vice versa) despite the fact that the United States was better at manufacturing both large and small jets, in real life nations can still gain from trade even if they are less productive in all industries than the countries they trade with.

GLOBAL COMPARISON **PAJAMA REPUBLICS**

A terrible industrial disaster made world headlines in 2013: a building housing five clothing factories in Bangladesh collapsed, killing more than a thousand garment workers trapped inside. Attention soon focused on the substandard working conditions in those factories, as well as the many violations of building codes and safety procedures—including those required by Bangladeshi law—that set the stage for the tragedy.

While the story provoked a justified outcry, it also highlighted the remarkable rise of Bangladesh's clothing industry, which has become a major player in world markets—second only to China in total exports—and a desperately needed source of income and employment in a very poor country.

It's not that Bangladesh has especially high productivity in clothing manufacturing. In fact, recent estimates by the consulting firm McKinsey and Company suggest that it's about a quarter less productive than China. Rather, it has even lower productivity in other industries, giving it a comparative advantage in clothing manufacturing. This is typical in poor countries, which often rely heavily on clothing exports during the early phases of their economic development. An official from one such country once joked, "We are not a banana republic—we are a pajama republic."

The figure plots the per capita income of several such "pajama republics" (the total income of the country divided by the size of the population) against the share of total exports accounted for by clothing; per capita income is measured as a percentage of the U.S.

level in order to give you a sense of just how poor these countries are. As you can see, they are very poor indeed—and the poorer they are, the more they depend on clothing exports.

It's worth pointing out, by the way, that relying on clothing exports is by no means necessarily a bad thing, despite tragedies like the Bangladesh factory disaster. Indeed, Bangladesh, although still desperately poor, is more than twice as rich as it was two decades ago, when it began its dramatic rise as a clothing exporter. (Also see the upcoming Economics in Action on Bangladesh.)

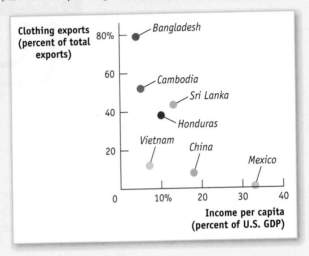

Data from: WTO.

Transactions: The Circular-Flow Diagram

The model economies that we've studied so far—each containing only one firm—are huge simplifications. We've also greatly simplified trade between the United States and Brazil, assuming that they engage only in the simplest of economic transactions, **barter,** in which one party directly trades a good or service for another good or service without using money. In a modern economy, simple barter is rare: usually people trade goods or services for money—pieces of colored paper with no inherent value—and then trade those pieces of colored paper for the goods or services they want. That is, they sell goods or services and buy other goods or services.

And they both sell and buy a lot of different things. The U.S. economy is a vastly complex entity, with more than a hundred million workers employed by millions of companies, producing millions of different goods and services. Yet you can learn some very important things about the economy by considering the simple graphic shown in Figure 2-6, the **circular-flow diagram.** This diagram represents the transactions that take place in an economy by two kinds of flows around a circle: flows of physical things such as goods, services, labor, or raw materials in one direction, and flows of money that pay for these physical things in the opposite direction. In this case the physical flows are shown in blue, the money flows in green.

The simplest circular-flow diagram illustrates an economy that contains only two kinds of inhabitants: **households** and **firms.** A household consists of either an individual or a group of people (usually, but not necessarily, a family) that share their income. A firm is an organization that produces goods and services for sale—and that employs members of households.

Trade takes the form of **barter** when people directly exchange goods or services that they have for goods or services that they want.

The **circular-flow diagram** represents the transactions in an economy by flows around a circle.

A **household** is a person or a group of people that share their income.

A **firm** is an organization that produces goods and services for sale.

FIGURE 2-6 The Circular-Flow Diagram

This diagram represents the flows of money and of goods and services in the economy. In the markets for goods and services, households purchase goods and services from firms, generating a flow of money to the firms and a flow of goods and services to the households. The money flows back to households as firms purchase factors of production from the households in factor markets.

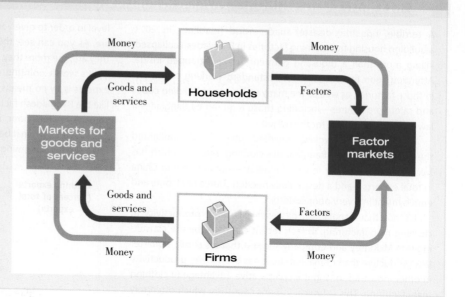

As you can see in Figure 2-6, there are two kinds of markets in this simple economy. On the left side, there are **markets for goods and services** in which households buy the goods and services they want from firms. This produces a flow of goods and services to households and a return flow of money to firms.

On the right side, there are **factor markets** in which firms buy the resources they need to produce goods and services. Recall from earlier that the main factors of production are land, labor, physical capital, and human capital.

The factor market most of us know best is the labor market, in which workers sell their services. In addition, we can think of households as owning and selling the other factors of production to firms. For example, when a firm buys physical capital in the form of machines, the payment ultimately goes to the households that own the machine-making firm. In this case, the transactions occur in the *capital market,* the market in which capital is bought and sold. As we'll examine in detail later, factor markets ultimately determine an economy's **income distribution,** how the total income created in an economy is allocated between less skilled workers, highly skilled workers, and the owners of capital and land.

The circular-flow diagram ignores a number of real-world complications in the interests of simplicity. A few examples:

- In the real world, the distinction between firms and households isn't always that clear-cut. Consider a small, family-run business—a farm, a shop, a small hotel. Is this a firm or a household? A more complete picture would include a separate box for family businesses.

- Many of the sales firms make are not to households but to other firms; for example, steel companies sell mainly to other companies such as auto manufacturers, not to households. A more complete picture would include these flows of goods, services, and money within the business sector.

- The figure doesn't show the government, which in the real world diverts quite a lot of money out of the circular flow in the form of taxes but also injects a lot of money back into the flow in the form of spending.

Figure 2-6, in other words, is by no means a complete picture either of all the types of inhabitants of the real economy or of all the flows of money and physical items that take place among these inhabitants.

Despite its simplicity, the circular-flow diagram is a very useful aid to thinking about the economy.

Firms sell goods and services that they produce to households in **markets for goods and services.**

Firms buy the resources they need to produce goods and services in **factor markets.**

An economy's **income distribution** is the way in which total income is divided among the owners of the various factors of production.

ECONOMICS >> *in Action*

Rich Nation, Poor Nation

Try taking off your clothes—at a suitable time and in a suitable place, of course—and taking a look at the labels inside that say where they were made. It's a very good bet that much, if not most, of your clothes were manufactured overseas, in a country that is much poorer than the United States—say, in El Salvador, Sri Lanka, or Bangladesh.

Why are these countries so much poorer than we are? The immediate reason is that their economies are much less *productive*—firms in these countries are just not able to produce as much from a given quantity of resources as comparable firms in the United States or other wealthy countries. Why countries differ so much in productivity is a deep question—indeed, one of the main questions that preoccupy economists. But in any case, the difference in productivity is a fact.

But if the economies of these countries are so much less productive than ours, how is it that they make so much of our clothing? Why don't we do it for ourselves?

The answer is "comparative advantage." Just about every industry in Bangladesh is much less productive than the corresponding industry in the United States. But the productivity difference between rich and poor countries varies across goods; it is very large in the production of sophisticated goods like aircraft but not that large in the production of simpler goods like clothing. So Bangladesh's position with regard to clothing production is like Embraer's position with respect to producing small jets: it's not as good at it as Boeing, but it's the thing Embraer does comparatively well.

Bangladesh, though it is at an absolute disadvantage compared with the United States in almost everything, has a comparative advantage in clothing production. This means that both the United States and Bangladesh are able to consume more because they specialize in producing different things, with Bangladesh supplying our clothes and the United States supplying Bangladesh with more sophisticated goods.

Although less productive than American workers, Bangladeshi workers have a comparative advantage in clothing production.

>> Check Your Understanding 2-1

Solutions appear at back of book.

1. True or false? Explain your answer.
   a. An increase in the amount of resources available to Boeing for use in producing Dreamliners and small jets does not change its production possibility frontier.
   b. A technological change that allows Boeing to build more small jets for any amount of Dreamliners built results in a change in its production possibility frontier.
   c. The production possibility frontier is useful because it illustrates how much of one good an economy must give up to get more of another good regardless of whether resources are being used efficiently.

2. In Italy, an automobile can be produced by 8 workers in one day and a washing machine by 3 workers in one day. In the United States, an automobile can be produced by 6 workers in one day and a washing machine by 2 workers in one day.
   a. Which country has an absolute advantage in the production of automobiles? In washing machines?
   b. Which country has a comparative advantage in the production of washing machines? In automobiles?
   c. What pattern of specialization results in the greatest gains from trade between the two countries?

>> Quick Review

• Most economic **models** are "thought experiments" or simplified representations of reality that rely on the **other things equal assumption.**

• The **production possibility frontier** model illustrates the concepts of efficiency, opportunity cost, and economic growth.

• Every person and every country has a **comparative advantage** in something, giving rise to gains from trade. Comparative advantage is often confused with **absolute advantage.**

• In the simplest economies people **barter** rather than transact with money. The **circular-flow diagram** illustrates transactions within the economy as flows of goods and services, **factors of production,** and money between **households** and **firms.** These transactions occur in **markets for goods and services** and **factor markets.** Ultimately, factor markets determine the economy's **income distribution.**

3. Using the numbers from Table 2-1, explain why the United States and Brazil are willing to engage in a trade of 10 large jets for 15 small jets.

4. Use the circular-flow diagram to explain how an increase in the amount of money spent by households results in an increase in the number of jobs in the economy. Describe in words what the circular-flow diagram predicts.

‖ Using Models

Economics, we have now learned, is mainly a matter of creating models that draw on a set of basic principles but add some more specific assumptions that allow the modeler to apply those principles to a particular situation. But what do economists actually *do* with their models?

Positive versus Normative Economics

Imagine that you are an economic adviser to the governor of your state. What kinds of questions might the governor ask you to answer?

Well, here are three possible questions:

1. How much revenue will the tolls on the state turnpike yield next year?
2. How much would that revenue increase if the toll were raised from $1 to $1.50?
3. Should the toll be raised, bearing in mind that a toll increase will reduce traffic and air pollution near the road but will impose some financial hardship on frequent commuters?

There is a big difference between the first two questions and the third one. The first two are questions about facts. Your forecast of next year's toll collection will be proved right or wrong when the numbers actually come in. Your estimate of the impact of a change in the toll is a little harder to check—revenue depends on other factors besides the toll, and it may be hard to disentangle the causes of any change in revenue. Still, in principle there is only one right answer.

But the question of whether tolls should be raised may not have a "right" answer—two people who agree on the effects of a higher toll could still disagree about whether raising the toll is a good idea. For example, someone who lives near the turnpike but doesn't commute on it will care a lot about noise and air pollution but not so much about commuting costs. A regular commuter who doesn't live near the turnpike will have the opposite priorities.

This example highlights a key distinction between two roles of economic analysis. Analysis that tries to answer questions about the way the world works, which have definite right and wrong answers, is known as **positive economics.** In contrast, analysis that involves saying how the world *should* work is known as **normative economics.** To put it another way, positive economics is about description; normative economics is about prescription.

Positive economics occupies most of the time and effort of the economics profession. And models play a crucial role in almost all positive economics. As we mentioned earlier, the U.S. government uses a computer model to assess proposed changes in national tax policy, and many state governments have similar models to assess the effects of their own tax policy.

It's worth noting that there is a subtle but important difference between the first and second questions we imagined the governor asking. Question 1 asked for a simple prediction about next year's revenue—a **forecast.** Question 2 was a "what if" question, asking how revenue would change if the tax law were changed. Economists are often called upon to answer both types of questions, but models are especially useful for answering "what if" questions.

The answers to such questions often serve as a guide to policy, but they are still predictions, not prescriptions. That is, they tell you what will happen if a policy were changed; they don't tell you whether or not that result is good.

Positive economics is the branch of economic analysis that describes the way the economy actually works.

Normative economics makes prescriptions about the way the economy should work.

A **forecast** is a simple prediction of the future.

Suppose your economic model tells you that the governor's proposed increase in highway tolls will raise property values in communities near the road but will hurt people who must use the turnpike to get to work. Does that make this proposed toll increase a good idea or a bad one? It depends on whom you ask. As we've just seen, someone who is very concerned with the communities near the road will support the increase, but someone who is very concerned with the welfare of drivers will feel differently. That's a value judgment—it's not a question of economic analysis.

Still, economists often do engage in normative economics and give policy advice. How can they do this when there may be no "right" answer?

One answer is that economists are also citizens, and we all have our opinions. But economic analysis can often be used to show that some policies are clearly better than others, regardless of anyone's opinions.

Suppose that policies A and B achieve the same goal, but policy A makes everyone better off than policy B—or at least makes some people better off without making other people worse off. Then A is clearly more efficient than B. That's not a value judgment: we're talking about how best to achieve a goal, not about the goal itself.

For example, two different policies have been used to help low-income families obtain housing: rent control, which limits the rents landlords are allowed to charge, and rent subsidies, which provide families with additional money to pay rent. Almost all economists agree that subsidies are the more efficient policy. And so the great majority of economists, whatever their personal politics, favor subsidies over rent control.

When policies can be clearly ranked in this way, then economists generally agree. But it is no secret that economists sometimes disagree.

When and Why Economists Disagree

Economists have a reputation for arguing with each other. Where does this reputation come from, and is it justified?

One important answer is that media coverage tends to exaggerate the real differences in views among economists. If nearly all economists agree on an issue—for example, the proposition that rent controls lead to housing shortages—reporters and editors are likely to conclude that it's not a story worth covering, leaving the professional consensus unreported. But an issue on which prominent economists take opposing sides—for example, whether cutting taxes right now would help the economy—makes a news story worth reporting. So you hear much more about the areas of disagreement within economics than you do about the large areas of agreement.

It is also worth remembering that economics is, unavoidably, often tied up in politics. On a number of issues powerful interest groups know what opinions they want to hear; they therefore have an incentive to find and promote economists who profess those opinions, giving these economists a prominence and visibility out of proportion to their support among their colleagues.

While the appearance of disagreement among economists exceeds the reality, it remains true that economists often *do* disagree about important things. For example, some well respected economists argue vehemently that the U.S. government should replace the income tax with a *value-added tax* (a national sales tax, which is the main source of government revenue in many European countries). Other equally respected economists disagree. Why this difference of opinion?

One important source of differences lies in values: as in any diverse group of individuals, reasonable people can differ. In comparison to an income tax, a value-added tax typically falls more heavily on people of modest means. So an economist

"If all the economists in the world were laid end to end, they still couldn't reach a conclusion," goes an economist joke. But do economists really disagree that much? Not according to an ongoing survey. The Booth School of Business at the University of Chicago has assembled a panel of 42 economists, all with exemplary professional reputations, representing a mix of regions, schools, and political affiliations. They are regularly polled on questions of policy or political interest, often ones on which there are bitter divides among politicians or the general public.

Yet the survey shows much more agreement among economists than rumor would have it, even on supposedly controversial topics. For example, 85% of the panel agreed that trade with China makes most Americans better off and nearly the same percentage agreed that Americans who work in the production of competing goods, like clothing, are made worse off by trade with China. Roughly the same

percentage (82%) disagreed with the proposition that rent control increases the supply of quality, affordable housing.

In the first case, the panel overwhelmingly agreed with a position widely considered liberal in American politics, while in the second case they agreed with one widely considered politically conservative.

Disagreements tended to involve untested economic policies. There was, for example, an almost even split over whether new Federal Reserve tactics aimed at boosting the economy would work. Ideology played a limited role in these disagreements: Economists known to be liberals did have slightly different positions, on average, from those known to be conservatives, but the differences weren't nearly as large as those among the general public.

So economists do disagree quite a lot on some issues, especially in macroeconomics. But there is a large area of common ground.

These four economists are on the panel (clockwise from top left): Amy Finkelstein of MIT, Roland Fryer of Harvard, Hilary Hoynes of UC Berkeley, and Raj Chetty of Harvard.

who values a society with more social and income equality for its own sake will tend to oppose a value-added tax. An economist with different values will be less likely to oppose it.

A second important source of differences arises from economic modeling. Because economists base their conclusions on models, which are simplified representations of reality, two economists can legitimately disagree about which simplifications are appropriate—and therefore arrive at different conclusions.

Suppose that the U.S. government were considering introducing a value-added tax. Economist A may rely on a model that focuses on the administrative costs of tax systems—that is, the costs of monitoring, processing papers, collecting the tax, and so on. This economist might then point to the well-known high costs of administering a value-added tax and argue against the change. But economist B may think that the right way to approach the question is to ignore the administrative costs and focus on how the proposed law would change savings behavior. This economist might point to studies suggesting that value-added taxes promote higher consumer saving, a desirable result.

Because the economists have used different models—that is, made different simplifying assumptions—they arrive at different conclusions. And so the two economists may find themselves on different sides of the issue.

ECONOMICS >> *in Action*
Economists: What Are They Good For?

On campus, your interactions with economists may be limited to your instructors. But that's just one example of what professional economists do. Data collection is one of their most important functions and economists have been doing it for nearly six thousand years.

Today, accurate data collection is vitally important for the functioning of governments and businesses. Because virtually every policy decision must take economic effects into consideration, economists are employed to collect data and assist with policy formulation.

The far-reaching impact that government economists can have is illustrated by events in China, which experienced an economic slowdown in 2016. Just how much the Chinese economy had slowed was an important piece of information for policy makers and business leaders around the world to know. Yet some questioned the accuracy of the official Chinese economic statistics, believing that the country had grown faster than the government's ability to collect data. The questions surrounding the Chinese statistics created a lot of uncertainty in forecasts of future global economic activity and may have lead firms to invest less than they would have otherwise.

In the United States, government agencies employ about half of the country's professional economists; this is according to the Bureau of Labor Statistics (BLS), a government agency devoted to gathering economic statistics on workers and employment. Specifically, economists:

- Serve on the Council of Economic Advisers, an agency that advises the president on economic matters.
- Can be found in the Congressional Budget Office (CBO), where they help prepare budget forecasts for Congress, the Department of Commerce, where they analyze economic issues about American business, and the Department of Labor, where they analyze economic issues regarding American workers.
- Dominate the staff of the Federal Reserve, a government agency that controls the economy's money supply and oversees banks.
- Play an important role in two international organizations: the International Monetary Fund (IMF), which provides advice and loans to countries experiencing economic difficulties, and the World Bank, which provides advice and loans to promote long-term economic development.

Many economists are employed by private businesses, including financial and investment firms where they buy and sell assets in financial markets or provide analyses of the future behavior of financial markets.

Trade associations, such as the National Restaurant Association, employ economists to help their members forecast future demand for their products. And consulting firms, such as McKinsey, sell economic analysis and advice to other businesses.

To keep up with professional economists at work, there are many lively websites to visit, including the IMF's at www.imf.org, a business-oriented site like www.economy.com, and economists' blogs, like Mark Thoma's (www.economistsview.typepad.com) or, yes, our own blog, at www.krugman.blogs.nytimes.com.

>> Check Your Understanding 2-2
Solutions appear at back of book.

1. Which of the following is a positive statement? Which is a normative statement?
   a. Society should take measures to prevent people from engaging in dangerous personal behavior.
   b. People who engage in dangerous personal behavior impose higher costs on society through higher medical costs.

2. True or false? Explain your answer.
   a. Policy choice A and policy choice B attempt to achieve the same social goal. Policy choice A, however, results in a much less efficient use of resources than policy choice B. Therefore, economists are more likely to agree on choosing policy choice B.
   b. When two economists disagree on the desirability of a policy, it's typically because one of them has made a mistake.

>> Quick Review

- **Positive economics**—the focus of most economic research—is the analysis of the way the world works, in which there are definite right and wrong answers. It often involves making **forecasts.** But in **normative economics,** which makes prescriptions about how things ought to be, inevitably involves value judgments.

- Economists do disagree—though not as much as legend has it—for two main reasons. One, they may disagree about which simplifications to make in a model. Two, economists may disagree—like everyone else—about values.

Efficiency, Opportunity Cost, and the Logic of Lean Production

Gilles Rolle/REA/Redux Pictures

Boeing is back at the drawing board. In 2015, after releasing the Boeing 777x, an update to the widely popular 777, they announced plans to redevelop their production process. Boeing hoped to extend the extremely successful process known as *lean production* to incorporate robotics and standardize production further, leading to what Boeing calls *advanced manufacturing*.

Lean manufacturing, pioneered by Toyota Motors of Japan, is based on the practice of having parts arrive on the factory floor just as they are needed for production. This reduces the amount of parts Boeing holds in inventory as well as the amount of the factory floor needed for production. To help move from lean production to advanced manufacturing Boeing has turned to Toyota, hiring some of their top engineers.

Boeing first adopted lean manufacturing in 1999 in the manufacture of the 737, the most popular commercial airplane. By 2005, after constant refinement, it achieved a 50% reduction in the time it takes to produce a plane and a nearly 60% reduction in parts inventory. An important feature is a continuously moving assembly line, moving products from one assembly team to the next at a steady pace and eliminating the need for workers to wander across the factory floor from task to task or in search of tools and parts.

Toyota's lean production techniques have been the most widely adopted, revolutionizing manufacturing worldwide. In simple terms, lean production is focused on organization and communication. Workers and parts are organized so as to ensure a smooth and consistent workflow that minimizes wasted effort and materials. Lean production is also designed to be highly responsive to changes in the desired mix of output—for example, quickly producing more sedans and fewer minivans according to changes in customer demand.

Toyota's methods were so successful that they transformed the global auto industry and severely threatened once-dominant American automakers. Until the 1980s, the "Big Three"—Chrysler, Ford, and General Motors—dominated the American auto industry, with virtually no foreign-made cars sold in the United States. In the 1980s, however, Toyotas became increasingly popular due to their high quality and relatively low price—so popular that the Big Three eventually prevailed upon the U.S. government to protect them by restricting the sale of Japanese autos in the U.S. Over time, Toyota responded by building assembly plants in the United States, bringing along its lean production techniques, which then spread throughout American manufacturing.

QUESTIONS FOR THOUGHT

1. What is the opportunity cost associated with having a worker wander across the factory floor from task to task or in search of tools and parts?

2. Explain how lean manufacturing improves the economy's efficiency in allocation.

3. Before lean manufacturing innovations, Japan mostly sold consumer electronics to the United States. How did lean manufacturing innovations alter Japan's comparative advantage vis-à-vis the United States?

4. How do you think the shift in the location of Toyota's production from Japan to the United States has altered the pattern of comparative advantage in automaking between the two countries?

SUMMARY

1. Almost all economics is based on **models,** "thought experiments" or simplified versions of reality, many of which use mathematical tools such as graphs. An important assumption in economic models is the **other things equal assumption,** which allows analysis of the effect of a change in one factor by holding all other relevant factors unchanged.

2. One important economic model is the **production possibility frontier.** It illustrates *opportunity cost* (showing how much less of one good can be produced if more of the other good is produced); *efficiency* (an economy is efficient in production if it produces on the production possibility frontier and efficient in allocation if it produces the mix of goods and services that people want to consume); and *economic growth* (an outward shift of the production possibility frontier). There are two basic sources of growth: an increase in **factors of production**—resources such as land, labor, capital, and human capital, inputs that are not used up in production—and improved **technology.**

3. Another important model is **comparative advantage,** which explains the source of gains from trade between individuals and countries. Everyone has a comparative advantage in something—some good or service in which that person has a lower opportunity cost than everyone else. But it is often confused with **absolute advantage,** an ability to produce a particular good or service better than anyone else. This confusion leads some to erroneously conclude that there are no gains from trade between people or countries.

4. In the simplest economies people **barter**—trade goods and services for one another—rather than trade them for money, as in a modern economy. The **circular-flow diagram** represents transactions within the economy as flows of goods, services, and money between **households** and **firms.** These transactions occur in **markets for goods and services** and **factor markets,** markets for factors of production—land, labor, physical capital, and human capital. It is useful in understanding how spending, production, employment, income, and growth are related in the economy. Ultimately, factor markets determine the economy's **income distribution,** how an economy's total income is allocated to the owners of the factors of production.

5. Economists use economic models for both **positive economics,** which describes how the economy works, and for **normative economics,** which prescribes how the economy *should* work. Positive economics often involves making **forecasts.** Economists can determine correct answers for positive questions but typically not for normative questions, which involve value judgments. The exceptions are when policies designed to achieve a certain objective can be clearly ranked in terms of efficiency.

6. There are two main reasons economists disagree. One, they may disagree about which simplifications to make in a model. Two, economists may disagree—like everyone else—about values.

KEY TERMS

Model, p. 26
Other things equal assumption, p. 26
Production possibility frontier, p. 27
Factors of production, p. 31
Technology, p. 32
Comparative advantage, p. 34

Absolute advantage, p. 36
Barter, p. 37
Circular-flow diagram, p. 37
Household, p. 37
Firm, p. 37
Markets for goods and services, p. 38

Factor markets, p. 38
Income distribution, p. 38
Positive economics, p. 40
Normative economics, p. 40
Forecast, p. 40

interactive activity

PROBLEMS

1. Two important industries on the island of Bermuda are fishing and tourism. According to data from the Food and Agriculture Organization of the United Nations and the Bermuda Department of Statistics, in 2014 the 315 registered fishermen in Bermuda caught 497 metric tons of marine fish. And the 2,446 people employed by hotels produced 580,209 hotel stays (measured by the number of visitor arrivals). Suppose that this production point is efficient in production. Assume also that the opportunity cost of 1 additional metric ton of fish is 2,000 hotel stays and that this opportunity cost is constant (the opportunity cost does not change).

   a. If all 315 registered fishermen were to be employed by hotels (in addition to the 2,446 people already working in hotels), how many hotel stays could Bermuda produce?

   b. If all 2,446 hotel employees were to become fishermen (in addition to the 315 fishermen already working in the fishing industry), how many metric tons of fish could Bermuda produce?

c. Draw a production possibility frontier for Bermuda, with fish on the horizontal axis and hotel stays on the vertical axis, and label Bermuda's actual production point for the year 2014.

2. According to data from the U.S. Department of Agriculture's National Agricultural Statistics Service, 124 million acres of land in the United States were used for wheat or corn farming in a recent year. Of those 124 million acres, farmers used 50 million acres to grow 2.158 billion bushels of wheat and 74 million acres to grow 11.807 billion bushels of corn. Suppose that U.S. wheat and corn farming is efficient in production. At that production point, the opportunity cost of producing 1 additional bushel of wheat is 1.7 fewer bushels of corn. However, because farmers have increasing opportunity costs, additional bushels of wheat have an opportunity cost greater than 1.7 bushels of corn. For each of the following production points, decide whether that production point is (i) feasible and efficient in production, (ii) feasible but not efficient in production, (iii) not feasible, or (iv) unclear as to whether or not it is feasible.

a. Farmers use 40 million acres of land to produce 1.8 billion bushels of wheat, and they use 60 million acres of land to produce 9 billion bushels of corn. The remaining 24 million acres are left unused.

b. From their original production point, farmers transfer 40 million acres of land from corn to wheat production. They now produce 3.158 billion bushels of wheat and 10.107 bushels of corn.

c. Farmers reduce their production of wheat to 2 billion bushels and increase their production of corn to 12.044 billion bushels. Along the production possibility frontier, the opportunity cost of going from 11.807 billion bushels of corn to 12.044 billion bushels of corn is 0.666 bushel of wheat per bushel of corn.

3. In the ancient country of Roma, only two goods, spaghetti and meatballs, are produced. There are two tribes in Roma, the Tivoli and the Frivoli. By themselves, the Tivoli each month can produce either 30 pounds of spaghetti and no meatballs, or 50 pounds of meatballs and no spaghetti, or any combination in between. The Frivoli, by themselves, each month can produce 40 pounds of spaghetti and no meatballs, or 30 pounds of meatballs and no spaghetti, or any combination in between.

a. Assume that all production possibility frontiers are straight lines. Draw one diagram showing the monthly production possibility frontier for the Tivoli and another showing the monthly production possibility frontier for the Frivoli. Show how you calculated them.

b. Which tribe has the comparative advantage in spaghetti production? In meatball production?

In A.D. 100 the Frivoli discover a new technique for making meatballs that doubles the quantity of meatballs they can produce each month.

c. Draw the new monthly production possibility frontier for the Frivoli.

d. After the innovation, which tribe now has an absolute advantage in producing meatballs? In producing spaghetti? Which has the comparative advantage in meatball production? In spaghetti production?

4. One July, the United States sold aircraft worth $1 billion to China and bought aircraft worth only $19,000 from China. During the same month, however, the United States bought $83 million worth of men's trousers, slacks, and jeans from China but sold only $8,000 worth of trousers, slacks, and jeans to China. Using what you have learned about how trade is determined by comparative advantage, answer the following questions.

a. Which country has the comparative advantage in aircraft production? In production of trousers, slacks, and jeans?

b. Can you determine which country has the absolute advantage in aircraft production? In production of trousers, slacks, and jeans?

5. Peter Pundit, an economics reporter, states that the European Union (EU) is increasing its productivity very rapidly in all industries. He claims that this productivity advance is so rapid that output from the EU in these industries will soon exceed that of the United States and, as a result, the United States will no longer benefit from trade with the EU.

a. Do you think Peter Pundit is correct or not? If not, what do you think is the source of his mistake?

b. If the EU and the United States continue to trade, what do you think will characterize the goods that the EU sells to the United States and the goods that the United States sells to the EU?

6. You are in charge of allocating residents to your dormitory's baseball and basketball teams. You are down to the last four people, two of whom must be allocated to baseball and two to basketball. The accompanying table gives each person's batting average and free-throw average.

Name	Batting average	Free-throw average
Kelley	70%	60%
Jackie	50%	50%
Curt	10%	30%
Gerry	80%	70%

a. Explain how you would use the concept of comparative advantage to allocate the players. Begin by establishing each player's opportunity cost of free throws in terms of batting average.

b. Why is it likely that the other basketball players will be unhappy about this arrangement but the other baseball players will be satisfied? Nonetheless, why would an economist say that this is an efficient way to allocate players for your dormitory's sports teams?

7. The inhabitants of the fictional economy of Atlantis use money in the form of cowry shells. Draw a circular-flow diagram showing households and firms. Firms produce potatoes and fish, and households buy potatoes and fish. Households also provide the land and labor to firms. Identify where in the flows of cowry shells or physical things (goods and services, or resources) each of the following impacts would occur. Describe how this impact spreads around the circle.

   a. A devastating hurricane floods many of the potato fields.

   b. A very productive fishing season yields a very large number of fish caught.

   c. The inhabitants of Atlantis discover Shakira and spend several days a month at dancing festivals.

8. An economist might say that colleges and universities "produce" education, using faculty members and students as inputs. According to this line of reasoning, education is then "consumed" by households. Construct a circular-flow diagram to represent the sector of the economy devoted to college education: colleges and universities represent firms, and households both consume education and provide faculty and students to universities. What are the relevant markets in this diagram? What is being bought and sold in each direction? What would happen in the diagram if the government decided to subsidize 50% of all college students' tuition?

9. Your dormitory roommate plays loud music most of the time; you, however, would prefer more peace and quiet. You suggest that she buy some headphones. She responds that although she would be happy to use headphones, she has many other things that she would prefer to spend her money on right now. You discuss this situation with a friend who is an economics major. The following exchange takes place:

   He: How much would it cost to buy headphones?

   You: $15.

   He: How much do you value having some peace and quiet for the rest of the semester?

   You: $30.

   He: It is efficient for you to buy the headphones and give them to your roommate. You gain more than you lose; the benefit exceeds the cost. You should do that.

   You: It just isn't fair that I have to pay for the headphones when I'm not the one making the noise.

   a. Which parts of this conversation contain positive statements and which parts contain normative statements?

   b. Construct an argument supporting your viewpoint that your roommate should be the one to change her behavior. Similarly, construct an argument from the viewpoint of your roommate that you should be the one to buy the headphones. If your dormitory has a policy that gives residents the unlimited right to play music, whose argument is likely to win? If your dormitory has a rule that a person must stop playing music whenever a roommate complains, whose argument is likely to win?

10. A representative of the American clothing industry recently made the following statement: "Workers in Asia often work in sweatshop conditions earning only pennies an hour. American workers are more productive and as a result earn higher wages. In order to preserve the dignity of the American workplace, the government should enact legislation banning imports of low-wage Asian clothing."

   a. Which parts of this quote are positive statements? Which parts are normative statements?

   b. Is the policy that is being advocated consistent with the preceding statements about the wages and productivities of American and Asian workers?

   c. Would such a policy make some Americans better off without making any other Americans worse off? That is, would this policy be efficient from the viewpoint of all Americans?

   d. Would low-wage Asian workers benefit from or be hurt by such a policy?

11. Are the following statements true or false? Explain your answers.

   a. "When people must pay higher taxes on their wage earnings, it reduces their incentive to work" is a positive statement.

   b. "We should lower taxes to encourage more work" is a positive statement.

   c. Economics cannot always be used to completely decide what society ought to do.

   d. "The system of public education in this country generates greater benefits to society than the cost of running the system" is a normative statement.

   e. All disagreements among economists are generated by the media.

12. Evaluate the following statement: "It is easier to build an economic model that accurately reflects events that have already occurred than to build an economic model to forecast future events." Do you think this is true or not? Why? What does this imply about the difficulties of building good economic models?

13. Economists who work for the government are often called on to make policy recommendations. Why do you think it is important for the public to be able to differentiate normative statements from positive statements in these recommendations?

14. The mayor of Gotham City, worried about a potential epidemic of deadly influenza this winter, asks an economic adviser the following series of questions. Determine whether a question requires the economic adviser to make a positive assessment or a normative assessment.

   a. How much vaccine will be in stock in the city by the end of November?

   b. If we offer to pay 10% more per dose to the pharmaceutical companies providing the vaccines, will they provide additional doses?

c. If there is a shortage of vaccine in the city, whom should we vaccinate first—the elderly or the very young? (Assume that a person from one group has an equal likelihood of dying from influenza as a person from the other group.)

d. If the city charges $25 per shot, how many people will pay?

e. If the city charges $25 per shot, it will make a profit of $10 per shot, money that can go to pay for inoculating poor people. Should the city engage in such a scheme?

15. Assess the accuracy of the following statement: "If economists just had enough data, they could solve all policy questions in a way that maximizes the social good. There would be no need for divisive political debates, such as whether the government should provide free medical care for all." Frame your answer using the concepts of positive and normative economics.

WORK IT OUT Interactive step-by-step help with solving this problem can be found online.

---

16. Atlantis is a small, isolated island in the South Atlantic. The inhabitants grow potatoes and catch fish. The accompanying table shows the maximum annual output combinations of potatoes and fish that can be produced. Obviously, given their limited resources and available technology, as they use more of their resources for potato production, there are fewer resources available for catching fish.

Maximum annual output options	Quantity of potatoes (pounds)	Quantity of fish (pounds)
A	1,000	0
B	800	300
C	600	500
D	400	600
E	200	650
F	0	675

a. Draw a production possibility frontier with potatoes on the horizontal axis and fish on the vertical axis illustrating these options, showing points A–F.

b. Can Atlantis produce 500 pounds of fish and 800 pounds of potatoes? Explain. Where would this point lie relative to the production possibility frontier?

c. What is the opportunity cost of increasing the annual output of potatoes from 600 to 800 pounds?

d. What is the opportunity cost of increasing the annual output of potatoes from 200 to 400 pounds?

e. Can you explain why the answers to parts c and d are not the same? What does this imply about the slope of the production possibility frontier?

Graphs in Economics

Getting the Picture

Whether you're reading about economics in the *Wall Street Journal* or in your economics textbook, you will see many graphs. Visual images can make it much easier to understand verbal descriptions, numerical information, or ideas. In economics, graphs are the type of visual image used to facilitate understanding. To fully understand the ideas and information being discussed, you need to be familiar with how to interpret and construct these visual aids. This appendix explains how to do this.

Graphs, Variables, and Economic Models

One reason to attend college is that a bachelor's degree provides access to higher-paying jobs. Additional degrees, such as MBAs or law degrees, increase earnings even more. If you were to read an article about the relationship between educational attainment and income, you would probably see a graph showing the income levels for workers with different amounts of education. And this graph would depict the idea that, in general, more education increases income.

This graph, like most of those in economics, would depict the relationship between two economic variables. A **variable** is a quantity that can take on more than one value, such as the number of years of education a person has, the price of a can of soda, or a household's income.

As you learned in this chapter, economic analysis relies heavily on *models*, simplified descriptions of real situations. Most economic models describe the relationship between two variables, simplified by holding constant other variables that may affect the relationship.

For example, an economic model might describe the relationship between the price of a can of soda and the number of cans of soda that consumers will buy, assuming that everything else affecting consumers' purchases of soda stays constant. This type of model can be described mathematically or verbally, but illustrating the relationship in a graph makes it easier to understand, as you'll see next.

How Graphs Work

Most graphs in economics are based on a grid built around two perpendicular lines that show the values of two variables, helping you visualize the relationship between them. So a first step in understanding the use of such graphs is to see how this system works.

Two-Variable Graphs

Figure 2A-1 shows a typical two-variable graph. It illustrates the data in the accompanying table on outside temperature and the number of sodas a typical vendor can expect to sell at a baseball stadium during one game. The first column shows the values of outside temperature (the first variable) and the second column shows the values of the number of sodas sold (the second variable). Five combinations or pairs of the two variables are shown, each denoted by *A* through *E* in the third column.

Now let's turn to graphing the data in this table. In any two-variable graph, one variable is called the *x*-variable and the other is called the *y*-variable. Here

A quantity that can take on more than one value is called a **variable.**

FIGURE 2A-1 Plotting Points on a Two-Variable Graph

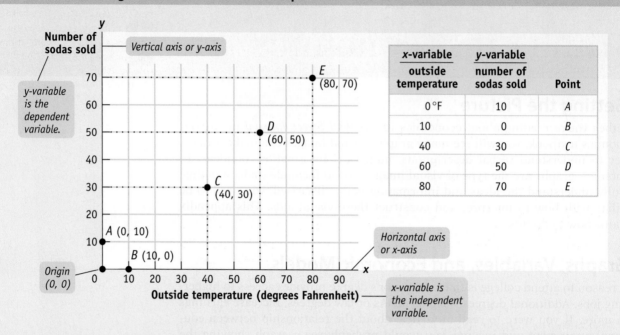

x-variable outside temperature	y-variable number of sodas sold	Point
0 °F	10	A
10	0	B
40	30	C
60	50	D
80	70	E

The data from the table are plotted where outside temperature (the independent variable) is measured along the horizontal axis and number of sodas sold (the dependent variable) is measured along the vertical axis. Each of the five combinations of temperature and sodas sold is represented by a point: *A, B, C, D,* and *E*. Each point in the graph is identified by a pair of values. For example, point *C* corresponds to the pair (40, 30)—an outside temperature of 40°F (the value of the *x*-variable) and 30 sodas sold (the value of the *y*-variable).

> The line along which values of the *x*-variable are measured is called the **horizontal axis** or ***x*-axis.** The line along which values of the *y*-variable are measured is called the **vertical axis** or ***y*-axis.** The point where the axes of a two-variable graph meet is the **origin.**
>
> A **causal relationship** exists between two variables when the value taken by one variable directly influences or determines the value taken by the other variable. In a causal relationship, the determining variable is called the **independent variable;** the variable it determines is called the **dependent variable.**

we have made outside temperature the *x*-variable and number of sodas sold the *y*-variable. The solid horizontal line in the graph is called the **horizontal axis** or ***x*-axis,** and values of the *x*-variable—outside temperature—are measured along it. Similarly, the solid vertical line in the graph is called the **vertical axis** or ***y*-axis,** and values of the *y*-variable—number of sodas sold—are measured along it.

At the **origin,** the point where the two axes meet, each variable is equal to zero. As you move rightward from the origin along the *x*-axis, values of the *x*-variable are positive and increasing. As you move up from the origin along the *y*-axis, values of the *y*-variable are positive and increasing.

You can plot each of the five points *A* through *E* on this graph by using a pair of numbers—the values that the *x*-variable and the *y*-variable take on for a given point. In Figure 2A-1, at point *C*, the *x*-variable takes on the value 40 and the *y*-variable takes on the value 30. You plot point *C* by drawing a line straight up from 40 on the *x*-axis and a horizontal line across from 30 on the *y*-axis. We write point *C* as (40, 30). We write the origin as (0, 0).

Looking at point *A* and point *B* in Figure 2A-1, you can see that when one of the variables for a point has a value of zero, it will lie on one of the axes. If the value of the *x*-variable is zero, the point will lie on the vertical axis, like point *A*. If the value of the *y*-variable is zero, the point will lie on the horizontal axis, like point *B*.

Most graphs that depict relationships between two economic variables represent a **causal relationship,** a relationship in which the value taken by one variable directly influences or determines the value taken by the other variable. In a causal relationship, the determining variable is called the **independent variable;** the variable it determines is called the **dependent variable.** In our example of soda sales, the outside temperature is the independent variable. It directly influences the number of sodas that are sold, the dependent variable in this case.

By convention, we put the independent variable on the horizontal axis and the dependent variable on the vertical axis. Figure 2A-1 is constructed consistent with this convention; the independent variable (outside temperature) is on the horizontal axis and the dependent variable (number of sodas sold) is on the vertical axis.

An important exception to this convention is in graphs showing the economic relationship between the price of a product and quantity of the product: although price is generally the independent variable that determines quantity, it is always measured on the vertical axis.

> A **curve** is a line on a graph that depicts a relationship between two variables. It may be either a straight line or a curved line. If the curve is a straight line, the variables have a **linear relationship.** If the curve is not a straight line, the variables have a **nonlinear relationship.**

Curves on a Graph

Panel (a) of Figure 2A-2 contains some of the same information as Figure 2A-1, with a line drawn through the points *B, C, D,* and *E.* Such a line on a graph is called a **curve,** regardless of whether it is a straight line or a curved line. If the curve that shows the relationship between two variables is a straight line, or linear, the variables have a **linear relationship.** When the curve is not a straight line, or nonlinear, the variables have a **nonlinear relationship.**

A point on a curve indicates the value of the *y*-variable for a specific value of the *x*-variable. For example, point *D* indicates that at a temperature of 60°F, a vendor can expect to sell 50 sodas. The shape and orientation of a curve reveal the

---

FIGURE 2A-2 Drawing Curves

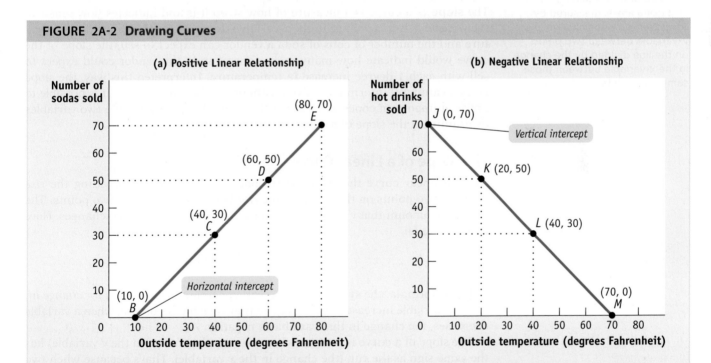

The curve in panel (a) illustrates the relationship between the two variables, outside temperature and number of sodas sold. The two variables have a positive linear relationship: positive because the curve has an upward tilt, and linear because it is a straight line. It implies that an increase in the *x*-variable (outside temperature) leads to an increase in the *y*-variable (number of sodas sold). The curve in panel (b) is also a straight line, but it tilts downward. The two variables here, outside temperature and number of hot drinks sold, have a negative linear relationship: an increase in the *x*-variable (outside temperature) leads to a decrease in the *y*-variable (number of hot drinks sold). The curve in panel (a) has a horizontal intercept at point *B,* where it hits the horizontal axis. The curve in panel (b) has a vertical intercept at point *J,* where it hits the vertical axis, and a horizontal intercept at point *M,* where it hits the horizontal axis.

Two variables have a **positive relationship** when an increase in the value of one variable is associated with an increase in the value of the other variable. It is illustrated by a curve that slopes upward from left to right.

Two variables have a **negative relationship** when an increase in the value of one variable is associated with a decrease in the value of the other variable. It is illustrated by a curve that slopes downward from left to right.

The **horizontal intercept** of a curve is the point at which it hits the horizontal axis; it indicates the value of the *x*-variable when the value of the *y*-variable is zero.

The **vertical intercept** of a curve is the point at which it hits the vertical axis; it shows the value of the *y*-variable when the value of the *x*-variable is zero.

The **slope** of a line or curve is a measure of how steep it is. The slope of a line is measured by "rise over run"—the change in the *y*-variable between two points on the line divided by the change in the *x*-variable between those same two points.

general nature of the relationship between the two variables. The upward tilt of the curve in panel (a) of Figure 2A-2 means that vendors can expect to sell more sodas at higher outside temperatures.

When variables are related this way—that is, when an increase in one variable is associated with an increase in the other variable—the variables are said to have a **positive relationship.** It is illustrated by a curve that slopes upward from left to right. Because this curve is also linear, the relationship between outside temperature and number of sodas sold illustrated by the curve in panel (a) of Figure 2A-2 is a positive linear relationship.

When an increase in one variable is associated with a decrease in the other variable, the two variables are said to have a **negative relationship.** It is illustrated by a curve that slopes downward from left to right, like the curve in panel (b) of Figure 2A-2. Because this curve is also linear, the relationship it depicts is a negative linear relationship. Two variables that might have such a relationship are the outside temperature and the number of hot drinks a vendor can expect to sell at a baseball stadium.

Return for a moment to the curve in panel (a) of Figure 2A-2 and you can see that it hits the horizontal axis at point *B*. This point, known as the **horizontal intercept,** shows the value of the *x*-variable when the value of the *y*-variable is zero. In panel (b) of Figure 2A-2, the curve hits the vertical axis at point *J*. This point, called the **vertical intercept,** indicates the value of the *y*-variable when the value of the *x*-variable is zero.

‖ A Key Concept: The Slope of a Curve

The **slope** of a curve is a measure of how steep it is and indicates how sensitive the *y*-variable is to a change in the *x*-variable. In our example of outside temperature and the number of cans of soda a vendor can expect to sell, the slope of the curve would indicate how many more cans of soda the vendor could expect to sell with each 1 degree increase in temperature. Interpreted this way, the slope gives meaningful information. Even without numbers for *x* and *y*, it is possible to arrive at important conclusions about the relationship between the two variables by examining the slope of a curve at various points.

The Slope of a Linear Curve

Along a linear curve the slope, or steepness, is measured by dividing the *rise* between two points on the curve by the *run* between those same two points. The rise is the amount that *y* changes, and the run is the amount that *x* changes. Here is the formula:

$$\frac{\text{Change in } y}{\text{Change in } x} = \frac{\Delta y}{\Delta x} = \text{Slope}$$

In the formula, the symbol Δ (the Greek uppercase delta) stands for *change in*. When a variable increases, the change in that variable is positive; when a variable decreases, the change in that variable is negative.

The slope of a curve is positive when the rise (the change in the *y*-variable) has the same sign as the run (the change in the *x*-variable). That's because when two numbers have the same sign, the ratio of those two numbers is positive. The curve in panel (a) of Figure 2A-2 has a positive slope: along the curve, both the *y*-variable and the *x*-variable increase.

The slope of a curve is negative when the rise and the run have different signs. That's because when two numbers have different signs, the ratio of those two numbers is negative. The curve in panel (b) of Figure 2A-2 has a negative slope: along the curve, an increase in the *x*-variable is associated with a decrease in the *y*-variable.

Figure 2A-3 illustrates how to calculate the slope of a linear curve. Let's focus first on panel (a). From point *A* to point *B* the value of the *y*-variable changes from

FIGURE 2A-3 Calculating the Slope

(a) Negative Constant Slope

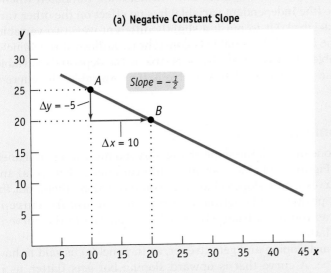

(b) Positive Constant Slope

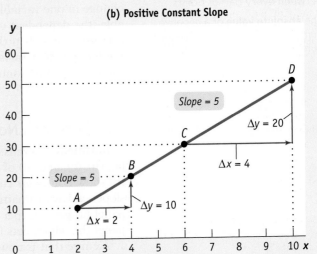

Panels (a) and (b) show two linear curves. Between points A and B on the curve in panel (a), the change in y (the rise) is -5 and the change in x (the run) is 10. So the slope from A to B is $\frac{\Delta y}{\Delta x} = \frac{-5}{10} = -\frac{1}{2} = -0.5$, where the negative sign indicates that the curve is downward sloping. In panel (b), the curve has a slope from A to B of $\frac{\Delta y}{\Delta x} = \frac{10}{2} = 5$. The slope from C to D is $\frac{\Delta y}{\Delta x} = \frac{20}{4} = 5$.

The slope is positive, indicating that the curve is upward sloping. Furthermore, the slope between A and B is the same as the slope between C and D, making this a linear curve. The slope of a linear curve is constant: it is the same regardless of where it is measured along the curve.

25 to 20 and the value of the x-variable changes from 10 to 20. So the slope of the line between these two points is:

$$\frac{\text{Change in } y}{\text{Change in } x} = \frac{\Delta y}{\Delta x} = \frac{-5}{10} = -\frac{1}{2} = -0.5$$

Because a straight line is equally steep at all points, the slope of a straight line is the same at all points. In other words, a straight line has a constant slope. You can check this by calculating the slope of the linear curve between points A and B and between points C and D in panel (b) of Figure 2A-3.

Between A and B: $\qquad\qquad \frac{\Delta y}{\Delta x} = \frac{10}{2} = 5$

Between C and D: $\qquad\qquad \frac{\Delta y}{\Delta x} = \frac{20}{4} = 5$

Horizontal and Vertical Curves and Their Slopes

When a curve is horizontal, the value of the y-variable along that curve never changes—it is constant. Everywhere along the curve, the change in y is zero. Now, zero divided by any number is zero. So, regardless of the value of the change in x, the slope of a horizontal curve is always zero.

If a curve is vertical, the value of the x-variable along the curve never changes—it is constant. Everywhere along the curve, the change in x is zero. This means that the slope of a vertical curve is a ratio with zero in the denominator. A ratio with zero in the denominator is equal to infinity—that is, an infinitely large number. So the slope of a vertical curve is equal to infinity.

A **nonlinear curve** is one in which the slope is not the same between every pair of points.

The **absolute value** of a negative number is the value of the negative number without the minus sign.

A vertical or a horizontal curve has a special implication: it means that the x-variable and the y-variable are unrelated. Two variables are unrelated when a change in one variable (the independent variable) has no effect on the other variable (the dependent variable). Or to put it a slightly different way, two variables are unrelated when the dependent variable is constant regardless of the value of the independent variable. If, as is usual, the y-variable is the dependent variable, the curve is horizontal. If the dependent variable is the x-variable, the curve is vertical.

The Slope of a Nonlinear Curve

A **nonlinear curve** is one in which the slope changes as you move along it. Panels (a), (b), (c), and (d) of Figure 2A-4 show various nonlinear curves. Panels (a) and (b) show nonlinear curves whose slopes change as you move along them, but the slopes always remain positive. Although both curves tilt upward, the curve in panel (a) gets steeper as you move from left to right in contrast to the curve in panel (b), which gets flatter.

A curve that is upward sloping and gets steeper, as in panel (a), is said to have *positive increasing* slope. A curve that is upward sloping but gets flatter, as in panel (b), is said to have *positive decreasing* slope.

When we calculate the slope along these nonlinear curves, we obtain different values for the slope at different points. How the slope changes along the curve determines the curve's shape. For example, in panel (a) of Figure 2A-4, the slope of the curve is a positive number that steadily increases as you move from left to right, whereas in panel (b), the slope is a positive number that steadily decreases.

The slopes of the curves in panels (c) and (d) are negative numbers. Economists often prefer to express a negative number as its **absolute value,** which is the value of the negative number without the minus sign. In general, we denote the absolute value of a number by two parallel bars around the number; for example, the absolute value of −4 is written as $|-4| = 4$.

In panel (c), the absolute value of the slope steadily increases as you move from left to right. The curve therefore has *negative increasing* slope. And in panel (d), the absolute value of the slope of the curve steadily decreases along the curve. This curve therefore has *negative decreasing* slope.

Calculating the Slope Along a Nonlinear Curve

We've just seen that along a nonlinear curve, the value of the slope depends on where you are on that curve. So how do you calculate the slope of a nonlinear curve? We will focus on two methods: the *arc method* and the *point method*.

The Arc Method of Calculating the Slope An arc of a curve is some piece or segment of that curve. For example, panel (a) of Figure 2A-4 shows an arc consisting of the segment of the curve between points A and B. To calculate the slope along a nonlinear curve using the arc method, you draw a straight line between the two end-points of the arc. The slope of that straight line is a measure of the average slope of the curve between those two endpoints.

You can see from panel (a) of Figure 2A-4 that the straight line drawn between points A and B increases along the x-axis from 6 to 10 (so that $\Delta x = 4$) as it increases along the y-axis from 10 to 20 (so that $\Delta y = 10$). Therefore the slope of the straight line connecting points A and B is:

$$\frac{\Delta y}{\Delta x} = \frac{10}{4} = 2.5$$

This means that the average slope of the curve between points A and B is 2.5.

FIGURE 2A-4   Nonlinear Curves

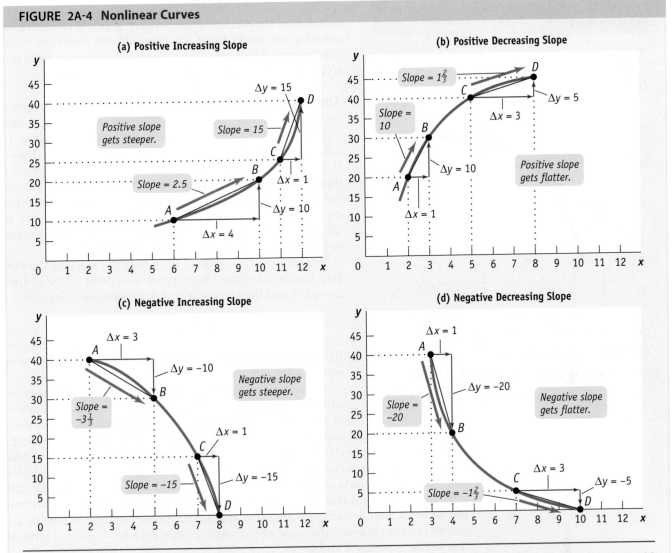

In panel (a) the slope of the curve from A to B is $\frac{y}{x} = \frac{10}{4} = 2.5$, and from C to D it is $\frac{\Delta y}{\Delta x} = \frac{15}{1} = 15$. The slope is positive and increasing; the curve gets steeper as you move to the right. In panel (b) the slope of the curve from A to B is $\frac{\Delta y}{\Delta x} = \frac{10}{1} = 10$, and from C to D it is $\frac{\Delta y}{\Delta x} = \frac{5}{3} = 1\frac{2}{3}$. The slope is positive and decreasing; the curve gets flatter as you move to the right. In panel (c) the slope from A to B is $\frac{\Delta y}{\Delta x} = \frac{-10}{3} = -3\frac{1}{3}$, and from C to D it is $\frac{\Delta y}{\Delta x} = \frac{-15}{1} = -15$. The slope is negative and increasing;

the curve gets steeper as you move to the right. And in panel (d) the slope from A to B is $\frac{\Delta y}{\Delta x} = \frac{-20}{1} = -20$, and from C to D it is $\frac{\Delta y}{\Delta x} = \frac{-5}{3} = -1\frac{2}{3}$. The slope is negative and decreasing; the curve gets flatter as you move to the right. The slope in each case has been calculated by using the arc method—that is, by drawing a straight line connecting two points along a curve. The average slope between those two points is equal to the slope of the straight line between those two points.

Now consider the arc on the same curve between points C and D. A straight line drawn through these two points increases along the x-axis from 11 to 12 ($\Delta x = 1$) as it increases along the y-axis from 25 to 40 ($\Delta y = 15$). So the average slope between points C and D is:

$$\frac{\Delta y}{\Delta x} = \frac{15}{1} = 15$$

FIGURE 2A-5 Calculating the Slope Using the Point Method

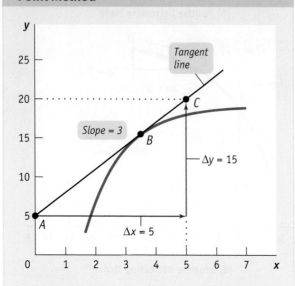

Here a tangent line has been drawn, a line that just touches the curve at point *B*. The slope of this line is equal to the slope of the curve at point *B*. The slope of the tangent line, measuring from *A* to *C*, is $\frac{\Delta y}{\Delta x} = \frac{15}{5} = 3$.

Therefore the average slope between points *C* and *D* is larger than the average slope between points *A* and *B*. These calculations verify what we have already observed—that this upward-tilted curve gets steeper as you move from left to right and therefore has positive increasing slope.

The Point Method of Calculating the Slope The point method calculates the slope of a nonlinear curve at a specific point on that curve. Figure 2A-5 illustrates how to calculate the slope at point *B* on the curve. First, we draw a straight line that just touches the curve at point *B*. Such a line is called a **tangent line:** the fact that it just touches the curve at point *B* and does not touch the curve at any other point on the curve means that the straight line is *tangent* to the curve at point *B*. The slope of this tangent line is equal to the slope of the nonlinear curve at point *B*.

You can see from Figure 2A-5 how the slope of the tangent line is calculated: from point *A* to point *C*, the change in *y* is 15 and the change in *x* is 5, generating a slope of:

$$\frac{\Delta y}{\Delta x} = \frac{15}{5} = 3$$

By the point method, the slope of the curve at point *B* is equal to 3.

A natural question to ask at this point is how to determine which method to use—the arc method or the point method—in calculating the slope of a nonlinear curve. The answer depends on the curve itself and the data used to construct it.

You use the arc method when you don't have enough information to be able to draw a smooth curve. For example, suppose that in panel (a) of Figure 2A-4 you have only the data represented by points *A*, *C*, and *D* and don't have the data represented by point *B* or any of the rest of the curve. Clearly, then, you can't use the point method to calculate the slope at point *B*; you would have to use the arc method to approximate the slope of the curve in this area by drawing a straight line between points *A* and *C*.

But if you have sufficient data to draw the smooth curve shown in panel (a) of Figure 2A-4, then you could use the point method to calculate the slope at point *B*—and at every other point along the curve as well.

Maximum and Minimum Points

The slope of a nonlinear curve can change from positive to negative or vice versa. When the slope of a curve changes from positive to negative, it creates what is called a *maximum* point of the curve. When the slope of a curve changes from negative to positive, it creates a *minimum* point.

Panel (a) of Figure 2A-6 illustrates a curve in which the slope changes from positive to negative as you move from left to right. When *x* is between 0 and 50, the slope of the curve is positive. At *x* equal to 50, the curve attains its highest point—the largest value of *y* along the curve. This point is called the **maximum** of the curve. When *x* exceeds 50, the slope becomes negative as the curve turns downward. Many important curves in economics, such as the curve that represents how the profit of a firm changes as it produces more output, are hill-shaped like this.

In contrast, the curve shown in panel (b) of Figure 2A-6 is U-shaped: it has a slope that changes from negative to positive. At *x* equal to 50, the curve reaches its lowest point—the smallest value of *y* along the curve. This point is called the

A **tangent line** is a straight line that just touches, or is tangent to, a nonlinear curve at a particular point. The slope of the tangent line is equal to the slope of the nonlinear curve at that point.

A nonlinear curve may have a **maximum** point, the highest point along the curve. At the maximum, the slope of the curve changes from positive to negative.

FIGURE 2A-6 Maximum and Minimum Points

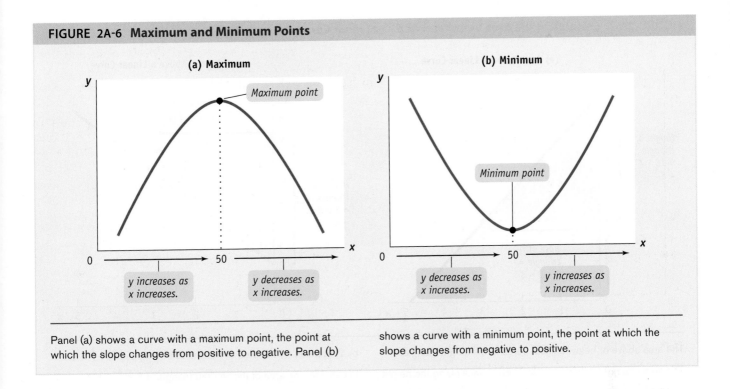

Panel (a) shows a curve with a maximum point, the point at which the slope changes from positive to negative. Panel (b) shows a curve with a minimum point, the point at which the slope changes from negative to positive.

minimum of the curve. Various important curves in economics, such as the curve that represents how per-unit the costs of some firms change as output increases, are U-shaped like this.

Calculating the Area Below or Above a Curve

Sometimes it is useful to be able to measure the size of the area below or above a curve. For the sake of simplicity, we'll only calculate the area below or above a linear curve.

How large is the shaded area below the linear curve in panel (a) of Figure 2A-7? First note that this area has the shape of a right triangle. A right triangle is a triangle that has two sides that make a right angle with each other. We will refer to one of these sides as the *height* of the triangle and the other side as the *base* of the triangle. For our purposes, it doesn't matter which of these two sides we refer to as the base and which as the height.

Calculating the area of a right triangle is straightforward: multiply the height of the triangle by the base of the triangle, and divide the result by 2. The height of the triangle in panel (a) of Figure 2A-7 is $10 - 4 = 6$. And the base of the triangle is $3 - 0 = 3$. So the area of that triangle is

$$\frac{6 \times 3}{2} = 9$$

How about the shaded area above the linear curve in panel (b) of Figure 2A-7? We can use the same formula to calculate the area of this right triangle. The height of the triangle is $8 - 2 = 6$. And the base of the triangle is $4 - 0 = 4$. So the area of that triangle is

$$\frac{6 \times 4}{2} = 12$$

A nonlinear curve may have a **minimum** point, the lowest point along the curve. At the minimum, the slope of the curve changes from negative to positive.

FIGURE 2A-7 Calculating the Area Below and Above a Linear Curve

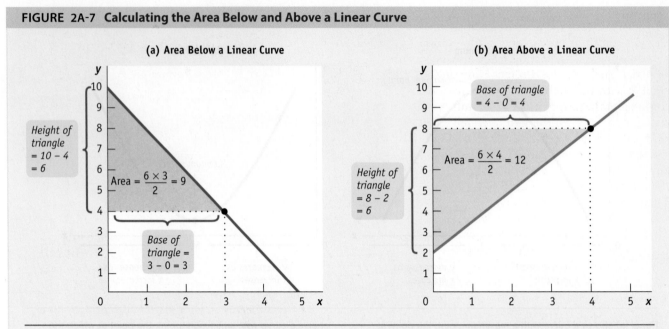

(a) Area Below a Linear Curve

Height of triangle = 10 − 4 = 6

Area = $\dfrac{6 \times 3}{2}$ = 9

Base of triangle = 3 − 0 = 3

(b) Area Above a Linear Curve

Base of triangle = 4 − 0 = 4

Area = $\dfrac{6 \times 4}{2}$ = 12

Height of triangle = 8 − 2 = 6

The area above or below a linear curve forms a right triangle.

The area of a right triangle is calculated by multiplying the height of the triangle by the base of the triangle, and dividing the result

by 2. In panel (a) the area of the shaded triangle is $6 \times \dfrac{3}{2} = 9$.

In panel (b) the area of the shaded triangle is $6 \times \dfrac{4}{2} = 12$.

Graphs That Depict Numerical Information

Graphs can also be used as a convenient way to summarize and display data without assuming some underlying causal relationship. Graphs that simply display numerical information are called *numerical graphs*. Here we will consider four types of numerical graphs: *time-series graphs, scatter diagrams, pie charts,* and *bar graphs*. These are widely used to display real, empirical data about different economic variables because they often help economists and policy makers identify patterns or trends in the economy. But as we will also see, you must be aware of both the usefulness and the limitations of numerical graphs to avoid misinterpreting them or drawing unwarranted conclusions from them.

Types of Numerical Graphs

You have probably seen graphs that show what has happened over time to economic variables such as the unemployment rate or stock prices. A **time-series graph** has successive dates on the horizontal axis and the values of a variable that occurred on those dates on the vertical axis.

For example, Figure 2A-8 shows real gross domestic product (GDP) per capita—a rough measure of a country's standard of living—in the United States from 1947 to 2016. A line connecting the points that correspond to real GDP per capita for each calendar quarter during those years gives a clear idea of the overall trend in the standard of living over these years.

Figure 2A-9 is an example of a different kind of numerical graph. It represents information from a sample of 186 countries on the standard of living, again measured by GDP per capita, and the amount of carbon emissions per capita, a measure of environmental pollution. Each point here indicates an average resident's standard of living and his or her annual carbon emissions for a given country.

A **time-series graph** has dates on the horizontal axis and values of a variable that occurred on those dates on the vertical axis.

The points lying in the upper right of the graph, which show combinations of a high standard of living and high carbon emissions, represent economically advanced countries such as the United States. (The country with the highest carbon emissions, at the top of the graph, is Qatar.) Points lying in the bottom left of the graph, which show combinations of a low standard of living and low carbon emissions, represent economically less advanced countries such as Afghanistan and Sierra Leone.

The pattern of points indicates that there is a positive relationship between living standard and carbon emissions per capita: on the whole, people create more pollution in countries with a higher standard of living.

This type of graph is called a **scatter diagram,** in which each point corresponds to an actual observation of the *x*-variable and the *y*-variable. In scatter diagrams, a curve is typically fitted to the scatter of points; that is, a curve is drawn that approximates as closely as possible the general relationship between the variables. As you can see, the fitted line in Figure 2A-9 is upward sloping, indicating the underlying positive relationship between the two variables. Scatter diagrams are often used to show how a general relationship can be inferred from a set of data.

A **pie chart** shows the share of a total amount that is accounted for by various components, usually expressed in percentages. For example, Figure 2A-10

FIGURE 2A-8 Time-Series Graph

The U.S. Standard of Living, 1947–2016

Time-series graphs show successive dates on the *x*-axis and values for a variable on the *y*-axis. This time-series graph shows real gross domestic product per capita, a measure of a country's standard of living, in the United States from 1947 to early 2016.

Data from: The Federal Reserve Bank of St. Louis.

A **scatter diagram** shows points that correspond to actual observations of the *x*- and *y*-variables. A curve is usually fitted to the scatter of points.

A **pie chart** shows how some total is divided among its components, usually expressed in percentages.

FIGURE 2A-9 Scatter Diagram

In a scatter diagram, each point represents the corresponding values of the *x*- and *y*-variables for a given observation. Here, each point indicates the GDP per capita and the amount of carbon emissions per capita for a given country for a sample of 186 countries. The upward-sloping fitted line here is the best approximation of the general relationship between the two variables.

Data from: World Development Indicators.

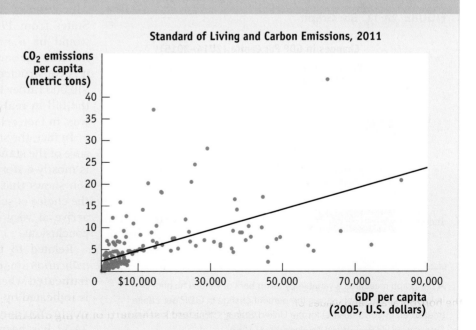

Standard of Living and Carbon Emissions, 2011

FIGURE 2A-10 Pie Chart

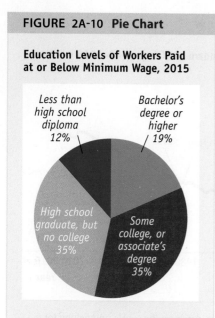

Education Levels of Workers Paid at or Below Minimum Wage, 2015

- Less than high school diploma 12%
- Bachelor's degree or higher 19%
- High school graduate, but no college 35%
- Some college, or associate's degree 35%

A pie chart shows the percentages of a total amount that can be attributed to various components. This pie chart shows the percentages of workers with given education levels who were paid at or below the federal minimum wage in 2015. (Numbers don't add due to rounding.)

Data from: Bureau of Labor Statistics.

is a pie chart that depicts the education levels of workers who in 2015 were paid the federal minimum wage or less. As you can see, the majority of workers paid at or below the minimum wage had no college degree. Only 19% of workers who were paid at or below the minimum wage had a bachelor's degree or higher.

Bar graphs use bars of various heights or lengths to indicate values of a variable. In the bar graph in Figure 2A-11, the bars show the percent change in GDP per capita from 2014 to 2015 for the United States, China, and Indonesia. Exact values of the variable that is being measured may be written at the end of the bar, as in this figure. For instance, GDP per capita for China increased by 6.7% between 2014 and 2015. But even without the precise values, comparing the heights or lengths of the bars can give useful insight into the relative magnitudes of the different values of the variable.

Problems in Interpreting Numerical Graphs

Although we've explained that graphs are visual images that make ideas or information easier to understand, graphs can be constructed (intentionally or unintentionally) in ways that are misleading and can lead to inaccurate conclusions. This section raises some issues to be aware of when you are interpreting graphs.

Features of Construction Before drawing any conclusions about what a numerical graph implies, pay close attention to the scale, or size of increments, shown on the axes. Small increments tend to visually exaggerate changes in the variables, whereas large increments tend to visually diminish them. So the scale used in construction of a graph can influence your interpretation of the significance of the changes it illustrates—perhaps in an unwarranted way.

Take, for example, Figure 2A-12, which shows real GDP per capita in the United States from 1981 to 1982 using increments of $500. You can see that real GDP per capita fell from $28,957 to $27,859. A decrease, sure, but is it as enormous as the scale chosen for the vertical axis makes it seem?

If you go back and reexamine Figure 2A-8, which shows real GDP per capita in the United States from 1947 to 2016, you can see that this would be a misguided conclusion. Figure 2A-8 includes the same data shown in Figure 2A-12, but it is constructed with a scale having increments of $10,000 rather than $500. From it you can see that the fall in real GDP per capita from 1981 to 1982 was, in fact, relatively insignificant.

In fact, the story of real GDP per capita—a measure of the standard of living—in the United States is mostly a story of ups, not downs. This comparison shows that if you are not careful to factor in the choice of scale in interpreting a graph, you can arrive at very different, and possibly misguided, conclusions.

Related to the choice of scale is the use of *truncation* in constructing a graph. An axis is **truncated** when part of the range is omitted. This is indicated by two slashes (//) in the axis near the origin. You can see that the vertical axis of Figure 2A-12 has been truncated—some of the range of values from 0 to $27,000 have been omitted and

FIGURE 2A-11 Bar Graph

Changes in GDP Per Capita (2014–2015)

	Percent change in GDP per capita	Change in GDP per capita
United States	1.6%	$745
China	6.7%	$243
Indonesia	3.7%	$66

A bar graph measures a variable by using bars of various heights or lengths. This bar graph shows the percent change in GDP per capita (measured in 2005 dollars) for the United States, China, and Indonesia.

Data from: World Bank, World Development Indicators.

FIGURE 2A-12   Interpreting Graphs: The Effect of Scale

Some of the same data for the years 1981 and 1982 used in Figure 2A-8 are represented here, except that here they are shown using increments of $500 rather than increments of $10,000. As a result of this change in scale, changes in the standard of living look much larger in this figure compared to Figure 2A-8.

Data from: Bureau of Economic Analysis.

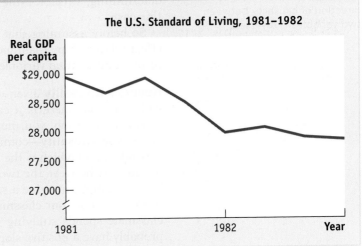

The U.S. Standard of Living, 1981–1982

a // appears in the axis. Truncation saves space in the presentation of a graph and allows smaller increments to be used in constructing it. As a result, changes in the variable depicted on a graph that has been truncated appear larger compared to a graph that has not been truncated and that uses larger increments.

You must also consider exactly what a graph is illustrating. For example, in Figure 2A-11, you should recognize that what is being shown are *percent* changes in the number of unemployed, not *numerical* changes. The growth rate for China increased by the highest percentage, 6.7% in this example. If you were to confuse numerical changes with percent changes, you would erroneously conclude the country with the greatest change in GDP per capita was China.

In fact, a correct interpretation of Figure 2A-11 shows that the greatest dollar change in GDP per capita was for the United States: GDP per capita increased by $745 for the United States, which is greater than the increase in GDP per capita for China, which is $243 in this example. Although there was a higher percentage increase in GDP per capita for China, the dollar increase for China from 2014 to 2015 was smaller than the change for the United States, leading to a smaller change in GDP per capita for China than the United States. The same can be said for Indonesia, where GDP per capita grew by 3.7%, but that only resulted in a $66 increase in actual GDP per capita.

Omitted Variables From a scatter diagram that shows two variables moving either positively or negatively in relation to each other, it is easy to conclude that there is a causal relationship. But relationships between two variables are not always due to direct cause and effect. Quite possibly an observed relationship between two variables is due to the *unobserved* effect of a third variable on each of the other two variables.

An unobserved variable that, through its influence on other variables, creates the erroneous appearance of a direct causal relationship among those variables is called an **omitted variable.** For example, in New England, a greater amount of snowfall during a given week will typically cause people to buy more snow shovels. It will also cause people to buy more de-icer fluid. But if you omitted the influence of the snowfall and simply plotted the number of snow shovels sold versus the number of bottles of de-icer fluid sold, you would produce a scatter diagram that showed an upward tilt in the pattern of points, indicating a positive relationship between snow shovels sold and de-icer fluid sold.

To attribute a causal relationship between these two variables, however, is misguided; more snow shovels sold do not cause more de-icer fluid to be sold,

A **bar graph** uses bars of varying heights or lengths to show the comparative sizes of different observations of a variable.

An axis is **truncated** when some of the values on the axis are omitted, usually to save space.

An **omitted variable** is an unobserved variable that, through its influence on other variables, creates the erroneous appearance of a direct causal relationship among those variables.

The error of **reverse causality** is committed when the true direction of causality between two variables is reversed.

or vice versa. They move together because they are both influenced by a third, determining, variable—the weekly snowfall, which is the omitted variable in this case.

So before assuming that a pattern in a scatter diagram implies a cause-and-effect relationship, it is important to consider whether the pattern is instead the result of an omitted variable. Or to put it succinctly: correlation is not causation.

Reverse Causality Even when you are confident that there is no omitted variable and that there is a causal relationship between two variables shown in a numerical graph, you must also be careful that you don't make the mistake of **reverse causality**—coming to an erroneous conclusion about which is the dependent and which is the independent variable by reversing the true direction of causality between the two variables.

For example, imagine a scatter diagram that depicts the grade point averages (GPAs) of 20 of your classmates on one axis and the number of hours that each classmate spends studying on the other. A line fitted between the points will probably have a positive slope, showing a positive relationship between GPA and hours of studying. We could reasonably infer that hours spent studying is the independent variable and that GPA is the dependent variable. But you could make the error of reverse causality: you could infer that a high GPA causes a student to study more, whereas a low GPA causes a student to study less.

As you've just seen, it is important to understand how graphs can mislead or be interpreted incorrectly. Policy decisions, business decisions, and political arguments are often based on interpretation of the types of numerical graphs we've just discussed. Problems of misleading features of construction, omitted variables, and reverse causality can lead to important and undesirable consequences.

PROBLEMS

interactive activity

1. Study the four accompanying diagrams. Consider the following statements and indicate which diagram matches each statement. Which variable would appear on the horizontal and which on the vertical axis? In each of these statements, is the slope positive, negative, zero, or infinity?

Panel (a)　　Panel (b)

Panel (c)　　Panel (d)

a. If the price of movies increases, fewer consumers go to see movies.

b. More experienced workers typically have higher incomes than less experienced workers.

c. Whatever the temperature outside, Americans consume the same number of hot dogs per day.

d. Consumers buy more frozen yogurt when the price of ice cream goes up.

e. Research finds no relationship between the number of diet books purchased and the number of pounds lost by the average dieter.

f. Regardless of its price, Americans buy the same quantity of salt.

2. During the Reagan administration, economist Arthur Laffer argued in favor of lowering income tax rates in order to increase tax revenues. Like most economists, he believed that at tax rates above a certain level, tax revenue would fall because high taxes would discourage some people from working and that people would refuse to work at all if they received no income after paying taxes. This relationship between tax rates and tax revenue is graphically summarized in what is widely known as the Laffer curve. Plot the Laffer curve relationship assuming that it has the shape of a nonlinear curve. The following questions will help you construct the graph.

a. Which is the independent variable? Which is the dependent variable? On which axis do you therefore measure the income tax rate? On which axis do you measure income tax revenue?

b. What would tax revenue be at a 0% income tax rate?

c. The maximum possible income tax rate is 100%. What would tax revenue be at a 100% income tax rate?

d. Estimates now show that the maximum point on the Laffer curve is (approximately) at a tax rate of 80%. For tax rates less than 80%, how would you describe the relationship between the tax rate and tax revenue, and how is this relationship reflected in the slope? For tax rates higher than 80%, how would you describe the relationship between the tax rate and tax revenue, and how is this relationship reflected in the slope?

3. In the accompanying figures, the numbers on the axes have been lost. All you know is that the units shown on the vertical axis are the same as the units on the horizontal axis.

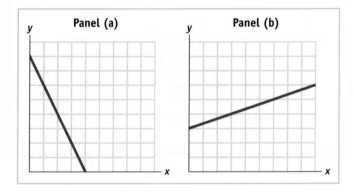

a. In panel (a), what is the slope of the line? Show that the slope is constant along the line.

b. In panel (b), what is the slope of the line? Show that the slope is constant along the line.

4. Answer each of the following questions by drawing a schematic diagram.

a. Taking measurements of the slope of a curve at three points farther and farther to the right along the horizontal axis, the slope of the curve changes from −0.3, to −0.8, to −2.5, measured by the point method. Draw a schematic diagram of this curve. How would you describe the relationship illustrated in your diagram?

b. Taking measurements of the slope of a curve at five points farther and farther to the right along the horizontal axis, the slope of the curve changes from 1.5, to 0.5, to 0, to −0.5, to −1.5, measured by the point method. Draw a schematic diagram of this curve. Does it have a maximum or a minimum?

5. For each of the accompanying diagrams, calculate the area of the shaded right triangle.

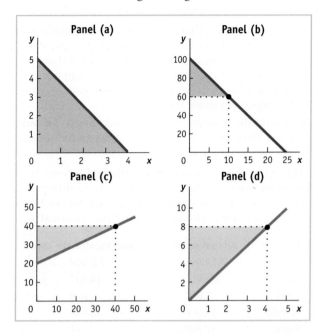

6. The base of a right triangle is 10, and its area is 20. What is the height of this right triangle?

7. The accompanying table shows the relationship between workers' hours of work per week and their hourly wage rate. Apart from the fact that they receive a different hourly wage rate and work different hours, these five workers are otherwise identical.

Name	Quantity of labor (hours per week)	Wage rate (per hour)
Athena	30	$15
Boris	35	30
Curt	37	45
Diego	36	60
Emily	32	75

a. Which variable is the independent variable? Which is the dependent variable?

b. Draw a scatter diagram illustrating this relationship. Draw a (nonlinear) curve that connects the points. Put the hourly wage rate on the vertical axis.

c. As the wage rate increases from $15 to $30, how does the number of hours worked respond according to the relationship depicted here? What is the average slope of the curve between Athena's and Boris's data points using the arc method?

d. As the wage rate increases from $60 to $75, how does the number of hours worked respond according to the relationship depicted here? What is the average slope of the curve between Diego's and Emily's data points using the arc method?

8. An insurance company has found that the severity of property damage in a fire is positively related to the number of firefighters arriving at the scene.

   a. Draw a diagram that depicts this finding with number of firefighters on the horizontal axis and amount of property damage on the vertical axis. What is the argument made by this diagram? Suppose you reverse what is measured on the two axes. What is the argument made then?

   b. Should the insurance company ask the city to send fewer firefighters to any fire in order to reduce its payouts to policy holders?

9. This table illustrates annual salaries and income tax owed by five individuals. Despite receiving different annual salaries and owing different amounts of income tax, these five individuals are otherwise identical.

Name	Annual salary	Annual income tax owed
Susan	$22,000	$3,304
Eduardo	63,000	14,317
John	3,000	454
Camila	94,000	23,927
Peter	37,000	7,020

   a. If you were to plot these points on a graph, what would be the average slope of the curve between the points for Eduardo's and Camila's salaries and taxes using the arc method? How would you interpret this value for slope?

   b. What is the average slope of the curve between the points for John's and Susan's salaries and taxes using the arc method? How would you interpret that value for slope?

   c. What happens to the slope as salary increases? What does this relationship imply about how the level of income taxes affects a person's incentive to earn a higher salary?

WORK IT OUT Interactive step-by-step help with solving this problem can be found online.

---

10. Studies have found a relationship between a country's yearly rate of economic growth and the yearly rate of increase in airborne pollutants. It is believed that a higher rate of economic growth allows a country's residents to have more cars and travel more, thereby releasing more airborne pollutants.

   a. Which variable is the independent variable? Which is the dependent variable?

   b. Suppose that in the country of Sudland, when the yearly rate of economic growth fell from 3.0% to 1.5%, the yearly rate of increase in airborne pollutants fell from 6% to 5%. What is the average slope of a nonlinear curve between these points using the arc method?

   c. Assume that when the yearly rate of economic growth rose from 3.5% to 4.5%, the yearly rate of increase in airborne pollutants rose from 5.5% to 7.5%. What is the average slope of a nonlinear curve between these two points using the arc method?

   d. How would you describe the relationship between the two variables here?

3 Supply and Demand

A NATURAL GAS BOOM

IN JUST FIVE YEARS, from 2010 to 2015, Karnes County went from producing a relatively small amount of oil and natural gas to the largest producing county in Texas. What accounted for the swift change was hydraulic fracturing, or fracking.

The adoption of new drilling technologies has led to cheaper natural gas, but not without controversy and environmental costs.

In those few years, Karnes County also went through an extreme cycle of boom and bust as the price of oil plunged from $100 a barrel in 2014 to under $45 a barrel in 2015, while the price of natural gas (per thousand cubic feet) went from nearly $8 to under $2. What accounted for this reversal of fortune? Once again, it was fracking. *Fracking* is a method of extracting natural gas (and to a lesser extent, oil) from deposits trapped between layers of shale rock thousands of feet underground using powerful jets of chemical-laden water. For almost a century in the United States vast deposits of natural gas within these shale formations lay untapped because drilling for them was too difficult.

Until recently, that is. A few decades ago, new drilling technologies were developed that made it possible to reach these deeply embedded deposits. But what finally pushed energy companies to invest in these new extraction technologies was the high price of natural gas over the last decade—a quadrupling from 2002 to 2006. Two principal factors explain the high prices: the demand for natural gas and the supply of natural gas.

First, the demand side. In 2002, the U.S. economy was mired in recession; with economic activity low and job losses high, people and businesses cut their energy consumption. For example, to save money, homeowners turned down their thermostats in winter and turned them up in the summer. But by 2006, the U.S. economy came roaring back, and natural gas consumption rose.

Second, the supply side. In 2005, Hurricane Katrina devastated the American Gulf Coast, site of most of the country's natural gas production at the time. So by 2006 the demand for natural gas surged while supply was severely curtailed. As a result, natural gas prices peaked at around $14 per thousand cubic feet, up from around $2 in 2002.

Fast-forward to 2013: natural gas prices once again fell to $2 per thousand cubic feet. But this time a slow economy was not the principal explanation, it was the impact of new technologies on oil and natural gas production. To illustrate, the United States produced 8.13 trillion cubic feet of natural gas from shale deposits in 2012, nearly doubling the total from 2010. That total increased to nearly 10 trillion cubic feet of natural gas in 2015, making the United States the world's largest producer of both oil and natural gas—overtaking both Russia and Saudi Arabia. Despite a brief surge in the winter of 2013–2014 due to high demand for heating fuel during a very cold winter, by late 2015 the price fell to under $2 as fracking technology advanced and more drilling expanded production.

The benefits of much lower natural gas prices have led to lower heating costs for consumers, and have cascaded through American industries. For example, electricity-generating power plants are switching from coal to natural gas, and mass-transit vehicles are switching from gasoline to natural gas. The effect has been so significant that many European manufacturers, paying four times more for gas than their U.S. rivals, have been forced to relocate plants to American soil to survive. In addition, the revived U.S. natural gas industry has directly created tens of thousands of new jobs.

Yet the benefits of natural gas have been accompanied by deep reservations and controversy over the environmental effects of fracking. While there are clear environmental benefits from the switch to natural gas (which burns cleaner than the other, heavily polluting fossil fuels, gasoline and coal), fracking has sparked another set of environmental worries. One is the potential for contamination of local groundwater by chemicals used in fracking. Another is that cheap natural gas may discourage the adoption of more expensive renewable energy sources like solar and wind power, furthering our dependence upon fossil fuel.

The debate over fracking has been highly charged and is ongoing. We, the authors, do not espouse one side or the other, believing that science as well as economics should provide guidance about the best course to follow.

But let's return to the topic of supply and demand. How, exactly, does the high price of natural gas nearly a decade ago translate into today's switch to vehicles powered by natural gas? The short answer is that it's a matter of supply and demand. But what does that mean? Many people use "supply and demand" as a sort of catchphrase to mean "the laws of the marketplace at work." To economists, however, the concept of supply and demand has a precise meaning: it is a *model of how a market behaves* that is extremely useful for understanding many—but not all—markets.

In this chapter, we lay out the pieces that make up the *supply and demand model,* put them together, and show how this model can be used. ●

Supply and Demand: A Model of a Competitive Market

Natural gas sellers and natural gas buyers constitute a market—a group of producers and consumers who exchange a good or service for payment. In this chapter, we'll focus on a particular type of market known as a *competitive market*. A **competitive market** is a market in which there are many buyers and sellers of the same good or service. More precisely, the key feature of a competitive market is that no individual's actions have a noticeable effect on the price at which the good or service is sold. It's important to understand, however, that this is not an accurate description of every market.

For example, it's not an accurate description of the market for cola beverages. That's because in this market, Coca-Cola and Pepsi account for such a large proportion of total sales that they are able to influence the price at which cola beverages are bought and sold. But it is an accurate description of the market for natural gas. The global marketplace for natural gas is so huge that even the biggest U.S. driller for natural gas—Exxon Mobil—accounts for such a small share of total global transactions that it is unable to influence the price at which natural gas is bought and sold.

It's a little hard to explain why competitive markets are different from other markets until we've seen how a competitive market works. So let's take a rain check—we'll return to that issue at the end of this chapter. For now, let's just say that it's easier to model competitive markets than other markets. When taking an exam, it's always a good strategy to begin by answering the easier questions. In this book, we're going to do the same thing. So we will start with competitive markets.

When a market is competitive, its behavior is well described by the **supply and demand model.** Because many markets are competitive, the supply and demand model is a very useful one indeed.

There are five key elements in this model:

• The *demand curve*

• The *supply curve*

• The set of factors that cause the demand curve to shift and the set of factors that cause the supply curve to shift

• The *market equilibrium*, which includes the *equilibrium price* and *equilibrium quantity*

• The way the market equilibrium changes when the supply curve or demand curve shifts

To understand the supply and demand model, we will examine each of these elements.

The Demand Curve

How much natural gas will American consumers want to buy in a given year? You might at first think that we can answer this question by adding up the amounts each American household and business consumes in that year. But that's not

A **competitive market** is a market in which there are many buyers and sellers of the same good or service, none of whom can influence the price at which the good or service is sold.

The **supply and demand model** is a model of how a competitive market behaves.

enough to answer the question, because how much natural gas Americans want to buy depends upon the price of natural gas.

When the price of natural gas falls, as it did from 2006 to 2015, consumers will generally respond to the lower price by using more natural gas—for example, by turning up their thermostats to keep their houses warmer in the winter or switching to vehicles powered by natural gas. In general, the amount of natural gas, or of any good or service that people want to buy, depends upon the price. The higher the price, the less of the good or service people want to purchase; alternatively, the lower the price, the more they want to purchase.

So the answer to the question "How many units of natural gas do consumers want to buy?" depends on the price of a unit of natural gas. If you don't yet know what the price will be, you can start by making a table of how many units of natural gas people would want to buy at a number of different prices. Such a table is known as a *demand schedule*. This, in turn, can be used to draw a *demand curve*, which is one of the key elements of the supply and demand model.

A **demand schedule** shows how much of a good or service consumers will want to buy at different prices.

The Demand Schedule and the Demand Curve

A **demand schedule** is a table showing how much of a good or service consumers will want to buy at different prices. At the right of Figure 3-1, we show a hypothetical demand schedule for natural gas. It's expressed in BTUs (British thermal units), a commonly used measure of quantity of natural gas. It's a hypothetical demand schedule—it doesn't use actual data on American demand for natural gas.

FIGURE 3-1   The Demand Schedule and the Demand Curve

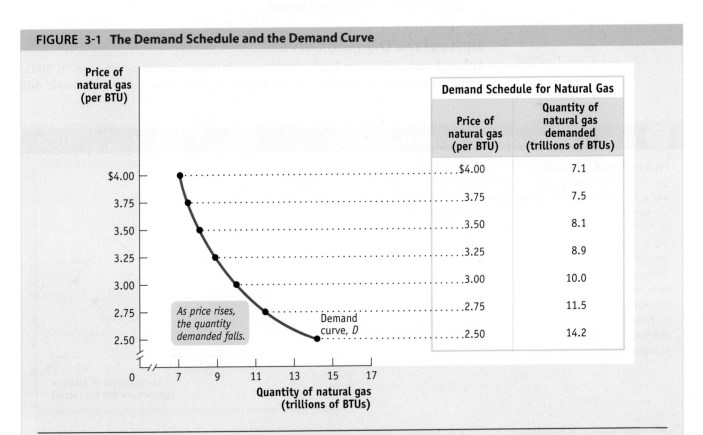

Demand Schedule for Natural Gas	
Price of natural gas (per BTU)	Quantity of natural gas demanded (trillions of BTUs)
$4.00	7.1
3.75	7.5
3.50	8.1
3.25	8.9
3.00	10.0
2.75	11.5
2.50	14.2

The demand schedule for natural gas yields the corresponding demand curve, which shows how much of a good or service consumers want to buy at any given price. The demand curve and the demand schedule reflect the law of demand: as price rises, the quantity demanded falls. Similarly, a fall in price raises the quantity demanded. As a result, the demand curve is downward sloping.

The **quantity demanded** is the actual amount of a good or service consumers are willing to buy at some specific price.

A **demand curve** is a graphical representation of the demand schedule. It shows the relationship between quantity demanded and price.

The **law of demand** says that a higher price for a good or service, other things equal, leads people to demand a smaller quantity of that good or service.

According to the table, if a BTU of natural gas costs $3, consumers will want to purchase 10 trillion BTUs of natural gas over the course of a year. If the price is $3.25 per BTU, they will want to buy only 8.9 trillion BTUs; if the price is only $2.75 per BTU, they will want to buy 11.5 trillion BTUs. The higher the price, the fewer BTUs of natural gas consumers will want to purchase. So, as the price rises, the **quantity demanded** of natural gas—the actual amount consumers are willing to buy at some specific price—falls.

The graph in Figure 3-1 is a visual representation of the information in the table. (You might want to review the discussion of graphs in economics in the appendix to Chapter 2.) The vertical axis shows the price of a BTU of natural gas and the horizontal axis shows the quantity of natural gas in trillions of BTUs. Each point on the graph corresponds to one of the entries in the table. The curve that connects these points is a **demand curve.** A demand curve is a graphical representation of the demand schedule, another way of showing the relationship between the quantity demanded and price.

Note that the demand curve shown in Figure 3-1 slopes downward. This reflects the inverse relationship between price and the quantity demanded: a higher price reduces the quantity demanded, and a lower price increases the quantity demanded. We can see this from the demand curve in Figure 3-1. As price falls, we move down the demand curve and quantity demanded increases. And as price increases, we move up the demand curve and quantity demanded falls.

In the real world, demand curves almost always *do* slope downward. (The exceptions are so rare that for practical purposes we can ignore them.) Generally, the proposition that a higher price for a good, *other things equal*, leads people to demand a smaller quantity of that good is so reliable that economists are willing to call it a "law"—the **law of demand.**

Shifts of the Demand Curve

Although natural gas prices in 2006 were higher than they had been in 2002, U.S. consumption of natural gas was higher in 2006. How can we reconcile this

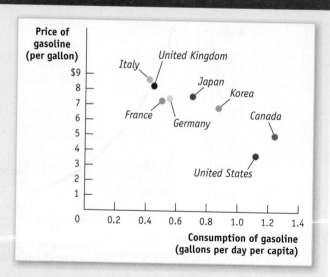

 GLOBAL COMPARISON   **PAY MORE, PUMP LESS**

For a real-world illustration of the law of demand, consider how gasoline consumption varies according to the prices consumers pay at the pump. Because of high taxes, gasoline and diesel fuel are more than twice as expensive in most European countries and in many East Asian countries than in the United States. According to the law of demand, this should lead Europeans to buy less gasoline than Americans—and they do. As you can see from the figure, per person, Europeans consume less than half as much fuel as Americans, mainly because they drive smaller cars with better mileage.

Prices aren't the only factor affecting fuel consumption, but they're probably the main cause of the difference between European and American fuel consumption per person.

Data from: World Development Indicators and U.S. Energy Information Administration, 2013.

fact with the law of demand, which says that a higher price reduces the quantity demanded, other things equal?

The answer lies in the crucial phrase *other things equal*. In this case, other things weren't equal: the U.S. economy had changed between 2002 and 2006 in ways that increased the amount of natural gas demanded at any given price. For one thing, the U.S. economy was much stronger in 2006 than in 2002. Figure 3-2 illustrates this phenomenon using the demand schedule and demand curve for natural gas. (As before, the numbers in Figure 3-2 are hypothetical.)

The table in Figure 3-2 shows two demand schedules. The first is the demand schedule for 2002, the same as shown in Figure 3-1. The second is the demand schedule for 2006. It differs from the 2002 schedule because of the stronger U.S. economy, leading to an increase in the quantity of natural gas demanded at any given price. So at each price the 2006 schedule shows a larger quantity demanded than the 2002 schedule. For example, the quantity of natural gas consumers wanted to buy at a price of $3 per BTU increased from 10 trillion to 12 trillion BTUs per year; the quantity demanded at $3.25 per BTU went from 8.9 trillion to 10.7 trillion, and so on.

What is clear from this example is that the changes that occurred between 2002 and 2006 generated a *new* demand schedule, one in which the quantity demanded was greater at any given price than in the original demand schedule. The two curves in Figure 3-2 show the same information graphically. As you can see, the demand schedule for 2006 corresponds to a new demand curve, D_2, that is to the right of the demand schedule for 2002, D_1. This **shift of the demand curve** shows the change in the quantity demanded at any given price, represented by the change in position of the original demand curve D_1 to its new location at D_2.

A **shift of the demand curve** is a change in the quantity demanded at any given price, represented by the shift of the original demand curve to a new position, denoted by a new demand curve.

FIGURE 3-2 An Increase in Demand

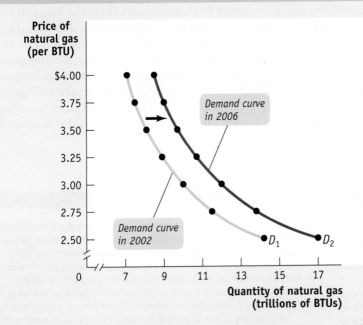

Demand Schedules for Natural Gas		
Price of natural gas (per BTU)	Quantity of natural gas demanded (trillions of BTUs)	
	in 2002	in 2006
$4.00	7.1	8.5
3.75	7.5	9.0
3.50	8.1	9.7
3.25	8.9	10.7
3.00	10.0	12.0
2.75	11.5	13.8
2.50	14.2	17.0

A strong economy is one factor that increases the demand for natural gas—a rise in the quantity demanded at any given price. This is represented by the two demand schedules—one showing the demand in 2002 when the economy was weak, the other showing the demand in 2006, when the economy was strong—and their corresponding demand curves. The increase in demand shifts the demand curve to the right.

FIGURE 3-3 Movement Along the Demand Curve versus Shift of the Demand Curve

The rise in quantity demanded when going from point *A* to point *B* reflects a movement along the demand curve: it is the result of a fall in the price of the good. The rise in quantity demanded when going from point *A* to point *C* reflects a shift of the demand curve: it is the result of a rise in the quantity demanded at any given price.

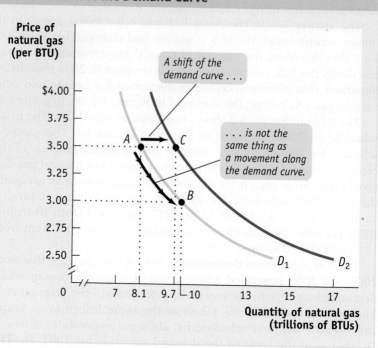

A **movement along the demand curve** is a change in the quantity demanded of a good arising from a change in the good's price.

It's crucial to make the distinction between such shifts of the demand curve and **movements along the demand curve,** changes in the quantity demanded of a good arising from a change in that good's price. Figure 3-3 illustrates the difference.

The movement from point *A* to point *B* is a movement along the demand curve: the quantity demanded rises due to a fall in price as you move down D_1. Here, a fall in the price of natural gas from $3.50 to $3 per BTU generates a rise in the quantity demanded from 8.1 trillion to 10 trillion BTUs per year. But the quantity demanded can also rise when the price is unchanged if there is an *increase in demand*—a rightward shift of the demand curve. This is illustrated in Figure 3-3 by the shift of the demand curve from D_1 to D_2. Holding the price constant at $3.50 per BTU, the quantity demanded rises from 8.1 trillion BTUs at point *A* on D_1 to 9.7 trillion BTUs at point *C* on D_2.

DEMAND VERSUS QUANTITY DEMANDED

When economists say "an increase in demand," they mean a rightward shift of the demand curve, and when they say "a decrease in demand," they mean a leftward shift of the demand curve—that is, when they're being careful.

In ordinary speech most people, including professional economists, use the word *demand* casually. For example, an economist might say "the demand for air travel has doubled over the past 15 years, partly because of falling airfares" when he or she really means that the *quantity demanded* has doubled.

It's OK to be a bit sloppy in ordinary conversation. But when you're doing economic analysis, it's important to make the distinction between changes in the quantity demanded, which involve movements along a demand curve, and shifts of the demand curve (see Figure 3-3 for an illustration). Sometimes students end up writing something like this: "If demand increases, the price will go up, but that will lead to a fall in demand, which pushes the price down . . ." and then go around in circles.

If you make a clear distinction between changes in *demand,* which mean shifts of the demand curve, and changes in *quantity demanded,* which means movement along the demand curve, you can avoid a lot of confusion.

When economists say "the demand for X increased" or "the demand for Y decreased," they mean that the demand curve for X or Y shifted—not that the quantity demanded rose or fell because of a change in the price.

Understanding Shifts of the Demand Curve

Figure 3-4 illustrates the two basic ways in which demand curves can shift.

1. When economists talk about an increase in demand, they mean a *rightward* shift of the demand curve: at any given price, consumers demand a larger quantity of the good or service than before. This is shown by the rightward shift of the original demand curve D_1 to D_2.

2. When economists talk about a decrease in demand, they mean a *leftward* shift of the demand curve: at any given price, consumers demand a smaller quantity of the good or service than before. This is shown by the leftward shift of the original demand curve D_1 to D_3.

What caused the demand curve for natural gas to shift? As we mentioned earlier, the reason was the stronger U.S. economy in 2006 compared to 2002. If you think about it, you can come up with other factors that would be likely to shift the demand curve for natural gas. For example, suppose that the price of heating oil rises. This will induce some consumers, who heat their homes and businesses in winter with heating oil, to switch to natural gas instead, increasing the demand for natural gas.

Economists believe that there are five principal factors that shift the demand curve for a good or service:

- Changes in the prices of related goods or services
- Changes in income
- Changes in tastes
- Changes in expectations
- Changes in the number of consumers

FIGURE 3-4   Shifts of the Demand Curve

Any event that increases demand shifts the demand curve to the right, reflecting a rise in the quantity demanded at any given price. Any event that decreases demand shifts the demand curve to the left, reflecting a fall in the quantity demanded at any given price.

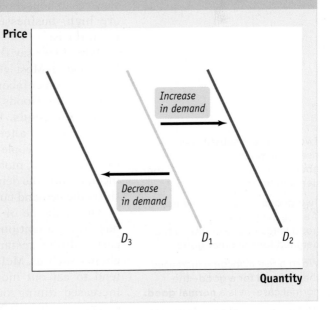

Although this is not an exhaustive list, it contains the five most important factors that can shift demand curves. When we say that the quantity of a good or service demanded falls as its price rises, *other things equal*, we are in fact stating that the factors that shift demand are remaining unchanged. Let's now explore how those factors shift the demand curve.

Changes in the Prices of Related Goods or Services Heating oil is what economists call a *substitute* for natural gas. A pair of goods are **substitutes** if a rise in the price of one good (heating oil) makes consumers more likely to buy the other good (natural gas). Substitutes are usually goods that in some way serve a similar function: coffee and tea, muffins and doughnuts, train rides and air flights. A rise in the price of the alternative good induces some consumers to purchase the original good *instead* of it, shifting demand for the original good to the right.

But sometimes a rise in the price of one good makes consumers *less* willing to buy another good. Such pairs of goods are known as **complements.** Complements are usually goods that in some sense are consumed together: computers and software, cappuccinos and cookies, cars and gasoline. Because consumers like to consume a good and its complement together, a change in the price of one of the goods will affect the demand for its complement. In particular, when the price of one good rises, the demand for its complement decreases, shifting the demand curve for the complement to the left. So, for example, when the price of gasoline began to rise in 2009 from under $3 per gallon to close to $4 per gallon in 2011, the demand for gas-guzzling cars fell.

Changes in Income Why did the stronger economy in 2006 lead to an increase in the demand for natural gas compared to the demand during the weak economy of 2002? Because with the stronger economy, Americans had more income, making them more likely to purchase more of *most* goods and services at any given price. For example, with a higher income you are likely to keep your house warmer in the winter than if your income is low.

And, the demand for natural gas, a major source of fuel for electricity-generating power plants, is tied to the demand for other goods and services. For example, businesses must consume power in order to provide goods and services to households. So when the economy is strong and household incomes are high, businesses will consume more electricity and, indirectly, more natural gas.

Why do we say that people are likely to purchase more of "most goods," not "all goods"? Most goods are **normal goods**—the demand for them increases when consumer income rises. However, the demand for some products falls when income rises. Goods for which demand decreases when income rises are known as **inferior goods.** Usually an inferior good is considered less desirable than more expensive alternatives—such as a bus ride versus a taxi ride. When they can afford to, people stop buying an inferior good and switch their consumption to the preferred, more expensive alternative. So when a good is inferior, a rise in income shifts the demand curve to the left. And, not surprisingly, a fall in income shifts the demand curve to the right.

One example of the distinction between normal and inferior goods that has drawn attention in the business press is the difference between so-called casual-dining restaurants such as Applebee's or Olive Garden and fast-food chains such as McDonald's and KFC. When their incomes rise, Americans tend to eat out more at casual-dining restaurants. However, some of this increased dining out comes at the expense of fast-food venues—to some extent, people visit McDonald's less once they can afford to move upscale. So casual dining is a normal good, whereas fast-food consumption appears to be an inferior good.

Two goods are **substitutes** if a rise in the price of one of the goods leads to an increase in the demand for the other good.

Two goods are **complements** if a rise in the price of one good leads to a decrease in the demand for the other good.

When a rise in income increases the demand for a good—the normal case—it is a **normal good.**

When a rise in income decreases the demand for a good, it is an **inferior good.**

Changes in Tastes Why do people want what they want? Fortunately, we don't need to answer that question—we just need to acknowledge that people have certain preferences, or tastes, that determine what they choose to consume and that these tastes can change. Economists usually lump together changes in demand due to trends, beliefs, cultural shifts, and so on under the heading of changes in tastes or preferences.

For example, once upon a time men wore hats. Up until around World War II, a respectable man wasn't fully dressed unless he wore a dignified hat along with his suit. But the returning troops adopted a more informal style, perhaps due to the rigors of the war. And President Eisenhower, who had been supreme commander of Allied Forces before becoming president, often went hatless. After World War II, it was clear that the demand curve for hats had shifted leftward, reflecting a decrease in the demand for hats.

Economists have relatively little to say about the forces that influence consumers' tastes. (Although marketers and advertisers have plenty to say about them!) However, a change in tastes has a predictable impact on demand. When tastes change in favor of a good, more people want to buy it at any given price, so the demand curve shifts to the right. When tastes change against a good, fewer people want to buy it at any given price, so the demand curve shifts to the left.

Changes in Expectations When consumers have some choice about when to make a purchase, current demand for a good is often affected by expectations about its future price. For example, savvy shoppers often wait for seasonal sales—say, buying next year's holiday gifts during the post-holiday markdowns. In this case, expectations of a future drop in price lead to a decrease in demand today. Alternatively, expectations of a future rise in price are likely to cause an increase in demand today.

In addition, the fall in gas prices in recent years to around $2 per BTU has spurred more consumers to switch to natural gas from other fuel types than when natural gas fell to $2 per BTU in 2002. But why are consumers more willing to switch now? Because in 2002, consumers didn't expect the fall in the price of natural gas to last—and they were right.

In 2002, natural gas prices fell because of the weak economy. That situation changed in 2006 when the economy came roaring back and the price of natural gas rose dramatically. In contrast, consumers have come to expect that the more recent fall in the price of natural gas will not be temporary because it is based on a permanent change: the ability to tap much larger deposits of natural gas.

Expected changes in future income can also lead to changes in demand: if you expect your income to rise in the future, you will typically borrow today and increase your demand for certain goods; if you expect your income to fall in the future, you are likely to save today and reduce your demand for some goods.

Changes in the Number of Consumers Another factor that can cause a change in demand is a change in the number of consumers of a good or service. For example, population growth in the United States eventually leads to higher demand for natural gas as more homes and businesses need to be heated in the winter and cooled in the summer.

Let's introduce a new concept: the **individual demand curve,** which shows the relationship between quantity demanded and price for an individual consumer. For example, suppose that the Gonzalez family is a consumer of natural gas for heating and cooling their home. Panel (a) of Figure 3-5 shows how many BTUs of natural gas they will buy per year at any given price. The Gonzalez family's individual demand curve is $D_{Gonzalez}$.

An **individual demand curve** illustrates the relationship between quantity demanded and price for an individual consumer.

FIGURE 3-5 Individual Demand Curves and the Market Demand Curve

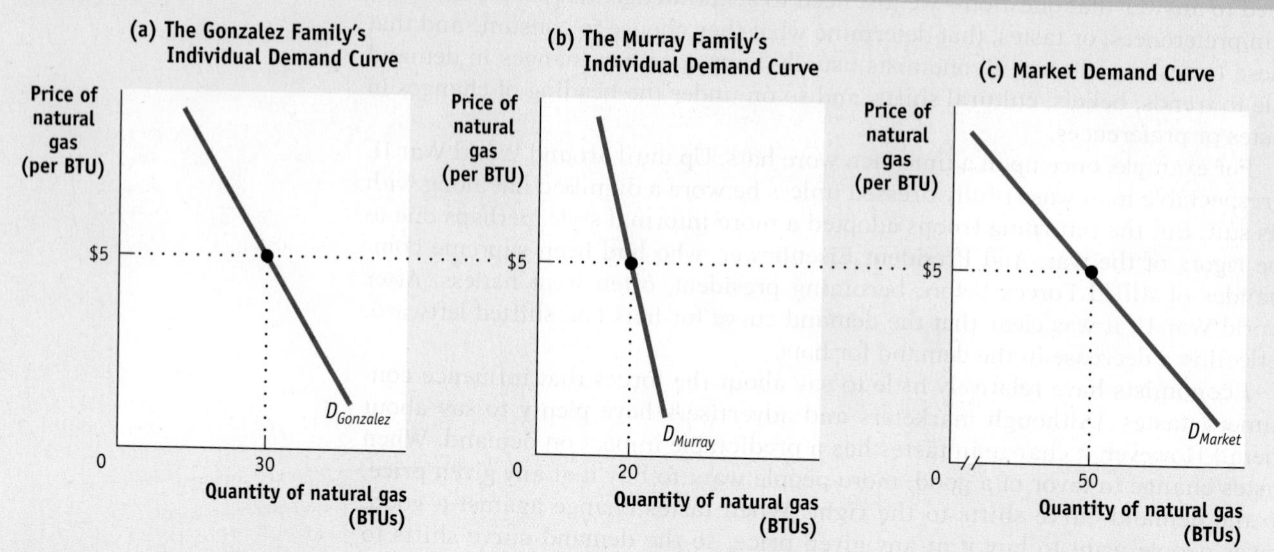

The Gonzalez family and the Murray family are the only two consumers of natural gas in the market. Panel (a) shows the Gonzalez family's individual demand curve: the number of BTUs they will buy per year at any given price. Panel (b) shows the Murray family's individual demand curve. Given that the Gonzalez family and the Murray family are the only two consumers, the *market demand curve,* which shows the quantity of BTUs demanded by all consumers at any given price, is shown in the panel (c). The market demand curve is the *horizontal sum* of the individual demand curves of all consumers. In this case, at any given price, the quantity demanded by the market is the sum of the quantities demanded by the Gonzalez family and the Murray family.

The *market demand curve* shows how the combined quantity demanded by all consumers depends on the market price of the good. (Most of the time when economists refer to the demand curve they mean the market demand curve.) The market demand curve is the *horizontal sum* of the individual demand curves of all consumers in that market.

To see what we mean by the term *horizontal sum,* assume for a moment that there are only two consumers of natural gas, the Gonzalez family and the Murray family. The Murray family consumes natural gas to fuel their natural gas–powered car. The Murray family's individual demand curve, D_{Murray}, is shown in panel (b). Panel (c) shows the market demand curve. At any given price, the quantity demanded by the market is the sum of the quantities demanded by the Gonzalez family and the Murray family. For example, at a price of $5 per BTU, the Gonzalez family demands 30 BTUs of natural gas per year and the Murray family demands 20 BTUs per year. So the quantity demanded by the market is 50 BTUs per year, as seen on the market demand curve, D_{Market}.

Clearly, the quantity demanded by the market at any given price is larger with the Murray family present than it would be if the Gonzalez family were the only consumer. The quantity demanded at any given price would be even larger if we added a third consumer, then a fourth, and so on. So an increase in the number of consumers leads to an increase in demand.

For a review of the factors that shift demand, see Table 3-1.

TABLE 3-1 Factors That Shift Demand

When this happens . . .	. . . demand increases	But when this happens . . .	. . . demand decreases
When the price of a substitute rises . . .	. . . demand for the original good increases.	When the price of a substitute falls . . .	. . . demand for the original good decreases.
When the price of a complement falls . . .	. . . demand for the original good increases.	When the price of a complement rises . . .	. . . demand for the original good decreases.
When income rises . . .	. . . demand for a normal good increases.	When income falls . . .	. . . demand for a normal good decreases.
When income falls . . .	. . . demand for an inferior good increases.	When income rises . . .	. . . demand for an inferior good decreases.
When tastes change in favor of a good . . .	. . . demand for the good increases.	When tastes change against a good . . .	. . . demand for the good decreases.
When the price is expected to rise in the future . . .	. . . demand for the good increases today.	When the price is expected to fall in the future . . .	. . . demand for the good decreases today.
When the number of consumers rises . . .	. . . market demand for the good increases.	When the number of consumers falls . . .	. . . market demand for the good decreases.

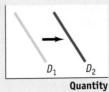
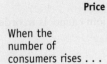
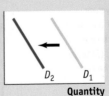

Cities can reduce traffic congestion by raising the price of driving.

ECONOMICS >> *in Action*
Beating the Traffic

All big cities have traffic problems, and many local authorities try to discourage driving in the crowded city center. If we think of an auto trip to the city center as a good that people consume, we can use the economics of demand to analyze anti-traffic policies.

One common strategy is to reduce the demand for auto trips by lowering the prices of substitutes. Many metropolitan areas subsidize bus and rail service, hoping to lure commuters out of their cars. An alternative is to raise the price of complements: several major U.S. cities impose high taxes on commercial parking garages and impose short time limits on parking meters, both to raise revenue and to discourage people from driving into the city.

A few major cities—including Singapore, London, Oslo, Stockholm, and Milan—have been willing to adopt a direct and politically controversial approach: reducing congestion by raising the price of driving. Under *congestion pricing*, a charge is imposed on cars entering the city center during business hours. Drivers buy passes, which are then debited electronically as they drive by monitoring stations. Compliance is monitored with cameras that photograph license plates.

In 2012, Moscow adopted a modest charge for parking in certain areas in an attempt to reduce its traffic jams, considered the worst of all major cities. After the approximately $1.60 charge was applied, city officials estimated that Moscow traffic decreased by 4%.

The standard cost of driving into London is currently £11.50 (about $19). Drivers who don't pay and are caught pay a fine of £130 (about $215) for each transgression.

Not surprisingly, studies have shown that after the implementation of congestion pricing, traffic does decrease. In the 1990s, London had some of the worst traffic in Europe. The introduction of its congestion charge in 2003 immediately reduced traffic in the city center by about 15%. And there has been increased use of substitutes, such as public transportation, bicycles, and ride-sharing. From 2001 to 2011, bike trips in London increased by 79%, and bus usage was up by 30%.

And less congestion led not just to fewer accidents, but to a lower *rate* of accidents as fewer cars jostled for space. One study found that from 2000 to 2010 the number of accidents per mile driven in London fell by 40%. Stockholm experienced effects similar to those in London: traffic fell by 22% in 2013 compared to pre-congestion charge levels, transit times fell by one-third to one-half, and air quality measurably improved.

>> Check Your Understanding 3-1
Solutions appear at back of book.

1. Explain whether each of the following events represents (i) a *shift of* the demand curve or (ii) a *movement along* the demand curve.
   a. A store owner finds that customers are willing to pay more for umbrellas on rainy days.
   b. When Circus Cruise Lines offered reduced prices for summer cruises in the Caribbean, their number of bookings increased sharply.
   c. People buy more long-stem roses the week of Valentine's Day, even though the prices are higher than at other times during the year.
   d. A sharp rise in the price of gasoline leads many commuters to join carpools in order to reduce their gasoline purchases.

|| The Supply Curve

Some deposits of natural gas are easier to tap than others. Before the widespread use of fracking, drillers would limit their natural gas wells to deposits that lay in easily reached pools beneath the earth. How much natural gas they would tap from existing wells, and how extensively they searched for new deposits and drilled new wells, depended on the price they expected to get for the natural gas. The higher the price, the more they would tap existing wells as well as drill and tap new wells.

So just as the quantity of natural gas that consumers want to buy depends upon the price they have to pay, the quantity that producers of natural gas, or of any good or service, are willing to produce and sell—the **quantity supplied—** depends upon the price they are offered.

The **quantity supplied** is the actual amount of a good or service people are willing to sell at some specific price.

A **supply schedule** shows how much of a good or service would be supplied at different prices.

A **supply curve** shows the relationship between quantity supplied and price.

The Supply Schedule and the Supply Curve

The table in Figure 3-6 shows how the quantity of natural gas made available varies with the price—that is, it shows a hypothetical **supply schedule** for natural gas.

A supply schedule works the same way as the demand schedule shown in Figure 3-1: in this case, the table shows the number of BTUs of natural gas producers are willing to sell at different prices. At a price of $2.50 per BTU, producers are willing to sell only 8 trillion BTUs of natural gas per year. At $2.75 per BTU, they're willing to sell 9.1 trillion BTUs. At $3, they're willing to sell 10 trillion BTUs, and so on.

In the same way that a demand schedule can be represented graphically by a demand curve, a supply schedule can be represented by a **supply curve,** as shown in Figure 3-6. Each point on the curve represents an entry from the table.

Suppose that the price of natural gas rises from $3 to $3.25; we can see that the quantity of natural gas producers are willing to sell rises from 10 trillion to 10.7 trillion BTUs. This is the normal situation for a supply curve, that a higher price leads to a higher quantity supplied. So just as demand curves normally slope downward, supply curves normally slope upward: the higher the price being offered, the more of any good or service producers will be willing to sell.

FIGURE 3-6 The Supply Schedule and the Supply Curve

Supply Schedule for Natural Gas	
Price of natural gas (per BTU)	Quantity of natural gas supplied (trillions of BTUs)
$4.00	11.6
3.75	11.5
3.50	11.2
3.25	10.7
3.00	10.0
2.75	9.1
2.50	8.0

The supply schedule for natural gas is plotted to yield the corresponding supply curve, which shows how much of a good producers are willing to sell at any given price. The supply curve and the supply schedule reflect the fact that supply curves are usually upward sloping: the quantity supplied rises when the price rises.

A **shift of the supply curve** is a change in the quantity supplied of a good or service at any given price. It is represented by the change of the original supply curve to a new position, denoted by a new supply curve.

A **movement along the supply curve** is a change in the quantity supplied of a good arising from a change in the good's price.

Shifts of the Supply Curve

Innovations in the technology of drilling natural gas deposits have led to a huge increase in U.S. production of natural gas—a 40% increase in daily production from 2005 through 2014. Figure 3-7 illustrates these events in terms of the supply schedule and the supply curve for natural gas. The table in Figure 3-7 shows two supply schedules. The schedule before improved natural gas–drilling technology was adopted is the same one as in Figure 3-6. The second schedule shows the supply of natural gas *after* the improved technology was adopted.

Just as a change in demand schedules leads to a shift of the demand curve, a change in supply schedules leads to a **shift of the supply curve**—a change in the quantity supplied at any given price. This is shown in Figure 3-7 by the shift of the supply curve before the adoption of new natural gas–drilling technology, S_1, to its new position after the adoption of new natural gas–drilling technology, S_2. Notice that S_2 lies to the right of S_1, a reflection of the fact that quantity supplied rises at any given price.

As in the analysis of demand, it's crucial to draw a distinction between such shifts of the supply curve and **movements along the supply curve**—changes in the quantity supplied arising from a change in price. We can see this difference in Figure 3-8. The movement from point A to point B is a movement along the supply curve: the quantity supplied rises along S_1 due to a rise in price. Here, a rise in price from $3 to $3.50 leads to a rise in the quantity supplied from 10 trillion to 11.2 trillion BTUs of natural gas. But the quantity supplied can also rise when the price is unchanged if there is an increase in supply—a rightward shift of the supply curve. This is shown by the rightward shift of the supply curve from S_1 to S_2. Holding the price constant at $3, the quantity supplied rises from 10 trillion BTUs at point A on S_1 to 12 billion pounds at point C on S_2.

FIGURE 3-7 An Increase in Supply

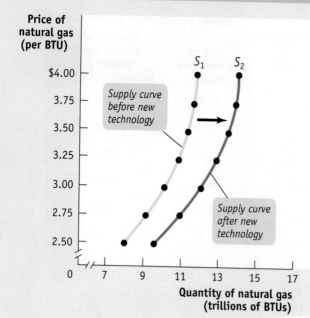

Supply Schedules for Natural Gas		
Price of natural gas (per BTU)	Quantity of natural gas supplied (trillions of BTUs)	
	Before new technology	After new technology
$4.00	11.6	13.9
3.75	11.5	13.8
3.50	11.2	13.4
3.25	10.7	12.8
3.00	10.0	12.0
2.75	9.1	10.9
2.50	8.0	9.6

The adoption of an improved natural gas–drilling technology generated an increase in supply—a rise in the quantity supplied at any given price. This event is represented by the two supply schedules—one showing supply before the new technology was adopted, the other showing supply after the new technology was adopted—and their corresponding supply curves. The increase in supply shifts the supply curve to the right.

FIGURE 3-8   Movement Along the Supply Curve versus Shift of the Supply Curve

The increase in quantity supplied when going from point *A* to point *B* reflects a movement along the supply curve: it is the result of a rise in the price of a good. The increase in quantity supplied when going from point *A* to point *C* reflects a shift of the supply curve: it is the result of an increase in the quantity supplied at any given price.

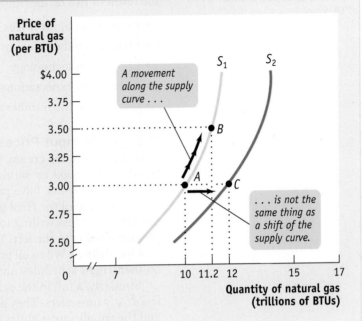

Understanding Shifts of the Supply Curve

Figure 3-9 illustrates the two basic ways in which supply curves can shift. When economists talk about an "increase in supply," they mean a *rightward* shift of the supply curve: at any given price, producers supply a larger quantity of the good than before. This is shown in Figure 3-9 by the rightward shift of the original supply curve S_1 to S_2. And when economists talk about a "decrease in supply," they mean a *leftward* shift of the supply curve: at any given price, producers supply a smaller quantity of the good than before. This is represented by the leftward shift of S_1 to S_3.

FIGURE 3-9   Shifts of the Supply Curve

Any event that increases supply shifts the supply curve to the right, reflecting a rise in the quantity supplied at any given price. Any event that decreases supply shifts the supply curve to the left, reflecting a fall in the quantity supplied at any given price.

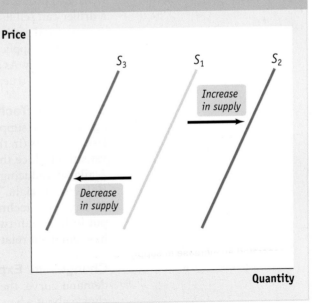

An **input** is a good or service that is used to produce another good or service.

Economists believe that shifts of the supply curve for a good or service are mainly the result of five factors (though, as with demand, there are other possible causes):

- Changes in input prices
- Changes in the prices of related goods or services
- Changes in technology
- Changes in expectations
- Changes in the number of producers

Changes in Input Prices To produce output, you need inputs. For example, to make vanilla ice cream, you need vanilla beans, cream, sugar, and so on. An **input** is any good or service that is used to produce another good or service. Inputs, like outputs, have prices. And an increase in the price of an input makes the production of the final good more costly for those who produce and sell it. So producers are less willing to supply the final good at any given price, and the supply curve shifts to the left. That is, supply decreases. For example, fuel is a major cost for airlines. When oil prices surged in 2007–2008, airlines began cutting back on their flight schedules and some went out of business.

Similarly, a fall in the price of an input makes the production of the final good less costly for sellers. They are more willing to supply the good at any given price, and the supply curve shifts to the right. That is, supply increases.

Changes in the Prices of Related Goods or Services A single producer often produces a mix of goods rather than a single product. For example, an oil refinery produces gasoline from crude oil, but it also produces heating oil and other products from the same raw material. When a producer sells several products, the quantity of any one good it is willing to supply at any given price depends on the prices of its other co-produced goods.

This effect can run in either direction. An oil refiner will supply less gasoline at any given price when the price of heating oil rises, shifting the supply curve for gasoline to the left. But it will supply more gasoline at any given price when the price of heating oil falls, shifting the supply curve for gasoline to the right. This means that gasoline and other co-produced oil products are *substitutes in production* for refiners.

In contrast, due to the nature of the production process, other goods can be *complements in production*. Producers of natural gas often find that natural gas wells also produce oil as a by-product of extraction. The higher the price at which a driller can sell its oil, the more willing it will be to drill natural gas wells and the more natural gas it will supply at any given price. Higher oil prices then lead to more natural gas supplied at any given price because oil and natural gas can be tapped simultaneously. As a result, oil is a complement in the production of natural gas. The reverse is also true: natural gas is a complement in the production of oil.

Changes in Technology As the opening story illustrates, changes in technology affect the supply curve. Technology improvements enable producers to spend less on inputs (in this case, drilling equipment, labor, land purchases, and so on), yet still produce the same amount of output. When a better technology becomes available, reducing the cost of production, supply increases and the supply curve shifts to the right.

Improved technology enabled natural gas producers to more than double output in less than two years. Technology is also the main reason that natural gas has remained relatively cheap, even as demand has grown.

Changes in Expectations Just as changes in expectations can shift the demand curve, they can also shift the supply curve. When suppliers have some choice about when they put their good up for sale, changes in the expected future price of the good can lead a supplier to supply less or more of the good today.

Consider the fact that gasoline and other oil products are often stored for significant periods of time at oil refineries before being sold to consumers. In fact, storage is normally part of producers' business strategy. Knowing that the demand for gasoline peaks in the summer, oil refiners normally store some of their gasoline produced during the spring for summer sale. Similarly, knowing that the demand for heating oil peaks in the winter, they normally store some of their heating oil produced during the fall for winter sale.

In each case, there's a decision to be made between selling the product now versus storing it for later sale. The choice a producer makes depends on a comparison of the current price and the expected future price. This example illustrates how changes in expectations can alter supply: an increase in the anticipated future price of a good or service reduces supply today, a leftward shift of the supply curve. But a fall in the anticipated future price increases supply today, a rightward shift of the supply curve.

Changes in the Number of Producers Just as changes in the number of consumers affect the demand curve, changes in the number of producers affect the supply curve. Let's examine the **individual supply curve,** by looking at panel (a) in Figure 3-10. The individual supply curve shows the relationship between quantity supplied and price for an individual producer. For example, suppose that Louisiana Drillers is a natural gas producer and that panel (a) of Figure 3-10 shows the quantity of BTUs it will supply per year at any given price. Then $S_{Louisiana}$ is its individual supply curve.

The *market supply curve* shows how the combined total quantity supplied by all individual producers in the market depends on the market price of that good. Just as the market demand curve is the horizontal sum of the individual demand curves of all consumers, the market supply curve is the horizontal sum of the individual supply curves of all producers. Assume for a moment that there are only two natural gas producers, Louisiana Drillers and Allegheny Natural Gas. Allegheny's individual supply curve is shown in panel (b). Panel (c) shows the

An **individual supply curve** illustrates the relationship between quantity supplied and price for an individual producer.

FIGURE 3-10 The Individual Supply Curve and the Market Supply Curve

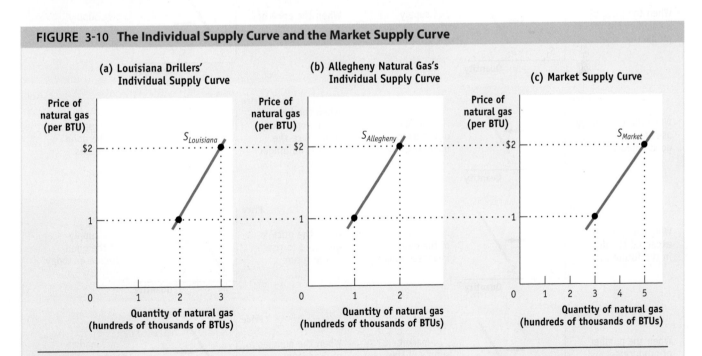

Panel (a) shows the individual supply curve for Louisiana Drillers $S_{Louisiana}$, the quantity it will sell at any given price. Panel (b) shows the individual supply curve for Allegheny Natural Gas, $S_{Allegheny}$. The market supply curve, which shows the quantity of natural gas supplied by all producers at any given price is shown in panel (c). The market supply curve is the horizontal sum of the individual supply curves of all producers.

market supply curve. At any given price, the quantity supplied to the market is the sum of the quantities supplied by Louisiana Drillers and Allegheny Natural Gas. For example, at a price of around $2 per BTU, Louisiana Drillers supplies 200,000 BTUs and Allegheny Natural Gas supplies 100,000 BTUs per year, making the quantity supplied to the market 300,000 BTUs.

Clearly, the quantity supplied to the market at any given price is larger when Allegheny Natural Gas is also a producer than it would be if Louisiana Drillers were the only supplier. The quantity supplied at a given price would be even larger if we added a third producer, then a fourth, and so on. So an increase in the number of producers leads to an increase in supply and a rightward shift of the supply curve.

For a review of the factors that shift supply, see Table 3-2.

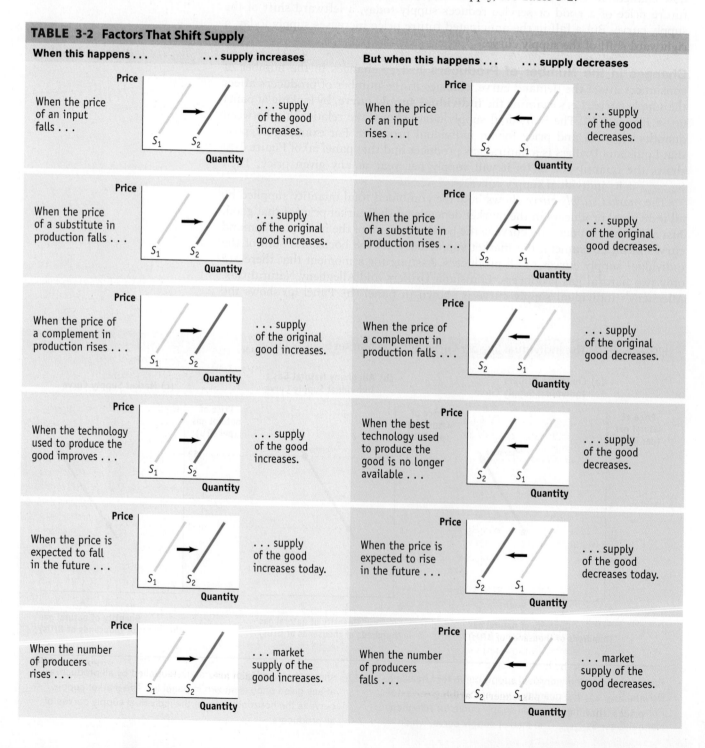

TABLE 3-2 Factors That Shift Supply

When this happens . . .	. . . supply increases	But when this happens . . .	. . . supply decreases
When the price of an input falls . . .	. . . supply of the good increases.	When the price of an input rises . . .	. . . supply of the good decreases.
When the price of a substitute in production falls . . .	. . . supply of the original good increases.	When the price of a substitute in production rises . . .	. . . supply of the original good decreases.
When the price of a complement in production rises . . .	. . . supply of the original good increases.	When the price of a complement in production falls . . .	. . . supply of the original good decreases.
When the technology used to produce the good improves . . .	. . . supply of the good increases.	When the best technology used to produce the good is no longer available . . .	. . . supply of the good decreases.
When the price is expected to fall in the future . . .	. . . supply of the good increases today.	When the price is expected to rise in the future . . .	. . . supply of the good decreases today.
When the number of producers rises . . .	. . . market supply of the good increases.	When the number of producers falls . . .	. . . market supply of the good decreases.

ECONOMICS >> *in Action*
Only Creatures Small and Pampered

Not so long ago, every rural community had a farm veterinarian who tended to cows, pigs, sheep, horses, and the occasional house pet. The life of a farm veterinarian was often arduous and dangerous (such as enduring a kick in the head from an angry steer), with long hours and sporadic payment from financially stretched farmers. Yet a farm veterinarian was considered a critical member of the community, saving valuable animals and helping farmers survive financially.

But that was then and this is now; rural areas have been losing their large-animal vets for more than 25 years. The source of the problem is competition. As the number of household pets has increased and the incomes of pet owners have grown, the demand for pet veterinarians has increased sharply. As a result, vets are drawn away from the business of caring for farm animals into the more lucrative, safer, and less time-consuming business of caring for pets. One vet who began her career caring for farm animals switched to a pet practice after "doing a C-section on a cow and it's 50 bucks. Do a C-section on a Chihuahua and you get $300. It's the money. I hate to say that."

Higher spending on pets means fewer veterinarians are available to tend to farm animals.

How can we translate this into supply and demand curves? Farm veterinary services and pet veterinary services are like gasoline and fuel oil: they're related goods that are substitutes in production. A veterinarian typically specializes in one type of practice or the other, and that decision often depends on the going price for the service. America's growing pet population, combined with the increased willingness of doting owners to spend on their companions' care, has driven up the price of pet veterinary services. As a result, fewer and fewer veterinarians have gone into farm animal practice. So the supply curve of farm veterinarians has shifted leftward—fewer farm veterinarians are offering their services at any given price.

In the end, farmers understand that it is all a matter of dollars and cents—they get fewer veterinarians because they are unwilling to pay more. As one farmer, who had recently lost an expensive cow due to the unavailability of a veterinarian, stated, "The fact that there's nothing you can do, you accept it as a business expense now. You didn't used to. If you have livestock, sooner or later you're going to have deadstock." (Although we should note that this farmer could have chosen to pay more for a vet who would have then saved his cow.)

>> Check Your Understanding 3-2
Solutions appear at back of book.

1. Explain whether each of the following events represents (i) a *shift of* the supply curve or (ii) a *movement along* the supply curve.
   a. More homeowners put their houses up for sale during a real estate boom that causes house prices to rise.
   b. Many strawberry farmers open temporary roadside stands during harvest season, even though prices are usually low at that time.
   c. Immediately after the school year begins, fast-food chains must raise wages, which represent the price of labor, to attract workers.
   d. Many construction workers temporarily move to areas that have suffered hurricane damage, lured by higher wages.
   e. Since new technologies have made it possible to build larger cruise ships (which are cheaper to run per passenger), Caribbean cruise lines offer more cabins, at lower prices, than before.

>> Quick Review

• The **supply schedule** shows how the **quantity supplied** depends on the price. The **supply curve** illustrates this relationship.

• Supply curves are normally upward sloping: at a higher price, producers are willing to supply more of a good or service.

• A change in price results in a **movement along the supply curve** and a change in the quantity supplied.

• Increases or decreases in supply lead to **shifts of the supply curve.** An increase in supply is a rightward shift: the quantity supplied rises for any given price. A decrease in supply is a leftward shift: the quantity supplied falls for any given price.

• The five main factors that can shift the supply curve are changes in (1) **input** prices, (2) prices of related goods or services, (3) technology, (4) expectations, and (5) number of producers.

• The market supply curve is the horizontal sum of the **individual supply** curves of all producers in the market.

A competitive market is in equilibrium when price has moved to a level at which the quantity of a good or service demanded equals the quantity of that good or service supplied. The price at which this takes place is the **equilibrium price,** also referred to as the **market-clearing price.** The quantity of the good or service bought and sold at that price is the **equilibrium quantity.**

Supply, Demand, and Equilibrium

We have now covered the first three key elements in the supply and demand model: the demand curve, the supply curve, and the set of factors that shift each curve. The next step is to put these elements together to show how they can be used to predict the actual price at which the good is bought and sold, as well as the actual quantity transacted.

What determines the price at which a good or service is bought and sold? What determines the quantity transacted of the good or service? In Chapter 1 we learned the general principle that *markets move toward equilibrium*, a situation in which no individual would be better off taking a different action. In the case of a competitive market, we can be more specific: a competitive market is in equilibrium when the price has moved to a level at which the quantity of a good demanded equals the quantity of that good supplied. At that price, no individual seller could make herself better off by offering to sell either more or less of the good and no individual buyer could make himself better off by offering to buy more or less of the good. In other words, at the market equilibrium, price has moved to a level that exactly matches the quantity demanded by consumers to the quantity supplied by sellers.

The price that matches the quantity supplied and the quantity demanded is the **equilibrium price;** the quantity bought and sold at that price is the **equilibrium quantity.** The equilibrium price is also known as the **market-clearing price:** it is the price that "clears the market" by ensuring that every buyer willing to pay that price finds a seller willing to sell at that price, and vice versa. So how do we find the equilibrium price and quantity?

Finding the Equilibrium Price and Quantity

The easiest way to determine the equilibrium price and quantity in a market is by putting the supply curve and the demand curve on the same diagram. Since the supply curve shows the quantity supplied at any given price and the demand curve shows the quantity demanded at any given price, the price at which the two curves cross is the equilibrium price: the price at which quantity supplied equals quantity demanded.

Figure 3-11 combines the demand curve from Figure 3-1 and the supply curve from Figure 3-6. They *intersect* at point *E*, which is the equilibrium of this market; $3 is the equilibrium price and 10 trillion BTUs is the equilibrium quantity.

Let's confirm that point *E* fits our definition of equilibrium. At a price of $3 per BTU, natural gas producers are willing to sell 10 trillion BTUs a year and natural gas consumers want to buy 10 trillion BTUs a year. So at the price of $3 per BTU, the quantity of natural gas supplied equals the quantity demanded. Notice that at any other price the market would not clear: every willing buyer would not be able to find a willing seller, or vice versa. More specifically, if the

PITFALLS

BOUGHT AND SOLD?

We have been talking about the price at which a good or service is bought *and* sold, as if the two were the same. But shouldn't we make a distinction between the price received by sellers and the price paid by buyers? In principle, yes; but it is helpful at this point to sacrifice a bit of realism in the interest of simplicity—by assuming away the difference between the prices received by sellers and those paid by buyers.

In reality, there is often a *middleman*—someone who brings buyers and sellers together. The middleman buys from suppliers, then sells to consumers at a markup. For example, natural gas brokers buy natural gas from drillers, and then sell the natural gas to gas companies who distribute it to households and firms. The drillers generally receive less than the gas companies pay per BTU of gas. But no mystery there: that difference is how natural gas brokers make a living.

In many markets, however, the difference between the buying and selling price is quite small. So it's not a bad approximation to think of the price paid by buyers as being the *same* as the price received by sellers. And that is what we assume in this chapter.

FIGURE 3-11 **Market Equilibrium**

Market equilibrium occurs at point *E*, where the supply curve and the demand curve intersect. In equilibrium, the quantity demanded is equal to the quantity supplied. In this market, the equilibrium price is $3 per BTU and the equilibrium quantity is 10 trillion BTUs per year.

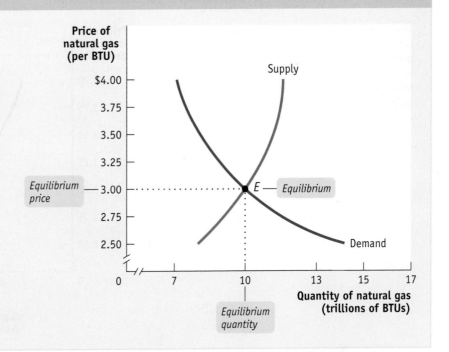

price were more than $3, the quantity supplied would exceed the quantity demanded; if the price were less than $3, the quantity demanded would exceed the quantity supplied.

The model of supply and demand, then, predicts that given the demand and supply curves shown in Figure 3-11, 10 trillion BTUs would change hands at a price of $3 per BTU. But how can we be sure that the market will arrive at the equilibrium price? We begin by answering three simple questions:

1. Why do all sales and purchases in a market take place at the same price?
2. Why does the market price fall if it is above the equilibrium price?
3. Why does the market price rise if it is below the equilibrium price?

1. Why Do All Sales and Purchases in a Market Take Place at the Same Price?

There are some markets where the same good can sell for many different prices, depending on who is selling or who is buying. For example, have you ever bought a souvenir in a tourist trap and then seen the same item on sale somewhere else for a lower price? Because tourists don't know which shops offer the best deals and don't have time for comparison shopping, sellers in tourist areas can charge different prices for the same good.

But in any market where the buyers and sellers have both been around for some time, sales and purchases tend to converge at a generally uniform price, so we can safely talk about *the* market price. It's easy to see why. Suppose a seller offered a potential buyer a price noticeably above what the buyer knew other people to be paying. The buyer would clearly be better off shopping elsewhere—unless the seller were prepared to offer a better deal.

Conversely, a seller would not be willing to sell for significantly less than the amount he knew most buyers were paying; he would be better off waiting to get a more reasonable customer. So in any well-established, ongoing market, all sellers

FIGURE 3-12 Price Above Its Equilibrium Level Creates a Surplus

The market price of $3.50 is above the equilibrium price of $3. This creates a surplus: at a price of $3.50, producers would like to sell 11.2 trillion BTUs but consumers want to buy only 8.1 trillion BTUs, so there is a surplus of 3.1 trillion BTUs. This surplus will push the price down until it reaches the equilibrium price of $3.

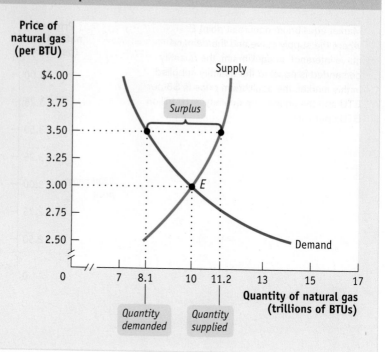

receive and all buyers pay approximately the same price. This is what we call the *market price.*

2. Why Does the Market Price Fall If It Is Above the Equilibrium Price?

Suppose the supply and demand curves are as shown in Figure 3-11 but the market price is above the equilibrium level of $3—say, $3.50. This situation is illustrated in Figure 3-12. Why can't the price stay there?

As the figure shows, at a price of $3.50 there would be more BTUs of natural gas available than consumers wanted to buy: 11.2 trillion BTUs versus 8.1 trillion BTUs. The difference of 3.1 trillion BTUs is the **surplus**—also known as the *excess supply*—of natural gas at $3.50.

This surplus means that some natural gas producers are frustrated: at the current price, they cannot find consumers who want to buy their natural gas. The surplus offers an incentive for those frustrated would-be sellers to offer a lower price in order to poach business from other producers and entice more consumers to buy. The result of this price cutting will be to push the prevailing price down until it reaches the equilibrium price. So the price of a good will fall whenever there is a surplus—that is, whenever the market price is above its equilibrium level.

3. Why Does the Market Price Rise If It Is Below the Equilibrium Price?

Now suppose the price is below its equilibrium level—say, at $2.75 per BTU, as shown in Figure 3-13. In this case, the quantity demanded, 11.5 trillion BTUs, exceeds the quantity supplied, 9.1 trillion BTUs, implying that there are would-be buyers who cannot find natural gas: there is a **shortage**, also known as an *excess demand*, of 2.4 trillion BTUs.

There is a **surplus** of a good or service when the quantity supplied exceeds the quantity demanded. Surpluses occur when the price is above its equilibrium level.

There is a **shortage** of a good or service when the quantity demanded exceeds the quantity supplied. Shortages occur when the price is below its equilibrium level.

FIGURE 3-13 Price Below Its Equilibrium Level Creates a Shortage

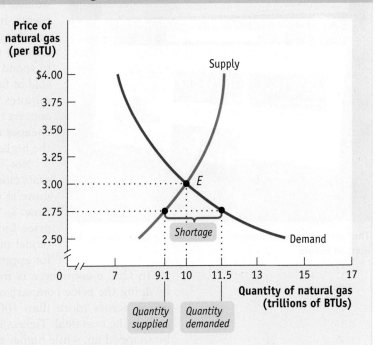

The market price of $2.75 is below the equilibrium price of $3. This creates a shortage: consumers want to buy 11.5 trillion BTUs, but only 9.1 trillion BTUs are for sale, so there is a shortage of 2.4 trillion BTUs. This shortage will push the price up until it reaches the equilibrium price of $3.

When there is a shortage, there are frustrated would-be buyers—people who want to purchase natural gas but cannot find willing sellers at the current price. In this situation, either buyers will offer more than the prevailing price or sellers will realize that they can charge higher prices. Either way, the result is to drive up the prevailing price.

This bidding up of prices happens whenever there are shortages—and there will be shortages whenever the price is below its equilibrium level. So the market price will always rise if it is below the equilibrium level.

Using Equilibrium to Describe Markets

We have now seen that a market tends to have a single price, the equilibrium price. If the market price is above the equilibrium level, the ensuing surplus leads buyers and sellers to take actions that lower the price. And if the market price is below the equilibrium level, the ensuing shortage leads buyers and sellers to take actions that raise the price. So the market price always *moves toward* the equilibrium price, the price at which there is neither surplus nor shortage.

ECONOMICS >> *in Action*
The Price of Admission

The market equilibrium, so the theory goes, is pretty egalitarian because the equilibrium price applies to everyone. That is, all buyers pay the same price—the equilibrium price—and all sellers receive that same price. But is this realistic?

The market for concert tickets is an example that seems to contradict the theory—there's one price at the box office, and there's another price (typically much higher) for the same event online where people who already have tickets resell them, such as StubHub.com or eBay. For example, compare the box office price for a Demi Lovato concert in Houston, Texas, in September 2016 to the StubHub.com price for seats in the same location: $99.95 versus $169.99.

The competitive market model determines the price you pay for concert tickets.

Puzzling as this may seem, there is no contradiction once we take opportunity costs and tastes into account. For major events, buying tickets from the box office means waiting in very long lines. Ticket buyers who use online resellers have decided that the opportunity cost of their time is too high to spend waiting in line. And tickets for major events being sold at face value by online box offices often sell out within minutes. In this case, some people who want to go to the concert badly but have missed out on the opportunity to buy cheaper tickets from the online box office are willing to pay the higher online reseller price.

Not only that, by comparing prices across sellers for seats close to one another, you can see that markets really do move to equilibrium. For example, for a seat in Section 107, Row 3, StubHub.com's price is $169.99 while ScoreBig's price for a nearby seat is $168. As the competitive market model predicts, units of the same good will end up selling for approximately the same price.

In fact, e-commerce is making markets move to equilibrium more quickly by doing the price comparisons for you. The website Seat Geek compares ticket prices across more than 100 ticket resellers, allowing customers to instantly choose the best deal. Tickets that are priced lower than those of competitors will be snapped up, while higher priced tickets will languish unsold.

And tickets on StubHub.com can sell for less than the face value for events with little appeal, while they can skyrocket for events in high demand. For example, in 2016 some fans paid over $20,000 to watch the Chicago Cubs win their first World Series Championship in 108 years. Even StubHub.com's chief executive says the site is "the embodiment of supply-and-demand economics."

So the theory of competitive markets isn't just speculation. If you want to experience it for yourself, try buying tickets to a concert (or the World Series).

>> **Check Your Understanding 3-3**

Solutions appear at back of book.

1. In the following three situations, the market is initially in equilibrium. Explain the changes in either supply or demand that result from each event. After each event described below, does a surplus or shortage exist at the original equilibrium price? What will happen to the equilibrium price as a result?
   a. 2015 was a very good year for California wine-grape growers, who produced a bumper crop.
   b. After a hurricane, Florida hoteliers often find that many people cancel their upcoming vacations, leaving them with empty hotel rooms.
   c. After a heavy snowfall, many people want to buy second-hand snowblowers at the local tool shop.

Changes in Supply and Demand

The huge fall in the price of natural gas from $14 to $2 per BTU from 2006 to 2013 may have come as a surprise to consumers, but to suppliers it was no surprise at all. Suppliers knew that advances in drilling technology had opened up vast reserves of natural gas that had been too costly to tap in the past. And, predictably, an increase in supply reduces the equilibrium price.

The adoption of improved drilling technology is an example of an event that shifted the supply curve for a good without having an effect on the demand curve. There are many such events. There are also events that shift the demand curve without shifting the supply curve. For example, a medical report that chocolate is good for you increases the demand for chocolate but does not affect the supply. Events often shift either the supply curve or the demand curve, but not both; it is therefore useful to ask what happens in each case.

We have seen that when a curve shifts, the equilibrium price and quantity change. We will now concentrate on exactly how the shift of a curve alters the equilibrium price and quantity.

What Happens When the Demand Curve Shifts

Heating oil and natural gas are substitutes: if the price of heating oil rises, the demand for natural gas will increase, and if the price of heating oil falls, the demand for natural gas will decrease. But how does the price of heating oil affect the *market equilibrium* for natural gas?

Figure 3-14 shows the effect of a rise in the price of heating oil on the market for natural gas. The rise in the price of heating oil increases the demand for natural gas. Point E_1 shows the equilibrium corresponding to the original demand curve, with P_1 the equilibrium price and Q_1 the equilibrium quantity bought and sold.

An increase in demand is indicated by a *rightward* shift of the demand curve from D_1 to D_2. At the original market price P_1, this market is no longer in equilibrium: a shortage occurs because the quantity demanded exceeds the quantity supplied. So the price of natural gas rises and generates an increase in the quantity supplied, an upward *movement along the supply curve.* A new equilibrium is established at point E_2, with a higher equilibrium price, P_2, and higher equilibrium quantity, Q_2. This sequence of events reflects a general principle: *When demand for a good or service increases, the equilibrium price and the equilibrium quantity of the good or service both rise.*

What would happen in the reverse case, a fall in the price of heating oil? A fall in the price of heating oil reduces the demand for natural gas, shifting the demand curve to the *left.* At the original price, a surplus occurs as quantity supplied exceeds quantity demanded. The price falls and leads to a decrease in the quantity supplied, resulting in a lower equilibrium price and a lower equilibrium quantity. This illustrates another general principle: *When demand for a good or service decreases, the equilibrium price and the equilibrium quantity of the good or service both fall.*

FIGURE 3-14 Equilibrium and Shifts of the Demand Curve

The original equilibrium in the market for natural gas is at E_1, at the intersection of the supply curve and the original demand curve, D_1. A rise in the price of heating oil, a substitute, shifts the demand curve rightward to D_2. A shortage exists at the original price, P_1, causing both the price and quantity supplied to rise, a movement along the supply curve. A new equilibrium is reached at E_2, with a higher equilibrium price, P_2, and a higher equilibrium quantity, Q_2. When demand for a good or service increases, the equilibrium price and the equilibrium quantity of the good or service both rise.

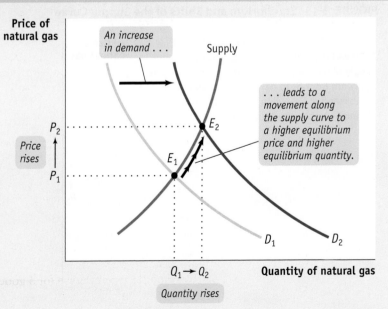

To summarize how a market responds to a change in demand: *An increase in demand leads to a rise in both the equilibrium price and the equilibrium quantity. A decrease in demand leads to a fall in both the equilibrium price and the equilibrium quantity.*

What Happens When the Supply Curve Shifts

For most goods and services, it is a bit easier to predict changes in supply than changes in demand. Physical factors that affect supply, like weather or the availability of inputs, are easier to get a handle on than the fickle tastes that affect demand. Still, with supply as with demand, what we can best predict are the *effects* of shifts of the supply curve.

As we mentioned in the opening story, improved drilling technology significantly increased the supply of natural gas from 2006 onward. Figure 3-15 shows how this shift affected the market equilibrium. The original equilibrium is at E_1, the point of intersection of the original supply curve, S_1, with an equilibrium price P_1 and equilibrium quantity Q_1. As a result of the improved technology, supply increases and S_1 shifts *rightward* to S_2. At the original price P_1, a surplus of natural gas now exists and the market is no longer in equilibrium. The surplus causes a fall in price and an increase in the quantity demanded, a downward movement along the demand curve. The new equilibrium is at E_2, with an equilibrium price P_2 and an equilibrium quantity Q_2. In the new equilibrium E_2, the price is lower and the equilibrium quantity is higher than before. This can be stated as a general principle: *When supply of a good or service increases, the equilibrium price of the good or service falls and the equilibrium quantity of the good or service rises.*

What happens to the market when supply falls? A fall in supply leads to a *leftward* shift of the supply curve. At the original price a shortage now exists; as a result, the equilibrium price rises and the quantity demanded falls. This describes what happened to the market for natural gas after Hurricane Katrina damaged natural gas production in the Gulf of Mexico in 2006. We can formulate a general principle: *When supply of a good or service decreases, the equilibrium price of the good or service rises and the equilibrium quantity of the good or service falls.*

To summarize how a market responds to a change in supply: *An increase in supply leads to a fall in the equilibrium price and a rise in the equilibrium quantity. A decrease in supply leads to a rise in the equilibrium price and a fall in the equilibrium quantity.*

PITFALLS

WHICH CURVE IS IT, ANYWAY?

When the price of some good or service changes, in general, we can say that this reflects a change in either supply or demand. But it is easy to get confused about which one. A helpful clue is the direction of change in the quantity. If the quantity sold changes in the *same* direction as the price—for example, if both the price and the quantity rise—this suggests that the demand curve has shifted. If the price and the quantity move in *opposite* directions, the likely cause is a shift of the supply curve.

FIGURE 3-15   Equilibrium and Shifts of the Supply Curve

The original equilibrium in the market is at E_1. Improved technology causes an increase in the supply of natural gas and shifts the supply curve rightward from S_1 to S_2. A new equilibrium is established at E_2, with a lower equilibrium price, P_2, and a higher equilibrium quantity, Q_2.

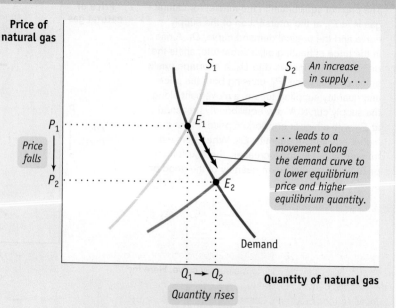

Simultaneous Shifts of Supply and Demand Curves

Finally, it sometimes happens that events shift *both* the demand and supply curves at the same time. This is not unusual; in real life, supply curves and demand curves for many goods and services shift quite often because the economic environment continually changes.

Figure 3-16 illustrates two examples of simultaneous shifts. In both panels there is an increase in supply—that is, a rightward shift of the supply curve from S_1 to S_2—representing, for example, adoption of an improved drilling technology. Notice that the rightward shift in panel (a) is larger than the one in panel (b): we can suppose that panel (a) represents a small, incremental change in technology while panel (b) represents a big advance in technology.

Both panels show a decrease in demand—that is, a leftward shift from D_1 to D_2. Also notice that the leftward shift in panel (a) is relatively larger than the one in panel (b): we can suppose that panel (a) reflects the effect on demand of a deep recession in the overall economy, while panel (b) reflects the effect of a mild winter.

In both cases the equilibrium price falls from P_1 to P_2 as the equilibrium moves from E_1 to E_2. But what happens to the equilibrium quantity, the quantity of natural gas bought and sold? In panel (a) the decrease in demand is large relative to the increase in supply, and the equilibrium quantity falls as a result. In panel (b) the increase in supply is large relative to the decrease in demand, and the equilibrium quantity rises as a result. That is, when demand decreases and supply increases, the actual quantity bought and sold can go either way depending on *how much* the demand and supply curves have shifted.

In general, when supply and demand shift in opposite directions, we can't predict what the ultimate effect will be on the quantity bought and sold. What we can say is that a curve that shifts a disproportionately greater distance than the

FIGURE 3-16   Simultaneous Shifts of the Demand and Supply Curves

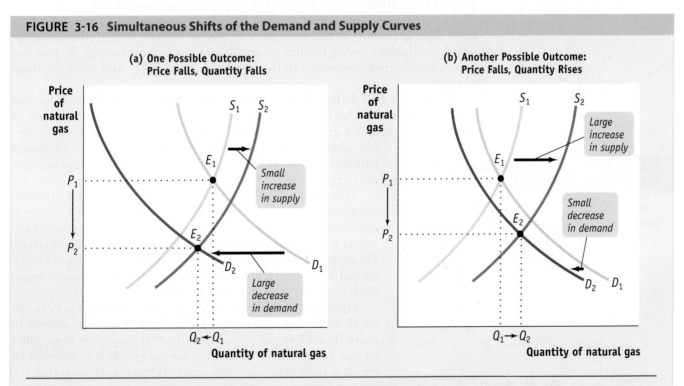

In panel (a) there is a simultaneous leftward shift of the demand curve and a rightward shift of the supply curve. Here the decrease in demand is relatively larger than the increase in supply, so the equilibrium quantity falls as the equilibrium price

also falls. In panel (b) there is also a simultaneous leftward shift of the demand curve and rightward shift of the supply curve. Here the increase in supply is large relative to the decrease in demand, so the equilibrium quantity rises as the equilibrium price falls.

other curve will have a disproportionately greater effect on the quantity bought and sold. That said, we can make the following prediction about the outcome when the supply and demand curves shift in opposite directions:

- When demand decreases and supply increases, the equilibrium price falls but the change in the equilibrium quantity is ambiguous.
- When demand increases and supply decreases, the equilibrium price rises but the change in the equilibrium quantity is ambiguous.

But suppose that the demand and supply curves shift in the same direction. This is what has happened in the United States, as the economy made a gradual recovery from the recession of 2008, resulting in an increase in both demand and supply. Can we safely make any predictions about the changes in price and quantity? In this situation, the change in quantity bought and sold can be predicted, but the change in price is ambiguous. The two possible outcomes when the supply and demand curves shift in the same direction are as follows:

- When both demand and supply increase, the equilibrium quantity rises but the change in equilibrium price is ambiguous.
- When both demand and supply decrease, the equilibrium quantity falls but the change in equilibrium price is ambiguous.

ECONOMICS >> *in Action*
The Cotton Panic and Crash of 2011

When fear of a future price increase strikes a large enough number of consumers, it can become a self-fulfilling prophecy. Much to the dismay of owners of cotton textile mills, this is exactly what happened in early 2011, when a huge surge in the price of raw cotton peaked, followed by an equally spectacular fall.

In such cases, consumers become their own worst enemy by engaging in *panic buying:* rushing to purchase more of a good because its price has gone up, which precipitates only a further price rise and more panic buying. So how did cotton buyers find themselves in this predicament in 2011? And what got them out of it?

The process had, in fact, been started years earlier. By 2010, demand for cotton had rebounded sharply from lows set during the global financial crisis of 2007–2008. In addition, greater demand for cotton clothing in countries with rapidly growing middle classes, like China, added to the increased demand for cotton. This had the effect of shifting the demand curve rightward.

At the same time there were significant supply reductions to the global market for cotton. India, the second largest exporter of cotton (an *exporter* sells goods to foreign buyers), restricted the sale of its cotton abroad to aid its own textile mills. And Pakistan, China, and Australia, also big cotton growers, experienced widespread flooding that significantly reduced their cotton crops. Both of these events shifted the supply curve leftward.

Figure 3-17, shows that while cotton had traded at between $0.35 and $0.60 per pound from 2000 to 2010, it surged to more than $2.40 per pound in early 2011—up more than 200% in one year. As high prices for cotton sparked panic buying, the demand curve shifted further rightward, intensifying the buying frenzy.

Yet by the end of 2011, cotton prices plummeted to $0.86 per pound. What happened? A number of things, illustrating the forces of supply and demand. First, demand fell as clothing

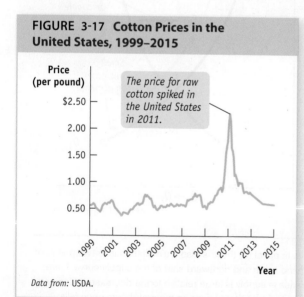

FIGURE 3-17 Cotton Prices in the United States, 1999–2015

The price for raw cotton spiked in the United States in 2011.

Data from: USDA.

manufacturers, unwilling to pass on huge price increases to their customers, shifted to less expensive fabrics like polyester. Second, supply increased as farmers planted more acreage of cotton in hopes of garnering high prices. As the effects of supply and demand became obvious, buyers stopped panicking and cotton prices finally fell back down to earth.

>> Check Your Understanding 3-4
Solutions appear at back of book.

1. For each of the following, determine (i) the market in question; (ii) whether a shift in demand or supply occurred, the direction of the shift, and what induced the shift; and (iii) the effect of the shift on the equilibrium price and the equilibrium quantity.
   a. As U.S. gasoline prices fell during the 1990s, more people bought large cars.
   b. As technological innovation has lowered the cost of recycling used paper, fresh paper made from recycled stock is used more frequently.
   c. When a local cable company offers cheaper on-demand films, local movie theaters have more unfilled seats.

2. When a new, faster computer chip is introduced, demand for computers using the older, slower chips decreases. Simultaneously, computer makers increase their production of computers containing the old chips in order to clear out their stocks of old chips.
   a. Draw two diagrams of the market for computers containing the old chips: one in which the equilibrium quantity falls in response to these events and one in which the equilibrium quantity rises.
   b. What happens to the equilibrium price in each diagram?

Competitive Markets—and Others

Earlier in this chapter we defined a competitive market and explained that the supply and demand framework is a model of competitive markets. But why does it matter whether or not a market is competitive? Now that we've seen how the supply and demand model works, we can offer some explanation.

To understand why competitive markets are different from other markets, compare the problems facing two individuals: a wheat farmer who must decide whether to grow more wheat and the president of a giant aluminum company—say, Alcoa—who must decide whether to produce more aluminum.

For the wheat farmer, the question is simply whether the extra wheat can be sold at a price high enough to justify the extra production cost. The farmer need not worry about whether producing more wheat will affect the price of the wheat he or she was already planning to grow. That's because the wheat market is competitive. There are thousands of wheat farmers, and one farmer's decision will not impact the market price.

But for the Alcoa executive, the aluminum market is *not* competitive. There are only a few big producers, including Alcoa, and each of them is well aware that its actions *do* have a noticeable impact on the market price. This adds a whole new level of complexity to the decisions producers have to make. Alcoa can't decide whether or not to produce more aluminum just by asking whether the additional product will sell for more than it costs to make. The company also has to ask whether producing more aluminum will drive down the market price and reduce its *profit*, its net gain from producing and selling its output.

When a market is competitive, individuals can base decisions on less complicated analyses than those used in a noncompetitive market. This in turn means that it's easier for economists to build a model of a competitive market than of a noncompetitive market.

This doesn't mean that economic analysis has nothing to say about noncompetitive markets. On the contrary, economists can offer some very important insights into how other kinds of markets work. But those insights require other models.

Uber Gives Riders a Lesson in Supply and Demand

Created in 2009 by two young entrepreneurs, Garrett Camp and Travis Kalanick, Uber was designed to alleviate a common frustration: how to find a taxi when there aren't any available. In a densely populated city like New York City, finding a taxi is relatively easy on most days—stand on a corner, stick out your arm, and before long a taxi will stop to pick you up. And you know exactly what taxi fare rates will be before you step into the car, because they are set by city regulators.

But at other times, it is not so easy to find a taxi, and you can wait a very long time for one—for example, on rainy days or during rush hour. As you wait, you will probably notice empty taxis passing you by—drivers who have quit working for the day and are headed home. Moreover, there are times when it is simply impossible to hail a taxi—such as during a snowstorm or on New Year's Eve.

Uber was created to address this problem. Using an app, Uber connects people who want a ride to drivers with cars. It also registers drivers, sets fares, and automatically collects payment from a registered rider's credit card. Uber then keeps 25% of the fare, with the rest going to the driver. In 2016, Uber was operating in 73 countries and in more than 450 cities, and booked $10.8 billion in rides.

In New York City, Uber fares are roughly comparable to regular taxi fares *during normal driving hours*. The qualification *during normal driving hours* is important because at other times Uber's rates fluctuate. When there are more people looking for a ride than cars available, Uber uses what it calls *surge pricing*: setting the rate higher until everyone who wants a car at the going price can get one. For example, during a snowstorm or on New Year's Eve, Uber rides cost around 9 to 10 times the standard price. Enraged, some Uber customers have accused it of price gouging.

But according to Kalanick, Uber's surge pricing is simply a method of keeping customers happy because the surge price is calculated to leave as few people as possible without a ride. As he explains, "We do not own cars nor do we employ drivers. Higher prices are required to get cars on the road and keep them on the road during the busiest times." However, with more drivers joining Uber's fleet, drivers are finding that it takes longer hours to make sufficient income. So in cities like San Diego, that don't have an existing fleet of taxis, Uber drivers have banded together to take "synchronized breaks" during peak hours, such as Saturday nights. These breaks cause prices to surge, which prompts the drivers to jump into their cars. Clearly these Uber drivers know how supply and demand works.

QUESTIONS FOR THOUGHT

1. What accounts for the fact that before Uber's arrival, there were typically enough taxis available for everyone who wanted one on good weather days, but not enough available on bad weather days?

2. How does Uber's surge pricing solve the problem? Assess Kalanick's claim that the price is set to leave as few people possible without a ride.

3. Use a supply and demand diagram to illustrate how Uber drivers can cause prices to surge by taking coordinated breaks. Why is this strategy unlikely to work in New York, a large city with an established fleet of taxis?

SUMMARY

1. The **supply and demand model** illustrates how a **competitive market,** one with many buyers and sellers, none of whom can influence the market price, works.

2. The **demand schedule** shows the **quantity demanded** at each price and is represented graphically by a **demand curve.** The **law of demand** says that demand curves slope downward; that is, a higher price for a good or service leads people to demand a smaller quantity, other things equal.

3. A **movement along the demand curve** occurs when a price change leads to a change in the quantity demanded. When economists talk of increasing or decreasing demand, they mean **shifts of the demand curve**—a change in the quantity demanded at any given price. An increase in demand causes a rightward shift of the demand curve. A decrease in demand causes a leftward shift.

4. There are five main factors that shift the demand curve:
   • A change in the prices of related goods or services, such as **substitutes** or **complements**
   • A change in income: when income rises, the demand for **normal goods** increases and the demand for **inferior goods** decreases
   • A change in tastes
   • A change in expectations
   • A change in the number of consumers

5. The market demand curve for a good or service is the horizontal sum of the **individual demand curves** of all consumers in the market.

6. The **supply schedule** shows the **quantity supplied** at each price and is represented graphically by a **supply curve.** Supply curves usually slope upward.

7. A **movement along the supply curve** occurs when a price change leads to a change in the quantity supplied. When economists talk of increasing or decreasing supply, they mean **shifts of the supply curve**—a change

in the quantity supplied at any given price. An increase in supply causes a rightward shift of the supply curve. A decrease in supply causes a leftward shift.

8. There are five main factors that shift the supply curve:
   • A change in **input** prices
   • A change in the prices of related goods and services
   • A change in technology
   • A change in expectations
   • A change in the number of producers

9. The market supply curve for a good or service is the horizontal sum of the **individual supply curves** of all producers in the market.

10. The supply and demand model is based on the principle that the price in a market moves to its **equilibrium price,** or **market-clearing price,** the price at which the quantity demanded is equal to the quantity supplied. This quantity is the **equilibrium quantity.** When the price is above its market-clearing level, there is a **surplus** that pushes the price down. When the price is below its market-clearing level, there is a **shortage** that pushes the price up.

11. An increase in demand increases both the equilibrium price and the equilibrium quantity; a decrease in demand has the opposite effect. An increase in supply reduces the equilibrium price and increases the equilibrium quantity; a decrease in supply has the opposite effect.

12. Shifts of the demand curve and the supply curve can happen simultaneously. When they shift in opposite directions, the change in equilibrium price is predictable but the change in equilibrium quantity is not. When they shift in the same direction, the change in equilibrium quantity is predictable but the change in equilibrium price is not. In general, the curve that shifts the greater distance has a greater effect on the changes in equilibrium price and quantity.

KEY TERMS

Competitive market, p. 66
Supply and demand model, p. 66
Demand schedule, p. 67
Quantity demanded, p. 68
Demand curve, p. 68
Law of demand, p. 68
Shift of the demand curve, p. 69
Movement along the demand
   curve, p. 70

Substitutes, p. 72
Complements, p. 72
Normal good, p. 72
Inferior good, p. 72
Individual demand curve, p. 73
Quantity supplied, p. 77
Supply schedule, p. 77
Supply curve, p. 77
Shift of the supply curve, p. 78

Movement along the supply curve,
   p. 78
Input, p. 80
Individual supply curve, p. 81
Equilibrium price, p. 84
Market-clearing price, p. 84
Equilibrium quantity, p. 84
Surplus, p. 86
Shortage, p. 86

PROBLEMS

1. A study conducted by Yahoo! revealed that chocolate is the most popular flavor of ice cream in America. For each of the following, indicate the possible effects on demand, supply, or both as well as equilibrium price and quantity of chocolate ice cream.

   a. A severe drought in the Midwest causes dairy farmers to reduce the number of milk-producing cattle in their herds by a third. These dairy farmers supply cream that is used to manufacture chocolate ice cream.

   b. A new report by the American Medical Association reveals that chocolate does, in fact, have significant health benefits.

   c. The discovery of cheaper synthetic vanilla flavoring lowers the price of vanilla ice cream.

   d. New technology for mixing and freezing ice cream lowers manufacturers' costs of producing chocolate ice cream.

2. In a supply and demand diagram, draw the shift of the demand curve for hamburgers in your hometown due to the following events. In each case, show the effect on equilibrium price and quantity.

   a. The price of tacos increases.

   b. All hamburger sellers raise the price of their french fries.

   c. Income falls in town. Assume that hamburgers are a normal good for most people.

   d. Income falls in town. Assume that hamburgers are an inferior good for most people.

   e. Hot dog stands cut the price of hot dogs.

3. The market for many goods changes in predictable ways according to the time of year, in response to events such as holidays, vacation times, seasonal changes in production, and so on. Using supply and demand, explain the change in price in each of the following cases. Note that supply and demand may shift simultaneously.

   a. Lobster prices usually fall during the summer peak lobster harvest season, despite the fact that people like to eat lobster during the summer more than at any other time of year.

   b. The price of a Christmas tree is lower after Christmas than before but fewer trees are sold.

   c. The price of a round-trip ticket to Paris on Air France falls by more than $200 after the end of school vacation in September. This happens despite the fact that generally worsening weather increases the cost of operating flights to Paris, and Air France therefore reduces the number of flights to Paris at any given price.

4. Show in a diagram the effect on the demand curve, the supply curve, the equilibrium price, and the equilibrium quantity of each of the following events.

   a. The market for newspapers in your town

   Case 1: The salaries of journalists go up.

   Case 2: There is a big news event in your town, which is reported in the newspapers.

   b. The market for Seattle Seahawks cotton T-shirts

   Case 1: The Seahawks win the Super Bowl.

   Case 2: The price of cotton increases.

   c. The market for bagels

   Case 1: People realize how fattening bagels are.

   Case 2: People have less time to make themselves a cooked breakfast.

   d. The market for the Krugman and Wells economics textbook

   Case 1: Your professor makes it required reading for all of his or her students.

   Case 2: Printing costs for textbooks are lowered by the use of synthetic paper.

5. Let's assume that each person in the United States consumes an average of 37 gallons of soft drinks (nondiet) at an average price of $2 per gallon and that the U.S. population is 294 million. At a price of $1.50 per gallon, each individual consumer would demand 50 gallons of soft drinks. From this information about the individual demand schedule, calculate the market demand schedule for soft drinks for the prices of $1.50 and $2 per gallon.

6. Suppose that the supply schedule of Maine lobsters is as follows:

Price of lobster (per pound)	Quantity of lobster supplied (pounds)
$25	800
20	700
15	600
10	500
5	400

Suppose that Maine lobsters can be sold only in the United States. The U.S. demand schedule for Maine lobsters is as follows:

Price of lobster (per pound)	Quantity of lobster demanded (pounds)
$25	200
20	400
15	600
10	800
5	1,000

a. Draw the demand curve and the supply curve for Maine lobsters. What are the equilibrium price and quantity of lobsters?

Now suppose that Maine lobsters can be sold in France. The French demand schedule for Maine lobsters is as follows:

Price of lobster (per pound)	Quantity of lobster demanded (pounds)
$25	100
20	300
15	500
10	700
5	900

b. What is the demand schedule for Maine lobsters now that French consumers can also buy them? Draw a supply and demand diagram that illustrates the new equilibrium price and quantity of lobsters. What will happen to the price at which fishermen can sell lobster? What will happen to the price paid by U.S. consumers? What will happen to the quantity consumed by U.S. consumers?

7. Find the flaws in reasoning in the following statements, paying particular attention to the distinction between shifts of and movements along the supply and demand curves. Draw a diagram to illustrate what actually happens in each situation.

a. "A technological innovation that lowers the cost of producing a good might seem at first to result in a reduction in the price of the good to consumers. But a fall in price will increase demand for the good, and higher demand will send the price up again. It is not certain, therefore, that an innovation will really reduce price in the end."

b. "A study shows that eating a clove of garlic a day can help prevent heart disease, causing many consumers to demand more garlic. This increase in demand results in a rise in the price of garlic. Consumers, seeing that the price of garlic has gone up, reduce their demand for garlic. This causes the demand for garlic to decrease and the price of garlic to fall. Therefore, the ultimate effect of the study on the price of garlic is uncertain."

8. The following table shows a demand schedule for a normal good.

Price	Quantity demanded
$23	70
21	90
19	110
17	130

a. Do you think that the increase in quantity demanded (say, from 90 to 110 in the table) when price decreases (from $21 to $19) is due to a rise in consumers' income? Explain clearly (and briefly) why or why not.

b. Now suppose that the good is an inferior good. Would the demand schedule still be valid for an inferior good?

c. Lastly, assume you do not know whether the good is normal or inferior. Devise an experiment that would allow you to determine which one it was. Explain.

9. In recent years, the number of car producers in China has increased rapidly. In fact, China now has more car brands than the United States. In addition, car sales have climbed every year and automakers have increased their output at even faster rates, causing fierce competition and a decline in prices. At the same time, Chinese consumers' incomes have risen. Assume that cars are a normal good. Draw a diagram of the supply and demand curves for cars in China to explain what has happened in the Chinese car market.

10. Aaron Hank is a star hitter for the Bay City baseball team. He is close to breaking the major league record for home runs hit during one season, and it is widely anticipated that in the next game he will break that record. As a result, tickets for the team's next game have been a hot commodity. But today it is announced that, due to a knee injury, he will not in fact play in the team's next game. Assume that season ticketholders are able to resell their tickets if they wish. Use supply and demand diagrams to explain your answers to parts a and b.

a. Show the case in which this announcement results in a lower equilibrium price and a lower equilibrium quantity than before the announcement.

b. Show the case in which this announcement results in a lower equilibrium price and a higher equilibrium quantity than before the announcement.

c. What accounts for whether case a or case b occurs?

d. Suppose that a scalper had secretly learned before the announcement that Aaron Hank would not play in the next game. What actions do you think he would take?

11. Fans of music often bemoan the high price of concert tickets. One rock superstar has argued that it isn't worth hundreds, even thousands, of dollars to hear him and his band play. Let's assume this star sold out arenas around the country at an average ticket price of $75.

a. How would you evaluate the argument that ticket prices are too high?

b. Suppose that due to this star's protests, ticket prices were lowered to $50. In what sense is this price too low? Draw a diagram using supply and demand curves to support your argument.

c. Suppose the superstar really wanted to bring down ticket prices. Since he and his band control the supply of their services, what do you recommend they do? Explain using a supply and demand diagram.

d. Suppose the band's next album was a total dud. Do you think they would still have to worry about ticket prices being too high? Why or why not? Draw a supply and demand diagram to support your argument.

e. Suppose the group announced their next tour was going to be their last. What effect would this likely have on the demand for and price of tickets? Illustrate with a supply and demand diagram.

12. After several years of decline, the market for hand-made acoustic guitars is making a comeback. These guitars are usually made in small workshops employing relatively few highly skilled luthiers. Assess the impact on the equilibrium price and quantity of hand-made acoustic guitars as a result of each of the following events. In your answers indicate which curve(s) shift(s) and in which direction.

a. Environmentalists succeed in having the use of Brazilian rosewood banned in the United States, forcing luthiers to seek out alternative, more costly woods.

b. A foreign producer reengineers the guitar-making process and floods the market with identical guitars.

c. Music featuring handmade acoustic guitars makes a comeback as audiences tire of heavy metal and alternative rock music.

d. The country goes into a deep recession and the income of the average American falls sharply.

13. *Demand twisters:* Sketch and explain the demand relationship in each of the following statements.

a. I would never buy a Taylor Swift album! You couldn't even give me one for nothing.

b. I generally buy a bit more coffee as the price falls. But once the price falls to $2 per pound, I'll buy out the entire stock of the supermarket.

c. I spend more on orange juice even as the price rises. (Does this mean that I must be violating the law of demand?)

d. Due to a tuition rise, most students at a college find themselves with less disposable income. Almost all of them eat more frequently at the school cafeteria and less often at restaurants, even though prices at the cafeteria have risen, too. (This one requires that you draw both the demand and the supply curves for school cafeteria meals.)

14. Will Shakespeare is a struggling playwright in sixteenth-century London. As the price he receives for writing a play increases, he is willing to write more plays. For the following situations, use a diagram to illustrate how each event affects the equilibrium price and quantity in the market for Shakespeare's plays.

a. The playwright Christopher Marlowe, Shakespeare's chief rival, is killed in a bar brawl.

b. The bubonic plague, a deadly infectious disease, breaks out in London.

c. To celebrate the defeat of the Spanish Armada, Queen Elizabeth declares several weeks of festivities, which involves commissioning new plays.

15. This year, the small town of Middling experiences a sudden doubling of the birth rate. After three years, the birth rate returns to normal. Use a diagram to illustrate the effect of these events on the following.

a. The market for an hour of babysitting services in Middling this year

b. The market for an hour of babysitting services 14 years into the future, after the birth rate has returned to normal, by which time children born today are old enough to work as babysitters

c. The market for an hour of babysitting services 30 years into the future, when children born today are likely to be having children of their own

16. Use a diagram to illustrate how each of the following events affects the equilibrium price and quantity of pizza.

a. The price of mozzarella cheese rises.

b. The health hazards of hamburgers are widely publicized.

c. The price of tomato sauce falls.

d. The incomes of consumers rise, and pizza is an inferior good.

e. Consumers expect the price of pizza to fall next week.

17. Although he was a prolific artist, Pablo Picasso painted only 1,000 canvases during his "Blue Period." Picasso is now dead, and all of his Blue Period works are currently on display in museums and private galleries throughout Europe and the United States.

a. Draw a supply curve for Picasso Blue Period works. Why is this supply curve different from ones you have seen?

b. Given the supply curve from part a, the price of a Picasso Blue Period work will be entirely dependent on what factor(s)? Draw a diagram showing how the equilibrium price of such a work is determined.

c. Suppose rich art collectors decide that it is essential to acquire Picasso Blue Period art for their collections. Show the impact of this on the market for these paintings.

18. Draw the appropriate curve in each of the following cases. Is it like or unlike the curves you have seen so far? Explain.

a. The demand for cardiac bypass surgery, given that the government pays the full cost for any patient

b. The demand for elective cosmetic plastic surgery, given that the patient pays the full cost

c. The supply of reproductions of Rembrandt paintings

19. In each of the following, what is the mistake that underlies the statement? Explain the mistake in terms of supply and demand and the factors that influence them.

a. Consumers are illogical because they are buying more Starbucks beverages in 2016 despite the fact that Starbucks has raised prices from 10 to 30 cents per drink.

b. Consumers are illogical because they buy less at Cost-U-Less Warehouse Superstore when their incomes go up.

c. Consumers are illogical for buying an iPhone 7 when an iPhone 5 costs less.

20. In 2016 the price of oil fell to a 12-year low. For drivers, the cost of driving fell significantly as gasoline prices plunged. For the airline industry, the cost of operation also fell significantly because jet fuel is a major expense.

a. Draw a supply and demand diagram that illustrates the effect of a fall in the price of jet fuel on the supply of air travel.

b. Draw a supply and demand diagram that illustrates the effect of a fall in the price of oil on the demand for air travel. (*Hint:* think about this in terms of the substitutes for air travel, like driving.)

c. Put the diagrams from parts a and b together. What happens to the equilibrium price and quantity of air travel?

Despite the fall in the cost of driving, many more Americans chose to fly to their destinations during 2014 to 2016, as incomes rose and people splurged on vacations that had been postponed during the Great Recession.

d. Using your results from part c, modify your diagram to illustrate an outcome in which the equilibrium price of air travel rises as people take more vacations by air.

WORK IT OUT Interactive step-by-step help with solving this problem can be found online.

21. The accompanying table gives the annual U.S. demand and supply schedules for pickup trucks.

Price of truck	Quantity of trucks demanded (millions)	Quantity of trucks supplied (millions)
$20,000	20	14
25,000	18	15
30,000	16	16
35,000	14	17
40,000	12	18

a. Plot the demand and supply curves using these schedules. Indicate the equilibrium price and quantity on your diagram.

b. Suppose the tires used on pickup trucks are found to be defective. What would you expect to happen in the market for pickup trucks? Show this on your diagram.

c. Suppose that the U.S. Department of Transportation imposes costly regulations on manufacturers that cause them to reduce supply by one-third at any given price. Calculate and plot the new supply schedule and indicate the new equilibrium price and quantity on your diagram.

4 Price Controls and Quotas: Meddling with Markets

BIG CITY, NOT SO BRIGHT IDEAS

IN 2015, A REAL ESTATE DEVELOPER purchased a New York City apartment building and wanted to evict three elderly tenants who had lived in their apartment for decades.

In New York City, an affordable and available rental apartment is hard to find.

But inducing the tenants to leave was no easy matter because their apartment was one of 27,000 units covered by New York's *rent control* law. The law prevents landlords from raising rents or evicting tenants in rent-controlled apartments except when specifically given permission by a city agency. In fact, under the law it would have been virtually impossible to evict these tenants against their will.

So, how was the situation resolved? After intense negotiations, the three tenants finally agreed to move after receiving a payment of $25 million from the developer. Yes, *$25 million.*

Why was the developer willing to pay so much? Because in New York City's highly lucrative housing market, with its shortage of places to live, the developer stood to make a lot more money by constructing a larger building with apartments that are not rent controlled and that will rent for very high prices. Some developers argue that the difficulty they have dislodging rent-controlled tenants in New York limits their ability to build more housing, leading to a shortage of all apartments, whether affordable or expensive.

Rent control is a type of *market intervention*, a policy imposed by government to prevail over the market forces of supply and demand—in this case, over the market forces of the supply and demand for New York City rental apartments.

Although rent control laws were introduced during World War II in many major American cities to protect the interests of tenants, the problems they create have led most cities to discard them. New York City and San Francisco are notable exceptions, although rent control covers only a small and diminishing proportion of rental apartments in both cities.

In Chapter 3 we learned the principle that a market moves to equilibrium—that the market price rises or falls to the level at which the quantity of a good that people are willing to supply is equal to the quantity that other people demand. However, when governments intervene in markets, they try to defy that principle.

As we will learn in this chapter, when a government tries to dictate either a market price or a market quantity that's different from the equilibrium price or quantity, the market strikes back in predictable ways. The shortage of apartments is one example of what happens when the logic of the market is defied: a market intervention like rent control keeps the price of apartment rentals below market equilibrium level, creating a shortage and other serious problems. And, as we'll see, those problems inevitably create winners and losers.

Our ability to predict what will happen when governments try to defy supply and demand shows the power and usefulness of supply and demand analysis.

We will also examine another form of market intervention used in New York and other cities—a licensing system for taxis that reduces the number of taxis offering rides below the market equilibrium level. Originally intended to protect the interests of both drivers and customers, like rent control, it led to a shortage of taxis. Although in recent years the rise of companies like Uber and Lyft has upended market interventions in the taxi industry and moved it closer to market equilibrium. We address this development in the chapter and in the Business Case at end of chapter.

Although there are specific winners and losers from market intervention, we will learn how and why society as a whole loses—a result that has led economists to be generally skeptical of market interventions except in certain well-defined situations. ●

Price controls are legal restrictions on how high or low a market price may go. They can take two forms: a **price ceiling,** a maximum price sellers are allowed to charge for a good or service, or a **price floor,** a minimum price buyers are required to pay for a good or service.

Why Governments Control Prices

As we know from Chapter 3, a market moves to equilibrium—the market price moves to the level at which the quantity supplied equals the quantity demanded. But this equilibrium price does not necessarily please either buyers or sellers.

After all, buyers would always like to pay less if they could, and sometimes they can make a strong moral or political case that they should pay lower prices. For example, what if the equilibrium between supply and demand for apartments in a major city leads to rental rates that an average working person can't afford? In that case, a government might well be under pressure to impose limits on the rents landlords can charge.

Sellers, however, would always like to get more money for what they sell, and sometimes they can make a strong moral or political case that they should receive higher prices. For example, consider the labor market: the price for an hour of a worker's time is the wage rate. What if the equilibrium between supply and demand for less skilled workers leads to wage rates that yield an income below the poverty level? In that case, a government might well be pressured to require employers to pay a rate no lower than some specified minimum wage.

In other words, there is often a strong political demand for governments to intervene in markets. And powerful interests can make a compelling case that a market intervention favoring them is "fair." When a government intervenes to regulate prices, we say that it imposes **price controls.** These controls typically take the form either of an upper limit, a **price ceiling,** or a lower limit, a **price floor.**

Unfortunately, it's not that easy to tell a market what to do. As we will now see, when a government tries to legislate prices—whether it legislates them down by imposing a price ceiling or up by imposing a price floor—there are certain predictable and unpleasant side effects.

We make an important assumption in this chapter: the markets in question are efficient before price controls are imposed. But markets can sometimes be inefficient—for example, a market dominated by a monopolist, a single seller that has the power to influence the market price. When markets are inefficient, price controls don't necessarily cause problems and can potentially move the market closer to efficiency.

In practice, however, price controls are often imposed on efficient markets—like the New York apartment market. And so the analysis in this chapter applies to many important real-world situations.

Price Ceilings

Aside from rent control, there are not many price ceilings in the United States today. But at times they have been widespread. Price ceilings are typically imposed during crises—wars, harvest failures, natural disasters—because these events often lead to sudden price increases that hurt many people but produce big gains for a lucky few.

The U.S. government imposed ceilings on many prices during World War II: the war sharply increased demand for raw materials, such as aluminum and steel, and price controls prevented those with access to these raw materials from earning huge profits. Price controls on oil were imposed in 1973, when an embargo by Arab oil-exporting countries seemed likely to generate huge profits for U.S. oil companies. Price controls were instituted again in 2012 by New York and New Jersey authorities in the aftermath of Hurricane Sandy, as gas shortages led to rampant price-gouging.

Rent control in New York is, as we mention in the opening story, a legacy of World War II: it was imposed because wartime production led to an economic boom that increased demand for apartments at a time when the labor and raw materials that might have been used to build them were being used to win the war instead. Although most price controls were removed soon after the war ended, New York's rent limits were retained and gradually extended to buildings not previously covered, leading to some very strange situations.

You can rent a one-bedroom apartment in Manhattan on fairly short notice—if you are able and willing to pay several thousand dollars a month and live in a less desirable area. Yet some people pay only a small fraction of this for comparable apartments, and others pay hardly more for bigger apartments in better locations.

Aside from producing great deals for some renters, however, what are the broader consequences of New York's rent-control system? To answer this question, we turn to the model we developed in Chapter 3: the supply and demand model.

Modeling a Price Ceiling

To see what can go wrong when a government imposes a price ceiling on an efficient market, consider Figure 4-1, which shows a simplified model of the market for apartments in New York. For the sake of simplicity, we imagine that all apartments are exactly the same and so would rent for the same price in an unregulated market.

The table in Figure 4-1 shows the demand and supply schedules; the demand and supply curves are shown on the left. We show the quantity of apartments on the horizontal axis and the monthly rent per apartment on the vertical axis. You can see that in an unregulated market the equilibrium would be at point E: 2 million apartments would be rented for $1,000 each per month.

Now suppose that the government imposes a price ceiling, limiting rents to a price below the equilibrium price—say, no more than $800.

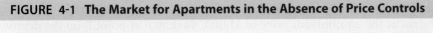

FIGURE 4-1   The Market for Apartments in the Absence of Price Controls

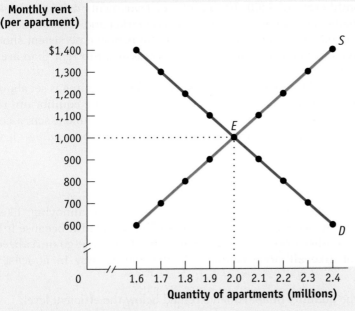

Monthly rent (per apartment)	Quantity of apartments (millions)	
	Quantity demanded	Quantity supplied
$1,400	1.6	2.4
1,300	1.7	2.3
1,200	1.8	2.2
1,100	1.9	2.1
1,000	2.0	2.0
900	2.1	1.9
800	2.2	1.8
700	2.3	1.7
600	2.4	1.6

Without government intervention, the market for apartments reaches equilibrium at point E with a market rent of $1,000 per month and 2 million apartments rented.

FIGURE 4-2 The Effects of a Price Ceiling

The black horizontal line represents the government-imposed price ceiling on rents of $800 per month. This price ceiling reduces the quantity of apartments supplied to 1.8 million, point A, and increases the quantity demanded to 2.2 million, point B. This creates a persistent shortage of 400,000 units: 400,000 people who want apartments at the legal rent of $800 but cannot get them.

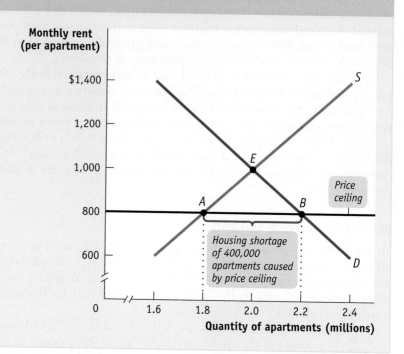

Figure 4-2 shows the effect of the price ceiling, represented by the line at $800. At the enforced rental rate of $800, landlords have less incentive to offer apartments, so they won't be willing to supply as many as they would at the equilibrium rate of $1,000. They will choose point A on the supply curve, offering only 1.8 million apartments for rent, 200,000 fewer than in the unregulated market.

At the same time, more people will want to rent apartments at a price of $800 than at the equilibrium price of $1,000; as shown at point B on the demand curve, at a monthly rent of $800 the quantity of apartments demanded rises to 2.2 million, 200,000 more than in the unregulated market and 400,000 more than are actually available at the price of $800. So there is now a persistent shortage of rental housing: at that price, 400,000 more people want to rent than are able to find apartments.

Do price ceilings always cause shortages? No. If a price ceiling is set above the equilibrium price, it won't have any effect. Suppose that the equilibrium rental rate on apartments is $1,000 per month and the city government sets a ceiling of $1,200. Who cares? In this case, the price ceiling won't be *binding*—it won't actually constrain market behavior—and it will have no effect.

How a Price Ceiling Causes Inefficiency

The housing shortage shown in Figure 4-2 is not merely annoying: like any shortage induced by price controls, it can be seriously harmful because it leads to inefficiency. In other words, there are gains from trade that go unrealized.

Rent control, like all price ceilings, creates inefficiency in at least four distinct ways.

1. It reduces the quantity of apartments rented below the efficient level.
2. It typically leads to inefficient allocation of apartments among would-be renters.
3. It leads to wasted time and effort as people search for apartments.
4. It leads landlords to maintain apartments in inefficiently low quality or condition.

In addition to inefficiency, price ceilings give rise to illegal behavior as people try to circumvent them. We'll now look at each of these inefficiencies caused by price ceilings.

Inefficiently Low Quantity Because a price ceiling reduces the price of a good, it reduces the quantity that sellers are willing to supply. In addition, buyers can't buy more units of a good than sellers are willing to sell. So a price ceiling reduces the quantity of a good bought and sold below the market equilibrium quantity.

Because rent control reduces the number of apartments supplied, it reduces the number of apartments rented, too. The low quantity sold is an inefficiency due to missed opportunities: price ceilings prevent mutually beneficial transactions from occurring, transactions that would benefit both buyers and sellers. Figure 4-3 shows the inefficiently low quantity of apartments supplied with rent control.

Inefficient Allocation to Consumers Rent control doesn't just lead to too few apartments being available. It can also lead to misallocation of the apartments that are available: people who badly need a place to live may not be able to find an apartment, but some apartments may be occupied by people with much less urgent needs.

In the case shown in Figure 4-2, 2.2 million people would like to rent an apartment at $800 per month, but only 1.8 million apartments are available. Of those 2.2 million who are seeking an apartment, some want one badly and are willing to pay a high price to get it. Others have a less urgent need and are only willing to pay a low price, perhaps because they have alternative housing.

An efficient allocation of apartments would reflect these differences: people who really want an apartment will get one and people who aren't all that anxious to find an apartment won't. In an inefficient distribution of apartments,

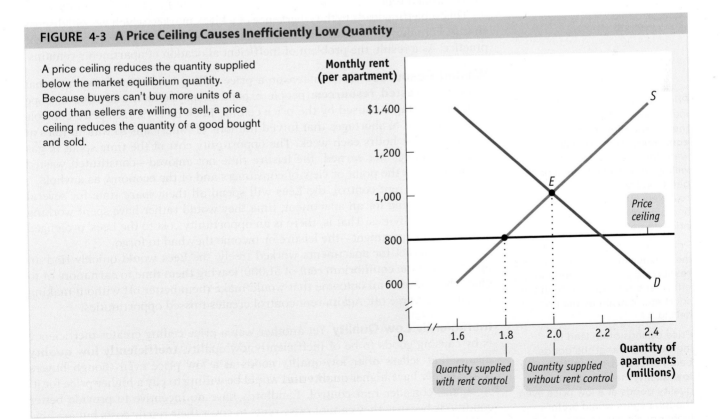

FIGURE 4-3 A Price Ceiling Causes Inefficiently Low Quantity

A price ceiling reduces the quantity supplied below the market equilibrium quantity. Because buyers can't buy more units of a good than sellers are willing to sell, a price ceiling reduces the quantity of a good bought and sold.

the opposite will happen: some people who are not especially anxious to find an apartment will get one and others who are very anxious to find an apartment won't.

Because people usually get apartments through luck or personal connections under rent control, it generally results in an **inefficient allocation to consumers** of the few apartments available.

To see the inefficiency involved, consider the plight of the Lees, a family with young children who have no alternative housing and would be willing to pay up to $1,500 for an apartment—but are unable to find one. Also consider George, a retiree who lives most of the year in Florida but still has a lease on the New York apartment he moved into 40 years ago. George pays $800 per month for this apartment, but if the rent were even slightly more—say, $850—he would give it up and stay with his children when he visits New York.

This allocation of apartments—George has one and the Lees do not—is a missed opportunity: there is a way to make the Lees and George both better off at no additional cost. The Lees would be happy to pay George, say, $1,200 a month to sublease his apartment, which he would happily accept since the apartment is worth no more than $849 a month to him. George would prefer the money he gets from the Lees to keeping his apartment; the Lees would prefer to have the apartment rather than the money. So both would be made better off by this transaction—and nobody else would be made worse off.

Generally, if people who really want apartments could sublease them from people who are less eager to live there, both those who gain apartments and those who trade their occupancy for money would be better off. However, subletting is illegal under rent control because it would occur at prices above the price ceiling.

The fact that subletting is illegal doesn't mean it never happens. In fact, chasing down illegal subletting is a major business for New York private investigators who are hired to prove that the legal tenants in rent-controlled apartments actually live somewhere else, and have sublet their apartments at two or three times the controlled rent.

This subletting leads to the emergence of a black market, which we will discuss shortly. For now, just note that landlords and legal agencies actively discourage the practice. As a result, the problem of inefficient allocation of apartments remains.

Wasted Resources Another reason a price ceiling causes inefficiency is that it leads to **wasted resources**: people expend money, effort, and time to cope with the shortages caused by the price ceiling. Back in 1979, U.S. price controls on gasoline led to shortages that forced millions of Americans to wait in lines at gas stations for hours each week. The opportunity cost of the time spent in gas lines—the wages not earned, the leisure time not enjoyed—constituted wasted resources from the point of view of consumers and of the economy as a whole.

Because of rent control, the Lees will spend all their spare time for several months searching for an apartment, time they would rather have spent working or in family activities. That is, there is an opportunity cost to the Lees' prolonged search for an apartment—the leisure or income they had to forgo.

If the market for apartments worked freely, the Lees would quickly find an apartment at the equilibrium rent of $1,000, leaving them time to earn more or to enjoy themselves—an outcome that would make them better off without making anyone else worse off. Again, rent control creates missed opportunities.

Inefficiently Low Quality Yet another way a price ceiling creates inefficiency is by causing goods to be of inefficiently low quality. **Inefficiently low quality** means that sellers offer low-quality goods at a low price even though buyers would rather have higher quality and would be willing to pay a higher price for it.

Again, consider rent control. Landlords have no incentive to provide better conditions because they cannot raise rents to cover their repair costs but are able to find tenants easily. In many cases, tenants would be willing to pay much more

Price ceilings often lead to inefficiency in the form of **inefficient allocation to consumers**: some people who want the good badly and are willing to pay a high price don't get it, and some who care relatively little about the good and are only willing to pay a low price do get it.

Price ceilings typically lead to inefficiency in the form of **wasted resources**: people expend money, effort, and time to cope with the shortages caused by the price ceiling.

Price ceilings often lead to inefficiency in that the goods being offered are of **inefficiently low quality**: sellers offer low-quality goods at a low price even though buyers would prefer a higher quality at a higher price.

FOR INQUIRING MINDS   **Mumbai's Rent-Control Millionaires**

Mumbai, India, like New York City, has rent-controlled apartments. Currently, about 60% of apartments in Mumbai's city center are rent-controlled. Although Mumbai is half a world away from New York City, the economics of rent control works just the same: rent control leads to shortages, low quality, inefficient allocation to consumers, wasted resources, and black markets.

Mumbai landlords, who often pay more in taxes and maintenance than what they receive in rent, sometimes simply abandon their properties to decay. In a

famous case, three people were killed when a dilapidated rent-controlled apartment building collapsed after 58 tenants, with nowhere else to go, camped out and refused to leave. And a black market in rent-controlled apartments thrives in Mumbai as old tenants sell the right to occupy apartments to new tenants.

And like New York, Mumbai has its "rent-control millionaires." One renter, Mea Kadwani, lived in a 2,600 square foot apartment, paying just $20 per month in an area where apartments not under rent

control often go for $2,000 a month. He refused to leave when his roof collapsed, and after three years of negotiations was paid $2.5 million to vacate the apartment so that a luxury building could be constructed.

With its shortage of land for development, and its desirability as a place to live for the rapidly expanding number of high-income Indians, Mumbai has thousands of rent-controlled tenants who have become millionaires upon vacating their apartments.

for improved conditions than it would cost for the landlord to provide them—for example, the upgrade of an outdated electrical system that cannot safely run air conditioners or computers. But any additional payment for such improvements would be legally considered a rent increase, which is prohibited.

Indeed, rent-controlled apartments are notoriously badly maintained, rarely painted, subject to frequent electrical and plumbing problems, sometimes even hazardous to inhabit. As one former manager of Manhattan buildings described: "At unregulated apartments we'd do most things that the tenants requested. But on the rent-regulated units, we did absolutely only what the law required. . . . We had a perverse incentive to make those tenants unhappy."

This whole situation is a missed opportunity—some tenants would be happy to pay for better conditions, and landlords would be happy to provide them for payment. But such an exchange would occur only if the market were allowed to operate freely.

Black Markets In addition to these four inefficiencies there is a final aspect of price ceilings: the incentive they provide for illegal activities, specifically the emergence of **black markets.** We have already described one kind of black market activity—illegal subletting by tenants. But it does not stop there. Clearly, there is a temptation for a landlord to say to a potential tenant, "Look, you can have the place if you slip me an extra few hundred in cash each month"—and for the tenant to agree if he or she is one of those people who would be willing to pay much more than the maximum legal rent.

What's wrong with black markets? In general, it's a bad thing if people break any law, because it encourages disrespect for the law in general. Worse yet, in this case illegal activity worsens the position of those who are honest. If the Lees are scrupulous about upholding the rent-control law but other people—who may need an apartment less than the Lees—are willing to bribe landlords, the Lees may never find an apartment.

So Why Are There Price Ceilings?

We have seen three common results of price ceilings:

- A persistent shortage of the good
- Inefficiency arising from this persistent shortage in the form of inefficiently low quantity transacted, inefficient allocation of the good to consumers, resources wasted in searching for the good, and the inefficiently low quality of the good offered for sale
- The emergence of illegal, black market activity

A **black market** is a market in which goods or services are bought and sold illegally—either because it is illegal to sell them at all or because the prices charged are legally prohibited by a price ceiling.

Given these unpleasant consequences of price ceilings, why do governments still sometimes impose them? Why does rent control, in particular, persist in New York?

One answer is that although price ceilings may have adverse effects, they do benefit some people. In practice, New York's rent-control rules—which are more complex than our simple model—hurt most residents but give a small minority of renters much cheaper housing than they would get in an unregulated market. And those who benefit from the controls are typically better organized and more vocal than those who are harmed by them.

Also, when price ceilings have been in effect for a long time, buyers may not have a realistic idea of what would happen without them. In our previous example, the rental rate in an unregulated market (Figure 4-1) would be only 25% higher than in the regulated market (Figure 4-2): $1,000 instead of $800. But how would renters know that? Indeed, they might have heard about black market transactions at much higher prices—the Lees or some other family paying George $1,200 or more—and would not realize that these black market prices are much higher than the price that would prevail in a fully unregulated market.

A last answer is that government officials often do not understand supply and demand analysis! It is a great mistake to suppose that economic policies in the real world are always sensible or well informed.

ECONOMICS >> *in Action*
Why Price Controls in Venezuela Proved Useless

Venezuela's food shortages show how price controls dispropor-tionately hurt the people they were designed to benefit.

By all accounts, Venezuela is a rich country as one of the world's top producers of oil. But despite its wealth, by 2016, price controls had so distorted its economy that the country was struggling to feed its citizens. Basic items like toilet paper, rice, coffee, corn, flour, milk, and meat were chronically lacking.

Venezuelans lined up for hours to purchase price-controlled goods at state-run stores, but often came away empty handed. "Empty shelves and no one to explain why a rich country has no food. It's unacceptable," said Jesús López, a 90-year old farmer.

The origins of the shortages can be traced to policies espoused by Venezuela's former president, Hugo Chavez. First elected in 1989 on a platform that promised to favor the poor and working classes over the country's economic elite, Chavez implemented price controls on basic food-stuffs. Prices were set so low that farmers reduced production, so that by 2006 shortages were severe. As a result, Venezuela went from being self-sufficient in food in 1989 to importing more than 70% of its food by 2016.

At the same time, generous government programs for the poor and working class created higher demand. The reduced supply of goods due to price controls combined with higher demand led to sharply rising prices for black market goods that, in turn, generated even greater demand for goods sold at the controlled prices. Smuggling became rampant, as a bottle of milk sold across the border in Colombia for seven or eight times the controlled price in Venezuela. Not surprisingly, fresh milk was rarely seen in Venezuelan markets.

The irony of the situation is that the policies put in place to help the poor and working classes have disproportionately hurt them. By 2016, a basket of basic foodstuffs on the black market cost six times the Venezuelan minimum monthly salary and people were spending up to 12 hours at a time in line. As one shopper in a low-income area said, "It fills me with rage to have to spend the one free day I have wasting my time for a bag of rice. I end up paying more at the resellers [the black market]. In the end, all these price controls proved useless."

By late 2016, the lack of basic necessities—food and medicine—coupled with soaring crime, led to a mass exodus from Venezuela to neighboring countries. As one woman said, "I'm leaving with nothing. But I have to do this. Otherwise, we will just die hungry here."

>> Check Your Understanding 4-1

Solutions appear at back of book.

1. On game days, homeowners near Middletown University's stadium used to rent parking spaces in their driveways to fans at a going rate of $11. A new town ordinance now sets a maximum parking fee of $7. Use the accompanying supply and demand diagram to explain how each of the following corresponds to a price-ceiling concept.

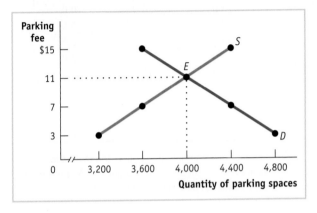

   a. Some homeowners now think it's not worth the hassle to rent out spaces.
   b. Some fans who used to carpool to the game now drive alone.
   c. Some fans can't find parking and leave without seeing the game.

   Explain how each of the following adverse effects arises from the price ceiling.

   d. Some fans now arrive several hours early to find parking.
   e. Friends of homeowners near the stadium regularly attend games, even if they aren't big fans. But some serious fans have given up because of the parking situation.
   f. Some homeowners rent spaces for more than $7 but pretend that the buyers are nonpaying friends or family.

2. True or false? Explain your answer. A price ceiling below the equilibrium price of an otherwise efficient market does the following:
   a. Increases quantity supplied
   b. Makes some people who want to consume the good worse off
   c. Makes all producers worse off

‖ Price Floors

Sometimes governments intervene to push market prices up instead of down. *Price floors* have been widely legislated for agricultural products, such as wheat and milk, as a way to support the incomes of farmers. Historically, there were also price floors—legally mandated minimum prices—on such services as trucking and air travel, although these were phased out by the U.S. government in the 1970s.

If you have ever worked in a fast-food restaurant, you are likely to have encountered a price floor: governments in the United States and many other countries maintain a lower limit on the hourly wage rate of a worker's labor; that is, a floor on the price of labor called the **minimum wage.**

Just like price ceilings, price floors are intended to help some people but generate predictable and undesirable side effects. Figure 4-4 shows hypothetical supply and demand curves for butter. Left to itself, the market would move to equilibrium at point *E*, with 10 million pounds of butter bought and sold at a price of $1 per pound.

>> Quick Review

• **Price controls** take the form of either legal maximum prices—**price ceilings**—or legal minimum prices—**price floors.**

• A price ceiling below the equilibrium price benefits successful buyers but causes predictable adverse effects such as persistent shortages, which lead to four types of inefficiencies: **inefficiently low quantity transacted, inefficient allocation to consumers, wasted resources,** and **inefficiently low quality.**

• Price ceilings also lead to **black markets,** as buyers and sellers attempt to evade the price controls.

The **minimum wage** is a legal floor on the wage rate, which is the market price of labor.

FIGURE 4-4 The Market for Butter in the Absence of Government Controls

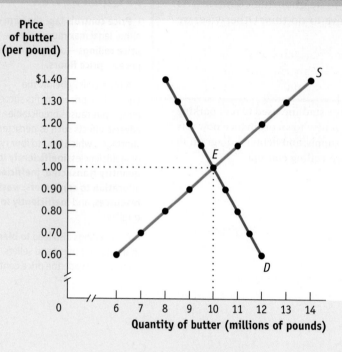

Price of butter (per pound)	Quantity of butter (millions of pounds)	
	Quantity demanded	Quantity supplied
$1.40	8.0	14.0
1.30	8.5	13.0
1.20	9.0	12.0
1.10	9.5	11.0
1.00	10.0	10.0
0.90	10.5	9.0
0.80	11.0	8.0
0.70	11.5	7.0
0.60	12.0	6.0

Without government intervention, the market for butter reaches equilibrium at a price of $1 per pound with 10 million pounds of butter bought and sold.

Now suppose that the government, in order to help dairy farmers, imposes a price floor on butter of $1.20 per pound. Its effects are shown in Figure 4-5, where the line at $1.20 represents the price floor. At a price of $1.20 per pound, producers would want to supply 12 million pounds (point *B* on the supply curve) but consumers would want to buy only 9 million pounds (point *A* on the demand curve). So the price floor leads to a persistent surplus of 3 million pounds of butter.

FIGURE 4-5 The Effects of a Price Floor

The black horizontal line represents the government-imposed price floor of $1.20 per pound of butter. The quantity of butter demanded falls to 9 million pounds, and the quantity supplied rises to 12 million pounds, generating a persistent surplus of 3 million pounds of butter.

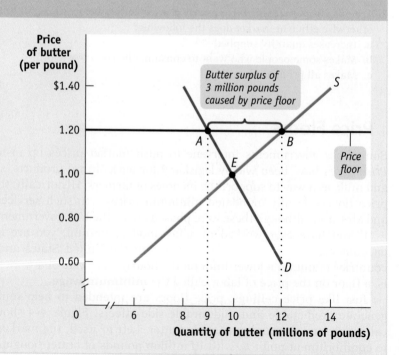

Does a price floor always lead to an unwanted surplus? No. Just as in the case of a price ceiling, the floor may not be binding—that is, it may be irrelevant. If the equilibrium price of butter is $1 per pound but the floor is set at only $0.80, the floor has no effect.

But suppose that a price floor is binding: what happens to the unwanted surplus? The answer depends on government policy. In the case of agricultural price floors, governments buy up unwanted surplus. As a result, the U.S. government has at times found itself warehousing thousands of tons of butter, cheese, and other farm products. (The European Commission, which administers price floors for a number of European countries, once found itself the owner of a so-called butter mountain, equal in weight to the entire population of Austria.) The government then has to find a way to dispose of these unwanted goods.

Some countries pay exporters to sell products at a loss overseas; this is standard procedure for the European Union. The United States gives surplus food away to citizens in need as well as to schools, which use the products in school lunches. In some cases, governments have actually destroyed the surplus production.

When the government is not prepared to purchase the unwanted surplus, a price floor means that would-be sellers cannot find buyers. This is what happens when there is a price floor on the wage rate paid for an hour of labor, the minimum wage: when the minimum wage is above the equilibrium wage rate, some people who are willing to work—that is, sell labor—cannot find buyers—that is, employers—willing to give them jobs.

How a Price Floor Causes Inefficiency

The persistent surplus that results from a price floor creates missed opportunities—inefficiencies—that resemble those created by the shortage that results from a price ceiling. Like a price ceiling, a price floor creates inefficiency in at least four ways:

1. It causes inefficiently low quantity.
2. It leads to an inefficient allocation of sales among sellers.
3. It leads to a waste of resources.
4. It leads to sellers providing an inefficiently high-quality level.

In addition to inefficiency, like a price ceiling, a price floor leads to illegal behavior as people break the law to sell below the legal price.

Inefficiently Low Quantity Because a price floor raises the price of a good to consumers, it reduces the quantity of that good demanded; because sellers can't sell more units of a good than buyers are willing to buy, a price floor reduces the quantity of a good bought and sold below the market equilibrium quantity. Notice that this is the *same* effect as a price ceiling. You might be tempted to think that a price floor and a price ceiling have opposite effects, but both have the effect of reducing the quantity of a good bought and sold (see the accompanying Pitfalls).

As in the case of a price ceiling, the low quantity sold is an inefficiency due to missed opportunities: price floors prevent mutually beneficial transactions from occurring, transactions that would benefit both buyers and sellers. Figure 4-6 shows the inefficiently low quantity of butter sold with a price floor on the price of butter.

Inefficient Allocation of Sales Among Sellers Like a price ceiling, a price floor can lead to *inefficient allocation*—in this case, an **inefficient allocation of sales among sellers:** sellers who are willing to sell at the lowest price are unable to make sales, while sales go to sellers who are only willing to sell at a higher price.

Price floors can lead to **inefficient allocation of sales among sellers:** sellers who are willing to sell at the lowest price are unable to make sales while sales go to sellers who are only willing to sell at a higher price.

FIGURE 4-6 A Price Floor Causes Inefficiently Low Quantity

A price floor reduces the quantity demanded below the market equilibrium quantity. Because sellers can't sell more units of a good than buyers are willing to buy, a price floor reduces the quantity of a good bought and sold.

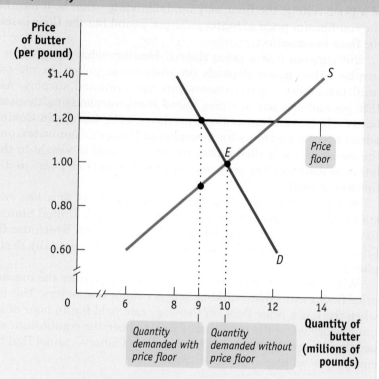

One historical example of the inefficient allocation of selling opportunities caused by a price floor was the labor market situation in many European countries from the 1980s onward. A high minimum wage led to a two-tier labor system, composed of the fortunate who had good jobs in the formal labor market, and the rest who were locked out without any prospect of ever finding a good job.

Either unemployed or underemployed in dead-end jobs in the black market for labor, the unlucky ones were disproportionately young, from the ages of 18 to early 30s. Although eager for good jobs in the formal sector and willing to accept less than the minimum wage—that is, willing to sell their labor for a lower price—it was illegal for employers to pay them less than the minimum wage.

The inefficiency of unemployment and underemployment was compounded as a generation of young people was unable to get adequate job training, develop careers, and save for their future. These young people were also more likely to engage in crime. And many of these countries saw their best and brightest young people emigrate, leading to a permanent reduction in the future performance of their economies. The social losses grew to such an extent that in recent years European countries have undertaken labor market reforms that have significantly reduced the problem.

PITFALLS

CEILINGS, FLOORS, AND QUANTITIES

A price ceiling pushes the price of a good *down*. A price floor pushes the price of a good *up*. So it's easy to assume that the effects of a price floor are the opposite of the effects of a price ceiling. In particular, if a price ceiling reduces the quantity of a good bought and sold, doesn't a price floor increase the quantity?

No, it doesn't. In fact, both floors and ceilings reduce the quantity bought and sold. Why? When the quantity of a good supplied isn't equal to the quantity demanded, the actual quantity sold is determined by the "short side" of the market—whichever quantity is less. If sellers don't want to sell as much as buyers want to buy, it's the sellers who determine the actual quantity sold, because buyers can't force unwilling sellers to sell. If buyers don't want to buy as much as sellers want to sell, it's the buyers who determine the actual quantity sold, because sellers can't force unwilling buyers to buy.

Wasted Resources Also like a price ceiling, a price floor generates inefficiency by *wasting resources*. The most graphic examples involve government purchases of the unwanted surpluses of agricultural products caused by price floors. The surplus production is sometimes destroyed, which is pure waste; in other cases, the stored produce goes, as officials euphemistically put it, "out of condition" and must be thrown away.

Price floors also lead to wasted time and effort. Consider the minimum wage. Would-be workers who spend many hours searching for jobs, or waiting in line in the hope of getting jobs, play the same role in the case of price floors as hapless families searching for apartments in the case of price ceilings.

Price floors often lead to inefficiency in that goods of **inefficiently high quality** are offered: sellers offer high-quality goods at a high price, even though buyers would prefer a lower quality at a lower price.

Inefficiently High Quality Again like price ceilings, price floors lead to inefficiency in the quality of goods produced.

We saw that when there is a price ceiling, suppliers produce products that are of inefficiently low quality: buyers prefer higher-quality products and are willing to pay for them, but sellers refuse to improve the quality of their products because the price ceiling prevents their being compensated for doing so. This same logic applies to price floors, but in reverse: suppliers offer goods of **inefficiently high quality.**

How can this be? Isn't high quality a good thing? Yes, but only if it is worth the cost. Suppose that suppliers spend a lot to make goods of very high quality but that this quality isn't worth much to consumers, who would rather receive the money spent on that quality in the form of a lower price. This represents a missed opportunity: suppliers and buyers could make a mutually beneficial deal in which buyers got goods of lower quality for a much lower price.

A good example of the inefficiency of excessive quality comes from the days when transatlantic airfares were set artificially high by international treaty. Forbidden to compete for customers by offering lower ticket prices, airlines instead offered expensive services, like lavish in-flight meals that went largely uneaten—an especially wasteful practice, considering that what passengers really wanted was less food and lower airfares.

Since the deregulation of U.S. airlines in the 1970s, American passengers have experienced a large decrease in ticket prices accompanied by a decrease in the quality of in-flight service—smaller seats, lower-quality food, and so on. Everyone complains about the service—but thanks to lower fares, the number of people flying on U.S. carriers has grown from 130 billion passenger miles when deregulation began to approximately 631 billion in 2015.

🌐 **GLOBAL COMPARISON**   **CHECK OUT OUR LOW, LOW WAGES!**

The minimum wage rate in the United States, as you can see in this graph, is actually quite low compared with that in other rich countries. Since minimum wages are set in national currency—the British minimum wage is set in British pounds, the French minimum wage is set in euros, and so on—the comparison depends on the exchange rate on any given day. As of 2016, Australia had a minimum wage nearly twice as high as the U.S. rate, with France, Canada, and Ireland not far behind.

You can see one effect of this difference in the supermarket checkout line. In the United States there is usually someone to bag your groceries—someone typically paid the minimum wage or at best slightly more. In Europe, where hiring a bagger is a lot more expensive, you're almost always expected to do the bagging yourself.

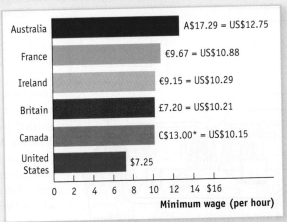

Australia	A$17.29 = US$12.75
France	€9.67 = US$10.88
Ireland	€9.15 = US$10.29
Britain	£7.20 = US$10.21
Canada	C$13.00* = US$10.15
United States	$7.25

Minimum wage (per hour)

Data from: Organization for Economic Cooperation and Development (OECD).
*The Canadian minimum wage varies by province from C$10.50 to C$13.00.

Illegal Activity In addition to the four inefficiencies we analyzed, like price ceilings, price floors provide incentives for illegal activity. For example, in countries where the minimum wage is far above the equilibrium wage rate, workers desperate for jobs sometimes agree to work off the books for employers who conceal their employment from the government—or bribe the government inspectors. This practice, known in Europe as *black labor*, is especially common in Southern European countries such as Italy and Spain.

So Why Are There Price Floors?

To sum up, a price floor creates various negative side effects:

- A persistent surplus of the good
- Inefficiency arising from the persistent surplus in the form of inefficiently low quantity transacted, inefficient allocation of sales among sellers, wasted resources, and an inefficiently high level of quality offered by suppliers
- The temptation to engage in illegal activity, particularly bribery and corruption of government officials

So why do governments impose price floors when they have so many negative side effects? The reasons are similar to those for imposing price ceilings. Government officials often disregard warnings about the consequences of price floors either because they believe that the relevant market is poorly described by the supply and demand model or, more often, because they do not understand the model. Above all, just as price ceilings are often imposed because they benefit some influential buyers of a good, price floors are often imposed because they benefit some influential sellers.

ECONOMICS >> *in Action*
The Rise and Fall of the Unpaid Intern

The best-known example of a price floor is the minimum wage. Most economists believe, however, that the minimum wage has relatively little effect on the overall job market in the United States, mainly because the floor is set so low. In 1964, the U.S. minimum wage was 53% of the average wage of blue-collar production workers; by 2015, it had fallen to about 35%. However, there is one sector of the U.S. job market where it appears that the minimum wage can indeed be binding: the market for interns.

Starting in 2011, a spate of lawsuits brought by former unpaid interns claiming they were cheated out of wages brought the matter to public attention. A common thread in these complaints was that interns were assigned grunt work with no educational value, such as tracking lost cell phones. In other cases, unpaid interns complained that they were given the work of full-salaried employees. And by 2015, many of those lawsuits proved successful: Condé Nast Publications settled for $5.8 million, Sirius XM Radio settled for $1.3 million, and Viacom Media settled for $7.2 million.

As a result, unless their programs can clearly demonstrate an educational component such as course credit, companies have to pay their interns minimum wage or shut down their programs altogether.

Some observers worry that the end of the unpaid internship means that programs that once offered valuable training will be lost. But as one lawyer commented, "The law says that when you work, you have to get paid [at least the minimum wage]."

"We have an opening for a part-time unpaid intern, which could lead to a full-time unpaid internship."

>> Check Your Understanding 4-2

Solutions appear at back of book.

1. The state legislature mandates a price floor for gasoline of P_F per gallon. Assess the following statements and illustrate your answer using the figure provided.

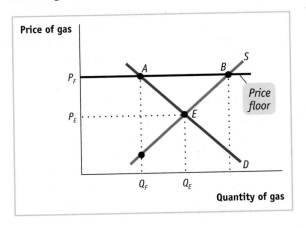

a. Proponents of the law claim it will increase the income of gas station owners. Opponents claim it will hurt gas station owners because they will lose customers.

b. Proponents claim consumers will be better off because gas stations will provide better service. Opponents claim consumers will be generally worse off because they prefer to buy gas at cheaper prices.

c. Proponents claim that they are helping gas station owners without hurting anyone else. Opponents claim that consumers are hurt and will end up doing things like buying gas in a nearby state or on the black market.

‖ Controlling Quantities

In the 1930s, New York City instituted a system of licensing for taxicabs: only taxis with a "medallion" were allowed to pick up passengers, hailing them from the street. Because this system was intended to assure quality, medallion owners were supposed to maintain certain standards, including safety and cleanliness. A total of 11,787 medallions were issued, with taxi owners paying $10 for each medallion.

In 1995, there were still only 11,787 licensed taxicabs in New York, even though the city had meanwhile become the financial capital of the world, a place where hundreds of thousands of people in a hurry tried to hail a cab every day. By 2015, the number of licensed cabs had risen to only 13,635. And until recently, this restriction on the number of New York City taxi medallions made them a very valuable item: if you want to operate a taxi in the city, you must lease a medallion from someone or buy one.

Yet restrictions on the number of taxis induced people to try to circumvent them, eventually leading to the emergence of mobile-app-based car services like Uber and Lyft. Their cars aren't hailed from the street like taxis—in fact, their drivers are forbidden from picking up riders from the street. Instead, riders quickly arrange trips by tapping their smartphones, directing available drivers to their location. Of course, the ubiquity of smartphones also contributed to the emergence of these car services.

Since 2013, Uber and Lyft have had a significant effect on the market for car rides in New York City and most other major cities. But let's postpone the discussion of those effects until we learn more about how the market worked when only licensed taxicabs could operate.

A taxi medallion is a form of **quantity control,** or **quota,** by which the government regulates the quantity of a good that can be bought and sold rather than the price at which it is transacted. It is another way that government intervenes in markets along with price ceilings and price floors. The total amount of the good that can be transacted under the quantity control is called the **quota limit.** Typically, the government limits quantity in a market by issuing **licenses;** only people with a license can legally supply the good.

A taxi medallion is just such a license. The government of New York City limits the number of taxi rides that can be sold by limiting the number of taxis to only those who hold medallions. More generally, quantity controls, or quotas, set an

A **quantity control,** or **quota,** is an upper limit on the quantity of some good that can be bought or sold. The total amount of the good that can be legally transacted is the **quota limit.**

A **license** gives its owner the right to supply a good.

upper limit on the quantity of a good that can be transacted. For example, quotas have been used frequently to limit the size of the catch of endangered fish stocks. In this case, quotas are implemented for good economic reasons: to protect endangered fish stocks.

But some quotas are implemented for bad economic reasons, typically for the purpose of enriching the quota holder. For example, quantity controls introduced to address a temporary problem such as assuring that only safe and clean taxis are allowed to operate, become difficult to remove later, once the problem has disappeared, because quota holders benefit from them and exert political pressure.

The Anatomy of Quantity Controls

To understand why a New York taxi medallion is worth so much money, we consider a simplified version of the market for taxi rides, shown in Figure 4-7. Just as we assumed in the analysis of rent control that all apartments are the same, we now suppose that all taxi rides are the same—ignoring the real-world complication that some taxi rides are longer, and so more expensive, than others.

The table in the figure shows supply and demand schedules. The equilibrium—indicated by point *E* in the figure and by the shaded entries in the table—is a fare of $5 per ride, with 10 million rides taken per year. (You'll see in a minute why we present the equilibrium this way.)

The New York medallion system limits the number of taxis, but each taxi driver can offer as many rides as he or she can manage. (Now you know why New York taxi drivers are so aggressive!) To simplify our analysis, however, we will assume that a medallion system limits the number of taxi rides that can legally be given to 8 million per year.

Until now, we have derived the demand curve by answering questions of the form: "How many taxi rides will passengers want to take if the price is $5 per ride?" But it is possible to reverse the question and ask instead: "At what price will consumers want to buy 10 million rides per year?" The price at which consumers want to buy a given quantity—in this case, 10 million rides at $5 per ride—is

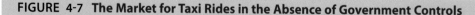

FIGURE 4-7 The Market for Taxi Rides in the Absence of Government Controls

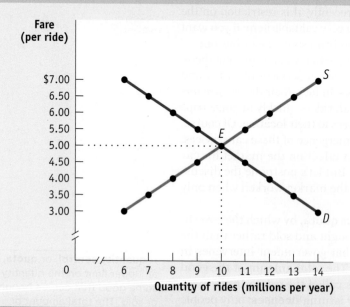

Fare (per ride)	Quantity of rides (millions per year)	
	Quantity demanded	Quantity supplied
$7.00	6	14
6.50	7	13
6.00	8	12
5.50	9	11
5.00	10	10
4.50	11	9
4.00	12	8
3.50	13	7
3.00	14	6

Without government intervention, the market reaches equilibrium with 10 million rides taken per year at a fare of $5 per ride.

the **demand price** of that quantity. You can see from the demand schedule in Figure 4-7 that the demand price of 6 million rides is $7 per ride, the demand price of 7 million rides is $6.50 per ride, and so on.

Similarly, the supply curve represents the answer to questions of the form: "How many taxi rides would taxi drivers supply at a price of $5 each?" But we can also reverse this question to ask: "At what price will suppliers be willing to supply 10 million rides per year?" The price at which suppliers will supply a given quantity—in this case, 10 million rides at $5 per ride—is the **supply price** of that quantity. We can see from the supply schedule in Figure 4-7 that the supply price of 6 million rides is $3 per ride, the supply price of 7 million rides is $3.50 per ride, and so on.

Now we are ready to analyze a quota. We have assumed that the city government limits the quantity of taxi rides to 8 million per year. Medallions, each of which carries the right to provide a certain number of taxi rides per year, are made available to selected people in such a way that a total of 8 million rides will be provided. Medallion-holders may then either drive their own taxis or rent their medallions to others for a fee.

Figure 4-8 shows the resulting market for taxi rides, with the black vertical line at 8 million rides per year representing the quota limit. Because the quantity of rides is limited to 8 million, consumers must be at point *A* on the demand curve, corresponding to the shaded entry in the demand schedule: the demand price of 8 million rides is $6 per ride. Meanwhile, taxi drivers must be at point *B* on the supply curve, corresponding to the shaded entry in the supply schedule: the supply price of 8 million rides is $4 per ride.

But how can the price received by taxi drivers be $4 when the price paid by taxi riders is $6? The answer is that in addition to the market in taxi rides, there is also a market in medallions. Medallion-holders may not always want to drive

> The **demand price** of a given quantity is the price at which consumers will demand that quantity.
>
> The **supply price** of a given quantity is the price at which producers will supply that quantity.

FIGURE 4-8   Effect of a Quota on the Market for Taxi Rides

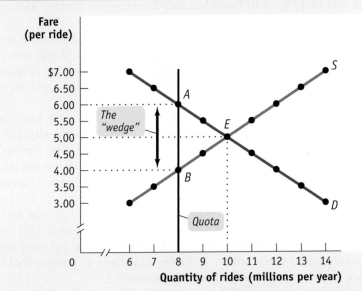

Fare (per ride)	Quantity of rides (millions per year)	
	Quantity demanded	Quantity supplied
$7.00	6	14
6.50	7	13
6.00	8	12
5.50	9	11
5.00	10	10
4.50	11	9
4.00	12	8
3.50	13	7
3.00	14	6

The table shows the demand price and the supply price corresponding to each quantity: the price at which that quantity would be demanded and supplied, respectively. The city government imposes a quota of 8 million rides by selling licenses for only 8 million rides, represented by the black vertical line. The price paid by consumers rises to $6 per ride, the demand price of 8 million rides, shown by point *A*. The supply price of 8 million rides is only $4 per ride, shown by point *B*. The difference between these two prices is the quota rent per ride, the earnings that accrue to the owner of a license. The quota rent drives a wedge between the demand price and the supply price and discourages mutually beneficial transactions.

A quantity control, or quota, drives a **wedge** between the demand price and the supply price of a good; that is, the price paid by buyers ends up being higher than that received by sellers.

The difference between the demand and supply price at the quota limit is the **quota rent,** the earnings that accrue to the license-holder from ownership of the right to sell the good. It is equal to the market price of the license when the licenses are traded.

their taxis: they may be ill or on vacation. Those who do not want to drive their own taxis will sell the right to use the medallion to someone else.

So we need to consider two sets of transactions here, and so two prices: (1) the transactions in taxi rides and the price at which these will occur, and (2) the transactions in medallions and the price at which these will occur. It turns out that since we are looking at two markets, the $4 and $6 prices will both be right.

To see how this all works, consider two imaginary New York taxi drivers, Sunil and Harriet. Sunil has a medallion but can't use it because he's recovering from a severely sprained wrist. So he's looking to rent his medallion out to someone else. Harriet doesn't have a medallion but would like to rent one. Furthermore, at any point in time there are many other people like Harriet who would like to rent a medallion. Suppose Sunil agrees to rent his medallion to Harriet. To make things simple, assume that any driver can give only one ride per day and that Sunil is renting his medallion to Harriet for one day. What rental price will they agree on?

To answer this question, we need to look at the transactions from the viewpoints of both drivers. Once she has the medallion, Harriet knows she can make $6 per day—the demand price of a ride under the quota. And she is willing to rent the medallion only if she makes at least $4 per day—the supply price of a ride under the quota. So Sunil cannot demand a rent of more than $2—the difference between $6 and $4. And if Harriet offered Sunil less than $2—say, $1.50—there would be other eager drivers willing to offer him more, up to $2. So, in order to get the medallion, Harriet must offer Sunil at least $2. Since the rent can be no more than $2 and no less than $2, it must be exactly $2.

It is no coincidence that $2 is exactly the difference between $6, the demand price of 8 million rides, and $4, the supply price of 8 million rides. In every case in which the supply of a good is legally restricted, there is a **wedge** between the demand price of the quantity transacted and the supply price of the quantity transacted.

This wedge, illustrated by the double-headed arrow in Figure 4-8, has a special name: the **quota rent.** It is the earnings that accrue to the license-holder from ownership of a valuable commodity, the license. In the case of Sunil and Harriet, the quota rent of $2 goes to Sunil because he owns the license, and the remaining $4 from the total fare of $6 goes to Harriet.

So Figure 4-8 also illustrates the quota rent in the market for New York taxi rides. The quota limits the quantity of rides to 8 million per year, a quantity at which the demand price of $6 exceeds the supply price of $4. The wedge between these two prices, $2, is the quota rent that results from the restrictions placed on the quantity of taxi rides in this market.

But wait a second. What if Sunil doesn't rent out his medallion? What if he uses it himself? Doesn't this mean that he gets a price of $6? No, not really. Even if Sunil doesn't rent out his medallion, he could have rented it out, which means that the medallion has an *opportunity cost* of $2: if Sunil decides to use his own medallion and drive his own taxi rather than renting his medallion to Harriet, the $2 represents his opportunity cost of not renting out his medallion. That is, the $2 quota rent is now the rental income he forgoes by driving his own taxi.

In effect, Sunil is in two businesses—the taxi-driving business and the medallion-renting business. He makes $4 per ride from driving his taxi and $2 per ride from renting out his medallion. It doesn't make any difference that in this particular case he has rented his medallion to himself!

So regardless of whether the medallion owner uses the medallion himself or herself, or rents it to others, it is a valuable asset. And this is represented in the going price for a New York City taxi medallion: in 2013, medallions regularly sold for over $1 million. At that time, an owner of a medallion who leased it to a driver could expect to earn about $2,500 per month, or a 3% return—an attractive rate of return compared to other investments.

Notice, by the way, that quotas—like price ceilings and price floors—don't always have a real effect. If the quota were set at 12 million rides—that is, above the equilibrium quantity in an unregulated market—it would have no effect because it would not be binding.

The Costs of Quantity Controls

Like price controls, quantity controls can have some predictable and undesirable side effects. The first is the by-now-familiar problem of inefficiency due to missed opportunities: quantity controls prevent mutually beneficial transactions from occurring, transactions that would benefit both buyers and sellers.

Looking back at Figure 4-8, you can see that starting at the quota limit of 8 million rides, New Yorkers would be willing to pay at least $5.50 per ride when 9 million rides are offered, 1 million more than the quota, and that taxi drivers would be willing to provide those rides as long as they got at least $4.50 per ride. These are rides that would have taken place if there were no quota limit.

The same is true for the next 1 million rides: New Yorkers would be willing to pay at least $5 per ride when the quantity of rides is increased from 9 to 10 million, and taxi drivers would be willing to provide those rides as long as they got at least $5 per ride. Again, these rides would have occurred without the quota limit.

Only when the market has reached the unregulated market equilibrium quantity of 10 million rides are there no "missed-opportunity rides." The quota limit of 8 million rides has caused 2 million "missed-opportunity rides."

Generally, *as long as the demand price of a given quantity exceeds the supply price, there is a missed opportunity*. A buyer would be willing to buy the good at a price that the seller would be willing to accept, but such a transaction does not occur because it is forbidden by the quota.

And because there are transactions that people would like to make but are not allowed to, quantity controls generate an incentive to circumvent them. In the days before Uber and Lyft, a substantial number of unlicensed taxis simply defied the law and picked up passengers without a medallion. These unregulated, unlicensed taxis contributed to a disproportionately large share of accidents in the city.

However, Uber and Lyft cars legally circumvent the restriction that a car without a medallion can't be hailed from the street. By 2016, Uber had 35,000 drivers in New York City, significantly more cars than the 13,635 licensed taxicabs.

Clearly, the quantity restriction on New York City taxicabs has been substantially undermined. In effect, the quota line in Figure 4-8 has shifted rightward, closer to the equilibrium quantity, with the entry of Uber and Lyft.

In the past few years, as quota rents to owners of a taxi medallion have fallen, the prices of taxi medallions have fallen significantly as well. We analyze these events in more detail in this chapter's Business Case. As owners of medallions are learning, the market eventually strikes back.

In sum, quantity controls typically create the following undesirable side effects:

- Inefficiencies, or missed opportunities, in the form of mutually beneficial transactions that don't occur
- Incentives for illegal activities

ECONOMICS >> *in Action*
Crabbing, Quotas, and Saving Lives in Alaska

Alaskan king and snow crab are considered delicacies worldwide. And crab fishing is one of the most important industries in the Alaskan economy. So many were justifiably concerned when, in 1983, the annual crab catch fell by 90% due to overfishing. In response, marine biologists set a *total allowable catch quota system*, which limited the amount of crab that could be harvested annually in order to allow the crab population to return to a healthy, sustainable level.

Notice, by the way, that the Alaskan crab quota is an example of a quota that was justified by broader economic and environmental considerations—unlike the New York taxicab quota, which has long since lost any economic rationale. Another important difference is that, unlike New York taxicab medallions, owners of Alaskan crab boats did not have the ability to buy or sell individual quotas.

Jean-Erick PASQUIER/Getty Images

The quota-share system protects Alaska's crab population and saves the lives of crabbers.

So although depleted crab stocks eventually recovered with the total catch quota system in place, there was another, unintended and deadly consequence.

The Alaskan crabbing season is fairly short, running roughly from October to January, and it can be further shortened by bad weather. By the 1990s, Alaskan crab fishermen were engaging in "fishing derbies," made famous by the Discovery Channel's *Deadliest Catch*. To stay within the quota limit when the crabbing season began, boat crews rushed to fish for crab in dangerous, icy, rough water, straining to harvest in a few days a haul that could be worth several hundred thousand dollars. As a result, boats often became overloaded and capsized. Crews were pushed too hard, with many fatalities from hypothermia or drowning.

According to federal statistics, at the time Alaskan crab fishing was among the most dangerous of jobs, with an average of 7.3 deaths a year, about 80 times the fatality rate for an average worker. And after the brief harvest, the market for crab was flooded with supply, lowering the prices fishermen received.

In 2006 fishery regulators instituted another quota system called *quota share*—aimed at protecting crabbers as well as Alaska's crabs. Under individual quota share, each boat received a quota to fill during the three-month season. Moreover, the individual quotas could be sold or leased. These changes transformed the industry as owners of bigger boats bought the individual quotas of smaller boats, shrinking the number of crabbing boats dramatically: from over 250 a few years earlier to about 80 in 2016. Bigger boats are much less likely to capsize, improving crew safety.

In addition, by extending the fishing season, the quota-share system boosted the crab population and crab prices. In 2004, under the old system, the quota was reached in just 3 days, while in 2010 it took 20 days. With more time to fish, fishermen could make sure that juvenile and female crabs were returned to the sea rather than harvested. And with a longer fishing season, the catch comes to market more gradually, eliminating the downward plunge in prices when supply hits the market. In 2015, snow crab sold for close to $7 per pound, up from close to $3 per pound in 2005.

Predictably, an Alaskan crab fisherman earns more money under the quota-share system than under the total catch quota system. As one observer said in 2012, "The information we have on crabbers' income is anecdotal, but crewmen we surveyed said they're making about $100,000 a year and captains twice that. That's a lot more than a few years ago."

>> Quick Review

• **Quantity controls,** or **quotas,** are government-imposed limits on how much of a good may be bought or sold. The quantity allowed for sale is the **quota limit.** The government then issues a **license**—the right to sell a given quantity of a good under the quota.

• When the quota limit is smaller than the equilibrium quantity in an unregulated market, the **demand price** is higher than the **supply price**—there is a **wedge** between them at the quota limit.

• This wedge is the **quota rent,** the earnings that accrue to the license-holder from ownership of the right to sell the good—whether by actually supplying the good or by renting the license to someone else. The market price of a license equals the quota rent.

• Like price controls, quantity controls create inefficiencies and encourage illegal activity.

>> Check Your Understanding 4-3

Solutions appear at back of book.

1. Suppose that the supply and demand for taxi rides is given by Figure 4-7 but the quota is set at 6 million rides instead of 8 million. Find the following and indicate them on Figure 4-7.
   a. The price of a ride
   b. The quota rent
   c. Suppose the quota limit on taxi rides is increased to 9 million. What happens to the quota rent?

2. Assume that the quota limit is 8 million rides. Suppose demand decreases due to a decline in tourism. What is the smallest parallel leftward shift in demand that would result in the quota no longer having an effect on the market? Illustrate your answer using Figure 4-7.

Why Taxi Medallion Lenders Are Feeling Like Roadkill

Prachatason Frederic/Alamy Stock Photo

In 2015, four loan companies filed a strongly worded lawsuit against the City of New York, accusing it of failing to protect the taxi industry's quantity-controlled status. The four companies, Melrose, Progressive, LOMTO, and Montauk, are among the largest lenders to purchasers of taxi medallions. They lend money to those who want to buy a medallion but don't have the sizable amount of cash required to do so, and to borrowers who pledge the medallions as collateral for their loans. That is, if the borrower can't repay the loan, the companies take ownership of the medallion to satisfy the debt by reselling it to someone else.

And for a long time, lending money to finance the purchase of medallions was a very good business—almost as good as printing money, some said. Over two decades, from 1990 to 2013, the value of a New York City taxi medallion rose 720%, making it a better investment than stocks, oil, or gold. As a result, loan companies saw

very little downside risk to lending for taxi medallions. And they had steady business: as the price of a taxi medallion rose, buyers wanted to borrow more money. The lender Melrose, for example, lent a total of $1.56 billion for 3,110 medallions.

But by 2015, these lending companies were deeply worried. The prices of a taxi medallion began to fall from a high of $1.3 million in 2013 to as little as $250,000 in 2016, *if* a buyer could be found. Monthly taxi pickups in New York City dropped from 14 million to 12 million over a two-year span from June 2013 to June 2015, while Uber ridership increased tenfold, to 3.5 million. And, meter revenue from taxicabs was down more than 9% from March 2014 to March 2015. As the four lenders stated in their lawsuit, arguing for more protection of taxicabs, "borrowers are falling behind in their loan payments and loans will soon fail."

Soon afterward, the fight between the taxicab industry and Uber turned political as a bill was introduced in the New York City Council to limit the number of Uber vehicles on city streets. Uber responded with a $3 million lobbying and advertising blitz. In the end, the bill didn't pass—a victory for Uber. However, Uber is still restricted from picking up fares hailed from the street.

QUESTIONS FOR THOUGHT

1. How did lenders benefit from the restriction on the number of New York City taxi medallions?

2. Use a graph to illustrate the effect of the entry of Uber on the incomes of taxicab drivers. Assume that Uber cars cannot pick up fares hailed from the street and that there are some people who prefer to hail cabs rather than use an app. How does your graph change if that restriction is lifted?

3. Why has the fight between Uber and the taxicab industry turned political?

SUMMARY

1. Even when a market is efficient, governments often intervene to pursue greater fairness or to please a powerful interest group. Interventions can take the form of **price controls** or quantity controls, both of which generate predictable and undesirable side effects consisting of various forms of inefficiency and illegal activity.

2. A **price ceiling,** a maximum market price below the equilibrium price, benefits successful buyers but creates persistent shortages. Because the price is maintained below the equilibrium price, the quantity demanded is increased and the quantity supplied is decreased compared to the equilibrium quantity. This leads to predictable problems: inefficiently low quantity transacted, **inefficient allocation to consumers, wasted resources,** and **inefficiently low quality.** It also encourages illegal activity as people turn to **black markets** to get the good. Because of these problems, price ceilings have generally lost favor as an economic policy tool. But some governments continue to impose them either because they don't understand the effects or because the price ceilings benefit some influential group.

3. A **price floor,** a minimum market price above the equilibrium price, benefits successful sellers but creates persistent surplus. Because the price is maintained above the equilibrium price, the quantity

demanded is decreased and the quantity supplied is increased compared to the equilibrium quantity. This leads to predictable problems: inefficiencies in the form of inefficiently low quantity transacted, **inefficient allocation of sales among sellers,** wasted resources, and **inefficiently high quality.** It also encourages illegal activity and black markets. The most well known kind of price floor is the **minimum wage,** but price floors are also commonly applied to agricultural products.

4. **Quantity controls,** or **quotas,** limit the quantity of a good that can be bought or sold. The quantity allowed for sale is the **quota limit.** The government issues **licenses** to individuals, the right to sell a given quantity of the good. The owner of a license earns a **quota rent,** earnings that accrue from ownership of the right to sell the good. It is equal to the difference between the **demand price** at the quota limit, what consumers are willing to pay for that quantity, and the **supply price** at the quota limit, what suppliers are willing to accept for that quantity. Economists say that a quota drives a **wedge** between the demand price and the supply price; this wedge is equal to the quota rent. Quantity controls lead to inefficiencies in the form of mutually beneficial transactions that do not occur; they also encourage illegal activity.

KEY TERMS

Price controls, p. 102
Price ceiling, p. 102
Price floor, p. 102
Inefficient allocation to consumers, p. 106
Wasted resources, p. 106
Inefficiently low quality, p. 106

Black market, p. 107
Minimum wage, p. 109
Inefficient allocation of sales among sellers, p. 111
Inefficiently high quality, p. 113
Quantity control, p. 115
Quota, p. 115

Quota limit, p. 115
License, p. 115
Demand price, p. 117
Supply price, p. 117
Wedge, p. 118
Quota rent, p. 118

PROBLEMS

interactive activity

1. In order to ingratiate himself with voters, the mayor of Gotham City decides to lower the price of taxi rides. Assume, for simplicity, that all taxi rides are the same distance and therefore cost the same. The accompanying table shows the demand and supply schedules for taxi rides.

Fare (per ride)	Quantity of rides (millions per year)	
	Quantity demanded	Quantity supplied
$7.00	10	12
6.50	11	11
6.00	12	10
5.50	13	9
5.00	14	8
4.50	15	7

a. Assume that there are no restrictions on the number of taxi rides that can be supplied (there is no medallion system). Find the equilibrium price and quantity.

b. Suppose that the mayor sets a price ceiling at $5.50. How large is the shortage of rides? Illustrate with a diagram. Who loses and who benefits from this policy?

c. Suppose that the stock market crashes and, as a result, people in Gotham City are poorer. This reduces the quantity of taxi rides demanded by 6 million rides per year at any given price. What effect will the mayor's new policy have now? Illustrate with a diagram.

d. Suppose that the stock market rises and the demand for taxi rides returns to normal (that is, returns to the demand schedule given in the table). The mayor now decides to ingratiate himself with taxi drivers. He announces a policy in which operating licenses are given to existing taxi drivers; the number of licenses is restricted such that only 10 million rides per year can be given. Illustrate the effect of this policy on the market, and indicate the resulting price and quantity transacted. What is the quota rent per ride?

2. In the late eighteenth century, the price of bread in New York City was controlled, set at a predetermined price above the market price.

a. Draw a diagram showing the effect of the policy. Did the policy act as a price ceiling or a price floor?

b. What kinds of inefficiencies were likely to have arisen when the controlled price of bread was above the market price? Explain in detail.

One year during this period, a poor wheat harvest caused a leftward shift in the supply of bread and therefore an increase in its market price. New York bakers found that the controlled price of bread in New York was below the market price.

c. Draw a diagram showing the effect of the price control on the market for bread during this one-year period. Did the policy act as a price ceiling or a price floor?

d. What kinds of inefficiencies do you think occurred during this period? Explain in detail.

3. In 2014, the U.S. House of Representatives approved a new farm bill establishing the Margin Protection Program (MPP) for dairy producers. The MPP supports dairy farmers when the margin between feed costs and milk prices falls below $0.08 per pound. Current feed costs are $0.10 per pound, which means the program creates a price floor for milk at $0.18 per pound. At that price, in 2015, the quantity of milk supplied is 240 billion pounds, and the quantity demanded is 140 billion pounds. To support the price of milk at the price floor, the U.S. Department of Agriculture (USDA) has to buy up 100 billion pounds of surplus milk. The supply and demand curves in the following diagram illustrate the market for milk.

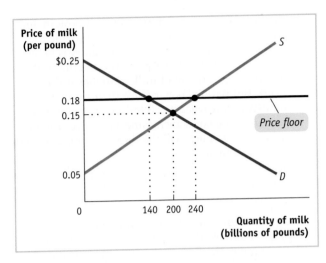

a. In the absence of a price floor, how much consumer surplus is created? How much producer surplus? What is the total surplus (producer surplus plus consumer surplus)?

b. With the price floor at $0.18 per pound of milk, consumers buy 140 billion pounds of milk. How much consumer surplus is created now?

c. With the price floor at $0.18 per pound of milk, producers sell 240 billion pounds of milk (some to consumers and some to the USDA). How much producer surplus is created now?

d. How much money does the USDA spend to buy surplus milk?

e. Taxes must be collected to pay for the purchases of surplus milk by the USDA. As a result, total surplus is reduced by the amount the USDA spent buying surplus milk. Using your answers from parts b, c, and d, what is the total surplus when there is a price floor? How does this total surplus compare to the total surplus without a price floor from part a?

4. The accompanying table shows hypothetical demand and supply schedules for milk per year. The U.S. government decides that the incomes of dairy farmers should be maintained at a level that allows the traditional family dairy farm to survive. So it implements a price floor of $1 per pint by buying surplus milk until the market price is $1 per pint.

Price of milk (per pint)	Quantity of milk (millions of pints per year)	
	Quantity demanded	Quantity supplied
$1.20	550	850
1.10	600	800
1.00	650	750
0.90	700	700
0.80	750	650

a. How much surplus milk will be produced as a result of this policy?

b. What will be the cost to the government of this policy?

c. Since milk is an important source of protein and calcium, the government decides to provide the surplus milk it purchases to elementary schools at a price of only $0.60 per pint. Assume that schools will buy any amount of milk available at this low price. But parents now reduce their purchases of milk at any price by 50 million pints per year because they know their children are getting milk at school. How much will the dairy program now cost the government?

d. Explain how inefficiencies in the form of inefficient allocation to sellers and wasted resources arise from this policy.

5. European governments tend to make greater use of price controls than does the U.S. government. For example, the French government sets minimum starting yearly wages for new hires who have completed *le bac,* certification roughly equivalent to a high school diploma. The demand schedule for new hires with *le bac* and the supply schedule for similarly credentialed new job seekers are given in the accompanying table. The price here—given in euros, the currency used in France—is the same as the yearly wage.

Wage (per year)	Quantity demanded (new job offers per year)	Quantity supplied (new job seekers per year)
€45,000	200,000	325,000
40,000	220,000	320,000
35,000	250,000	310,000
30,000	290,000	290,000
25,000	370,000	200,000

a. In the absence of government interference, what are the equilibrium wage and number of graduates hired per year? Illustrate with a diagram. Will there be anyone seeking a job at the equilibrium wage who is unable to find one—that is, will there be anyone who is involuntarily unemployed?

b. Suppose the French government sets a minimum yearly wage of €35,000. Is there any involuntary unemployment at this wage? If so, how much? Illustrate with a diagram. What if the minimum wage is set at €40,000? Also illustrate with a diagram.

c. Given your answer to part b and the information in the table, what do you think is the relationship between the level of involuntary unemployment and the level of the minimum wage? Who benefits from such a policy? Who loses? What is the missed opportunity here?

6. In many European countries high minimum wages have led to high levels of unemployment and underemployment, and a two-tier labor system. In the formal labor market, workers have good jobs that pay at least the minimum wage. In the informal, or black market for labor, workers have poor jobs and receive less than the minimum wage.

a. Draw a demand and supply diagram showing the effect of the imposition of a minimum wage on the overall market for labor, with wage on the vertical axis and hours of labor on the horizontal axis. Your supply curve should represent the hours of labor offered by workers according to the wage, and the demand curve should represent the hours of labor demanded by employers according to the wage. What type of shortage is created? Illustrate on your diagram the size of the shortage.

b. Assume that the imposition of the high minimum wage causes a contraction in the economy so that employers in the formal sector cut their production and their demand for workers. Illustrate the effect of this on the overall market for labor. What happens to the shortage? Illustrate with a diagram.

c. Assume that the workers who cannot get a job paying at least the minimum wage move into the informal labor market where there is no minimum wage. What happens to the size of the informal market for labor as a result of the economic contraction? What happens to the equilibrium wage in the informal labor market? Illustrate with a supply and demand diagram for the informal market.

7. For the last 80 years the U.S. government has used price supports to provide income assistance to American farmers. To implement these price supports, at times the government has used price floors, which it maintains by buying up the surplus farm products. At other times, it has used target prices, a policy by which the government gives the farmer an amount equal to the difference between the market price and the target price for each unit sold. Consider the market for corn depicted in the accompanying diagram.

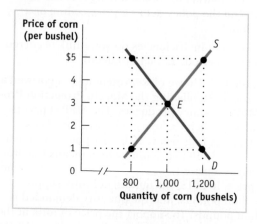

a. If the government sets a price floor of $5 per bushel, how many bushels of corn are produced? How many are purchased by consumers? By the government? How much does the program cost the government? How much revenue do corn farmers receive?

b. Suppose the government sets a target price of $5 per bushel for any quantity supplied up to 1,000 bushels. How many bushels of corn are purchased by consumers and at what price? By the government? How much does the program cost the government? How much revenue do corn farmers receive?

c. Which of these programs (in parts a and b) costs corn consumers more? Which program costs the government more? Explain.

d. Is one of these policies less inefficient than the other? Explain.

8. The waters off the North Atlantic coast were once teeming with fish. But because of overfishing by the commercial fishing industry, the stocks of fish became seriously depleted. In 1991, the National Marine Fishery Service of the U.S. government implemented a quota to allow fish stocks to recover. In 2016 the quota limited the amount of swordfish caught per year by all U.S.-licensed fishing boats to 7 million pounds. As soon as the U.S. fishing fleet had met the quota limit, the swordfish catch was closed down for the rest of the year. The accompanying table gives the hypothetical demand and supply schedules for swordfish caught in the United States per year.

Price of swordfish (per pound)	Quantity of swordfish (millions of pounds per year)	
	Quantity demanded	Quantity supplied
$20	6	15
18	7	13
16	8	11
14	9	9
12	10	7

a. Use a diagram to show the effect of the quota on the market for swordfish in 1991.

b. How do you think fishermen will change how they fish in response to this policy?

9. In Maine, you must have a license to harvest lobster commercially; these licenses are issued yearly. The state of Maine is concerned about the dwindling supplies of lobsters found off its coast. The state fishery department has decided to place a yearly quota of 80,000 pounds of lobsters harvested in all Maine waters. It has also decided to give licenses this year only to those fishermen who had licenses last year. The accompanying diagram shows the demand and supply curves for Maine lobsters.

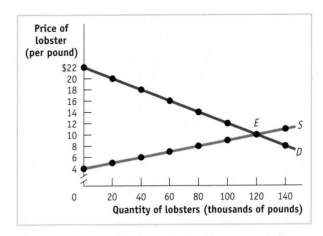

a. In the absence of government restrictions, what are the equilibrium price and quantity?

b. What is the *demand price* at which consumers wish to purchase 80,000 pounds of lobsters?

c. What is the *supply price* at which suppliers are willing to supply 80,000 pounds of lobsters?

d. What is the *quota rent* per pound of lobster when 80,000 pounds are sold?

e. Explain a transaction that benefits both buyer and seller but is prevented by the quota restriction.

10. The Venezuelan government has imposed a price ceiling on the retail price of roasted coffee beans. The accompanying diagram shows the market for coffee beans. In the absence of price controls, the equilibrium is at point E, with an equilibrium price of P_E and an equilibrium quantity bought and sold of Q_E.

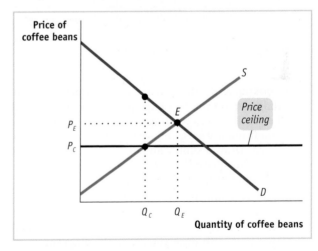

a. Show the consumer and producer surplus before the introduction of the price ceiling.

After the introduction of the price ceiling, the price falls to P_C and the quantity bought and sold falls to Q_C.

b. Show the consumer surplus after the introduction of the price ceiling (assuming that the consumers with the highest willingness to pay get to buy the available coffee beans; that is, assuming that there is no inefficient allocation to consumers).

c. Show the producer surplus after the introduction of the price ceiling (assuming that the producers with the lowest cost get to sell their coffee beans; that is, assuming that there is no inefficient allocation of sales among producers).

d. Using the diagram, show how much of what was producer surplus before the introduction of the price ceiling has been transferred to consumers as a result of the price ceiling.

11. The accompanying diagram shows data from the U.S. Bureau of Labor Statistics on the average price of an airline ticket in the United States from 1975 until 1985, adjusted to eliminate the effect of *inflation* (the general increase in the prices of all goods over time). In 1978, the United States Airline Deregulation Act removed the price floor on airline fares, and it also allowed the airlines greater flexibility to offer new routes.

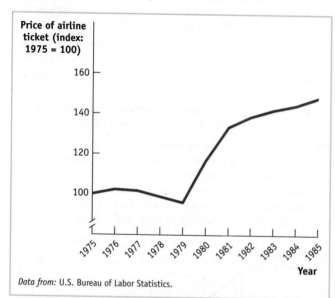

Data from: U.S. Bureau of Labor Statistics.

a. Looking at the data on airline ticket prices in the diagram, do you think the price floor that existed before 1978 was binding or nonbinding? That is, do you think it was set above or below the equilibrium price? Draw a supply and demand diagram, showing where the price floor that existed before 1978 was in relation to the equilibrium price.

b. Most economists agree that the average airline ticket price per mile traveled actually *fell* as a result of the Airline Deregulation Act. How might you reconcile that view with what you see in the diagram?

12. Many college students attempt to land internships before graduation to burnish their resumes, gain experience in a chosen field, or try out possible careers. The hope shared by all of these prospective interns is that they will find internships that pay more than typical summer jobs, such as waiting tables or flipping burgers.

a. With wage measured on the vertical axis and number of hours of work on the horizontal axis, draw a supply and demand diagram for the market for interns in which the minimum wage is nonbinding at the market equilibrium.

b. Assume that a market downturn reduces the demand for interns by employers. However, many students are willing and eager to work in unpaid internships. As a result, the new market equilibrium wage is equal to zero. Draw another supply and demand diagram to illustrate this new market equilibrium.

WORK IT OUT Interactive step-by-step help with solving this problem can be found online.

---

13. Suppose it is decided that rent control in New York City will be abolished and that market rents will now prevail. Assume that all rental units are identical and so are offered at the same rent. To address the plight of residents who may be unable to pay the market rent, an income supplement will be paid to all low-income households equal to the difference between the old controlled rent and the new market rent.

a. Use a diagram to show the effect on the rental market of the elimination of rent control. What will happen to the quality and quantity of rental housing supplied?

b. Use a second diagram to show the additional effect of the income-supplement policy on the market. What effect does it have on the market rent and quantity of rental housing supplied in comparison to your answers to part a?

c. Are tenants better or worse off as a result of these policies? Are landlords better or worse off? Is society as a whole better or worse off?

d. From a political standpoint, why do you think cities have been more likely to resort to rent control rather than a policy of income supplements to help low-income people pay for housing?

International Trade

THE EVERYWHERE PHONE

WHAT DO AMERICANS DO with their time? The answer, increasingly, is that they stare at small screens. According to one survey, the average American spent almost three hours a day looking at a smartphone (especially an iPhone) or a tablet, slightly more time than is spent watching TV.

Bloomberg/Getty Images

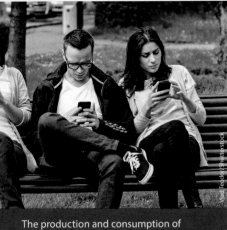

Vlad Teodor/Shutterstock

The production and consumption of smartphones are examples of today's hyperglobal world with its soaring levels of international trade.

Where do these small screens come from? Specifically, where does an iPhone come from?

Apple, which sells the iPhone, is an American company. But if you said that iPhones come from America, you're mostly wrong: Apple develops products, but contracts almost all of the manufacturing of those products to other companies, which are mainly overseas. But it's not really right to answer "China," either, even though that's where iPhones are assembled. You see, assembly—the last phase of iPhone production, in which the pieces are put together in the familiar metal-and-glass case—only accounts for a small fraction of the phone's value.

In fact, a study of the iPhone estimated that of the average factory price of $229 per phone, only around $10 stayed in the Chinese economy. A substantially larger amount went to Korean manufacturers, who supplied the display and memory chips. There were also substantial outlays for raw materials, sourced all over the world. And the biggest share of the price—more than half—consisted of Apple's profit margin, which was largely a reward for research, development, and design.

So where do iPhones come from? Lots of places. And the case of the iPhone isn't unusual: the car you drive, the clothing you wear, even the food you eat are generally the end products of complex *supply chains* that span the globe.

Has this always been true? Yes and no. Large-scale international trade isn't new. By the early twentieth century, middle-class residents of London already ate bread made from Canadian wheat and beef from the Argentine Pampas, while wearing clothing woven from Australian wool and Egyptian cotton. In recent decades, however, new technologies for transportation and communication have interacted with pro-trade policies to produce an era of *hyperglobalization* in which international trade has soared thanks to complex chains of production like the one that puts an iPhone in front of your nose. As a result, now, more than ever before, we must have a full picture of international trade to understand how national economies work.

This chapter examines the economics of international trade. We start from the model of comparative advantage, which, as we saw in Chapter 2, explains why there are gains from international trade. We will briefly recap that model here, then turn to a more detailed examination of the causes and consequences of globalization. ●

WHAT YOU WILL LEARN

- What is comparative advantage and why does it lead to international trade?
- What are the sources of comparative advantage?
- Who gains and who loses from international trade?
- Why do trade protections like **tariffs** and **import quotas** create inefficiency?
- Why do governments engage in **trade protection** and how do **international trade agreements** counteract this?

Goods and services purchased from other countries are **imports;** goods and services sold to other countries are **exports.**

Globalization is the phenomenon of growing economic linkages among countries.

Comparative Advantage and International Trade

The United States buys smartphones—and many other goods and services— from other countries. At the same time, it sells many goods and services to other countries. Goods and services purchased from abroad are **imports;** goods and services sold abroad are **exports.**

As illustrated by the opening story, international trade plays an increasingly important role in the world economy. Panel (a) of Figure 5-1 shows the ratio of goods crossing national borders to *world GDP*—the total value of goods and services produced in the world as a whole—since 1870. As you can see, the long-term trend has been upward, although there have been some periods of declining trade—for example, the sharp but brief dip in trade during the global financial crisis of 2008 and its aftermath.

Panel (b) shows imports and exports as a percentage of GDP for a number of countries. It shows that foreign trade is significantly more important for many other countries than it is for the United States.

Foreign trade isn't the only way countries interact economically. In the modern world, investors from one country often invest funds in another nation; many companies are multinational, with subsidiaries operating in several countries; and a growing number of people work in a country different from the one in which they were born. The growth of all these forms of economic linkages among countries is often called **globalization.**

Globalization isn't a new phenomenon. As you can see from panel (a) of Figure 5-1, there was rapid growth in trade between 1870 and the beginning of

FIGURE 5-1 The Growing Importance of International Trade

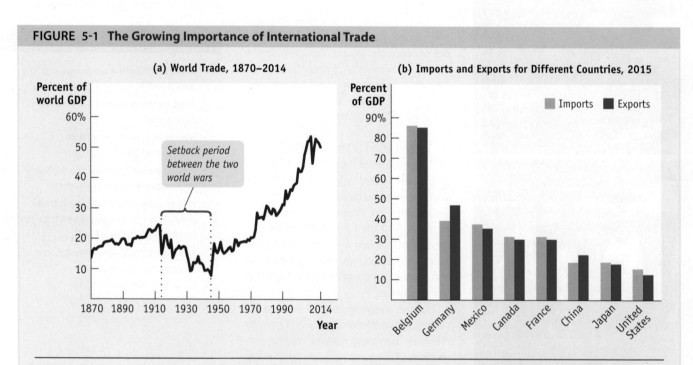

Panel (a) shows the long-term history of the ratio of world trade to world production. The trend has been generally upward, thanks to technological progress in transportation and communication, although there was a long setback during the period between the two world wars. Panel (b) demonstrates that international trade is significantly more important to many other countries than it is to the United States.

Data from: [panel (a)] Klasing, M. J., and P. Milionis, "Quantifying the Evolution of World Trade, 1870–1949," *Journal of International Economics* (2013); and Feenstra, Robert C., Robert Inklaar, and Marcel P. Timmer, "The Next Generation of the Penn World Table" *American Economic Review* 105, no. 10 (2015): 3150–3182, available for download at www.ggdc.net/pwt; [panel (b)] World Development Indicators.

World War I, as railroads and steamships effectively made shipping goods long distances faster and cheaper, effectively shrinking the world. This growth of trade was accompanied by large-scale international investment and migration. However, globalization went into reverse for almost 40 years after World War I, as governments imposed limits on trade of the kind analyzed later in this chapter. And by several measures, globalization didn't return to 1913 levels until the 1980s.

Since then, however, there has been a further dramatic increase in international linkages, sometimes referred to as **hyperglobalization,** exemplified by the way manufacture of iPhones and other high-tech goods involves supply chains of production that span the globe, and in which each stage of a good's production takes place in a different country—all made possible by advances in communication and transportation technology. (For a real-life example, see this chapter's Business Case.)

One big question in international economics is whether hyperglobalization will continue in the decades ahead. As you can see from looking closely at Figure 5-1, the big rise in the ratio of exports to world GDP leveled off around 2005. Since then, there have been many reports about companies deciding that the money they saved by buying goods from suppliers thousands of miles away is more than offset by the disadvantages of long shipping times and other inconveniences. (Even now, it takes around two weeks for a container ship from China to arrive in California, and a month to reach the East Coast.) As a result, there has been some move toward *reshoring*, bringing production closer to markets. If this turns out to be a major trend, world trade could level off or even decline as a share of world GDP, although it would remain very important.

To understand why international trade occurs and why economists believe it is beneficial to the economy, we will first review the concept of comparative advantage.

Hyperglobalization is the phenomenon of extremely high levels of international trade.

Production Possibilities and Comparative Advantage, Revisited

To produce phones, any country must use resources—land, labor, and capital—that could have been used to produce other things. The potential production of other goods a country must forgo to produce a phone is the opportunity cost of that phone.

In some cases, it's easy to see why the opportunity cost of producing a good is especially low in a given country. Consider, for example, shrimp—much of which now comes from seafood farms in Vietnam and Thailand. It's a lot easier to produce shrimp in Vietnam, where the climate is nearly ideal and there's plenty of coastal land suitable for shellfish farming, than it is in the United States.

Conversely, other goods are not produced as easily in Vietnam as in the United States. For example, Vietnam doesn't have the base of skilled workers and technological know-how that makes the United States so good at producing high-technology goods. So the opportunity cost of a ton of shrimp, in terms of other goods such as aircraft, is much less in Vietnam than it is in the United States.

In other cases, matters are a bit less obvious. It's as easy to assemble smartphones in the United States as it is in China, and Chinese electronics workers are, if anything, less productive than their U.S. counterparts. But Chinese workers are a lot less productive than U.S. workers in other areas, such as automobile and chemical production. This means that diverting a Chinese worker into assembling phones reduces output of other goods less than diverting a U.S. worker into assembling phones. That is, the opportunity cost of smartphone assembly in China is less than it is in the United States.

The opportunity cost of smartphone assembly in China is lower, giving it a comparative advantage.

Notice that we said the opportunity cost of phone *assembly*. As we've seen, most of the value of a "Chinese made" phone actually comes from other countries. For the sake of exposition, however, let's ignore that complication and consider a hypothetical case in which China makes phones from scratch.

So we say that China has a comparative advantage in producing smartphones. Let's repeat the definition of comparative advantage from Chapter 2: *A country has a comparative advantage in producing a good or service if the opportunity cost of producing the good or service is lower for that country than for other countries.*

Figure 5-2 provides a hypothetical numerical example of comparative advantage in international trade. We assume that only two goods are produced and consumed, phones and Caterpillar heavy trucks. (The U.S. doesn't export many ordinary trucks, but Caterpillar, which makes earth-moving equipment, is a major exporter.) And we assume that there are only two countries in the world, the United States and China. The figure shows hypothetical production possibility frontiers for the United States and China.

As in Chapter 2, we simplify the model by assuming that the production possibility frontiers are straight lines, as shown in Figure 2-1, rather than the more realistic bowed-out shape in Figure 2-2. The straight-line shape implies that the opportunity cost of a phone in terms of trucks in each country is constant—it does not depend on how many units of each good the country produces. The analysis of international trade under the assumption that opportunity costs are constant, which makes production possibility frontiers straight lines, is known as the **Ricardian model of international trade,** named after the English economist David Ricardo, who introduced this analysis in the early nineteenth century.

In Figure 5-2 we show a situation in which the United States can produce 100,000 trucks if it produces no phones, or 100 million phones if it produces no trucks. Thus, the slope of the U.S. production possibility frontier, or *PPF*, is $-100,000/100 = -1,000$. That is, to produce an additional million phones, the United States must forgo the production of 1,000 trucks. Likewise, to produce one more truck, the United States must forgo 1,000 phones (equal to 1 million phones divided by 1,000 trucks).

FIGURE 5-2 Comparative Advantage and the Production Possibility Frontier

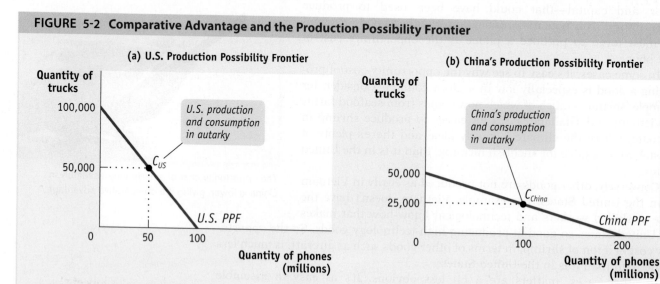

The U.S. opportunity cost of 1 million phones in terms of trucks is 1,000: for every 1 million phones, 1,000 trucks must be forgone. The Chinese opportunity cost of 1 million phones in terms of trucks is 250: for every additional 1 million phones, only 250 trucks must be forgone. As a result, the United States has a comparative advantage in truck production, and China has a comparative advantage in phone production. In autarky, each country is forced to consume only what it produces: 50,000 trucks and 50 million phones for the United States; 25,000 trucks and 100 million phones for China.

Similarly, China can produce 50,000 trucks if it produces no phones or 200 million phones if it produces no trucks. Thus, the slope of China's *PPF* is −50,000/200 = −250. That is, to produce an additional million phones, China must forgo the production of 250 trucks. Likewise, to produce one more truck, China must forgo 4,000 phones (1 million phones divided by 250 trucks).

Economists use the term **autarky** to refer to a situation in which a country does not trade with other countries. We assume that in autarky the United States chooses to produce and consume 50 million phones and 50,000 trucks. We also assume that in autarky China produces 100 million phones and 25,000 trucks.

The trade-offs facing the two countries when they don't trade are summarized in Table 5-1. As you can see, the United States has a comparative advantage in the production of trucks because it has a lower opportunity cost in terms of phones than China has: producing a truck costs the United States only 1,000 phones, while it costs China 4,000 phones. Correspondingly, China has a comparative advantage in phone production: 1 million phones costs only 250 trucks, while it costs the United States 1,000 trucks.

As we learned in Chapter 2, each country can do better by engaging in trade than it could by not trading. A country can accomplish this by specializing in the production of the good in which it has a comparative advantage and exporting that good, while importing the good in which it has a comparative disadvantage.

Let's see how this works.

> **Autarky** is a situation in which a country does not trade with other countries.

TABLE 5-1 U.S. and Chinese Opportunity Costs of Phones and Trucks

	U.S. Opportunity Cost		Chinese Opportunity Cost
1 million phones	1,000 trucks	>	250 trucks
1 truck	1,000 phones	<	4,000 phones

The Gains from International Trade

Figure 5-3 illustrates how both countries can gain from specialization and trade, by showing a hypothetical rearrangement of production and consumption that allows *each* country to consume more of *both* goods. Again, panel (a) represents the United States and panel (b) represents China. In each panel we indicate again the autarky production and consumption assumed in Figure 5-2.

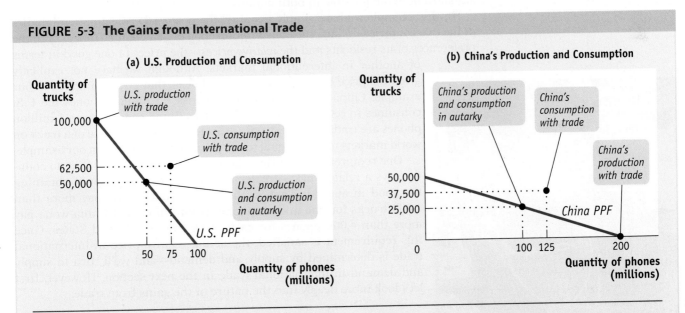

FIGURE 5-3 The Gains from International Trade

Trade increases world production of both goods, allowing both countries to consume more. Here, each country specializes its production as a result of trade: the United States concentrates on producing trucks, and China concentrates on producing phones. Total world production of both goods rises, which means that it is possible for both countries to consume more of both goods.

TABLE 5-2 How the United States and China Gain from Trade

		In Autarky		With Trade		
		Production	Consumption	Production	Consumption	Gains from trade
United States	**Million phones**	50	50	0	75	+25
	Trucks	50,000	50,000	100,000	62,500	+12,500
China	**Million phones**	100	100	200	125	+25
	Trucks	25,000	25,000	0	37,500	+12,500

Once trade becomes possible, however, everything changes. With trade, each country can move to producing only the good in which it has a comparative advantage—trucks for the United States and phones for China. Because the world production of both goods is now higher than in autarky, trade makes it possible for each country to consume more of both goods.

Table 5-2 sums up the changes as a result of trade and shows why both countries can gain. The left part of the table shows the autarky situation, before trade, in which each country must produce the goods it consumes. The right part of the table shows what happens as a result of trade. After trade, the United States specializes in the production of trucks, producing 100,000 trucks and no phones; China specializes in the production of phones, producing 200 million phones and no trucks.

The result is a rise in total world production of both goods. As you can see in the table, gains from trade enable the United States to consume both more trucks (12,500 more) and phones (25 million more) than before, even though it no longer produces phones, because it can import phones from China. China can also consume more of both goods (12,500 more trucks and 25 million more phones), even though it no longer produces trucks, because it can import trucks from the United States.

The key to this mutual gain is the fact that trade liberates both countries from self-sufficiency—from the need to produce the same mixes of goods they consume. Because each country can concentrate on producing the good in which it has a comparative advantage, total world production rises, making a higher standard of living possible in both nations.

In this example we have simply assumed the post-trade consumption bundles of the two countries. In fact, the consumption choices of a country reflect both the preferences of its residents and the *relative prices*—the prices of one good in terms of another in international markets. Although we have not explicitly given the price of trucks in terms of phones, that price is implicit in our example: China sells the United States the 75 million phones the U.S. consumes in return for the 37,500 trucks China consumes, so 1 million phones are traded for 500 trucks. This tells us that the price of a truck on world markets must be equal to the price of 2,000 phones in our example.

One requirement that the relative price must satisfy is that no country pays a relative price greater than its opportunity cost of obtaining the good in autarky. That is, the United States won't pay more than 1,000 trucks for one million phones from China, and China won't pay more than 4,000 phones for each truck from the United States. Once this requirement is satisfied, the actual relative price in international trade is determined by supply and demand—and we'll turn to supply and demand in international trade in the next section. However, first let's look more deeply into the nature of the gains from trade.

Comparative Advantage versus Absolute Advantage

It's easy to accept the idea that Vietnam and Thailand have a comparative advantage in shrimp production: they have a tropical climate

The tropical climates of Vietnam and Thailand give them a comparative advantage in shrimp production.

that's better suited to shrimp farming than that of the United States (even along the Gulf Coast), and they have a lot of usable coastal area. So the United States imports shrimp from Vietnam and Thailand. In other cases, however, it may be harder to understand why we import certain goods from abroad.

U.S. imports of phones from China are a case in point. There's nothing about China's climate or resources that makes it especially good at assembling electronic devices. In fact, it almost surely would take fewer hours of labor to assemble a smartphone or a tablet in the United States than in China.

Why, then, do we buy phones assembled in China? Because the gains from trade depend on *comparative advantage,* not absolute advantage. Yes, it would take less labor to assemble a phone in the United States than in China. That is, the productivity of Chinese electronics workers is less than that of their U.S. counterparts. But what determines comparative advantage is not the amount of resources used to produce a good but the opportunity cost of that good—here, the quantity of other goods forgone in order to produce a phone. And the opportunity cost of phones is lower in China than in the United States.

Here's how it works: Chinese workers have low productivity compared with U.S. workers in the electronics industry. But Chinese workers have even lower productivity compared with U.S. workers in other industries. Because Chinese labor productivity in industries other than electronics is relatively very low, producing a phone in China, even though it takes a lot of labor, does not require forgoing the production of large quantities of other goods.

In the United States, the opposite is true: very high productivity in other industries (such as automobiles) means that assembling electronic products in the United States, even though it doesn't require much labor, requires sacrificing lots of other goods. So the opportunity cost of producing electronics is less in China than in the United States. Despite its lower labor productivity, China has a comparative advantage in the production of many consumer electronics, although the United States has an absolute advantage.

The source of China's comparative advantage in consumer electronics is reflected in global markets by the wages Chinese workers are paid. That's because a country's wage rates, in general, reflect its labor productivity. In countries where labor is highly productive in many industries, employers are willing to pay high wages to attract workers, so competition among employers leads to an overall high wage rate. In countries where labor is less productive, competition for workers is less intense and wage rates are correspondingly lower.

As the Global Comparison shows, there is indeed a strong relationship between overall levels of productivity and wage rates around the world. Because China has generally low productivity, it has a relatively low wage rate. Low wages, in turn, give China a cost advantage in producing goods where its productivity is only moderately low, like consumer electronics. As a result, it's cheaper to produce these goods in China than in the United States.

The kind of trade that takes place between low-wage, low-productivity economies like China and high-wage, high-productivity economies like the United States gives rise to two common misperceptions. One, the *pauper labor fallacy,* is the belief that when a country with high wages imports goods produced by workers who are paid low wages, this must hurt the standard of living of workers in the importing country. The other, the *sweatshop labor fallacy,* is the belief that trade must be bad for workers in poor exporting countries because those workers are paid very low wages by our standards.

Both fallacies miss the nature of gains from trade: it's to the advantage of both countries if the poorer, lower-wage country exports goods in which it has a comparative advantage, even if its cost advantage in these goods depends on low wages. That is, both countries are able to achieve a higher standard of living through trade.

It's particularly important to understand that buying a good made by someone who is paid much lower wages than most U.S. workers doesn't necessarily

GLOBAL COMPARISON   PRODUCTIVITY AND WAGES AROUND THE WORLD

Is it true that both the pauper labor argument and the sweatshop labor argument are fallacies? Yes, it is. The real explanation for low wages in poor countries is low overall productivity.

The graph shows estimates of labor productivity, measured by the value of output (GDP) per worker, and wages, measured by the hourly compensation of the average worker, for several countries in 2014. Both productivity and wages are expressed as percentages of U.S. productivity and wages; for example, productivity and wages in Japan were 62% and 73%, respectively, of their U.S. levels. You can see the strong positive relationship between productivity and wages. The relationship isn't perfect. For example, Norway has higher wages than its productivity might lead you to expect. But simple comparisons of wages give a misleading sense of labor costs in poor countries: their low wage advantage is mostly offset by low productivity.

Data from: The Conference Board.

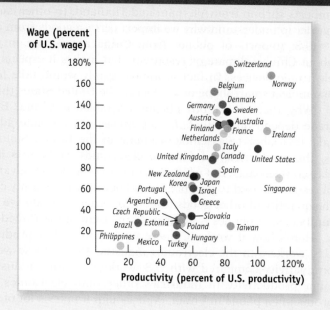

imply that you're taking advantage of that person. It depends on the alternatives. Because workers in poor countries have low productivity across the board, they are offered low wages whether they produce goods exported to America or goods sold in local markets. A job that looks terrible by rich-country standards can be a step up for someone in a poor country.

International trade that depends on low-wage exports can nonetheless raise the exporting country's standard of living. This is especially true of very-low-wage nations. For example, Bangladesh and similar countries would be much poorer than they are—their citizens might even be starving—if they weren't able to export goods such as clothing based on their low wage rates.

Sources of Comparative Advantage

International trade is driven by comparative advantage, but where does comparative advantage come from? Economists who study international trade have found three main sources of comparative advantage: international differences in *climate*, international differences in *factor endowments*, and international differences in *technology*.

Differences in Climate One key reason the opportunity cost of producing shrimp in Vietnam and Thailand is less than in the United States is that shrimp need warm water—Vietnam has plenty of that, but America doesn't. In general, differences in climate play a significant role in international trade. Tropical countries export tropical products like coffee, sugar, bananas, and shrimp. Countries in the temperate zones export crops like wheat and corn. Some trade is even driven by the difference in seasons between the northern and southern hemispheres: winter deliveries of Chilean grapes and New Zealand apples have become commonplace in U.S. and European supermarkets.

Differences in Factor Endowments The United States does more trade with Canada than with any other country (China comes in second). Among other things, Canada sells us a lot of forest products—lumber and products derived from lumber, like pulp and paper. These exports don't reflect the special skill of

A greater endowment of forestland gives Canada a comparative advantage in forest products.

Johner Images/Alamy

Canadian lumberjacks. Canada has a comparative advantage in forest products because its forested area is much greater compared to the size of its labor force than the ratio of forestland to the labor force in the United States.

Forestland, like labor and capital, is a *factor of production:* an input used to produce goods and services. (Recall from Chapter 2 that the factors of production are land, labor, physical capital, and human capital.) Due to history and geography, the mix of available factors of production differs among countries, providing an important source of comparative advantage. The relationship between comparative advantage and factor availability is found in an influential model of international trade, the *Heckscher–Ohlin model,* developed by two Swedish economists in the first half of the twentieth century.

Two key concepts in the model are *factor abundance* and *factor intensity.* Factor abundance refers to how large a country's supply of a factor is relative to its supply of other factors. **Factor intensity** refers to the ranking of goods according to which factor is used in relatively greater quantities in production compared to other factors. So oil refining is a capital-intensive good because it tends to use a high ratio of capital to labor, but phone production is a labor-intensive good because it tends to use a high ratio of labor to capital.

According to the **Heckscher–Ohlin model,** *a country that has an abundant supply of a factor of production will have a comparative advantage in goods whose production is intensive in that factor.* So a country that has a relative abundance of capital will have a comparative advantage in capital-intensive industries such as oil refining, but a country that has a relative abundance of labor will have a comparative advantage in labor-intensive industries such as phone production.

The basic intuition behind this result is simple and based on opportunity cost.

- The opportunity cost of a given factor—the value that the factor would generate in alternative uses—is low for a country when it is relatively abundant in that factor.

- Relative to the United States, China has an abundance of low-skilled labor.

- As a result, the opportunity cost of the production of low-skilled, labor-intensive goods is lower in China than in the United States.

World trade in clothing is the most dramatic example of the validity of the Heckscher–Ohlin model in practice. Clothing production is a labor-intensive activity: it doesn't take much physical capital, nor does it require a lot of human capital in the form of highly educated workers. So you would expect labor-abundant countries such as China and Bangladesh to have a comparative advantage in clothing production. And they do.

The fact that international trade is the result of differences in factor endowments helps explain another fact: international specialization of production is often *incomplete.* That is, a country often maintains some domestic production of a good that it imports. A good example of this is the United States and oil. Saudi Arabia exports oil to the United States because Saudi Arabia has an abundant supply of oil relative to its other factors of production; the United States exports medical devices to Saudi Arabia because it has an abundant supply of expertise in medical technology relative to its other factors of production. But the United States also produces some oil domestically because the size of its domestic oil reserves in Texas and Alaska (and now, increasingly, its oil shale reserves elsewhere) makes it economical to do so.

In our supply and demand analysis in the next section, we'll consider incomplete specialization by a country to be the norm. We should emphasize, however, that the fact that countries often incompletely specialize does not in any way change the conclusion that there are gains from trade.

The **factor intensity** of a good is a measure of which factor is used in relatively greater quantities than other factors in production.

According to the **Heckscher–Ohlin model,** a country has a comparative advantage in a good whose production is intensive in the factors that are abundantly available in that country.

Differences in Technology In the 1970s and 1980s, Japan became by far the world's largest exporter of automobiles, selling large numbers to the United States and the rest of the world. Japan's comparative advantage in automobiles wasn't the result of climate. Nor can it easily be attributed to differences in factor endowments: aside from a scarcity of land, Japan's mix of available factors is quite similar to that in other advanced countries. Instead, Japan's comparative advantage in automobiles was based on the superior production techniques developed by its manufacturers, which allowed them to produce more cars with a given amount of labor and capital than their American or European counterparts.

Japan's comparative advantage in automobiles was a case of comparative advantage caused by differences in technology—the techniques used in production.

The causes of differences in technology are somewhat mysterious. Sometimes they seem to be based on knowledge accumulated through experience—for example, Switzerland's comparative advantage in watches reflects a long tradition of watchmaking. Sometimes they are the result of a set of innovations that for some reason occur in one country but not in others.

Technological advantage, however, is often transitory. By adopting *lean production* (techniques designed to improve manufacturing productivity through increased efficiency), American auto manufacturers have closed much of the gap in productivity with their Japanese competitors. In addition, Europe's aircraft industry has closed a similar gap with the U.S. aircraft industry. At any given point in time, however, differences in technology are a major source of comparative advantage.

ECONOMICS >> *in Action*
How Hong Kong Lost Its Shirts

The rise of Hong Kong was one of the most improbable-sounding economic success stories of the twentieth century. When a communist regime took over China in 1949, Hong Kong—which was still at that point a British colony—became in effect a city without a hinterland, largely cut off from economic relations with the territory just over the border. Since Hong Kong had until that point made a living largely by serving as a point of entry into China, you might have expected the city to languish. Instead, however, Hong Kong prospered, to such an extent that today the city—now returned to China, but governed as a special autonomous region—has a GDP per capita comparable to that of the United States.

During much of its ascent, Hong Kong's rise rested, above all, on its clothing industry. In 1980 Hong Kong's garment and textile sectors employed almost 450,000 workers, close to 20% of total employment. These workers overwhelmingly made apparel—shirts, trousers, dresses, and more—for export, especially to the United States.

Since then, however, the Hong Kong clothing industry has fallen sharply in size—in fact, it has almost disappeared. So, too, have Hong Kong's apparel exports. Figure 5-4 shows Hong Kong's share of U.S. apparel imports since 1989, along with the share of a relative newcomer to the industry, Bangladesh. As you can see, Hong Kong has more or less dropped off the chart, while Bangladesh's share has risen significantly in recent years.

Why did Hong Kong lose its comparative advantage in making shirts, pants, and so on? It wasn't because the city's garment workers became less productive. Instead, it was because the city got better at other things. Apparel production is a labor-intensive, relatively low-tech industry; comparative advantage in that industry has historically always rested with poor, labor-abundant economies. Hong Kong no longer fits that description; Bangladesh does. Hong Kong's garment industry was a victim of the city's success.

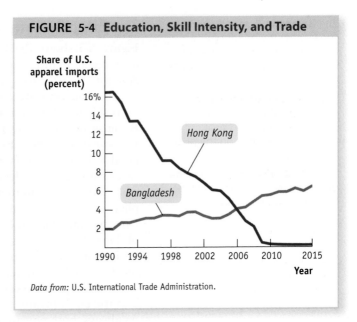

FIGURE 5-4 Education, Skill Intensity, and Trade

Share of U.S. apparel imports (percent)

Data from: U.S. International Trade Administration.

>> Check Your Understanding 5-1

Solutions appear at back of book.

1. In the United States, the opportunity cost of 1 ton of corn is 50 bicycles. In China, the opportunity cost of 1 bicycle is 0.01 ton of corn.
   a. Determine the pattern of comparative advantage.
   b. In autarky, the United States can produce 200,000 bicycles if no corn is produced, and China can produce 3,000 tons of corn if no bicycles are produced. Draw each country's production possibility frontier assuming constant opportunity cost, with tons of corn on the vertical axis and bicycles on the horizontal axis.
   c. With trade, each country specializes its production. The United States consumes 1,000 tons of corn and 200,000 bicycles; China consumes 3,000 tons of corn and 100,000 bicycles. Indicate the production and consumption points on your diagrams, and use them to explain the gains from trade.

2. Explain the following patterns of trade using the Heckscher–Ohlin model.
   a. France exports wine to the United States, and the United States exports movies to France.
   b. Brazil exports shoes to the United States, and the United States exports shoe-making machinery to Brazil.

‖ Supply, Demand, and International Trade

Simple models of comparative advantage are helpful for understanding the fundamental causes of international trade. However, to analyze the effects of international trade at a more detailed level and to understand trade policy, it helps to return to the supply and demand model. We'll start by looking at the effects of imports on domestic producers and consumers, then turn to the effects of exports.

>> Quick Review

• **Imports** and **exports** account for a growing share of the U.S. economy and the economies of many other countries.

• The growth of international trade and other international linkages is known as **globalization.** Extremely high levels of international trade are known as **hyperglobalization.**

• International trade is driven by comparative advantage. **The Ricardian model of international trade** shows that trade between two countries makes both countries better off than they would be in **autarky**—that is, there are gains from international trade.

• The main sources of comparative advantage are international differences in climate, factor endowments, and technology.

• The **Heckscher–Ohlin model** shows how comparative advantage can arise from differences in factor endowments: goods differ in their **factor intensity,** and countries tend to export goods that are intensive in the factors they have in abundance.

The **domestic demand curve** shows how the quantity of a good demanded by domestic consumers depends on the price of that good.

The **domestic supply curve** shows how the quantity of a good supplied by domestic producers depends on the price of that good.

The **world price** of a good is the price at which that good can be bought or sold abroad.

The Effects of Imports

Figure 5-5 shows the U.S. market for phones, ignoring international trade for a moment. It introduces a few new concepts: the *domestic demand curve*, the *domestic supply curve*, and the domestic or autarky price.

The **domestic demand curve** shows how the quantity of a good demanded by residents of a country depends on the price of that good. Why "domestic"? Because people living in other countries may demand the good, too. Once we introduce international trade, we need to distinguish between purchases of a good by domestic consumers and purchases by foreign consumers. So the domestic demand curve reflects only the demand of residents of our own country.

Similarly, the **domestic supply curve** shows how the quantity of a good supplied by producers inside our own country depends on the price of that good. Once we introduce international trade, we need to distinguish between the supply of domestic producers and foreign supply—supply brought in from abroad.

In autarky, with no international trade in phones, the equilibrium in this market would be determined by the intersection of the domestic demand and domestic supply curves, point A. The equilibrium price of phones would be P_A, and the equilibrium quantity of phones produced and consumed would be Q_A. As always, both consumers and producers gain from the existence of the domestic market.

Economists refer to the net gain that buyers receive from the purchase of a good as *consumer surplus*. Likewise, *producer surplus* is the net gain to sellers from selling a good. *Total surplus* is the sum of consumer and producer surplus. We analyze these three concepts in this chapter's appendix. In autarky, consumer surplus would be equal to the area of the blue-shaded triangle in Figure 5-5. Producer surplus would be equal to the area of the red-shaded triangle. And total surplus would be equal to the sum of these two shaded triangles.

Now let's imagine opening up this market to imports. To do this, we must make an assumption about the supply of imports. The simplest assumption, which we will adopt here, is that unlimited quantities of phones can be purchased from abroad at a fixed price, known as the world price of phones. Figure 5-6 shows a situation in which the **world price** of a phone, P_W, is lower than the price of a phone that would prevail in the domestic market in autarky, P_A.

FIGURE 5-5 Consumer and Producer Surplus in Autarky

In the absence of trade, the domestic price is P_A, the autarky price at which the domestic supply curve and the domestic demand curve intersect. The quantity produced and consumed domestically is Q_A. Consumer surplus is represented by the blue-shaded area, and producer surplus is represented by the red-shaded area.

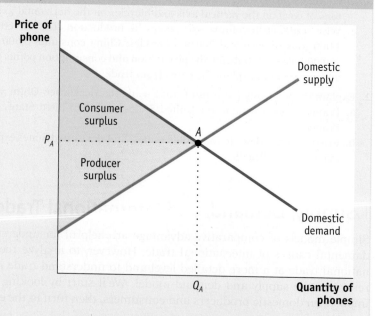

Given that the world price is below the domestic price of a phone, it is profitable for importers to buy phones abroad and resell them domestically. The imported phones increase the supply of phones in the domestic market, driving down the domestic market price. Phones will continue to be imported until the domestic price falls to a level equal to the world price.

The result is shown in Figure 5-6. Because of imports, the domestic price of a phone falls from P_A to P_W. The quantity of phones demanded by domestic consumers rises from Q_A to Q_D, and the quantity supplied by domestic producers falls from Q_A to Q_S. The difference between the domestic quantity demanded and the domestic quantity supplied, $Q_D - Q_S$, is filled by imports.

Now let's turn to the effects of imports on consumer surplus and producer surplus. Because imports of phones lead to a fall in their domestic price, consumer surplus rises and producer surplus falls. Figure 5-7 shows how this works. We label four areas: W, X, Y, and Z. The autarky consumer surplus we identified in Figure 5-5 corresponds to W, and the autarky producer surplus corresponds to the sum of X and Y. The fall in the domestic price to the world price leads to an increase in consumer surplus; it increases by X and Z, so consumer surplus now equals the sum of W, X, and Z. At the same time, producers lose X in surplus, so producer surplus now equals only Y.

The table in Figure 5-7 summarizes the changes in consumer and producer surplus when the phone market is opened to imports. Consumers gain surplus equal to the areas $X + Z$. Producers lose surplus equal to X. So the sum of producer and consumer surplus—the total surplus generated in the phone market—increases by Z. As a result of trade, consumers gain and producers lose, but the gain to consumers exceeds the loss to producers.

This is an important result. We have just shown that opening up a market to imports leads to a net gain in total surplus, which is what we should have expected given the proposition that there are gains from international trade.

However, we have also learned that although the country as a whole gains, some groups—in this case, domestic producers of phones—lose as a result of international trade. As we'll see shortly, the fact that international trade typically creates losers as well as winners is crucial for understanding the politics of trade policy.

FIGURE 5-6 The Domestic Market with Imports

Here the world price of phones, P_W, is below the autarky price, P_A. When the economy is opened to international trade, imports enter the domestic market, and the domestic price falls from the autarky price, P_A, to the world price, P_W. As the price falls, the domestic quantity demanded rises from Q_A to Q_D and the domestic quantity supplied falls from Q_A to Q_S. The difference between domestic quantity demanded and domestic quantity supplied at P_W, the quantity $Q_D - Q_S$, is filled by imports.

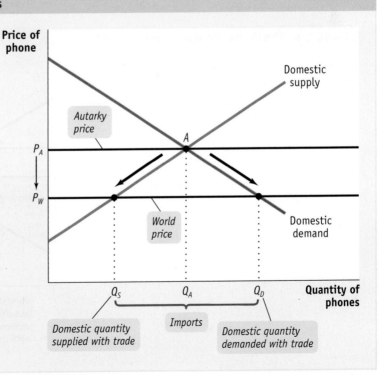

FIGURE 5-7 The Effects of Imports on Surplus

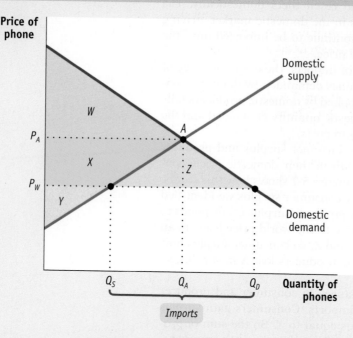

	Changes in surplus	
	Gain	**Loss**
Consumer surplus	$X + Z$	
Producer surplus		$-X$
Change in total surplus	$+Z$	

When the domestic price falls to P_W as a result of international trade, consumers gain additional surplus (areas $X + Z$) and producers lose surplus (area X).

Because the gains to consumers outweigh the losses to producers, there is an increase in the total surplus in the economy as a whole (area Z).

The Effects of Exports

Figure 5-8 shows the effects on a country when it exports a good, in this case trucks. For this example, we assume that unlimited quantities of trucks can be sold abroad at a given world price, P_W, which is higher than the price that would prevail in the domestic market in autarky, P_A.

FIGURE 5-8 The Domestic Market with Exports

Here the world price, P_W, is greater than the autarky price, P_A. When the economy is opened to international trade, some of the domestic supply is now exported. The domestic price rises from the autarky price, P_A, to the world price, P_W. As the price rises, the domestic quantity demanded falls from Q_A to Q_D and the domestic quantity supplied rises from Q_A to Q_S. The portion of domestic production that is not consumed domestically, $Q_S - Q_D$, is exported.

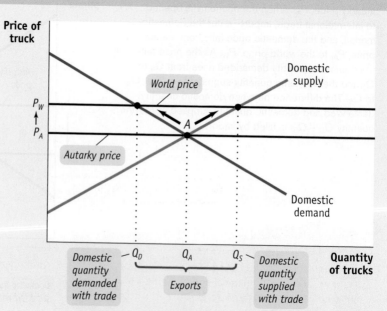

The higher world price makes it profitable for exporters to buy trucks domestically and sell them overseas. The purchases of domestic trucks drive the domestic price up until it is equal to the world price. As a result, the quantity demanded by domestic consumers falls from Q_A to Q_D and the quantity supplied by domestic producers rises from Q_A to Q_S. This difference between domestic production and domestic consumption, $Q_S - Q_D$, is exported.

Like imports, exports lead to an overall gain in total surplus for the exporting country but also create losers as well as winners. Figure 5-9 shows the effects of truck exports on producer and consumer surplus. In the absence of trade, the price of each truck would be P_A. Consumer surplus in the absence of trade is the sum of areas W and X, and producer surplus is area Y. As a result of trade, price rises from P_A to P_W, consumer surplus falls to W, and producer surplus rises to $Y + X + Z$. So producers gain $X + Z$, consumers lose X, and, as shown in the table accompanying the figure, the economy as a whole gains total surplus in the amount of Z.

We have learned, then, that imports of a particular good hurt domestic producers of that good but help domestic consumers, whereas exports of a particular good hurt domestic consumers of that good but help domestic producers. In each case, the gains are larger than the losses.

International Trade and Wages

So far we have focused on the effects of international trade on producers and consumers in a particular industry. For many purposes this is a very helpful approach. However, producers and consumers are not the only parts of society affected by trade—so are the owners of factors of production. In particular, the owners of labor, land, and capital employed in producing goods that are exported, or goods that compete with imported goods, can be deeply affected by trade.

Moreover, the effects of trade aren't limited to just those industries that export or compete with imports because *factors of production can often move between*

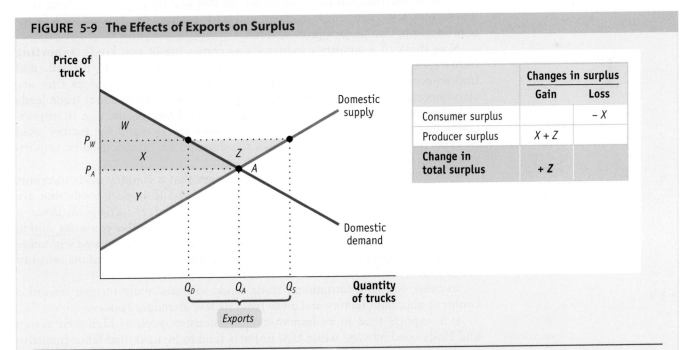

FIGURE 5-9 The Effects of Exports on Surplus

	Changes in surplus	
	Gain	**Loss**
Consumer surplus		– X
Producer surplus	X + Z	
Change in total surplus	**+ Z**	

When the domestic price rises to P_W as a result of trade, producers gain additional surplus (area $X + Z$) but consumers lose surplus (area X). Because the gains to producers outweigh the losses to consumers, there is an increase in the total surplus in the economy as a whole (area Z).

Exporting industries produce goods and services that are sold abroad.

Import-competing industries produce goods and services that are also imported.

industries. So now we turn our attention to the long-run effects of international trade on income distribution—how a country's total income is allocated among its various factors of production.

To begin our analysis, consider the position of Maria, who is initially employed as an accountant in an industry that is shrinking as a result of growing international trade. Suppose, for example, that she works in the U.S. apparel (clothing) industry, which formerly employed millions of people but has largely been displaced by imports from low-wage countries. Maria is likely to find a new job in another industry, such as health care, which has been expanding rapidly over time. How will the move affect her earnings?

The answer is, there probably won't be much effect. According to the U.S. Bureau of Labor Statistics, accountants earn roughly the same amount in health care that they do in what's left of the apparel industry—about $65,000 a year. So we shouldn't think of Maria as a producer of apparel who is hurt by competition from imports. Instead, we should think of her as a worker with particular skills who is affected by imports mainly by the extent to which those imports change the wages of accountants in the economy as a whole.

The wage rate of accountants is a *factor price*—the price employers have to pay for the services of a factor of production. One key question about international trade is how it affects factor prices—not just narrowly defined factors of production like accountants, but broadly defined factors such as capital, unskilled labor, and college-educated labor.

Earlier in this chapter we described the Heckscher–Ohlin model of trade, which states that comparative advantage is determined by a country's factor endowment. This model also suggests how international trade affects factor prices in a country: compared to autarky, international trade tends to raise the prices of factors that are abundantly available and reduce the prices of factors that are scarce.

We won't work this out in detail, but the idea is simple. The prices of factors of production, like the prices of goods and services, are determined by supply and demand. If international trade increases the demand for a factor of production, that factor's price will rise; if international trade reduces the demand for a factor of production, that factor's price will fall.

Now think of a country's industries as consisting of two kinds: **exporting industries,** which produce goods and services that are sold abroad, and **import-competing industries,** which produce goods and services that are also imported from abroad. Compared with autarky, international trade leads to higher production in exporting industries and lower production in import-competing industries. This indirectly increases the demand for factors used by exporting industries and decreases the demand for factors used by import-competing industries.

In addition, the Heckscher–Ohlin model says that a country tends to export goods that are intensive in its abundant factors and to import goods that are intensive in its scarce factors. *So international trade tends to increase the demand for factors that are abundant in our country compared with other countries, and to decrease the demand for factors that are scarce in our country compared with other countries. As a result, the prices of abundant factors tend to rise, and the prices of scarce factors tend to fall as international trade grows.*

In other words, international trade tends to redistribute income toward a country's abundant factors and away from its less abundant factors.

U.S. exports tend to be human-capital-intensive (such as high-tech design and Hollywood movies) while U.S. imports tend to be unskilled-labor-intensive (such as phone assembly and clothing production). This suggests that the effect of international trade on the U.S. factor markets is to raise the wage rate of highly educated American workers and reduce the wage rate of unskilled American workers.

This effect has been a source of much concern in recent years. Wage inequality—the gap between the wages of high-paid and low-paid workers—has increased substantially over the last 30 years. Some economists believe that growing international trade is an important factor in that trend. If international trade has the effects predicted by the Heckscher–Ohlin model, its growth raises the wages of highly educated American workers, who already have relatively high wages, and lowers the wages of less educated American workers, who already have relatively low wages.

But keep in mind another phenomenon: trade reduces the income inequality between countries as poor countries improve their standard of living by exporting to rich countries.

How important are these effects? In some historical episodes, the impacts of international trade on factor prices have been very large. As we explain in the following Economics in Action, the opening of transatlantic trade in the late nineteenth century had a large negative impact on land rents in Europe, hurting landowners but helping workers and owners of capital.

The effects of trade on wages in the United States have generated considerable controversy in recent years. Most economists who have studied the issue agree that growing imports of labor-intensive products from newly industrializing economies, and the export of high-technology goods in return, have helped cause a widening wage gap between highly educated and less educated workers in this country. However, most economists believe that it is only one of several forces explaining the growth in American wage inequality.

ECONOMICS >> *in Action*
Trade, Wages, and Land Prices in the Nineteenth Century

Beginning around 1870, there was an explosive growth of world trade in agricultural products, based largely on the steam engine. Steam-powered ships could cross the ocean much more quickly and reliably than sailing ships. Until about 1860, steamships had higher costs than sailing ships, but after that costs dropped sharply. At the same time, steam-powered rail transport made it possible to bring grain and other bulk goods cheaply from the interior to ports. The result was that land-abundant countries—the United States, Canada, Argentina, and Australia—began shipping large quantities of agricultural goods to the densely populated, land-scarce countries of Europe.

This opening up of international trade led to higher prices of agricultural products, such as wheat, in exporting countries and a decline in their prices in importing countries. Notably, the difference between wheat prices in the midwestern United States and England plunged.

The change in agricultural prices created winners and losers on both sides of the Atlantic as factor prices adjusted. In England, land prices fell by half compared with average wages; landowners found their purchasing power sharply reduced, but workers benefited from cheaper food. In the United States, the reverse happened: land prices doubled compared with wages. Landowners did very well, but workers found the purchasing power of their wages dented by rising food prices.

International trade redistributes income toward a country's abundant factors and away from its less abundant factors.

>> Check Your Understanding 5-2

Solutions appear at back of book.

1. Due to a strike by truckers, trade in food between the United States and Mexico is halted. In autarky, the price of Mexican grapes is lower than that of U.S. grapes. Using a diagram of the U.S. domestic demand curve and the U.S. domestic supply curve for grapes, explain the effect of the strike on the following.
   a. U.S. grape consumers' surplus
   b. U.S. grape producers' surplus
   c. U.S. total surplus

2. What effect do you think the strike will have on Mexican grape producers? Mexican grape pickers? Mexican grape consumers? U.S. grape pickers?

‖ The Effects of Trade Protection

Ever since David Ricardo laid out the principle of comparative advantage in the early nineteenth century, most economists have advocated **free trade.** That is, they have argued that government policy should not attempt either to reduce or to increase the levels of exports and imports that occur naturally as a result of supply and demand.

Despite the free-trade arguments of economists, however, many governments use taxes and other restrictions to limit imports. Less frequently, governments offer subsidies to encourage exports. Policies that limit imports, usually with the goal of protecting domestic producers in import-competing industries from foreign competition, are known as **trade protection** or simply as **protection.**

Let's look at the two most common protectionist policies, *tariffs* and *import quotas*, then turn to the reasons governments follow these policies.

The Effects of a Tariff

A **tariff** is a form of excise tax, one that is levied only on sales of imported goods. For example, the U.S. government could declare that anyone bringing in phones must pay a tariff of $100 per unit. In the distant past, tariffs were an important source of government revenue because they were relatively easy to collect. But in the modern world, tariffs are usually intended to discourage imports and protect import-competing domestic producers rather than as a source of government revenue.

The tariff raises both the price received by domestic producers and the price paid by domestic consumers. Suppose, for example, that our country imports phones, and a phone costs $200 on the world market. As we saw earlier, under free trade the domestic price would also be $200. But if a tariff of $100 per unit is imposed, the domestic price will rise to $300, because it won't be profitable to import phones unless the price in the domestic market is high enough to compensate importers for the cost of paying the tariff.

Figure 5-10 illustrates the effects of a tariff on imports of phones. As before, we assume that P_W is the world price of a phone. Before the tariff is imposed, imports have driven the domestic price down to P_W, so that pre-tariff domestic production is Q_S, pre-tariff domestic consumption is Q_D, and pre-tariff imports are $Q_D - Q_S$.

Now suppose that the government imposes a tariff on each phone imported. As a consequence, it is no longer profitable to import phones unless the domestic price received by the importer is greater than or equal to the world price plus the tariff. So the domestic price rises to P_T, which is equal to the world price, P_W, plus the tariff. Domestic production rises to Q_{ST}, domestic consumption falls to Q_{DT}, and imports fall to $Q_{DT} - Q_{ST}$.

FIGURE 5-10 The Effect of a Tariff

A tariff raises the domestic price of the good from P_W to P_T. The domestic quantity demanded shrinks from Q_D to Q_{DT}, and the domestic quantity supplied increases from Q_S to Q_{ST}. As a result, imports—which had been $Q_D - Q_S$ before the tariff was imposed—shrink to $Q_{DT} - Q_{ST}$ after the tariff is imposed.

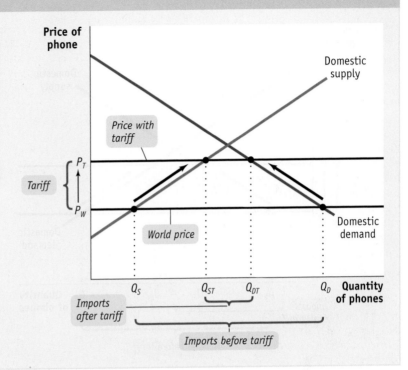

A tariff, then, raises domestic prices, leading to increased domestic production and reduced domestic consumption compared to the situation under free trade. Figure 5-11 shows the effects on surplus. There are three effects:

1. The higher domestic price increases producer surplus, a gain equal to area A.
2. The higher domestic price reduces consumer surplus, a reduction equal to the sum of areas A, B, C, and D.
3. The tariff yields revenue to the government. How much revenue? The government collects the tariff—which, remember, is equal to the difference between P_T and P_W on each of the $Q_{DT} - Q_{ST}$ units imported. So total revenue is $(P_T - P_W) \times (Q_{DT} - Q_{ST})$. This is equal to area C.

The welfare effects of a tariff are summarized in the table in Figure 5-11. Producers gain, consumers lose, and the government gains. But consumer losses are greater than the sum of producer and government gains, leading to a net reduction in total surplus equal to areas $B + D$.

An excise tax creates inefficiency, or deadweight loss, because it prevents mutually beneficial trades from occurring. The same is true of a tariff, where the deadweight loss imposed on society is equal to the loss in total surplus represented by areas $B + D$.

Tariffs generate deadweight losses because they create inefficiencies in two ways:

1. Some mutually beneficial trades go unexploited: some consumers who are willing to pay more than the world price, P_W, do not purchase the good, even though P_W is the true cost of a unit of the good to the economy. The cost of this inefficiency is represented in Figure 5-11 by area D.
2. The economy's resources are wasted on inefficient production: some producers whose cost exceeds P_W produce the good, even though an additional unit of the good can be purchased abroad for P_W. The cost of this inefficiency is represented in Figure 5-11 by area B.

FIGURE 5-11 A Tariff Reduces Total Surplus

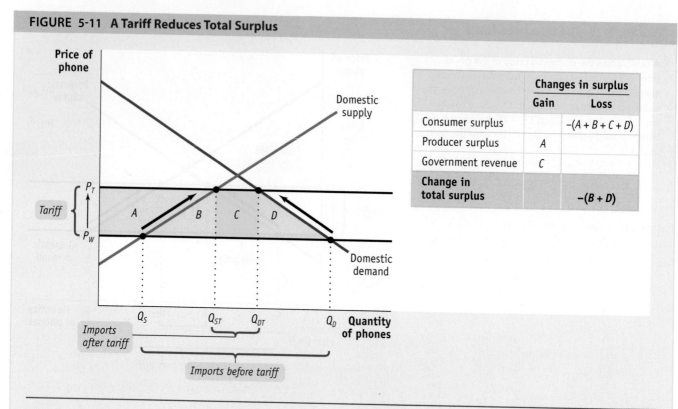

When the domestic price rises as a result of a tariff, producers gain additional surplus (area *A*), the government gains revenue (area *C*), and consumers lose surplus (areas *A + B + C + D*).

Because the losses to consumers outweigh the gains to producers and the government, the economy as a whole loses surplus (areas *B* and *D*).

The Effects of an Import Quota

An **import quota,** another form of trade protection, is a legal limit on the quantity of a good that can be imported. For example, a U.S. import quota on Chinese phones might limit the quantity imported each year to 50 million units. Import quotas are usually administered through licenses: a number of licenses are issued, each giving the license-holder the right to import a limited quantity of the good each year.

A quota on sales has the same effect as an excise tax, with one difference: the money that would otherwise have accrued to the government as tax revenue under an excise tax becomes license-holders' revenue under a quota—also known as quota rents. (*Quota rent* is defined in Chapter 4.) Similarly, an import quota has the same effect as a tariff, with one difference: the money that would otherwise have been government revenue becomes quota rents to license-holders.

Look again at Figure 5-11. An import quota that limits imports to $Q_{DT} - Q_{ST}$ will raise the domestic price of phones by the same amount as the tariff we considered previously. That is, it will raise the domestic price from P_W to P_T. However, area *C* will now represent quota rents rather than government revenue.

Who receives import licenses and so collects the quota rents? In the case of U.S. import protection, the answer may surprise you: the most important import licenses—mainly for clothing, and to a lesser extent for sugar—are granted to foreign governments.

Because the quota rents for most U.S. import quotas go to foreigners, the cost to the nation of such quotas is larger than that of a comparable tariff (a tariff that leads to the same level of imports). In Figure 5-11 the net loss to the United States from such an import quota would be equal to areas *B + C + D*, the difference between consumer losses and producer gains.

An **import quota** is a legal limit on the quantity of a good that can be imported.

ECONOMICS >> *in Action*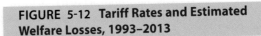
Trade Protection in the United States

The United States today generally follows a policy of free trade, both in comparison with other countries and in comparison with its own history. Most imports are subject to either no tariff or to a low tariff. So what are the major exceptions to this rule?

Most of the remaining protection involves just two industries: clothing and sugar. Until 2005, trade in clothing and textiles around the world—not just in the United States—was limited by an elaborate system of import quotas. The end of that system led to a sharp drop in welfare losses (as shown in Figure 5-12), but the United States maintains relatively high tariffs on clothing imports.

The U.S. government also maintains a system of import quotas on sugar, which raise sugar's price above world levels and cost consumers several hundred million dollars a year.

The most important thing to know about current U.S. trade protection is how limited it really is, and how little cost it imposes on the economy. Every two years the U.S. International Trade Commission, a government agency, produces estimates of the impact of "significant trade restrictions" on U.S. welfare. As Figure 5-12 shows, over the past two decades both average tariff levels and the cost of trade restrictions as a share of national income, which weren't all that big to begin with, have fallen sharply.

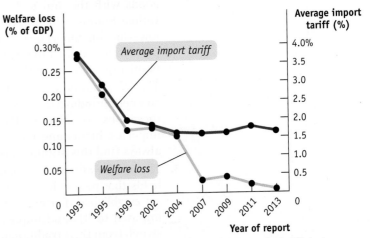

FIGURE 5-12 Tariff Rates and Estimated Welfare Losses, 1993–2013

Data from: U.S. International Trade Commission (2013); Federal Reserve Bank of St. Louis; and World Development Indicators.

>> Check Your Understanding 5-3
Solutions appear at back of book.

1. Suppose the world price of butter is $0.50 per pound and the domestic price in autarky is $1.00 per pound. Use a diagram similar to Figure 5-10 to show the following.
   a. If there is free trade, domestic butter producers want the government to impose a tariff of no less than $0.50 per pound. Compare the outcome with a tariff of $0.25 per pound.
   b. What happens if a tariff greater than $0.50 per pound is imposed?
2. Suppose the government imposes an import quota rather than a tariff on butter. What quota limit would generate the same quantity of imports as a tariff of $0.50 per pound?

‖ The Political Economy of Trade Protection

We have seen that international trade produces mutual benefits to the countries that engage in it. We have also seen that tariffs and import quotas, although they produce winners as well as losers, reduce total surplus. Yet many countries continue to impose tariffs and import quotas as well as to enact other protectionist measures.

To understand why trade protection takes place, we will first look at some common justifications for protection. Then we will look at the politics of trade protection. Finally, we will look at an important feature of trade protection in today's world: tariffs and import quotas are the subject of international negotiation and are policed by international organizations.

>> Quick Review

- Most economists advocate **free trade**, although many governments engage in **trade protection** of import-competing industries. The two most common protectionist policies are tariffs and import quotas. In rare instances, governments subsidize exporting industries.

- A **tariff** is a tax on imports. It raises the domestic price above the world price, leading to a fall in trade and domestic consumption and a rise in domestic production. Domestic producers and the government gain, but domestic consumer losses more than offset this gain, leading to deadweight loss.

- An **import quota** is a legal quantity limit on imports. Its effect is like that of a tariff, except that revenues—the quota rents—accrue to the license holder, not to the domestic government.

Arguments for Trade Protection

Advocates for tariffs and import quotas offer three common arguments:

1. The *national security* argument is based on the proposition that overseas sources of goods are vulnerable to disruption in times of international conflict; therefore, a country should protect domestic suppliers of crucial goods with the aim to be self-sufficient in those goods. In the 1960s, the United States—which had begun to import oil as domestic oil reserves ran low—had an import quota on oil, justified on national security grounds. Some people have argued that we should again have policies to discourage imports of oil, especially from the Middle East.

2. The *job creation* argument points to the additional jobs created in import-competing industries as a result of trade protection. Economists argue that these jobs are offset by the jobs lost elsewhere, such as industries that use imported inputs and now face higher input costs. But noneconomists don't always find this argument persuasive.

3. The *infant industry* argument, often raised in newly industrializing countries, holds that new industries require a temporary period of trade protection to get established. For example, in the 1950s many countries in Latin America imposed tariffs and import quotas on manufactured goods, in an effort to switch from their traditional role as exporters of raw materials to a new status as industrial countries.

In theory, the argument for infant industry protection can be compelling, particularly in high-tech industries that increase a country's overall skill level. Reality, however, is more complicated: it is most often industries that are politically influential that gain protection. In addition, governments tend to be poor predictors of the best emerging technologies. Finally, it is often very difficult to wean an industry from protection when it should be mature enough to stand on its own.

The Politics of Trade Protection

In reality, much trade protection has little to do with the arguments just described. Instead, it reflects the political influence of import-competing producers.

We've seen that a tariff or import quota leads to gains for import-competing producers and losses for consumers. Producers, however, usually have much more influence over trade policy decisions. The producers who compete with imports of a particular good are usually a smaller, more cohesive group than the consumers of that good.

An example is the import quota on sugar. This quota hurts millions of consumers, but by and large they don't even know it exists. Meanwhile, it benefits a few thousand growers, who are very aware of these benefits and hire lobbyists to keep those benefits coming.

It would be nice to say that the main reason trade protection is so limited is that economists have convinced governments of the virtues of free trade. A more important reason, however, is the role of *international trade agreements*.

International Trade Agreements and the World Trade Organization

When a country engages in trade protection, it hurts two groups. We've already emphasized the adverse effect on domestic consumers, but protection also hurts foreign export industries. This means that countries care about one anothers' trade policies: the Canadian lumber industry, for example, has a strong interest in keeping U.S. tariffs on forest products low.

Because countries care about one anothers' trade policies, they enter into **international trade agreements:** treaties in which a country promises to engage in less trade protection against the exports of another country in return for a promise by the other country to do the same for its own exports. Most world trade is now governed by such agreements.

Some international trade agreements involve just two countries or a small group of countries. For example, the United States, Canada, and Mexico are joined together by the **North American Free Trade Agreement,** or **NAFTA.** This agreement was signed in 1993, and by 2008 it had removed most barriers to trade among the three nations.

Most European countries are part of an even more comprehensive agreement, the **European Union,** or **EU.** Unlike members of NAFTA, the 28 members of the EU agree to charge the same tariffs on goods imported from other countries. The EU also sets rules on policies other than trade, most notably requiring that each member nation freely accept migrants from any other member, while collecting fees from member nations to pay for things like agricultural subsidies. These rules and fees are often unpopular and controversial. In June 2016, Britain held a referendum on whether to leave the EU—a proposal popularly known as *Brexit* (an abbreviation for "British exit"), which was approved by a narrow majority of voters. Negotiations over the details of Britain's exit from the EU, and its future relationship with it, were still in progress as this book went to press.

There are also global trade agreements covering most of the world. Such global agreements are overseen by the **World Trade Organization,** or **WTO,** an international organization composed of member countries—164 of them currently, accounting for the bulk of world trade. The WTO plays two roles:

1. It provides the framework for the massively complex negotiations involved in a major international trade agreement (the full text of the last major agreement, approved in 1994, was 24,000 pages long).

2. The WTO resolves disputes between its members that typically arise when one country claims that another country's policies violate its previous agreements.

An example of the WTO at work is the dispute between the United States and Brazil over American subsidies to its cotton farmers. These subsidies, in the amount of $3 billion to $4 billion a year, are illegal under WTO rules. Brazil argued that they artificially reduced the price of American cotton on world markets and hurt Brazilian cotton farmers. In 2005 the WTO ruled against the United States and in favor of Brazil, and the United States responded by cutting some export subsidies on cotton. However, in 2007 the WTO ruled that the United States had not done enough to fully comply, such as eliminating government loans to cotton farmers. In 2010, after Brazil threatened, in turn, to impose import tariffs on U.S.-manufactured goods, the two sides agreed to a framework for the solution to the cotton dispute.

Both Vietnam and Thailand are members of the WTO. Yet the United States has, on and off, imposed tariffs on shrimp imports from these countries. The reason this is possible is that WTO rules do allow trade protection under certain circumstances. One circumstance is where the foreign competition is "unfair" under certain technical criteria. Trade protection is also allowed as a temporary measure when a sudden surge of imports threatens to disrupt a domestic industry.

The WTO is sometimes, with great exaggeration, described as a world government. In fact, it has no army, no police, and no direct enforcement power. The grain of truth in that description is that when a country joins the WTO, it agrees to accept the organization's judgments—and these judgments apply not only to tariffs and import quotas but also to domestic policies that the organization considers trade protection disguised under another name. So in joining the WTO a country does give up some of its sovereignty.

International trade agreements are treaties in which a country promises to engage in less trade protection against the exports of other countries in return for a promise by other countries to do the same for its own exports.

The **North American Free Trade Agreement,** or **NAFTA,** is a trade agreement among the United States, Canada, and Mexico.

The **European Union,** or **EU,** is a customs union among 28 European nations.

The **World Trade Organization,** or **WTO,** oversees international trade agreements and rules on disputes between countries over those agreements.

Offshore outsourcing takes place when businesses hire people in another country to perform various tasks.

Challenges to Globalization

The forward march of globalization over the past century is generally considered a major political and economic success. Economists and policy makers alike have viewed growing world trade, in particular, as a good thing.

We would be remiss, however, if we failed to acknowledge that many people are having second thoughts about globalization. To a large extent, these second thoughts reflect two concerns shared by many economists: worries about the effects of globalization on inequality and worries that new developments, in particular the growth in *offshore outsourcing*, are increasing economic insecurity.

Inequality We've already mentioned the implications of international trade for factor prices, such as wages: when wealthy countries like the United States export skill-intensive products like aircraft while importing labor-intensive products like clothing, they can expect to see the wage gap between more educated and less educated domestic workers widen. Forty years ago, this wasn't a significant concern, because most of the goods wealthy countries imported from poorer countries were raw materials or goods where comparative advantage depended on climate. Today, however, many manufactured goods are imported from relatively poor countries, with a potentially much larger effect on the distribution of income.

Trade with Asia, in particular, raises concerns among groups trying to maintain wages in rich countries. Despite its rapid economic growth and rising wages in recent years, China is still a very low-wage country compared with the United States, with hourly compensation in manufacturing only around 10% of the U.S. level. Other manufacturing exporters, such as India, Bangladesh, and Vietnam, have wage levels less than half of China's. It's hard to argue against the proposition that imports from these countries put downward pressure on the wages of less skilled U.S. workers.

Outsourcing Chinese exports to the United States overwhelmingly consist of labor-intensive manufactured goods. However, some U.S. workers have recently found themselves facing a new form of international competition. *Outsourcing*, in which a company hires another company to perform some task, such as running the corporate computer system, is a long-standing business practice. Until recently, however, outsourcing was normally done locally, with a company hiring another company in the same city or country.

Now, modern telecommunications increasingly make it possible to engage in **offshore outsourcing,** in which businesses hire people in another country to perform various tasks. The classic example is call centers: the person answering the phone when you call a company's 1-800 help line may well be in India, which has taken the lead in attracting offshore outsourcing. Offshore outsourcing has also spread to fields such as software design and even health care: the radiologist examining your X-rays, like the person giving you computer help, may be on another continent.

Although offshore outsourcing has come as a shock to some U.S. workers, such as programmers whose jobs have been outsourced to India, it's still relatively small compared with more traditional trade. Some economists have warned that millions or even tens of millions of workers who have never thought they could face foreign competition for their jobs may face unpleasant surprises in the not-too-distant future. However, the recent rise of reshoring jobs, as described earlier, could mitigate some of those job losses.

Nevada Wier/Getty Images

Offshore outsourcing has the potential to disrupt the job prospects of millions of U.S. workers.

Do these new challenges to globalization undermine the argument that international trade is a good thing? The great majority of economists would argue that the gains from reducing trade protection still exceed the losses. However, it has become more important than before to make sure that the gains from international trade are widely spread. And the politics of international trade are becoming increasingly difficult as the extent of trade has grown.

ECONOMICS >> *in Action*

Solar Disputes

Solar energy has become big business. Rapidly improving technology has drastically reduced solar power's cost compared with more conventional forms of energy, especially the cost of solar panels—the blue rectangles you can now see all across America. But who will produce tomorrow's solar panels? That's still an open question—and international trade policy will have a role in determining the answer.

In 2012 the U.S. Department of Commerce accused Chinese companies of "dumping" solar panels in the U.S. market—that is, selling them below cost. To protect the U.S. industry, the department imposed so-called anti-dumping duties—tariffs—on Chinese panels. China responded, in part, by switching part of its production to Taiwan, in effect bypassing the tariffs, so two years later the United States imposed additional tariffs on solar panels coming from Taiwan. And in 2016, the U.S. Department of Commerce imposed tariffs of 24% to 33% on imports from major Chinese manufacturers.

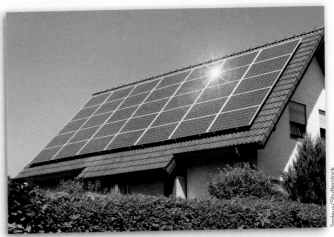

International trade policy is central to the ongoing dispute between the United States and China over solar panels.

What motivated these protectionist actions? One answer is the infant industry argument. The modern solar panel industry is very new, based on a technology that is rapidly evolving. It's not far-fetched to argue that whichever country or countries get a head start, perhaps via government subsidies and/or unfair business practices, might end up dominating the industry once it matures. So you can make a public-interest case for actions to keep U.S. producers in the race.

At the same time, however, business self-interest tied to political influence was clearly also a factor. The campaign against Chinese solar panel exports was spearheaded by SolarWorld, a company with a factory in Oregon and a clear interest in putting barriers in the way of its competitors.

One interesting final note about globalization: while SolarWorld does employ U.S. workers, it is a German-owned company headquartered in Bonn.

>> Check Your Understanding 5-4

Solutions appear at back of book.

1. In 2015, the United States proposed a tariff on steel imports from China. Steel is an input in a large number and variety of U.S. industries. Explain why political lobbying to eliminate these tariffs is more likely to be effective than political lobbying to eliminate tariffs on consumer goods such as sugar or clothing.

2. Over the years, the WTO has increasingly found itself adjudicating trade disputes that involve not just tariffs or quota restrictions but also restrictions based on quality, health, and environmental considerations. Why do you think this has occurred? What method would you, as a WTO official, use to decide whether a quality, health, or environmental restriction is in violation of a free-trade agreement?

>> Quick Review

• The three major justifications for trade protection are national security, job creation, and protection of infant industries.

• Despite the deadweight losses, import protections are often imposed because groups representing import-competing industries are more influential than groups of consumers.

• To further trade liberalization, countries engage in **international trade agreements.** Some agreements are among a small number of countries, such as the **North American Free Trade Agreement (NAFTA)** and the **European Union (EU).** The **World Trade Organization (WTO)** oversees global trade agreements and referees trade disputes between members.

• Resistance to globalization has emerged in response to a surge in imports from relatively poor countries and the **offshore outsourcing** of many jobs that had been considered safe from foreign competition.

Li & Fung: From Guangzhou to You

It's a very good bet that as you read this, you're wearing something manufactured in Asia. And if you are, it's also a good bet that the Hong Kong company Li & Fung was involved in getting your garment designed, produced, and shipped to your local store. From Levi's to Walmart, Li & Fung is a critical conduit from factories around the world to the shopping mall nearest you.

The company was founded in 1906 in Guangzhou, China. According to Victor Fung, the company's chairman, his grandfather's "value added" was that he spoke English, allowing him to serve as an interpreter in business deals between Chinese and foreigners. When Mao's Communist Party seized control in mainland China, the company moved to Hong Kong. There, as Hong Kong's market economy took off during the 1960s and 1970s, Li & Fung grew as an export broker,

bringing together Hong Kong manufacturers and foreign buyers.

The real transformation of the company came, however, as Asian economies grew and changed. Hong Kong's rapid growth led to rising wages, making Li & Fung increasingly uncompetitive in garments, its main business. So the company reinvented itself: rather than being a simple broker, it became a "supply chain manager." Not only would it allocate production of a good to a manufacturer, it would also break production down, allocate production of the inputs, and then allocate final assembly of the good among its 12,000+ suppliers around the globe. Sometimes production would be done in sophisticated economies like those of Hong Kong or even Japan, where wages are high but so is quality and productivity; sometimes it would be done in less advanced locations like mainland China or Thailand, where labor is less productive but cheaper.

For example, suppose you own a U.S. retail chain and want to sell garment-washed blue jeans. Rather than simply arrange for production of the jeans, Li & Fung will work with you on their design, providing you with the latest production and style information, like what materials and colors are trendy. After the design has been finalized, Li & Fung will arrange for the creation of a prototype, find the most cost-effective way to manufacture it,

and then place an order on your behalf. Through Li & Fung, the yarn might be made in Korea and dyed in Taiwan, and the jeans sewn in Thailand or mainland China. And because production is taking place in so many locations, Li & Fung provides transport logistics as well as quality control.

Li & Fung has been enormously successful. In 2016, the company had a market value of $5.4 billion. The company also had nearly $20 billion in business turnover, with offices and distribution centers in more than 40 countries.

QUESTIONS FOR THOUGHT

1. Why do you think it was profitable for Li & Fung to go beyond brokering exports to becoming a supply chain manager, breaking down the production process and sourcing the inputs from various suppliers across many countries?

2. What principle do you think underlies Li & Fung's decisions on how to allocate production of a good's inputs and its final assembly among various countries?

3. Why do you think a retailer prefers to have Li & Fung arrange international production of its jeans rather than purchase them directly from a jeans manufacturer in mainland China?

4. What is the source of Li & Fung's success? Is it based on human capital, on ownership of a natural resource, or on ownership of capital?

SUMMARY

1. International trade is of growing importance to the United States and of even greater importance to most other countries. International trade, like trade among individuals, arises from comparative advantage: the opportunity cost of producing an additional unit of a good is lower in some countries than in others. Goods and services purchased from abroad are **imports;** those sold abroad are **exports.** Foreign trade, like other economic linkages between countries, has been growing rapidly, a phenomenon called **globalization. Hyperglobalization,** the phenomenon of extremely high levels of international trade, has occurred as advances in communication and transportation technology have allowed supply chains of production to span the globe.

2. The **Ricardian model of international trade** assumes that opportunity costs are constant. It shows that there are gains from trade: two countries are better off with trade than in **autarky.**

3. In practice, comparative advantage reflects differences between countries in climate, factor endowments, and technology. The **Heckscher–Ohlin model** shows how differences in factor endowments determine comparative advantage: goods differ in **factor intensity,** and countries tend to export goods that are intensive in the factors they have in abundance.

4. The **domestic demand curve** and the **domestic supply curve** determine the price of a good in autarky. When international trade occurs, the domestic price is driven to equality with the **world price,** the price at which the good is bought and sold abroad.

5. If the world price is below the autarky price, a good is imported. This leads to an increase in consumer surplus, a fall in producer surplus, and a gain in total surplus. If the world price is above the autarky price, a good is exported. This leads to an increase in producer surplus, a fall in consumer surplus, and a gain in total surplus.

6. International trade leads to expansion in **exporting industries** and contraction in **import-competing industries.** This raises the domestic demand for abundant factors of production, reduces the demand for scarce factors, and so affects factor prices, such as wages.

7. Most economists advocate **free trade,** but in practice many governments engage in **trade protection.** The two most common forms of **protection** are tariffs and quotas. In rare occasions, export industries are subsidized.

8. A **tariff** is a tax levied on imports. It raises the domestic price above the world price, hurting consumers, benefiting domestic producers, and generating government revenue. As a result, total surplus falls. An **import quota** is a legal limit on the quantity of a good that can be imported. It has the same effects as a tariff, except that the revenue goes not to the government but to those who receive import licenses.

9. Although several popular arguments have been made in favor of trade protection, in practice the main reason for protection is probably political: import-competing industries are well organized and well informed about how they gain from trade protection, while consumers are unaware of the costs they pay. Still, U.S. trade is fairly free, mainly because of the role of **international trade agreements,** in which countries agree to reduce trade protection against one anothers' exports. The **North American Free Trade Agreement (NAFTA)** and the **European Union (EU)** cover a small number of countries. In contrast, the **World Trade Organization (WTO)** covers a much larger number of countries, accounting for the bulk of world trade. It oversees trade negotiations and adjudicates disputes among its members.

10. In the past few years, many concerns have been raised about the effects of globalization. One issue is the increase in income inequality due to the surge in imports from relatively poor countries over the past 20 years. Another concern is the increase in **offshore outsourcing,** as many jobs that were once considered safe from foreign competition have been moved abroad.

KEY TERMS

PROBLEMS

interactive activity

1. Both Canada and the United States produce lumber and footballs with constant opportunity costs. The United States can produce either 10 tons of lumber and no footballs, or 1,000 footballs and no lumber, or any combination in between. Canada can produce either 8 tons of lumber and no footballs, or 400 footballs and no lumber, or any combination in between.

   a. Draw the U.S. and Canadian production possibility frontiers in two separate diagrams, with footballs on the horizontal axis and lumber on the vertical axis.

   b. In autarky, if the United States wants to consume 500 footballs, how much lumber can it consume at most? Label this point A in your diagram. Similarly, if Canada wants to consume 1 ton of lumber, how many footballs can it consume in autarky? Label this point C in your diagram.

   c. Which country has the absolute advantage in lumber production?

   d. Which country has the comparative advantage in lumber production?

   Suppose each country specializes in the good in which it has the comparative advantage, and there is trade.

   e. How many footballs does the United States produce? How much lumber does Canada produce?

   f. Is it possible for the United States to consume 500 footballs and 7 tons of lumber? Label this point B in your diagram. Is it possible for Canada at the same time to consume 500 footballs and 1 ton of lumber? Label this point D in your diagram.

2. For each of the following trade relationships, explain the likely source of the comparative advantage of each of the exporting countries.

   a. The United States exports software to Venezuela, and Venezuela exports oil to the United States.

   b. The United States exports airplanes to China, and China exports clothing to the United States.

   c. The United States exports wheat to Colombia, and Colombia exports coffee to the United States.

3. According to data from the U.S. Census Bureau, since 2000, the value of U.S. imports of men's and boy's apparel from China has more than tripled from a relatively small $244 million in 2000 to $926 million in 2014. What prediction does the Heckscher–Ohlin model make about the wages received by labor in China?

4. Shoes are labor-intensive and satellites are capital-intensive to produce. The United States has abundant capital. China has abundant labor. According to the Heckscher–Ohlin model, which good will China export? Which good will the United States export? In the United States, what will happen to the price of labor (the wage) and to the price of capital?

5. Before the North American Free Trade Agreement (NAFTA) gradually eliminated import tariffs on goods, the autarky price of tomatoes in Mexico was below the world price and in the United States was above the world price. Similarly, the autarky price of poultry in Mexico was above the world price and in the United States was below the world price. Draw diagrams with domestic supply and demand curves for each country and each of the two goods. (You will need to draw four diagrams, total.) As a result of NAFTA, the United States now imports tomatoes from Mexico and the United States now exports poultry to Mexico. How would you expect the following groups to be affected?

   a. Mexican and U.S. consumers of tomatoes. Illustrate the effect on consumer surplus in your diagram.

   b. Mexican and U.S. producers of tomatoes. Illustrate the effect on producer surplus in your diagram.

   c. Mexican and U.S. tomato workers.

   d. Mexican and U.S. consumers of poultry. Illustrate the effect on consumer surplus in your diagram.

   e. Mexican and U.S. producers of poultry. Illustrate the effect on producer surplus in your diagram.

   f. Mexican and U.S. poultry workers.

6. The accompanying table indicates the U.S. domestic demand schedule and domestic supply schedule for commercial jet airplanes. Suppose that the world price of a commercial jet airplane is $100 million.

Price of jet (millions)	Quantity of jets demanded	Quantity of jets supplied
$120	100	1,000
110	150	900
100	200	800
90	250	700
80	300	600
70	350	500
60	400	400
50	450	300
40	500	200

   a. In autarky, how many commercial jet airplanes does the United States produce, and at what price are they bought and sold?

   b. With trade, what will the price for commercial jet airplanes be? Will the United States import or export airplanes? How many?

7. The accompanying table shows the U.S. domestic demand schedule and domestic supply schedule for oranges. Suppose that the world price of oranges is $0.30 per orange.

Consumer and Producer Surplus

The concepts of *consumer surplus* and *producer surplus* are extremely useful for analyzing a wide variety of economic issues. They let us calculate how much benefit producers and consumers receive from the existence of a market. They also allow us to calculate how the welfare of consumers and producers is affected by changes in market prices. Such calculations play a crucial role in evaluating economic policies, and they are especially useful in understanding the effects of trade.

All we need in order to calculate consumer surplus are the demand and supply curves for a good. That is, the supply and demand model isn't just a model of how a competitive market works—it's also a model of how much consumers and producers gain from participating in that market. Our starting point is the market in used textbooks, a big business in terms of dollars and cents—several billion dollars each year. More importantly for us, it is useful for developing the concepts of consumer and producer surplus.

Consumer Surplus and the Demand Curve

Let's look at the market for used textbooks, starting with the buyers. The key point, as we'll see in a minute, is that the demand curve is derived from their tastes or preferences—and that those same preferences also determine how much they gain from the opportunity to buy used books.

Willingness to Pay and the Demand Curve

A used book is not as good as a new book—it will be battered and coffee-stained, may include someone else's highlighting, and may not be completely up to date. How much this bothers you depends on your preferences. Some potential buyers would prefer to buy the used book even if it is only slightly cheaper than a new one; others would buy the used book only if it is considerably cheaper.

Let's define a potential buyer's **willingness to pay** as the maximum price at which he or she would buy a good, in this case a used textbook. An individual won't buy the book if it costs more than this amount but is eager to do so if it costs less. If the price is just equal to an individual's willingness to pay, he or she is indifferent between buying and not buying.

Table 5A-1 shows five potential buyers of a used book that costs $100 new, listed in order of their willingness to pay. At one extreme is Aleisha, who will buy a second-hand book even if the price is as high as $59. Brad is less willing to have

TABLE 5A-1 Consumer Surplus If the Price of a Used Textbook = $30

Potential buyer	Willingness to pay	Price paid	Individual consumer surplus = Willingness to pay − Price paid
Aleisha	$59	$30	$29
Brad	45	30	15
Claudia	35	30	5
Darren	25	—	—
Edwina	10	—	—
All buyers			**Total consumer surplus = $49**

A consumer's **willingness to pay** for a good is the maximum price at which he or she would buy that good.

a used book and will buy one only if the price is $45 or less. Claudia is willing to pay only $35 and Darren, only $25. And Edwina, who really doesn't like the idea of a used book, will buy one only if it costs no more than $10.

How many of these five students will actually buy a used book? It depends on the price. If the price of a used book is $55, only Aleisha buys one; if the price is $40, Aleisha and Brad both buy used books, and so on. So the information in the table on willingness to pay also defines the *demand schedule* for used textbooks.

Willingness to Pay and Consumer Surplus

Suppose that the campus bookstore makes used textbooks available at a price of $30. In that case Aleisha, Brad, and Claudia will buy books. Do they gain from their purchases, and if so, how much?

The answer, shown in Table 5A-1, is that each student who purchases a book does achieve a net gain but that the amount of the gain differs among students.

Aleisha would have been willing to pay $59, so her net gain is $59 – $30 = $29. Brad would have been willing to pay $45, so his net gain is $45 – $30 = $15. Claudia would have been willing to pay $35, so her net gain is $35 – $30 = $5. Darren and Edwina, however, won't be willing to buy a used book at a price of $30, so they neither gain nor lose.

The net gain that a buyer achieves from the purchase of a good is called that buyer's **individual consumer surplus.** What we learn from this example is that whenever a buyer pays a price less than his or her willingness to pay, the buyer achieves some individual consumer surplus.

The sum of the individual consumer surpluses achieved by all the buyers of a good is known as the **total consumer surplus** achieved in the market. In Table 5A-1, the total consumer surplus is the sum of the individual consumer surpluses achieved by Aleisha, Brad, and Claudia: $29 + $15 + $5 = $49.

Economists often use the term **consumer surplus** to refer to both individual and total consumer surplus. We will follow this practice; it will always be clear in context whether we are referring to the consumer surplus achieved by an individual or by all buyers.

Total consumer surplus can be represented graphically. As explained in Chapter 3, we can use the demand schedule to derive the market demand curve shown in Figure 5A-1. Because we are considering only a small number of consumers, this curve doesn't look like the smooth demand curves of Chapter 3, where markets contained hundreds or thousands of consumers. Instead, this demand curve is stepped, with alternating horizontal and vertical segments.

Each horizontal segment or step corresponds to one potential buyer's willingness to pay. Each step in that demand curve is one book wide and represents one consumer. For example, the height of Aleisha's step is $59, her willingness to pay. This step forms the top of a rectangle, with $30—the price she actually pays for a book—forming the bottom. The area of Aleisha's rectangle, ($59 – $30) × 1 = $29, is her consumer surplus from purchasing one book at $30. So the individual consumer surplus Aleisha gains is the *area of the dark blue rectangle* shown in Figure 5A-1.

In addition to Aleisha, Brad and Claudia will also each buy a book when the price is $30. Like Aleisha, they benefit from their purchases, though not as much, because they each have a lower willingness to pay. Figure 5A-1 also shows the consumer surplus gained by Brad and Claudia; again, this can be measured by the areas of the appropriate rectangles. Darren and Edwina, because they do not buy books at a price of $30, receive no consumer surplus.

The total consumer surplus achieved in this market is just the sum of the individual consumer surpluses received by Aleisha, Brad, and Claudia. So total consumer surplus is equal to the combined area of the three rectangles—the entire shaded area in Figure 5A-1. Another way to say this: total consumer surplus is equal to the area below the demand curve but above the price.

Individual consumer surplus is the net gain to an individual buyer from the purchase of a good. It is equal to the difference between the buyer's willingness to pay and the price paid.

Total consumer surplus is the sum of the individual consumer surpluses of all the buyers of a good in a market.

The term **consumer surplus** is often used to refer both to individual and to total consumer surplus.

FIGURE 5A-1 Consumer Surplus in the Used-Textbook Market

At a price of $30, Aleisha, Brad, and Claudia each buy a book but Darren and Edwina do not. Aleisha, Brad, and Claudia receive individual consumer surpluses equal to the difference between their willingness to pay and the price, illustrated by the areas of the shaded rectangles. Both Darren and Edwina have a willingness to pay less than $30, so they are unwilling to buy a book in this market; they receive zero consumer surplus. The total consumer surplus is given by the entire shaded area—the sum of the individual consumer surpluses of Aleisha, Brad, and Claudia—equal to $29 + $15 + $5 = $49.

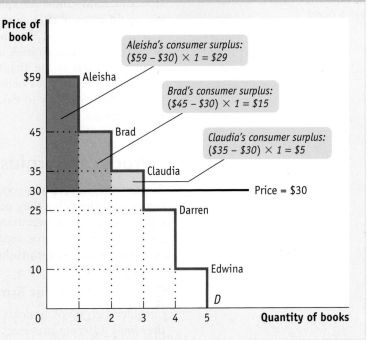

This illustrates the following general principle: *The total consumer surplus generated by purchases of a good at a given price is equal to the area below the demand curve but above that price.* The same principle applies regardless of the number of consumers.

For large markets, such as the market for smartphones that was used in the chapter, this graphical representation of consumer surplus becomes extremely helpful. Consider, for example, the sales of iPads to millions of potential buyers. Each potential buyer has a maximum price that he or she is willing to pay. With so many potential buyers, the demand curve will be smooth, like the one shown in Figure 5A-2.

FIGURE 5A-2 Consumer Surplus

The demand curve for iPads is smooth because there are many potential buyers. At a price of $500, 1 million iPads are demanded. The consumer surplus at this price is equal to the shaded area: the area below the demand curve but above the price. This is the total net gain to consumers generated from buying and consuming iPads when the price is $500.

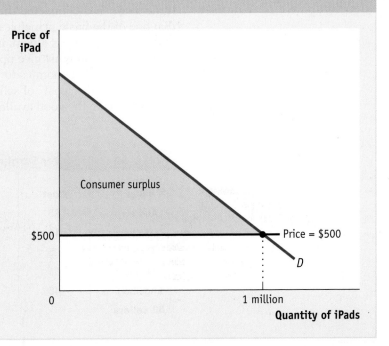

A seller's **cost** is the lowest price at which he or she is willing to sell a good.

Suppose that at a price of $500, a total of 1 million iPads are purchased. How much do consumers gain from being able to buy those 1 million iPads? We could answer that question by calculating the consumer surplus of each individual buyer and then adding these numbers up to arrive at a total. But it is much easier just to look at Figure 5A-2 and use the fact that total consumer surplus is equal to the shaded area. As in our original example, consumer surplus is equal to the area below the demand curve but above the price. (To refresh your memory on how to calculate the area of a right triangle, see the appendix to Chapter 2.)

Producer Surplus and the Supply Curve

Just as some buyers of a good would have been willing to pay more for their purchase than the price they actually pay, some sellers of a good would have been willing to sell it for less than the price they actually receive. So just as there are consumers who receive consumer surplus from buying in a market, there are producers who receive producer surplus from selling in a market.

Cost and Producer Surplus

Consider a group of students who are potential sellers of used textbooks. Because they have different preferences, the various potential sellers differ in the price at which they are willing to sell their books. Table 5A-2 shows the prices at which several different students would be willing to sell. Andrew is willing to sell the book as long as he can get at least $5; Betty won't sell unless she can get at least $15; Carlos, unless he can get $25; Donna, unless she can get $35; Engelbert, unless he can get $45.

The lowest price at which a potential seller is willing to sell has a special name in economics: it is called the seller's **cost.** So Andrew's cost is $5, Betty's is $15, and so on.

Using the term *cost*, which people normally associate with the monetary cost of producing a good, may sound a little strange when applied to sellers of used textbooks. The students don't have to manufacture the books, so it doesn't cost the student who sells a used textbook anything to make that book available for sale, does it?

Yes, it does. A student who sells a book won't have it later, as part of his or her personal collection. So there is an *opportunity* cost to selling a textbook, even if the owner has completed the course for which it was required. And remember that one of the basic principles of economics is that the true measure of the cost of doing something is always its opportunity cost. That is, the real cost of something is what you must give up to get it.

So it is good economics to talk of the minimum price at which someone will sell a good as the "cost" of selling that good, even if he or she doesn't spend any money to make the good available for sale. Of course, in most real-world markets

TABLE 5A-2 Producer Surplus When the Price of a Used Textbook = $30

Potential seller	Cost	Price received	Individual producer surplus = Price received − Cost
Andrew	$5	$30	$25
Betty	15	30	15
Carlos	25	30	5
Donna	35	—	—
Engelbert	45	—	—
All sellers			**Total producer surplus = $45**

the sellers are also those who produce the good and therefore *do* spend money to make it available for sale. In this case, the cost of making the good available for sale includes monetary costs, but it may also include other opportunity costs.

Getting back to the example, suppose that Andrew sells his book for $30. Clearly he has gained from the transaction: he would have been willing to sell for only $5, so he has gained $25. This net gain, the difference between the price he actually gets and his cost—the minimum price at which he would have been willing to sell—is known as his **individual producer surplus.**

As in the case of consumer surplus, we can add the individual producer surpluses of sellers to calculate the **total producer surplus,** the total net gain to all sellers in the market. Economists use the term **producer surplus** to refer to either individual or total producer surplus. Table 5A-2 shows the net gain to each of the students who would sell a used book at a price of $30: $25 for Andrew, $15 for Betty, and $5 for Carlos. The total producer surplus is $25 + $15 + $5 = $45.

As with consumer surplus, the producer surplus gained by those who sell books can be represented graphically. Just as we derived the demand curve from the willingness to pay of different consumers, we derive the supply curve from the cost of different producers. The step-shaped curve in Figure 5A-3 shows the supply curve implied by the cost shown in Table 5A-2. Each step in that supply curve is one book wide and represents one seller. The height of Andrew's step is $5, his cost. This forms the bottom of a rectangle, with $30, the price he actually receives for his book, forming the top. The area of this rectangle, ($30 − $5) × 1 = $25, is his producer surplus. So the producer surplus Andrew gains from selling his book is the *area of the red rectangle* shown in the figure.

Let's assume that the campus bookstore is willing to buy all the used copies of this book that students are willing to sell at a price of $30. Then, in addition to Andrew, Betty and Carlos will also sell their books. They will also benefit from their sales, though not as much as Andrew, because they have higher costs. Andrew, as we have seen, gains $25. Betty gains a smaller amount: since her cost is $15, she gains only $15. Carlos gains even less, only $5.

Again, as with consumer surplus, we have a general rule for determining the total producer surplus from sales of a good: *The total producer surplus from sales of a good at a given price is the area above the supply curve but below that price.*

Individual producer surplus is the net gain to an individual seller from selling a good. It is equal to the difference between the price received and the seller's cost.

Total producer surplus is the sum of the individual producer surpluses of all the sellers of a good in a market.

Economists use the term **producer surplus** to refer both to individual and to total producer surplus.

FIGURE 5A-3 Producer Surplus in the Used-Textbook Market

At a price of $30, Andrew, Betty, and Carlos each sell a book but Donna and Engelbert do not. Andrew, Betty, and Carlos get individual producer surpluses equal to the difference between the price and their cost, illustrated here by the shaded rectangles. Donna and Engelbert each have a cost that is greater than the price of $30, so they are unwilling to sell a book and so receive zero producer surplus. The total producer surplus is given by the entire shaded area, the sum of the individual producer surpluses of Andrew, Betty, and Carlos, equal to $25 + $15 + $5 = $45.

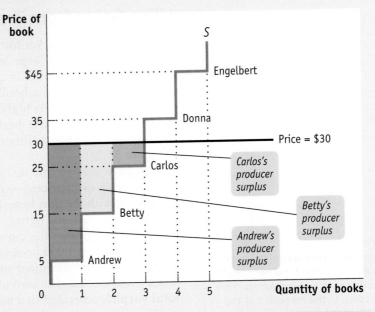

FIGURE 5A-4 Producer Surplus

Here is the supply curve for wheat. At a price of $5 per bushel, farmers supply 1 million bushels. The producer surplus at this price is equal to the shaded area: the area above the supply curve but below the price. This is the total gain to producers—farmers in this case—from supplying their product when the price is $5.

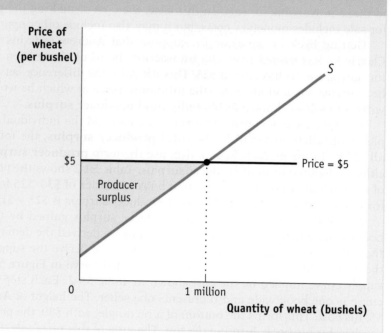

This rule applies both to examples like the one shown in Figure 5A-3, where there are a small number of producers and a step-shaped supply curve, and to more realistic examples, where there are many producers and the supply curve is smooth.

Consider, for example, the supply of wheat. Figure 5A-4 shows how producer surplus depends on the price per bushel. Suppose that, as shown in the figure, the price is $5 per bushel and farmers supply 1 million bushels. What is the benefit to the farmers from selling their wheat at a price of $5? Their producer surplus is equal to the shaded area in the figure—the area above the supply curve but below the price of $5 per bushel.

‖ The Gains from Trade

Let's return to the market for used textbooks, but now consider a much bigger market—say, one at a large state university. There are many potential buyers and sellers, so the market is competitive. Let's line up incoming students who are potential buyers of a book in order of their willingness to pay, so that the entering student with the highest willingness to pay is potential buyer number 1, the student with the next highest willingness to pay is number 2, and so on. Then we can use their willingness to pay to derive a demand curve like the one in Figure 5A-5.

Similarly, we can line up outgoing students, who are potential sellers of the book, in order of their cost—starting with the student with the lowest cost, then the student with the next lowest cost, and so on—to derive a supply curve like the one shown in the same figure.

As we have drawn the curves, the market reaches equilibrium at a price of $30 per book, and 1,000 books are bought and sold at that price. The two shaded triangles show the consumer surplus (blue) and the producer surplus (red) generated by this market. The sum of consumer and producer surplus is known as the **total surplus** generated in a market.

The striking thing about this picture is that both consumers and producers gain—that is, both consumers and producers are better off because there is a

The **total surplus** generated in a market is the total net gain to consumers and producers from trading in the market. It is the sum of the producer and the consumer surplus.

FIGURE 5A-5 Total Surplus

In the market for used textbooks, the equilibrium price is $30 and the equilibrium quantity is 1,000 books. Consumer surplus is given by the blue area, the area below the demand curve but above the price. Producer surplus is given by the red area, the area above the supply curve but below the price. The sum of the blue and the red areas is total surplus, the total benefit to society from the production and consumption of the good.

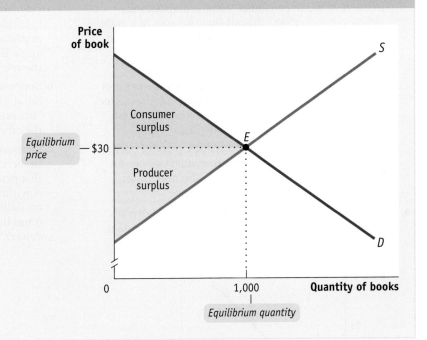

market in this good. But this should come as no surprise—it illustrates another core principle of economics that you learned about in earlier chapters: *There are gains from trade.* These gains from trade are the reason everyone is better off participating in a market economy than they would be if each individual tried to be self-sufficient.

PROBLEMS

1. Determine the amount of consumer surplus generated in each of the following situations.

   a. Leon goes to the clothing store to buy a new T-shirt, for which he is willing to pay up to $10. He picks out one he likes with a price tag of exactly $10. When he is paying for it, he learns that the T-shirt has been discounted by 50%.

   b. Alberto goes to the music store hoping to find a used copy of Nirvana's *Nevermind* for up to $30. The store has one copy of the record selling for $30, which he purchases.

   c. After soccer practice, Stacey is willing to pay $2 for a bottle of mineral water. The 7-Eleven sells mineral water for $2.25 per bottle, so she declines to purchase it.

2. Determine the amount of producer surplus generated in each of the following situations.

   a. Gordon lists his old Lionel electric trains on eBay. He sets a minimum acceptable price, known as his reserve price, of $75. After five days of bidding, the final high bid is exactly $75. He accepts the bid.

   b. So-Hee advertises her car for sale in the used-car section of the student newspaper for $2,000, but she

is willing to sell the car for any price higher than $1,500. The best offer she gets is $1,200, which she declines.

   c. Sanjay likes his job so much that he would be willing to do it for free. However, his annual salary is $80,000.

3. You are the manager of Fun World, a small amusement park. The accompanying diagram shows the demand curve of a typical customer at Fun World.

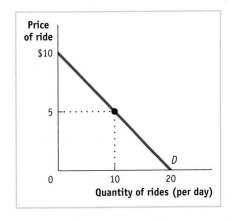

a. Suppose that the price of each ride is $5. At that price, how much consumer surplus does an individual consumer get? (Recall that the area of a right triangle is ½ × the height of the triangle × the base of the triangle.)

b. Suppose that Fun World considers charging an admission fee, even though it maintains the price of each ride at $5. What is the maximum admission fee it could charge? (Assume that all potential customers have enough money to pay the fee.)

c. Suppose that Fun World lowered the price of each ride to zero. How much consumer surplus does an individual consumer get? What is the maximum admission fee Fun World could charge?

4. The accompanying diagram illustrates a taxi driver's individual supply curve (assume that each taxi ride is the same distance).

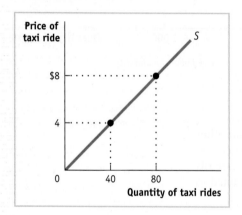

a. Suppose the city sets the price of taxi rides at $4 per ride, and at $4 the taxi driver is able to sell as many taxi rides as he desires. What is this taxi driver's producer surplus? (Recall that the area of a right triangle is ½ × the height of the triangle × the base of the triangle.)

b. Suppose that the city keeps the price of a taxi ride set at $4, but it decides to charge taxi drivers a "licensing fee." What is the maximum licensing fee the city could extract from this taxi driver?

c. Suppose that the city allowed the price of taxi rides to increase to $8 per ride. Again assume that, at this price, the taxi driver sells as many rides as he is willing to offer. How much producer surplus does an individual taxi driver now get? What is the maximum licensing fee the city could charge this taxi driver?

6

Macroeconomics: The Big Picture

🌐 GREEK TRAGEDIES

IN THE SUMMER OF 2015, 28-year-old Christina Tsimpida was ready to give up on her native country. The Athens lawyer's office where she worked had shut, laying off all its employees, and despite being highly qualified, she had no leads on where to find another job. She was not alone: in 2015 very few young Greeks were able to get jobs of any kind. The Greek *unemployment rate*—the percentage of Greeks seeking work who had been unable to find it—averaged 25% in 2015, and the unemployment rate among young workers exceeded 45%.

Macroeconomics seeks to understand and even prevent episodes like the 2015 recession in Greece, when millions faced unemployment and long lines for unemployment benefits.

Yet it wasn't always like that. In the mid-2000s, Greek unemployment was only a third as high as it was in 2015, and someone with Tsimpida's education would have been virtually assured of a job. But then Greece plunged into a severe economic downturn, a *recession*, which led to a collapse in employment. Many businesses went bust and people suffered economic hardship. And Greece wasn't alone. Much of the world, including the United States, plunged into a deep recession after 2007, which came to be known as the *Great Recession*. By 2015 the United States had mostly recovered, but much of Europe had not.

Yet, as bad as things were during the Great Recession, the global economy had seen much worse. Beginning in 1929, a severe global economic slump known as the *Great Depression* hit and lasted over a decade, until the start of World War II in 1940. The Great Recession was less severe than the Great Depression for many reasons. But one significant factor was that economists had learned something about what to do from the earlier catastrophe. As the Great Depression began in 1929, political leaders and their economic advisers had no idea what policies might help or hinder recovery.

Microeconomics, which is concerned with the consumption and production decisions of individual consumers and producers and with the allocation of scarce resources among industries, was already a well-developed branch of economics. But *macroeconomics*, which focuses on the behavior of the economy as a whole, was still in its infancy. In contrast, by 2007 macroeconomics had advanced enough that economists knew what needed to be done when the Great Recession hit.

In normal economic times, when there is no recession or depression, workers who lose their jobs are able to find employment somewhere else. However, the Great Depression was no normal time: in the United States the unemployment rate hit 25% and the value of the economy's output (GDP) fell by 26%. Economists realized that they needed to understand the nature of the catastrophe that had overtaken the United States and much of the rest of the world in order to extricate themselves, as well as to learn how to avoid such economic disasters in the future. To this day, the effort to understand economic slumps and find ways to prevent them is at the core of macroeconomics. Over time, however, macroeconomics has broadened its reach to encompass a number of other subjects, such as long-run economic growth, inflation, and international macroeconomics.

This chapter offers an overview of macroeconomics. We start with a general description of the difference between macroeconomics and microeconomics, then briefly describe some of the field's major concerns. ●

WHAT YOU WILL LEARN

- What is the difference between macroeconomics and microeconomics?
- What are **business cycles** and why do policy makers try to diminish their severity?
- How does **long-run economic growth** determine a country's standard of living?
- What are **inflation** and **deflation,** and why is **price stability** preferred?
- Why does **international macroeconomics** matter, and how do economies interact through **trade deficits** and **trade surpluses?**

The Nature of Macroeconomics

Macroeconomics differs from microeconomics by focusing on the behavior of the economy as a whole.

Macroeconomic Questions

Table 6-1 lists some typical economic questions from the perspectives of micro-economists in the left column, and macroeconomists in the right column. By comparing the questions, you can begin to get a sense of the difference between microeconomics and macroeconomics.

As these questions illustrate, microeconomics focuses on how decisions are made by individuals and firms and the consequences of those decisions. For example, we use microeconomics to determine how much it would cost a university or college to offer a new course, which includes the instructor's salary, the cost of class materials, and so on. The school can then decide whether to offer the course by weighing the costs and benefits.

TABLE 6-1 Microeconomic versus Macroeconomic Questions

Microeconomic Questions	Macroeconomic Questions
Should I go to business school or take a job right now?	How many people are employed in the economy as a whole this year?
What determines the salary Google offers to Cherie Camajo, a new MBA?	What determines the overall salary levels paid to workers in a given year?
What determines the cost to a university or college of offering a new course?	What determines the overall level of prices in the economy as a whole?
What government policies should be adopted to make it easier for low-income students to attend college?	What government policies should be adopted to promote employment and growth in the economy as a whole?
What determines whether Citibank opens a new office in Shanghai?	What determines the overall trade in goods, services, and financial assets between the United States and the rest of the world?

Macroeconomics, in contrast, examines the *overall* behavior of the economy—how the actions of all the individuals and firms in the economy interact to produce a particular economy-wide level of economic performance. For example, macroeconomics is concerned with the general level of prices in the economy and how high or how low it is relative to the general level of prices last year, rather than with the price of one particular good or service.

You might imagine that macroeconomic questions can be answered simply by adding up microeconomic answers. For example, the model of supply and demand introduced in Chapter 3 tells us how the equilibrium price of an individual good or service is determined in a competitive market. So you might think that applying supply and demand analysis to every good and service in the economy, then summing the results, is the way to understand the overall level of prices in the economy as a whole.

But that is incorrect: although basic concepts such as supply and demand are essential to macroeconomics, answering macroeconomic questions requires an additional set of tools and an expanded frame of reference.

Macroeconomics: The Whole Is Greater Than the Sum of Its Parts

If you drive on a highway, you probably know what a rubber-necking traffic jam is and why it is so annoying. Someone pulls over to the side of the road, perhaps to fix a flat tire, and, pretty soon, a long traffic jam occurs as drivers slow down to take a look.

What makes it so annoying is that the length of the traffic jam is greatly out of proportion to the minor event that precipitated it. Because some drivers hit their brakes in order to rubber-neck, the drivers behind them must also hit their brakes, those behind them must do the same, and so on. The accumulation of all the individual hitting of brakes eventually leads to a long, wasteful traffic jam as each driver slows down a little bit more than the driver ahead. In other words, each person's response leads to an amplified response by the next person.

Understanding a rubber-necking traffic jam gives us some insight into one very important way in which macroeconomics differs from microeconomics: many thousands or millions of individual actions compound upon one another to produce an outcome that isn't simply the sum of those individual actions.

Consider, for example, what macroeconomists call the *paradox of thrift:* when families and businesses are worried about the possibility of economic hard times, they prepare by cutting their spending. This reduction in spending depresses the economy as consumers spend less and businesses react by laying off workers. As a result, families and businesses may end up worse off than if they hadn't tried to act responsibly by cutting their spending.

This is a paradox because seemingly virtuous behavior—preparing for hard times by saving more—ends up harming everyone. And there is a flip-side to this story: when families and businesses are feeling optimistic about the future, they spend more today. This stimulates the economy, leading businesses to hire more workers, which further expands the economy. Seemingly profligate behavior leads to good times for all.

A key insight of macroeconomics, then, is that the combined effect of individual decisions can have results that are very different from what any one individual intended, results that are sometimes perverse. The behavior of the macroeconomy is, indeed, greater than the sum of individual actions and market outcomes.

Just as individual actions on the road can unintentionally lead to a traffic jam, individual actions in the economy can produce an unintended macroeconomic effect.

Macroeconomics: Theory and Policy

To a much greater extent than microeconomists, macroeconomists are concerned with questions about *policy,* about what the government can do to make macroeconomic performance better. This policy focus was strongly shaped by history, in particular by the Great Depression of the 1930s.

Before the 1930s, economists tended to regard the economy as **self-regulating:** they believed that problems such as unemployment would be corrected through the working of the invisible hand and that government attempts to improve the economy's performance would be ineffective at best—and would probably make things worse.

The Great Depression changed all that. The sheer scale of the catastrophe, which left a quarter of the U.S. workforce without jobs and threatened the political stability of many countries, created a demand for action. It also led to a major effort on the part of economists to understand economic slumps and find ways to prevent them.

In 1936 the British economist John Maynard Keynes (pronounced "canes") published *The General Theory of Employment, Interest, and Money,* a book that transformed macroeconomics. According to **Keynesian economics,** a depressed economy is the result of inadequate spending. In addition, Keynes argued that government intervention can help a depressed economy through *monetary policy* and *fiscal policy.* **Monetary policy** uses changes in the quantity of money to alter interest rates, which in turn affect the level of overall spending. **Fiscal policy** uses changes in taxes and government spending to affect overall spending.

In general, Keynes established the idea that managing the economy is a government responsibility. Keynesian ideas continue to have a strong influence on both economic theory and public policy: in 2008 and 2009, Congress, the White House, and the Federal Reserve (a quasi-governmental agency that manages U.S. monetary policy) took steps to fend off an economic slump that were clearly Keynesian in spirit, as described in the following Economics in Action.

In a **self-regulating economy,** problems such as unemployment are resolved without government intervention, through the working of the invisible hand.

According to **Keynesian economics,** economic slumps are caused by inadequate spending, and they can be mitigated by government intervention.

Monetary policy uses changes in the quantity of money to alter interest rates and affect overall spending.

Fiscal policy uses changes in government spending and taxes to affect overall spending.

ECONOMICS >> *in Action*

Fending Off Depression

In 2008 the world economy experienced a severe financial crisis reminiscent of the early days of the Great Depression. Major banks teetered on the edge of collapse and world trade slumped. In reviewing the 2009 data, the economic historians Barry Eichengreen and Kevin O'Rourke pointed out that "globally we are tracking or even doing worse than the Great Depression."

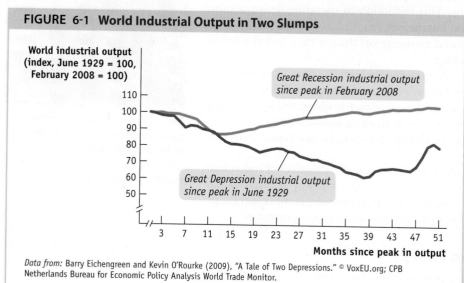

FIGURE 6-1 World Industrial Output in Two Slumps

Great Recession industrial output since peak in February 2008

Great Depression industrial output since peak in June 1929

World industrial output (index, June 1929 = 100, February 2008 = 100)

Months since peak in output

Data from: Barry Eichengreen and Kevin O'Rourke (2009), "A Tale of Two Depressions." © VoxEU.org; CPB Netherlands Bureau for Economic Policy Analysis World Trade Monitor.

But the worst did not, in the end, come to pass. Figure 6-1 shows one of Eichengreen and O'Rourke's measures of economic activity, world industrial production, during the Great Depression (the bottom line) and during the Great Recession (the top line). During the first year the two crises were indeed comparable. But fortunately, 11 months into the Great Recession, world production leveled off and turned around. In contrast, three years into the Great Depression world production continued to fall. Why the difference?

At least part of the answer is that policy makers responded very differently. During the Great Depression, it was widely argued that the slump should be allowed to run its course. Any attempt to mitigate the ongoing catastrophe, declared Joseph Schumpeter—the Austrian-born Harvard economist now famed for his work on innovation—would "leave the work of depression undone." In the early 1930s, some countries' monetary authorities actually raised interest rates in the face of the slump, while governments cut spending and raised taxes—actions that deepened the recession.

In the aftermath of the 2008 crisis, by contrast, interest rates were slashed, and a number of countries, the United States included, used temporary increases in spending and reductions in taxes in an attempt to sustain spending. Governments also moved to shore up their banks with loans, aid, and guarantees.

Many of these measures were controversial, to say the least. But most economists believe that by responding actively to the Great Recession—and doing so using the knowledge gained from the study of macroeconomics—governments helped avoid a global economic catastrophe.

>> Quick Review

• Microeconomics focuses on decision making by individuals and firms and the consequences of the decisions made. Macroeconomics focuses on the overall behavior of the economy.

• The combined effect of individual actions can have unintended consequences and lead to worse or better macroeconomic outcomes for everyone.

• Before the 1930s, economists tended to regard the economy as **self-regulating.** After the Great Depression, **Keynesian economics** provided the rationale for government intervention through **monetary policy** and **fiscal policy** to help a depressed economy.

>> Check Your Understanding 6-1

Solutions appear at back of book.

1. Which of the following questions involve microeconomics, and which involve macroeconomics? In each case, explain your answer.
   a. Why did consumers switch to smaller cars in 2008?
   b. Why did overall consumer spending slow down in 2008?
   c. Why did the standard of living rise more rapidly in the first generation after World War II than in the second?
   d. Why have starting salaries for students with economics degrees risen sharply of late?
   e. What determines the choice between rail and road transportation?

f. Why did laptops get much cheaper between 2000 and 2017?

g. Why did inflation fall in the 2010s?

2. In 2008, problems in the financial sector led to a drying up of credit around the country: home-buyers were unable to get mortgages, students were unable to get student loans, car-buyers were unable to get car loans, and so on.

a. Explain how the drying up of credit can lead to compounding effects throughout the economy and result in an economic slump.

b. If you believe the economy is self-regulating, what would you advocate that policy makers do?

c. If you believe in Keynesian economics, what would you advocate that policy makers do?

The Business Cycle

The Great Depression was by far the worst economic crisis in U.S. history. Although the economy managed to avoid catastrophe in the decades that followed, it has experienced many ups and downs.

It's true that the ups have consistently been bigger than the downs: a chart of any of the major numbers used to track the U.S. economy shows a strong upward trend over time. For example, panel (a) of Figure 6-2 shows total U.S. private-sector employment (the total number of jobs offered by private businesses) measured along the left vertical axis, with the data from 1985 to 2017 given by the purple line. The graph also shows the index of industrial production (a measure of the total output of U.S. factories) measured along the right vertical axis, with the data from 1985 to 2017 given by the red line. Both private-sector employment

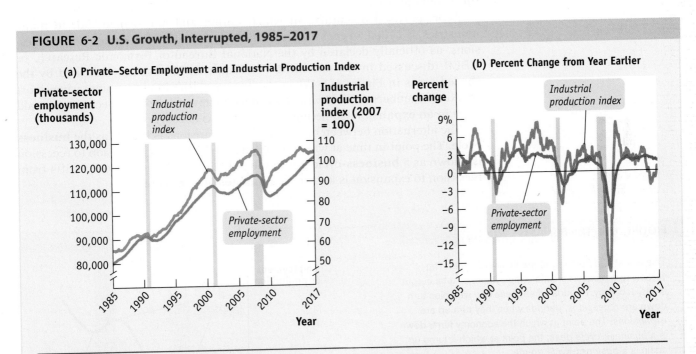

FIGURE 6-2 U.S. Growth, Interrupted, 1985–2017

Panel (a) shows two important economic numbers, the industrial production index and total private-sector employment. Both numbers grew substantially from 1985 to 2017, but they didn't grow steadily. Instead, both suffered from three downturns associated with recessions, which are indicated by the shaded areas in the figure. Panel (b) emphasizes those downturns by showing the annual rate of change of industrial production and employment, that is, the percentage increase over the past year. The simultaneous downturns in both numbers during the three recessions are clear.

Data from: Federal Reserve Bank of St. Louis.

Recessions, or contractions, are periods of economic downturn when output and employment are falling.

Expansions, or recoveries, are periods of economic upturn when output and employment are rising.

The **business cycle** is the short-run alternation between recessions and expansions.

The point at which the economy turns from expansion to recession is a **business-cycle peak.**

The point at which the economy turns from recession to expansion is a **business-cycle trough.**

and industrial production were much higher at the end of this period than at the beginning, and in most years both measures rose.

But they didn't rise steadily. As you can see from the figure, there were three periods—in the early 1990s, in the early 2000s, and again beginning in late 2007—when both employment and industrial output stumbled. Panel (b) emphasizes these stumbles by showing the *rate of change* of employment and industrial production over the previous year. For example, the percent change in employment for October 2009 was –0.6 because employment in October 2009 was 0.6% lower than it had been in October 2008. The three big downturns stand out clearly. What's more, a detailed look at the data makes it clear that in each period the stumble wasn't confined to only a few industries: in each downturn, just about every sector of the U.S. economy cut back on production and on the number of people employed.

The economy's forward march, in other words, isn't smooth. And the uneven pace of the economy's progress, its ups and downs, is one of the main preoccupations of macroeconomics.

Charting the Business Cycle

Figure 6-3 shows a stylized representation of the way the economy evolves over time. The vertical axis shows either employment or an indicator of how much the economy is producing, such as industrial production or *real gross domestic product (real GDP),* a measure of the economy's overall output that we'll learn about in the next chapter. As the data in Figure 6-2 suggest, these two measures tend to move together. Their common movement is the starting point for a major theme of macroeconomics: the economy's alternation between short-run downturns and upturns.

A broad-based downturn, in which output and employment fall in many industries, is called a **recession** (sometimes referred to as a *contraction*). Recessions, as officially declared by the National Bureau of Economic Research, or NBER (discussed in the upcoming For Inquiring Minds), are indicated by the shaded areas in Figure 6-2. When the economy isn't in a recession, when most economic numbers are following their normal upward trend, the economy is said to be in an **expansion** (sometimes referred to as a *recovery*).

The alternation between recessions and expansions is known as the **business cycle.** The point in time at which the economy shifts from expansion to recession is known as a **business-cycle peak;** the point at which the economy shifts from recession to expansion is known as a **business-cycle trough.**

FIGURE 6-3 The Business Cycle

This is a stylized picture of the business cycle. The vertical axis measures either employment or total output in the economy. Periods when these two variables turn down are *recessions;* periods when they turn up are *expansions.* The point at which the economy turns down is a *business-cycle peak;* the point at which it turns up again is a *business-cycle trough.*

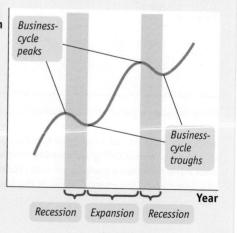

The business cycle is an enduring feature of the economy. Table 6-2 shows the official list of business-cycle peaks and troughs. As you can see, there have been recessions and expansions for at least the past 160 years. Whenever there is a prolonged expansion, as there was in the 1960s and again in the 1990s, books and articles come out proclaiming the end of the business cycle. Such proclamations have always proved wrong: the cycle always comes back.

The Pain of Recession

Not many people complain about the business cycle when the economy is expanding. Recessions, however, create a great deal of pain.

The most important effect of a recession is its effect on the ability of workers to find and hold jobs. The most widely used indicator of conditions in the labor market is the *unemployment rate*. We'll explain how that rate is calculated in Chapter 8, but for now it's enough to say that a high unemployment rate tells us that jobs are scarce and a low unemployment rate tells us that jobs are easy to find.

Figure 6-4 shows the unemployment rate from 1987 to 2017. As you can see, the U.S. unemployment rate surged during and after each recession but eventually fell during periods of expansion. The rising unemployment rate in 2008 was a sign that a new recession might be under way, which was later confirmed by the NBER to have begun in December 2007.

Because recessions cause many people to lose their jobs and make it hard to find new ones, they hurt the standard of living of many families. Recessions are usually associated with a rise in the number of people living below the poverty line, an increase in the number of people who lose their houses because they can't afford the mortgage payments, and a fall in the percentage of Americans with health insurance coverage.

You should not think, however, that workers are the only group that suffers during a recession. Recessions are also bad for firms: profits fall during recessions, and many small businesses fail.

All in all, then, recessions are bad for almost everyone. Can anything be done to reduce their frequency and severity?

TABLE 6-2 The History of the Business Cycle

Business-Cycle Peak	Business-Cycle Trough
no prior data available	December 1854
June 1857	December 1858
October 1860	June 1861
April 1865	December 1867
June 1869	December 1870
October 1873	March 1879
March 1882	May 1885
March 1887	April 1888
July 1890	May 1891
January 1893	June 1894
December 1895	June 1897
June 1899	December 1900
September 1902	August 1904
May 1907	June 1908
January 1910	January 1912
January 1913	December 1914
August 1918	March 1919
January 1920	July 1921
May 1923	July 1924
October 1926	November 1927
August 1929	March 1933
May 1937	June 1938
February 1945	October 1945
November 1948	October 1949
July 1953	May 1954
August 1957	April 1958
April 1960	February 1961
December 1969	November 1970
November 1973	March 1975
January 1980	July 1980
July 1981	November 1982
July 1990	March 1991
March 2001	November 2001
December 2007	June 2009

Data from: National Bureau of Economic Research.

FIGURE 6-4 The U.S. Unemployment Rate, 1987–2017

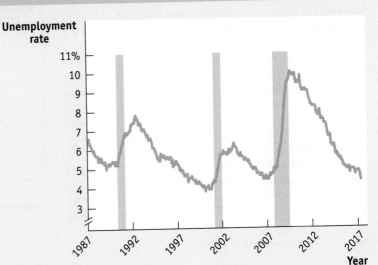

The unemployment rate, a measure of joblessness, rises sharply during recessions and usually falls during expansions.

Data from: Bureau of Labor Statistics.

FOR INQUIRING MINDS **Defining Recessions and Expansions**

You may be wondering exactly how recessions and expansions are defined. The truth is that there are no exact definitions!

In many countries, economists adopt the rule that a recession is a period of at least two consecutive quarters (a quarter is three months) during which the total output of the economy shrinks. The two-consecutive-quarters requirement is designed to avoid classifying brief hiccups in the economy's performance, with no lasting significance, as recessions.

Sometimes, however, this seems too strict. For example, three months of sharply declining output, then three months of slightly positive growth, then another three months of rapid decline, should surely be considered a recession.

In the United States, the task of determining when a recession begins and ends is assigned to an independent panel of experts at the National Bureau of Economic Research (NBER). This panel looks at a variety of economic indicators, then makes a judgment call.

Sometimes this judgment is controversial. In fact, there is lingering controversy over the 2001 recession. According to the NBER, that recession began in March 2001 and ended in November 2001 when output began rising. Some critics argued that the recession began several months earlier, when industrial production began falling. Other critics argue that the recession didn't end in 2001 because employment continued to fall and the job market remained weak for another year and a half.

Taming the Business Cycle

"I can't move in with my parents. They moved in with my grandparents."

Modern macroeconomics largely came into being as a response to the worst recession in history—the 43-month downturn that began in 1929 and continued into 1933, ushering in the Great Depression. The havoc wreaked by the 1929–1933 recession spurred economists to search both for understanding and for solutions: they wanted to know how such things could happen and how to prevent them.

As explained earlier, the work of John Maynard Keynes suggested that monetary and fiscal policies could be used to mitigate the effects of recessions, and to this day governments turn to Keynesian policies when recession strikes. Later work, notably that of another great macroeconomist, Milton Friedman, led to a consensus that it's important to rein in booms as well as to fight slumps. So modern policy makers try to "smooth out" the business cycle. They haven't been completely successful, as a look back at Figure 6-2 makes clear. It's widely believed, however, that policy guided by macroeconomic analysis has helped make the economy more stable.

GLOBAL COMPARISON SLUMPS ACROSS THE ATLANTIC

This figure shows manufacturing production from 2007 to 2016 in two of the world's biggest economies: the United States and the euro area, the group of European countries that share a common currency, the euro. As you can see, both economies suffered a severe downturn in 2008–2009.

More or less simultaneous recessions in different countries are, in fact, quite common. But that doesn't mean that economies always or even usually move in lockstep. As you can see from the figure, both the euro area and the United States began to recover in mid-2009. The U.S. economy continued to recover steadily, although more slowly than most would have liked. But the euro area entered a new recession in 2011, due in part to a wrong turn in economic policy.

What we learn, then, is that the business cycle is to some extent an international phenomenon. But individual countries can diverge from each other for a variety of reasons, including differences in policy and in the underlying structure of their economies.

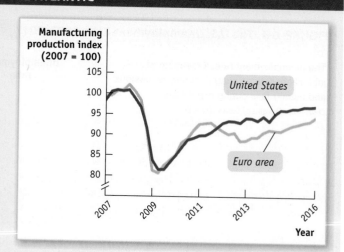

Data from: Federal Reserve Bank of St. Louis.

Although the business cycle is one of the main concerns of macroeconomics and historically played a crucial role in fostering the development of the field, macroeconomists are also concerned with other issues, which we examine next.

ECONOMICS >> *in Action*
Comparing Recessions

The alternation of recessions and expansions seems to be an enduring feature of economic life. However, not all business cycles are created equal. In particular, some recessions have been much worse than others.

Let's compare the two most recent U.S. recessions: the 2001 recession and the Great Recession of 2007–2009. These recessions differed in duration: the first lasted only eight months, the second more than twice as long. Even more important, however, they differed greatly in depth.

In Figure 6-5 we compare the depth of the recessions by looking at what happened to industrial production over the months after the recession began. In each case, production is measured as a percentage of its level at the recession's start. Thus the line for the 2007–2009 recession shows that industrial production eventually fell to about 85% of its initial level.

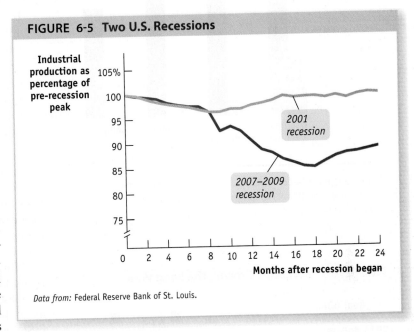

FIGURE 6-5 Two U.S. Recessions

Data from: Federal Reserve Bank of St. Louis.

Clearly, the 2007–2009 recession hit the economy vastly harder than the 2001 recession. Indeed, by comparison to many recessions, the 2001 slump was very mild.

Of course, this was no consolation to the millions of American workers who lost their jobs, even in that mild recession.

>> Check Your Understanding 6-2
Solutions appear at back of book.

1. Why do we talk about business cycles for the economy as a whole, rather than just talking about the ups and downs of particular industries?

2. Describe who gets hurt in a recession, and how.

> ## >> Quick Review
>
> • The **business cycle,** the short-run alternation between **recessions** and **expansions,** is a major concern of modern macroeconomics.
>
> • The point at which expansion shifts to recession is a **business-cycle peak.** The point at which recession shifts to expansion is a **business-cycle trough.**

‖ Long-Run Economic Growth

In 1960, most Americans believed, rightly, that they were better off than the citizens of any other nation, past or present. Yet they were quite poor by today's standards. Figure 6-6 shows the percentage of American homes equipped with selected appliances in 1960 and 2011: in 1960 only a minority of households had a washing machine, very few had air conditioning, and of course nobody had smartphones or computers. And if we turn the clock back to, say, 1900, we find that life for many Americans was startlingly primitive by today's standards.

Why are the vast majority of Americans today able to afford conveniences that many Americans lacked in 1960? The answer is **long-run economic growth,** the sustained rise in the quantity of goods and services the economy produces. Figure 6-7 shows estimates of real GDP per capita, a measure of total output

Long-run economic growth is the sustained upward trend in the economy's output over time.

FIGURE 6-6 The Fruits of Long-Run Growth in America

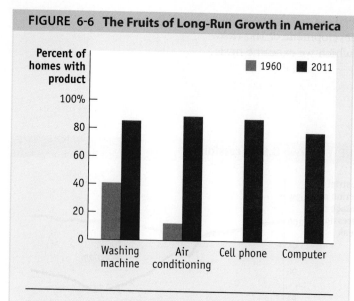

Americans have become able to afford many more material goods over time thanks to long-run economic growth.

Data from: U.S. Census.

FIGURE 6-7 Economic Growth, the Long View

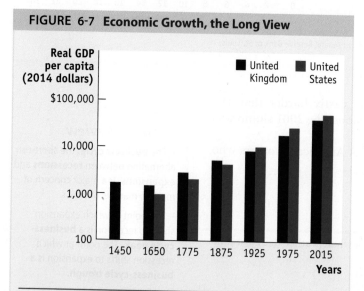

Over the long run, real GDP per capita has increased in both Britain and the United States. For about 300 years, real GDP per capita was greater in Britain. But early in the twentieth century, the United States surpassed Britain, becoming the richer country.

Data from: Maddison Data Project, The Conference Board Total Economy Database™, January 2016.

per person, for two countries—the United States and Britain—for selected years going back to the Middle Ages. Both countries have experienced an enormous long-run rise in production per person, dwarfing the ups and downs of the business cycle.

Two points are, however, worth noting:

1. Long-run economic growth is a modern invention: Britain doesn't seem to have been any richer in 1650 than it was two centuries earlier, and overall world incomes didn't start rising until around 1890.

2. Countries don't necessarily grow at the same rate. Britain was once substantially richer than the United States, but was overtaken by a rapidly growing America after 1875.

Long-run economic growth is fundamental to many of the most pressing economic questions today. Responses to key policy questions, such as the country's ability to bear the future costs of government programs such as Social Security and Medicare, depend in part on how fast the U.S. economy grows over the next few decades.

More broadly, the public's sense that the country is making progress depends crucially on success in achieving long-run growth. When growth slows, as it did in the 1970s, it can help feed a national mood of pessimism. In particular, *long-run growth per capita*—a sustained upward trend in output per person—is the key to higher wages and a rising standard of living. A major concern of macroeconomics—and the theme of Chapter 9—is trying to understand the forces behind long-run growth.

Long-run growth is an even more urgent concern in poorer, less developed countries. In these countries, which would like to achieve a higher standard of living, the question of how to accelerate long-run growth is the central concern of economic policy.

As we'll see, macroeconomists don't use the same models to think about long-run growth that they use to think about the business cycle. It's important to keep both sets of models in mind, because what is good in the long run can be bad in the short run, and vice versa. For example, we've already mentioned the paradox of thrift: an attempt by households to increase their savings can cause a recession. But a higher level of savings, as we'll see in Chapter 10, plays a crucial role in encouraging long-run economic growth.

ECONOMICS >> *in Action*
A Tale of Two Countries

Many countries have experienced long-run growth, but not all have done equally well. One of the most informative contrasts is between Canada and Argentina, two countries that, at the beginning of the twentieth century, seemed to be in a good economic position.

From today's vantage point, it's surprising to realize that Canada and Argentina looked rather similar before World War I. Both were major exporters of agricultural products; both attracted large numbers of European immigrants; both also attracted large amounts of European investment, especially in the railroads that opened up their agricultural hinterlands. Economic historians believe that the average level of per capita income was comparable in the two countries as late as the 1930s.

After World War II, however, Argentina's economy performed poorly, largely due to political instability and bad macroeconomic policies. Argentina experienced several periods of extremely high inflation, during which the cost of living soared. Meanwhile, Canada made steady progress. Thanks to the fact that Canada has achieved sustained long-run growth since 1930, but Argentina has not, Canada's standard of living today is almost as high as that of the United States—and is about two and a half times as high as Argentina's.

>> Check Your Understanding 6-3
Solutions appear at back of book.

1. Many poor countries have high rates of population growth. What does this imply about the long-run growth rates of overall output that they must achieve in order to generate a higher standard of living per person?

2. Argentina used to be as rich as Canada; now it's much poorer. Does this mean that Argentina is poorer than it was in the past? Explain.

Inflation and Deflation

In January 1980 the average production worker in the United States was paid $6.57 an hour. By January 2017, the average hourly earnings for such a worker had risen to $21.84 an hour. Three cheers for economic progress!

But wait. American workers were paid much more in 2017, but they also faced a much higher cost of living. In January 1980, a dozen eggs cost only about $0.88; by January 2017, that was up to $1.60. The price of a loaf of white bread went from about $0.50 to $1.35. And the price of a gallon of gasoline rose from just $1.13 to $2.35.

Figure 6-8 compares the percentage increase in hourly earnings between 1980 and 2017 with the increases in the prices of some standard items: the average worker's paycheck went farther in terms of some goods, but less far in terms of others. Overall, the 213% rise in the cost of living from 1980 to 2017 wiped out

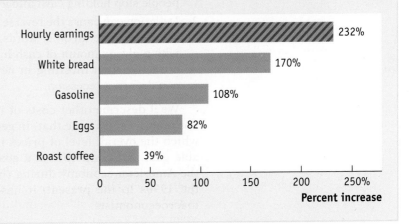

FIGURE 6-8 Rising Prices

Between 1980 and 2017, American workers' hourly earnings rose by 232%. But the prices of just about all the goods bought by workers also rose, some by more, some by less. Overall, the rising cost of living offset most of the rise in the average U.S. worker's wage.

Data from: Bureau of Labor Statistics.

	Percent increase
Hourly earnings	232%
White bread	170%
Gasoline	108%
Eggs	82%
Roast coffee	39%

A rising overall level of prices is **inflation.**

A falling overall level of prices is **deflation.**

The economy has **price stability** when the overall level of prices changes slowly or not at all.

almost all of the wage gains of the typical American worker during that period. In other words, once inflation is taken into account, the living standard of the typical American worker barely rose from 1980 to the present.

The point is that between 1980 and 2017 the economy experienced substantial **inflation:** a rise in the overall level of prices. Understanding the causes of inflation and its opposite, **deflation**—a fall in the overall level of prices—is another main concern of macroeconomics.

The Causes of Inflation and Deflation

You might think that changes in the overall level of prices are just a matter of supply and demand. For example, higher gasoline prices reflect the higher price of crude oil, and higher crude oil prices reflect such factors as the exhaustion of major oil fields, growing demand from China and other emerging economies as more people grow rich enough to buy cars, and so on. Can't we just add up what happens in each of these markets to find out what happens to the overall level of prices?

The answer is no, we can't. Supply and demand can only explain why a particular good or service becomes more expensive *relative to other goods and services.* It can't explain why, for example, the price of chicken has risen over time in spite of the fact that chicken production has become more efficient (you don't want to know) and that chicken has become substantially cheaper compared to other goods.

What causes the overall level of prices to rise or fall? As we'll learn in Chapter 8, in the short run, movements in inflation are closely related to the business cycle. When the economy is depressed and jobs are hard to find, inflation tends to fall; when the economy is booming, inflation tends to rise. For example, prices of most goods and services fell sharply during the terrible recession of 1929–1933.

In the long run, by contrast, the overall level of prices is mainly determined by changes in the money supply, the total quantity of assets that can be readily used to make purchases. As we'll see in Chapter 16, hyperinflation, in which prices rise by thousands or hundreds of thousands of percent, invariably occurs when governments print money to pay a large part of their bills.

The Pain of Inflation and Deflation

Both inflation and deflation can pose problems for the economy. Here are two examples:

1. Inflation discourages people from holding onto cash, because cash loses value over time if the overall price level is rising. That is, the amount of goods and services you can buy with a given amount of cash falls. In extreme cases, people stop holding cash altogether and turn to barter.
2. Deflation can cause the reverse problem. If the price level is falling, cash gains value over time. In other words, the amount of goods and services you can buy with a given amount of cash increases. So holding on to it can become more attractive than investing in new factories and other productive assets. This can deepen a recession.

We'll describe other costs of inflation and deflation in Chapters 8 and 16. For now, let's just note that, in general, economists regard **price stability**—in which the overall level of prices is changing, if at all, only slowly—as a desirable goal. Price stability is a goal that seemed far out of reach for much of the American economy during the post–World War II period. However, from the 1990s to the present, it has been achieved to the satisfaction of most macroeconomists.

ECONOMICS >> *in Action*
A Fast (Food) Measure of Inflation

The original McDonald's opened in 1948. It offered fast service—it was, indeed, the original fast-food restaurant. And it was also very inexpensive: hamburgers cost $0.15, $0.25 with fries. By 2016, a hamburger at a typical McDonald's cost more than six times as much, about $1.00. Has McDonald's lost touch with its fast-food roots? Have burgers become luxury cuisine?

No—in fact, compared with other consumer goods, a burger is a better bargain today than it was in 1948. Burger prices were about 6.5 times as high in 2016 as they were in 1948. But the consumer price index, the most widely used measure of the cost of living, was about 10 times as high in 2016 as it was in 1948.

Even though a burger costs six times more than it did when McDonald's first opened, it's still a good bargain compared to other consumer goods.

>> Check Your Understanding 6-4
Solutions appear at back of book.

1. Which of these sound like inflation, which sound like deflation, and which are ambiguous?
   a. Gasoline prices are up 10%, food prices are down 20%, and the prices of most services are up 1–2%.
   b. Gas prices have doubled, food prices are up 50%, and most services seem to be up 5% or 10%.
   c. Gas prices haven't changed, food prices are way down, and services have gotten cheaper, too.

International Imbalances

The United States is an **open economy:** an economy that trades goods and services with other countries. There have been times when that trade was more or less balanced—when the United States sold about as much to the rest of the world as it bought. But this isn't one of those times.

In 2015, the United States ran a big **trade deficit**—that is, the value of the goods and services U.S. residents bought from the rest of the world was a lot larger than the value of the goods and services American producers sold to customers abroad. Meanwhile, some other countries were in the opposite position, selling much more to foreigners than they bought.

Figure 6-9 shows the exports and imports of goods for three important economies in 2015. As you can see, the United States imported much more than it exported, but Germany and China did the reverse: they each ran a **trade surplus.** A country runs a trade surplus when the value of the goods and services it buys from the rest of the world is smaller than the value of the goods and services it sells abroad. Was America's trade deficit a sign that something was wrong with our economy—that we weren't able to make things that people in other countries wanted to buy?

No, not really. Trade deficits and their opposite, trade surpluses, are macroeconomic phenomena. They're the result of situations in which the whole is very different from the sum of its parts. You might think that countries with highly productive workers or widely desired products and services to sell run trade surpluses but countries with unproductive workers or poor-quality products and services run deficits. But the reality is that there's no simple relationship between the success of an economy and whether it runs trade surpluses or deficits.

>> Quick Review

• A dollar today doesn't buy what it did in 1980, because the prices of most goods have risen. This rise in the overall price level has wiped out most if not all of the wage increases received by the typical American worker over the past 34 years.

• One area of macroeconomic study is in the overall level of prices. Because either **inflation** or **deflation** can cause problems for the economy, economists typically advocate maintaining **price stability.**

An **open economy** is an economy that trades goods and services with other countries.

A country runs a **trade deficit** when the value of goods and services bought from foreigners is more than the value of goods and services it sells to them. It runs a **trade surplus** when the value of goods and services bought from foreigners is less than the value of the goods and services it sells to them.

FIGURE 6-9 Unbalanced Trade

In 2015, the goods and services the United States bought from the other countries were worth considerably more than the goods and services we sold abroad. Germany and China were in the reverse position. Trade deficits and trade surpluses reflect macroeconomic forces, especially differences in savings and investment spending.

Data from: International Monetary Fund, International Financial Statistics.

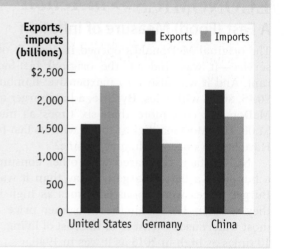

In Chapter 2 we learned that international trade is the result of comparative advantage: countries export goods they're relatively good at producing and import goods they're not as good at producing. That's why the United States exports wheat and imports coffee. What the concept of comparative advantage doesn't explain, however, is why the value of a country's imports is sometimes much larger than the value of its exports, or vice versa.

So what does determine whether a country runs a trade surplus or a trade deficit? In Chapter 18 we'll learn the surprising answer: the determinants of the overall balance between exports and imports lie in decisions about savings and investment spending—spending on goods like machinery and factories that are in turn used to produce goods and services for consumers. Countries with high investment spending relative to savings run trade deficits; countries with low investment spending relative to savings run trade surpluses.

ECONOMICS >> *in Action* 🌐
Greece's Costly Surplus

In 1999 Greece took a momentous step: it gave up its national currency, the drachma, in order to adopt the euro, a shared currency intended to promote closer economic and political union among the nations of Europe. How did this affect Greece's international trade?

Figure 6-10 shows Greece's current account balance—a broad definition of its trade balance—from 1999 to 2016. A negative current account balance, as shown here, means the country is running a trade deficit. As you can see, after Greece switched to the euro it began running large trade deficits, which at their peak equaled almost 16% of the total value of goods and services Greece produced. After 2008, however, the trade deficit began shrinking rapidly, and by 2013 Greece was running a small surplus.

Did this mean that Greece's economy was doing badly in the mid-2000s, and better thereafter? Just the opposite. When Greece adopted the euro, foreign investors became highly optimistic about its prospects, and money poured into the country, fueling rapid economic

FIGURE 6-10 Greece's Current Account Balance, 1999–2016

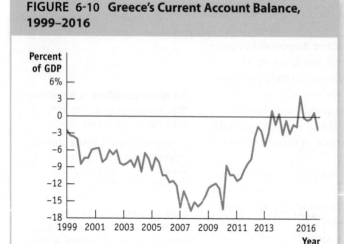

Data from: OECD, Main Economic Indicators.

expansion. Unfortunately, this optimism eventually evaporated, and the inflows of foreign capital dried up. One consequence was that Greece could no longer run large trade deficits, and by 2013 was forced into running a surplus. Another consequence was a severe recession, leading to very high unemployment—including the unemployment of Christina Tsimpida, the jobless graduate described at the start of this chapter.

>> *Check Your Understanding* 6-5

Solutions appear at back of book.

1. Which of the following reflect comparative advantage, and which reflect macroeconomic forces?
   a. Thanks to the development of huge oil sands in the province of Alberta, Canada has become an exporter of oil and an importer of manufactured goods.
   b. Like many consumer goods, the Apple iPad is assembled in China, although many of the components are made in other countries.
   c. Since 2002, Germany has been running huge trade surpluses, exporting much more than it imports.
   d. The United States, which had roughly balanced trade in the early 1990s, began running large trade deficits later in the decade, as the technology boom took off.

>> *Quick Review*

• Comparative advantage can explain why an **open economy** exports some goods and services and imports others, but it can't explain why a country imports more than it exports, or vice versa.

• **Trade deficits** and **trade surpluses** are macroeconomic phenomena, determined by decisions about investment spending and savings.

BUSINESS CASE | The Business Cycle and the Decline of Montgomery Ward

Chicago History Museum/Getty Images

Before there was the internet, there was mail order, and for rural and small-town America that meant, above all, the Montgomery Ward catalog. Starting in 1872, that catalog made it possible for families far from the big city to buy goods their local store wasn't likely to stock—everything from bicycles to pianos. In 1896 Sears, Roebuck and Co. introduced a competing catalog, and in the 1920s both companies opened physical stores around the country. The two firms struggled for dominance right up to World War II. After that, however, Montgomery Ward fell far behind. By 2000, it had closed all of its stores.

Why did Montgomery Ward falter? One key factor was that its management misjudged postwar prospects. The 1930s were a difficult time for retailers in general because of the catastrophic economic impact of the Great Depression. Figure 6-11 shows an index of department store sales, which plunged after 1930 and hadn't fully recovered by 1940. Montgomery Ward coped with this tough environment by cutting back: closing some stores, cutting costs, and accumulating a lot of cash. This strategy served the company well, restoring profitability and putting it in a very strong financial position.

Unfortunately for the company, it made the mistake of returning to this strategy after World War II—and the postwar environment was nothing like the environment of the 1930s. Overall department store sales surged: by 1960 they were more than four times their 1940 level. Sears and other retailers expanded to meet this surge in demand, especially in the rapidly growing suburbs. But Montgomery Ward, expecting the 1930s to return, just sat on its cash; it didn't open any new stores until 1959. By failing to expand with the market, Montgomery Ward suffered what turned out to be an irretrievable loss of market share, reputation, and name recognition.

Nothing in business is forever. Eventually Sears too entered a long, slow decline. First it was overtaken by newer retailers like Walmart, whose big box stores didn't sell large appliances but generally sold other goods more cheaply than Sears, in part by using information technology to hold costs down. More recently, the rise of online shopping has hurt traditional retailers of all kinds. But Montgomery Ward's self-inflicted defeat in the years after World War II nonetheless shows how important it is for businesses to understand what is happening in the broader economic environment—that is, to take macroeconomics into account.

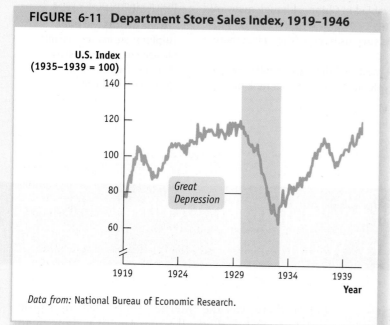

FIGURE 6-11 Department Store Sales Index, 1919–1946

U.S. Index
(1935–1939 = 100)

Great Depression

Data from: National Bureau of Economic Research.

QUESTIONS FOR THOUGHT

1. Why was it profitable for Montgomery Ward to close some of its stores during the Great Depression?

2. Use Figure 6-1 to compare the nature of the Great Depression to the Great Recession. What about the Great Depression made Montgomery Ward's decision not to expand in the 1940s appear rational? Would the same decision be rational now, in the aftermath of the Great Recession? Explain.

3. The National Retail Federation provides various economic forecasts on its website, http://research.nrffoundation.com. Click on the link "Retail and Economy" and you will see five categories. Explain why, in light of this case, it is important for a retailer to have each of the five categories of information provided.

SUMMARY

1. Macroeconomics is the study of the behavior of the economy as a whole, which can be different from the sum of its parts. Macroeconomics differs from microeconomics in the type of questions it tries to answer. Macroeconomics also has a strong policy focus: **Keynesian economics,** which emerged during the Great Depression, advocates the use of **monetary policy** and **fiscal policy** to fight economic slumps. Prior to the Great Depression, the economy was thought to be **self-regulating.**

2. One key concern of macroeconomics is the **business cycle,** the short-run alternation between **recessions,** periods of falling employment and output, and **expansions,** periods of rising employment and output. The point at which expansion turns to recession is a **business-cycle peak.** The point at which recession turns to expansion is a **business-cycle trough.**

3. Another key area of macroeconomic study is **long-run economic growth,** the sustained upward trend in the economy's output over time. Long-run economic growth is the force behind long-term increases in living standards and is important for financing some economic programs. It is especially important for poorer countries.

4. When the prices of most goods and services are rising, so that the overall level of prices is going up, the

economy experiences **inflation.** When the overall level of prices is going down, the economy is experiencing **deflation.** In the short run, inflation and deflation are closely related to the business cycle. In the long run, prices tend to reflect changes in the overall quantity of money. Because both inflation and deflation can cause problems, economists and policy makers generally aim for **price stability.**

5. Although comparative advantage explains why **open economies** export some things and import others, macroeconomic analysis is needed to explain why countries run **trade surpluses** or **trade deficits.** The determinants of the overall balance between exports and imports lie in decisions about savings and investment spending.

KEY TERMS

Self-regulating economy, p. 169
Keynesian economics, p. 169
Monetary policy, p. 169
Fiscal policy, p. 169
Recession, p. 172
Expansion, p. 172

Business cycle, p. 172
Business-cycle peak, p. 172
Business-cycle trough, p. 172
Long-run economic growth, p. 175
Inflation, p. 178
Deflation, p. 178

Price stability, p. 178
Open economy, p. 179
Trade deficit, p. 179
Trade surplus, p. 179

PROBLEMS

interactive activity

1. Which of the following questions are relevant for the study of macroeconomics and which for microeconomics?

   a. How will Ms. Martin's tips change when a large manufacturing plant near the restaurant where she works closes?

   b. What will happen to spending by consumers when the economy enters a downturn?

   c. How will the price of oranges change when a late frost damages Florida's orange groves?

   d. How will wages at a manufacturing plant change when its workforce is unionized?

   e. What will happen to U.S. exports as the dollar becomes less expensive in terms of other currencies?

   f. What is the relationship between a nation's unemployment rate and its inflation rate?

2. When one person saves more, that person's wealth is increased, meaning that he or she can consume more in the future. But when everyone saves more, everyone's income falls, meaning that everyone must consume less today. Explain this seeming contradiction.

3. Before the Great Depression, the conventional wisdom among economists and policy makers was that the economy is largely self-regulating.

   a. Is this view consistent or inconsistent with Keynesian economics? Explain.

   b. What effect did the Great Depression have on conventional wisdom?

   c. Contrast the response of policy makers during the 2007–2009 recession to the actions of policy makers during the Great Depression. What would have been the likely outcome of the 2007–2009 recession if policy makers had responded in the same fashion as policy makers during the Great Depression?

4. How do economists in the United States determine when a recession begins and when it ends? How do other countries determine whether or not a recession is occurring?

5. The U.S. Department of Labor reports statistics on employment and earnings that are used as key indicators by many economists to gauge the health of the economy. Figure 6-4 plots historical data on the unemployment rate each month. Noticeably, the numbers were high during the recessions in the early 1990s, in 2001, and in the aftermath of the Great Recession, 2008–2017.

   a. Locate the latest data on the national unemployment rate. (*Hint:* Go to the Bureau of Labor Statistics at www.bls.gov, in the search bar enter "Employment Situation Summary," and select the subsequent page.)

   b. Compare the current numbers with those during the early 1990s, 2001, and during 2008–2017, as well as with the periods of relatively high economic growth just before the recessions. Are the current numbers indicative of a recessionary trend?

6. In the 1990s there were some dramatic economic events that came to be known as the *Asian financial crisis*. A decade later similar events came to be known as the *global financial crisis*. The accompanying figure shows the growth rate of real GDP in the United States and Japan from 1995 to 2014. Using the graph, explain why the two sets of events are referred to this way.

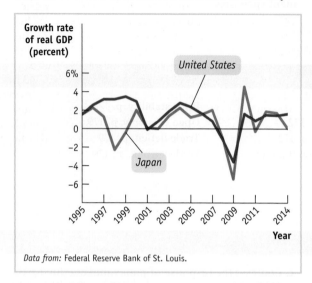

Data from: Federal Reserve Bank of St. Louis.

7. Access the Discovering Data exercise for Chapter 6 online to answer the following questions.

 a. What is the percentage decline in industrial production for Greece from 2007 to 2009? What is it from 2007 to 2014?

 b. What country has the largest decline in industrial production from 2007 to 2009? Rank the countries, in order, from the largest decline in industrial production to the smallest.

 c. Find the decline in industrial production from 2007 to 2009 for each of the countries.

 d. What country experienced the fastest recovery from the financial crisis? The slowest recovery?

 e. How long did it take Germany to fully recover from the financial crisis? How long did it take the United States?

8. a. What three measures of the economy tend to move together during the business cycle? Which way do they move during an upturn? During a downturn?

 b. Who in the economy is hurt during a recession? How?

 c. How did Milton Friedman alter the consensus that had developed in the aftermath of the Great Depression on how the economy should be managed? What is the current goal of policy makers in managing the economy?

9. Why do we consider a business-cycle expansion different from long-run economic growth? Why do we care about the size of the long-run growth rate of real GDP relative to the size of the growth rate of the population?

10. In 1798, Thomas Malthus's *Essay on the Principle of Population* was published. In it, he wrote: "Population, when unchecked, increases in a geometrical ratio. Subsistence increases only in an arithmetical ratio. . . . This implies a strong and constantly operating check on population from the difficulty of subsistence." Malthus was saying that the growth of the population is limited by the amount of food available to eat; people will live at the subsistence level forever. Why didn't Malthus's description apply to the world after 1800?

11. Each year, *The Economist* publishes data on the price of the Big Mac in different countries and exchange rates. The accompanying table shows some data from 2007 and 2016. Use this information to answer the following questions.

	2007		2016	
Country	Price of Big Mac (in local currency)	Price of Big Mac (in U.S. dollars)	Price of Big Mac (in local currency)	Price of Big Mac (in U.S. dollars)
Argentina	peso8.25	$2.65	peso33.0	$2.39
Canada	C$3.63	$3.08	C$5.84	$4.14
Euro area	€2.94	$3.82	€3.72	$4.00
Japan	¥280	$2.31	¥370	$3.12
United States	$3.22	$3.22	$4.93	$4.93

 a. Where was it cheapest to buy a Big Mac in U.S. dollars in 2007?

 b. Where was it cheapest to buy a Big Mac in U.S. dollars in 2016?

 c. Using the increase in the local currency price of the Big Mac in each country to measure the percent change in the overall price level from 2007 to 2016, which nation experienced the most inflation? Did any of the nations experience deflation?

12. The accompanying figure illustrates the trade deficit of the United States since 1987. The United States has been consistently and, on the whole, increasingly importing more goods than it has been exporting. One of the countries it runs a trade deficit with is China. Which of the following statements are valid possible explanations of this fact? Explain.

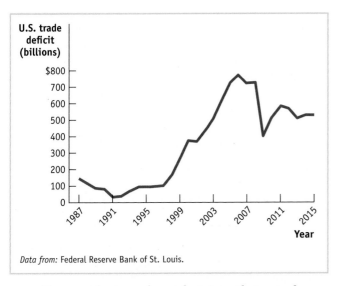

Data from: Federal Reserve Bank of St. Louis.

a. Many products, such as televisions, that were formerly manufactured in the United States are now manufactured in China.

b. The wages of the average Chinese worker are far lower than the wages of the average American worker.

c. Investment spending in the United States is high relative to its level of savings.

13. College tuition has risen significantly in the last few decades. For the sake of this problem, let's assume that over the last 20 years the cost of college, including total tuition, room, and board paid by full-time undergraduate students went from $2,871 to $16,789 at public institutions, a 485% price increase, and from $6,330 to $33,716 at private institutions, a 433% increase. Over the same time, average personal income after taxes rose from $9,785 to $39,409 per year, an increase of 302%. Have these tuition increases made it more difficult for the average student to afford college tuition?

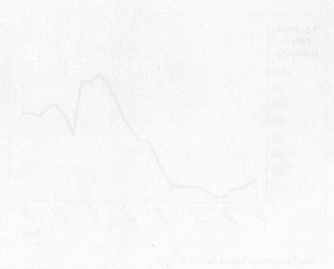

7

GDP and the CPI: Tracking the Macroeconomy

🌐 CHINA HITS THE BIG TIME

WE OPENED THIS BOOK with a portrait of the Pearl River Delta, the huge urban complex in southeastern China that, taken as a whole, is now the world's biggest city. The world's biggest city also has a very big economy, larger than that of many nations. And China as a whole, by some measures, now has the world's largest economy. Other measures show that the U.S. economy is still larger.

China has become an economic superpower, surpassing Japan.

But what does it mean to have the largest economy in the world? If you compare China with the United States, you find that they do quite different things. China, for example, produces much of the world's clothing, while the U.S. clothing industry has largely disappeared. On the other hand, America produces around half of the world's passenger jets, while China is just getting into the aircraft industry. So you might think that trying to compare the sizes of the two economies

would be a matter of comparing apples and oranges—well, pajamas and Boeings, but you get the idea.

In fact, however, economists routinely do compare the sizes of economies across both space and time—for example, they compare the size of the U.S. economy with that of China, and they also compare the size of the U.S. economy today with its size in the past. They do this using a measure known as *gross domestic product,* or GDP, the total value of goods and services produced in a country, and a closely related measure, *real GDP,* which corrects GDP for annual price changes. When number-crunchers say that one country's economy has overtaken the other's, they mean that China's real GDP has surpassed that of the United States (or that the United States' real GDP has surpassed that of China).

GDP and real GDP are two of the most important measures used to track the macroeconomy—that is, to quantify movements in the overall level of output and prices. Measures like GDP and *price indexes* play an important role in formulating economic policy, since policy makers need to know what's going on, and anecdotes are no substitute for hard data. Measures are also important for business decisions—to such an extent that, as the Business Case at the end of the chapter illustrates, corporations and other players seek independent estimates when they don't trust official numbers.

In this chapter, we explain how macroeconomists measure key aspects of the economy. We first explore ways to measure the economy's total output and total income. We then turn to the problem of how to measure the level of prices and the change in prices in the economy. ●

WHAT YOU WILL LEARN

- How do economists use aggregate measures to track the performance of the economy?
- What is **gross domestic product,** or **GDP,** and how is it calculated?
- What is the difference between **real GDP** and **nominal GDP,** and why is real GDP the appropriate measure of real economic activity?
- What is a **price index,** and how is it used to calculate the **inflation rate?**

The **national income and product accounts,** or **national accounts,** keep track of the flows of money between different sectors of the economy.

Government purchases of goods and services are total expenditures on goods and services by federal, state, and local governments.

Consumer spending is household spending on goods and services.

Investment spending is spending on productive physical capital—such as machinery and construction of buildings—and on changes to inventories.

Goods and services sold to other countries are **exports.** Goods and services purchased from other countries are **imports.**

‖ The National Accounts

Almost all countries calculate a set of numbers known as the *national income and product accounts.* In fact, the accuracy of a country's accounts is a remarkably reliable indicator of its state of economic development—in general, the more reliable the accounts, the more economically advanced the country. When international economic agencies seek to help a less developed country, typically the first order of business is to send a team of experts to audit and improve the country's accounts.

In the United States, these numbers are calculated by the Bureau of Economic Analysis, a division of the U.S. government's Department of Commerce. The **national income and product accounts,** often referred to simply as the **national accounts,** keep track of the spending of consumers, sales of producers, business investment spending, government purchases, and a variety of other flows of money between different sectors of the economy. Let's see how they work.

Following the Money: The Expanded Circular-Flow Diagram

To understand the principles behind the national accounts, it helps to look at Figure 7-1, which is an expanded version of the circular-flow diagram we introduced in Chapter 2 (see Figure 2-6). Figure 7-1 shows the flows of money through the economy. For the purposes of this chapter, however, we will only focus on the left side of the diagram, where green arrows represent the "real" economy—flows of money associated with the production and sales of goods and services. We'll turn to the "financial" economy, represented by the blue arrows, in Chapter 10—borrowing, lending, and other money flows—that are crucial but have only an indirect effect on production.

As Figure 7-1 shows, spending on goods and services—flows of money *into* the markets for goods and services—comes from four distinct kinds of buyer:

1. Governments at the local, state, and federal level spend tax revenue in two broad areas: **government purchases of goods and services** like education or defense, where the government buys things for its own use, and *transfer payments* like Social Security, where the government gives money to households. For now, in this chapter, we will focus only on government purchases.

2. Households—that's your family, ours, and tens of millions of others. Households engage in **consumer spending** by purchasing goods and services through the markets for goods and services from firms or imports from the rest of the world.

3. Firms—firms buy goods and services from each other when they engage in **investment spending,** spending on productive capital, such as machinery and construction of buildings.

4. Rest of the World—a fourth source of spending comes from **exports,** goods and services sold to residents of other countries.

All four of these money flows involve spending on goods and services. However, some of the goods and services purchased by a country's residents are produced abroad. For example, many consumer goods sold in the United States are made in China. Goods and services that are purchased by households, governments, or firms, but produced by residents of another country, are known as **imports.** The purchase of imports leads to a flow of money *out* of the market for goods and services and *out* of the economy.

Suppose we add up consumer spending on goods and services, investment spending, government purchases of goods and services, and the value of exports, then subtract the value of imports. This gives us a measure of the overall market value of the goods and services the economy produces. That measure has a name: it's a country's *gross domestic product.* But before we can formally define gross domestic product, or GDP, we have to examine an important distinction

FIGURE 7-1   An Expanded Circular-Flow Diagram: The Flows of Money Through the Economy

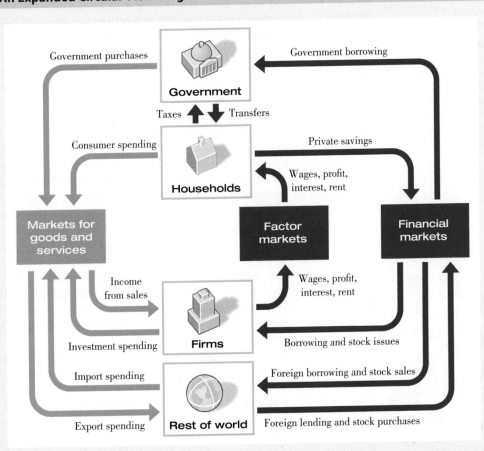

A circular flow of money connects the four sectors of the economy: government, households, firms, and the rest of the world, via three types of markets: markets for goods and services, factor markets, and financial markets. Money flows from firms to households in the form of wages, profit, interest, and rent through the factor markets. Households use that money to pay taxes to the government, save it in the form of private savings that flows to the financial markets, or to pay for consumer spending on goods and services from firms or imports from the rest of the world. The government uses tax revenue to purchase goods and services from firms or the rest of the world. It can also use tax revenue to transfer money to households in the form of subsidies or the social safety net

(Social Security or unemployment insurance payments, for example). Firms use the money they receive from the financial markets via borrowing or issuing stocks or bonds to pay for investment spending, which involves spending on goods and services such as machinery and building construction, which will increase their production in the future. Finally, the rest of the world purchases the economy's exports. To understand national income accounting, we focus on the flows to and from the markets for goods and services, which represent the "real" economy, shown on the left side of the diagram, in green. The right side of the diagram, in blue, represents the "financial" economy, which we will examine in Chapter 10.

---

between classes of goods and services: the difference between *final goods and services,* on one side, and *intermediate goods and services* on the other.

Gross Domestic Product

A consumer's purchase of a new car from a dealer is one example of a sale of **final goods and services:** goods and services sold to the final, or end, user. But an automobile manufacturer's purchase of steel from a steel foundry or glass from a glassmaker is an example of purchasing **intermediate goods and services:** goods and services that are inputs for production of final goods and services. In the case of intermediate goods and services, the purchaser—another firm—is *not* the final user.

Final goods and services are goods and services sold to the final, or end, user.

Intermediate goods and services are goods and services—bought from one firm by another firm—that are inputs for production of final goods and services.

Gross domestic product, or **GDP,** is the total value of all final goods and services produced in the economy during a given year.

Aggregate spending, the sum of consumer spending, investment spending, government purchases of goods and services, and exports minus imports, is the total spending on domestically produced final goods and services in the economy.

Gross domestic product, or **GDP,** is the total value of all *final goods and services* produced in an economy during a given period, usually a year. In 2016 the GDP of the United States was $18,566 billion, or about $57,409 per person. If you are an economist trying to construct a country's national accounts, *one way to calculate GDP is to calculate it directly: survey firms and add up the total value of their production of final goods and services.* We'll soon explain why intermediate goods, and some other types of goods as well, are not included in the calculation of GDP.

But adding up the total value of final goods and services produced isn't the only way of calculating GDP. There are two other ways. One way is based on total spending on final goods and services. Since GDP is equal to the total value of final goods and services produced in the economy, it must also equal the flow of funds received by firms from sales in the goods and services market.

If you look again at the circular-flow diagram in Figure 7-1, you will see the arrow going from markets for goods and services to firms. The flow of funds out of the markets for goods and services to firms is equal to the total flow of funds into the markets for goods and services from other sectors. And as you can see from Figure 7-1, the total flow of funds into the markets for goods and services is total or **aggregate spending** on domestically produced final goods and services—the sum of consumer spending, investment spending, government purchases of goods and services, and exports minus imports. *So a second way of calculating GDP is to add up aggregate spending on domestically produced final goods and services in the economy.*

The third way of calculating GDP is based on total income earned in the economy. Firms, and the factors of production that they employ, are owned by households. So firms must ultimately pay out what they earn to households. The flow from firms to the factor markets is the factor income paid out by firms to households in the form of wages, profit, interest, and rent. Since all the income earned by firms belongs to someone—if it doesn't go to workers or bondholders, it counts as profits that accrue to shareholders—the value of the flow of factor income from firms to households must be equal to the flow of money into firms from the markets for goods and services. And this last value, we know, is the total value of production in the economy—GDP.

Why is GDP equal to the total value of factor income paid by firms in the economy to households? Because each sale in the economy must accrue to someone as income—either as wages, profit, interest, or rent. *So a third way of calculating GDP is to sum the total factor income earned by households from firms in the economy.*

"You wouldn't think there'd be much money in potatoes, chickens, and woodchopping, but it all adds up."

Frank Cotham The New Yorker Collection/The Cartoon Bank

Calculating GDP

We've just explained the three methods for calculating GDP:

1. adding up total value of all final goods and services produced
2. adding up spending on all domestically produced goods and services
3. adding up total factor income earned by households from firms in the economy

Government statisticians use all three methods. To illustrate how these three methods work, we will consider a simplified hypothetical economy, shown in Figure 7-2. This economy consists of three firms—American Motors, Inc., which produces one car per year; American Steel, Inc., which produces the steel that goes into the car; and American Ore, Inc., which mines the iron ore that goes into the steel. So GDP is $21,500, the value of the one car per year the economy produces. Let's look at how the three different methods of calculating GDP yield the same result.

FIGURE 7-2 Calculating GDP

In this simplified hypothetical economy consisting of three firms, GDP can be calculated in three different ways: (1) measuring GDP as the value of production of final goods and services, by summing each firm's value added; (2) measuring GDP as aggregate spending on domestically produced final goods and services; and (3) measuring GDP as factor income earned by households from firms in the economy.

2. Aggregate spending on domestically produced final goods and services = $21,500

	American Ore, Inc.	American Steel, Inc.	American Motors, Inc.	Total factor income
Value of sales	$4,200 (ore)	$9,000 (steel)	$21,500 (car)	
Intermediate goods	0	4,200 (iron ore)	9,000 (steel)	
Wages	2,000	3,700	10,000	$15,700
Interest payments	1,000	600	1,000	2,600
Rent	200	300	500	1,000
Profit	1,000	200	1,000	2,200
Total expenditure by firm	4,200	9,000	21,500	
Value added per firm = Value of sales − Cost of intermediate goods	4,200	4,800	12,500	

3. Total payments to factors = $21,500

1. Value of production of final goods and services, sum of value added = $21,500

Measuring GDP as the Value of Production of Final Goods and Services

The first method for calculating GDP is to add up the value of all the final goods and services produced in the economy—a calculation that excludes the value of intermediate goods and services. Why are intermediate goods and services excluded? After all, don't they represent a very large and valuable portion of the economy?

To understand why only final goods and services are included in GDP, look at the simplified economy described in Figure 7-2. Should we measure the GDP of this economy by adding up the total sales of the iron ore producer, the steel producer, and the auto producer? If we did, we would in effect be counting the value of the steel twice—once when it is sold by the steel plant to the auto plant, and again when the steel auto body is sold to a consumer as a finished car. And we would be counting the value of the iron ore *three* times—once when it is mined and sold to the steel company, a second time when it is made into steel and sold to the auto producer, and a third time when the steel is made into a car and sold to the consumer.

So counting the full value of each producer's sales would cause us to count the same items several times and artificially inflate the calculation of GDP. For example, in Figure 7-2, the total value of all sales, intermediate and final, is $34,700: $21,500 from the sale of the car, plus $9,000 from the sale of the steel, plus $4,200 from the sale of the iron ore. Yet we know that GDP is only $21,500. The way we avoid double-counting is to count only each producer's **value added** in the calculation of GDP: the difference between the value of its sales and the value of the intermediate goods and services it purchases from other businesses.

That is, we subtract the cost of inputs—the intermediate goods—at each stage of the production process. In this case, the value added of the auto producer is the dollar value of the cars it manufactures *minus* the cost of the steel it buys, or $12,500. The value added of the steel producer is the dollar value of the steel it

The **value added** of a producer is the value of its sales minus the value of its purchases of intermediate goods and services.

Steel is an intermediate good because it is sold to other product manufacturers, such as automakers, and rarely to final buyers, such as consumers.

produces *minus* the cost of the ore it buys, or $4,800. Only the ore producer, which we have assumed doesn't buy any inputs, has value added equal to its total sales, $4,200. The sum of the three producers' value added is $21,500, equal to GDP.

Measuring GDP as Spending on Domestically Produced Final Goods and Services

Another way to calculate GDP is by adding up aggregate spending on domestically produced final goods and services. That is, GDP can be measured by the flow of funds into firms. Like the method that estimates GDP as the value of domestic production of final goods and services, this measurement must be carried out in a way that avoids double-counting.

In terms of our steel and auto example, we don't want to count both consumer spending on a car (represented in Figure 7-2 by $21,500, the sales price of the car) and the auto producer's spending on steel (represented in Figure 7-2 by $9,000, the price of a car's worth of steel). If we counted both, we would be counting the steel embodied in the car twice. We solve this problem by counting only the value of sales to *final buyers*, such as consumers, firms that purchase investment goods, the government, or foreign buyers. In other words, in order to avoid double-counting of spending, we omit sales of inputs from one business to another when estimating GDP using spending data. You can see from Figure 7-2 that aggregate spending on final goods and services—the finished car—is $21,500.

As we've already pointed out, the national accounts *do* include investment spending by firms as a part of final spending. That is, an auto company's purchase of steel to make a car isn't considered a part of final spending, but the company's purchase of new machinery for its factory *is* considered a part of final spending. What's the difference? Steel is an input that is used up in production; machinery will last for a number of years. Since purchases of capital goods that will last for a considerable time aren't closely tied to current production, the national accounts consider such purchases a form of final sales.

In later chapters, we will make use of the proposition that GDP is equal to aggregate spending on domestically produced goods and services by final buyers. We will also develop models of how final buyers decide how much to spend. With that in mind, we'll now examine the types of spending that make up GDP.

FOR INQUIRING MINDS | **Our Imputed Lives**

An old line says that when a person marries the household cook, GDP falls. And it's true: when someone provides services for pay, those services are counted as a part of GDP. But the services family members provide to each other are not. Some economists have produced alternative measures that try to "impute" the value of household work—that is, assign an estimate of what the market value of that work would have been if it had been paid for. But the standard measure of GDP doesn't contain that imputation.

GDP estimates do, however, include an imputation for the value of owner-occupied housing. That is, if you buy the home you were formerly renting, GDP does not go down. It's true that because

you no longer pay rent to your landlord, the landlord no longer sells a service to you—namely, use of the house or apartment. But the statisticians make an estimate of what you would have paid if you rented your dwelling, whether it's an apartment or a house. For the purposes of the statistics, it's as if you were renting from yourself.

If you think about it, this makes a lot of sense. In a home-owning country like the United States, the pleasure we derive from our houses is an important part of the standard of living. So to be accurate, estimates of GDP must take into account the value of housing that is occupied by owners as well as the value of rental housing.

The value of the services that family members provide to each other is not counted as part of GDP.

Look again at the markets for goods and services in Figure 7-1, and you will see that one component of sales by firms is consumer spending. Let's denote consumer spending with the symbol *C*. Figure 7-1 also shows three other components of sales: sales of investment goods to other businesses, or investment spending, which we will denote by *I*; government purchases of goods and services, which we will denote by *G*; and sales to foreigners—that is, exports—which we will denote by *X*.

In reality, not all of this final spending goes toward domestically produced goods and services. We must take account of spending on imports, which we will denote by *IM*. Income spent on imports is income not spent on domestic goods and services—it is income that has "leaked" across national borders. So to accurately value domestic production using spending data, we must subtract out spending on imports to arrive at spending on domestically produced goods and services. Putting this all together gives us the following equation that breaks GDP down by the four sources of aggregate spending:

(7-1) $GDP = C + I + G + X - IM$

We'll be seeing a lot of Equation 7-1 in later chapters.

Measuring GDP as Factor Income Earned from Firms in the Economy A final way to calculate GDP is to add up all the income earned by factors of production from firms in the economy—the wages earned by labor; the interest paid to those who lend their savings to firms and the government; the rent earned by those who lease their land or structures to firms; and dividends, the profits paid to the shareholders, the owners of the firms' physical capital.

Figure 7-2 shows how this calculation works for our simplified economy. The numbers shaded in the column at far right show the total wages, interest, and rent paid by all these firms as well as their total profit. Summing up all of these items yields total factor income of $21,500—again, equal to GDP.

PITFALLS

GDP: WHAT'S IN AND WHAT'S OUT

It's easy to confuse what is included in and excluded from GDP. For example, investment spending—spending on productive physical capital (including construction of residential and commercial structures), and changes to inventories (goods and raw materials held to facilitate business operations)—is included in GDP. But spending on intermediate goods and services, like the steel used to make cars, is not. Why?

The answer is that we only include items that are newly produced (unlike, say, used cars), and aren't used up in production (like the steel in new cars). Here's a table summarizing what's in or out.

IN	OUT
Investment spending Spending on productive physical capital (including construction of residential and commercial structures) and changes to inventories	**Spending on intermediate goods and services** Inputs for production of final goods and services
Capital spending Considered part of investment spending	**Used goods** To include them would be to double-count: counting them once when sold as new and again when sold as used
Domestically produced final goods and services Includes capital goods and new construction of structures produced by firms (also includes owner-occupied home-based businesses like child care provided by households, and educational and other such services provided by the government)	**Financial assets like stocks and bonds** They don't represent either the production or the sale of final goods and services: a *bond* represents a promise to repay with interest; a *stock* represents a proof of ownership
	Import Spending Spending on goods and services produced outside the country are not part of domestic production and are excluded

We won't emphasize factor income as much as the other two methods of calculating GDP. It's important to keep in mind, however, that all the money spent on domestically produced goods and services generates factor income to households.

The Components of GDP Now that we know how GDP is calculated in principle, let's see what it looks like in practice.

Figure 7-3 shows the first two methods of calculating GDP side by side. The height of each bar above the horizontal axis represents the GDP of the U.S. economy in 2016: $18,566 billion. Each bar is divided to show the breakdown of that total in terms of where the value was added and how the money was spent.

In the left bar in Figure 7-3, we see the breakdown of GDP by value added according to sector, the first method of calculating GDP. Of the $18,566 billion, $14,003 billion consisted of value added by businesses. Another $2,358 billion of value added was added by households and institutions; a large part of that was the imputed services of owner-occupied housing, described in the For Inquiring Minds "Our Imputed Lives." Finally, $2,204 billion consisted of value added by government, in the form of military, education, and other government services.

The right bar in Figure 7-3 corresponds to the second method of calculating GDP, showing the breakdown by the four types of aggregate spending. The total length of the right bar is longer than the total length of the left bar, a difference of $500 billion (which, as you can see, is the amount by which the right bar extends below the horizontal axis). That's because the total length of the right bar represents total spending in the economy, spending on both domestically produced and foreign-produced final goods and services. Within the bar, consumer spending (*C*), which is 68.7% of GDP, dominates overall spending.

FIGURE 7-3 U.S. GDP in 2016: Two Methods of Calculating GDP

The two bars show two equivalent ways of calculating GDP. The height of each bar above the horizontal axis represents $18,566 billion, U.S. GDP in 2016. The left bar shows the breakdown of GDP according to the value added of each sector of the economy: government, households, and firms. The right bar shows the breakdown of GDP according to the four types of aggregate spending: *C* + *I* + *G* + *X* − *IM*. The right bar has a total length of $18,566 billion + $500 billion = $19,066 billion. The $500 billion, shown as the area extending below the horizontal axis, is the amount of total spending absorbed by net exports, which were negative in 2016. (Numbers may not add due to rounding.)

Data from: Bureau of Economic Analysis.

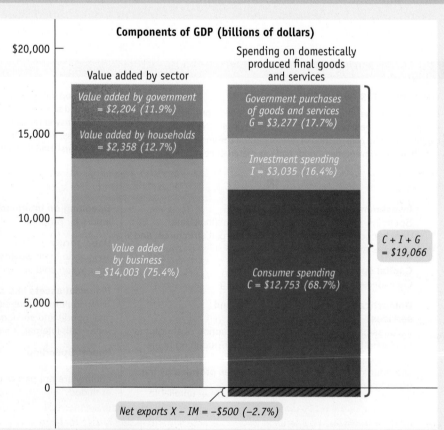

But some of that spending was absorbed by foreign-produced goods and services. In 2016, **net exports,** the difference between the value of exports and the value of imports ($X - IM$ in Equation 7-1) was negative—the United States was a net importer of foreign goods and services. The 2016 value of $X - IM$ was –$500 billion, or –2.7% of GDP. Thus, a portion of the right bar extends below the horizontal axis by $500 billion to represent the amount of total spending that was absorbed by net imports and so did not lead to higher U.S. GDP. Investment spending (I) constituted 16.4% of GDP; government purchases of goods and services (G) constituted 17.7% of GDP.

Net exports are the difference between the value of exports and the value of imports.

What GDP Tells Us

Now we've seen the various ways that gross domestic product is calculated. But what does the measurement of GDP tell us?

The most important use of GDP is as a measure of the size of the economy. For example, suppose you want to compare the economies of different nations. A natural approach is to compare their GDPs. In 2016, as we've seen, U.S. GDP was $18,566 billion, China's GDP was $11,392 billion, and the combined GDP of the 28 countries that make up the European Union was $16,518 billion.

But wait—didn't we open this chapter by stating that by some measures, China has the world's largest economy, while other measures show that the U.S. economy is still larger? Well, it turns out that one must be careful when using GDP numbers in comparing countries, and especially when making comparisons over time. That's because part of the increase in the value of GDP over time represents increases in the *prices* of goods and services rather than an increase in output. For example, U.S. GDP was $8,608 billion in 1997 and had more than doubled to $18,566 billion by 2016. But the U.S. economy didn't actually double in size over that period. To measure actual changes in aggregate output, we need a modified version of GDP that is adjusted for price changes, known as *real GDP*.

A similar issue arises when comparing the United States and China, because many goods and services sold inside China are much cheaper than they are in the United States, and estimates that take this into account find that China's real GDP is bigger than the unadjusted number suggests. We'll see next how real GDP is calculated.

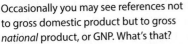

FOR INQUIRING MINDS   **Gross What?**

Occasionally you may see references not to gross domestic product but to gross *national* product, or GNP. What's that?

If you look at Figure 7-1 carefully, you may realize that there's a possibility that is missing from the figure. According to the figure, all factor income goes to domestic households. But what happens when profits are paid to foreigners who own stock in General Motors or Apple? And where do the profits earned by American companies operating overseas fit in?

The answer is, they're in *GNP*, which is defined as the total factor income earned by residents of a country. It *excludes* factor income earned by foreigners, like profits paid to foreign investors who own American stocks and payments

to foreigners who work temporarily in the United States. And it *includes* factor income earned abroad by Americans, like the profits of Apple's European operations that accrue to Apple's American shareholders and the wages of Americans who work abroad temporarily.

In the early days of national income accounting, economists usually used GNP rather than GDP as a measure of the economy's size. They switched to GDP mainly because it's considered a better indicator of short-run movements in production and because data on international flows of factor income are considered somewhat unreliable.

In practice, it doesn't make much difference which measure is used for large

economies like that of the United States, where the flows of net factor income to other countries are relatively small. In 2015, America's GNP was about 1.2% larger than its GDP, mainly because of the overseas profit of U.S. companies. However, for smaller countries, which are likely to be hosts to a number of foreign companies, GDP and GNP can diverge significantly. For example, much of Ireland's industry is owned by American corporations, whose profit must be deducted from Ireland's GNP. In addition, Ireland has become a host to many temporary workers from poorer regions of Europe, whose wages must also be deducted from Ireland's GNP. As a result, in 2015 Ireland's GNP was only 80% of its GDP.

>> Quick Review

- A country's **national income and product accounts**, or **national accounts**, track flows of money among economic sectors.

- There are four flows of money into the markets for goods and services: **consumer spending, government purchases of goods and services, exports**, and **investment spending**.

- Part of spending on goods and services flows out of the country via **imports**. The rest becomes sales by domestic producers.

- **Gross domestic product**, or **GDP**, can be calculated in three different ways: add up the **value added** by all firms; add up all spending on domestically produced **final goods and services**, an amount equal to **aggregate spending**; or add up all factor income paid by firms. **Intermediate goods and services** are not included in the calculation of GDP.

>> Check Your Understanding 7-1

Solutions appear at back of book.

1. Explain why the three methods of calculating GDP produce the same estimate of GDP.

2. What are the various sectors to which firms make sales? What are the various ways in which households are linked with other sectors of the economy?

3. Consider the first row of Figure 7-2 and suppose you mistakenly believed that total value added was $30,500, the sum of the sales price of a car and a car's worth of steel. What items would you be counting twice?

Real GDP: A Measure of Aggregate Output

The U.S. economy had a pretty good year in 2016: the nation gained 2.2 million jobs, while the unemployment rate fell from 5 to 4.7 percent. It was certainly a better year than 1982, when a severe recession reduced employment by 2 million and sent unemployment soaring. Strange to say, however, gross domestic product rose slightly faster in 1982 (3.8%) than it did in 2016 (2.9%). How is that possible? The answer is that back in 1982 GDP was rising for a bad reason—inflation, which raised the prices of the goods and services America produced—not because the economy was actually growing. Inflation was much lower in 2016, so the rise in GDP really did correspond to economic progress.

In order to accurately measure the economy's growth, we need a measure of **aggregate output:** the total quantity of final goods and services the economy produces. The measure that is used for this purpose is known as *real GDP*. By tracking real GDP over time, we avoid the problem of changes in prices distorting the value of changes in production of goods and services over time. Let's look first at how real GDP is calculated, then at what it means.

Calculating Real GDP

To understand how real GDP is calculated, imagine an economy in which only two goods, apples and oranges, are produced and in which both goods are sold only to final consumers. The outputs and prices of the two fruits for two consecutive years are shown in Table 7-1.

The first thing we can say about these data is that the value of sales increased from year 1 to year 2. In the first year, the total value of sales was (2,000 billion × $0.25) + (1,000 billion × $0.50) = $1,000 billion; in the second it was (2,200 billion × $0.30) + (1,200 billion × $0.70) = $1,500 billion, which is 50% larger. But it is also clear from the table that this increase in the dollar value of GDP overstates the real growth in the economy. Although the quantities of both apples and oranges increased, the prices of both apples and oranges also rose. So part of the 50% increase in the dollar value of GDP from year 1 to year 2 simply reflects higher prices, not higher production of output.

To estimate the true increase in aggregate output produced, we have to ask: how much would GDP have gone up if prices had *not* changed? To answer this question, we need to find the value of output in year 2 expressed in year 1 prices. In year 1 the price of apples was $0.25 each and the price of oranges $0.50 each. So year 2 output *at year 1 prices* is (2,200 billion × $0.25) + (1,200 billion × $0.50) = $1,150 billion. And output in year 1 at year 1 prices was $1,000 billion. So in this example GDP measured in year 1 prices rose 15%—from $1,000 billion to $1,150 billion.

Now we can define **real GDP:** it is the total value of final goods and services produced in the economy during a year, calculated as

Aggregate output is the economy's total quantity of output of final goods and services.

Real GDP is the total value of all final goods and services produced in the economy during a given year, calculated using the prices of a selected base year.

TABLE 7-1 Calculating GDP and Real GPD in a Simple Economy

	Year 1	Year 2
Quantity of apples (billions)	2,000	2,200
Price of apple	$0.25	$0.30
Quantity of oranges (billions)	1,000	1,200
Price of orange	$0.50	$0.70
GDP (billions of dollars)	$1,000	$1,500
Real GDP (billions of year 1 dollars)	$1,000	$1,150

if prices had stayed constant at the level of some given base year. A real GDP number always comes with information about what the base year is.

A GDP number that has not been adjusted for changes in prices is calculated using the prices in the year in which the output is produced. Economists call this measure **nominal GDP,** GDP at current prices. If we had used nominal GDP to measure the true change in output from year 1 to year 2 in our apples and oranges example, we would have overstated the true growth in output: we would have claimed it to be 50%, when in fact it was only 15%. By comparing output in the two years using a common set of prices—the year 1 prices in this example—we are able to focus solely on changes in the quantity of output by eliminating the influence of changes in prices.

Table 7-2 shows a real-life version of our apples and oranges example. The second column shows nominal GDP in 2003, 2009, and 2015. The third column shows real GDP for each year in 2009 dollars. For 2009 the two numbers are the same. But real GDP in 2003 expressed in 2009 dollars was higher than nominal GDP in 2003, reflecting the fact that prices were in general higher in 2009 than in 2003. Real GDP in 2015 expressed in 2009 dollars, however, was less than nominal GDP in 2015 because prices in 2009 were lower than in 2015.

TABLE 7-2 Nominal versus Real GDP in 2003, 2009, and 2015		
	Nominal GDP (billions of current dollars)	Real GDP (billions of 2009 dollars)
2003	$11,511	$13,271
2009	14,419	14,419
2015	18,037	16,397

You might have noticed that there is an alternative way to calculate real GDP using the data in Table 7-1. Why not measure it using the prices of year 2 rather than year 1 as the base-year prices? This procedure seems equally valid. According to that calculation, real GDP in year 1 at year 2 prices is (2,000 billion × $0.30) + (1,000 billion × $0.70) = $1,300 billion; real GDP in year 2 at year 2 prices is $1,500 billion, the same as nominal GDP in year 2. So using year 2 prices as the base year, the growth rate of real GDP is equal to ($1,500 billion – $1,300 billion)/$1,300 billion = 0.154, or 15.4%. This is slightly higher than the figure we got from the previous calculation, in which year 1 prices were the base-year prices. In that calculation, we found that real GDP increased by 15%. Neither answer, 15.4% versus 15%, is more "correct" than the other.

In reality, the government economists who put together the U.S. national accounts have adopted a method to measure the change in real GDP known as chain-linking, which uses the average between the GDP growth rate calculated using an early base year and the GDP growth rate calculated using a late base year. As a result, U.S. statistics on real GDP are always expressed in **chained dollars.**

What Real GDP Doesn't Measure

GDP, nominal or real, is a measure of a country's aggregate output. Other things equal, a country with a larger population will have higher GDP simply because there are more people working. So if we want to compare GDP across countries but want to eliminate the effect of differences in population size, we use the measure **GDP per capita**—GDP divided by the size of the population, equivalent to the average GDP per person.

Real GDP per capita can be a useful measure in some circumstances, such as in a comparison of labor productivity between countries. However, despite the fact that it is a rough measure of the average real output per person, real GDP per capita has well-known limitations as a measure of a country's living standards. Every once in a while economists are accused of believing that growth in real GDP per capita is the only thing that matters—that is, thinking that increasing real GDP per capita is a goal in itself. In fact, economists rarely make that mistake; the idea that economists care only about real GDP per capita is a sort of urban legend.

Let's take a moment to be clear about why a country's real GDP per capita is not a sufficient measure of human welfare in that country and why growth in real GDP per capita is not an appropriate policy goal in itself.

Nominal GDP is the value of all final goods and services produced in the economy during a given year, calculated using the prices current in the year in which the output is produced.

Chained dollars is the method of calculating changes in real GDP using the average between the growth rate calculated using an early base year and the growth rate calculated using a late base year.

GDP per capita is GDP divided by the size of the population; it is equivalent to the average GDP per person.

GLOBAL COMPARISON **GDP AND THE MEANING OF LIFE**

"I've been rich and I've been poor," the actress Mae West famously declared. "Believe me, rich is better." But is the same true for countries?

This figure shows two pieces of information for a number of countries: how rich they are, as measured by GDP per capita, and how people assess their well-being. Well-being was measured by a Gallup world survey that asked people to rate their lives at the current time and their expectations for the next five years. The graph shows the percentage of people who rated their well-being as "thriving." The figure seems to tell us three things:

1. *Rich is better.* Richer countries on average have higher well-being than poor countries.
2. *Money matters less as you grow richer.* As GDP rises, the average gain in life satisfaction gets smaller and smaller.

For example, the rise in GDP per capita from lower-income Italy to middle-income Belgium is about the same as from middle-income Belgium to the high-income United States. But the increase in life satisfaction is much greater going from Italy to Belgium compared to going from Belgium to the United States.

3. *Money isn't everything.* Israelis, though rich by world standards, are poorer than Americans—but they seem more satisfied with their lives. Japan is richer than most other nations, but scores low on the survey of well-being.

These results are consistent with the observation that high GDP per capita makes it easier to achieve a good life but that countries aren't equally successful in taking advantage of that possibility.

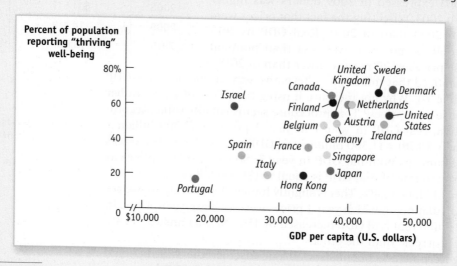

Data from: Gallup; World Bank.

One way to think about this issue is to say that an increase in real GDP means an expansion in the economy's production possibility frontier. Because the economy has increased its productive capacity, society can achieve more things. But whether society actually makes good use of that increased potential to improve living standards is another matter. To put it in a slightly different way, your income may be higher this year than last year, but whether you use that higher income to improve your quality of life is your choice.

So let's say it again: real GDP per capita is a measure of an economy's average aggregate output per person—and so of what it *can* do. It is not a sufficient goal in itself because it doesn't address how a country uses that output to affect living standards. A country with a high GDP can afford for its citizens to be healthy, to be well educated, and in general, to have a good quality of life. But there is not a one-to-one match between GDP and the quality of life.

ECONOMICS >> *in Action*
Miracle in Venezuela?

The South American nation of Venezuela has a distinction that may surprise you: in recent years, it has had one of the world's fastest-growing nominal GDPs. Between 2013 and 2016, in fact, Venezuelan nominal GDP grew at an estimated 1,200%—compared with growth of only 11% in the United States.

So is Venezuela experiencing an economic miracle? On the contrary, its economy is a mess, partly because the price of oil—the country's main export—has plunged and partly because of erratic government policies that have disrupted production and led to widespread shortages of basic consumer goods. In fact, *real* GDP fell by an estimated 19% from 2013 to 2016. But those shortages have led to surging prices (especially on the black market, but even official prices are rising rapidly). Furthermore, the government, having lost much of its revenue thanks to falling oil exports, has started to pay some of its bills simply by printing money, leading to accelerating inflation.

In other words, Venezuela is an extreme illustration of the importance of distinguishing between nominal and real GDP: it's producing fewer and fewer goods and services, but nominal GDP is soaring because the prices of the goods and services it does manage to produce are rising at triple-digit rates.

>> Check Your Understanding 7-2

Solutions appear at back of book.

1. Assume there are only two goods in the economy, french fries and onion rings. In 2015, 1,000,000 servings of french fries were sold at $0.40 each and 800,000 servings of onion rings at $0.60 each. From 2015 to 2016 the price of french fries rose by 25% and the servings sold fell by 10%; the price of onion rings fell by 15% and the servings sold rose by 5%.
   a. Calculate nominal GDP in 2015 and 2016. Calculate real GDP in 2016 using 2015 prices.
   b. Why would an assessment of growth using nominal GDP be misguided?
2. From 2010 to 2015, the price of electronic equipment fell dramatically and the price of housing rose dramatically. What are the implications of this in deciding whether to use 2010 or 2015 as the base year in calculating 2013 real GDP?

Price Indexes and the Aggregate Price Level

In late 2016, drivers had something to celebrate: gasoline prices had tumbled to an average of $2.25 per gallon, down 38% from their peak, two and a half years earlier. But while driving was getting cheaper, having someplace to live when you arrived was getting more expensive: by the end of 2016, average rents were 10% higher than they had been when gas was its most expensive. So was the cost of living going up or down?

Clearly, there was a need for a single number summarizing what was happening to consumer prices. Just as macroeconomists find it useful to have a single number representing the overall level of output, they also find it useful to have a single number representing the overall level of prices: the **aggregate price level.** Yet a huge variety of goods and services are produced and consumed in the economy. How can we summarize the prices of all these goods and services with a single number? The answer lies in the concept of a *price index*—a concept best introduced with an example.

Market Baskets and Price Indexes

Suppose that a frost in Florida destroys most of the citrus harvest. As a result, the price of an orange rises from $0.20 to $0.40, the price of a grapefruit rises from $0.60 to $1.00, and the price of a lemon rises from $0.25 to $0.45. How much has the price of citrus fruit increased?

One way to answer that question is to state three numbers—the changes in prices for oranges, grapefruit, and lemons. But this is a very cumbersome method. Rather than having to recite three numbers in an effort to track changes in the prices of citrus fruit, we would prefer to have some kind of overall measure of the *average* price change.

To measure average price changes for consumer goods and services, economists track changes in the cost of a typical consumer's *consumption bundle*—the typical basket of goods and services purchased before the price changes.

The **aggregate price level** is a measure of the overall level of prices in the economy.

TABLE 7-3 Calculating the Cost of a Market Basket

	Pre-frost	Post-frost
Price of orange	$0.20	$0.40
Price of grapefruit	0.60	1.00
Price of lemon	0.25	0.45
Cost of market basket (200 oranges, 50 grapefruit, 100 lemons)	(200 × $0.20) + (50 × $0.60) + (100 × $0.25) = $95.00	(200 × $0.40) + (50 × $1.00) + (100 × $0.45) = $175.00

A hypothetical consumption bundle, used to measure changes in the overall price level, is known as a **market basket.** Suppose that before the frost a typical consumer bought 200 oranges, 50 grapefruit, and 100 lemons over the course of a year, our market basket for this example.

Table 7-3 shows the pre-frost and post-frost cost of this market basket. Before the frost, it cost $95; after the frost, the same bundle of goods cost $175. Since $175/$95 = 1.842, the post-frost basket costs 1.842 times the cost of the pre-frost basket, a cost increase of 84.2%. In this example, the average price of citrus fruit has increased 84.2% since the base year as a result of the frost, where the base year is the initial year used in the measurement of the price change.

Economists use the same method to measure changes in the overall price level over time. For example, to measure the change in the overall price level from 2010 (the base year) to 2016, they compare the cost of purchasing the market basket in 2010 to the cost in 2016. They use a simplification to avoid tracking the market basket in the intervening years (2011 to 2015). So they *normalize* the measure of the aggregate price level, meaning that they set the cost of the market basket equal to 100 in the chosen base year. Working with a market basket and a base year, and after normalizing, we arrive at a **price index,** a normalized measure of the overall price level. It is always cited along with the year for which the aggregate price level is being measured and the base year. A price index can be calculated using the following formula:

(7-2) $\text{Price index in a given year} = \dfrac{\text{Cost of market basket in a given year}}{\text{Cost of market basket in base year}} \times 100$

In our example, the citrus fruit market basket cost $95 in the base year, the year before the frost. So by Equation 7-2 we define the price index for citrus fruit as (cost of market basket in a given year/$95) × 100, yielding an index of 100 for the period before the frost and 184.2 after the frost. You should note that the price index for the base year always results in a price index equal to 100. This is because the price index in the base year is equal to: (cost of market basket in base year/cost of market basket in base year) × 100 = 100.

Thus, the price index makes it clear that the average price of citrus has risen 84.2% as a consequence of the frost. Because of its simplicity and intuitive appeal, the method we've just described is used to calculate a variety of price indexes to track average price changes among a variety of different groups of goods and services. For example, the *consumer price index,* which we'll discuss shortly, is the most widely used measure of the aggregate price level, the overall price level of final consumer goods and services across the economy.

Price indexes are also the basis for measuring inflation. The **inflation rate** is the annual percent change in an official price index. The inflation rate from year 1 to year 2 is calculated using the following formula, where we assume that year 1 and year 2 are consecutive years.

(7-3) $\text{Inflation rate} = \dfrac{\text{Price index in year 2} - \text{Price index in year 1}}{\text{Price index in year 1}} \times 100$

Typically, a news report that cites "the inflation rate" is referring to the annual percent change in the consumer price index.

A **market basket** is a hypothetical set of consumer purchases of goods and services.

A **price index** measures the cost of purchasing a given market basket in a given year, where that cost is normalized so that it is equal to 100 in the selected base year.

The **inflation rate** is the percent change per year in a price index—typically the consumer price index.

The Consumer Price Index

The most widely used measure of prices in the United States is the **consumer price index** (often referred to simply as the **CPI**), which is intended to show how the cost of all purchases by a typical urban family has changed over time. It is calculated by surveying market prices for a market basket that is constructed to represent the consumption of a typical family of four living in a typical American city. The base period for the index is currently 1982–1984; that is, the index is calculated so that the average of consumer prices in 1982–1984 is 100.

The market basket used to calculate the CPI is far more complex than the three-fruit market basket we just described. In fact, to calculate the CPI, the Bureau of Labor Statistics sends its employees out to survey supermarkets, gas stations, hardware stores, and so on—some 23,000 retail outlets in 87 cities. Every month it tabulates about 80,000 prices, on everything from romaine lettuce to a medical check-up.

Figure 7-4 shows the weight of major categories in the consumer price index as of December 2016. For example, motor fuel, mainly gasoline, accounted for 3% of the CPI. On the other hand, housing accounted for more than 40% of the CPI. So that 38% plunge in gasoline prices in 2016 reduced the CPI by roughly 1% (0.38 × 3%), while the much smaller percentage rise in housing costs of 10% actually had a bigger positive effect on the overall price index of 4%.

Figure 7-5 shows how the CPI has changed since measurement began in 1913. Since 1940, the CPI has risen steadily, although its annual percent increases in recent years have been much smaller than those of the 1970s and early 1980s. (A logarithmic scale is used so that equal percent changes in the CPI have the same slope.)

The United States is not the only country that calculates a consumer price index. In fact, nearly every country has one. As you might expect, the market baskets that make up these indexes differ quite a lot from country to country. In poor countries, where people must spend a high proportion of their income just to feed themselves, food makes up a large share of the price index. Among high-income countries, differences in consumption patterns lead to differences in the price indexes: the Japanese price index puts a larger weight on raw fish and a smaller weight on beef than ours does, and the French price index puts a larger weight on wine.

> The **consumer price index,** or **CPI,** measures the cost of the market basket of a typical urban American family.
>
> The **producer price index,** or **PPI,** measures changes in the prices of goods purchased by producers.

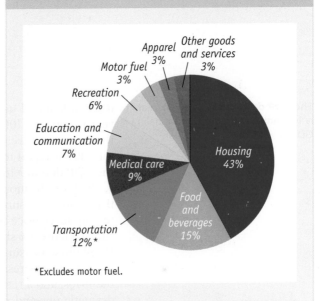

FIGURE 7-4 The Makeup of the Consumer Price Index in 2016

*Excludes motor fuel.

This chart shows the percentage shares of major types of spending in the CPI as of December 2016. Housing, food, transportation, and motor fuel made up about 73% of the CPI market basket. (Numbers don't add to 100% due to rounding.)

Data from: Bureau of Labor Statistics.

Other Price Measures

There are two other price measures that are also widely used to track economy-wide price changes. One is the **producer price index** (or **PPI,** which used to be known as the *wholesale price index*). As its name suggests, the producer price index measures the cost of a typical basket of goods and services—containing raw commodities such as steel, electricity, coal, and so on—purchased by producers. Because commodity producers are relatively quick to change prices when they perceive a change in overall demand for their goods, the PPI often responds to inflationary or deflationary pressures more quickly than the CPI. As a result, a change in the PPI is often regarded as an early warning signal of changes in the inflation rate.

The other widely used price measure is the *GDP deflator;* it isn't exactly a price index, although it serves the same purpose. Recall in our discussion of Table 7-2 we distinguished between *nominal GDP* (GDP in current prices) and *real GDP*

FIGURE 7-5 The CPI, 1913–2017

Since 1940, the CPI has risen steadily. But the annual percentage increases in recent years have been much smaller than those of the 1970s and early 1980s. (The vertical axis is measured on a logarithmic scale so that equal percent changes in the CPI have the same slope.)

Data from: Bureau of Labor Statistics.

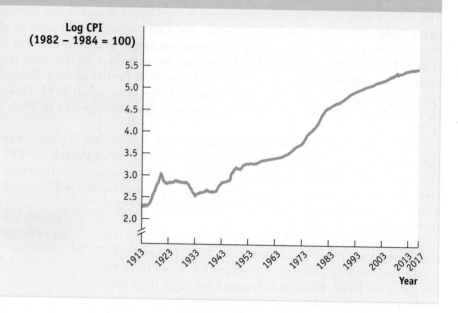

The GDP deflator for a given year is 100 times the ratio of nominal GDP to real GDP in that year.

(GDP calculated using the prices of a base year). The **GDP deflator** for a given year is equal to 100 times the ratio of nominal GDP for that year to real GDP for that year. Since real GDP is currently expressed in 2009 dollars, the GDP deflator for 2009 is equal to 100. If nominal GDP doubles but real GDP does not change, the GDP deflator indicates that the aggregate price level doubled.

Perhaps the most important point about the different inflation rates generated by these three measures of prices is that they usually move closely together (although the producer price index tends to fluctuate more than either of the other two measures). Figure 7-6 shows the annual percent changes in the three indexes since 1930. By all three measures, the U.S. economy experienced deflation during the early years of the Great Depression, inflation during World War II, accelerating inflation during the 1970s, and a return to relative price stability in the 1990s. Notice, by the way, the dramatic ups and downs in producer prices from 2000 to 2016 on the graph; this

FIGURE 7-6 The CPI, the PPI, and the GDP Deflator

As the figure shows, the three different measures of inflation, the PPI (orange), the CPI (green), and the GDP deflator (purple), usually move closely together. Each reveals a drastic acceleration of inflation during the 1970s and a return to relative price stability in the 1990s. With the exception of a brief period of deflation in 2009, prices have remained stable from 2000 to 2016.

Data from: Bureau of Labor Statistics; Bureau of Economic Analysis.

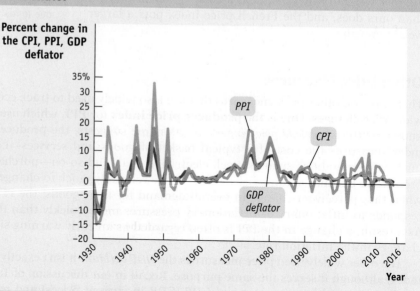

reflects large swings in energy and food prices, which play a much bigger role in the PPI than they do in either the CPI or the GDP deflator.

ECONOMICS >> *in Action*
Indexing to the CPI

Although GDP is a very important number for shaping economic policy, official statistics on GDP don't have a direct effect on people's lives. The CPI, by contrast, has a direct and immediate impact on millions of Americans.

The reason is that many payments are tied, or *indexed*, to the CPI—the amount paid rises or falls when the CPI rises or falls.

The practice of indexing payments to consumer prices goes back to the dawn of the United States as a nation. In 1780 the Massachusetts State Legislature recognized that the pay of its soldiers fighting the British needed to be increased because of inflation that occurred during the Revolutionary War. The legislature adopted a formula that made a soldier's pay proportional to the cost of a market basket, consisting of 5 bushels of corn, 68 $^4/_7$ pounds of beef, 10 pounds of sheep's wool, and 16 pounds of shoe leather.

Today, 60 million people receive payments from Social Security, a national retirement program that accounts for almost a quarter of current total federal spending—more than the defense budget. The amount of an individual's Social Security payment is determined by a formula that reflects each person's previous payments into the system and other factors. In addition, all Social Security payments are adjusted each year to offset any increase in consumer prices over the previous year. The CPI is used to calculate the official estimate of the inflation rate used to adjust these payments yearly. So every percentage point added to the official estimate of the rate of inflation adds 1% to the checks received by tens of millions of individuals.

Other government payments, such as disability benefits, are also indexed to the CPI. In addition, income tax brackets, the bands of income levels that determine a taxpayer's income tax rate, are indexed to the CPI. (Individuals in a higher income bracket pay a higher income tax rate in a progressive tax system like ours.) Indexing also extends to the private sector, where some private contracts, including some wage settlements, contain cost-of-living allowances (called COLAs) that adjust payments in proportion to changes in the CPI.

Because the CPI plays such an important and direct role in people's lives, it's a politically sensitive number. The Bureau of Labor Statistics, which calculates the CPI, takes great care in collecting and interpreting price and consumption data. It uses a complex method in which households are surveyed to determine what they buy and where they shop, and a carefully selected sample of stores are surveyed to get representative prices.

A small change in the CPI has large consequences for those dependent on Social Security payments.

>> Check Your Understanding 7-3

Solutions appear at back of book.

1. Consider Table 7-3 but suppose that the market basket is composed of 100 oranges, 50 grapefruit, and 200 lemons. How does this change the pre-frost and post-frost price indexes? Explain. Generalize your explanation to how the construction of the market basket affects the price index.

2. For each of the following events, how would an economist using a 10-year-old market basket create a bias in measuring the change in the cost of living today?
   a. A typical family owns more cars than it would have a decade ago. Over that time, the average price of a car has increased more than the average prices of other goods.
   b. Virtually no households had broadband internet access 20 years ago. Now many households have it, and the price has regularly fallen each year.

3. The consumer price index in the United States (base period 1982–1984) was 237.486 in 2015 and 242.821 in 2016. Calculate the inflation rate from 2015 to 2016.

>> Quick Review

• Changes in the **aggregate price level** are measured by the cost of buying a particular **market basket** during different years. A **price index** for a given year is the cost of the market basket in that year normalized so that the price index equals 100 in a selected base year.

• The **inflation rate** is calculated as the percent change in a price index. The most commonly used price index is the **consumer price index**, or **CPI**, which tracks the cost of a basket of consumer goods and services. The **producer price index**, or **PPI**, does the same for goods and services used as inputs by firms. The **GDP deflator** measures the aggregate price level as the ratio of nominal to real GDP times 100. These three measures normally behave quite similarly.

Betting on Bad Numbers

DON EMMERT/Getty Images

In early 2016 the *Wall Street Journal* reported that a number of big financial players, including the legendary speculator George Soros, had taken an interest in the future performance of the Chinese economy. Although China had achieved spectacular economic growth over the past 25 years, much of the *smart money* (cash invested or wagered by those considered to be experts) in the global financial system thought that boom times in China were over and that an economic crisis was looming. They believed that a weak Chinese economy would be especially devastating because Chinese companies had borrowed heavily during the boom times. Some even warned of political instability as tens of millions of Chinese citizens found their new-found prosperity slipping away.

That same year, global financial speculators placed their money in assets that would do well if the Chinese economy took a plunge.

What was the basis of this pessimism? And why did it merit betting hundreds of millions of dollars on it? Although official Chinese statistics did indicate some slowing of growth, they also showed a relatively robust growth rate of 6.9% in 2015 and forecast similar growth for 2016. Yet, this is what the smart money in global markets knew: nobody believed China's official numbers.

In fact, many in China knew this as well. In an unguarded moment, a rising Chinese official named Li Keqiang (shown in the accompanying photo) told the U.S. ambassador that China's official GDP figures were "man-made." That is, he effectively admitted they were concocted by Chinese officials to fit the optimistic story about the state of the economy that the government was communicating to its citizens. Li Keqiang also explained that in trying to understand the state of the Chinese economy he used three indicators that were easy to track and that weren't part of the Chinese national account: railway shipments, electricity consumption, and loans disbursed by banks. The revelation of this conversation made a splash around the world because it confirmed what many observers believed. Mr. Li knew what he was talking about. He soon went on to become China's Prime Minister, and if he didn't believe his own government's numbers, why should anyone else?

For businesses with interests in China, it is standard operating procedure to turn to independent estimates of Chinese GDP growth produced by a variety of researchers at places like Citibank, the British consulting firm Lombard Street Research, and the Conference Board, a research-oriented business association. Many of these estimates make use of some variation of the "Li Keqiang index"; that is, they rely on the data Li Keqiang uses, as well as other indicators like data on trade with neighboring countries like South Korea that have a reputation for clean statistics. For example, a fall in Chinese imports of components used in the production of goods from South Korea—which is also a fall in South Korea's exports to China—is a good indication of a slump in Chinese manufacturing.

So how much did these independent estimates differ from the official statistics? They generally suggested a much sharper slowdown than was indicated by the numbers coming from the Chinese government. Was this discrepancy enough to justify big bets against China? At the time of writing, it's too early to know.

QUESTIONS FOR THOUGHT

1. Why would an economic downturn cause problems for Chinese companies that borrowed heavily?

2. How do the three statistics that Li Keqiang cited fit into the three different ways to calculate GDP?

3. What business problems might China's untrustworthy numbers create?

SUMMARY

1. Economists keep track of the flows of money between sectors with the **national income and product accounts,** or **national accounts.** Demand for goods and services comes from **consumer spending, investment spending,** and **government purchases of goods and services. Exports** generate an inflow of funds into the country from the rest of the world, but **imports** lead to an outflow of funds to the rest of the world.

2. **Gross domestic product,** or **GDP,** measures the value of all **final goods and services** produced in the economy. It does not include the value of **intermediate goods and services,** but it does include **net exports** $(X - IM)$. It can be calculated in three ways: add up the **value added** by all producers; add up all spending on domestically produced final goods and services, leading to the equation $GDP = C + I + G + X - IM,$ also known as **aggregate spending;** or add up all the income paid by domestic firms to factors of production. These three methods are equivalent because in the economy as a whole, total income paid by domestic firms to factors of production must equal total spending on domestically produced final goods and services.

3. **Real GDP** is the value of the final goods and services produced calculated using the prices of a selected base year. Except in the base year, real GDP is not the same as **nominal GDP,** the value of **aggregate output** calculated using current prices. Analysis of the growth rate of aggregate output must use real GDP because doing so eliminates any change in the value of aggregate output due solely to price changes. Real **GDP per capita** is a measure of average aggregate output per person but is not in itself an appropriate policy goal. U.S. statistics on real GDP are always expressed in **chained dollars.**

4. To measure the **aggregate price level,** economists calculate the cost of purchasing a **market basket.** A **price index** is the ratio of the current cost of that market basket to the cost in a selected base year, multiplied by 100.

5. The **inflation rate** is the yearly percent change in a price index, typically based on the **consumer price index,** or **CPI,** the most common measure of the aggregate price level. A similar index for goods and services purchased by firms is the **producer price index,** or **PPI.** Finally, economists also use the **GDP deflator,** which measures the price level by calculating the ratio of nominal GDP to real GDP times 100.

KEY TERMS

PROBLEMS

interactive activity

1. At right is a simplified circular-flow diagram for the economy of Micronia. (Note that there is no investment and no transfers in Micronia.)

a. What is the value of GDP in Micronia?

b. What is the value of net exports?

c. What is the value of disposable income?

d. Does the total flow of money out of households—the sum of taxes paid and consumer spending—equal the total flow of money into households?

e. How does the government of Micronia finance its purchases of goods and services?

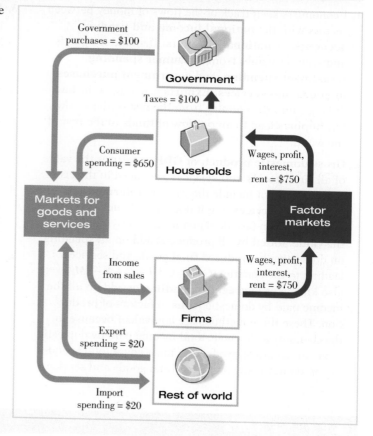

2. A more complex circular-flow diagram for the economy of Macronia is shown at right.

a. What is the value of GDP in Macronia?

b. What is the value of net exports?

c. What is the value of disposable income?

d. Does the total flow of money out of households—the sum of taxes paid, consumer spending, and private savings—equal the total flow of money into households?

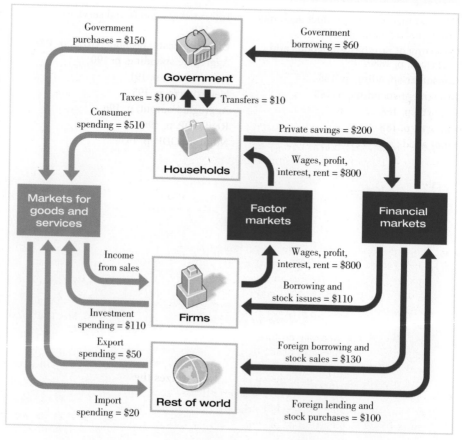

3. The components of GDP in the accompanying table were produced by the Bureau of Economic Analysis.

Category	Components of GDP in 2015 (billions of dollars)
Consumer spending	
Durable goods	$1,328.7
Nondurable goods	2,650.1
Services	8,293.1
Private investment spending	
Fixed investment spending	2,911.4
Nonresidential	2,301.9
Structures	497.2
Equipment and intellectual property products	1,804.7
Residential	609.5
Change in private inventories	109.2
Net exports	
Exports	2,253.4
Imports	2,782.3
Government purchases of goods and services and investment spending	
Federal	1,224.6
National defense	740.8
Nondefense	483.9
State and local	1,958.8

a. Calculate 2015 consumer spending.

b. Calculate 2015 private investment spending.

c. Calculate 2015 net exports.

d. Calculate 2015 government purchases of goods and services and government investment spending.

e. Calculate 2015 gross domestic product.

f. Calculate 2015 consumer spending on services as a percentage of total consumer spending.

g. Calculate 2015 exports as a percentage of imports.

h. Calculate 2015 government purchases on national defense as a percentage of federal government purchases of goods and services.

4. The small economy of Pizzania produces three goods (bread, cheese, and pizza), each produced by a separate company. The bread and cheese companies produce all the inputs they need to make bread and cheese, respectively. The pizza company uses the bread and cheese from the other companies to make its pizzas. All three companies employ labor to help produce their goods, and the difference between the value of goods sold and the sum of labor and input costs is the firm's profit. The accompanying table summarizes the activities of the three companies when all the bread and cheese produced are sold to the pizza company as inputs in the production of pizzas.

	Bread company	Cheese company	Pizza company
Cost of inputs	$0	$0	$50 (bread) 35 (cheese)
Wages	15	20	75
Value of output	50	35	200

a. Calculate GDP as the value added in production.

b. Calculate GDP as spending on final goods and services.

c. Calculate GDP as factor income.

5. In the economy of Pizzania (from Problem 4), bread and cheese produced are sold both to the pizza company for inputs in the production of pizzas and to consumers as final goods. The accompanying table summarizes the activities of the three companies.

	Bread company	Cheese company	Pizza company
Cost of inputs	$0	$0	$50 (bread) 35 (cheese)
Wages	25	30	75
Value of output	100	60	200

a. Calculate GDP as the value added in production.

b. Calculate GDP as spending on final goods and services.

c. Calculate GDP as factor income.

6. Which of the following transactions will be included in GDP for the United States?

a. Coca-Cola builds a new bottling plant in the United States.

b. Delta sells one of its existing airplanes to Korean Air.

c. Ms. Moneybags buys an existing share of Disney stock.

d. A California winery produces a bottle of Chardonnay and sells it to a customer in Montreal, Canada.

e. An American buys a bottle of French perfume in Tulsa.

f. A book publisher produces too many copies of a new book; the books don't sell this year, so the publisher adds the surplus books to inventories.

7. Access the Discovering Data exercise for Chapter 7 online to answer the following questions.

a. What was GDP for the United States last year?

b. Calculate the absolute change in U.S. GDP between last year and the year before.

c. Which component of GDP was the largest last year? Which was the smallest? What is the most recent year in which net exports were positive?

d. What happened to the size of government spending during the 1940s? What factors likely caused the shift?

e. How has each of the four components, as a percent of GDP, changed since the 1940s?

8. The accompanying table shows data on nominal GDP (in billions of dollars), real GDP (in billions of 2009 dollars), and population (in thousands) of the United States in 1965, 1975, 1985, 1995, 2005, and 2015. The U.S. price level rose consistently over the period 1965–2015.

Year	Nominal GDP (billions of dollars)	Real GDP (billions of 2009 dollars)	Population (thousands)
1965	$743.7	$3,976.7	194,250
1975	1,688.9	5,385.4	215,891
1985	4,346.7	7,593.8	238,416
1995	7,664.1	10,174.8	266,458
2005	13,093.7	14,234.2	296,115
2015	17,947.0	16,348.9	321,601

a. Why is real GDP greater than nominal GDP for all years until 2005 and lower for 2015?

b. Calculate the percent change in real GDP from 1965 to 1975, 1975 to 1985, 1985 to 1995, 1995 to 2005, and 2005 to 2015. Which period had the highest growth rate?

c. Calculate real GDP per capita for each of the years in the table.

d. Calculate the percent change in real GDP per capita from 1965 to 1975, 1975 to 1985, 1985 to 1995, 1995 to 2005, and 2005 to 2015. Which period had the highest growth rate?

e. How do the percent change in real GDP and the percent change in real GDP per capita compare? Which is larger? Do we expect them to have this relationship?

9. Eastland College is concerned about the rising price of textbooks that students must purchase. To better identify the increase in the price of textbooks, the dean asks you, the Economics Department's star student, to create an index of textbook prices. The average student purchases three English, two math, and four economics textbooks per year. The prices of these books are given in the accompanying table.

	2014	2015	2016
English textbook	$100	$110	$114
Math textbook	140	144	148
Economics textbook	160	180	200

a. What is the percent change in the price of an English textbook from 2014 to 2016?

b. What is the percent change in the price of a math textbook from 2014 to 2016?

c. What is the percent change in the price of an economics textbook from 2014 to 2016?

d. Using 2015 as a base year, create a price index for these books for all years.

e. What is the percent change in the price index from 2014 to 2016?

10. The consumer price index, or CPI, measures the cost of living for a typical urban household by multiplying the price for each category of expenditure (housing, food, and so on) times a measure of the importance of that expenditure in the average consumer's market basket and summing over all categories. However, using data from the consumer price index, we can see that changes in the cost of living for different types of consumers can vary a great deal. Let's compare the cost of living for a hypothetical retired person and a hypothetical college student. Let's assume that the market basket of a retired person is allocated in the following way: 10% on housing, 15% on food, 5% on transportation, 60% on medical care, 0% on education, and 10% on recreation. The college student's market basket is allocated as follows: 5% on housing, 15% on food, 20% on transportation, 0% on medical care, 40% on education, and 20% on recreation. The accompanying table shows the May 2016 CPI for each of the relevant categories.

	CPI May 2016
Housing	242.8
Food	248.0
Transportation	194.6
Medical care	460.5
Education	246.9
Recreation	117.2

Calculate the overall CPI for the retired person and for the college student by multiplying the CPI for each of the categories by the relative importance of that category to the individual and then summing each of the categories. The CPI for all items in May 2016 was 239.4. How do your calculations for a CPI for the retired person and the college student compare to the overall CPI?

11. Go to the Bureau of Labor Statistics home page at www.bls.gov. Place the cursor over the "Economic Releases" tab and then click on "Major Economic Indicators" in the drop-down menu that appears. Once on the "Major Economic Indicators" page, click on "Consumer Price Index." On that page, under "Table of Contents," click on "Table 1: Consumer Price Index for All Urban Consumers." Using the "unadjusted" figures, determine what the CPI was for the previous month. How did it change from the previous month? How does the CPI compare to the same month one year ago?

12. The accompanying table provides the annual real GDP (in billions of 2009 dollars) and nominal GDP (in billions of dollars) for the United States.

  a. Calculate the GDP deflator for each year.

  b. Use the GDP deflator to calculate the inflation rate for all years except 2009.

	2009	**2010**	**2011**	**2012**	**2013**	**2014**	**2015**
Real GDP (billions of 2009 dollars)	14,418.7	14,783.8	15,020.6	15,354.6	15,583.3	15,961.7	16,348.9
Nominal GDP (billions of dollars)	14,418.7	14,964.4	15,517.9	16,155.3	16,663.2	17,348.1	17,947.0

13. The accompanying table contains two price indexes for the years 2013, 2014, and 2015: the GDP deflator and the CPI. For each price index, calculate the inflation rate from 2013 to 2014 and from 2014 to 2015.

Year	GDP deflator	CPI
2013	106.929	232.964
2014	108.686	236.715
2015	109.775	236.995

14. The cost of a college education in the United States is rising at a rate faster than inflation. The following table shows the average cost of a college education in the United States during the academic year that began in 2014 and the academic year that began in 2015 for public and private colleges. Assume the costs listed in the table are the only costs experienced by the various college students in a single year.

  a. Calculate the cost of living for an average college student in each category for 2014 and 2015.

  b. Calculate an inflation rate for each type of college student between 2014 and 2015.

	Cost of college education during academic year beginning 2014 (averages in 2014 dollars)			
	Tuition and fees	**Room and board**	**Books and supplies**	**Other expenses**
Two-year public college: commuter	$3,161	$7,810	$1,378	$3,809
Four-year public college: in-state, on-campus	8,199	9,495	1,250	3,203
Four-year public college: out-of-state, on-campus	22,203	9,495	1,250	3,203
Four-year private college: on-campus	30,177	10,506	1,251	2,488
	Cost of college education during academic year beginning 2015 (averages in 2015 dollars)			
	Tuition and fees	**Room and board**	**Books and supplies**	**Other expenses**
Two-year public college: commuter	$3,270	$7,918	$1,422	$3,761
Four-year public college: in-state, on-campus	8,445	9,760	1,275	3,272
Four-year public college: out-of-state, on-campus	23,107	9,760	1,275	3,272
Four-year private college: on-campus	31,177	10,827	1,248	2,511

WORK IT OUT Interactive step-by-step help with solving this problem can be found online.

15. The economy of Britannica produces three goods: computers, pens, and pizza. The accompanying table shows the prices and output of the three goods for the years 2014, 2015, and 2016.

   a. What is the percent change in production of each of the goods from 2014 to 2015 and from 2015 to 2016?

   b. What is the percent change in prices of each of the goods from 2014 to 2015 and from 2015 to 2016?

   c. Calculate nominal GDP in Britannica for each of the three years. What is the percent change in nominal GDP from 2014 to 2015 and from 2015 to 2016?

   d. Calculate real GDP in Britannica using 2014 prices for each of the three years. What is the percent change in real GDP from 2014 to 2015 and from 2015 to 2016?

	Computers		Pens		Pizzas	
Year	Price	Quantity	Price	Quantity	Price	Quantity
2014	$900	10	$10	100	$15	2
2015	1,000	10.5	12	105	16	2
2016	1,050	12	14	110	17	3

8 | Unemployment and Inflation

LIFTOFF

THERE ARE MANY official committees with impressive-sounding names but little impact on world events. The Federal Open Market Committee (FOMC), most certainly, is not one of them. The FOMC is part of the Federal Reserve system, a semi-autonomous federal agency that is responsible for making and implementing U.S. monetary policy.

The chair of the Federal Reserve balances the goals of low unemployment and price stability when deciding whether to give the economy more gas or hit the brakes.

The FOMC may have a drab-sounding name, but the decisions it makes eight times a year are critical, not just for the U.S. economy, but for the global economy as well. The committee, a 12-member panel under the directorship of the chair of the Federal Reserve, meets every six weeks to decide key aspects of monetary policy; when it announces its decisions, global financial markets move, sometimes dramatically. And the FOMC meeting that took place on December 16 and 17 of 2015, with Janet Yellen (shown in the photo) as Fed chair, was among the most consequential in the Federal Reserve's history.

The most important decision the FOMC makes is setting the level of the *federal funds rate*, the key benchmark interest rate for the U.S. economy. The critical importance of the federal funds rate was illustrated in 2008, when a financial crisis sent the U.S. economy into free fall. In the eye of the storm, the FOMC took the extraordinary step of cutting the federal funds rate to zero in order to stabilize financial markets and the economy. This dramatic action helped prevent the crisis from turning into a full replay of the Great Depression. Moreover, the FOMC made it clear to all observers that it would provide economic life support as long as it was needed. In fact, although the Great Recession, precipitated by the financial crisis, finally ended in 2009, the FOMC kept the federal funds rate at zero for another six years. So when the FOMC finally raised the federal funds rate to 0.5% at that December 2015 meeting, it was a clear signal that the Federal Reserve thought the U.S. economy was finally on the mend.

After seven long years, what new evidence convinced the FOMC that it was time for a rate increase? The answer mainly came down to two numbers: the unemployment rate and the inflation rate. Unemployment had surged during the Great Recession, peaking at 10% in October 2009. By late 2015 the rate was down to a historically low 5%. In addition, the FOMC believed that inflation, while still low by historical standards, was on the rise. These two pieces of evidence convinced the FOMC that it was time to "move off of zero." And, as we'll explain shortly, while having a zero federal funds rate was undoubtedly critical for the economy's recovery, having a zero federal funds rate for too long inflicts damage on the economy.

As the FOMC knows, high unemployment and high inflation are the two great evils of macroeconomics: high unemployment incurs human and economic waste because willing workers can't find jobs. High inflation undermines the monetary system through rapidly rising prices. So the two principal goals of macroeconomic policy are low unemployment and price stability, usually defined as a low but positive rate of inflation. Sometimes these twin goals can be in conflict: at those times, macroeconomic policy makers must make a trade-off based on judgment and guesswork. At other times, such as during the extraordinary events of 2008, they aren't in conflict, and the making of macroeconomic policy is more straightforward.

In this chapter, we'll explore the dynamics of unemployment and inflation in the economy. We'll learn how they are measured and why accurate measurement is a critical function of government. From there we will go on to understand why low unemployment and price stability are the main goals of macroeconomic policy. Yet, as we just noted, sometimes those goals are in conflict; at other times they are not. It is the ability to cope with the dramatic shifts in the U.S. macroeconomy that makes the FOMC one of the most important committees in the world. ●

WHAT YOU WILL LEARN

- How is **unemployment** measured and how is the **unemployment rate** calculated?
- What is the significance of the unemployment rate for the economy?
- What is the relationship between the unemployment rate and economic growth?
- What factors determine the **natural rate of unemployment**?
- What are the economic costs of inflation?
- How do inflation and deflation create winners and losers?
- Why do policy makers try to maintain a stable rate of inflation?

Employment is the number of people currently employed in the economy, either full time or part time.

Unemployment is the number of people who are actively looking for work but aren't currently employed.

The **labor force** is equal to the sum of employment and unemployment.

The **labor force participation rate** is the percentage of the population aged 16 or older that is in the labor force.

The Unemployment Rate

Figure 8-1 shows the U.S. unemployment rate from 1948 to 2017; as you can see, unemployment soared during the Great Recession of 2007–2009 and fell only gradually in the years that followed. What did the elevated unemployment rate mean, and why was it such a big factor in people's lives? To understand why policy makers pay so much attention to employment and unemployment, we need to understand how they are both defined and measured.

Defining and Measuring Unemployment

It's easy to define employment: you're employed if and only if you have a job. **Employment** is the total number of people currently employed, either full time or part time.

Unemployment, however, is a more subtle concept. Just because a person isn't working doesn't mean that we consider that person unemployed. For example, as of April 2017, there were 44.8 million retired workers in the United States receiving Social Security checks. Most of them were probably happy that they were no longer working, so we wouldn't consider someone who has settled into a comfortable, well-earned retirement to be unemployed. There were also 14 million disabled U.S. workers receiving benefits because they were unable to work. Again, although they weren't working, we wouldn't normally consider them to be unemployed.

The U.S. Census Bureau, the federal agency tasked with collecting data on unemployment, considers the unemployed to be those who are "jobless, looking for jobs, and available for work." Retired people don't count because they aren't looking for jobs; the disabled don't count because they aren't available for work. More specifically, an individual is considered unemployed if he or she doesn't currently have a job and has been actively seeking a job during the past four weeks. So **unemployment** is defined as the total number of people who are actively looking for work but aren't currently employed.

A country's **labor force** is the sum of employment and unemployment—that is, of people who are currently working and people who are currently looking for work, respectively. The **labor force participation rate**, defined as the percentage of the working-age population that is in the labor force, is calculated as follows:

$$\textbf{(8-1)} \quad \text{Labor force participation rate} = \frac{\text{Labor force}}{\text{Population age 16 and older}} \times 100$$

FIGURE 8-1 The U.S. Unemployment Rate, 1948–2017

The unemployment rate has fluctuated widely over time. It always rises during recessions, which are shown by the shaded bars. It usually, but not always, falls during periods of economic expansion.

Data from: Bureau of Labor Statistics; National Bureau of Economic Research.

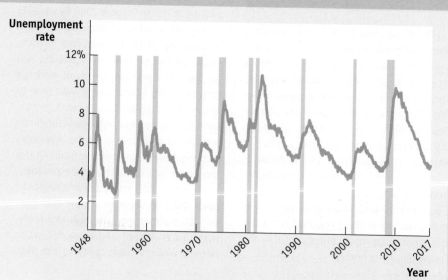

The **unemployment rate,** defined as the percentage of the total number of people in the labor force who are unemployed, is calculated as follows:

$$(8\text{-}2) \quad \text{Unemployment rate} = \frac{\text{Number of unemployed workers}}{\text{Labor force}} \times 100$$

To estimate the numbers that go into calculating the unemployment rate, the U.S. Census Bureau carries out a monthly survey called the Current Population Survey, which involves interviewing a random sample of approximately 60,000 American families. People are asked whether they are currently employed. If they are not employed, they are asked whether they have been looking for a job during the past four weeks. The results are then scaled up, using estimates of the total population, to estimate the total number of employed and unemployed Americans.

The Significance of the Unemployment Rate

In general, the unemployment rate is a good indicator of how easy or difficult it is to find a job given the current state of the economy. When the unemployment rate is low, nearly everyone who wants a job can find one. In 2000, when the unemployment rate averaged just 4%, jobs were so abundant that employers spoke of a "mirror test" for getting a job: if you were breathing (therefore your breath would fog a mirror), you could find work. By contrast, in 2010, with the unemployment rate above 9% all year, it was very hard to find work. In fact, there were almost five times as many Americans seeking work as there were job openings.

Although the unemployment rate is a good indicator of current labor market conditions, it's not a literal measure of the percentage of people who want a job but can't find one. That's because in some ways the unemployment rate exaggerates the difficulty people have in finding jobs. But in other ways, the opposite is true—a low unemployment rate can conceal deep frustration over the lack of job opportunities.

How the Unemployment Rate Can Overstate the True Level of Unemployment If you are searching for work, it's normal to take at least a few weeks to find a suitable job. Yet a worker who is quite confident of finding a job, but has not yet accepted a position, is counted as unemployed. As a consequence, the unemployment rate never falls to zero, even in boom times when jobs are plentiful. Even in the buoyant labor market of 2000, when it was easy to find work, the unemployment rate was still 4%. Later in this chapter, we'll discuss in greater depth the reasons that measured unemployment persists even when jobs are abundant.

How the Unemployment Rate Can Understate the True Level of Unemployment Frequently, people who would like to work but aren't working still don't get counted as unemployed. In particular, an individual who has given up looking for a job for the time being because there are no jobs available—say, a laid-off steelworker in a deeply depressed steel town—isn't counted as unemployed because he or she has not been searching for a job during the previous four weeks. Individuals who want to work but have told government researchers that they aren't currently searching because they see little prospect of finding a job given the state of the job market are called **discouraged workers.** Because it does not count discouraged workers, the measured unemployment rate may understate the percentage of people who want to work but are unable to find jobs.

Discouraged workers are part of a larger group—**marginally attached workers.** These are people who say they would like to have a job and have looked for work in the recent past but are not currently looking for work. They are also not included when calculating the unemployment rate. Finally, another category of workers who are frustrated in their ability to find work but aren't counted as unemployed are the **underemployed:** workers who would like to find full-time jobs but are currently working part time "for economic reasons"—that is, they can't find a full-time job. Again, they aren't counted in the unemployment rate.

The **unemployment rate** is the percentage of the total number of people in the labor force who are unemployed.

Discouraged workers are nonworking people who are capable of working but have given up looking for a job given the state of the job market.

Marginally attached workers would like to be employed and have looked for a job in the recent past but are not currently looking for work.

Underemployment is the number of people who work part time because they cannot find full-time jobs.

FIGURE 8-2 Alternative Measures of Unemployment, 1994–2017

The unemployment number usually quoted in the news media counts someone as unemployed only if he or she has been looking for work during the past four weeks. Broader measures also count discouraged workers, marginally attached workers, and the underemployed. These broader measures show a higher unemployment rate, but they move closely in parallel with the standard rate.

Data from: Bureau of Labor Statistics.

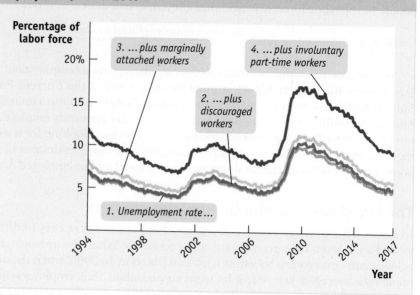

The *Bureau of Labor Statistics* is the federal agency that calculates the official unemployment rate. It also calculates broader "measures of labor underutilization" that include the three categories of frustrated workers. Figure 8-2 shows what happens to the measured unemployment rate once discouraged workers, other marginally attached workers, and the underemployed are counted. The broadest measure of unemployment and underemployment, known as *U-6*, is the sum of these three measures plus the unemployed. It is substantially higher than the rate usually quoted by the news media. But U-6 and the unemployment rate move very much in parallel, so changes in the unemployment rate remain a good guide to what's happening in the overall labor market, including frustrated workers.

Finally, it's important to realize that the unemployment rate varies greatly among demographic groups. Other things equal, jobs are generally easier to find for more experienced workers and for workers during their prime working years, that is, from ages 25 to 54. For younger workers, as well as workers nearing retirement age, jobs are typically harder to find, other things equal.

Figure 8-3 shows unemployment rates for different groups in 2007, when the overall unemployment rate was low by historical standards, in 2010, when the

FIGURE 8-3 Unemployment Rates of Different Groups in 2007, 2010, and 2017

Unemployment rates vary greatly among different demographic groups. For example, although the overall unemployment rate in May 2017 was 4.3%, the unemployment rate among African-American teenagers was 27.3%. As a result, even during periods of low overall unemployment, unemployment remains a serious problem for some groups.

Data from: Bureau of Labor Statistics.

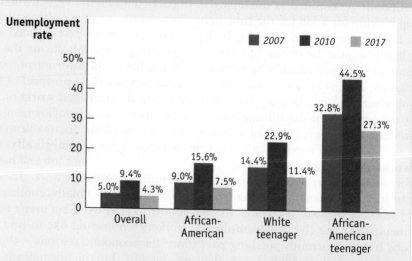

rate was high in the aftermath of the Great Recession, and in May 2017, when it had come down to pre-crisis levels. As you can see, the unemployment rate for African-American workers is consistently much higher than the national average; the unemployment rate for White teenagers (ages 16–19) is normally even higher; and the unemployment rate for African-American teenagers is higher still. (Bear in mind that a teenager isn't considered unemployed, even if he or she isn't working, unless that teenager is looking for work but can't find it.) So even at times when the overall unemployment rate is relatively low, jobs are hard to find for some groups.

So you should interpret the unemployment rate as an indicator of overall labor market conditions, not as an exact, literal measure of the percentage of people unable to find jobs. The unemployment rate is, however, a very good indicator: its ups and downs closely reflect economic changes that have a significant impact on people's lives. Let's turn now to the causes of these fluctuations.

Growth and Unemployment

Compared to Figure 8-1, Figure 8-4 shows the U.S. unemployment rate over a somewhat shorter period, from 1979 through 2017. The shaded bars represent periods of recession. As you can see, during every recession, without exception, the unemployment rate rose. The severe recession of 2007–2009, like the earlier one of 1981–1982, led to a huge rise in unemployment.

Correspondingly, during periods of economic expansion the unemployment rate usually falls. The long economic expansion of the 1990s eventually brought the unemployment rate to 4.0%, and the recovery from the Great Recession eventually brought unemployment down to under 5.0%. However, it's important to recognize that *economic expansions aren't always periods of falling unemployment.* Look at the periods immediately following the recessions of 1990–1991 and 2001 in Figure 8-4. In each case the unemployment rate continued to rise for more than a year after the recession was officially over. The explanation in both cases is that although the economy was growing, it was not growing fast enough to reduce the unemployment rate.

Figure 8-5 is a scatter diagram showing U.S. data for the period from 1949 to 2016. The horizontal axis measures the annual rate of growth in real GDP—the percent by which each year's real GDP changed compared to the previous year's real GDP. (Notice that there were ten years in which growth was negative—that is,

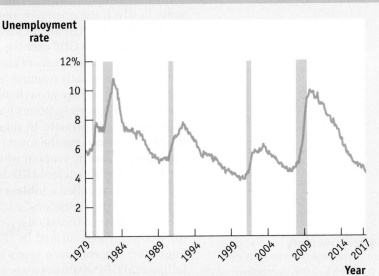

FIGURE 8-4 Unemployment and Recessions, 1979–2017

This figure shows a close-up of the unemployment rate for the past three decades, with the shaded bars indicating recessions. It's clear that unemployment always rises during recessions and *usually* falls during expansions. But in both the early 1990s and the early 2000s, unemployment continued to rise for some time after the recession was officially declared over.

Data from: Bureau of Labor Statistics; National Bureau of Economic Research.

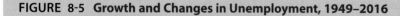

FIGURE 8-5 Growth and Changes in Unemployment, 1949–2016

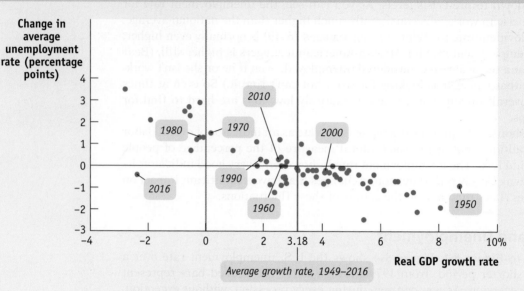

Each dot shows the growth rate of the economy and the change in the unemployment rate for a specific year between 1949 and 2016. For example, in 2000 the economy grew 4.1% and the unemployment rate fell 0.2 percentage points, from 4.2% to 4.0%.

In general, the unemployment rate fell when growth was above its average rate of 3.18% a year and rose when growth was below average. Unemployment always rose when real GDP fell.

Data from: Bureau of Labor Statistics; Bureau of Economic Analysis.

real GDP shrank.) The vertical axis measures the *change* in the average unemployment rate over the previous year in percentage points—last year's unemployment rate minus this year's unemployment rate. Each dot represents the observed growth rate of real GDP and change in the unemployment rate for a given year. For example, in 2000 the average unemployment rate fell to 4.0% from 4.2% in 1999; this is shown as a value of −0.2 along the vertical axis for the year 2000. Over the same period, real GDP grew by 4.1%; this is the value shown along the horizontal axis for the year 2000.

The downward trend of the scatter diagram in Figure 8-5 shows that there is a generally strong negative relationship between growth in the economy and the rate of unemployment. Years of high growth in real GDP were also years in which the unemployment rate fell, and years of low or negative growth in real GDP were years in which the unemployment rate rose.

The green vertical line in Figure 8-5 at the value of 3.18% indicates the average growth rate of real GDP over the period from 1949 to 2016. Points lying to the right of the vertical line are years of above-average growth. In these years, the value on the vertical axis is usually negative, meaning that the unemployment rate fell. That is, years of above-average growth were usually years in which the unemployment rate was falling. Conversely, points lying to the left of the green vertical line were years of below-average growth. In these years, the value on the vertical axis is usually positive, meaning that the unemployment rate rose. That is, years of below-average growth were usually years in which the unemployment rate was rising.

A period in which real GDP is growing at a below-average rate and unemployment is rising is called a **jobless recovery** or a *growth recession*. Since 1990, there have been three recessions, each of which was followed by a period of jobless recovery. But true recessions, periods when real GDP falls, are especially painful for workers. As illustrated by the points to the left of the purple vertical line in Figure 8-5 (representing years in which the real GDP growth rate is negative), falling real GDP is always associated with a rising rate of unemployment, causing a great deal of hardship for families.

A **jobless recovery** is a period in which the real GDP growth rate is positive but the unemployment rate is still rising.

ECONOMICS >> *in Action*

Failure to Launch

In March 2010, when the U.S. job situation was near its worst, the *Harvard Law Record* published a brief note titled "Unemployed law student will work for $160K plus benefits." In a self-mocking tone, the author admitted to having graduated from Harvard Law School the previous year but not landing a job offer. "What mark on our résumé is so bad that it outweighs the crimson H?" the note asked.

The answer, of course, is that it wasn't about the résumé—it was about the economy. Times of high unemployment are especially hard on new graduates, who often find it hard to get any kind of full-time job.

How bad was it around the time that note was written? Figure 8-6 shows the unemployment rate by gender, for college graduates aged 20 to 24, from 2000 to 2017. The negative impact of the Great Recession was much worse than that of the previous slump shown, the recession of 2000–2001. The downturn slammed the construction and manufacturing sectors especially hard, sending the unemployment rate for men into the double digits. The public and service sectors, where women are disproportionately employed, fared somewhat better. But women still saw their unemployment rate rise to over 8%. The effects of the Great Recession were prolonged, with unemployment still well above pre-crisis levels in 2015, seven years after the recession began.

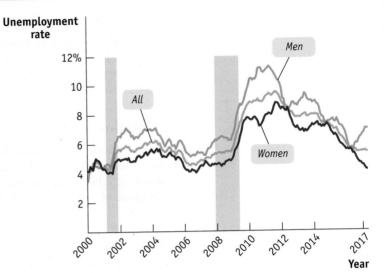

FIGURE 8-6 Unemployment Rate for College Graduates Ages 20–24, 2000–2017

Data from: Bureau of Labor Statistics.

>> Check Your Understanding 8-1

Solutions appear at back of book.

1. Suppose employment websites develop new software that enables job-seekers to find suitable jobs more quickly and employers to better screen potential employees. What effect will this have on the unemployment rate over time? Also suppose that these websites encourage job-seekers who had given up their searches to begin looking again. What effect will this have on the unemployment rate?

2. In which of the following cases is a worker counted as unemployed? Explain.
   a. Rosa, an older worker who has been laid off and who gave up looking for work months ago
   b. Anthony, a schoolteacher who is not working during his three-month summer break
   c. Kanako, an investment banker who has been laid off and is currently searching for another position
   d. Sergio, a classically trained musician who can only find work playing for local parties
   e. Natasha, a graduate student who went back to school because jobs were scarce

3. Which of the following are consistent with the observed relationship between growth in real GDP and changes in the unemployment rate as shown in Figure 8-5? Which are not?
   a. A rise in the unemployment rate accompanies a fall in real GDP.
   b. An exceptionally strong business recovery is associated with a greater percentage of the labor force being employed.
   c. Negative real GDP growth is associated with a fall in the unemployment rate.

>> Quick Review

• The **labor force,** equal to **employment** plus **unemployment,** does not include discouraged workers. Nor do labor statistics contain data on **underemployment.** The **labor force participation rate** is the percentage of the population age 16 and over in the labor force.

• The **unemployment rate** is an indicator of the state of the labor market, not an exact measure of the percentage of workers who can't find jobs. It can overstate the true level of unemployment because workers often spend time searching for a job even when jobs are plentiful. But it can also understate the true level of unemployment because it excludes **discouraged workers, marginally attached workers,** and **underemployed** workers.

• There is a strong negative relationship between growth in real GDP and changes in the unemployment rate. When growth is above average, the unemployment rate generally falls. When growth is below average, the unemployment rate generally rises—a period called a **jobless recovery** that typically follows a deep recession.

The Natural Rate of Unemployment

Fast economic growth tends to reduce the unemployment rate. So how low can the unemployment rate go? You might be tempted to say zero, but that isn't feasible. Over the past half-century, the national unemployment rate has never dropped below 2.9%.

How can there be so much unemployment even when many businesses are having a hard time finding workers? To answer this question, we need to examine the nature of labor markets and why they normally lead to substantial measured unemployment even when jobs are plentiful. Our starting point is the observation that even in the best of times, jobs are constantly being created and destroyed.

Job Creation and Job Destruction

Even during good times, most Americans know someone who has lost his or her job. In January 2017, the U.S. unemployment rate was only 4.8%, relatively low by historical standards. Yet in that month there were 5.2 million *job separations*—terminations of employment that occur because a worker is either fired or quits voluntarily.

There are many reasons for such job loss. One is structural change in the economy: industries rise and fall as new technologies emerge and consumers' tastes change. For example, employment in coal mining has declined to a small fraction of its one-time high due to both automation and a switch to other sources of energy. However, structural change also brings the creation of new jobs: employment in solar power surged after 2010 as a combination of rapidly improving technology and tax incentives led to a rapid growth in the use of solar panels. Poor management performance or bad luck at individual companies also leads to job loss for employees. For example, in early 2017, Macy's announced the closure of 68 stores and the layoff of 10,000 workers. Sears announced the closure of 150 stores. Meanwhile, online retailers like Amazon continued to expand.

Continual job creation and destruction are features of modern economies, making a naturally occurring amount of unemployment inevitable. Within this naturally occurring amount, there are two types of unemployment—*frictional* and *structural*.

"At this point, I'm just happy to still have a job"

Frictional Unemployment

When a worker loses a job involuntarily due to job destruction, he or she often doesn't take the first new job offered. For example, suppose a skilled programmer, laid off because her software company's product line was unsuccessful, sees an online job posting for a receptionist. She might apply and get the job—but that would be foolish. Instead, she should take the time to look for a job that takes advantage of her skills and pays accordingly. In addition, individual workers are constantly leaving jobs voluntarily, typically for personal reasons—family moves, dissatisfaction, and better job prospects elsewhere.

Economists say that workers who spend time looking for employment are engaged in **job search.** If all workers and all jobs were alike, job search wouldn't be necessary; if information about jobs and workers was perfect, job search would be very quick. In practice, however, it's normal for a worker who loses a job, or a young worker seeking a first job, to spend at least a few weeks searching.

Frictional unemployment is unemployment due to the time workers spend in job search. A certain amount of frictional unemployment is inevitable due to the constant process of economic change. As we just mentioned, during the low-unemployment month of January 2017 there were nonetheless more than

Workers who spend time looking for employment are engaged in job search.

Frictional unemployment is unemployment due to the time workers spend in job search.

FIGURE 8-7   Labor Market Flows in January 2017

Even in January 2017, a low-unemployment month, large numbers of workers moved into and out of both employment and unemployment.

Data from: Bureau of Labor Statistics.

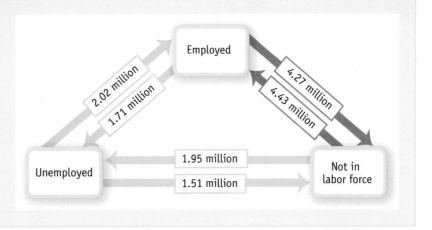

5.2 million job separations, in which workers left or lost their jobs. Total employment grew because these separations were more than offset by almost 5.4 million hires. Inevitably, some of the workers who left or lost their jobs spent at least some time unemployed, as did some of the workers newly entering the labor force.

Figure 8-7 shows the average monthly flows of workers among three states: employed, unemployed, and not in the labor force during January 2017. What the figure suggests is how much churning is constantly taking place in the labor market. An inevitable consequence of that churning is a significant number of workers who haven't yet found their next job—that is, frictional unemployment.

A limited amount of frictional unemployment is relatively harmless and may even be a good thing. The economy is more productive if workers take the time to find jobs that are well matched to their skills, and workers who are unemployed for a brief period while searching for the right job don't experience great hardship. In fact, when there is a low unemployment rate, periods of unemployment tend to be quite short, suggesting that much of the unemployment is frictional.

Figure 8-8 shows the composition of unemployment in May 2017. Nearly 31% of the unemployed had been unemployed for less than 5 weeks, and only 41% had been unemployed for 15 or more weeks. Only about one in four unemployed workers were considered to be *long-term unemployed*—those unemployed for 27 or more weeks.

In periods of higher unemployment, however, workers tend to be jobless for longer periods of time, suggesting that a smaller share of unemployment is frictional. Figure 8-9 shows the fraction of the unemployed who had been out of work for six months or more from 2007 to 2017. It jumped to 45% after the Great Recession, but came gradually down as the economy recovered.

FIGURE 8-8   Distribution of the Unemployed by Duration of Unemployment, May 2017

When the unemployment rate is low, most unemployed workers are unemployed for only a short period. In May 2017, 31% of the unemployed had been unemployed for less than 5 weeks and 59% for less than 15 weeks. The short duration of unemployment for most workers suggests that much of the unemployment was frictional.

Data from: Bureau of Labor Statistics.

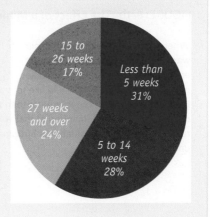

Structural Unemployment

Frictional unemployment exists even when the number of people seeking jobs is equal to the number of jobs being offered—that is, the existence of frictional unemployment doesn't mean that there is a surplus of labor. Sometimes, however,

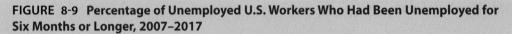

Before the Great Recession, relatively few U.S. workers had been unemployed for long periods. However, the percentage of long-term unemployed shot up after 2007, and came down only gradually.

Data from: Bureau of Labor Statistics.

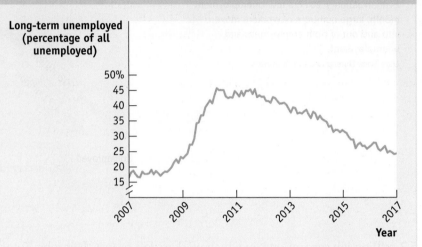

there is a *persistent surplus* of job-seekers in a particular labor market, even when the economy is at the peak of the business cycle. There may be more workers with a particular skill than there are jobs available using that skill, or there may be more workers in a particular geographic region than there are jobs available in that region. **Structural unemployment** is unemployment that results when there are more people seeking jobs in a particular labor market than there are jobs available at the current wage rate.

The supply and demand model tells us that the price of a good, service, or factor of production tends to move toward an equilibrium level that matches the quantity supplied with the quantity demanded. This is equally true, in general, of labor markets.

Figure 8-10 shows a typical market for labor. The labor demand curve indicates that when the price of labor—the wage rate—increases, employers demand less labor. The labor supply curve indicates that when the price of labor increases,

In **structural unemployment,** more people are seeking jobs in a particular labor market than there are jobs available at the current wage rate, even when the economy is at the peak of the business cycle.

FIGURE 8-10 The Effect of a Minimum Wage on a Labor Market

When the government sets a minimum wage, W_F, that exceeds the market equilibrium wage rate in that market, W_E, the number of workers who would like to work at that minimum wage, Q_S, is greater than the number of workers demanded at that wage rate, Q_D. This surplus of labor is structural unemployment.

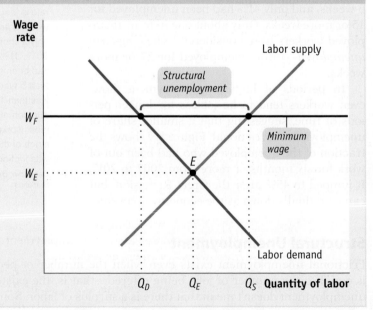

more workers are willing to supply labor at the prevailing wage rate. These two forces coincide to lead to an equilibrium wage rate for any given type of labor in a particular location. That equilibrium wage rate is shown as W_E.

Even at the equilibrium wage rate W_E, there will still be some frictional unemployment. That's because there will always be some workers engaged in job search even when the number of jobs available is equal to the number of workers seeking jobs. But there wouldn't be any structural unemployment in this labor market. *Structural unemployment occurs when the wage rate is, for some reason, persistently above W_E.* Several factors can lead to a wage rate in excess of W_E, the most important being minimum wages, labor unions, *efficiency wages,* the side effects of government policies, and mismatches between employees and employers.

Minimum Wages A minimum wage is a government-mandated floor on the price of labor. In the United States, the national minimum wage in early 2017 was $7.25 an hour. A number of state and local governments also determine the minimum wage within their jurisdictions, typically for the purpose of setting it higher than the federal level. For example, the city of Seattle has set a minimum wage at $15 an hour. For many American workers, the minimum wage is irrelevant; the market equilibrium wage for these workers is well above the national price floor. But for less skilled workers, the minimum wage may be binding—it affects the wages that people are actually paid and can lead to structural unemployment in particular markets for labor. Other wealthy countries have higher minimum wages; for example, in 2017 the French minimum wage was 9.76 euros an hour, or around $10.58. In these countries, there are more workers for whom the minimum wage is binding.

California's minimum wage will be raised incrementally to $15 by 2022.

Figure 8-10 shows the effect of a binding minimum wage. In this market, there is a legal floor on wages, W_F, which is above the equilibrium wage rate, W_E. This leads to a persistent surplus in the labor market: the quantity of labor supplied, Q_S, is larger than the quantity demanded, Q_D. In other words, more people want to work than can find jobs at the minimum wage, leading to structural unemployment.

Given that minimum wages—that is, binding minimum wages—generally lead to structural unemployment, you might wonder why governments impose them. The rationale is to help ensure that people who work can earn enough income to afford at least a minimally comfortable lifestyle. However, this may come at a cost, because it may eliminate the opportunity to work for some workers who would have willingly worked for lower wages. As illustrated in Figure 8-10, not only are there more sellers of labor than there are buyers, but there are also fewer people working at a minimum wage (Q_D) than there would have been with no minimum wage at all (Q_E).

Although economists broadly agree that a high minimum wage has the employment-reducing effects shown in Figure 8-10, there is widespread although not universal agreement that this isn't a good description of how the U.S. minimum wage actually works. The minimum wage in the United States is quite low compared with that in other wealthy countries, and as already noted, it isn't binding for the vast majority of workers.

In addition, researchers have produced evidence suggesting that minimum wage increases don't seem to be associated with employment declines and may actually lead to higher employment when, as was the case in the United States at one time, the minimum wage is low compared to average wages. They argue that firms employing a large percentage of workers in a particular market can keep wages low by restricting their hiring. Under these conditions, a moderate rise in the minimum wage will not lead to a loss of jobs. Most economists, however, agree that a sufficiently high minimum wage *does* lead to structural unemployment.

Labor Unions The actions of *labor unions* can have effects similar to those of minimum wages, leading to structural unemployment. By bargaining collectively for all of a firm's workers, unions can often win higher wages from employers than workers would have obtained by bargaining individually. This process, known as *collective bargaining*, is intended to tip the scales of bargaining power more toward workers and away from employers. Labor unions exercise bargaining power by threatening firms with a *labor strike*, a collective refusal to work. The threat of a strike can have serious consequences for firms. In such cases, workers acting collectively can exercise more power than they could if acting individually.

Employers have acted to counter the bargaining power of unions by threatening and enforcing *lockouts*—periods in which union workers are locked out and rendered unemployed—while hiring replacement workers.

When workers have increased bargaining power, they tend to demand and receive higher wages. Unions also bargain over benefits, such as health care and pensions, which we can think of as additional wages. Indeed, economists who study the effects of unions on wages find that unionized workers earn higher wages and more generous benefits than non-union workers with similar skills. The result of these increased wages can be the same as the result of a minimum wage: labor unions push the wage that workers receive above the equilibrium wage. Like a binding minimum wage, this leads to structural unemployment. In the United States, however, due to a low level of unionization, the amount of unemployment generated by union demands is likely to be very small. And in countries such as Germany and Japan, unions and management collaborate on devising more efficient work practices that support higher equilibrium wages.

Efficiency Wages Actions by firms can contribute to structural unemployment. Firms may choose to pay **efficiency wages**—wages that employers set above the equilibrium wage rate as an incentive for their workers to perform better.

Employers may feel the need for such incentives for several reasons. For example, employers often have difficulty observing directly how hard an employee works. They can, however, elicit more work effort by paying above-market wages: employees receiving these higher wages are more likely to work harder to ensure that they aren't fired, which would cause them to lose their higher wages.

When many firms pay efficiency wages, the result is a pool of workers who want jobs but can't find them. So the use of efficiency wages by firms leads to structural unemployment.

Side Effects of Government Policies In addition, government policies designed to help workers who lose their jobs can lead to structural unemployment as an unintended side effect. Most economically advanced countries provide benefits to laid-off workers as a way to tide them over until they find a new job. In the United States, these benefits typically replace only about 45% of a worker's income and expire after 26 weeks. (Benefits were extended in some cases to 99 weeks during the period of high unemployment in 2009–2011). In other countries, particularly in Europe, benefits are more generous and last longer. The drawback to this generosity is that it reduces a worker's incentive to quickly find a new job. During the 1980s, it was often argued that unemployment benefits in some European countries were one of the causes of *Eurosclerosis*, persistently high unemployment that afflicted a number of European economies.

Mismatches Between Employees and Employers It takes time for workers and firms to adjust to shifts in the economy. The result can be a mismatch between what employees have to offer and what employers are looking for. A skills mismatch is one form; for example, in the aftermath of the housing bust

Efficiency wages are wages that employers set above the equilibrium wage rate as an incentive for better employee performance.

of 2009, there were more construction workers looking for jobs than were available. Another form is geographic, as in Michigan, which has had a long-standing surplus of workers after its auto industry declined. Until the mismatch is resolved through a big enough fall in wages of the surplus workers that induces retraining or relocation, there will be structural unemployment.

The Natural Rate of Unemployment

Because some frictional unemployment is inevitable and because many economies also suffer from structural unemployment, a certain amount of unemployment is normal, or "natural." Actual unemployment fluctuates around this normal level. The **natural rate of unemployment** is the normal unemployment rate around which the actual unemployment rate fluctuates. It is the rate of unemployment that arises from the effects of frictional plus structural unemployment.

Cyclical unemployment is the deviation of the actual rate of unemployment from the natural rate; that is, it is the difference between the actual and natural rates of unemployment. As the name suggests, cyclical unemployment is the share of unemployment that arises from the downturns of the business cycle.

We'll see in Chapter 16 that an economy's natural rate of unemployment is a critical policy variable because a government cannot keep the unemployment rate persistently below the natural rate without leading to accelerating inflation.

We can summarize the relationships between the various types of unemployment as follows:

(8-3) Natural unemployment =
Frictional unemployment + Structural unemployment

(8-4) Actual unemployment =
Natural unemployment + Cyclical unemployment

Perhaps because of its name, people often imagine that the natural rate of unemployment is a constant that doesn't change over time and can't be affected by government policy. Neither proposition is true. Let's take a moment to stress two facts:

1. The natural rate of unemployment changes over time.
2. It can be affected by government policies.

Changes in the Natural Rate of Unemployment

Private-sector economists and government agencies need estimates of the natural rate of unemployment both to make forecasts and to conduct policy analyses. Almost all these estimates show that the U.S. natural rate rises and falls over time. For example, the Congressional Budget Office, the independent agency that conducts budget and economic analyses for Congress, believes that the U.S. natural rate of unemployment was 5.3% in 1950, rose to 6.3% by the end of the 1970s, but fell to 5% by 2017. European countries have experienced even larger swings in their natural rates of unemployment.

What causes the natural rate of unemployment to change? The most important factors are changes in labor force characteristics, changes in labor market institutions, and changes in government policies. Let's look briefly at each factor.

Changes in Labor Force Characteristics In May 2017 the rate of unemployment in the United States was 4.3%. Young workers, however, had much higher unemployment rates: 14.3% for teenagers and 6.7% for workers aged 20 to 24. Workers aged 25 to 54 had an unemployment rate of only 3.8%.

The **natural rate of unemployment** is the unemployment rate that arises from the effects of frictional plus structural unemployment.

Cyclical unemployment is the deviation of the actual rate of unemployment from the natural rate due to downturns in the business cycle.

In general, unemployment rates tend to be lower for experienced than for inexperienced workers. Because experienced workers tend to stay in a given job longer than do inexperienced ones, they have lower frictional unemployment. Also, because older workers are more likely than young workers to be family breadwinners, they have a stronger incentive to find and keep jobs.

One reason the natural rate of unemployment rose during the 1970s was a large rise in the number of new workers—children of the post–World War II baby boom entered the labor force, as well as a rising percentage of women. As Figure 8-11 shows, both the percentage of the labor force less than 25 years old and the percentage of women in the labor force grew rapidly in the 1970s. By the end of the 1990s, however, the share of women in the labor force had leveled off, and the percentage of workers under 25 had fallen sharply. As a result, the labor force as a whole is more experienced today than it was in the 1970s, one likely reason that the natural rate of unemployment is lower today than in the 1970s.

Changes in Labor Market Institutions As we pointed out earlier, unions that negotiate wages above the equilibrium level can be a source of structural unemployment. Some economists believe that the high natural rate of unemployment in Europe is caused, in part, by strong labor unions. In the United States, a sharp fall in union membership after 1980 may have been one reason the natural rate of unemployment fell between the 1970s and the 1990s.

Other institutional changes may also be at work. For example, some labor economists believe that temporary employment agencies have reduced frictional unemployment by helping match workers to jobs. Likewise, the proliferation of companies like TaskRabbit may have reduced frictional unemployment by operating as an online marketplace matching freelance workers with temporary jobs (as explained in this chapter's Business Case).

Technological change, coupled with labor market institutions, can also affect the natural rate of unemployment. Technological change tends to increase the demand for skilled workers who are familiar with the relevant technology and reduce the demand for unskilled workers. Economic theory predicts that wages should increase for skilled workers and decrease for unskilled workers as technology advances. But if wages for unskilled workers cannot go down—say, due to a binding minimum wage—increased structural unemployment, and therefore a higher natural rate of unemployment, will result during periods of faster technological change.

Changes in Government Policies A high minimum wage can cause structural unemployment. Generous unemployment benefits can increase both structural

---

FIGURE 8-11 The Changing Makeup of the U.S. Labor Force, 1948–2017

In the 1970s the percentage of women in the labor force rose rapidly, as did the percentage of those under age 25. These changes reflected the entry of large numbers of women into the paid labor force for the first time and the fact that baby boomers were reaching working age. The natural rate of unemployment may have risen because many of these workers were relatively inexperienced. Today, the labor force is much more experienced, which is one possible reason the natural rate has fallen since the 1970s.

Data from: Bureau of Labor Statistics.

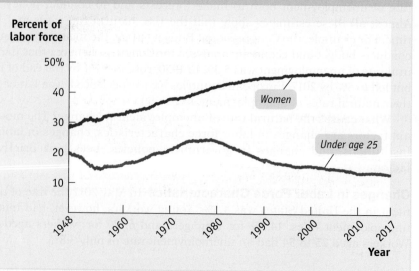

and frictional unemployment. So government policies intended to help workers can have the undesirable side effect of raising the natural rate of unemployment.

Some government policies, however, may reduce the natural rate. Two examples are job training and employment subsidies. *Job-training programs* are supposed to provide unemployed workers with skills that widen the range of jobs they can perform. *Employment subsidies* are payments either to workers or to employers that provide a financial incentive to accept or offer jobs.

ECONOMICS >> *in Action*
Structural Unemployment in Spain

Spain went through some dramatic ups and downs after 2000 when huge inflows of money from Germany and other northern European countries fed a giant housing boom. Then, after 2008, the boom went bust, causing both GDP and employment to slump, and unemployment to soar to more than 26%. We'll have more to say about this story later in the book. But right now we want to note a somewhat unusual aspect of Spain's experience: even during the height of the boom, unemployment was high by U.S. standards, bottoming out at about 8%. This suggests that Spain's natural rate of unemployment is very high, and several independent estimates do in fact put it in the range of 16% to 17%.

Why is Spain's natural rate so high? Researchers at the International Monetary Fund, the European Central Bank, and other institutions emphasize the role of laws that make it very hard to fire full-time workers, which in turn often allows these "insiders," many of whom are unionized, to demand relatively high wages even in the face of high unemployment among other workers. If these researchers are right, Spain is experiencing something like the possible effect of labor unions in causing structural unemployment.

Spain's seemingly high structural unemployment isn't unique: a number of other European countries seem to have similar issues, although none to such an extreme degree. For example, both Ireland and Portugal have a natural rate of unemployment over 10%. The important point to remember is that labor market institutions can differ greatly even among advanced economies, and that the result can be big differences in economic performance.

>> Check Your Understanding 8-2
Solutions appear at back of book.

1. Explain the following statements.
   a. Frictional unemployment is higher when the pace of technological advance quickens.
   b. Structural unemployment is higher when the pace of technological advance quickens.
   c. Frictional unemployment accounts for a larger share of total unemployment when the unemployment rate is low.

2. Why does collective bargaining have the same general effect on unemployment as a minimum wage? Illustrate your answer with a diagram.

3. Suppose that at the peak of the business cycle the United States dramatically increases benefits for unemployed workers. Explain what will happen to the natural rate of unemployment.

|| Inflation and Deflation

As we mentioned in the opening story, macroeconomic policy makers are usually focused on two big evils, unemployment and inflation. It's easy to see why high unemployment is a problem. But why is inflation something to worry about? Why do policy makers even now get anxious about inflation going too high? The answer is that inflation can impose costs on the economy—but not in the way most people think.

> ## >> Quick Review
>
> • **Frictional unemployment** occurs because unemployed workers engage in **job search**, making some amount of unemployment inevitable.
>
> • A variety of factors—minimum wages, unions, **efficiency wages**, the side effects of government policies such as unemployment benefits, and mismatches between employees and employers—lead to **structural unemployment**.
>
> • Frictional plus structural unemployment equals natural unemployment, yielding a **natural rate of unemployment.** In contrast, **cyclical unemployment** changes with the business cycle. Actual unemployment is equal to the sum of natural unemployment and cyclical unemployment.
>
> • The natural rate of unemployment can shift over time, due to changes in labor force characteristics and institutions. Government policies designed to help workers are believed to be one reason for high natural rates of unemployment in Europe.

The Level of Prices Doesn't Matter...

The most common complaint about *inflation*, which is an increase in the price level, is that it makes everyone poorer—after all, a given amount of money buys less. But inflation does not make everyone poorer. To see why, it's helpful to imagine what would happen if the United States did something other countries have done from time to time—replacing the dollar with a new currency.

An example of this kind of currency conversion happened in 2002, when France, like a number of other European countries, replaced its national currency, the franc, with the new pan-European currency, the euro. People turned in their franc coins and notes, and received euro coins and notes in exchange, at a rate of precisely 6.55957 francs per euro. At the same time, all contracts were restated in euros at the same rate of exchange. For example, if a French citizen had a home mortgage debt of 500,000 francs, this became a debt of 500,000/6.55957 = 76,224.51 euros. If a worker's contract specified that he or she should be paid 100 francs per hour, it became a contract specifying a wage of 100/6.55957 = 15.2449 euros per hour, and so on.

You could imagine doing the same thing here, replacing the dollar with a "new dollar" at a rate of exchange of, say, 7 to 1. If you owed $140,000 on your home, that would become a debt of 20,000 new dollars. If you had a wage rate of $14 an hour, it would become 2 new dollars an hour, and so on. This would bring the overall U.S. price level back to about what it was in 1962, when John F. Kennedy was president.

So would everyone be richer as a result because prices would be only one-seventh as high? Of course not. Prices would be lower, but so would wages and incomes in general. If you cut a worker's wage to one-seventh of its previous value, but also cut all prices to one-seventh of their previous level, the worker's **real wage**—the wage rate divided by the price level—hasn't changed. In fact, bringing the overall price level back to what it was during the Kennedy administration would have no effect on overall purchasing power because doing so would reduce income exactly as much as it reduced prices.

Conversely, the rise in prices that has actually taken place since the early 1960s hasn't made America poorer because it has also raised incomes by the same amount: **real incomes**—incomes divided by the price level—haven't been affected by the rise in overall prices.

The moral of this story is that the *level* of prices doesn't matter: the United States would be no richer than it is now if the overall level of prices was still as low as it was in 1961; conversely, the rise in prices over the past 50 years hasn't made us poorer.

...But the Rate of Change of Prices Does

The conclusion that the level of prices doesn't matter might seem to imply that the inflation rate doesn't matter either. But that's not true.

To see why, it's crucial to distinguish between the *level of prices* and the *inflation rate:* the percent increase in the overall level of prices per year. Recall from Chapter 7 that the inflation rate is defined as follows:

$$\text{Inflation rate} = \frac{\text{Price index in year 2 – Price index in year 1}}{\text{Price index in year 1}} \times 100$$

Figure 8-12 highlights the difference between the price level and the inflation rate in the United States over the last half-century, with the price level measured along the left vertical axis and the inflation rate measured along the right vertical axis. In the 2000s, the overall level of prices in America was much higher than it had been in 1960—but that, as we've learned, didn't matter. The inflation rate in the 2000s, however, was much lower than in the 1970s—and that almost certainly made the economy richer than it would have been if high inflation had continued.

The **real wage** is the wage rate divided by the price level.

Real income is income divided by the price level.

FIGURE 8-12 The Price Level versus the Inflation Rate, 1960–2017

With the exception of 2009, over the past half-century the price level has continuously increased. But the *inflation rate*—the rate at which prices are rising—has had both ups and downs. And in 2009, the inflation rate briefly turned negative, a phenomenon called *deflation*.
Data from: Bureau of Labor Statistics.

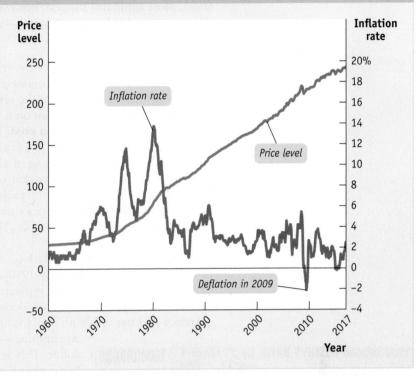

Economists believe that high rates of inflation impose significant economic costs. The most important of these costs are *shoe-leather costs, menu costs,* and *unit-of-account costs.* We'll discuss each in turn.

Shoe-Leather Costs People hold money—cash in their wallets and bank deposits—for convenience in making transactions. A high inflation rate, however, discourages people from holding money because the purchasing power of the cash in your wallet and the funds in your bank account steadily erode as the overall level of prices rises. This leads people to move funds into assets they believe will hold value and to reduce the amount of money they hold, often at considerable economic cost. For example, when Venezuelan *hyperinflation* hit 800% in 2016 (meaning prices doubled every 18 days), people began holding cigarettes and electronic currency (like Bitcoin) instead of Venezuelan currency.

During the most famous of all inflations, the German *hyperinflation* of 1921–1923, merchants employed runners to take their cash to the bank many times a day to convert it into something that would hold its value, such as a stable foreign currency. In such cases, to avoid having the purchasing power of their money eroded, people use up valuable resources, such as the labor of the German runners, that can be used productively elsewhere. During the German hyperinflation, so many banking transactions were taking place that the number of employees at German banks nearly quadrupled—from around 100,000 in 1913 to 375,000 in 1923.

More recently, Brazil experienced hyperinflation during the early 1990s; during that episode, the Brazilian banking sector grew so large that it accounted for 15% of GDP, more than twice the size of the financial sector in the United States measured as a share of GDP. The large increase in the Brazilian banking sector needed to cope with the consequences of inflation represented a loss of real resources to its society.

Increased costs of transactions caused by inflation are known as **shoe-leather costs,** an allusion to the wear and tear caused by the extra running around that takes place when people are trying to avoid holding money. Shoe-leather costs are substantial in economies with very high inflation, as anyone who has lived

Shoe-leather costs are the increased costs of transactions caused by inflation.

in such an economy—say, one suffering inflation of 100% or more per year—can attest. Most estimates suggest, however, that the shoe-leather costs of inflation at the rates seen in the United States—which in peacetime has never had inflation above 15%—are quite small.

Menu Costs In a modern economy, most of the things we buy have a listed price. There's a price listed under each item on a supermarket shelf, a price listed for goods sold on any online retailer's website, such as Amazon or Zappos, and a price listed for each dish on a restaurant's menu. Changing a listed price has a real cost, called a **menu cost.** Although the potential burden imposed by menu costs have diminished in advanced economies as more sales have shifted online and prices can be changed electronically, they still exist. For example, to change prices in a supermarket or a clothing store requires sending clerks to change the listed price with each item. In the face of inflation, of course, firms are forced to change prices more often than they would if the aggregate price level was more or less stable. This means higher costs for the economy as a whole.

In times of very high inflation, menu costs can be substantial. During the Brazilian inflation of the early 1990s, for instance, supermarket workers reportedly spent half of their time replacing old price stickers with new ones. When inflation is high, merchants may decide to stop listing prices in terms of the local currency and use either an artificial unit—in effect, measuring prices relative to one another—or a more stable currency, such as the U.S. dollar. This is exactly what the Israeli real estate market began doing in the mid-1980s: prices were quoted in U.S. dollars, even though payment was made in Israeli shekels. And this is also what happened in Zimbabwe when, in May 2008, official estimates of the inflation rate reached 1,694,000%. By 2009, the government had suspended the Zimbabwean dollar, allowing Zimbabweans to buy and sell goods using foreign currencies.

Menu costs are also present in low-inflation economies, but they are not severe. In low-inflation economies, businesses might update their prices only sporadically—not daily or even more frequently, as is the case in high-inflation or hyperinflation economies.

When one hundred trillion dollar bills are in circulation as they were in Zimbabwe, menu costs are substantial.

Unit-of-Account Costs In the Middle Ages, contracts were often specified "in kind": a tenant might, for example, be obliged to provide his landlord with a certain number of cattle each year (the phrase *in kind* actually comes from an ancient word for *cattle*). This may have made sense at the time, but it would be an awkward way to conduct modern business. Instead, we state contracts in monetary terms: a renter owes a certain number of dollars per month, a company that issues a bond promises to pay the bondholder the dollar value of the bond when it comes due, and so on. We also tend to make our economic calculations in dollars: a family planning its budget, or a small business owner trying to figure out how well the business is doing, makes estimates of the amount of money coming in and going out.

This role of the dollar as a basis for contracts and calculation is called the *unit-of-account* role of money. It's an important aspect of the modern economy. Yet it's a role that can be degraded by inflation, which causes the purchasing power of a dollar to change over time—a dollar next year is worth less than a dollar this year. The effect, many economists argue, is to reduce the quality of economic decisions: the economy as a whole makes less efficient use of its resources because of the uncertainty caused by changes in the unit of account, the dollar. The **unit-of-account costs** of inflation are the costs arising from the way inflation makes money a less reliable unit of measurement.

The **menu cost** is the real cost of changing a listed price.

The **unit-of-account costs** of inflation are the costs arising from the way inflation makes money a less reliable unit of measurement.

Unit-of-account costs may be particularly important in the tax system because inflation can distort the measures of income on which taxes are collected. Here's an example: assume that the inflation rate is 10%, so the overall level of prices rises 10% each year. Suppose that a business buys an asset, such as a piece of land, for $100,000, then resells it a year later for $110,000. In a fundamental sense, the business didn't make a profit on the deal: in real terms, it got no more for the land than it paid for it. But U.S. tax law would say that the business made a capital gain of $10,000, and it would have to pay taxes on that phantom gain.

During the 1970s, when the United States had relatively high inflation, the distorting effects of inflation on the tax system were a serious problem. Some businesses were discouraged from productive investment spending because they found themselves paying taxes on phantom gains. Meanwhile, some unproductive investments became attractive because they led to phantom losses that reduced tax bills. When inflation fell in the 1980s—and tax rates were reduced—these problems became much less important.

Winners and Losers from Inflation

As we've just learned, a high inflation rate imposes overall costs on the economy. In addition, inflation can produce winners and losers within the economy. The main reason inflation sometimes helps some people while hurting others is that economic transactions often involve contracts that extend over a period of time, such as loans, and these contracts are normally specified in nominal—that is, in dollar—terms.

In the case of a loan, the borrower receives a certain amount of funds at the beginning, and the loan contract specifies the *interest rate* on the loan and when it must be paid off. The **interest rate** is the return a lender receives for allowing borrowers the use of their savings for one year, calculated as a percentage of the amount borrowed.

But what that dollar is worth in real terms—that is, in terms of purchasing power—depends greatly on the rate of inflation over the intervening years of the loan. Economists summarize the effect of inflation on borrowers and lenders by distinguishing between the *nominal* interest rate and the *real* interest rate. The **nominal interest rate** is the interest rate in dollar terms—for example, the interest rate on a student loan. The **real interest rate** is the nominal interest rate minus the rate of inflation. For example, if a loan carries an interest rate of 8%, but there is 5% inflation, the real interest rate is 8% − 5% = 3%.

When a borrower and a lender enter into a loan contract, the contract is normally written in dollar terms—that is, the interest rate it specifies is a nominal interest rate. (And in later chapters, when we say the interest rate we will mean the nominal interest rate unless noted otherwise.) But each party to a loan contract has an expectation about the future rate of inflation and therefore an expectation about the real interest rate on the loan. If the actual inflation rate is *higher* than expected, borrowers gain at the expense of lenders: borrowers will repay their loans with funds that have a lower real value than had been expected. Conversely, if the inflation rate is *lower* than expected, lenders will gain at the expense of borrowers: borrowers must repay their loans with funds that have a higher real value than had been expected.

In modern America, home mortgages are the most important source of gains and losses from inflation. While some mortgage interest rates are linked to the inflation rate, the vast majority are not, creating big winners and losers when inflation rates have changed unexpectedly. Americans who took out mortgages in the early 1970s quickly found the real cost of their payments reduced by higher-than-expected inflation. In contrast, those who took out mortgages in the early 1990s lost. The inflation rate fell to lower-than-expected levels in the following years and raised the cost of their payments.

The **interest rate** on a loan is the price, calculated as a percentage of the amount borrowed, that lenders charge borrowers the use of their savings for one year.

The **nominal interest rate** is the interest rate expressed in dollar terms.

The **real interest rate** is the nominal interest rate minus the rate of inflation.

Disinflation is the process of bringing the inflation rate down.

Because gains for some and losses for others result from inflation that is either higher or lower than expected, yet another problem arises: uncertainty about the future inflation rate discourages people from entering into any form of long-term contract. This is an additional cost of high inflation, because high rates of inflation are usually unpredictable. In countries with high and uncertain inflation, long-term loans are rare, which makes it difficult in many cases to make long-term investments.

One last point: unexpected *deflation*—a surprise fall in the price level—creates winners and losers, too. Between 1929 and 1933, as the U.S. economy plunged into the Great Depression, the consumer price index fell by 35%. This meant that debtors, including many farmers and homeowners, saw a sharp rise in the real value of their debts, which led to widespread bankruptcy and helped create a banking crisis, as lenders found their customers unable to pay back their loans. And as you can see in Figure 8-12, deflation occurred again in 2009, when the inflation rate fell to –2% at the trough of a deep recession. Like the Great Depression (but to a much lesser extent), the unexpected deflation of 2009 imposed heavy costs on debtors. We will discuss the effects of deflation in more detail in Chapter 16.

Inflation Is Easy; Disinflation Is Hard

There is not much evidence that a rise in the inflation rate from 2% to 5% would do a great deal of harm to the economy. Still, policy makers generally move forcefully to bring inflation back down when it creeps above 2% or 3%. Why? Because experience shows that bringing the inflation rate down—a process called **disinflation**—is very difficult and costly once a higher rate of inflation has become well established in the economy.

Figure 8-13 shows what happened during two major episodes of disinflation in the United States, in the mid-1970s and in the early 1980s. The horizontal axis shows the unemployment rate. The vertical axis shows *core inflation* over the previous year, a measure that excludes volatile food and energy prices and is widely considered a better measure of underlying inflation than overall consumer prices. Each marker represents the inflation rate and the unemployment rate for one month. In each episode, unemployment and inflation followed a sort of clockwise spiral, with high inflation gradually falling in the face of an extended period of very high unemployment.

FIGURE 8-13 The Cost of Disinflation

There were two major periods of disinflation in modern U.S. history, in the mid-1970s and the early 1980s. This figure shows the track of the unemployment rate and the core inflation rate, which excludes food and energy, during these two episodes. In each case bringing inflation down required a temporary but very large increase in the unemployment rate, demonstrating the high cost of disinflation.

Data from: Bureau of Labor Statistics.

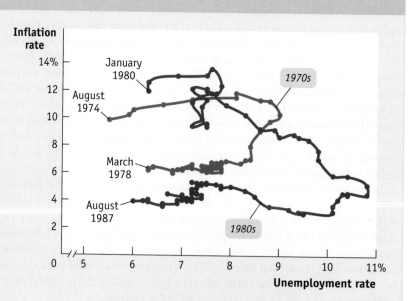

According to many economists, these periods of high unemployment that temporarily depressed the economy were necessary to reduce inflation that had become deeply embedded in the economy. The best way to avoid having to put the economy through a wringer to reduce inflation, however, is to avoid having a serious inflation problem in the first place. So policy makers respond forcefully to signs that inflation may be accelerating as a form of preventive medicine for the economy.

ECONOMICS >> *in Action*
Israel's Experience with Inflation

It's often hard to see the costs of inflation clearly because serious inflation problems are often associated with other problems that disrupt economic life, notably war or political instability (or both). In the mid-1980s, however, Israel experienced a "clean" inflation: there was no war, the government was stable, and there was order in the streets. Yet a series of policy errors led to very high inflation, with prices often rising more than 10% a month.

As it happens, one of the authors spent a month visiting at Tel Aviv University at the height of the inflation, so we can give a first-hand account of the effects.

During a period of high inflation in the mid-1980s, Israelis held very little cash, forcing them to make repeated trips to banks.

First, the shoe-leather costs of inflation were substantial. At the time, debit cards had not yet been introduced. So Israelis spent a lot of time in lines at the bank, moving money in and out of accounts that provided high enough interest rates to offset inflation. People walked around with very little cash in their wallets; they had to go to the bank whenever they needed to make even a moderately large cash payment. Banks responded by opening a lot of branches, a costly business expense.

Second, although menu costs weren't that visible to a visitor, what you could see were the efforts businesses made to minimize them. For example, restaurant menus often didn't list prices. Instead, they listed numbers that you had to multiply by another number, written on a chalkboard and changed every day, to figure out the price of a dish.

Finally, it was hard to make decisions because prices changed so much and so often. It was a common experience to walk out of a store because prices were 25% higher than at one's usual shopping destination, only to discover that prices had just been increased 25% there, too.

>> Check Your Understanding 8-3
Solutions appear at back of book.

1. The widespread use of technology has revolutionized the banking industry, making it much easier for customers to access and manage their assets. Does this mean that the shoe-leather costs of inflation are higher or lower than they used to be?

2. Most people in the United States have grown accustomed to a modest inflation rate of around 2% to 3%. Who would gain and who would lose if inflation unexpectedly came to a complete stop over the next 15 or 20 years?

>> *Quick Review*

- The **real wage** and **real income** are unaffected by the level of prices.

- Inflation, like unemployment, is a major concern of policy makers—so much so that in the past they have accepted high unemployment as the price of reducing inflation.

- While the overall level of prices is irrelevant, high rates of inflation impose real costs on the economy: **shoe-leather costs, menu costs,** and **unit-of-account costs.**

- The **interest rate** is the return a lender receives for use of his or her funds for a year. The **real interest rate** is equal to the **nominal interest rate** minus the inflation rate. As a result, unexpectedly high inflation helps borrowers and hurts lenders. With high and uncertain inflation, people will often avoid long-term investments.

- **Disinflation** is very costly, so policy makers try to avoid getting into situations of high inflation in the first place.

"Moving is the worst. Yard work is the worst. Building IKEA furniture is the worst." So began a 2015 report on TaskRabbit, a company founded in 2008 (under the name RunMyErrand), that helps people hire others to do their chores. As of 2017 there were about 30,000 of these freelancers, whom the company calls Taskers, and TaskRabbit operated in 23 major U.S. cities and London.

Why would becoming a Tasker seem appealing to some workers? The great majority of Taskers are part-time workers, who want flexibility in their employment; the company's pitch to potential Taskers contains the slogan "Work. Life. Balanced." and features testimonials from workers who combined employment with parenting, careers in the arts, and so on.

Working part-time for a variety of clients isn't a new phenomenon. On urban street corners across America, workers still line up early each morning in the hope of getting day jobs in industries like construction, where the need for workers fluctuates, sometimes unpredictably. For more skilled workers, there are numerous online resources as well as temporary staffing agencies like Allegis Group that provide workers on a subcontracting basis, from a few days to months at a time. And some people still find temporary jobs by calling numbers listed in classified ads, or even going door to door.

But TaskRabbit—founded the year after Apple introduced its first iPhone—tries to use the ubiquity of smartphones to simplify the process. Originally it was set up as a kind of auction market, in which potential employers and workers placed bids, but since 2014 it has relied on a streamlined system that is very similar to the way car services like Uber or Lyft match riders with willing drivers. TaskRabbit's apps let those seeking help make their needs known simply by tapping on one of a few common chores; potential workers can then offer to do jobs that match the locations and skills they have put in their profiles, again simply by tapping on jobs that appear on their smartphones. (They have already specified their hourly rate.) The process takes a lot less time and effort than standing on street corners, pounding the pavement, performing online job searches, or even calling the numbers from old-style classified ads.

How big a deal are enterprises like TaskRabbit? Some observers suggest that we're seeing the rise of a *gig economy*, in which large numbers of people freelance, moving from job to job rather than being formal employees of a large firm. There's probably some hype in these pronouncements, but real change does seem to be happening. In fact, one recent study concludes that the number of people with alternative work arrangements such as freelancing grew 50% from 2005 to 2015, accounting for *all* net U.S. job growth over that period. As of 2016, the share of independent workers in the U.S. economy was estimated at 22% to 30% of the workforce.

QUESTIONS FOR THOUGHT

1. How is the matching of job-seekers and employers through services like TaskRabbit likely to affect frictional unemployment?

2. What is the likely effect of such services on the number of people considered to be in the labor force?

3. Some analysts suggest that most freelancers have other jobs, and only do gig economy work on the side. How does that statement help explain the lack of clear evidence for a growing gig economy?

SUMMARY

1. The two principal objectives of macroeconomic policy are price stability (a low, but positive, level of inflation) and low unemployment.

2. **Employment** is the number of people employed; **unemployment** is the number of people unemployed and actively looking for work. Their sum is equal to the **labor force,** and the **labor force participation rate** is the percentage of the population age 16 or older that is in the labor force.

3. The **unemployment rate,** the percentage of the labor force that is unemployed and actively looking for work, can both overstate and understate the true level of unemployment. It can overstate because it counts as unemployed those who are continuing to search for a job despite having been offered one. It can understate because it ignores frustrated workers, such as **discouraged workers, marginally attached workers,** and the **underemployed.** In addition, the unemployment rate varies greatly among different groups in the population; it is typically higher for younger workers and for workers near retirement age than for workers in their prime working years.

4. The unemployment rate is affected by the business cycle. The unemployment rate generally falls when the growth rate of real GDP is above average and generally increases when the growth rate of real GDP is below average. A **jobless recovery,** a period in which real GDP is growing but unemployment rises, often follows recessions.

5. Job creation and destruction, as well as voluntary job separations, lead to **job search** and **frictional unemployment.** In addition, a variety of factors such as minimum wages, unions, **efficiency wages,** government policies designed to help laid-off workers, and mismatch between employees and employers result in

a situation in which there is a surplus of labor at the market wage rate, creating **structural unemployment.** As a result, the **natural rate of unemployment,** the sum of frictional and structural unemployment, is well above zero, even when jobs are plentiful.

6. The actual unemployment rate is equal to the natural rate of unemployment, the share of unemployment that is independent of the business cycle, plus **cyclical unemployment,** the share of unemployment that depends on fluctuations in the business cycle.

7. The natural rate of unemployment changes over time, largely in response to changes in labor force characteristics, labor market institutions, and government policies.

8. Inflation does not, as many assume, make everyone poorer by raising the level of prices. That's because wages and incomes are adjusted to take into account a rising price level, leaving **real wages** and **real income** unaffected. However, a high inflation rate imposes overall costs on the economy: **shoe-leather costs, menu costs,** and **unit-of-account costs.**

9. Inflation can produce winners and losers within the economy, because long-term contracts are generally written in dollar terms. The **interest rate** specified in a loan is typically a **nominal interest rate,** which differs from the **real interest rate** due to inflation. A higher-than-expected inflation rate is good for borrowers and bad for lenders. A lower-than-expected inflation rate is good for lenders and bad for borrowers.

10. Many believe policies that depress the economy and produce high unemployment are necessary to reduce embedded inflation. Because **disinflation** is very costly, policy makers try to prevent inflation from becoming excessive in the first place.

KEY TERMS

Employment, p. 212
Unemployment, p. 212
Labor force, p. 212
Labor force participation rate, p. 212
Unemployment rate, p. 213
Discouraged workers, p. 213
Marginally attached workers, p. 213
Underemployment, p. 213

Jobless recovery, p. 216
Job search, p. 218
Frictional unemployment, p. 218
Structural unemployment, p. 220
Efficiency wages, p. 222
Natural rate of unemployment, p. 223
Cyclical unemployment, p. 223
Real wage, p. 226

Real income, p. 226
Shoe-leather costs, p. 227
Menu costs, p. 228
Unit-of-account costs, p. 228
Interest rate, p. 229
Nominal interest rate, p. 229
Real interest rate, p. 229
Disinflation, p. 230

PROBLEMS

1. Each month, usually on the first Friday of the month, the Bureau of Labor Statistics releases the Employment Situation Summary for the previous month. Go to www.bls.gov and find the latest report. On the Bureau of Labor Statistics home page, at the top of the page, select the "Economic Releases" tab, find "Latest Releases," and select "Employment Situation." You will find the Employment Situation Summary listed at the top. How does the current unemployment rate compare to the rate one month earlier? How does the current unemployment rate compare to the rate one year earlier?

2. In general, how do changes in the unemployment rate vary with changes in real GDP? After several quarters of a severe recession, explain why we might observe a decrease in the official unemployment rate. Explain why we could see an increase in the official unemployment rate after several quarters of a strong expansion.

3. In each of the following situations, what type of unemployment is Melanie facing?

   a. After completing a complex programming project, Melanie is laid off. Her prospects for a new job requiring similar skills are good, and she has signed up with a programmer placement service. She has passed up offers for low-paying jobs.

   b. When Melanie and her co-workers refused to accept pay cuts, her employer outsourced their programming tasks to workers in another country. This phenomenon is occurring throughout the programming industry.

   c. Due to the current slump, Melanie has been laid off from her programming job. Her employer promises to rehire her when business picks up.

4. Part of the information released in the Employment Situation Summary concerns how long individuals have been unemployed. Go to www.bls.gov to find the latest report. Use the same technique as in Problem 1 to find the Employment Situation Summary. Near the end of the Employment Situation, click on Table A-12, titled "Unemployed persons by duration of unemployment." Use the seasonally adjusted numbers to answer the following questions.

   a. How many workers were unemployed less than 5 weeks? What percentage of all unemployed workers do these workers represent? How do these numbers compare to the previous month's data?

   b. How many workers were unemployed for 27 or more weeks? What percentage of all unemployed workers do these workers represent? How do these numbers compare to the previous month's data?

   c. How long has the average worker been unemployed (average duration, in weeks)? How does this compare to the average for the previous month's data?

   d. Comparing the latest month for which there are data with the previous month, has the problem of long-term unemployment improved or deteriorated?

5. A country's labor force is the sum of the number of employed and unemployed workers. The accompanying table provides data on the size of the labor force and the number of unemployed workers for different regions of the United States.

Region	Labor force (thousands)		Unemployed (thousands)	
	July 2015	**July 2016**	**July 2015**	**July 2016**
Northeast	28,397	28,565	1,459	1,377
South	57,297	58,022	2,978	2,720
Midwest	34,489	34,996	1,627	1,585
West	36,949	37,543	2,099	1,985

Data from: Bureau of Labor Statistics.

   a. Calculate the number of workers employed in each of the regions in July 2015 and July 2016. Use your answers to calculate the change in the total number of workers employed between July 2015 and July 2016.

   b. For each region, calculate the growth in the labor force from July 2015 to July 2016.

   c. Compute unemployment rates in the different regions of the country in July 2015 and July 2016.

   d. What can you infer about the fall in unemployment rates over this period? Was it caused by a net gain in the number of jobs or by a large fall in the number of people seeking jobs?

6. Access the Discovering Data exercise for Chapter 8 Problem 6 online to answer the following questions.

   a. What is the current federal minimum wage?

   b. In what year was the federal minimum wage last increased?

   c. What is the current value for the real minimum wage?

   d. In what year was the real minimum wage the highest? The lowest?

   e. In general, since 1970, how has the purchasing power of the minimum wage changed over time?

7. In which of the following cases is it more likely for efficiency wages to exist? Why?

   a. Jane and her boss work as a team selling ice cream.

   b. Jane sells ice cream without any direct supervision by her boss.

   c. Jane speaks Korean and sells ice cream in a neighborhood in which Korean is the primary language. It is difficult to find another worker who speaks Korean.

8. How will the following changes affect the natural rate of unemployment?

a. The government reduces the time during which an unemployed worker can receive unemployment benefits.

b. More teenagers focus on their studies and do not look for jobs until after college.

c. Greater access to the internet leads both potential employers and potential employees to use the internet to list and find jobs.

d. Union membership declines.

9. With its tradition of a job for life for most citizens, Japan once had a much lower unemployment rate than that of the United States; from 1960 to 1995, the unemployment rate in Japan exceeded 3% only once. However, since the crash of its stock market in 1989 and slow economic growth in the 1990s, the job-for-life system has broken down and unemployment rose to more than 5% in 2003.

a. Explain the likely effect of the breakdown of the job-for-life system in Japan on the Japanese natural rate of unemployment.

b. As the accompanying diagram shows, the rate of growth of real GDP picked up in Japan after 2001 and before the global economic crisis of 2007–2009. Explain the likely effect of this increase in real GDP growth on the unemployment rate. Was the likely cause of the change in the unemployment rate during this period a change in the natural rate of unemployment or a change in the cyclical unemployment rate?

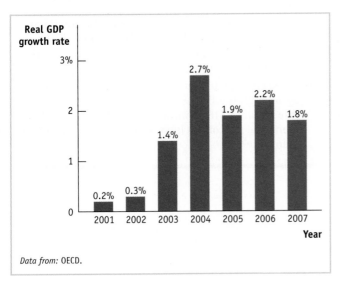

Data from: OECD.

10. In the following examples, is inflation creating winners and losers at no net cost to the economy or is inflation imposing a net cost on the economy? If a net cost is being imposed, which type of cost is involved?

a. When inflation is expected to be high, workers get paid more frequently and make more trips to the bank.

b. Lanwei is reimbursed by her company for her work-related travel expenses. Sometimes, however, the company takes a long time to reimburse her. So when inflation is high, she is less willing to travel for her job.

c. Hector Homeowner has a mortgage with a fixed nominal 6% interest rate that he took out five years ago. Over the years, the inflation rate has crept up unexpectedly to its present level of 7%.

d. In response to unexpectedly high inflation, the manager of Cozy Cottages of Cape Cod must reprint and resend expensive color brochures correcting the price of rentals this season.

11. The accompanying diagram shows the interest rate on one-year loans and inflation during 2001–2016 in the economy of Albernia. When would one-year loans have been especially attractive and why?

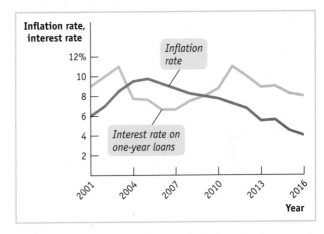

12. The accompanying table provides the inflation rate in the year 2005 and the average inflation rate over the period 2006–2015 for seven different countries.

Country	Inflation rate in 2005	Average inflation rate in 2006–2015
Brazil	6.87%	5.70%
China	1.82	2.89
France	1.90	1.47
Indonesia	10.46	6.82
Japan	−0.27	0.32
Turkey	8.18	8.30
United States	3.37	1.96

Data from: IMF.

a. Given the expected relationship between average inflation and menu costs, rank the countries in descending order of menu costs using average inflation over the period 2006–2015.

b. Rank the countries in order of inflation rates that most favored borrowers with ten-year loans that were taken out in 2005. Assume that the loans were agreed upon with the expectation that the inflation rate for 2006 to 2015 would be the same as the inflation rate in 2005.

c. Did borrowers who took out ten-year loans in Japan gain or lose overall versus lenders? Explain.

13. Access the Discovering Data exercise for Chapter 8 Problem 13 online to answer the following questions.

   a. What is the current level of employment for individuals without a high school diploma?

   b. How much has employment changed for high school graduates from 2007 through 2016?

   c. Since 2007, which education group has experienced the largest increase in employment?

   d. Since the end of the Great Recession in 2009, how has employment changed for the different education levels? Calculate the net gain (or loss) of jobs for each category to answer.

   e. What percent of the employed had a bachelor's degree in January 1992? What percent has a bachelor's degree today?

   f. Calculate the change in the share of employment by education level since 1992.

14. The accompanying diagram shows the inflation rate in the United Kingdom from 1980 to 2016.

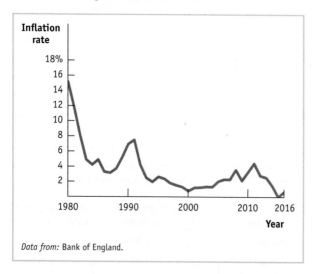

Data from: Bank of England.

   a. Between 1980 and 1985, policy makers in the United Kingdom worked to lower the inflation rate. What would you predict happened to unemployment between 1980 and 1985?

   b. Policy makers in the United Kingdom react forcefully when the inflation rate rises above a target rate of 2%. Why would it be harmful if inflation rose from 0.7% (the level in 2016) to, say, a level of 5%?

WORK IT OUT Interactive step-by-step help with solving this problem can be found online.

15. There is only one labor market in Profunctia. All workers have the same skills, and all firms hire workers with these skills. Use the accompanying diagram, which shows the supply of and demand for labor, to answer the following questions. Illustrate each answer with a diagram.

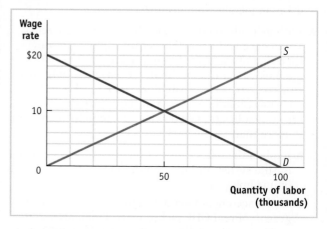

   a. What is the equilibrium wage rate in Profunctia? At this wage rate, what are the level of employment, the size of the labor force, and the unemployment rate?

   b. If the government of Profunctia sets a minimum wage equal to $12, what will be the level of employment, the size of the labor force, and the unemployment rate?

   c. If unions bargain with the firms in Profunctia and set a wage rate equal to $14, what will be the level of employment, the size of the labor force, and the unemployment rate?

   d. If the concern for retaining workers and encouraging high-quality work leads firms to set a wage rate equal to $16, what will be the level of employment, the size of the labor force, and the unemployment rate?

9 Long-Run Economic Growth

 ## AIRPOCALYPSE NOW

ON JANUARY 2, 2017, a video shot in Beijing went viral. It was a time-lapse recording showing a "wall of smog" overrunning China's capital, with blue skies quickly giving way to an almost complete lack of visibility. Unfortunately, the event wasn't all that exceptional. Severe pollution alerts have become common in Beijing and other major Chinese cities.

Rapid, uncontrolled economic growth has resulted in much higher living standards in China but at the cost of very high levels of pollution.

ZUMA Press, Inc/Alamy

The *New York Times* has referred to the oppressive smog as an "airpocalypse." The severe air pollution that has become commonplace in China's cities makes the smog that used to afflict Los Angeles and other U.S. cities seem mild by comparison. The smog in U.S. cities is mostly gone now thanks to pollution regulations.

It goes without saying that the situation in China is a bad thing, and must be dealt with. But it is also a byproduct of a very good thing: China's extraordinary economic growth in the past few decades, which has raised literally hundreds of millions of people out of abject poverty. These newly enriched masses want what everyone wants if they can afford it: better food, better housing, and consumer goods—including, in many cases, cars. As recently as 2007 there were fewer than 60 million motor vehicles in China, around 1 for every 20 people. By 2016 that number had tripled. Unfortunately, the growth in China's car population has run ahead of its pollution controls. And the result, combined with the emissions of the country's burgeoning industry, is epochal smog.

Despite its troubling environmental problems, China has made enormous economic strides over the past few decades. Indeed, its recent history is probably the world's most impressive example to date of *long-run economic growth*—a sustained increase in output per capita. Yet despite its impressive performance, in terms of per capita income, China is still playing catch-up with economically advanced countries like the United States and Japan. China is still a relatively poor country because these other nations began the process of long-run economic growth many decades ago. In the case of the United States and European countries, long-run economic growth began more than a century ago.

Many economists have argued that long-run economic growth— why it happens and how to achieve it—is the single most important issue in macroeconomics because of its direct effect on living standards.

In this chapter, we present some facts about long-run growth, look at the factors that economists believe determine the pace at which long-run growth takes place, and examine how government policies can help or hinder growth. We will also address questions about the environmental sustainability of long-run growth. ●

WHAT YOU WILL LEARN

- Why is long-run economic growth measured as the increase in real GDP per capita? How has real GDP per capita changed over time in different countries?

- Why is **productivity** the key to long-run economic growth? How is productivity driven by **physical capital, human capital,** and **technological progress?**

- Why do long-run growth rates differ so much among countries?

- How does growth vary among several important regions of the world? Why does the **convergence hypothesis** apply to economically advanced countries?

- How do scarcity of natural resources and environmental degradation pose a challenge to **sustainable long-run economic growth?**

Comparing Economies Across Time and Space

Before we analyze the sources of long-run economic growth, it's useful to have a sense of just how much the U.S. economy has grown over time and how large the gaps are between wealthy countries like the United States and countries that have yet to achieve comparable growth. So let's take a look at the numbers.

Real GDP per Capita

The key statistic used to track economic growth is *real GDP per capita*—real GDP divided by the population size. We focus on GDP because, as we learned in Chapter 7, GDP measures the total value of an economy's production of final goods and services as well as the income earned in that economy in a given year. We use *real* GDP because we want to separate changes in the quantity of goods and services from the effects of a rising price level. We focus on real GDP *per capita* because we want to isolate the effect of changes in the population. For example, other things equal, an increase in the population lowers the standard of living for the average person—there are now more people to share a given amount of real GDP. An increase in real GDP that only matches an increase in population leaves the average standard of living unchanged.

Although we also learned in Chapter 7 that growth in real GDP per capita should not be a policy goal in and of itself, it does serve as a very useful summary measure of a country's economic progress over time. Figure 9-1 shows real GDP per capita for the United States, India, and China, measured in 1990 dollars, from 1900 to 2015. The vertical axis is drawn on a logarithmic scale so that equal percent changes in real GDP per capita across countries are the same size in the graph.

To give a sense of how much the U.S. economy grew during the last century, Table 9-1 shows real GDP per capita at selected years, expressed two ways: as a percentage of the 1900 level and as a percentage of the 2015 level. In 1920, the U.S. economy already produced 136% as much per person as it did in 1900. In 2015,

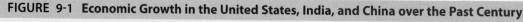

FIGURE 9-1 Economic Growth in the United States, India, and China over the Past Century

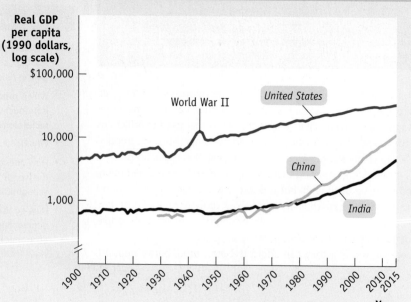

Real GDP per capita from 1900 to 2015, measured in 1990 dollars, is shown for the United States, India, and China. Equal percent changes in real GDP per capita are drawn the same size. As the steeper slopes of the lines representing China and India show, since 1980 India and China had a much higher growth rate than the United States. The standard of living achieved in the United States in 1900 was attained by China in 2000 and by India in 2015 (approximately for both). Note that the break in China data from 1940 to 1950 is due to war.

Data from: Angus Maddison, *Statistics on World Population, GDP, and Per Capita GDP, 1–2008AD,* http://www.ggdc.net/maddison; The Conference Board Total Economy Database™, May 2016, http://www.conference-board.org/data/economydatabase/.

it produced 804% as much per person as it did in 1900, more than an eight-fold increase. Alternatively, in 1900 the U.S. economy produced only 12% as much per person as it did in 2015.

The income of the typical family normally grows more or less in proportion to per capita income. For example, a 1% increase in real GDP per capita corresponds, roughly, to a 1% increase in the income of the median or typical family—a family at the center of the income distribution. In 2015, the median American household had an income of about $56,500. Since Table 9-1 tells us that real GDP per capita in 1900 was only 12% of its 2015 level, a typical family in 1900 probably had a purchasing power only 12% as large as the purchasing power of a typical family in 2015. That's around $6,780 in today's dollars, representing a standard of living that we would now consider severe poverty. Today's typical American family, if transported back to the United States of 1900, would feel quite a lot of deprivation.

Yet many people in the world have a standard of living equal to or lower than that of the average American at the beginning of the last century. That's the message about China and India in Figure 9-1: despite dramatic economic growth in China over the last three decades and the more recent acceleration of economic growth in India, China has only recently exceeded the standard of living that the United States enjoyed in the early twentieth century, while India has matched it only recently. And much of the world today is poorer than China or India.

You can get a sense of how poor much of the world remains by looking at Figure 9-2, a map of the world in which countries are classified according to their 2015 levels of GDP per capita, in U.S. dollars. As you can see, large parts of the world have very low incomes. Generally speaking, the countries of Europe and North America, as well as a few in the Pacific, have high incomes. Many Asian countries, including China and India, have experienced rapid economic growth, moving them into the middle income groups. Africa, however, is dominated by countries with GDP less than $5,000 per capita. In fact, about 25% of the world's

TABLE 9-1 U.S. Real GDP per Capita

Year	Percentage of 1900 real GDP per capita	Percentage of 2015 real GDP per capita
1900	100%	12%
1920	136	17
1940	171	21
1980	454	56
2000	704	21
2015	804	100

Data from: Angus Maddison, *Statistics on World Population, GDP, and Per Capita GDP, 1–2008AD,* "The First Update of the Madison Project: Reestimating Growth Before 1820" http://www.ggdc.net/maddison; The Conference Board Total Economy Database, May 2016. http://www.conference-board.org/data/economydatabase.

FIGURE 9-2 Incomes Around the World, 2015

Although the countries of Europe and North America—along with a few in the Pacific—have high incomes, much of the world is still very poor. Today, about a quarter of the world's population lives in countries with a lower standard of living than the United States had a century ago.

Data from: World Development Indicators, World Bank.

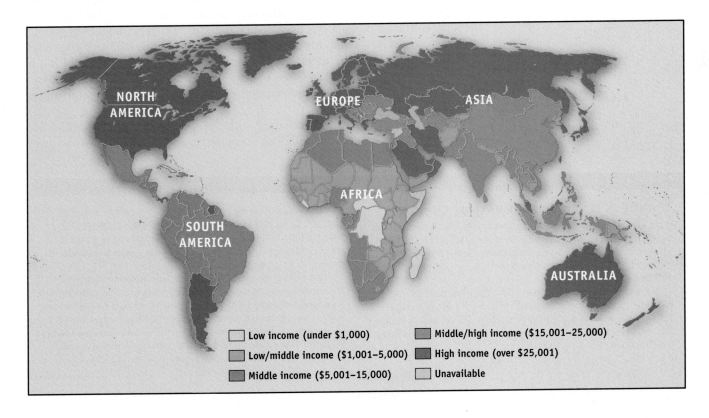

Low income (under $1,000)

Low/middle income ($1,001–5,000)

Middle income ($5,001–15,000)

Middle/high income ($15,001–25,000)

High income (over $25,001)

Unavailable

According to the **Rule of 70,** the time it takes a variable that grows gradually over time to double is approximately 70 divided by that variable's annual growth rate.

people live in countries with a lower standard of living than the United States had a century ago.

Growth Rates

How did the United States manage to produce over eight times as much per person in 2015 than in 1900? A little bit at a time. Long-run economic growth is normally a gradual process in which real GDP per capita grows at most a few percent per year. From 1900 to 2015, real GDP per capita in the United States increased an average of 1.9% each year.

To have a sense of the relationship between the annual growth rate of real GDP per capita and the long-run change in real GDP per capita, it's helpful to keep in mind the **Rule of 70,** a mathematical formula that tells us how long it takes real GDP per capita, or any other variable that grows gradually over time, to double. The approximate answer is:

$$\textbf{(9-1)} \quad \text{Number of years for variable to double} = \frac{70}{\text{Annual growth rate of variable}}$$

(Note that the Rule of 70 can only be applied to a positive growth rate.) So if real GDP per capita grows at 1% per year, it will take 70 years to double. If it grows at 2% per year, it will take only 35 years to double. In fact, U.S. real GDP per capita rose on average 1.9% per year over the last century.

Applying the Rule of 70 to this information implies that it should have taken 37 years for real GDP per capita to double; it would have taken 111 years—three periods of 37 years each—for U.S. real GDP per capita to double three times. That is, the Rule of 70 implies that over the course of 111 years, U.S. real GDP per capita should have increased by a factor of $2 \times 2 \times 2 = 8$. And this does turn out to be a pretty good approximation of reality. Between 1900 and 2015—a period of 115 years—real GDP per capita rose just over eightfold.

Figure 9-3 shows the average annual rate of growth of real GDP per capita for selected countries from 1980 to 2015. Some countries were notable success stories: for example, China, though still quite poor, has made spectacular progress. India, although not matching China's performance, has also achieved impressive growth. The same is true for Bangladesh, as discussed in the following Economics in Action.

Some countries, though, have had very disappointing growth. Argentina was once considered a wealthy nation. In the early years of the twentieth century, it was in the same league as the United States and Canada. But since then it has lagged far behind more dynamic economies. And still others, like Zimbabwe, have slid backward.

What explains these differences in growth rates? To answer that question, we need to examine the sources of long-run economic growth, which we turn to next.

PITFALLS

CHANGE IN LEVELS VERSUS RATE OF CHANGE

When studying economic growth, it's vitally important to understand the difference between a change in level and a rate of change. When we say that real GDP "grew," we mean that the level of real GDP increased. For example, we might say that U.S. real GDP grew during 2015 by $415 billion.

If we knew the level of U.S. real GDP in 2014, we could also represent the amount of 2015 growth in terms of a rate of change. For example, if U.S. real GDP in 2014 had been $15,982 billion, then U.S. real GDP in 2015 would have been $15,982 billion + $415 billion = $16,397 billion.

We could calculate the rate of change, or the growth rate, of U.S. real GDP during 2015 as: (($16,397 billion − $15,982 billion)/$15,982 billion) × 100 = ($415 billion/$15,982 billion) × 100 = 2.6%. Statements about economic growth over a period of years almost always refer to changes in the growth rate.

When talking about growth or growth rates, economists often use phrases that appear to mix the two concepts and so can be confusing. For example, when we say that "U.S. growth fell during the 1970s," we are really saying that the U.S. growth rate of real GDP was lower in the 1970s in comparison to the 1960s. When we say that "growth accelerated during the early 1990s," we are saying that the growth rate increased year after year in the early 1990s—for example, going from 3% to 3.5% to 4%.

FIGURE 9-3 Comparing Recent Growth Rates

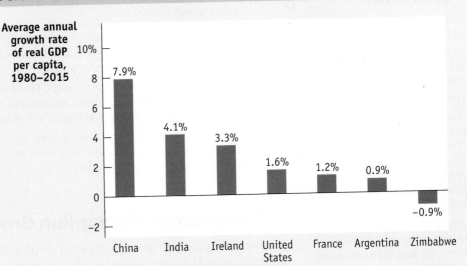

The average annual rate of growth of real GDP per capita from 1980 to 2015 is shown here for selected countries. China and, to a lesser extent, India and Ireland achieved impressive growth. The United States and France had moderate growth. Once considered an economically advanced country, Argentina had more sluggish growth. Still others, such as Zimbabwe, slid backward.

Data from: World Development Indicators.

Average annual growth rate of real GDP per capita, 1980–2015

China 7.9%
India 4.1%
Ireland 3.3%
United States 1.6%
France 1.2%
Argentina 0.9%
Zimbabwe −0.9%

ECONOMICS >> *in Action*

An Economic Breakthrough in Bangladesh

Western news media rarely mention Bangladesh: it's not a political hot spot, it doesn't have oil, and it's overshadowed by its immense neighbor, India. Yet it is home to more than 160 million people—and although it is still very poor, it is nonetheless one of the greatest economic success stories of the past generation.

As recently as the 1980s, real GDP per capita in Bangladesh—which achieved independence from Pakistan in 1971, after a brutal war—was barely higher than it had been in 1950, when the country was so poor that it literally lived on the edge of starvation. In the early 1990s, however, the nation began a process of political and economic reform, making the transition from military rule to democracy, freeing up markets, and achieving monetary and fiscal stability. And growth took off, most notably with the rise of Bangladesh as a major exporter of clothing to Western markets. Real GDP per capita grew at over 3% per year, from the late 1980s through 2010, doubling over the 20-year period from 1990 to 2010.

Although Bangladesh remains a very poor country, a high growth rate has improved living standards over the last 25 years.

By 2015 real GDP per capita was almost 2½ times what it had been in 1990. Other measures also showed dramatic improvements in the quality of life: life expectancy rose by a dozen years, child mortality fell by 70%, school enrollment rose sharply, especially for girls.

Make no mistake, Bangladesh is still incredibly poor by American standards. Wages are very low although rising, while working conditions are often terrible and dangerous—a point highlighted in 2013, when a factory complex collapsed, killing more than a thousand workers. But compared with its own past, Bangladesh has achieved a lot of progress—and demonstrated that economic growth brings real human benefits, too.

>> *Check Your Understanding* **9-1**
Solutions appear at back of book.

1. Why do economists use real GDP per capita to measure economic progress rather than some other measure, such as nominal GDP per capita or real GDP?

2. Apply the Rule of 70 to the data in Figure 9-3 to determine how many years it will take each of the countries listed there (except Zimbabwe) to double its real GDP per capita. Would India's real GDP per capita exceed that of the United States in the future if growth rates remain as shown in Figure 9-3? Why or why not?

3. Although China and India currently have growth rates much higher than the U.S. growth rate, the typical Chinese or Indian household is far poorer than the typical American household. Explain why.

The Sources of Long-Run Growth

Long-run economic growth depends almost entirely on one ingredient: rising *productivity*. However, a number of factors affect the growth of productivity. Let's look first at why productivity is the key ingredient and then examine what affects it.

The Crucial Importance of Productivity

Sustained economic growth occurs only when the amount of output produced by the average worker increases steadily. The term **labor productivity**, or **productivity** for short, is used to refer either to output per worker or, in some cases, to output per hour. (The number of hours worked by an average worker differs to some extent across countries, although this isn't an important factor in the difference between living standards in, say, India and the United States.)

In this book we'll focus on output per worker. For the economy as a whole, productivity—output per worker—is simply real GDP divided by the number of people working.

You might wonder why we say that higher productivity is the only source of long-run growth. Can't an economy also increase its real GDP per capita by putting more of the population to work? The answer is, yes, but . . . .

For short periods of time, an economy can experience a burst of growth in output per capita by putting a higher percentage of the population to work. That happened in the United States during World War II, when millions of women who previously worked only in the home entered the paid workforce. The percentage of adult civilians employed outside the home rose from 50% in 1941 to 58% in 1944, and you can see the resulting bump in real GDP per capita during those years in Figure 9-1.

Over the longer run, however, the rate of employment growth is never very different from the rate of population growth. Over the course of the twentieth century, for example, the population of the United States rose at an average rate of 1.3% per year and employment rose 1.5% per year. Real GDP per capita rose 1.9% per year; of that, 1.7%—that is, almost 90% of the total—was the result of rising productivity. In general, overall real GDP can grow because of population growth, but any large increase in real GDP *per capita* must be the result of increased output *per worker*. That is, it must be due to higher productivity.

So increased productivity is the key to long-run economic growth. But what leads to higher productivity?

Explaining Growth in Productivity

There are three main reasons why the average U.S. worker today produces far more than his or her counterpart a century ago. First, the modern worker has far more *physical capital*, such as machinery and office space, to work with. Second,

Labor productivity, often referred to simply as **productivity,** is output per worker.

the modern worker is much better educated and so possesses much more *human capital*. Finally, modern firms have the advantage of a century's accumulation of technical advancements reflecting a great deal of *technological progress*.

Let's look at each of these factors in turn.

Increase in Physical Capital Economists define **physical capital** as manufactured resources such as buildings and machines. Physical capital makes workers more productive. For example, a worker operating a backhoe can dig a lot more feet of trench per day than one equipped only with a shovel.

The average U.S. private-sector worker today is backed up by more than $350,000 worth of physical capital—far more than a U.S. worker had 100 years ago and far more than the average worker in most other countries has today.

Increase in Human Capital It's not enough for a worker to have good equipment—he or she must also know what to do with it. **Human capital** refers to the improvement in labor created by the education and knowledge embodied in the workforce.

The human capital of the United States has increased dramatically over the past century. A century ago, although most Americans were able to read and write, very few had an extensive education. In 1910, only 13.5% of Americans over 25 had graduated from high school and only 3% had four-year college degrees. By 2015, the percentages were 88% and 33%, respectively. It would be impossible to run today's economy with a population as poorly educated as that of a century ago.

Analyses based on *growth accounting*, described later in this chapter, suggest that education—and its effect on productivity—is an even more important determinant of growth than increases in physical capital.

Technological Progress Probably the most important driver of productivity growth is **technological progress,** which is broadly defined as an advance in the technical means of the production of goods and services. We'll see shortly how economists measure the impact of technology on growth.

Workers today are able to produce more than those in the past, even with the same amount of physical and human capital, because technology has advanced over time. It's important to realize that economically important technological progress need not be flashy or rely on cutting-edge science.

Historians have noted that past economic growth has been driven not only by major inventions, such as the railroad or the semiconductor chip, but also by thousands of modest innovations, such as the flat-bottomed paper bag, patented in 1870, which made packing groceries and many other goods much easier, and the Post-it® note, introduced in 1981, which has had surprisingly large benefits for office productivity.

Experts attribute much of the productivity surge that took place in the United States late in the twentieth century to new technology adopted by service-producing companies like Walmart rather than to high-technology companies.

Accounting for Growth: The Aggregate Production Function

Productivity is higher, other things equal, when workers are equipped with more physical capital, more human capital, better technology, or any combination of the three. But can we put numbers to these effects? To do this, economists make use of estimates of the **aggregate production function,** which shows how productivity depends on the quantities of physical capital per worker and human capital per worker as well as the state of technology.

In general, all three factors tend to rise over time, as workers are equipped with more machinery, receive more education, and benefit from technological

Physical capital consists of human-made resources such as buildings and machines.

Human capital is the improvement in labor created by the education and knowledge embodied in the workforce.

Technological progress is an advance in the technical means of the production of goods and services.

The **aggregate production function** is a hypothetical function that shows how productivity (real GDP per worker) depends on the quantities of physical capital per worker and human capital per worker as well as the state of technology.

An aggregate production function exhibits **diminishing returns to physical capital** when, holding the amount of human capital per worker and the state of technology fixed, each successive increase in the amount of physical capital per worker leads to a smaller increase in productivity.

advances. What the aggregate production function does is allow economists to disentangle the effects of these three factors on overall productivity.

An example of an aggregate production function applied to real data comes from a comparative study of Chinese and Indian economic growth by the economists Barry Bosworth and Susan Collins of the Brookings Institution. They used the following aggregate production function:

GDP per worker = $T \times$ (Physical capital per worker)$^{0.4} \times$ (Human capital per worker)$^{0.6}$

where T represented an estimate of the level of technology and they assumed that each year of education raises workers' human capital by 7%. Using this function, they tried to explain why China grew faster than India between 1978 and 2004. About half the difference, they found, was due to China's higher levels of investment spending, which raised its level of physical capital per worker faster than India's. The other half was due to faster Chinese technological progress.

In analyzing historical economic growth, economists have discovered a crucial fact about the estimated aggregate production function: it exhibits **diminishing returns to physical capital.** That is, when the amount of human capital per worker and the state of technology are held fixed, each successive increase in the amount of physical capital per worker leads to a smaller increase in productivity.

Figure 9-4 and the table to its right give a hypothetical example of how the level of physical capital per worker might affect the level of real GDP per worker, holding human capital per worker and the state of technology fixed. In this example, we measure the quantity of physical capital in dollars.

To see why the relationship between physical capital per worker and productivity exhibits diminishing returns, think about how having farm equipment

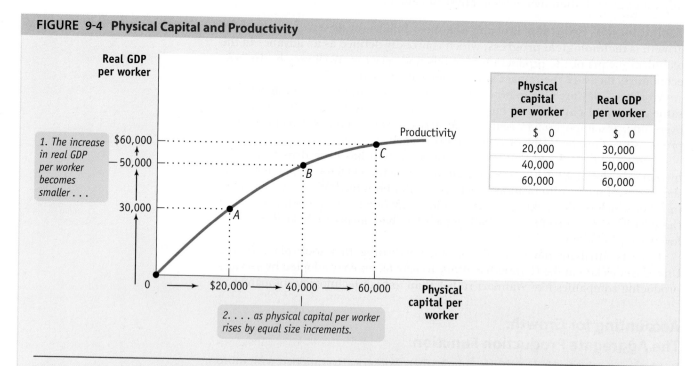

FIGURE 9-4 Physical Capital and Productivity

Physical capital per worker	Real GDP per worker
$ 0	$ 0
20,000	30,000
40,000	50,000
60,000	60,000

1. The increase in real GDP per worker becomes smaller . . .

2. . . . as physical capital per worker rises by equal size increments.

The aggregate production function shows how, in this case, holding human capital per worker and technology fixed, productivity increases as physical capital per worker rises. Other things equal, a greater quantity of physical capital per worker leads to higher real GDP per worker but is subject to diminishing returns: each successive addition to physical capital per worker produces a smaller increase in productivity. Starting at the origin, 0, a $20,000 increase in physical capital per worker leads to an increase in real GDP per worker of $30,000, indicated by point A. Starting from point A, another $20,000 increase in physical capital per worker leads to an increase in real GDP per worker but only of $20,000, indicated by point B. Finally, a third $20,000 increase in physical capital per worker leads to only a $10,000 increase in real GDP per worker, indicated by point C.

affects the productivity of farmworkers. A little bit of equipment makes a big difference: a worker equipped with a tractor can do much more than a worker without one. And a worker using more expensive equipment will, other things equal, be more productive: a worker with a $40,000 tractor will normally be able to cultivate more farmland in a given amount of time than a worker with a $20,000 tractor because the more expensive machine will be more powerful, perform more tasks, or both.

But will a worker with a $40,000 tractor, holding human capital and technology constant, be twice as productive as a worker with a $20,000 tractor? Probably not: there's a huge difference between not having a tractor at all and having even an inexpensive tractor; there's much less difference between having an inexpensive tractor and having a better tractor. And we can be sure that a worker with a $200,000 tractor won't be 10 times as productive: a tractor can be improved only so much. Because the same is true of other kinds of equipment, the aggregate production function shows diminishing returns to physical capital.

Diminishing returns to physical capital imply a relationship between physical capital per worker and output per worker like the one shown in Figure 9-4. As the productivity curve for physical capital and the accompanying table illustrate, more physical capital per worker leads to more output per worker. But each $20,000 increment in physical capital per worker adds less to productivity.

As you can see from the table, there is a big payoff for the first $20,000 of physical capital: real GDP per worker rises by $30,000. The second $20,000 of physical capital also raises productivity, but not by as much: real GDP per worker goes up by only $20,000. The third $20,000 of physical capital raises real GDP per worker by only $10,000. By comparing points along the curve you can also see that as physical capital per worker rises, output per worker also rises—but at a diminishing rate.

Going from the origin at 0 to point *A*, a $20,000 increase in physical capital per worker, leads to an increase of $30,000 in real GDP per worker. Going from point *A* to point *B*, a second $20,000 increase in physical capital per worker, leads to an increase of only $20,000 in real GDP per worker. And from point *B* to point *C*, a $20,000 increase in physical capital per worker, increased real GDP per worker by only $10,000.

It's important to realize that diminishing returns to physical capital is an "other things equal" phenomenon: additional amounts of physical capital are less productive *when the amount of human capital per worker and the technology are held fixed*. Diminishing returns may disappear if we increase the amount of human capital per worker, or improve the technology, or both at the same time the amount of physical capital per worker is increased.

For example, a worker with a $40,000 tractor who has also been trained in the most advanced cultivation techniques may in fact be more than twice as productive as a worker with only a $20,000 tractor and no additional human capital.

But diminishing returns to any one input—regardless of whether it is physical capital, human capital, or number of workers—is a pervasive characteristic of production. Typical estimates suggest that in practice a 1% increase in the quantity of physical capital per worker increases output per worker by only one-third of 1%, or 0.33%.

In practice, all the factors contributing to higher productivity rise during the course of economic growth: both physical capital and human capital per worker increase, and technology advances as well. To disentangle the effects of these factors, economists use **growth accounting,** which estimates the contribution of each major factor in the aggregate production function to economic growth. For example, suppose the following are true:

- The amount of physical capital per worker grows 3% per year.
- According to estimates of the aggregate production function, each 1% rise in physical capital per worker, holding human capital and technology constant, raises output per worker by one-third of 1%, or 0.33%.

Growth accounting estimates the contribution of each major factor in the aggregate production function to economic growth.

IT MAY BE DIMINISHED . . . BUT IT'S STILL POSITIVE

It's important to understand what diminishing returns to physical capital means and what it doesn't mean. As we've already explained, it's an "other things equal" statement: holding the amount of human capital per worker and the technology fixed, each successive increase in the amount of physical capital per worker results in a smaller increase in real GDP per worker.

But this doesn't mean that real GDP per worker eventually falls as more and more physical capital is added. It's just that the *increase* in real GDP per worker gets smaller and smaller, albeit remaining at or above zero. So an increase in physical capital per worker will never reduce productivity.

But due to diminishing returns, at some point increasing the amount of physical capital per worker no longer produces an economic payoff: at this point the increase in output is so small that it is not worth the cost of the additional physical capital.

In that case, we would estimate that growing physical capital per worker is responsible for 3% × 0.33 = 1 percentage point of productivity growth per year. A similar but more complex procedure is used to estimate the effects of growing human capital. The procedure is more complex because there aren't simple dollar measures of the quantity of human capital.

Growth accounting allows us to calculate the effects of greater physical and human capital on economic growth. But how can we estimate the effects of technological progress? We do so by estimating what is left over after the effects of physical and human capital have been taken into account. For example, let's imagine that there was no increase in human capital per worker so that we can focus on changes in physical capital and in technology.

In Figure 9-5, the lower curve shows the same hypothetical relationship between physical capital per worker and output per worker shown in Figure 9-4. Let's assume that this was the relationship given the technology available in 1945. The upper curve also shows a relationship between physical capital per worker and productivity, but this time given the technology available in 2015. (We've

FIGURE 9-5 Technological Progress and Productivity Growth

Technological progress raises productivity at any given level of physical capital per worker, and therefore shifts the aggregate production function upward. Here we hold human capital per worker fixed. We assume that the lower curve (the same curve as in Figure 9-4) reflects technology in 1945 and the upper curve reflects technology in 2015. Holding technology and human capital fixed, tripling physical capital per worker from $20,000 to $60,000 leads to a doubling of real GDP per worker, from $30,000 to $60,000. This is shown by the movement from point A to point C, reflecting an approximately 1% per year rise in real GDP per worker. In reality, technological progress raised productivity at any given level of physical capital—shown here by the upward shift of the curve—and the actual rise in real GDP per worker is shown by the movement from point A to point D. Real GDP per worker grew 2% per year, leading to a quadrupling during the period. The extra 1% in growth of real GDP per worker is due to higher total factor productivity.

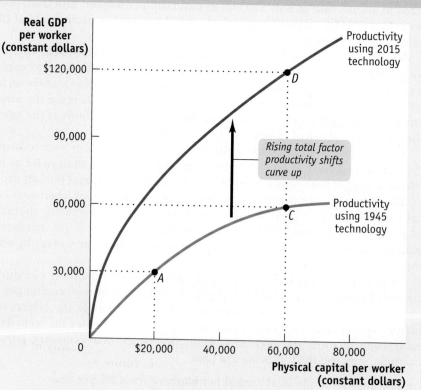

chosen a 70-year stretch to allow us to use the Rule of 70.) The 2015 curve is shifted up compared to the 1945 curve because technologies developed over the previous 70 years make it possible to produce more output for a given amount of physical capital per worker than was possible with the technology available in 1945. (Note that the two curves are measured in constant dollars.)

Let's assume that between 1945 and 2015 the amount of physical capital per worker rose from $20,000 to $60,000. If this increase in physical capital per worker had taken place without any technological progress, the economy would have moved from A to C: output per worker would have risen, but only from $30,000 to $60,000, or 1% per year (using the Rule of 70 tells us that a 1% growth rate over 70 years doubles output). In fact, however, the economy moved from A to D: output rose from $30,000 to $120,000, or 2% per year. There was an increase in both physical capital per worker and technological progress, which shifted the aggregate production function.

In this case, 50% of the annual 2% increase in productivity—that is, 1% in annual productivity growth—is due to higher **total factor productivity,** the amount of output that can be produced with a given amount of factor inputs. So when total factor productivity increases, the economy can produce more output with the same quantity of physical capital, human capital, and labor.

Most estimates find that increases in total factor productivity are central to a country's economic growth. We believe that observed increases in total factor productivity in fact measure the economic effects of technological progress. All of this implies that technological change is crucial to economic growth.

The Bureau of Labor Statistics estimates the growth rate of both labor productivity and total factor productivity for nonfarm business in the United States. According to the Bureau's estimates, over the period from 1948 to 2016 American labor productivity rose 2.2% per year. Less than half of that rise, approximately 49%, is explained by increases in physical and human capital per worker; the rest is explained by rising total factor productivity—that is, by technological progress.

> **Total factor productivity** is the amount of output that can be achieved with a given amount of factor inputs.

What About Natural Resources?

In our discussion so far, we haven't mentioned natural resources, which certainly have an effect on productivity. Other things equal, countries that are abundant in valuable natural resources, such as highly fertile land or rich mineral deposits, have higher real GDP per capita than less fortunate countries.

The most obvious modern example is the Middle East, where enormous oil deposits have made a few sparsely populated countries very rich. For example, Kuwait has about the same level of real GDP per capita as Germany, but Kuwait's wealth is based on oil, not manufacturing, the source of Germany's high output per worker.

But other things are often not equal. In the modern world, natural resources are a much less important determinant of productivity than human or physical capital for the great majority of countries. For example, some nations with very high real GDP per capita, such as Japan, have very few natural resources. Some resource-rich nations, such as Nigeria (which has sizable oil deposits), are very poor.

Historically, natural resources played a much more prominent role in determining productivity. In the nineteenth century, the countries with the highest real GDP per capita were those abundant in rich farmland and mineral deposits: the United States, Canada, Argentina, and Australia. As a consequence, natural resources figured prominently in the development of economic thought.

In a famous book published in 1798, *An Essay on the Principle of Population,* the English economist Thomas Malthus made the fixed quantity of land in the world the basis of a pessimistic prediction about future productivity. As population grew, he pointed out, the amount of land per worker would decline. And this, other things equal, would cause productivity to fall.

His view, in fact, was that improvements in technology or increases in physical capital would lead only to temporary improvements in productivity because they would always be offset by the pressure of rising population and more workers on the supply of land. In the long run, he concluded, the great majority of people were condemned to living on the edge of starvation. Only then would death rates be high enough and birth rates low enough to prevent rapid population growth from outstripping productivity growth.

It hasn't turned out that way, although many historians believe that Malthus's prediction of falling or stagnant productivity was valid for much of human history. Population pressure probably did prevent large productivity increases until the eighteenth century. But in the time since Malthus wrote his book, any negative effects on productivity from population growth have been far outweighed by other, positive factors—advances in technology, increases in human and physical capital, and the opening up of enormous amounts of cultivable land in the New World.

It remains true, however, that we live on a finite planet, with limited supplies of resources such as oil and limited ability to absorb environmental damage. We address the concerns these limitations pose for economic growth in the final section of this chapter.

ECONOMICS >> *in Action*
The Rise, Fall, and Return of the Productivity Paradox

We live in an era of revolutionary technological change—or that's what everyone says. And to be fair, there are good reasons for the excitement. After all, your smartphone is thousands of times faster and can store millions of times more data as the computers available to the astronauts who landed on the moon. But is the dramatic increase in computing power translating into equally dramatic economic growth? Economists have been asking that question for decades—and the answer still isn't clear.

From today's perspective, the cutting-edge technologies introduced in the 1980s—desktop computers that could display text in any color you wanted as long as it was green, cell phones the size of small bricks, and so on—look pretty primitive. But they were a big improvement on what came before. Yet the economic payoff was surprisingly hard to see.

As Figure 9-6 shows, the big technological changes of the 1980s took place in the middle of a prolonged slump in the growth of total factor productivity. During the 21 years from 1974 to 1995, the average annual growth rate of total factor productivity was only 0.6%, a little over a quarter of what it had been during the previous 25 years. In 1987 Robert Solow, the Nobel-winning father of the modern theory of economic growth, famously noted that "you can see the computer age everywhere but in the productivity statistics." What was going on?

Some economists argued that the explanation of the so-called *productivity paradox* was that there's a big difference between having a new technology and knowing what to do with it. They predicted that computers would eventually pay off once business practices evolved to take advantage of personal computers, local area networks, and the internet.

And this optimistic view was seemingly borne out by developments in the mid-1990s. Total factor productivity surged after around 1995, with much of the surge taking place in formerly staid sectors like retailing, where companies like Walmart took advantage of information technology

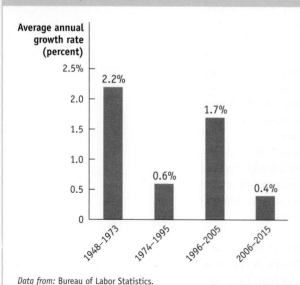

FIGURE 9-6 The Rise and Fall of Total Factor Productivity, 1948–2015

Average annual growth rate (percent)

2.2%
1.7%
0.6%
0.4%

1948–1973 1974–1995 1996–2005 2006–2015

Data from: Bureau of Labor Statistics.

to achieve big efficiency gains in seemingly prosaic areas like inventory management (using bar-code technology, as illustrated in this chapter's Business Case). The productivity paradox was over. Or was it?

After the spike from 1996 to 2005, growth in total factor productivity slowed to a crawl after 2005. Once again, new technology seemed to be everywhere: smartphones, tablets, and high-speed wireless internet were post-2005 developments. Despite these innovations, the productivity paradox was back with a vengeance.

The larger lesson here is that advances in technology can be exciting and ultimately very useful, but it may take many years of figuring out how to use them before there is a significant impact on living standards.

>> Check Your Understanding 9-2
Solutions appear at back of book.

1. Predict the effect of each of the following events on the growth rate of productivity.
   a. The amounts of physical and human capital per worker are unchanged, but there is significant technological progress.
   b. The amount of physical capital per worker grows at a steady pace, but the level of human capital per worker and technology are unchanged.

2. Output in the economy of Erewhon has grown 3% per year over the past 30 years. The labor force has grown at 1% per year, and the quantity of physical capital has grown at 4% per year. The average education level hasn't changed. Estimates by economists say that each 1% increase in physical capital per worker, other things equal, raises productivity by 0.3%. (*Hint:* % change in (X/Y) = % change in X – % change in Y.)
   a. How fast has productivity in Erewhon grown?
   b. How fast has physical capital per worker grown?
   c. How much has growing physical capital per worker contributed to productivity growth? What percentage of productivity growth is that?
   d. How much has technological progress contributed to productivity growth? What percentage of productivity growth is that?

3. Multinomics, Inc., is a large company with many offices around the country. It has just adopted a new computer system that will affect virtually every function performed within the company. Why might a period of time pass before employees' productivity is improved by the new computer system? Why might there be a temporary decrease in employees' productivity?

>> Quick Review
- Long-run increases in living standards arise almost entirely from growing **labor productivity,** often simply referred to as **productivity.**

- An increase in **physical capital** is one source of higher productivity, but it is subject to **diminishing returns to physical capital.**

- **Human capital** and **technological progress** are also sources of increases in productivity.

- The **aggregate production function** is used to estimate the sources of increases in productivity. **Growth accounting** has shown that rising **total factor productivity,** interpreted as the effect of technological progress, is central to long-run economic growth.

- Natural resources are less important today than physical and human capital as sources of productivity growth in most economies.

Why Growth Rates Differ

In 1820, according to estimates by the economic historian Angus Maddison, Mexico had somewhat higher real GDP per capita than Japan. Today, Japan has higher real GDP per capita than most European nations and Mexico is a relatively poor country, though by no means among the poorest. The difference? Over the long run—since 1820—real GDP per capita grew at 1.9% per year in Japan but at only 1.3% per year in Mexico.

As this example illustrates, even small differences in growth rates have large consequences over the long run. So why do growth rates differ across countries and across periods of time?

Explaining Differences in Growth Rates

As one might expect, economies with rapid growth tend to be economies that add physical capital, increase their human capital, or experience rapid technological progress. Striking economic success stories, like Japan in the 1950s and 1960s or China more recently, tend to be countries that do all three:

1. Rapidly add to their physical capital through high savings and investment spending.
2. Upgrade their educational level.
3. Make fast technological progress.

Evidence also points to the importance of government policies, property rights, political stability, and good governance in fostering the sources of growth. (We'll look at the role of government in the next section.)

Savings and Investment Spending One reason for differences in growth rates between countries is that some countries are increasing their stock of physical capital much more rapidly than others, through high rates of investment spending. In the 1960s, Japan was the fastest-growing major economy; it also spent a much higher share of its GDP on investment goods than did other major economies. In recent years, China has been the fastest-growing major economy, and it similarly spends a very large share of its GDP on investment goods. In 2015, investment spending was 43% of China's GDP, compared with only 20% in the United States.

The money for high investment spending comes from savings. In the next chapter we'll analyze how financial markets channel savings into investment spending. For now, however, the key point is that investment spending must be paid for either out of savings from domestic households or by savings from foreign households—that is, an inflow of foreign capital.

Foreign capital has played an important role in the long-run economic growth of some countries, including the United States, which relied heavily on foreign funds during its early industrialization. For the most part, however, countries that invest a large share of their GDP are able to do so because they have high domestic savings. In fact, China in 2015 saved an even higher percentage of its GDP than it invested at home. The extra savings were invested abroad, largely in the United States.

One reason for differences in growth rates, then, is that countries add different amounts to their stocks of physical capital because they have different rates of savings and investment spending.

Education Just as countries differ substantially in the rate at which they add to their physical capital, there have been large differences in the rate at which countries add to their human capital through education.

A case in point is the comparison between Argentina and China. In both countries the adult literacy rate has risen steadily over time, but it has risen much faster in China.

Figure 9-7 shows the percentage of people over the age of 15 who can both read and write in China, which we have highlighted as an example of spectacular long-run growth, and in Argentina, a country whose growth has been disappointing. Thirty-five years ago, Argentina had a much more educated population, while many Chinese were still illiterate. Today, the average educational level and adult literacy rate in China is still slightly below that in Argentina— but that's mainly because there are still many elderly adults in China who never received basic education. In terms of secondary and tertiary education, China has outstripped once-rich Argentina.

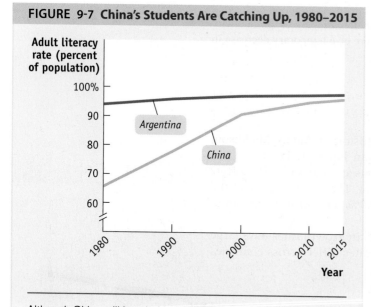

FIGURE 9-7 China's Students Are Catching Up, 1980–2015

Although China still lags behind Argentina in adult literacy, it is rapidly catching up. China's success at adding human capital is one key to the spectacular rise in its long-run growth rate in recent decades.

Data from: World Development Indicators, World Bank.

Research and Development   The advance of technology is a key force behind economic growth. What drives technological progress?

Scientific advances make new technologies possible. To take the most spectacular example in today's world, the semiconductor chip—which is the basis for all modern information technology—could not have been developed without the theory of quantum mechanics in physics.

But science alone is not enough: scientific knowledge must be translated into useful products and processes. And that often requires devoting a lot of resources to **research and development,** or **R&D,** spending to create new technologies and apply them to practical use.

Although some research and development is conducted by governments, much R&D is paid for by the private sector. The United States became the world's leading economy in large part because American businesses were among the first to make systematic research and development a part of their operations. In fact, it was Thomas Edison who created the first modern industrial research laboratory, as described in the following For Inquiring Minds.

Developing new technology is one thing; applying it is another. There have often been notable differences in the pace at which different countries take advantage of new technologies. For example, since 2000, Italy has suffered a significant decline in its total factor productivity, while the United States has moved ahead (see the Economics in Action on Italy at the end of this section). The sources of these national differences are the subject of a great deal of economic research.

The Role of Government in Promoting Economic Growth

Governments can play an important role in promoting—or blocking—all three sources of long-term economic growth: physical capital, human capital, and technological progress. They can either affect growth directly through subsidies to factors that enhance growth, or by creating an environment that either fosters or hinders growth.

Government Policies   Government policies can increase the economy's growth rate through four main channels.

1. GOVERNMENT SUBSIDIES TO INFRASTRUCTURE   Governments play an important direct role in building **infrastructure:** roads, power lines, ports, information networks, and other large-scale physical capital projects that provide a foundation for economic activity. Although some infrastructure is provided by private companies, much of it is either provided by the government or requires a great deal of government regulation and support.

Research and development, or **R&D,** is spending to create and implement new technologies.

Roads, power lines, ports, information networks, and other underpinnings for economic activity are known as **infrastructure.**

FOR INQUIRING MINDS   **Inventing R&D**

Thomas Edison is best known as the inventor of the lightbulb and the phonograph. But his biggest invention may surprise you: he invented research and development.

Before Edison's time, there had, of course, been many inventors. Some of them worked in teams. But in 1875 Edison created something new: his Menlo Park, New Jersey, laboratory. It employed 25 men full time to generate new products and processes for business. In other words,

he did not set out to pursue a particular idea and then cash in. He created an organization whose purpose was to create new ideas year after year.

You could say that before Edison's lab, technology just sort of happened: people came up with ideas, but businesses didn't plan to make continuous technological progress. Now R&D operations, often much bigger than Edison's original team, are standard practice throughout the business world.

Edison in his lab in 1888 with a work in progress: the phonograph.

Ireland is often cited as an example of the importance of government-provided infrastructure. After the government invested in an excellent telecommunications infrastructure in the 1980s, Ireland became a favored location for high-technology companies from abroad and its economy took off in the 1990s.

Poor infrastructure, such as a power grid that frequently fails and cuts off electricity, is a major obstacle to economic growth in many countries. To provide good infrastructure, an economy must not only be able to afford it, but it must also have the political discipline to maintain it.

Perhaps the most crucial infrastructure is something we, in an advanced country, rarely think about: basic public health measures in the form of a clean water supply and disease control. Poor health infrastructure is a major obstacle to economic growth in poor countries, especially those in Africa.

2. GOVERNMENT SUBSIDIES TO EDUCATION In contrast to physical capital, which is mainly created by private investment spending, much of an economy's human capital is the result of government spending on education. In the United States, various levels of government fund the bulk of primary and secondary education. Government funding subsidizes a significant share of higher education as well: over 70% of students attend public colleges and universities. In addition, the federal government significantly subsidizes research performed at private colleges and universities.

Differences in the rate at which countries add to their human capital largely reflect government policy. As we saw in Figure 9-7, the adult literacy rate in China has been increasing more rapidly than in Argentina. This isn't because China is richer than Argentina; until recently, China was, on average, poorer than Argentina. Instead, it reflects the fact that the Chinese government has made education and raising the literacy rate high priorities.

3. GOVERNMENT SUBSIDIES TO R&D Technological progress is largely the result of private initiative. But in the more advanced countries, important R&D is done by government agencies as well. For example, the internet grew out of a system, the Advanced Research Projects Agency Network (ARPANET), created by the U.S. Defense department, then extended to educational institutions by the National Science Foundation.

4. MAINTAINING A WELL-FUNCTIONING FINANCIAL SYSTEM Governments play an important indirect role in making high rates of private investment spending possible. Both the amount of savings and the ability of an economy to direct savings into productive investment spending depend on the economy's institutions, especially its financial system. A well-regulated and well-functioning financial system is very important for economic growth because in most countries it is the principal way in which savings are channeled into investment spending.

If a country's citizens trust their banks, they will place their savings in bank deposits, which the banks will then lend to their business customers. But if people distrust their banks, they will hoard gold or foreign currency, keeping their savings in safe deposit boxes or under the mattress, where it cannot be turned into productive investment spending. A well-functioning financial system requires appropriate government regulation to assure depositors that their funds are protected from loss.

Protection of Property Rights *Property rights* are the rights of owners of valuable items to dispose of those items as they choose. A subset, *intellectual property rights*, are the rights of an innovator to accrue the rewards of her innovation. The state of property rights generally, and intellectual property rights in particular, are important factors in explaining differences in growth rates across economies. Why? Because no one would bother to spend the effort and resources required to innovate if someone else could appropriate that innovation and capture the rewards. So, for innovation to flourish, intellectual property rights must receive protection.

Sometimes this is accomplished by the nature of the innovation: it may be too difficult or expensive to copy. But, generally, the government has to protect intellectual property rights. A *patent* is a government-created temporary monopoly given to an innovator for the use or sale of his or her innovation. It's a temporary rather than permanent monopoly because while it's in society's interests to give an innovator an incentive to invent, it's also in society's interests to eventually encourage competition.

Political Stability and Good Governance There's not much point in investing in a business if rioting mobs are likely to destroy it, or in saving your money if someone with political connections can steal it. Political stability and good governance (including the protection of property rights) are essential ingredients in fostering economic growth in the long run.

Long-run economic growth in successful economies, like that of the United States, has been possible because there are good laws, institutions that enforce those laws, and a stable political system that maintains those institutions. The law must say that your property is really yours so that someone else can't take it away. The courts and the police must be honest so that they can't be bribed to ignore the law. And the political system must be stable so that laws don't change capriciously.

Americans take these preconditions for granted, but they are by no means guaranteed. Aside from the disruption caused by war or revolution, many countries find that their economic growth suffers due to corruption among the government officials who should be enforcing the law. For example, until 1991 the Indian government imposed many bureaucratic restrictions on businesses, which often had to bribe government officials to get approval for even routine activities—a tax on business, in effect. Economists have argued that a reduction in this burden of corruption is one reason Indian growth has been much faster in recent years.

Even when the government isn't corrupt, excessive government intervention can be a brake on economic growth. If large parts of the economy are supported by wasteful government subsidies, protected from imports, subject to unnecessary monopolization, or otherwise insulated from competition, productivity tends to suffer because of a lack of incentives. As we'll see in the next section, excessive government intervention is one often-cited explanation for slow growth in Latin America.

ECONOMICS >> *in Action*
What's the Matter with Italy?

Italy was once considered a remarkable economic success story. A century ago it was still a poor country—so poor that in the late nineteenth and early twentieth century millions of Italians emigrated to the United States and other destinations in search of a better life. After World War II, however, Italy experienced decades of rapid growth, with real GDP per capita quadrupling between 1950 and 1990. By the end of that growth spurt, as you can see from Figure 9-8, Italy was significantly richer than Britain, the nation that had led the Industrial Revolution.

But at that point Italian growth stalled. Real GDP per capita was stagnant after the late 1990s, and began falling after 2008, as Italy's economy suffered a severe downturn as a result of the European debt crisis. What went wrong?

Part of the answer involves slow growth of the factors of production. Italy's low birth rate has meant a rapidly aging population, with a declining

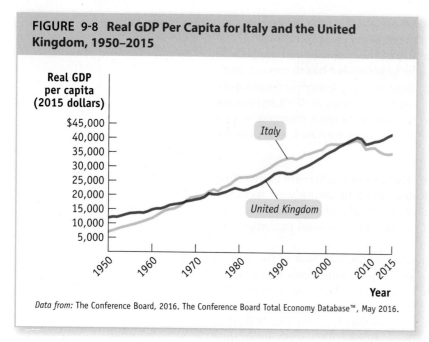

FIGURE 9-8 Real GDP Per Capita for Italy and the United Kingdom, 1950–2015

Data from: The Conference Board, 2016. The Conference Board Total Economy Database™, May 2016.

percentage of working age adults. Italy has also lagged in education, with the lowest college-educated share of the population in the European Union. Italy also seems to be having trouble taking advantage of technological progress. In fact, measured total factor productivity in Italy has declined since 2000. Why?

Some economists suggest that the explanation may lie in its business culture. There is widespread criticism, in particular, of Italian management practices. The claim is that promotion and financial rewards all too often reflect seniority rather than performance, giving few incentives to adopt new technology and best business practices.

Underlying this low-performance culture may be a lack of effective competition in many markets, which means that even badly run companies can stay in business indefinitely. The absence of competition within the Italian economy points to a government policy failure, perhaps arising from the relationship between established firms and government being too cozy. In an economy dominated by established firms, there's little incentive to invest or innovate. Italy's troubles show that even countries with a history of economic success can stumble. Achieving economic growth, it turns out, isn't easy.

>> Check Your Understanding 9-3

Solutions appear at back of book.

1. Explain the link between a country's growth rate, its investment spending as a percent of GDP, and its domestic savings.

2. U.S. centers of academic biotechnology research have closer connections with private biotechnology companies than do their European counterparts. What effect might this have on the pace of innovation and development of new drugs in the United States versus Europe?

3. During the 1990s in the former Soviet Union a lot of property was seized and controlled by those in power. How might this have affected the country's growth rate at that time? Explain.

>> Quick Review

• Countries differ greatly in their growth rates of real GDP per capita due to differences in the rates at which they accumulate physical capital and human capital as well as differences in technological progress. A prime cause of differences in growth rates is differences in rates of domestic savings and investment spending as well as differences in education levels, and **research and development,** or **R&D,** levels. R&D largely drives technological progress.

• Government actions can promote or hinder the sources of long-term growth.

• Government policies that directly promote growth are subsidies to **infrastructure,** particularly public health infrastructure, subsidies to education, subsidies to R&D, and the maintenance of a well-functioning financial system.

• Governments improve the environment for growth by protecting property rights (particularly intellectual property rights through patents), by providing political stability, and through good governance. Poor governance includes corruption and excessive government intervention.

Success, Disappointment, and Failure

As we've seen, rates of long-run economic growth differ quite a lot around the world. Now let's look at three regions of the world that have had quite different experiences with economic growth over the last few decades.

Figure 9-9 shows trends since 1960 in real GDP per capita in 2010 dollars for three countries: Argentina, Nigeria, and South Korea. (As in Figure 9-1, the vertical axis is drawn in logarithmic scale.) We have chosen these countries because each is a particularly striking example of what has happened in its region. South Korea's amazing rise is part of a broad "economic miracle" in East Asia. Argentina's slow progress, interrupted by repeated setbacks, is more or less typical of the disappointing growth that has characterized Latin America. And Nigeria's unhappy story until fairly recently—with little growth in real GDP until after 2000—was, unfortunately, an experience shared by many African countries.

FIGURE 9-9   Success and Disappointment

Real GDP per capita from 1960 to 2015, measured in 2010 dollars, is shown for Argentina, South Korea, and Nigeria, using a logarithmic scale. South Korea and some other East Asian countries have been highly successful at achieving economic growth. Argentina, like much of Latin America, has had several setbacks, slowing its growth. Nigeria's standard of living in 2015 was only barely higher than it had been in 1960, an experience shared by many African countries. Neither Argentina nor Nigeria exhibited much growth over the 55-year period, although both have had significantly higher growth in recent years.

Data from: World Development Indicators.

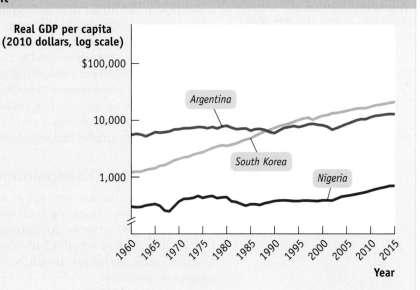

East Asia's Miracle

In 1960 South Korea was a very poor country. In fact, in 1960 its real GDP per capita was lower than that of India today. But, as you can see from Figure 9-9, beginning in the early 1960s South Korea began an extremely rapid economic ascent: real GDP per capita grew about 7% per year for more than 30 years. Today South Korea, though still somewhat poorer than Europe or the United States, looks very much like an economically advanced country.

South Korea's economic growth is unprecedented in history: it took the country only 35 years to achieve growth that required centuries elsewhere. Yet South Korea is only part of a broader phenomenon, often referred to as the East Asian economic miracle. High growth rates first appeared in South Korea, Taiwan, Hong Kong, and Singapore but then spread across the region, most notably to China. Since 1975, the whole region has increased real GDP per capita by 6% per year, more than three times America's historical rate of growth.

How have the Asian countries achieved such high growth rates? The answer is that all of the sources of productivity growth have been firing on all cylinders. Very high savings rates, the percentage of GDP that is saved nationally in any given year, have allowed the countries to significantly increase the amount of physical capital per worker. Very good basic education has permitted a rapid improvement in human capital. And these countries have experienced substantial technological progress.

Why were such high rates of growth unheard of in the past? Most economic analysts think that East Asia's growth spurt was possible because of its *relative* backwardness. That is, by the time that East Asian economies began to move into the modern world, they could benefit from adopting the technological advances that had been generated in technologically advanced countries such as the United States.

In 1900, the United States could not have moved quickly to a modern level of productivity because much of the technology that powers the modern economy, from jet planes to computers, hadn't been invented yet. In 1970, South Korea probably still had lower labor productivity than the United States had in 1900, but it could rapidly upgrade its productivity by adopting technology that had been developed in the United States, Europe, and Japan over the previous century. This was aided by a huge investment in human capital through widespread schooling.

According to the **convergence hypothesis,** international differences in real GDP per capita tend to narrow over time.

The East Asian experience demonstrates that economic growth can be especially fast in countries that are playing catch-up to other countries with higher GDP per capita. On this basis, many economists have suggested a general principle known as the **convergence hypothesis.** It says that differences in real GDP per capita among countries tend to narrow over time because countries that start with lower real GDP per capita tend to have higher growth rates. We'll look at the evidence on the convergence hypothesis in the upcoming Economics in Action.

Even before we get to that evidence, however, we can say right away that starting with a relatively low level of real GDP per capita is no guarantee of rapid growth, as the examples of Latin America and Africa both demonstrate.

Latin America's Disappointment

In 1900, Latin America was not considered an economically backward region. Natural resources, including both minerals and cultivable land, were abundant. Some countries, notably Argentina, attracted millions of immigrants from Europe in search of a better life. Measures of real GDP per capita in Argentina, Uruguay, and southern Brazil were comparable to those in economically advanced countries.

Since about 1920, however, growth in Latin America has been disappointing. As Figure 9-9 shows in the case of Argentina, growth has been disappointing for many decades, until 2000 when it finally began to increase. The fact that South Korea is now much richer than Argentina would have seemed inconceivable a few generations ago.

Why did Latin America stagnate? Comparisons with East Asian success stories suggest several factors. The rates of savings and investment spending in Latin America have been much lower than in East Asia, partly as a result of irresponsible government policy that has eroded savings through high inflation, bank failures, and other disruptions. Education—especially broad basic education—has been underemphasized: even Latin American nations rich in natural resources often failed to channel that wealth into their educational systems. And political instability, leading to irresponsible economic policies, has taken a toll.

In the 1980s, many economists came to believe that Latin America was suffering from excessive government intervention in markets. They recommended opening the economies to imports, selling off government-owned companies, and, in general, freeing up individual initiative. The hope was that this would produce an East Asian–type economic surge. So far, however, only one Latin American nation, Chile, has achieved sustained rapid growth.

Africa's Troubles and Promise

Africa south of the Sahara is home to more than 1 billion people, more than 3 times the population of the United States. On average, they are very poor, nowhere close to U.S. living standards 100 or even 200 years ago. And economic progress has been both slow and uneven, as the example of Nigeria, the most populous nation in the region, suggests. In fact, real GDP per capita in sub-Saharan Africa actually fell 13% from 1980 to 1994, although it has recovered since then. The consequence of this poor growth performance has been intense and continuing poverty.

This is a very disheartening story. What explains it?

Several factors are probably crucial. Perhaps first and foremost is the problem of political instability. In the years after 1975, large parts of Africa experienced devastating civil wars (often with outside powers backing rival sides) that killed millions of people and made productive

Slow and uneven economic growth in sub-Saharan Africa has led to extreme and ongoing poverty for many of its people.

investment spending impossible. The threat of war and general anarchy also inhibited other important preconditions for growth, such as education and provision of necessary infrastructure.

Property rights are also a major problem. The lack of legal safeguards means that property owners are often subject to extortion because of government corruption, making them averse to owning property or improving it. This is especially damaging in a country that is very poor.

While many economists see political instability and government corruption as the leading causes of underdevelopment in Africa, some—most notably Jeffrey Sachs of Columbia University and the United Nations—believe the opposite. They argue that Africa is politically unstable because it is poor. And Africa's poverty, they go on to claim, stems from its extremely unfavorable geographic conditions—much of the continent is landlocked, hot, infested with tropical diseases, and cursed with poor soil.

Sachs, along with economists from the World Health Organization, has highlighted the importance of health problems in Africa. In poor countries, worker productivity is often severely hampered by malnutrition and disease. In particular, tropical diseases such as malaria can only be controlled with an effective public health infrastructure, something that is lacking in much of Africa. At the time of writing, economists are studying certain regions of Africa to determine whether modest amounts of aid given directly to residents for the purposes of increasing crop yields, reducing malaria, and increasing school attendance can produce self-sustaining gains in living standards.

Although the example of African countries represents a warning that long-run economic growth cannot be taken for granted, there are some signs of hope. As we saw in Figure 9-9, Nigeria's per capita GDP, after decades of stagnation, turned upward after 2000, and it achieved an average annual growth rate of 3.0% from 2008 through 2015.

Left Behind by Growth?

Historically, rising real GDP per capita has translated into rising real income for the great majority of a nation's residents. However, there's no guarantee that this will happen. In fact, if the share of the nation's income going to a particular group of citizens falls over time, that group may be left behind while others benefit from growth. That group may even suffer a decline in their real income while the overall income of the nation is rising.

This isn't just a theoretical possibility. In the United States, and to a lesser extent in other wealthy countries, the share of income going to families near the top of the income distribution, and especially to the 1% of families with the highest incomes, has grown substantially since 1980. Figure 9-10 shows one consequence of this rise in inequality. The figure compares the growth since 1953 of real per capita GDP in the United States and the real income of the *median family*—the family at the exact middle of the income scale, with half of all families richer and half poorer. Both numbers are shown as indexes, with 1953 = 100.

Until 1980 the two numbers grew at nearly the same rate because the distribution of income was quite stable. After 1980, however, a growing share of income went to a relatively small number of people at the top. As a result, the income of the median family—which arguably reflects the experience of the typical American—rose much more slowly than real GDP per capita. Many American families, in other words, were to some extent left behind by economic growth.

It is important, however, to acknowledge two qualifications to this trend in the United States. First, in the broad sweep of history it is still true that economic growth raises the standard of living of the great majority of the population. Second, it would be wrong to imagine that global economic growth, even in

FIGURE 9-10 The Growing Income Divide, 1953–2015

In the United States, from 1953 through 1980, both real per capita GDP and the real income of the median family grew at nearly identical rates because the distribution of income was quite stable. After 1980, however, the share of national income going to the richest Americans rose significantly. And while real GDP per capita continued to grow, real median income—the income earned by families in the middle of the income distribution—lagged behind. This means that since 1980 many of those families in the middle have been left behind by economic growth.

Data from: U.S. Census; FRED.

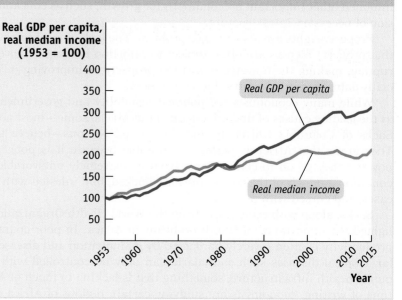

recent decades, has mainly benefited a well-off minority. On the contrary, from a worldwide perspective the most conspicuous aspect of recent growth has been the rise of a *global middle class*—rapidly rising incomes among hundreds of millions of previously poor people in China and other emerging economies.

ECONOMICS >> in Action
Are Economies Converging?

In the 1950s, much of Europe seemed quaint and backward to American visitors, and Japan seemed very poor. Today, a visitor to Paris or Tokyo sees a city that looks about as rich as New York. Although real GDP per capita is still somewhat higher in the United States, the differences in the standards of living among the United States, Europe, and Japan are relatively small.

Many economists have argued that this convergence in living standards is normal; the convergence hypothesis says that relatively poor countries should have higher rates of growth of real GDP per capita than relatively rich countries. And if we look at today's relatively well-off countries, the convergence hypothesis seems to be true.

Panel (a) of Figure 9-11 shows data for a number of today's wealthy economies measured in 2015 dollars. On the horizontal axis is real GDP per capita in 1955; on the vertical axis is the average annual growth rate of real GDP per capita from 1955 to 2015. There is a clear negative relationship as can be seen from the line fitted through the points. The United States was the richest country in this group in 1955 and had the slowest rate of growth. Japan, Ireland, and Spain were the poorest countries in 1955 and had the fastest rates of growth. These data suggest that the convergence hypothesis is true.

But economists who looked at similar data realized that these results depend on the countries selected. If you look at successful economies that have a high standard of living today, you find that real GDP per capita has converged. But looking across the world as a whole, including countries that remain poor, there is little evidence of convergence.

Panel (b) of Figure 9-11 illustrates this point using data for regions rather than individual countries (other than the United States). In 1955, East Asia and Africa were both very poor regions. Over the next 60 years, the East Asian regional economy grew quickly, as the convergence hypothesis would have predicted, but

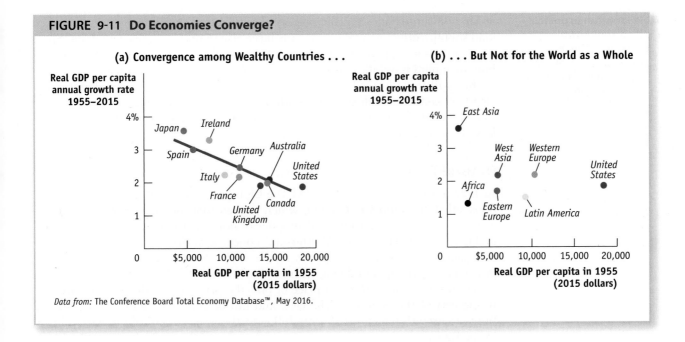

FIGURE 9-11   Do Economies Converge?

(a) Convergence among Wealthy Countries . . .

(b) . . . But Not for the World as a Whole

Data from: The Conference Board Total Economy Database™, May 2016.

the African regional economy grew very slowly. In 1955, Western Europe had higher real GDP per capita than Latin America. But, contrary to the convergence hypothesis, the Western European regional economy grew much more quickly over the next 60 years, widening the gap between the regions rather than narrowing it, as the hypothesis would predict.

So the convergence hypothesis isn't all wrong. Economists still believe that countries with relatively low real GDP per capita tend to have higher rates of growth than countries with relatively high real GDP per capita, *other things equal.* But other things—education, infrastructure, rule of law, and so on—are often not equal. Statistical studies find that when you adjust for differences in these other factors, poorer countries do tend to have higher growth rates. This result is known as *conditional convergence.*

Because other factors differ, however, there is no clear tendency toward convergence in the world economy as a whole. Western Europe, North America, and parts of Asia are becoming more similar in real GDP per capita, but the gap between these regions and the rest of the world is growing.

>> Check Your Understanding 9-4

Solutions appear at back of book.

1. Some economists think the high rates of growth of productivity achieved by many Asian economies cannot be sustained. Why might they be right? What would have to happen for them to be wrong?

2. Consider Figure 9-11, panel (b). Based on the data there, which regions support the convergence hypothesis? Which do not? Explain.

3. Some economists think the best way to help African countries is for wealthier countries to provide more funds for basic infrastructure. Others think this policy will have no long-run effect unless African countries have the financial and political means to maintain this infrastructure. What policies would you suggest?

‖ Is World Growth Sustainable?

Earlier in the chapter we described the views of Thomas Malthus, the early-nineteenth-century economist who warned that the pressure of population growth would tend to limit the standard of living. Malthus was right about the past: for

>> Quick Review

• East Asia's spectacular growth was generated by high savings and investment spending rates, emphasis on education, and adoption of technological advances from other countries.

• Poor education, political instability, and irresponsible government policies are major factors in the slow growth of Latin America.

• In sub-Saharan Africa, severe instability, war, and poor infrastructure—particularly affecting public health—resulted in a catastrophic failure of growth. But economic performance in recent years has been much better than in preceding years.

• The **convergence hypothesis** seems to hold only when other things that affect economic growth—such as education, infrastructure, property rights, and so on—are held equal.

Sustainable long-run economic growth is long-run growth that can continue in the face of the limited supply of natural resources and with less negative impact on the environment.

around 58 centuries, from the origins of civilization until his own time, limited land supplies effectively prevented any large rise in real incomes per capita. Since then, however, technological progress and rapid accumulation of physical and human capital have allowed the world to defy Malthusian pessimism.

But will this always be the case? Some skeptics have expressed doubt about whether **sustainable long-run economic growth** is possible—that is, growth that can continue in the face of the limited supply of natural resources and with less negative impact on the environment.

Natural Resources and Growth, Revisited

In 1972 a group of scientists called The Club of Rome made a big splash with a book titled *The Limits to Growth*, which argued that long-run economic growth wasn't sustainable due to limited supplies of nonrenewable resources such as oil and natural gas. These "neo-Malthusian" concerns at first seemed to be validated by a sharp rise in resource prices in the 1970s. Since then, however, resource prices have gone up and down, with no clear trend.

Figure 9-12 shows the real price of oil—the price of oil adjusted for inflation in the rest of the economy. The rise, and fall of concern about resource-based limits to growth have more or less followed the rise and fall of oil prices shown in the figure.

Differing views about the impact of limited natural resources on long-run economic growth turn on the answers to three questions:

1. How large are the supplies of key natural resources?
2. How effective will technology be at finding alternatives to natural resources?
3. Can long-run economic growth continue in the face of resource scarcity?

It's mainly up to geologists to answer the first question. Unfortunately, there's wide disagreement among the experts, especially about the prospects for future oil production. Some analysts believe there is enough untapped oil in the ground for world oil production to continue to rise for several decades. Others, including a number of oil company executives, believe that the growing difficulty of finding new oil fields will cause oil production to stop growing and eventually begin a gradual decline in the fairly near future. Some analysts believe that we have already reached that point.

FIGURE 9-12 The Real Price of Oil, 1950–2017

The real prices of natural resources, like oil, rose dramatically in the 1970s and then fell just as dramatically in the 1980s. In 2005 the real prices of natural resources have soared, but by late 2014 real oil prices returned to the levels last seen in the 1990s.

Data from: Energy Information Administration; FRED.

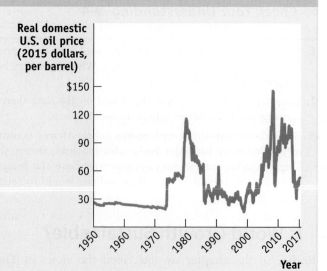

The answer to the second question, whether there are alternatives to natural resources, will come from engineers. However, there are already many alternative natural resources being exploited. Since 2005 there have been dramatic developments in energy production, with large amounts of previously unreachable oil and gas extracted through fracking, and with a huge decline in the cost of electricity generated by wind and solar power.

The third question, whether economies can continue to grow in the face of resource scarcity, is mainly a question for economists. And most, though not all, economists are optimistic. They believe that modern economies can find ways to work around limits on the supply of natural resources. One reason for this optimism is the fact that resource scarcity leads to high resource prices. These high prices, in turn, provide strong incentives to conserve the scarce resource and find alternatives. For example, after the sharp oil price increases of the 1970s, American consumers turned to smaller, more fuel-efficient cars as U.S. industry greatly intensified its efforts to reduce energy bills.

Given such responses to prices, economists generally tend to see resource scarcity as a problem that modern economies handle fairly well, and not as a fundamental limit to long-run economic growth. Environmental issues, however, pose a more difficult problem for economies because dealing with them requires effective political action.

Economic Growth and the Environment

Economic growth, other things equal, tends to increase the adverse impact of human activity on the environment, including an increase in pollution, the loss of wildlife habitats, the extinction of species, and reduced biodiversity. As we saw in this chapter's opening story, China's spectacular economic growth has also brought a spectacular increase in air pollution in its cities.

In analyzing economic growth and its environmental impact, it is useful to distinguish between *local* environmental degradation, which affects a geographically limited area, and *global* environmental degradation, which is far-reaching, with worldwide impact. As we'll see, it has proven to be far more difficult to address global environmental degradation and, in particular, the problem of *climate change.*

In fact, the improved air quality in the cities of today's advanced economies indicates that local environmental harm can be greatly reduced when there is sufficient political will and resources are devoted to finding a solution. Decades ago, before regulations virtually eliminated the use of coal heat, air pollution in London was so bad that it killed 4,000 people over two weeks in 1952. And as recounted in the opening story, the smog that once afflicted Los Angeles has disappeared thanks to regulations mandating cleaner-burning gasoline. In both of these cases, government intervention and expending some resources made everyone better off.

However, tackling climate change—a problem of global environmental degradation—has been a much harder problem to solve because policies must be implemented on a global scale, requiring the cooperation of many countries. There is broad scientific consensus that burning fossil fuels—coal, oil, and natural gas—leads to increasing levels of carbon dioxide in the atmosphere. Carbon dioxide is a type of *greenhouse gas.* Such gases trap the sun's energy, raising the planet's temperature, and lead to climate change, which, in turn, imposes high human, economic, and environmental costs. These costs include extreme weather, increased flooding, the disruption of agriculture, including crop failures, and more. A recent estimate put the cost of unmitigated climate change at 20% of world gross domestic product by 2100. Moreover, these costs tend to fall more heavily on poor countries.

The problem of climate change is linked to economic growth: the larger the economy, the more homes, factories, and vehicles, will have to be powered,

Under the **Paris Agreement** of 2015, 196 countries agreed to reduce their greenhouse gas emissions in an effort to limit the rise in the earth's temperature to no more than 2 degrees centigrade.

typically by burning fossil fuels. At present, world energy consumption is overwhelmingly dependent upon fossil fuels, which account for 81.4% of total consumption, while clean, renewable sources account for only 2.6%. Why? Because historically, fossil fuels have been cheaper to use. Most of today's wealthy countries grew their economies through industrialization and the burning of fossil fuels over the last century. To reduce the global emission of greenhouse gases, developed countries and large rapidly developing countries, such as China and India, will have to undertake a transition from a heavy reliance on fossil fuels to greater use of clean, renewable energy sources such as wind and solar power. We refer to this process as the *great energy transition*.

Until recently, effective action against climate change had been stymied by disagreement among countries on how to pay the cost of shifting from fossil fuel to clean energy sources. As Figure 9-13 shows, today's wealthy economies have historically been responsible for most of the carbon dioxide emissions—and carbon dioxide alone accounts for almost 76% of all global greenhouse gas emissions. But newly emerging economies like China and India are responsible for the recent growth. Inevitably, rich countries are reluctant to pay the price of reducing emissions only to have their efforts frustrated by rapidly growing emissions from new players. But relatively poor countries like China and India consider it unfair that they should be expected to bear the burden of protecting an environment threatened by the past actions of rich nations.

In 2015, in acknowledgement of the seriousness of the problem, 196 countries came together under the **Paris Agreement,** committing to reduce their emissions of greenhouse gases in an effort to limit the rise in the earth's temperature to no more than 2 degrees centigrade. The linchpin of the agreement was cooperation between China, India, and the United States. China and India agreed to limit their emissions, and the United States, along with other rich countries, committed to develop various forms of public and private financing to help poorer countries pay the cost.

Is it possible to maintain long-run growth while averting the effects of climate change? The answer, according to most economists who have studied the issue, is yes. While there will be economic costs, those costs have been falling as technological innovation in clean energy sources advances. The best available estimates show that even a large reduction in greenhouse gas emissions over the next few

---

FIGURE 9-13 Climate Change and Growth

Greenhouse gas emissions are positively related to growth. As shown here by the United States and Europe, wealthy countries have historically been responsible for the great bulk of carbon dioxide emissions—which make up more than three quarters of all greenhouse gas emissions—because of their richer and faster-growing economies. As China and other emerging economies have grown, they began to emit much more carbon dioxide. China has since overtaken the United States and Europe in emissions.

Data from: Energy Information Administration.

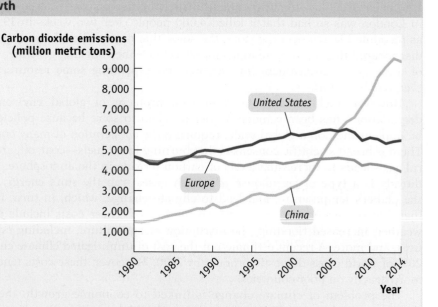

decades would cause only a modest reduction in the long-term rise in real GDP per capita.

To achieve long-run economic growth with environmental protection, governments will need to use regulations and environmental standards, and institute policies that create market incentives to encourage individuals and firms to make the transition to clean energy sources. Finally, governments—both rich and poor—will need to continue to cooperate with one another. Getting political consensus around the necessary policies will be key.

The answer is blowing in the wind.

ECONOMICS >> *in Action*

What Is the Cost of Limiting Carbon?

You may be surprised to learn that taking action against climate change in the United States doesn't necessarily require new legislation. Under U.S. law, the Environmental Protection Agency (EPA) is obliged to regulate pollutants that endanger public health, and in 2007 the Supreme Court ruled that carbon dioxide emissions meet that criterion.

So the EPA initiated a series of steps to limit carbon emissions. First, it set new fuel-efficiency standards to reduce emissions from motor vehicles. Then, it introduced rules limiting emissions from new power plants. Finally, in June 2014 it announced plans to limit emissions from existing power plants. This was a crucial step because coal-burning power plants account for a large part of carbon emissions, both in the United States and in other countries.

But how will the new rules affect the U.S. economy? Critics have argued that the EPA rules would cripple economic growth. For the most part, however, economists disagree. The EPA's own analysis suggests that by 2030 its rules would cost the U.S. economy about $9 billion annually in today's dollars—equivalent to 0.05% of the $19 trillion of goods and services produced annually—a trivial sum.

Still, the EPA's proposed rules would, at best, make a small dent in the problem of climate change. How much would a program that really deals with the problem cost? In 2014 the United Nations International Panel on Climate Change (IPCC) estimated that global measures limiting the rise in temperatures to 2 degrees centigrade would impose gradually rising costs, reaching about 5% of output by the year 2100. The impact on the world's rate of economic growth would, however, be small—a reduction of approximately 0.06 percentage points each year. The IPCC's numbers were more or less in line with other estimates. Most independent studies have found that environmental protection need not greatly reduce growth.

Why this optimism? At a fundamental level, the key insight is that given the right incentives modern economies can find many ways to reduce emissions, ranging from the use of renewable energy sources (which have grown much cheaper) to inducing consumers to choose goods with lower environmental impact. Economic growth and environmental damage don't have to go together.

>> Check Your Understanding 9-5

Solutions appear at back of book.

1. Are economists typically more concerned about the limits to growth imposed by environmental degradation or those imposed by resource scarcity? Explain, noting the role of negative externalities (costs imposed by individuals or firms on others without the requirement to pay compensation), in your answer.

2. What is the link between greenhouse gas emissions and growth? What is the expected effect on growth from emissions reduction? Why is international burden sharing of greenhouse gas emissions reduction a contentious problem?

>> Quick Review

• Economists generally believe that environmental degradation poses a greater challenge to **sustainable long-run economic growth** than resource scarcity. They also generally believe that modern economies can find ways to alleviate limits to growth from natural resource scarcity through the price response that promotes conservation and the creation of alternatives.

• Economic growth tends to harm the environment unless actions are taken to protect it. Local environmental degradation can be addressed through political will and resources. Global environmental degradation is harder to address because it requires cooperation across many countries.

• The accumulation of *greenhouse gases,* a by-product of burning fossil fuels, has led to *climate change,* the raising of the earth's temperature. In order to avert the impact of climate change, effective government intervention is required.

• Developed countries and large countries that are rapidly growing need to shift from a heavy reliance on fossil fuels to using clean, energy sources like solar and wind power. This will come at a modest cost to the rise in real GDP per capita, a cost that is falling as technological innovation in clean energy sources advances.

• In the **Paris Agreement** of 2015, 196 countries agreed to reduce their greenhouse gas emissions in an effort to limit the rise in the earth's temperature.

Raising the Bar(code)

When we think about innovation and technological progress, we tend to focus on the dramatic changes: cars replacing horses and buggies, electric light bulbs replacing gaslights, computers replacing adding machines and typewriters. However, much more progress is incremental and almost invisible to most people, yet has huge effects over time. Consider, for example, the simple bar-code scanner.

Bar codes were first used commercially in 1974, when a 10-pack of Wrigley's chewing gum was rung up with a scanner produced by the National Cash Register Corporation (now NCR Corp). Since then bar codes and their two-dimensional descendants—visual patterns that are meaningless to human eyes but are instantly recognizable by scanners and smartphones—have become ubiquitous, used to identify and route everything from shipping containers to airline passengers.

The benefits from machine-readable labels are enormous, extending well beyond what consumers in the checkout line can see. For example, retailers use them to continuously track sales, telling them when to reorder merchandise and restock shelves, what to keep in their warehouses, how productive individual workers are, and more. Grocery retailing is a labor-intensive industry, and economists estimate that the adoption of bar-code technology reduced labor costs by as much as 40%. Ultimately, bar-code technology helped drive the computerization of the entire retail industry.

You might think, then, that NCR, which remains a major player in point-of-service technologies like scanners, ATMs, and so forth, made a fortune from its leading role in this technology revolution. But while the company has done well, scanner sales in the early years weren't enormous: the adoption of bar-code scanners was relatively slow compared with the spread of smartphones a couple of decades later. Only about a third of supermarkets adopted them in the first decade after that historic pack of gum.

Why? To realize the full potential of bar-code technology, both retailers and firms had to spend substantial money upfront to buy the scanners and the information-processing systems they served. Equally important, manufacturers had to install the equipment to put bar codes on their products. This created a chicken-and-egg problem, with retailers waiting to have more scanner-readable products available and manufacturers waiting for more scanner-ready stores.

Over time this problem was resolved as retailers and manufacturers made the necessary investments, setting the stage for widespread use of information technology. In fact, after around 1990 retailing became one of the leading sources of overall productivity growth in the U.S. economy.

Adoption was slower in Europe. In the United States, big stores were the first to install scanners, and the technology fostered greater concentration of retailing at the expense of small, mom-and-pop stores that couldn't afford to implement scanner technology. In Europe, however, government policies—especially land-use policy—protected these stores.

Eventually, however, Europe began to follow the trend, too. Bar-code technology has spread from the United States to become almost universal, at least in advanced economies.

QUESTIONS FOR THOUGHT

1. Bar-code technology spurred a lot of investment in retailing. How did it alter the retailing production function? What would a similar amount of investment have accomplished without the new technology?

2. The spread of bar codes was delayed in the United States because everyone was waiting for someone else to move. What policy could have been adopted to address the delays? Would it have been a good idea?

3. Use the case to explain why international growth rates vary.

4. Despite initial barriers, bar codes have spread globally. What does this imply about differences in economic growth across countries?

SUMMARY

1. Growth is measured as changes in real GDP per capita in order to eliminate the effects of changes in the price level and changes in population size. Levels of real GDP per capita vary greatly around the world: About a quarter of the world's population lives in countries that are still poorer than the United States was in 1900. GDP per capita in the United States is about 8 times as high as it was in 1900.

2. Growth rates of real GDP per capita also vary widely. According to the **Rule of 70,** the number of years it takes for real GDP per capita to double is equal to 70 divided by the annual growth rate of real GDP per capita.

3. The key to long-run economic growth is rising **labor productivity,** or just **productivity,** which is output per worker. Increases in productivity arise from increases in **physical capital** per worker and **human capital** per worker as well as **technological progress.** The **aggregate production function** shows how real GDP per worker depends on these three factors. Other things equal, there are **diminishing returns to physical capital:** holding human capital per worker and technology fixed, each successive addition to physical capital per worker yields a smaller increase in productivity than the one before. Equivalently, more physical capital per worker results in a lower, but still positive, increase in productivity. **Growth accounting,** which estimates the contribution of each factor to a country's economic growth, has shown that rising **total factor productivity,** the amount of output produced from a given amount of factor inputs, is key to long-run growth. It is usually interpreted as the effect of technological progress. In contrast to earlier times, natural resources are a less significant source of productivity growth in most countries today.

4. The large differences in countries' growth rates are largely due to differences in their rates of accumulation of physical and human capital as well as differences in technological progress. Although inflows of foreign savings from abroad help, a prime factor is differences in domestic savings and investment spending rates, since most countries that have high investment spending on physical capital finance it by high domestic savings. Technological progress is largely a result of **research and development, or R&D.**

5. Governments can help or hinder growth. Government policies that directly foster growth are subsidies to **infrastructure,** particularly public health infrastructure, subsidies to education and R&D, and maintenance of a well-functioning financial system that channels savings into investment spending, education, and R&D. Governments can enhance the environment for growth by protecting property rights (particularly intellectual property rights through patents), by being politically stable, and by providing good governance. Poor governance includes corruption and excessive government intervention.

6. The world economy contains examples of success and failure in the effort to achieve long-run economic growth. East Asian economies have done many things right and achieved very high growth rates. The low growth rates of Latin American and African economies over many years led economists to believe that the **convergence hypothesis,** the claim that differences in real GDP per capita across countries narrow over time, fits the data only when factors that affect growth, such as education, infrastructure, and favorable government policies and institutions, are held equal across countries. In recent years, there has been an uptick in growth among some Latin American and sub-Saharan African countries, largely due to a boom in commodity exports.

7. Economists generally believe that environmental degradation poses a greater challenge to **sustainable long-run economic growth** than does natural resource scarcity. Addressing environmental degradation requires effective governmental intervention, but the problem of natural resource scarcity is often well handled by the market price response.

8. Climate change is linked to growth and there is broad consensus that government action is needed to address it. To avert the impact of climate change, countries will need to shift from a heavy reliance on fossil fuel to using clean, renewable energy sources— what we call the great energy transition. This will come at a modest cost to the rise in real GDP per capita, a cost that is falling as technological innovation in clean energy sources advances. Countries also need to cooperate with each other to realize the terms of the 2015 **Paris Agreement,** in which 196 signatory countries agreed to reduce their greenhouse gas emissions in an effort to limit the rise in earth's temperature.

PROBLEMS

interactive activity

1. The accompanying table shows data from the World Bank, World Development Indicators, for real GDP per capita in 2010 U.S. dollars for Argentina, Ghana, South Korea, and the United States for 1960, 1980, 2000, and 2015.

a. Complete the table by expressing each year's real GDP per capita as a percentage of its 1960 and 2015 levels.

b. How does the growth in living standards from 1960 to 2015 compare across these four nations? What might account for these differences?

	Argentina			Ghana			South Korea			United States		
		Percentage of			Percentage of			Percentage of			Percentage of	
Year	Real GDP per capita (2010 dollars)	1960 real GDP per capita	2015 real GDP per capita	Real GDP per capita (2010 dollars)	1960 real GDP per capita	2015 real GDP per capita	Real GDP per capita (2010 dollars)	1960 real GDP per capita	2015 real GDP per capita	Real GDP per capita (2010 dollars)	1960 real GDP per capita	2015 real GDP per capita
1960	$5,853	?	?	$1,053	?	?	$1,103	?	?	$17,037	?	?
1980	8,408	?	?	901	?	?	3,911	?	?	28,734	?	?
2000	8,544	?	?	975	?	?	15,105	?	?	45,056	?	?
2015	12,128	?	?	1,696	?	?	25,023	?	?	51,486	?	?

2. The following table shows the average annual growth rate in real GDP per capita for Argentina, Ghana, and South Korea using data from the World Bank, World Development Indicators, for the past few decades.

	Average annual growth rate of real GDP per capita		
Years	Argentina	Ghana	South Korea
1965–1975	1.92%	−1.13%	8.29%
1975–1985	−1.42	−2.29	7.08
1985–1995	1.54	1.70	8.06
1995–2005	1.14	2.16	4.28
2005–2015	3.11	4.45	3.02

a. For each 10-year period and for each country, use the Rule of 70 where possible to calculate how long it would take for that country's real GDP per capita to double.

b. Suppose that the average annual growth rate that each country achieved over the period 2005–2015 continues indefinitely into the future. Starting from 2015, use the Rule of 70 to calculate, where possible, the year in which a country will have doubled its real GDP per capita.

3. The following table provides approximate statistics on per capita income levels and growth rates for regions defined by income levels. According to the Rule of 70, starting in 2015 the high-income countries are projected to double their per capita GDP in approximately 70 years, in 2085. Throughout this question, assume constant growth rates for each of the regions are equal to their average value between 2000 and 2015.

Region	Real GDP per capita (2015)	Average annual growth rate of real GDP per capita (2000–2015)
High-income countries	$41,038	1.0%
Middle-income countries	4,584	4.4
Low-income countries	588	2.3

Data from: World Bank.

a. Calculate the ratio of per capita GDP in 2015 of the following:

   i. Middle-income to high-income countries

   ii. Low-income to high-income countries

   iii. Low-income to middle-income countries

b. Calculate the number of years it will take the low-income and middle-income countries to double their per capita GDP.

c. Calculate the per capita GDP of each of the regions in 2085. (*Hint:* How many times does their per capita GDP double in 70 years, the number of years from 2015 to 2085?)

d. Repeat part a with the projected per capita GDP in 2085.

e. Compare your answers to parts a and d. Comment on the change in economic inequality between the regions.

4. The country of Androde is currently using Method 1 for its production function. By chance, scientists stumble onto a technological breakthrough that will enhance Androde's productivity. This technological breakthrough is reflected in another production function, Method 2. The accompanying table shows combinations of physical capital per worker and output per worker for both methods, assuming that human capital per worker is fixed.

Method 1		Method 2	
Physical capital per worker	**Real GDP per worker**	**Physical capital per worker**	**Real GDP per worker**
0	0.00	0	0.00
50	35.36	50	70.71
100	50.00	100	100.00
150	61.24	150	122.47
200	70.71	200	141.42
250	79.06	250	158.11
300	86.60	300	173.21
350	93.54	350	187.08
400	100.00	400	200.00
450	106.07	450	212.13
500	111.80	500	223.61

a. Using the data in the accompanying table, draw the two production functions in one diagram. Androde's current amount of physical capital per worker is 100. In your figure, label that point A.

b. Starting from point A, over a period of 70 years, the amount of physical capital per worker in Androde rises to 400. Assuming Androde still uses Method 1, in your diagram, label the resulting point of production B. Using the Rule of 70, calculate by how many percent per year output per worker has grown.

c. Now assume that, starting from point A, over the same period of 70 years, the amount of physical capital per worker in Androde rises to 400, but that during that time period, Androde switches to Method 2. In your diagram, label the resulting point of production C. Using the Rule of 70, calculate by how many percent per year output per worker has grown now.

d. As the economy of Androde moves from point A to point C, what share of the annual productivity growth is due to higher total factor productivity?

5. The Bureau of Labor Statistics regularly releases the "Productivity and Costs" report for the previous month. Go to www.bls.gov and find the latest report. (On the Bureau of Labor Statistics home page, from the tab "Subjects," select the link to "Productivity: Labor Productivity & Costs"; then, from the heading "LPC News Releases," find the most recent "Productivity and Costs" report.) What were the percent changes in business and nonfarm business productivity for the previous quarter? How does the percent change in that quarter's productivity compare to the percent change from the same quarter a year ago?

6. What roles do physical capital, human capital, technology, and natural resources play in influencing long-run economic growth of aggregate output per capita?

7. How have U.S. policies and institutions influenced the country's long-run economic growth?

8. Over the next 100 years, real GDP per capita in Groland is expected to grow at an average annual rate of 2.0%. In Sloland, however, growth is expected to be somewhat slower, at an average annual growth rate of 1.5%. If both countries have a real GDP per capita today of $20,000, how will their real GDP per capita differ in 100 years? [*Hint:* A country that has a real GDP today of x and grows at $y\%$ per year will achieve a real GDP of $\$x \times (1 + (y/100))^z$ in z years. We assume that $0 \leq y < 100$.]

9. The accompanying table shows data from the World Bank, World Development Indicators, for real GDP per capita (2010 U.S. dollars) in France, Japan, the United Kingdom, and the United States in 1960 and 2015. Complete the table. Have these countries converged economically?

	1960		2015	
	Real GDP per capita (2010 dollars)	**Percentage of U.S. real GDP per capita**	**Real GDP per capita (2010 dollars)**	**Percentage of U.S. real GDP per capita**
France	$12,992	?	$41,330	?
Japan	8,369	?	44,657	?
United Kingdom	13,869	?	40,933	?
United States	17,037	?	51,486	?

10. The accompanying table shows data from the World Bank, World Development Indicators for real GDP per capita (2010 U.S. dollars) for Argentina, Ghana, South Korea, and the United States in 1960 and 2015. Complete the table. Have these countries converged economically?

	1960		2015	
	Real GDP per capita (2010 dollars)	Percentage of U.S. real GDP per capita	Real GDP per capita (2010 dollars)	Percentage of U.S. real GDP per capita
Argentina	$5,853	?	$12,128	?
Ghana	1,053	?	1,696	?
South Korea	1,103	?	25,023	?
United States	17,037	?	51,486	?

11. Access the Discovering Data exercise for Chapter 9 online to answer the following questions.

  a. What was the ratio of Japanese GDP per capita relative to the United States in 1950 and 1991?

  b. Why has Japan's GDP converged to that of the United States?

  c. Rank the country in order of richest to poorest (with 1 being the richest) in 1960 and 2010?

  d. What was the ratio of GDP per capita for Spain relative to the United States in 1960 and 2010?

  e. Which two countries experienced the fastest rate of convergence from 1960 through 2010?

  f. Why are lower income countries, like Korea in 1960, able to grow faster than rich countries?

  g. If countries continue along a similar path, will Japan, Korea, Chile, or Spain be the first country to reach the level of real GDP per capita in the United States?

12. Why would you expect real GDP per capita in California and Pennsylvania to exhibit convergence but not in California and Baja California, a state of Mexico that borders the United States? What changes would allow California and Baja California to converge?

13. According to the U.S. Energy Information Administration, the proven oil reserves existing in the world in 2015 consisted of 1,663 billion barrels. In that year, the U.S. Energy Information Administration reported that the world daily oil production was 80.58 million barrels a day.

  a. At this rate, for how many years will the proven oil reserves last? Discuss the Malthusian view in the context of the number you just calculated.

  b. In order to do the calculations in part a, what did you assume about the total quantity of oil reserves over time? About oil prices over time? Are these assumptions consistent with the Malthusian view on resource limits?

  c. Discuss how market forces may affect the amount of time the proven oil reserves will last, assuming that no new oil reserves are discovered and that the demand curve for oil remains unchanged.

14. The accompanying table shows the annual growth rate for the years 2000–2014 in per capita emissions of carbon dioxide (CO_2) and the annual growth rate in real GDP per capita for selected countries.

Country	2000–2014 Average annual growth rate	
	Real GDP per capita	CO_2 emissions per capita
Argentina	1.69%	1.17%
Bangladesh	4.33	4.47
Canada	0.96	0.01
China	9.24	7.48
Germany	1.20	−0.41
Ireland	1.30	−2.56
Japan	0.70	0.11
South Korea	3.51	2.32
Mexico	0.67	0.42
Nigeria	5.03	−1.30
Russia	4.16	1.35
South Africa	1.64	−0.02
United Kingdom	1.02	−2.20
United States	0.85	−1.27

Data from: Energy Information Administration; World Bank.

  a. Rank the countries in terms of their growth in CO_2 emissions, from highest to lowest. What five countries have the highest growth rate in emissions? What five countries have the lowest growth rate in emissions?

  b. Now rank the countries in terms of their growth in real GDP per capita, from highest to lowest. What five countries have the highest growth rate? What five countries have the lowest growth rate?

  c. Would you infer from your results that CO_2 emissions are linked to growth in output per capita?

  d. Do high growth rates necessarily lead to high CO_2 emissions?

WORK IT OUT Interactive step-by-step help with solving this problem can be found online.

15. You are hired as an economic consultant to the countries of Albernia and Brittania. Each country's current relationship between physical capital per worker and output per worker is given by the curve labeled "Productivity$_1$" in the accompanying diagram. Albernia is at point A and Brittania is at point B.

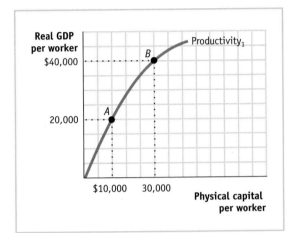

a. In the relationship depicted by the curve Productivity$_1$, what factors are held fixed? Do these countries experience diminishing returns to physical capital per worker?

b. Assuming that the amount of human capital per worker and the technology are held fixed in each country, can you recommend a policy to generate a doubling of real GDP per capita in Albernia?

c. How would your policy recommendation change if the amount of human capital per worker could be changed? Assume that an increase in human capital doubles the output per worker when physical capital per worker equals $10,000. Draw a curve on the diagram that represents this policy for Albernia.

10 Savings, Investment Spending, and the Financial System

PAYING FOR A HIDDEN EMPIRE

AMAZON.COM IS THE WORLD'S LARGEST and most famous *e-tailer*. Millions of people routinely visit its website to buy everything from books to electronics to pet supplies. Unlike traditional retailers, Amazon doesn't operate physical, brick-and-mortar stores; the customer's interaction with the company is virtual. You click a mouse or tap your smartphone, and a few days later the item you want shows up at your door, seemingly untouched by human hands.

Through the financial system Amazon obtained billions of dollars to finance its expansion, making it the world's largest e-tailer.

But the impression one sometimes has of a disembodied organization that summons consumer goods out of thin air is misleading: Amazon is by no means a virtual company, existing only in cyberspace. Behind those convenient online interactions and deliveries lies a vast, if mostly hidden, physical empire of server farms handling data and warehouses. In fact, that network of physical facilities is widely regarded as a key factor in Amazon's growth. In particular, the warehouses ("fulfillment centers,"

in Amazon-speak), close to major markets and containing a huge inventory of popular products, are what allow the firm to offer one- or two-day delivery on many items. And this superiority in distribution—some of you may have bought your textbook from Amazon!—gives the company a big competitive advantage.

We don't know exactly how much Amazon has spent to build this hidden physical empire, but the cost has surely run to many billions of dollars. Where did that money come from?

Not from reinvestment of the company's profits: Amazon, founded in 1994, basically earned no profits until 2016. But the company was able to convince outside investors that it would eventually become highly profitable. And the prospect of future profits was enough to bring in large amounts of money from outside investors.

Some of these investors bought equity—essentially shares in those expected future profits. Unusually for a technology company—but following standard practice for many traditional companies—Amazon also moved, early in its history, to sell debt: promises to pay investors a fixed amount each year, whatever happens. Those debt sales were controversial at the time, but are now widely viewed as having given Amazon a crucial advantage over competitors, who weren't able to make the same kind of investment in physical plant, especially those warehouses.

Amazon, then, was able to get the money it needed for massive investment spending long before that spending could yield financial results. It was, in a way, a kind of financial miracle—but while Amazon is an exceptional case, the same kind of financial miracle happens all the time in modern economies.

The long-run growth we analyzed in the previous chapter depends crucially on a set of markets and institutions, collectively known as the *financial system*, that channels the funds of savers into productive investment spending. Without this system, businesses like Amazon would not be able to purchase much of the physical capital that is an important source of productivity growth. And savers would be forced to accept a lower return on their funds.

Historically, financial systems channeled funds into investment spending projects such as railroads and factories. Today, financial systems channel funds into new sources of growth such as green technology, social media, and investments in human capital. Without a well-functioning financial system, a country will suffer stunted economic growth.

In this chapter, we begin by focusing on the economy as a whole. We will examine the relationship between savings and investment spending. Next, we go behind this relationship and analyze the financial system, the means by which savings is transformed into investment spending.

We'll see how the financial system works by creating assets, markets, and institutions that increase the welfare of both savers (those with funds to invest) and borrowers (those with investment spending projects to finance). Finally, we examine the behavior of financial markets and why they often resist economists' attempts at explanation. ●

WHAT YOU WILL LEARN

- What is the relationship between savings and investment spending?
- How does the **loanable funds market** match savers with borrowers?
- What are the purposes of the four principal types of **financial assets: loans, bonds, stocks,** and **bank deposits?**
- How do **financial intermediaries** help investors achieve **diversification?**
- What are the competing views about how asset prices are determined and why asset market fluctuations can be a source of macroeconomic instability?

According to the **savings–investment spending identity,** savings and investment spending are always equal for the economy as a whole.

Matching Up Savings and Investment Spending

We learned in the previous chapter that two of the essential ingredients in economic growth are increases in the economy's levels of *human capital* and *physical capital*. Human capital is largely provided by governments through public education. (In countries with a large private education sector, like the United States, private post-secondary education is also an important source of human capital.) But physical capital, with the exception of infrastructure, is mainly created through private investment spending—that is, spending by firms rather than by the government.

Who pays for private investment spending? In some cases it's the people or corporations that actually do the spending—for example, a family that owns a business might use its own savings to buy new equipment or a new building, or a corporation might reinvest some of its own profits to build a new factory. In the modern economy, however, individuals and firms that create physical capital often do it with other people's money—money that they borrow or raise by selling stock.

You may recall Figure 7-1, which showed an extended version of the circular flow of funds through the economy. In Chapter 7 we focused on the left side of that diagram, the green arrows showing flows of money into and out of the markets for goods and services. In this chapter we focus on the blue arrows on the right side of the diagram, specifically those flowing into and out of the *financial markets*, markets in which the government, firms, and individuals trade, not goods, but promises to pay in the future.

To understand financial markets and how investment spending is financed, we need to look first at how savings and investment spending are related for the economy as a whole. Then we will examine how savings are allocated among investment spending projects.

The Savings–Investment Spending Identity

The most basic point to understand about savings and investment spending is that they are always equal. This is not a theory; it's a fact of accounting called the **savings–investment spending identity.**

To see why the savings–investment spending identity must be true, let's look again at the national income accounting that we learned in Chapter 7. Recall that GDP is equal to total spending on domestically produced final goods and services, and that we can write the following equation (which is the same as Equation 7-1):

(10-1) $\text{GDP} = C + I + G + X - IM$

where C is spending by consumers, I is investment spending, G is government purchases of goods and services, X is the value of exports to other countries, and IM is spending on imports from other countries.

The Savings–Investment Spending Identity in a Closed Economy
In a closed economy, there are no exports or imports. So $X = 0$ and $IM = 0$, which makes Equation 10-1 simpler. As we learned in Chapter 7, the overall income of this simplified economy would, by definition, equal total spending. Why? Recall one of the basic principles of economics from Chapter 1, that one person's spending is another person's income: the only way people can earn income is by selling something to someone else, and every dollar spent in the economy creates income for somebody. This is represented by Equation 10-2: on the left, GDP represents total income earned in the economy, and on the right, $C + I + G$ represents total spending in the economy:

PITFALLS

INVESTMENT VERSUS INVESTMENT SPENDING

When macroeconomists use the term *investment spending,* they almost always mean "spending on new physical capital." This can be confusing, because in ordinary life we often say that someone who buys stocks or purchases an existing building is "investing." The important point to keep in mind is that only spending that adds to the economy's stock of physical capital is "investment spending." In contrast, the act of purchasing an asset such as a share of stock or a bond is "making an investment."

(10-2) $GDP = C + I + G$
Total income = Total spending

Now, what can be done with income? It can either be spent on consumption—consumer spending (C) plus government purchases of goods and services (G)—or saved (S). So it must be true that:

(10-3) $GDP = C + G + S$
Total income = Consumption spending + Savings

where S is savings. Meanwhile, as Equation 10-2 tells us, total spending consists of either consumption spending ($C + G$) or investment spending (I):

(10-4) $GDP = C + G + I$
Total income = Consumption spending + Investment spending

Putting Equations 10-3 and 10-4 together, we get:

(10-5) $C + G + S = C + G + I$
Consumption spending + savings = Consumption spending +
Investment spending

Subtract consumption spending ($C + G$) from both sides, and we get:

(10-6) $S = I$
Savings = Investment spending

As we said, then, it's a basic accounting fact that savings equals investment spending for the economy as a whole.

Now, let's take a closer look at savings. Households are not the only parties that can save in an economy. In any given year, the government can save, too, if it collects more tax revenue than it spends. When this occurs, the difference is called a **budget surplus** and is equivalent to savings by government.

If, alternatively, government spending exceeds tax revenue, there is a **budget deficit**—a negative budget surplus. In this case, we often say that the government is *dissaving:* by spending more than its tax revenues, the government is engaged in the opposite of savings. One way to finance a budget deficit is by borrowing. **Government borrowing** is the total amount of funds borrowed by federal, state, and local governments in the financial markets.

We'll define the term **budget balance** to refer to both cases, with the understanding that the budget balance can be positive (a budget surplus) or negative (a budget deficit). The budget balance is defined as:

(10-7) $S_{Government} = T - G - TR$

Where T is the value of tax revenues and TR is the value of government transfers. The budget balance is equivalent to savings by government—if it's positive, the government is saving; if it's negative, the government is dissaving. **National savings,** which we just called savings, for short, is equal to the sum of the budget balance and private savings, where private savings is disposable income (income plus government transfers minus taxes) minus consumption. It is given by:

(10-8) $S_{National} = S_{Government} + S_{Private}$

So Equations 10-6 and 10-8 tell us that, in a closed economy, the savings–investment spending identity has the following form:

(10-9) $S_{National} = I$
National savings = Investment spending

The Savings–Investment Spending Identity in an Open Economy

In an open or international economy, goods and money can flow into and out of the country. This changes the savings–investment spending identity because savings

The **budget surplus** is the difference between tax revenue and government spending when tax revenue exceeds government spending.

The **budget deficit** is the difference between tax revenue and government spending when government spending exceeds tax revenue.

Government borrowing is the total amount of funds borrowed by federal, state, and local governments in the financial markets.

The **budget balance** is the difference between tax revenue and government spending.

National savings, the sum of private savings and the budget balance, is the total amount of savings generated within the economy.

THE DIFFERENT KINDS OF CAPITAL

It's important to understand clearly the three different kinds of capital: physical capital, human capital, and financial capital (as explained in the previous chapter):

1. *Physical capital* consists of manufactured resources such as buildings and machines.
2. *Human capital* is the improvement in the labor force generated by education and knowledge.
3. *Financial capital* is funds from savings that are available for investment spending. A country that has a positive net capital inflow is experiencing a flow of funds into the country from abroad that can be used for investment spending.

need not be spent on investment spending projects in the same country in which the savings are generated. That's because the savings of people who live in any one country can be used to finance investment spending that takes place in other countries. So any given country can receive *inflows* of funds—foreign savings that finance investment spending in that country. Any given country can also generate *outflows* of funds—domestic savings that finance investment spending in another country.

The net effect of international inflows and outflows of funds on the total savings available for investment spending in any given country is known as the **net capital inflow** into that country, equal to the total inflow of foreign funds minus the total outflow of domestic funds to other countries. Like the budget balance, a net capital inflow can be negative—that is, more capital can flow out of a country than flows into it. In recent years, the United States has experienced a consistent positive net capital inflow from foreigners, who view our economy as an attractive place to put their savings. In 2016, for example, net capital inflows into the United States were $481.2 billion.

It's important to note that, from a national perspective, a dollar generated by national savings and a dollar generated by capital inflow are not equivalent. Yes, they can both finance the same dollar's worth of investment spending. But any dollar borrowed from a saver must eventually be repaid with interest. A dollar that comes from national savings is repaid with interest to someone domestically—either a private party or the government.

But a dollar that comes as capital inflow must be repaid with interest to a foreigner. So a dollar of investment spending financed by a capital inflow comes at a higher *national* cost—the interest that must eventually be paid to a foreigner—than a dollar of investment spending financed by national savings.

The fact that a net capital inflow represents funds borrowed from foreigners is an important aspect of the savings–investment spending identity in an international economy. Consider an individual who spends more than his or her income; that person must borrow the difference from others. Similarly, a country that spends more on imports than it earns from exports must borrow the difference from foreigners. And that difference, the amount of funds borrowed from foreigners, is the country's net capital inflow. As we explain more fully in Chapter 18, this means the net capital inflow into a country is equal to the difference between imports and exports:

(10-10)
$$NCI = IM - X$$
Net capital inflow = Imports – Exports

Rearranging Equation 10-1 we get:

(10-11) $I = (GDP - C - G) + (IM - X)$

Using Equation 10-3 we know that $GDP - C - G$ is equal to national savings, so that:

(10-12) $I = S_{National} + (IM - X) = S_{National} + NCI$
Investment spending = National savings + Net capital inflow

So the application of the savings–investment spending identity to an economy that is open to inflows or outflows of capital means that investment spending is equal to savings, where savings is equal to national savings *plus* net capital inflow. That is, in an economy with a positive net capital inflow, some investment spending is funded by the savings of foreigners. And in an economy with a negative net capital inflow (that is, more capital is flowing out than flowing in), some portion of national savings is funding investment spending in other countries.

Net capital inflow is the total inflow of funds into a country minus the total outflow of funds out of a country.

U.S. investment spending in 2016 totaled $3,657.2 billion. Private savings totaled $3,756.6 billion, and government savings equaled –$330.4 billion, leading to national savings of $3,426.2 billion. Net capital inflow was $481.2 billion. Notice that these numbers don't quite add up. Because data collection isn't perfect, there is a statistical discrepancy of –$250.2 billion, the amount that national savings plus net capital inflow exceeded investment spending. We know this is a data error because the savings–investment spending identity must hold.

Figure 10-1 shows what the savings–investment spending identity looked like in 2016 for two of the world's major economies, those of the United States and Germany. To make the two economies easier to compare, we've measured savings and investment spending as percentages of GDP. In each panel the orange bars on the left show total investment spending and the multicolored bars on the right show the components of savings. U.S. investment spending was 19.7% of GDP, financed by a combination of private savings (23.0% of GDP) and positive net capital inflow (2.6% of GDP) and partly offset by a government budget deficit (–4.4% of GDP). German investment spending was lower as a percentage of GDP, at 19.2%. It was financed by a higher level of private savings as a percentage of GDP (27.1%), and a small government budget surplus (0.8% of GDP), but was offset by a negative capital inflow or capital outflow (–8.5% of GDP).

The economy's savings finance its investment spending. But how are these funds that are available for investment spending allocated among various projects? That is, what determines which projects get financed (such as Amazon's fulfillment centers) and which don't? We'll see shortly that funds get allocated to investment spending projects using a familiar method: by the market, via supply and demand.

FIGURE 10-1 The Savings–Investment Spending Identity in Open Economies: The United States and Germany, 2016

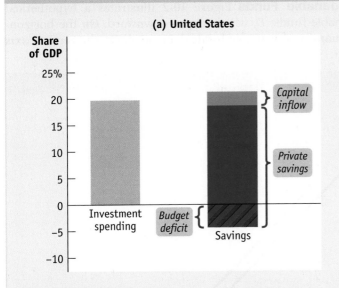
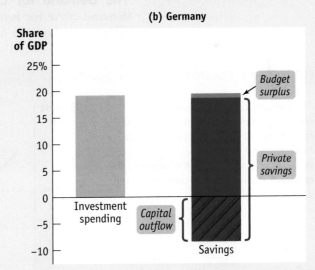

U.S. investment spending in 2016 (equal to 19.7% of GDP) was financed by a combination of private savings (23.0% of GDP) and a capital inflow (2.6% of GDP), which were partially offset by a government budget deficit (–4.4% of GDP).
German investment spending in 2016 was slightly lower as a percentage of GDP (19.2%). It was financed by a higher level of private savings as a percentage of GDP (27.1%), and a small government budget surplus (0.8% of GDP), but was offset by a capital outflow (–8.5% of GDP). Bars may not equal due to statistical discrepancy.

Data from: International Monetary Fund.

The loanable funds market is a hypothetical market that illustrates the market outcome of the demand for funds generated by borrowers and the supply of funds provided by lenders.

The Market for Loanable Funds

For the economy as a whole, savings always equals investment spending. In a closed economy, savings is equal to national savings. In an international or open economy, savings is equal to national savings plus capital inflow. At any given time, however, savers, the people with funds to lend, are usually not the same as borrowers, the people who want to borrow to finance their investment spending. How are savers and borrowers brought together?

Savers and borrowers are matched up with one another in much the same way producers and consumers are matched up: through markets governed by supply and demand.

To understand this, it helps to consider a somewhat simplified version of reality. In the actual economy, there are a large number of different financial markets. These include markets for *bonds* and *loans*, which are both promises to pay a fixed amount whatever happens, and *stocks*, which give investors a share of future profits. However, economists often work with a simplified model in which they assume that there is just one market that brings together those who want to lend money (savers) and those who want to borrow (firms with investment spending projects).

This hypothetical market is known as the **loanable funds market.** The price that is determined in the loanable funds market is the interest rate, denoted by *r*. As we noted in Chapter 8, loans typically specify a nominal interest rate. So although we call *r* "the interest rate," it is with the understanding that *r* is a nominal interest rate—an interest rate that is unadjusted for inflation.

We're not quite done simplifying things. There are, in reality, many different kinds of interest rates, because there are many different kinds of loans—short-term loans, long-term loans, loans made to corporate borrowers, loans made to governments, and so on. In the interest of simplicity, we'll ignore those differences and assume that there is only one type of loan.

OK, now we're ready to analyze how savings and investment get matched up.

The Demand for Loanable Funds Figure 10-2 illustrates a hypothetical demand curve for loanable funds, *D*, which slopes downward. On the horizontal axis we show the quantity of loanable funds demanded. On the vertical axis

FIGURE 10-2 The Demand for Loanable Funds

The demand curve for loanable funds slopes downward: the lower the interest rate, the greater the quantity of loanable funds demanded. Here, reducing the interest rate from 12% to 4% increases the quantity of loanable funds demanded from $150 billion to $450 billion.

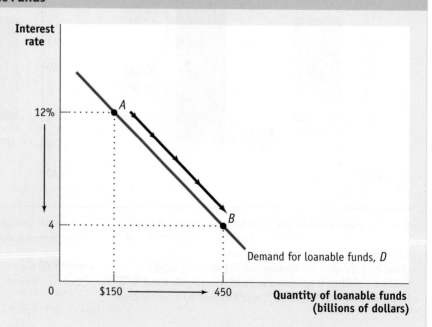

we show the interest rate, which is the "price" of borrowing. But why does the demand curve for loanable funds slope downward?

To answer this question, consider what a firm is doing when it engages in investment spending—say, by buying new equipment. Investment spending means laying out money right now, expecting that this outlay will lead to higher profits at some point in the future. In fact, however, the promise of a dollar five or ten years from now is worth less than an actual dollar right now. So an investment is worth making only if it generates a future return that is *greater* than the monetary cost of making the investment today. How much greater?

To answer that, we need to take into account the **present value** of the future return the firm expects to get. We examine the concept of *present value* in the accompanying For Inquiring Minds. Then, in the chapter's appendix, we show how the concept of present value can be applied to dollars earned multiple years in the future. The appendix also addresses how present value is used to calculate the prices of shares of stock and bonds.

> The **present value** of X is the amount of money needed today in order to receive X at a future date given the interest rate.

FOR INQUIRING MINDS   **Using Present Value**

An understanding of the concept of present value shows why the demand curve for loanable funds slopes downward. A simple way to grasp the essence of present value is to consider an example that illustrates the difference in value between having a sum of money today and having the same sum of money a year from now.

Suppose that exactly one year from today you will graduate, and you want to reward yourself by taking a trip that will cost $1,000. In order to have $1,000 a year from now, how much do you need today? It's not $1,000, and the reason why has to do with the interest rate.

Let's call the amount you need today X. We'll use r to represent the interest rate you receive on funds deposited in the bank. If you put X into the bank today and earn interest rate r on it, then after one year, the bank will pay you $X \times (1 + r)$. If what the bank will pay you a year from now is equal to $1,000, then the amount you need today is

$$X \times (1 + r) = \$1,000$$

You can apply some basic algebra to find that

$$X = \$1,000/(1 + r)$$

Notice that the value of X depends on the interest rate r, which is always greater than 0. This fact implies that X is always *less than* $1,000. For example, if r = 5% (that is, r = 0.05), then X = $952.38. In other words, having $952.38 today is equivalent to having $1,000 a year from now when the interest rate is 5%. That is, $952.38 is the value of $1,000 today given an interest rate of 5%.

Now we can define the *present value* of X: it is the amount of money needed today in order to receive X in the future given the interest rate. In this numerical example, $952.38 is the present value of $1,000 received one year from now given an interest rate of 5%.

The concept of present value also applies to decisions made by firms. Think about a firm that has two potential investment projects in mind, each of which will yield $1,000 a year from now. However, each project has different initial costs—say, one requires that the firm borrow $900 right now and the other requires that the firm borrow $950. Which, if any, of these projects is worth borrowing money to finance and undertake?

The answer depends on the interest rate, which determines the present value of $1,000 a year from now. If the interest rate is 10%, the present value of $1,000 delivered a year from now is $909. In other words, at an interest rate of 10%, a $909 loan requires a repayment of $1,000 in a year's time. A loan less than $909 requires a repayment less than $1,000, while a loan of more than $909 requires a repayment of more than $1,000. So only the first project, which has an initial cost of less than $909, is profitable, because its return in a year's time is more than the amount of the loan repayment.

With an interest rate of 10%, the return on any project costing more than $909 is less than the amount the firm has to repay on its loan and is therefore unprofitable. If the interest rate is only 5%, however, the present value of $1,000 rises to $952. At this interest rate, both projects are profitable, because $952 exceeds both projects' initial cost. So a firm will borrow more and engage in more investment spending when the interest rate is lower.

Meanwhile, similar calculations will be taking place at other firms. So a lower interest rate will lead to higher investment spending in the economy as a whole: the demand curve for loanable funds slopes downward.

When making financial decisions, individuals and firms must always keep in mind that having $1,000 today is worth more than having $1,000 a year from now.

In present value calculations, we use the interest rate to determine how the value of a dollar in the future compares to the value of a dollar today. But the fact is that future dollars are worth less than a dollar today, and they are worth even less when the interest rate is higher.

The intuition behind present value calculations is simple. The interest rate measures the opportunity cost of investment spending that results in a future return: instead of spending money on an investment spending project, a company could simply put the money into the bank and earn interest on it. And the higher the interest rate, the more attractive it is to simply put money into the bank and let it earn interest instead of investing it in an investment spending project.

In other words, the higher the interest rate, the higher the opportunity cost of investment spending. And, the higher the opportunity cost of investment spending, the lower the number of investment spending projects firms want to carry out, and therefore the lower the quantity of loanable funds demanded. It is this insight that explains why the demand curve for loanable funds is downward sloping.

When businesses engage in investment spending, they spend money right now in return for an expected payoff in the future. To evaluate whether a particular investment spending project is worth undertaking, a business must compare the present value of the future payoff with the current cost of that project. If the present value of the future payoff is greater than the current cost, a project is profitable and worth investing in. If the interest rate falls, then the present value of any given project rises, so more projects pass that test. If the interest rate rises, then the present value of any given project falls, and fewer projects pass that test.

So total investment spending, and hence the demand for loanable funds to finance that spending, is negatively related to the interest rate. Thus, the demand curve for loanable funds slopes downward. You can see this in Figure 10-2. When the interest rate falls from 12% to 4%, the quantity of loanable funds demanded rises from $150 billion (point A) to $450 billion (point B).

The Supply of Loanable Funds Figure 10-3 shows a hypothetical supply curve for loanable funds, S. Again, the interest rate plays the same role that the price plays in ordinary supply and demand analysis. But why is this curve upward sloping?

FIGURE 10-3 The Supply of Loanable Funds

The supply curve for loanable funds slopes upward: the higher the interest rate, the greater the quantity of loanable funds supplied. Here, increasing the interest rate from 4% to 12% increases the quantity of loanable funds supplied from $150 billion to $450 billion.

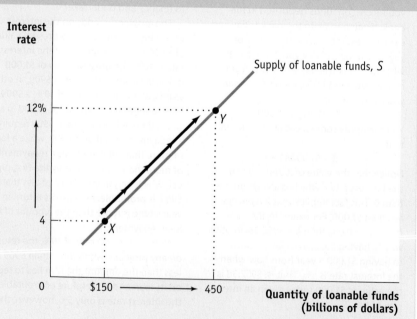

The answer is that loanable funds are supplied by savers, and savers incur an opportunity cost when they lend to a business: the funds could instead be spent on consumption—say, a nice vacation. Whether a given saver becomes a lender by making funds available to borrowers depends on the interest rate received in return. By saving your money today and earning interest on it, you are rewarded with higher consumption in the future when the loan you made is repaid with interest. So it is a good assumption that more people are willing to forgo current consumption and make a loan to a borrower when the interest rate is higher.

As a result, our hypothetical supply curve of loanable funds slopes upward. In Figure 10-3, lenders will supply $150 billion to the loanable funds market at an interest rate of 4% (point X); if the interest rate rises to 12%, the quantity of loanable funds supplied will rise to $450 billion (point Y).

The Equilibrium Interest Rate The interest rate at which the quantity of loanable funds supplied equals the quantity of loanable funds demanded is called the **equilibrium interest rate.** As you can see in Figure 10-4, the equilibrium interest rate, r^*, and the total quantity of lending, Q^*, are determined by the intersection of the supply and demand curves, at point E.

Here, the equilibrium interest rate is 8%, at which $300 billion is lent and borrowed. In this equilibrium, only investment spending projects that are profitable if the interest rate is 8% or higher are funded. Projects that are profitable only when the interest rate falls below 8% are not funded. Correspondingly, only lenders who are willing to accept an interest rate of 8% or less will have their offers to lend funds accepted; lenders who demand an interest rate higher than 8% do not have their offers to lend accepted.

Figure 10-4 shows how the market for loanable funds matches up desired savings with desired investment spending: in equilibrium, the quantity of funds that savers want to lend is equal to the quantity of funds that firms want to borrow. The figure also shows that this match-up is efficient, in two senses. First, the right investments get made: the investment spending projects that are actually financed have higher payoffs (in terms of present value) than those that do not get financed. Second, the right people do the saving and lending: the savers who actually lend funds are willing to lend for lower interest rates than those who do not.

> The interest rate at which the quantity of loanable funds supplied equals the quantity of loanable funds demanded is the **equilibrium interest rate.**

FIGURE 10-4 Equilibrium in the Loanable Funds Market

At the equilibrium interest rate, the quantity of loanable funds supplied equals the quantity of loanable funds demanded. Here, the equilibrium interest rate is 8%, with $300 billion of funds lent and borrowed. Lenders who demand an interest rate of 8% or lower have their offers of loans accepted; those who demand a higher interest rate do not. Projects that are profitable at an interest rate of 8% or higher are funded; those that are profitable only when the interest rate falls below 8% are not.

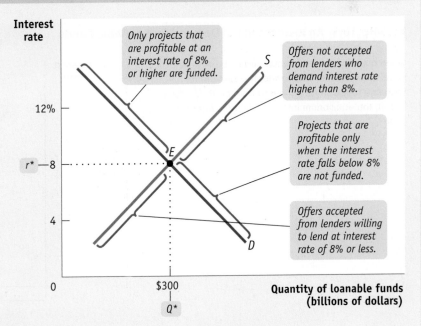

The insight that the loanable funds market leads to an efficient use of savings, although drawn from a highly simplified model, has important implications for real life. As we'll see shortly, it is the reason that a well-functioning financial system increases an economy's long-run economic growth rate.

Before we get to that, let's look at how the market for loanable funds responds to shifts of demand and supply. As in the standard model of supply and demand, where the equilibrium price changes in response to shifts of the demand or supply curves, here, the equilibrium interest rate changes when there are shifts of the demand curve for loanable funds, the supply curve for loanable funds, or both.

Shifts of the Demand for Loanable Funds Let's start by looking at the causes and effects of changes in demand.

The factors that can cause the demand curve for loanable funds to shift include the following:

1. *Changes in perceived business opportunities.* A change in beliefs about the payoff of investment spending can increase or decrease the amount of desired spending at any given interest rate. For example, during the 1990s there was great excitement over the business possibilities created by the internet, which had just begun to be widely used. As a result, businesses rushed to buy computer equipment, put fiber-optic cables in the ground, launch websites, and so on. This shifted the demand for loanable funds to the right. By 2001, the failure of many dot-com businesses had led to disillusionment with technology-related investment; this shifted the demand for loanable funds back to the left.

2. *Changes in government borrowing.* A government runs a budget deficit when, in a given year, it spends more than it receives. A government that runs budget deficits can be a major source of demand for loanable funds. For example, in 2009 the U.S. federal government was running a budget deficit in excess of $1.413 trillion, but by 2016 the federal deficit had been cut by $1 trillion to a little more than $330 billion. The federal government greatly reduced its borrowing needs. This change in the federal budget position had the effect, other things equal, of shifting the demand curve for loanable funds to the left.

Figure 10-5 shows the effects of an increase in the demand for loanable funds. S is the supply of loanable funds, and D_1 is the initial demand curve. The initial

---

FIGURE 10-5 An Increase in the Demand for Loanable Funds

If the quantity of funds demanded by borrowers rises at any given interest rate, the demand for loanable funds shifts rightward from D_1 to D_2. As a result, the equilibrium interest rate rises from r_1 to r_2.

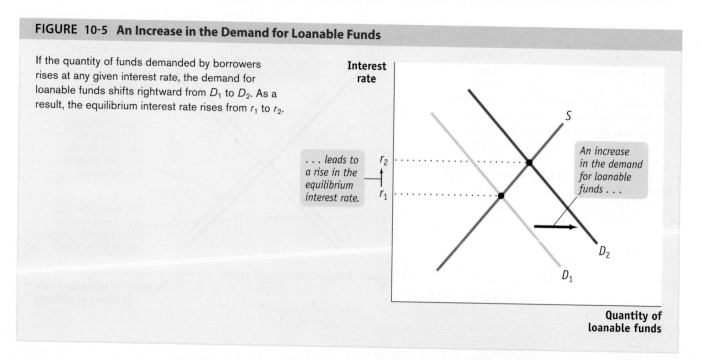

equilibrium interest rate is r_1. An increase in the demand for loanable funds means that the quantity of funds demanded rises at any given interest rate, so the demand curve shifts rightward to D_2. As a result, the equilibrium interest rate rises to r_2.

The fact that an increase in the demand for loanable funds leads, other things equal, to a rise in the interest rate has one especially important implication: it tells us that increasing or persistent government budget deficits are cause for concern because an increase in the government's deficit shifts the demand curve for loanable funds to the right, which leads to a higher interest rate. If the interest rate rises, businesses will cut back on their investment spending.

So, other things equal, a rise in the government budget deficit tends to reduce overall investment spending. Economists call the negative effect of government budget deficits on investment spending **crowding out.** Concerns about crowding out are one key reason to worry about increasing or persistent budget deficits.

However, it's important to add a qualification here: crowding out may not occur if the economy is depressed. When the economy is operating far below full employment, government spending can lead to higher incomes, and these higher incomes lead to increased savings at any given interest rate. Higher savings allows the government to borrow without raising interest rates. Many economists believe, for example, that the large budget deficits that the U.S. government ran from 2008 to 2013 in the face of a depressed economy caused little if any crowding out.

Shifts of the Supply of Loanable Funds Like the demand for loanable funds, the supply of loanable funds can shift. Among the factors that can cause the supply of loanable funds to shift are the following:

1. *Changes in private savings behavior.* A number of factors can cause the level of private savings to change at any given interest rate. For example, between 2008 and 2012 declining home prices in the United States made many homeowners feel poorer, making them decrease their spending and save more. This had the effect of shifting the supply curve of loanable funds to the right.

2. *Changes in net capital inflows.* Capital flows into and out of a country can change as investors' perceptions of that country change. For example, Greece experienced large net capital inflows after the creation of the euro, Europe's common currency, in 1999, because investors believed that Greece's adoption of the euro as its currency had made it a safe place to put their funds. By 2009, however, worries about the Greek government's solvency (and the discovery that it had been understating its debt) led to a collapse in investor confidence, and the net inflow of funds dried up. The effect of shrinking capital inflows was to shift the supply curve in the Greek loanable funds market to the left.

   In the mid-2000s, the United States received large net capital inflows, with much of the money coming from China and the Middle East. Those inflows helped fuel a big increase in residential investment spending—newly constructed homes—from 2003 to 2006. As a result of the bursting of the U.S. housing bubble in 2006–2007 and the subsequent deep recession, those inflows began to trail off in 2008.

Figure 10-6 shows the effects of an increase in the supply of loanable funds. D is the demand for loanable funds, and S_1 is the initial supply curve. The initial equilibrium interest rate is r_1. An increase in the supply of loanable funds means that the quantity of funds supplied rises at any given interest rate, so the supply curve shifts rightward to S_2. As a result, the equilibrium interest rate falls to r_2.

A Global Market for Loanable Funds? As we've noted, international capital flows can be an important influence on interest rates. What determines these capital flows? Most of the time, capital flows from countries where interest rates are relatively low to countries where interest rates are relatively high. And the result of these flows is to raise interest rates where they were low, and reduce rates where they were high.

Crowding out occurs when a government budget deficit drives up the interest rate and leads to reduced investment spending.

FIGURE 10-6 An Increase in the Supply of Loanable Funds

If the quantity of funds supplied by lenders rises at any given interest rate, the supply of loanable funds shifts rightward from S_1 to S_2. As a result, the equilibrium interest rate falls from r_1 to r_2.

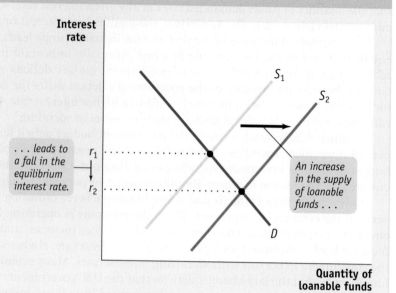

. . . leads to a fall in the equilibrium interest rate.

An increase in the supply of loanable funds . . .

Quantity of loanable funds

A **global loanable funds market** arises when international capital flows are so large that they equalize interest rates across countries.

For some purposes, it is useful to think about what would happen if this process went all the way—if international capital flows are so large that they had the effect of completely equalizing interest rates across countries. In that case we could talk about a **global loanable funds market.**

Figure 10-7 shows how such a market would work. We imagine a world consisting of only two countries, the United States and Britain. Panel (a) shows the loanable funds market in the United States, where the equilibrium in the absence of international capital flows is at point E_{US}, with an interest rate of 6%. Panel (b) shows the loanable funds market in Britain, where the equilibrium in the absence of international capital flows is at point E_B, with an interest rate of 2%.

FIGURE 10-7 Loanable Funds Markets in a Two-Country World

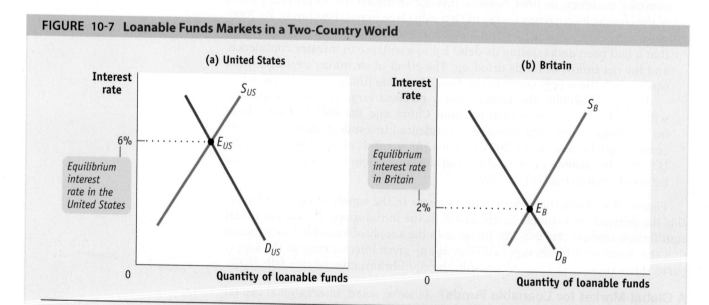

Here we show two countries, the United States and Britain, each with its own loanable funds market. The equilibrium interest rate is 6% in the U.S. market but only 2% in the British market. This creates an incentive for capital to flow from Britain to the United States.

Will the actual interest rate in the United States remain at 6% and that in Britain at 2%? Not if it is easy for British residents to make loans to Americans. In that case, British lenders, attracted by high U.S. interest rates, will send some of their loanable funds to the United States. This capital inflow will increase the quantity of loanable funds supplied to American borrowers, pushing the U.S. interest rate down. It will also reduce the quantity of loanable funds supplied to British borrowers, pushing the British interest rate up. So international capital flows will narrow the gap between U.S. and British interest rates.

Let's further suppose that British lenders consider a loan to an American to be just as good as a loan to one of their own compatriots, and that American borrowers regard a debt to a British lender as no more costly than a debt to an American lender. In that case, the flow of funds from Britain to the United States will continue until the gap between their interest rates is eliminated. In other words, when residents of the two countries believe that foreign assets and foreign liabilities are as good as domestic ones, then international capital flows will equalize the interest rates in the two countries.

Figure 10-8 shows how an international equilibrium in the loanable funds markets arises. In this case, the equilibrium interest rate is 4% in both the United States and Britain. At this interest rate, the quantity of loanable funds demanded by American borrowers exceeds the quantity of loanable funds supplied by American lenders. This gap is filled by "imported" funds—a capital inflow from Britain. At the same time, the quantity of loanable funds supplied by British lenders is greater than the quantity of loanable funds demanded by British borrowers. This excess is "exported" in the form of a capital outflow to the United States. A global loanable funds market arises as the two markets are in equilibrium at a common interest rate of 4%. At that rate, the total quantity of loans demanded by borrowers across the two markets is equal to the total quantity of loans supplied by lenders across the two markets.

In short, international flows of capital are like international flows of goods and services. Capital moves from places where it would be cheap in the absence of international capital flows to places where it would be expensive in the absence of such flows.

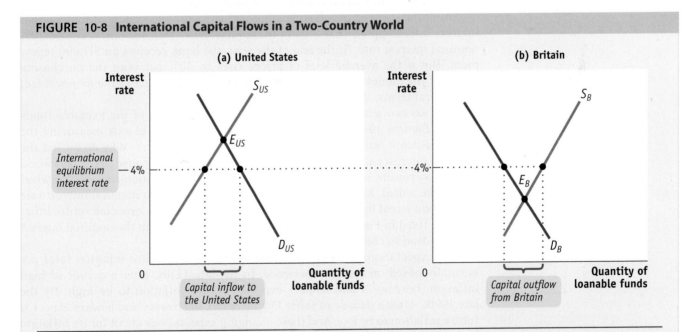

FIGURE 10-8 International Capital Flows in a Two-Country World

(a) United States

(b) Britain

British lenders lend to borrowers in the United States, leading to equalization of interest rates at 4% in both countries. At that rate, American borrowing exceeds American lending; the difference is made up by capital inflows to the United States. Meanwhile, British lending exceeds British borrowing; the excess is a capital outflow from Britain.

In practice, this picture is complicated by various factors. In particular, countries use different currencies—America uses dollars, Britain uses pounds—and when you compare the interest rate on loans in dollars with the rate on loans in pounds, you need to take into account the possibility that the value of a pound in dollars can change over time. Still, the concept of a global market for loanable funds is very useful for some purposes, and we will return to that concept in later chapters.

Inflation and Interest Rates   Anything that shifts either the supply of loanable funds curve or the demand for loanable funds curve changes the interest rate. Historically, major changes in interest rates have been driven by many factors, including changes in government policy and technological innovations that created new investment opportunities.

However, arguably the most important factor affecting interest rates over time—the reason, for example, that interest rates today are much lower than they were in the late 1970s and early 1980s—is changing expectations about future inflation, which shift both the supply and the demand for loanable funds.

To understand the effect of expected future inflation on interest rates, recall our discussion in Chapter 8 of the way inflation creates winners and losers—for example, the way that higher than expected U.S. inflation in the 1970s and 1980s reduced the real value of homeowners' mortgages, which was good for the homeowners but bad for the banks. We also learned that economists summarize the effect of inflation on borrowers and lenders by distinguishing between the *nominal interest rate* and the *real interest rate*, where the difference is:

$$\text{Real interest rate} = \text{Nominal interest rate} - \text{Inflation rate}$$

The true cost of borrowing is the real interest rate, not the nominal interest rate. To see why, suppose a firm borrows $10,000 for one year at a 10% nominal interest rate. At the end of the year, it must repay $11,000—the amount borrowed plus the interest. But suppose that over the course of the year the average level of prices increases by 10%, so that the real interest rate is zero. Then the $11,000 repayment has the same purchasing power as the original $10,000 loan. In real terms, the borrower has received a zero-interest loan.

Similarly, the true payoff to lending is the real interest rate, not the nominal interest rate. Suppose that a bank makes a $10,000 loan for one year at a 10% nominal interest rate. At the end of the year, the bank receives an $11,000 repayment. But if the average level of prices rises by 10% per year, the purchasing power of the money the bank gets back is no more than that of the money it lent out. In real terms, the bank has made a zero-interest loan.

Now we can add an important detail to our analysis of the loanable funds market. Figures 10-5 and 10-6 are drawn with the vertical axis measuring the *nominal interest rate for a given expected future inflation rate*. Why do we use the nominal interest rate rather than the real interest rate? Because in the real world neither borrowers nor lenders know what the future inflation rate will be when they make a deal. Actual loan contracts therefore specify a nominal interest rate rather than a real interest rate. Because we are holding the expected future inflation rate fixed in Figures 10-5 and 10-6, however, changes in the nominal interest rate also lead to changes in the real interest rate.

The expectations of borrowers and lenders about future inflation rates are normally based on recent experience. In the late 1970s, after a decade of high inflation, borrowers and lenders expected future inflation to be high. By the late 1990s, after a decade of fairly low inflation, borrowers and lenders expected future inflation to be low. And these changing expectations about future inflation had a strong effect on the nominal interest rate, largely explaining why nominal interest rates were much lower in the early years of the twenty-first century than they were in the early 1980s.

Let's look at how changes in the expected future rate of inflation are reflected in the loanable funds model.

FIGURE 10-9 The Fisher Effect

D_0 and S_0 are the demand and supply curves for loanable funds when the expected future inflation rate is 0%. At an expected inflation rate of 0%, the equilibrium nominal interest rate is 4%. An increase in expected future inflation pushes both the demand and supply curves upward by 1 percentage point for every percentage point increase in expected future inflation. D_{10} and S_{10} are the demand and supply curves for loanable funds when the expected future inflation rate is 10%. The 10 percentage point increase in expected future inflation raises the equilibrium nominal interest rate to 14%. The expected real interest rate remains at 4%, and the equilibrium quantity of loanable funds also remains unchanged.

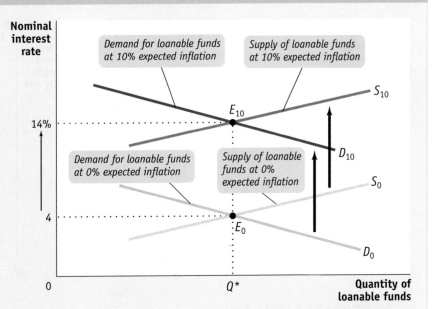

In Figure 10-9, the curves S_0 and D_0 show the supply and demand for loanable funds given that the expected future rate of inflation is 0%. In that case, equilibrium is at E_0, and the equilibrium nominal interest rate is 4%. Because expected future inflation is 0%, the equilibrium expected real interest rate over the life of the loan is also 4%.

Now suppose that the expected future inflation rate rises to 10%. The demand curve for loanable funds shifts upward to D_{10}: borrowers are now willing to borrow as much at a nominal interest rate of 14% as they were previously willing to borrow at 4%. That's because with a 10% inflation rate, a 14% nominal interest rate corresponds to a 4% real interest rate.

Similarly, the supply curve of loanable funds shifts upward to S_{10}: lenders require a nominal interest rate of 14% to persuade them to lend as much as they would previously have lent at 4%. The new equilibrium is at E_{10}: the result of an expected future inflation rate of 10% is that the equilibrium nominal interest rate rises from 4% to 14%.

This situation can be summarized as a general principle, known as the **Fisher effect** (after the American economist Irving Fisher, who proposed it in 1930): *the expected real interest rate is unaffected by changes in expected future inflation.*

According to the Fisher effect, an increase in expected future inflation drives up the nominal interest rate, where each additional percentage point of expected future inflation drives up the nominal interest rate by 1 percentage point. The central point is that both lenders and borrowers base their decisions on the expected real interest rate. As a result, a change in the expected rate of inflation does not affect the equilibrium quantity of loanable funds or the expected real interest rate; all it affects is the equilibrium nominal interest rate.

According to the **Fisher effect,** an increase in expected future inflation drives up the nominal interest rate, leaving the expected real interest rate unchanged.

ECONOMICS >> *in Action*
Sixty Years of U.S. Interest Rates

There have been some large movements in U.S. interest rates dating back to the 1950s. These movements clearly show how both changes in expected future inflation and changes in the expected return on investment spending move interest rates.

FIGURE 10-10 Changes in U.S. Interest Rates Over Time

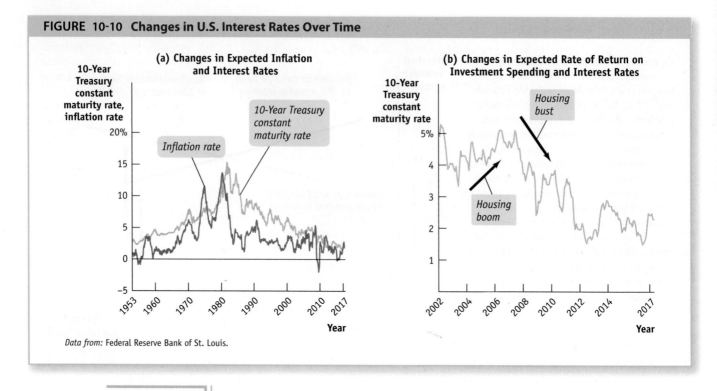

Data from: Federal Reserve Bank of St. Louis.

>> **Quick Review**

• The **savings–investment spending identity** is an accounting fact: savings is equal to investment spending for the economy as a whole.

• The government is a source of savings when it runs a positive **budget balance,** a **budget surplus.** It is a source of dissavings when it runs a negative budget balance, a **budget deficit,** which can be financed by **government borrowing**—the total amount of funds borrowed by federal, state, and local governments in the financial markets.

• Savings is equal to **national savings** plus **net capital inflow,** which may be either positive or negative.

• To make the correct comparison when costs or benefits arrive at different times, you must transform any dollars realized in the future into their **present value.**

• The **loanable funds market** matches savers to borrowers. In equilibrium, only investment spending projects with an expected return greater than or equal to the **equilibrium interest rate** are funded.

• Because government borrowing competes with private borrowers in the loanable funds market, a government deficit can cause **crowding out,** which is less likely if the economy is in a slump.

Panel (a) of Figure 10-10 illustrates the first effect. It shows the average interest rate on bonds issued by the U.S. government—specifically, bonds for which the government promises to repay the full amount after 10 years—from 1953 to 2017, along with the rate of consumer price inflation over the same period. As you can see, the big story about interest rates is the way they soared in the 1970s, before coming back down in the 1980s.

It's not hard to see why that happened: inflation shot up during the 1970s, leading to widespread expectations that high inflation would continue. And as we've seen, a higher expected inflation rate raises the equilibrium interest rate. As the inflation rate came down in the 1980s, so did expectations of future inflation, and this brought interest rates down as well.

Panel (b) illustrates the second effect: changes in the expected return on investment spending and interest rates, with a "close-up" of interest rates from 2002 to 2017. Notice the rise in interest rates during the middle years of the last decade, followed by a sharp drop. We know from other evidence (such as surveys of investor opinion) that the expected rate of inflation didn't change much over those years. What happened, instead, was the boom and bust in housing: interest rates rose as demand for housing soared, pushing the demand curve for loanable funds to the right, then fell as the housing boom collapsed, shifting the demand curve for loanable funds back to the left.

Throughout this whole process, total savings was equal to total investment spending, and the rise and fall of the interest rate played a key role in matching lenders with borrowers.

>> **Check Your Understanding 10-1**
Solutions appear at back of book.

1. Use a diagram of the loanable funds market to illustrate the effect of the following events on the equilibrium interest rate and investment spending.
   a. An economy is opened to international movements of capital, and a net capital inflow occurs.
   b. Retired people generally save less than working people at any interest rate. The proportion of retired people in the population goes up.

2. Explain what is wrong with the following statement: "Savings and investment spending may not be equal in the economy as a whole because when the interest rate rises, households will want to save more money than businesses will want to invest."

3. Suppose that expected inflation rises from 3% to 6%.
   a. How will the real interest rate be affected by this change?
   b. How will the nominal interest rate be affected by this change?
   c. What will happen to the equilibrium quantity of loanable funds?

• Capital flows allow countries to export their savings to borrowers in other countries. Capital flows from a country with a lower interest rate to a country with a higher interest rate, reducing the difference in those rates. If capital flows are large, a **global loanable funds market** arises, equalizing interest rates across countries.

• Higher expected future inflation raises the nominal interest rate through the **Fisher effect,** leaving the real interest rate unchanged.

The Financial System

A well-functioning financial system that brings together the funds of investors and the vision of entrepreneurs has made the rise of Amazon possible. But to think that this is an exclusively modern phenomenon would be misguided. Financial markets raised the funds that were used to develop colonial markets in India, to build canals across Europe, and to finance the Napoleonic wars in the eighteenth and early nineteenth centuries. Capital inflows financed the early economic development of the United States, funding investment spending in mining, railroads, and canals. In fact, many of the principal features of financial markets and assets have been well understood in Europe and the United States since the eighteenth century. These features are no less relevant today. So let's begin by understanding exactly what is traded in financial markets.

Financial markets are where households invest their current savings and their accumulated savings, or **wealth,** by purchasing *financial assets.* A **financial asset** is a paper claim that entitles the buyer to future income from the seller. For example, when a saver lends funds to a company, the loan is a financial asset sold by the company that entitles the lender (the buyer of the financial asset) to future income from the company.

A household can also invest its current savings or wealth by purchasing a **physical asset,** a tangible object that can be used to generate future income such as a preexisting house or preexisting piece of equipment. Purchasing a physical asset gives the owner the right to dispose of the object as he or she wishes (for example, rent it or sell it).

Recall that the purchase of a financial or physical asset is typically called investing. So if you purchase a preexisting piece of equipment—say, a used airliner—you are investing in a physical asset. In contrast, if you spend funds that *add* to the stock of physical capital in the economy—say, purchasing a newly manufactured airplane—you are engaging in investment spending.

If you get a loan from your local bank—say, to buy a new car—you and the bank are creating a financial asset: your loan. A *loan* is one important kind of financial asset in the real world, one that is owned by the lender—in this case, your local bank. In creating that loan, you and the bank are also creating a **liability,** a requirement to pay income in the future.

So although your loan is a financial asset from the bank's point of view, it is a liability from your point of view. In addition to loans, there are three other important kinds of financial assets: *stocks, bonds,* and *bank deposits.* Because a financial asset is a claim to future income that someone has to pay, it is also someone else's liability. We'll explain in detail shortly who bears the liability for each type of financial asset.

These four types of financial assets—loans, stocks, bonds, and bank deposits—exist because the economy has developed a set of specialized markets, like the stock market and the bond market, and specialized institutions, like banks, that facilitate the flow of funds from lenders to borrowers. Taken together, these institutions and markets are known as the **financial system.**

A well-functioning financial system is a critical ingredient in achieving long-run growth because it encourages greater savings and investment spending. It also ensures that savings and investment spending are undertaken efficiently. To

Financial markets are where households invest their current and accumulated savings. A household's **wealth** is the value of its accumulated savings.

A **financial asset** is a paper claim that entitles the buyer to future income from the seller.

A **physical asset** is a tangible object that can be used to generate future income.

A **liability** is a requirement to pay income in the future.

The **financial system** is the collection of markets and institutions that facilitate the flow of funds from lenders to borrowers.

Transaction costs are the expenses of negotiating and executing a deal.

Financial risk is uncertainty about future outcomes that involve financial losses or gains.

understand how this occurs, we first need to know what tasks the financial system needs to accomplish. Then we can see how the job gets done.

Three Tasks of a Financial System

Our earlier analysis of the loanable funds market ignored three important problems facing borrowers and lenders: *transaction costs, risk,* and the desire for *liquidity.* The three tasks of a financial system are to reduce these problems in a cost-effective way that enhances the efficiency of financial markets and makes it more likely that lenders and borrowers will make mutually beneficial trades—trades that make society as a whole richer. We'll turn now to examining how financial assets are designed and how institutions are developed to cope with these problems.

Task 1: Reducing Transaction Costs The expenses of actually putting together and executing a deal are known as **transaction costs.** For example, arranging a loan requires spending time and money negotiating the terms of the deal, verifying the borrower's ability to pay, drawing up and executing legal documents, and so on.

Suppose a large business decided that it wanted to raise $1 billion for investment spending. No individual would be willing to lend that much. And negotiating individual loans from thousands of different people, each willing to lend a modest amount, would impose very large total costs because each individual transaction would incur a cost. Total costs would be so large that the entire deal would probably be unprofitable for the business.

Fortunately, that's not necessary: when large businesses want to borrow money, they either go to a bank or sell bonds in the bond market. Obtaining a loan from a bank avoids large transaction costs by involving only a single borrower and a single lender. We'll explain more about how bonds work in the next section. For now, it is enough to know that the principal reason a bond market exists is to allow companies to borrow large sums of money without incurring large transaction costs.

Task 2: Reducing Risk Another problem that real-world borrowers and lenders face is **financial risk,** uncertainty about future outcomes that involve financial losses or gains. Financial risk, or simply risk, is a problem because the future is uncertain, containing the potential for losses as well as gains. For example, owning and driving a car entails the financial risk of a costly accident. Most people view potential losses and gains in an *asymmetrical* way: most people experience the loss in welfare from losing a given amount of money more intensely than they experience the increase in welfare from gaining the same amount of money.

A person who is more sensitive to a loss than to a gain of an equal dollar amount is called *risk-averse.* Most people are risk-averse, although to differing degrees. For example, people who are wealthy are typically less risk-averse than those who are not so well-off.

A well-functioning financial system helps people reduce their exposure to risk, which risk-averse people would like to do. Suppose the owner of a business expects to make a greater profit if she buys additional capital equipment, but she isn't completely sure that this will happen. She could pay for the equipment by using her savings or selling her house. But if the profit is significantly less than expected, she will have lost her savings, her house, or both. That is, she would be exposing herself to a lot of risk due to uncertainty about how well or poorly the business performs. (This is why business owners, who typically have a significant portion of their own personal wealth tied up in their businesses, are usually more tolerant of risk than the average person.)

So, being risk-averse, this business owner wants to share the risk of purchasing new capital equipment with someone, even if that requires sharing some of the profit if all goes well. She can do this by selling shares of her company to other people and using the money she receives from selling shares, rather than money from the sale of her other assets, to finance the equipment purchase. By selling shares in her company, she reduces her personal losses if the profit is less than expected: she won't have lost her other assets. But if things go well, the shareholders earn a share of the profit as a return on their investment.

By selling a share of her business, the owner has achieved *diversification:* she has been able to invest in several things in a way that lowers her total risk. She has maintained her investment in her bank account, a financial asset; in owner-ship of her house, a physical asset; and in ownership of the unsold portion of her business, a financial asset. These investments are likely to carry some risk of their own; for example, her bank may fail or her house may burn down (though in the modern United States it is likely that she is partly protected against these risks by insurance).

But even in the absence of insurance, she is better off having maintained investments in these different assets because their different risks are *unrelated,* or *independent, events.* This means, for example, that her house is no more likely to burn down if her business does poorly and that her bank is no more likely to fail if her house burns down.

To put it another way, if one asset performs poorly, it is very likely that her other assets will be unaffected and, as a result, her total risk of loss has been reduced. But if she had invested all her wealth in her business, she would have faced the prospect of losing everything if the business had performed poorly. By engaging in **diversification**—investing in several assets with unrelated, or inde-pendent, risks—our business owner has lowered her total risk of loss.

The desire of individuals to manage and reduce their total risk by engaging in diversification is why we have stocks and a stock market, as we'll explain in detail in the next section.

Task 3: Providing Liquidity The financial system also exists to provide inves-tors with *liquidity*, a concern that—like risk—arises because the future is uncer-tain. Suppose that, having made a loan, a lender suddenly finds himself in need of cash—say, to meet a medical emergency. Unfortunately, if that loan was made to a business that used it to buy new equipment, the business cannot repay the loan on short notice to satisfy the lender's need to recover his money. Knowing in advance that there is a danger of needing to get his money back before the term of the loan is up, our lender might be reluctant to lock up his money by lending it to a business.

An asset is **liquid** if it can be quickly converted into cash with relatively little loss of value, **illiquid** if it cannot. As we'll see, stocks and bonds are a partial answer to the problem of liquidity. Banks provide an additional way for individuals to hold liquid assets and still finance illiquid investment spending projects, such as buying capital equipment for a business.

To help lenders and borrowers make mutually beneficial deals, then, the econ-omy needs ways to reduce transaction costs, to reduce and manage risk through diversification, and to provide liquidity. How does it achieve these tasks?

Types of Financial Assets

Recall that in the modern economy there are four main types of financial assets: *loans, bonds, stocks,* and *bank deposits.* In addition, financial innovation has allowed the creation of a wide range of *loan-backed securities.* Each asset serves a somewhat different purpose. We'll examine loans, bonds, stocks, and loan-backed securities now, reserving our discussion of bank deposits until the following section.

Loans A lending agreement made between an individual lender and an individ-ual borrower is a **loan.** Most people encounter loans in the form of a student loan

An individual can engage in **diversification** by investing in several different assets so that the possible losses are independent events.

An asset is **liquid** if it can be quickly converted into cash with relatively little loss of value.

An asset is **illiquid** if it cannot be quickly converted into cash with relatively little loss of value.

A **loan** is a lending agreement between an individual lender and an individual borrower.

A **bond** is borrowing in the form of an IOU that pays interest.

A **default** occurs when a borrower fails to make payments as specified by the loan or bond contract.

A **loan-backed security** is an asset created by pooling individual loans and selling shares in that pool.

A **stock** is a share in the ownership of a company held by a shareholder.

or a bank loan to finance the purchase of a car or a house. And small businesses usually use bank loans to buy new equipment.

The good aspect of loans is that a given loan is usually tailored to the needs of the borrower. Before a small business can get a loan, it usually has to discuss its business plans, its profits, and so on with the lender. This results in a loan that meets the borrower's needs and ability to pay.

The bad aspect of loans is that making a loan to an individual person or a business typically involves a lot of transaction costs, such as the cost of negotiating the terms of the loan, investigating the borrower's credit history and ability to repay, and so on. To minimize these costs, large borrowers such as major corporations and governments often take a more streamlined approach: they sell (or issue) bonds.

Bonds An IOU issued by a borrower is known as a **bond.** Normally, the seller of the bond promises to pay a fixed sum of interest each year and to repay the principal—the value stated on the face of the bond—to the owner of the bond on a particular date. So a bond is a financial asset from its owner's point of view and a liability from its issuer's point of view.

A bond issuer sells a number of bonds with a given interest rate and maturity date to whoever is willing to buy them, a process that avoids costly negotiation of the terms of a loan with many individual lenders.

Bond purchasers can acquire information free of charge on the quality of the bond issuer, such as the bond issuer's credit history, from bond-rating agencies rather than incurring the expense of investigating it themselves. A particular concern for investors is the possibility of **default,** the risk that the bond issuer will fail to make payments as specified by the bond contract. Once a bond's risk of default has been rated, it can be sold on the bond market as a more or less standardized product, one with clearly defined terms and quality. In general, bonds with a higher default risk must pay a higher interest rate to attract investors.

Another important advantage of bonds is that they are easy to resell. This provides liquidity to bond purchasers. Indeed, a bond will often pass through many hands before it finally comes due. Loans, in contrast, are much more difficult to resell because, unlike bonds, they are not standardized: they differ in size, quality, terms, and so on. This makes them a lot less liquid than bonds.

Loan-Backed Securities Assets created by pooling individual loans and selling shares in that pool (a process called *securitization*) are called **loan-backed securities.** This type of asset has become extremely popular over the past two decades. While mortgage-backed securities—in which thousands of individual home mortgages are pooled and shares are sold to investors—are the best-known example, securitization has also been widely applied to student loans, credit card loans, and auto loans.

These loan-backed securities are traded on financial markets like bonds; they are preferred by investors because they provide more diversification and liquidity than individual loans. However, with so many loans packaged together, it can be difficult to assess the true quality of the asset. That difficulty came to haunt investors during the financial crisis of 2008, when the bursting of the housing bubble led to widespread defaults on mortgages and large losses for holders of supposedly "safe" mortgage-backed securities, pain that spread throughout the entire financial system.

Stocks A share in the ownership of a company is a **stock.** A share of stock is a financial asset from its owner's point of view and a liability from the company's point of view. Not all companies sell shares of their stock; privately held companies are owned by an individual or a few partners, who get to keep all of the company's profit. Most large companies, however, do sell stock. For example, Microsoft has nearly 8 billion shares outstanding; if you buy one of those shares, you are entitled to one-eight billionth of the company's profit, as well as 1 of 8 billion votes on company decisions.

Why does Microsoft, historically a very profitable company, allow you to buy a share in its ownership? Why didn't Bill Gates and Paul Allen, the two founders of Microsoft, keep complete ownership for themselves and just sell bonds for their investment spending needs? The reason, as we have just learned, is risk: few individuals are risk-tolerant enough to face the risk involved in being the sole owner of a large company.

Reducing the risk that business owners face, however, is not the only way in which the existence of stocks improves society's welfare: it also improves the welfare of investors who buy stocks. Shareowners are able to enjoy the higher returns over time that stocks generally offer in comparison to bonds. Over the past century, stocks have typically yielded about 7% after adjusting for inflation; bonds have yielded only about 2%. But as investment companies warn you, "past performance is no guarantee of future results."

And there is a downside: owning the stock of a given company is riskier than owning a bond issued by the same company. Why? Loosely speaking, a bond is a promise while a stock is a hope: by law, a company must pay what it owes its lenders before it distributes any profit to its shareholders. And if the company should fail (that is, be unable to pay its interest obligations and declare bankruptcy), its physical and financial assets go to its bondholders—its lenders—while its shareholders generally receive nothing. So although a stock generally provides a higher return to an investor than a bond, it also carries higher risk.

But the financial system has devised ways to help investors as well as business owners simultaneously manage risk and enjoy somewhat higher returns. It does that through the services of institutions known as *financial intermediaries*.

Financial Intermediaries

A **financial intermediary** is an institution that transforms funds gathered from many individuals into financial assets. The most important types of financial intermediaries are *mutual funds, pension funds, life insurance companies,* and *banks*. About three-quarters of the financial assets Americans own are held through these intermediaries rather than directly.

Mutual Funds As we've seen, owning shares of a company entails accepting risk in return for a higher potential reward. But it should come as no surprise that stock investors can lower their total risk by engaging in diversification. By owning a *diversified portfolio* of stocks—a group of stocks in which risks are unrelated to, or offset by, one another—rather than concentrating investment in the shares of a single company or a group of related companies, investors can reduce their risk.

In addition, financial advisers, aware that most people are risk-averse, almost always advise their clients to diversify not only their stock portfolio but also their entire wealth by holding other assets in addition to stock—assets such as bonds and cash. (And, for good measure, to have plenty of insurance in case of accidental losses.)

However, for individuals who don't have a large amount of money to invest— say, $1 million or more—building a diversified stock portfolio can incur high transaction costs (particularly fees paid to stockbrokers) because they are buying a few shares of a lot of companies. Fortunately for such investors, *mutual funds* help solve the problem of achieving diversification without high transaction costs.

A **mutual fund** is a financial intermediary that creates a stock portfolio by buying and holding shares in companies and then selling shares of the stock portfolio to individual investors. By buying these shares, investors with a relatively small amount of money to invest can indirectly hold a diversified portfolio,

A **financial intermediary** is an institution that transforms the funds it gathers from many individuals into financial assets.

A **mutual fund** is a financial intermediary that creates a stock portfolio and then resells shares of this portfolio to individual investors.

Table 10-1 Fidelity 500 Index Fund, Top Holdings (as of December 2016)

Company	Percent of mutual fund assets invested in a company
Apple Inc.	3.03%
Microsoft Corp.	2.39
Exxon Mobil Corp.	1.84
Johnson & Johnson	1.55
Berkshire Hathaway Inc. B	1.52
Amazon.com Inc.	1.50
JPMorgan Chase & Co.	1.47
General Electric Co.	1.40
Facebook Inc. A	1.40
Wells Fargo & Co.	1.22

Data from: Fidelity Investments.

achieving a better return for any given level of risk than they could otherwise achieve. Table 10-1 shows an example of a diversified mutual fund, the Fidelity 500 Index Fund. It shows the percentage of investors' money invested in the stocks of the largest companies in the mutual fund's portfolio.

Many mutual funds also perform market research on the companies they invest in. This is important because there are thousands of stock-issuing U.S. companies (not to mention foreign companies), each differing in terms of its likely profitability, dividend payments, and so on. It would be extremely time-consuming and costly for an individual investor to do adequate research on even a small number of companies. Mutual funds save transaction costs by doing this research for their customers.

The mutual fund industry represents a huge portion of the modern U.S. economy, not just of the U.S. financial system. In total, U.S. mutual funds had assets of $16.2 trillion at the end of 2016. In 2016, the largest mutual fund company was Fidelity, with $5.4 trillion in assets in June 2016.

We should mention, by the way, that mutual funds charge fees for their services. These fees are quite small for mutual funds that simply hold a diversified portfolio of stocks without trying to pick winners. But the fees charged by mutual funds that claim to have special expertise in investing your money can be quite high.

Pension Funds and Life Insurance Companies In addition to mutual funds, many Americans have holdings in **pension funds,** nonprofit institutions that collect the savings of their members and invest those funds in a wide variety of assets, providing their members with income when they retire. Although pension funds are subject to some special rules and receive special treatment for tax purposes, they function much like mutual funds. They invest in a diverse array of financial assets, allowing their members to achieve more cost-effective diversification and market research than they would be able to achieve individually. At the end of 2016, pension funds in the United States held more than $19 trillion in assets.

Americans also have substantial holdings in the policies of **life insurance companies,** which guarantee a payment to the policyholder's beneficiaries (typically, the family) when the policyholder dies. By enabling policyholders to cushion their beneficiaries from financial hardship arising from their death, life insurance companies also improve welfare by reducing risk.

Banks Recall the problem of liquidity: other things equal, people want assets that can be readily converted into cash. Bonds and stocks are much more liquid than physical assets or loans, yet the transaction cost of selling bonds or stocks to meet a sudden expense can be large. Furthermore, for many small and moderate-size companies, the cost of issuing bonds and stocks is too large given the modest amount of money they seek to raise. A *bank* is an institution that helps resolve the conflict between lenders' needs for liquidity and the financing needs of borrowers who don't want to use the stock or bond markets.

A bank works by first accepting funds from *depositors:* when you put your money in a bank, you are essentially becoming a lender by lending the bank your money. In return, you receive credit for a **bank deposit**—a claim on the bank, which is obliged to give you your cash if and when you demand it. So a bank deposit is a financial asset owned by the depositor and a liability of the bank that holds it.

A **pension fund** is a type of mutual fund that holds assets in order to provide retirement income to its members.

A **life insurance company** sells policies that guarantee a payment to a policyholder's beneficiaries when the policyholder dies.

A **bank deposit** is a claim on a bank that obliges the bank to give the depositor his or her cash when demanded.

GLOBAL COMPARISON CORPORATE BONDS IN THE UNITED STATES AND THE EURO AREA

A business that wants to borrow funds could do this two ways: by selling bonds to investors or by getting loans from banks. There are advantages and disadvantages to each strategy.

On the one hand, issuing bonds tends to be cheaper than borrowing from a bank, because it eliminates the middleman. Also, banks often place conditions on loans, restricting the borrower's freedom to conduct its business as it chooses. On the other hand, bank loans can be less risky than issuing bonds. If a borrower gets into difficulty, its bank will typically be supportive, offering more time to repay if a good plan is in place to fix their problems. Bond holders are much less flexible.

It's a tough choice—and interestingly, companies in the United States and their counterparts in Europe generally make different choices. The figure shows the value of bonds issued by nonfinancial corporations in the United States and in the euro area, the group of European countries using the euro as a common currency, both expressed as a percentage of GDP in 2016. U.S. companies issue more bonds than their European counterparts, who rely much more on bank borrowing.

Why the difference? Generally, American companies are more inclined to take risks. Also, European households are more inclined than U.S. households to leave large sums in bank accounts. As a result, European banks have more money to lend than their American counterparts.

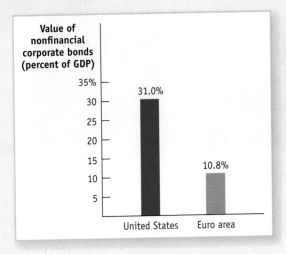

Data from: BIS Statistics Explorer.

A bank, however, keeps only a fraction of its customers' deposits in the form of ready cash. Most of its deposits are lent out to businesses, buyers of new homes, and other borrowers. These loans come with a long-term commitment by the bank to the borrower: as long as the borrower makes his or her payments on time, the loan cannot be recalled by the bank and converted into cash. So a bank enables those who wish to borrow for long lengths of time to use the funds of those who wish to lend but simultaneously want to maintain the ability to get their cash back on demand.

More formally, a **bank** is a financial intermediary that provides liquid financial assets in the form of deposits to lenders and uses their funds to finance the illiquid investment spending needs of borrowers. In essence, a bank is engaging in a kind of mismatch: lending for long periods of time while subject to the condition that its depositors could demand their funds back at any time. How can it manage that?

The bank counts on the fact that, on average, only a small fraction of its depositors will want their cash at the same time. On any given day, some people will make withdrawals and others will make new deposits; these will roughly cancel each other out. So the bank needs to keep only a limited amount of cash on hand to satisfy its depositors.

In addition, if a bank becomes financially incapable of paying its depositors, individual bank deposits are guaranteed to depositors up to $250,000 by the Federal Deposit Insurance Corporation, or FDIC, a federal agency. This reduces the risk to a depositor of holding a bank deposit, in turn reducing the incentive to withdraw funds if concerns about the financial state of the bank should arise. So, under normal conditions, banks need hold only a fraction of their depositors' cash.

By reconciling the needs of savers for liquid assets with the needs of borrowers for long-term financing, banks play a key economic role. As the following Economics in Action explains, the creation of a well-functioning banking system was a key turning point in South Korea's economic success.

A **bank** is a financial intermediary that provides liquid assets in the form of bank deposits to lenders and uses those funds to finance the illiquid investment spending needs of borrowers.

ECONOMICS >> *in Action*
Banks and the South Korean Miracle

South Korea's experience with banks shows how important a good financial system is to economic growth.

South Korea, now a very rich modern country, is one of the great success stories of economic growth. In the early 1960s, it was a very poor nation. Then it experienced spectacularly high rates of economic growth. And South Korean banks had a lot to do with it.

In the early 1960s, South Korea's banking system was a mess. Interest rates on deposits were set very low by government regulation at a time when the country was experiencing high inflation. So savers didn't want to put their money in a bank, fearing that much of their purchasing power would be eroded by rising prices. Instead, they engaged in current consumption by spending their money on goods and services. Or they used their wealth to buy physical assets such as real estate and gold. Because savers refused to make bank deposits, businesses found it very hard to borrow money to finance investment spending.

In 1965, the South Korean government reformed the country's banks and increased interest rates to a level that was attractive to savers. Over the next five years the value of bank deposits increased sevenfold, and the national savings rate—the percentage of GDP going into national savings—more than doubled. The rejuvenated banking system made it possible for South Korean businesses to launch a great investment spending boom, a key element in the country's growth surge.

Many other factors besides banking were involved in South Korea's success, but the country's experience does show how important a good financial system is to economic growth.

>> Quick Review

- **Financial markets** are where households can invest their current savings or their **wealth** by purchasing either **financial assets** or **physical assets.** A financial asset is a seller's liability.

- A well-functioning **financial system** reduces **transaction costs,** reduces **financial risk** by enabling **diversification,** and provides **liquid** assets, which investors prefer to **illiquid** assets.

- The four main types of financial assets are **loans, bonds, stocks,** and **bank deposits.** A recent innovation is **loan-backed securities,** which are more liquid and more diversified than individual loans. Bonds with a higher **default** risk typically must pay a higher interest rate.

- The most important types of **financial intermediaries** are **mutual funds, pension funds, life insurance companies,** and banks.

- A **bank** accepts bank deposits, which obliges it to return depositors' cash on demand, and lends those funds to borrowers for long lengths of time.

>> Check Your Understanding 10-2
Solutions appear at back of book.

1. Rank the following assets in terms of (i) level of transaction costs, (ii) level of risk, (iii) level of liquidity.
   a. A bank deposit with a guaranteed interest rate
   b. A share of a highly diversified mutual fund, which can be quickly sold
   c. A share of the family business, which can be sold only if you find a buyer and all other family members agree to the sale

2. What relationship would you expect to find between the level of development of a country's financial system and its level of economic development? Explain in terms of the country's level of savings and level of investment spending.

‖ Financial Fluctuations

We've learned that the financial system is an essential part of the economy; without stock markets, bond markets, and banks, long-run economic growth would be hard to achieve. Yet the news isn't entirely good: the financial system sometimes doesn't function well and instead is a source of instability in the short run.

In fact, the financial consequences of a sharp fall in housing prices became a major problem for economic policy makers starting in the summer of 2007. By the fall of 2008, it was clear that the U.S. economy faced a severe slump as it adjusted to the consequences of greatly reduced home values, and unemployment stayed elevated for years. We could easily write a whole book on asset market fluctuations. In fact, many people have. Here, we briefly discuss the causes of asset price fluctuations.

The Demand for Stocks

Once a company issues shares of stock to investors, those shares can then be resold to other investors in the stock market. And thanks to cable TV and the internet, you can easily spend all day watching stock market fluctuations—the movement up and down of the prices of individual stocks—as well as summary measures of stock prices like the Dow Jones Industrial Average. These fluctuations reflect changes in supply and demand by investors. But what causes the supply and demand for stocks to shift?

Remember that stocks are financial assets: they are shares in the ownership of a company. Unlike a good or service, whose value to its owner comes from its consumption, the value of an asset comes from its ability to generate higher future consumption of goods or services.

A financial asset allows higher future consumption in two ways. First, many financial assets provide regular income to their owners in the form of interest payments or dividends. But many companies don't pay dividends; instead, they retain their earnings to finance future investment spending. Investors purchase non-dividend-paying stocks in the belief that they will earn income from selling the stock in the future at a profit, the second way of generating higher future income. Even in the cases of a bond or a dividend-paying stock, investors will not want to purchase an asset that they believe will sell for less in the future than today, because such an asset will reduce their wealth when they sell it.

So the value of a financial asset today depends on investors' beliefs about the future value or price of the asset. If investors believe that it will be worth more in the future, they will demand more of the asset today at any given price; consequently, today's equilibrium price of the asset will rise. Conversely, if investors believe the asset will be worth less in the future, they will demand less today at any given price; consequently, today's equilibrium price of the asset will fall. Today's stock prices will change according to changes in investors' expectations about future stock prices.

FOR INQUIRING MINDS   How Now, Dow Jones?

Financial news reports often lead with the day's stock market action, as measured by changes in the Dow Jones Industrial Average, the S&P 500, and the NASDAQ.

All three are stock market indices. Like the consumer price index, they are numbers constructed as a summary of average prices—in this case, prices of stocks.

- The Dow, created by the financial analysis company Dow Jones, is an index of the prices of stock in 30 leading companies.

- The S&P 500 is an index of 500 companies, created by Standard and Poor's, another financial company.

- The NASDAQ is compiled by the National Association of Securities Dealers, which trades the stocks of smaller new companies.

Because these indices contain different groups of stocks, they track somewhat different things. The Dow, because it contains only 30 of the largest companies, tends to reflect traditional business powerhouses. The NASDAQ is heavily influenced by technology stocks. The S&P 500, a broad measure, is in between.

These indexes give investors a quick, snapshot view of how stocks from certain sectors of the economy are doing. And the price of a stock embodies investors' expectations about the future prospects of the underlying company. By implication, an index composed of stocks drawn from companies in a particular sector embodies investors' expectations of the future prospects of that sector of the economy.

The numbers tell the tale.

Suppose an event occurs that leads to a rise in the expected future price of a company's shares—say, for example, Apple announces that it forecasts higher than expected profitability due to torrential sales of the latest version of the iPhone. Demand for Apple shares will increase. At the same time, existing shareholders will be less willing to supply their shares to the market at any given price, leading to a decrease in the supply of Apple shares. And as we know, an increase in demand or a decrease in supply (or both) leads to a rise in price.

Alternatively, suppose that an event occurs that leads to a fall in the expected future price of a company's shares—say, Home Depot announces that it expects lower profitability because a slump in home sales has depressed the demand for home improvements. Demand for Home Depot shares will decrease. At the same time, supply will increase because existing shareholders will be more willing to supply their Home Depot shares to the market. Both changes lead to a fall in the stock price.

So stock prices are determined by the supply and demand for shares—which, in turn, depend on investors' expectations about the future stock price.

Stock prices are also affected by changes in the attractiveness of substitute assets, like bonds. As we learned early on, the demand for a particular good decreases when purchasing a substitute good becomes more attractive—say, due to a fall in its price. The same lesson holds true for stocks: when purchasing bonds becomes more attractive due to a rise in interest rates, stock prices will fall. And when purchasing bonds becomes less attractive due to a fall in interest rates, stock prices will rise.

The Demand for Other Assets

Everything we've just said about stocks applies to other assets as well, including physical assets. Consider the demand for commercial real estate—office buildings, shopping malls, and other structures that provide space for business activities. An investor who buys an office building does so for two reasons. First, because space in the building can be rented out, the owner of the building receives income in the form of rents. Second, the investor may expect the building to rise in value, meaning that it can be sold at a higher price at some future date.

As in the case of stocks, the demand for commercial real estate also depends on the attractiveness of substitute assets, especially bonds. When interest rates rise, the demand for commercial real estate decreases; when interest rates fall, the demand for commercial real estate increases.

Most Americans don't own commercial real estate. Only half of the population owns any stock, even indirectly through mutual funds, and for most of those people, stock ownership is well under $50,000. However, at the end of 2015 about 63% of American households owned another kind of asset: their own homes. What determines housing prices?

You might wonder whether home prices can be analyzed the same way we analyze stock prices or the price of commercial real estate. After all, stocks pay dividends, commercial real estate yields rents, but when a family lives in its own home, no money changes hands.

In economic terms, however, that doesn't matter very much. To a large extent, the benefit of owning your own home is the fact that you don't have to pay rent to someone else—or, to put it differently, it's as if you were paying rent to yourself. In fact, the U.S. government includes *implicit rent*—an estimate of the amount that homeowners, in effect, pay to themselves—in its estimates of GDP. The amount people are willing to pay for a house depends in part on the implicit rent they expect to receive from that house.

The demand for housing, like the demand for other assets, also depends on what people expect to happen to future prices: they're willing to pay more for a house if they believe they can sell it at a higher price sometime in the future.

Last but not least, the demand for houses depends on interest rates: a rise in the interest rate increases the cost of a mortgage and leads to a decrease in housing demand; a fall in the interest rate reduces the cost of a mortgage and causes an increase in housing demand.

All asset prices, then, are determined by a similar set of factors. But we haven't yet fully answered the question of what determines asset prices because we haven't explained what determines investors' *expectations* about future asset prices.

Asset Price Expectations

There are two principal competing views about how asset price expectations are determined. One view, which comes from traditional economic analysis, emphasizes the rational reasons why expectations *should* change. The other, widely held by market participants and also supported by some economists, emphasizes the irrationality of market participants.

The Efficient Markets Hypothesis Suppose you were trying to assess what Home Depot's stock is really worth. To do this, you would look at the *fundamentals*, the underlying determinants of the company's future profits. These would include factors like the changing shopping habits of the American public and the prospects for home remodeling. You would also want to compare the earnings you could expect to receive from Home Depot with the likely returns on other financial assets, such as bonds.

According to one view of asset prices, the value you would come up with after a careful study of this kind would, in fact, turn out to be the price at which Home Depot stock is already selling in the market. Why? Because all publicly available information about Home Depot's fundamentals is already embodied in its stock price. Any difference between the market price and the value suggested by a careful analysis of the underlying fundamentals indicates a profit opportunity to smart investors, who then sell Home Depot stock if it looks overpriced and buy it if it looks underpriced.

The **efficient markets hypothesis** is the general form of this view; it means that asset prices always embody all publicly available information. One implication of the efficient markets hypothesis is that at any point in time, stock prices are fairly valued: they reflect all currently available information about fundamentals. So they are neither overpriced nor underpriced.

Another implication of the efficient markets hypothesis is that the prices of stocks and other assets should change only in response to new information about the underlying fundamentals. Since new information is by definition unpredictable—if it were predictable, it wouldn't be new information—movements in asset prices are also unpredictable. As a result, the movement of, say, stock prices will follow a **random walk**—the general term for the movement over time of an unpredictable variable.

The efficient markets hypothesis plays an important role in understanding how financial markets work. Most investment professionals and many economists, however, regard it as an oversimplification. Investors, they claim, aren't that rational.

Irrational Markets? Many people who actually trade in the markets, such as individual investors and professional money managers, are skeptical of the efficient markets hypothesis. They believe that markets often behave irrationally and that a smart investor can engage in successful *market timing*—buying stocks when they are underpriced and selling them when they are overpriced.

Although economists are generally skeptical about claims that there are sure-fire ways to outsmart the market, many have also challenged the efficient markets hypothesis. It's important to understand, however, that finding particular examples where the market got it wrong does not disprove the efficient markets hypothesis. If the price of Home Depot stock plunges from $40 to $10 because of a sudden change in buying patterns, this doesn't mean that the market was inefficient in originally pricing the stock at $40. The fact that buying patterns were

According to the **efficient markets hypothesis,** asset prices embody all publicly available information.

A **random walk** is the movement over time of an unpredictable variable.

FOR INQUIRING MINDS **Behavioral Finance**

Individuals often make irrational—sometimes predictably irrational—choices that leave them worse off economically than would other, feasible alternatives. People also have a habit of repeating the same decision-making mistakes. This kind of behavior is the subject of *behavioral economics,* which includes the rapidly growing subfield of *behavioral finance,* the study of how investors in financial markets often make predictably irrational choices. In fact, the 2013 Nobel Prize in Economics was awarded to Yale professor Robert Shiller (along with two others), for his work showing how financial markets exhibit clear signs of irrationality.

Like most people, investors depart from rationality in systematic ways. In particular, they are prone to

- *Overconfidence:* having a misguided faith that they are able to spot a winning stock
- *Loss aversion:* being unwilling to sell an unprofitable asset and accept the loss
- A *herd mentality:* buying an asset when its price has already been driven high and selling it when its price has already been driven low

This irrational behavior raises an important question: can investors who *are* rational make a lot of money at the expense of those investors who aren't—for example, by buying a company's stock if irrational fears make it cheap?

The answer to this question is sometimes yes and sometimes no. Some professional investors have made huge profits by betting against irrational moves in the market—buying when there is irrational selling and selling when there is irrational buying. For example, the billionaire hedge fund manager John Paulson made $4 billion by betting against subprime mortgages during the U.S. housing bubble of 2007–2008 because he understood that these financial assets were being sold at inflated prices.

But sometimes even a rational investor cannot profit from market irrationality. For example, a money manager has to obey customers' orders to buy or sell even when those actions are irrational. Likewise, it can be much safer for professional money managers to follow the herd: if they do that and their investments go badly, they have the career-saving excuse that no one foresaw a problem. But if they've gone against the herd and their investments go south, they are likely to be fired for making poor choices. So rational investors can even exacerbate the irrational moves in financial markets.

Some observers of historical trends hypothesize that financial markets alternate between periods of complacency and forgetfulness, which breed bubbles as investors irrationally believe that prices can only go up, followed by a crash, which in turn leads investors to avoid financial markets altogether and renders asset prices irrationally cheap.

Clearly, the events of the past 15 years, with a huge housing bubble followed by extreme turmoil in financial markets, have given researchers in the area of behavioral finance a lot of material to work with.

about to change wasn't publicly available information, so it wasn't embodied in the earlier stock price.

Serious challenges to the efficient markets hypothesis focus instead either on evidence of systematic misbehavior of market prices or on evidence that individual investors don't behave in the way the theory suggests. For example, some economists believe they have found strong evidence that stock prices fluctuate more than can be explained by news about fundamentals.

Others believe they have strong evidence that individual investors behave in systematically irrational ways. For example, people seem to expect that a stock that has risen in the past will keep on rising, even though the efficient markets hypothesis tells us there is no reason to expect this. The same appears to be true of other assets, especially housing: the great housing bubble, described in the Economics in Action that follows this section, arose in large part because homebuyers assumed that home prices would continue rising in the future.

Asset Prices and Macroeconomics

How should macroeconomists and policy makers deal with the fact that asset prices fluctuate a lot and that these fluctuations can have important economic effects? This question has become one of the major problems facing macroeconomic policy.

On one side, policy makers are reluctant to assume that the market is wrong—that asset prices are either too high or too low. In part, this reflects the efficient markets hypothesis, which says that any information that is publicly available is already accounted for in asset prices. More generally, it's hard to make the case that government officials are better judges of appropriate prices than private investors who are putting their own money on the line.

On the other side, the past 20 years were marked by not one but two huge asset bubbles, each of which created major macroeconomic problems when it burst. In the late 1990s the prices of technology stocks, including but not limited to dot-com internet firms, soared to hard-to-justify heights. When the bubble burst, these stocks lost, on average, two-thirds of their value in a short time, helping to cause the 2001 recession and a period of high unemployment. A few years later there was a major bubble in housing prices. The collapse of this bubble in 2008 triggered a severe financial crisis followed by a deep recession, and the lingering effects of the crisis afflicted the U.S. economy years later.

These events have prompted much debate over whether and how to limit financial instability. We discuss financial regulation and the efforts to make it more effective in Chapter 14.

ECONOMICS >> *in Action*
The Great American Housing Bubble

Between 2000 and 2006, there was a huge increase in the price of houses in America. By the summer of 2006, home prices were well over twice as high as they had been in January 2000 in a number of major U.S. cities, including Los Angeles, San Diego, San Francisco, Washington, Miami, Las Vegas, and New York.

In 2004, as the increase in home prices accelerated, a number of economists (including the authors of this text) argued that this price increase was excessive—that it was a bubble, a rise in asset prices driven by unrealistic expectations about future prices.

It was certainly true that home prices rose much more than the cost of renting a comparable place to live. Panel (a) of Figure 10-11 compares a widely used index of U.S. housing prices with the U.S. government's index of the cost of renting, both shown as index numbers with January 2000 = 100. Home prices shot up, even though rental rates grew only gradually.

Yet there were also a number of economists who argued that the rise in housing prices was completely justified. They pointed, in particular, to the fact that interest rates were unusually low in the years of rapid price increases, and they argued that low interest rates combined with other factors, such as growing population, explained the surge in prices. Alan Greenspan, then chairman of the Federal Reserve, conceded in 2005 that there might be some "froth" in the markets but denied that there was any national bubble.

Unfortunately, it turned out that the skeptics were right. Greenspan himself would later concede that there had, in fact, been a huge national bubble. In 2006, as home prices began to level off, it became apparent that many buyers had held unrealistic expectations about future prices. As home prices began to fall, expectations of future increases in home prices were revised downward, precipitating a sudden and dramatic collapse in prices. And with home prices falling, the demand for housing fell drastically, as illustrated by panel (b) of Figure 10-11.

FIGURE 10-11 The Great American Housing Bubble

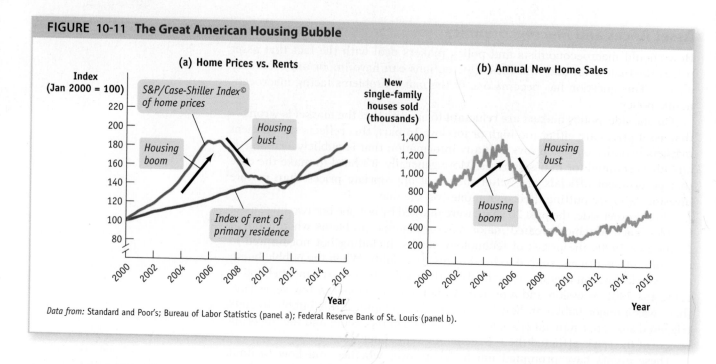

Data from: Standard and Poor's; Bureau of Labor Statistics (panel a); Federal Reserve Bank of St. Louis (panel b).

>> Quick Review

• Financial market fluctuations can be a source of short-run macroeconomic instability.

• Asset prices are driven by supply and demand as well as by the desirability of competing assets like bonds. Supply and demand also reflect expectations about future asset prices. One view of expectations is the **efficient markets hypothesis,** which leads to the view that stock prices follow a **random walk.**

• Market participants and some economists question the efficient markets hypothesis. In practice, policy makers don't assume that they can outsmart the market, but they also don't assume that markets will always behave rationally.

The implosion in housing, in turn, created numerous economic difficulties, including severe stress on the banking system.

>> Check Your Understanding 10-3

Solutions appear at back of book.

1. What is the likely effect of each of the following events on the stock price of a company? Explain your answers.

   a. The company announces that although profits are low this year, it has discovered a new line of business that will generate high profits next year.

   b. The company announces that although it had high profits this year, those profits will be less than had been previously announced.

   c. Other companies in the same industry announce that sales are unexpectedly slow this year.

   d. The company announces that it is on track to meet its previously forecast profit target.

2. Assess the following statement: "Although many investors may be irrational, it is unlikely that over time they will behave irrationally in exactly the same way—such as always buying stocks the day after the Dow has risen by 1%."

Grameen Bank: Banking Against Poverty

An old joke says that a banker will only lend you money if you don't need it. So when Guadalupe Perez found it hard to pay the rent for her party decoration store in Queens, New York, as the Great Recession hurt her business, she normally would have been forced to close her doors. Instead she was able to turn for help to Grameen America, obtaining a loan to tide her over. "It opened up a way for me to keep my business," she said. "It was a loan that I could pay little by little; I felt it was a good choice for me." And she returned to Grameen, borrowing several more times to expand her store and invest in more inventory.

Grameen America is a subsidiary of Grameen Bank in Bangladesh, which pioneered the business of *microcredit*, providing small loans to poor individuals. It was created in the mid-1970s by Mohammed Yunus, a Bangladeshi economist with a PhD from Vanderbilt University. Regular banks require a borrower to have an established credit history and/or assets that are put up as collateral for the loan (and will be seized if the loan isn't repaid on time)—requirements that a poor person can rarely meet.

Instead, Grameen Bank relies on collective responsibility to ensure that its loans are repaid: each borrower is part of a five-member group that approves each other's loan and provides oversight. The group doesn't have any legal obligation to repay the loan, but in practice the group usually does take financial responsibility if a borrower gets into difficulties. If everyone in the group repays on time, each member is able to borrow a larger amount the next time.

Grameen operates in over 100 countries, from the United States to Uganda. The great majority of its customers are rural women seeking to escape poverty by starting small businesses. Since its inception it has lent over $15 billion to well over eight million women.

Even in a rich country like the United States, *microlending*—defined as a loan less than $50,000—has become a booming business. Since 2008, when it was founded, through 2016 Grameen America has made over $265,000 in loans and dispensed nearly $591 million. The company estimates that borrowers have increased their income by an average of $1,200 annually.

However, microcredit isn't a panacea. Multiple studies have found that while microcredit does increase small-business investment, its impacts in reducing poverty and improving family well-being are limited. And in some cases it leads to excessive debt. Still, the overall impact of microcredit is positive, especially when combined with other efforts to expand access to the financial system.

Fittingly, in 2006 Yunus and Grameen received the Nobel Peace Prize for their contributions to development and poverty reduction.

QUESTIONS FOR THOUGHT

1. What market inefficiency is being exploited by Grameen Bank? What is the source of this inefficiency?

2. What tasks of a financial system does microlending perform?

3. What do you predict is the effect of Grameen Bank's lending on a community?

SUMMARY

1. Investment in physical capital is necessary for long-run economic growth. So in order for an economy to grow, it must channel savings into investment spending.

2. According to the **savings–investment spending identity,** savings and investment spending are always equal for the economy as a whole. The government is a source of savings when it runs a positive **budget balance,** also known as a **budget surplus;** it is a source of dissavings when it runs a negative budget balance, also known as a **budget deficit.** One way a government can finance a budget deficit is by borrowing. **Government borrowing** is the total amount of funds borrowed by federal, state, and local governments in the financial markets. In a closed economy, savings is equal to **national savings,** the sum of private savings plus the budget balance. In an open or international economy, savings is equal to national savings plus **net capital inflow** of foreign savings. When a negative net capital inflow occurs, some portion of national savings is funding investment spending in other countries.

3. The hypothetical **loanable funds market** shows how loans from savers are allocated among borrowers with investment spending projects. At the **equilibrium interest rate** the quantity of loans demanded equals the quantity of loans offered. Only those investment projects with an expected return greater or equal to the equilibrium interest rate are funded. By showing how gains from trade between lenders and borrowers are maximized, the loanable funds market shows why a well-functioning **financial system** leads to greater long-run economic growth. Increasing or persistent government budget deficits can lead to **crowding out:** higher interest rates and reduced investment spending. Changes in perceived business opportunities and in government borrowing shift the demand curve for loanable funds; changes in private savings and capital inflows shift the supply curve.

4. In order to evaluate a project in which the return, X, is realized in the future, you must transform X into its **present value** using the interest rate, r. The present value of $1 received one year from now is $1/(1 + r)$, the amount of money you must lend out today to have $1 one year from now. The present value of a given project rises as the interest rate falls and falls as the interest rate rises. This tells us that the demand curve for loanable funds is downward sloping.

5. Capital flows narrow differences in interest rates across countries by flowing from low interest rate countries to high interest rate countries. When flows are large, a **global loanable funds market** arises in which interest rates are equalized across countries.

6. Because neither borrowers nor lenders can know the future inflation rate, loans specify a nominal interest rate rather than a real interest rate. For a given expected future inflation rate, shifts of the demand and supply curves of loanable funds result in changes in the underlying real interest rate, leading to changes in the nominal interest rate. According to the **Fisher effect,** an increase in expected future inflation raises the nominal interest rate one-to-one so that the expected real interest rate remains unchanged.

7. **Financial markets** are where households invest their current savings or **wealth**—their accumulated savings—by purchasing assets. Assets come in the form of either a **financial asset,** a paper claim that entitles the buyer to future income from the seller, or a **physical asset,** a tangible object that can generate future income. A financial asset is also a **liability** from the point of view of its seller. There are four main types of financial assets: **loans, bonds, stocks,** and **bank deposits.** Each of them serves a different purpose in addressing the three fundamental tasks of a financial system: reducing **transaction costs**—the cost of making a deal; reducing **financial risk**—uncertainty about future outcomes that involves financial gains and losses; and providing **liquid** assets—assets that can be quickly converted into cash without much loss of value (in contrast to **illiquid** assets, which are not easily converted).

8. Although many small and moderate borrowers use bank loans to fund investment spending, larger companies typically issue bonds. Bonds with a higher risk of **default** must typically pay a higher interest rate. Business owners reduce their risk by selling stock. Although stocks usually generate a higher return than bonds, investors typically wish to reduce their risk by engaging in **diversification,** owning a wide range of assets whose returns are based on unrelated, or independent, events. Most people are risk-averse, more sensitive to a loss than to an equal-size gain. **Loan-backed securities,** a recent innovation, are assets created by pooling individual loans and selling shares of that pool to investors. Because they are more diversified and more liquid than individual loans, bonds are preferred by investors. It can be difficult, however, to assess a bond's quality.

9. **Financial intermediaries**—institutions such as **mutual funds, pension funds, life insurance companies,** and **banks**—are critical components of the financial system. Mutual funds and pension funds allow small investors to diversify, and life insurance companies reduce risk.

10. A bank allows individuals to hold liquid bank deposits that are then used to finance illiquid loans. Banks can perform this mismatch because on average only a small fraction of depositors withdraw their funds at any one time. A well-functioning banking sector is a key ingredient of long-run economic growth.

11. Asset market fluctuations can be a source of short-run macroeconomic instability. Asset prices are determined by supply and demand as well as by the desirability of competing assets, like bonds: when the interest rate rises, prices of stocks and physical assets such as real estate generally fall, and vice versa. Expectations drive the supply of and demand for assets: expectations of higher future prices push today's asset prices higher, and expectations of lower future prices drive them lower. One view of how expectations are formed is the **efficient markets hypothesis,** which holds that the prices of assets embody all publicly available information. It implies that fluctuations are inherently unpredictable—they follow a **random walk.**

12. Many market participants and economists believe that, based on actual evidence, financial markets are not as rational as the efficient markets hypothesis claims. Such evidence includes the fact that stock price fluctuations are too great to be driven by fundamentals alone. Likewise, policy makers do not believe that markets always behave rationally or that they can outsmart them.

KEY TERMS

Savings–investment spending identity, p. 272
Budget surplus, p. 273
Budget deficit, p. 273
Government borrowing, p. 273
Budget balance, p. 273
National savings, p. 273
Net capital inflow, p. 274
Loanable funds market, p. 276
Present value, p. 277
Equilibrium interest rate, p. 279
Crowding out, p. 281
Global loanable funds market, p. 282

Fisher effect, p. 285
Financial markets, p. 287
Wealth, p. 287
Financial asset, p. 287
Physical asset, p. 287
Liability, p. 287
Financial system, p. 287
Transaction costs, p. 288
Financial risk, p. 288
Diversification, p. 289
Liquid, p. 289
Illiquid, p. 289
Loan, p. 289

Bond, p. 290
Default, p. 290
Loan-backed securities, p. 290
Stock, p. 290
Financial intermediary, p. 291
Mutual fund, p. 291
Pension fund, p. 292
Life insurance company, p. 292
Bank deposit, p. 292
Bank, p. 293
Efficient markets hypothesis, p. 297
Random walk, p. 297

PROBLEMS

interactive activity

1. Given the following information about the closed economy of Brittania, what is the level of investment spending and private savings, and what is the budget balance? What is the relationship among the three? Is national savings equal to investment spending? There are no government transfers.

   GDP = $1,000 million T = $50 million

   C = $850 million G = $100 million

2. Given the following information about the international economy of Regalia, what is the level of investment spending and private savings, and what are the budget balance and net capital inflow? What is the relationship among the four? There are no government transfers. [*Hint:* Net capital inflow equals the value of imports (IM) minus the value of exports (X).]

   GDP = $1,000 million G = $100 million

   C = $850 million X = $100 million

   T = $50 million IM = $125 million

3. The accompanying table shows the percentage of GDP accounted for by private savings, investment spending, and net capital inflow in the economies of Capsland and Marsalia. Capsland is currently experiencing a positive net capital inflow and Marsalia, a negative net capital inflow. What is the budget balance (as a percentage of GDP) in both countries? Are Capsland and Marsalia running a budget deficit or surplus?

	Capsland	Marsalia
Investment spending as a percentage of GDP	20%	20%
Private savings as a percentage of GDP	10	25
Net capital inflow as a percentage of GDP	5	−2

4. Assume the economy is open to capital inflows and outflows and therefore net capital inflow equals imports (*IM*) minus exports (*X*). Calculate each of the following.

a. $X = \$125$ million
   $IM = \$80$ million
   Budget balance = $-\$200$ million
   $I = \$350$ million
   Calculate private savings.

b. $X = \$85$ million
   $IM = \$135$ million
   Budget balance = $\$100$ million
   Private savings = $\$250$ million
   Calculate *I*.

c. $X = \$60$ million
   $IM = \$95$ million
   Private savings = $\$325$ million
   $I = \$300$ million
   Calculate the budget balance.

d. Private savings = $\$325$ million
   $I = \$400$ million
   Budget balance = $\$10$ million
   Calculate $IM - X$.

5. The government is running a budget balance of zero when it decides to increase education spending by $200 billion and finance the spending by selling bonds. The accompanying diagram shows the market for loanable funds before the government sells the bonds. Assume that there are no capital inflows or outflows. How will the equilibrium interest rate and the equilibrium quantity of loanable funds change? Is there any crowding out in the market?

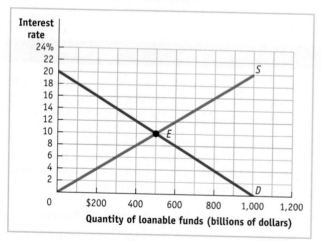
Quantity of loanable funds (billions of dollars)

6. Congress estimated that the cost of increasing support and expanding pre-kindergarten education and infant and toddler childcare would cost $28 billion in 2014. Since the U.S. government was running a budget deficit at the time, assume that the new pre-K funding was financed by government borrowing, which increases the demand for loanable funds without affecting supply. This question considers the likely effect of this government expenditure on the interest rate.

a. Draw typical demand (D_1) and supply (S_1) curves for loanable funds without the cost of the expanded pre-K programs accounted for. Label the vertical axis "Interest rate" and the horizontal axis "Quantity of loanable funds." Label the equilibrium point (E_1) and the equilibrium interest rate (r_1).

b. Now draw a new diagram with the cost of the expanded pre-K programs included in the analysis. Shift the demand curve in the appropriate direction. Label the new equilibrium point (E_2) and the new equilibrium interest rate (r_2).

c. How does the equilibrium interest rate change in response to government expenditure on the expanded pre-K programs? Explain.

7. Explain why equilibrium in the loanable funds market maximizes efficiency.

8. How would you respond to a friend who claims that the government should eliminate all purchases that are financed by borrowing because such borrowing crowds out private investment spending?

9. Boris Borrower and Lynn Lender agree that Lynn will lend Boris $10,000 and that Boris will repay the $10,000 with interest in one year. They agree to a nominal interest rate of 8%, reflecting a real interest rate of 3% on the loan and a commonly shared expected inflation rate of 5% over the next year.

a. If the inflation rate is actually 4% over the next year, how does that lower-than-expected inflation rate affect Boris and Lynn? Who is better off?

b. If the actual inflation rate is 7% over the next year, how does that affect Boris and Lynn? Who is better off?

10. Using the accompanying diagram, explain what will happen to the market for loanable funds when there is a fall of 2 percentage points in the expected future inflation rate. How will the change in the expected future inflation rate affect the equilibrium quantity of loanable funds?

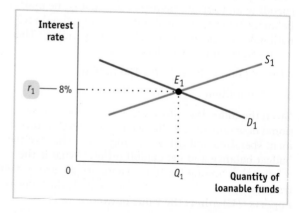

11. The accompanying diagram shows data for the interest rate on 10-year euro area government bonds and inflation rate for the euro area for 1996 through 2016, as reported by the European Central Bank. How would you describe the relationship between the two? How does the pattern compare to that of the United States in Figure 10-10?

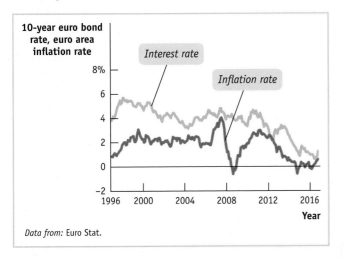

Data from: Euro Stat.

12. For each of the following, is it an example of investment spending, investing in financial assets, or investing in physical assets?

a. Rupert Moneybucks buys 100 shares of existing Coca-Cola stock.

b. Rhonda Moviestar spends $10 million to buy a mansion built in the 1970s.

c. Ronald Basketballstar spends $10 million to build a new mansion with a view of the Pacific Ocean.

d. Rawlings builds a new plant to make catcher's mitts.

e. Russia buys $100 million in U.S. government bonds.

13. Explain how a well-functioning financial system increases savings and investment spending, holding the budget balance and any capital flows fixed.

14. What are the important types of financial intermediaries in the U.S. economy? What are the primary assets of these intermediaries, and how do they facilitate investment spending and saving?

15. Explain the effect on a company's stock price today of each of the following events, other things held constant.

a. The interest rate on bonds falls.

b. Several companies in the same sector announce surprisingly higher sales.

c. A change in the tax law passed last year reduces this year's profit.

d. The company unexpectedly announces that due to an accounting error, it must amend last year's accounting statement and reduce last year's reported profit by $5 million. It also announces that this change has no implications for future profits.

16. Sallie Mae is a quasi-governmental agency that packages individual student loans into pools of loans and sells shares of these pools to investors as Sallie Mae bonds.

a. What is this process called? What effect will it have on investors compared to situations in which they could only buy and sell individual student loans?

b. What effect do you think Sallie Mae's actions will have on the ability of students to get loans?

c. Suppose that a very severe recession hits and, as a consequence, many graduating students cannot get jobs and default on their student loans. What effect will this have on Sallie Mae bonds? Why is it likely that investors now believe Sallie Mae bonds to be riskier than expected? What will be the effect on the availability of student loans?

WORK IT OUT Interactive step-by-step help with solving this problem can be found online.

17. Use the market for loanable funds shown in the accompanying diagram to explain what happens to private savings, private investment spending, and the interest rate if each of the following events occur. Assume that there are no capital inflows or outflows.

a. The government reduces the size of its deficit to zero.

b. At any given interest rate, consumers decide to save more. Assume the budget balance is zero.

c. At any given interest rate, businesses become very optimistic about the future profitability of investment spending. Assume the budget balance is zero.

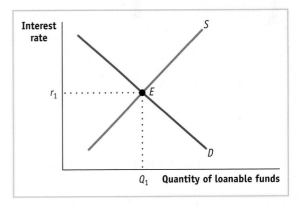

Toward a Fuller Understanding of Present Value

In this appendix we will show how you can expand the use of present value calculations to understand how businesses make investment spending decisions and how investors determine the prices of existing financial assets like stocks and bonds. We begin by showing how to apply present value calculations for one-year and multi-year projects. Then we show how to calculate the present value of a project that has revenues and costs arising in the future. Finally, we use present value to calculate the prices of financial assets like bonds and stocks.

The key point to keep in mind is that when businesses engage in investment spending, the lower the equilibrium interest rate, the greater the payoff from a project, other things equal. As a result, when the interest rate falls, more businesses will spend on investment projects. Likewise, consider an existing financial asset like a stock or bond that promises to deliver payments to its owner in the future. When the equilibrium interest rate falls, the value today of those promised future payments goes up. As a result, the prices of those existing financial assets will rise in financial markets.

How to Calculate the Present Value of One-Year Projects

Recall that the symbol r represents the interest rate, either as a percentage or decimal (that is, $r = 5\% = 0.05$). Rather than work with units of $1,000, we will calculate present value for the simplest case, units of $1.

If you lend X, at the end of one year you will receive:

(10A-1) $X \times (1 + r) =$ Amount received at end of year in return for lending X

From Equation 10A-1, we can calculate how much you would have to lend today in order to receive $1 a year from now. To do that we set Equation 10A-1 equal to $1 and solve for X:

(10A-2) $X \times (1 + r) = \$1$

Solving for X by dividing both sides of Equation 10A-2 by $(1 + r)$ gives:

(10A-3) $X = \$1/(1 + r)$

As we explained in the chapter, X is the present value of $1 given an interest rate of r: it is the amount of money you would need today in order to generate a given amount of money one year from now given the interest rate r. Because r is greater than zero, X is less than $1; $1 to be delivered in the future is worth less than $1 delivered today.

Also recall from the chapter that as the interest rate goes up, the present value of a dollar delivered in the future falls. For example, the present value of $1 when $r = 0.02$ is $\$1/(1 + 0.02) = \$1/1.02 = \$0.98$, and the present value of $1 when $r = 0.10$ is $\$1/(1 + 0.10) = \$1/1.10 = \$0.91$.

How to Calculate the Present Value of Multiyear Projects

Let's represent the value of $1 to be received two years from now as X_{2yrs}. If you lend out X_{2yrs} today for two years, you will receive:

(10A-4) $X_{2yrs} \times (1 + r)$ at the end of one year which you then reinvest to receive:

(10A-5) $X_{2\text{yrs}} \times (1 + r) \times (1 + r) = X_{2\text{yrs}} \times (1 + r)^2$ at the end of two years

From Equation 10A-5 we can calculate how much you would have to lend today in order to receive $1 two years from now:

(10A-6) $X_{2\text{yrs}} (1 + r)^2 = \$1$

To solve for $X_{2\text{yrs}}$, divide both sides of Equation 10A-6 by $(1 + r)^2$ to arrive at:

(10A-7) $X_{2\text{yrs}} = \$1/(1 + r)^2$

For example, if $r = 0.10$, then $X_{2\text{yrs}} = \$1/(1.10)^2 = \$1/1.21 = \$0.83$.

Equation 10A-7 points the way toward the general expression for present value, where $1 is paid after N years. It is

(10A-8) $X_{N\text{yrs}} = \$1/(1 + r)^N$

In other words, the present value of $1 to be received N years from now is equal to $\$1/(1 + r)^N$.

How to Calculate the Present Value of Projects with Revenues and Costs

Suppose you have to choose one of three projects to undertake. Project A gives you an immediate payoff of $100. Project B costs you $10 now and pays $115 a year from now. Project C gives you an immediate payoff of $119 but requires you to pay $20 a year from now. We will assume that $r = 0.10$.

In order to compare these three projects, you must evaluate costs and revenues that are expended or realized at different times. It is here, of course, that the concept of present value is extremely handy: by using present value to convert any dollars realized in the future into today's value, you can factor out differences in time. Once differences in time are factored out, you can compare the three projects by calculating each one's *net present value*, the present value of current and future revenues minus the present value of current and future costs. The best project to undertake is the one with the highest net present value.

Table 10A-1 shows how to calculate the net present value of each of the three projects. The second and third columns show how many dollars are realized and when they are realized; costs are indicated by a minus sign. The fourth column shows the equations used to convert the flows of dollars into their present value, and the fifth column shows the actual amounts of the total net present value for each of the three projects.

For instance, to calculate the net present value of project B, you need to calculate the present value of $115 received one year from now. The present value of $1 received one year from now is $\$1/(1 + r)$. So the present value of $115 received one year from now is $115 \times \$1/(1 + r) = \$115/(1 + r)$. The net present value of project B is the present value of current and future revenues minus the present value of current and future costs: $-\$10 + \$115/(1 + r)$.

From the fifth column, we can immediately see that, at an interest rate of 10%, project C is the best project. It has the highest net present value, $100.82, which is higher than the net present value of project A ($100) and much higher than the net present value of project B ($94.55).

TABLE 10A-1 **The Net Present Value of Three Hypothetical Projects**

Project	Dollars realized today	Dollars realized one year from today	Present value formula	Net present value given $r = 0.10$
A	$100	—	$100	$100.00
B	−$10	$115	−$10 + $115/(1 + r)	$94.55
C	$119	−$20	$119 − $20/(1 + r)	$100.82

This example shows how important the concept of present value is. If we had failed to use the present value calculations and had instead simply added up the revenues and costs, we would have been misled into believing that project B was the best project and C was the worst one.

How to Calculate the Price of a Bond Using Present Value

In Chapters 7 and 10 we learned that a buyer of a bond is entitled to receive a fixed sum of interest each year over the life of the bond and, at the end, a repayment of *principal* (the face value of the bond: the amount lent when the bond was issued). Let's illustrate how we can use present value to price a bond with a simple example.

Suppose that today you are offered the chance to purchase a bond issued by Facebook. It was issued two years ago to mature in seven years' time. That is, it pays interest for seven years total, at the end of which the principal is repaid. As of today, then, the bond will pay interest for five more years. Assume that the principal on this Facebook bond is $1,000. Also assume that when it was issued it paid an interest rate of 6%, equal to the current market equilibrium interest rate at the time. So the amount of interest that the owner of this bond receives every year is $1,000 × 0.06 = $60. This annual interest payment is known generally as the *coupon*.

To determine today's price of this bond we need to calculate the present value of the future interest payments from this bond based on *today's* market equilibrium interest rate. Suppose that the market equilibrium interest rate has dropped from 6% when the bond was issued two years ago to 5% today. Then the present value of this bond is equal to the present value of the annual $60 coupon for the remaining five years plus the present value of the repayment of the $1,000 principal at the end of the five years:

(10A-9) At today's market equilibrium $r = 5\%$,
$$\text{Present value} = \$60/(1 + 0.05) + \$60/(1 + 0.05)^2 + \$60/(1 + 0.05)^3$$
$$+ \$60/(1 + 0.05)^4 + \$60/(1 + 0.05)^5 + \$1,000/(1 + 0.05)^5$$
$$= \$1,043.30$$

(Your calculated value may be slightly different due to rounding error.)

This means that, as of today, you should be willing to pay no more than $1,043.30 for this Facebook bond. At a higher price you would be better off spending your $1,043.30 on a newly issued bond that pays an interest rate of 5% for the next five years. This example illustrates a general rule: when determining the price of a preexisting bond, the interest rate used to calculate that price is the *current market equilibrium interest rate* (5% in this example), not the interest rate that was current when the bond was originally issued (6% in this example).

To gain further understanding, let's calculate what the present value of that same bond would be today if the equilibrium interest rate had not fallen and had instead remained at 6%:

(10A-10) At market equilibrium $r = 6\%$,
$$\text{Present value} = \$60/(1 + 0.06) + \$60/(1 + 0.06)^2 + \$60/(1 + 0.06)^3$$
$$+ \$60/(1 + 0.06)^4 + \$60/(1 + 0.06)^5 + \$1,000/(1 + 0.06)^5$$
$$= \$1,000.00$$

(Again, your calculated value may be slightly different due to rounding error.)

Equation 10A-10 illustrates a general principle: when the current market equilibrium interest rate is unchanged from when the bond was issued, then the present value of the bond is equal to its face value, regardless of how many periods are left until it matures. You can check this for yourself by recalculating the present value for the bond when $r = 6\%$ and four years are left to maturity. Your answer should be approximately $1,000.00.

By comparing Equations 10A-9 and 10A-10, you can see that the price of the bond goes up when the market equilibrium interest rate falls. Conversely, the price of a bond falls when the market equilibrium interest rate goes up.

In the real world there is an additional complicating factor when pricing a bond: risk. Some bonds are riskier than others because the bond issuer is perceived to be less likely to repay bondholders in full. A high-risk bond will sell at a lower price than a low-risk bond with the same maturity, face value, and annual coupon payments. That lower price compensates the owner of the high-risk bond for the risk she faces of not being repaid in full.

Ignoring the problem of risk, the general formula for bond pricing is as follows, where n is the number of years to maturity, C is the annual coupon, F is the face value, and i is the current market equilibrium interest rate on comparable bonds:

(10A-11) Bond price $= C/(1 + i) + C/(1 + i)^2 + \ldots + C(1 + i)^{n-1} + C(1 + i)^n + F(1 + i)^n$

We can conclude that when the market interest rate on comparable bonds rises, the price of existing bonds falls; when the market interest rate on comparable bonds falls, the price of existing bonds rises.

How to Calculate the Price of a Share of Stock Using Present Value

While a bond entitles its owner to interest payments, a share of stock entitles its owner to a share of the company's profits. That's because a share of stock represents ownership of a portion of the company. As we explained in Chapter 7, a share of a company's profits paid to a shareholder is called a *dividend*. So a share entitles its owner to a series of payments of future dividends, and we can use the present value formula to find the price of a share of stock:

(10A-12) Stock price $= \text{Dividend}/(1 + r) + \text{Dividend}/(1 + r)^2 + \text{Dividend}/(1 + r)^3 + \ldots$

In the formula, r is the interest rate in the market for loanable funds. Unlike the formula for a bond price in Equation 10A-11, there is no end date, n, in the formula for a stock because a share entitles its owner to dividend payments indefinitely.

It's possible to simplify Equation 10A-12 if we assume that the company's profits grow at a constant rate every year, and its dividends grow at a constant rate. Then the stock price formula becomes:

(10A-13) Stock price $= \text{Dividend}/(r - \textit{Growth rate})$

Like bond pricing, stock pricing comes with real-world complicating factors for investors to consider: First, dividends paid by most businesses are highly variable (much more than bond payments) because profits vary from year to year. So stock prices are based upon *expected* future dividend payments. Second, the stock market is affected by rumors, fads, and other types of irrational behavior, so stock prices fluctuate far more than bond prices.

PROBLEMS

interactive activity

1. You have won the state lottery. There are two ways in which you can receive your prize. You can either have $1 million in cash now, or you can have $1.2 million that is paid out as follows: $300,000 now, $300,000 in one year's time, $300,000 in two years' time, and $300,000 in three years' time. The interest rate is 20%. How would you prefer to receive your prize?

2. The drug company Pfizer is considering whether to invest in the development of a new cancer drug.

Development will require an initial investment of $10 million now; beginning one year from now, the drug will generate annual profits of $4 million for three years.

a. If the interest rate is 12%, should Pfizer invest in the development of the new drug? Why or why not?

b. If the interest rate is 8%, should Pfizer invest in the development of the new drug? Why or why not?

WORK IT OUT **Interactive step-by-step help with solving this problem can be found online.**

3. Suppose that a major city's main thoroughfare, which is also an interstate highway, will be completely closed to traffic for two years, from January 2014 to December 2015, for reconstruction at a cost of $535 million. If the construction company were to keep the highway open for traffic during construction, the highway reconstruction project would take much longer and be more expensive. Suppose that construction would take four years if the highway were kept open, at a total cost of $800 million. The state department of transportation had to make its decision in 2013, one year before the start of construction (so that the first payment was one year away). So the department of transportation had the following choices:

(i) Close the highway during construction, at an annual cost of $267.5 million per year for two years.

(ii) Keep the highway open during construction, at an annual cost of $200 million per year for four years.

a. Suppose the interest rate is 10%. Calculate the present value of the costs incurred under each plan. Which reconstruction plan is less expensive?

b. Now suppose the interest rate is 80%. Calculate the present value of the costs incurred under each plan. Which reconstruction plan is now less expensive?

11 Income and Expenditure

HARD TIMES IN HELSINKI

HELSINKI, THE CAPITAL OF FINLAND, was a cheerful-looking place in 2016, with plenty of chic shops and trendy restaurants. Yet times were tough for many Finns and many Finnish businesses. The unemployment rate was above 9%, almost twice its level in the United States. Retail sales were depressed: Stockmann, Finland's iconic department store, was losing a million euros a week.

After Finland's exports of Nokia phones and wood products plunged, the effects spread throughout the economy and multiplied, leading to an economic bust.

In fact, the scale of Finland's economic setback was startling: real GDP per capita was down almost 10% from its peak in 2008. What went wrong?

The answer, surprisingly, was that Finland was hurt by new developments in digital technology. In the early 2000s, the Finnish firm Nokia was one of the world's leading producers of cell phones, and a huge contributor to the Finnish economy. But Nokia failed to keep up when the iPhone and other smartphones took over most of the mobile phone business, and its sales collapsed.

Nor was Nokia's decline the only adverse shock. Outside Helsinki, Finland is basically one big forest, and exports of paper, made from wood pulp, have long been key to its economic success. In fact, Nokia began as a wood pulp producer. But the digital revolution has many people staring at screens instead of reading documents on paper, and Finnish paper exports have been in decline.

The fall in exports explains why Finland's economy has been facing hard times. But a fall in exports doesn't tell us why retail sales are also down. Why are Finns spending less in department stores?

The answer is that when Finnish exports took a hit, this reduced household incomes, which led families to spend less on other goods and services. The fall in spending meant another round of income cuts among those who produced the goods and services people weren't buying. And the process didn't stop there: as incomes fell, consumer spending fell even further, leading to further declines in incomes, leading to further cuts, and so on.

Finland's troubles illustrate the way booms and busts happen for the economy as a whole. The business cycle is often driven by ups or downs in one particular kind of spending—either exports, as is the case in Finland, or investment spending. These first-round changes in spending then lead to changes in consumer spending, which magnify—or, as economists usually say, *multiply*—the effect of the initial changes on the economy as a whole.

In this chapter we'll study how this process works, showing how *multiplier* analysis helps us understand the business cycle. As a first step, we introduce the concept of the multiplier informally. ●

WHAT YOU WILL LEARN

- What is the importance of the **multiplier,** which summarizes how initial changes in spending lead to further changes?
- What is the **aggregate consumption function?**
- How do expected future income and aggregate wealth affect consumer spending?
- What determines investment spending and why do we need to distinguish between **planned investment spending** and **unplanned inventory investment?**
- How does the inventory adjustment process move the economy to a new equilibrium after a change in demand?
- Why is investment spending considered a leading indicator of the future state of the economy?

‖ The Multiplier: An Informal Introduction

The story of the slump in Finland involves a sort of chain reaction in which an initial rise or fall in aggregate spending leads to changes in income, which lead to further changes in aggregate spending, and so on. Let's examine that chain reaction more closely, this time thinking through the effects of changes in aggregate spending in the economy as a whole.

For the sake of this analysis, we'll initially make four simplifying assumptions that will have to be reconsidered later.

1. We assume that *producers are willing to supply additional output at a fixed price.* That is, if consumers or businesses buying investment goods decide to spend an additional $1 billion, that will translate into the production of $1 billion worth of additional goods and services without driving up the overall level of prices. As a result, *changes in aggregate spending translate into changes in aggregate output,* as measured by real GDP. As we'll learn in the next chapter, this assumption isn't too unrealistic in the short run, but it needs to be changed when we think about the long-run effects of changes in demand.

2. We take the interest rate as given.

3. We assume that there is no government spending and no taxes.

4. We assume that exports and imports are zero (which is obviously a departure from our Finnish example, but in a later section we'll see how to bring trade back).

Given these simplifying assumptions, consider what happens if there is a change in investment spending. For example, imagine that for some reason home builders decide to spend an extra $100 billion on home construction over the next year.

The direct effect of this increase in investment spending will be to increase income and the value of aggregate output by the same amount. That's because each dollar spent on home construction translates into a dollar's worth of income for construction workers, suppliers of building materials, electricians, and so on. If the process stopped there, the increase in housing investment spending would raise overall income by exactly $100 billion.

But the process doesn't stop there. The increase in aggregate output leads to an increase in disposable income that flows to households in the form of profits and wages. The increase in households' disposable income leads to a rise in consumer spending, which, in turn, induces firms to increase output yet again. This generates another rise in disposable income, which leads to another round of consumer spending increases, and so on. So there are multiple rounds of increases in aggregate output.

How large is the total effect on aggregate output if we sum the effect from all these rounds of spending increases? To answer this question, we need to introduce the concept of the **marginal propensity to consume,** or **MPC:** the increase in consumer spending when disposable income rises by $1. When consumer spending changes because of a rise or fall in disposable income, *MPC* is the change in consumer spending divided by the change in disposable income:

$$\textbf{(11-1)} \quad MPC = \frac{\Delta \text{ Consumer spending}}{\Delta \text{ Disposable income}}$$

where the symbol Δ (delta) means "change in." For example, if consumer spending goes up by $6 billion when disposable income goes up by $10 billion, *MPC* is $6 billion/$10 billion = 0.6.

Because consumers normally spend part but not all of an additional dollar of disposable income, *MPC* is a number between 0 and 1. The additional disposable income that consumers don't spend is saved; the **marginal propensity to save,** or **MPS,** is the fraction of an additional dollar of disposable income that is saved. *MPS* is equal to $1 - MPC$.

The **marginal propensity to consume,** or **MPC,** is the increase in consumer spending when disposable income rises by $1.

The **marginal propensity to save,** or **MPS,** is the increase in household savings when disposable income rises by $1.

Because we assumed that there are no taxes and no international trade, each $1 increase in aggregate spending raises both real GDP and disposable income by $1. So the $100 billion increase in investment spending initially raises real GDP by $100 billion. This leads to a second-round increase in consumer spending, which raises real GDP by a further $MPC \times$ $100 billion. It is followed by a third-round increase in consumer spending of $MPC \times MPC \times$ $100 billion, and so on. After an infinite number of rounds, the total effect on real GDP is:

$$
\begin{array}{llll}
\text{Increase in investment spending} & = & \text{\$100 billion} \\
+ \text{ Second-round increase in consumer spending} & = MPC & \times \text{\$100 billion} \\
+ \text{ Third-round increase in consumer spending} & = MPC^2 & \times \text{\$100 billion} \\
+ \text{ Fourth-round increase in consumer spending} & = MPC^3 & \times \text{\$100 billion} \\
& \vdots & \vdots
\end{array}
$$

Total increase in real GDP $= (1 + MPC + MPC^2 + MPC^3 + \ldots) \times$ $100 billion

So the $100 billion increase in investment spending sets off a chain reaction in the economy. The net result of this chain reaction is that a $100 billion increase in investment spending leads to a change in real GDP that is a *multiple* of the size of that initial change in spending.

How large is this multiple? It's a mathematical fact that an infinite series of the form $1 + x + x^2 + x^3 + \ldots$, where x is between 0 and 1, is equal to $1/(1 - x)$. So the total effect of a $100 billion increase in investment spending, I, taking into account all the subsequent increases in consumer spending (and assuming no taxes and no international trade), is given by:

(11-2) Total increase in real GDP from a $100 billion rise in I

$$
= \frac{1}{1 - MPC} \times \text{\$100 billion}
$$

Let's consider a numerical example in which $MPC = 0.6$: each $1 in additional disposable income causes a $0.60 rise in consumer spending. In that case, a $100 billion increase in investment spending raises real GDP by $100 billion in the first round. The second-round increase in consumer spending raises real GDP by another $0.6 \times$ $100 billion, or $60 billion. The third-round increase in consumer spending raises real GDP by another $0.6 \times$ $60 billion, or $36 billion. Table 11-1 shows the successive stages of increases, where "..." means the process goes on an infinite number of times. In the end, real GDP rises by $250 billion as a consequence of the initial $100 billion rise in investment spending:

$$
\frac{1}{1 - 0.6} \times \text{\$100 billion} = 2.5 \times \text{\$100 billion} = \text{\$250 billion}
$$

Notice that even though there are an infinite number of rounds of expansion of real GDP, the total rise in real GDP is limited to $250 billion. The reason is that at each stage some of the rise in disposable income "leaks out" because it is saved. How much of an additional dollar of disposable income is saved depends on MPS, the marginal propensity to save.

We've described the effects of a change in investment spending, but the same analysis can be applied to any other change in aggregate spending. The important thing is to distinguish between the initial change in aggregate spending, before real GDP rises, and the additional change in aggregate spending caused by the change in real GDP as the chain reaction unfolds. For example, suppose that a boom in housing prices makes consumers feel richer and that, as a result, they become willing to spend more at any given level of disposable income. This will lead to an initial rise in consumer spending, before real GDP rises. But it

TABLE 11-1 Rounds of Increases in Real GDP When $MPC = 0.6$

Rounds	Increase in real GDP (billions)	Total increase in real GDP (billions)
First	$100	$100
Second	60	160
Third	36	196
Fourth	21.6	217.6
...	...	...
Final	0	250

An **autonomous change in aggregate spending** is an initial change in the desired level of spending by firms, households, or government at a given level of real GDP.

The **multiplier** is the ratio of the total change in real GDP caused by an autonomous change in aggregate spending to the size of that autonomous change.

will also lead to second and later rounds of higher consumer spending as real GDP rises.

An initial rise or fall in aggregate spending at a given level of real GDP is called an **autonomous change in aggregate spending.** It's autonomous—which means self-governing—because it's the cause, not the result, of the chain reaction we've just described. Formally, the **multiplier** is the ratio of the total change in real GDP caused by an autonomous change in aggregate spending to the size of that autonomous change.

If we let ΔAAS stand for autonomous change in aggregate spending and ΔY stand for the change in real GDP, then the multiplier is equal to $\Delta Y/\Delta AAS$. And we've already seen how to find the value of the multiplier. Assuming no taxes and no trade, the change in real GDP caused by an autonomous change in spending is:

$$\textbf{(11-3)} \quad \Delta Y = \frac{1}{1 - MPC} \times \Delta AAS$$

So the multiplier is:

$$\textbf{(11-4)} \quad \text{Multiplier} = \frac{\Delta Y}{\Delta AAS} = \frac{1}{1 - MPC}$$

Notice that the size of the multiplier depends on MPC. If the marginal propensity to consume is high, so is the multiplier. This is true because the size of MPC determines how large each round of expansion is compared with the previous round. To put it another way, the higher MPC is, the less disposable income leaks out into savings at each round of expansion.

In later chapters we'll use the concept of the multiplier to analyze the effects of fiscal and monetary policies. We'll also see that the formula for the multiplier changes when we introduce various complications, including taxes and foreign trade. First, however, we need to look more deeply at what determines consumer spending.

ECONOMICS >> *in Action*
To Shale and Back

For most of America, recovery from the severe recession of 2007–2009 was disappointingly slow. But a few parts of the country experienced rapid growth—and none more rapid than North Dakota, whose economy grew 35% between 2010 and 2012. That's an annual growth rate of nearly 17%, more than five times the growth of the U.S. economy as a whole.

There's no mystery about the North Dakota boom: it was all about shale oil. Fracking made it possible to extract oil from the Bakken shale, which underlies the state. Oil companies and other investors rushed in, along with thousands of oil-field workers, more than doubling the output of the mining sector in just two years.

But as Figure 11-1 shows, mining and related industries weren't the only sectors growing fast. North Dakota also saw much faster growth than other states in a number of areas, notably retail and wholesale trade, banking, and utilities. Why?

The answer was the multiplier. As high-paying shale-related jobs surged, so did consumer spending—much of which ended up in the hands of local shops, bank branches, companies supplying electricity and heating oil, and so on. These local suppliers, in turn, hired more workers, whose incomes added to consumer spending and fed additional rounds of expansion.

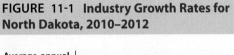

FIGURE 11-1 Industry Growth Rates for North Dakota, 2010–2012

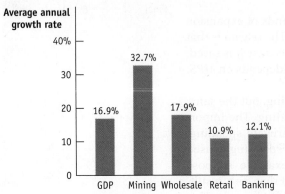

Data from: Bureau of Economic Analysis.

Obviously this extraordinary growth couldn't last. In fact, North Dakota's boom slowed sharply after 2012, and by 2015, as a glut of oil drove prices down, state employment was falling. But the boom was fun while it lasted, and it also gave an excellent example of the multiplier at work.

>> *Check Your Understanding* 11-1

Solutions appear at back of book.

1. Explain why a decline in investment spending caused by a change in business expectations leads to a fall in consumer spending.

2. What is the multiplier if the marginal propensity to consume is 0.5? What is it if *MPC* is 0.8?

3. As a percentage of GDP, savings accounts for a larger share of the economy in the country of Scania compared to the country of Amerigo. Which country is likely to have the larger multiplier? Explain.

‖ Consumer Spending

Should you splurge on a restaurant meal or save money by eating at home? Should you buy a new car and, if so, how expensive a model? Should you redo that bathroom or live with it for another year? In the real world, households are constantly confronted with such choices—not just about the consumption mix but also about how much to spend in total.

These choices, in turn, have a powerful effect on the economy: consumer spending normally accounts for two-thirds of total spending on final goods and services. In particular, as we've just seen, the decision about how much of an additional dollar in income to spend—the marginal propensity to consume—determines the size of the multiplier, which determines the ultimate effect on the economy of autonomous changes in spending.

But what determines how much consumers spend?

Current Disposable Income and Consumer Spending

The most important factor affecting a family's consumer spending is its current disposable income—income after taxes are paid and government transfers are received. It's obvious from daily life that people with high disposable incomes on average drive more expensive cars, live in more expensive houses, and spend more on meals and clothing than people with lower disposable incomes. And the relationship between current disposable income and spending is clear in the data.

The Bureau of Labor Statistics (BLS) collects annual data on family income and spending. Families are grouped by levels of before-tax income, and after-tax income for each group is also reported. Since the income figures include transfers from the government, what the BLS calls a household's after-tax income is equivalent to its current disposable income.

Figure 11-2 is a scatter diagram illustrating the relationship between household current disposable income and household consumer spending for American households by income group in 2015. For example, point *A* shows that in 2015 the middle fifth of the population had an average current disposable income of $46,807 and average spending of $45,912. The pattern of the dots slopes upward from left to right, making it clear that households with higher current disposable income had higher consumer spending.

It's very useful to represent the relationship between an individual household's current disposable income and its consumer spending with an equation. The **consumption function** is an equation showing how an individual household's consumer

People with lower disposable incomes may avoid higher-priced brand-name goods in favor of generics that cost less.

FIGURE 11-2 Current Disposable Income and Consumer Spending for American Households in 2015

For each income group of households, average current disposable income in 2015 is plotted versus average consumer spending in 2015. For example, the middle income group, with current disposable income of $37,638, to $62,587, is represented by point *A*, indicating a household average current disposable income of $46,807 and average household consumer spending of $45,912. The data clearly show a positive relationship between current disposable income and consumer spending: families with higher current disposable income have higher consumer spending.

Data from: Bureau of Labor Statistics.

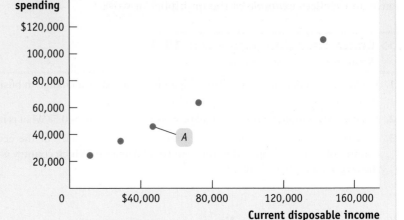

The **consumption function** is an equation showing how an individual household's consumer spending varies with the household's current disposable income.

spending varies with the household's current disposable income. The simplest version of a consumption function is a linear equation:

(11-5) $c = a + MPC \times yd$

where lowercase letters indicate variables measured for an individual household.

In this equation, c is individual household consumer spending and yd is individual household current disposable income. Recall that *MPC*, the marginal propensity to consume, is the amount by which consumer spending rises if current disposable income rises by $1. Finally, a is a constant term—individual household *autonomous consumer spending*, the amount of spending a household would do if it had zero disposable income. We assume that a is greater than zero because a household with zero disposable income is able to fund some consumption by borrowing or using its savings.

Notice, by the way, that we're using y for income. That's standard practice in macroeconomics, even though *income* isn't actually spelled "yncome." The reason is that I is reserved for investment spending.

Recall that we expressed *MPC* as the ratio of a change in consumer spending to the change in current disposable income. We've rewritten it for an individual household as Equation 11-6:

(11-6) $MPC = \Delta c / \Delta yd$

Multiplying both sides of Equation 11-6 by Δyd, we get:

(11-7) $MPC \times \Delta yd = \Delta c$

Equation 11-7 tells us that when yd goes up by $1, c goes up by $MPC \times $1.

Figure 11-3 shows what Equation 11-5 looks like graphically, plotting yd on the horizontal axis and c on the vertical axis. Individual household autonomous consumer spending, a, is the value of c when yd is zero—it is the vertical *intercept* of the consumption function, *cf*. *MPC* is the *slope* of the line, measured by rise over run. If current disposable income rises by Δyd, household consumer spending, c, rises by Δc. Since *MPC* is defined as $\Delta c / \Delta yd$, the slope of the consumption function is:

(11-8) Slope of consumption function
    = Rise over run
    = $\Delta c / \Delta yd$
    = *MPC*

In reality, actual data has never fit Equation 11-5 perfectly, but the fit can be pretty good. Figure 11-4 shows the data from Figure 11-2 again, together with a

FIGURE 11-3 The Consumption Function

The consumption function relates a household's current disposable income to its consumer spending. The vertical intercept, *a*, is individual household autonomous consumer spending: the amount of a household's consumer spending if its current disposable income is zero. The slope of the consumption function line, *cf*, is the marginal propensity to consume, or *MPC*: of every additional $1 of current disposable income, $MPC \times \$1$ is spent.

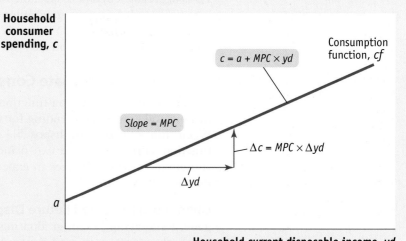

line drawn to fit the data as closely as possible. According to the data on households' consumer spending and current disposable income, the best estimate of *a* is $16,070 and of *MPC* is 0.67. So the consumption function fitted to the data is:

$$c = \$16,070 + 0.67 \times yd$$

That is, the data suggest a marginal propensity to consume of approximately 0.67. This implies that the marginal propensity to save (*MPS*)—the amount of an additional $1 of disposable income that is saved—is approximately 0.33, and the multiplier is approximately 1/0.33 = 3.00.

It's important to realize that Figure 11-4 shows a *microeconomic* relationship between the current disposable income of individual households and their spending on goods and services. However, macroeconomists assume that a similar relationship holds *for the economy as a whole*: that there is a relationship, called the **aggregate consumption function,** between aggregate current disposable income and aggregate consumer spending. We'll assume that it has the same form as the household-level consumption function:

(11-9) $C = A + MPC \times YD$

The **aggregate consumption function** is the relationship for the economy as a whole between aggregate current disposable income and aggregate consumer spending.

FIGURE 11-4 A Consumption Function Fitted to Data

The data from Figure 11-2 are reproduced here, along with a line drawn to fit the data as closely as possible. For American households in 2015, the best estimate of the average household's autonomous consumer spending, *a*, is $16,070 and the best estimate of *MPC* is 0.67.

Data from: Bureau of Labor Statistics.

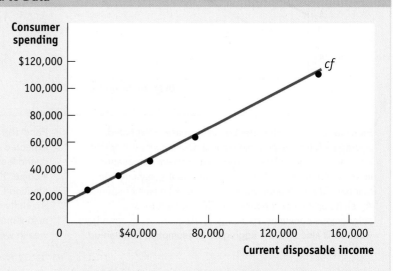

Here, C is aggregate consumer spending (called just "consumer spending"); YD is aggregate current disposable income (called, for simplicity, just "disposable income"); and A is aggregate autonomous consumer spending, the amount of consumer spending when YD equals zero. This is the relationship represented in Figure 11-5 by CF, analogous to cf in Figure 11-3.

Shifts of the Aggregate Consumption Function

The aggregate consumption function shows the relationship between disposable income and consumer spending for the economy as a whole, other things equal. When things other than disposable income change, the aggregate consumption function shifts. There are two principal causes of shifts of the aggregate consumption function: changes in expected future disposable income and changes in aggregate wealth.

Changes in Expected Future Disposable Income Suppose you land a really good, well-paying job on graduating from college in May—but the job, and the paychecks, won't start until September. So your disposable income hasn't risen yet. Even so, it's likely that you will start spending more on final goods and services right away—maybe buying nicer work clothes than you originally planned—because you know that higher income is coming.

Conversely, suppose you have a good job but learn that the company is planning to downsize your division, raising the possibility that you may lose your job and have to take a lower-paying one somewhere else. Even though your disposable income hasn't gone down yet, you might well cut back on spending even while still employed, to save for a rainy day.

Both of these examples show how expectations about future disposable income can affect consumer spending. The two panels of Figure 11-5, which plot

FIGURE 11-5 Shifts of the Aggregate Consumption Function

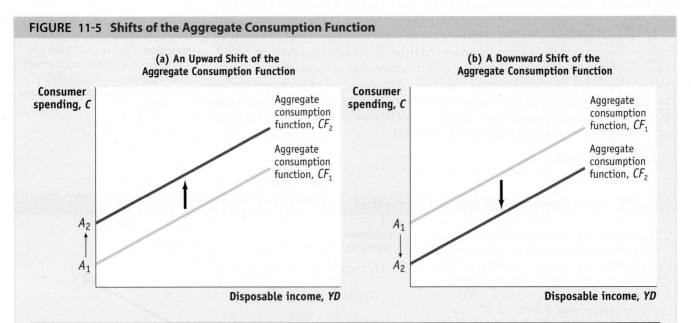

Panel (a) illustrates the effect of an increase in expected aggregate future disposable income. Consumers will spend more at every given level of aggregate current disposable income, YD. As a result, the initial aggregate consumption function CF_1, with aggregate autonomous consumer spending A_1, shifts up to a new position at CF_2 and aggregate autonomous consumer spending A_2. An increase in aggregate wealth will also shift the aggregate consumption function up.

Panel (b), in contrast, illustrates the effect of a reduction in expected aggregate future disposable income. Consumers will spend less at every given level of aggregate current disposable income, YD. Consequently, the initial aggregate consumption function CF_1, with aggregate autonomous consumer spending A_1, shifts down to a new position at CF_2 and aggregate autonomous consumer spending A_2. A reduction in aggregate wealth will have the same effect.

disposable income against consumer spending, show how changes in expected future disposable income affect the aggregate consumption function. In both panels, CF_1 is the initial aggregate consumption function. Panel (a) shows the effect of good news: information that leads consumers to expect higher disposable income in the future than they did before.

Consumers will now spend more at any given level of current disposable income, YD, corresponding to an increase in A, aggregate autonomous consumer spending, from A_1 to A_2. The effect is to shift the aggregate consumption function up, from CF_1 to CF_2. Panel (b) shows the effect of bad news: information that leads consumers to expect lower disposable income in the future than they did before. Consumers will now spend less at any given level of current disposable income, YD, corresponding to a fall in A from A_1 to A_2. The effect is to shift the aggregate consumption function down, from CF_1 to CF_2.

In a famous 1957 book, *A Theory of the Consumption Function*, Milton Friedman showed that taking the effects of expected future income into account explains an otherwise puzzling fact about consumer behavior. If we look at consumer spending during any given year, we find that people with high current income save a larger fraction of their income than those with low current income. (This is obvious from the data in Figure 11-4: people with higher incomes spend considerably less than their income; those with lower incomes spend more than their income.) You might think this implies that the overall savings rate will rise as the economy grows and average current incomes rise; in fact, however, this hasn't happened.

Friedman pointed out that when we look at individual incomes in a given year, there are systematic differences between current and expected future income that create a positive relationship between current income and the savings rate. On one side, people with low current incomes are often having an unusually bad year. For example, they may be workers who have been laid off but will probably find new jobs eventually. They are people whose expected future income is higher than their current income, so it makes sense for them to have low or even negative savings. On the other side, people with high current incomes in a given year are often having an unusually good year. For example, they may have investments that happened to do extremely well. They are people whose expected future income is lower than their current income, so it makes sense for them to save most of their windfall.

When the economy grows, by contrast, current and expected future incomes rise together. Higher current income tends to lead to higher savings today, but higher expected future income tends to lead to less savings today. As a result, there's a weaker relationship between current income and the savings rate.

Friedman argued that consumer spending ultimately depends mainly on the income people expect to have over the long term rather than on their current income. This argument is known as the *permanent income hypothesis*.

Changes in Aggregate Wealth Imagine two individuals, Maria and Mark, both of whom expect to earn $30,000 this year. Suppose, however, that they have different histories. Maria has been working steadily for the past 10 years, owns her own home, and has $200,000 in the bank. Mark is the same age as Maria, but he has been in and out of work, hasn't managed to buy a house, and has very little in savings. In this case, Maria has something that Mark doesn't have: *wealth*. Even though they have the same disposable income, other things equal, you'd expect Maria to spend more on consumption than Mark. That is, wealth has an effect on consumer spending.

The effect of wealth on spending is emphasized by an influential economic model of how consumers make choices about spending versus saving called the *life-cycle hypothesis*. According to this hypothesis, consumers plan their spending over a lifetime, not just in response to their current disposable income. As a result, people try to smooth their consumption over their lifetimes—they save some of their current disposable income during their years of peak earnings (typically occurring during a worker's 40s and 50s) and during their retirement live off the wealth they accumulated while working.

We won't go into the details of this hypothesis but will simply point out that it implies an important role for wealth in determining consumer spending. For example, a middle-aged couple who have accumulated a lot of wealth—who have paid off the mortgage on their house and already own plenty of stocks and bonds— will, other things equal, spend more on goods and services than a couple who have the same current disposable income but still need to save for their retirement.

Because wealth affects household consumer spending, changes in wealth across the economy can shift the aggregate consumption function. A rise in aggregate wealth—say, because of a booming stock market—increases the vertical intercept A, aggregate autonomous consumer spending. This, in turn, shifts the aggregate consumption function up in the same way as does an expected increase in future disposable income. A decline in aggregate wealth—say, because of a fall in housing prices as occurred in 2008—reduces A and shifts the aggregate consumption function down.

ECONOMICS >> *in Action*
Famous First Forecasting Failures

The Great Depression created modern macroeconomics. It also gave birth to the modern field of *econometrics*—the use of statistical techniques to fit economic models to empirical data. The aggregate consumption function was one of the first things econometricians studied. And, sure enough, they quickly experienced one of the first major failures of economic forecasting: consumer spending after World War II was much higher than estimates of the aggregate consumption function based on prewar data would have predicted.

Figure 11-6 tells the story. Panel (a) shows aggregate data on disposable income and consumer spending from 1929 to 1941, measured in billions of 2005 dollars.

FIGURE 11-6 Changes in the Aggregate Consumption Function Over Time

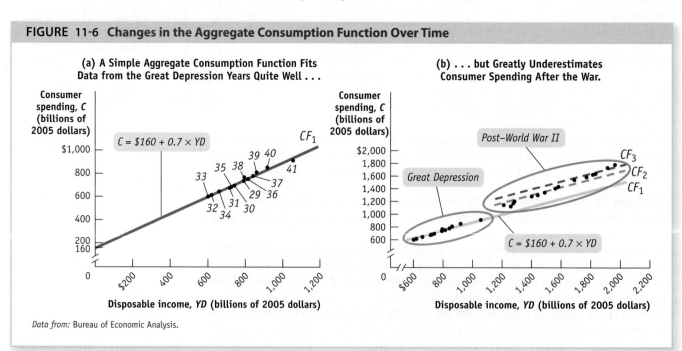

Data from: Bureau of Economic Analysis.

A simple linear consumption function, CF_1, seems to fit the data very well. And many economists thought this relationship would continue to hold in the future. But panel (b) shows what actually happened in later years. The points in the circle at the left are the data from the Great Depression shown in panel (a). The points in the circle at the right are data from 1946 to 1960. (Data from 1942 to 1945 aren't included because rationing during World War II prevented consumers from spending normally.)

The solid line in the figure, CF_1, is the consumption function fitted to 1929–1941 data. As you can see, post–World War II consumer spending was much higher than the relationship from the Depression years would have predicted. For example, in 1960 consumer spending was 13.5% higher than the level predicted by CF_1.

Why was extrapolating from the earlier relationship so misleading? The answer is that from 1946 onward, both expected future disposable income and aggregate wealth were steadily rising. Consumers grew increasingly confident that the Great Depression wouldn't reemerge and that the post–World War II economic boom would continue. At the same time, wealth was steadily increasing. As indicated by the dashed lines in panel (b), CF_2 and CF_3, the increases in expected future disposable income and in aggregate wealth shifted the aggregate consumption function up a number of times.

In macroeconomics, failure—whether of economic policy or of economic prediction—often leads to intellectual progress. The embarrassing failure of early estimates of the aggregate consumption function to predict post–World War II consumer spending led to important progress in our understanding of consumer behavior.

>> Check Your Understanding 11-2

Solutions appear at back of book.

1. Suppose the economy consists of three people: Angelina, Felicia, and Marina. The table shows how their consumer spending varies as their current disposable income rises by $10,000.

   a. Derive each individual's consumption function, where *MPC* is calculated for a $10,000 change in current disposable income.

   b. Derive the aggregate consumption function.

Current disposable income	Consumer spending		
	Angelina	Felicia	Marina
$0	$8,000	$6,500	$7,250
10,000	12,000	14,500	14,250

2. Suppose that problems in the capital markets make consumers unable either to borrow or to put money aside for future use. What implication does this have for the effects of expected future disposable income on consumer spending?

‖ Investment Spending

Although consumer spending is much larger than investment spending, booms and busts in investment spending tend to drive the business cycle. In fact, most recessions originate as a fall in investment spending. Figure 11-7 illustrates this point; it shows the annual percent change of investment spending and consumer spending in the United States, measured in real terms, during six recessions from 1973 to 2009. As you can see, swings in investment spending are much more dramatic than those in consumer spending. In addition, due to the multiplier process, economists believe that declines in consumer spending are usually the result of a process that begins with a slump in investment spending. Soon we'll examine in more detail how a slump in investment spending generates a fall in consumer spending through the multiplier process.

Before we do that, however, let's analyze the factors that determine investment spending, which are somewhat different from those that determine consumer spending. The most important ones are the interest rate and expected future

FIGURE 11-7 Fluctuations in Investment Spending and Consumer Spending

The bars illustrate the annual percent change in investment spending and consumer spending during six recent recessions. As the lengths of the bars show, swings in investment spending were much larger in percentage terms than those in consumer spending. This pattern has led economists to believe that recessions typically originate as a slump in investment spending.

Data from: Bureau of Economic Analysis.

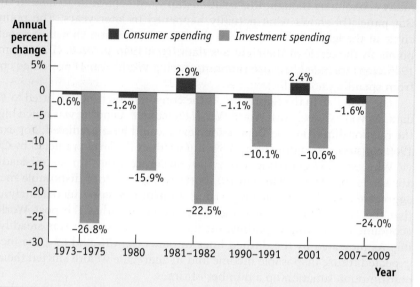

real GDP. We'll also revisit a fact that we noted in Chapter 10: the level of investment spending businesses *actually* carry out is sometimes not the same level as **planned investment spending,** the investment spending that firms *intend* to undertake during a given period.

Planned investment spending depends on three principal factors that we'll analyze next.

1. The interest rate
2. The expected future level of real GDP
3. The current level of production capacity

First, we'll analyze the effect of the interest rate.

1. The Interest Rate and Investment Spending

Interest rates have their clearest effect on one particular form of investment spending: spending on residential construction—that is, on the construction of homes. The reason is straightforward: home builders only build houses they think they can sell, and houses are more affordable—and so more likely to sell—when the interest rate is low.

Consider a family that needs to borrow $150,000 to buy a house. At an interest rate of 7.5%, a 30-year home mortgage will mean payments of $1,048 per month. At an interest rate of 5.5%, those payments would be only $851 per month, making houses significantly more affordable. As described in the upcoming Economics in Action, interest rates actually did drop from roughly 7.5% to 5.5% between the late 1990s and 2003, helping set off a huge housing boom.

Interest rates also affect other forms of investment spending. Firms with investment spending projects will only go ahead with a project if they expect a rate of return higher than the cost of the funds they would have to borrow to finance that project. As we saw in Chapter 10, if the interest rate rises, fewer projects will pass that test, and as a result investment spending will be lower.

You might think that the trade-off a firm faces is different if it can fund its investment project with its past profits rather than through borrowing. Past profits used to finance investment spending are called *retained earnings*. But even if a firm pays for investment spending out of retained earnings, the trade-off it must make in deciding whether or not to fund a project remains the same because it

Planned investment spending is the investment spending that businesses intend to undertake during a given period.

must take into account the opportunity cost of its funds. For example, instead of purchasing new equipment, the firm could lend out the funds and earn interest. The forgone interest earned is the opportunity cost of using retained earnings to fund an investment project.

So the trade-off the firm faces when comparing a project's rate of return to the market interest rate has not changed when it uses retained earnings rather than borrowed funds, which means that regardless of whether a firm funds investment spending through borrowing or retained earnings, a rise in the market interest rate makes any given investment project less profitable.

Conversely, a fall in the interest rate makes some investment projects that were unprofitable before profitable at the now lower interest rate. So some projects that had been unfunded before will be funded now.

So planned investment spending—spending on investment projects that firms voluntarily decide whether or not to undertake—is negatively related to the interest rate. Other things equal, a higher interest rate leads to a lower level of planned investment spending.

2. Expected Future Real GDP, Production Capacity, and Investment Spending

Suppose a firm has enough capacity to continue to produce the amount it is currently selling but doesn't expect its sales to grow in the future. Then it will engage in investment spending only to replace existing equipment and structures that wear out or are rendered obsolete by new technologies. But if, instead, the firm expects its sales to grow rapidly in the future, it will find its existing production capacity insufficient for its future production needs. So the firm will undertake investment spending to meet those needs. This implies that, other things equal, firms will undertake more investment spending when they expect their sales to grow.

Now suppose that the firm currently has considerably more capacity than necessary to meet current production needs. Even if it expects sales to grow, it won't have to undertake investment spending for a while—not until the growth in sales catches up with its excess capacity. This illustrates the fact that, other things equal, the current level of productive capacity has a negative effect on investment spending: other things equal, the higher the current capacity, the lower is investment spending.

If we combine the effects on investment spending of both growth in expected future sales and the size of current production capacity, we can see one situation in which we can be reasonably sure that firms will undertake high levels of investment spending: when they expect sales to grow rapidly. In that case, even excess production capacity will soon be used up, leading firms to resume investment spending.

What is an indicator of high expected growth of future sales? It's a high expected future growth rate of real GDP. A higher expected future growth rate of real GDP results in a higher level of planned investment spending, but a lower expected future growth rate of real GDP leads to lower planned investment spending. This relationship is summarized in a proposition known as the **accelerator principle.** As explained in the upcoming Economics in Action, in 2006, when expectations of future real GDP growth turned negative, planned investment spending—and, in particular, residential investment spending—plunged, accelerating the economy's slide into recession. Generally, the effects of the accelerator principle play an important role in *investment spending slumps*, periods of low investment spending.

3. Inventories and Unplanned Investment Spending

Most firms maintain **inventories,** stocks of goods held to satisfy future sales. Firms hold inventories so they can quickly satisfy buyers—a consumer can purchase an item off the shelf rather than waiting for it to be manufactured.

According to the **accelerator principle,** a higher growth rate of real GDP leads to higher planned investment spending, but a lower growth rate of real GDP leads to lower planned investment spending.

Inventories are stocks of goods held to satisfy future sales.

Inventory investment is the value of the change in total inventories held in the economy during a given period.

Unplanned inventory investment is an unintended swing in inventory that occurs when actual sales are higher or lower than expected sales.

Actual investment spending is the sum of planned investment spending and unplanned inventory investment.

In addition, businesses often hold inventories of their inputs to be sure they have a steady supply of necessary materials and spare parts. At the end of March 2017, the overall value of inventories in the U.S. economy was estimated at $1.84 trillion, just under 10% of GDP.

A firm that increases its inventories is engaging in a form of investment spending. Suppose, for example, that the U.S. auto industry produces 800,000 cars per month but sells only 700,000. The remaining 100,000 cars are added to the inventory at auto company warehouses or car dealerships, ready to be sold in the future. **Inventory investment** is the value of the change in total inventories held in the economy during a given period. Unlike other forms of investment spending, inventory investment can actually be negative. If, for example, the auto industry reduces its inventory over the course of a month, we say that it has engaged in negative inventory investment.

To understand inventory investment, think about a manager stocking the canned goods section of a supermarket. The manager tries to keep the store fully stocked so that shoppers can almost always find what they're looking for. But the manager does not want the shelves too heavily stocked because shelf space is limited and products can spoil. Similar considerations apply to many firms and typically lead them to manage their inventories carefully.

However, sales fluctuate. And because firms cannot always accurately predict sales, they often find themselves holding more or less inventories than they had intended. These unintended swings in inventories due to unforeseen changes in sales are called **unplanned inventory investment.** They represent investment spending, positive or negative, that occurred but was unplanned.

So in any given period, **actual investment spending** is equal to planned investment spending plus unplanned inventory investment. If we let $I_{Unplanned}$ represent unplanned inventory investment, $I_{Planned}$ represent planned investment spending, and I represent actual investment spending, then the relationship among all three can be represented as:

(11-10) $I = I_{Unplanned} + I_{Planned}$

When the economy slumps, as it did in 2009, consumer spending plunges and inventory—such as cars at auto dealers—goes unsold, leading to a rise in unplanned inventory investment.

To see how unplanned inventory investment can occur, let's continue to focus on the auto industry and make the following assumptions. First, let's assume that the industry must determine each month's production volume in advance, before it knows the volume of actual sales. Second, let's assume that it anticipates selling 800,000 cars next month and that it plans neither to add to nor subtract from existing inventories. In that case, it will produce 800,000 cars to match anticipated sales.

Now imagine that next month's actual sales are less than expected, only 700,000 cars. As a result, the value of 100,000 cars will be added to investment spending as unplanned inventory investment.

The auto industry will, of course, eventually adjust to this slowdown in sales and the resulting unplanned inventory investment. The industry will probably cut next month's production volume in order to reduce inventories.

In fact, economists who study macroeconomic variables in an attempt to determine the future path of the economy pay careful attention to changes in inventory levels. Rising inventories typically indicate positive unplanned inventory investment and a slowing economy, as sales are less than had been forecast. Falling inventories typically indicate negative unplanned inventory investment and a growing economy, as sales are greater than forecast.

In the next section, we will see how production adjustments in response to fluctuations in sales and inventories ensure that the value of final goods and services actually produced is equal to desired purchases of those final goods and services.

ECONOMICS >> *in Action*

Interest Rates and U.S. Housing

As we just learned, interest rates typically have their biggest effects on one particular category of investment spending: home construction. And it's possible to see that effect clearly in the business cycle after 2000: there was a huge housing boom from 2000 until 2006, driven to an important extent by low interest rates. That boom ended with a crash, but there was eventually a recovery—again driven to an important extent by low rates.

Figure 11-8 shows the interest rate on 30-year home mortgages—the traditional way to borrow money for a home purchase—and the number of housing starts, the number of homes for which construction is started per month, from 1995 to mid-2017, in the United States. Panel (a), which shows the mortgage rate, gives you an idea of how much interest rates fell. In the second half of the 1990s, mortgage rates generally fluctuated between 7% and 8%; by 2003, they were down to between 5% and 6%. These lower rates were largely the result of Federal Reserve policy: the Fed cut rates in response to the 2001 recession and continued cutting them into 2003 out of concern that the economy's recovery was too weak to generate sustained job growth.

The low interest rates led to a large increase in residential investment spending, reflected in a surge of housing starts, shown in panel (b). This rise in investment spending drove an overall economic expansion, both through its direct effects and through the multiplier process.

Unfortunately, the housing boom eventually turned into too much of a good thing. By 2006, it was clear that the U.S. housing market was experiencing a bubble: people were buying housing based on unrealistic expectations about future price increases. When the bubble burst, housing—and the U.S. economy—took a fall. The fall was so severe that even when the Fed cut rates to near zero, and mortgage rates consequently dropped to below 5% beginning

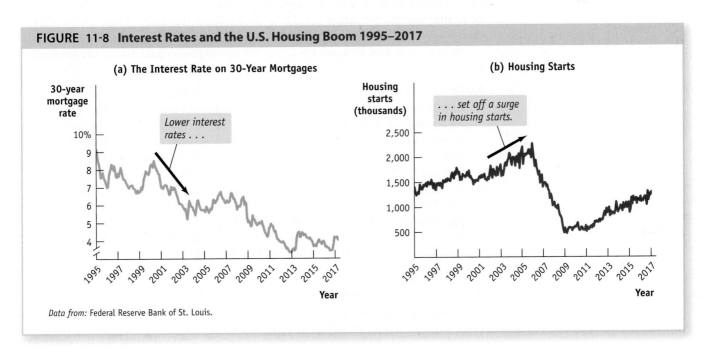

FIGURE 11-8   Interest Rates and the U.S. Housing Boom 1995–2017

(a) The Interest Rate on 30-Year Mortgages

(b) Housing Starts

Data from: Federal Reserve Bank of St. Louis.

in 2009, housing starts merely stabilized. Eventually, however, housing starts staged a significant comeback, although not to boom levels, thanks to those low borrowing costs.

>> *Check Your Understanding* **11-3**
Solutions appear at back of book.

1. For each event, explain whether planned investment spending or unplanned inventory investment will change and in what direction.
   a. An unexpected increase in consumer spending
   b. A sharp rise in the cost of business borrowing
   c. A sharp increase in the economy's growth rate of real GDP
   d. An unanticipated fall in sales

2. Historically, investment spending has experienced more extreme upward and downward swings than consumer spending. Why do you think this is so? (*Hint:* Consider the marginal propensity to consume and the accelerator principle.)

3. Consumer spending was sluggish in late 2007, and economists worried that an *inventory overhang*—a high level of unplanned inventory investment throughout the economy—would make it difficult for the economy to recover anytime soon. Explain why an inventory overhang might, like the existence of too much production capacity, depress current economic activity.

The Income–Expenditure Model

Earlier in this chapter, we described how autonomous changes in spending—such as a fall in investment spending when a housing bubble bursts—lead to a multistage process through the actions of the multiplier that magnifies the effect of these changes on real GDP. We will now examine this multistage process more closely.

We'll see that the multiple rounds of changes in real GDP are accomplished through changes in the amount of output produced by firms—changes that they make in response to changes in their inventories. We'll come to understand why inventories play a central role in macroeconomic models of the economy in the short run as well as why economists pay particular attention to the behavior of firms' inventories when trying to understand the likely future state of the economy.

Before we begin, let's quickly recap the assumptions underlying the multiplier process.

1. *Changes in overall spending lead to changes in aggregate output.* We assume that producers are willing to supply additional output at a fixed price level. As a result, changes in spending translate into changes in output rather than moves of the overall price level up or down. A fixed aggregate price level also implies that there is no difference between nominal GDP and real GDP. So we can use the two terms interchangeably in this chapter.

2. *The interest rate is fixed.* We'll take the interest rate as predetermined and unaffected by the factors we analyze in the model. As in the case of the aggregate price level, what we're really doing here is leaving the determinants of the interest rate outside the model. As we'll see, the model can still be used to study the effects of a change in the interest rate.

3. *Taxes, government transfers, and government purchases are all zero.*

4. *Exports and imports are both zero.*

In all subsequent chapters, we will drop the assumption that the aggregate price level is fixed. The Chapter 13 appendix addresses how taxes affect the multiplier process. We'll discuss how foreign trade enters the picture briefly later in this chapter, and bring it fully into the model in Chapter 18.

Planned Aggregate Spending and Real GDP

In an economy with no government and no foreign trade, there are only two sources of aggregate spending: consumer spending, C, and investment spending, I. And since we assume that there are no taxes or transfers, aggregate disposable income is equal to GDP (which, since the aggregate price level is fixed, is the same as real GDP): the total value of final sales of goods and services ultimately accrues to households as income. So in this highly simplified economy, there are two basic equations of national income accounting:

(11-11) $GDP = C + I$

(11-12) $YD = GDP$

As we learned earlier, the aggregate consumption function shows the relationship between disposable income and consumer spending. Let's continue to assume that the aggregate consumption function is of the same form as in Equation 11-9:

(11-13) $C = A + MPC \times YD$

In our simplified model, we will also assume planned investment spending, $I_{Planned}$, is fixed.

We need one more concept before putting the model together: **planned aggregate spending,** the total amount of planned spending in the economy. Unlike firms, households don't take unintended actions like unplanned inventory investment. So planned aggregate spending is equal to the sum of consumer spending and planned investment spending. We denote planned aggregate spending by $AE_{Planned}$, so:

(11-14) $AE_{Planned} = C + I_{Planned}$

The level of planned aggregate spending in a given year depends on the level of real GDP in that year. To see why, let's look at a specific example, shown in Table 11-2. We assume that the aggregate consumption function is:

(11-15) $C = 300 + 0.6 \times YD$

Real GDP, YD, C, $I_{Planned}$, and $AE_{Planned}$ are all measured in billions of dollars, and we assume that the level of planned investment, $I_{Planned}$, is fixed at $500 billion per year. The first column shows possible levels of real GDP. The second column shows disposable income, YD, which in our simplified model is equal to real GDP. The third column shows consumer spending, C, equal to $300 billion plus 0.6 times disposable income, YD. The fourth column shows planned investment spending, $I_{Planned}$, which we have assumed is $500 billion regardless of the level of real GDP. Finally, the last column shows planned aggregate spending, $AE_{Planned}$, the sum of aggregate consumer spending, C, and planned investment spending, $I_{Planned}$. (To economize on notation, we'll assume that it is understood from now on that all the variables in Table 11-2 are measured in billions of dollars per year.)

As you can see, a higher level of real GDP leads to a higher level of disposable income: every 500 increase in real GDP raises YD by 500, which in turn raises C by $500 \times 0.6 = 300$ and $AE_{Planned}$ by 300.

TABLE 11-2 Equilibrium When Real GDP = YD = $AE_{Planned}$

Real GDP	YD	C	$I_{Planned}$	$AE_{Planned}$
		(billions of dollars)		
$0	$0	$300	$500	$800
500	500	600	500	1,100
1,000	1,000	900	500	1,400
1,500	1,500	1,200	500	1,700
2,000	2,000	1,500	500	2,000
2,500	2,500	1,800	500	2,300
3,000	3,000	2,100	500	2,600
3,500	3,500	2,400	500	2,900

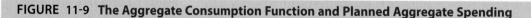

FIGURE 11-9 The Aggregate Consumption Function and Planned Aggregate Spending

The lower line, *CF*, is the aggregate consumption function constructed from the data in Table 11-2. The upper line, $AE_{Planned}$, is the planned aggregate spending line, also constructed from the data in Table 11-2. It is equivalent to the aggregate consumption function shifted up by $500 billion, the amount of planned investment spending, $I_{Planned}$.

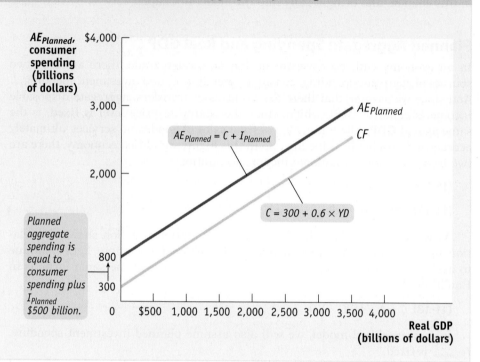

Figure 11-9 illustrates the information in Table 11-2 graphically. Real GDP is measured on the horizontal axis. *CF* is the aggregate consumption function; it shows how consumer spending depends on real GDP. $AE_{Planned}$, the planned aggregate spending line, corresponds to the aggregate consumption function shifted up by 500 (the amount of $I_{Planned}$). It shows how planned aggregate spending depends on real GDP. Both lines have a slope of 0.6, equal to *MPC*, the marginal propensity to consume.

But this isn't the end of the story. Table 11-2 reveals that real GDP equals planned aggregate spending, $AE_{Planned}$, only when the level of real GDP is at 2,000. Real GDP does not equal $AE_{Planned}$ at any other level. Is that possible? Didn't we learn in Chapter 7, with the circular-flow diagram, that total spending on final goods and services in the economy is equal to the total value of output of final goods and services? The answer is that for *brief* periods of time, planned aggregate spending can differ from real GDP because of the role of *unplanned* aggregate spending—$I_{Unplanned}$, unplanned inventory investment.

But as we'll see next, the economy moves over time to a situation in which there is no unplanned inventory investment, a situation called *income–expenditure equilibrium*. And when the economy is in income–expenditure equilibrium, planned aggregate spending on final goods and services equals aggregate output.

Income–Expenditure Equilibrium

For all but one value of real GDP shown in Table 11-2, real GDP is either more or less than $AE_{Planned}$, the sum of consumer spending and *planned* investment spending. For example, when real GDP is 1,000, consumer spending, *C*, is 900 and planned investment spending is 500, making planned aggregate spending 1,400. This is 400 *more* than the corresponding level of real GDP. Now consider what happens when real GDP is 2,500; consumer spending, *C*, is 1,800 and planned investment spending is 500, making planned aggregate spending only 2,300, which is 200 *less* than real GDP.

As we've just explained, planned aggregate spending can be different from real GDP only if there is unplanned inventory investment, $I_{Unplanned}$, in the economy. Let's examine Table 11-3, which includes the numbers for real GDP and for planned aggregate spending from Table 11-2. It also includes the levels of unplanned inventory investment, $I_{Unplanned}$, that each combination of real GDP and planned aggregate spending implies. For example, if real GDP is 2,500, planned aggregate spending is only 2,300. This 200 excess of real GDP over $AE_{Planned}$ must consist of positive unplanned inventory investment. This can happen only if firms have overestimated sales and produced too much, leading to unintended additions to inventories.

More generally, any level of real GDP in excess of 2,000 corresponds to a situation in which firms are producing more than consumers and other firms want to purchase, creating an unintended increase in inventories.

Conversely, a level of real GDP below 2,000 implies that planned aggregate spending is *greater* than real GDP. For example, when real GDP is 1,000, planned aggregate spending is much larger, at 1,400. The 400 excess of $AE_{Planned}$ over real GDP corresponds to negative unplanned inventory investment equal to –400. More generally, any level of real GDP below 2,000 implies that firms have underestimated sales, leading to a negative level of unplanned inventory investment in the economy.

By putting together Equations 11-10, 11-11, and 11-14, we can summarize the general relationships among real GDP, planned aggregate spending, and unplanned inventory investment as follows:

(11-16) $GDP = C + I$
$$= C + I_{Planned} + I_{Unplanned}$$
$$= AE_{Planned} + I_{Unplanned}$$

So whenever real GDP exceeds $AE_{Planned}$, $I_{Unplanned}$ is positive; whenever real GDP is less than $AE_{Planned}$, $I_{Unplanned}$ is negative.

But firms will act to correct their mistakes. We've assumed that they don't change their prices, but they *can* adjust their output. Specifically, they will reduce production if they have experienced an unintended rise in inventories or increase production if they have experienced an unintended fall in inventories. And these responses will eventually eliminate the unanticipated changes in inventories and move the economy to a point at which real GDP is equal to planned aggregate spending.

Staying with our example, if real GDP is 1,000, negative unplanned inventory investment will lead firms to increase production, leading to a rise in real GDP. In fact, this will happen whenever real GDP is less than 2,000—that is, whenever real GDP is less than planned aggregate spending. Conversely, if real GDP is 2,500, positive unplanned inventory investment will lead firms to reduce production, leading to a fall in real GDP. This will happen whenever real GDP is greater than planned aggregate spending.

The only situation in which firms won't have an incentive to change output in the next period is when aggregate output, measured by real GDP, is equal to planned aggregate spending in the current period, an outcome known as **income–expenditure equilibrium.** In Table 11-3, income–expenditure equilibrium is achieved when real GDP is 2,000, the only level of real GDP at which unplanned inventory investment is zero. From now on, we'll denote the real GDP level at which income–expenditure equilibrium occurs as Y^* and call it the **income–expenditure equilibrium GDP.**

Figure 11-10 illustrates the concept of income–expenditure equilibrium graphically. Real GDP is on the horizontal axis and planned aggregate spending, $AE_{Planned}$, is on the vertical axis. There are two lines in the figure. The solid line is the planned aggregate spending line. It shows how $AE_{Planned}$, equal to $C + I_{Planned}$, depends on real GDP; it has a slope of 0.6, equal to the marginal propensity to consume, *MPC*, and a vertical intercept equal to $A + I_{Planned}$ (300 + 500 = 800). The dashed line, which goes through the origin with a slope of 1 (often called a 45-degree line), shows all the possible points at which planned aggregate spending is equal to real GDP.

TABLE 11-3 Equilibrium When $I_{Unplanned} = 0$

Real GDP	$AE_{Planned}$	$I_{Unplanned}$
(billions of dollars)		
$0	$800	–$800
500	1,100	–600
1,000	1,400	–400
1,500	1,700	–200
2,000	2,000	0
2,500	2,300	200
3,000	2,600	400
3,500	2,900	600

The economy is in **income–expenditure equilibrium** when aggregate output, measured by real GDP, is equal to planned aggregate spending.

Income–expenditure equilibrium GDP is the level of real GDP at which real GDP equals planned aggregate spending.

FIGURE 11-10 Income–Expenditure Equilibrium

Income–expenditure equilibrium occurs at E, the point where the planned aggregate spending line, $AE_{Planned}$, crosses the 45-degree line. At E, the economy produces real GDP of $2,000 billion per year, the only point at which real GDP equals planned aggregate spending, $AE_{Planned}$, and unplanned inventory investment, $I_{Unplanned}$, is zero. This is the level of income–expenditure equilibrium GDP, Y^*. At any level of real GDP less than Y^*, $AE_{Planned}$ exceeds real GDP. As a result, unplanned inventory investment, $I_{Unplanned}$, is negative and firms respond by increasing production. At any level of real GDP greater than Y^*, real GDP exceeds $AE_{Planned}$. Unplanned inventory investment, $I_{Unplanned}$, is positive and firms respond by reducing production.

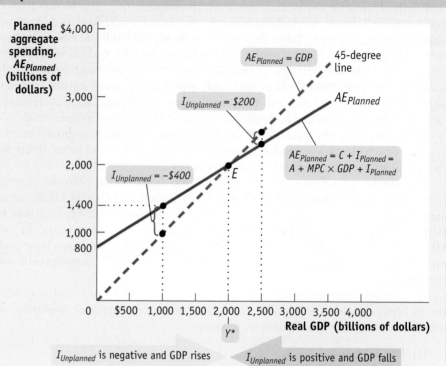

This line allows us to easily spot the point of income–expenditure equilibrium, which must lie on both the 45-degree line and the planned aggregate spending line. So the point of income–expenditure equilibrium is at E, where the two lines cross. And the income–expenditure equilibrium GDP, Y^*, is 2,000—the same outcome we derived in Table 11-3.

Now consider what happens if the economy isn't in income–expenditure equilibrium. We can see from Figure 11-10 that whenever real GDP is less than Y^*, the planned aggregate spending line lies above the 45-degree line and $AE_{Planned}$ exceeds real GDP. In this situation, $I_{Unplanned}$ is negative: as shown in the figure, at a real GDP of 1,000, $I_{Unplanned}$ is −400. As a consequence, real GDP will rise. In contrast, whenever real GDP is greater than Y^*, the planned aggregate expenditure line lies below the 45-degree line. Here, $I_{Unplanned}$ is positive: as shown, at a real GDP of 2,500, $I_{Unplanned}$ is 200. The unanticipated accumulation of inventory leads to a fall in real GDP.

The type of diagram shown in Figure 11-10, which identifies income–expenditure equilibrium as the point at which the planned aggregate spending line crosses the 45-degree line, has a special place in the history of economic thought. Known as the **Keynesian cross,** it was developed by Paul Samuelson, one of the greatest economists of the twentieth century (as well as a Nobel Prize winner), to explain the ideas of John Maynard Keynes, the founder of macroeconomics as we know it.

The Multiplier Process and Inventory Adjustment

We've just learned about a very important feature of the macroeconomy: when planned spending by households and firms does not equal the current aggregate output by firms, this difference shows up in changes in inventories. The response of firms to those inventory changes moves real GDP over time to the point at which real GDP and planned aggregate spending are equal. That's why, as we

The **Keynesian cross** diagram identifies income-expenditure equilibrium as the point where the planned aggregate spending line crosses the 45-degree line.

mentioned earlier, changes in inventories are considered a leading indicator of future economic activity.

Now that we understand how real GDP moves to achieve income–expenditure equilibrium for a given level of planned aggregate spending, let's turn to understanding what happens when there is *a shift of the planned aggregate spending line*. How does the economy move from the initial point of income–expenditure equilibrium to a new point of income–expenditure equilibrium? And what are the possible sources of changes in planned aggregate spending?

In our simple model there are only two possible sources of a shift of the planned aggregate spending line: a change in planned investment spending, $I_{Planned}$, or a shift of the aggregate consumption function, *CF*. For example, a change in $I_{Planned}$ can occur because of a change in the interest rate. (Remember, we're assuming that the interest rate is fixed by factors that are outside the model. But we can still ask what happens when the interest rate changes.) A shift of the aggregate consumption function (that is, a change in its vertical intercept, *A*) can occur because of a change in aggregate wealth—say, due to a rise in house prices. When the planned aggregate spending line shifts—when there is a change in the level of planned aggregate spending at any given level of real GDP—there is an autonomous change in planned aggregate spending.

Recall that an autonomous change in planned aggregate spending is a change in the desired level of spending by firms, households, and government at any given level of real GDP (although we've assumed away the government for the time being). How does an autonomous change in planned aggregate spending affect real GDP in income–expenditure equilibrium?

Table 11-4 and Figure 11-11 start from the same numerical example we used in Table 11-3 and Figure 11-10. They also show the effect of an autonomous increase in planned aggregate spending of 400—what happens when planned aggregate spending is 400 higher at each level of real GDP.

Look first at Table 11-4. Before the autonomous increase in planned aggregate spending, the level of real GDP at which planned aggregate spending is equal to real GDP, Y^*, is 2,000. After the autonomous change, Y^* has risen to 3,000. The same result is visible in Figure 11-11. The initial income–expenditure equilibrium is at E_1, where Y_1^* is 2,000. The autonomous rise in planned aggregate spending shifts the planned aggregate spending line up, leading to a new income–expenditure equilibrium at E_2, where Y_2^* is 3,000.

The fact that the rise in income–expenditure equilibrium GDP, from 2,000 to 3,000, is much larger than the autonomous increase in aggregate spending, which is only 400, has a familiar explanation: the multiplier process. In the specific example we have just described, an autonomous increase in planned aggregate spending of 400 leads to an increase in Y^* from 2,000 to 3,000, a rise of 1,000. So the multiplier in this example is 1,000/400 = 2.5.

We can examine in detail what underlies the multistage multiplier process by looking more closely at Figure 11-11. First, starting from E_1, the autonomous increase in planned aggregate spending leads to a gap between planned aggregate spending and real GDP. This is represented by the vertical distance between *X*, at 2,400, and E_1, at 2,000. This gap illustrates an unplanned fall in inventory investment: $I_{Unplanned} = -400$. Firms respond by increasing production, leading to a rise in real GDP from Y_1^*. The rise in real GDP translates into an increase in disposable income, *YD*.

That's the first stage in the chain reaction. But it doesn't stop there—the increase in *YD* leads to a rise in consumer spending, *C*, which sets off a second-round rise in real GDP. This in turn leads to a further rise in disposable income

TABLE 11-4 Real GDP Before and After Autonomous Spending Increases by 400 ($MPC = 0.6$)		
Real GDP	$AE_{Planned}$ **before autonomous change**	$AE_{Planned}$ **after autonomous change**
	(billions of dollars)	
$0	$800	$1,200
500	1,100	1,500
1,000	1,400	1,800
1,500	1,700	2,100
2,000	2,000	2,400
2,500	2,300	2,700
3,000	2,600	3,000
3,500	2,900	3,300
4,000	3,200	3,600

FIGURE 11-11 The Multiplier

This figure illustrates the change in Y^* caused by an autonomous increase in planned aggregate spending. The economy is initially at equilibrium point E_1 with an income–expenditure equilibrium GDP, Y_1^*, equal to 2,000. An autonomous increase in $AE_{Planned}$ of 400 shifts the planned aggregate spending line upward by 400. The economy is no longer in income–expenditure equilibrium: real GDP is equal to 2,000 but $AE_{Planned}$ is now 2,400, represented by point X. The vertical distance between the two planned aggregate spending lines, equal to 400, represents $I_{Unplanned} = -400$—the negative inventory investment that the economy now experiences. Firms respond by increasing production, and the economy eventually reaches a new income–expenditure equilibrium at E_2 with a higher level of income–expenditure equilibrium GDP, Y_2^*, equal to 3,000.

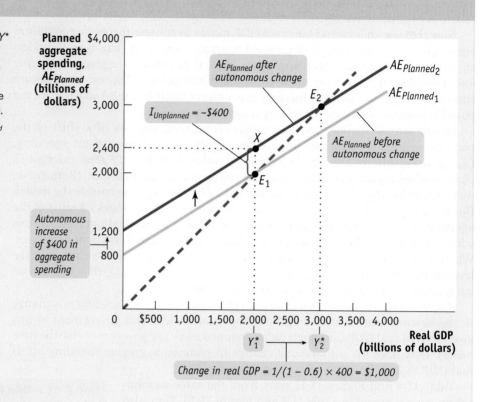

and consumer spending, and so on. And we could play this process in reverse: an autonomous fall in aggregate spending will lead to a chain reaction of reductions in real GDP and consumer spending.

We can summarize these results in an equation, where $\Delta AAE_{Planned}$ represents the autonomous change in $AE_{Planned}$, and $\Delta Y^* = Y_2^* - Y_1^*$, the subsequent change in income–expenditure equilibrium GDP:

(11-17) $\Delta Y^* = \text{Multiplier} \times \Delta AAE_{Planned} = \dfrac{1}{1 - MPC} \times \Delta AAE_{Planned}$

Recalling that the multiplier, $1/(1 - MPC)$, is greater than 1, Equation 11-17 tells us that the change in income–expenditure equilibrium GDP, ΔY^*, is several times larger than the autonomous change in planned aggregate spending, $\Delta AAE_{Planned}$. It also helps us recall an important point: because the marginal propensity to consume is less than 1, each increase in disposable income and each corresponding increase in consumer spending is smaller than in the previous round. That's because at each round some of the increase in disposable income leaks out into savings.

As a result, although real GDP grows at each round, the increase in real GDP diminishes from each round to the next. At some point the increase in real GDP is negligible, and the economy converges to a new income–expenditure equilibrium GDP at Y_2^*.

The Paradox of Thrift In an earlier chapter we mentioned the paradox of thrift to illustrate the fact that in macroeconomics the outcome of many individual actions can generate a result that is different from and worse than the simple sum of those individual actions. In the paradox of thrift, households and firms cut their spending in anticipation of future tough economic times. These actions depress the economy, leaving households and firms worse off than if they hadn't acted virtuously to prepare for tough times. It is called a paradox because what's usually "good" (saving to provide for your family in hard times) is "bad" (because it can make everyone worse off).

Using the multiplier, we can now see exactly how this scenario unfolds. Suppose that there is a slump in consumer spending or investment spending, or both, just like the slump in residential construction investment spending leading up to the 2007–2009 recession. This causes a fall in income–expenditure equilibrium GDP that is several times larger than the original fall in spending. The fall in real GDP leaves consumers and producers worse off than they would have been if they hadn't cut their spending.

Conversely, prodigal behavior is rewarded: if consumers or producers increase their spending, the resulting multiplier process makes the increase in income–expenditure equilibrium GDP several times larger than the original increase in spending. So lavish spending makes consumers and producers better off than if they had been cautious spenders.

Lavish spending after a slump makes everyone better off thanks to the multiplier effect.

It's important to realize that our result that the multiplier is equal to $1/(1 - MPC)$ depends on the simplifying assumption that there are no taxes or transfers, so that disposable income is equal to real GDP. In the Chapter 13 appendix, we'll bring taxes into the picture, which makes the expression for the multiplier more complicated and the multiplier itself smaller.

But the general principle we just learned remains valid: an autonomous change in planned aggregate spending leads to a change in income–expenditure equilibrium GDP, both directly and through an induced change in consumer spending.

As we've seen, declines in planned investment spending are usually the major factor causing recessions, because historically they have been the most common source of autonomous reductions in aggregate spending. The tendency of the consumption function to shift upward over time, which as noted earlier in the Economics in Action, "Famous First Forecasting Failures," means that autonomous changes in both planned investment spending and consumer spending play important roles in expansions. But regardless of the source, there are multiplier effects in the economy that magnify the size of the initial change in aggregate spending.

What About Exports and Imports?

The simple version of the income–expenditure model that we have just laid out assumes that there is no international trade. But, as you may have noticed, the opening story for this chapter deviates in an important way from this simple version of the model. Finland's problems were largely the result of a sharp drop in exports as Nokia phone sales dropped and the demand for paper declined. And in a basic sense the boom in North Dakota, described in an earlier Economics in Action, also involved trade—North Dakota's shale oil is sold to other states and countries, not to local consumers.

So how does bringing exports and imports back in change the story? The answer is that the basic multiplier story continues to work, with two modifications.

First, income earned from exports is a source of spending on domestically produced goods and services, just like consumption and investment. Changes in exports act just like autonomous changes in spending, like an investment boom or slump. In Finland's case, the slump in exports led to a direct fall in Finnish income. This then led to a decline in demand for consumer goods, which led to a further decline in income, and so on, exactly the way a decline in investment spending leads via the multiplier process to an economic downturn.

Second, the multiplier process itself is made somewhat weaker thanks to foreign trade: when consumer spending rises or falls, part of that change is reflected in changes in spending on imports, which don't affect a nation's own income. Suppose, for example, that U.S. consumer spending rises by $1 billion. If the U.S. didn't engage in foreign trade, all of that rise in spending would translate directly into a rise in U.S. GDP. In reality, however, a significant part of the total—say $200 million—will be a rise in spending on goods produced in Canada, Mexico, China, or elsewhere. And this spending *isn't* part of U.S. GDP. As economists sometimes put it, part of any spending change "leaks" abroad.

The effect of this leakage is to reduce the size of the multiplier. The extent to which the multiplier falls depends on how much of an additional dollar of spending falls on imports rather than domestic goods—the *marginal propensity to import*. In the case of the United States, which is a very large economy with only limited international trade, leaks from imports have only a modest effect on the size of the multiplier. In small countries that engage in a lot of trade, trade may greatly reduce the multiplier.

One final point about the effect of trade: it creates interdependence among national economies, because each country's exports are some other country's imports. Suppose that the U.S. economy enters a recession. This will lead, other things equal, to a decline in the amount we spend on goods produced in Canada, which means a decline in Canadian exports. And this spillover will tend to drag Canada's economy down too. More broadly, the trade links between economies are one reason business cycles are often international, even global, in scope: many countries tend to have recessions and recoveries at the same time.

One thing is important to realize, however, about exports and imports: while they can change the size of the multiplier, they don't change the fundamental story about how aggregate spending rises and falls.

ECONOMICS >> *in Action*
Inventories and the End of a Recession

A very clear example of the role of inventories in the multiplier process took place in late 2001, as that year's recession came to an end. The driving force behind the recession was a slump in business investment spending. It took several years before investment spending bounced back in the form of a housing boom. By late 2001 the economy had begun to recover, largely due to an increase in consumer spending—especially on durable goods such as automobiles.

Initially, this increase in consumer spending caught manufacturers by surprise. Figure 11-12 shows changes in real GDP, real consumer spending, and real inventories in each quarter of 2001 and 2002. Notice the surge in consumer spending in the fourth quarter of 2001. Initially, it didn't lead to significant GDP growth because it was offset by a plunge in inventories. But in the first quarter of 2002, producers greatly increased their production, leading to a jump in real GDP.

FIGURE 11-12 Inventories and the End of a Recession

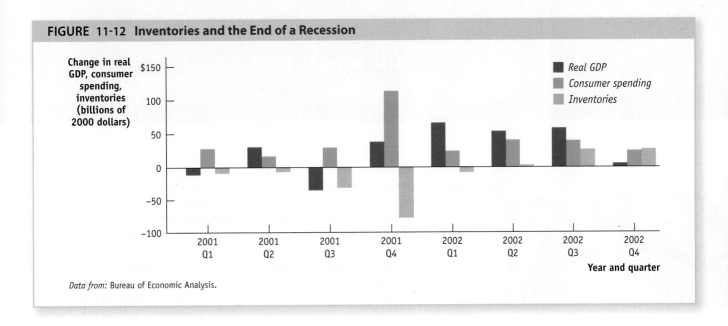

Data from: Bureau of Economic Analysis.

>> Check Your Understanding 11-4

Solutions appear at back of book.

1. Although economists believe that recessions typically begin as slumps in investment spending, they also believe that consumer spending eventually slumps during a recession. Explain why.

2. **a.** Use a diagram like Figure 11-11 to show what happens when there is an autonomous fall in planned aggregate spending. Describe how the economy adjusts to a new income–expenditure equilibrium.

   b. Suppose Y^* is originally $500 billion, the autonomous reduction in planned aggregate spending is $300 million ($0.3 billion), and $MPC = 0.5$. Calculate Y^* after such a change.

>> Quick Review

• The economy is in **income–expenditure equilibrium** when **planned aggregate spending** is equal to real GDP.

• At any output level greater than **income–expenditure equilibrium GDP,** real GDP exceeds planned aggregate spending and inventories are rising. At any lower output level, real GDP falls short of planned aggregate spending and inventories are falling.

• After an autonomous change in planned aggregate spending, the economy moves to a new income–expenditure equilibrium through the inventory adjustment process, as illustrated by the **Keynesian cross.** Because of the multiplier effect, the change in income–expenditure equilibrium GDP is a multiple of the autonomous change in aggregate spending.

• The multiplier effect is modified but not fundamentally changed by international trade. Changes in imports operate in the same way as changes in consumption and investment spending. Imports create leakages of spending, which make the size of the multiplier smaller than it is in an economy with no imports.

What's Good for America Is Good for GM

With the economy in a steep nosedive in 2009, the U.S. government took many stabilization measures, some of which were highly controversial. The decision to use taxpayer's funds to bail out General Motors, which was teetering on the edge of bankruptcy, was among the most controversial. To keep the company afloat, the U.S. government gave it $49.5 billion in loans that were then converted into stock, giving the government temporary ownership of 61% of the company.

General Motors—or GM, as it was often called in its heyday—was once an American icon, so dominant that in the 1950s the company's president, who had been nominated as Secretary of Defense, famously claimed that any conflict of interest was inconceivable: "I thought what was good for our country was good for General Motors, and vice versa."

By 2009 the fate of GM and the fate of America seemed less intertwined. Still, the case for the bailout rested crucially on the belief that GM's problems weren't entirely self-made, that the company was in trouble because the U.S. economy was in trouble, and that national recovery would make a big difference to the automaker's fortune too.

On the face of it, this interdependence wasn't entirely obvious: the 2007–2009 recession was driven by a housing bust and troubles in the banking sector, not by developments in the auto industry. But multiplier effects had indeed led to a plunge in auto sales, as shown in Figure 11-13. And sure enough, as the economy began to recover, auto sales made up most of their lost ground, with GM sharing in the industry's resurgence.

Did saving GM justify the bailout? The company's recovery meant that taxpayers got most of their money back—but not all of it. Recall that the government loan of almost $50 billion was converted into GM stock. Over time, the government sold off its stake for roughly $40 billion—leaving taxpayers with a $10 billion loss.

Defenders of the bailout nonetheless declared it a success, because it resuscitated the U.S. auto industry and saved many jobs, not just in the auto companies and their suppliers, but in the many businesses whose sales depend on the incomes of workers employed in the auto industry. In the summer of 2009 the unemployment rate in Michigan, still America's automotive heartland, rose above 14%—but it then began a rapid decline, falling below the national average to 4.5% by the summer of 2016. Few would argue that the speedy recovery in employment in Michigan would have happened without the auto bailout.

In the end, GM bounced back because the U.S. economy recovered; what was good for America was indeed still good for General Motors. And what was good for General Motors was clearly good for Michigan—and maybe, arguably, for America as a whole.

QUESTIONS FOR THOUGHT

1. Why did a national slump that began with housing affect companies like General Motors?

2. Why was it reasonable in June 2009 to predict that auto sales would improve in the near future?

3. How does this story about General Motors help explain how a slump in housing—a relatively small part of the U.S. economy—could produce such a deep national recession?

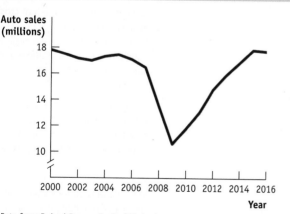

FIGURE 11-13 U.S. Auto Sales 2000–2016

Auto sales (millions)

Year

Data from: Federal Reserve Bank of St. Louis.

SUMMARY

1. An **autonomous change in aggregate spending** leads to a chain reaction in which the total change in real GDP is equal to the **multiplier** times the initial change in aggregate spending. The size of the multiplier, $1/(1 - MPC)$, depends on the **marginal propensity to consume, MPC,** the fraction of an additional dollar of disposable income spent on consumption. The larger the MPC, the larger the multiplier and the larger the change in real GDP for any given autonomous change in aggregate spending. The **marginal propensity to save, MPS,** is equal to $1 - MPC$.

2. The **consumption function** shows how an individual household's consumer spending is determined by its current disposable income. The **aggregate consumption function** shows the relationship for the entire economy. According to the life-cycle hypothesis, households try to smooth their consumption over their lifetimes. As a result, the aggregate consumption function shifts in response to changes in expected future disposable income and changes in aggregate wealth.

3. **Planned investment spending** depends negatively on the interest rate and on existing production capacity; it depends positively on expected future real GDP. The **accelerator principle** says that investment spending is greatly influenced by the expected growth rate of real GDP.

4. Firms hold **inventories** of goods so that they can satisfy consumer demand quickly. **Inventory investment** is positive when firms add to their inventories, negative when they reduce them. Often, however, changes in inventories are unintended. They arise when expected sales and actual sales don't match. The result is unplanned inventory investment. **Actual investment spending** is the sum of planned investment spending and unplanned inventory investment.

5. In **income–expenditure equilibrium, planned aggregate spending,** which in a simplified model with no government and no trade is the sum of consumer spending and planned investment spending, is equal to real GDP. At the **income–expenditure equilibrium GDP,** or Y^*, unplanned inventory investment is zero. When planned aggregate spending is larger than Y^*, unplanned inventory investment is negative; there is an unanticipated reduction in inventories and firms increase production. When planned aggregate spending is less than Y^*, unplanned inventory investment is positive; there is an unanticipated increase in inventories and firms reduce production. The **Keynesian cross** shows how the economy self-adjusts to income–expenditure equilibrium through inventory adjustments.

6. After an autonomous change in planned aggregate spending, the inventory adjustment process moves the economy to a new income–expenditure equilibrium. The change in income–expenditure equilibrium GDP arising from an autonomous change in spending is equal to $(1/(1 - MPC)) \times \Delta AAE_{Planned}$.

7. When trade is introduced, the basic multiplier story continues to work but it is modified in two ways: first, income earned from exports is a source of spending on domestically produced goods and services, just like consumption and investment; and second, imports reduce the size of the multiplier.

KEY TERMS

Marginal propensity to consume (*MPC*), p. 314
Marginal propensity to save (*MPS*), p. 314
Autonomous change in aggregate spending, p. 316
Multiplier, p. 316

Consumption function, p. 318
Aggregate consumption function, p. 319
Planned investment spending, p. 324
Accelerator principle, p. 325
Inventories, p. 325
Inventory investment, p. 326

Unplanned inventory investment, p. 326
Actual investment spending, p. 326
Planned aggregate spending, p. 329
Income–expenditure equilibrium, p. 331
Income–expenditure equilibrium GDP, p. 331
Keynesian cross, p. 332

PROBLEMS

interactive activity

1. Due to an increase in consumer wealth, there is a $40 billion autonomous increase in consumer spending in the economies of Westlandia and Eastlandia. Assuming that the aggregate price level is constant, the interest rate is fixed in both countries, and there are no taxes and no foreign trade, complete the accompanying tables to show the various rounds of increased spending that will occur in both economies if the marginal propensity to consume is 0.5 in Westlandia and 0.75 in Eastlandia. What do your results indicate about the relationship between the size of the marginal propensity to consume and the multiplier?

	Westlandia	
Rounds	Incremental change in GDP	Total change in GDP
1	ΔC = $40 billion	?
2	$MPC \times \Delta C$ = ?	?
3	$MPC \times MPC \times \Delta C$ = ?	?
4	$MPC \times MPC \times MPC \times \Delta C$ = ?	?
...	...	...
Total change in GDP	$(1/(1 - MPC)) \times \Delta C$ = ?	

	Eastlandia	
Rounds	Incremental change in GDP	Total change in GDP
1	ΔC = $40 billion	?
2	$MPC \times \Delta C$ = ?	?
3	$MPC \times MPC \times \Delta C$ = ?	?
4	$MPC \times MPC \times MPC \times \Delta C$ = ?	?
...	...	...
Total change in GDP	$(1/(1 - MPC)) \times \Delta C$ = ?	

2. Assuming that the aggregate price level is constant, the interest rate is fixed, and there are no taxes and no foreign trade, what will be the change in GDP if the following events occur?

   a. There is an autonomous increase in consumer spending of $25 billion; the marginal propensity to consume is $2/3$.

   b. Firms reduce investment spending by $40 billion; the marginal propensity to consume is 0.8.

   c. The government increases its purchases of military equipment by $60 billion; the marginal propensity to consume is 0.6.

3. Economists observed the only five residents of a very small economy and estimated each one's consumer spending at various levels of current disposable income. The accompanying table shows each resident's consumer spending at three income levels.

Individual consumer spending by	Individual current disposable income		
	$0	$20,000	$40,000
Andre	$1,000	$15,000	$29,000
Barbara	2,500	12,500	22,500
Casey	2,000	20,000	38,000
Declan	5,000	17,000	29,000
Elena	4,000	19,000	34,000

   a. What is each resident's consumption function? What is the marginal propensity to consume for each resident?

   b. What is the economy's aggregate consumption function? What is the marginal propensity to consume for the economy?

4. From 2009 to 2014, Eastlandia experienced large fluctuations in both aggregate consumer spending and disposable income, but wealth, the interest rate, and expected future disposable income did not change. The accompanying table shows the level of aggregate consumer spending and disposable income in millions of dollars for each of these years. Use this information to answer the following questions.

Year	Disposable income (millions of dollars)	Consumer spending (millions of dollars)
2009	$100	$180
2010	350	380
2011	300	340
2012	400	420
2013	375	400
2014	500	500

   a. Plot the aggregate consumption function for Eastlandia.

   b. What is the marginal propensity to consume? What is the marginal propensity to save?

   c. What is the aggregate consumption function?

5. The Bureau of Economic Analysis reported that, in real terms, overall consumer spending increased by $345.8 billion in 2015.

   a. If the marginal propensity to consume is 0.50, by how much will real GDP change in response?

   b. If there are no other changes to autonomous spending other than the increase in consumer spending in part a, and unplanned inventory investment, $I_{Unplanned}$, decreased by $100 billion, what is the change in real GDP?

c. GDP at the end of 2014 was $15,982.3 billion. If GDP were to increase by the amount calculated in part b, what would be the percent increase in GDP?

6. During the early 2000s, the Case–Shiller U.S. Home Price Index, a measure of average home prices, rose continuously until it peaked in March 2006. From March 2006 to May 2009, the index lost 32% of its value. Meanwhile, the stock market experienced similar ups and downs. From March 2003 to October 2007, the Standard and Poor's 500 (S&P 500) stock index, a broad measure of stock market prices, almost doubled, from 800.73 to a high of 1,565.15. From that time until March 2009, the index fell by almost 60%, to a low of 676.53. How do you think the movements in home prices both influenced the growth in real GDP during the first half of the decade and added to the concern about maintaining consumer spending after the collapse in the housing market that began in 2006? To what extent did the movements in the stock market hurt or help consumer spending?

7. How will planned investment spending change as the following events occur?

a. The interest rate falls as a result of Federal Reserve policy.

b. The U.S. Environmental Protection Agency decrees that corporations must upgrade or replace their machinery in order to reduce their emissions of sulfur dioxide.

c. Baby boomers begin to retire in large numbers and reduce their savings, resulting in higher interest rates.

8. Explain how each of the following actions will affect the level of planned investment spending and unplanned inventory investment. Assume the economy is initially in income–expenditure equilibrium.

a. The Federal Reserve raises the interest rate.

b. There is a rise in the expected growth rate of real GDP.

c. A sizable inflow of foreign funds into the country lowers the interest rate.

9. In an economy with no government and no foreign sectors, autonomous consumer spending is $250 billion, planned investment spending is $350 billion, and the marginal propensity to consume is ⅔.

a. Plot the aggregate consumption function and planned aggregate spending.

b. What is unplanned inventory investment when real GDP equals $600 billion?

c. What is Y^*, income–expenditure equilibrium GDP?

d. What is the value of the multiplier?

e. If planned investment spending rises to $450 billion, what will be the new Y^*?

10. An economy has a marginal propensity to consume of 0.5, and Y^*, income–expenditure equilibrium GDP, equals $500 billion. Given an autonomous increase in planned investment of $10 billion, show the rounds of increased spending that take place by completing the accompanying table. The first and second rows are filled in for you. In the first row, the increase of planned investment spending of $10 billion raises real GDP and YD by $10 billion, leading to an increase in consumer spending of $5 billion ($MPC \times$ change in disposable income) in row 2, raising real GDP and YD by a further $5 billion.

Rounds	Change in $I_{Planned}$ or C	Change in real GDP	Change in YD
		(billions of dollars)	
1	$\Delta I_{Planned}$ = $10.00	$10.00	$10.00
2	ΔC = $5.00	$5.00	$5.00
3	ΔC = ?	?	?
4	ΔC = ?	?	?
5	ΔC = ?	?	?
6	ΔC = ?	?	?
7	ΔC = ?	?	?
8	ΔC = ?	?	?
9	ΔC = ?	?	?
10	ΔC = ?	?	?

a. What is the total change in real GDP after the 10 rounds? What is the value of the multiplier? What would you expect the total change in Y^* to be based on the multiplier formula? How do your answers to the first and third questions compare?

b. Redo the table starting from round 2, assuming the marginal propensity to consume is 0.75. What is the total change in real GDP after 10 rounds? What is the value of the multiplier? As the marginal propensity to consume increases, what happens to the value of the multiplier?

11. Although the United States is one of the richest nations in the world, it is also the world's largest debtor nation. We often hear that the problem is the nation's low savings rate. Suppose policy makers attempt to rectify this by encouraging greater savings in the economy. What effect will their successful attempts have on real GDP?

12. The U.S. economy slowed significantly in early 2008, and policy makers were extremely concerned about growth. To boost the economy, Congress passed several relief packages (the Economic Stimulus Act of 2008 and the American Recovery and Reinvestment Act of 2009) that combined would deliver about $700 billion in government spending. Assume, for the sake of argument, that this spending was in the form of payments made directly to consumers. The objective was to boost the economy by increasing the disposable income of American consumers.

a. Calculate the initial change in aggregate consumer spending as a consequence of this policy measure if the marginal propensity to consume (MPC) in the United States is 0.5. Then calculate the resulting change in real GDP arising from the $700 billion in payments.

b. Illustrate the effect on real GDP with the use of a graph depicting the income–expenditure equilibrium. Label the vertical axis "Planned aggregate spending, $AE_{Planned}$" and the horizontal axis "Real GDP." Draw two planned aggregate expenditure curves ($AE_{Planned1}$ and $AE_{Planned2}$) and a 45-degree line to show the effect of the autonomous policy change on the equilibrium.

WORK IT OUT **Interactive step-by-step help with solving this problem can be found online.**

13. a. The accompanying table shows gross domestic product (GDP), disposable income (YD), consumer spending (C), and planned investment spending ($I_{Planned}$) in an economy. Assume there is no government or foreign sector in this economy. Complete the table by calculating planned aggregate spending ($AE_{Planned}$) and unplanned inventory investment ($I_{Unplanned}$).

b. What is the aggregate consumption function?

c. What is Y^*, income–expenditure equilibrium GDP?

d. What is the value of the multiplier?

e. If planned investment spending falls to $200 billion, what will be the new Y^*?

f. If autonomous consumer spending rises to $200 billion, what will be the new Y^*?

GDP	YD	C	$I_{Planned}$	$AE_{Planned}$	$I_{Unplanned}$
			(billions of dollars)		
$0	$0	$100	$300	?	?
400	400	400	300	?	?
800	800	700	300	?	?
1,200	1,200	1,000	300	?	?
1,600	1,600	1,300	300	?	?
2,000	2,000	1,600	300	?	?
2,400	2,400	1,900	300	?	?
2,800	2,800	2,200	300	?	?
3,200	3,200	2,500	300	?	?

Deriving the Multiplier Algebraically

This appendix shows how to derive the multiplier algebraically. First, recall that in this chapter planned aggregate spending, $AE_{Planned}$, is the sum of consumer spending, C, which is determined by the consumption function, and planned investment spending, $I_{Planned}$. That is, $AE_{Planned} = C + I_{Planned}$. Rewriting this equation to express all its terms fully, we have:

(11A-1) $AE_{Planned} = A + MPC \times YD + I_{Planned}$

Because there are no taxes or government transfers in this model, disposable income is equal to GDP, so Equation 11A-1 becomes:

(11A-2) $AE_{Planned} = A + MPC \times GDP + I_{Planned}$

The income–expenditure equilibrium GDP, Y^*, is equal to planned aggregate spending:

(11A-3) $Y^* = AE_{Planned}$
$= A + MPC \times Y^* + I_{Planned}$
in income–expenditure equilibrium

Just two more steps. Subtract $MPC \times Y^*$ from both sides of Equation 11A-3:

(11A-4) $Y^* - MPC \times Y^* = Y^* \times (1 - MPC) = A + I_{Planned}$

Finally, divide both sides by $(1 - MPC)$:

(11A-5) $Y^* = \dfrac{A + I_{Planned}}{1 - MPC}$

Equation 11A-5 tells us that a \$1 autonomous change in planned aggregate spending—a change in either A or $I_{Planned}$—causes a \$1/(1 - MPC) change in income–expenditure equilibrium GDP, Y^*. The multiplier in our simple model is therefore:

(11A-6) Multiplier = $1/(1 - MPC)$

PROBLEMS

1. Complete the following table by calculating the value of the multiplier and identifying the change in Y^* due to the change in autonomous spending. How does the value of the multiplier change with the marginal propensity to consume?

MPC	Value of multiplier	Change in spending	Change in Y*
0.5	?	$\Delta C = +$ \$50 million	?
0.6	?	$\Delta I = -$ \$10 million	?
0.75	?	$\Delta C = -$ \$25 million	?
0.8	?	$\Delta I = +$ \$20 million	?
0.9	?	$\Delta C = -$ \$2.5 million	?

WORK IT OUT Interactive step-by-step help with solving this problem can be found online.

2. In an economy without government purchases, transfers, or taxes, and without imports or exports, aggregate autonomous consumer spending is \$500 billion, planned investment spending is \$250 billion, and the marginal propensity to consume is 0.5.

   a. Write the expression for planned aggregate spending as in Equation 11A-1.

   b. Solve for Y^* algebraically.

   c. What is the value of the multiplier?

   d. How will Y^* change if autonomous consumer spending falls to \$450 billion?

12 | Aggregate Demand and Aggregate Supply

DIFFERENT GENERATIONS, DIFFERENT POLICIES

UNEMPLOYMENT AND INFLATION are the two great evils of macroeconomics, and policy makers do their best to keep both under control. Sometimes, however, this task isn't straightforward, as we learned in Chapter 8: Policies to control inflation can worsen unemployment and policies aimed at reducing unemployment can cause inflation. So at times it's hard to know whether inflation or unemployment poses the bigger risk to the economy.

Policy makers at the Federal Reserve found themselves facing such a quandary in 2011, when the unemployment rate, at around 9%, was very high by historical standards, but inflation had spiked to almost 4%, twice the widely accepted policy target of 2%. So should policy remain expansionary, to fight unemployment, or should it be contractionary, to reduce inflation?

In the end, the Fed decided to keep its foot on the gas and continue with a strongly expansionary monetary policy—it reduced interest rates with the goal of boosting the economy. Fed officials believed that the inflation surge was a blip caused by a temporary rise in oil prices, and would soon dissipate. Time proved them right: once the oil price rise ran its course, inflation quickly fell back below 2%. The Fed's counterpart in Europe, the European Central Bank, or ECB, faced a similar situation: a 10% unemployment rate and 3% inflation. Yet it made the opposite policy choice: contractionary monetary policy—raising interest rates with the goal of slowing the economy.

In response to increased inflation in 2011, Fed chair Bernanke made the right policy choice, while ECB president Trichet did not. The *AD–AS* model explains why.

Why did these two central banks, facing similar circumstances, move in opposite directions? Differences in the ages of the two bank leaders may provide a clue: Jean-Claude Trichet, President of the ECB, was 68, while Ben Bernanke, the chairman of the Fed, was 57. To many readers, the closeness of their ages suggests that the two men are more alike than different. But for these policy makers, the 11-year difference in age was significant because it corresponds to differences in the kinds of economic problems that dominated when each man was coming of age.

In fact, Neil Irwin of the *New York Times* has found a strong correlation between the ages of policy makers and their policy stances. Those like Mr. Trichet, who spent their young adulthood during the high-inflation 1970s, were more likely to call for interest-rate hikes and tightening monetary policy to head off inflation than were younger policy makers, like Mr. Bernanke, who, in contrast, were more concerned about unemployment and growth.

Bernanke understood that an economic slump can arise from different types of shocks. This understanding requires a model of the economy that can distinguish between different types of short-run economic fluctuations, a model that extends beyond the income–expenditure framework we studied in the previous chapter.

So why was Bernanke right in this case? Because the recessions of the 1970s were very different from the severe slump that began in 2007 and was still afflicting the economy in 2011. The recessions of the 1970s were largely caused by *supply shocks*, while the Great Recession of 2007–2009 was the result of a *demand shock*. (We discuss supply and demand shocks at length in the chapter.)

To develop this model, called the *AD–AS model*, we'll proceed in three steps. First, we'll develop the concept of *aggregate demand*. Then we'll turn to the parallel concept of *aggregate supply*. Finally, we'll put the two concepts together. ●

WHAT YOU WILL LEARN

- How does the **aggregate demand curve** illustrate the relationship between the aggregate price level and the quantity of aggregate output demanded?
- How does the **aggregate supply curve** illustrate the relationship between the aggregate price level and the quantity of aggregate output supplied?
- Why is the aggregate supply curve different in the short run compared to the long run?
- How is the *AD–AS* **model** used to analyze economic fluctuations?
- How can monetary policy and fiscal policy stabilize the economy?

The **aggregate demand curve** shows the relationship between the aggregate price level and the quantity of aggregate output demanded by households, businesses, the government, and the rest of the world.

Aggregate Demand

The Great Depression, the great majority of economists agree, was the result of a massive negative demand shock. What does that mean? In Chapter 3 we explained that when economists talk about a fall in the demand for a particular good or service, they're referring to a leftward shift of the demand curve. Similarly, when economists talk about a negative demand shock to the economy as a whole, they're referring to a leftward shift of the **aggregate demand curve**, a curve that shows the relationship between the aggregate price level and the quantity of aggregate output demanded by households, firms, the government, and the rest of the world.

Figure 12-1 shows what the aggregate demand curve may have looked like in 1933, at the end of the 1929–1933 recession. The horizontal axis shows the total quantity of domestic goods and services demanded, measured in 2009 dollars. We use real GDP to measure aggregate output and will often use the two terms interchangeably.

The vertical axis shows the aggregate price level, measured by the GDP deflator. With these variables on the axes, we can draw a curve, *AD*, showing how much aggregate output would have been demanded at any given aggregate price level. Since *AD* is meant to illustrate aggregate demand in 1933, one point on the curve corresponds to actual data for 1933, when the aggregate price level was 7.3 and the total quantity of domestic final goods and services purchased was $778 billion in 2009 dollars.

As drawn in Figure 12-1, the aggregate demand curve is downward sloping, indicating a negative relationship between the aggregate price level and the quantity of aggregate output demanded. A higher aggregate price level, other things equal, reduces the quantity of aggregate output demanded; a lower aggregate price level, other things equal, increases the quantity of aggregate output demanded. According to Figure 12-1, if the price level in 1933 had been 4.2 instead of 7.3, the total quantity of domestic final goods and services demanded would have been $1,000 billion in 2009 dollars instead of $778 billion.

The first key question about the aggregate demand curve is: why should the curve be downward sloping?

FIGURE 12-1 The Aggregate Demand Curve

The aggregate demand curve shows the relationship between the aggregate price level and the quantity of aggregate output demanded. The curve is downward sloping due to the wealth effect of a change in the aggregate price level and the interest rate effect of a change in the aggregate price level. Corresponding to the actual 1933 data, here the total quantity of goods and services demanded at an aggregate price level of 7.3 is $778 billion in 2009 dollars. According to our hypothetical curve, however, if the aggregate price level had been only 4.2, the quantity of aggregate output demanded would have risen to $1,000 billion.

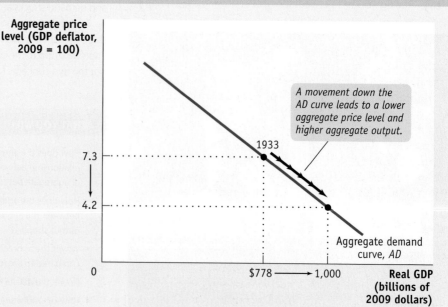

Why Is the Aggregate Demand Curve Downward Sloping?

In Figure 12-1, the curve *AD* is downward sloping. Why? Recall the basic equation of national income accounting:

(12-1) GDP = $C + I + G + X - IM$

where *C* is consumer spending, *I* is investment spending, *G* is government purchases of goods and services, *X* is exports to other countries, and *IM* is imports. If we measure these variables in constant dollars—that is, in prices of a base year—then $C + I + G + X - IM$ is the quantity of domestically produced final goods and services demanded during a given period. *G* is decided by the government, but the other variables are private-sector decisions. To understand why the aggregate demand curve slopes downward, we need to understand why a rise in the aggregate price level reduces *C*, *I*, and *X − IM*.

You might think that the downward slope of the aggregate demand curve is a natural consequence of the *law of demand* defined back in Chapter 3. That is, since the demand curve for any one good is downward sloping, isn't it natural that the demand curve for aggregate output is also downward sloping? This turns out, however, to be a misleading parallel. The demand curve for any individual good shows how the quantity demanded depends on the price of that good, *holding the prices of other goods and services constant*. The main reason the quantity of a good demanded falls when the price of that good rises—that is, the quantity of a good demanded falls as we move up the demand curve—is that people switch their consumption to other goods and services.

But when we consider movements up or down the aggregate demand curve, we're considering *a simultaneous change in the prices of all final goods and services*. Furthermore, changes in the composition of goods and services in consumer spending aren't relevant to the aggregate demand curve: if consumers decide to buy fewer clothes but more cars, this doesn't necessarily change the total quantity of final goods and services they demand.

Why, then, does a rise in the aggregate price level lead to a fall in the quantity of all domestically produced final goods and services demanded? There are two main reasons: the *wealth effect* and the *interest rate effect* of a change in the aggregate price level.

The Wealth Effect An increase in the aggregate price level, other things equal, reduces the purchasing power of many assets. Consider, for example, someone who has $5,000 in a bank account. If the aggregate price level were to rise by 25%, what used to cost $5,000 would now cost $6,250, and would no longer be affordable. And what used to cost $4,000 would now cost $5,000, so that the $5,000 in the bank account would now buy only as much as $4,000 would have bought previously. With the loss in purchasing power, the owner of that bank account would probably scale back his or her consumption plans. Millions of other people would respond the same way, leading to a fall in spending on final goods and services, because a rise in the aggregate price level reduces the purchasing power of everyone's bank account.

Correspondingly, a fall in the aggregate price level increases the purchasing power of consumers' assets and leads to more consumer demand. The **wealth effect of a change in the aggregate price level** is the effect on consumer spending caused by the effect of a change in the aggregate price level on the purchasing power of consumers' assets. Because of the wealth effect, consumer spending, *C*, falls when the aggregate price level rises, leading to a downward-sloping aggregate demand curve.

The Interest Rate Effect Economists use the term *money* in its narrowest sense to refer to cash and bank accounts on which people can use a debit card and write checks. People and firms hold money because it reduces the cost and

The **wealth effect of a change in the aggregate price level** is the effect on consumer spending caused by the effect of a change in the aggregate price level on the purchasing power of consumers' assets.

The **interest rate effect of a change in the aggregate price level** is the effect on consumer spending and investment spending caused by the effect of a change in the aggregate price level on the purchasing power of consumers' and firms' money holdings.

inconvenience of making transactions. An increase in the aggregate price level, other things equal, reduces the purchasing power of a given amount of money holdings. To purchase the same basket of goods and services as before, people and firms now need to hold more money. So, in response to an increase in the aggregate price level, the public tries to increase its money holdings, either by borrowing more or by selling assets such as bonds. This reduces the funds available for lending to other borrowers and drives interest rates up.

In Chapter 10 we learned that a rise in the interest rate reduces investment spending because it makes the cost of borrowing higher. It also reduces consumer spending because households save more of their disposable income. So a rise in the aggregate price level depresses investment spending, *I*, and consumer spending, *C*, through its effect on the purchasing power of money holdings, an effect known as the **interest rate effect of a change in the aggregate price level.** This also leads to a downward-sloping aggregate demand curve.

We'll have a lot more to say about money and interest rates in Chapter 15 on monetary policy. We'll also see, in Chapter 18, which covers international macroeconomics, that a higher interest rate indirectly tends to reduce exports (*X*) and increase imports (*IM*). For now, the important point is that the aggregate demand curve is downward sloping due to both the wealth effect and the interest rate effect of a change in the aggregate price level.

The Aggregate Demand Curve and the Income–Expenditure Model

In the preceding chapter we introduced the *income–expenditure model*, which shows how the economy arrives at *income–expenditure equilibrium*. Now we've introduced the aggregate demand curve, which relates the overall demand for goods and services to the overall price level. How do these concepts fit together?

Recall that one of the assumptions of the income–expenditure model is that the aggregate price level is fixed. We now drop that assumption. We can still use the income–expenditure model, however, to ask what aggregate spending would be *at any given aggregate price level*, which is precisely what the aggregate demand curve shows. So the *AD* curve is actually derived from the income–expenditure model. Economists sometimes say that the income–expenditure model is "embedded" in the *AD–AS* model.

Figure 12-2 shows, once again, how income–expenditure equilibrium is determined. Real GDP is on the horizontal axis; real planned aggregate spending is on the vertical axis. Other things equal, planned aggregate spending, equal to consumer spending plus planned investment spending, rises with real GDP. This is illustrated by the upward-sloping lines $AE_{Planned_1}$ and $AE_{Planned_2}$. Income–expenditure equilibrium, as we learned in Chapter 11, is at the point where the line representing planned aggregate spending crosses the 45-degree line. For example, if $AE_{Planned_1}$ is the relationship between real GDP and planned aggregate spending, then income–expenditure equilibrium is at point E_1, corresponding to a level of real GDP equal to Y_1.

We've just seen, however, that changes in the aggregate price level change the level of planned aggregate spending *at any given level of real GDP*. This means that when the aggregate price level changes, the $AE_{Planned}$ curve shifts. For example, suppose that the aggregate price level falls. As a result of both the wealth effect and the interest rate effect, the fall in the aggregate price level will lead to higher planned aggregate spending at any given level of real GDP. So the $AE_{Planned}$ curve will shift up, as illustrated in Figure 12-2 by the shift from $AE_{Planned_1}$ to $AE_{Planned_2}$. The increase in planned aggregate spending leads to a multiplier process that moves the income–expenditure equilibrium from point E_1 to point E_2, raising real GDP from Y_1 to Y_2.

Figure 12-3 shows how this result can be used to derive the aggregate demand curve. In Figure 12-3, we show a fall in the aggregate price level from P_1 to P_2.

FIGURE 12-2 How Changes in the Aggregate Price Level Affect Income–Expenditure Equilibrium

Income–expenditure equilibrium occurs at the point where the curve $AE_{Planned}$, which shows real aggregate planned spending, crosses the 45-degree line. A fall in the aggregate price level causes the $AE_{Planned}$ curve to shift from $AE_{Planned1}$ to $AE_{Planned2}$, leading to a rise in income–expenditure equilibrium GDP from Y_1 to Y_2.

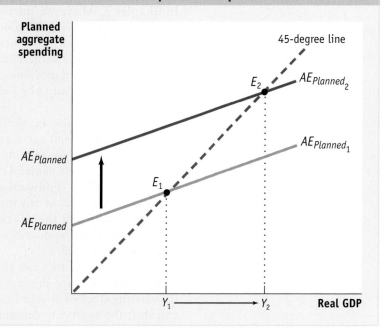

We see in Figure 12-2 that a fall in the aggregate price level would lead to an upward shift of the $AE_{Planned}$ curve and hence a rise in real GDP. We can see this same result in Figure 12-3 as a movement along the AD curve: as the aggregate price level falls, real GDP rises from Y_1 to Y_2.

So the aggregate demand curve doesn't replace the income–expenditure model. Instead, it's a way to summarize what the income–expenditure model says about the effects of changes in the aggregate price level.

In practice, economists often use the income–expenditure model to analyze short-run economic fluctuations, even though strictly speaking it should be seen as a component of a more complete model. In the short run, in particular, this is usually a reasonable shortcut.

FIGURE 12-3 The Income–Expenditure Model and the Aggregate Demand Curve

Figure 12-2 shows how a fall in the aggregate price level shifts the planned aggregate spending curve up, leading to a rise in real GDP. Here we see that same result as a movement along the aggregate demand curve. If the aggregate price level falls from P_1 to P_2, real GDP rises from Y_1 to Y_2. The AD curve is therefore downward sloping.

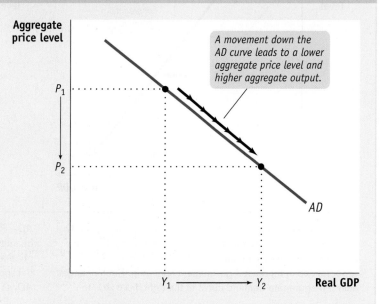

Shifts of the Aggregate Demand Curve

In Chapter 3, where we introduced the analysis of supply and demand in the market for an individual good or service, we stressed the importance of the distinction between *movements along* the demand curve and *shifts of* the demand curve. The same distinction applies to the aggregate demand curve. Figure 12-1 shows a *movement along* the aggregate demand curve, a change in the aggregate quantity of goods and services demanded as the aggregate price level changes.

But there can also be *shifts of* the aggregate demand curve, changes in the quantity of goods and services demanded at any given price level, as shown in Figure 12-4. When we talk about an increase in aggregate demand, we mean a shift of the aggregate demand curve to the right, as shown in panel (a) by the shift from AD_1 to AD_2. A rightward shift occurs when the quantity of aggregate output demanded increases at any given aggregate price level. A decrease in aggregate demand means that the AD curve shifts to the left, as in panel (b). A leftward shift implies that the quantity of aggregate output demanded falls at any given aggregate price level.

A number of factors can shift the aggregate demand curve. Among the most important factors are changes in expectations, changes in wealth, and the size of the existing stock of physical capital. In addition, both fiscal and monetary policy can shift the aggregate demand curve. All five factors set the multiplier process in motion. By causing an initial rise or fall in real GDP, they change disposable income, which leads to additional changes in aggregate spending, which lead to further changes in real GDP, and so on. For an overview of factors that shift the aggregate demand curve, see upcoming Table 12-1.

Changes in Expectations Both consumer spending and planned investment spending depend in part on people's expectations about the future. Consumers base their spending not only on the income they have now but also on the income they expect to have in the future. Firms base their planned investment

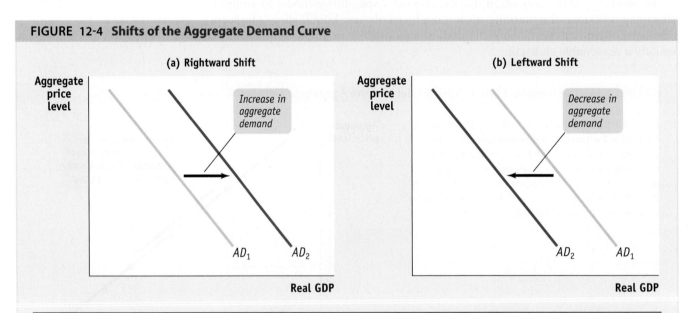

FIGURE 12-4 Shifts of the Aggregate Demand Curve

(a) Rightward Shift

Aggregate price level

Increase in aggregate demand

AD_1 AD_2

Real GDP

(b) Leftward Shift

Aggregate price level

Decrease in aggregate demand

AD_2 AD_1

Real GDP

Panel (a) shows the effect of events that increase the quantity of aggregate output demanded at any given aggregate price level, such as improvements in business and consumer expectations or increased government spending. Such changes shift the aggregate demand curve to the right, from AD_1 to

AD_2. Panel (b) shows the effect of events that decrease the quantity of aggregate output demanded at any given aggregate price level, such as a fall in wealth caused by a stock market decline. This shifts the aggregate demand curve leftward from AD_1 to AD_2.

TABLE 12-1 Factors That Shift Aggregate Demand

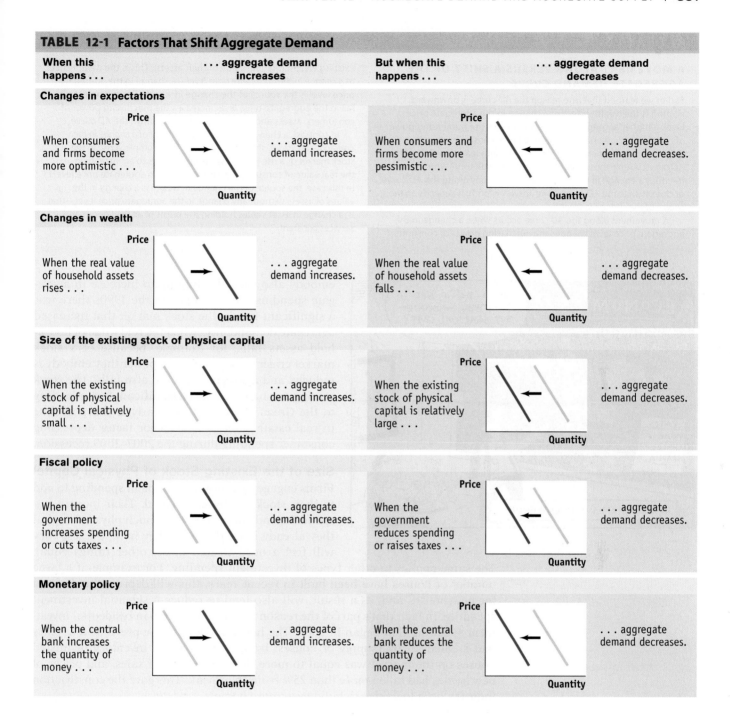

When this happens . . .	. . . aggregate demand increases	But when this happens . . .	. . . aggregate demand decreases
Changes in expectations			
When consumers and firms become more optimistic . . .	. . . aggregate demand increases.	When consumers and firms become more pessimistic . . .	. . . aggregate demand decreases.
Changes in wealth			
When the real value of household assets rises . . .	. . . aggregate demand increases.	When the real value of household assets falls . . .	. . . aggregate demand decreases.
Size of the existing stock of physical capital			
When the existing stock of physical capital is relatively small . . .	. . . aggregate demand increases.	When the existing stock of physical capital is relatively large . . .	. . . aggregate demand decreases.
Fiscal policy			
When the government increases spending or cuts taxes . . .	. . . aggregate demand increases.	When the government reduces spending or raises taxes . . .	. . . aggregate demand decreases.
Monetary policy			
When the central bank increases the quantity of money . . .	. . . aggregate demand increases.	When the central bank reduces the quantity of money . . .	. . . aggregate demand decreases.

spending not only on current conditions but also on the sales they expect to make in the future. As a result, changes in expectations can push consumer spending and planned investment spending up or down. If consumers and firms become more optimistic, aggregate spending rises; if they become more pessimistic, aggregate spending falls.

In fact, short-run economic forecasters pay careful attention to surveys of consumer and business sentiment. In particular, forecasters watch the Consumer Confidence Index, a monthly measure calculated by the Conference Board, and the Michigan Consumer Sentiment Index, a similar measure calculated by the University of Michigan.

Changes in Wealth Consumer spending depends in part on the value of household assets. When the real value of these assets rises, the purchasing power they

A MOVEMENT ALONG VERSUS A SHIFT OF THE AGGREGATE DEMAND CURVE

Earlier we learned that one reason the *AD* curve is downward sloping is the wealth effect of a change in the aggregate price level: a higher aggregate price level reduces the purchasing power of households' assets and leads to a fall in consumer spending, *C*. But we've just learned that changes in wealth lead to a shift of the *AD* curve. Aren't those two principles contradictory? Which one is it—does a change in wealth move the economy along the *AD* curve or does it shift the *AD* curve? The answer is both: *it depends on the source of the change in wealth.*

A movement along the *AD* curve occurs when a change in the aggregate price level changes the purchasing power of consumers'

existing wealth (the real value of their assets). This is the *wealth effect of a change in the aggregate price level*—a change in the aggregate price level is the source of the change in wealth. For example, a fall in the aggregate price level increases the purchasing power of consumers' assets and leads to a movement down the *AD* curve.

In contrast, a change in wealth *independent of a change in the aggregate price level* shifts the *AD* curve. For example, a rise in the stock market or a rise in real estate values leads to an increase in the real value of consumers' assets at any given aggregate price level. In this case, the source of the change in wealth is a change in the values of assets without any change in the aggregate price level—that is, a change in asset values holding the prices of all final goods and services constant.

embody also rises, leading to an increase in aggregate spending. For example, in the 1990s there was a significant rise in the stock market that increased aggregate demand. And when the real value of household assets falls, for example, because of a stock market crash—the purchasing power they embody is reduced and aggregate demand also falls. The stock market crash of 1929 was a significant factor leading to the Great Depression. Similarly, a sharp decline in real estate values was a major factor depressing consumer spending during the 2007–2009 recession.

Size of the Existing Stock of Physical Capital

Firms engage in planned investment spending to add to their stock of physical capital. Their incentive to spend depends in part on how much physical capital they already have: the more they have, the less they will feel a need to add more, other things equal. The same applies to other types of investment spending. For example, if a large number of houses have been built in recent years, this will depress the demand for new houses and, as a result, will also tend to reduce residential investment spending. In fact, that's part of the reason for the deep slump in residential investment spending that began in 2006. The housing boom of the previous few years had created an oversupply of houses: by spring 2009, the inventory of unsold houses on the market was equal to more than 14 months of sales, and prices of new homes had fallen more than 25% from their peak. This gave the construction industry little incentive to build even more homes.

Government Policies and Aggregate Demand

One of the key insights of macroeconomics is that the government can have a powerful influence on aggregate demand and that, in some circumstances, this influence can be used to improve economic performance.

The two main ways the government can influence the aggregate demand curve are through fiscal policy and monetary policy. We'll briefly discuss their influence on aggregate demand, leaving a full-length discussion for upcoming chapters.

Fiscal Policy The use of either government spending—government purchases of final goods and services and government transfers—or tax policy to stabilize the economy is known as fiscal policy. In practice, governments often respond to recessions by increasing spending, cutting taxes, or both. They often respond to inflation by reducing spending or increasing taxes.

The effect of government purchases of final goods and services, *G*, on the aggregate demand curve is *direct* because government purchases are themselves a component of aggregate demand. So an increase in government purchases shifts the aggregate demand curve to the right and a decrease shifts it to the left. History's most dramatic example of how increased government purchases affect aggregate demand was the effect of wartime government spending during World War II.

Because of the war, U.S. federal purchases surged 400%. This increase in purchases is usually credited with ending the Great Depression. In the 1990s Japan used large public works projects—such as government-financed construction of roads, bridges, and dams—in an effort to increase aggregate demand in the face of a slumping economy. Similarly, in 2009, in the wake of the Great Recession, the United States began spending more than $100 billion on infrastructure projects such as improving highways, bridges, public transportation, and more, to stimulate overall spending.

In contrast, changes in either tax rates or government transfers influence the economy *indirectly* through their effect on disposable income. A lower tax rate means that consumers get to keep more of what they earn, increasing their disposable income. An increase in government transfers also increases consumers' disposable income. In either case, this increases consumer spending and shifts the aggregate demand curve to the right. A higher tax rate or a reduction in transfers reduces the amount of disposable income received by consumers. This reduces consumer spending and shifts the aggregate demand curve to the left.

Monetary Policy We opened this chapter by talking about the problems faced by the Federal Reserve in 2011. The Federal Reserve controls monetary policy—the use of changes in the quantity of money or the interest rate to stabilize the economy. We've just discussed how a rise in the aggregate price level, by reducing the purchasing power of money holdings, causes a rise in the interest rate. That, in turn, reduces both investment spending and consumer spending.

But what happens if the quantity of money in the hands of households and firms changes? In modern economies, the quantity of money in circulation is largely determined by the decisions of a *central bank* created by the government. As we'll learn in Chapter 14, the Federal Reserve, the U.S. central bank, is a special institution that is neither exactly part of the government nor exactly a private institution. When the central bank increases the quantity of money in circulation, households and firms have more money, which they are willing to lend out. The effect is to drive the interest rate down at any given aggregate price level, leading to higher investment spending and higher consumer spending.

That is, increasing the quantity of money shifts the aggregate demand curve to the right. Reducing the quantity of money has the opposite effect: households and firms have fewer money holdings than before, leading them to borrow more and lend less. This raises the interest rate, reduces investment spending and consumer spending, and shifts the aggregate demand curve to the left.

ECONOMICS >> *in Action*
Moving Along the Aggregate Demand Curve, 1979–1980

When looking at data, it's often hard to distinguish between changes in spending that represent *movements along* the aggregate demand curve and *shifts of* the aggregate demand curve. One telling exception, however, is what happened right after the oil crisis of 1979. Faced with a sharp increase in the aggregate price level—the rate of consumer price inflation reached 14.8% in March of 1980—the

During the 1979 oil crisis, the interest rate effect from a rise in the aggregate price level pushed the economy up the *AD* curve, leading to a fall in aggregate output.

Federal Reserve stuck to a policy of increasing the quantity of money slowly. The aggregate price level was rising steeply, but the quantity of money circulating in the economy was growing slowly. The net result was that the purchasing power of the quantity of money in circulation fell.

This led to an increase in the demand for borrowing and a surge in interest rates. The *prime rate*, which is the interest rate banks charge their best customers, climbed above 20%. High interest rates, in turn, caused both consumer spending and investment spending to fall: in 1980 purchases of durable consumer goods like cars fell by 5.3% and real investment spending fell by 8.9%.

In other words, in 1979–1980 the economy responded just as we'd expect if it were moving upward along the aggregate demand curve from right to left: due to the wealth effect and the interest rate effect of a change in the aggregate price level, the quantity of aggregate output demanded fell as the aggregate price level rose. This does not explain, of course, why the aggregate price level rose. But as we'll see in the upcoming section on the *AD–AS* model, the answer to that question lies in the behavior of the *short-run aggregate supply curve*.

>> *Quick Review*

• The **aggregate demand curve** is downward sloping because of the **wealth effect of a change in the aggregate price level** and the **interest rate effect of a change in the aggregate price level.**

• The aggregate demand curve shows how income–expenditure equilibrium GDP changes when the aggregate price level changes.

• Changes in consumer spending caused by changes in wealth and expectations about the future shift the aggregate demand curve. Changes in investment spending caused by changes in expectations and by the size of the existing stock of physical capital also shift the aggregate demand curve.

• Fiscal policy affects aggregate demand directly through government purchases and indirectly through changes in taxes or government transfers. Monetary policy affects aggregate demand indirectly through changes in the interest rate.

>> *Check Your Understanding* **12-1**

Solutions appear at back of book.

1. Determine the effect on aggregate demand of each of the following events. Explain whether it represents a movement along the aggregate demand curve (up or down) or a shift of the curve (leftward or rightward).
   a. A rise in the interest rate caused by a change in monetary policy
   b. A fall in the real value of money in the economy due to a higher aggregate price level
   c. News of a worse-than-expected job market next year
   d. A fall in tax rates
   e. A rise in the real value of assets in the economy due to a lower aggregate price level
   f. A rise in the real value of assets in the economy due to a surge in real estate values

‖ Aggregate Supply

Between 1929 and 1933, there was a sharp fall in aggregate demand—a reduction in the quantity of goods and services demanded at any given price level. One consequence of the economy-wide decline in demand was a fall in the prices of most goods and services. By 1933, the GDP deflator (one of the price indexes we defined in Chapter 7) was 26% below its 1929 level, and other indexes were down by similar amounts. A second consequence was a decline in the output of most goods and services: by 1933, real GDP was 27% below its 1929 level. A third consequence, closely tied to the fall in real GDP, was a surge in the unemployment rate from 3% to 25%.

The association between the plunge in real GDP and the plunge in prices wasn't an accident. Between 1929 and 1933, the U.S. economy was moving down its **aggregate supply curve,** which shows the relationship between the economy's aggregate price level (the overall price level of final goods and services in the economy) and the total quantity of final goods and services, or aggregate output, producers are willing to supply. (As you will recall, we use real GDP to measure aggregate output. So we'll often use the two terms interchangeably.) More specifically, between 1929 and 1933 the U.S. economy moved down its *short-run aggregate supply curve*.

The **aggregate supply curve** shows the relationship between the aggregate price level and the quantity of aggregate output supplied in the economy.

The Short-Run Aggregate Supply Curve

The period from 1929 to 1933 demonstrated that there is a positive relationship in the short run between the aggregate price level and the quantity of aggregate output supplied. That is, a rise in the aggregate price level is associated with a rise in the quantity of aggregate output supplied, other things equal; a fall in the aggregate price level is associated with a fall in the quantity of aggregate output supplied, other things equal. To understand why this positive relationship exists, consider the most basic question facing a producer: is producing a unit of output profitable or not? Let's define profit per unit:

(12-2) Profit per unit of output =
Price per unit of output − Production cost per unit of output

Thus, the answer to the question depends on whether the price the producer receives for a unit of output is greater or less than the cost of producing that unit of output. At any given point in time, many of the costs producers face are fixed per unit of output and can't be changed for an extended period of time. Typically, the largest source of inflexible production cost is the wages paid to workers. *Wages* here refers to all forms of worker compensation, such as employer-paid health care and retirement benefits in addition to earnings.

Wages are typically an inflexible production cost because the dollar amount of any given wage paid, called the **nominal wage,** is often determined by contracts that were signed some time ago. And even when there are no formal contracts, there are often informal agreements between management and workers, making companies reluctant to change wages in response to economic conditions. For example, companies usually will not reduce wages during poor economic times—unless the downturn has been particularly long and severe—for fear of generating worker resentment. Correspondingly, they typically won't raise wages during better economic times—until they are at risk of losing workers to competitors—because they don't want to encourage workers to routinely demand higher wages.

As a result of both formal and informal agreements, then, the economy is characterized by **sticky wages:** nominal wages that are slow to fall even in the face of high unemployment and slow to rise even in the face of labor shortages. It's important to note, however, that nominal wages cannot be sticky forever: ultimately, formal contracts and informal agreements will be renegotiated to take into account changed economic circumstances. As the Pitfalls at the end of this section explains, how long it takes for nominal wages to become flexible is an integral component of what distinguishes the short run from the long run.

To understand how the fact that many costs are fixed in nominal terms gives rise to an upward-sloping short-run aggregate supply curve, it's helpful to know that prices are set somewhat differently in different kinds of markets. In *perfectly competitive markets,* producers take prices as given; in *imperfectly competitive markets,* producers have some ability to choose the prices they charge. In both kinds of markets, there is a short-run positive relationship between prices and output, but for slightly different reasons.

Let's start with the behavior of producers in perfectly competitive markets; remember, they take the price as given. Imagine that, for some reason, the aggregate price level falls, which means that the price received by the typical producer of a final good or service falls. Because many production costs are fixed in the short run, production cost per unit of output doesn't fall by the same proportion as the fall in the price of output. So the profit per unit of output declines, leading perfectly competitive producers to reduce the quantity supplied in the short run.

The **nominal wage** is the dollar amount of the wage paid.

Sticky wages are nominal wages that are slow to fall even in the face of high unemployment and slow to rise even in the face of labor shortages.

The **short-run aggregate supply curve** shows the relationship between the aggregate price level and the quantity of aggregate output supplied that exists in the short run, the time period when many production costs can be taken as fixed.

On the other hand, suppose that for some reason the aggregate price level rises. As a result, the typical producer receives a higher price for its final good or service. Again, many production costs are fixed in the short run, so production cost per unit of output doesn't rise by the same proportion as the rise in the price of a unit. And since the typical perfectly competitive producer takes the price as given, profit per unit of output rises and output increases.

Now consider an imperfectly competitive producer that is able to set its own price. If there is a rise in the demand for this producer's product, it will be able to sell more at any given price. Given stronger demand for its products, it will probably choose to increase its prices as well as its output, as a way of increasing profit per unit of output. In fact, industry analysts often talk about variations in an industry's *pricing power:* when demand is strong, firms with pricing power are able to raise prices—and they do.

Conversely, if there is a fall in demand, firms will normally try to limit the fall in their sales by cutting prices.

Both the responses of firms in perfectly competitive industries and those of firms in imperfectly competitive industries lead to an upward-sloping relationship between aggregate output and the aggregate price level. The positive relationship between the aggregate price level and the quantity of aggregate output producers are willing to supply during the time period when many production costs, particularly nominal wages, can be taken as fixed is illustrated by the **short-run aggregate supply curve.** The positive relationship between the aggregate price level and aggregate output in the short run gives the short-run aggregate supply curve its upward slope.

Figure 12-5 shows a hypothetical short-run aggregate supply curve, *SRAS,* that matches actual U.S. data for 1929 and 1933. On the horizontal axis is aggregate output (or, equivalently, real GDP)—the total quantity of final goods and services supplied in the economy—measured in 2009 dollars. On the vertical axis is the aggregate price level as measured by the GDP deflator, with the value for the year 2009 equal to 100. In 1929, the aggregate price level was 9.9 and real GDP was $1,057 billion. In 1933, the aggregate price level was 7.3 and real GDP was only $778 billion. The movement down the *SRAS* curve corresponds to the deflation and fall in aggregate output experienced over those years.

FIGURE 12-5 The Short-Run Aggregate Supply Curve

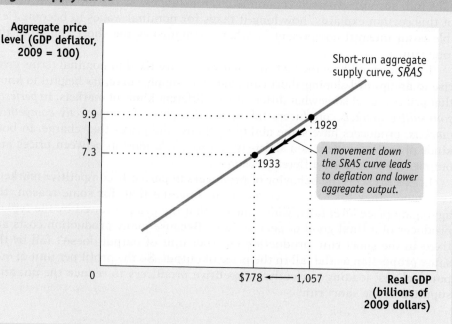

The short-run aggregate supply curve shows the relationship between the aggregate price level and the quantity of aggregate output supplied in the short run, the period in which many production costs such as nominal wages are fixed. It is upward sloping because a higher aggregate price level leads to higher profit per unit of output and higher aggregate output given fixed nominal wages. Here we show numbers corresponding to early in the Great Depression, from 1929 to 1933. When deflation occurred and the aggregate price level fell from 9.9 (in 1929) to 7.3 (in 1933), firms responded by reducing the quantity of aggregate output supplied from $1,057 billion to $778 billion measured in 2009 dollars.

Most macroeconomists agree that the picture shown in Figure 12-5 is correct: there is, other things equal, a positive short-run relationship between the aggregate price level and aggregate output. But many would argue that the details are a bit more complicated.

So far we've stressed a difference in the behavior of the aggregate price level and the behavior of nominal wages. That is, we've said that the aggregate price level is flexible but nominal wages are sticky in the short run. Although this assumption is a good way to explain why the short-run aggregate supply curve is upward sloping, empirical data on wages and prices don't wholly support a sharp distinction between flexible prices of

final goods and services and sticky nominal wages.

On one side, some nominal wages are in fact flexible even in the short run because some workers are not covered by a contract or informal agreement with their employers. Since some nominal wages are sticky but others are flexible, we observe that the *average nominal wage*—the nominal wage averaged over all workers in the economy—falls when there is a steep rise in unemployment. For example, nominal wages fell substantially in the early years of the Great Depression.

On the other side, some prices of final goods and services are sticky rather than flexible. For example, some firms,

particularly the makers of luxury or name-brand goods, are reluctant to cut prices even when demand falls. Instead they prefer to cut output even if their profit per unit hasn't declined.

These complications, as we've said, don't change the basic picture. When the aggregate price level falls, some producers cut output because the nominal wages they pay are sticky. And some producers don't cut their prices in the face of a falling aggregate price level, preferring instead to reduce their output. In both cases, the positive relationship between the aggregate price level and aggregate output is maintained. So, in the end, the short-run aggregate supply curve is still upward sloping.

Shifts of the Short-Run Aggregate Supply Curve

Figure 12-5 shows a *movement along* the short-run aggregate supply curve, as the aggregate price level and aggregate output fell from 1929 to 1933. But there can also be *shifts of* the short-run aggregate supply curve, as shown in Figure 12-6. Panel (a) shows a *decrease in short-run aggregate supply*—a leftward shift of the short-run aggregate supply curve. Aggregate supply decreases when producers reduce the quantity of aggregate output they are willing to supply at any given aggregate price level. Panel (b) shows an *increase in short-run aggregate*

FIGURE 12-6 Shifts of the Short-Run Aggregate Supply Curve

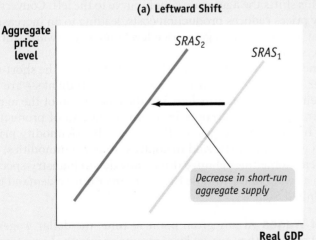

(a) Leftward Shift

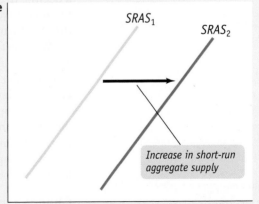

(b) Rightward Shift

Panel (a) shows a decrease in short-run aggregate supply: the short-run aggregate supply curve shifts leftward from $SRAS_1$ to $SRAS_2$, and the quantity of aggregate output supplied at any given aggregate price level falls. Panel (b) shows an increase in short-run aggregate supply: the short-run aggregate supply curve shifts rightward from $SRAS_1$ to $SRAS_2$, and the quantity of aggregate output supplied at any given aggregate price level rises.

supply—a rightward shift of the short-run aggregate supply curve. Aggregate supply increases when producers increase the quantity of aggregate output they are willing to supply at any given aggregate price level.

To understand why the short-run aggregate supply curve can shift, it's important to recall that producers make output decisions based on their profit per unit of output. The short-run aggregate supply curve illustrates the relationship between the aggregate price level and aggregate output: because some production costs are fixed in the short run, a change in the aggregate price level leads to a change in producers' profit per unit of output and, in turn, leads to a change in aggregate output.

But other factors besides the aggregate price level can affect profit per unit and, in turn, aggregate output. It is changes in these other factors that will shift the short-run aggregate supply curve.

To develop some intuition, suppose that something happens that raises production costs—say, an increase in the price of oil. At any given price of output, a producer now earns a smaller profit per unit of output. As a result, producers reduce the quantity supplied at any given aggregate price level, and the short-run aggregate supply curve shifts to the left. If, in contrast, something happens that lowers production costs—say, a fall in the nominal wage—a producer now earns a higher profit per unit of output at any given price of output. This leads producers to increase the quantity of aggregate output supplied at any given aggregate price level, and the short-run aggregate supply curve shifts to the right.

Now we'll discuss some of the important factors that affect producers' profit per unit and so can lead to shifts of the short-run aggregate supply curve. These factors include changes in commodity prices, changes in nominal wages, and changes in productivity.

Changes in Commodity Prices In this chapter's opening story, we saw how the views of Jean-Claude Trichet, the president of the ECB, were shaped by the high inflation of the 1970s. The origins of that inflationary period lay in a sharp and sustained increase in the price of a very important commodity—oil. The high price of oil sharply raised costs for producers around the world.

A *commodity* is a standardized input bought and sold in bulk quantities. An increase in the price of a commodity, such as oil, raises production costs across the economy and reduces the quantity of aggregate output supplied at any given aggregate price level. This shifts the aggregate supply curve to the left. Conversely, a decline in commodity prices reduces production costs, leading to an increase in the quantity supplied at any given aggregate price level and a rightward shift of the short-run aggregate supply curve.

Why isn't the influence of commodity prices already captured by the short-run aggregate supply curve? Because commodities—unlike, say, soft drinks—are not a final good. Hence their prices are not included in the calculation of the aggregate price level. Further, commodities represent a significant cost of production to most suppliers, just like nominal wages do. So changes in commodity prices have large impacts on production costs. And in contrast to noncommodities, the prices of commodities can sometimes change drastically due to industry-specific shocks to supply—such as wars in the Middle East or rising Chinese demand that leaves less oil for the United States.

Changes in Nominal Wages At any given point in time, the dollar wages of many workers are fixed because they are set by contracts or informal agreements made in the past. Nominal wages can change, however, once enough time has passed for contracts and informal agreements to be renegotiated.

Suppose, for example, that there is an economy-wide rise in the cost of health care insurance premiums paid by employers as part of employees' wages. From the employers' perspective, this is equivalent to a rise in nominal wages because it is an increase in employer-paid compensation. So this rise in nominal wages increases production costs and shifts the short-run aggregate supply curve to the left.

Conversely, suppose there is an economy-wide fall in the cost of such premiums. This is equivalent to a fall in nominal wages from the point of view of employers; it reduces production costs and shifts the short-run aggregate supply curve to the right.

An important historical fact is that during the 1970s the surge in the price of oil had the indirect effect of also raising nominal wages. This "knock-on" effect occurred because many wage contracts included *cost-of-living allowances* that automatically raised the nominal wage when consumer prices increased. Through this channel, the surge in the price of oil—which led to an increase in overall consumer prices—ultimately caused a rise in nominal wages.

So the economy, in the end, experienced two leftward shifts of the aggregate supply curve: the first generated by the initial surge in the price of oil, the second generated by the induced increase in nominal wages. The negative effect on the economy of rising oil prices was greatly magnified through the cost-of-living allowances in wage contracts. Today, cost-of-living allowances in wage contracts are rare.

Changes in Productivity An increase in productivity means that a worker can produce more units of output with the same quantity of inputs. For example, the introduction of bar-code scanners in retail stores greatly increased the ability of a single worker to stock, inventory, and resupply store shelves. As a result, the cost to a store of "producing" a dollar of sales fell and profit rose. And, correspondingly, the quantity supplied increased. (Think of Walmart and the increase in the number of its stores as an increase in aggregate supply.) So a rise in productivity, whatever the source, increases producers' profits and shifts the short-run aggregate supply curve to the right.

Conversely, a fall in productivity—say, due to new regulations that require workers to spend more time filling out forms—reduces the number of units of output a worker can produce with the same quantity of inputs. Consequently, the cost per unit of output rises, profit falls, and quantity supplied falls. This shifts the short-run aggregate supply curve to the left.

For a summary of the factors that shift the short-run aggregate supply curve, see Table 12-2.

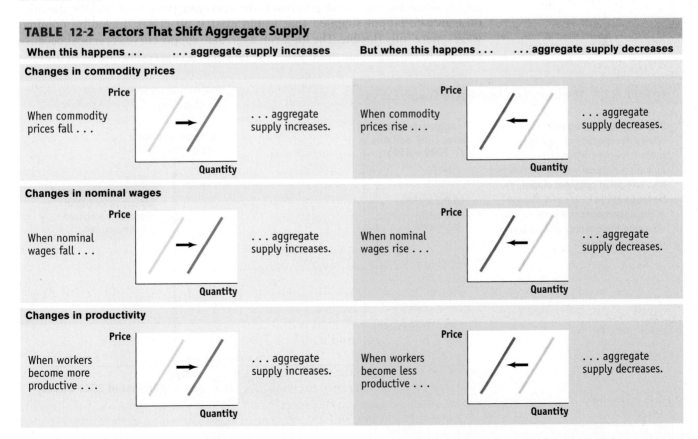

TABLE 12-2 Factors That Shift Aggregate Supply			
When this happens . . .	**. . . aggregate supply increases**	**But when this happens . . .**	**. . . aggregate supply decreases**
Changes in commodity prices			
When commodity prices fall . . .	. . . aggregate supply increases.	When commodity prices rise . . .	. . . aggregate supply decreases.
Changes in nominal wages			
When nominal wages fall . . .	. . . aggregate supply increases.	When nominal wages rise . . .	. . . aggregate supply decreases.
Changes in productivity			
When workers become more productive . . .	. . . aggregate supply increases.	When workers become less productive . . .	. . . aggregate supply decreases.

The **long-run aggregate supply curve** shows the relationship between the aggregate price level and the quantity of aggregate output supplied that would exist if all prices, including nominal wages, were fully flexible.

The Long-Run Aggregate Supply Curve

We've just seen that in the short run a fall in the aggregate price level leads to a decline in the quantity of aggregate output supplied because nominal wages are sticky in the short run. But, as mentioned earlier, contracts and informal agreements are renegotiated in the long run. So in the long run, nominal wages—like the aggregate price level—are flexible, not sticky. This fact greatly alters the long-run relationship between the aggregate price level and aggregate supply. In fact, in the long run the aggregate price level has *no* effect on the quantity of aggregate output supplied.

To see why, let's conduct a thought experiment. Imagine that you could wave a magic wand—or maybe a magic bar-code scanner—and cut *all prices* in the economy in half at the same time. By "all prices" we mean the prices of all inputs, including nominal wages, as well as the prices of final goods and services. What would happen to aggregate output, given that the aggregate price level has been halved and all input prices, including nominal wages, have been halved?

The answer is: nothing. Consider Equation 12-2 again: each producer would receive a lower price for its product, but costs would fall by the same proportion. As a result, every unit of output profitable to produce before the change in prices would still be profitable to produce after the change in prices. So a halving of *all* prices in the economy has no effect on the economy's aggregate output. In other words, changes in the aggregate price level now have no effect on the quantity of aggregate output supplied.

In reality, of course, no one can change all prices by the same proportion at the same time. But now, we'll consider the *long run, the period of time over which all prices are fully flexible.* In the long run, inflation or deflation has the same effect as someone changing all prices by the same proportion. *As a result, changes in the aggregate price level do not change the quantity of aggregate output supplied in the long run.* That's because changes in the aggregate price level will, in the long run, be accompanied by equal proportional changes in *all* input prices, including nominal wages.

The **long-run aggregate supply curve,** illustrated in Figure 12-7 by the curve *LRAS*, shows the relationship between the aggregate price level and the quantity of aggregate output supplied that would exist if all prices, including nominal wages, were fully flexible. The long-run aggregate supply curve is vertical because changes in the aggregate price level have *no* effect on aggregate output in the long

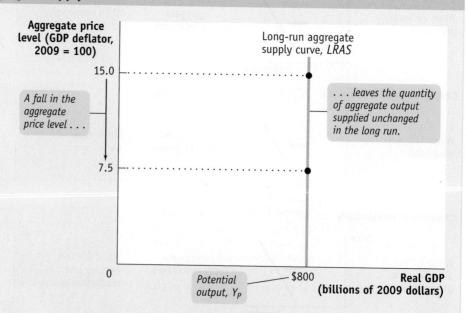

FIGURE 12-7　The Long-Run Aggregate Supply Curve

The long-run aggregate supply curve shows the quantity of aggregate output supplied when all prices, including nominal wages, are flexible. It is vertical at potential output, Y_P, because in the long run a change in the aggregate price level has no effect on the quantity of aggregate output supplied.

Aggregate price level (GDP deflator, 2009 = 100)

Long-run aggregate supply curve, *LRAS*

15.0

A fall in the aggregate price level . . .

. . . leaves the quantity of aggregate output supplied unchanged in the long run.

7.5

Potential output, Y_P

$800

Real GDP (billions of 2009 dollars)

run. At an aggregate price level of 15.0, the quantity of aggregate output supplied is $800 billion in 2009 dollars. If the aggregate price level falls by 50% to 7.5, the quantity of aggregate output supplied is unchanged in the long run at $800 billion in 2009 dollars.

It's important to understand not only that the *LRAS* curve is vertical but also that its position along the horizontal axis represents a significant measure. The horizontal intercept in Figure 12-7, where *LRAS* touches the horizontal axis ($800 billion in 2009 dollars), is the economy's **potential output**, Y_P: the level of real GDP the economy would produce if all prices, including nominal wages, were fully flexible.

In reality, the actual level of real GDP is almost always either above or below potential output. We'll see why later in this chapter, when we discuss the *AD–AS* model. Still, an economy's potential output is an important number because it defines the trend around which actual aggregate output fluctuates from year to year.

In the United States, the Congressional Budget Office, or CBO, estimates annual potential output for the purpose of federal budget analysis. In Figure 12-8, the CBO's estimates of U.S. potential output from 1990 to 2016 are represented by the orange line and the actual values of U.S. real GDP over the same period are represented by the blue line. Years shaded purple on the horizontal axis correspond to periods in which actual aggregate output fell short of potential output; years shaded green correspond to periods in which actual aggregate output exceeded potential output.

As you can see, U.S. potential output has risen steadily over time—implying a series of rightward shifts of the *LRAS* curve. What has caused these rightward shifts? The answer lies in the factors related to long-run growth that we discussed

Potential output is the level of real GDP the economy would produce if all prices, including nominal wages, were fully flexible.

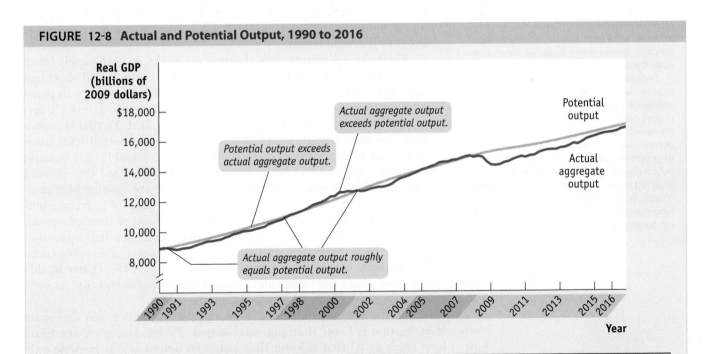

FIGURE 12-8 Actual and Potential Output, 1990 to 2016

This figure shows the performance of actual and potential output in the United States from 1990 to 2016. The orange line shows estimates of U.S. potential output, produced by the Congressional Budget Office, and the blue line shows actual aggregate output. The purple-shaded years are periods in which actual aggregate output fell below potential output, and the years shaded green are periods in which actual aggregate output exceeded potential output. As shown, significant shortfalls occurred in the recessions of the early 1990s and after 2000. Actual aggregate output was significantly above potential output in the boom of the late 1990s, and a huge shortfall occurred after the recession of 2007–2009.

Data from: Congressional Budget Office; Bureau of Economic Analysis; Federal Reserve Bank of St. Louis.

in Chapter 9, such as increases in physical capital and human capital as well as technological progress. Over the long run, as the size of the labor force and the productivity of labor both rise, the level of real GDP that the economy is capable of producing also rises. Indeed, one way to think about long-run economic growth is that it is the growth in the economy's potential output. We generally think of the long-run aggregate supply curve as shifting to the right over time as an economy experiences long-run growth.

From the Short Run to the Long Run

As you can see in Figure 12-8, the economy normally produces more or less than potential output: actual aggregate output was below potential output in the early 1990s, above potential output in the late 1990s, below potential output for most of the 2000s, and significantly below potential output after the recession of 2007–2009. So the economy is normally on its short-run aggregate supply curve—but not on its long-run aggregate supply curve. So why is the long-run curve relevant? Does the economy ever move from the short run to the long run? And if so, how?

The first step to answering these questions is to understand that the economy is always in one of only two states with respect to the short-run and long-run aggregate supply curves. It can be on both curves simultaneously by being at a point where the curves cross (as in the few years in Figure 12-8 in which actual aggregate output and potential output roughly coincided). Or it can be on the short-run aggregate supply curve but not the long-run aggregate supply curve (as in the years in which actual aggregate output and potential output *did not* coincide).

But that is not the end of the story. If the economy is on the short-run but not the long-run aggregate supply curve, the short-run aggregate supply curve will shift over time until the economy is at a point where both curves cross—a point where actual aggregate output is equal to potential output.

Figure 12-9 illustrates how this process works. In both panels *LRAS* is the long-run aggregate supply curve, $SRAS_1$ is the initial short-run aggregate supply curve, and the aggregate price level is at P_1. In panel (a) the economy starts at the initial production point, A_1, which corresponds to a quantity of aggregate output supplied, Y_1, that is higher than potential output, Y_P. Producing an aggregate output level (such as Y_1) that is higher than potential output (Y_P) is possible only because nominal wages haven't yet fully adjusted upward. Until this upward adjustment in nominal wages occurs, producers are earning high profits and producing a high level of output. But a level of aggregate output higher than potential output means a low level of unemployment. Because jobs are abundant and workers are scarce, nominal wages will rise over time, gradually shifting the short-run aggregate supply curve leftward. Eventually it will be in a new position, such as $SRAS_2$. (Later in this chapter, we'll show where the short-run aggregate supply curve ends up. As we'll see, that depends on the aggregate demand curve as well.)

In panel (b), the initial production point, A_1, corresponds to an aggregate output level, Y_1, that is lower than potential output, Y_P. Producing an aggregate output level (such as Y_1) that is lower than potential output (Y_P) is possible only because nominal wages haven't yet fully adjusted downward. Until this downward adjustment occurs, producers are earning low (or negative) profits and producing a low level of output. An aggregate output level lower than potential output means high unemployment. Because workers are abundant and jobs are scarce, nominal wages will fall over time, shifting the short-run aggregate supply curve gradually to the right. Eventually it will be in a new position, such as $SRAS_2$.

We'll see shortly that these shifts of the short-run aggregate supply curve will return the economy to potential output in the long run.

FIGURE 12-9   From the Short Run to the Long Run

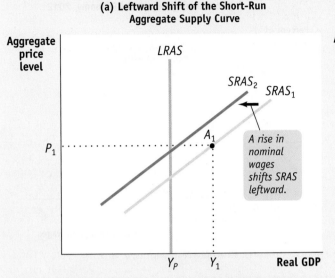

(a) Leftward Shift of the Short-Run Aggregate Supply Curve

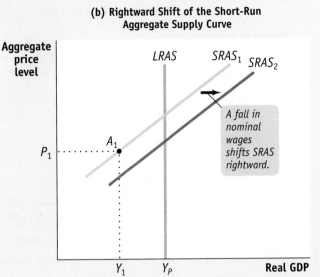

(b) Rightward Shift of the Short-Run Aggregate Supply Curve

In panel (a), the initial short-run aggregate supply curve is $SRAS_1$. At the aggregate price level, P_1, the quantity of aggregate output supplied, Y_1, exceeds potential output, Y_P. Eventually, low unemployment will cause nominal wages to rise, leading to a leftward shift of the short-run aggregate supply

curve from $SRAS_1$ to $SRAS_2$. In panel (b), the reverse happens: at the aggregate price level, P_1, the quantity of aggregate output supplied is less than potential output. High unemployment eventually leads to a fall in nominal wages over time and a rightward shift of the short-run aggregate supply curve.

ECONOMICS >> *in Action*

Sticky Wages in the Great Recession

We've asserted that the aggregate supply curve is upward-sloping in the short run mainly because of *sticky wages*—in particular, because employers are reluctant to cut nominal wages (and workers are unwilling to accept wage cuts) even when labor is in excess supply. But what is the evidence for wage stickiness?

The answer is that we can look at what happens to wages at times when we might have expected to see many workers facing wage cuts because similar workers are unemployed and would be willing to work for less. If wages are sticky, what we would expect to find at such times is that many workers' wages don't change at all: there's no reason for employers to give them a raise, but because wages are sticky, they don't face cuts either.

And that is exactly what you find during and after the Great Recession of 2007–2009. Figure 12-10 shows an especially striking illustration: the case of Portugal, which suffered a severe, prolonged slump starting in 2008, with the unemployment rate peaking at more than 17% in early 2013.

Panel (a) shows the distribution of Portuguese wage changes—the percentage of all workers whose wage went up by a given amount—in prosperous times, namely 1984, when the economy was doing fairly well and there was also significant inflation. As you can see, most workers were getting raises of between 15% and 20%, but they were spread over a significant range. Panel (b), by contrast, shows the distribution of wage changes in 2012, when the Portuguese economy was deeply depressed and inflation was near zero. Under those circumstances you might have expected to see widespread wage cuts. But employers are reluctant to cut wages. So what we saw instead was that most workers' wages, nearly 80%, were completely flat, as shown by the spike you see at zero. That is, because wages were sticky, most wages were neither rising nor falling.

FIGURE 12-10 Distribution Wage Changes in Portugal

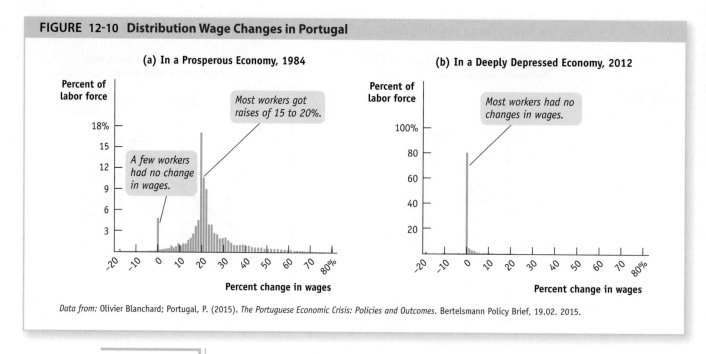

Data from: Olivier Blanchard; Portugal, P. (2015). *The Portuguese Economic Crisis: Policies and Outcomes.* Bertelsmann Policy Brief, 19.02. 2015.

>> *Quick Review*

• The **aggregate supply curve** illustrates the relationship between the aggregate price level and the quantity of aggregate output supplied.

• The **short-run aggregate supply curve** is upward sloping: a higher aggregate price level leads to higher aggregate output given that **nominal wages** are **sticky.**

• Changes in commodity prices, nominal wages, and productivity shift the short-run aggregate supply curve.

• In the long run, all prices are flexible, and changes in the aggregate price level have no effect on aggregate output. The **long-run aggregate supply curve** is vertical at **potential output.**

• If actual aggregate output exceeds potential output, nominal wages eventually rise and the short-run aggregate supply curve shifts leftward. If potential output exceeds actual aggregate output, nominal wages eventually fall and the short-run aggregate supply curve shifts rightward.

In the *AD–AS* **model,** the aggregate supply curve and the aggregate demand curve are used together to analyze economic fluctuations.

>> *Check Your Understanding* **12-2**

Solutions appear at back of book.

1. Determine the effect on short-run aggregate supply for each of the following events. Explain whether it represents a movement along the *SRAS* curve or a shift of the *SRAS* curve.
   a. A rise in the consumer price index (CPI) leads producers to increase output.
   b. A fall in the price of oil leads producers to increase output.
   c. A rise in legally mandated retirement benefits paid to workers leads producers to reduce output.

2. Suppose the economy is initially at potential output and the quantity of aggregate output supplied increases. What information would you need to determine whether this was due to a movement along the *SRAS* curve or a shift of the *LRAS* curve?

The *AD–AS* Model

From 1929 to 1933, the U.S. economy moved down the short-run aggregate supply curve as the aggregate price level fell. In contrast, from 1979 to 1980 the U.S. economy moved up the aggregate demand curve as the aggregate price level rose. In each case, the cause of the movement along the curve was a shift of the other curve. In 1929–1933, it was a leftward shift of the aggregate demand curve—a major fall in consumer spending. In 1979–1980, it was a leftward shift of the short-run aggregate supply curve—a dramatic fall in short-run aggregate supply caused by the surging price of oil. Although the aggregate price level did not fall during the the Great Recession, economists agree that it was caused by a leftward shift of the aggregate demand curve, similar to the 1929–1933 episode.

So to understand the behavior of the economy, we must put the aggregate supply curve and the aggregate demand curve together. The result is the *AD–AS* **model,** the basic model we use to understand economic fluctuations.

Short-Run Macroeconomic Equilibrium

We'll begin our analysis by focusing on the short run. Figure 12-11 shows the aggregate demand curve and the short-run aggregate supply curve on the same diagram. The point at which the *AD* and *SRAS* curves intersect, E_{SR}, is the

FIGURE 12-11 The *AD–AS* Model

The *AD–AS* model combines the aggregate demand curve and the short-run aggregate supply curve. Their point of intersection, E_{SR}, is the point of short-run macroeconomic equilibrium where the quantity of aggregate output demanded is equal to the quantity of aggregate output supplied. P_E is the short-run equilibrium aggregate price level, and Y_E is the short-run equilibrium level of aggregate output.

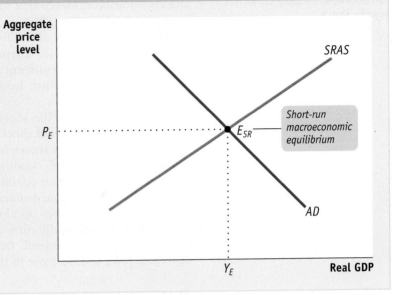

short-run macroeconomic equilibrium: the point at which the quantity of aggregate output supplied is equal to the quantity demanded by domestic households, businesses, the government, and the rest of the world. The aggregate price level at E_{SR}, P_E, is the **short-run equilibrium aggregate price level.** The level of aggregate output at E_{SR}, Y_E, is the **short-run equilibrium aggregate output.**

In the supply and demand model we saw that a shortage of any individual good causes its market price to rise but a surplus of the good causes its market price to fall. These forces ensure that the market reaches equilibrium. The same logic applies to short-run macroeconomic equilibrium. If the aggregate price level is above its equilibrium level, the quantity of aggregate output supplied exceeds the quantity of aggregate output demanded. This leads to a fall in the aggregate price level and pushes it toward its equilibrium level.

If the aggregate price level is below its equilibrium level, the quantity of aggregate output supplied is less than the quantity of aggregate output demanded. This leads to a rise in the aggregate price level, again pushing it toward its equilibrium level. In the discussion that follows, we'll assume that the economy is always in short-run macroeconomic equilibrium.

We'll also make another important simplification based on the observation that in reality there is a long-term upward trend in both aggregate output and the aggregate price level. We'll assume that a fall in either variable really means a fall compared to the long-run trend. For example, if the aggregate price level normally rises 4% per year, a year in which the aggregate price level rises only 3% would count, for our purposes, as a 1% decline. In fact, since the Great Depression there have been very few years in which the aggregate price level of any major nation actually declined—Japan's period of deflation since 1995 is one of the few exceptions. There have, however, been many cases in which the aggregate price level fell relative to the long-run trend.

Short-run equilibrium aggregate output and the short-run equilibrium aggregate price level can change either because of shifts of the *AD* curve or because of shifts of the *SRAS* curve. Let's look at each case in turn.

Shifts of Aggregate Demand: Short-Run Effects

An event that shifts the aggregate demand curve, such as a change in expectations or wealth, the effect of the size of the existing stock of physical capital, or the use of fiscal or monetary policy, is known as a **demand shock.** The Great Depression

The economy is in **short-run macroeconomic equilibrium** when the quantity of aggregate output supplied is equal to the quantity demanded.

The **short-run equilibrium aggregate price level** is the aggregate price level in the short-run macroeconomic equilibrium.

Short-run equilibrium aggregate output is the quantity of aggregate output produced in the short-run macroeconomic equilibrium.

An event that shifts the aggregate demand curve is a **demand shock.**

An event that shifts the short-run aggregate supply curve is a **supply shock.**

was caused by a negative demand shock, the collapse of wealth and of business and consumer confidence that followed the stock market crash of 1929 and the banking crisis of 1930–1931.

The Depression was ended by a positive demand shock—the huge increase in government purchases during World War II. In 2008 the U.S. economy experienced another significant negative demand shock as the housing market turned from boom to bust, leading consumers and firms to scale back their spending.

Figure 12-12 shows the short-run effects of negative and positive demand shocks. A negative demand shock shifts the aggregate demand curve, *AD*, to the left, from AD_1 to AD_2, as shown in panel (a). The economy moves down along the *SRAS* curve from E_1 to E_2, leading to lower short-run equilibrium aggregate output and a lower short-run equilibrium aggregate price level. A positive demand shock shifts the aggregate demand curve, *AD*, to the right, as shown in panel (b). Here, the economy moves up along the *SRAS* curve, from E_1 to E_2. This leads to higher short-run equilibrium aggregate output and a higher short-run equilibrium aggregate price level. Demand shocks cause aggregate output and the aggregate price level to move in the same direction.

Shifts of the *SRAS* Curve

An event that shifts the short-run aggregate supply curve, such as a change in commodity prices, nominal wages, or productivity, is known as a **supply shock.** A *negative* supply shock raises production costs and reduces the quantity producers are willing to supply at any given aggregate price level, leading to a leftward shift of the short-run aggregate supply curve. The U.S. economy experienced severe negative supply shocks following disruptions to world oil supplies in 1973 and 1979.

In contrast, a *positive* supply shock reduces production costs and increases the quantity supplied at any given aggregate price level, leading to a rightward shift of the short-run aggregate supply curve. The United States experienced a

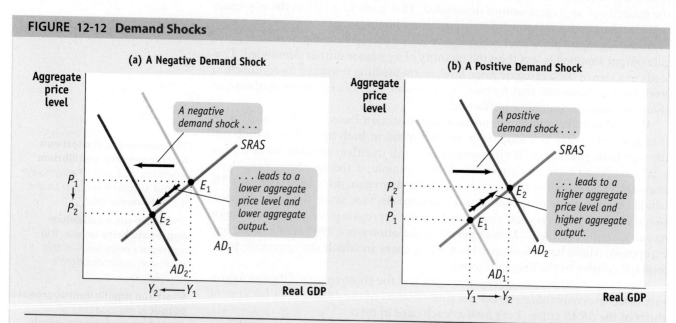

FIGURE 12-12 Demand Shocks

(a) A Negative Demand Shock

Aggregate price level / Real GDP

A negative demand shock . . .

SRAS

. . . leads to a lower aggregate price level and lower aggregate output.

E_1
E_2
P_1
P_2
AD_1
AD_2
$Y_2 \longleftarrow Y_1$

(b) A Positive Demand Shock

Aggregate price level / Real GDP

A positive demand shock . . .

SRAS

. . . leads to a higher aggregate price level and higher aggregate output.

E_2
E_1
P_2
P_1
AD_2
AD_1
$Y_1 \longrightarrow Y_2$

A demand shock shifts the aggregate demand curve, moving the aggregate price level and aggregate output in the same direction. In panel (a), a negative demand shock shifts the aggregate demand curve leftward from AD_1 to AD_2, reducing the aggregate price level from P_1 to P_2 and aggregate output from Y_1 to Y_2. In panel (b), a positive demand shock shifts the aggregate demand curve rightward, increasing the aggregate price level from P_1 to P_2 and aggregate output from Y_1 to Y_2.

positive supply shock between 1995 and 2000, when the increasing use of the internet and other information technologies caused productivity growth to surge.

The effects of a negative supply shock are shown in panel (a) of Figure 12-13. The initial equilibrium is at E_1, with aggregate price level P_1 and aggregate output Y_1. The disruption in the oil supply causes the short-run aggregate supply curve to shift to the left, from $SRAS_1$ to $SRAS_2$. As a consequence, aggregate output falls and the aggregate price level rises, an upward movement along the AD curve. At the new equilibrium, E_2, the short-run equilibrium aggregate price level, P_2, is higher, and the short-run equilibrium aggregate output level, Y_2, is lower than before.

The combination of inflation and falling aggregate output shown in panel (a) has a special name: **stagflation,** for "stagnation plus inflation." Stagflation is unpleasant: falling aggregate output leads to rising unemployment, while the purchasing power of consumers is squeezed by rising prices. Stagflation in the 1970s created a mood of economic pessimism, and deeply affected those who lived through it, like Jean-Claude Trichet. It also, as we'll see, poses a dilemma for policy makers.

A positive supply shock, shown in panel (b), has exactly the opposite effects. A rightward shift of the $SRAS$ curve from $SRAS_1$ to $SRAS_2$ results in a rise in aggregate output and a fall in the aggregate price level, a downward movement along the AD curve. The favorable supply shocks of the late 1990s led to a combination of full employment and declining inflation. That is, the aggregate price level fell compared with the long-run trend. This combination produced, for a time, a great wave of national optimism.

The distinctive feature of supply shocks, both negative and positive, is that, unlike demand shocks, they cause the aggregate price level and aggregate output to move in *opposite* directions.

There's another important contrast between supply shocks and demand shocks. As we've seen, monetary policy and fiscal policy enable the government to shift the AD curve, meaning that governments are in a position to create the

Stagflation is the combination of inflation and falling aggregate output.

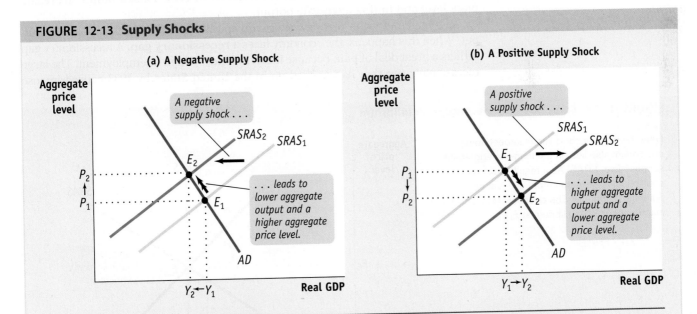

FIGURE 12-13   Supply Shocks

(a) A Negative Supply Shock

A negative supply shock . . .

$SRAS_2$ $SRAS_1$

. . . leads to lower aggregate output and a higher aggregate price level.

AD

$Y_2 \leftarrow Y_1$ Real GDP

(b) A Positive Supply Shock

A positive supply shock . . .

$SRAS_1$ $SRAS_2$

. . . leads to higher aggregate output and a lower aggregate price level.

AD

$Y_1 \rightarrow Y_2$ Real GDP

A supply shock shifts the short-run aggregate supply curve, moving the aggregate price level and aggregate output in opposite directions. Panel (a) shows a negative supply shock, which shifts the short-run aggregate supply curve leftward and causes *stagflation*—lower aggregate output and a higher aggregate price level. Here the short-run aggregate supply curve shifts from $SRAS_1$ to $SRAS_2$, and the economy moves from E_1 to E_2. The

aggregate price level rises from P_1 to P_2, and aggregate output falls from Y_1 to Y_2. Panel (b) shows a positive supply shock, which shifts the short-run aggregate supply curve rightward, generating higher aggregate output and a lower aggregate price level. The short-run aggregate supply curve shifts from $SRAS_1$ to $SRAS_2$, and the economy moves from E_1 to E_2. The aggregate price level falls from P_1 to P_2, and aggregate output rises from Y_1 to Y_2.

The economy is in **long-run macroeconomic equilibrium** when the point of short-run macroeconomic equilibrium is on the long-run aggregate supply curve.

There is a **recessionary gap** when aggregate output is below potential output.

kinds of shocks shown in Figure 12-12. It's much harder for governments to shift the *AS* curve. Are there good policy reasons to shift the *AD* curve? We'll turn to that question soon. First, however, let's look at the difference between short-run macroeconomic equilibrium and *long-run macroeconomic equilibrium*.

Long-Run Macroeconomic Equilibrium

Figure 12-14 combines the aggregate demand curve with both the short-run and long-run aggregate supply curves. The aggregate demand curve, *AD*, crosses the short-run aggregate supply curve, *SRAS*, at E_{LR}. Here we assume that enough time has elapsed that the economy is also on the long-run aggregate supply curve, *LRAS*. As a result, E_{LR} is at the intersection of all three curves—*SRAS*, *LRAS*, and *AD*. So short-run equilibrium aggregate output is equal to potential output, Y_P. Such a situation, in which the point of short-run macroeconomic equilibrium is on the long-run aggregate supply curve, is known as **long-run macroeconomic equilibrium.**

To see the significance of long-run macroeconomic equilibrium, let's consider what happens if a demand shock moves the economy away from long-run macroeconomic equilibrium. In Figure 12-15, we assume that the initial aggregate demand curve is AD_1 and the initial short-run aggregate supply curve is $SRAS_1$. So the initial macroeconomic equilibrium is at E_1, which lies on the long-run aggregate supply curve, *LRAS*. The economy, then, starts from a point of short-run and long-run macroeconomic equilibrium, and short-run equilibrium aggregate output equals potential output at Y_1.

Now suppose that for some reason—such as a sudden worsening of business and consumer expectations—aggregate demand falls and the aggregate demand curve shifts leftward to AD_2. This results in a lower equilibrium aggregate price level at P_2 and a lower equilibrium aggregate output level at Y_2 as the economy settles in the short run at E_2. The short-run effect of such a fall in aggregate demand is what the U.S. economy experienced in 1929–1933: a falling aggregate price level and falling aggregate output.

Aggregate output in this new short-run equilibrium, E_2, is below potential output. When this happens, the economy faces a **recessionary gap.** A recessionary gap inflicts a great deal of pain because it corresponds to high unemployment. The large recessionary gap that had opened up in the United States by 1933 caused intense

FIGURE 12-14 Long-Run Macroeconomic Equilibrium

Here the point of short-run macroeconomic equilibrium also lies on the long-run aggregate supply curve, *LRAS*. As a result, short-run equilibrium aggregate output is equal to potential output, Y_P. The economy is in long-run macroeconomic equilibrium at E_{LR}.

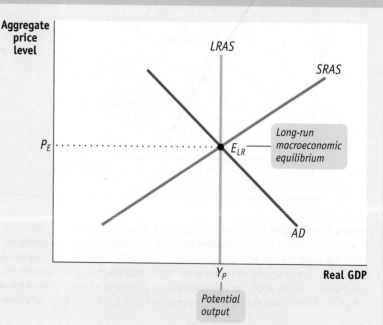

FIGURE 12-15 Short-Run versus Long-Run Effects of a Negative Demand Shock

In the long run the economy is self-correcting: demand shocks have only a short-run effect on aggregate output. Starting at E_1, a negative demand shock shifts AD_1 leftward to AD_2. In the short run the economy moves to E_2 and a recessionary gap arises: the aggregate price level declines from P_1 to P_2, aggregate output declines from Y_1 to Y_2, and unemployment rises. But in the long run nominal wages fall in response to high unemployment at Y_2, and $SRAS_1$ shifts rightward to $SRAS_2$. Aggregate output rises from Y_2 to Y_1, and the aggregate price level declines again, from P_2 to P_3. Long-run macroeconomic equilibrium is eventually restored at E_3.

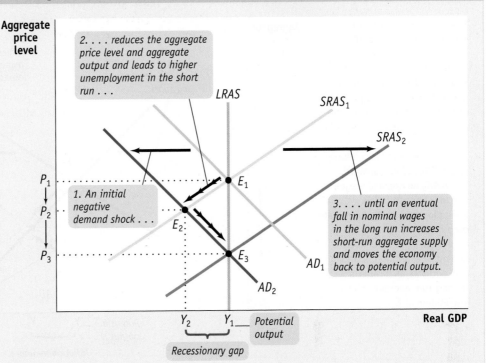

social and political turmoil. And the devastating recessionary gap that opened up in Germany at the same time played an important role in Hitler's rise to power.

But this isn't the end of the story. In the face of high unemployment, nominal wages eventually fall, as do any other sticky prices, ultimately leading producers to increase output. As a result, a recessionary gap causes the short-run aggregate supply curve to gradually shift to the right over time. This process continues until $SRAS_1$ reaches its new position at $SRAS_2$, bringing the economy to equilibrium at E_3, where AD_2, $SRAS_2$, and $LRAS$ all intersect. At E_3, the economy is back in long-run macroeconomic equilibrium; it is back at potential output Y_1 but at a lower aggregate price level, P_3, reflecting a long-run fall in the aggregate price level. In the end, the economy is *self-correcting* in the long run.

What if, instead, there was an increase in aggregate demand? The results are shown in Figure 12-16, where we again assume that the initial aggregate demand curve is AD_1 and the initial short-run aggregate supply curve is $SRAS_1$, so that the initial macroeconomic equilibrium, at E_1, lies on the long-run aggregate supply curve, $LRAS$. Initially, then, the economy is in long-run macroeconomic equilibrium.

FOR INQUIRING MINDS   Where's the Deflation?

The *AD–AS* model says that either a negative demand shock or a positive supply shock should lead to a fall in the aggregate price level—that is, deflation. However, since 1949, an actual fall in the aggregate price level has been a rare occurrence in the United States. Similarly, most other countries have had little or no experience with deflation. Japan, which experienced sustained mild deflation in the late 1990s and the early part of the next decade, is

the big (and much discussed) exception. What happened to deflation?

The basic answer is that since World War II economic fluctuations have largely taken place around a long-run inflationary trend. Before the war, it was common for prices to fall during recessions, but since then negative demand shocks have largely been reflected in a *decline in the rate of inflation* rather than an actual fall in prices. For example, the rate of consumer price

inflation fell from more than 3% at the beginning of the 2001 recession to 1.1% a year later, but it never went below zero.

All of this changed during the recession of 2007–2009. The negative demand shock that followed the 2008 financial crisis was so severe that, for most of 2009, consumer prices in the United States indeed fell. But the deflationary period didn't last long: beginning in 2010, prices again rose, at a rate of between 1% and 4% per year.

FIGURE 12-16 Short-Run versus Long-Run Effects of a Positive Demand Shock

Starting at E_1, a positive demand shock shifts AD_1 rightward to AD_2, and the economy moves to E_2 in the short run. This results in an inflationary gap as aggregate output rises from Y_1 to Y_2, the aggregate price level rises from P_1 to P_2, and unemployment falls to a low level. In the long run, $SRAS_1$ shifts leftward to $SRAS_2$ as nominal wages rise in response to low unemployment at Y_2. Aggregate output falls back to Y_1, the aggregate price level rises again to P_3, and the economy self-corrects as it returns to long-run macroeconomic equilibrium at E_3.

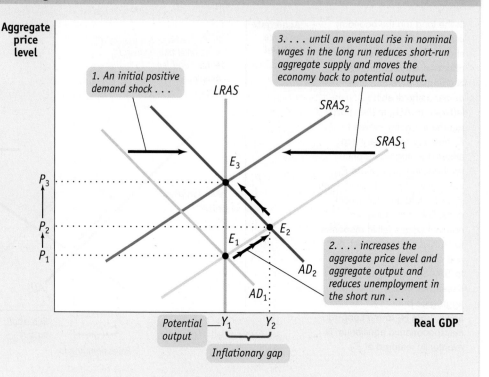

1. An initial positive demand shock . . .

3. . . . until an eventual rise in nominal wages in the long run reduces short-run aggregate supply and moves the economy back to potential output.

2. . . . increases the aggregate price level and aggregate output and reduces unemployment in the short run . . .

Now suppose that aggregate demand rises, and the AD curve shifts rightward to AD_2. This results in a higher aggregate price level, at P_2, and a higher aggregate output level, at Y_2, as the economy settles in the short run at E_2. Aggregate output in this new short-run equilibrium is above potential output, and unemployment is low in order to produce this higher level of aggregate output. When this happens, the economy experiences an **inflationary gap.**

As in the case of a recessionary gap, the story doesn't end here. In the face of low unemployment, nominal wages will rise, as will other sticky prices. An inflationary gap causes the short-run aggregate supply curve to shift gradually to the left as producers reduce output in the face of rising nominal wages. This process continues until $SRAS_1$ reaches its new position at $SRAS_2$, bringing the economy to equilibrium at E_3, where AD_2, $SRAS_2$, and $LRAS$ all intersect. At E_3, the economy is back in long-run macroeconomic equilibrium. It is back at potential output, but at a higher price level, P_3, reflecting a long-run rise in the aggregate price level. Again, the economy is self-correcting in the long run.

To summarize the analysis of how the economy responds to recessionary and inflationary gaps, we can focus on the **output gap,** the percentage difference between actual aggregate output and potential output. The output gap is calculated as follows:

There is an **inflationary gap** when aggregate output is above potential output.

The **output gap** is the percentage difference between actual aggregate output and potential output.

The economy is **self-correcting** when shocks to aggregate demand affect aggregate output in the short run, but not the long run.

(12-3) $\text{Output gap} = \dfrac{\text{Actual aggregate output} - \text{Potential output}}{\text{Potential output}} \times 100$

Our analysis says that the output gap always tends toward zero.

If there is a recessionary gap, so that the output gap is negative, nominal wages eventually fall, moving the economy back to potential output and bringing the output gap back to zero. If there is an inflationary gap, so that the output gap is positive, nominal wages eventually rise, also moving the economy back to potential output and again bringing the output gap back to zero. So in the long run the economy is **self-correcting:** shocks to aggregate demand affect aggregate output in the short run but not the long run.

ECONOMICS >> *in Action* 🌐

Supply Shocks versus Demand Shocks in Practice

How often do supply shocks and demand shocks, respectively, cause recessions? The verdict of most, though not all, macroeconomists is that recessions are mainly caused by demand shocks. But when a negative supply shock does happen, the resulting recession tends to be particularly severe.

Let's get specific. Officially there have been twelve recessions in the United States since World War II. However, two of these, in 1979–1980 and 1981–1982, are often treated as a single *double-dip recession* (that is, a recession followed by a temporary recovery, then followed by another recession), bringing the total number down to eleven. Of these eleven recessions, only two—the recession of 1973–1975 and the double-dip recession of 1979–1982—showed the distinctive combination of falling aggregate output and a surge in the price level that we call stagflation. In each case, the cause of the supply shock was political turmoil in the Middle East—the Arab–Israeli war of 1973 and the Iranian revolution of 1979—that disrupted world oil supplies and sent oil prices skyrocketing. In fact, economists sometimes refer to the two slumps as "OPEC I" and "OPEC II," after the Organization of Petroleum Exporting Countries, the world oil cartel. A third recession that began in 2007 and lasted until 2009 was at least partially exacerbated, if not at least partially caused, by a spike in oil prices.

So eight of eleven postwar recessions were purely the result of demand shocks, not supply shocks. The few supply-shock recessions, however, were the worst as measured by the unemployment rate. Figure 12-17 shows the U.S. unemployment rate since 1948, with the dates of the 1973 Arab–Israeli war and the 1979 Iranian revolution marked on the graph. Some of the highest unemployment rates since World War II came after these big negative supply shocks.

There's a reason the aftermath of a supply shock tends to be particularly severe for the economy: macroeconomic policy has a much harder time dealing with supply shocks than with demand shocks. We'll see in a moment why supply shocks present such a problem.

>> Check Your Understanding 12-3

Solutions appear at back of book.

1. Describe the short-run effects of each of the following shocks on the aggregate price level and on aggregate output.
   a. The government sharply increases the minimum wage, raising the wages of many workers.
   b. Solar energy firms launch a major program of investment spending.
   c. Congress raises taxes and cuts spending.
   d. Severe weather destroys crops around the world.

2. A rise in productivity increases potential output, but some worry that demand for the additional output will be insufficient even in the long run. How would you respond?

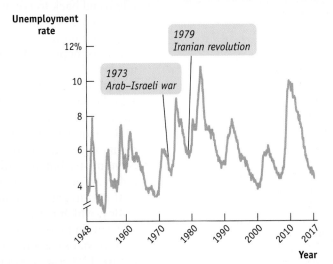

FIGURE 12-17   Negative Supply Shocks Are Relatively Rare but Nasty

Data from: Bureau of Labor Statistics; Federal Reserve Bank of St Louis.

>> *Quick Review*

• The **AD–AS model** is used to study economic fluctuations.

• **Short-run macroeconomic equilibrium** occurs at the intersection of the short-run aggregate supply and aggregate demand curves. This determines the **short-run equilibrium aggregate price level** and the level of **short-run equilibrium aggregate output.**

• A **demand shock,** a shift of the *AD* curve, causes the aggregate price level and aggregate output to move in the same direction. A **supply shock,** a shift of the *SRAS* curve, causes them to move in opposite directions. **Stagflation** is the consequence of a negative supply shock.

• A fall in nominal wages occurs in response to a **recessionary gap,** and a rise in nominal wages occurs in response to an **inflationary gap.** Both move the economy to **long-run macroeconomic equilibrium,** where the *AD, SRAS,* and *LRAS* curves intersect.

• The **output gap** always tends toward zero because the economy is **self-correcting** in the long run.

Stabilization policy is the use of government policy to reduce the severity of recessions and rein in excessively strong expansions.

Macroeconomic Policy

We've just seen that the economy is self-correcting in the long run: it will eventually trend back to potential output. Most macroeconomists believe, however, that the process of self-correction typically takes a decade or more. In particular, if aggregate output is below potential output, the economy can suffer an extended period of depressed aggregate output and high unemployment before it returns to normal.

This belief is the background to one of the most famous quotations in economics: John Maynard Keynes's declaration, "In the long run we are all dead." We explain the context in which he made this remark in the upcoming For Inquiring Minds.

Economists usually interpret Keynes as having recommended that governments not wait for the economy to correct itself. Instead, it is argued by many economists, but not all, that the government should use monetary and fiscal policy to get the economy back to potential output in the aftermath of a shift of the aggregate demand curve. This is the rationale for an active **stabilization policy,** which is the use of government policy to reduce the severity of recessions and rein in excessively strong expansions.

Can stabilization policy improve the economy's performance? If we reexamine Figure 12-8, the answer certainly appears to be yes. Under active stabilization policy, the U.S. economy returned to potential output in 1996 after an approximately five-year recessionary gap. Likewise, in 2001 it also returned to potential output after an approximately four-year inflationary gap. These periods are much shorter than the decade or more that economists believe it would take for the economy to self-correct in the absence of active stabilization policy. In fact, recovery from the Great Recession took longer—seven years—partly because of political constraints on fiscal policy. And recovery would have taken even longer if Ben Bernanke had not undertaken strongly expansionary monetary policy, as recounted in the opening story. However, as we'll see shortly, the ability to improve the economy's performance is not always guaranteed. It depends on the kinds of shocks the economy faces.

Policy in the Face of Demand Shocks

Imagine that the economy experiences a negative demand shock, like the one shown in Figure 12-15. As we've discussed in this chapter, monetary and fiscal policy shift the aggregate demand curve. If policy makers react quickly to the fall in aggregate demand, they can use monetary or fiscal policy to shift the aggregate

---

FOR INQUIRING MINDS **Keynes and the Long Run**

The British economist Sir John Maynard Keynes (1883–1946), probably more than any other single economist, created the modern field of macroeconomics. We'll look at his role, and the controversies that still swirl around some aspects of his thought, in a later chapter on macroeconomic events and ideas. But for now let's just look at his most famous quote.

In 1923 Keynes published *A Tract on Monetary Reform,* a small book on the economic problems of Europe after World War I. In it he decried the tendency of many of his colleagues to focus on

how things work out in the long run—as in the long-run macroeconomic equilibrium we have just analyzed—while ignoring the often very painful and possibly disastrous things that can happen along the way. Here's a fuller version of the quote:

This long run is a misleading guide to current affairs. In the long run we are all dead. Economists set themselves too easy, too useless a task if in tempestuous seasons they can only tell us that when the storm is long past the sea is flat again.

Bettmann/Getty Images

Keynes focused the attention of economists of his day on the short run.

demand curve back to the right. And if policy were able to perfectly anticipate shifts of the aggregate demand curve, it could short-circuit the whole process shown in Figure 12-15. Instead of going through a period of low aggregate output and falling prices, the government could manage the economy so that it would stay at E_1.

Why might a policy that short-circuits the adjustment shown in Figure 12-15 and maintains the economy at its original equilibrium be desirable? For two reasons.

1. The temporary fall in aggregate output that would happen without policy intervention is a bad thing, particularly because such a decline is associated with high unemployment.

2. As explained in Chapter 8, price stability is generally regarded as a desirable goal. So preventing deflation—a fall in the aggregate price level—is a good thing.

Does this mean that policy makers should always act to offset declines in aggregate demand? Not necessarily. As we'll see in later chapters, some policy measures to increase aggregate demand, especially those that increase budget deficits, may have long-term costs in terms of lower long-run growth. Furthermore, in the real world policy makers aren't perfectly informed, and the effects of their policies aren't perfectly predictable. This creates the danger that stabilization policy will do more harm than good; that is, attempts to stabilize the economy may end up creating more instability. We'll describe the long-running debate over macroeconomic policy in Chapter 17. Despite these qualifications, most economists believe that a good case can be made for using macroeconomic policy to offset major negative shocks to the *AD* curve.

Should policy makers also try to offset positive shocks to aggregate demand? It may not seem obvious that they should. After all, even though inflation may be a bad thing, isn't more output and lower unemployment a good thing? Not necessarily.

Most economists now believe that any short-run gains from an inflationary gap must be paid back later. So policy makers today usually try to offset positive as well as negative demand shocks. For reasons we'll explain in Chapter 15, attempts to eliminate recessionary gaps and inflationary gaps usually rely on monetary rather than fiscal policy. In 2007 and 2008 the Federal Reserve sharply cut interest rates in an attempt to head off a rising recessionary gap; earlier in the decade, when the U.S. economy seemed headed for an inflationary gap, it raised interest rates to generate the opposite effect.

But how should macroeconomic policy respond to supply shocks?

Responding to Supply Shocks

Back in panel (a) of Figure 12-13 we showed the effects of a negative supply shock: in the short run such a shock leads to lower aggregate output but a higher aggregate price level. As we've noted, policy makers can respond to a negative *demand* shock by using monetary and fiscal policy to return aggregate demand to its original level. But what can or should they do about a negative *supply* shock?

In contrast to the aggregate demand curve, there are no easy policies that shift the short-run aggregate supply curve. That is, there is no government policy that can easily affect producers' profitability and so compensate for shifts of the short-run aggregate supply curve. So the policy response to a negative supply shock cannot aim to simply push the curve that shifted back to its original position.

And if you consider using monetary or fiscal policy to shift the aggregate demand curve in response to a supply shock, the right response isn't obvious. Two bad things are happening simultaneously: a fall in aggregate output, leading to a rise in unemployment, *and* a rise in the aggregate price level. Any policy that shifts the aggregate demand curve helps one problem only by making the other worse. If the government acts to increase aggregate demand and limit the rise in unemployment, it reduces the decline in output but causes even more inflation. If it acts to reduce aggregate demand, it curbs inflation but causes a further rise in unemployment.

It's a trade-off with no good answer. In the end, the United States and other economically advanced nations suffering from the supply shocks of the 1970s eventually chose to stabilize prices even at the cost of higher unemployment. This was the same policy that Jean-Claude Trichet adopted in 2011, when he chose to forgo expansionary monetary policy after he mistook a temporary blip in oil prices as a supply shock.

ECONOMICS >> *in Action*
Is Stabilization Policy Stabilizing?

We've described the theoretical rationale for stabilization policy as a way of responding to demand shocks. But does stabilization policy actually stabilize the economy? We can try to answer this question by looking at the long-term historical record.

Before World War II, the U.S. government didn't really have a stabilization policy, largely because macroeconomics as we know it didn't exist, and there was no consensus about what to do. Since World War II, and especially since 1960, active stabilization policy has become standard practice.

So, has the economy actually become more stable since the government began trying to stabilize it? The answer is a qualified yes. It's qualified for two reasons. One is that data from the pre–World War II era are less reliable than modern data. The other is that the severe and protracted slump that began in 2007 has shaken confidence in the effectiveness of government policy. Still, there seems to have been a reduction in the size of fluctuations.

Figure 12-18 shows the number of unemployed as a percentage of the nonfarm labor force since 1890. (We focus on nonfarm workers because farmers, though they often suffer economic hardship, are rarely reported as unemployed.) Even ignoring the huge spike in unemployment during the Great Depression, unemployment seems to have varied a lot more before World War II than after. It's also worth noticing that the peaks in postwar unemployment, in 1975, 1982, and to some extent in 2010, corresponded to major supply shocks—the kind of shock for which stabilization policy has no good answer.

It's possible that the greater stability of the economy reflects good luck rather than policy. But on the face of it, the evidence suggests that stabilization policy is indeed stabilizing.

FIGURE 12-18 Has Stabilization Policy Been Stabilizing?

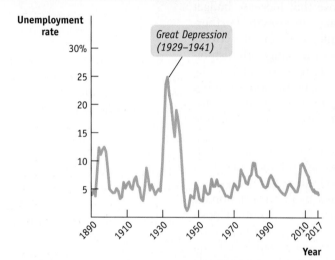

Data from: Christina Romer, "Spurious Volatility in Historical Unemployment Data." *Journal of Political Economy* 94, no. 1 (1986): 1–37 (years 1890–1928); Bureau of Labor Statistics (years 1929–2017).

>> Quick Review

• **Stabilization policy** is the use of fiscal or monetary policy to offset demand shocks. There can be drawbacks, however. Such policies may lead to a long-term rise in the budget deficit and lower long-run growth because of crowding out. And, due to incorrect predictions, a misguided policy can increase economic instability.

• Negative supply shocks pose a policy dilemma because fighting the slump in aggregate output worsens inflation and fighting inflation worsens the slump.

>> Check Your Understanding 12-4
Solutions appear at back of book.

1. Suppose someone says, "Using monetary or fiscal policy to pump up the economy is counterproductive—you get a brief high, but then you have the pain of inflation."
   a. Explain what this means in terms of the *AD–AS* model.
   b. Is this a valid argument against stabilization policy? Why or why not?

2. In 2008, in the aftermath of the collapse of the housing bubble and a sharp rise in the price of commodities, particularly oil, there was much internal disagreement within the Fed about how to respond, with some advocating lowering interest rates and others contending that this would set off a rise in inflation. Explain the reasoning behind each one of these views in terms of the *AD–AS* model.

Toyota Makes Its Move

If you or someone you know bought a new car recently, the odds are pretty good that it was manufactured by one of two Japanese companies, Toyota or Honda. Together, these companies account for about a quarter of total passenger car sales. But this was not always the case. In 1973, the two companies accounted for a mere 2.6% of U.S. auto sales. Over the course of the 1970s and early 1980s, the Japanese share quadrupled. Why?

Toyota did a lot of things right: during the 1960s it had perfected the technique of so-called *just-in-time production* or *lean manufacturing*, a production system that yielded lower costs, higher productivity, and higher quality compared to American production techniques. (You may recall our discussion of lean production in the Chapter 2 Business Case.)

But Toyota was lucky as well. During the 1970s, Americans began to switch from enormous sedans to smaller cars, a market that American car companies had neglected. The few choices they did offer were of poor quality, and included the AMC Gremlin and Ford Pinto, among others. In contrast, Toyota, having long produced small, reliable, fuel-efficient cars for Japan, its home market, was ready to fill the gap.

But why the shift to smaller, fuel-efficient cars? One answer is that the United States experienced a series of severe recessions, which could have induced consumers to seek cheaper alternatives to traditional big cars. As it turns out, however, other recessions have not led to major downsizing in car purchases. Figure 12-19 shows the average number of miles per gallon for new passenger cars since 1975, which has generally trended upward, but increased at a much faster rate in the mid to late 1970s and early 1980s, before stabilizing in the early 1990s—this despite the fact that many consumers were buying more fuel efficient cars at that time. And, as you can see, there was only a slight increase in average mileage after 2007, even though the Great Recession that began that year was deeper and more prolonged than any slump since the 1930s.

So what was different in the 1970s? At that time, two bad things were happening: unemployment was rising sharply, but so was the price of gasoline. After 2007, as unemployment soared, gas prices fluctuated but eventually came down to levels well below those before the recession. So people bought fewer cars, but not, by and large, smaller cars.

The point is that Toyota got its big break not just by producing good cars, but also by producing the particular kind of good car that suited consumers during the economic troubles of the 1970s.

QUESTIONS FOR THOUGHT

1. Why do you think gas prices rose in the recessions of the 1970s but fell after the Great Recession?

2. What does this say about the causes of the recessions in each case?

3. In the 1970s, Toyota was able to increase its American sales despite interest rates on auto loans surging as high as 17.5%. In contrast, after 2007, auto loan rates fell to their lowest levels in history; car sales also declined. Explain why. (*Hint:* Examine the connection between inflation and interest rates on loans.)

FIGURE 12-19 Average Miles per Gallon for New Cars, 1975–2016

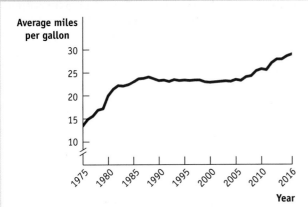

Data from: Environmental Protection Agency.

SUMMARY

1. The **aggregate demand curve** shows the relationship between the aggregate price level and the quantity of aggregate output demanded.

2. The aggregate demand curve is downward sloping for two reasons. The first is the **wealth effect of a change in the aggregate price level**—a higher aggregate price level reduces the purchasing power of households' wealth and reduces consumer spending. The second is the **interest rate effect of a change in the aggregate price level**—a higher aggregate price level reduces the purchasing power of households' and firms' money holdings, leading to a rise in interest rates and a fall in investment spending and consumer spending.

3. The aggregate demand curve shifts because of changes in expectations, changes in wealth not due to changes in the aggregate price level, and the effect of the size of the existing stock of physical capital. Policy makers can use fiscal policy and monetary policy to shift the aggregate demand curve.

4. The **aggregate supply curve** shows the relationship between the aggregate price level and the quantity of aggregate output supplied.

5. The **short-run aggregate supply curve** is upward sloping because **nominal wages** are **sticky** in the short run: a higher aggregate price level leads to higher profit per unit of output and increased aggregate output in the short run.

6. Changes in commodity prices, nominal wages, and productivity lead to changes in producers' profits and shift the short-run aggregate supply curve.

7. In the long run, all prices, including nominal wages, are flexible and the economy produces at its **potential output.** If actual aggregate output exceeds potential output, nominal wages will eventually rise in response to low unemployment and aggregate output will fall. If potential output exceeds actual aggregate output, nominal wages will eventually fall in response to high unemployment and aggregate output will rise. So the **long-run aggregate supply curve** is vertical at potential output.

8. In the **AD–AS model,** the intersection of the short-run aggregate supply curve and the aggregate demand curve is the point of **short-run macroeconomic equilibrium.** It determines the **short-run equilibrium aggregate price level** and the level of **short-run equilibrium aggregate output.**

9. Economic fluctuations occur because of a shift of the aggregate demand curve (a *demand shock*) or the short-run aggregate supply curve (a *supply shock*). A **demand shock** causes the aggregate price level and aggregate output to move in the same direction as the economy moves along the short-run aggregate supply curve. A **supply shock** causes them to move in opposite directions as the economy moves along the aggregate demand curve. A particularly nasty occurrence is **stagflation**—inflation and falling aggregate output—which is caused by a negative supply shock.

10. Demand shocks have only short-run effects on aggregate output because the economy is **self-correcting** in the long run. In a **recessionary gap,** an eventual fall in nominal wages moves the economy to **long-run macroeconomic equilibrium,** where aggregate output is equal to potential output. In an **inflationary gap,** an eventual rise in nominal wages moves the economy to long-run macroeconomic equilibrium. We can use the **output gap,** the percentage difference between actual aggregate output and potential output, to summarize how the economy responds to recessionary and inflationary gaps. Because the economy tends to be self-correcting in the long run, the output gap always tends toward zero.

11. The high cost—in terms of unemployment—of a recessionary gap and the future adverse consequences of an inflationary gap lead many economists to advocate active **stabilization policy:** using fiscal or monetary policy to offset demand shocks. There can be drawbacks, however, because such policies may contribute to a long-term rise in the budget deficit and crowding out of private investment, leading to lower long-run growth. Also, poorly timed policies can increase economic instability.

12. Negative supply shocks pose a policy dilemma: a policy that counteracts the fall in aggregate output by increasing aggregate demand will lead to higher inflation, but a policy that counteracts inflation by reducing aggregate demand will deepen the output slump.

KEY TERMS

PROBLEMS

interactive activity

1. A fall in the value of the dollar against other curren-cies makes U.S. final goods and services cheaper to foreigners even though the U.S. aggregate price level stays the same. As a result, foreigners demand more American aggregate output. Your study partner says that this represents a movement down the aggregate demand curve because foreigners are demanding more in response to a lower price. You, however, insist that this represents a rightward shift of the aggregate demand curve. Who is right? Explain.

2. Your study partner is confused by the upward-sloping short-run aggregate supply curve and the vertical long-run aggregate supply curve. How would you explain this?

3. Suppose that in Wageland all workers sign annual wage contracts each year on January 1. No matter what happens to prices of final goods and services during the year, all workers earn the wage specified in their annual contract. This year, prices of final goods and services fall unexpectedly after the contracts are signed. Answer the following questions using a diagram and assume that the economy starts at potential output.

   a. In the short run, how will the quantity of aggregate output supplied respond to the fall in prices?

   b. What will happen when firms and workers renegoti-ate their wages?

4. The economy is at point *A* in the accompanying dia-gram. Suppose that the aggregate price level rises from P_1 to P_2. How will aggregate supply adjust in the short run and in the long run to the increase in the aggregate price level? Illustrate with a diagram.

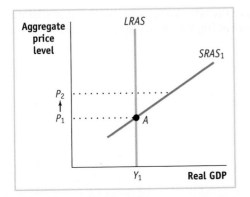

5. Suppose that all households hold all their wealth in assets that automatically rise in value when the aggregate price level rises (an example of this is what is called an "inflation-indexed bond"—a bond whose interest rate, among other things, changes one-for-one with the inflation rate). What happens to the wealth effect of a change in the aggregate price level as a result of this allocation of assets? What happens to the slope of the aggregate demand curve? Will it still slope downward? Explain.

6. Suppose that the economy is currently at potential output. Also suppose that you are an economic policy maker and that a college economics student asks you to rank, if possible, your most preferred to least pre-ferred type of shock: positive demand shock, negative demand shock, positive supply shock, negative supply shock. How would you rank them and why?

7. Explain whether the following government policies affect the aggregate demand curve or the short-run aggregate supply curve and how.

   a. The government reduces the minimum nominal wage.

   b. The government increases Temporary Assistance to Needy Families (TANF) payments, government transfers to families with dependent children.

   c. To reduce the budget deficit, the government announces that households will pay much higher taxes beginning next year.

   d. The government reduces military spending.

8. In Wageland, all workers sign annual wage contracts each year on January 1. In late January, a new com-puter operating system is introduced that increases labor productivity dramatically. Explain how Wage-land will move from one short-run macroeconomic equilibrium to another. Illustrate with a diagram.

9. The Conference Board publishes the Consumer Con-fidence Index (CCI) every month based on a survey of 5,000 representative U.S. households. It is used by many economists to track the state of the economy. A press release by the Board on December 27, 2016, stated: "The Conference Board Consumer Confi-dence Index®, which had increased considerably in

November, posted another gain in December. The Index now stands at 113.7 (1985 = 100), up from 109.4 in November."

a. As an economist, is this news encouraging for economic growth?

b. Explain your answer to part a with the help of the *AD–AS* model. Draw a typical diagram showing two equilibrium points (E_1) and (E_2). Label the vertical axis "Aggregate price level" and the horizontal axis "Real GDP." Assume that all other major macroeconomic factors remain unchanged.

c. How should the government respond to this news if the economy is below potential output? If it is above potential output?

10. There were two major shocks to the U.S. economy in 2007, leading to the severe recession of 2007–2009. One shock was related to oil prices; the other was the slump in the housing market. This question analyzes the effect of these two shocks on GDP using the *AD–AS* framework.

a. Draw typical aggregate demand and short-run aggregate supply curves. Label the horizontal axis "Real GDP" and the vertical axis "Aggregate price level." Label the equilibrium point E_1, the equilibrium quantity Y_1, and equilibrium price P_1.

b. Data taken from the Department of Energy indicate that the average price of crude oil in the world increased from $54.63 per barrel on January 5, 2007, to $92.93 on December 28, 2007. Would an increase in oil prices cause a demand shock or a supply shock? Redraw the diagram from part a to illustrate the effect of this shock by shifting the appropriate curve.

c. The Housing Price Index, published by the Office of Federal Housing Enterprise Oversight, calculates that U.S. home prices fell by an average of 3.0% in the 12 months between January 2007 and January 2008. Would the fall in home prices cause a supply shock or demand shock? Redraw the diagram from part b to illustrate the effect of this shock by shifting the appropriate curve. Label the new equilibrium point E_3, the equilibrium quantity Y_3, and equilibrium price P_3.

d. Compare the equilibrium points E_1 and E_3 in your diagram for part c. What was the effect of the two shocks on real GDP and the aggregate price level (increase, decrease, or indeterminate)?

11. Using aggregate demand, short-run aggregate supply, and long-run aggregate supply curves, explain the process by which each of the following economic

events will move the economy from one long-run macroeconomic equilibrium to another. Illustrate with diagrams. In each case, what are the short-run and long-run effects on the aggregate price level and aggregate output?

a. There is a decrease in households' wealth due to a decline in the stock market.

b. The government lowers taxes, leaving households with more disposable income, with no corresponding reduction in government purchases.

12. Using aggregate demand, short-run aggregate supply, and long-run aggregate supply curves, explain the process by which each of the following government policies will move the economy from one long-run macroeconomic equilibrium to another. Illustrate with diagrams. In each case, what are the short-run and long-run effects on the aggregate price level and aggregate output?

a. There is an increase in taxes on households.

b. There is an increase in the quantity of money.

c. There is an increase in government spending.

13. The economy is in short-run macroeconomic equilibrium at point E_1 in the accompanying diagram. Based on the diagram, answer the following questions.

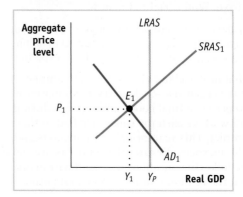

a. Is the economy facing an inflationary or a recessionary gap?

b. What policies can the government implement that might bring the economy back to long-run macroeconomic equilibrium? Illustrate with a diagram.

c. If the government did not intervene to close this gap, would the economy return to long-run macroeconomic equilibrium? Explain and illustrate with a diagram.

d. What are the advantages and disadvantages of the government implementing policies to close the gap?

14. In the accompanying diagram, the economy is in long-run macroeconomic equilibrium at point E_1 when an oil shock shifts the short-run aggregate supply curve to $SRAS_2$. Based on the diagram, answer the following questions.

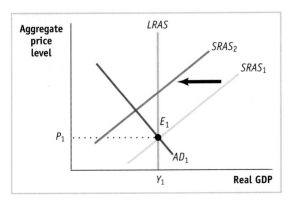

a. How do the aggregate price level and aggregate output change in the short run as a result of the oil shock? What is this phenomenon known as?

b. What fiscal or monetary policies can the government use to address the effects of the supply shock? Use a diagram that shows the effect of policies chosen to address the change in real GDP. Use another diagram to show the effect of policies chosen to address the change in the aggregate price level.

c. Why do supply shocks present a dilemma for government policy makers?

15. The late 1990s in the United States were characterized by substantial economic growth with low inflation; that is, real GDP increased with little, if any, increase in the aggregate price level. Explain this experience using aggregate demand and aggregate supply curves. Illustrate with a diagram.

WORK IT OUT **Interactive step-by-step help with solving this problem can be found online.**

---

16. In each of the following cases, in the short run, determine whether the events cause a shift of a curve or a movement along a curve. Determine which curve is involved and the direction of the change.

a. As a result of an increase in the value of the dollar in relation to other currencies, American producers now pay less in dollar terms for foreign steel, a major commodity used in production.

b. An increase in the quantity of money by the Federal Reserve increases the quantity of money that people wish to lend, lowering interest rates.

c. Greater union activity leads to higher nominal wages.

d. A fall in the aggregate price level increases the purchasing power of households' and firms' money holdings. As a result, they borrow less and lend more.

13 Fiscal Policy

SPENDING OUR WAY OUT OF A RECESSION

THE U.S. ECONOMY entered the downturn that would eventually be dubbed the Great Recession at the end of 2007, but it didn't fall off a cliff until the fall of 2008, when it took a terrifying plunge, losing more than 6 million jobs over the 10 months between August 2008 and June 2009. Policy makers scrambled on multiple fronts to stabilize the situation, such as cutting interest rates and rushing emergency aid to troubled banks.

In making fiscal policy, timing is crucial. Expansionary fiscal policy was appropriate during the deeply depressed economy of 2009. But it is counterproductive if undertaken when the economy is strong, as it was in 2017.

However, advisers to newly elected President Obama believed that these measures were insufficient to do any more than limit the bleeding. They believed that in order to restore the jobs being lost, the economy needed a boost—a *stimulus*—from the federal government's budget, in the form of increased spending and tax cuts.

The president took their advice, and the American Recovery and Reinvestment Act was signed into law on February 17, 2009. It increased federal spending, temporarily expanded federal assistance programs like food stamps and unemployment insurance, provided aid to financially strapped state and local governments, and cut some taxes. It came with a total price tag of about $840 billion, mostly falling in the first two years, when it peaked at about 10% of the federal budget. Policy makers argued that this stimulus package would provide crucial support to the severely depressed economy and accelerate the pace of recovery.

It was a classic example of *fiscal policy:* changes in taxes and government spending to stabilize the economy by shifting the aggregate demand curve. In this case the fiscal policy was *expansionary*, designed to shift the aggregate demand curve out; fiscal policies that shift the aggregate demand curve in are *contractionary*.

Fiscal policy is often controversial. In 2009, some observers believed it was a mistake to increase government spending at a time of widespread distress. One member of Congress spoke for many when he declared that the government should spend *less* in hard times: "American families are tightening their belts, but they don't see government tightening its belt." There were also concerns that the stimulus would widen the budget deficit. But most economists believe that expansionary fiscal policy is appropriate when the economy is depressed.

The qualification—"when the economy is depressed"—is important. In 2017, eight years after the Obama stimulus, the new Trump administration proposed measures that in some respects looked similar to the Obama stimulus: tax cuts and additional spending on infrastructure. While some economists supported these proposals, most did not—including many who supported the Obama stimulus. Weren't they being inconsistent? In reality, no: in early 2009 the U.S. economy was deeply depressed and was heading further downward. By contrast, in early 2017 the economy was growing strongly and appeared close to full employment. The economists who declined to support the proposed Trump stimulus knew that stimulus, delivered at the wrong time, was likely to be counterproductive to the economy. They understood that, in making fiscal policy, timing is crucial.

In this chapter we'll see how fiscal policy fits into the models of economic fluctuation we studied in Chapters 11 and 12. We will also see why budget deficits and government debt can be problems, and why short-run and long-run considerations can pull fiscal policy in opposite directions. ●

WHAT YOU WILL LEARN

- What is fiscal policy and why is it an essential tool in managing economic fluctuations?

- Which policies constitute **expansionary fiscal policy** and which constitute **contractionary fiscal policy**?

- Why does fiscal policy have a multiplier effect and how is this effect influenced by **automatic stabilizers**?

- Why do governments calculate the **cyclically adjusted budget balance**?

- Why can a large **public debt** and **implicit liabilities** of the government be a cause for concern?

Fiscal Policy: The Basics

Modern governments in economically advanced countries spend a great deal of money and collect a lot in taxes. Figure 13-1 shows government spending and tax revenue as percentages of GDP for a selection of high-income countries in 2016. As you can see, the French government sector is relatively large, accounting for more than half of the French economy. The government of the United States plays a smaller role in the economy than those of Canada and most European countries. But that role is still sizable, with the government playing a major role in the U.S. economy. As a result, changes in the federal budget—changes in government spending or in taxation—can have large effects on the American economy.

To analyze these effects, we begin by showing how taxes and government spending affect the economy's flow of income. Then we can see how changes in spending and tax policy affect aggregate demand.

Taxes, Purchases of Goods and Services, Government Transfers, and Borrowing

In Figure 7-1 we showed the circular flow of income and spending in the economy as a whole. One of the sectors represented in that figure was the government. Funds flow *into* the government in the form of taxes and government borrowing; funds flow *out* in the form of government purchases of goods and services and government transfers to households.

What kinds of taxes do Americans pay, and where does the money go? Figure 13-2 shows the composition of U.S. tax revenue in 2016. Taxes, of course, are required payments to the government. In the United States, taxes are collected at the national level by the federal government; at the state level by each state government; and at local levels by counties, cities, and towns. At the federal level, the taxes that generate the greatest revenue are income taxes on both personal income and corporate profits as well as *social insurance* taxes, which we'll explain shortly. At the state and local levels, the picture is more complex: these governments rely on a mix of sales taxes, property taxes, income taxes, and fees of various kinds.

Overall, taxes on personal income and corporate profits accounted for 47% of total government revenue in 2016; social insurance taxes accounted for 24%; and a variety of other taxes, collected mainly at the state and local levels, accounted for the rest.

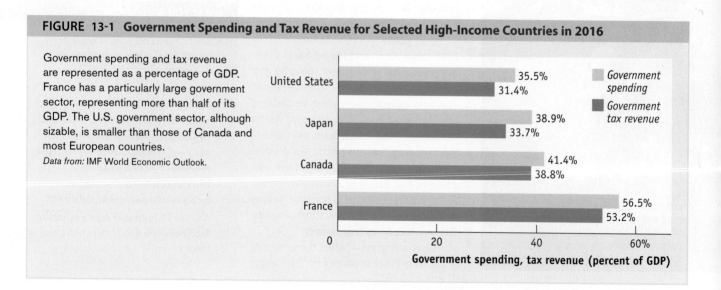

FIGURE 13-1 Government Spending and Tax Revenue for Selected High-Income Countries in 2016

Government spending and tax revenue are represented as a percentage of GDP. France has a particularly large government sector, representing more than half of its GDP. The U.S. government sector, although sizable, is smaller than those of Canada and most European countries.

Data from: IMF World Economic Outlook.

United States — Government spending 35.5%, Government tax revenue 31.4%
Japan — Government spending 38.9%, Government tax revenue 33.7%
Canada — Government spending 41.4%, Government tax revenue 38.8%
France — Government spending 56.5%, Government tax revenue 53.2%

Government spending, tax revenue (percent of GDP)

Figure 13-3 shows the composition of total U.S. government spending in 2016, which takes two broad forms. One form is purchases of goods and services. This includes everything from ammunition for the military to the salaries of public school teachers (who are treated in the national accounts as providers of a service—education). The big items here are national defense and education. The category "Other goods and services" consists mainly of state and local spending on a variety of services, from police and firefighters to highway construction and maintenance.

The other form of government spending is government transfers, which are payments by the government to households for which no good or service is provided in return. In the United States, as well as in Canada and Europe, government transfers represent a very large proportion of the budget. Most U.S. government spending on transfer payments is accounted for by four programs:

- Social Security, which provides guaranteed income to older Americans, disabled Americans, and the surviving spouses and dependent children of deceased or retired beneficiaries

- Medicare, which covers much of the cost of health care for Americans over age 65

- Medicaid, which covers much of the cost of health care for Americans with low incomes

- The Affordable Care Act (ACA), which seeks to make health insurance available and affordable to all Americans

The term **social insurance** is used to describe government programs that are intended to protect families against economic hardship. These include Social Security, Medicare, Medicaid, and the ACA, as well as smaller programs such as unemployment insurance and food stamps. The ACA works through a system of regulated private insurance markets, subsidies, and an expansion of Medicaid eligibility, and is much smaller than the other three large programs. Social insurance programs in the United States are largely paid for with special, dedicated taxes on wages—the social insurance taxes mentioned earlier. The ACA is an exception: it is funded mainly by taxes on private health insurance purchases.

How do tax policy and government spending affect the economy? The answer is that taxation and government spending have a strong effect on total aggregate spending in the economy.

The Government Budget and Total Spending

Let's recall the basic equation of national income accounting:

(13-1) $GDP = C + I + G + X - IM$

The left-hand side of this equation is GDP, the value of all final goods and services produced in the economy. The right-hand side is aggregate spending, total spending on final goods and services produced in the economy. It is the sum of consumer spending (C), investment spending (I), government purchases of goods and services (G), and the value of exports (X) minus the value of imports (IM). It includes all the sources of aggregate demand.

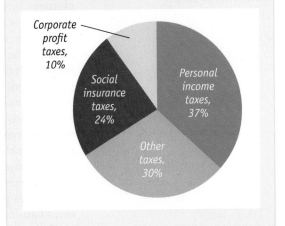

FIGURE 13-2 Sources of Tax Revenue in the United States, 2016

Personal income taxes, taxes on corporate profits, and social insurance taxes account for most government tax revenue. The rest is a mix of property taxes, sales taxes, and other sources of revenue. (Percentages do not add to 100 due to rounding.)

Data from: Bureau of Economic Analysis.

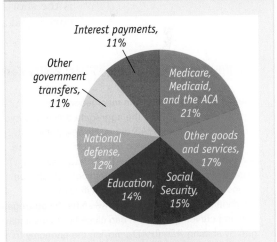

FIGURE 13-3 Government Spending in the United States, 2016

The two types of government spending are purchases of goods and services and government transfers. The biggest items in government purchases are national defense and education. The biggest items in government transfers are Social Security, Medicare, Medicaid, and the Affordable Care Act. (Percentages do not add to 100 due to rounding.)

Data from: Bureau of Economic Analysis.

Social insurance programs are government programs intended to protect families against economic hardship.

The government directly controls one of the variables on the right-hand side of Equation 13-1: government purchases of goods and services (G). But that's not the only effect fiscal policy has on aggregate spending in the economy. Through changes in taxes and transfers, it also influences consumer spending (C) and, in some cases, investment spending (I).

To see why the budget affects consumer spending, recall that *disposable income*, the total income households have available to spend, is equal to the total income they receive from wages, dividends, interest, and rent, *minus* taxes, *plus* government transfers. So either an increase in taxes or a reduction in government transfers *reduces* disposable income. And a fall in disposable income, other things equal, leads to a fall in consumer spending. Conversely, either a decrease in taxes or an increase in government transfers *increases* disposable income. And a rise in disposable income, other things equal, leads to a rise in consumer spending.

The government's ability to affect investment spending is a more complex story, which we won't discuss in detail. The important point is that the government taxes profits, and changes in the rules that determine how much a business owes can increase or reduce the incentive to spend on investment goods.

Because the government itself is one source of spending in the economy, and because taxes and transfers can affect spending by consumers and firms, the government can use changes in taxes or government spending to *shift the aggregate demand curve*. And as we saw in Chapter 12, there are sometimes good reasons to shift the aggregate demand curve.

Expansionary and Contractionary Fiscal Policy

Why would the government want to shift the aggregate demand curve? Because it wants to close either a recessionary gap, created when aggregate output falls below potential output, or an inflationary gap, created when aggregate output exceeds potential output.

Figure 13-4 shows the case of an economy facing a recessionary gap. SRAS is the short-run aggregate supply curve, LRAS is the long-run aggregate supply curve, and AD_1 is the initial aggregate demand curve. At the initial short-run

---

FIGURE 13-4 Expansionary Fiscal Policy Can Close a Recessionary Gap

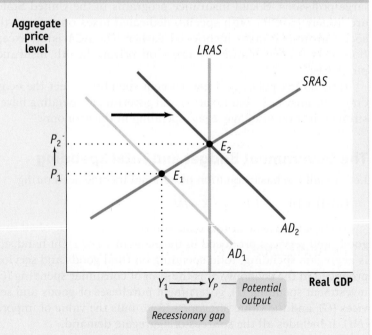

The economy is in short-run macroeconomic equilibrium at E_1, where the aggregate demand curve, AD_1, intersects the *SRAS* curve. However, it is not in long-run macroeconomic equilibrium. At E_1, there is a recessionary gap of $Y_P - Y_1$. An expansionary fiscal policy—an increase in government purchases of goods and services, a reduction in taxes, or an increase in government transfers—shifts the aggregate demand curve rightward. It can close the recessionary gap by shifting AD_1 to AD_2, moving the economy to a new short-run macroeconomic equilibrium, E_2, which is also a long-run macroeconomic equilibrium.

macroeconomic equilibrium, E_1, aggregate output is Y_1, below potential output, Y_P. What the government would like to do is increase aggregate demand, shifting the aggregate demand curve rightward to AD_2. This would increase aggregate output, making it equal to potential output. Fiscal policy that increases aggregate demand, called **expansionary fiscal policy,** normally takes one of three forms:

1. An increase in government purchases of goods and services
2. A cut in taxes
3. An increase in government transfers

The 2009 stimulus (or the Recovery Act) was a combination of all three: a direct increase in federal spending and aid to state governments to help them maintain spending, tax cuts for most families, and increased aid to the unemployed.

Figure 13-5 shows the opposite case—an economy facing an inflationary gap. Again, *SRAS* is the short-run aggregate supply curve, *LRAS* is the long-run aggregate supply curve, and AD_1 is the initial aggregate demand curve. At the initial equilibrium, E_1, aggregate output is Y_1, above potential output, Y_P. As we'll explain in later chapters, policy makers often try to head off inflation by eliminating inflationary gaps. To eliminate the inflationary gap shown in Figure 13-5, fiscal policy must reduce aggregate demand and shift the aggregate demand curve leftward to AD_2. This reduces aggregate output and makes it equal to potential output. Fiscal policy that reduces aggregate demand, called **contractionary fiscal policy,** is the opposite of expansionary fiscal policy. It is implemented in three possible ways:

1. A reduction in government purchases of goods and services
2. An increase in taxes
3. A reduction in government transfers

A classic example of contractionary fiscal policy occurred in 1968, when U.S. policy makers grew worried about rising inflation. President Lyndon Johnson imposed a temporary 10% surcharge on taxable income—everyone's income taxes

> **Expansionary fiscal policy** is fiscal policy that increases aggregate demand.
>
> **Contractionary fiscal policy** is fiscal policy that reduces aggregate demand.

FIGURE 13-5 Contractionary Fiscal Policy Can Close an Inflationary Gap

The economy is in short-run macroeconomic equilibrium at E_1, where the aggregate demand curve, AD_1, intersects the *SRAS* curve. But it is not in long-run macroeconomic equilibrium. At E_1, there is an inflationary gap of $Y_1 - Y_P$. A contractionary fiscal policy—such as reduced government purchases of goods and services, an increase in taxes, or a reduction in government transfers—shifts the aggregate demand curve leftward. It closes the inflationary gap by shifting AD_1 to AD_2, moving the economy to a new short-run macroeconomic equilibrium, E_2, which is also a long-run macroeconomic equilibrium.

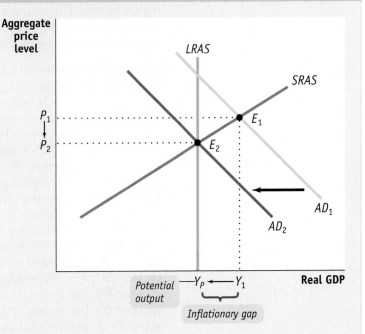

were increased by 10%. He also tried to scale back government purchases of goods and services, which had risen dramatically because of the cost of the Vietnam War.

Can Expansionary Fiscal Policy Actually Work?

In practice, the use of fiscal policy—in particular, the use of expansionary fiscal policy in the face of a recessionary gap—is often controversial. We'll examine the origins of these controversies in detail in Chapter 17. But for now, let's quickly summarize the major points of the debate over expansionary fiscal policy, so we can understand when the critiques are justified and when they are not.

There are three main arguments against the use of expansionary fiscal policy.

- Government spending always crowds out private spending
- Government borrowing always crowds out private investment spending
- Government budget deficits lead to reduced private spending

The first of these claims is wrong in principle, but it has nonetheless played a prominent role in public debates. The second is valid under some, but not all, circumstances. The third argument, although it raises some important issues, isn't a good reason to believe that expansionary fiscal policy doesn't work.

Claim 1: "Government Spending Always Crowds Out Private Spending"
Some claim that expansionary fiscal policy can never raise aggregate spending and therefore can never raise aggregate income, with reasons that go something like this: "Every dollar that the government spends is a dollar taken away from the private sector. So any rise in government spending must be offset by an equal fall in private spending." In other words, every dollar spent by the government *crowds out*, or displaces, a dollar of private spending.

But the statement is wrong because it assumes that resources in the economy are always fully employed and, as a result, the aggregate income earned in the economy is always a fixed sum—which isn't true. In reality, whether or not government spending crowds out private spending depends upon the state of the economy. In particular, when the economy is suffering from a recessionary gap, there are unemployed resources in the economy, and output, and therefore income, is below its potential level. Expansionary fiscal policy during these periods puts unemployed resources to work and generates higher spending and higher income. Government spending crowds out private spending only when the economy is operating at full employment. So the argument that expansionary fiscal policy always crowds out private spending is wrong in principle.

Claim 2: "Government Borrowing Always Crowds Out Private Investment Spending"
In Chapter 10, we discussed the possibility that government borrowing uses funds that would have otherwise been used for private investment spending—that is, it crowds out private investment spending. So how valid is the argument that government borrowing always reduces private investment spending?

Much like Claim 1, Claim 2 is wrong because whether crowding out occurs depends upon whether the economy is depressed or not. If the economy is not depressed, then increased government borrowing, by increasing the demand for loanable funds, can raise interest rates and crowd out private investment spending. However, if the economy is depressed, crowding out is much less likely to occur. When the economy is at far less than full employment, a fiscal expansion will lead to higher incomes, which in turn leads to increased savings at any given interest rate. This larger pool of savings allows the government to borrow without driving up interest rates. The stimulus of 2009 was a case in point: despite high levels of government borrowing, U.S. interest rates stayed near historic lows. In the end, government borrowing crowds out private investment spending only when the economy is operating at full employment (which is why most economists declined to endorse the Trump administration's 2017 fiscal expansion proposals).

Claim 3: "Government Budget Deficits Lead to Reduced Private Spending" Other things equal, expansionary fiscal policy leads to a larger budget deficit and greater government debt. And higher debt will eventually require the government to raise taxes to pay it off. So, according to the third argument against expansionary fiscal policy, consumers, anticipating that they must pay higher taxes in the future to pay off today's government debt, will cut their spending today in order to save money. This argument, first made by nineteenth-century economist David Ricardo, is known as *Ricardian equivalence*. It is an argument often taken to imply that expansionary fiscal policy will have no effect on the economy because far-sighted consumers will undo any attempts at expansion by the government. (And will also undo any contractionary fiscal policy, for that matter.)

In reality, however, it's doubtful that consumers behave with such foresight and budgeting discipline. Most people, when provided with extra cash (generated by the fiscal expansion), will spend at least some of it. So even fiscal policy that takes the form of temporary tax cuts or transfers of cash to consumers probably does have an expansionary effect.

Moreover, it's possible to show that even with Ricardian equivalence, a temporary rise in government spending that involves direct purchases of goods and services—such as a program of road construction—would still lead to a boost in total spending in the near term. That's because even if consumers cut back their current spending in anticipation of higher future taxes, their reduced spending will take place over an extended period as consumers save over time to pay the future tax bill. Meanwhile, the additional government spending will be concentrated in the near future, when the economy needs it.

So although the effects emphasized by Ricardian equivalence may reduce the impact of fiscal expansion, the claim that it makes fiscal expansion completely ineffective is neither consistent with how consumers actually behave nor a reason to believe that increases in government spending have no effect. So, in the end, it's not a valid argument against expansionary fiscal policy.

In Sum The extent to which we should expect expansionary fiscal policy to work depends upon the circumstances. Recall our conclusion in the chapter opening story: in making fiscal policy, timing is critical. When the economy has a recessionary gap—as it did when the 2009 stimulus was passed—economics tells us that this is just the kind of situation in which expansionary fiscal policy helps the economy. However, when the economy is already at full employment, as it was very close to in 2017, expansionary fiscal policy is the wrong policy and will lead to crowding out, an overheated economy, and higher inflation.

A Cautionary Note: Lags in Fiscal Policy

Looking back at Figures 13-4 and 13-5, it may seem obvious that the government should actively use fiscal policy—always adopting an expansionary fiscal policy when the economy faces a recessionary gap and always adopting a contractionary fiscal policy when the economy faces an inflationary gap. But many economists caution against an extremely active stabilization policy, arguing that a government that tries too hard to stabilize the economy—through either fiscal policy or monetary policy—can end up making the economy less stable.

We'll leave discussion of the warnings associated with monetary policy to Chapter 15. In the case of fiscal policy, one key reason for caution is that there are important *time lags* between when the policy is decided upon and when it is implemented. To understand the nature of these lags, consider the three things that have to happen before the government increases spending to fight a recessionary gap.

1. The government has to realize that the recessionary gap exists: economic data take time to collect and analyze, and recessions are often recognized only

months after they have begun. As we've seen, the Great Recession is generally considered to have begun in December 2007, but as late as September 2008 some economists were still questioning whether the recession was real.

2. The government has to develop a spending plan, which can itself take months, particularly if politicians take time debating how the money should be spent and passing legislation.

3. It takes time to spend money. For example, a road construction project begins with activities such as surveying that don't involve spending large sums. It may be quite some time before the big spending begins. The Recovery Act was passed in the first quarter of 2009, but much of its effect on federal spending, especially purchases of goods and services, didn't come until 2011.

Because of these lags, an attempt to increase spending to fight a recessionary gap may take so long to get going that the economy has already recovered on its own. In fact, the recessionary gap may have turned into an inflationary gap by the time expansionary fiscal policy takes effect. In that case, expansionary fiscal policy will make things worse instead of better.

This doesn't mean that fiscal policy should never be actively used. In early 2009 there was good reason to believe that the slump facing the U.S. economy would be both deep and long and that a fiscal stimulus designed to arrive over the next year or two would almost surely push aggregate demand in the right direction. In fact, as we'll see later in this chapter, the 2009 stimulus arguably faded out too soon, leaving the economy still deeply depressed when it ended. But the problem of lags makes the actual use of both fiscal and monetary policy harder than you might think from a simple analysis like the one we have just given.

ECONOMICS >> *in Action*
A Tale of Two Stimuli

There were some broad similarities between the Obama stimulus of 2009 and proposals that were floated by the Trump administration soon after it took office in early 2017. We touch on both stimulus plans in the opening story. In both cases, a new administration was suggesting tax cuts (although not increased transfers) and increased spending on infrastructure. Yet many economists who supported the Obama stimulus were dubious about the Trump plan, because the state of the economy had changed.

Figure 13-6 shows two indicators that played an important role in policy discussions at both times. One is the unemployment rate. The other is the *quits rate*, the fraction of workers voluntarily leaving their jobs each month. This rate is widely viewed as an indication of how good the labor market is: workers are reluctant to quit if they believe new jobs are very hard to find. For this reason, the quits rate is a useful backup to the unemployment rate: if you're unsure whether the unemployment rate is giving an accurate read on the situation, you can check whether the quits rate is telling the same story.

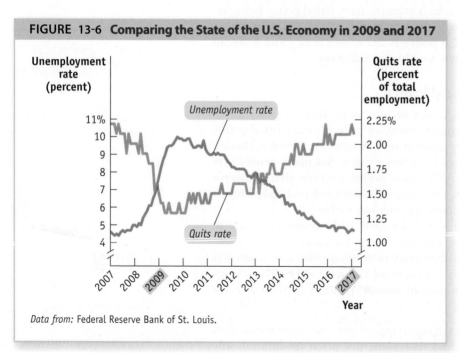

FIGURE 13-6 Comparing the State of the U.S. Economy in 2009 and 2017

Data from: Federal Reserve Bank of St. Louis.

What you can see from Figure 13-6 is that in early 2009 the United States showed all the signs of a deeply depressed economy, in the grip of an accelerating plunge, with unemployment high and rising and the quits rate low and falling. By early 2017, however, the data were telling the opposite story: a low unemployment rate and a high quits rate indicated that jobs were relatively plentiful.

This difference meant that the case for expansionary fiscal policy was much weaker in 2017 than it has been in 2009: under 2017 conditions it was, in fact, likely that increased government spending would crowd out private spending, and that increased government borrowing would crowd out private investment. It was possible to favor the Trump administration's proposals for a variety of reasons. But the macroeconomics of fiscal policy made the potential downside much higher than in 2009.

>> Check Your Understanding 13-1

Solutions appear at back of book.

1. In each of the following cases, determine whether the policy is an expansionary or contractionary fiscal policy.
   a. Several military bases around the country, which together employ tens of thousands of people, are closed.
   b. The number of weeks an unemployed person is eligible for unemployment benefits is increased.
   c. The federal tax on gasoline is increased.
2. Explain why federal disaster relief, which quickly disburses funds to victims of natural disasters such as hurricanes, floods, and large-scale crop failures, will stabilize the economy more effectively after a disaster than relief that must be legislated.
3. Is the following statement true or false? Explain. "When the government expands, the private sector shrinks; when the government shrinks, the private sector expands."

‖ Fiscal Policy and the Multiplier

An expansionary fiscal policy, like the 2009 stimulus, pushes the aggregate demand curve to the right. A contractionary fiscal policy pushes the aggregate demand curve to the left. For policy makers, however, knowing the direction of the shift isn't enough: they need estimates of *how much* a given policy will shift the aggregate demand curve. To get these estimates, they use the concept of the multiplier, which we learned about in Chapter 11.

Multiplier Effects of an Increase in Government Purchases of Goods and Services

Suppose that a government decides to spend $50 billion building bridges and roads. The government's purchases of goods and services will directly increase total spending on final goods and services by $50 billion. But as we learned in Chapter 11, there will also be an indirect effect: the government's purchases will start a chain reaction throughout the economy. The firms that produce the goods and services purchased by the government earn revenues that flow to households in the form of wages, profits, interest, and rent. This increase in disposable income leads to a rise in consumer spending. The rise in consumer spending, in turn, induces firms to increase output, leading to a further rise in disposable income, which leads to another round of consumer spending increases, and so on.

As we know, the *multiplier* is the ratio of the change in real GDP caused by an autonomous change in aggregate spending to the size of that autonomous change. An increase in government purchases of goods and services is a prime example of such an autonomous increase in aggregate spending.

Expansionary or contractionary fiscal policy will start a chain reaction throughout the economy.

Grafissimo/Getty Images

In Chapter 11 we considered a simple case in which there are no taxes or international trade, so that any change in GDP accrues entirely to households. We also assumed that the aggregate price level is fixed, so that any increase in nominal GDP is also a rise in real GDP, and that the interest rate is fixed. In that case the multiplier is $1/(1 - MPC)$. Recall that MPC is the *marginal propensity to consume*, the fraction of an additional dollar in disposable income that is spent. For example, if the marginal propensity to consume is 0.5, the multiplier is $1/(1 - 0.5) = 1/0.5 = 2$. Given a multiplier of 2, a $50 billion increase in government purchases of goods and services would increase real GDP by $100 billion. Of that $100 billion, $50 billion is the initial effect from the increase in G, and the remaining $50 billion is the subsequent effect arising from the increase in consumer spending.

What happens if government purchases of goods and services are instead reduced? The math is exactly the same, except that there's a minus sign in front: if government purchases of goods and services fall by $50 billion and the marginal propensity to consume is 0.5, real GDP falls by $100 billion.

Multiplier Effects of Changes in Government Transfers and Taxes

Expansionary or contractionary fiscal policy need not take the form of changes in government purchases of goods and services. Governments can also change transfer payments or taxes. In general, however, a change in government transfers or taxes shifts the aggregate demand curve by *less* than an equal-sized change in government purchases, resulting in a smaller effect on real GDP.

To see why, imagine that instead of spending $50 billion on building bridges, the government simply hands out $50 billion in the form of government transfers. In this case, there is no direct effect on aggregate demand, as there was with government purchases of goods and services. Real GDP goes up because households spend some of that $50 billion—but they won't spend it all.

Table 13-1 shows a hypothetical comparison of two expansionary fiscal policies assuming an MPC equal to 0.5: one in which the government directly purchases $50 billion in goods and services and one in which the government makes transfer payments instead, sending out $50 billion in checks to consumers. In each case there is a first-round effect on real GDP, either from purchases by the government or from purchases by the consumers who received the checks, followed by a series of additional rounds as rising real GDP raises disposable income.

However, the first-round effect of the transfer program is smaller. Because we have assumed that the MPC is 0.5, only $25 billion of the $50 billion is spent, with the other $25 billion saved. And as a result, all the further rounds are smaller, too. In the end, the transfer payment increases real GDP by only $50 billion, equal to $MPC \times 1/(1 - MPC)$. In comparison, a $50 billion increase in government purchases produces a $100 billion increase in real GDP, equal to $1/(1 - MPC)$.

Overall, when expansionary fiscal policy takes the form of a rise in transfer payments, real GDP may rise by either more or less than the initial government outlay—that is, the multiplier may be either more or less than 1 depending upon the size of the MPC. In Table 13-1, with an MPC equal to 0.5, the multiplier is exactly 1: a $50 billion rise in transfer payments increases real GDP by $50 billion. If the MPC is less than 0.5, so that a smaller share of the initial transfer is spent, the multiplier

TABLE 13-1 Hypothetical Effects of a Fiscal Policy When $MPC = 0.5$

Effect on real GDP	$50 billion rise in government purchases of goods and services	$50 billion rise in government transfer payments
First round	$50 billion	$25 billion
Second round	$25 billion	$12.5 billion
Third round	$12.5 billion	$6.25 billion
.	.	.
.	.	.
.	.	.
Total effect	$100 billion	$50 billion
Total effect in terms of multiplier	$\Delta Y = \Delta G \times 1/(1 - MPC)$	$\Delta Y = \Delta TR \times MPC \times 1/(1 - MPC)$

on that transfer is *less* than 1. If a larger share of the initial transfer is spent, the multiplier is *more* than 1.

A tax cut has an effect similar to the effect of a transfer. It increases disposable income, leading to a series of increases in consumer spending. But the overall effect is smaller than that of an equal-sized increase in government purchases of goods and services: the autonomous increase in aggregate spending is smaller because households save part of the amount of the tax cut.

We should also note that taxes introduce a further complication—they typically change the size of the multiplier. That's because in the real world governments rarely impose **lump-sum taxes,** in which the amount of tax a household owes is independent of its income. With lump-sum taxes there is no change in the multiplier. Instead, the great majority of tax revenue is raised via taxes that are not lump-sum, and so tax revenue depends upon the level of real GDP. As we'll discuss shortly, and analyze in detail in this chapter's appendix, non-lump-sum taxes reduce the size of the multiplier.

In practice, economists often argue that the size of the multiplier determines *who* among the population should get tax cuts or increases in government transfers. For example, compare the effects of an increase in unemployment benefits to a cut in taxes on profits distributed to shareholders as dividends. Consumer surveys suggest that the average unemployed worker will spend a higher share of any increase in his or her disposable income than would the average recipient of dividend income. That is, people who are unemployed tend to have a higher *MPC* than people who own a lot of stocks because the latter tend to be wealthier and tend to save more of any increase in disposable income. If that's true, a dollar spent on unemployment benefits increases aggregate demand more than a dollar's worth of dividend tax cuts.

> **Lump-sum taxes** are taxes that don't depend on the taxpayer's income.

How Taxes Affect the Multiplier

When we introduced the analysis of the multiplier in Chapter 11, we simplified matters by assuming that a $1 increase in real GDP raises disposable income by $1. In fact, however, government taxes capture some part of the increase in real GDP that occurs in each round of the multiplier process, since most government taxes depend positively on real GDP. As a result, disposable income increases by considerably less than $1 once we include taxes in the model.

The increase in government tax revenue when real GDP rises isn't the result of a deliberate decision or action by the government. It's a consequence of the way the tax laws are written, which causes most sources of government revenue to increase *automatically* when real GDP goes up. For example, income tax receipts increase when real GDP rises because the amount each individual owes in taxes depends positively on his or her income, and households' taxable income rises when real GDP rises. Sales tax receipts increase when real GDP rises because people with more income spend more on goods and services. And corporate profit tax receipts increase when real GDP rises because profits increase when the economy expands.

The effect of these automatic increases in tax revenue is to reduce the size of the multiplier. Remember, the multiplier is the result of a chain reaction in which higher real GDP leads to higher disposable income, which leads to higher consumer spending, which leads to further increases in real GDP. The fact that the government siphons off some of any increase in real GDP means that at each stage of this process, the increase in consumer spending is smaller than it would be if taxes weren't part of the picture. The result is to reduce the multiplier.

In fact, the effect of taxes on the multiplier is very similar to the effect of international trade, which also reduces the multiplier. In one case the multiplier process is weakened because at each stage some spending "leaks" into imports; in the other case, income "leaks" into taxes. The appendix to this chapter shows how to derive the multiplier when taxes that depend positively on real GDP are taken into account.

Automatic stabilizers are government spending and taxation rules that cause fiscal policy to be automatically expansionary when the economy contracts and automatically contractionary when the economy expands.

Discretionary fiscal policy is fiscal policy that is the result of deliberate actions by policy makers rather than rules.

Many macroeconomists believe it's a good thing that taxes reduce the multiplier. In the previous chapter we argued that most, though not all, recessions are the result of negative demand shocks. The same mechanism that makes tax revenue increase when the economy expands makes tax revenue decrease when the economy contracts. Since tax receipts decrease when real GDP falls, the effects of these negative demand shocks are smaller than in a world in which there were no taxes. The decrease in tax revenue reduces the adverse effect of the initial fall in aggregate demand.

The automatic decrease in government tax revenue generated by a fall in real GDP—caused by a decrease in the amount of taxes households pay—acts like an automatic expansionary fiscal policy implemented in the face of a recession. Similarly, when the economy expands, the government finds itself automatically pursuing a contractionary fiscal policy—a tax increase. Government spending and taxation rules that cause fiscal policy to be automatically expansionary when the economy contracts and automatically contractionary when the economy expands, without requiring any deliberate action by policy makers, are called **automatic stabilizers.**

The rules that govern tax collection aren't the only automatic stabilizers, although they are the most important ones. Some types of government transfers also play a stabilizing role. For example, more people receive unemployment insurance when the economy is depressed than when it is booming. The same is true of Medicaid and food stamps. So transfer payments tend to rise when the economy is contracting and fall when the economy is expanding. Like changes in tax revenue, these automatic changes in transfers tend to reduce the size of the multiplier because the total change in disposable income that results from a given rise or fall in real GDP is smaller.

As in the case of government tax revenue, many macroeconomists believe that it's a good thing that government transfers reduce the multiplier. Expansionary and contractionary fiscal policies that are the result of automatic stabilizers are widely considered helpful to macroeconomic stabilization because they blunt the extremes of the business cycle.

But what about fiscal policy that *isn't* the result of automatic stabilizers? **Discretionary fiscal policy** is the direct result of deliberate actions by policy makers rather than automatic adjustment. For example, during a recession, the government may pass legislation that cuts taxes and increases government spending in order to stimulate the economy. In general, economists tend to support the use of discretionary fiscal policy only in the case of a severe recession or sustained economic weakness.

During the Great Depression, the Works Progress Administration (WPA), an example of discretionary fiscal policy, put millions of unemployed Americans to work constructing bridges, roads, buildings, dams, and parks.

ECONOMICS >> *in Action*
Austerity and the Multiplier

We've explained the logic of the fiscal multiplier, but what empirical evidence do economists have about multiplier effects in practice? Until a few years ago, the answer would have been that we didn't have nearly as much evidence as we'd like.

The problem was that large changes in fiscal policy are fairly rare, and usually happen at the same time other things are taking place, making it hard to separate the effects of spending and taxes from those of other factors. For example, the U.S. government drastically increased spending during World War II. But it also instituted rationing of many consumer goods and restricted construction of new homes in order to conserve resources for the war effort. So it is hard to distinguish the effects of the increase in government spending from the transformation of a peacetime economy to a war economy.

However, recent events offer considerable new evidence. In the wake of the Global Financial Crisis of 2009, several European governments found themselves facing debt crises. As loans they had taken out came due, these governments were either unable to raise new funds or were forced to pay extremely high interest rates. As a result, they had to turn to the rest of Europe for aid. In an attempt to reduce budget deficits, a condition of this aid was *austerity*—sharp cuts in spending plus tax increases. Austerity is a form of contractionary fiscal policy. So by comparing the economic performance of countries forced into austerity with the performance of countries that weren't, we get a relatively clear view of the effects of changes in spending and taxes.

Figure 13-7 compares the amount of austerity imposed in a number of countries between 2009 and 2015 to the growth in their GDP over the same period. Austerity is measured on the horizontal axis by the change in the *cyclically adjusted budget balance*, defined later in this chapter. As you can see, Greece stands out. It was forced to impose severe spending cuts and suffered a huge fall in output. But even without Greece there is a clear negative relationship. A line fitted through the scatterplot has a slope of –1.8. That is, the figure suggests that spending cuts and tax increases had an average multiplier of 1.8. Put another way, a contractionary fiscal policy that took $1 out of the economy resulted in a $1.80 fall in GDP.

Economists have offered a number of qualifications and caveats to this result, given that this wasn't truly a controlled experiment. Yet, recent experience strongly supports the proposition that fiscal policy does indeed move GDP in the predicted direction, with a multiplier of more than 1.

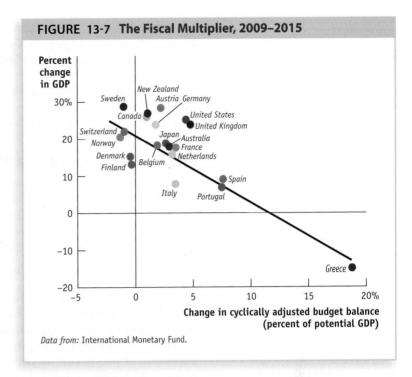

FIGURE 13-7 The Fiscal Multiplier, 2009–2015

Data from: International Monetary Fund.

>> Check Your Understanding 13-2

Solutions appear at back of book.

1. Explain why a $500 million increase in government purchases of goods and services will generate a larger rise in real GDP than a $500 million increase in government transfers.

2. Explain why a $500 million reduction in government purchases of goods and services will generate a larger fall in real GDP than a $500 million reduction in government transfers.

3. The country of Boldovia has no unemployment insurance benefits and a tax system using only lump-sum taxes. The neighboring country of Moldovia has generous unemployment benefits and a tax system in which residents must pay a percentage of their income. Which country will experience greater variation in real GDP in response to demand shocks, positive and negative? Explain.

>> **Quick Review**

- The amount by which changes in government purchases raise real GDP is determined by the multiplier.

- Changes in taxes and government transfers also move real GDP, but by less than equal-sized changes in government purchases.

- Taxes reduce the size of the multiplier unless they are **lump-sum taxes.**

- Taxes and some government transfers act as **automatic stabilizers** as tax revenue responds positively to changes in real GDP and some government transfers respond negatively to changes in real GDP. Many economists believe that it is a good thing that they reduce the size of the multiplier. In contrast, economists tend to support the use of **discretionary fiscal policy** only during severe recessions or periods of sustained economic weakness.

The Budget Balance

Headlines about the government's budget tend to focus on just one point: whether the government is running a surplus or a deficit and, in either case, how big. People usually think of surpluses as good: when the federal government ran a record surplus in 2000, many people regarded it as a cause for celebration. Conversely, people usually think of deficits as bad: when the U.S. federal government ran record deficits from 2009 to 2011, many people regarded it as a cause for concern.

How do surpluses and deficits fit into the analysis of fiscal policy? Are deficits ever a good thing and surpluses a bad thing? To answer those questions, let's look at the causes and consequences of surpluses and deficits.

The Budget Balance as a Measure of Fiscal Policy

What do we mean by surpluses and deficits? The budget balance, which was defined in Chapter 10, is the difference between the government's revenue, in the form of tax revenue, and its spending, both on goods and services and on government transfers, in a given year. That is, the budget balance—savings by government—is defined by Equation 13-2 (which is the same as Equation 10-7):

$$\textbf{(13-2)} \quad S_{Government} = T - G - TR$$

where T is the value of tax revenues, G is government purchases of goods and services, and TR is the value of government transfers. As we've learned, a budget surplus is a positive budget balance and a budget deficit is a negative budget balance.

Other things equal, expansionary fiscal policies—increased government purchases of goods and services, higher government transfers, or lower taxes—reduce the budget balance for that year. That is, expansionary fiscal policies make a budget surplus smaller or a budget deficit bigger. Conversely, contractionary fiscal policies—reduced government purchases of goods and services, lower government transfers, or higher taxes—increase the budget balance for that year, making a budget surplus bigger or a budget deficit smaller.

You might think this means that changes in the budget balance can be used to measure fiscal policy. In fact, economists often do just that: they use changes in the budget balance as a "quick-and-dirty" way to assess whether current fiscal policy is expansionary or contractionary. But they always keep in mind two reasons this quick-and-dirty approach is sometimes misleading:

1. Two different changes in fiscal policy that have equal-sized effects on the budget balance may have quite unequal effects on the economy. As we have already seen, changes in government purchases of goods and services have a larger effect on real GDP than equal-sized changes in taxes and government transfers.

2. Often, changes in the budget balance are themselves the result, not the cause, of fluctuations in the economy.

To understand the second point, we need to examine the effects of the business cycle on the budget.

The Business Cycle and the Cyclically Adjusted Budget Balance

Historically there has been a strong relationship between the federal government's budget balance and the business cycle. The budget tends to move into deficit when the economy experiences a recession, but deficits tend to get smaller or even turn into surpluses when the economy is expanding. Figure 13-8 shows the federal budget deficit as a percentage of GDP from 1964 to 2016. Shaded areas indicate recessions; unshaded areas indicate expansions. As you can see, the federal budget deficit increased around the time of each recession and usually declined during expansions. In fact, in the late stages of the long expansion from 1991 to 2000, the deficit actually became negative—the budget deficit became a budget surplus.

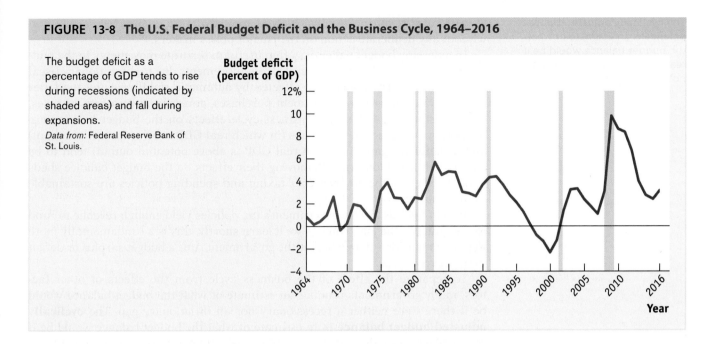

FIGURE 13-8 The U.S. Federal Budget Deficit and the Business Cycle, 1964–2016

The budget deficit as a percentage of GDP tends to rise during recessions (indicated by shaded areas) and fall during expansions.

Data from: Federal Reserve Bank of St. Louis.

The relationship between the business cycle and the budget balance is even clearer if we compare the budget deficit as a percentage of GDP with the unemployment rate, as we do in Figure 13-9. The budget deficit almost always rises when the unemployment rate rises and falls when the unemployment rate falls.

Is this relationship between the business cycle and the budget balance evidence that policy makers engage in discretionary fiscal policy, using expansionary fiscal policy during recessions and contractionary fiscal policy during expansions? Not necessarily. To a large extent the relationship in Figure 13-9 reflects automatic stabilizers at work. As we saw earlier in the discussion of automatic stabilizers, government tax revenue tends to rise and some government transfers, like unemployment benefit payments, tend to fall when the economy expands. Conversely, government tax revenue tends to fall and some government transfers tend to rise when the economy contracts. So the budget tends to move

FIGURE 13-9 The U.S. Federal Budget Deficit and the Unemployment Rate, 1964–2016

There is a close relationship between the budget balance and the business cycle: a recession moves the budget balance toward deficit, but an expansion moves it toward surplus. Here, the unemployment rate serves as an indicator of the business cycle, and we should expect to see a higher unemployment rate associated with a higher budget deficit. This is confirmed by the figure: the budget deficit as a percentage of GDP moves closely in tandem with the unemployment rate.

Data from: Federal Reserve Bank of St. Louis.

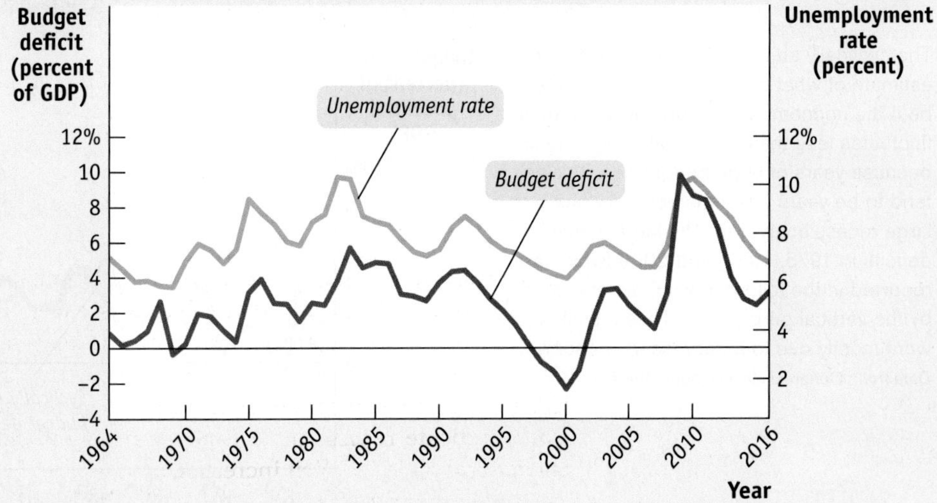

The **cyclically adjusted budget balance** is an estimate of what the budget balance would be if real GDP were exactly equal to potential output.

toward surplus during expansions and toward deficit during recessions even without any deliberate action on the part of policy makers.

In assessing budget policy, it's often useful to separate movements in the budget balance due to the business cycle from movements due to discretionary fiscal policy changes. The former are affected by automatic stabilizers and the latter by deliberate changes in government purchases, government transfers, or taxes. It's important to realize that business-cycle effects on the budget balance are temporary: both recessionary gaps (in which real GDP is below potential output) and inflationary gaps (in which real GDP is above potential output) tend to be eliminated in the long run. Removing their effects on the budget balance sheds light on whether the government's taxing and spending policies are sustainable in the long run.

In other words, do the government's tax policies yield enough revenue to fund its spending in the long run? As we'll learn shortly, this is a fundamentally more important question than whether the government runs a budget surplus or deficit in the current year.

To separate the effect of the business cycle from the effects of other factors, many governments produce an estimate of what the budget balance would be if there were neither a recessionary nor an inflationary gap. The **cyclically adjusted budget balance** is an estimate of what the budget balance would be if real GDP were exactly equal to potential output. It takes into account the extra tax revenue the government would collect and the transfers it would save if a recessionary gap were eliminated—or the revenue the government would lose and the extra transfers it would make if an inflationary gap were eliminated.

Figure 13-10 shows the actual budget deficit and the Congressional Budget Office estimate of the cyclically adjusted budget deficit, both as a percentage of potential GDP, from 1965 to 2016. As you can see, the cyclically adjusted budget deficit doesn't fluctuate as much as the actual budget deficit. In particular, large actual deficits, such as those of 1975, 1983, and 2009 (indicated by the purple lines), are mostly due to a depressed economy.

Should the Budget Be Balanced?

Persistent budget deficits can cause problems for both the government and the economy. Yet politicians are often tempted to run deficits because this allows them to cater to voters by cutting taxes without cutting spending or by increasing

---

FIGURE 13-10 The Actual Budget Deficit versus the Cyclically Adjusted Budget Deficit, 1965–2016

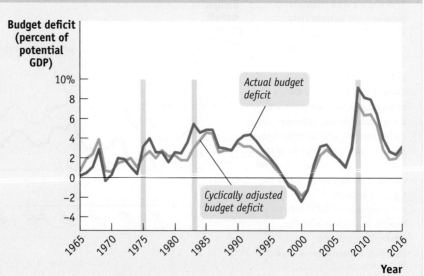

The cyclically adjusted budget deficit is an estimate of what the budget deficit would be if the economy was at potential output. It fluctuates less than the actual budget deficit because years of large budget deficits also tend to be years when the economy has a large recessionary gap. The large actual deficits in 1975, 1983, and 2009 (which are reported in the following year) are indicated by the vertical purple lines. These deficits were mostly due to a depressed economy.

Data from: Congressional Budget Office.

spending without increasing taxes. As a result, there are occasional attempts by policy makers to force fiscal discipline by introducing legislation—even a constitutional amendment—forbidding the government from running budget deficits. This is usually stated as a requirement that the budget be balanced—that revenues at least equal spending each fiscal year. Would it be a good idea to require a balanced budget annually?

Most economists don't think so. They believe that the government should only balance its budget on average—that it should be allowed to run deficits in bad years, offset by surpluses in good years. They don't believe the government should be forced to run a balanced budget *every year* because this would undermine the role of taxes and transfers as automatic stabilizers.

As we've learned, the tendency of tax revenue to fall and transfers to rise when the economy contracts helps to limit the size of recessions. But falling tax revenue and rising transfer payments generated by a downturn in the economy push the budget toward deficit. If constrained by a balanced-budget rule, the government would have to respond to this deficit with contractionary fiscal policies that would tend to deepen a recession.

Yet policy makers concerned about excessive deficits sometimes feel that rigid rules prohibiting—or at least setting an upper limit on—deficits are necessary. In fact, as the following Economics in Action explains, state and local governments do have such rules, which had a major impact on fiscal policy during the Great Recession and in its aftermath.

ECONOMICS >> *in Action*
Trying to Balance Budgets in a Recession

When the Great Recession struck, the U.S. federal government's budget deficit increased from just $160 billion to $1.4 trillion, partly because of stimulus measures but mainly because of automatic stabilizers: revenue fell sharply, while some expenditures, especially unemployment benefits, rose. Many observers worried about this deficit, but most economists thought that trying to balance the budget in the face of a recession would actually make that recession worse.

When it comes to government spending in America, however, the federal government isn't the only player. State and local governments account for about 40% of total government spending, and most government employment. (Most government employees are in positions that deliver essential services, such as schoolteachers, police officers, and firefighters.) And almost all of these state and local governments have rules requiring that they balance their budgets all the time.

There are a number of reasons for these rules, which make sense for each individual state or city. Taken together, however, the rules mean that for a large part of government in America, automatic stabilizers don't work. In fact, state and local governments cut back sharply in the face of a depressed economy, especially after 2010, when federal aid from the 2009 stimulus ended. Figure 13-11 shows the number of state and local employees from 2000 to 2016; as you can see, from 2009 until 2013 (the period shaded in purple), there were large cuts, mainly layoffs of teachers, in the face of falling revenues.

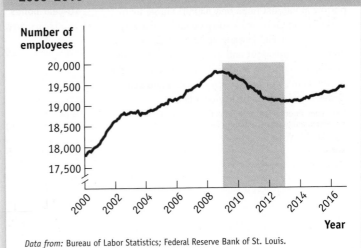

FIGURE 13-11 State and Local Government Employment, 2000–2016

Data from: Bureau of Labor Statistics; Federal Reserve Bank of St. Louis.

These actions at the state and local levels didn't fully offset the effects of automatic stabilizers at the federal level, but they still probably caused the recession to be deeper and the recovery slower than it would have been if we didn't have multiple levels of government, with the lower levels required to run balanced budgets.

>> Check Your Understanding 13-3

Solutions appear at back of book.

1. Why is the cyclically adjusted budget balance a better measure of whether government policies are sustainable in the long run than the actual budget balance?

2. Explain why states required by their constitutions to balance their budgets are likely to experience more severe economic fluctuations than states not held to that requirement.

Long-Run Implications of Fiscal Policy

At the end of 2009, the government of Greece ran into a financial wall. Like most other governments in Europe (and the U.S. government, too), the Greek government was running a large budget deficit, which meant that it needed to keep borrowing more funds, both to cover its expenses and to pay off existing loans as they came due. But governments, like countries or individuals, can only borrow if lenders believe it's likely that they will eventually be willing or able to repay their debts. By 2009 many lenders had lost faith in Greece's financial future, and were no longer willing to lend to the Greek government. Those few who were willing to lend demanded very high interest rates to compensate them for the risk of loss.

Figure 13-12 compares interest rates on 10-year bonds issued by the governments of Greece and Germany. At the beginning of 2007, Greece could borrow at almost the same rate as Germany, widely considered a very safe borrower. In 2009 its borrowing costs started to climb, and by the end of 2011 Greece had to pay an interest rate around 10 times the rate Germany paid.

What precipitated the crisis? In 2009 it became clear that the Greek government had used creative accounting to hide just how much debt it had already taken on. Government debt is, after all, a promise to make future payments to lenders. By 2010 it seemed likely that the Greek government had already promised more than it could possibly deliver.

FIGURE 13-12 Greek and German Long-Term Interest Rates

As late as 2008, the government of Greece could borrow at interest rates only slightly higher than those facing Germany, widely considered a very safe borrower. But in early 2009, as it became clear that both Greek debt and deficits were larger than previously reported, lenders lost confidence in the government's ability to repay its debts and sent Greek borrowing costs skyrocketing.

Data from: Federal Reserve Bank of St. Louis; OECD "Main Economic Indicators Complete Database."

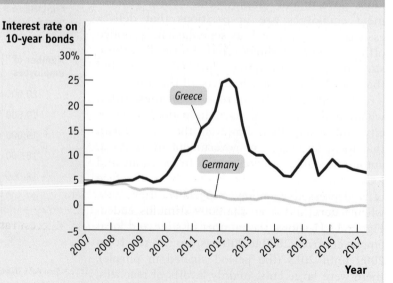

Lenders became deeply worried that the level of Greek government debt was unsustainable—that is, it was unlikely to repay what was owed. As a result, Greece found itself largely shut out of private debt markets. In order to prevent a government collapse, it received emergency loans from other European nations and the International Monetary Fund. But these loans came with the requirement that the Greek government undertake austerity, by making severe spending cuts and sharply raising taxes. Austerity in Greece wreaked havoc with the economy, imposed severe economic hardship on citizens, and led to massive social unrest.

The 2009 crisis in Greece shows why no discussion of fiscal policy is complete without taking into account the long-run implications of government budget surpluses and deficits, especially the implications for government debt. We now turn to those long-run implications.

Deficits, Surpluses, and Debt

When a family spends more than it earns over the course of a year, it has to raise the extra funds either by selling assets or by borrowing. And if a family borrows year after year, it will eventually end up with a lot of debt.

The same is true for governments. With a few exceptions, governments don't raise large sums by selling assets such as national parkland. Instead, when a government spends more than the tax revenue it receives—when it runs a budget deficit—it almost always borrows the extra funds. And governments that run persistent budget deficits end up with substantial debts.

To interpret the numbers that follow, you need to know a slightly peculiar feature of federal government accounting. For historical reasons, the U.S. government does not keep books by calendar years. Instead, budget totals are kept by **fiscal years,** which run from October 1 to September 30 and are labeled by the calendar year in which they end. For example, fiscal 2016 began on October 1, 2015, and ended on September 30, 2016.

At the end of fiscal 2016, the U.S. federal government had total debt equal to $19.5 trillion. However, part of that debt represented special accounting rules specifying that the federal government as a whole owes funds to certain government programs, especially Social Security. We'll explain those rules shortly. For now, however, let's focus on **public debt:** federal government debt held by individuals and institutions outside the government. At the end of fiscal 2016, the federal government's public debt was "only" $14.1 trillion, or 76% of GDP. Federal public debt at the end of 2016 was larger than at the end of 2015 because the government ran a deficit in 2016: a government that runs persistent budget deficits will experience a rising level of public debt. Why is this a problem?

Potential Dangers Posed by Rising Government Debt

There are two reasons to be concerned when a government runs persistent budget deficits that result in government debt that rises over time.

1. Crowding Out When the economy is at full employment and the government borrows funds in the financial markets, it is competing with firms that plan to borrow funds for investment spending. As a result, the government's borrowing may crowd out private investment spending, increasing interest rates and reducing the economy's long-run rate of growth.

2. Financial Pressure and Default Today's deficits, by increasing the government's debt, place financial pressure on future budgets. The impact of current

A **fiscal year** runs from October 1 to September 30 and is labeled according to the calendar year in which it ends.

Public debt is government debt held by individuals and institutions outside the government.

PITFALLS

DEFICITS VERSUS DEBT

Confusing *deficits* with *debt* is a common mistake. Let's review the difference.

A *deficit* is the difference between the amount of money a government spends and the amount it receives in taxes over a given period—usually, though not always, a year. Deficit numbers always come with a statement about the time period to which they apply, as in "the U.S. budget deficit *in fiscal 2016* was $587 billion."

A *debt* is the sum of money a government owes at a particular point in time. Debt numbers usually come with a specific date, as in "U.S. public debt *at the end of fiscal 2016* was $14.1 trillion."

Deficits and debt are linked, because government debt grows when governments run deficits. But they aren't the same thing, and they can even tell different stories. For example, Italy, which found itself in debt trouble in 2011, had a fairly small deficit by historical standards, but it had very high debt, a legacy of past policies.

deficits on future budgets is straightforward. Like individuals, governments must pay their bills, including interest payments on their accumulated debt. When a government is deeply in debt, those interest payments can be substantial. In fiscal 2016, the U.S. federal government paid 1.3% of GDP, or $241 billion, in interest on its debt. The more heavily indebted government of Italy paid interest of 4% of its GDP in 2016, according to estimates.

Other things equal, a government paying large sums in interest must raise more revenue from taxes or spend less than it would otherwise be able to afford—or it must borrow even more to cover the gap. And a government that borrows to pay interest on its outstanding debt pushes itself even deeper into debt. This process can eventually push a government to the point where lenders question its ability to repay. Like a consumer who has maxed out his or her credit cards, it will find that lenders are unwilling to lend any more funds. The result can be that the government defaults on its debt—it stops paying what it owes. Default is often followed by deep financial and economic turmoil.

Americans aren't used to the idea of government default, but it does happen. In the 1990s Argentina, a relatively high-income developing country, was widely praised for its economic policies—and it was able to borrow large sums from foreign lenders. By 2001, however, Argentina's interest payments were spiraling out of control, and the country defaulted. It eventually reached a settlement with most of its lenders under which it paid less than a third of the amount originally due.

Default creates havoc in a country's financial markets and badly shakes public confidence in both the government and the economy. Argentina's debt default was accompanied by a crisis in the country's banking system and a very severe recession. And even if a highly indebted government avoids default, a heavy debt burden typically forces it to slash spending or raise taxes, politically unpopular

---

 GLOBAL COMPARISON   **THE AMERICAN WAY OF DEBT**

How does the public debt of the United States stack up internationally? In dollar terms, we're number one—but this isn't very informative, since the U.S. economy and so the government's tax base are much larger than those of all but a few other nations. A more informative comparison is the ratio of public debt to GDP.

The figure shows the *net public debt* of a number of rich countries as a percentage of GDP at the end of 2016. Net public debt is government debt minus any assets governments may have—an adjustment that can make a big difference. What you see here is that the United States is more or less in the middle of the pack.

It may not surprise you that Greece heads the list, and most of the other high net debt countries are European nations that have been making headlines for their debt problems. Interestingly, however, Japan is also high on the list because it has used massive public spending to prop up its economy ever since the 1990s. Investors, however, still consider Japan a reliable government, so its borrowing costs remain low despite high net debt.

In contrast to the other countries, Norway has a large *negative* net public debt

thanks to oil. Norway is one of the world's largest oil exporters. Instead of spending its oil revenues immediately, the government of Norway has used them to build up an investment fund for future needs following the lead of traditional oil producers like Saudi Arabia. As a result, Norway has a huge stock of government assets rather than a large government debt.

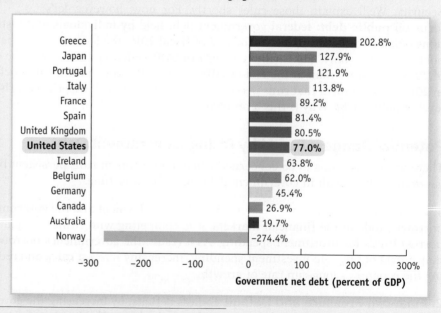

Country	Government net debt (percent of GDP)
Greece	202.8%
Japan	127.9%
Portugal	121.9%
Italy	113.8%
France	89.2%
Spain	81.4%
United Kingdom	80.5%
United States	**77.0%**
Ireland	63.8%
Belgium	62.0%
Germany	45.4%
Canada	26.9%
Australia	19.7%
Norway	−274.4%

Government net debt (percent of GDP)

Data from: International Monetary Fund; World Economic Outlook, October 2016; Congressional Budget Office.

measures that can also damage the economy. In some cases, austerity measures intended to reassure lenders that the government can indeed pay end up depressing the economy so much that lender confidence continues to fall.

If it has its own currency, a government that has trouble borrowing can print money to pay its bills. But doing so can lead to another problem: inflation. In fact, budget problems are the main cause of very severe inflation. Governments do not want to find themselves in a position where the choice is between defaulting on their debts and inflating those debts away by printing money.

Concerns about the long-run effects of deficits need not rule out the use of expansionary fiscal policy to stimulate the economy when it is depressed. However, these concerns do mean that governments should try to offset budget deficits in bad years with budget surpluses in good years. In other words, governments should run a budget that is approximately balanced over time. Have they actually done so?

> The **debt–GDP ratio** is the government's debt as a percentage of GDP.

Deficits and Debt in Practice

Figure 13-13 shows the U.S. federal government's budget deficit and how its debt changed from 1940 to 2016. Panel (a) shows the federal deficit as a percentage of GDP. As you can see, the federal government ran huge deficits during World War II. It briefly ran surpluses after the war, but it has normally run deficits ever since, especially after 1980. This seems inconsistent with the advice that governments should offset deficits in bad times with surpluses in good times.

However, panel (b) of Figure 13-13 shows that for most of the period these persistent deficits didn't lead to runaway debt. To assess the ability of governments to pay their debt, we use the **debt–GDP ratio,** the government's debt as a percentage of GDP. We use this measure, rather than simply looking at the size of the debt, because GDP, which measures the size of the economy as a whole, is a good indicator of the potential taxes the government can collect. If the government's debt grows more slowly than GDP, the burden of paying that debt is actually falling compared with the government's potential tax revenue. Under these conditions

FIGURE 13-13 U.S. Federal Deficits and Debt

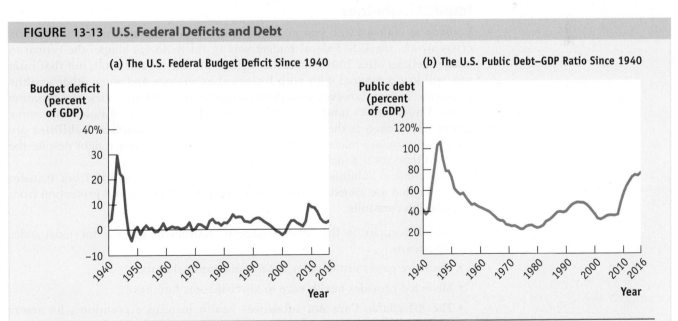

Panel (a) shows the U.S. federal budget deficit as a percentage of GDP from 1940 to 2016. The U.S. government ran huge deficits during World War II and has run smaller deficits ever since. Panel (b) shows the U.S. debt–GDP ratio. Comparing panels (a) and (b), you can see that in many years the debt–GDP ratio has declined in spite of government deficits. This seeming paradox reflects the fact that the debt–GDP ratio can fall, even when debt is rising, as long as GDP grows faster than debt.

Data from: Office of Management and Budget; Federal Reserve Bank of St. Louis.

As you can see from Figure 13-13, the U.S. government paid for World War II by borrowing on a huge scale. By the war's end, the public debt was more than 100% of GDP, and many people worried about how it could ever be paid off.

The truth is that it never was paid off. In 1946 public debt was $242 billion; that

number dipped slightly in the next few years, as the United States ran postwar budget surpluses, but the government budget went back into deficit in 1950 with the start of the Korean War. By 1962 the public debt was back up to $248 billion.

But by that time nobody was worried about the fiscal health of the U.S.

government because the debt–GDP ratio had fallen by more than half. The reason? Vigorous economic growth, plus mild inflation, led to a rapid rise in GDP. The experience was a clear lesson in the peculiar fact that modern governments can run deficits forever, as long as they aren't too large.

the underlying economy is strong enough to generate future surpluses, allowing the government to pay off its debt, at a time of its own choosing, and avoid the potential dangers of financial pressure and default.

What we see from panel (b) is that although the federal debt grew in almost every year, the debt–GDP ratio fell for 30 years after the end of World War II. This shows that the debt–GDP ratio can fall, even when debt is rising, as long as GDP grows faster than debt. The accompanying For Inquiring Minds, explains how sufficiently high levels of growth and/or inflation can allow a government that runs persistent budget deficits to nevertheless have a declining debt–GDP ratio.

Still, a government that runs persistent *large* deficits will have a rising debt–GDP ratio when debt grows faster than GDP. In the aftermath of the financial crisis of 2008, the U.S. government began running deficits much larger than anything seen since World War II, and the debt–GDP ratio began rising sharply. Similar surges in the debt–GDP ratio could be seen in a number of other countries after 2008. Economists and policy makers agreed that this was not a sustainable trend, that governments would need to get their spending and revenues back in line.

Implicit Liabilities

Looking at Figure 13-13, you might be tempted to conclude that until the 2008 crisis struck, the U.S. federal budget was in fairly decent shape: the return to budget deficits after 2001 caused the debt–GDP ratio to rise a bit, but that ratio was still low compared with both historical experience and some other wealthy countries. In fact, however, experts on long-run budget issues view the situation of the United States (and other countries such as Japan and Italy) with some alarm. The reason is the problem of *implicit liabilities*. **Implicit liabilities** are spending promises made by governments that are effectively a debt despite the fact that they are not included in the usual debt statistics.

The implicit liabilities of the U.S. government arise mainly from transfer programs that are aimed at providing security in retirement and protection from large health care bills:

- Social Security is the main source of retirement income for most older Americans.

- Medicare pays most of older Americans' medical costs.

- Medicaid provides health care to lower-income families.

- The Affordable Care Act subsidizes health insurance premiums for many low- to moderate-income families who are ineligible for Medicaid.

Implicit liabilities are spending promises made by governments that are effectively a debt despite the fact that they are not included in the usual debt statistics.

In each of these cases, the government has promised to provide transfer payments to future as well as current beneficiaries. So these programs represent a future debt that must be honored, even though the debt does not currently show up in the usual statistics. Together, these programs currently account for approximately half of federal spending.

The implicit liabilities created by these transfer programs worry fiscal experts. Figure 13-14 shows why. It shows actual 2016 spending on Social Security and major health care programs, measured as a percentage of GDP, together with Congressional Budget Office projections for spending in 2046. According to these projections, spending on Social Security will rise substantially over the next few decades and spending on the major health care programs will soar. Why?

In the case of Social Security, the answer is demography. Social Security is a pay-as-you-go system: current workers pay payroll taxes that fund the benefits of current retirees. So the ratio of the number of retirees drawing benefits to the number of workers paying into Social Security has a major impact on the system's finances.

There was a huge surge in the U.S. birth rate between 1946 and 1964, the years of what is commonly called the *baby boom*. Most baby boomers are currently of working age—which means they are paying taxes, not collecting benefits. But some are starting to retire, and as more and more of them do so, they will stop earning taxable income and start collecting benefits.

As a result, the ratio of retirees receiving benefits to workers paying into the Social Security system will rise. In 2016 there were 36 retirees receiving benefits for every 100 workers paying into the system. By 2046, according to the Social Security Administration, that number will rise to 47. So as baby boomers move into retirement, benefit payments will continue to rise relative to the size of the economy.

The aging of the baby boomers, by itself, poses only a moderately sized long-run fiscal problem. The projected rise in health care spending is a much more serious concern. These projections also reflect the aging of the population, both because more people will be eligible for Medicare and because older people tend to have higher medical costs. But the main story behind projections of higher health care spending is the long-run tendency of such spending to rise faster than overall spending, for both government-funded and privately funded health care.

To some extent, the implicit liabilities of the U.S. government are already reflected in debt statistics. We mentioned earlier that the government had a total debt of $19.5 trillion at the end of fiscal 2016 but that only $14.1 trillion of that total was owed to the public. The main explanation for that discrepancy is that both Social Security and part of Medicare (the hospital insurance program) are supported by *dedicated taxes:* their expenses are paid out of special taxes on wages. At times, these dedicated taxes yield more revenue than is needed to pay current benefits.

In particular, since the mid-1980s the Social Security system has been taking in more revenue than it currently needs in order to prepare for the retirement of the baby boomers. This surplus in the Social Security system has been used to accumulate a *Social Security trust fund*, which was $2.8 trillion at the end of fiscal 2016.

The money in the trust fund is held in the form of U.S. government bonds, which are included in the $19.5 trillion in total debt. You could say that there's something funny about counting bonds in the Social Security trust fund as part of government debt. After all, these bonds are owed by one part of the government (the government outside the Social Security system) to another part of the government (the Social Security system itself). But the debt corresponds to a real, if implicit, liability: promises by the government to pay future retirement benefits. So many economists argue that the gross debt of $18.1 trillion, the sum of public debt and government debt held by Social Security and other trust funds, is a more accurate indication of the government's fiscal health than the smaller amount owed to the public alone.

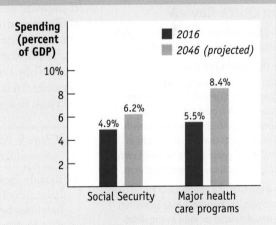

FIGURE 13-14 Future Demands on the Federal Budget

This figure shows actual spending on social insurance programs as a percentage of GDP in 2016 and Congressional Budget Office projections for these same programs in 2046. Partly as a result of an aging population, these programs will become much more expensive over time. But, it is the significant increases in health care spending that will pose the most serious problem for the federal budget in the future.

Data from: Congressional Budget Office.

ECONOMICS >> *in Action*

Reducing Implicit Liabilities

As we've seen, implicit government liabilities are a lot like a hidden form of debt. But they do differ from ordinary debts in one important way: unlike debts, which must be either repaid or defaulted on, implicit liabilities can be brought down by government policies that reduce future spending.

TABLE 13-2 Congressional Budget Office Budget Projections for 2035 (percent of GDP)

Implicit liabilities	2010 projection	2016 projection
Social Security spending	6.2%	6.2%
Major health care programs	10.9%	7.3%
Debt held by public	**185%**	**110%**

In fact, something like that has happened to U.S. implicit liabilities, where there has been a big change in the outlook since 2010, as shown in Table 13-2. The table compares two projections of the U.S. fiscal situation in 2035, made by the Congressional Budget Office (CBO) in 2010 and then in 2016. In 2010, the CBO's outlook (according to the most widely used scenario) was quite grim: rising spending on social insurance, the office suggested, would lead to soaring debt. By 2016 the outlook, though far from reassuring, was much less catastrophic: debt would rise to "only" 110% of GDP.

Why the change? As you can see in the table, it was mainly about health care costs. Projections for Social Security hadn't changed at all. However, after 2010 medical costs grew much more slowly than they had in previous years, leading the CBO to revise its expectations of future health care spending down.

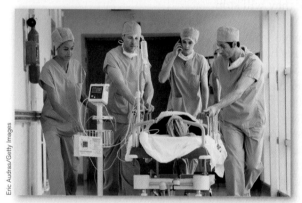

The cost-control measures of the Affordable Care Act offer an example of how increased efficiency in the provision of government services lowers implicit liabilities.

But why did health costs grow more slowly? Part of the answer probably has to do with a variety of cost-control measures that were included in the Affordable Care Act, which expanded government aid to many of the previously uninsured. One measure, for example, offered hospitals rewards if they found ways to save the government money, and penalized them if patients were readmitted too frequently with the same problems. Individually, these measures may not sound like much, but many health economists believe that their combined effect has been substantial.

The lesson from this story is that while implicit liabilities are a very important issue, they don't necessarily mean that governments must raise taxes or reduce services. In some cases, these liabilities can be reduced by providing government services in a smarter, more efficient way.

>> Quick Review

• Large and persistent budget deficits lead to increases in **public debt.**

• Public debt that rises year after year can lead to financial pressure and government default. In less extreme cases, it can crowd out investment spending, reducing long-run growth. This suggests that budget deficits in bad **fiscal years** should be offset with budget surpluses in good fiscal years.

• However, if a country has rising GDP, economists believe it may safely run annual deficits as long as the **debt–GDP ratio** is stable or falling because GDP is growing faster than the debt.

• In addition to their official public debt, modern governments have implicit liabilities. The U.S. government has large **implicit liabilities** in the form of Social Security, Medicare, Medicaid, and the Affordable Care Act (ACA). With large implicit liabilities, a stable debt–GDP ratio may give a misleading sense of security.

>> Check Your Understanding 13-4

Solutions appear at back of book.

1. Explain how each of the following events would affect the public debt or implicit liabilities of the U.S. government, other things equal. Would the public debt or implicit liabilities be greater or smaller?
   a. A higher growth rate of real GDP
   b. Retirees live longer
   c. A decrease in tax revenue
   d. Government borrowing to pay interest on its current public debt

2. Suppose the economy is in a slump and the current public debt is quite large. Explain the trade-off of short-run versus long-run objectives that policy makers face when deciding whether or not to engage in deficit spending.

3. Explain how a contractionary fiscal policy like austerity can make it more likely that a government is unable to pay its debts.

Eric Audras/Getty Images

Here Comes the Sun

The Solana power plant covers three square miles of the Arizona desert in Gila Bend, about 70 miles from Phoenix. Whereas most solar installations rely on photovoltaic panels that convert light directly into electricity, Solana uses a system of mirrors to concentrate the sun's heat on black pipes, which convey that heat to tanks of molten salt. The heat in the salt is, in turn, used to generate electricity. The advantage of this arrangement is that the plant can keep generating power long after the sun has gone down, greatly enhancing its efficiency.

Solana is one of only a small number of concentrated thermal solar plants operating or under construction, and as Figure 13-15 shows, solar power has been rapidly rising in importance, with the amount of solar-generated electricity increasing over 800% between 2008 and 2016. There are a number of reasons for this sudden rise, but the 2009 stimulus—which put substantial sums into the promotion of green energy—was a major factor. Solana, in particular, was built by the Spanish company Abengoa with the aid of a $1.45 billion federal loan guarantee. Abengoa also received $1.2 billion for a similar plant in the Mojave Desert.

While Solana is a good example of stimulus spending at work, it is also a good example of why such spending tends to be politically difficult. There were many protests over federal loans to a non-American firm, although Abengoa had the necessary technology, and the construction jobs created by the project were, of course, in the United States. Also, the long-term financial viability of solar power projects depends in part on whether government subsidies and other policies favoring renewable energy will continue, which isn't certain.

In terms of the goals of the stimulus, however, Solana seems to have done what it was supposed to: it generated jobs at a time when borrowing was cheap and many construction workers were unemployed.

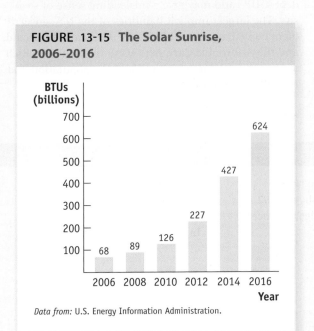

FIGURE 13-15 The Solar Sunrise, 2006–2016

Data from: U.S. Energy Information Administration.

QUESTIONS FOR THOUGHT

1. How did the political reaction to government funding for the Solana project differ from the reaction to more conventional government spending projects such as roads and schools? What does the case tell us about how to assess the value of a fiscal stimulus project?

2. In the chapter we talked about the problem of lags in discretionary fiscal policy. What does the Solana case tell us about this issue?

3. Is the depth of a recession a good or a bad time to undertake an energy project? Why or why not?

SUMMARY

1. The government plays a large role in the economy, collecting a large share of GDP in taxes and spending a large share both to purchase goods and services and to make transfer payments, largely for **social insurance.** *Fiscal policy* is the use of taxes, government transfers, or government purchases of goods and services to shift the aggregate demand curve.

2. Government purchases of goods and services directly affect aggregate demand, and changes in taxes and government transfers affect aggregate demand indirectly by changing households' disposable income. **Expansionary fiscal policy** shifts the aggregate demand curve rightward; **contractionary fiscal policy** shifts the aggregate demand curve leftward.

3. Only when the economy is at full employment is there potential for crowding out of private spending and private investment spending by expansionary fiscal policy. The argument that expansionary fiscal policy won't work because of Ricardian equivalence—that consumers will cut back spending today to offset expected future tax increases—appears to be untrue in practice. What is clearly true is that very active fiscal policy may make the economy less stable due to time lags in policy formulation and implementation.

4. Fiscal policy has a multiplier effect on the economy, the size of which depends on the fiscal policy. Except in the case of lump-sum taxes, taxes reduce the size of the multiplier. Expansionary fiscal policy leads to an increase in real GDP, and contractionary fiscal policy leads to a reduction in real GDP. Because part of any change in taxes or transfers is absorbed by savings in the first round of spending, changes in government purchases of goods and services have a more powerful effect on the economy than equal-sized changes in taxes or transfers.

5. Rules governing taxes—with the exception of **lump-sum taxes**—and some transfers act as **automatic stabilizers,** reducing the size of the multiplier and automatically reducing the size of fluctuations in the business cycle. In contrast, **discretionary fiscal policy** arises from deliberate actions by policy makers rather than from the business cycle.

6. Some of the fluctuations in the budget balance are due to the effects of the business cycle. In order to separate the effects of the business cycle from the effects of discretionary fiscal policy, governments estimate the **cyclically adjusted budget balance,** an estimate of the budget balance if the economy were at potential output.

7. U.S. government budget accounting is calculated on the basis of **fiscal years.** Persistently large budget deficits have long-run consequences because they lead to an increase in **public debt.** As a result, two potential dangers may arise: crowding out, which reduces long-run economic growth, and financial pressure leading to default, which brings economic and financial turmoil.

8. A widely used measure of fiscal health is the **debt–GDP ratio.** This number can remain stable or fall even in the face of persistent budget deficits if GDP rises over time. With large **implicit liabilities,** a stable debt–GDP ratio may give a misleading sense of security. The largest implicit liabilities of the U.S. government come from Social Security, Medicare, Medicaid, and the Affordable Care Act (ACA), the costs of which are increasing due to the aging of the population and rising medical costs.

KEY TERMS

Social insurance, p. 384
Expansionary fiscal policy, p. 385
Contractionary fiscal policy, p. 385
Lump-sum taxes, p. 391

Automatic stabilizers, p. 392
Discretionary fiscal policy, p. 392
Cyclically adjusted budget balance, p. 396

Fiscal year, p. 399
Public debt, p. 399
Debt–GDP ratio, p. 401
Implicit liabilities, p. 402

PROBLEMS

interactive activity

1. The accompanying diagram shows the current macroeconomic situation for the economy of Albernia. You have been hired as an economic consultant to help the economy move to potential output, Y_P.

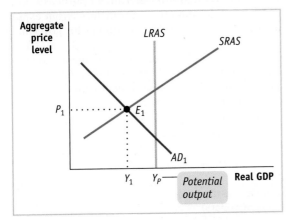

a. Is Albernia facing a recessionary or inflationary gap?

b. Which type of fiscal policy—expansionary or contractionary—would move the economy of Albernia to potential output, Y_P? What are some examples of such policies?

c. Illustrate the macroeconomic situation in Albernia with a diagram after the successful fiscal policy has been implemented.

2. The accompanying diagram shows the current macroeconomic situation for the economy of Brittania; real GDP is Y_1, and the aggregate price level is P_1. You have been hired as an economic consultant to help the economy move to potential output, Y_P.

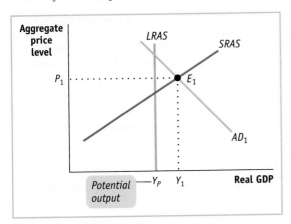

a. Is Brittania facing a recessionary or inflationary gap?

b. Which type of fiscal policy—expansionary or contractionary—would move the economy of Brittania to potential output, Y_P? What are some examples of such policies?

c. Illustrate the macroeconomic situation in Brittania with a diagram after the successful fiscal policy has been implemented.

3. An economy is in long-run macroeconomic equilibrium when each of the following aggregate demand shocks occurs. What kind of gap—inflationary or recessionary—will the economy face after the shock, and what type of fiscal policies would help move the economy back to potential output? How would your recommended fiscal policy shift the aggregate demand curve?

a. A stock market boom increases the value of stocks held by households.

b. Firms come to believe that a recession in the near future is likely.

c. Anticipating the possibility of war, the government increases its purchases of military equipment.

d. The quantity of money in the economy declines and interest rates increase.

4. During a 2008 interview, then German Finance Minister Peer Steinbrueck said, "We have to watch out that in Europe and beyond, nothing like a combination of downward economic [growth] and high inflation rates emerges—something that experts call stagflation." Such a situation can be depicted by the movement of the short-run aggregate supply curve from its original position, $SRAS_1$, to its new position, $SRAS_2$, with the new equilibrium point E_2 in the accompanying figure. In this question, we try to understand why stagflation is particularly hard to fix using fiscal policy.

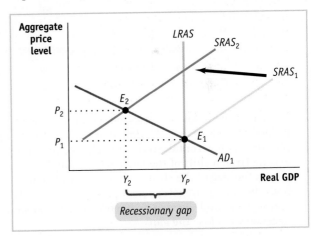

a. What would be the appropriate fiscal policy response to this situation if the primary concern of the government was to maintain economic growth? Illustrate the effect of the policy on the equilibrium point and the aggregate price level using the diagram.

b. What would be the appropriate fiscal policy response to this situation if the primary concern of the government was to maintain price stability? Illustrate the effect of the policy on the equilibrium point and the aggregate price level using the diagram.

c. Discuss the effectiveness of the policies in parts a and b in fighting stagflation.

5. Show why a $10 billion reduction in government purchases of goods and services will have a larger effect on real GDP than a $10 billion reduction in government transfers by completing the accompanying table for an economy with a marginal propensity to consume (*MPC*) of 0.6. The first and second rows of the table are filled in for you: on the left side of the table, in the first row, the $10 billion reduction in government purchases decreases real GDP and disposable income, *YD*, by $10 billion, leading to a reduction in consumer spending of $6 billion (*MPC* × change in disposable income) in row 2. However, on the right side of the table, the $10 billion reduction in transfers has no effect on real GDP in round 1 but does lower *YD* by $10 billion, resulting in a decrease in consumer spending of $6 billion in round 2.

a. When government purchases decrease by $10 billion, what is the sum of the changes in real GDP after the 10 rounds?

b. When the government reduces transfers by $10 billion, what is the sum of the changes in real GDP after the 10 rounds?

c. Using the formula for the multiplier for changes in government purchases and for changes in transfers, calculate the total change in real GDP due to the $10 billion decrease in government purchases and the $10 billion reduction in transfers. What explains the difference? [*Hint:* The multiplier for government purchases of goods and services is $1/(1 - MPC)$. But since each $1 change in government transfers only leads to an initial change in real GDP of $MPC \times$ $1, the multiplier for government transfers is $MPC/(1 - MPC)$.]

Rounds	Decrease in *G* = −$10 billion (billions of dollars)			Decrease in *TR* = −$10 billion (billions of dollars)		
	Change in *G* or *C*	Change in real GDP	Change in *YD*	Change in *TR* or *C*	Change in real GDP	Change in *YD*
1	ΔG = −$10.00	−$10.00	−$10.00	ΔTR = −$10.00	−$0.00	−$10.00
2	ΔC = −6.00	−6.00	−6.00	ΔC = −6.00	−6.00	−6.00
3	ΔC = ?	?	?	ΔC = ?	?	?
4	ΔC = ?	?	?	ΔC = ?	?	?
5	ΔC = ?	?	?	ΔC = ?	?	?
6	ΔC = ?	?	?	ΔC = ?	?	?
7	ΔC = ?	?	?	ΔC = ?	?	?
8	ΔC = ?	?	?	ΔC = ?	?	?
9	ΔC = ?	?	?	ΔC = ?	?	?
10	ΔC = ?	?	?	ΔC = ?	?	?

6. In each of the following cases, either a recessionary or inflationary gap exists. Assume that the aggregate supply curve is horizontal, so that the change in real GDP arising from a shift of the aggregate demand curve equals the size of the shift of the curve. Calculate both the change in government purchases of goods and services and the change in government transfers necessary to close the gap.

a. Real GDP equals $100 billion, potential output equals $160 billion, and the marginal propensity to consume is 0.75.

b. Real GDP equals $250 billion, potential output equals $200 billion, and the marginal propensity to consume is 0.5.

c. Real GDP equals $180 billion, potential output equals $100 billion, and the marginal propensity to consume is 0.8.

7. Most macroeconomists believe it is a good thing that taxes act as automatic stabilizers and lower the size of the multiplier. However, a smaller multiplier means that the change in government purchases of goods and services, government transfers, or taxes needed to close an inflationary or recessionary gap is larger. How can you explain this apparent inconsistency?

8. The government's budget surplus in Macroland has risen consistently over the past five years. Two government policy makers disagree as to why this has happened. One argues that a rising budget surplus indicates a growing economy; the other argues that it shows that the government is using contractionary fiscal policy. Can you determine which policy maker is correct? If not, why not?

9. Figure 13-10 shows the actual budget deficit and the cyclically adjusted budget deficit as a percentage of GDP in the United States from 1965 to 2016. Assuming that potential output was unchanged, use this figure to determine which of the years from 1990 to 2016 the government used expansionary fiscal policy and in which years it used contractionary fiscal policy.

10. You are an economic adviser to a candidate for national office. She asks you for a summary of the economic consequences of a balanced-budget rule for the federal government and for your recommendation on whether she should support such a rule. How do you respond?

11. In 2016, the policy makers of the economy of Eastlandia projected the debt–GDP ratio and the ratio of the budget deficit to GDP for the economy for the next 10 years under different scenarios for growth in the government's deficit. Real GDP is currently $1,000 billion per year and is expected to grow by 3% per year, the public debt is $300 billion at the beginning of the year, and the deficit is $30 billion in 2016.

Year	Real GDP (billions of dollars)	Debt (billions of dollars)	Budget deficit (billions of dollars)	Debt (percent of real GDP)	Budget deficit (percent of real GDP)
2016	$1,000	$300	$30	?	?
2017	1,030	?	?	?	?
2018	1,061	?	?	?	?
2019	1,093	?	?	?	?
2020	1,126	?	?	?	?
2021	1,159	?	?	?	?
2022	1,194	?	?	?	?
2023	1,230	?	?	?	?
2024	1,267	?	?	?	?
2025	1,305	?	?	?	?
2026	1,344	?	?	?	?

a. Complete the accompanying table to show the debt–GDP ratio and the ratio of the budget deficit to GDP for the economy if the government's budget deficit remains constant at $30 billion over the next 10 years. (Remember that the government's debt will grow by the previous year's deficit.)

b. Redo the table to show the debt–GDP ratio and the ratio of the budget deficit to GDP for the economy if the government's budget deficit grows by 3% per year over the next 10 years.

c. Redo the table again to show the debt–GDP ratio and the ratio of the budget deficit to GDP for the economy if the government's budget deficit grows by 20% per year over the next 10 years.

d. What happens to the debt–GDP ratio and the ratio of the budget deficit to GDP for the economy over time under the three different scenarios?

12. Your study partner argues that the distinction between the government's budget deficit and debt is similar to the distinction between consumer savings and wealth. He also argues that if you have large budget deficits, you must have a large debt. In what ways is your study partner correct and in what ways is he incorrect?

13. Access the Discovering Data exercise for Chapter 13 online to answer these questions.

a. Which of these six countries—United States, France, Italy, Greece, Germany, and United Kingdom—had the largest amount of government debt as a percent of GDP as of 2015? Which had the smallest?

b. Calculate the percentage change in government debt from 2007 through 2015 for the same six countries. Which country experienced the largest percentage increase in government inflation debt from 2007 through 2015? Which experienced the smallest?

c. Using the six countries as a reference point, what conclusions can you draw about the relationship between government debt and economic growth?

14. In which of the following cases does the size of the government's debt and the size of the budget deficit indicate potential problems for the economy?

a. The government's debt is relatively low, but the government is running a large budget deficit as it builds a high-speed rail system to connect the major cities of the nation.

b. The government's debt is relatively high due to a recently ended deficit-financed war, but the government is now running only a small budget deficit.

c. The government's debt is relatively low, but the government is running a budget deficit to finance the interest payments on the debt.

d. The government's debt is relatively high and the government is running a budget deficit to finance new infrastructure spending.

15. How did or would the following affect the current public debt and implicit liabilities of the U.S. government?

a. In 2003, Congress passed and President Bush signed the Medicare Modernization Act, which provides seniors and individuals with disabilities with a prescription drug benefit. Some of the benefits under this law took effect immediately, but others will not begin until sometime in the future.

b. The age at which retired persons can receive full Social Security benefits is raised to age 70 for future retirees.

c. Social Security benefits for future retirees are limited to those with low incomes.

d. Because the cost of health care is increasing faster than the overall inflation rate, annual increases in Social Security benefits are increased by the annual increase in health care costs rather than the overall inflation rate.

e. The Affordable Care Act (ACA), which went into effect in 2014, created incentives for hospitals to find ways to save the government money.

16. Unlike households, governments are often able to sustain large debts. For example, in 2016, the U.S. government's total debt reached $19.5 trillion, approximately equal to 106.1% of GDP. At the time, according to the U.S. Treasury, the average interest rate paid by the government on its debt was 1.3%. However, running budget deficits becomes hard when very large debts are outstanding.

   a. Calculate the dollar cost of the annual interest on the government's total debt assuming the interest rate and debt figures cited above.

   b. If the government operates on a balanced budget before interest payments are taken into account, at what rate must GDP grow in order for the debt–GDP ratio to remain unchanged?

   c. Calculate the total increase in national debt if the government incurs a deficit of $600 billion in 2017.

   d. At what rate would nominal GDP have to grow in order for the debt–GDP ratio to remain unchanged when the deficit in 2017 is $600 billion?

   e. Why is the debt–GDP ratio the preferred measure of a country's debt rather than the dollar value of the debt? Why is it important for a government to keep this number under control?

WORK IT OUT Interactive step-by-step help with solving this problem can be found online.

17. The accompanying table shows how consumers' marginal propensities to consume in a particular economy are related to their level of income.

Income range	Marginal propensity to consume
$0–$20,000	0.9
$20,001–$40,000	0.8
$40,001–$60,000	0.7
$60,001–$80,000	0.6
Above $80,000	0.5

   a. Suppose the government engages in increased purchases of goods and services. For each of the income groups in the table, what is the value of the multiplier— that is, what is the "bang for the buck" from each dollar the government spends on government purchases of goods and services in each income group?

   b. If the government needed to close a recessionary or inflationary gap, at which group should it primarily aim its fiscal policy of changes in government purchases of goods and services?

Taxes and the Multiplier

In the chapter, we described how taxes that depend positively on real GDP reduce the size of the multiplier and act as an automatic stabilizer for the economy. Let's look a little more closely at the mathematics of how this works.

Specifically, let's assume that the government "captures" a fraction t of any increase in real GDP in the form of taxes, where t, the tax rate, is a fraction between 0 and 1. And let's repeat the exercise we carried out in Chapter 11, where we consider the effects of a $100 billion increase in investment spending. The same analysis holds for *any* autonomous increase in aggregate spending—in particular, it is also true for increases in government purchases of goods and services.

The $100 billion increase in investment spending initially raises real GDP by $100 billion (the first round). In the absence of taxes, disposable income would rise by $100 billion. But because part of the rise in real GDP is collected in the form of taxes, disposable income only rises by $(1 - t) \times \$100$ billion. The second-round increase in consumer spending, which is equal to the marginal propensity to consume (MPC) multiplied by the rise in disposable income, is $(MPC \times (1 - t)) \times \$100$ billion. This leads to a third-round increase in consumer spending of $(MPC \times (1 - t)) \times (MPC \times (1 - t)) \times \$100$ billion, and so on. So the total effect on real GDP is

Increase in investment spending $\quad = \quad$ $100 billion

$+$ Second-round increase in consumer spending $= (MPC \times (1 - t)) \times \$100$ billion

$+$ Third-round increase in consumer spending $\quad = (MPC \times (1 - t))^2 \times \$100$ billion

$+$ Fourth-round increase in consumer spending $\quad = (MPC \times (1 - t))^3 \times \$100$ billion

$$
\begin{array}{ccc}
\cdot & & \cdot \\
\cdot & & \cdot \\
\cdot & & \cdot
\end{array}
$$

$$\text{Total increase in real GDP} = [1 + (MPC \times (1 - t)) + (MPC \times (1 - t))^2$$
$$+ (MPC \times (1 - t))^3 + \ldots] \times \$100 \text{ billion}$$

As explained in Chapter 11, an infinite series of the form $1 + x + x^2 + \ldots$, with $0 < x < 1$, is equal to $1/(1 - x)$. In this example, $x = (MPC \times (1 - t))$. So the total effect of a $100 billion increase in investment spending, taking into account all the subsequent increases in consumer spending, is to raise real GDP by:

$$\frac{1}{1 - (MPC \times (1 - t))} \times \$100 \text{ billion}$$

When we calculated the multiplier assuming away the effect of taxes, we found that it was $1/(1 - MPC)$. But when we assume that a fraction t of any change in real GDP is collected in the form of taxes, the multiplier is:

$$\text{Multiplier} = \frac{1}{1 - (MPC \times (1 - t))}$$

This is always a smaller number than $1/(1 - MPC)$, and its size diminishes as t grows. Suppose, for example, that $MPC = 0.6$. In the absence of taxes, this implies a multiplier of $1/(1 - 0.6) = 1/0.4 = 2.5$. But now let's assume that $t = 1/3$, that is, that 1/3 of any increase in real GDP is collected by the government. Then the multiplier is:

$$\frac{1}{1 - (0.6 \times (1 - 1/3))} = \frac{1}{1 - (0.6 \times 2/3)} = \frac{1}{1 - 0.4} = \frac{1}{0.6} = 1.667$$

PROBLEMS

interactive activity

1. An economy has a marginal propensity to consume of 0.6, real GDP equals $500 billion, and the government collects 20% of GDP in taxes. If government purchases increase by $10 billion, show the rounds of increased spending that take place by completing the accompanying table. The first and second rows are filled in for you. In the first row, the increase in government purchases of $10 billion raises real GDP by $10 billion, taxes increase by $2 billion, and YD increases by $8 billion; in the second row, the increase in YD of $8 billion increases consumer spending by $4.80 billion ($MPC \times$ change in disposable income).

Rounds	Change in G or C	Change in real GDP	Change in taxes	Change in YD
	(billions of dollars)			
1	$\Delta G = \$10.00$	$10.00	$2.00	$8.00
2	$\Delta C = 4.80$	4.80	0.96	3.84
3	$\Delta C = ?$	?	?	?
4	$\Delta C = ?$	?	?	?
5	$\Delta C = ?$	?	?	?
6	$\Delta C = ?$	?	?	?
7	$\Delta C = ?$	?	?	?
8	$\Delta C = ?$	?	?	?
9	$\Delta C = ?$	?	?	?
10	$\Delta C = ?$	?	?	?

a. What is the total change in real GDP after the 10 rounds? What is the value of the multiplier? What would you expect the total change in real GDP to be, based on the multiplier formula? How do your two answers compare?

b. Redo the accompanying table, assuming the marginal propensity to consume is 0.75 and the government collects 10% of the rise in real GDP in taxes. What is the total change in real GDP after 10 rounds? What is the value of the multiplier? How do your two answers compare?

WORK IT OUT **Interactive step-by-step help with solving this problem can be found online.**

2. Calculate the change in government purchases of goods and services necessary to close the recessionary or inflationary gaps in the following cases. Assume that the short-run aggregate supply curve is horizontal, so that the change in real GDP arising from a shift of the aggregate demand curve equals the size of the shift of the curve.

a. Real GDP equals $100 billion, potential output equals $160 billion, the government collects 20% of any change in real GDP in the form of taxes, and the marginal propensity to consume is 0.75.

b. Real GDP equals $250 billion, potential output equals $200 billion, the government collects 10% of any change in real GDP in the form of taxes, and the marginal propensity to consume is 0.5.

c. Real GDP equals $180 billion, potential output equals $100 billion, the government collects 25% of any change in real GDP in the form of taxes, and the marginal propensity to consume is 0.8.

Money, Banking, and the Federal Reserve System

NOT SO FUNNY MONEY

"THE PRODUCT IS CAREFULLY CREATED in rural facilities throughout the Peruvian countryside using cheap labor, then hoarded in stash houses controlled by violent gangs in Lima. Once there, the goods are packed into parcels, loaded onto planes or hidden inside luggage, pottery, hollowed-out Bibles, sneakers, children's toys or massive shipping containers bound for major U.S. ports of entry, such as Miami." So began a 2016 *Washington Post* report on Operation Sunset, a huge raid carried out by Peruvian authorities in cooperation with the U.S. Secret Service. But what was the target of this raid? It wasn't a drug bust; it was a fake money bust.

In recent years, Peru has become a major source for the production of counterfeit U.S. currency; the so-called "Peruvian note" is considered to be the best counterfeit in the business. Workers employed by criminal syndicates meticulously add decorative details to printed bills by hand, creating high-quality fakes that are very hard to detect.

The funny thing is that elaborately decorated pieces of paper have little or no intrinsic value. Indeed, a $100 bill printed with blue or orange ink wouldn't be worth the paper it was printed on.

But if the ink on that piece of paper is just the right shade of green, people will think that it's *money* and will accept it as payment for very real goods and services. Why? Because they believe, correctly, that they can do the same thing: exchange that piece of green paper for real goods and services.

In fact, here's a riddle: If a fake $100 bill from Peru enters the United States and is successfully exchanged for a good or service with nobody ever realizing it's a fake, who gets hurt? Accepting a fake $100 bill isn't like buying a car that turns out to be a lemon or a meal that turns out to be inedible. As long as the bill's counterfeit nature remains undiscovered, it will pass from hand to hand just like a real $100 bill.

The answer to the riddle is that the actual victims of the counterfeiting are U.S. taxpayers, because counterfeit dollars reduce the revenues available to pay for the operations of the U.S. government. Accordingly, the Secret Service diligently monitors the integrity of U.S. currency, promptly investigating any reports of counterfeit dollars. The efforts of the Secret Service attest to the fact that money isn't like ordinary goods and services, and it certainly is not like a piece of colored paper.

In this chapter we'll look at what money is, the role that it plays, the workings of a modern monetary system, and the institutions that sustain and regulate it, including the *Federal Reserve*. ●

Money is the essential channel that links the various parts of the modern economy.

WHAT YOU WILL LEARN

- What are the various roles that **money** plays and what forms does it take?

- Why is the level of the **money supply** so important to the state of the economy?

- How do the actions of private banks and the Federal Reserve determine the **money supply?**

- How does the Federal Reserve use **open-market operations** to change the **monetary base?**

Money is any asset that can easily be used to purchase goods and services.

Currency in circulation is cash held by the public.

Checkable bank deposits are bank accounts which can be accessed using checks, debit cards, and digital payments.

The **money supply** is the total value of financial assets in the economy that are considered money.

The Meaning of Money

In everyday conversation, people often use the word *money* to mean wealth. If you ask, "How much money does Bill Gates, the founder of Microsoft, have?" the answer will be something like, "Oh, $80 billion or so, but who's counting?" That is, the number will include the value of the stocks, bonds, real estate, and other assets he owns.

But the economist's definition of money doesn't include all forms of wealth. The dollar bills in your wallet are money; other forms of wealth—such as cars, houses, and stock certificates—aren't money. What, according to economists, distinguishes money from other forms of wealth?

What Is Money?

Money is defined in terms of what it does: **money** is any asset that can easily be used to purchase goods and services. In Chapter 10 we defined an asset as *liquid* if it can easily be converted into cash. Money consists of cash itself, which is liquid by definition, as well as other assets that are highly liquid.

You can see the distinction between money and other assets by asking yourself how you pay for your morning jolt of java. The person at the register will accept dollar bills in return for a double mocha latte—but he or she won't accept stock certificates or a collection of vintage baseball cards. If you want to convert stock certificates or vintage baseball cards into a latte, you have to sell them—trade them for money—and then use the money to buy your drink.

Of course, the vast majority of stores allow you to buy goods with a debit card linked to your bank account, and many of us pay larger bills (like tuition) with checks written on our accounts. Does that make your bank account money, even if you haven't converted it into cash? Yes. **Currency in circulation**—actual cash in the hands of the public—is considered money. So are **checkable bank deposits**—bank accounts which can be accessed using checks, debit cards, and digital payments.

Some definitions of money include assets other than currency and checkable bank deposits. There are two widely used definitions of the **money supply,** the total value of financial assets in the economy that are considered money.

Without a liquid asset like money, making purchases would be much harder.

1. The narrower definition of money considers only the most liquid assets to be money: currency in circulation, checkable bank deposits, and traveler's checks. (Once popular, traveler's checks are rarely used now, but are still included in the Fed's definition of the money supply.)

2. The broader definition includes three categories just noted plus other assets that are "almost" checkable, such as savings account deposits that can easily be transferred into a checking account with a phone call or a few taps on a smartphone. Both definitions of the money supply, however, make a distinction between those assets that can easily be used to purchase goods and services and those that can't.

Money plays a crucial role in generating *gains from trade* because it makes indirect exchange possible. Think of what happens when a cardiac surgeon buys a new refrigerator. The surgeon has valuable services to offer—namely, heart operations. The owner of the store has valuable goods to offer—refrigerators and other appliances. It would be extremely difficult for both parties if, instead of using money, they had to directly barter the goods and services they sell. In a barter system, a cardiac surgeon and an appliance store owner could trade only if the store owner happened to want a heart operation and the surgeon happened to want a new refrigerator.

This is known as the problem of finding a *double coincidence of wants:* in a barter system, two parties can trade only when each wants what the other has to offer. Money solves this problem: individuals can trade what they have to offer for money and trade money for what they want.

Because the ability to make transactions with money rather than relying on bartering makes it easier to achieve gains from trade, the existence of money increases welfare, even though money does not directly produce anything.

Let's take a closer look at the roles money plays in the economy.

> A **medium of exchange** is an asset that individuals acquire for the purpose of trading goods and services rather than for their own consumption.
>
> A **store of value** is a means of holding purchasing power over time.

Roles of Money

Money plays three main roles in any modern economy: it is a *medium of exchange*, a *store of value*, and a *unit of account*.

1. Medium of Exchange Our cardiac surgeon/refrigerator example illustrates the role of money as a **medium of exchange**—an asset that individuals use to trade for goods and services rather than for consumption. People can't eat dollar bills; rather, they use dollar bills to trade for edible goods and their accompanying services.

In normal times, the official money of a given country—the dollar in the United States, the peso in Mexico, and so on—is also the medium of exchange in virtually all transactions in that country. During troubled economic times, however, other goods or assets often play that role instead. For example, during economic turmoil people often turn to other countries' moneys as the medium of exchange: U.S. dollars have played this role in troubled Latin American countries, as have euros in troubled Eastern European countries. In a famous example, cigarettes functioned as the medium of exchange in World War II prisoner-of-war camps: even nonsmokers traded goods and services for cigarettes because the cigarettes could in turn be easily traded for other items. Inmates at federal penitentiaries, where smoking is now banned, reportedly use canned mackerel for many transactions. During the extreme German inflation of 1923, goods such as eggs and lumps of coal became, briefly, mediums of exchange.

2. Store of Value In order to act as a medium of exchange, money must also be a **store of value**—a means of holding purchasing power over time. To see why this is necessary, imagine trying to operate an economy in which ice-cream cones were the medium of exchange. Such an economy would quickly suffer from, well, monetary meltdown: your medium of exchange would often turn into a sticky

---

🌐 GLOBAL COMPARISON   THE BIG MONEYS

Americans tend to think of the dollar as the world's leading currency—and it does remain the currency most likely to be accepted in payment around the globe. But there are other important currencies, too. One simple measure of a currency's importance is the value of the quantity of that currency in circulation. This figure shows the value, in billions of dollars, of the quantity of four major currencies in circulation as of April 2017. The euro, used by a group of countries whose combined economies are roughly comparable in size to America's, is used almost as often as the dollar. China, with its rapidly growing economy, has a currency (the yuan) that isn't far behind the euro. And Japan's yen isn't far behind the big three, despite its much smaller economy, largely because the Japanese make much more use of cash, as opposed to checks, credit cards, or debit cards, than either Europeans or Americans.

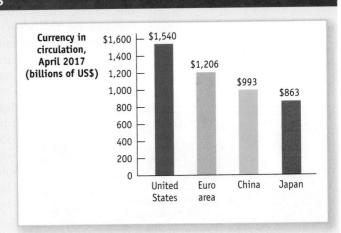

Data from: Federal Reserve Bank of St. Louis; European Central Bank; Bank of Japan; The People's Bank of China.

A **unit of account** is a measure used to set prices and make economic calculations.

Commodity money is a good used as a medium of exchange that has intrinsic value in other uses.

Commodity-backed money is a medium of exchange with no intrinsic value whose ultimate value is guaranteed by a promise that it can be converted into valuable goods.

puddle before you could use it to buy something else. (As we'll see in Chapter 16, one of the problems caused by high inflation is that, in effect, it causes the value of money to "melt.") Of course, money is by no means the only store of value. Any asset that holds its purchasing power over time is a store of value. So the store-of-value role is a necessary but not distinctive feature of money.

3. Unit of Account Finally, money normally serves as the **unit of account**—the commonly accepted measure individuals use to set prices and make economic calculations. To understand the importance of this role, consider a historical fact: during the Middle Ages, peasants typically were required to provide land-owners with goods and labor rather than money. A peasant might, for example, be required to work on the lord's land one day a week and hand over one-fifth of his harvest.

Today, rents, like other prices, are almost always specified in money terms. That makes things much clearer: imagine how hard it would be to decide which apartment to rent if modern landlords followed medieval practice. Suppose, for example, that Mr. Smith says he'll let you have a place if you clean his house twice a week and bring him a pound of steak every day, whereas Ms. Jones wants you to clean her house just once a week but wants four pounds of chicken every day. Who's offering the better deal? It's hard to say. If, instead, Smith wants $600 a month and Jones wants $700, the comparison is easy. In other words, without a commonly accepted measure, the terms of a transaction are harder to determine, making it more difficult to make transactions and achieve gains from trade.

Types of Money

In some form or another, money has been in use for thousands of years. For most of that period, people used **commodity money:** the medium of exchange was a good, normally gold or silver, that had intrinsic value in other uses. These alternative uses gave commodity money value independent of its role as a medium of exchange. For example, cigarettes, which served as money in World War II prisoner-of-war camps, were also valuable because many prisoners smoked. Gold was valuable because it was used for jewelry and ornamentation, aside from the fact that it was minted into coins.

By 1776, the year in which the United States declared independence and Adam Smith published *The Wealth of Nations*, there was widespread use of paper money in addition to gold or silver coins. Unlike modern dollar bills, however, this paper money consisted of notes issued by private banks, which promised to exchange their notes for gold or silver coins on demand. So the paper currency that initially replaced commodity money was **commodity-backed money,** a medium of exchange with no intrinsic value whose ultimate value was guaranteed by a promise that it could always be converted into valuable goods on demand.

The big advantage of commodity-backed money over simple commodity money, like gold and silver coins, was that it tied up fewer valuable resources. Although a note-issuing bank still had to keep some gold and silver on hand, it had to keep only enough to satisfy demands for redemption of its notes. And it could rely on the fact that on a normal day only a fraction of its paper notes would be redeemed. So the bank needed to keep only a portion of the total value of its notes in circulation in the form of gold and silver in its vaults. It could then lend out the remaining gold and silver to those who wished to use it. This allowed society to use the remaining gold and silver for other purposes, all with no loss in the ability to achieve gains from trade.

Goods with value, like gold and silver, were used as a medium of exchange for centuries.

By issuing paper notes to function as money instead of gold and silver coins, banks were able to free up valuable resources.

In a famous passage in *The Wealth of Nations,* Adam Smith described paper money as a "waggon-way through the air." Smith was making an analogy between money and an imaginary highway that did not absorb valuable land beneath it. An actual highway provides a useful service but at a cost: land that could be used to grow crops is instead paved over. If the highway could be built through the air, it wouldn't destroy useful land. As Smith understood, when banks replaced gold and silver money with paper notes, they accomplished a similar feat: they reduced the amount of real resources used by society to provide the functions of money.

At this point you may ask: why make any use at all of gold and silver in the monetary system, even to back paper money? In fact, today's monetary system goes even further than the system Smith admired, having eliminated any role for gold and silver. A U.S. dollar bill isn't commodity money, and it isn't even commodity-backed. Rather, its value arises entirely from the fact that it is generally accepted as a means of payment, a role that is ultimately decreed by the U.S. government. Money whose value derives entirely from its official status as a means of exchange is known as **fiat money** because it exists by government fiat, a historical term for a policy declared by a ruler.

Fiat money has two major advantages over commodity-backed money. First, it is even more of a "waggon-way through the air"—creating it doesn't use up any real resources beyond the paper it's printed on. Second, the supply of money can be adjusted based on the needs of the economy, instead of being determined by the amount of gold and silver prospectors happen to discover.

Fiat money, though, poses some risks. In the opening story, we described one such risk—counterfeiting. Counterfeiters usurp a privilege of the U.S. government, which has the sole legal right to print dollar bills. And the benefit that counterfeiters get by exchanging fake bills for real goods and services comes at the expense of the U.S. federal government, which covers a small but nontrivial part of its own expenses by issuing new currency to meet a growing demand for money.

The larger risk is that governments that can create money whenever they feel like it will be tempted to abuse the privilege. In Chapter 16 we'll learn how governments sometimes rely too heavily on printing money to pay their bills, leading to high inflation. In this chapter, however, we'll stay focused on the question of what money is and how it is managed.

Measuring the Money Supply

The Federal Reserve calculates the size of two **monetary aggregates,** overall measures of the money supply, which differ in how strictly money is defined. The two aggregates are known, rather cryptically, as M1 and M2. (There used to be a third aggregate named—you guessed it—M3, but in 2006 the Federal Reserve concluded that measuring it was no longer useful.)

M1, the narrowest definition, contains only currency in circulation (also known as cash), checkable bank deposits, and traveler's checks. M2 adds several other kinds of assets, often referred to as **near-moneys**—financial assets that aren't directly usable as a medium of exchange but can be readily converted into cash or checkable bank deposits, such as savings accounts. Examples are time deposits such as small-denomination *certificates of deposit (CDs),* which aren't checkable but can be withdrawn at any time before their maturity date by paying a penalty. Because currency and checkable deposits are directly usable as a medium of exchange, M1 is the most liquid measure of money.

Figure 14-1 shows the actual composition of M1 and M2 as of April 2017, in billions of dollars. M1 was valued at $3,428.7 billion, with about 43% accounted for by currency in circulation, almost all the rest accounted for by checkable bank deposits, and a tiny slice accounted for by traveler's checks. In turn, M1 made up 26% of M2, valued at $13,431.3 billion. M2 consists of M1 plus other types of assets: two types of bank deposits, known as savings deposits and time deposits,

Fiat money is a medium of exchange whose value derives entirely from its official status as a means of payment.

A **monetary aggregate** is an overall measure of the money supply.

Near-moneys are financial assets that can't be directly used as a medium of exchange but can be readily converted into cash or checkable bank deposits.

PITFALLS

WHAT'S NOT IN THE MONEY SUPPLY

Financial assets like stocks and bonds are not part of the money supply under any definition because they're not liquid enough.

M1 consists, roughly speaking, of assets you can use to buy groceries or a cup of coffee: currency, checkable deposits, and traveler's checks. M2 is broader, because it includes things like savings accounts that can easily and quickly be converted into M1. For example, you can switch funds between your savings and checking accounts at an ATM or using your smartphone.

By contrast, converting a stock or a bond into cash requires selling the stock or bond— something that usually takes some time and involves paying a broker's fee. That makes these assets much less liquid than bank deposits. So stocks and bonds, unlike bank deposits, aren't considered money.

FIGURE 14-1 Monetary Aggregates, April 2017

The Federal Reserve uses two definitions of the money supply, M1 and M2. As panel (a) shows, more than half of M1 consists of checkable bank deposits with currency in circulation making up virtually all of the rest. M2, as panel (b) shows, has a much broader definition: it includes M1 plus a range of other deposits and deposit-like assets, making it almost four times as large.

Data from: Federal Reserve Bank of St. Louis.

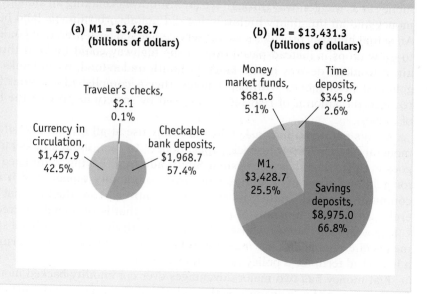

(a) M1 = $3,428.7
(billions of dollars)

Traveler's checks, $2.1 0.1%
Currency in circulation, $1,457.9 42.5%
Checkable bank deposits, $1,968.7 57.4%

(b) M2 = $13,431.3
(billions of dollars)

Money market funds, $681.6 5.1%
Time deposits, $345.9 2.6%
M1, $3,428.7 25.5%
Savings deposits, $8,975.0 66.8%

both of which are considered noncheckable, plus money market funds, which are mutual funds that invest only in liquid assets and bear a close resemblance to bank deposits. These near-moneys pay interest, although cash (currency in circulation) does not, and they typically pay higher interest rates than any offered on checkable bank deposits.

FOR INQUIRING MINDS 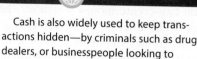 **From Bucks to Bitcoin**

There is $1.5 trillion of currency in circulation in the United States, or $4,500 for every man, woman, and child. Most individuals don't carry this amount in their wallets. So where is all the cash?

It can be found in cash registers. Businesses as well as individuals need to hold cash.

The largest proportion of these huge currency holdings—approximately 60%—is in the hands of foreign residents who so distrust their national currencies that the U.S. dollar has become a widely accepted medium of exchange and store of value.

Cash is also widely used to keep transactions hidden—by criminals such as drug dealers, or businesspeople looking to avoid paying taxes on their income.

The desire to shield transactions from the eyes of authorities helps to explain the growth of Bitcoin, a virtual currency created in 2009. It is basically a computing algorithm that creates electronic tokens that are accepted by some as currency.

But what leads people to place faith in a virtual currency—to accept it in place of "real" money? As with the dollar, faith in

Bitcoin arose from the belief that someone else, at a later date, would accept it in exchange for something real. As long as there are people who want to hide transactions, that's not an unreasonable belief. Bitcoin has become increasingly popular as merchants have started to accept it to avoid credit card fees.

One drawback to Bitcoin is its susceptibility to hacking. Despite that, the attractions of Bitcoin, and another new virtual currency, Ethereum, are so great that their combined value in June 2017 was approximately $75 billion.

ECONOMICS >> *in Action*
The History of the Dollar

U.S. dollar bills are pure fiat money: they have no intrinsic value, and they are not backed by anything that does. But American money wasn't always like that. In the early days of European settlement, the colonies that would become the United States used commodity money, partly consisting of gold and silver coins minted in Europe. But such coins were scarce on this side of the Atlantic, so the colonists relied on a variety of other forms of commodity money. For example, settlers in Virginia used tobacco as money and settlers in the Northeast used *wampum*, a type of clamshell.

Later in American history, commodity-backed paper money came into widespread use. But this wasn't paper money as we now know it, issued by the U.S. government and bearing the signature of the Secretary of the Treasury. Before the Civil War, the U.S. government didn't issue any paper money. Instead, dollar bills were issued by private banks, which promised that their bills could be redeemed for gold or silver coins on demand. These promises weren't always credible because banks sometimes failed, leaving holders of their bills with worthless pieces of paper. Understandably, people were reluctant to accept currency from any bank rumored to be in financial trouble. In this private money system, some dollars were less valuable than others.

A curious legacy of that time was notes issued by the Citizens' Bank of Louisiana, based in New Orleans, that became among the most widely used bank notes in the southern states. These notes were printed in English on one side and French

Not until the Civil War did the U.S. government issue official paper money.

on the other. (At the time, many people in New Orleans, originally a colony of France, spoke French.) Thus, the $10 bill read *Ten* on one side and *Dix*, the French word for *ten*, on the other. These $10 bills became known as *dixies*, probably the source of the nickname of the U.S. South.

The U.S. government began issuing official paper money, called *greenbacks*, in 1862 as a way to pay for the ongoing Civil War. At first greenbacks had no fixed value in terms of commodities. After 1873, the U.S. government guaranteed the value of a dollar in terms of gold, effectively turning dollars into commodity-backed money.

In 1933, when President Franklin D. Roosevelt broke the link between dollars and gold, his own federal budget director—who feared that the public would lose confidence in the dollar if it wasn't ultimately backed by gold—declared ominously, "This will be the end of Western civilization." It wasn't. The link between the dollar and gold was restored a few years later, then dropped again—seemingly for good—in August 1971. Despite the warnings of doom, the U.S. dollar went on to become the world's most widely used currency.

>> Check Your Understanding 14-1

Solutions appear at back of book.

1. Suppose you hold a gift card, good for certain products at participating stores. Is this gift card money? Why or why not?

2. Although most bank accounts pay some interest, depositors can get a higher interest rate by buying a certificate of deposit, or CD. The difference between a CD and a checking account is that the depositor pays a penalty for withdrawing the money before the CD comes due—a period of months or even years. Small CDs are counted in M2 but not in M1. Explain why they are not part of M1.

3. Explain why a system of commodity-backed money uses resources more efficiently than a system of commodity money.

>> Quick Review

• **Money** is any asset that can easily be used to purchase goods and services. **Currency in circulation** and **checkable bank deposits** are both part of the **money supply.**

• Money plays three roles: a **medium of exchange,** a **store of value,** and a **unit of account.**

• Historically, money took the form first of **commodity money,** then of **commodity-backed money.** Today the dollar is pure **fiat money.**

• The money supply is measured by two **monetary aggregates:** M1 and M2. M1 consists of currency in circulation, checkable bank deposits, and traveler's checks. M2 consists of M1 plus various kinds of **near-moneys.**

The Monetary Role of Banks

Roughly 43% of M1, the narrowest definition of the money supply, consists of currency in circulation—$1 bills, $5 bills, and so on. It's obvious where currency comes from: it's printed by the U.S. Treasury. But the rest of M1 consists of checkable bank deposits, and savings deposits account for the great bulk of M2, the broader definition of the money supply. By either measure, then, bank deposits are a major component of the money supply. And this fact brings us to our next topic: the monetary role of banks.

Bank reserves are the currency banks hold in their vaults plus their deposits at the Federal Reserve.

A **T-account** is a tool for analyzing a business's financial position by showing, in a single table, the business's assets (on the left) and liabilities (on the right).

What Banks Do

As we learned in Chapter 10, a bank is a *financial intermediary* that uses liquid assets in the form of bank deposits to finance the illiquid investments of borrowers. Banks can create liquidity because it isn't necessary for a bank to keep all of the funds deposited with it in the form of highly liquid assets. Except in the case of a *bank run*—which we'll get to shortly—all of a bank's depositors won't want to withdraw their funds at the same time. So a bank can provide its depositors with liquid assets yet still invest much of the depositors' funds in illiquid assets, such as mortgages and business loans.

Banks can't, however, lend out all the funds placed in their hands by depositors because they have to satisfy any depositor who wants to withdraw his or her funds. In order to meet these demands, a bank must keep substantial quantities of liquid assets on hand. In the modern U.S. banking system, these assets take the form either of currency in the bank's vault or deposits held in the bank's own account at the Federal Reserve. As we'll see shortly, the latter can be converted into currency more or less instantly. Currency in bank vaults and bank deposits held at the Federal Reserve are called **bank reserves.** Because bank reserves are in bank vaults and at the Federal Reserve, not held by the public, they are not part of currency in circulation.

To understand the role of banks in determining the money supply, we start by introducing a simple tool for analyzing the financial position of a bank or business: a **T-account.** A T-account summarizes the financial position of a bank or business in a single table that shows assets on the left and liabilities on the right.

Figure 14-2 shows the T-account for a hypothetical business that *isn't* a bank—Samantha's Smoothies. According to Figure 14-2, Samantha's Smoothies owns a building worth $30,000 and has $15,000 worth of smoothie-making equipment. These are assets, so they're on the left side of the table. To finance its opening, the business borrowed $20,000 from a local bank. That's a liability, so the loan is on the right side of the table. By looking at the T-account, you can immediately see what Samantha's Smoothies owns and what it owes. Oh, and it's called a T-account because the lines in the table make a T-shape.

Samantha's Smoothies is an ordinary, nonbank business. Now let's look at the T-account for a hypothetical bank, First Street Bank, which is the repository of $1 million in bank deposits.

Figure 14-3 shows First Street Bank's financial position. The loans First Street Bank has made are on the left side because they're assets: they represent funds that those who have borrowed from the bank are expected to repay. The bank's only other assets, in this simplified example, are its reserves, which, as we've learned, can take the form either of cash in the bank's vault or deposits at the Federal Reserve. On the right side are the bank's liabilities, which in this example consist entirely of deposits made by customers at First Street Bank. These are liabilities because they represent funds that must ultimately be repaid to depositors.

Notice that in this example First Street Bank's assets are larger than its liabilities. And that's the way it is supposed to be. Banks are required by law to maintain assets larger by a specific percentage than their liabilities.

FIGURE 14-2 A T-Account for Samantha's Smoothies

A T-account summarizes a business's financial position. Its assets, in this case consisting of a building and some smoothie-making machinery, are on the left side. Its liabilities, consisting of the money it owes to a local bank, are on the right side.

Assets		Liabilities	
Building	$30,000	Loan from bank	$20,000
Smoothie-making machines	$15,000		

FIGURE 14-3 Assets and Liabilities of First Street Bank

First Street Bank's assets consist of $1,200,000 in loans and $100,000 in reserves. Its liabilities consist of $1,000,000 in deposits—money owed to people who have placed funds in First Street's hands.

Assets		Liabilities	
Loans	$1,200,000	Deposits	$1,000,000
Reserves	$100,000		

In this example, First Street Bank holds reserves equal to 10% of its customers' bank deposits. The fraction of bank deposits that a bank holds as reserves is its **reserve ratio.** In the modern American system, the Federal Reserve—which, among other things, regulates banks operating in the United States—sets a minimum required reserve ratio that banks must maintain. To understand why banks are regulated, let's consider a problem banks can face: bank runs.

The **reserve ratio** is the fraction of bank deposits that a bank holds as reserves.

A **bank run** is a phenomenon in which many of a bank's depositors try to withdraw their funds due to fears of a bank failure.

The Problem of Bank Runs

A bank can lend out most of the funds deposited in its care because in normal times only a small fraction of its depositors want to withdraw their funds on any given day. But what would happen if, for some reason, all or at least a large fraction of its depositors did try to withdraw their funds during a short period of time, such as a couple of days?

If a significant share of its depositors demanded their money back at the same time, the bank wouldn't be able to raise enough cash to meet those demands. The reason is that banks convert most of their depositors' funds into loans made to borrowers; that's how banks earn revenue—by charging interest on loans.

Bank loans, however, are illiquid: they can't easily be converted into cash on short notice. To see why, imagine that First Street Bank has lent $100,000 to Drive-A-Peach Used Cars, a local dealership. To raise cash to meet demands for withdrawals, First Street Bank can sell its loan to Drive-A-Peach to someone else—another bank or an individual investor. But if First Street Bank tries to sell the loan quickly, potential buyers will be wary: they will suspect that First Street Bank wants to sell the loan because there is something wrong and the loan might not be repaid. As a result, First Street Bank can sell the loan quickly only by offering it for sale at a deep discount—say, a discount of 40%, for a sale price of $60,000.

The upshot is that if a significant number of First Street Bank's depositors suddenly decided to withdraw their funds, the bank's efforts to raise the necessary cash quickly would force it to sell off its assets very cheaply. Inevitably, this leads to a *bank failure:* the bank would be unable to pay off its depositors in full.

What might start this whole process? That is, what might lead First Street Bank's depositors to rush to pull their money out? A plausible answer is a spreading rumor that the bank is in financial trouble. Even if depositors aren't sure the rumor is true, they are likely to play it safe and get their money out while they still can. And it gets worse: a depositor who simply thinks that *other* depositors are going to panic and try to get their money out will realize that this could "break the bank." So he or she joins the rush. In other words, fear about a bank's financial condition can be a self-fulfilling prophecy: depositors who believe that other depositors will rush to the exit will rush to the exit themselves.

A **bank run** is a phenomenon in which many of a bank's depositors try to withdraw their funds due to fears of a bank failure. Moreover, bank runs aren't bad only for the bank in question and its depositors. Historically, they have often proved contagious, with a run on one bank leading to a loss of faith in other banks, causing additional bank runs.

Deposit insurance guarantees that a bank's depositors will be paid even if the bank can't come up with the funds, up to a maximum amount per account.

Reserve requirements are rules set by the Federal Reserve that determine the minimum reserve ratio for banks.

The **discount window** is an arrangement in which the Federal Reserve stands ready to lend money to banks in trouble.

The upcoming Economics in Action describes an actual case of just such a contagion, the wave of bank runs that swept across the United States in the early 1930s. In response to that experience and similar experiences in other countries, the United States and most other modern governments established a system of bank regulations that protect depositors and prevent most bank runs.

Bank Regulation

Should you worry about losing money in the United States due to a bank run? As long as it's a conventional bank, the answer is no. After the banking crises of the 1930s, the United States and most other countries put into place a system designed to protect depositors and the economy as a whole against bank runs. This system has four main features: *deposit insurance, capital requirements, reserve requirements*, and, in addition, banks have access to the *discount window*, a source of cash when it's needed.

1. Deposit Insurance Almost all banks in the United States advertise themselves as a "member of the FDIC"—the Federal Deposit Insurance Corporation. The FDIC provides **deposit insurance,** a guarantee that depositors will be paid even if the bank can't come up with the funds, up to a maximum amount per account. The FDIC currently guarantees the first $250,000 per depositor, per insured bank.

It's important to realize that deposit insurance doesn't just protect depositors if a bank actually fails. The insurance also eliminates the main reason for bank runs: since depositors know their funds are safe even if a bank fails, they have no incentive to rush to pull them out because of a rumor that the bank is in trouble.

2. Capital Requirements Although deposit insurance protects the banking system against bank runs, it creates a well-known incentive problem. Because depositors are protected from loss, they have no incentive to monitor their bank's financial health, allowing risky behavior by the bank to go undetected. At the same time, the owners of banks have an incentive to engage in overly risky investment behavior, such as making questionable loans at high interest rates. That's because if all goes well, the owners profit; if things go badly, the government covers the losses through federal deposit insurance.

To reduce the incentive for excessive risk taking, regulators require that bank owners hold substantially more assets than the value of bank deposits. That way, the bank still has assets larger than its deposits even if some of its loans go bad, and losses will accrue against the bank's assets, not the government. The excess of a bank's assets over its bank deposits and other liabilities is called the *bank's capital*. For example, First Street Bank has capital of $300,000, equal to ($1,200,000 + $100,0000) − $1,000,000. This is equivalent to $300,000/($1,200,000 + $100,000) = 23% of the total value of its assets. In practice, banks' capital is required to equal at least 7% of the value of their assets.

3. Reserve Requirements Another regulation used to reduce the risk of bank runs is **reserve requirements,** rules set by the Federal Reserve that specify the minimum reserve ratio for banks. For example, in the United States, the minimum reserve ratio for checkable bank deposits is 10%.

4. The Discount Window One final protection against bank runs is the fact that the Federal Reserve, which we'll discuss more thoroughly later in this chapter, stands ready to lend money to banks in trouble, an arrangement known as the **discount window.** The ability to borrow money means a bank can avoid being forced to sell its assets at fire-sale prices in order to satisfy the demands of a sudden rush of depositors demanding cash. Instead, it can turn to the Fed and borrow the funds it needs to pay off depositors.

Limits to Regulation's Reach: Shadow Banking The modern U.S. banking system is well-protected against old-fashioned bank runs. Unfortunately, as many investors learned to their horror in 2008, although old-fashioned bank runs may be a thing of the past, new-fashioned bank runs—which look very different, but have many of the same effects—can still happen.

How is that possible? The answer lies in a variety of financial arrangements that aren't exactly banking in the traditional sense, but serve more or less the same purposes as conventional banking, and can pose serious risks. These arrangements, referred to as *shadow banking*, are undertaken by nondepository financial firms, including investment banks, insurance companies, hedge fund companies, and money market fund companies. Because they don't accept deposits, firms in the shadow banking sector aren't fully covered by the protections or regulations that have made conventional, depository banking so safe. We'll say more about shadow banking later in the chapter.

ECONOMICS >> *in Action*

It's a Wonderful Banking System

Around Christmastime, it's a sure thing that when flipping channels you will encounter the 1946 film *It's a Wonderful Life*, featuring Jimmy Stewart as George Bailey, a small-town banker whose life is saved by an angel. The movie's climactic scene is a run on Bailey's bank, as fearful depositors rush to take their funds out.

When the movie was made, such scenes were still fresh memories for Americans who lived through the Great Depression. There was a wave of bank runs in late 1930, a second wave in the spring of 1931, and a third wave in early 1933. By the end, more than a third of the nation's banks had failed. To bring the panic to an end, on March 6, 1933, the newly inaugurated president, Franklin Delano Roosevelt, declared a national *bank holiday*, closing all banks for a week to give bank regulators time to close unhealthy banks and certify healthy ones.

Since then, regulation has protected the United States and other wealthy countries against most bank runs. In fact, the scene in *It's a Wonderful Life* was already out of date when the movie was made. But recent decades have seen several waves of bank runs in developing countries. For example, bank runs played a role in an economic crisis that swept Southeast Asia in 1997–1998 and in the severe economic crisis in Argentina that began in late 2001. And a panic with strong resemblance to a wave of bank runs swept world financial markets in 2008.

Notice that we said *most bank runs*. There are some limits on deposit insurance; in particular, in the United States currently only the first $250,000 of an individual depositor's funds in an insured bank is covered. As a result, there can still be a run on a bank perceived as troubled. In fact, that's exactly what happened in July 2008 to IndyMac, a Pasadena-based lender that had made a large number of questionable home loans. As questions about IndyMac's financial soundness were raised, depositors began pulling out funds, forcing federal regulators to step in and close the bank. In Britain the limits on deposit insurance are much lower, which exposed the bank Northern Rock to a classic bank run in September 2007. Unlike the bank runs of the 1930s, however, most depositors at both IndyMac and Northern Rock got all their funds back—and the panics at these banks didn't spread to other institutions.

Panicky IndyMac depositors lined up to pull their money out of the troubled California bank in July 2008.

>> Check Your Understanding 14-2
Solutions appear at back of book.

1. Suppose you are a depositor at First Street Bank. You hear a rumor that the bank has suffered serious losses on its loans. Every depositor knows that the rumor isn't true, but each thinks that most other depositors believe the rumor. Why, in the absence of deposit insurance, could this lead to a bank run? How does deposit insurance change the situation?

2. A con artist has a great idea: he'll open a bank without investing any capital and lend all the deposits at high interest rates to real estate developers. If the real estate market booms, the loans will be repaid and he'll make high profits. If the real estate market goes bust, the loans won't be repaid and the bank will fail—but he will not lose any of his own wealth. How would modern bank regulation frustrate his scheme?

Determining the Money Supply

Without banks, there would be no checkable deposits, so the quantity of currency in circulation would equal the money supply. In that case, the money supply would be solely determined by whoever controls government minting and printing presses. But banks do exist, and through their creation of checkable bank deposits they affect the money supply in two ways.

1. Banks remove some currency from circulation: dollar bills that are sitting in bank vaults, as opposed to sitting in people's wallets, aren't part of the money supply.

2. Much more importantly, banks create money by accepting deposits and making loans—that is, they make the money supply larger than just the value of currency in circulation.

Our next topic is how banks create money and what determines the amount of money they create.

How Banks Create Money

To see how banks create money, let's examine what happens when someone decides to deposit currency in a bank. Consider the example of Silas, a miser, who keeps a shoebox full of cash under his bed. Suppose Silas realizes that it would be safer, as well as more convenient, to deposit that cash in the bank and to use his debit card when shopping. Assume that he deposits $1,000 into a checkable account at First Street Bank. What effect will Silas's actions have on the money supply?

Panel (a) of Figure 14-4 shows the initial effect of his deposit. First Street Bank credits Silas with $1,000 in his account, so the economy's checkable bank deposits rise by $1,000. Meanwhile, Silas's cash goes into the vault, raising First Street's reserves by $1,000 as well.

This initial transaction has no effect on the money supply. Currency in circulation, part of the money supply, falls by $1,000; checkable bank deposits, also part of the money supply, rise by the same amount.

But this is not the end of the story, because First Street Bank can now lend out part of Silas's deposit. Assume that it holds 10% of Silas's deposit—$100—in reserves and lends the rest out in cash to Silas's neighbor, Maya. The effect of this second stage is shown in panel (b). First Street's deposits remain unchanged, and so does the value of its assets. But the composition of its assets changes: by making the loan, it reduces its reserves by $900, so that they are only $100 larger than they were before Silas made his deposit. In the place of the $900 reduction in reserves, the bank has acquired an IOU, its $900 cash loan to Maya.

FIGURE 14-4 Effect on the Money Supply of Turning Cash into a Checkable Deposit at First Street Bank

(a) Initial Effect Before Bank Makes a New Loan

Assets		Liabilities	
Loans	No change	Checkable	
Reserves	+$1,000	deposits	+$1,000

(b) Effect When Bank Makes a New Loan

Assets		Liabilities	
Loans	+$900	No change	
Reserves	−$900		

When Silas deposits $1,000 (which had been stashed under his bed) into a checkable bank account, there is initially no effect on the money supply: currency in circulation falls by $1,000, but checkable bank deposits rise by $1,000. The corresponding entries on the bank's T-account, depicted in panel (a), show deposits initially rising by $1,000 and the bank's reserves initially rising by $1,000. In the second stage, depicted in panel (b), the bank holds 10% of Silas's deposit ($100) as reserves and lends out the rest ($900) to Maya. As a result, its reserves fall by $900 and its loans increase by $900. Its liabilities, including Silas's $1,000 deposit, are unchanged. The money supply, the sum of checkable bank deposits and currency in circulation, has now increased by $900—the $900 now held by Maya.

So by putting $900 of Silas's cash back into circulation by lending it to Maya, First Street Bank has, in fact, increased the money supply. That is, the sum of currency in circulation and checkable bank deposits has risen by $900 compared to what it had been when Silas's cash was still under his bed. Although Silas is still the owner of $1,000, now in the form of a checkable deposit, Maya has the use of $900 in cash from her borrowings.

And this may not be the end of the story. Suppose that Maya uses her cash to buy a television from Acme Merchandise. What does Anne Acme, the store's owner, do with the cash? If she holds on to it, the money supply doesn't increase any further. But suppose she deposits the $900 into a checkable bank deposit—say, at Second Street Bank. Second Street Bank, in turn, will keep only part of that deposit in reserves, lending out the rest, creating still more money.

Assume that Second Street Bank, like First Street Bank, keeps 10% of any bank deposit in reserves and lends out the rest. Then it will keep $90 in reserves and lend out $810 of Anne's deposit to another borrower, further increasing the money supply.

Table 14-1 shows the process of money creation we have described so far. To simplify the table we will assume that, at first, the money supply consists only of Silas's $1,000. After he deposits the cash into a checkable bank deposit and the bank makes a loan, the money supply rises to $1,900. After the second deposit and the second loan, the money supply rises to $2,710. And the process will, of course, continue from there. (Although we have considered the case in which Silas places his cash in a checkable bank deposit, the results would be the same if he put it into any type of near-money.)

This process of money creation may sound familiar. In Chapter 11 we described the *multiplier process*: an initial increase in real GDP leads to a rise in consumer spending, which leads to a further rise in real GDP, which leads to a further rise in consumer spending, and so on. What we have here is another kind of multiplier—the *money multiplier*. We'll now see what determines the size of this multiplier.

TABLE 14-1 How Banks Create Money

	Currency in circulation	Checkable bank deposits	Money supply
First stage Silas keeps his cash under his bed.	$1,000	$0	$1,000
Second stage Silas deposits cash in First Street Bank, which lends out $900 to Maya, who then pays it to Anne Acme.	900	1,000	1,900
Third stage Anne Acme deposits $900 in Second Street Bank, which lends out $810 to another borrower.	810	1,900	2,710

Excess reserves are a bank's reserves over and above its required reserves.

Reserves, Bank Deposits, and the Money Multiplier

In tracing out the effect of Silas's deposit in Table 14-1, we assumed that the funds a bank lends out always end up being deposited either in the same bank or in another bank—so funds disbursed as loans come back to the banking system, even if not to the lending bank itself.

In reality, some of these loaned funds may be held by borrowers in their wallets and not deposited in a bank, meaning that some of the loaned amount "leaks" out of the banking system. Such leaks reduce the size of the money multiplier, just as leaks of real income into savings reduce the size of the real GDP multiplier. (Bear in mind, however, that the leak here comes from the fact that borrowers keep some of their funds in currency, rather than the fact that consumers save some of their income.)

"There's money in there that could be used for other purposes."

But let's set that complication aside for a moment and consider how the money supply is determined in a checkable-deposits-only monetary system, where funds are always deposited in bank accounts and none are held in wallets as currency. That is, in our checkable-deposits-only monetary system, any and all funds borrowed from a bank are immediately deposited into a checkable bank account. We'll assume that banks are required to satisfy a minimum reserve ratio of 10% and that every bank lends out all of its **excess reserves,** reserves over and above the amount needed to satisfy the minimum reserve ratio.

Now suppose that for some reason a bank suddenly finds itself with $1,000 in excess reserves. What happens? The answer is that the bank will lend out that $1,000, which will end up as a checkable bank deposit somewhere in the banking system, launching a money multiplier process very similar to the process shown in Table 14-1.

In the first stage, the bank lends out its excess reserves of $1,000, which becomes a checkable bank deposit somewhere. The bank that receives the $1,000 deposit keeps 10%, or $100, as reserves and lends out the remaining 90%, or $900, which again becomes a checkable bank deposit somewhere. The bank receiving this $900 deposit again keeps 10%, which is $90, as reserves and lends out the remaining $810. The bank receiving this $810 keeps $81 in reserves and lends out the remaining $729, and so on. As a result of this process, the total increase in checkable bank deposits is equal to a sum that looks like:

$$\$1,000 + \$900 + \$810 + \$729 + \dots$$

We'll use the symbol rr for the reserve ratio. More generally, the total increase in checkable bank deposits that is generated when a bank lends out $1,000 in excess reserves is:

(14-1) Increase in checkable bank deposits from $1,000 in excess reserves =
$\$1,000 + (\$1,000 \times (1 - rr)) + (\$1,000 \times (1 - rr)^2) + (\$1,000 \times (1 - rr)^3) + \dots$

As we saw in Chapter 11, an infinite series of this form can be simplified to:

(14-2) Increase in checkable bank deposits from $1,000 in excess reserves =
$\$1,000/rr$

Given a reserve ratio of 10%, or 0.1, a $1,000 increase in excess reserves will increase the total value of checkable bank deposits by $1,000/0.1 = $10,000. In fact, in a checkable-deposits-only monetary system, the total value of checkable bank deposits will be equal to the value of bank reserves divided by the reserve ratio. Or to put it a different way, if the reserve ratio is 10%, each $1 of reserves held by a bank supports $1/$rr$ = $1/0.1 = $10 of checkable bank deposits.

The Money Multiplier in Reality

In reality, the determination of the money supply is more complicated than our simple model suggests because it depends not only on the ratio of reserves to bank deposits but also on the fraction of the money supply that individuals choose to hold in the form of currency. In fact, we already saw this in our example of Silas depositing the cash under his bed: when he chose to hold a checkable bank deposit instead of currency, he set in motion an increase in the money supply.

To define the money multiplier in practice, it's important to recognize that the Federal Reserve controls the *sum* of bank reserves and currency in circulation, called the *monetary base*, but it does not control the allocation of that sum between bank reserves and currency in circulation. Consider Silas and his deposit one more time: by taking the cash from under his bed and depositing it in a bank, he reduced the quantity of currency in circulation but increased bank reserves by an equal amount—leaving the *monetary base*, on net, unchanged. The **monetary base,** which is the quantity the monetary authorities control, is the sum of currency in circulation and reserves held by banks.

The monetary base is different from the money supply in two ways.

1. Bank reserves, which are part of the monetary base, aren't considered part of the money supply. A $1 bill in someone's wallet is considered money because it's available for an individual to spend, but a $1 bill held as bank reserves in a bank vault or deposited at the Federal Reserve isn't considered part of the money supply because it's not available for spending.

2. Checkable bank deposits, which are part of the money supply because they are available for spending, aren't part of the monetary base.

Figure 14-5 illustrates the two concepts. The circle on the left represents the monetary base, consisting of bank reserves plus currency in circulation. The circle on the right represents the money supply, consisting mainly of currency in circulation plus checkable or near-checkable bank deposits. As the figure indicates, currency in circulation is part of both the monetary base and the money supply. But bank reserves aren't part of the money supply, and checkable or near-checkable bank deposits aren't part of the monetary base. In practice, most of the monetary base actually consists of currency in circulation, which also makes up about half of the money supply.

Now we can formally define the **money multiplier:** it's the ratio of the money supply to the monetary base. Before the financial crisis of 2008, it was about 1.6, as calculated from official Federal Reserve statistics. After the crisis, it fell to about 0.7. Even before the crisis it was a lot smaller than 1/0.1 = 10, which would

The **monetary base** is the sum of currency in circulation and bank reserves.

The **money multiplier** is the ratio of the money supply to the monetary base.

FIGURE 14-5 The Monetary Base and the Money Supply

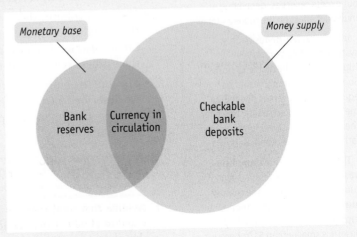

The monetary base is equal to bank reserves plus currency in circulation. It is different from the money supply, consisting mainly of checkable or near-checkable bank deposits plus currency in circulation. Each dollar of bank reserves backs several dollars of bank deposits. As a result, in normal economic times, the money supply is larger than the monetary base, making the circle at right larger than the circle on the left. However, in extraordinary economic times, as in the aftermath of the 2008 financial crisis, the monetary base grew, overtaking the money supply, making the circle at right smaller than the circle on the left.

The collapse of Lehman Brothers and the ensuing financial crisis prompted the Federal Reserve to dramatically increase the monetary base in order to stabilize the economy.

be the money multiplier in a checkable-deposits-only system with a reserve ratio of 10% (the minimum required ratio for most checkable deposits in the United States).

The reason the actual money multiplier has been smaller than 10 is that people hold significant amounts of cash, and a dollar of currency in circulation, unlike a dollar in reserves, doesn't support multiple dollars of the money supply. In fact, before the crisis currency in circulation accounted for more than 90% of the monetary base.

At the beginning of 2009, currency in circulation had dropped to only 40% of the monetary base. Nearly a decade later, in 2017, the percentage remained the same. What happened? Basically, the Federal Reserve dramatically expanded the monetary base in response to the financial crisis. The Fed undertook this action in an effort to stabilize the economy after Lehman Brothers, a key financial institution, failed in September 2008. However, banks, saw few opportunities for safe, profitable lending at the time. So rather than lending out the increase in the monetary base, they parked it at the Federal Reserve in the form of deposits that counted as part of the monetary base. As a result, currency in circulation no longer dominated the monetary base, as the surge in deposits at the Fed made the monetary base larger than M1. As a result, the actual money multiplier fell to less than 1 as banks held much more than the required 10% in reserves at the Fed. In May 2017, the money multiplier stood at 0.9.

ECONOMICS >> *in Action*
Multiplying Money Down

TABLE 14-2 The Effects of Bank Runs, 1929–1933

	Currency in circulation	Checkable bank deposits	M1
	(billions of dollars)		
1929	$3.90	$22.74	$26.64
1933	5.09	14.82	19.91
Percent change	+31%	−35%	−25%

Data from: U.S. Census Bureau (1975), *Historical Statistics of the United States.*

In our hypothetical example illustrating how banks create money, we described Silas the miser taking the currency from under his bed and turning it into a checkable bank deposit. This led to an increase in the money supply, as banks engaged in successive waves of lending backed by Silas's funds. It follows that if something happened to make Silas revert to old habits, taking his money out of the bank and putting it back under his bed, the result would be less lending and, ultimately, a decline in the money supply. That's exactly what happened as a result of the bank runs of the 1930s.

Table 14-2 shows what happened between 1929 and 1933, as bank failures shook the public's confidence in the banking system:

- The second column shows the public's holdings of currency. This increased sharply, as many Americans decided that money under the bed was safer than money in the bank after all.

- The third column shows the value of checkable bank deposits. This fell sharply, through the multiplier process, when individuals pulled their cash out of banks. Loans also fell because banks that survived the waves of bank runs increased their excess reserves, just in case another wave began.

- The fourth column shows the value of M1, the first of the monetary aggregates we described earlier. It fell sharply because the total reduction in checkable or near-checkable bank deposits was much larger than the increase in currency in circulation.

>> Quick Review

- Banks create money when they lend out **excess reserves,** generating a multiplier effect on the money supply.

- In a checkable-deposits-only system, $1 of bank reserves supports $1/rr checkable deposits. So the money supply would be equal to bank reserves divided by the reserve ratio. In reality, however, the public holds some funds as cash rather than in checkable deposits.

- The Fed controls the **monetary base,** equal to bank reserves plus currency in circulation. The **money multiplier** is equal to the money supply divided by the monetary base. It is smaller than $1/rr because people hold some funds as cash.

>> Check Your Understanding 14-3
Solutions appear at back of book.

1. Assume that total reserves are equal to $200 and total checkable bank deposits are equal to $1,000. Also assume that the public does not hold any currency. Now suppose that the required reserve ratio falls from 20% to 10%. Trace out how this leads to an expansion in bank deposits.

2. Take the example of Silas depositing his $1,000 in cash into First Street Bank and assume that the required reserve ratio is 10%. But now assume that each time someone receives a bank loan, he or she keeps half the loan in cash. Explain the resulting expansion in the money supply.

A **central bank** is an institution that oversees and regulates the banking system and controls the monetary base.

The Federal Reserve System

Who's in charge of ensuring that banks maintain enough reserves? Who decides how large the monetary base will be? The answer, in the United States, is an institution known as the Federal Reserve (or, informally, as the *Fed*). The Federal Reserve is a **central bank**—an institution that oversees and regulates the banking system and controls the monetary base.

Other central banks include the Bank of England, the People's Bank of China, the Bank of Japan, and the European Central Bank, or ECB. The ECB acts as a common central bank for 19 European countries: Austria, Belgium, Cyprus, Estonia, Finland, France, Germany, Greece, Ireland, Italy, Latvia, Lithuania, Luxembourg, Malta, the Netherlands, Portugal, Slovakia, Slovenia, and Spain. The world's oldest central bank is Sweden's Sveriges Riksbank, which awards the Nobel Prize in economics.

The Structure of the Fed

The legal status of the Fed, which was created in 1913, is unusual: it is not exactly part of the U.S. government, but it is not really a private institution either. Strictly speaking, the Federal Reserve system consists of two parts: the Board of Governors and the 12 regional Federal Reserve Banks.

The Board of Governors, which oversees the entire system from its offices in Washington, D.C., is constituted like a government agency: its seven members are appointed by the president and must be approved by the Senate. However, they are appointed for 14-year terms, to insulate them from political pressure in their conduct of monetary policy. (Why this is a potential problem will become clear in the next chapter, when we discuss inflation.)

Although the chair is appointed more frequently—every four years—it's traditional for chairs to be reappointed and serve much longer terms. For example, William McChesney Martin was chair of the Fed from 1951 until 1970. Alan Greenspan, appointed in 1987, served as the Fed's chair until 2006. Ben Bernanke, Greenspan's successor, served until 2014. And Bernanke's successor, Janet Yellen, is up for reappointment in 2018.

The 12 Federal Reserve Banks each serve a region of the country, providing various banking and supervisory services. One of their jobs, for example, is to audit the books of private-sector banks to ensure their financial health. Each regional bank is run by a board of directors chosen from the local banking and business community. The Federal Reserve Bank of New York plays a special role: it carries out *open-market operations*, usually the main tool of monetary policy. Figure 14-6 shows the 12 Federal Reserve districts and the city in which each regional Federal Reserve Bank is located.

Decisions about monetary policy are made by the Federal Open Market Committee, which consists of the Board of Governors plus five of the regional bank presidents. The president of the Federal Reserve Bank of New York is always on the committee, and the other four seats rotate among the 11 other regional bank presidents. The chairman of the Board of Governors normally also serves as the chairman of the Open Market Committee.

The effect of this complex structure is to create an institution that is ultimately accountable to the voting public because the Board of Governors is chosen by the president and confirmed by the Senate, all of whom are themselves elected officials. But the long terms served by board members, as well as the indirectness of their appointment process, largely insulate them from short-term political pressures.

FIGURE 14-6 The Federal Reserve System

The Federal Reserve System consists of the Board of Governors in Washington, D.C., plus 12 regional Federal Reserve Banks. This map shows each of the 12 Federal Reserve districts.

Data from: Board of Governors of the Federal Reserve System.

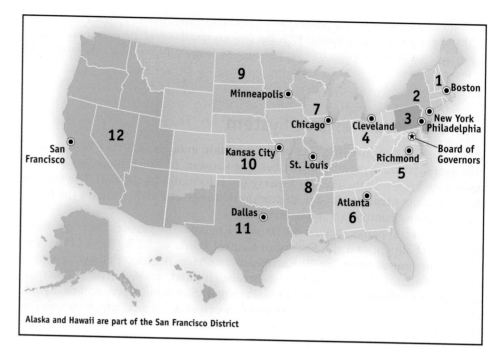

Alaska and Hawaii are part of the San Francisco District

What the Fed Does: Reserve Requirements and the Discount Rate

The Fed has three main policy tools at its disposal: *reserve requirements,* the *discount rate,* and, most importantly, *open-market operations.*

In our discussion of bank runs, we noted that the Fed sets a minimum reserve ratio requirement, currently equal to 10% for checkable bank deposits. Banks that fail to maintain at least the required reserve ratio on average over a two-week period face penalties.

What does a bank do if it looks as if it has insufficient reserves to meet the Fed's reserve requirement? Normally, it borrows additional reserves from other banks via the **federal funds market,** a financial market that allows banks that fall short of the reserve requirement to borrow reserves (usually just overnight) from banks that are holding excess reserves. The interest rate in this market is determined by supply and demand—but the supply and demand for bank reserves are both strongly affected by Federal Reserve actions. As we'll see in the next chapter, the **federal funds rate,** the interest rate at which funds are borrowed and lent in the federal funds market, plays a key role in modern monetary policy.

Alternatively, banks in need of reserves can borrow from the Fed itself via the *discount window.* The **discount rate** is the rate of interest the Fed charges on those loans. Normally, the discount rate is set 1 percentage point above the federal funds rate in order to discourage banks from turning to the Fed when they are in need of reserves. Beginning in the fall of 2007, however, the Fed reduced the spread between the federal funds rate and the discount rate as part of its response to an ongoing financial crisis, described in the upcoming Economics in Action. As a result, by the spring of 2008 the discount rate was only 0.25 percentage point above the federal funds rate. And in mid-2017, the discount rate was still only 0.60 percentage point above the federal funds rate.

In order to alter the money supply, the Fed can change reserve requirements, the discount rate, or both. If the Fed reduces reserve requirements, banks will normally lend a larger percentage of their deposits, leading to more loans and an increase in the money supply via the money multiplier. Alternatively, if the Fed increases reserve requirements, banks are forced to reduce their lending, leading to a fall in the money supply via the money multiplier.

The **federal funds market** allows banks that fall short of the reserve requirement to borrow funds from banks with excess reserves.

The **federal funds rate** is the interest rate at which funds are borrowed and lent in the federal funds market.

The **discount rate** is the rate of interest the Fed charges on loans to banks.

If the Fed reduces the spread between the discount rate and the federal funds rate, the cost to banks of being short of reserves falls. Banks respond by increasing their lending, and the money supply increases via the money multiplier. If the Fed increases the spread between the discount rate and the federal funds rate, bank lending falls—and so will the money supply via the money multiplier.

Under current practice, however, the Fed doesn't use changes in reserve requirements to actively manage the money supply. The last significant change in reserve requirements was in 1992. The Fed normally doesn't use the discount rate either, although, as we mentioned earlier, there was a temporary surge in lending through the discount window beginning in 2007 in response to a financial crisis. Ordinarily, monetary policy is conducted almost exclusively using the Fed's third policy tool: open-market operations.

> An **open-market operation** is a purchase or sale of government debt by the Fed.

Open-Market Operations

Like the banks it oversees, the Federal Reserve has assets and liabilities. The Fed's assets normally consist of holdings of debt issued by the U.S. government, mainly short-term U.S. government bonds with a maturity of less than one year, known as U.S. Treasury bills. Remember, the Fed isn't exactly part of the U.S. government, so U.S. Treasury bills held by the Fed are a liability of the government but an asset of the Fed. The Fed's liabilities consist of currency in circulation and bank reserves. Figure 14-7 summarizes the normal assets and liabilities of the Fed in the form of a T-account.

In an **open-market operation** the Federal Reserve buys or sells U.S. Treasury bills, normally through a transaction with *commercial banks* (banks that accept deposits and make loans), and *investment banks* (that create and trade assets but don't accept deposits). The Fed never buys U.S. Treasury bills directly from the federal government. There's a good reason for this: when a central bank buys government debt directly from the government, it is lending directly to the government—in effect, the central bank is printing money to finance the government's budget deficit. This has historically been a formula for disastrously high levels of inflation.

The two panels of Figure 14-8 show the changes in the financial position of both the Fed and commercial banks that result from open-market operations. When the Fed buys U.S. Treasury bills from a commercial bank, it pays by crediting the bank's reserve account by an amount equal to the value of the Treasury bills. This is illustrated in panel (a): the Fed buys $100 million of U.S. Treasury bills from commercial banks, which increases the monetary base by $100 million because it increases bank reserves by $100 million. When the Fed sells U.S. Treasury bills to commercial banks, it debits the banks' accounts, reducing their reserves. This is shown in panel (b), where the Fed sells $100 million of U.S. Treasury bills. Here, bank reserves and the monetary base decrease.

You might wonder where the Fed gets the funds to purchase U.S. Treasury bills from banks. The answer is that it simply creates them with a mouse click—or the stroke of a pen—that credits the banks' accounts with extra reserves. (The Fed prints money to pay for Treasury bills only when banks want the additional

FIGURE 14-7 The Federal Reserve's Assets and Liabilities

The Federal Reserve holds its assets mostly in short-term government bonds called U.S. Treasury bills. Its liabilities are the monetary base—currency in circulation plus bank reserves.

Assets	Liabilities
Government debt (Treasury bills)	Monetary base (currency in circulation + bank reserves)

FIGURE 14-8 Open-Market Operations by the Federal Reserve

(a) An Open-Market Purchase of $100 Million

Federal Reserve	Assets		Liabilities	
	Treasury bills	+$100 million	Monetary base	+$100 million

Commercial banks	Assets		Liabilities	
	Treasury bills	−$100 million	No change	
	Reserves	+$100 million		

(b) An Open-Market Sale of $100 Million

Federal Reserve	Assets		Liabilities	
	Treasury bills	−$100 million	Monetary base	−$100 million

Commercial banks	Assets		Liabilities	
	Treasury bills	+$100 million	No change	
	Reserves	−$100 million		

In panel (a), the Federal Reserve increases the monetary base by purchasing U.S. Treasury bills from private commercial banks in an open-market operation. Here, a $100 million purchase of U.S. Treasury bills by the Federal Reserve is paid for by a $100 million addition to private bank reserves, generating a $100 million increase in the monetary base. This will ultimately lead to an increase in the money supply via the money multiplier as banks lend out some of these new reserves. In panel (b), the Federal Reserve reduces the monetary base by selling U.S. Treasury bills to private commercial banks in an open-market operation. Here, a $100 million sale of U.S. Treasury bills leads to a $100 million reduction in private bank reserves, resulting in a $100 million decrease in the monetary base. This will ultimately lead to a fall in the money supply via the money multiplier as banks reduce their loans in response to a fall in their reserves.

reserves in the form of currency.) Remember, the modern dollar is fiat money, which isn't backed by anything. So the Fed can create additional monetary base at its own discretion.

The change in bank reserves caused by an open-market operation doesn't directly affect the money supply. Instead, it starts the money multiplier in motion. After the $100 million increase in reserves shown in panel (a) of Figure 14-8,

---

FOR INQUIRING MINDS   Who Gets the Interest on the Fed's Assets?

The Fed owns a lot of assets—Treasury bills—that it bought from commercial banks in exchange for additions to the monetary base in the form of credits to banks' reserve accounts. These assets pay interest. Yet the Fed's liabilities consist mainly of the monetary base, liabilities on which the Fed normally *doesn't* pay interest. So the Fed is, in effect, an institution that has the privilege of borrowing funds at a zero interest rate and lending them out at a positive interest rate. That sounds like a pretty profitable business. And the U.S. taxpayers get the profits.

The Fed keeps some of the interest it receives to finance its operations but turns most of it over to the U.S. Treasury. For example, in 2016 the total income of the Federal Reserve system was $92.7 billion, almost all in the form of interest on its assets, of which $92.0 billion was returned to the Treasury.

Let's look again at our opening story and the impact of those forged dollars printed in Peru. When, say, a fake $20 bill enters circulation, it has the same economic effect as a real $20 bill printed by the U.S. government. That is, as long as nobody catches the forgery, the fake bill serves, for all practical purposes, as part of the monetary base.

Meanwhile, the Fed decides on the size of the monetary base based on economic considerations—in particular, the Fed normally doesn't let the monetary base get too large because that can cause higher inflation. So every fake $20 bill that enters circulation means that the Fed prints one less real $20 bill. When the Fed prints a $20 bill legally, however, it gets Treasury bills in return—and the interest on those bills helps pay for the U.S. government's expenses. So a counterfeit $20 bill reduces the amount of Treasury bills the Fed can acquire and thereby reduces the interest payments going to the Fed and the U.S. Treasury. Taxpayers, then, bear the real cost of counterfeiting.

commercial banks will (under normal circumstances) lend out all of their additional reserves, immediately increasing the money supply by $100 million. Some of those loans would be deposited back into the banking system, increasing reserves again and permitting a further round of loans, and so on, leading to a rise in the money supply. An open-market sale has the reverse effect: bank reserves fall, requiring banks to reduce their loans, leading to a fall in the money supply.

Although economists often say, loosely, that the Fed controls the money supply—checkable deposits plus currency in circulation, that statement is not completely accurate. *The Fed literally only controls the monetary base—bank reserves plus currency in circulation. But by increasing or reducing the monetary base, the Fed can exert a powerful influence on both the money supply and interest rates.* This influence is the basis of monetary policy, the subject of the next chapter.

The European Central Bank

We've seen that the Fed is only one of a number of central banks around the world, and it's much younger than Sweden's Sveriges Riksbank and Britain's Bank of England. In general, other central banks operate in much the same way as the Fed. That's especially true of the only other central bank that rivals the Fed in terms of importance to the world economy: the European Central Bank.

The European Central Bank (ECB) was created in January 1999 when 11 European nations abandoned their national currencies, adopted the euro as their common currency, and placed their joint monetary policy in the ECB's hands. More countries have joined since then, with Lithuania becoming the nineteenth European nation to adopt the euro in 2015. The ECB instantly became an extremely important institution: although no single European nation has an economy anywhere near as large as that of the United States, the combined economies of the eurozone, the group of countries that have adopted the euro as their currency, are roughly as big as the U.S. economy. As a result, the ECB and the Fed are the two giants of the monetary world.

Like the Fed, the ECB has a special status: it's not a private institution, but it's not exactly a government agency either. In fact, it can't be a government agency because there is no pan-European government! Luckily for puzzled Americans, there are strong analogies between European central banking and the Federal Reserve system.

First of all, the ECB, which is located in the German city of Frankfurt, isn't really the counterpart of the whole Federal Reserve system: it's the equivalent of the Board of Governors in Washington. The European counterparts of the regional Federal Reserve Banks are Europe's national central banks: the Bank of France, the Bank of Italy, and so on. Until 1999, each of these national banks was its country's equivalent to the Fed. For example, the Bank of France controlled the French monetary base.

Today these national banks, like regional Feds, provide various financial services to local banks and businesses and conduct open-market operations, but the making of monetary policy has moved upstream to the ECB. Still, the various European national central banks aren't small institutions: in total, they employ more than 50,000 people; in 2016, the ECB employed about 3,000 people.

In the eurozone, each country chooses who runs its own national central bank. The ECB's Executive Board is the counterpart of the Fed's Board of Governors; its members are chosen by unanimous consent of the eurozone national governments. The counterpart of the Federal Open Market Committee is the ECB's Governing Council. Just as the Fed's Open Market Committee consists of the Board of Governors plus a rotating group of regional Fed presidents, the ECB's Governing Council consists of the Executive Board plus the heads of the national central banks.

The ECB is like the Fed in two ways: it is ultimately answerable to voters, and it tries to maintain its independence from short-term political pressures.

ECONOMICS >> *in Action*
The Fed's Balance Sheet, Normal and Abnormal

Figure 14-7 showed a simplified version of the Fed's balance sheet. Here, liabilities consisted entirely of the monetary base and assets consisted entirely of Treasury bills. This is an oversimplification because the Fed's operations are more complicated in reality and its balance sheet contains a number of additional things. But, in normal times, Figure 14-7 is a reasonable approximation: the monetary base typically accounts for 90% of the Fed's liabilities, and 90% of its assets are in the form of claims on the U.S. Treasury (as in Treasury bills).

But in late 2007 it became painfully clear that we were no longer in normal times. The source of the turmoil was the bursting of a huge housing bubble, which led to massive losses for financial institutions that had made mortgage loans or held mortgage-related assets. This led to a widespread loss of confidence in the financial system.

Not only were conventional deposit-taking commercial banks in trouble, but so were nondepository financial institutions like investment banks and insurance companies that make up the shadow banking sector. Because they carried a lot of debt, faced huge losses from the collapse of the housing bubble, and held illiquid assets, panic hit the shadow banking sector. Within hours the financial system was frozen as financial institutions experienced what were essentially bank runs.

For example, in 2008, many investors became worried about the health of Bear Stearns, a Wall Street investment bank that engaged in complex financial deals, buying and selling financial assets with borrowed funds. When confidence in Bear Stearns dried up, the firm was unable to raise the funds needed to deliver on its end of these deals and it quickly spiraled into collapse. This was followed by the collapse of another investment bank, Lehman Brothers, and set off widespread panic in financial markets.

The Fed sprang into action to contain what was becoming a meltdown across the entire financial sector. It greatly expanded its discount window—making huge loans to deposit-taking banks as well as nondepository financial institutions. This gave financial institutions the liquidity that the financial market had denied them. And as these firms took advantage of the ability to borrow cheaply from the Fed, they pledged their assets on hand as collateral—a motley collection of real estate loans, business loans, and so on.

Examining Figure 14-9, we see that starting in mid-2008, the Fed sharply reduced its holdings of traditional securities like Treasury bills, as its "lending to financial institutions" skyrocketed—referring to discount window lending, but also to loans the Fed made directly to firms like Bear Stearns. "Liquidity to key credit markets" covers purchases by the Fed of assets like corporate bonds, which was necessary to keep interest rates on loans to firms from soaring. Finally, "Federal agency debt" is the debt of Fannie Mae and Freddie Mac, the government-sponsored home mortgage agencies, which the Fed was also compelled to buy in order to prevent collapse in the mortgage market.

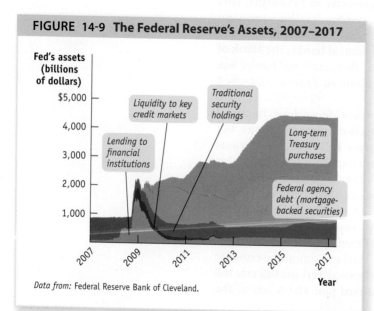

FIGURE 14-9 The Federal Reserve's Assets, 2007–2017

Fed's assets (billions of dollars)

Liquidity to key credit markets

Traditional security holdings

Long-term Treasury purchases

Lending to financial institutions

Federal agency debt (mortgage-backed securities)

Data from: Federal Reserve Bank of Cleveland.

Year

As the crisis subsided in late 2009, the Fed didn't return to its traditional asset holdings. Instead, it shifted into long-term Treasury bills and increased its purchases of Federal agency debt. The whole episode was very unusual—a major departure from the way the Fed normally conducts business, but one that it deemed necessary to stave off financial and economic collapse. It was also a graphic illustration of the fact that the Fed does much more than just determine the size of the monetary base.

>> Check Your Understanding 14-4

Solution appears at back of book.

1. Assume that any money lent by a bank is always deposited back in the banking system as a checkable deposit, that the reserve ratio is 10%, and that banks don't hold excess reserves. Explain the effects of a $100 million open-market purchase of U.S. Treasury bills by the Fed on the value of checkable bank deposits. What is the size of the money multiplier?

The Evolution of the American Banking System

Up to this point, we have been describing the U.S. banking system and how it works. To fully understand that system, however, it is helpful to understand how and why it was created—a story that is closely intertwined with the story of how and when things went wrong. The key elements of twenty-first-century U.S. banking weren't created out of thin air: efforts to change both the regulations that govern banking and the Federal Reserve system that resulted from the 2008 crisis have propelled financial reform to the forefront. This reform promises to continue reshaping the financial system well into future years.

The Crisis in American Banking in the Early Twentieth Century

The creation of the Federal Reserve system in 1913 marked the beginning of the modern era of American banking. From 1864 until 1913, American banking was dominated by a federally regulated system of national banks. They alone were allowed to issue currency, and the currency notes they issued were printed by the federal government with uniform size and design. How much currency a national bank could issue depended on its capital. Although this system was an improvement on the earlier period in which banks issued their own notes with no uniformity and virtually no regulation, the national banking regime still suffered numerous bank failures and major financial crises—at least one and often two per decade.

The main problem afflicting the system was that the money supply was not sufficiently responsive: it was difficult to shift currency around the country to respond quickly to local economic changes. (In particular, there was often a tug-of-war between New York City banks and rural banks for adequate amounts of currency.) Rumors that a bank had insufficient currency to satisfy demands for withdrawals would quickly lead to a bank run. A bank run would then spark a contagion, setting off runs at other nearby banks, sowing widespread panic and devastation in the local economy. In response, bankers in some locations pooled their resources to create local clearinghouses that would jointly guarantee a member's liabilities in the event of a panic, and some state governments began offering deposit insurance on their banks' deposits.

Despite these recurrent crises, calls for monetary reform went unheeded until the Panic of 1907, which led to a four-year national recession, drove home just how vulnerable the system had become.

The Pierpont Morgan Library/Art Resource, NY

In both the Panic of 1907 and the financial crisis of 2008, large losses from risky speculation destabilized the banking system.

This crisis originated in institutions in New York known as *trusts*, bank-like institutions that accepted deposits but that were originally intended to manage only inheritances and estates for wealthy clients. Because these trusts were supposed to engage only in low-risk activities, they were less regulated, had lower reserve requirements, and had lower cash reserves than national banks, allowing them to pay their depositors higher returns. As a result, trusts grew rapidly: by 1907, the total assets of trusts in New York City were as large as those of national banks. Meanwhile, the trusts declined to join the New York Clearinghouse, a consortium of New York City national banks that guaranteed one anothers' soundness.

The Panic of 1907 began with the failure of the Knickerbocker Trust, a large New York City trust that failed when it suffered massive losses in unsuccessful stock market speculation. Quickly, other New York trusts came under pressure, and frightened depositors began queuing in long lines to withdraw their funds. The New York Clearinghouse declined to step in and lend to the trusts, and even healthy trusts came under serious assault. Within two days, a dozen major trusts had gone under. Credit markets froze, and the stock market fell dramatically as stock traders were unable to get credit to finance their trades and business confidence evaporated.

Fortunately, New York City's wealthiest man, the banker J. P. Morgan, quickly stepped in to stop the panic. Understanding that the crisis was spreading and would soon engulf healthy institutions, trusts and banks alike, he worked with other bankers, wealthy men such as John D. Rockefeller, and the U.S. Secretary of the Treasury to shore up the reserves of banks and trusts so they could withstand the onslaught of withdrawals. Once people were assured that they could withdraw their money, the panic ceased. Although the panic itself lasted little more than a week, it and the stock market collapse decimated the economy. A four-year recession ensued, with production falling 11% and unemployment rising from 3% to 8%.

Responding to Banking Crises: The Creation of the Federal Reserve

Concerns over the frequency of banking crises and the unprecedented role of J. P. Morgan in saving the financial system prompted the federal government to initiate banking reform. In 1913 the national banking system was eliminated and the Federal Reserve system was created as a way to compel all deposit-taking institutions to hold adequate reserves and to open their accounts to inspection by regulators. The Panic of 1907 convinced many that the time for centralized control of bank reserves had come. In addition, the Federal Reserve was given the sole right to issue currency in order to make the money supply sufficiently responsive to satisfy economic conditions around the country.

Although the new regime standardized and centralized the holding of bank reserves, it did not eliminate the potential for bank runs because banks' reserves were still less than the total value of their deposits. The potential for more bank runs became a reality during the Great Depression. Plunging commodity prices hit American farmers particularly hard, precipitating a series of bank runs in 1930, 1931, and 1933, each of which started at midwestern banks and then spread throughout the country.

After the failure of a particularly large bank in 1930, federal officials realized that the economy-wide effects compelled them to take a less hands-off approach and to intervene more vigorously. In 1932, the Reconstruction Finance

Corporation (RFC) was established and given the authority to make loans to banks in order to stabilize the banking sector. Also, the Glass-Steagall Act of 1933, which created federal deposit insurance and increased the ability of banks to borrow from the Federal Reserve system, was passed. However, the beast had not yet been tamed. Banks became fearful of borrowing from the RFC because doing so signaled weakness to the public.

As noted earlier, during the catastrophic bank run of 1933, the new president, Franklin Delano Roosevelt, was inaugurated. He immediately declared a "bank holiday," closing all banks until regulators could get a handle on the problem.

In March 1933, emergency measures were adopted that gave the RFC extraordinary powers to stabilize and restructure the banking industry by providing capital to banks through either loans or outright purchases of bank shares. With the new rules, regulators closed nonviable banks and recapitalized viable ones by allowing the RFC to buy preferred shares in banks (shares that gave the U.S. government more rights than regular shareholders) and by greatly expanding banks' ability to borrow from the Federal Reserve. By 1933, the RFC had invested over $18 billion (2017 dollars) in bank capital—one-third of the total capital of all banks in the United States at that time—and purchased shares in almost one-half of all banks. The RFC loaned more than $36 billion (2017 dollars) to banks during this period.

Economic historians uniformly agree that the banking crises of the early 1930s greatly exacerbated the severity of the Great Depression, rendering monetary policy ineffective as the banking sector broke down and currency, withdrawn from banks and stashed under beds, reduced the money supply.

Although the powerful actions of the RFC stabilized the banking industry, new legislation was needed to prevent future banking crises. The Glass-Steagall Act of 1933 separated banks into two categories, **commercial banks,** depository banks that are covered by deposit insurance, and nondepository **investment banks,** which engaged in creating and trading financial assets such as stocks and corporate bonds and which were not covered by deposit insurance.

Regulation Q prevented commercial banks from paying interest on checking accounts in the belief that this would promote unhealthy competition between banks. In addition, investment banks were much more lightly regulated than commercial banks. The most important measure for the prevention of bank runs, however, was the adoption of federal deposit insurance (with an original limit of $2,500 per deposit).

These measures were clearly successful, and the United States enjoyed a long period of financial and banking stability. As memories of the bad old days dimmed, Depression-era bank regulations were lifted. In 1980, Regulation Q was eliminated; by 1999, the Glass-Steagall Act had been so weakened that offering services like trading financial assets was no longer off-limits to commercial banks.

The Savings and Loan Crisis of the 1980s

Along with banks, the banking industry also included **savings and loans** (also called S&Ls or **thrifts**), institutions designed to accept savings and turn them into long-term mortgages for home-buyers. S&Ls were covered by federal deposit insurance and were tightly regulated for safety. However, trouble hit in the 1970s, as high inflation led savers to withdraw their funds from low-interest-paying S&L accounts and put them into higher-interest-paying money market accounts. In addition, the high inflation rate severely eroded the value of the S&Ls' assets, the long-term mortgages they held on their books.

In order to improve S&Ls' competitive position vis-à-vis banks, Congress eased regulations to allow S&Ls to undertake much more risky investments in

A **commercial bank** accepts deposits and is covered by deposit insurance.

An **investment bank** trades in financial assets and does not accept deposits, so it is not covered by deposit insurance.

A **savings and loan (thrift)** is another type of deposit-taking bank, usually specialized in issuing home loans.

Bank-like activities undertaken by nondepository financial firms such as investment banks and hedge funds, but without regulatory oversight or protection, are known as **shadow banking**.

addition to long-term home mortgages. However, the new freedom did not bring with it increased oversight, leaving S&Ls with less oversight than banks. Not surprisingly, during the real estate boom of the 1970s and 1980s, S&Ls engaged in overly risky real estate lending. Also, corruption occurred as some S&L executives used their institutions as private piggy banks.

During the late 1970s and early 1980s, political interference from Congress kept insolvent S&Ls open when a bank in a comparable situation would have been quickly shut down by regulators. By the early 1980s, numerous S&Ls had failed. Because accounts were covered by federal deposit insurance, the liabilities of a failed S&L became liabilities of the federal government, and depositors had to be paid from taxpayer funds. From 1986 through 1995, the federal government closed over 1,000 failed S&Ls, costing U.S. taxpayers over $124 billion.

In a classic case of shutting the barn door after the horse has escaped, in 1989 Congress put in place comprehensive oversight of S&L activities. It also empowered Fannie Mae and Freddie Mac to take over much of the home mortgage lending previously done by S&Ls. *Fannie Mae* and *Freddie Mac* are quasi-governmental agencies created during the Great Depression to make homeownership more affordable for low- and moderate-income households. The S&L crisis led to a steep slowdown in the finance and real estate industries, leading to the recession of the early 1990s.

Back to the Future: The Financial Crisis of 2008 and Its Aftermath

The bank regulations introduced in the 1930s led to a long era of relative financial stability. But by the early twenty-first century a new problem had emerged: these regulations didn't cover **shadow banking**—activities, as we explained earlier, that don't look like traditional banking but serve similar purposes while posing significant risks. In 2008 shadow banking was at the center of a crisis that in important ways resembled the crisis of the 1930s.

Shadow Banking and Its Vulnerabilities The details of shadow banking can be complex. However, much of the shadow banking system involves financial intermediaries—nondepository financial firms like investment banks, insurance companies, hedge funds, and money market funds. These firms borrow short-term—often taking out loans that must be repaid the next day—and use the borrowed funds to buy relatively illiquid assets to put up as collateral. This looks like banking to those lending funds to intermediaries, because their loans are a lot like bank deposits. For example, a corporation with extra cash on hand might lend that extra cash on an overnight basis to a Wall Street investment bank. That way it can get a higher interest rate than if it parked the funds in ordinary bank deposits, and under normal circumstances it can still count on having access to the money with only one day's notice.

Meanwhile, the financial intermediary doesn't have to keep enough cash on hand to repay all of its debts every day. Many of the lenders will simply roll over their loans each day, relending the funds. And when a lender does demand repayment, the borrower will simply raise the cash from another lender. So the shadow banking firm's relationship to its lenders is a lot like a conventional bank's relationship with its depositors, except for two significant differences: there is no deposit insurance and there is much less regulation of what the intermediary does.

It is a system that can work seamlessly in normal times, but it can also go terribly wrong as it did when the housing bubble it helped to create burst in 2007, leading to the Great Recession.

Subprime Lending and the Housing Bubble The story of the 2008 crisis begins with low interest rates: by 2003, U.S. interest rates were at historically low levels, partly because of Federal Reserve policy and partly because of large inflows of capital from other countries, especially China. These low interest rates helped cause a boom in housing, which in turn pulled the U.S. economy out of recession. As housing boomed, however, financial institutions took on greater risks that were not well understood.

Traditionally, people were only able to borrow money to buy homes if they could show that they had sufficient income to meet the mortgage payments. Home loans to people who don't meet the usual criteria for borrowing, called **subprime lending,** were only a minor part of overall lending. But in the booming housing market of 2003–2006, subprime lending started to seem like a safe bet. According to conventional thinking, since housing prices kept rising, borrowers who were unable to make their mortgage payments could always pay off their mortgages by selling their homes. As a result, subprime lending exploded.

Who was making these subprime loans? For the most part, it was not traditional banks that were lending out depositors' money. Instead, most of the loans were made by *loan originators*, companies specializing in making subprime loans and quickly selling them off to other investors in the shadow banking market. Large-scale sales of subprime mortgages were made possible by **securitization:** the assembly of pools of loans and sale of shares of the income from these pools. Again, according to conventional thinking, these shares were considered relatively safe investments, based on the belief that large numbers of home-buyers were unlikely to default on their payments at the same time.

But that's exactly what happened. The housing boom turned out to be a bubble, and when home prices started falling in late 2006, significant numbers of subprime borrowers were unable either to meet their mortgage payments or sell their houses for enough to pay off their mortgages. As a result, they defaulted and investors in securities backed by subprime mortgages suffered heavy losses.

These securities were largely held by shadow banking institutions, but also by some traditional, depository banks. Like the trusts that played a key role in the Panic of 1907, these largely unregulated shadow banks offered higher returns to investors but left them extremely vulnerable in a crisis. Without the safety net of deposit insurance, mortgage-related losses led to a collapse of trust in the financial system.

Figure 14-10 shows one measure of the severity of the loss of trust: the quantity of *asset-backed commercial paper,* an important asset class in shadow banking. In the mid-2000s this paper—backed by short-term loans taken out using assets often created by securitization of mortgages and other

> **Subprime lending** is lending to home-buyers who don't meet the usual criteria for qualifying for a loan.
>
> In **securitization,** a pool of loans is assembled and shares of that pool are sold to investors.

"Honey we're homeless."

Leo Cullum, The New Yorker Collection/The Cartoon Bank

FIGURE 14-10 Measuring Lost Trust

In the mid-2000s the use of asset-backed commercial paper, short-term loans created by securitization of mortgages and other debts, and an important component of shadow banking, grew rapidly in volume. But it went into rapid decline after the housing boom went bust, a sign of extreme financial stress as liquidity in the financial system dried up.

Data from: Federal Reserve Bank of St. Louis.

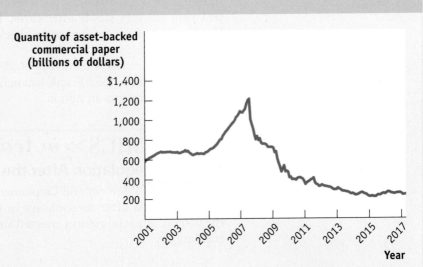

debts—grew rapidly in volume. After the housing bust, it went into rapid decline, a sign of extreme financial stress. Although this was not a 1930s-style crash in the money supply in an official sense, it functioned in much the same way because commercial paper was an essential source of liquidity in the financial system.

Crisis and Response Starting in 2007, the bursting of the housing bubble, followed by large losses on the part of financial firms and the collapse in trust in the financial system, led to major disruptions for the economy as a whole. All firms—financial and nonfinancial—found it difficult to borrow, even for short-term operations. Individuals found home loans unavailable and credit card limits reduced. Prices of many assets tumbled, severely reducing household wealth.

Overall, the negative economic effect of the financial crisis bore a strong and extremely troubling resemblance to the banking crisis of the early 1930s, which sparked the Great Depression. Policy makers, noticing the resemblance, tried to prevent a repeat performance. Beginning in August 2007, the Federal Reserve provided liquidity to stop a cascade of defaults, by lending funds to a wide range of institutions and buying commercial paper. The Fed and the Treasury Department also stepped in to rescue individual firms that were deemed too crucial to be allowed to fail, such as the investment bank Bear Stearns and the insurance company AIG.

In September 2008, however, under political pressure to punish "irresponsible bankers," policy makers allowed one major investment bank, Lehman Brothers, to fail. They quickly regretted the decision. Within days of Lehman's failure, widespread panic gripped the financial markets. In response, the U.S. government intervened further to support the financial system. The U.S. Treasury injected capital directly into banks—supplying them with cash in return for shares. The effect was to partly *nationalize* the financial system (take public ownership). The Federal Reserve engaged in novel forms of open-market operations, such as providing massive liquidity through discount window lending and buying a large quantity of other assets—mainly long-term government debt and the debt of Fannie Mae and Freddie Mac (as shown in Figure 14-9 by the huge surge in Fed assets after September 2008).

The Aftermath of the Crisis After many terrifying months, in the fall of 2010 the financial system stabilized, and major institutions had repaid much of the money the federal government had injected during the crisis. However, the recovery of the banks was not matched by a successful turnaround for the overall economy. Although the recession that began in December 2007 officially ended in June 2009, with unemployment reaching a high of 10% in October 2009, unemployment fell very slowly afterwards. It took nearly nine years, until May 2016, for the unemployment rate to fall back to where it had been before the start of the Great Recession.

Like earlier crises, the crisis of 2008 led to changes in banking regulation, most notably the Dodd-Frank financial regulatory reform act discussed in the following Economics in Action.

ECONOMICS >> *in Action*
Financial Regulation After the 2008 Crisis

The Wall Street Reform and Consumer Protection Act of 2010—generally known as Dodd-Frank, after its sponsors in the Senate and House, respectively—was the biggest financial reform enacted since the 1930s. How did it change financial regulation?

For traditional depository banks, the main change was the creation of a new agency, the Bureau of Consumer Financial Protection. Its mission was to protect borrowers from being exploited through seemingly attractive financial deals they didn't understand.

The main thrust of Dodd-Frank, however, was the regulation of shadow banking institutions. Under the law, a financial institution could be designated as "systematically important"—that is, like Lehman Brothers, it was important enough to the financial system that it could trigger a banking crisis, even though it wasn't a depository bank.

Under Dodd-Frank, these systemically important institutions were subjected to depository bank–style regulation, such as relatively high capital requirements and limits on risk taking. In addition, the federal government asserted *resolution authority*, the right to seize troubled nondepository financial institutions in much the same way that it seized troubled banks.

The Wall Street Reform and Consumer Protection Act of 2010, known as Dodd-Frank, extended old-fashioned bank regulation to today's more complex financial system.

Dodd-Frank also mandated that most *derivatives*, complex financial instruments that also played a significant role in the 2008 crisis, could be bought and sold on public exchanges in order to make them more transparent and reduce risk.

Overall, the purpose of Dodd-Frank was to extend the spirit of old-fashioned bank regulation to the more complex financial system of the twenty-first century. How well is it working? Relatively well, according to the evidence so far:

- The new rules on systemically important institutions seem to have reduced the incentive to create shadow banks that bypass regulations on conventional banks. An example is the case of GE Capital, an unregulated bank owned by General Electric. Although it was the main source of profits for its parent company, General Electric sold it off in the wake of Dodd-Frank.

- Resolution authority seems to have led to a reduction in the so-called *too big to fail subsidy:* the lower cost of borrowing enjoyed by big financial institutions compared to smaller ones because it was assumed that only the big ones would be bailed out in a crisis.

- The Consumer Financial Protection Bureau is widely considered to have been quite effective at punishing and deterring financial fraud.

That said, we won't know how effective Dodd-Frank has been until the next period of financial turbulence.

>> Check Your Understanding 14-5

Solutions appear at back of book.

1. What are the similarities between the Panic of 1907, the S&L crisis, and the crisis of 2008?

2. Why did the creation of the Federal Reserve fail to prevent the bank runs of the Great Depression? What measures stopped the bank runs?

3. Why were extraordinary measures needed to deal with the financial crisis of 2008?

>> Quick Review

- The Federal Reserve system was created in response to the Panic of 1907.

- Widespread bank runs in the early 1930s resulted in greater bank regulation and the creation of federal deposit insurance. Banks were separated into two categories: **commercial** (covered by deposit insurance) and **investment** (not covered).

- In the **savings and loan (thrift)** crisis of the 1970s and 1980s, insufficiently regulated S&Ls incurred huge losses from risky speculation in housing.

- Unregulated **shadow banking** activities created a vulnerability in the financial system. In the mid-2000s, **securitization** spread loans from **subprime lending** throughout the shadow banking sector, and among some traditional banks, leading to a financial crisis when the housing bubble burst. The Federal Reserve and U.S. Treasury undertook extraordinary steps to stabilize financial markets.

- In 2010, Congress passed the Dodd-Frank Act. The law extended both financial regulations—to avoid another financial crisis—and protections against consumer financial fraud.

The Perfect Gift: Cash or a Gift Card?

It's always nice when someone shows his or her appreciation by giving you a gift. Over the past few years, more people have been showing their appreciation by giving gift cards, prepaid plastic cards issued by a retailer that can be redeemed for merchandise. The best-selling single item for more than 80% of the top 100 American retailers, says GiftCardUSA.com, is their gift cards.

What could be more simple and useful than allowing the recipient to choose what he or she wants? And isn't a gift card more personal than cash or a check?

Yet a number of firms are now making a profit from the fact that gift card recipients are often willing to sell their cards at a discount—sometimes at a fairly sizable discount—to turn them into cold, impersonal dollars and cents. Meanwhile, other people are willing to buy those cards, and turn them into goods they want.

Cardcash.com is one such site. At the time of writing, it offers to pay cash to a seller of a Walmart gift card equivalent to 89% of the card's face value. For example, the seller of a Walmart card with a value of $100 would receive $89. Cardcash.com profits by reselling the card at a premium over what it paid. So it would sell a Walmart gift card for more than 89% of its face value.

The amount of cash offered to sellers of cards will vary by retailer. Cardcash offers cash equal to only 69% of a Gap card's face value, for example.

Many consumers will sell at a sizable discount to turn gift cards into cash. But retailers promote the use of gift cards over cash because much of the value of gift cards issued never gets used, a phenomenon known as *breakage*.

How does breakage occur? People lose cards. Or they spend only $47 of a $50 gift card, and never return to the store to spend that last $3. Also, retailers have imposed fees on the use of cards or made them subject to expiration dates, which customers forget about. And if a retailer goes out of business, the value of outstanding gift cards disappears with it.

In addition to breakage, retailers benefit when customers intent on using up the value of their gift card find that it is too difficult to spend exactly the amount of the card. Instead, they end up spending even more than the card's face value, sometimes even more than they would have without the gift card.

Gift cards are so beneficial to retailers that instead of rewarding customer loyalty with rebate checks (once a common practice), they have switched to dispensing gift cards. As one commentator noted in explaining why retailers prefer gift cards to rebate checks, "Nobody neglects to spend cash."

QUESTIONS FOR THOUGHT

1. Why are gift card owners willing to sell their cards for a cash amount less than their face value?

2. Why do gift cards for Walmart sell for a smaller discount than those for the Gap?

3. Use your answer from Question 2 to explain why cash never "sells" at a discount.

4. Explain why retailers prefer to reward loyal customers with gift cards instead of rebate checks.

5. There are now laws restricting retailers' ability to impose fees and expiration dates on their gift cards and mandate greater disclosure of their terms. Why do you think Congress enacted this legislation?

SUMMARY

1. **Money** is any asset that can easily be used to purchase goods and services. **Currency in circulation** and **checkable bank deposits** are both considered part of the **money supply**. Money plays three roles: it is a **medium of exchange** used for transactions, a **store of value** that holds purchasing power over time, and a **unit of account** in which prices are stated.

2. Over time, **commodity money,** which consists of goods possessing value aside from their role as money, such as gold and silver coins, was replaced by **commodity-backed money,** such as paper currency backed by gold. Today the dollar is pure **fiat money,** whose value derives solely from its official role.

3. The Federal Reserve calculates two measures of the money supply. M1 is the narrowest **monetary aggregate,** containing only currency in circulation, traveler's checks, and checkable bank deposits. M2 includes a wider range of assets called **near-moneys,** mainly other forms of bank deposits, that can easily be converted into checkable bank deposits.

4. Banks allow depositors immediate access to their funds, but they also lend out most of the funds deposited in their care. To meet demands for cash, they maintain **bank reserves** composed of both currency held in vaults and deposits at the Federal Reserve. The **reserve ratio** is the ratio of bank reserves to bank deposits. A **T-account** summarizes a bank's financial position, with loans and reserves counted as assets and deposits counted as liabilities.

5. Banks have sometimes been subject to **bank runs,** most notably in the early 1930s. To avert this danger, depositors are now protected by **deposit insurance,** bank owners face capital requirements that reduce the incentive to make overly risky loans with depositors' funds, and banks must satisfy **reserve requirements.**

6. When currency is deposited in a bank, it starts a multiplier process in which banks lend out **excess reserves,** leading to an increase in the money supply—so banks create money. If the entire money supply consisted of checkable bank deposits, the money supply would be equal to the value of reserves divided by the reserve ratio. In reality, much of the **monetary base** consists of currency in circulation, and the **money multiplier** is the ratio of the money supply to the monetary base.

7. The monetary base is controlled by the Federal Reserve, the **central bank** of the United States. The Fed regulates banks and sets reserve requirements. To meet those requirements, banks borrow and lend reserves in the **federal funds market** at the **federal funds rate.** Through the **discount window** facility, banks can borrow from the Fed at the **discount rate.**

8. **Open-market operations** by the Fed are the principal tool of monetary policy: the Fed can increase or reduce the monetary base by buying U.S. Treasury bills from banks or selling U.S. Treasury bills to banks.

9. In response to the Panic of 1907, the Fed was created to centralize the holding of reserves, inspect banks' books, and make the money supply sufficiently responsive to varying economic conditions.

10. The Great Depression sparked widespread bank runs in the early 1930s, which greatly worsened and lengthened it. Federal deposit insurance was created, and the government recapitalized banks by lending to them and by buying shares of banks. By 1933, banks had been separated into two categories: **commercial banks** (which accept deposits and are covered by deposit insurance) and **investment banks** (which don't accept deposits and are not covered). Public acceptance of deposit insurance finally stopped the bank runs of the Great Depression.

11. The **savings and loan (thrift)** crisis of the 1980s arose because insufficiently regulated S&Ls engaged in overly risky speculation and incurred huge losses. Depositors in failed S&Ls were compensated with taxpayer funds because they were covered by deposit insurance. The crisis caused steep losses in the financial and real estate sectors, resulting in a recession in the early 1990s.

12. The emergence of **shadow banking**, bank-like activities undertaken by nondepository financial firms which were not subject to regulatory oversight or protection, made the financial system once again vulnerable to bank-run type panics. In the mid-2000s, **securitization** of mortgage loans from **subprime lending** spread through the shadow banking sector and among some traditional depository banks. When the housing bubble burst in 2007, losses by financial institutions led to panic and a widespread collapse of the financial system in 2008. To prevent another Great Depression, the Federal Reserve and U.S. Treasury undertook extraordinary actions to provide support to the financial system, such as injecting capital into banks through the purchase of bank shares, providing massive liquidity through discount window lending, and buying large amounts of long-term government debt and government-sponsored agency debt. By 2010, the financial system had stabilized but the economy did not fully recover until 2016.

13. In 2010, Congress passed a financial regulation reform act, known as Dodd-Frank, in order to prevent another crisis. Its main purpose was to extend old-fashioned bank regulation to today's more complex financial system. It also extended protection for consumers against financial fraud.

KEY TERMS

Money, p. 414
Currency in circulation, p. 414
Checkable bank deposits, p. 414
Money supply, p. 414
Medium of exchange, p. 415
Store of value, p. 415
Unit of account, p. 416
Commodity money, p. 416
Commodity-backed money, p. 416
Fiat money, p. 417
Monetary aggregate, p. 417

Near-moneys, p. 417
Bank reserves, p. 420
T-account, p. 420
Reserve ratio, p. 421
Bank run, p. 421
Deposit insurance, p. 422
Reserve requirements, p. 422
Discount window, p. 422
Excess reserves, p. 426
Monetary base, p. 427
Money multiplier, p. 427

Central bank, p. 429
Federal funds market, p. 430
Federal funds rate, p. 430
Discount rate, p. 430
Open-market operation, p. 431
Commercial bank, p. 437
Investment bank, p. 437
Savings and loan (thrift), p. 437
Shadow banking, p. 438
Subprime lending, p. 439
Securitization, p. 439

PROBLEMS

interactive activity

1. For each of the following transactions, what is the initial effect (increase or decrease) on M1? On M2?

   a. You sell a few shares of stock and put the proceeds into your savings account.

   b. You sell a few shares of stock and put the proceeds into your checking account.

   c. You transfer money from your savings account to your checking account.

   d. You discover $0.25 under the floor mat in your car and deposit it in your checking account.

   e. You discover $0.25 under the floor mat in your car and deposit it in your savings account.

2. There are three types of money: commodity money, commodity-backed money, and fiat money. Which type of money is used in each of the following situations?

   a. Bottles of rum were used to pay for goods in colonial Australia.

   b. Salt was used in many European countries as a medium of exchange.

   c. For a brief time, Germany used paper money (the "Rye Mark") that could be redeemed for a certain amount of rye, a type of grain.

   d. The town of Ithaca, New York, prints its own currency, the Ithaca HOURS, which can be used to purchase local goods and services.

3. The following table shows the components of M1 and M2 in billions of dollars for the month of December in the years 2006 to 2016 reported by the Federal Reserve Bank of St. Louis. Complete the table by calculating M1, M2, currency in circulation as a percentage of M1, and currency in circulation as a percentage of M2. What trends or patterns about M1, M2, currency in circulation as a percentage of M1, and currency in circulation as a percentage of M2 do you see? What might account for these trends?

Year	Currency in circulation	Traveler's checks	Checkable deposits	Savings deposits	Time deposits	Money market funds	M1	M2	Currency in circulation as a percentage of M1	Currency in circulation as a percentage of M2
2006	$750.2	$6.7	$611.3	$3,694.9	$1,206.1	$772.2	?	?	?	?
2007	760.6	6.3	609.5	3,898.4	1,276.1	923.3	?	?	?	?
2008	816.3	5.5	785.1	4,089.4	1,457.9	1,012.5	?	?	?	?
2009	863.7	5.1	829.7	4,813.1	1,188.3	771.1	?	?	?	?
2010	918.8	4.7	919.0	5,331.3	933.2	668.1	?	?	?	?
2011	1,001.5	4.3	1,164.1	6,032.0	775.8	658.6	?	?	?	?
2012	1,090.5	3.8	1,367.0	6,685.0	643.7	638.6	?	?	?	?
2013	1,160.2	3.5	1,496.5	7,131.5	567.3	635.7	?	?	?	?
2014	1,252.2	2.9	1,675.0	7,580.9	519.0	616.9	?	?	?	?
2015	1,337.9	2.5	1,739.3	8,185.1	408.4	640.3	?	?	?	?
2016	1,418.4	2.2	1,902.0	8,842.3	371.6	712.6	?	?	?	?

Data from: Federal Reserve Bank of St. Louis.

4. Indicate whether each of the following is part of M1, M2, or neither:

a. $95 on your campus meal card

b. $0.55 in the change cup of your car

c. $1,663 in your savings account

d. $459 in your checking account

e. 100 shares of stock worth $4,000

f. A $1,000 line of credit on your Target credit card

5. Tracy Williams deposits $500 that was in her sock drawer into a checking account at the local bank. The reserve ratio is 10%.

a. How does the deposit initially change the T-account of the local bank? How does it change the money supply?

b. If the bank maintains a reserve ratio of 10%, how will it respond to the new deposit?

c. If every time the bank makes a loan, the loan results in a new checkable bank deposit in a different bank equal to the amount of the loan, by how much could the total money supply in the economy expand in response to Tracy's initial cash deposit of $500?

d. If every time the bank makes a loan, the loan results in a new checkable bank deposit in a different bank equal to the amount of the loan and the bank maintains a reserve ratio of 5%, by how much could the money supply expand in response to Tracy's initial cash deposit of $500?

6. Ryan Cozzens withdraws $400 from his checking account at the local bank and keeps it in his wallet.

a. How will the withdrawal change the T-account of the local bank and the money supply?

b. If the bank maintains a reserve ratio of 10%, how will it respond to the withdrawal? Assume that the bank responds to insufficient reserves by reducing the amount of deposits it holds until its level of reserves satisfies its required reserve ratio. The bank reduces its deposits by calling in some of its loans, forcing borrowers to pay back these loans by taking cash from their checking deposits (at the same bank) to make repayment.

c. If every time the bank decreases its loans, checkable bank deposits fall by the amount of the loan, by how much will the money supply in the economy contract in response to Ryan's withdrawal of $400?

d. If every time the bank decreases its loans, checkable bank deposits fall by the amount of the loan and the bank maintains a reserve ratio of 20%, by how much will the money supply contract in response to a withdrawal of $400?

7. The government of Eastlandia uses measures of monetary aggregates similar to those used by the United States, and the central bank of Eastlandia imposes a required reserve ratio of 10%. Given the following information, answer the questions below.

Bank deposits at the central bank = $200 million
Currency held by public = $150 million
Currency in bank vaults = $100 million

Checkable bank deposits = $500 million
Traveler's checks = $10 million

a. What is M1?

b. What is the monetary base?

c. Are the commercial banks holding excess reserves?

d. Can the commercial banks increase checkable bank deposits? If yes, by how much can checkable bank deposits increase?

8. In Westlandia, the public holds 50% of M1 in the form of currency, and the required reserve ratio is 20%. Estimate how much the money supply will increase in response to a new cash deposit of $500 by completing the accompanying table. (*Hint:* The first row shows that the bank must hold $100 in minimum reserves—20% of the $500 deposit—against this deposit, leaving $400 in excess reserves that can be loaned out. However, since the public wants to hold 50% of the loan in currency, only $400 × 0.5 = $200 of the loan will be deposited in round 2 from the loan granted in round 1.) How does your answer compare to an economy in which the total amount of the loan is deposited in the banking system and the public doesn't hold any of the loan in currency? What does this imply about the relationship between the public's desire for holding currency and the money multiplier?

Round	Deposits	Required reserves	Excess reserves	Loans	Held as currency
1	$500.00	$100.00	$400.00	$400.00	$200.00
2	200.00	?	?	?	?
3	?	?	?	?	?
4	?	?	?	?	?
5	?	?	?	?	?
6	?	?	?	?	?
7	?	?	?	?	?
8	?	?	?	?	?
9	?	?	?	?	?
Total after 10 rounds	?	?	?	?	?

9. What will happen to the money supply under the following circumstances in a checkable-deposits-only system?

a. The required reserve ratio is 25%, and a depositor withdraws $700 from his checkable bank deposit and holds it as cash.

b. The required reserve ratio is 5%, and a depositor withdraws $700 from his checkable bank deposit and holds it as cash.

c. The required reserve ratio is 20%, and a customer deposits $750 to her checkable bank deposit and holds it as cash.

d. The required reserve ratio is 10%, and a customer deposits $600 to her checkable bank deposit and holds it as cash.

10. Although the U.S. Federal Reserve doesn't use changes in reserve requirements to manage the money supply, the central bank of Albernia does. The commercial banks of Albernia have $100 million in reserves and $1,000 million in checkable deposits; the initial required reserve ratio is 10%. The commercial banks follow a policy of holding no excess reserves. The public holds no currency, only checkable deposits in the banking system.

a. How will the money supply change if the required reserve ratio falls to 5%?

b. How will the money supply change if the required reserve ratio rises to 25%?

11. Using Figure 14-6, find the Federal Reserve district in which you live. Go to www.federalreserve.gov/fomc/ and determine if the president of the regional Federal Reserve bank in your district is currently a voting member of the Federal Open Market Committee (FOMC).

12. Show the changes to the T-accounts for the Federal Reserve and for commercial banks when the Federal Reserve sells $30 million in U.S. Treasury bills. If the public holds a fixed amount of currency (so that all new loans create an equal amount of checkable bank deposits in the banking system) and the minimum reserve ratio is 5%, by how much will checkable bank deposits in the commercial banks change? By how much will the money supply change? Show the final changes to the T-account for the commercial banks when the money supply changes by this amount.

13. The Congressional Research Service estimates that at least $45 million of counterfeit U.S. $100 notes produced by the North Korean government are in circulation.

a. Why do U.S. taxpayers lose because of North Korea's counterfeiting?

b. As of December 2016, the interest rate earned on one-year U.S. Treasury bills was 0.87%. At a 0.87% rate of interest, what is the amount of money U.S. taxpayers are losing per year because of these $45 million in counterfeit notes?

14. As shown in Figure 14-9, the portion of the Federal Reserve's assets made up of U.S. Treasury bills has declined since 2007. Go to www.federalreserve.gov. On the top of page, under "Data" and "Money Stock and Reserve Balances," select the link "Factors Affecting Reserve Balances – H.4.1." Click on the link for the current release.

a. Under "Condition Statement of Federal Reserve Banks," find the row "Reserve Bank Credit." What is the total amount of reserve bank credit under "Average of Daily Figures" for the most current week ended? What is the amount displayed for "U.S. Treasury securities"? What percentage of the Federal Reserve's total reserve bank credit is currently made up of U.S. Treasury bills?

b. Do the Federal Reserve's assets consist primarily of U.S. Treasury securities, as they did in January 2007, the beginning of the graph in Figure 14-9, or does the Fed still own a large number of other assets, as it did in early 2017, the end of the graph in Figure 14-9?

15. The accompanying figure shows new U.S. housing starts, in thousands of units per month, between January 1980 and December 2016. The graph shows a large drop in new housing starts in 1984–1991 and 2006–2009. New housing starts are related to the availability of mortgages.

a. What caused the drop in new housing starts in 1984–1991?

b. What caused the drop in new housing starts in 2006–2009?

c. How could better regulation of financial institutions have prevented these two instances?

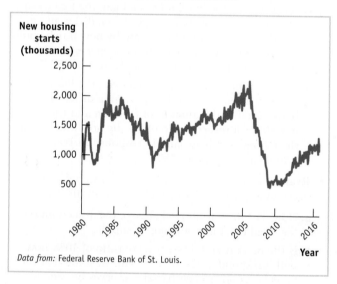

Data from: Federal Reserve Bank of St. Louis.

WORK IT OUT   **Interactive step-by-step help with solving this problem can be found online.**

---

16. Show the changes to the T-accounts for the Federal Reserve and for commercial banks when the Federal Reserve buys $50 million in U.S. Treasury bills. If the public holds a fixed amount of currency (so that all loans create an equal amount of deposits in the banking system), the minimum reserve ratio is 10%, and banks hold no excess reserves, by how much will deposits in the commercial banks change? By how much will the money supply change? Show the final changes to the T-account for commercial banks when the money supply changes by this amount.

15 | Monetary Policy

THE MOST POWERFUL PERSON IN GOVERNMENT

WHEN Nicholas Lemann, a writer for the *New Yorker* magazine, sought to write an article on arguably the most powerful person in the U.S. government, he didn't visit the White House. Instead, he visited the Federal Reserve in Washington, D.C., the home of the Fed's Board of Governors and its chairperson, Janet Yellen. As he later wrote, "There is an old saw that the Fed chair(person) is the most powerful person in the government. In the wake of the financial crisis, that may actually be an understatement."

Yet, at the Federal Reserve, unlike at the nearby White House, there is no pomp and circumstance: no aides dashing around, no splendidly dressed military guards, no ornate paintings on the walls, and no Secret Service. Instead, workers at the Fed are casually dressed—and often look like graduate students. For example, each day at the New York Federal Reserve Bank, where the Fed's financial operations are performed, billions of dollars worth of long-term U.S. government bonds are bought and sold in a small room with just five employees.

The chair of the Federal Reserve is arguably the most powerful position in the U.S. government.

Struck by the ordinariness of it all, Lemann wrote, "Can a spectacle so lacking in the indicia of importance—no pageantry, no emotions, not even speaking—really be the beating heart of capitalism?"

The answer is yes. The source of the power of the Fed chair and the Board of Governors comes from their ability to set *monetary policy*. It's hard to overstate the importance of the Fed's monetary policy to the U.S. economy—for price stability, for job creation, and for the smooth functioning of the financial system. Roughly half the recessions that have occurred since World War II can be attributed, at least partly, to policies undertaken by the Federal Reserve to fight inflation. And during many other periods, Fed policy played a critical role in fighting slumps and promoting recovery. More recently, during the financial crisis of 2008 and the ensuing Great Recession, the Fed was at the very center of the fight to keep the economy from plunging into an abyss.

How does the Fed accomplish all this? Through changes in the money supply and interest rates, which are implemented by its unassuming-looking employees trading billions of dollars daily in U.S. government bonds. (And, as we learned in Chapter 14, to a lesser extent, the Fed can influence the money supply by changing the reserve requirements for banks.)

In this chapter we'll learn how monetary policy works—how actions by the Federal Reserve can have a powerful effect on the economy. We'll start by looking at the *demand for money* from households and firms. Then we'll see how the Fed's ability to change the *supply of money* allows it to move interest rates in the short run and thereby affect real GDP. We'll look at U.S. monetary policy in practice and compare it to the monetary policy of other central banks. We'll conclude by examining monetary policy's long-run effects. ●

WHAT YOU WILL LEARN

- What is the **money demand curve?**
- Why does the **liquidity preference model** determine the interest rate in the short run?
- How does the Federal Reserve implement monetary policy?
- Why is monetary policy the main tool for stabilizing the economy?
- Why do economists believe in **monetary neutrality?**

A **certificate of deposit (CD)** is a bank-issued asset in which customers deposit funds for a specified amount of time and earn a specified interest rate.

The Demand for Money

In the previous chapter we learned about the various types of monetary aggregates: M1, the most commonly used definition of the money supply, consists of currency in circulation (cash), plus checkable bank deposits, plus traveler's checks; and M2, a broader definition of the money supply, consists of M1 plus deposits that can easily be transferred into checkable deposits. We also learned why people hold money—to make it easier to purchase goods and services. Now we'll go deeper, examining what determines how much money individuals and firms want to hold at any given time.

The Opportunity Cost of Holding Money

Most economic decisions involve trade-offs at the margin. That is, individuals decide how much of a good to consume by determining whether the benefit they'd gain from consuming a bit more of any given good is worth the cost. The same decision process is used when deciding how much money to hold.

Individuals and firms find it useful to hold some of their assets in the form of money because of the convenience cash provides: money can be used to make purchases directly, but other assets can't. But there is a price to be paid for that convenience: money normally yields no rate of return, or a lower rate of return, than nonmonetary assets.

As an example of how convenience makes it worth incurring some opportunity costs, consider the substantial sums that Americans hold in cash and in zero-interest bank accounts linked to debit cards or money transmitters like PayPal and Venmo. By doing so they forgo the interest that could have been earned by putting those funds into an interest-bearing asset like a certificate of deposit. A **certificate of deposit,** or **CD,** is a bank-issued asset allowing customers to deposit their funds for a specified amount of time, and, in return, the bank pays a specified interest rate. For example, as of March 2017 the bank Capital One was offering a five-year CD paying 2.30% annually and a one-year CD paying 1.30%. But CDs also carry a penalty if funds are withdrawn before the specified amount of time— whether five years or one year—has elapsed.

There is a price to be paid for the convenience of holding money.

So making sense of the demand for money is about understanding how individuals and firms trade off the benefit of holding monetary assets that provide convenience but little or no interest (like cash and zero-interest bank accounts) versus the benefit of holding nonmonetary assets—that provide more interest but less convenience (like CDs). And that trade-off is affected by the interest rate. (As before, when we say *the interest rate* it is with the understanding that we mean a nominal interest rate—that is, it's unadjusted for inflation.) Next, we'll examine how that trade-off changed dramatically from June 2007 to June 2009, when there was a big fall in interest rates.

Table 15-1 illustrates the opportunity cost of holding money in a specific month, June 2007. The first row shows the interest rate on one-month certificates of deposit—that is, the interest rate individuals could get if they were willing to tie their funds up for one month.

In June 2007, one-month CDs yielded 5.30%. The second row shows the interest rate on interest-bearing demand deposits. Funds in these accounts were more accessible than those in CDs, but the price of that convenience was a much lower interest rate, only 2.30%. Finally, the last row shows the interest rate on currency—cash in your wallet—which was, of course, zero.

TABLE 15-1 Selected Interest Rates, June 2007	
One-month certificates of deposit (CDs)	5.30%
Interest-bearing demand deposits	2.30%
Currency	0

Data from: Federal Reserve Bank of St. Louis.

Big Cheese Photo/Superstock

Table 15-1 shows the opportunity cost of holding money at one point in time, but the opportunity cost of holding money changes when the overall level of interest rates changes. Specifically, when the overall level of interest rates falls, the opportunity cost of holding money falls, too.

Table 15-2 illustrates this point by showing how selected interest rates changed between June 2007 and June 2009, a period when the Federal Reserve was slashing rates in an (unsuccessful) effort to fight off a rapidly worsening recession. A comparison between interest rates in those two months illustrates what happens when the opportunity cost of holding money falls sharply. Over the course of two years the federal funds rate, which is the rate the Fed controls most directly, fell by 5.05 percentage points. The interest rate on one-month CDs fell almost as much, 5.02 percentage points. These interest rates are **short-term interest rates**—rates on financial assets that come due, or mature, within less than a year.

TABLE 15-2 Interest Rates and the Opportunity Cost of Holding Money

	June 2007	June 2009
Federal funds rate	5.25%	0.20%
One-month certificates of deposit (CDs)	5.30%	0.28%
Interest-bearing demand deposits	2.30%	0.14%
Currency	0	0
CDs minus interest-bearing demand deposits (percentage points)	**3.00**	**0.14**
CDs minus currency (percentage points)	**5.30**	**0.28**

Data from: Federal Reserve Bank of St. Louis.

As short-term interest rates fell, the interest rates on money didn't fall by the same amount. The interest rate on currency, of course, remained at zero. The interest rate paid on demand deposits did fall, but by much less than short-term interest rates. As a comparison of the two columns of Table 15-2 shows, the opportunity cost of holding money fell. The last two rows of Table 15-2 summarize this comparison: they give the differences between the interest rates on demand deposits and between currency and the interest rate on CDs.

These differences—the opportunity cost of holding money rather than interest-bearing assets—declined sharply between June 2007 and June 2009. This reflects a general result: *the higher the short-term interest rate, the higher the opportunity cost of holding money; the lower the short-term interest rate, the lower the opportunity cost of holding money.*

The fact that the federal funds rate in Table 15-2 and the interest rate on one-month CDs fell by almost the same percentage is not an accident: all short-term interest rates tend to move together, with rare exceptions. The reason short-term interest rates tend to move together is that CDs and other short-term assets (like one-month and three-month U.S. Treasury bills) are in effect competing for the same business. Any short-term asset that offers a lower-than-average interest rate will be sold by investors, who will move their wealth into a higher-yielding short-term asset. The selling of the asset, in turn, forces its interest rate up, because investors must be rewarded with a higher rate in order to induce them to buy it.

Conversely, investors will move their wealth into any short-term financial asset that offers an above-average interest rate. The purchase of the asset drives its interest rate down when sellers find they can lower the rate of return on the asset and still find willing buyers. So interest rates on short-term financial assets tend to be roughly the same because no asset will consistently offer a higher-than-average or a lower-than-average interest rate.

Table 15-2 contains only short-term interest rates. At any given moment, **long-term interest rates**—rates of interest on financial assets that mature, or come due, a number of years into the future—may be different from short-term interest rates. The difference between short-term and long-term interest rates is sometimes important as a practical matter.

Moreover, it's short-term rates rather than long-term rates that affect money demand, because the decision to hold money involves trading off the convenience of holding cash versus the payoff from holding assets that mature in the short term—a year or less. For the moment, however, let's ignore the distinction between short-term and long-term rates and assume that there is only one interest rate.

Short-term interest rates are the interest rates on financial assets that mature within less than a year.

Long-term interest rates are interest rates on financial assets that mature a number of years in the future.

The **money demand curve** shows the relationship between the interest rate and the quantity of money demanded.

The Money Demand Curve

Because the overall level of interest rates affects the opportunity cost of holding money, the quantity of money individuals and firms want to hold is, other things equal, negatively related to the interest rate. In Figure 15-1, the horizontal axis shows the quantity of money demanded and the vertical axis shows the interest rate, r, which you can think of as a representative short-term interest rate such as the rate on one-month CDs. (As we discussed in Chapter 10, it is the nominal interest rate, not the real interest rate, that influences people's money allocation decisions. Hence, r in Figure 15-1 and all subsequent figures is the nominal interest rate.)

The relationship between the interest rate and the quantity of money demanded by the public is illustrated by the **money demand curve, MD**, in Figure 15-1. The money demand curve slopes downward because, other things equal, a higher interest rate increases the opportunity cost of holding money, leading the public to reduce the quantity of money it demands. For example, if the interest rate is very low—say, 1%—the interest forgone by holding money is relatively small. As a result, individuals and firms will tend to hold relatively large amounts of money to avoid the cost and nuisance of converting other assets into money when making purchases.

By contrast, if the interest rate is relatively high—say, 15%, a level it reached in the United States in the early 1980s—the opportunity cost of holding money is high. People will respond by keeping only small amounts in cash and deposits, converting assets into money only when needed.

You might ask why we draw the money demand curve with the interest rate—as opposed to rates of return on other assets, such as stocks or real estate—on the vertical axis. The answer is that for most people the relevant question in deciding how much money to hold is whether to put the funds in the form of other assets that can be turned fairly quickly and easily into money. Stocks don't fit that definition because there are significant transaction fees when you sell stock (which is why stock market investors are advised not to buy and sell too often). Real estate doesn't fit the definition either because selling real estate involves even larger fees and can take a long time as well. So the relevant comparison is with assets that are "close to" money—assets like CDs that are less liquid than money but more liquid than stocks or real estate.

FIGURE 15-1 The Money Demand Curve

The money demand curve illustrates the relationship between the interest rate and the quantity of money demanded. It slopes downward: a higher interest rate leads to a higher opportunity cost of holding money and reduces the quantity of money demanded. Correspondingly, a lower interest rate reduces the opportunity cost of holding money and increases the quantity of money demanded.

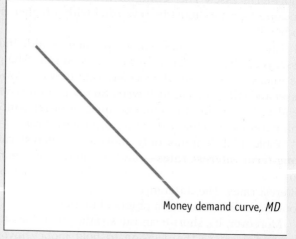

And as we've already seen, the interest rates on all these assets normally move closely together.

Shifts of the Money Demand Curve

A number of factors other than the interest rate affect the demand for money. When one of these factors changes, the money demand curve shifts. Figure 15-2 shows shifts of the money demand curve: an increase in the demand for money corresponds to a rightward shift of the *MD* curve, raising the quantity of money demanded at any given interest rate; a decrease in the demand for money corresponds to a leftward shift of the *MD* curve, reducing the quantity of money demanded at any given interest rate.

The most important factors causing the money demand curve to shift are changes in the aggregate price level, changes in real GDP, changes in credit markets and banking technology, and changes in institutions.

Changes in the Aggregate Price Level Americans keep a lot more cash on hand and funds in their checking accounts today than they did in the 1950s. One reason is that they have to if they want to be able to buy anything: almost everything costs more now than it did when you could get a burger, fries, and a drink at McDonald's for 45 cents and a gallon of gasoline for 29 cents. So, other things equal, higher prices increase the demand for money (a rightward shift of the *MD* curve), and lower prices decrease the demand for money (a leftward shift of the *MD* curve).

We can actually be more specific than this: other things equal, the demand for money is *proportional* to the price level. That is, if the aggregate price level rises by 20%, the quantity of money demanded at any given interest rate, such as r_1 in Figure 15-2, also rises by 20%—the movement from M_1 to M_2. Why? Because if the price of everything rises by 20%, it takes 20% more money to buy the same basket of goods and services. And if the aggregate price level falls by 20%, at any given interest rate the quantity of money demanded falls by 20%—shown by the movement from M_1 to M_3 at the interest rate r_1. As we'll see later, the fact that money demand is proportional to the price level has important implications for the long-run effects of monetary policy.

FIGURE 15-2 Increases and Decreases in the Demand for Money

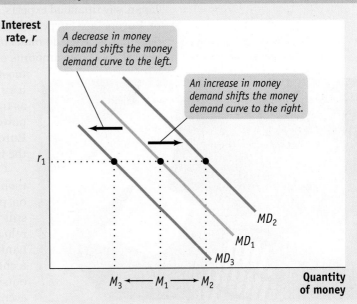

The demand curve for money shifts when non-interest-rate factors that affect the demand for money change. An increase in money demand shifts the money demand curve to the right, from MD_1 to MD_2, and the quantity of money demanded rises at any given interest rate. A decrease in money demand shifts the money demand curve to the left, from MD_1 to MD_3, and the quantity of money demanded falls at any given interest rate.

A decrease in money demand shifts the money demand curve to the left.

An increase in money demand shifts the money demand curve to the right.

A typical scene in a Belgian supermarket. Belgium is one of several nations at the forefront in moving toward a cashless society with a significant percentage of payments made via fingerprint scans (shown here) and smartphones used as virtual wallets.

Changes in Real GDP Households and firms hold money as a way to facilitate purchases of goods and services. The larger the quantity of goods and services they buy, the larger the quantity of money they will want to hold at any given interest rate. So an increase in real GDP—the total quantity of goods and services produced and sold in the economy—shifts the money demand curve rightward. A fall in real GDP shifts the money demand curve leftward.

Changes in Credit Markets and Banking Technology As late as the 1960s almost all small purchases—lunch, groceries, and more—were made using cash because alternatives were few. Since then, however, the need for cash has been greatly reduced by a series of innovations, from widely available credit cards to debit cards to apps like PayPal that let you pay with your smartphone (see the Business Case at end of chapter to learn more about money transmitters like PayPal and Venmo). ATMs and then online banking also made it much easier to transfer funds between accounts, so it became less necessary to hold a surplus of funds in checking accounts in order to make payments. All of these developments make it easier for people to make purchases and reduce the demand for money, shifting the demand curve for money to the left.

Changes in Institutions Changes in institutions can increase or decrease the demand for money. For example, until Regulation Q was eliminated in 1980, U.S. banks weren't allowed to offer interest on checking accounts. So the interest you would forgo by holding funds in a checking account instead of an interest-bearing asset made the opportunity cost of holding funds in checking accounts very high. When banking regulations changed, allowing banks to pay interest on checking account funds, the demand for money rose and shifted the money demand curve to the right.

ECONOMICS >> *in Action*
A Yen for Cash

Japan, say financial experts, is still a "cash society." Visitors from the United States or Europe are surprised at how little use the Japanese make of credit cards or debit cards. They do make many purchases with smartphones, yet they still carry remarkably large amounts of cash around in their wallets. Yet Japan is one of the most economically and technologically advanced countries, and superior to the United States in some areas such as transportation. So why do the citizens of this economic powerhouse often still do business the way Americans and Europeans did a generation ago? The answer highlights the factors affecting the demand for money.

One reason the Japanese use cash so much is that their institutions never made the switch to heavy reliance on plastic. For complex reasons, Japan's retail sector is still dominated by small mom-and-pop stores, which are reluctant to invest in information technology. Japan's banks have also been slow about pushing transaction technology; visitors are often surprised to find that ATMs outside of major metropolitan areas close early in the evening rather than staying open all night.

But there's another reason the Japanese hold so much cash: there's little opportunity cost to doing so. Short-term

No matter what they are shopping for, Japanese consumers tend to pay with cash rather than plastic.

interest rates in Japan have been below 1% since the mid-1990s. It also helps that the Japanese crime rate is quite low, so you are unlikely to have your wallet stolen. So why not hold cash?

>> Check Your Understanding 15-1

Solutions appear at back of book.

1. Explain how each of the following would affect the quantity of money demanded. Does the change cause a movement along the money demand curve or a shift of the money demand curve?

    a. Short-term interest rates rise from 5% to 30%.

    b. All prices fall by 10%.

    c. New wireless technology automatically charges supermarket purchases to credit cards, eliminating the need to stop at the cash register.

    d. In order to avoid paying a sharp increase in taxes, residents of Laguria shift their assets into overseas bank accounts. These accounts are harder for tax authorities to trace but also harder for their owners to tap and convert funds into cash.

2. Which of the following will increase the opportunity cost of holding cash or reduce it? Explain.

    a. In order to attract new customers, the new internet payment firm, PayBuddy, announces it will pay 0.5% interest on cash balances in a PayBuddy account.

    b. To attract more deposits, banks raise the interest paid on six-month CDs.

    c. In an effort to increase holiday sales, stores offer one-year zero-interest deals on purchases made with store credit cards.

Money and Interest Rates

Consistent with its statutory mandate, the Committee seeks to foster maximum employment and price stability. The Committee expects that, with gradual adjustments in the stance of monetary policy, economic activity will expand at a moderate pace, labor market conditions will strengthen somewhat further, and inflation will stabilize around 2 percent over the medium term. Near-term risks to the economic outlook appear roughly balanced. The Committee continues to closely monitor inflation indicators and global economic and financial developments.

In view of realized and expected labor market conditions and inflation, the Committee decided to raise the target range for the federal funds rate to ¾ to 1 percent. The stance of monetary policy remains accommodative, thereby supporting some further strengthening in labor market conditions and a sustained return to 2 percent inflation.

So read part of a press release from the Federal Reserve issued on March 15, 2017. We learned about the federal funds rate in Chapter 14: it's the rate at which banks lend reserves to each other to meet the required reserve ratio. As the statement implies, at each of its eight-times-a-year meetings, a group called the Federal Open Market Committee sets a target value for the federal funds rate. It's then up to Fed officials to achieve that target. This is done by the Open Market Desk at the Federal Reserve Bank of New York, which buys and sells short-term U.S. government debt, known as Treasury bills, to achieve that target.

As we've already seen, other short-term interest rates, such as the rates on CDs, move with the federal funds rate. So when the Fed raised its target for the federal funds rate in March 2017, many other short-term interest rates also rose by about the same amount.

How does the Fed go about achieving a *target federal funds rate?* And more to the point, how is the Fed able to affect interest rates at all?

The Equilibrium Interest Rate

Recall that, for simplicity, we're assuming there is only one interest rate paid on nonmonetary financial assets, both in the short run and in the long run. To understand how the interest rate is determined, consider Figure 15-3, which illustrates the **liquidity preference model of the interest rate;** this model says that the interest rate is determined by the supply and demand for money in the market for money. Figure 15-3 combines the money demand curve, *MD*, with the **money supply curve,** *MS*, which shows how the quantity of money supplied by the Federal Reserve varies with the interest rate.

The Federal Reserve can increase or decrease the money supply: it usually does this through *open-market operations,* buying or selling Treasury bills, but it can also lend via the *discount window* or change *reserve requirements.* Let's assume for simplicity that the Fed, using one or more of these methods, simply chooses the level of the money supply that it believes will achieve its interest rate target. Then the money supply curve is a vertical line, *MS* in Figure 15-3, with a horizontal intercept corresponding to the money supply chosen by the Fed, $\overline{M}$. The money market equilibrium is at *E*, where *MS* and *MD* cross. At this point the quantity of money demanded equals the money supply, $\overline{M}$, leading to an equilibrium interest rate of r_E.

To understand why r_E is the equilibrium interest rate, consider what happens if the money market is at a point like *L*, where the interest rate, r_L, is below r_E. At r_L the public wants to hold the quantity of money M_L, an amount larger than the actual money supply, $\overline{M}$. This means that at point *L*, the public wants to shift some of its wealth out of interest-bearing assets such as CDs into money.

This result has two implications.

1. The quantity of money demanded is *more* than the quantity of money supplied.
2. The quantity of interest-bearing nonmoney assets demanded is *less* than the quantity supplied.

So those trying to sell nonmoney assets will find that they have to offer a higher interest rate to attract buyers. As a result, the interest rate will be driven up from r_L until the public wants to hold the quantity of money that is actually available, $\overline{M}$. That is, the interest rate will rise until it is equal to r_E.

FIGURE 15-3 Equilibrium in the Money Market

The money supply curve, *MS*, is vertical at the money supply chosen by the Federal Reserve, $\overline{M}$. The money market is in equilibrium at the interest rate r_E: the quantity of money demanded by the public is equal to $\overline{M}$, the quantity of money supplied.

At a point such as *L*, the interest rate, r_L, is below r_E and the corresponding quantity of money demanded, M_L, exceeds the money supply, $\overline{M}$. In an attempt to shift their wealth out of nonmoney interest-bearing financial assets and raise their money holdings, investors drive the interest rate up to r_E. At a point such as *H*, the interest rate r_H exceeds r_E and the corresponding quantity of money demanded, M_H, is less than the money supply, $\overline{M}$. In an attempt to shift out of money holdings into nonmoney interest-bearing financial assets, investors drive the interest rate down to r_E.

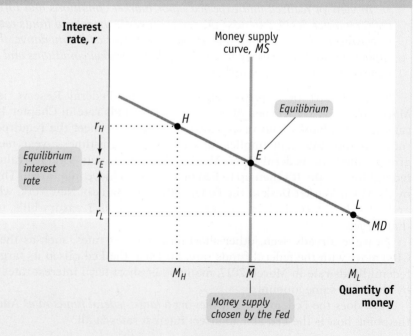

Now consider what happens if the money market is at a point such as H in Figure 15-3, where the interest rate r_H is above r_E. In that case the quantity of money demanded, M_H, is less than the quantity of money supplied, $\overline{M}$. Correspondingly, the quantity of interest-bearing nonmoney assets demanded is greater than the quantity supplied. Those trying to sell interest-bearing nonmoney assets will find that they can offer a lower interest rate and still find willing buyers. This leads to a fall in the interest rate from r_H. It falls until the public wants to hold the quantity of money that is actually available, $\overline{M}$. Again, the interest rate will end up at r_E.

Two Models of Interest Rates?

You might have noticed that this is the second time we have discussed the determination of the interest rate. In Chapter 10 we studied the *loanable funds model* of the interest rate; according to that model, the interest rate is determined by the equalization of the supply of funds from lenders and the demand for funds by borrowers in the market for loanable funds. But here we have described a seemingly different model in which the interest rate is determined by the equalization of the supply and demand for money in the money market. Which of these models is correct?

The answer is both. We explain how the models are consistent with each other in the appendix to this chapter. For now, let's put the loanable funds model to one side and concentrate on the liquidity preference model of the interest rate. The most important insight from this model is that it shows us how monetary policy—actions by the Federal Reserve and other central banks—works.

Monetary Policy and the Interest Rate

Let's examine how the Federal Reserve can use changes in the money supply to change the interest rate. Figure 15-4 shows what happens when the Fed increases the money supply from $\overline{M}_1$ to $\overline{M}_2$. The economy is originally in equilibrium at E_1, with an equilibrium interest rate of r_1 and money supply, $\overline{M}_1$. An increase in the money supply by the Fed to $\overline{M}_2$ shifts the money supply curve to the right, from MS_1 to MS_2, and leads to a fall in the equilibrium interest rate to r_2. Why? Because r_2 is the only interest rate at which the public is willing to hold the quantity of money actually supplied, $\overline{M}_2$.

FIGURE 15-4   The Effect of an Increase in the Money Supply on the Interest Rate

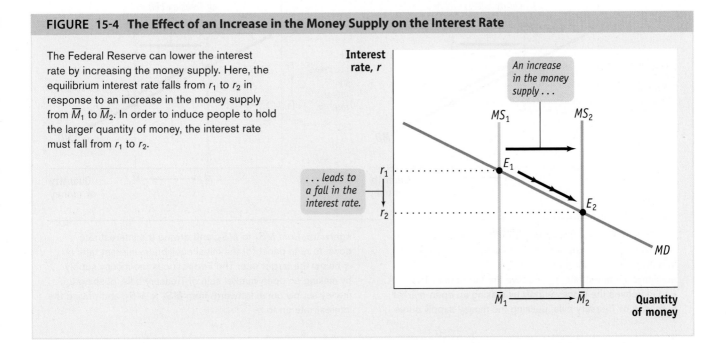

The Federal Reserve can lower the interest rate by increasing the money supply. Here, the equilibrium interest rate falls from r_1 to r_2 in response to an increase in the money supply from $\overline{M}_1$ to $\overline{M}_2$. In order to induce people to hold the larger quantity of money, the interest rate must fall from r_1 to r_2.

PITFALLS

SETTING INTEREST RATES OR THE MONEY SUPPLY: DIFFERENT LOOK, SAME STORY

Over the years, the Federal Reserve has changed the way in which monetary policy is implemented. In the late 1970s and early 1980s, it set a target level for the money supply and altered the monetary base to achieve that target. Under this operating procedure, the federal funds rate fluctuated freely. Today the Fed uses the reverse procedure, setting a target for the federal funds rate and allowing the money supply to fluctuate as it pursues that target.

A common mistake is to imagine that these changes in the way the Federal Reserve operates alter the way the money market works. That is, you'll sometimes hear people say that the interest rate no longer reflects the supply and demand for money because the Fed sets the interest rate.

In fact, the money market works the same way as always: the interest rate is determined by the supply and demand for money. The only difference is that now the Fed adjusts the supply of money to achieve its target interest rate. It's important not to confuse a change in the Fed's operating procedure with a change in the way the economy works.

So an increase in the money supply drives the interest rate down. Conversely, a reduction in the money supply drives the interest rate up. By adjusting the money supply up or down, the Fed can set the interest rate.

In practice, at each meeting the Federal Open Market Committee decides on the interest rate to prevail for the next six weeks, until its next meeting. The Fed sets a **target federal funds rate,** a desired level for the federal funds rate. This target is then enforced by the Open Market Desk of the Federal Reserve Bank of New York—in those two small rooms we mentioned in the opening story—which adjusts the money supply through the purchase and sale of Treasury bills until the actual federal funds rate equals the target rate. The other tools of monetary policy, lending through the discount window and changes in reserve requirements, aren't used on a regular basis (although the Fed used discount window lending in its efforts to address the 2008 financial crisis).

Figure 15-5 shows how this works. In both panels, r_T is the target federal funds rate. In panel (a), the initial money supply curve is MS_1 with money supply $\overline{M}_1$, and the equilibrium interest rate, r_1, is above the target rate. To lower the interest rate to r_T, the Fed makes an open-market purchase of Treasury bills. As we learned in Chapter 14, an open-market purchase of Treasury bills leads to an increase in the money supply via the money multiplier. This is illustrated in panel (a) by the rightward shift of the money supply curve from MS_1 to MS_2 and an increase in the money supply to $\overline{M}_2$. This drives the equilibrium interest rate down to the target rate, r_T.

Panel (b) shows the opposite case. Again, the initial money supply curve is MS_1 with money supply $\overline{M}_1$. But this time the equilibrium

FIGURE 15-5 Setting the Federal Funds Rate

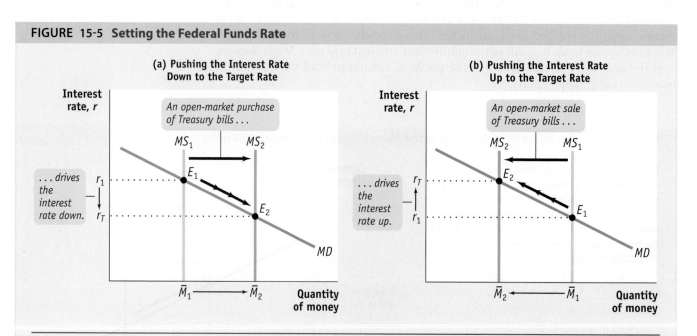

The Federal Reserve sets a target for the federal funds rate and uses open-market operations to achieve that target. In both panels the target rate is r_T. In panel (a) the initial equilibrium interest rate, r_1, is above the target rate. The Fed increases the money supply by making an open-market purchase of Treasury bills, pushing the money supply curve rightward, from MS_1 to MS_2, and driving the interest rate down to r_T. In panel (b) the initial equilibrium interest rate, r_1, is below the target rate. The Fed reduces the money supply by making an open-market sale of Treasury bills, pushing the money supply curve leftward, from MS_1 to MS_2, and driving the interest rate up to r_T.

interest rate, r_1, is below the target federal funds rate, r_T. In this case, the Fed will make an open-market sale of Treasury bills, leading to a fall in the money supply to $\overline{M}_2$ via the money multiplier. The money supply curve shifts leftward from MS_1 to MS_2, driving the equilibrium interest rate up to the target federal funds rate, r_T.

The **target federal funds rate** is the Federal Reserve's desired federal funds rate.

Long-Term Interest Rates

In early 2015, short-term interest rates were quite similar in the world's wealthy economies, because they were all close to zero. For example, in Germany the short-term interest rate was 0.05%, while in the United States it was 0.15%. But long-term interest rates—rates on bonds or loans that mature in several years—were quite different. The interest rate on 10-year German government bonds was 0.35%, but the corresponding rate for the United States was 1.97%.

Why were these long-term rates so different? Because long-term rates reflect expected future monetary policy, which in turn largely depend on the future economic outlook.

Consider the case of Millie, who has already decided to place $10,000 in U.S. government bonds for the next two years. However, she hasn't decided whether to put the money in one-year bonds, at a 4% rate of interest, or two-year bonds, at a 5% rate of interest. If she buys the one-year bond, then in one year, Millie will receive the $10,000 she paid for the bond (the *principal*) plus interest earned. If instead she buys the two-year bond, Millie will have to wait until the end of the second year to receive her principal and her interest.

You might think that the two-year bonds are a clearly better deal—but they may not be. Suppose that Millie expects the rate of interest on one-year bonds to rise sharply next year. If she puts her funds in one-year bonds this year, she will be able to reinvest the money at a much higher rate next year. And this could give her a two-year rate of return that is higher than if she put her funds into the two-year bonds today.

For example, if the rate of interest on one-year bonds rises from 4% this year to 8% next year, putting her funds in a one-year bond today and in another one-year bond a year from now will give her an annual rate of return over the next two years of about 6%, better than the 5% rate on two-year bonds.

The same considerations apply to all investors deciding between short-term and long-term bonds. If they expect short-term interest rates to rise, investors may buy short-term bonds even if long-term bonds bought today offer a higher interest rate today. If they expect short-term interest rates to fall, investors may buy long-term bonds even if short-term bonds bought today offer a higher interest rate today.

As the example suggests, long-term interest rates largely reflect the average expectation in the market about what's going to happen to short-term rates in the future. What was happening in 2015 was that investors expected the U.S. economy to recover much more strongly than the European economy. As a result, investors expected the Fed to raise rates over the next few years, while they didn't expect the ECB to similarly tighten monetary policy. Hence, the United States had higher long-term rates in 2015 compared to the ECB, even though the short-term rates of the two regions were almost the same.

Expected monetary policy is not, however, the whole story: risk is also a factor. Let's return to Millie's decision: whether to buy one-year or two-year bonds. Suppose that there is some chance she will need to cash in her investment after just one year—say, to meet an emergency medical bill. If she buys two-year bonds, she would have to sell those bonds to meet the unexpected expense. But what price will she get for those bonds? It depends on what has happened to interest rates in the rest of the economy. As we've learned, bond prices and interest rates move in opposite directions: if interest rates rise, bond prices fall, and vice versa.

Flagg, J. M. (ca. 1917.) *I want you for U.S. Army: nearest recruiting station/James Montgomery Flagg.* United States, ca. 1917. [Photograph] Retrieved from the Library of Congress, https://www.loc.gov/item/96507165/.

Advertising during the two world wars increased the demand for government long-term bonds from savers who might have been otherwise reluctant to tie up their funds for several years.

This means that Millie will face extra risk if she buys two-year rather than one-year bonds, because if a year from now bond prices fall and she must sell her bonds in order to raise cash, she will lose money on the bonds. Owing to this risk factor, long-term interest rates are, on average, higher than short-term rates in order to compensate long-term bond purchasers for the higher risk they face (although this relationship is reversed when short-term rates are unusually high).

As we will soon see, the fact that long-term rates don't necessarily move with short-term rates is sometimes an important consideration for monetary policy.

ECONOMICS >> *in Action*
Up the Down Staircase

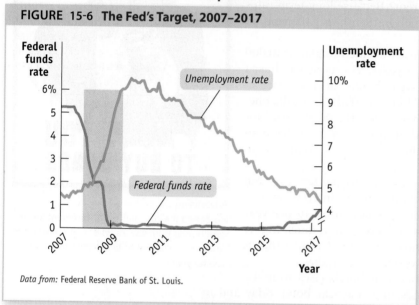

FIGURE 15-6 The Fed's Target, 2007–2017

Data from: Federal Reserve Bank of St. Louis.

We began this section with the Fed's March 2017 announcement that it was raising its target interest rate. By historical standards, however, the target rate was still very low. As Figure 15-6 shows, in early 2007, before the financial crisis, the target rate was 5.25%. But when the financial crisis hit in 2008, the Fed drastically cut rates in an effort to fight the Great Recession, and kept them close to zero for seven years.

Why did the Fed keep rates so low? Because a severe recession followed by a slow recovery kept unemployment—also shown in the figure—very high, while inflation stayed low, for a very long time. In effect, the Fed believed that it needed to keep the pedal to the metal.

By late 2015, however, the economy had clearly improved, with unemployment, in particular, down roughly to its pre-crisis level. And in December 2015 the Federal Open Market Committee began inching back toward a more historically normal monetary policy, a process still underway in March 2017. But "inching" is the word: in the aftermath of that March 2017 rate hike, the federal funds rate was still only a fraction of what it had been a decade earlier.

Why was the Fed moving so slowly? For one thing, while the economy had clearly recovered from the worst of the Great Recession, it was hardly experiencing an inflationary boom. In fact, the Fed's preferred measure of inflation was still a bit below its target.

Also, a significant number of economists worried that changes in the economic environment, in particular an aging population and slowing productivity growth, meant that maintaining full employment would require keeping interest rates more or less permanently low by historical standards. Investors seemed to agree: long-term interest rates in early 2017 were only about 2.50%, which implied that investors didn't expect the Fed to return to the kind of interest rates it used to target for the foreseeable future.

But was this expectation right? Should the Fed have moved more quickly—or not moved at all? Time will tell. But changes in the Fed's target over the period from 2007 to 2017 offer a clear illustration of the forces that drive monetary policy.

>> **Check Your Understanding 15-2**
Solutions appear at back of book.

1. There is an increase in the demand for money at every interest rate. Draw a diagram showing the effect of this on the equilibrium interest rate for a given money supply.

2. Now assume that the Fed is following a policy of targeting the federal funds rate. What will the Fed do in the situation described in Question 1 to keep the federal funds rate unchanged? Illustrate with a diagram.

3. Malia must decide whether to buy a one-year bond today and another one a year from now, or buy a two-year bond today. In which of the following scenarios is she better off taking the first action? The second action?
   a. This year, the interest on a one-year bond is 4%; next year, it will be 10%. The interest rate on a two-year bond is 5%.
   b. This year, the interest rate on a one-year bond is 4%; next year, it will be 1%. The interest rate on a two-year bond is 3%.

>> **Quick Review**

• According to the **liquidity preference model of the interest rate,** the equilibrium interest rate is determined by the money demand curve and the **money supply curve.**

• The Federal Reserve can move the interest rate through open-market operations that shift the money supply curve. In practice, the Fed sets a **target federal funds rate** and uses open-market operations to achieve that target.

• Long-term interest rates reflect expectations about what's going to happen to short-term rates in the future. Because of risk, long-term interest rates tend to be higher than short-term rates.

Monetary Policy and Aggregate Demand

We saw how fiscal policy can be used to stabilize the economy in Chapter 13. Now we will see how monetary policy, which we defined earlier as changes in the money supply, and the interest rate together can play the same role.

Expansionary and Contractionary Monetary Policy

In Chapter 12 we learned that monetary policy shifts the aggregate demand curve. We can now explain how that works: through the effect of monetary policy on the interest rate.

Figure 15-7 illustrates the process. Suppose, first, that the Federal Reserve wants to reduce interest rates, so it expands the money supply. As you can see in the top portion of the figure, a lower interest rate, in turn, will lead, other things equal, to more investment spending. This will in turn lead to higher consumer spending, through the multiplier process, and to an increase in aggregate output demanded. In the end, the total quantity of goods and services demanded at any given aggregate price level rises when the quantity of money increases, and the *AD* curve shifts to the right. Monetary policy that increases the demand for goods and services is known as **expansionary monetary policy.** (It is also commonly called *loose monetary policy*.)

Suppose, alternatively, that the Federal Reserve wants to increase interest rates, so it contracts the money supply. You can see this process illustrated in the bottom portion of the diagram. Contraction of the money supply leads to a higher interest rate. The higher interest rate leads to lower investment spending, then to lower consumer spending, and then to a decrease in aggregate output demanded. So the total quantity of goods and services demanded falls when the money supply is reduced, and the *AD* curve shifts to the left. Monetary policy that decreases the demand for goods and services is called **contractionary monetary policy.** (It is also commonly called *tight monetary policy*.)

Expansionary monetary policy is monetary policy that increases aggregate demand.

Contractionary monetary policy is monetary policy that decreases aggregate demand.

Monetary Policy in Practice

How does the Fed decide whether to use expansionary or contractionary monetary policy? And how does it decide how much is enough? As we've learned, policy makers try

"I told you the Fed should have tightened."

FIGURE 15-7 Expansionary and Contractionary Monetary Policy

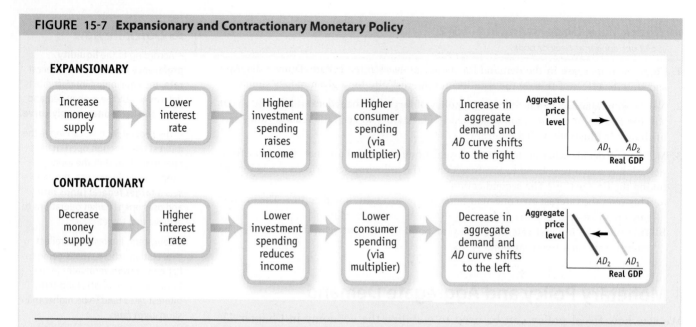

The top portion of the diagram shows what happens when the Fed adopts an expansionary monetary policy and increases the money supply. Interest rates fall, leading to higher investment spending, which raises income, which, in turn, raises consumer spending and shifts the *AD* curve to the right. The bottom portion shows what happens when the Fed adopts a contractionary monetary policy and reduces the money supply. Interest rates rise, leading to lower investment spending and a reduction in income. This lowers consumer spending and shifts the *AD* curve to the left.

to both fight recessions and ensure *price stability:* low (though usually not zero) inflation. Actual monetary policy reflects a combination of these goals.

The Fed and other central banks tend to engage in expansionary monetary policy when actual real GDP is below potential output. Panel (a) of Figure 15-8 shows the U.S. output gap, defined in Chapter 12 as the percentage difference between actual real GDP and potential output, versus the federal funds rate since 1985. (Recall that the output gap is positive when actual real GDP exceeds potential output.) As you can see, the Fed tends to raise interest rates when the output gap is rising (when the economy is developing an inflationary gap) and cut rates when the output gap is falling. (The exception is the period from 2009 to 2016 when the federal funds rate was stuck near zero, a phenomenon, called the zero *lower bound on interest rates*.)

The big exception was the late 1990s, when the Fed left rates steady for several years even as the economy developed a positive output gap (which went along with a low unemployment rate). One reason the Fed was willing to keep interest rates low in the late 1990s was that inflation was low.

Panel (b) of Figure 15-8 compares the inflation rate, measured as the rate of change in consumer prices excluding food and energy, with the federal funds rate. You can see how low inflation during the mid-1990s, the early 2000s, and the late 2000s helped encourage loose monetary policy in the late 1990s, in 2002–2003, and again beginning in 2008.

The Taylor Rule Method of Setting Monetary Policy

In 1993 Stanford economist John Taylor suggested that monetary policy should follow a simple rule that takes into account concerns about both the business cycle and inflation. He also suggested that actual monetary policy often looks as if the Federal Reserve was, in fact, more or less following the proposed rule. A **Taylor rule for monetary policy** is a rule for setting interest rates that takes into account the inflation rate and the output gap or, in some cases, the unemployment rate.

A widely cited example of a Taylor rule is a relationship among Fed policy, inflation, and unemployment estimated by economists at the Federal Reserve

A **Taylor rule for monetary policy** is a rule that sets the federal funds rate according to the level of the inflation rate and either the output gap or the unemployment rate.

FIGURE 15-8 Tracking Monetary Policy Using the Output Gap and Inflation

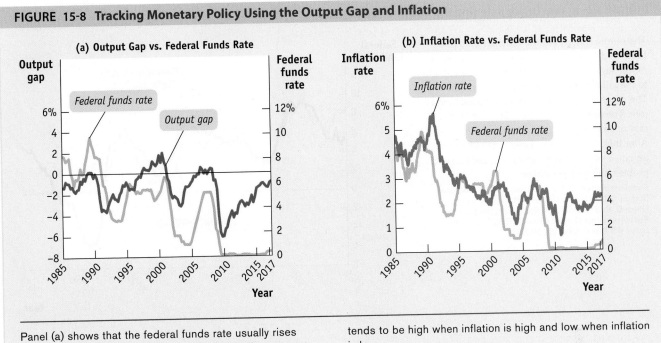

Panel (a) shows that the federal funds rate usually rises when the output gap is rising, and falls when the output gap is falling. Panel (b) illustrates that the federal funds rate tends to be high when inflation is high and low when inflation is low.

Data from: Federal Reserve Bank of St. Louis.

Bank of San Francisco. These economists found that between 1988 and 2008 the Fed's behavior was well summarized by the following Taylor rule:

$$\text{Federal funds rate} = 2.07 + 1.28 \times \text{inflation rate} - 1.95 \times \text{unemployment gap}$$

where the inflation rate was measured by the change over the previous year in consumer prices excluding food and energy, and the unemployment gap was the difference between the actual unemployment rate and Congressional Budget Office estimates of the natural rate of unemployment.

Figure 15-9 compares the federal funds rate predicted by this rule with the actual federal funds rate from 1985 to early 2017. As you can see, the Fed's decisions were quite close to those predicted by this particular Taylor rule from 1985 through the end of 2008. We'll talk about what happened after 2008 shortly.

Inflation Targeting

Until January 2012, the Fed did not explicitly commit itself to achieving a particular inflation rate. However, in January 2012, the Fed announced that it would set its policy to maintain an approximately 2% inflation rate per year. With that statement, the Fed joined a number of other central banks that have explicit inflation targets. So rather than using a Taylor rule to set monetary policy, they instead announce the inflation rate that they want to achieve—the *inflation target*—and set policy in an attempt to hit that target. This method of setting monetary policy, called **inflation targeting,** involves having the central bank announce the inflation rate it is trying to achieve and set policy in an attempt to hit that target. The central bank of New Zealand, which was the first country to adopt inflation targeting, specified a range for that target of 1% to 3%.

Other central banks commit themselves to achieving a specific number. For example, the Bank of England has committed to keeping inflation at 2%. In practice, there doesn't seem to be much difference between these versions: central banks with a target range for inflation seem to aim for the middle of that range, and central banks with a fixed target tend to give themselves considerable wiggle room.

Inflation targeting occurs when the central bank sets an explicit target for the inflation rate and sets monetary policy in order to hit that target.

FIGURE 15-9 The Taylor Rule and the Federal Funds Rate

The purple line shows the federal funds rate predicted by the San Francisco Fed's version of the Taylor rule, which relates the interest rate to the inflation rate and the unemployment rate. The green line shows the actual federal funds rate. The actual rate tracked the predicted rate quite closely through the end of 2008. After that, however, the Taylor rule called for negative interest rates, which is a difficult and problematic goal to achieve.

Data from: Bureau of Labor Statistics; Congressional Budget Office; Federal Reserve Bank of St. Louis; Glenn D. Rudebusch, "The Fed's Monetary Policy Response to the Current Crisis," *FRBSF Economic Letter* #2009–17 (May 22, 2009).

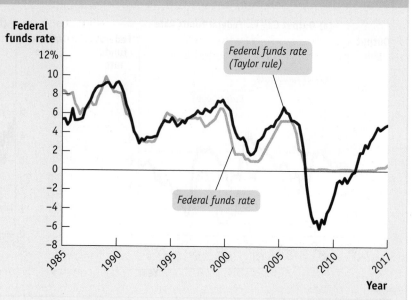

One major difference between inflation targeting and the Taylor rule method is that inflation targeting is forward-looking rather than backward-looking. That is, the Taylor rule method adjusts monetary policy in response to *past* inflation, but inflation targeting is based on a forecast of future inflation.

Advocates of inflation targeting argue that it has two key advantages over a Taylor rule: *transparency* and *accountability*. First, economic uncertainty is reduced because the central bank's plan is transparent: the public knows the objective of an inflation-targeting central bank. Second, the central bank's success can be judged by seeing how closely actual inflation rates have matched the inflation target, making central bankers accountable.

Critics of inflation targeting argue that it's too restrictive because there are times when other concerns—like the stability of the financial system—should take priority over achieving any particular inflation rate. Indeed, starting in late 2013 the Taylor rule rate and the federal funds rate diverged significantly, as the Fed kept the interest rate close to zero while the Taylor rule rate climbed. The Fed's actions were motivated by the fear that an interest rate rise could push the persistently weak economy back into turmoil and recession.

GLOBAL COMPARISON   INFLATION TARGETS

This figure shows the target inflation rates of six central banks that have adopted inflation targeting. The central bank of New Zealand introduced inflation targeting in 1990. Today it has an inflation target range of from 1% to 3%. The central banks of Canada and Sweden have the same target range but also specify 2% as the precise target. The central bank of Norway has a target of 2.5%, with an allowable range from 1.5% to 3.5%, while the central bank of Britain specifies an inflation target of 2%. Since 2012, the U.S. Federal Reserve also targets inflation at 2%.

In practice, these differences in detail don't seem to lead to significantly different results. New Zealand aims for the middle of its range, at 2% inflation; Britain, Norway, and the United States allow considerable wiggle room around their target inflation rates.

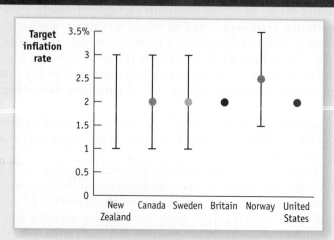

Data from: IMF.

Many American macroeconomists have had positive things to say about inflation targeting—including Ben Bernanke (the Fed chair from 2006 through early 2014). And in January 2012 the Fed declared that what it means by the "price stability" it seeks is 2% inflation, although there was no explicit commitment about when this inflation rate would be achieved.

The **zero lower bound for interest rates** means that interest rates cannot fall much below zero without causing significant problems.

The Zero Lower Bound Problem

As Figure 15-9 shows, a Taylor rule based on inflation and the unemployment rate does a good job of predicting Federal Reserve policy from 1985 through 2008. After that, however, things go awry, and for a simple reason: with very high unemployment and low inflation, the same Taylor rule called for an interest rate significantly less than zero, which is a difficult and problematic goal to achieve.

Negative interest rates are a problem because people always have the alternative of holding cash, which offers a zero interest rate. Why, then, would they ever buy a bond yielding an interest rate less than zero?

Until 2014 most economists believed that it was basically impossible for interest rates to go below zero. That year, however, the central bank of Switzerland did the previously unthinkable, setting rates slightly below zero. It turns out that even at a slightly negative interest rate, there are limits to how much cash the public is willing to hold, because storing cash is expensive: you need vaults that are secure against loss, both from potential theft and from threats like money-eating mice. (Yes, rodent control turns out to play some role in monetary policy.) By 2016, the Swiss equivalent of the federal funds rate was −0.75%, and both the European Central Bank and the Bank of Japan also had slightly negative rates. (Japan's situation, which economists refer to as being *up against the zero bound*, is addressed in Chapter 16.)

So the zero lower bound isn't an absolute limit. Still, no central bank has tried to push rates significantly below zero, say down to −3% or −6%, which is what the Taylor rule suggested for the United States in 2009 and 2010. This is explained partly because rates that low would clearly lead to hoarding of cash. Also, negative interest rates are widely believed to cause big problems for the banking system, with adverse effects on the economy as a whole. This set of circumstances leads to what is called the **zero lower bound for interest rates:** interest rates cannot fall much below zero without causing significant problems. So the Fed has never been willing to push rates below zero. This in turn means that when inflation is low and the economy is operating far below potential, normal monetary policy—open-market purchases of short-term government debt to expand the money supply—runs out of room to operate because short-term interest rates are already at or near zero. Economists refer to this situation as *running up against the zero lower bound*.

In November 2010 the Fed began an attempt to circumvent the problem caused by its inability to reduce interest rates further despite economic weakness, which went by the somewhat obscure name *quantitative easing*. Instead of purchasing only short-term government debt, it began buying longer-term government debt—five-year or six-year bonds, rather than three-month Treasury bills. And, as we know, long-term interest rates don't exactly follow short-term rates. At the time the Fed began this program, short-term rates were near zero, but rates on longer-term bonds were between 2% and 3%. The Fed hoped that direct purchases of these longer-term bonds would drive down interest rates on long-term debt, exerting an expansionary effect on the economy.

Later the Fed expanded the program further, also purchasing mortgage-backed securities, which normally offer somewhat higher rates than U.S. government debt. Here, too, the hope was that these rates could be driven down, with an expansionary effect on the economy. As with ordinary open-market operations, quantitative easing was undertaken by the Federal Reserve Bank of New York.

Was this policy effective? The Federal Reserve believes that it helped the economy. However, the pace of recovery remained disappointingly slow. Starting in 2016, the Fed began to slowly raise rates by an amount less than a Taylor rule would have predicted, reflecting the sluggish pace of the recovery.

FIGURE 15-10 When the Fed Wants a Recession

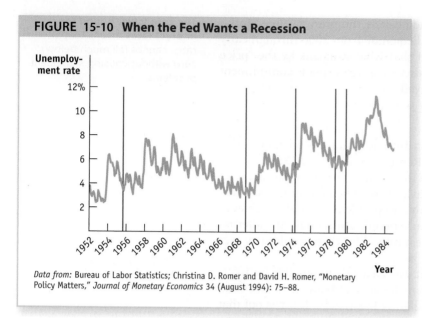

Data from: Bureau of Labor Statistics; Christina D. Romer and David H. Romer, "Monetary Policy Matters," *Journal of Monetary Economics* 34 (August 1994): 75–88.

ECONOMICS >> *in Action*
What the Fed Wants, the Fed Gets

What's the evidence that the Fed can actually cause an economic contraction or expansion? You might think that finding such evidence is just a matter of looking at what happens to the economy when interest rates go up or down. But it turns out that there's a big problem with that approach: the Fed usually changes interest rates in an attempt to tame the business cycle, raising rates if the economy is expanding and reducing rates if the economy is slumping. So in the actual data, it often looks as if low interest rates go along with a weak economy and high rates go along with a strong economy.

In a famous paper titled "Does Monetary Policy Matter?" macroeconomists Christina Romer and David Romer solved this problem by focusing on episodes in which monetary policy wasn't a reaction to the business cycle. Specifically, they used minutes from the Federal Open Market Committee and other sources to identify episodes "in which the Federal Reserve in effect decided to attempt to create a recession to reduce inflation." As we'll learn in Chapter 16, rather than just using monetary policy as a tool of macroeconomic stabilization, sometimes it is used to eliminate *embedded inflation*—inflation that people believe will persist into the future. In such a case, the Fed needs to create a recessionary gap—not just eliminate an inflationary gap—to wring embedded inflation out of the economy.

Figure 15-10 shows the unemployment rate between 1952 and 1984 and also identifies five dates on which, according to Romer and Romer, the Fed decided that it wanted a recession (the vertical lines). In four out of the five cases, the decision to contract the economy was followed, after a modest lag, by a rise in the unemployment rate. On average, Romer and Romer found, the unemployment rate rises by 2 percentage points after the Fed decides that unemployment needs to go up.

So yes, the Fed gets what it wants.

>> Quick Review

• The Federal Reserve can use **expansionary monetary policy** to increase aggregate demand and **contractionary monetary policy** to reduce aggregate demand. The Federal Reserve and other central banks generally try to tame the business cycle while keeping the inflation rate low but positive.

• Under a **Taylor rule for monetary policy,** the target federal funds rate rises when there is high inflation and either a positive output gap or very low unemployment; it falls when there is low or negative inflation and either a negative output gap or high unemployment.

• In contrast, some central banks set monetary policy by **inflation targeting,** a forward-looking policy rule, rather than by using the Taylor rule, a backward-looking policy rule. Although inflation targeting has the benefits of transparency and accountability, some think it is too restrictive. Until 2008, the Fed followed a loosely defined Taylor rule. Starting in early 2012, it began inflation targeting with a target of 2% per year.

• There is a **zero lower bound for interest rates**—they cannot fall much below zero without causing significant problems—that limits the effectiveness of monetary policy.

• Because it is subject to fewer lags than fiscal policy, monetary policy is the main tool for macroeconomic stabilization.

>> Check Your Understanding 15-3
Solutions appear at back of book.

1. Suppose the economy is currently suffering from an output gap and the Federal Reserve uses an expansionary monetary policy to close that gap. Describe the short-run effect of this policy on the following.
    a. The money supply curve
    b. The equilibrium interest rate
    c. Investment spending
    d. Consumer spending
    e. Aggregate output

2. In setting monetary policy, which central bank—one that operates according to a Taylor rule or one that operates by inflation targeting—is likely to respond more directly to a financial crisis? Explain.

|| Money, Output, and Prices in the Long Run

Through its expansionary and contractionary effects, monetary policy is generally the policy tool of choice to help stabilize the economy. However, not all actions by central banks are productive. In particular, central banks sometimes print money not to fight a recessionary gap but to help the government pay its bills, an action that typically destabilizes the economy.

What happens when a change in the money supply pushes the economy away from, rather than toward, long-run equilibrium? As we've learned, the economy is self-correcting in the long run: a demand shock has only a temporary effect on aggregate output. If the demand shock is the result of a change in the money supply, we can make a stronger statement: in the long run, changes in the quantity of money affect the aggregate price level, but they do not change real aggregate output or the interest rate. To see why, let's look at what happens if the central bank permanently increases the money supply.

Short-Run and Long-Run Effects of an Increase in the Money Supply

To analyze the long-run effects of monetary policy, it's helpful to think of the central bank as choosing a target for the money supply rather than the interest rate. In assessing the effects of an increase in the money supply, we return to the analysis of the long-run effects of an increase in aggregate demand, first introduced in Chapter 12.

Figure 15-11 shows the short-run and long-run effects of an increase in the money supply when the economy begins at potential output, Y_1. The initial short-run aggregate supply curve is $SRAS_1$, the long-run aggregate supply curve is $LRAS$, and the initial aggregate demand curve is AD_1. The economy's initial equilibrium is at E_1, a point of both short-run and long-run macroeconomic equilibrium because it is on both the short-run and the long-run aggregate supply curves. Real GDP is at potential output, Y_1.

Now suppose there is an increase in the money supply. Other things equal, an increase in the money supply reduces the interest rate, which increases investment spending, which leads to a further rise in consumer spending, and so on. So an increase in the money supply increases the quantity of goods and services

---

FIGURE 15-11   The Short-Run and Long-Run Effects of an Increase in the Money Supply

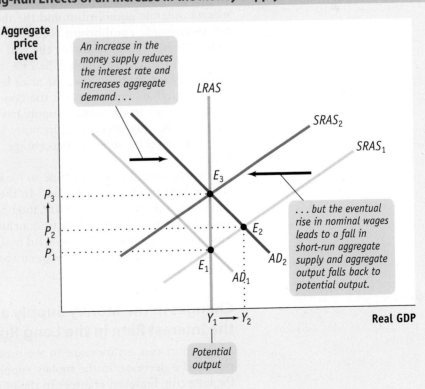

When the economy is already at potential output, an increase in the money supply generates a positive short-run effect, but no long-run effect, on real GDP.

Here, the economy begins at E_1, a point of short-run and long-run macroeconomic equilibrium. An increase in the money supply shifts the AD curve rightward, and the economy moves to a new short-run macroeconomic equilibrium at E_2 and a new real GDP of Y_2. But E_2 is not a long-run equilibrium: Y_2 exceeds potential output, Y_1, leading over time to an increase in nominal wages. In the long run, the increase in nominal wages shifts the short-run aggregate supply curve leftward, to a new position at $SRAS_2$.

The economy reaches a new short-run and long-run macroeconomic equilibrium at E_3 on the $LRAS$ curve, and output falls back to potential output, Y_1. When the economy is already at potential output, the only long-run effect of an increase in the money supply is an increase in the aggregate price level from P_1 to P_3.

According to the concept of **monetary neutrality,** changes in the money supply have no real effects on the economy.

demanded, shifting the *AD* curve rightward, to AD_2. In the short run, the economy moves to a new short-run macroeconomic equilibrium at E_2. The price level rises from P_1 to P_2, and real GDP rises from Y_1 to Y_2. That is, both the aggregate price level and aggregate output increase in the short run.

But the aggregate output level, Y_2, is above potential output. As a result, nominal wages will rise over time, causing the short-run aggregate supply curve to shift leftward. This process stops only when the *SRAS* curve ends up at $SRAS_2$ and the economy ends up at point E_3, a point of both short-run and long-run macroeconomic equilibrium. The long-run effect of an increase in the money supply, then, is that the aggregate price level has increased from P_1 to P_3, but aggregate output is back at potential output, Y_1. In the long run, a monetary expansion raises the aggregate price level but has no effect on real GDP.

We won't describe the effects of a monetary contraction in detail, but the same logic applies. In the short run, a fall in the money supply leads to a fall in aggregate output as the economy moves down the short-run aggregate supply curve. In the long run, however, the monetary contraction reduces only the aggregate price level, and real GDP returns to potential output.

Monetary Neutrality

How much does a change in the money supply change the aggregate price level in the long run? The answer is that a change in the money supply leads to an equal proportional change in the aggregate price level in the long run. For example, if the money supply falls 25%, the aggregate price level falls 25% in the long run; if the money supply rises 50%, the aggregate price level rises 50% in the long run.

How do we know this? Consider the following thought experiment: suppose all prices in the economy—prices of final goods and services and also factor prices, such as nominal wage rates—double. And suppose the money supply doubles at the same time. What difference does this make to the economy in real terms? The answer is none. All real variables in the economy—such as real GDP and the real value of the money supply (the amount of goods and services it can buy)—are unchanged. So there is no reason for anyone to behave any differently.

We can state this argument in reverse: if the economy starts out in long-run macroeconomic equilibrium and the money supply changes, restoring long-run macroeconomic equilibrium requires restoring all real values to their original values. This includes restoring the real value of the money supply to its original level. So if the money supply falls 25%, the aggregate price level must fall 25%; if the money supply rises 50%, the price level must rise 50%; and so on.

This analysis demonstrates the concept known as **monetary neutrality,** in which changes in the money supply have no real effects on the economy. In the long run, the only effect of an increase in the money supply is to raise the aggregate price level by an equal percentage. Economists argue that *money is neutral in the long run.*

This is, however, a good time to recall the dictum of John Maynard Keynes: "In the long run we are all dead." In the long run, changes in the money supply don't have any effect on real GDP, interest rates, or anything else except the price level. But it would be foolish to conclude from this that the Fed is irrelevant. Monetary policy does have powerful real effects on the economy in the short run, often making the difference between recession and expansion. And that matters a lot for society's welfare.

Changes in the Money Supply and the Interest Rate in the Long Run

In the short run, an increase in the money supply leads to a fall in the interest rate, and a decrease in the money supply leads to a rise in the interest rate. In the long run, however, changes in the money supply don't affect the interest rate.

FIGURE 15-12   The Long-Run Determination of the Interest Rate

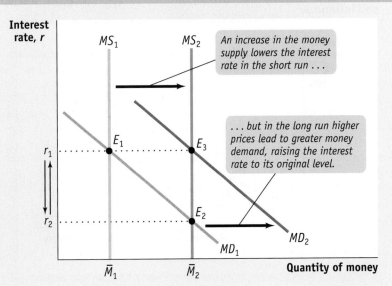

The economy is initially at E_1, a long-run macroeconomic equilibrium. In the short run, an increase in the money supply, from $\overline{M}_1$ to $\overline{M}_2$ pushes the interest rate down from r_1 to r_2. The economy moves to E_2, a short-run equilibrium. In the long run, however, the aggregate price level rises in proportion to the increase in the money supply, leading to an increase in money demand at any given interest rate in proportion to the increase in the aggregate price level, as shown by the shift from MD_1 to MD_2. The result is that the quantity of money demanded at any given interest rate rises by the same amount as the quantity of money supplied. The economy moves to long-run equilibrium at E_3 and the interest rate returns to r_1.

An increase in the money supply lowers the interest rate in the short run . . .

. . . but in the long run higher prices lead to greater money demand, raising the interest rate to its original level.

Figure 15-12 shows why. It shows the money supply curve and the money demand curve before and after the Fed increases the money supply. We assume that the economy is initially at E_1, in long-run macroeconomic equilibrium at potential output, and with money supply $\overline{M}_1$. The initial equilibrium interest rate, determined by the intersection of the money demand curve MD_1 and the money supply curve MS_1, is r_1.

Now suppose the money supply increases from $\overline{M}_1$ to $\overline{M}_2$. In the short run, the economy moves from E_1 to E_2 and the interest rate falls from r_1 to r_2. Over time, however, the aggregate price level rises, and this raises money demand, shifting the money demand curve rightward from MD_1 to MD_2. The economy moves to a new long-run equilibrium at E_3, and the interest rate rises to its original level at r_1.

And it turns out that the long-run equilibrium interest rate is the original interest rate, r_1. We know this for two reasons. First, due to monetary neutrality, in the long run the aggregate price level rises by the same proportion as the money supply; so if the money supply rises by, say, 50%, the price level will also rise by 50%. Second, the demand for money is, other things equal, proportional to the aggregate price level.

So a 50% increase in the money supply raises the aggregate price level by 50%, which increases the quantity of money demanded at any given interest rate by 50%. As a result, the quantity of money demanded at the initial interest rate, r_1, rises exactly as much as the money supply—so that r_1 is still the equilibrium interest rate. In the long run, then, changes in the money supply do not affect the interest rate.

ECONOMICS >> in Action
International Evidence of Monetary Neutrality

These days monetary policy is quite similar among wealthy countries. Each major nation (or, in the case of the euro, the euro area) has a central bank that is insulated from political pressure. All of these central banks try to keep the aggregate price level roughly stable, which usually means inflation of at most 2% to 3% per year.

But if we look at a longer period and a wider group of countries, we see large differences in the growth of the money supply. Between 1970 and the present, the money supply rose only a few percent per year in some countries, such as

FIGURE 15-13 The Long-Run Relationship Between Money and Inflation

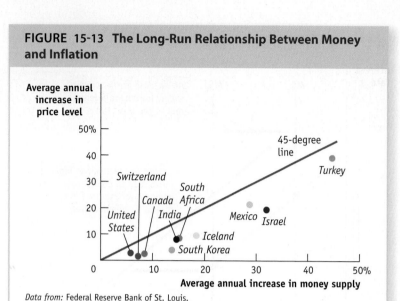

Data from: Federal Reserve Bank of St. Louis.

Switzerland and the United States, but rose much more rapidly in some poorer countries, such as South Africa and Mexico. These differences allow us to see whether it is really true that increases in the money supply lead, in the long run, to equal percent rises in the aggregate price level.

Figure 15-13 shows the annual percentage increases in the money supply and average annual increases in the aggregate price level—that is, the average rate of inflation—for a sample of countries during the period 1983–2015, with each point representing a country. If the relationship between increases in the money supply and changes in the aggregate price level were exact, the points would lie precisely on a 45-degree line.

In fact, the relationship isn't exact, because other factors besides money affect the aggregate price level. But the scatter of points clearly lies close to a 45-degree line, showing a more or less proportional relationship between money and the aggregate price level. That is, the data support the concept of monetary neutrality in the long run.

>> Quick Review

• According to the concept of **monetary neutrality,** changes in the money supply do not affect real GDP, they only affect the aggregate price level. Economists believe that money is neutral in the long run.

• In the long run, the equilibrium interest rate in the economy is unaffected by changes in the money supply.

>> Check Your Understanding 15-4

Solutions appear at back of book.

1. Assume the central bank increases the quantity of money by 25%, even though the economy is initially in both short-run and long-run macroeconomic equilibrium. Describe the effects, in the short run and in the long run (giving numbers where possible), on the following.
   a. Aggregate output
   b. Aggregate price level
   c. Interest rate

2. Why does monetary policy affect the economy in the short run but not in the long run?

Parking Your Money at PayPal

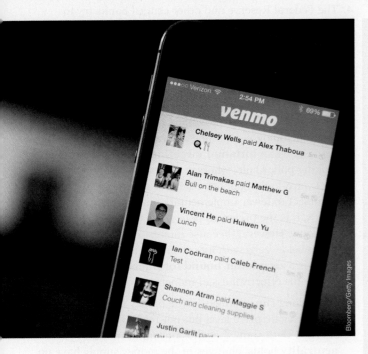

Bloomberg/Getty Images

Officially, PayPal, the electronic funds-transfer firm—which is also the owner of Venmo, a mobile-phone payment service that has become extremely popular—isn't considered a bank. Instead, regulators consider it a *money transmitter*, an entity that sends your money someplace rather than holding it and keeping it safe.

However, as users accumulate substantial sums in their PayPal accounts, that distinction has started to look questionable. Venmo users, in particular, often seem willing to let incoming payments sit in their accounts until the funds are spent. As a result, PayPal's accounts were estimated to total more than $13 billion in 2016. If those billions were considered bank deposits, PayPal would be considered among the 50 largest banks in the United States.

At first glance, leaving significant sums in PayPal accounts seems counterintuitive for two reasons. First, these accounts aren't protected by federal deposit insurance. Second, they pay no interest. But upon closer examination, this behavior makes good economic sense. People will typically hold only a tiny fraction of their wealth in their PayPal account, thereby making the lack of federal deposit insurance an acceptable risk. And interest rates on bank accounts are so low at the time of this writing (around 0.03% in Spring 2017) that losing that interest is a reasonable price to pay to avoid the hassle of moving funds back and forth between a bank account and a PayPal or Venmo account.

The result is that many people are behaving like one user quoted by the *Wall Street Journal*, who now waits a while before transferring funds out of her Venmo account to her regular bank account: "I'm starting to intentionally keep my money in there a bit longer."

But will PayPal/Venmo or something like it begin to make major inroads into traditional banking? Some analysts think so. Others suggest, however, that conventional banks will find ways to make mobile payments easier, and that rising interest rates will lure customers back to conventional bank deposits. Time will tell.

QUESTIONS FOR THOUGHT

1. PayPal accounts aren't counted as part of the money supply. Should they be? Why or why not?

2. In 2010, only around 25% of mobile phones in the United States were smartphones. In 2017, that number increased to more than 80%. How does this situation play into the PayPal story, and how does it fit into the broader pattern of monetary history?

3. How might future actions by the Federal Open Market Committee affect the future of PayPal and similar services?

SUMMARY

1. The **money demand curve** arises from a trade-off between the opportunity cost of holding money and the liquidity that money provides. Americans hold substantial sums in cash and in zero-interest bank accounts linked to debit cards or money transmitters like Paypal and Venmo. By doing so they forgo the interest that could have been earned by putting those funds into an interest-bearing asset like a **certificate of deposit (CD).** The opportunity cost of holding money depends on **short-term interest rates,** not **long-term interest rates.** Changes in the aggregate price level, real GDP, technology, and institutions shift the money demand curve.

2. According to the **liquidity preference model of the interest rate,** the interest rate is determined in the money market by the money demand curve and the **money supply curve.** The Federal Reserve can change the interest rate in the short run by shifting the money supply curve. In practice, the Fed uses open-market operations to achieve a **target federal funds rate,** which other short-term interest rates generally track. Although long-term interest rates don't necessarily move with short-term interest rates, they reflect expectations about what's going to happen to short-term rates in the future.

3. **Expansionary monetary policy** reduces the interest rate by increasing the money supply. This increases investment spending and consumer spending, which in turn increases aggregate demand and real GDP in the short run. **Contractionary monetary policy** raises the interest rate by reducing the money supply. This reduces investment spending and consumer spending, which in turn reduces aggregate demand and real GDP in the short run.

4. The Federal Reserve and other central banks try to stabilize the economy, limiting fluctuations of actual output around potential output, while also keeping inflation low but positive. Under a **Taylor rule for monetary policy,** the target federal funds rate rises when there is high inflation and either a positive output gap or very low unemployment; it falls when there is low or negative inflation and either a negative output gap or high unemployment. Some central banks, including the Fed, engage in **inflation targeting,** which is a forward-looking policy rule, whereas the Taylor rule method is a backward-looking policy rule. Because monetary policy is subject to fewer implementation lags than fiscal policy, it is the preferred policy tool for stabilizing the economy. However, because interest rates cannot fall much below zero without causing significant problems, there is a **zero lower bound for interest rates.** As a result, the effectiveness of monetary policy is limited.

5. In the long run, changes in the money supply affect the aggregate price level but not real GDP or the interest rate. Data show that the concept of **monetary neutrality** holds: changes in the money supply have no real effect on the economy in the long run.

KEY TERMS

Certificate of deposit (CD), p. 448
Short-term interest rates, p. 449
Long-term interest rates, p. 449
Money demand curve, p. 450
Liquidity preference model of the interest rate, p. 454

Money supply curve, p. 454
Target federal funds rate, p. 457
Expansionary monetary policy, p. 459
Contractionary monetary policy, p. 459
Taylor rule for monetary policy, p. 460

Inflation targeting, p. 461
Zero lower bound for interest rates, p. 463
Monetary neutrality, p. 466

PROBLEMS

interactive activity

1. Access the Discovering Data exercise for Chapter 15 Problem 1 online to answer the following questions.

   a. What is the target federal funds rate?

   b. Is the target federal funds rate different from the target federal funds rate in the previous FOMC statement? If yes, by how much does it differ?

   c. Does the statement comment on current macroeconomic conditions in the United States? How does it describe the U.S. economy?

2. How will the following events affect the demand for money? In each case, specify whether there is a shift of the demand curve or a movement along the demand curve and its direction.

   a. There is a fall in the interest rate from 12% to 10%.

   b. Thanksgiving arrives and, with it, the beginning of the holiday shopping season.

   c. Increasingly, merchants are adopting electronic payment systems that allow more consumers to use PayPal and Apple Pay to make purchases.

   d. The Fed engages in an open-market purchase of U.S. Treasury bills.

3. a. Go to www.treasurydirect.gov. Under "Individuals," go to "Treasury Securities & Programs." Click on "Treasury bills." Under "at a glance," click on "rates in recent auctions." What is the investment rate for the most recently issued 52-week T-bills?

b. Go to the website of your favorite bank. What is the interest rate for one-year CDs?

c. Why are the rates for one-year CDs higher than for 52-week Treasury bills?

4. Go to www.treasurydirect.gov. Under "Individuals," go to "Treasury Securities & Programs." Click on "Treasury notes." Under "at a glance," click on "rates in recent auctions." Use the list of Recent Note, Bond, and TIPS Auction Results to answer the following questions.

a. What are the interest rates on 2-year and 10-year notes?

b. How do the interest rates on the 2-year and 10-year notes relate to each other? Why is the interest rate on the 10-year note higher (or lower) than the interest rate on the 2-year note?

5. An economy is facing the recessionary gap shown in the accompanying diagram. To eliminate the gap, should the central bank use expansionary or contractionary monetary policy? How will the interest rate, investment spending, consumer spending, real GDP, and the aggregate price level change as monetary policy closes the recessionary gap?

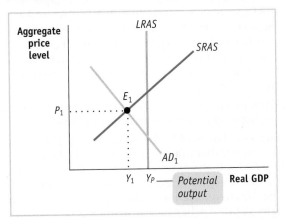

6. An economy is facing the inflationary gap shown in the accompanying diagram. To eliminate the gap, should the central bank use expansionary or contractionary monetary policy? How will the interest rate, investment spending, consumer spending, real GDP, and the aggregate price level change as monetary policy closes the inflationary gap?

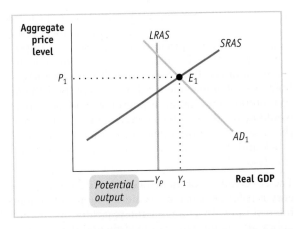

7. In the economy of Eastlandia, the money market is initially in equilibrium when the economy begins to slide into a recession.

a. Using the accompanying diagram, explain what will happen to the interest rate if the central bank of Eastlandia keeps the money supply constant at $\overline{M}_1$.

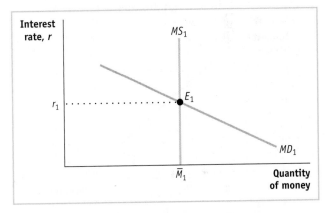

b. If the central bank is instead committed to maintaining an interest rate target of r_1, then as the economy slides into recession, how should the central bank react? Using your diagram from part a, demonstrate the central bank's reaction.

8. Suppose that the money market in Westlandia is initially in equilibrium and the central bank decides to decrease the money supply.

a. Using a diagram like the one in Problem 7, explain what will happen to the interest rate in the short run.

b. What will happen to the interest rate in the long run?

9. An economy is in long-run macroeconomic equilibrium with an unemployment rate of 5% when the government passes a law requiring the central bank to use monetary policy to lower the unemployment rate to 3% and keep it there. How could the central bank achieve this goal in the short run? What would happen in the long run? Illustrate with a diagram.

10. According to the European Central Bank website, the treaty establishing the European Community "makes clear that ensuring price stability is the most important contribution that monetary policy can make to achieve a favourable economic environment and a high level of employment." If price stability is the only goal of monetary policy, explain how monetary policy would be conducted during recessions. Analyze both the case of a recession that is the result of a demand shock and the case of a recession that is the result of a supply shock.

11. The effectiveness of monetary policy depends on how easy it is for changes in the money supply to change interest rates. By changing interest rates, monetary policy affects investment spending and the aggregate demand curve. The economies of Albernia and Brittania have very different money demand curves, as shown in the accompanying diagram. In which economy will changes in the money supply be a more effective policy tool? Why?

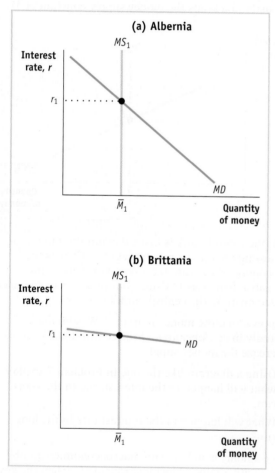

12. During the Great Depression, businesspeople in the United States were very pessimistic about the future of economic growth and reluctant to increase investment spending even when interest rates fell. How did this limit the potential for monetary policy to help alleviate the Depression?

13. Access the Discovering Data exercise for Chapter 15 Problem 13 online to answer the following questions.

   a. How does the relationship between the effective federal funds rate and the Taylor Rule change throughout the Great Recession?

   b. Compare the long-term and short-term interest rate before and after the Great Recession.

WORK IT OUT Interactive step-by-step help with solving this problem can be found online.

---

14. Because of the economic slowdown associated with the 2007–2009 recession, the Federal Open Market Committee of the Federal Reserve, between September 18, 2007, and December 16, 2008, lowered the federal funds rate in a series of steps from a high of 5.25% to a rate between zero and 0.25%. The idea was to provide a boost to the economy by increasing aggregate demand.

   a. Use the liquidity preference model to explain how the Federal Open Market Committee lowers the interest rate in the short run. Draw a typical graph that illustrates the mechanism. Label the vertical axis "Interest rate" and the horizontal axis "Quantity of money." Your graph should show two interest rates, r_1 and r_2.

   b. Explain why the reduction in the interest rate causes aggregate demand to increase in the short run.

   c. Suppose that in 2022 the economy is at potential output but that this is somehow overlooked by the Fed, which continues its monetary expansion. Demonstrate the effect of the policy measure on the *AD* curve. Use the *LRAS* curve to show that the effect of this policy measure on the *AD* curve, other things equal, causes the aggregate price level to rise in the long run. Label the vertical axis "Aggregate price level" and the horizontal axis "Real GDP."

In the liquidity preference model of the interest rate developed in Chapter 15, at the equilibrium interest rate the quantity of money demanded equals the quantity of money supplied. Yet, in the loanable funds model of the interest rate developed in Chapter 10, the equilibrium interest rate matches the quantity of loanable funds supplied by savers with the quantity of loanable funds demanded for investment spending. Can these two models of the interest rate be reconciled? Yes, they can. We will do this in two steps, focusing first on the short run and then on the long run.

The Interest Rate in the Short Run

As explained in the chapter, a fall in the interest rate leads to a rise in investment spending, I, which then leads to a rise in both real GDP and consumer spending, C. The rise in real GDP doesn't lead only to a rise in consumer spending, however. It also leads to a rise in savings: at each stage of the multiplier process, part of the increase in disposable income is saved. How much do savings rise?

In Chapter 10 we introduced the *savings–investment spending identity:* total savings in the economy is always equal to investment spending. *This tells us that when a fall in the interest rate leads to higher investment spending, the resulting increase in real GDP generates exactly enough additional savings to match the rise in investment spending.* To put it another way, after a fall in the interest rate, the quantity of savings supplied rises exactly enough to match the quantity of savings demanded. Understanding this relationship is the key to reconciling the two models of the interest rate.

Figure 15A-1 illustrates how the two models of the interest rate are reconciled in the short run. Panel (a) shows the liquidity preference model of the interest rate where MS_1 and MD_1 are the initial supply and demand curves for money, and r_1, the initial equilibrium interest rate, equalizes the quantity of money supplied to the quantity of money demanded in the money market. Panel (b) shows the loanable funds model of the interest rate where S_1 is the initial supply curve, D is the demand curve for loanable funds, and r_1, the initial equilibrium interest rate, equalizes the quantity of loanable funds supplied to the quantity of loanable funds demanded in the market for loanable funds.

In Figure 15A-1 both the money market and the market for loanable funds are initially in equilibrium at E_1 with the same interest rate, r_1. You might think that this would only happen by accident, but in fact it will always be true. To see why, consider what happens in panel (a), the money market, when the Fed increases the money supply from $\overline{M}_1$ to $\overline{M}_2$, pushing the money supply curve rightward, to MS_2, reducing the equilibrium interest rate in the market to r_2, and moving the economy to a short-run equilibrium at E_2.

What happens in panel (b), the market for loanable funds? In the short run, the fall in the interest rate due to the increase in the money supply leads to a rise in real GDP, which generates a rise in savings through the multiplier process. This rise in savings shifts the supply curve for loanable funds rightward, from S_1 to S_2, moving the equilibrium in the loanable funds market from E_1 to E_2 and reducing the equilibrium interest rate in the loanable funds market. Since the rise in savings must exactly match the rise in investment spending, the equilibrium rate in the loanable funds market must fall to r_2, the same as the new equilibrium interest rate in the money market.

FIGURE 15A-1 **The Short-Run Determination of the Interest Rate**

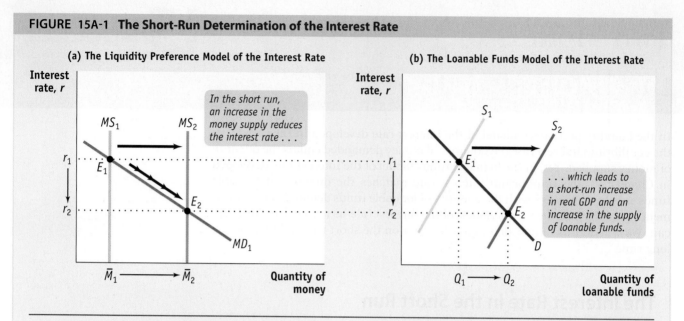

(a) The Liquidity Preference Model of the Interest Rate

(b) The Loanable Funds Model of the Interest Rate

In the short run, an increase in the money supply reduces the interest rate . . .

. . . which leads to a short-run increase in real GDP and an increase in the supply of loanable funds.

Panel (a) shows the liquidity preference model of the interest rate: the equilibrium interest rate matches the money supply to the quantity of money demanded. In the short run, the interest rate is determined in the money market, where an increase in the money supply, from $\overline{M}_1$ to $\overline{M}_2$, pushes the equilibrium interest rates down, from r_1 to r_2. Panel (b) shows the loanable funds model of the interest rate. The fall in the interest rate in the money market leads, through the multiplier effect, to an increase in real GDP and savings; to a rightward shift of the supply curve of loanable funds, from S_1 to S_2; and to a fall in the interest rate, from r_1 to r_2. As a result, the new equilibrium interest rate in the loanable funds market matches the new equilibrium interest rate in the money market at r_2.

In the short run, then, the supply and demand for money determine the interest rate, and the loanable funds market follows the lead of the money market until the equilibrium interest rate in the loanable funds market is the same as the equilibrium interest rate in the money market.

Notice our use of the phrase *in the short run*. Changes in aggregate demand affect aggregate output only in the short run. In the long run, aggregate output is equal to potential output. So our story about how a fall in the interest rate leads to a rise in aggregate output, which leads to a rise in savings, applies only to the short run.

In the long run, as we'll see next, the determination of the interest rate is quite different, because the roles of the two markets are reversed. In the long run, the loanable funds market determines the equilibrium interest rate, and it is the market for money that follows the lead of the loanable funds market.

‖ The Interest Rate in the Long Run

In the short run an increase in the money supply leads to a fall in the interest rate, and a decrease in the money supply leads to a rise in the interest rate. In the long run, however, changes in the money supply don't affect the interest rate.

Figure 15A-2 shows why. As in Figure 15A-1, panel (a) shows the liquidity preference model of the interest rate and panel (b) shows the supply and demand for loanable funds. We assume that in both panels the economy is initially at E_1, in long-run macroeconomic equilibrium at potential output with the money supply equal to $\overline{M}_1$. The demand curve for loanable funds is D, and the initial supply curve for loanable funds is S_1. The initial equilibrium interest rate in both markets is r_1.

FIGURE 15A-2   The Long-Run Determination of the Interest Rate

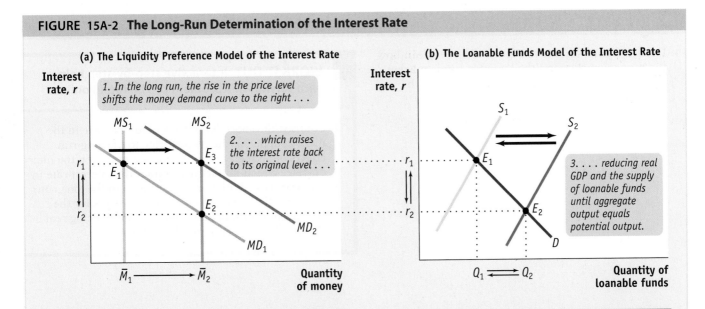

(a) The Liquidity Preference Model of the Interest Rate

1. In the long run, the rise in the price level shifts the money demand curve to the right . . .

2. . . . which raises the interest rate back to its original level . . .

Interest rate, r

MS_1 MS_2

r_1 E_1 E_3

r_2 E_2

MD_2

MD_1

$\overline{M}_1$ ⟶ $\overline{M}_2$

Quantity of money

(b) The Loanable Funds Model of the Interest Rate

Interest rate, r

S_1 S_2

r_1 E_1

3. . . . reducing real GDP and the supply of loanable funds until aggregate output equals potential output.

r_2 E_2

D

Q_1 ⇄ Q_2

Quantity of loanable funds

Panel (a) shows the liquidity preference model long-run adjustment to an increase in the money supply from $\overline{M}_1$ to $\overline{M}_2$; panel (b) shows the corresponding long-run adjustment in the loanable funds market. Both panels start from E_1, a long-run macroeconomic equilibrium at potential output and with interest rate r_1. As we discussed in Figure 15A-1, the increase in the money supply reduces the interest rate from r_1 to r_2, increases real GDP, and increases savings in the short run. This is shown in panels (a) and (b) as the movement from E_1 to E_2. In the long run, however, the increase in the money

supply raises wages and other nominal prices. This shifts the money demand curve in panel (a) from MD_1 to MD_2, leading to an increase in the interest rate from r_2 to r_1 as the economy moves from E_2 to E_3. The rise in the interest rate causes a fall in real GDP and a fall in savings, shifting the loanable funds supply curve back to S_1 from S_2 and moving the loanable funds market from E_2 back to E_1. In the long run, the equilibrium interest rate is determined by matching the supply of loanable funds to the demand for loanable funds that results when real GDP equals potential output.

Now suppose the money supply rises from $\overline{M}_1$ to $\overline{M}_2$. As in Figure 15A-1, this initially reduces the interest rate to r_2. According to the neutrality of money, in the long run the aggregate price level rises by the same proportion as the increase in the money supply. And we also know that a rise in the aggregate price level increases money demand by the same proportion. So in the long run the money demand curve shifts out to MD_2 as money demand responds to higher prices, and moves the equilibrium interest rate back to its original level, r_1.

Panel (b) of Figure 15A-2 shows what happens in the market for loanable funds. As before, an increase in the money supply leads to a short-run rise in real GDP, and this shifts the supply of loanable funds rightward from S_1 to S_2. In the long run, however, real GDP falls back to its original level as wages and other nominal prices rise. As a result, the supply of loanable funds, S, which initially shifted from S_1 to S_2, shifts back to S_1.

In the long run, then, changes in the money supply do not affect the interest rate. So what determines the interest rate in the long run, r_1, in Figure 15A-2? The answer is the supply and demand for loanable funds. More specifically, in the long run the equilibrium interest rate matches the supply and demand for loanable funds that arise at potential output.

PROBLEMS

interactive activity

1. Using a figure similar to Figure 15A-1, explain how the money market and the loanable funds market react to a reduction in the money supply in the short run.

WORK IT OUT Interactive step-by-step help with solving this problem can be found online.

2. Contrast the short-run effects of an increase in the money supply on the interest rate to the long-run effects of an increase in the money supply on the interest rate. Which market determines the interest rate in the short run? Which market does so in the long run? What are the implications of your answers for the effectiveness of monetary policy in influencing real GDP in the short run and the long run?

16 Inflation, Disinflation, and Deflation

🌐 BRINGING A SUITCASE TO THE BANK

THE AFRICAN NATION of Zimbabwe achieved a dubious distinction in 2008: it exhibited one of the highest inflation rates ever recorded, peaking at around 500 billion percent. Although the government kept introducing ever-larger denominations of the Zimbabwe dollar—for example, in May 2008 it introduced a half-billion-dollar bill—it still took a lot of currency to pay for the necessities of life: a stack of Zimbabwean cash worth $100 U.S. dollars weighed about 40 pounds. Zimbabwean currency was worth so little that some people withdrawing funds from banks brought suitcases along in order to be able to walk away with enough cash to pay for ordinary living expenses. In the end, the Zimbabwe dollar lost all value—literally. By October 2008, the currency had more or less vanished from circulation, replaced by U.S. dollars. More recently, euros, South African rands, and Chinese yuan have also circulated.

The Zimbabwe dollar was so devalued by extreme inflation in 2008 that this much currency was needed to pay for a single loaf of bread.

Zimbabwe's experience was shocking, but not unprecedented. In 1994 the inflation rate in Armenia hit 27,000%. In 1991 Nicaraguan inflation exceeded 60,000%. And Zimbabwe's experience was more or less matched by history's most famous example of extreme inflation, which took place in Germany in 1922–1923. Toward the end of the German hyperinflation, prices were rising 16% a *day*, which—through compounding—meant an increase of approximately 500 billion percent over the course of five months.

Germans became so reluctant to hold paper money, which lost value by the hour, that eggs and lumps of coal began to circulate as currency. Firms would pay their workers several times a day so that they could spend their earnings before they lost value (lending new meaning to the term *hourly wage*). Legend has it that men sitting down at a bar would order two beers at a time, out of fear that the price of a beer would rise before they could order a second round!

The United States has never experienced that kind of inflation. The worst U.S. inflation in modern times took place at the end of the 1970s. From 1978 to 1980 the U.S. inflation rate more than doubled, from 6.4% to 14.5%. Yet inflation at even that rate was profoundly troubling to the American public, and the policies the Federal Reserve pursued in order to get U.S. inflation back down to an acceptable rate led to a severe recession.

What causes inflation to rise and fall? In this chapter, we'll look at the underlying reasons for inflation. We'll see that the underlying causes of very high inflation, the type of inflation suffered by Zimbabwe, are quite different from the causes of more moderate inflation. We'll also learn why *disinflation*, a reduction in the inflation rate, is often very difficult. Finally, we'll discuss the special problems associated with a falling price level, or deflation. ●

WHAT YOU WILL LEARN

- Why can printing money lead to high rates of inflation and hyperinflation?
- How does the **Phillips curve** describe the short-run trade-off between inflation and unemployment?
- Why does the trade-off between inflation and unemployment cease in the long run?
- Why can even moderate levels of inflation be hard to end?
- Why is deflation a problem for economic policy makers?

‖ Money and Inflation

Moderate levels of inflation such as those experienced in the United States—even the double-digit inflation of the late 1970s—can have complex causes. But very high inflation is always associated with rapid increases in the money supply.

To understand why, we need to revisit the effect of changes in the money supply on the overall price level. Then we'll turn to the reasons governments sometimes increase the money supply very rapidly.

The Classical Model of Money and Prices

In the previous chapter we learned that in the short run, an increase in the money supply increases real GDP by lowering the interest rate and stimulating investment spending and consumer spending. However, in the long run, as nominal wages and other sticky prices rise, real GDP falls back to its original level. So in the long run, an increase in the money supply does not change real GDP. Instead, other things equal, it leads to an equal percent rise in the overall price level; that is, the prices of all goods and services in the economy, including nominal wages and the prices of intermediate goods, rise by the same percentage as the money supply. And when the overall price level rises, the aggregate price level—the prices of all final goods and services—rises as well.

As a result, a change in the *nominal* money supply, M, leads in the long run to a change in the aggregate price level that leaves the *real* quantity of money, M/P, at its original level, with no long-run effect on aggregate demand or real GDP. For example, when Turkey dropped six zeros from its currency, the Turkish lira, in January 2005, Turkish real GDP did not change. The only thing that changed was the number of zeros in prices: instead of something costing 2,000,000 lira, it cost 2 lira.

This is, to repeat, what happens in the long run. When analyzing large changes in the aggregate price level, however, macroeconomists often find it useful to ignore the distinction between the short run and the long run. Instead, they work with a simplified model in which the effect of a change in the money supply on the aggregate price level takes place instantaneously rather than over a long period of time. You might be concerned about this assumption, given that in previous chapters we've emphasized the difference between the short run and the long run. However, for reasons we'll explain shortly, this is a reasonable assumption to make in the case of high inflation.

A simplified model in which the real quantity of money, M/P, is always at its long-run equilibrium level is known as the **classical model of the price level** because it was commonly used by "classical" economists who wrote before the work of John Maynard Keynes. To understand the classical model and why it is useful in the context of high inflation, let's revisit the *AD–AS* model and what it says about the effects of an increase in the money supply. (Unless otherwise noted, we will always be referring to changes in the *nominal* supply of money.)

Figure 16-1 reviews the effects of an increase in the money supply according to the *AD–AS* model. The economy starts at E_1, a point of short-run and long-run macroeconomic equilibrium. It lies at the intersection of the aggregate demand curve, AD_1, and the short-run aggregate supply curve, $SRAS_1$. It also lies on the long-run aggregate supply curve, *LRAS*. At E_1, the equilibrium aggregate price level is P_1.

Now suppose there is an increase in the money supply. This is an expansionary monetary policy, which shifts the aggregate demand curve to the right, to AD_2, and moves the economy to a new short-run macroeconomic equilibrium at E_2. Over time, however, nominal wages adjust upward in response to the rise in the aggregate price level, and the *SRAS* curve shifts to the left, to $SRAS_2$. The new long-run macroeconomic equilibrium is at E_3, and real GDP returns to its initial level. As we learned in Chapter 15, the long-run increase in the aggregate price level from P_1 to P_3 is proportional to the increase in the money supply. As

According to the **classical model of the price level,** the real quantity of money is always at its long-run equilibrium level.

FIGURE 16-1 The Classical Model of the Price Level

Starting at E_1, an increase in the money supply shifts the aggregate demand curve rightward, as shown by the movement from AD_1 to AD_2. There is a new short-run macroeconomic equilibrium at E_2 and a higher price level at P_2. In the long run, nominal wages adjust upward and push the SRAS curve leftward to $SRAS_2$. The total percent increase in the price level from P_1 to P_3 is equal to the percent increase in the money supply. In the *classical model of the price level*, we ignore the transition period and think of the price level as rising to P_3 immediately. This is a good approximation under conditions of high inflation.

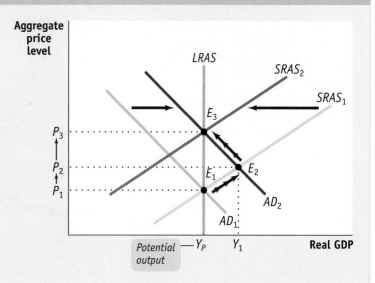

a result, in the long run changes in the money supply have no effect on the real quantity of money, *M/P*, or on real GDP. In the long run, money—as we learned—is *neutral.*

The classical model of the price level ignores the short-run movement from E_1 to E_2, assuming that the economy moves directly from one long-run equilibrium to another long-run equilibrium. In other words, it assumes that the economy moves directly from E_1 to E_3 and that real GDP never changes in response to a change in the money supply. In effect, in the classical model the effects of money supply changes are analyzed as if the short-run as well as the long-run aggregate supply curves were vertical.

This is a poor assumption during periods of low inflation, because it may take a while for workers and firms to react to a monetary expansion by raising wages and prices. As a result, under low inflation there is an upward-sloping SRAS curve, and changes in the money supply can indeed change real GDP in the short run.

In the face of high inflation, however, economists have observed that the short-run stickiness of nominal wages and prices tends to vanish. Workers and businesses, sensitized to inflation, are quick to raise their wages and prices in response to changes in the money supply. This implies that under high inflation, there is a quicker adjustment of wages and prices of intermediate goods than occurs in the case of low inflation. So the short-run aggregate supply curve shifts leftward more quickly, and there is a more rapid return to long-run equilibrium under high inflation. As a result, the classical model of the price level is much more likely to be a good approximation of reality for economies experiencing persistently high inflation.

The consequence of this rapid adjustment of all prices in the economy is that in countries with persistently high inflation, changes in the money supply are quickly translated into changes in the inflation rate. Let's look at Zimbabwe. Figure 16-2 shows the annual rate of growth in the money supply and the annual rate of change of consumer prices from 2003 through April 2008. As you can see, the surge in the growth rate of the money supply coincided closely with a roughly equal surge in the inflation rate. Note that to fit these very large percentage increases—several thousands of percent—onto the figure, we have drawn the vertical axis using a logarithmic scale that allows us to draw equal-size percent changes as the same size.

What leads a country to increase its money supply so much that the result is an inflation rate in the millions, or even billions, of percent?

FIGURE 16-2   Money Supply Growth and Inflation in Zimbabwe

This figure, drawn on a logarithmic scale, shows the annual rates of change of the money supply and the price level in Zimbabwe from 2003 through April 2008. The surges in the money supply were quickly reflected in a roughly equal surge in the price level.

Data from: International Monetary Fund.

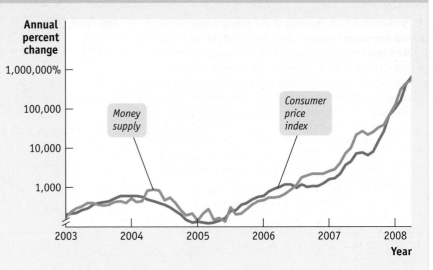

The Inflation Tax

Modern economies use fiat money—pieces of paper that have no intrinsic value but are accepted as a medium of exchange. In the United States and most other wealthy countries, the decision about how many pieces of paper to issue is placed in the hands of a central bank that is somewhat independent of the political process. However, this independence can always be taken away if politicians decide to seize control of monetary policy.

So what is to prevent a government from paying for some of its expenses not by raising taxes or borrowing but simply by printing money? Nothing. In fact, governments, including the U.S. government, do it all the time. How can the U.S. government do this, given that the Federal Reserve issues money, not the U.S. Treasury? The answer is that the Treasury and the Federal Reserve work in concert. The Treasury issues debt to finance the government's purchases of goods and services, and the Fed *monetizes* the debt by creating money and buying the debt back from the public through open-market purchases of Treasury bills. In effect, the U.S. government can and does raise revenue by printing money.

For example, in August 2008, the U.S. monetary base—bank reserves plus currency in circulation—was $18 billion larger than it had been a year earlier. This occurred because, over the course of that year, the Federal Reserve had issued $20 billion in money or its electronic equivalent and put it into circulation through open-market operations. To put it another way, the Fed created money out of thin air and used it to buy valuable government securities from the private sector. It's true that the U.S. government pays interest on debt owned by the Federal Reserve—but the Fed, by law, hands the interest payments it receives on government debt back to the Treasury, keeping only enough to fund its own operations. In effect, then, the Federal Reserve's actions enabled the government to pay off $18 billion in outstanding government debt by printing money.

An alternative way to look at this is to say that the right to print money is itself a source of revenue. Economists refer to the revenue generated by the government's right to print money as *seigniorage,* an archaic term that goes back to the Middle Ages. It refers to the right to stamp gold and silver into coins, and charge a fee for doing so, that medieval lords—*seigniors,* in Medieval France—reserved for themselves.

The **inflation tax** is the reduction in the value of money held by the public as a result of inflation.

Seigniorage normally accounts for only a tiny fraction (less than 1%) of the U.S. government's budget. Furthermore, concerns about seigniorage don't have any influence on the Federal Reserve's decisions about how much money to print; the Fed is worried about inflation and unemployment, not revenue. But this hasn't always been true, even in America: both North and South relied on seigniorage to help cover budget deficits during the Civil War. And there have been many occasions in history when governments turned to their printing presses as a crucial source of revenue.

According to the usual scenario, a government finds itself running a large budget deficit—and lacks either the competence or the political will to eliminate this deficit by raising taxes or cutting spending. Furthermore, the government can't borrow to cover the gap because potential lenders won't extend loans given the fear that the government's weakness will continue and leave it unable to repay its debts.

In such a situation, governments end up printing money to cover the budget deficit. But by printing money to pay its bills, a government increases the quantity of money in circulation. And as we've just seen, increases in the money supply sooner or later translate into equally large increases in the aggregate price level. So printing money to cover a budget deficit leads to inflation.

Who ends up paying for the goods and services the government purchases with newly printed money? The people who currently hold money pay. They pay because inflation erodes the purchasing power of their money holdings. In other words, a government imposes an **inflation tax,** the reduction in the value of the money held by the public, by printing money to cover its budget deficit and creating inflation.

It's helpful to think about what this tax represents. If the inflation rate is 5%, then a year from now $1 will buy goods and services worth only $0.95 today. So a 5% inflation rate in effect imposes a tax rate of 5% on the value of all money held by the public.

But why would any government push the inflation tax to rates of hundreds or thousands of percent? We turn next to the logic of hyperinflation.

The Logic of Hyperinflation

Inflation imposes a tax on individuals who hold money. And, like most taxes, it will lead people to change their behavior. In particular, when inflation is high, people will try to avoid holding money and will instead substitute real goods as well as interest-bearing assets for money. In the opening story, we described how, during the German hyperinflation, people began using eggs or lumps of coal as a medium of exchange. They did this because lumps of coal maintained their real value over time, but money didn't. Indeed, during the peak of German hyperinflation, people often burned paper money, which was less valuable than wood.

Moreover, people don't just reduce their nominal money holdings—they reduce their *real* money holdings, cutting the amount of money they hold so much that it actually has less purchasing power than the amount of money they would hold if inflation were low. They do this by using the money to buy goods that last over time or assets that hold

In the 1920s, hyperinflation made German currency worth so little that children made kites from banknotes.

their value, like gold. Why? Because the more real money holdings they have, the greater the real amount of resources the government captures from them through the inflation tax.

We are now ready to understand how countries can get themselves into situations of extreme inflation. High inflation arises when the government must print a large quantity of money, imposing a large inflation tax, to cover a large budget deficit.

Now, the seigniorage collected by the government over a short period—say, one month—is equal to the change in the money supply over that period. Let's use M to represent the money supply and use the symbol Δ to mean "monthly change in." Then:

(16-1) Seigniorage = ΔM

The money value of seigniorage, however, isn't very informative by itself. After all, the whole point of inflation is that a given amount of money buys less and less over time. So it's more useful to look at *real* seigniorage, the revenue created by printing money divided by the price level, P:

(16-2) Real seigniorage = $\Delta M/P$

Equation 16-2 can be rewritten by dividing and multiplying by the current level of the money supply, M, giving us:

(16-3) Real seigniorage = $(\Delta M/M) \times (M/P)$

or

Real seigniorage = Rate of growth of the money supply × Real money supply

But as we've just explained, in the face of high inflation the public reduces the real amount of money it holds, so the far right-hand term in Equation 16-3, M/P, gets smaller. Suppose that the government needs to print enough money to pay for a given quantity of goods and services—that is, it needs to collect a given *real* amount of seigniorage. Then, as the real money supply, M/P, falls as people hold smaller amounts of real money, the government has to respond by accelerating the rate of growth of the money supply, $\Delta M/M$. This will lead to an even higher rate of inflation. And people will respond to this new higher rate of inflation by reducing their real money holdings, M/P, yet again.

As the process becomes self-reinforcing, it can easily spiral out of control. Although the amount of real seigniorage that the government must ultimately collect to pay off its deficit does not change, the inflation rate the government needs to impose to collect that amount rises. So the government is forced to increase the money supply more rapidly, leading to an even higher rate of inflation, and so on.

Here's an analogy: imagine a city government that tries to raise a lot of money with a special fee on parking. The fee will raise the cost of parking in the city, and this will cause people to turn to easily available substitutes, such as walking or taking the bus. As the number of parked cars declines, the government finds that its tax revenue declines, and it must impose a higher fee to raise the same amount of revenue as before. You can imagine the ensuing vicious circle: the government imposes fees on parking, which leads to less parking, which causes the government to raise the fee on parking, which leads to even less parking, and so on.

Substitute the real money supply for parking and the inflation rate for the increase in the fee on parking, and you have the story of hyperinflation. A race develops between the government printing presses and the public: the presses churn out money at a faster and faster rate to try to compensate for the fact that the public is reducing its real money holdings. At some point the inflation rate explodes into hyperinflation, and people are unwilling to hold any money at all (and resort to trading in eggs and lumps of coal). The government is then forced to abandon its use of the inflation tax and shut down the printing presses.

ECONOMICS >> *in Action*

Zimbabwe's Inflation

Zimbabwe offers a recent example of a country experiencing very high inflation. Figure 16-2 showed that surges in Zimbabwe's money supply growth were matched by almost simultaneous surges in its inflation rate. But looking at rates of change doesn't give a true feel for just how much prices went up.

Figure 16-3 shows Zimbabwe's consumer price index from January 2000 to July 2008, with the January 2000 level set equal to 100. As in Figure 16-2, we also use a logarithmic scale. In a little over eight years, consumer prices rose by approximately 80 trillion percent.

Why did Zimbabwe's government pursue policies that led to runaway inflation? The reason boils down to political instability, which in turn had its roots in Zimbabwe's history. Until the 1970s, Zimbabwe had been ruled by its small white minority; even after the shift to majority rule, many of the country's farms remained in the hands of whites. Eventually Robert Mugabe, Zimbabwe's president, tried to solidify his position by seizing these farms and turning them over to his political supporters.

But because this seizure disrupted production, the result was to undermine the country's economy and its tax base. It became impossible for the government to balance its budget either by raising taxes or by cutting spending. At the same time, the regime's instability left Zimbabwe unable to borrow money in world markets. Like many others before it, Zimbabwe's government turned to the printing press to cover the gap—leading to massive inflation.

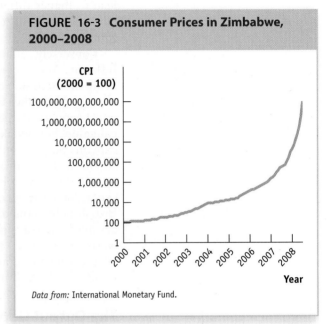

FIGURE 16-3 Consumer Prices in Zimbabwe, 2000–2008

Data from: International Monetary Fund.

>> Check Your Understanding 16-1

Solutions appear at back of book.

1. Suppose there is a large increase in the money supply in an economy that previously had low inflation. As a consequence, aggregate output expands in the short run. What does this say about situations in which the classical model of the price level applies?

2. Suppose that all wages and prices in an economy are indexed to inflation—that is, wages and prices are automatically adjusted to incorporate the latest inflation figures. Can there still be an inflation tax?

>> Quick Review

• The **classical model of the price level** does not distinguish between the short and the long run. It explains how increases in the money supply feed directly into inflation. It is a good description of reality only for countries with persistently high inflation or hyperinflation.

• Governments sometimes print money to cover a budget deficit. The resulting loss in the value of money is called the **inflation tax.**

• A high inflation rate causes people to reduce their real money holdings, leading to the printing of more money and higher inflation in order to collect the inflation tax. This can cause a self-reinforcing spiral into hyperinflation.

| Moderate Inflation and Disinflation

The governments of wealthy, politically stable countries, like the United States and Britain, don't find themselves forced to print money to pay their bills. Yet over the past 40 years, both countries, along with a number of other nations, have experienced uncomfortable episodes of inflation. In the United States, the inflation rate peaked at 14% at the beginning of the 1980s. In Britain, the inflation rate reached 26% in 1975. Why did policy makers allow this to happen?

The answer, in brief, is that in the short run, policies that produce a booming economy also tend to lead to higher inflation, and policies that reduce inflation tend to depress the economy. This creates both temptations and dilemmas for governments.

First, imagine yourself as a politician facing an election in a year or two, and suppose that inflation is fairly low at the moment. You might well be tempted to pursue expansionary policies that will push the unemployment rate down as a way to please voters, even if your economic advisers warn that this will eventually lead to higher inflation. You might also be tempted to find different economic advisers who will tell you not to worry: in politics, as in ordinary life, wishful thinking often prevails over realistic analysis.

Conversely, imagine yourself as a politician in an economy suffering from inflation. Your economic advisers will probably tell you that the only way to bring inflation down is to push the economy into a recession, which will lead to temporarily higher unemployment. Are you willing to pay that price? Maybe not.

This political dilemma—inflationary policies often produce short-term political gains, but policies to bring inflation down carry short-term political costs—explains how countries with no need to impose an inflation tax can end up with serious inflation problems. For example, that 26% rate of inflation in Britain was largely the result of the British government's decision in 1971 to pursue highly expansionary monetary and fiscal policies in order to gain a political advantage. British politicians disregarded warnings that these policies would be inflationary and were extremely reluctant to reverse course when it became clear that the warnings had been accurate.

But why do expansionary policies lead to inflation? To answer that question, we need to look first at the relationship between output and unemployment.

The Output Gap and the Unemployment Rate

In Chapter 12 we introduced the concept of *potential output*, the level of real GDP that the economy would produce once all prices had fully adjusted. Potential output typically grows steadily over time, reflecting long-run growth. However, as we learned from the aggregate demand–aggregate supply model, actual aggregate output fluctuates around potential output in the short run: a recessionary gap arises when actual aggregate output falls short of potential output; an inflationary gap arises when actual aggregate output exceeds potential output.

Recall that the percentage difference between the actual level of real GDP and potential output is called the *output gap*. A positive or negative output gap occurs when an economy is producing more than or less than what would be "expected" because all prices, including wages in the labor market, have not yet adjusted. And wages, as we've learned, are the prices in the labor market.

Meanwhile, we learned in Chapter 8 that the unemployment rate is composed of cyclical unemployment and natural unemployment, the portion of the unemployment rate unaffected by the business cycle. So there is a relationship between the unemployment rate and the output gap. This relationship is defined by two rules:

1. When actual aggregate output is equal to potential output, the actual unemployment rate is equal to the natural rate of unemployment.
2. When the output gap is positive (an inflationary gap), the unemployment rate is *below* the natural rate. When the output gap is negative (a recessionary gap), the unemployment rate is *above* the natural rate.

In other words, fluctuations of aggregate output around the long-run trend of potential output correspond to fluctuations of the unemployment rate around the natural rate.

This makes sense. When the economy is producing less than potential output—when the output gap is negative—it is not making full use of its productive resources. Among the resources that are not fully utilized is labor, the economy's most important resource. So we would expect a negative output gap to be associated with unusually high unemployment. Conversely, when the economy is producing more than potential output, it is temporarily using resources at higher-than-normal rates. With this positive output gap, we would expect to see lower-than-normal unemployment.

Figure 16-4 confirms this rule. Panel (a) shows the actual and natural rates of unemployment, as estimated by the Congressional Budget Office (CBO). Panel (b) shows two series. One is cyclical unemployment: the difference between the actual unemployment rate and the CBO estimate of the natural rate of unemployment, measured on the left. The other is the CBO estimate of the output gap, measured on the right. To make the relationship clearer, the output gap series is inverted—shown upside down—so that the line goes down if actual output rises above potential output and up if actual output falls below potential output.

As you can see, the two series move together quite closely, showing the strong relationship between the output gap and cyclical unemployment. Years of high cyclical unemployment, like 1982, 1992, or 2009, were also years of a strongly negative output gap. Years of low cyclical unemployment, like the late 1960s or 2000, were also years of a strongly positive output gap.

FIGURE 16-4 Cyclical Unemployment and the Output Gap

Panel (a) shows the actual U.S. unemployment rate from 1949 through 2017, together with the Congressional Budget Office estimate of the natural rate of unemployment. The actual rate fluctuates around the natural rate, often for extended periods. Panel (b) shows cyclical unemployment—the difference between the actual unemployment and the natural rate of unemployment—and the output gap, also estimated by the CBO. The unemployment rate is measured on the left vertical axis, and the output gap is measured with an inverted scale on the right vertical axis. With an inverted scale, it moves in the same direction as the unemployment rate: when the output gap is positive, the actual unemployment rate is below its natural rate. And when the output gap is negative, the actual unemployment rate is above its natural rate. The two series track one another closely, showing the strong relationship between the output gap and cyclical unemployment.

Data from: Federal Reserve Bank of St. Louis.

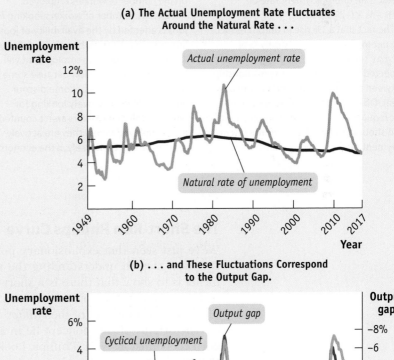

(a) The Actual Unemployment Rate Fluctuates Around the Natural Rate . . .

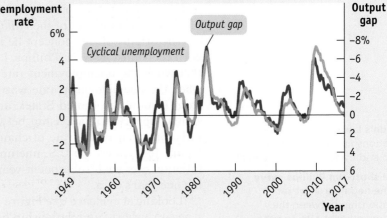

(b) . . . and These Fluctuations Correspond to the Output Gap.

FOR INQUIRING MINDS   Okun's Law

Although cyclical unemployment and the output gap move together, cyclical unemployment seems to move *less* than the output gap. For example, the output gap reached −8% in 1982, but the cyclical unemployment rate reached only 4%. This observation is the basis of an important relationship originally discovered by Arthur Okun, Lyndon Johnson's chief economic adviser.

Modern estimates of **Okun's law**—the negative relationship between the output gap and the cyclical unemployment rate—typically find that a rise in the output gap of 1 percentage point reduces the unemployment rate by about ½ of a percentage point.

For example, suppose that the natural rate of unemployment is 5.2% and that the economy is currently producing at only 98% of potential output. In that case, the output gap is −2%, and Okun's law predicts an unemployment rate of $5.2 - \frac{1}{2} \times (-2\%) = 6.2\%$.

The fact that a 1% rise in output reduces the unemployment rate by only ½ of 1% may seem puzzling: you might have expected to see a one-to-one relationship between the output gap and unemployment. Doesn't a 1% rise in aggregate output require a 1% increase in employment? And shouldn't that take 1% off the unemployment rate?

The answer is no: there are several well-understood reasons why the relationship isn't one-to-one. For one thing, companies often meet changes in demand in part by changing the number of hours their existing employees work. For example, a company that experiences a sudden increase in demand for its products may cope by asking (or requiring) its workers to put in longer hours, rather than by hiring more workers. Conversely, a company that sees sales drop will often reduce workers' hours rather than lay off employees. This behavior dampens the effect of output fluctuations on the number of workers employed.

Also, the number of workers looking for jobs is affected by the availability of jobs. Suppose that the number of jobs falls by 1 million. Measured unemployment will rise by less than 1 million because some unemployed workers become discouraged and give up actively looking for work. (Recall that workers aren't counted as unemployed unless they are actively seeking work.) Conversely, if the economy

adds 1 million jobs, some people who haven't been actively looking for work will begin doing so. As a result, measured unemployment will fall by less than 1 million.

Finally, the rate of growth of labor productivity generally accelerates during booms and slows down or even turns negative during busts. The reasons for this phenomenon are the subject of some dispute among economists. The consequence, however, is that the effects of booms and busts on the unemployment rate are dampened.

The Short-Run Phillips Curve

We've just seen that expansionary policies lead to a lower unemployment rate. Our next step in understanding the temptations and dilemmas facing governments is to show that there is a short-run trade-off between unemployment and inflation—lower unemployment tends to lead to higher inflation, and vice versa. The key concept is that of the *Phillips curve*.

The origins of this concept lie in a famous 1958 paper by the New Zealand–born economist A. W. H. Phillips. Looking at historical data for Britain, he found that when the unemployment rate was high, the wage rate tended to fall, and when the unemployment rate was low, the wage rate tended to rise. Using data from Britain, the United States, and elsewhere, other economists soon found a similar apparent relationship between the unemployment rate and the rate of inflation—that is, the rate of change in the aggregate price level. For example, Figure 16-5 shows the U.S. unemployment rate and the rate of consumer price inflation over each subsequent year from 1955 to 1968, with each dot representing one year's data.

Looking at evidence like Figure 16-5, many economists concluded that there is a negative short-run relationship between the unemployment rate and the inflation rate, which is called the **short-run Phillips curve,** or *SRPC*. (We'll explain

Okun's law is the negative relationship between the output gap and cyclical unemployment.

The **short-run Phillips curve** is the negative short-run relationship between the unemployment rate and the inflation rate.

FIGURE 16-5 Unemployment and Inflation, 1955–1968

Each dot shows the average U.S. unemployment rate for one year and the percentage increase in the consumer price index over the subsequent year. Data like this lay behind the initial concept of the Phillips curve.

Data from: Bureau of Labor Statistics.

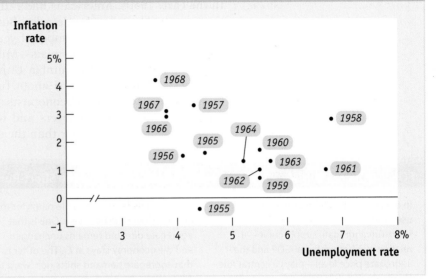

the difference between the short-run and the long-run Phillips curve soon.) Figure 16-6 shows a hypothetical short-run Phillips curve.

Early estimates of the short-run Phillips curve for the United States were very simple: they showed a negative relationship between the unemployment rate and the inflation rate, without taking account of any other variables. During the 1950s and 1960s, this simple approach seemed, for a while, to be adequate. And this simple relationship is clear in the data in Figure 16-5.

Even at the time, however, some economists argued that a more accurate short-run Phillips curve would include other factors. In Chapter 12 we discussed the effect of *supply shocks*, such as sudden changes in the price of oil, which shift the short-run aggregate supply curve. Such shocks also shift the short-run Phillips curve: surging oil prices were an important factor in the inflation of the 1970s and also played an important role in the acceleration of inflation in 2007–2008. In general, a negative supply shock shifts *SRPC* up as the inflation rate increases for every level of the unemployment rate, and a positive supply shock shifts it down as the inflation rate falls for every level of the unemployment rate. Both outcomes are shown in Figure 16-8.

FIGURE 16-6 The Short-Run Phillips Curve

The short-run Phillips curve, *SRPC*, slopes downward because the relationship between the unemployment rate and the inflation rate is negative.

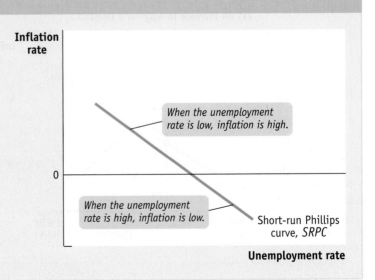

But supply shocks are not the only factors that can change the inflation rate. In the early 1960s, Americans had little experience with inflation because inflation rates had been low for decades. But by the late 1960s, after inflation had been steadily increasing for a number of years, Americans had come to expect future inflation. In 1968, two economists—Milton Friedman of the University of Chicago and Edmund Phelps of Columbia University—independently set forth a crucial hypothesis: that expectations about future inflation directly affect the present inflation rate. Today most economists accept that the *expected inflation rate*—the rate of inflation that employers and workers expect in the near future—is the most important factor, other than the unemployment rate, affecting inflation.

FOR INQUIRING MINDS   The Aggregate Supply Curve and the Short-Run Phillips Curve

In earlier chapters we made extensive use of the *AD–AS* model, in which the short-run aggregate supply curve—a relationship between real GDP and the aggregate price level—plays a central role. Now we've introduced the concept of the short-run Phillips curve, a relationship between the unemployment rate and the rate of inflation. How do these two concepts fit together?

We can get a partial answer to this question by looking at panel (a) of Figure 16-7, which shows how changes in the aggregate price level and the output gap depend on changes in aggregate demand. Assume that in year 1 the aggregate demand curve is AD_1, the long-run aggregate supply curve is *LRAS,* and the short-run aggregate supply curve is *SRAS.* The initial macroeconomic equilibrium is at E_1, where the price level is 100 and real GDP is $10 trillion. Notice that at E_1 real GDP is equal to potential output, so the output gap is zero.

Now consider two possible paths for the economy over the next year. One is that aggregate demand remains unchanged and the economy stays at E_1. The other is that aggregate demand shifts rightward to AD_2 and the economy moves to E_2.

At E_2, real GDP is $10.4 trillion, $0.4 trillion more than potential output— a 4% output gap. Meanwhile, at E_2 the aggregate price level is 102—a 2% increase. So panel (a) tells us that in this example, a zero output gap is associated with zero inflation and a 4% output gap is associated with 2% inflation.

Panel (b) shows what this implies for the relationship between unemployment and inflation. Assume that the natural rate of unemployment is 6% and that a rise of 1 percentage point in the output gap causes a fall of ½ percentage point in the unemployment rate per Okun's law, described in the previous For Inquiring Minds. In that case, the two cases shown in panel (a)—aggregate demand either unchanged

or rising—correspond to the two points in panel (b). At E_1, the unemployment rate is 6% and the inflation rate is 0%. At E_2, the unemployment rate is 4%—because an output gap of 4% reduces the unemployment rate by 4% × 0.5 = 2% below its natural rate of 6%—and the inflation rate is 2%. So there is a negative relationship between unemployment and inflation.

So does the short-run aggregate supply curve say exactly the same thing as the short-run Phillips curve? Not quite. The short-run aggregate supply curve seems to imply a relationship between the *change* in the unemployment rate and the inflation rate, but the short-run Phillips curve shows a relationship between the *level* of the unemployment rate and the inflation rate. Reconciling these views completely would go beyond the scope of this book. The important point is that the short-run Phillips curve is a concept that is closely related, though not identical, to the short-run aggregate supply curve.

FIGURE 16-7   The *AD–AS* Model and the Short-Run Phillips Curve

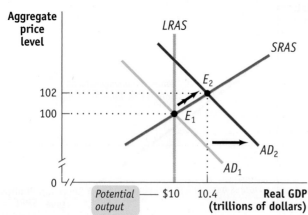
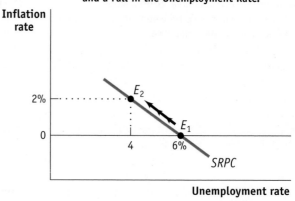

(a) An Increase in Aggregate Demand . . .

(b) . . . Leads to Both Inflation and a Fall in the Unemployment Rate.

FIGURE 16-8 The Short-Run Phillips Curve and Supply Shocks

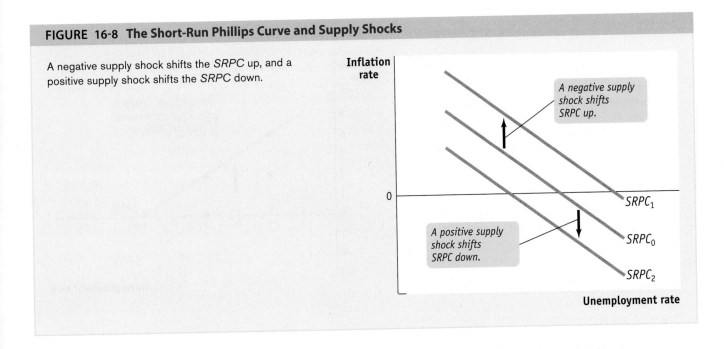

A negative supply shock shifts the *SRPC* up, and a positive supply shock shifts the *SRPC* down.

A negative supply shock shifts *SRPC* up.

A positive supply shock shifts *SRPC* down.

Inflation Expectations and the Short-Run Phillips Curve

The **expected rate of inflation** is the rate of inflation that employers and workers expect in the near future. One of the crucial discoveries of modern macroeconomics is that changes in the expected rate of inflation affect the short-run trade-off between unemployment and inflation and shift the short-run Phillips curve.

Why do changes in expected inflation affect the short-run Phillips curve? Put yourself in the position of a worker and employer about to sign a contract setting the worker's wages over the next year. For a number of reasons, the wage rate they agree to will be higher if everyone expects high inflation (including rising wages) than if everyone expects prices to be stable. The worker will want a wage rate that takes into account future declines in the purchasing power of earnings. He or she will also want a wage rate that won't fall behind the wages of other workers. And the employer will be more willing to agree to a wage increase now if hiring workers later will be even more expensive. Also, rising prices will make paying a higher wage rate more affordable for the employer because the employer's output will sell for more.

For these reasons, an increase in expected inflation shifts the short-run Phillips curve upward: the actual rate of inflation at any given unemployment rate is higher when the expected inflation rate is higher. In fact, macroeconomists believe that the relationship between changes in expected inflation and changes in actual inflation is one-to-one. That is, when the expected inflation rate increases, the actual inflation rate at any given unemployment rate will increase by the same amount. When the expected inflation rate falls, the actual inflation rate at any given level of unemployment will fall by the same amount.

Figure 16-9 shows how the expected rate of inflation affects the short-run Phillips curve. First, suppose that the expected rate of inflation is 0%. $SRPC_0$ is the short-run Phillips curve when the public expects 0% inflation. According to $SRPC_0$, the actual inflation rate will be 0% if the unemployment rate is 6%; it will be 2% if the unemployment rate is 4%.

Alternatively, suppose the expected rate of inflation is 2%. In that case, employers and workers will build this expectation into wages and prices: at any given unemployment rate, the actual inflation rate will be 2 percentage points higher than it would be if people expected 0% inflation. $SRPC_2$, which shows the Phillips curve when the expected inflation rate is 2%, is $SRPC_0$ shifted upward by 2 percentage points at every level of unemployment. According to $SRPC_2$, the

The **expected rate of inflation** is the inflation rate that businesses and workers are expecting in the near future.

FIGURE 16-9 Expected Inflation and the Short-Run Phillips Curve

An increase in expected inflation shifts the short-run Phillips curve up. $SRPC_0$ is the initial short-run Phillips curve with an expected inflation rate of 0%; $SRPC_2$ is the short-run Phillips curve with an expected inflation rate of 2%. Each additional percentage point of expected inflation raises the actual inflation rate at any given unemployment rate by 1 percentage point.

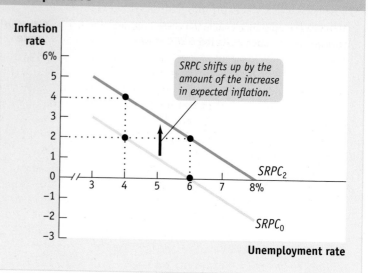

actual inflation rate will be 2% if the unemployment rate is 6%; it will be 4% if the unemployment rate is 4%.

What determines the expected rate of inflation? In general, people base their expectations about inflation on experience. If the inflation rate has hovered around 0% in the last few years, people will expect it to be around 0% in the near future. But if the inflation rate has averaged around 5% lately, people will expect inflation to be around 5% in the near future.

Since expected inflation is an important part of the modern discussion about the short-run Phillips curve, you might wonder why it was not in the original formulation of the Phillips curve. The answer lies in history. Think back to what we said about the early 1960s: at that time, people were accustomed to low inflation rates and reasonably expected that future inflation rates would also be low. It was only after 1965 that persistent inflation became a fact of life. So only then did economists begin to argue that expected inflation should play an important role in price setting.

Sure enough, the seemingly clear relationship between inflation and unemployment fell apart after 1969. Figure 16-10 plots the track of U.S. unemployment

FIGURE 16-10 Unemployment and Inflation, 1961–1990

In the 1970s, the short-run Phillips curve relationship that seemed to hold during the 1950s and 1960s broke down as the U.S. economy experienced a combination of high unemployment and high inflation. Economists believe this was the result of both negative supply shocks and the cumulative effect of several years of higher than expected inflation. Inflation came down during the 1980s, and the 1990s were a time of both low unemployment and low inflation.
Data from: Bureau of Labor Statistics.

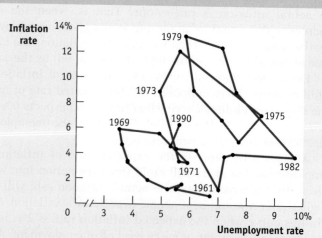

and inflation rates from 1961 to 1990. As you can see, the track looks more like a tangled piece of yarn than like a smooth curve.

Through much of the 1970s and early 1980s, the economy suffered from a combination of above-average unemployment rates coupled with inflation rates unprecedented in modern American history. This condition came to be known as *stagflation*—for stagnation combined with high inflation. In the late 1990s, by contrast, the economy was experiencing a blissful combination of low unemployment and low inflation. What explains these developments?

Part of the answer can be attributed to a series of negative supply shocks that the U.S. economy suffered during the 1970s. The price of oil, in particular, soared as wars and revolutions in the Middle East led to a reduction in oil supplies and as oil-exporting countries deliberately curbed production to drive up prices. Compounding the oil price shocks, there was also a slowdown in labor productivity growth. Both of these factors shifted the short-run Phillips curve upward. During the 1990s, by contrast, supply shocks were positive. Prices of oil and other raw materials were generally falling, and productivity growth accelerated. As a result, the short-run Phillips curve shifted downward.

Equally important, however, was the role of expected inflation. As mentioned earlier in the chapter, inflation accelerated during the 1960s. During the 1970s, the public came to expect high inflation, and this also shifted the short-run Phillips curve up. It took a sustained and costly effort during the 1980s to get inflation back down. The result, however, was that expected inflation was very low by the late 1990s, allowing actual inflation to be low even with low rates of unemployment.

ECONOMICS >> *in Action*
The Phillips Curve in the Great Recession

We've returned many times in the course of this book to the great global economic crisis that struck in 2008. This crisis caused a drastic rise in unemployment in many countries, especially in some (but not all) European nations, and unemployment remained high even years later. According to the logic of the Phillips curve, this surge in unemployment should have led to falling inflation, with the biggest declines in the worst-hit countries. And that is exactly what happened.

Figure 16-11 shows how unemployment rates and inflation rates in a number of European economies changed between 2007, the eve of the Great Recession, and 2013. Unemployment rose in every country except Germany, soaring in Ireland and the troubled economies of southern Europe. Inflation fell in 9 out of the 11 countries, and in the overall euro area. In Portugal, Ireland, Spain, and Greece, inflation fell by more than the euro area average. The relationship between unemployment and inflation isn't exact— relationships in economics rarely are. But the data are consistent with the notion of a short-run trade-off between unemployment and inflation. Incidentally, researchers at the Federal Reserve have found a similar relationship between unemployment and inflation among major U.S. cities, some of which were hit much harder by the housing bust than others.

FIGURE 16-11 Rising Unemployment and Falling Inflation in Europe, 2007–2013

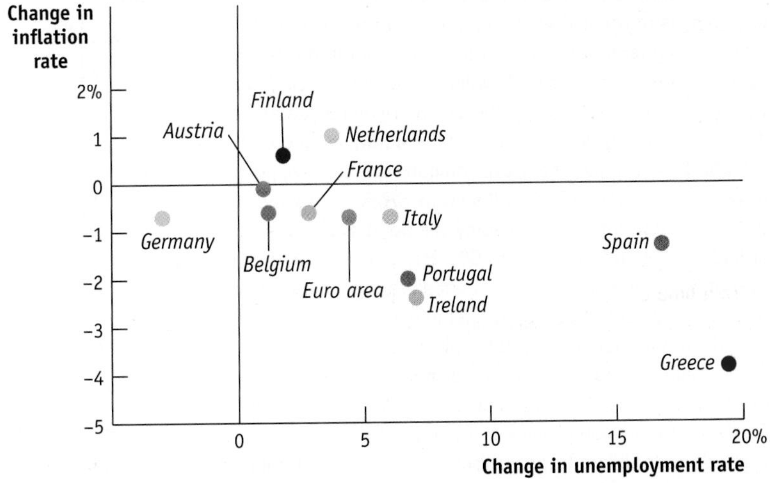

Change in inflation rate

- Germany
- Austria
- Finland
- Netherlands
- France
- Belgium
- Italy
- Euro area
- Portugal
- Ireland
- Spain
- Greece

Change in unemployment rate

Data from: IMF World Economic Outlook.

>> Check Your Understanding 16-2

Solutions appear at back of book.

1. Explain how the short-run Phillips curve illustrates the negative relationship between cyclical unemployment and the actual inflation rate for a given level of the expected inflation rate.

2. Which way does the short-run Phillips curve move in response to a fall in commodities prices? To a surge in commodities prices? Explain.

Inflation and Unemployment in the Long Run

The short-run Phillips curve says that at any given point in time, there is a trade-off between unemployment and inflation. According to this view, policy makers have a choice: they can choose whether or not to accept the price of high inflation in order to achieve low unemployment. In fact, during the 1960s, many economists believed that this trade-off represented a real choice.

However, this view was greatly altered by the later recognition that expected inflation affects the short-run Phillips curve. In the short run, expectations often diverge from reality. In the long run, however, any consistent rate of inflation will be reflected in expectations. If inflation is consistently high, as it was in the 1970s, people will come to expect more of the same; if inflation is consistently low, as it has been in recent years, that, too, will become part of expectations.

So what does the trade-off between inflation and unemployment look like in the long run, when actual inflation is incorporated into expectations? Most macroeconomists believe that there is, in fact, no long-run trade-off. That is, it is not possible to achieve lower unemployment in the long run by accepting higher inflation. To see why, we need to introduce another concept: the *long-run Phillips curve*.

The Long-Run Phillips Curve

Figure 16-12 reproduces the two short-run Phillips curves from Figure 16-9, $SRPC_0$ and $SRPC_2$. It also adds an additional short-run Phillips curve, $SRPC_4$, representing a 4% expected rate of inflation. In a moment, we'll explain the significance of the vertical long-run Phillips curve, $LRPC$.

FIGURE 16-12 The NAIRU and the Long-Run Phillips Curve

$SRPC_0$ is the short-run Phillips curve when the expected inflation rate is 0%. At a 4% unemployment rate, the economy is at point A with an actual inflation rate of 2%. The higher inflation rate will be incorporated into expectations, and the SRPC will shift upward to $SRPC_2$. If policy makers act to keep the unemployment rate at 4%, the economy will be at B and the actual inflation rate will rise to 4%. Inflationary expectations will be revised upward again, and SRPC will shift to $SRPC_4$. At a 4% unemployment rate, the economy will be at C and the actual inflation rate will rise to 6%. Here, an unemployment rate of 6% is the NAIRU, or nonaccelerating inflation rate of unemployment. As long as unemployment is at the NAIRU, the actual inflation rate will match expectations and remain constant. An unemployment rate below 6% requires ever-accelerating inflation. The long-run Phillips curve, $LRPC$, which passes through E_0, E_2, and E_4, is vertical: no long-run trade-off between unemployment and inflation exists.

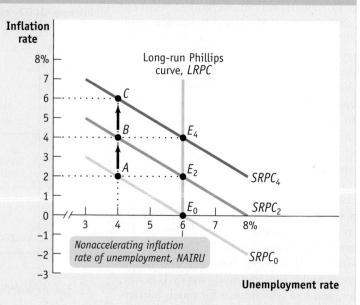

Suppose that the economy has, in the past, had a 0% inflation rate. In that case, the current short-run Phillips curve will be $SRPC_0$, reflecting a 0% expected inflation rate. If the unemployment rate is 6%, the actual inflation rate will be 0%.

Also suppose that policy makers decide to trade off lower unemployment for a higher rate of inflation. They use monetary policy, fiscal policy, or both to drive the unemployment rate down to 4%. This puts the economy at point A on $SRPC_0$, leading to an actual inflation rate of 2%.

Over time, the public will come to expect a 2% inflation rate. *This increase in inflationary expectations will shift the short-run Phillips curve upward to $SRPC_2$.* Now, when the unemployment rate is 6%, the actual inflation rate will be 2%. Given this new short-run Phillips curve, policies adopted to keep the unemployment rate at 4% will lead to a 4% actual inflation rate—point B on $SRPC_2$—rather than point A with a 2% actual inflation rate.

Eventually, the 4% actual inflation rate gets built into expectations about the future inflation rate, and the short-run Phillips curve shifts upward yet again to $SRPC_4$. To keep the unemployment rate at 4% would now require accepting a 6% actual inflation rate, point C on $SRPC_4$, and so on. In short, a persistent attempt to trade off lower unemployment for higher inflation leads to *accelerating* inflation over time.

To avoid accelerating inflation over time, the unemployment rate must be high enough that the actual rate of inflation matches the expected rate of inflation.

This is the situation at E_0 on $SRPC_0$: when the expected inflation rate is 0% and the unemployment rate is 6%, the actual inflation rate is 0%. It is also the situation at E_2 on $SRPC_2$: when the expected inflation rate is 2% and the unemployment rate is 6%, the actual inflation rate is 2%. And it is the situation at E_4 on $SRPC_4$: when the expected inflation rate is 4% and the unemployment rate is 6%, the actual inflation rate is 4%. This relationship between accelerating inflation and the unemployment rate is known as the *natural rate hypothesis*.

The unemployment rate at which inflation does not change over time—6% in Figure 16-12—is known as the **nonaccelerating inflation rate of unemployment, or NAIRU** for short. Keeping the unemployment rate below the NAIRU leads to ever-accelerating inflation and cannot be maintained. Most macroeconomists believe that there is a NAIRU and that there is no long-run trade-off between unemployment and inflation.

We can now explain the significance of the vertical line *LRPC*. It is the **long-run Phillips curve,** the relationship between unemployment and inflation in the long run, after expectations of inflation have had time to adjust to experience. It is vertical because any unemployment rate below the NAIRU leads to ever-accelerating inflation. In other words, the long-run Phillips curve shows that there are limits to expansionary policies, because an unemployment rate below the NAIRU cannot be maintained in the long run. Moreover, there is a corresponding point we have not yet emphasized: any unemployment rate above the NAIRU leads to decelerating inflation.

The Natural Rate of Unemployment, Revisited

Recall that the natural rate of unemployment is the portion of the unemployment rate unaffected by the swings of the business cycle. Now we have introduced the concept of the *NAIRU*. How do these two concepts relate to each other?

The answer is that the NAIRU is another name for the natural rate. The level of unemployment the economy needs in order to avoid accelerating inflation is equal to the natural rate of unemployment.

In fact, economists estimate the natural rate of unemployment by looking for evidence about the NAIRU from the behavior of the inflation rate and the unemployment rate over the course of the business cycle. For example, the way major European countries learned, to their dismay, that their natural rates of unemployment had risen 9% or more by around 1990, was through unpleasant

The **nonaccelerating inflation rate of unemployment,** or **NAIRU,** is the unemployment rate at which inflation does not change over time.

The **long-run Phillips curve** shows the relationship between unemployment and inflation after expectations of inflation have had time to adjust to experience.

The great disinflation of the 1980s wasn't unique to the United States. A number of other advanced countries also experienced high inflation during the 1970s, then brought inflation down during the 1980s at the cost of a severe recession. This figure shows the annual rate of inflation in Britain, Italy, and the United States from 1970 to 2016. All three nations experienced high inflation rates following the two oil price shocks of 1973 and 1979, with the U.S. inflation rate the least severe of the three. All three nations then weathered severe recessions in order to bring inflation down. Since the 1980s, inflation has remained low and stable in all wealthy nations.

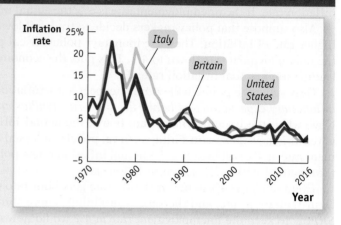

Data from: World Development Indicators, World Bank.

experience. In the late 1980s, and again in the late 1990s, European inflation began to accelerate as European unemployment rates, which had been above 9%, began to fall, approaching 8%.

In Figure 16-4 we cited Congressional Budget Office estimates of the U.S. natural rate of unemployment. The CBO has a model that predicts changes in the inflation rate based on the deviation of the actual unemployment rate from the natural rate. Given data on actual unemployment and inflation, this model can be used to deduce estimates of the natural rate—and that's where the CBO numbers come from. In 2017, the CBO estimate of the U.S. natural rate was 4.7%.

The Costs of Disinflation

Through experience, policy makers have found that bringing inflation down is a much harder task than increasing it. The reason is that once the public has come to expect continuing inflation, bringing inflation down is painful.

A persistent attempt to keep unemployment below the natural rate leads to accelerating inflation that becomes incorporated into expectations. To reduce inflationary expectations, policy makers need to run the process in reverse, adopting contractionary policies that keep the unemployment rate above the natural rate for an extended period of time. The process of bringing down inflation that has become embedded in expectations is known as *disinflation*, a concept discussed in Chapter 8.

Disinflation can be very expensive. As the following Economics in Action documents, the U.S. retreat from high inflation at the beginning of the 1980s appears to have cost the equivalent of about 18% of a year's real GDP, the equivalent of roughly $3 trillion today. The justification for paying these costs is that they lead to a permanent gain. Although the economy does not recover the short-term production losses caused by disinflation, it no longer suffers from the costs associated with persistently high inflation. In fact, the United States, Britain, and other wealthy countries that experienced inflation in the 1970s eventually decided that the benefit of bringing inflation down was worth the required suffering—the large reduction in real GDP in the short term.

Some economists argue that the costs of disinflation can be reduced if policy makers explicitly state their determination to reduce inflation. A clearly announced, credible policy of disinflation, they contend, can reduce expectations of future inflation and so shift the short-run Phillips curve downward. Some economists believe that the clear determination of the Federal Reserve to combat the inflation of the 1970s was credible enough that the costs of disinflation, huge though they were, were lower than they might otherwise have been.

ECONOMICS >> *in Action*
The Great Disinflation of the 1980s

As we've mentioned, the United States ended the 1970s with a high rate of inflation, at least by its own peacetime historical standards—14% in 1980. Part of this inflation was the result of one-time events, especially a world oil crisis. But expectations of future inflation at 10% or more per year appeared to be firmly embedded in the economy.

By the mid-1980s, however, inflation was running at about 4% per year. Panel (a) of Figure 16-13 shows the annual rate of change in the "core" consumer price index (CPI)—also called the *core inflation rate*. This index, which excludes volatile energy and food prices, is widely regarded as a better indicator of underlying inflation trends than the overall CPI. By this measure, inflation fell from about 12% at the end of the 1970s to about 4% by the mid-1980s.

How was this disinflation achieved? At great cost. Beginning in late 1979, the Federal Reserve imposed strongly contractionary monetary policies, which pushed the economy into a severe recession—at that point the worst since the Great Depression, although it would later be surpassed by the Great Recession of 2007–2009. Panel (b) shows the Congressional Budget Office estimate of the U.S. output gap from 1979 to 1989: by 1982, actual output was 7% below potential output, corresponding to an unemployment rate of more than 9%. Aggregate output didn't get back to potential output until 1987.

Our analysis of the Phillips curve tells us that a temporary rise in unemployment, like that of the 1980s, is needed to break the cycle of inflationary expectations. Once expectations of inflation are reduced, the economy can return to the natural rate of unemployment at a lower inflation rate. And that's just what happened.

But the cost was huge. If you add up the output gap over 1980–1987, you find that the economy sacrificed approximately 18% of an average year's output over the period. If we had to do the same thing today, that would mean giving up roughly $3 trillion worth of goods and services.

FIGURE 16-13 The Great Disinflation

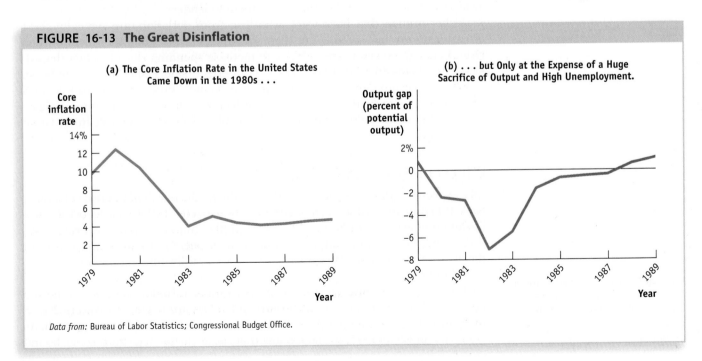

(a) The Core Inflation Rate in the United States Came Down in the 1980s . . .

(b) . . . but Only at the Expense of a Huge Sacrifice of Output and High Unemployment.

Data from: Bureau of Labor Statistics; Congressional Budget Office.

>> Quick Review

• Policies that keep the unemployment rate below the **NAIRU,** the **nonaccelerating rate of inflation,** will lead to accelerating inflation as inflationary expectations adjust to higher levels of actual inflation. The NAIRU is equal to the natural rate of unemployment.

• The **long-run Phillips curve** is vertical and shows that an unemployment rate below the NAIRU cannot be maintained in the long run. As a result, there are limits to expansionary policies.

• *Disinflation* imposes high costs—unemployment and lost output—on an economy. Governments adopt it to avoid the costs of persistently high inflation.

>> Check Your Understanding 16-3

Solutions appear at back of book.

1. Why is there no long-run trade-off between unemployment and inflation?

2. British economists believe that the natural rate of unemployment in their country rose sharply during the 1970s, from around 3% to as much as 10%. During that period, Britain experienced a sharp acceleration of inflation, which for a time went above 20%. How might these facts be related?

3. Why is disinflation so costly for an economy? Are there ways to reduce these costs?

Deflation

Before World War II, *deflation*—a falling aggregate price level—was almost as common as inflation. (We introduced deflation in Chapter 6.) In fact, the U.S. consumer price index on the eve of World War II was 30% lower than it had been in 1920. After World War II, inflation became the norm in all countries. But in the 1990s, deflation reappeared in Japan and proved difficult to reverse. Concerns about potential deflation played a crucial role in U.S. monetary policy in the early 2000s and again in the aftermath of the 2008 financial crisis.

Why is deflation a problem? And why is it hard to end?

Debt Deflation

Deflation, like inflation, produces both winners and losers—but in the opposite direction. Due to the falling price level, a dollar in the future has a higher real value than a dollar today. So lenders, who are owed money, gain under deflation because the real value of borrowers' payments increases. Borrowers lose because the real burden of their debt rises.

In a famous analysis at the beginning of the Great Depression, Irving Fisher (who first analyzed the *Fisher effect* of expected inflation on interest rates, described in Chapter 10) claimed that the effects of deflation on borrowers and lenders can worsen an economic slump. Deflation, in effect, takes real resources away from borrowers and redistributes them to lenders.

Fisher argued that borrowers, who lose from deflation, are typically short of cash and will be forced to cut their spending sharply when their debt burden rises. Lenders, however, are unlikely to increase spending sharply when the values of the loans they own rise. The overall effect, said Fisher, is that deflation reduces aggregate demand, deepening an economic slump, which, in a vicious circle, may lead to further deflation. The effect of deflation in reducing aggregate demand, known as **debt deflation,** probably played a significant role in the Great Depression.

Effects of Expected Deflation

Like expected inflation, expected deflation affects the nominal interest rate. Look back at Figure 10-9, which demonstrated how expected inflation affects the equilibrium interest rate. In Figure 10-9, the equilibrium nominal interest rate is 4% if the expected inflation rate is 0%. But, if the expected inflation rate is –3%—if the public expects deflation at 3% per year—the equilibrium nominal interest rate would fall to 1%.

But what would happen if the expected rate of inflation is –6%? Would the nominal interest rate fall to –2%, in which lenders are paying borrowers 2% on their debt? Probably not, because they could do better by simply holding cash. As explained in Chapter 15, we now know that there isn't a strict zero lower bound

Debt deflation is the reduction in aggregate demand arising from the increase in the real burden of outstanding debt caused by deflation.

because holding lots of cash is inconvenient. But the nominal rate clearly can't go more than a small amount below zero.

This restriction—called the zero lower bound problem—can limit the effectiveness of monetary policy. Suppose the economy is depressed, with output below potential output and the unemployment rate above the natural rate. Normally the central bank can respond by cutting interest rates to increase aggregate demand. If the nominal interest rate is already zero, however, the central bank cannot push it down any further. The central bank is up against the zero lower bound for the nominal interest rate. Banks refuse to lend and consumers and firms refuse to spend because, with a negative inflation rate and a 0% nominal interest rate, holding cash yields a positive real return: with falling prices, a given amount of cash buys more over time. Any further increases in the monetary base will either be held in bank vaults or held as cash by individuals and firms, without being spent.

A situation in which conventional monetary policy to fight a slump—cutting interest rates—can't be used because nominal interest rates can't be cut further is known as a **liquidity trap.** A liquidity trap can occur whenever there is a sharp reduction in demand for loanable funds—which is exactly what happened during the Great Depression. Figure 16-14 shows the interest rate on short-term U.S. government debt from 1920 to 2017. As you can see, during the period from 1933 to the post–World War II recovery, the U.S. economy was either close to or up against the zero lower bound. After World War II, when inflation became the norm around the world, the zero lower bound largely vanished as a problem, as the public came to expect inflation rather than deflation. As a result, economists largely lost interest in the issue.

But, as you can see, the zero lower bound emerged again as a result of the financial crisis of 2008. Once more, the interest rate on three-month U.S. Treasury bills was virtually zero. Yet for reasons not entirely clear, the United States did not experience deflation during the Great Recession. Sticky wages may have been the cause, since the United States did not experience a significant fall in nominal wages although unemployment shot up.

The recent history of the Japanese economy, shown in Figure 16-15, provides the best modern illustration of the problem of deflation and the liquidity trap. In the 1990s, after the bursting of a huge housing and stock bubble, the Japanese economy entered a period of sustained weakness in which wages and prices fell.

The economy is in a **liquidity trap** when conventional monetary policy is ineffective because the nominal interest rate is up against the zero lower bound.

FIGURE 16-14 The Zero Lower Bound in the U.S. Economy

This figure shows U.S. short-term interest rates, specifically the interest rate on three-month Treasury bills, from 1920 to 2017. As shown by the shaded bar at left, for much of the 1930s, interest rates were very close to zero, leaving little room for expansionary monetary policy. After World War II, persistent inflation generally kept interest rates well above zero. However, in late 2008, in the wake of the housing bubble bursting and the financial crisis, the interest rate on three-month Treasury bills was again virtually zero and stayed there for almost eight years—shown by the shaded bar at right.

Data from: National Bureau of Economic Research; Federal Reserve Bank of St. Louis.

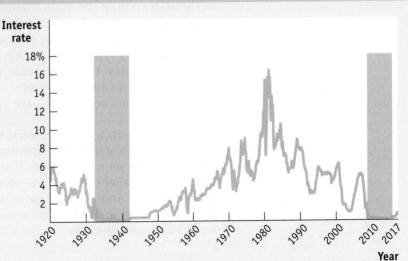

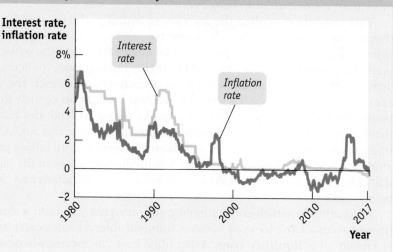

FIGURE 16-15 Deflation and the Liquidity Trap in the Japanese Economy

A prolonged economic slump in Japan led to deflation from the late 1990s on. The Bank of Japan responded by cutting interest rates—but eventually ran up against the zero lower bound where it remained in 2017, over 20 years later.

Data from: Federal Reserve Bank of St. Louis.

In an effort to fight the economic weakness, the Bank of Japan—the equivalent of the Federal Reserve—repeatedly cut interest rates. Eventually, it arrived at the ZIRP: the *zero interest rate policy*. The call money rate, the equivalent of the U.S. federal funds rate, was literally set equal to zero. Because the economy was still depressed, it would have been desirable to cut interest rates even further. But that wasn't possible: Japan was up against the zero lower bound. And it was still there in 2017, more than 20 years later!

In the aftermath of the 2008 financial crisis, the world's most important central banks—the U.S. Federal Reserve and the European Central Bank—found themselves facing much of the same problems as the Bank of Japan had faced since the 1990s: their economies remained depressed despite policy interest rates close to zero and inflation persistently below target. In 2014, neither the United States nor the euro area was experiencing actual deflation, but as the following Economics in Action describes, Europe did get alarmingly close.

ECONOMICS >> *in Action*

Is Europe Turning Japanese?

In the aftermath of the 2008 financial crisis, officials at the Federal Reserve were deeply worried about the possibility of *Japanification*—that is, they worried that, like Japan since the 1990s, the United States might find itself stuck in a deflationary trap. To avoid this possibility, they took some extraordinary measures, notably the large-scale purchases of assets—so-called *quantitative easing*—described in Chapter 15. By 2017, the danger of deflation in the United States seemed to have receded, and the Fed began to normalize its policy.

But Europe was a different story. Where the U.S. recovery from the recession of 2007–2009 was steady, if disappointingly slow, the euro area, held back by debt crises, slid back into recession in late 2011. Growth resumed in 2013, but as you can see from panel (a) of Figure 16-16, it only led to a modest decline in high unemployment. And as panel (b) of Figure 16-16 shows, in 2013–2017 inflation began sliding below 1%, leading to worries that Europe was on track to replicate Japan's economic situation.

FIGURE 16-16 Trouble in Europe, 2008–2017

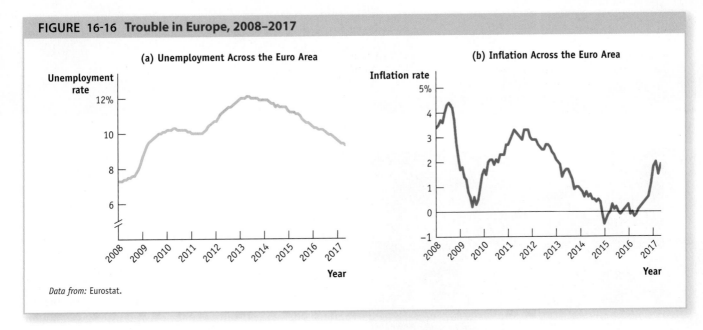

Data from: Eurostat.

While Europe was not yet experiencing sustained deflation as of 2017, it was, as the International Monetary Fund put it, suffering from *lowflation*—inflation persistently below target—and this created many of the same problems. In particular, lower-than-expected inflation was worsening the problems of highly indebted nations, like Portugal, Spain, and Greece.

And like the Bank of Japan a number of years earlier, the European Central Bank was finding it hard to devise an effective answer to the problem. Beginning in June 2014, the ECB took the extraordinary step of reducing one of its key policy rates, the interest rate it pays on deposits of private banks, to *minus 0.1 percent*—that is, it began actually charging banks a fee for holding their money. But below-target inflation persisted.

>> Check Your Understanding 16-4

Solution appears at back of book.

1. Why won't anyone lend money at a negative nominal rate of interest? How can this pose problems for monetary policy?

>> Quick Review

• Unexpected deflation helps lenders and hurts borrowers. This can lead to **debt deflation,** which has a contractionary effect on aggregate demand.

• Deflation makes it more likely that interest rates will end up against the zero lower bound. When this happens, the economy is in a **liquidity trap,** and monetary policy is ineffective.

Dining and Dollars in Buenos Aires

Back in 2014, the Adentro Dinner Club was among the best-reviewed restaurants in Buenos Aires, Argentina. In fact, it was fully booked well in advance—but not too far in advance. Why? Because Kelly Brenner and Gabriel Aguallo, the owners of the restaurant, didn't dare accept reservations, say, for two months ahead, because at the time of booking they couldn't know how much they would have to charge for a meal. In fact, that year many Argentinian restaurants had given up printing menus with prices, resorting to using chalkboards so that prices could be easily erased and revised.

In 2014, Argentina was in severe economic distress. Unable to either raise taxes or cut spending, its government ran intractable budget deficits but was unable to borrow on world markets. In addition, the country was suffering from a bout of high inflation, a problem that has occurred frequently in its history. Officially, the inflation rate was 24% that year, but independent analysts put the number closer to 40%.

Luckily for Brenner and Aguallo, most of their customers were American tourists, so they were able to charge in U.S. dollars. The purchasing power of dollars was much more predictable than that of Argentine pesos. This solution wasn't available to less prestigious businesses, however. The Argentine government imposed restrictions that made it difficult to convert pesos into foreign currency—even patrolling the border with currency-sniffing dogs. Only a small elite had access to dollars on a regular basis.

As of early 2017, the year-old government of Argentina's President, Mauricio Macri, was struggling to bring inflation under control. If you are a tourist in Argentina, don't bother looking for the Adentro Dining Club. It closed in 2015, when its owners decided to move to the United States.

QUESTIONS FOR THOUGHT

1. What was the relationship between inflation and the Argentine government's chronic budget deficits?

2. What were the implications of Argentina's inability to get its government deficits under control for Argentine businesses?

3. Why did the Argentine government try to stop Argentinians from converting pesos into foreign currency, such as dollars?

SUMMARY

1. In analyzing high inflation, economists use the **classical model of the price level,** which says that changes in the money supply lead to proportional changes in the aggregate price level even in the short run.

2. Governments sometimes print money in order to finance budget deficits. When they do, they impose an **inflation tax,** generating tax revenue equal to the inflation rate times the money supply, on those who hold money. Revenue from the real inflation tax, the inflation rate times the real money supply, is the real value of resources captured by the government. In order to avoid paying the inflation tax, people reduce their real money holdings and force the government to increase inflation to capture the same amount of real inflation tax revenue. In some cases, this leads to a vicious circle of a shrinking real money supply and a rising rate of inflation, leading to hyperinflation and a fiscal crisis.

3. The output gap is the percentage difference between the actual level of real GDP and potential output. A positive output gap is associated with lower-than-normal unemployment; a negative output gap is associated with higher-than-normal unemployment. The relationship between the output gap and cyclical unemployment is described by **Okun's law.**

4. Countries that don't need to print money to cover government deficits can still stumble into moderate inflation, either because of political opportunism or because of wishful thinking.

5. At a given point in time, there is a downward-sloping relationship between unemployment and inflation known as the **short-run Phillips curve.** This curve is shifted by changes in the **expected rate of inflation.** The **long-run Phillips curve,** which shows the relationship between unemployment and inflation once expectations have had time to adjust, is vertical. It defines the **nonaccelerating inflation rate of unemployment,** or **NAIRU,** which is equal to the natural rate of unemployment. *Stagflation,* a combination of high unemployment and high inflation, reflects an upward shift of the short-run Phillips curve.

6. Once inflation has become embedded in expectations, getting inflation back down can be difficult because *disinflation* can be very costly, requiring the sacrifice of large amounts of aggregate output and imposing high levels of unemployment. However, policy makers in the United States and other wealthy countries were willing to pay that price of bringing down the high inflation of the 1970s.

7. Deflation poses several problems. It can lead to **debt deflation,** in which a rising real burden of outstanding debt intensifies an economic downturn. Also, nominal interest rates are more likely to run up against the zero lower bound in an economy experiencing deflation. When this happens, the economy enters a **liquidity trap,** rendering conventional monetary policy ineffective.

KEY TERMS

Classical model of the price level, p. 478
Inflation tax, p. 481
Okun's law, p. 486

Short-run Phillips curve, p. 486
Expected rate of inflation, p. 489
Nonaccelerating inflation rate of unemployment (NAIRU), p. 493

Long-run Phillips curve, p. 493
Debt deflation, p. 496
Liquidity trap, p. 497

PROBLEMS

interactive activity

1. In the economy of Scottopia, policy makers want to lower the unemployment rate and raise real GDP by using monetary policy. Using the accompanying diagram, show why this policy will ultimately result in a higher aggregate price level but no change in real GDP.

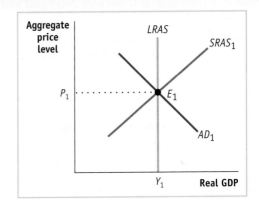

2. In the following examples, would the classical model of the price level be a useful model for analyzing how the economy behaves?

a. The economy has high unemployment and no history of inflation.

b. The economy has just experienced five years of hyperinflation.

c. Although the economy experienced inflation in the 10% to 20% range three years ago, prices have recently been stable and the unemployment rate has approximated the natural rate of unemployment.

3. Access the Discovering Data exercise for Chapter 16 online to answer the following questions.

a. How much did the monetary base change in the last year?

b. How did the change in the monetary base help in the government's efforts to finance its deficit?

c. Why is it important for the central bank to be independent of government policy makers?

4. Answer the following questions about the (real) inflation tax, assuming that the price level starts at 1.

a. Maria Moneybags keeps $1,000 in her sock drawer for a year. Over the year, the inflation rate is 10%. What is the real inflation tax paid by Maria for this year?

b. Maria continues to keep the $1,000 in her drawer for a second year. What is the real value of this $1,000 at the beginning of the second year? Over the year, the inflation rate is again 10%. What is the real inflation tax paid by Maria for the second year?

c. For a third year, Maria keeps the $1,000 in the drawer. What is the real value of this $1,000 at the beginning of the third year? Over the year, the inflation rate is again 10%. What is the real inflation tax paid by Maria for the third year?

d. After three years, what is the cumulative real inflation tax paid?

e. Redo parts a through d with an inflation rate of 25%. Why is hyperinflation such a problem?

5. The inflation tax is often used as a significant source of revenue in developing countries where the tax collection and reporting system is not well developed and tax evasion may be high.

a. Use the numbers in the accompanying table to calculate the inflation tax in the United States and India (Rp = rupees).

	Inflation in 2015	Money supply in 2015 (billions)	Central government receipts in 2015 (billions)
India	5.87%	Rp24,581	Rp12,409
United States	0.12%	$3,082	$3,515

Data from: Bureau of Economic Analysis; Controller General of Accounts (India); Reserve Bank of India; International Monetary Fund; The World Bank.

b. How large is the inflation tax for the two countries when calculated as a percentage of government receipts?

6. Concerned about the crowding-out effects of government borrowing on private investment spending, a candidate for president argues that the United States should just print money to cover the government's budget deficit. What are the advantages and disadvantages of such a plan?

7. The accompanying scatter diagram shows the relationship between the unemployment rate and the output gap in the United States from 1996 to 2016. Draw a straight line through the scatter of dots in the figure. Assume that this line represents Okun's law:

Unemployment rate = $b - (m \times \text{Output gap})$

where b is the vertical intercept and $-m$ is the slope

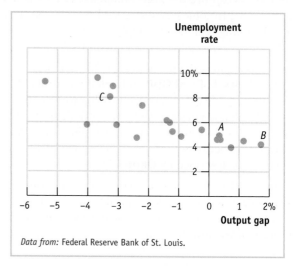

Data from: Federal Reserve Bank of St. Louis.

What is the unemployment rate when aggregate output equals potential output? What would the unemployment rate be if the output gap were 2%? What if the output gap were −3%? What do these results tell us about the coefficient m in Okun's law?

8. After experiencing a recession for the past two years, the residents of Albernia were looking forward to a decrease in the unemployment rate. Yet after six months of strong positive economic growth, the unemployment rate has fallen only slightly below what it was at the end of the recession. How can you explain why the unemployment rate did not fall as much although the economy was experiencing strong economic growth? (*Hint:* Reread the For Inquiring Minds box on Okun's law for help with answering this question.)

9. a. Go to www.bls.gov. Click on link "Subjects"; on the left, under "Inflation & Prices," click on the link "Consumer Price Index," then "CPI Tables," and then "Archived CPI Detailed Report Tables." Download the zip file for 2009 and open file cpid09av.pdf. What is the value of the percent change in the CPI from 2008 to 2009?

b. Now go to www.treasury.gov and click on "Resource Center." From there, click on "Data and Charts Center." Under the heading "Interest Rates," select "Daily Treasury Bill Rates" and select "2009" under "Select Time Period." Examine the data in "4 Weeks Bank Discount." What is the maximum? The minimum? Then do the same for 2007. How do the data for 2009 and 2007 compare? How would you relate this to your answer in part a? From the data on Treasury bill interest rates, what would you infer about the level of the inflation rate in 2007 compared to 2009? (You can check your answer by going back to the www.bls.gov website to find the percent change in the CPI from 2006 to 2007.)

c. How would you characterize the change in the U.S. economy from 2007 to 2009? What were the implications for the effectiveness of monetary policy?

10. The economy of Brittania has been suffering from high inflation with an unemployment rate equal to its natural rate. Policy makers would like to disinflate the economy with the lowest economic cost possible. Assume that the state of the economy is not the result of a negative supply shock. How can they try to minimize the unemployment cost of disinflation? Is it possible for there to be no cost of disinflation?

11. Who are the winners and losers when a mortgage company lends $100,000 to the Miller family to buy a house worth $105,000 and during the first year prices unexpectedly fall by 10%? What would you expect to happen if the deflation continued over the next few years? How would continuing deflation affect borrowers and lenders throughout the economy as a whole?

> **WORK IT OUT** **Interactive step-by-step help with solving this problem can be found online.**

12. Due to historical differences, countries often differ in how quickly a change in actual inflation is incorporated into a change in expected inflation. In a country such as Japan, which has had very little inflation in recent memory, it will take longer for a change in the actual inflation rate to be reflected in a corresponding change in the expected inflation rate. In contrast, in a country such as Zimbabwe, which has recently had very high inflation, a change in the actual inflation rate will immediately be reflected in a corresponding change in the expected inflation rate. What does this imply about the short-run and long-run Phillips curves in these two types of countries? What does this imply about the effectiveness of monetary and fiscal policy to reduce the unemployment rate?

17 Macroeconomics: Events and Ideas

OLD BOOKS AND NEW IDEAS

IN EARLY 2011, the Institute for New Economic Thinking hosted a conference devoted to analyzing the severe economic crisis that began with the financial crisis of 2008—an economic catastrophe that few had predicted. Mark Thoma, an economics professor at the University of Oregon, was one of the attendees. While at the conference, a joke he made on his influential blog quickly became a classic among macroeconomists: "I've learned that new economic thinking means reading old books."

Thoma hastened to add that he was finding the conference valuable. But as many economists recognized, he had a point. In many ways, the crisis of 2008 and its aftermath looked more like the Great Depression and the problems that faced the world in the 1930s than the problems that had preoccupied economists in the late twentieth century. And it turned out that there were valuable insights still to be found by studying economic history and rereading the work of economists who had confronted past economic difficulties.

Insights from the past are useful in a twenty-first century crisis: although specific circumstances change over time, there are similarities in how people and institutions behave. As we learned in Chapter 14, this was true of the Panic of 1907 and the financial crisis of 2008. Although these crises occurred over 100 years apart, the patterns of behavior that created them were similar.

Macroeconomic ideas evolve because circumstances change. Solutions that were appropriate when gold and silver were the only monies available are inappropriate in an age of debit cards, Paypal, and digital currency. However, macroeconomic ideas also evolve because there is a steady accumulation of research and evidence that can be applied to the kinds of economic phenomenon that recur over time. The lessons learned in one decade are made available for the benefit of future generations.

Because of the knowledge contained in those old macroeconomics books, the Great Recession didn't turn into a full replay of the Great Depression. Policy makers in 2008 knew more about the causes of depressions and how to fight them thanks to the research done in the aftermath of the Great Depression. Still, to understand the state of macroeconomic thinking today requires a trip through economic history and an understanding of the way economic ideas have evolved in the face of events.

In this chapter we'll trace the development of macroeconomic ideas over the past 85 years: the rise of Keynesian economics in response to the Great Depression, the challenges to policy activism that arose in response to the stagflation of the 1970s, and the controversies created by the Great Recession and its aftermath. ●

To tackle the Great Recession, policy makers were able to use the macroeconomic tools that evolved from the experience of the Great Depression.

WHAT YOU WILL LEARN

- Why was classical macroeconomics inadequate for the problems posed by the Great Depression?

- How did John Maynard Keynes and the experience of the Great Depression legitimize **macroeconomic policy activism**?

- What is **monetarism** and why did monetarists claim there are limits to the use of **discretionary monetary policy**?

- How did challenges lead to a revision of **Keynesian economics** and the emergence of the **new classical macroeconomics**?

- Why was the **Great Moderation consensus** undermined by the 2008 financial crisis, leading to fierce debates among economists and the emergence of two post–Great Recession policy camps?

‖ Classical Macroeconomics

The term *macroeconomics* appears to have been coined in 1933 by the Norwegian economist Ragnar Frisch. The date, during the worst year of the Great Depression, is no accident. Still, there were economists analyzing what we now consider macroeconomic issues—the behavior of the aggregate price level and aggregate output—before then.

Money and the Price Level

In Chapter 16, we described the *classical model of the price level*. According to the classical model, prices are flexible, making the aggregate supply curve vertical even in the short run. In this model, an increase in the money supply leads, other things equal, to an equal proportional rise in the aggregate price level, with no effect on aggregate output. As a result, increases in the money supply lead to inflation, and that's all. Before the 1930s, the classical model of the price level dominated economic thinking about the effects of monetary policy.

Did classical economists really believe that changes in the money supply affected only aggregate prices, without any effect on aggregate output? Probably not. Historians of economic thought argue that before 1930 most economists were aware that changes in the money supply affect aggregate output as well as aggregate prices in the short run—or, to use modern terms, they were aware that the short-run aggregate supply curve slopes upward. But they regarded such short-run effects as unimportant, stressing that it was the long run that mattered. It was this attitude that led John Maynard Keynes to scoff at the exclusive focus on the long run, in which, as he said, "we are all dead."

The Business Cycle

Despite their lack of interest in the short run, classical economists were aware that the economy did not grow smoothly. Some economic historians argue that the first true recession in the modern sense took place in Britain in 1825–1826, when an overheated boom in a canal-building collapsed. As the Industrial Revolution spread beyond Britain, so did the business cycle, which eventually became the object of systematic, quantitative study, pioneered by the American economist Wesley Mitchell. In 1920 Mitchell founded the National Bureau of Economic Research (NBER), an independent, nonprofit organization that to this day has the official role of declaring the beginnings of recessions and expansions. Thanks to Mitchell's work, the *measurement* of business cycles was well advanced by 1930. But there was no widely accepted *theory* of what caused business cycles or what to do about them.

In the absence of any clear theory, conflicts arose among policy makers over how to respond to a recession. Some economists favored expansionary monetary and fiscal policies to fight a recession. Others believed that such policies would worsen the slump or merely postpone the inevitable. For example, in 1934 Harvard's Joseph Schumpeter, now famous for his early recognition of the importance of technological change, warned that any attempt to alleviate the Great Depression with expansionary monetary policy "would, in the end, lead to a collapse worse than the one it was called in to remedy." When the Great Depression hit, policy was paralyzed by this lack of consensus.

Necessity was, however, the mother of invention. As we'll see next, the Great Depression provided an opportunity for economists to develop theories that could serve as a guide to policy.

The Great Depression and the Keynesian Revolution

The Great Depression demonstrated, once and for all, that economists cannot safely ignore the short run. Not only was the economic pain severe; it threatened to destabilize societies and political systems. In particular, the economic plunge helped Adolf Hitler rise to power in Germany, setting the stage for World War II.

The whole world wanted to know how this economic disaster could be happening and what should be done about it. But because there was no widely accepted theory of the business cycle, economists gave conflicting and often harmful advice. Some believed that only a huge change in the economic system—such as having the government take over much of private industry and replace markets with a command economy—could end the slump. Others argued that slumps were natural—even beneficial, helping to correct past excesses—and that nothing should be done.

Some economists, however, argued that slumps were destructive and should be cured. Moreover, they could be cured without compromising the market economy. The most compelling advocate for this view, the British economist John Maynard Keynes, compared the problems of the U.S. and British economies in 1930 to those of a car with a defective starter. Getting the economy running, he argued, would require only a modest repair, not a complete overhaul.

Nice metaphor. But what did he mean, specifically?

Keynes's Theory

In 1936 Keynes presented his analysis of the Great Depression—his explanation of what was wrong with the economy's starter—in a book titled *The General Theory of Employment, Interest, and Money*. In 1946 the great American economist and Nobel Prize winner Paul Samuelson wrote that "it is a badly written book, poorly organized. . . . Flashes of insight and intuition intersperse tedious algebra. . . . We find its analysis to be obvious and at the same time new. In short, it is a work of genius." Samuelson was correct on both counts: *The General Theory* isn't easy reading, yet it stands with Adam Smith's *The Wealth of Nations* as one of the most influential books on economics ever written.

As Samuelson's description indicates, Keynes's book offers a vast stew of ideas. *Keynesian economics* is principally based on two innovations. First, Keynes emphasized the importance of short-run effects of changes in aggregate demand on aggregate output, unlike the classicists who focused exclusively on the long-run determination of the aggregate price level.

Until *The General Theory* appeared most economists had treated short-run macroeconomics as a minor issue, a view satirized by Keynes's famous remark that, "In the long run, we are all dead." Keynes shifted the focus of attention of economists away from the unreachable long run to the world in which people actually live, one in which the short-run aggregate supply curve slopes upward and shifts in the aggregate demand curve affect aggregate output and employment as well as aggregate prices.

Figure 17-1 illustrates the difference between Keynesian and classical macroeconomics. Both panels of the figure show the short-run aggregate supply curve, *SRAS*; in both it is assumed that for some reason demand falls and the aggregate demand curve shifts leftward from AD_1 to AD_2—say, for example, in response to a fall in stock market prices that leads households to reduce consumer spending.

Panel (a) shows the classical view: in it, the short-run aggregate supply curve is vertical. Therefore the fall in aggregate demand leads to a fall in the aggregate price level, from P_1 to P_2, but leaves aggregate output unchanged. Panel (b) shows the Keynesian view: in it, the short-run aggregate supply curve slopes upward.

FIGURE 17-1 Classical versus Keynesian Macroeconomics

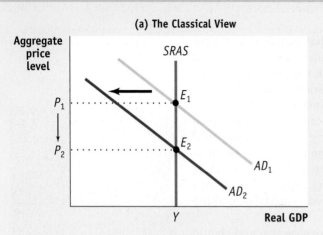

(a) The Classical View

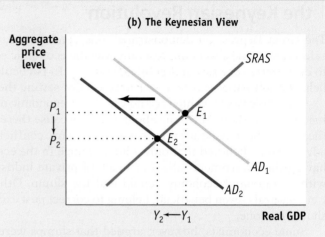

(b) The Keynesian View

One important difference between classical and Keynesian economics involves the short-run aggregate supply curve. Panel (a) shows the classical view: the *SRAS* curve is vertical, so shifts in aggregate demand affect the aggregate price level but not aggregate output. Panel (b) shows the Keynesian view: in the short run the *SRAS* curve slopes upward, so shifts in aggregate demand affect aggregate output as well as aggregate prices.

So a fall in aggregate demand leads to both a fall in the aggregate price level, from P_1 to P_2, and a fall in aggregate output, from Y_1 to Y_2.

As we've already explained, many classical macroeconomists would have agreed that panel (b) portrayed an accurate story in the short run—but they regarded the short run as unimportant. Keynes strongly disagreed, arguing that short-run economic problems caused great social distress and were in fact fixable. [Just to be clear, there isn't any diagram that looks like panel (b) of Figure 17-1 in Keynes's *General Theory*. But Keynes's discussion of aggregate supply, translated into modern terminology, clearly implies an upward-sloping *SRAS* curve.]

Keynes's second innovation concerned the question of what factors shifted the aggregate demand curve and caused business cycles. Classical economists attributed shifts in the demand curve almost exclusively to changes in the money supply. Keynes, by contrast, argued that other factors, especially changes in "animal spirits"—these days usually referred to with the bland term *business confidence*—are mainly responsible for business cycles.

Before Keynes, economists argued that as long as the money supply stayed constant, changes in factors like business confidence would have no effect on either the aggregate price level or aggregate output. Keynes offered a very different picture in which, for example, pessimism about future profits can lead to a fall in investment spending, and this can cause a recession.

Keynesian economics, a view of the business cycle informed by these innovations, has penetrated deeply into the public consciousness, to the extent that many people who have never heard of Keynes, or have heard of him but think they disagree with his theory, use Keynesian ideas all the time. For example, suppose that a business commentator says something like this: "Businesses are holding back on investment spending because they're worried about low consumer demand, and that's why recovery has stalled." Whether the commentator knows it or not, that statement is pure Keynesian economics.

Keynes himself more or less predicted that someday people would make use of his ideas without knowing that they were *Keynesians*. As he famously wrote in *The General Theory*, "Practical men, who believe themselves to be quite exempt from any intellectual influences, are usually the slaves of some defunct economist."

Keynesian economics rests on two main tenets: changes in aggregate demand affect aggregate output, employment, and prices; and changes in business confidence cause the business cycle.

Some political commentators use the term *Keynesian economics* as a synonym for left-wing economics. Because Keynes offered a rationale for some kinds of government activism, these commentators have gone on to claim that he was a leftist of some kind, maybe even a socialist. But the truth is more complicated.

As we explained, Keynesian ideas have actually been accepted among economists and policy makers across a broad range of the political spectrum. In 2004 the American president, George W. Bush, was a conservative, as was his top economist, N. Gregory Mankiw. But Mankiw is also a well-known promoter of Keynesian ideas.

In fact, Keynes was no socialist—and not much of a leftist. At the time *The General Theory* was published, the Depression had convinced many intellectuals that socialism was the only solution to the economy's woes. They believed that the Great Depression was the final crisis of the capitalist economic system

and that only a government takeover of industry could save the economy. Keynes, in contrast, argued that socialism was not the answer. Instead, he said, all the capitalist market system needed was a narrow technical fix. In essence, his ideas were pro-capitalist and politically conservative.

What is true is that the rise of Keynesian economics in the 1940s, 1950s, and 1960s accompanied a general enlargement of the role of government in the economy, and those who favored a larger role for government tended to be enthusiastic Keynesians. Conversely, a swing of the pendulum back toward free-market policies in the 1970s and 1980s was accompanied by a series of challenges to Keynesian ideas, which we will describe in this chapter.

Recent history shows that it is quite easy to find respected economists and policy makers who have conservative political preferences and who simultaneously respect Keynes's fundamental

contributions to macroeconomics. It is equally possible to find those of a liberal bent who question some of Keynes's ideas.

The ideas of John Maynard Keynes have been accepted across the political spectrum.

Policy to Fight Recessions

The greatest consequence of Keynes's work was that it legitimized **macroeconomic policy activism**—the use of monetary and fiscal policy to smooth out the business cycle.

It's true that some economists had called for macroeconomic activism before Keynes, in particular advocating monetary expansion to fight economic downturns. And some economists had even argued, as Keynes did, that temporary budget deficits were a good thing in times of recession. But macroeconomic policy activism at the time was considered deeply controversial and those who advocated it were fiercely attacked.

As a result, when some governments during the 1930s followed policies that we would now call Keynesian, they were carried out in a half-hearted way and were insufficient to turn the Great Depression around. In the United States, the administration of Franklin Roosevelt engaged in modest deficit spending in an effort to create jobs, actions which seemed to gain some traction in improving the economy. But, in 1937 Roosevelt gave in to advice from non-Keynesian economists who urged him to balance the federal budget and raise interest rates, even though the economy was still deeply depressed. The result was a renewed slump.

Over time, however, Keynesian ideas spread, and they were widely accepted among economists after World War II. There were, however, a series of challenges to those ideas, which led to a considerable shift in views even among those economists who continued to believe that Keynes was broadly right about the causes of recessions. Next we'll learn about those challenges and the schools, *new classical economics* and *new Keynesian economics*, that emerged.

Macroeconomic policy activism is the use of monetary and fiscal policy to smooth out the business cycle.

ECONOMICS >> *in Action*
The End of the Great Depression

It would make a good story if Keynes's ideas had led to a change in economic policy that brought the Great Depression to an end. Unfortunately, that's not what happened. Yet, the way the Depression finally ended helped convince the economics profession that Keynes was basically right.

What economists learned from Keynes's work was that economic recovery requires aggressive fiscal expansion—deficit spending on a sufficiently large scale to create jobs and push up aggregate demand. And that happened in the United States not because of intentional economic policy, but as the result of a very large war that required an enormous amount of government spending, World War II. The overwhelming evidence that it was government expenditures for World War II that lifted the economy out of the Great Depression finally ended the debate over the validity of Keynes's views.

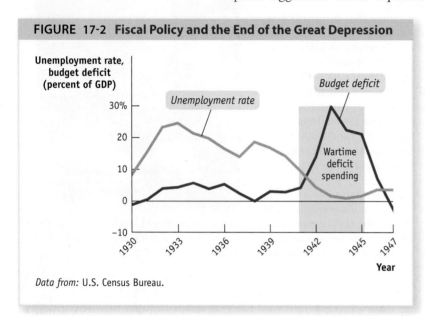

FIGURE 17-2 Fiscal Policy and the End of the Great Depression

Data from: U.S. Census Bureau.

Figure 17-2 shows the U.S. unemployment rate and the federal budget deficit as a share of GDP from 1930 to 1947. As you can see, deficit spending during the 1930s was on a modest scale. In 1940, as the risk of war grew larger, the United States began a large military buildup, building tanks, planes, military bases and the like, moving the budget deep into deficit. After the attack on Pearl Harbor on December 7, 1941, the country began deficit spending on an enormous scale: in fiscal 1943, which began in July 1942, the deficit was 30% of GDP. Today that would be equivalent to a deficit of $5.6 trillion.

What was clear to economists and policy makers was that with this enormous surge in government spending the economy, mired in the Great Depression for well over a decade, finally recovered in a sustainable way. World War II wasn't intended as a Keynesian fiscal policy. And it is hard to believe that any event, short of a world war, would have compelled the U.S. government to spend so much money. Yet unintentional as it was, World War II spending demonstrated that expansionary fiscal policy can lift the economy out of a deep slump.

>> Check Your Understanding 17-1
Solutions appear at back of book.

1. In their famous book *A Monetary History of the United States*, the economists Milton Friedman and Anna Schwartz argued that the Federal Reserve was responsible for the Great Depression, because it failed to pursue a sufficiently expansionary monetary policy. Why would a classical economist have thought that action by the Federal Reserve would not have made a difference in the length or depth of the Great Depression?

2. In a press release during the Great Recession, the National Federation of Independent Business, which calculates the Small Business Optimism Index, stated "The Small Business Optimism Index rose just 0.1 points in January. . . . Historically, optimism remains at recession levels. While small business owners appeared less pessimistic about the outlook for business conditions and real sales growth, that optimism did not materialize in hiring or increased inventories plans." Would this statement seem familiar to a Keynesian economist? Which conclusion would a Keynesian economist draw for the need for public policy?

>> Quick Review

• Classical macroeconomists focused on the long-run effects of monetary policy on the aggregate price level, ignoring any short-run effects on aggregate output.

• By the time of the Great Depression, the measurement of business cycles was well advanced, but there was no widely accepted theory about why they happened.

• The key innovations of **Keynesian economics** are an emphasis on the short run, in which the *SRAS* curve slopes upward rather than being vertical, and the belief that changes in business confidence shift the *AD* curve and thereby generate business cycles.

• Keynesian economics legitimized **macroeconomic policy activism.**

• Keynesian ideas are widely used even by people who haven't heard of Keynes or think they disagree with him.

‖ Challenges to Keynesian Economics

Keynes's ideas fundamentally changed the way economists think about business cycles. They did not, however, go unquestioned. In the wake of the success of government expenditures in ending the Great Depression, Keynesian economics faced a new series of challenges. As a result, by the 1980s the consensus of macroeconomists retreated somewhat from the strong version of Keynesianism that prevailed in the 1950s. In particular, many economists began to suggest limits to the effectiveness of macroeconomic policy activism.

The Revival of Monetary Policy

Many macroeconomists agree with Keynes's view that during a depression monetary policy would be relatively ineffective. We met this phenomenon in Chapter 16 in what we called the *liquidity trap*, a situation in which monetary policy is ineffective because the interest rate cannot be pushed any lower. In the 1930s, when Keynes wrote, interest rates were, in fact, very close to zero.

When the era of near-zero interest rates came to an end after World War II and the economy had recovered, the pendulum had swung so far in favor of Keynesian economics that many economists continued to emphasize fiscal policy and downplay the usefulness of monetary policy. Eventually, however, the pendulum swung partly back as macroeconomists eventually reassessed the importance of monetary policy.

A key milestone in this reassessment was the 1963 publication of *A Monetary History of the United States, 1867–1960* by Milton Friedman, of the University of Chicago, and Anna Schwartz, of the National Bureau of Economic Research. Friedman and Schwartz showed that business cycles had historically been associated with fluctuations in the money supply. In particular, the money supply fell sharply during the onset of the Great Depression. Friedman and Schwartz persuaded many, though not all, economists that the Great Depression could have been avoided if the Federal Reserve had acted to prevent the monetary contraction by increasing the monetary base. They persuaded most economists that monetary policy should play a key role in economic management.

Milton Friedman and co-author Anna Schwartz played a key role in convincing macroeconomists of the importance of monetary policy.

The revival of interest in monetary policy was significant because it suggested that the burden of managing the economy could be shifted away from fiscal policy—meaning that economic management could largely be taken out of the hands of politicians. This feature was attractive to many because fiscal policy necessarily involves political choices. If the government tries to stimulate the economy by cutting taxes, it must decide whose taxes will be cut. If it tries to stimulate the economy with government spending, it must decide what to spend the money on. As a result, management of the economy would often be bogged down by the political process if fiscal policy were the only tool available.

Monetary policy, in contrast, does not involve such political choices: when the central bank cuts interest rates to fight a recession, it cuts everyone's interest rate at the same time. So a shift from relying on fiscal policy to relying on monetary policy makes macroeconomics a more technical, less political undertaking. In fact, as we've learned, monetary policy in most major economies is set by an independent central bank that is insulated from the political process.

Monetarism

After the publication of *A Monetary History*, Milton Friedman led a movement that sought to eliminate all forms of macroeconomic policy activism—fiscal and

Monetarism asserts that GDP will grow steadily if the money supply grows steadily.

Discretionary monetary policy is the use of changes in the interest rate or the money supply to stabilize the economy.

A **monetary policy rule** is a formula that determines the central bank's actions.

monetary. Instead, he asserted that the best way to manage the economy was with non-activist or *nondiscretionary* monetary policy. **Monetarism** asserts that GDP will grow steadily if the money supply grows steadily. According to the monetarist policy prescription, the central bank should target a constant rate of growth of the money supply, such as 3% per year, and maintain that target regardless of any fluctuations in the economy.

It's important to realize that monetarism retained many Keynesian ideas. Like Keynes, Friedman asserted that the short run is important and that short-run changes in aggregate demand affect aggregate output as well as aggregate prices. Like Keynes, he argued that macroeconomic policy should have been much more expansionary during the Great Depression, even if he believed that only monetary policy was needed.

Monetarists argued, however, that in most cases activist macroeconomic policy to smooth out the business cycle actually makes things worse. In Chapter 13 we described how lags can cause problems for *discretionary fiscal policy*. For example, a government that tries to respond to recessions by increasing spending sometimes finds that by the time it realizes that a recession is underway, takes action, and gets results, the recession is over, and the spending increase feeds a boom instead of fighting a slump. According to monetarists, **discretionary monetary policy,** changes in the interest rate or the money supply by the central bank in order to stabilize the economy, faces similar problems and can easily make the economy less stable.

Friedman also argued that if the central bank followed his advice, adopting a non-activist monetary policy and refusing to change the money supply in response to fluctuations in the economy, fiscal policy would be much less effective than Keynesians believed due to *crowding out*—when government spending crowds out private investment spending. In Chapter 10 we analyzed how this can occur: government spending leads to deficits, which drive up interest rates and reduce investment spending. Friedman and others pointed out that if the money supply is held fixed while the government pursues an expansionary fiscal policy, crowding out will occur as the interest rate rises, limiting the effect of the fiscal expansion on aggregate demand.

Figure 17-3 illustrates this argument. Panel (a) shows aggregate output and the aggregate price level. AD_1 is the initial aggregate demand curve and $SRAS$ is the short-run aggregate supply curve. At the initial equilibrium, E_1, the level of aggregate output is Y_1 and the aggregate price level is P_1. Panel (b) shows the money market. MS is the money supply curve and MD_1 is the initial money demand curve, so the initial interest rate is r_1.

Now suppose the government increases purchases of goods and services. We know that this will shift the AD curve rightward, as illustrated by the shift from AD_1 to AD_2, and that aggregate output will rise, from Y_1 to Y_2, and the aggregate price level will rise, from P_1 to P_2. Both the rise in aggregate output and the rise in the aggregate price level will, however, increase the demand for money, shifting the money demand curve rightward from MD_1 to MD_2. This drives up the equilibrium interest rate to r_2.

Friedman's point was that this rise in the interest rate reduces investment spending, partially offsetting the initial rise in government spending. As a result, the rightward shift of the AD curve is smaller than the multiplier analysis in Chapter 13 indicated. And Friedman argued that with a constant rate of increase in the money supply, the multiplier is so small that there's not much point in using fiscal policy, even in a depressed economy.

As already noted, Friedman didn't favor activist monetary policy either, arguing that the problems of time lags that limit the ability of discretionary fiscal policy to stabilize the economy also apply to discretionary monetary policy. Friedman's solution was to make monetary policy nondiscretionary, to put it on autopilot. The central bank, he argued, should follow a **monetary policy rule,** a

FIGURE 17-3 Fiscal Policy with a Fixed Money Supply

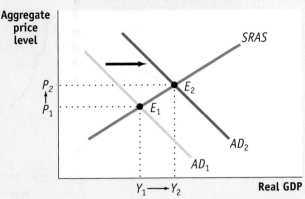

(a) The Increase in Aggregate Demand from an Expansionary Fiscal Policy Is Limited When the Money Supply Is Fixed . . .

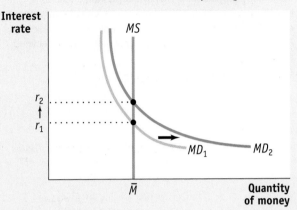

(b) . . . Because the Increase in Money Demand Drives up the Interest Rate, Crowding out Some Investment Spending.

In panel (a) an expansionary fiscal policy shifts the *AD* curve rightward, driving up both the aggregate price level and aggregate output. However, this leads to an increase in the demand for money. If the money supply is held fixed, as in panel (b), the increase in money demand drives up the interest rate, reducing investment spending and offsetting part of the fiscal expansion. So the shift of the *AD* curve is less than it would otherwise be: fiscal policy becomes less effective when the money supply is held fixed.

formula that determines its actions and leaves it relatively little discretion. During the 1960s and 1970s, most monetarists favored a monetary policy rule of slow, steady growth in the money supply.

Underlying this view was the concept of the **velocity of money,** the ratio of nominal GDP to the money supply. Monetarists believed, with considerable historical justification, that the velocity of money, *V*, was stable in the short run and changed only slowly in the long run. As a result, they claimed, steady growth in *M*, the money supply, by the central bank would ensure steady growth in spending, and therefore in GDP. Monetarism strongly influenced U.S. monetary policy in the late 1970s and early 1980s as the Fed tried to keep the rate of growth in the money supply constant. It quickly became clear, however, that this didn't ensure steady growth in the economy: the velocity of money wasn't stable enough for such a simple policy rule to work.

Figure 17-4 shows how events eventually undermined the monetarists' view. The figure shows the velocity of money, as measured by the ratio of nominal GDP to M1, from 1960 through mid-2017. As you can see, until 1980 velocity followed a fairly smooth and predictable upward trend. After that, however, the velocity of money began moving erratically, undermining the case for monetarism, and leading to a significant fall in its influence.

Consequently, traditional monetarists—those who believe that GDP will grow steadily if the money supply grows steadily—are hard to find among today's macroeconomists. As we'll see shortly, however, the concern that originally motivated the monetarists—that too much discretionary monetary policy can actually destabilize the economy—still has followers.

Limits to Macroeconomic Policy: Inflation and the Natural Rate of Unemployment

The problem of time lags in the implementation of activist macroeconomic policy was not the only criticism leveled at Keynesian economics. Another serious

The **velocity of money** is the ratio of nominal GDP to the money supply.

FIGURE 17-4 The Velocity of Money

From 1960 to 1980, the velocity of money followed a smooth and predictable upward trend, leading monetarists to believe that steady growth in the money supply would lead to a stable economy. After 1980, however, velocity began moving erratically, undermining the case for traditional monetarism. As a result, the influence of traditional monetarism declined significantly.

Data from: Federal Reserve Bank of St. Louis.

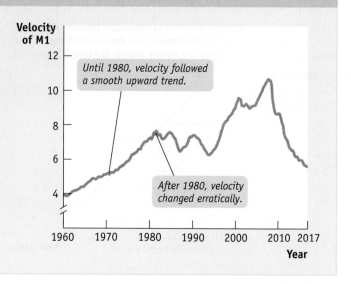

According to the **natural rate hypothesis,** because inflation is eventually embedded into expectations, to avoid accelerating inflation over time the unemployment rate should be kept stable around the natural rate.

concern arose over its effect on inflation. During the 1940s and 1950s, many Keynesian economists believed that expansionary fiscal policy could be used to achieve full employment on a permanent basis. By the 1960s, however, many economists realized that persistently expansionary policies could cause problems with inflation. Yet they still believed that governments could choose to keep unemployment low if they were willing to accept higher inflation.

In 1968, however, Milton Friedman and Edmund Phelps of Columbia University, working independently, argued that there isn't actually a long-run trade-off between unemployment and inflation. According to Friedman and Phelps's **natural rate hypothesis,** any attempt to keep unemployment below a minimum level would lead not just to inflation but to ever-rising inflation. The important point to recognize here is that if true, the natural rate hypothesis implies that Keynesian policies can't accomplish as much as macroeconomists previously believed. Because the government can't keep unemployment below the natural rate, its task is not to keep unemployment low but to keep it *stable around the natural rate*—to prevent large fluctuations in unemployment above or below the natural rate.

And the natural rate hypothesis was, in fact, accepted by most economists after the 1970s. The Friedman–Phelps hypothesis made a strong prediction: that the apparent trade-off between unemployment and inflation would not survive an extended period of rising prices. Once inflation was embedded into the public's expectations, it would continue even in the face of high unemployment.

Sure enough, that's exactly what happened in the 1970s. This accurate prediction was one of the triumphs of macroeconomic analysis. It convinced the great majority of economists that the natural rate hypothesis was correct, although some macroeconomists believe that at very low rates of inflation or deflation the hypothesis doesn't work.

The Political Business Cycle

One final challenge to Keynesian economics focused not on the validity of the economic analysis but on its political consequences. A number of economists and political scientists pointed out that activist macroeconomic policy lends itself to political manipulation.

Statistical evidence suggests that election results are strongly affected by the state of the economy in the months just before the election. In the United States,

Political manipulation in order to win votes is a danger of activist macroeconomic policy.

if the economy is growing rapidly and the unemployment rate is falling in the six months or so before Election Day, the incumbent party tends to be re-elected even if the economy performed poorly in the preceding three years. This creates an obvious temptation to abuse activist macroeconomic policy: pump up the economy in an election year, and pay the price in higher inflation and/or higher unemployment later. The consequence will be unnecessary instability in the economy, a **political business cycle** caused by the use of macroeconomic policy to serve political ends.

An often-cited example is the combination of expansionary fiscal and monetary policy that led to rapid growth in the U.S. economy just before the 1972 election and a sharp acceleration in inflation after the election. Kenneth Rogoff, a highly respected macroeconomist who served as chief economist at the International Monetary Fund, has proclaimed Richard Nixon, the president at the time, "the all-time hero of political business cycles."

As we've learned, one way to avoid a political business cycle is to place monetary policy in the hands of an independent central bank, insulated from political pressure. The political business cycle is also a reason to limit the use of discretionary fiscal policy to extreme circumstances like a liquidity trap.

> A **political business cycle** results when politicians use macroeconomic policy to serve political ends.

ECONOMICS >> *in Action*
The Fed's Flirtation with Monetarism

In the late 1970s and early 1980s the Federal Reserve flirted with monetarism. For most of its prior existence, the Fed had targeted interest rates, adjusting its target based on the state of the economy. In the late 1970s, however, the Fed adopted a monetary policy rule and began announcing target ranges for several measures of the money supply. It also stopped setting targets for interest rates. Most people interpreted these changes as a strong move toward monetarism.

In 1982, however, the Fed turned its back on monetarism. Since 1982 the Fed has pursued a discretionary monetary policy, which has led to large swings in the money supply. At the end of the 1980s, the Fed returned to conducting monetary policy by setting target levels for the interest rate.

Why did the Fed flirt with monetarism, then abandon it? The turn to monetarism largely reflected the events of the 1970s, when a sharp rise in inflation broke the perceived trade-off between inflation and unemployment and discredited traditional Keynesianism. The accuracy of Friedman's prediction of a worsening trade-off between inflation and unemployment increased his prestige and that of his followers. As a result, policy makers adopted Friedman's proposals.

The turn away from monetarism also reflected events: as we saw in Figure 17-4, the velocity of money, which had followed a smooth and predictable upward trend before 1980, became erratic after 1980. This made monetarism seem like a much less good idea.

>> Check Your Understanding 17-2
Solutions appear at back of book.

1. What are the limits of macroeconomic policy activism?
2. Starting in 2008, as the economy entered the Great Recession, unemployment soared while interest rates and investment spending fell sharply. The Fed accelerated the growth of M1 in response.
   a. What effect would these events have on the velocity of money? Do you think Milton Friedman would have agreed with the Fed's policy?
   b. Monetarists, like Friedman, generally believe that discretionary monetary policy and fiscal policy are ineffective. Do you think their objections to fiscal and monetary policy were valid during the Great Recession? Note that unemployment did not return to its pre-recession level until 2016.

>> Quick Review

- Early Keynesianism downplayed the effectiveness of monetary as opposed to fiscal policy, but later macroeconomists realized that monetary policy is effective except in the case of a liquidity trap.

- According to **monetarism,** due to time lags, both discretionary fiscal policy and **discretionary monetary policy** do more harm than good, and a simple **monetary policy rule** is the best way to stabilize the economy. Monetarists believed that the **velocity of money** was stable and therefore steady growth of the money supply would lead to steady growth of GDP. This doctrine was popular for a time but has fallen out of favor as its predictions failed to materialize.

- The **natural rate hypothesis,** now very widely accepted, places sharp limits on what macroeconomic policy can achieve. It implies that policy should aim to stabilize the unemployment rate around the natural rate.

- Concerns about a **political business cycle** suggest that the central bank should be independent and that discretionary fiscal policy should be avoided except in extreme circumstances like a liquidity trap.

New classical macroeconomics is an approach to the business cycle that returns to the classical view that shifts in the aggregate demand curve affect only the aggregate price level, not aggregate output.

Rational expectations is the view that individuals and firms make decisions optimally, using all available information.

Rational Expectations, Real Business Cycles, and New Classical Macroeconomics

As we have seen, one key difference between classical economics and Keynesian economics is that classical economists believed that the short-run aggregate supply curve is vertical, while Keynesian economics claims that the aggregate supply curve slopes upward in the short run. A consequence of the upward-sloping demand curve is that demand shocks—shifts in the aggregate demand curve—cause fluctuations in aggregate output.

However, the challenges to Keynesian economics that arose in the 1950s and 1960s from monetarists and from natural rate theorists didn't rely on classical economics ideas. The challengers accepted an upward-sloping aggregate supply curve—that an increase in aggregate demand leads to a rise in aggregate output in the short run and that a decrease in aggregate demand leads to a fall in aggregate output in the short run. Instead, they argued that the policy medicine advocated by traditional Keynesians, activist macroeconomic policy, would worsen the very disease they were trying to cure—economic fluctuations.

In the 1970s and 1980s, the classical view that shifts in the aggregate demand curve affect only the aggregate price level, not aggregate output, was revived in an approach known as **new classical macroeconomics.** It evolved in two stages. First, some economists challenged traditional arguments about the slope of the short-run aggregate supply curve based on the concept of *rational expectations*. Second, some economists suggested that changes in productivity cause economic fluctuations, a view known as *real business cycle theory*.

Rational Expectations

In the 1970s a concept known as *rational expectations* had a powerful impact on macroeconomics. **Rational expectations,** originally introduced by John Muth in 1961, claims that individuals and firms make decisions optimally, using all available information.

For example, workers and employers bargaining over long-term wage contracts need to take account of the expected inflation rate over the life of that contract. Rational expectations says that in making estimates of future inflation, they won't just look at past rates of inflation; they will also take into account currently available information about monetary and fiscal policy. Suppose that prices didn't rise last year, but that the monetary and fiscal policies announced by policy makers have made it clear that there will be substantial inflation over the next few years. According to rational expectations, long-term wage contracts will be adjusted today to reflect this future inflation, even though prices haven't yet risen.

Adopting the premise of rational expectations can significantly alter beliefs about the effectiveness of activist macroeconomic policy. According to the original version of the natural rate hypothesis, a government attempt to persistently push the unemployment rate below the natural rate would work in the short run but will eventually fail because higher inflation will get built into expectations. According to rational expectations, we should remove the word *eventually* and replace it with *immediately:* if the government tries to lower unemployment today at the cost of higher inflation in the future, inflation will shoot up immediately without even a temporary fall in unemployment. So, under rational expectations, government intervention fails in the short run and the long run.

In the 1970s Robert Lucas of the University of Chicago used the logic of rational expectations to argue that monetary policy can change the level of output and unemployment only if it comes as a surprise to the public. Otherwise, attempts to lower unemployment will simply result in higher prices. According to Lucas's **rational expectations model** of the economy, monetary policy isn't useful in stabilizing the economy after all. In 1995 Lucas won the Nobel Prize in economics for this work, which remains widely admired. However, many—perhaps most—macroeconomists, especially those advising policy makers, now believe that his conclusions were overstated. The Federal Reserve certainly thinks that it can play a useful role in economic stabilization.

Why, in the view of many macroeconomists, doesn't Lucas's rational expectations model of macroeconomics accurately describe how the economy actually behaves? **New Keynesian economics,** a set of ideas that became influential in the 1990s, provides an explanation. It argues that market imperfections interact to make many prices in the economy temporarily sticky. And with sticky prices, expected inflation can't rise quickly enough to offset activist macroeconomic policy.

For example, one new Keynesian argument points out that monopolists don't have to be too careful about setting prices exactly right: if they set a price a bit too high, they'll lose some sales but make more profit on each sale; if they set the price too low, they'll reduce the profit per sale but sell more. As a result, even small costs to changing prices can lead to substantial price stickiness and make the economy as a whole behave in a Keynesian fashion.

Over time, new Keynesian ideas combined with actual experience have reduced the practical influence of the rational expectations concept. Nonetheless, the idea of rational expectations served as a useful caution for macroeconomists who had become excessively optimistic about their ability to manage the economy.

Real Business Cycles

In Chapter 9 we introduced the concept of *total factor productivity,* the amount of output that can be generated with a given level of factor inputs. Total factor productivity grows over time, but that growth isn't smooth. In the 1980s a number of economists argued that slowdowns in productivity growth, which they attributed to pauses in technological progress, are the main cause of recessions. **Real business cycle theory** claims that fluctuations in the rate of growth of total factor productivity cause the business cycle.

Believing that the aggregate supply curve is vertical, real business cycle theorists attribute the source of business cycles to shifts of the aggregate supply curve. A recession occurs because technology regresses, leading to a slowdown in productivity growth which shifts the aggregate supply curve leftward. A recovery occurs because technology advances, leading to a pickup in productivity growth which shifts the aggregate supply curve rightward. In the early days of real business cycle theory, the theory's proponents denied that changes in aggregate demand—and, likewise, macroeconomic policy activism—had any effect on aggregate output.

This theory was strongly influential, reflected by the fact that two of the founders of real business cycle theory, Finn Kydland of Carnegie Mellon University and Edward Prescott of the Federal Reserve Bank of Minneapolis, won the 2004 Nobel Prize in economics. The current status of real business cycle theory, however, is similar to that of rational expectations. It is widely recognized for making a valuable contribution to our understanding of the economy, and for cautioning against an overemphasis on aggregate demand.

But many of the real business cycle theorists themselves now acknowledge that the actual economic data indicate that their models need an upward-sloping aggregate supply curve—and that this gives aggregate demand a potential role in determining aggregate output.

According to the **rational expectations model** of the economy, expected changes in monetary policy have no effect on unemployment and output and only affect the price level.

According to **new Keynesian economics,** market imperfections can lead to price stickiness for the economy as a whole.

Real business cycle theory claims that fluctuations in the rate of growth of total factor productivity cause the business cycle.

During the 1970s a group of economic writers began propounding what came to be known as *supply-side economics*. Proponents of this view believed that reducing tax rates, and so increasing the incentives to work and invest, would have a powerful positive effect on the growth rate of potential output. The supply-siders urged the government to cut taxes without worrying about matching spending cuts: economic growth, they argued, would offset any negative effects from budget deficits.

Some supply-siders even argued that a cut in tax *rates* would have such a miraculous effect on economic growth that tax *revenues*—the total amount taxpayers pay to the government—would actually rise. That is, some supply-siders argued that the United States was on the wrong side of the *Laffer curve,* a hypothetical relationship between tax rates and total tax revenue that slopes upward at low tax rates

but turns downward when tax rates are very high. Supply-side economics became popular with politicians, and in 1980 Ronald Reagan made supply-side economics the basis of his presidential campaign.

Because supply-side economics emphasizes supply rather than demand, and because the supply-siders are harshly critical of Keynesian economics, it would appear that it belongs in our discussion of new classical macroeconomics. But, in fact, supply-side economics is generally dismissed by economic researchers.

The main reason for this dismissal is lack of supporting evidence. Almost all economists agree that tax cuts increase incentives to work and invest. But attempts to estimate these incentive effects indicate that at current U.S. tax levels, the positive incentive effects aren't nearly strong enough to support

the strong claims made by supply-siders. In particular, the supply-side doctrine implies that large tax cuts, such as the Reagan tax cuts of the early 1980s, should sharply raise potential output, while tax hikes, like the Clinton tax hikes of 1993, should slow potential growth. Yet estimates by the Congressional Budget Office and others showed no sign of either.

Years later, in 2012, the state of Kansas provided the best evidence so far against the usefulness of supply-side economics. That year, Kansas passed large cuts in state taxes. Yet its economy tanked, with economic growth and job creation falling far below the national average, and its state deficit skyrocketed. In 2017, facing a state financial crisis and voters angry over cuts to state services, Kansas ended its experiment in supply-side economics and raised taxes.

ECONOMICS >> *in Action*
The 1970s in Reverse

When economists talk about the natural rate hypothesis, they usually frame it in terms of what happens if the government tries to keep unemployment low. The hypothesis says that sustained low unemployment will lead to ever-rising inflation. That is why most economists took the experience of stagflation in the 1970s as strong evidence that the natural rate hypothesis was right. However, the same logic says that sustained *high* unemployment should lead to ever-*falling* inflation, and eventually to accelerating *deflation.* So the experience of the Great Recession and aftermath, with unemployment remaining very high for years, offered a test of this prediction.

As it turned out, the prediction wasn't very successful. Inflation in the United States has generally been somewhat lower since the Great Recession than it was before, but the United States never entered a period of sustained or accelerating deflation. By 2014, prices were falling in some European countries with very high unemployment, but there was no sign of accelerating deflation.

The failure of deflation to materialize didn't come as a complete surprise, since some economists had long argued that the natural rate hypothesis breaks down at low inflation. However, that view became much more widespread after 2008 than it had been before—and it has an important implication. If high unemployment doesn't lead to ever-falling inflation, government policies to reduce unemployment may be effective even in the long run, as long as the unemployment target isn't too low. That is, an old-fashioned Keynesian view of macroeconomic policy, which says that it can permanently reduce unemployment even in the long run, may be right after all.

In that sense the era since the Great Recession was the 1970s in reverse, and Keynesian views gained strength in the light of experience.

1. In late 2008, as it became clear that the United States was experiencing a recession, the Fed reduced its target for the federal funds rate to near zero, as part of a larger aggressively expansionary monetary policy stance (including what the Fed called *quantitative easing*). Most observers agreed that the Fed's aggressive monetary expansion helped reduce the length and severity of the Great Recession.
   a. What would rational expectations theorists say about this conclusion?
   b. What would real business cycle theorists say?

The Great Moderation Consensus

The 1970s and the first half of the 1980s were a stormy period for the U.S. economy (and for other major economies, too). There was a severe recession in 1974–1975, then two back-to-back recessions in 1979–1982 that sent the unemployment rate to almost 11%. At the same time, the inflation rate soared into double digits—and then plunged. As we have seen, these events left a strong mark on macroeconomic thought.

After about 1985, however, the economy settled down. The recession of 1990–1991 was much milder than the 1974–1975 recession or the double-dip slump from 1979 to 1982, and the inflation rate generally stayed below 4%. The period of relative calm in the economy from 1985 to 2007 came to be known as the **Great Moderation.** And the calmness of the economy was to a large extent marked by a similar calm in macroeconomic policy discussion. In fact, it seemed that a broad consensus had emerged about several key macroeconomic issues.

The Great Moderation was, unfortunately, followed by the Great Recession, the severe and persistent slump that followed the 2008 financial crisis. We'll soon talk about the policy disputes caused by the Great Recession. But first, let's examine the apparent consensus that emerged during the Great Moderation, which we call the **Great Moderation consensus.** It combines a belief in monetary policy as the main tool of stabilization, with skepticism toward the use of fiscal policy, and an acknowledgement of the policy constraints imposed by the natural rate of unemployment and the political business cycle.

To understand where the Great Moderation consensus came from and what still remains in dispute, we'll look at how macroeconomists from the various schools have answered the five key questions about macroeconomic policy over the decades. Their answers are summarized in upcoming Table 17-1. Notice that classical and new classical macroeconomics said no to all five questions, basically because they didn't think macroeconomic policy could accomplish very much. But let's examine the questions one by one.

1. Is Expansionary Monetary Policy Helpful in Fighting Recessions?
Most macroeconomists now agree that monetary policy can be used to shift the aggregate demand curve and reduce economic instability. The classical view that changes in the money supply affect only aggregate prices, not aggregate output, has few supporters today. The view of early Keynesian economists—that changes in the money supply have little effect—has equally few supporters. Now it is generally agreed that monetary policy is ineffective only in the case of a liquidity trap.

2. Is Expansionary Fiscal Policy Effective in Fighting Recessions?
Most macroeconomists now agree that fiscal policy, like monetary policy, can shift the aggregate demand curve. Most macroeconomists also agree that the government should not seek to balance the budget regardless of the state of the economy:

The **Great Moderation** is the period from 1985 to 2007 when the U.S. economy experienced relatively small fluctuations and low inflation.

The **Great Moderation consensus** combines a belief in monetary policy as the main tool of stabilization, with skepticism toward the use of fiscal policy, and an acknowledgement of the policy constraints imposed by the natural rate of unemployment and the political business cycle.

they agree that the role of the budget as an automatic stabilizer helps keep the economy on an even keel.

3. Can Monetary and/or Fiscal Policy Reduce Unemployment in the Long Run? Almost all macroeconomists now accept the natural rate hypothesis, which leads them to accept sharp limits to what monetary and fiscal policy can accomplish. Effective monetary and fiscal policy, most macroeconomists believe, can limit the size of fluctuations of the actual unemployment rate around the natural rate, but they can't be used to keep unemployment below the natural rate.

4. Should Fiscal Policy Be Used in a Discretionary Way? During the Great Moderation many, but not all, macroeconomists came to believe that *discretionary fiscal policy* was usually counterproductive: the lags in adjusting fiscal policy mean that policies intended to fight a slump often intensify a boom. As a result, the macroeconomic consensus gave monetary policy the lead role in economic stabilization.

5. Should Monetary Policy Be Used in a Discretionary Way? The Great Moderation consensus rejected simple monetarism. Given large fluctuations in the velocity of money, it was clear that simply stabilizing the money supply wasn't enough to stabilize the economy. There was, however, some dispute about how central banks should conduct policy. Some macroeconomists argued for explicit rules—usually some version of the *Taylor rule* described in Chapter 15—that the central bank should follow at all times. Others argued for more discretion, for example allowing central banks to be aggressive about interest rate cuts when they had reason to believe a recession was looming. This was a technical debate, since both sides shared the same general view about how the economy worked. In any case, the debate was largely overtaken by events that followed the 2008 financial crisis.

‖ Modern Macroeconomics After the Great Recession

The Great Recession and its aftermath marked the end of the Great Moderation, and also the end of any sense that macroeconomists had entered an era of agreement over key policy questions. Once again, there were sharp disputes over appropriate monetary and fiscal policies. The main policy camps in the post–Great Recession era have come to be known as the *secular stagnationists* and the *inflation bears*. Their differences closely align with the differences between the Keynesians and new Keynesians on one side, and the classical and new classical on the other (as you can see in Table 17-1). A third view, the *theory of expansionary austerity*, also gained popularity in Europe, but was not considered a full-fledged policy camp. We examine these viewpoints next.

The Economic Environment Post Recession

As we know, expansionary monetary policy loses traction when the economy is in a liquidity trap (when interest rates are already close to zero). Macroeconomists knew this before the Great Recession, but they believed it wouldn't pose much of a problem. One influential Federal Reserve study concluded that as long as the inflation target was set at 2%, episodes in which interest rates hit zero would be rare—occurring about once every 20 years—and short-lived, lasting a year or less.

They were, however, much too optimistic. The U.S. economy entered a liquidity trap in 2008, and didn't begin to emerge until 2015. Europe was still in the trap in 2017, and so was Japan, which entered a liquidity trap in the mid-1990s. By historical standards, monetary policy looked extremely expansionary in all major economies. Yet rising inflation, the usual side effect of excessively expansionary monetary policy, was nowhere to be seen. In fact, almost all major central banks

TABLE 17-1 Five Key Questions About Macroeconomic Policy

	Classical and new classical	Keynesian and new Keynesian	Monetarism	Great Moderation consensus	Post–Great Recession era	
					Inflation bears	Secular stagnationists
1. Is expansionary monetary policy helpful in fighting recessions?	No	Not very	Yes	Yes, except in special circumstances	No	Not very
2. Is expansionary fiscal policy effective in fighting recessions?	No	Yes	No	Yes	No	Yes
3. Can monetary and/or fiscal policy reduce unemployment in the long run?	No	Yes	No	No	No	Yes
4. Should fiscal policy be used in a discretionary way?	No	Yes	No	No, except possibly in special circumstances	No	Yes
5. Should monetary policy be used in a discretionary way?	No	Yes	No	Disputed	No	Yes

kept undershooting their inflation targets; that is, they tried, but kept failing to get inflation up (generally to 2%). It was clear that limits on the ability of central banks to cut interest rates posed a much bigger problem than the Great Moderation consensus had imagined.

In response to this persistent liquidity trap, some influential economists argued that inadequate demand had become the new normal. Invoking a concept from the 1930s, they suggested that underlying factors such as declining population growth and, perhaps, a slowdown in technological progress had put the world's major economies in or on the edge of **secular stagnation,** a state in which the interest rate that is needed to achieve full employment is consistently below zero. (And as we learned in Chapter 15, it is very difficult to push interest rates consistently below zero.) Proponents of this view, the secular stagnationists, advocated an active fiscal policy and unconventional monetary policy to fight the Great Recession, aligning them with the Keynesian and new Keynesian viewpoints.

Whether or not one accepts the secular stagnation view, the persistence of the liquidity trap undermined a key pillar of the Great Moderation consensus, the view that monetary policy could and should do the job of stabilizing the economy. This was true even in the United States, which had returned more or less to full employment by 2016, but with interest rates so low that there was very little room to cut rates if recession should strike again.

The big question then became, how should policy makers behave in a world in which protracted periods of high unemployment seem likely, and interest rate cuts aren't an adequate response? Two issues in particular led to fierce debates.

1. Should fiscal policy be expansionary, to make up for the ineffectiveness of monetary policy, or should governments adopt fiscal austerity policies—cutting spending and raising taxes—to reassure investors about their solvency?

2. Should central banks unable to cut interest rates any further try to boost economies with unconventional policies such as buying risky assets?

Stimulus versus Austerity

In 2009 a number of governments, including that of the United States, responded to the Great Recession with expansionary fiscal policy, or **fiscal stimulus,** generally taking the form of a mix of temporary spending measures and temporary tax cuts. From the start, however, these efforts were highly controversial. There were arguments for and against, and a number of nations reversed course after 2010.

Secular stagnation occurs when the interest rate that is needed to achieve full employment is consistently below zero.

Fiscal stimulus is expansionary fiscal policy that takes the form of temporary spending measures and temporary tax cuts.

According to the **theory of expansionary austerity,** fiscal austerity will lead to an increase in output and employment by raising private-sector confidence.

Supporters of fiscal stimulus offered three main arguments for breaking with the normal presumption against discretionary fiscal policy and argued that:

1. Discretionary fiscal expansion was needed because the usual tool for stabilizing the economy, monetary policy, could no longer be used with interest rates near zero.

2. One typical concern about expansionary fiscal policy—that deficit spending would drive up interest rates, crowding out private investment spending—was unlikely to be a problem in a depressed economy, because interest rates were close to zero and were likely to stay there as long as the economy was depressed.

3. Another concern about discretionary fiscal policy—that, due to lags, it would take a long time to get going—was less of an issue given the likelihood that the economy would be depressed for an extended period.

These arguments generally won the day in early 2009. However, opponents of fiscal stimulus raised two main objections:

1. Households and firms would see any rise in government spending as a sign that tax burdens were likely to rise in the future, leading to a fall in private spending that would undo any positive effect. (This is the *Ricardian equivalence* argument covered in Chapter 13.)

2. Spending programs might undermine investors' faith in the government's ability to repay its debts, leading to an increase in long-term interest rates despite loose monetary policy.

In fact, by 2010 a number of economists were arguing that the best way to boost the economy was actually to *cut* government spending. According to this view, the **theory of expansionary austerity,** fiscal austerity will increase private-sector confidence, leading to higher spending by households and businesses, and thereby increasing output and employment. This theory—that what ails depressed economies is a lack of private confidence caused by fiscal spending—was especially popular in Europe.

Why were Europeans especially attracted to arguments for fiscal austerity? The differences in the behavior of bond markets in Europe were one explanation, as illustrated in Figure 17-5, which shows interest rates on long-term government bonds in the United States and in two major European economies, Italy and

---

FIGURE 17-5 Comparing Long-Term Interest Rates, 2007–2017

Due to the persistently weak economy, U.S. interest rates remained low after the Great Recession, despite large budget deficits. Some European countries like Italy and Spain, however, saw sharply rising borrowing costs in the aftermath of the Greek fiscal crisis. Although their economies were also extremely weak, their borrowing costs shot up because investors feared that these countries would not repay their debts.

Data from: Federal Reserve Bank of St. Louis.

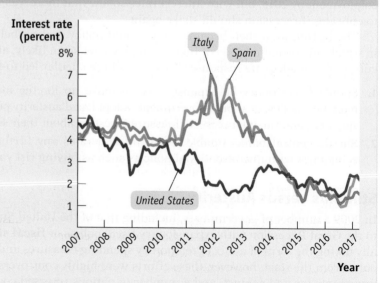

Spain. As you can see, interest rates on long-term U.S. government bonds have been consistently low by historical standards since the Great Recession; these low interest rates persisted despite big budget deficits from 2009 to 2012, indicating that individuals and institutions lending to the U.S. government weren't worried about being repaid. In the United States, borrowing costs remained low by historical standards despite large budget deficits in the first few years after the Great Recession. In Italy and Spain, however, borrowing costs shot up in 2010–2012.

In Europe, there were widespread doubts about whether governments would repay their debts in full. Europe's fiscal crisis began in Greece, which announced in late 2009 that it had been understating its deficits and debt, eventually forcing lenders to take substantial losses. Although Greece is a small economy—about the same size as the economy of Miami—its troubles led to a contagion with widespread loss of confidence as borrowing costs shot up in 2010–2012 in the much bigger economies of Italy and Spain. You can see this rate escalation in Figure 17-5.

In addition to the behavior of bond markets, soaring interest rates were probably the main motivation behind calls for fiscal austerity in Europe. Some experts argued that they presented a warning for the United States as well. For example, in June 2010, Alan Greenspan, then chairman of the Federal Reserve, published an article urging the United States to move rapidly to cut its budget deficit despite high unemployment, because otherwise it, too, might see interest rates shoot up.

Clearly, this did not happen and the United States never experienced a Greece-type crisis. By 2016—with the economy more or less back to full employment and the budget deficit back down to 3% of GDP—talk of a U.S. fiscal crisis had largely receded. What you may find more surprising is the sharp drop in Italian and Spanish borrowing costs after 2012. What restored investor confidence?

Many economists now argue that a major cause of the European debt crisis of 2010–2012 was that most European nations had abandoned their own independent currencies when adopting the euro. While there were a number of arguments in favor of the euro's creation, one unanticipated downside was that the loss of independent currrencies made governments more vulnerable to fiscal trouble.

Countries like the United States or Japan that borrow in their own currencies can't run out of cash, because they can always print money to pay the bills. Italy and Spain, which use the euro, cannot. This, some economists argued, put these countries at risk of suffering a *self-fulfilling debt crisis* in which investors panic about future repayment, causing a cash shortage that produces the very default they feared.

In 2012, the actions of the European Central Bank validated this line of reasoning—that without support, the eurozone countries could be pushed into a self-fulfilling debt crisis. That year the ECB declared that it would become the lender of last resort for the eurozone by directly buying the bonds of troubled governments in that area if necessary, thereby greatly reducing the fears of a liquidity crisis for these governments. As you can see in Figure 17-5, interest rates on Spanish and Italian debt fell sharply in 2012 after the announcement.

Meanwhile, the claim that fiscal austerity policies would actually boost economies by increasing confidence wasn't borne out in practice. Look back at Figure 13-7, which compares changes in the cyclically adjusted budget balance after 2009—one measure of fiscal austerity—with economic growth for a number of countries. From the figure, we estimate an average fiscal multiplier across Europe of 1.8, implying that $1 in fiscal contraction reduces GDP by $1.80. In addition to Greece, several nations in southern Europe pursued extreme austerity policies in the wake of the Greek crisis. Unsurprisingly, their economies shrank substantially.

While some economists still defend the theory of expansionary austerity, most now believe that experience since the Great Recession confirms a Keynesian view of the effects of fiscal policy.

According to the **inflation bear viewpoint,** expansionary monetary policy will cause inflation without raising output, even in a depressed economy.

The Fed's Unconventional Monetary Policy

A central bank that wants to increase aggregate demand normally does this by buying short-term government debt, pushing short-term interest rates down and causing spending to rise. By the fall of 2008, however, this conventional form of monetary policy had already reached its limit because the relevant interest rates were close to zero. In other words, policy makers were running up against the zero lower bound. The question then became whether there were other things the Federal Reserve and other central banks could do.

In 2008–2009 and again in the fall of 2010, the Fed pursued one such alternative, known as *quantitative easing,* which involved buying assets other than short-term government debt, notably long-term debt whose interest rate was still significantly above zero. This policy was controversial, facing criticism both from those who believed that the Fed was doing too much and from those who believed it was doing too little.

Those who believed that the Fed was doing too much were concerned about a surge in inflation. In November 2010 a number of the most prominent of Republican-leaning economists published an open letter to Ben Bernanke, then Fed chair, warning that the policy would "risk currency debasement and inflation." It's not hard to see why: quantitative easing led to a huge increase in the monetary base, and big increases in that base have historically often been associated with high inflation. Those adopting the **inflation bear viewpoint** believed that, despite the depressed state of the economy, expansionary monetary policy would cause inflation without raising output. Predicting that a bigger monetary base would simply result in higher prices, the inflation bears were closely aligned with classical and new classical macroeconomic viewpoints.

The Fed, however—drawing on the work of Keynesian-oriented economists including Bernanke himself—believed that the economy operated under a different set of rules when subject to liquidity-trap conditions, and that its policy posed little risk of a surge in prices. Events vindicated the Fed's position.

Figure 17-6 shows the U.S. monetary base and the consumer price index from 2007 to 2017, both expressed as indexes with December 2007 = 100. Fed policies led to a huge increase in the monetary base—almost 400 percent. But consumer prices barely budged. This was one of the clearest tests of rival economic views in history, and the inflation bear viewpoint was defeated hands down.

Yet, secular stagnationists argued that even if quantitative easing did not cause inflation, it was likely to be ineffective. They believed that long-term

---

FIGURE 17-6 Big Money, Small Inflation in the United States, 2007–2017
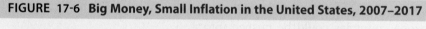

Quantitative easing led to a huge rise in the U.S. monetary base after the Great Recession, and some economists warned that this would in turn lead to high inflation. The Fed, however, argued that inflation risks were low, and, as you can see from the figure, was vindicated by events: the consumer price index stayed virtually flat, reflecting a very low inflation rate from 2008 onwards.

Data from: Federal Reserve Bank of St. Louis.

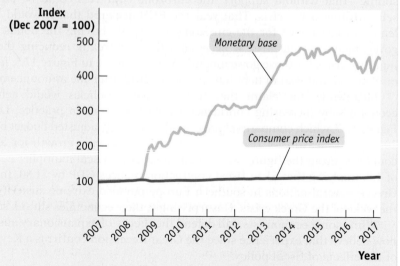

interest rates mainly reflected expectations about future short-term rates, and that even large purchases of long-term bonds by the Fed would have little impact. They called on the Fed for even more active policy and advocated for an official rise in the Fed's inflation target. Recall the distinction between the *nominal* interest rate, which is the number normally cited, and the *real* interest rate—the nominal rate minus expected inflation—which is what should matter for investment decisions. The secular stagnationists also argued that by promising to raise prices over, say, the next 10 years by an annual average rate of 3% or 4%, the Fed could push the real interest rate down even though the nominal rate was close to zero.

Such proposals, however, led to fierce disputes. The inflation bears pointed out that the Fed had fought hard to drive inflation expectations down and argued that changing course would undermine hard-won credibility. But the secular stagnationists argued that given the enormous economic and human damage being done by high unemployment, it was time for extraordinary measures, and fighting inflation should no longer be given first priority.

This dispute lost some of its intensity as the U.S. economy recovered: by 2016 unemployment was back to pre-crisis levels and inflation was near the Fed's target, making the need for new policy tools seem less urgent. But the argument hasn't gone away: secular stagnationists say that recovery took much longer than it should have, and warn that the Fed will be dangerously short of room to cut interest rates to avoid another liquidity trap when the next recession strikes.

"I'll pause for a moment so you can let this information sink in."

ECONOMICS >> *in Action*

Japan's Escape Attempt

After the 2008 financial crisis, most of the world's wealthy economies entered a new world of economic policy, with interest rates near zero and no room for conventional monetary expansion. Japan, however, was already there: Japanese short-term interest rates have been close to zero since the 1990s, and Japan has long suffered from slow deflation, which it never seemed able to end even during periods of economic recovery.

In 2012 Japan elected a new prime minister, Shinzo Abe, who decided to make a major effort to break out of deflation, an effort quickly dubbed *Abenomics*. Officially, Abenomics contained three "arrows":

1. Monetary expansion
2. Fiscal stimulus
3. *Structural reform* (which involved trying to remove rules and regulations that might be inhibiting Japanese growth)

Despite the limited success of Abenomics at home, Prime Minister Shinzo Abe would like to see his economic policies expanded to other nations to address risks facing the world economy.

In its first few years, however, only the first arrow was evident in force: in particular, modest increases in public spending were offset by a significant tax increase, which was motivated by long-run budget concerns but arguably undermined the attempt to raise inflation.

On the monetary side, the Bank of Japan engaged in huge purchases of unconventional assets (such as exchange traded funds and Japanese bonds),

>> Quick Review

• The **Great Moderation,** the period of economic calm from 1985 to 2007, produced the **Great Moderation consensus:** monetary policy should be the main stabilization tool, with an independent central bank to avoid the political business cycle; fiscal policy reserved for exceptional circumstances such as a liquidity trap; and limitations on policy activism imposed by the natural rate of unemployment. It broke down as monetary policy lost its effectiveness in the liquidity-trap conditions of the Great Recession and policy views divided into two camps.

• Believers in **secular stagnation** claimed that declining population growth and slower technological progress led to a state of persistent economic weakness in which the interest rate must remain consistently below zero to achieve full employment. They argued for expansionary fiscal policy, unconventional monetary policy, and a higher inflation target, aligning themselves with the Keynesians and new Keynesians.

• **Inflation bears** claimed that expansionary fiscal policy causes inflation in a depressed economy. They argued that the Fed's unconventional monetary policy would generate inflation without raising output, aligning themselves with the classical and new classical views.

• According to the **theory of expansionary austerity,** popular in Europe, lack of private-sector confidence that government debt would be repaid was the source of the economy's problems. Fiscal austerity caused substantial shrinkage of many European economies, dealing the theory a significant blow.

• Arguments over monetary policy faded as the U.S. economy recovered and inflation stayed low, disproving the inflation bear viewpoint. But they have not disappeared, as secular stagnationists claim that the Fed needs to raise its inflation target to avoid a liquidity trap when the next recession strikes.

and also repeatedly declared its determination to keep pursuing such policies until inflation reached 2%. Financial markets were initially impressed: stock prices rose dramatically, and the value of the yen against other currencies dropped, making Japanese manufacturing more competitive. The economy also began growing somewhat faster, and slow deflation gave way to slow inflation.

Nonetheless, after five years the results of Abenomics were widely viewed as disappointing. Most notably, inflation was still well below the 2% target. In response, Prime Minister Abe declared his intention to become even more aggressive, especially on the fiscal side. At the time of writing, however, Japan's experience seemed to show just how hard it can be to escape from persistent deflation.

Since Europe is still experiencing problems that somewhat resemble Japan's, and many economists worry that the United States might experience similar problems in the future, Japan's struggles also illustrate how far we've come from the confidence in economic management that prevailed during the Great Moderation.

>> Check Your Understanding 17-4
Solutions appear at back of book.

1. Why did the Great Recession lead to the decline of the Great Moderation consensus? What is the current state of consensus among most economists?

2. Why was there such a fierce debate over both the Fed's unconventional monetary policy and over the appropriate level of the Fed's inflation target?

SUMMARY

1. Classical macroeconomics asserted that monetary policy affected only the aggregate price level, not aggregate output, and that the short run was unimportant. By the 1930s, measurement of business cycles was a well-established subject, but there was no widely accepted theory of business cycles.

2. **Keynesian economics** attributed the business cycle to shifts of the aggregate demand curve, often the result of changes in business confidence. Keynesian economics also offered a rationale for **macroeconomic policy activism.**

3. In the decades that followed Keynes's work, economists came to agree that monetary policy as well as fiscal policy is effective under certain conditions. **Monetarism,** a doctrine that called for a **monetary policy rule** as opposed to **discretionary monetary policy** and that argued—based on a belief that the **velocity of money** was stable—that GDP would grow steadily if the money supply grew steadily, was influential for a time but was eventually rejected by many macroeconomists.

4. The **natural rate hypothesis** became almost universally accepted, limiting the role of macroeconomic policy to stabilizing the economy rather than seeking a permanently lower unemployment rate. Fears of a **political business cycle** led to a consensus that monetary policy should be insulated from politics.

5. **Rational expectations** claims that individuals and firms make decisions using all available information. According to the **rational expectations model** of the economy, only unexpected changes in monetary policy affect aggregate output and employment; expected changes merely alter the price level. **Real business cycle theory** claims that changes in the rate of growth of total factor productivity are the main cause of business cycles. Both of these versions of **new classical macroeconomics** received wide attention and respect, but policy makers and many economists haven't accepted the conclusion that monetary and fiscal policy are ineffective in changing aggregate output.

6. **New Keynesian economics** argues that market imperfections can lead to price stickiness, so that changes in aggregate demand have effects on aggregate output after all.

7. The **Great Moderation** from 1985 to 2007 generated the **Great Moderation consensus:** belief in monetary policy as the main tool of stabilization; skepticism toward use of fiscal policy, except possibly in exceptional circumstances such as a liquidity trap; and acknowledgement of the policy constraints imposed by the natural rate of unemployment and the political business cycle. But it broke down in the wake of the Great Recession as monetary policy lost its effectiveness under liquidity-trap conditions. Economists then largely divided into two camps: believers in **secular stagnation** and advocates of the **inflation bear viewpoint.**

8. *Secular stagnationists* believed that declining population growth and a slowdown in technological factors led to a state of persistent economic weakness, and that full employment could only be reached by pushing the interest rate consistently below zero. They advocated expansionary fiscal policy and unconventional monetary policy, as well as a higher inflation target, thus aligning themselves with Keynesian and new Keynesian viewpoints.

9. Adherents of the *inflation bear viewpoint* opposed the Fed's unconventional monetary policy, arguing that it would harm the economy by sparking inflation without raising output. They are aligned with the classical and new classical viewpoints because of their belief that expansionary monetary policy will cause inflation, even in a depressed economy.

10. In Europe, the **theory of expansionary austerity** became popular. Believing that what ailed the economy was a lack of private-sector confidence due to concern that government debts would not be repaid, policy makers cut government spending. The theory was dealt a significant blow when countries that adopted fiscal austerity saw their economies shrink substantially.

11. Concerns over crowding out and time lags were irrelevant given the length and severity of the Great Recession in the United States. Active fiscal policy was revived given the ineffectiveness of monetary policy in the liquidity-trap environment. Most economists returned to a Keynesian view on fiscal policy and low inflation disproved the inflation bear viewpoint. Disputes over monetary policy have not disappeared, although they diminished in intensity as the economy recovered. Secular stagnationists claim that unless the Fed raises its inflation target, it will have insufficient room to cut interest rates to avoid another liquidity trap when the next recession strikes.

KEY TERMS

Keynesian economics, p. 508
Macroeconomic policy activism, p. 509
Monetarism, p. 512
Discretionary monetary policy, p. 512
Monetary policy rule, p. 512
Velocity of money, p. 513
Natural rate hypothesis, p. 514

Political business cycle, p. 515
New classical macroeconomics, p. 516
Rational expectations, p. 516
Rational expectations model, p. 517
New Keynesian economics, p. 517
Real business cycle theory, p. 517

Great Moderation, p. 519
Great Moderation consensus, p. 519
Secular stagnation, p. 521
Fiscal stimulus, p. 521
Theory of expansionary austerity, p. 522
Inflation bear viewpoint, p. 524

PROBLEMS

interactive activity

1. Since the crash of its stock market in 1989, the Japanese economy has seen little economic growth and some deflation. The accompanying table from the Organization for Economic Cooperation and Development (OECD) shows some key macroeconomic data for Japan for 1991 (a "normal" year) and 1995–2003.

   a. From the data, determine the type of policies Japan's policy makers undertook at that time to promote growth.

   b. We can safely consider a short-term interest rate that is less than 0.1% to effectively be a 0% interest rate. What is this situation called? What does it imply about the effectiveness of monetary policy? Of fiscal policy?

Year	Real GDP annual growth rate	Short-term interest rate	Government debt (percent of GDP)	Government budget deficit (percent of GDP)
1991	3.4%	7.38%	64.8%	−1.81%
1995	1.9	1.23	87.1	4.71
1996	3.4	0.59	93.9	5.07
1997	1.9	0.60	100.3	3.79
1998	−1.1	0.72	112.2	5.51
1999	0.1	0.25	125.7	7.23
2000	2.8	0.25	134.1	7.48
2001	0.4	0.12	142.3	6.13
2002	−0.3	0.06	149.3	7.88
2003	2.5	0.04	157.5	7.67

2. The National Bureau of Economic Research (NBER) maintains the official chronology of past U.S. business cycles. Go to its website at www.nber.org/cycles/cyclesmain.html to answer the following questions.

   a. How many business cycles have occurred since the end of World War II in 1945?

   b. What was the average duration of a business cycle when measured from the end of one expansion (its peak) to the end of the next? That is, what was the average duration of a business cycle in the period from 1945 to 2009?

   c. When was the last announcement by the NBER's Business Cycle Dating Committee, and what was it?

3. The fall of its military rival, the Soviet Union, in 1989 allowed the United States to significantly reduce its defense spending in subsequent years. Using the data in the following table from the Economic Report of the President, replicate Figure 17-2 for the 1990–2000 period. Given the strong economic growth in the United States during the late 1990s, why would a Keynesian see the reduction in defense spending during the 1990s as a good thing?

Year	Budget deficit (percent of GDP)	Unemployment rate
1990	3.9%	5.6%
1991	4.5	6.8
1992	4.7	7.5
1993	3.9	6.9
1994	2.9	6.1
1995	2.2	5.6
1996	1.4	5.4
1997	0.3	4.9
1998	−0.8	4.5
1999	−1.4	4.2
2000	−2.4	4.0

4. In the modern world, central banks are free to increase or reduce the money supply as they see fit. However, some people harken back to the "good old days" of the gold standard. Under the gold standard, the money supply could expand only when the amount of available gold increased.

a. Under the gold standard, if the velocity of money were stable when the economy was expanding, what would have had to happen to keep prices stable?

b. Why would modern macroeconomists consider the gold standard a bad idea?

5. The chapter notes that Kenneth Rogoff proclaimed Richard Nixon "the all-time hero of political business cycles." Using the following table of data from the Economic Report of the President, explain why Nixon may have earned that title. (*Note:* Nixon entered office in January 1969 and was reelected in November 1972. He resigned in August 1974.)

Year	Government receipts (billions of dollars)	Government spending (billions of dollars)	Government budget balance (billions of dollars)	M1 growth	M2 growth	3-month Treasury bill rate
1969	$186.9	$183.6	$3.2	3.3%	3.7%	6.68%
1970	192.8	195.6	−2.8	5.1	6.6	6.46
1971	187.1	210.2	−23.0	6.5	13.4	4.35
1972	207.3	230.7	−23.4	9.2	13.0	4.07
1973	230.8	245.7	−14.9	5.5	6.6	7.04

6. The economy of Albernia is facing a recessionary gap, and the leader of that nation calls together its best economists representing the classical, Keynesian, monetarist, real business cycle, Great Moderation consensus, expansionary austerity, and secular stagnationist views of the macroeconomy. Explain what policies each economist would recommend and why.

7. Which of the following policy recommendations are consistent with the classical, Keynesian, monetarist, and/or Great Moderation consensus, and, expansionary austerity, and secular stagnationist views of the macroeconomy?

a. Since the long-run growth of GDP is 2%, the money supply should grow at 2%.

b. Decrease government spending in order to decrease inflationary pressure.

c. Increase the money supply in order to alleviate a recessionary gap.

d. Always maintain a balanced budget.

e. Decrease the budget deficit as a percent of GDP when facing a recessionary gap.

f. Pursue large, expansionary fiscal policies during a liquidity trap.

g. Maintain a 3% to 4% inflation rate today, which is necessary to fight future recessions.

8. Using a graph like Figure 17-3, show how a monetarist can argue that a contractionary fiscal policy need not lead to a fall in real GDP given a fixed money supply. Explain.

9. Monetarists believed for a period of time that the velocity of money was stable within a country. However, with financial innovation, the velocity began shifting around erratically after 1980. As would be expected, the velocity of money is different across countries depending upon the sophistication of their financial systems—velocity of money tends to be higher in countries with developed financial systems. The following table provides money supply and GDP information in 2016 for six countries.

Country	National currency	M1 (billions in national currency)	Nominal GDP (billions in national currency)
Egypt	Egyptian pounds	540	1,838
South Korea	Korean won	734,412	1,466,788
Thailand	Thai baht	1,864	9,501
United States	U.S. dollars	3,327	16,397
Kenya	Kenyan pounds	1,309	4,050
India	Indian rupees	20,059	113,575

Data from: Central Bank of Egypt; Bank of Korea; Bank of Thailand; Federal Reserve Bank of St. Louis; Central Bank of Kenya; Reserve Bank of India.

a. Calculate the velocity of money for each of the countries. The following table shows GDP per capita for each of these countries in 2016 in U.S. dollars.

Country	Nominal GDP per capita (U.S. dollars)
Egypt	$3,685
South Korea	27,539
Thailand	5,899
United States	57,436
Kenya	1,516
India	1,723

Data from: IMF.

b. Rank the countries in descending order of per capita GDP and velocity of money. Do wealthy countries or poor countries tend to "turn over" their money more times per year? Would you expect wealthy countries to have more sophisticated financial systems?

10. In response to the Great Recession, the Federal Reserve took drastic and largely untested measures to stabilize both the financial system and the macroeconomy. These measures caused the monetary base to increase from approximately $850 billion to over $4 trillion. What would an economist from each of the following viewpoints—classical, Keynesian, monetarist, real business cycle, Great Moderation consensus, inflation bears, and secular stagnationists—predict about the effect of these policies, and why? Indicate whether each school would support the Fed's actions.

18

International Macroeconomics

SWITZERLAND DOESN'T WANT YOUR MONEY

PARKING YOUR MONEY in a Swiss bank is no way to get rich, given the low interest rates Swiss bankers offer. Since 2013, in fact, Swiss banks have paid negative interest on deposits, charging customers for the service of keeping their funds.

The Swiss National Bank undertook extraordinary actions to protect the Swiss economy from massive inflows of foreign money.

But for generations, Swiss bank accounts have been seen as a way to *stay* rich, a safe place to store your wealth. In the troubled years that followed the 2008 financial crisis, the Swiss reputation for safety became especially important. European investors, in particular, poured enormous sums of money into Swiss banks.

And the Swiss hated it. The inflow of foreign funds led to a surge in the value of the Swiss franc that wreaked havoc with Swiss exports.

At the beginning of 2008, one Swiss franc traded for about 0.6 euro. By mid-2011, the franc was trading for around 0.9 euro, a 50% appreciation. That meant that Swiss exporters, other things equal, had seen a 50% rise in their labor costs relative to competitors elsewhere in Europe. Thanks to its reputation for quality, Switzerland has been remarkably successful over the years at selling goods to the world

market, despite high labor costs. Nobody expects to get a bargain on Swiss watches or Swiss chocolate. But a 50% appreciation of the Swiss franc pushed Swiss exporters to the breaking point.

So what was to be done? Starting in early 2009, the Swiss National Bank, Switzerland's equivalent of the Federal Reserve, began selling Swiss francs on the foreign exchange market in an attempt to hold down its value. In return, the Swiss National Bank received other currencies, mainly dollars and euros, which it added to its reserves. We're talking about a *lot* of sales: over a period of 2½ years, the bank added $180 billion to its foreign exchange reserves, equal to a third of Switzerland's GDP—the equivalent for the United States of selling $5 trillion.

Yet even that wasn't enough to stop the Swiss franc's rise. In September 2011, as the franc seemed headed for a value of 1 euro or more, the Swiss National Bank announced that it would do whatever it took—that is, sell an unlimited amount of francs—to keep the franc below a maximum of 0.833 euro per franc. That announcement finally seemed to halt the franc's rise.

What the extraordinary efforts of the Swiss National Bank illustrated was the importance of a dimension of macroeconomics that we haven't emphasized so far—the fact that modern national economies trade large quantities of goods, services, and assets with the rest of the world. *International macroeconomics* is a branch of macroeconomics that deals with the relationships between national economies (it is sometimes referred to as *open-economy macroeconomics*). As the Swiss story illustrates, economic interactions with the rest of the world can have a profound impact on a domestic economy.

In this chapter we'll learn about some of the key issues in international macroeconomics: the determinants of a country's *balance of payments*, the factors affecting *exchange rates*, the different forms of *exchange rate policy* adopted by various countries, and the relationship between exchange rates and macroeconomic policy. ●

WHAT YOU WILL LEARN

- What are the **balance of payments accounts?**
- What determines international capital flows?
- What roles do the **foreign exchange market** and the **exchange rate** play?
- How do **real exchange rates** affect the **current account?**
- Why do countries choose different **exchange rate regimes,** such as **fixed exchange rates** and **floating exchange rates?**
- How should domestic macroeconomic policy be adjusted as a consequence of international economic considerations?

A country's **balance of payments accounts** are a summary of the country's transactions with other countries for a given year.

Capital Flows and the Balance of Payments

In 2016 people living in the United States sold trillions of dollars' worth of stuff to people living in other countries and bought trillions' of dollars worth of stuff in return. What kind of stuff? All kinds. Residents of the United States (including firms operating in the United States) sold airplanes, bonds, software licenses, wheat, and many other items to residents of other countries. U.S. residents bought cars, stocks, oil, and many other items from residents of other countries.

How can we keep track of these transactions? In Chapter 7 we learned that economists keep track of the domestic economy using the national income and product accounts. Economists keep track of international transactions using a different but related set of numbers, the *balance of payments accounts*.

Balance of Payments Accounts

A country's **balance of payments accounts** are a summary of the country's transactions with other countries for a given year.

To understand the basic idea behind the balance of payments accounts, let's consider a small-scale example: not a country, but a family farm. Let's say that we know the following about how last year went financially for the Costas, who own a small artichoke farm in California:

- They made $100,000 by selling artichokes.

- They spent $70,000 on running the farm, including purchases of new farm machinery, and another $40,000 buying food, paying utility bills, replacing their worn-out car, and so on.

- They received $500 in interest on their bank account but paid $10,000 in interest on their mortgage.

- They took out a new $25,000 loan to help pay for farm improvements but didn't use all the money immediately. So they put the remaining $5,500 in the bank.

TABLE 18-1 The Costas' Financial Year

	Sources of cash	Uses of cash	Net
Sales and purchases of goods and services	Artichoke sales: $100,000	Farm operation and living expenses: $110,000	−$10,000
Interest payments	Interest received on bank account: $500	Interest paid on mortgage: $10,000	−$9,500
Loans and deposits	Funds received from new loan: $25,000	Funds deposited in bank: $5,500	+$19,500
Total	$125,500	$125,500	$0

How could we summarize the Costas' transactions for the year? One way would be with a table like Table 18-1, which shows sources of cash coming in and uses of cash going out, characterized under a few broad headings. The first row of Table 18-1 shows sales and purchases of goods and services: sales of artichokes; purchases of groceries, heating oil, that new car, and so on. The second row shows interest payments: the interest the Costas received from their bank account and the interest they paid on their mortgage. The third row shows loans and deposits: cash coming in from a loan and cash deposited in the bank.

In each row we show the net inflow of cash from that type of transaction. So the net in the first row is −$10,000, because the Costas spent $10,000 more than they earned. The net in the second row is −$9,500, the difference between the interest the Costas received on their bank account and the interest they paid on the mortgage. The net in the third row is $19,500: the Costas brought in $25,000 with their new loan but put only $5,500 of that sum in the bank.

The last row shows the sum of cash coming in from all sources and the sum of all cash used. These sums are equal, by definition: every dollar has a source, and every dollar received gets used somewhere. (What if the Costas hid money under the mattress? Then that would be counted as another "use" of cash.)

A country's balance of payments accounts is a table that summarizes the country's transactions with the rest of the world for a given year in a manner very similar to the way we just summarized the Costas' financial year.

Table 18-2 shows a simplified version of the U.S. balance of payments accounts for 2016. Where the Costas family's accounts show sources and uses of cash, a country's balance of payments accounts show payments from foreigners—sources of cash for the United States as a whole—and payments to foreigners—uses of cash for the United States as a whole.

Row 1 of Table 18-2 shows payments that arise from U.S. sales to foreigners and U.S. purchases from foreigners of goods and services in 2016. For example, the number in the second column of row 1, $2,212 billion, incorporates items such as the value of U.S. wheat exports and the fees foreigners paid to U.S. consulting companies in 2016. The number in the third column of row 1, $2,713 billion, incorporates items such as the value of U.S. oil imports and the fees U.S. companies paid to Indian call centers—the people who often answer your 1-800 calls—in 2016.

Row 2 shows U.S. *factor income* in 2016—the income that foreigners paid to American residents

TABLE 18-2 The U.S. Balance of Payments in 2016 (billions of dollars)

		Payments from foreigners	Payments to foreigners	Net
1	Sales and purchases of goods and services	$2,212	$2,713	–$501
2	Factor income	802	621	181
3	Transfers	128	289	–161
	Current account (1 + 2 + 3)			–481
4	Asset sales and purchases (financial account)	759	353	406
	Financial account (4)			406
	Statistical discrepancy			–75

Data from: Bureau of Economic Analysis.

for the use of American-owned factors of production, as well as income paid by Americans to foreigners for the use of foreign-owned factors of production. Factor income mostly consists of investment income, such as interest paid by Americans on loans from overseas, profits of American-owned corporations that operate overseas, and the like. For example, the profits earned by Disneyland Paris, which is owned by the U.S.-based Walt Disney Company, are included in the $802 billion figure in the second column of row 2. The profits earned by the U.S. operations of Japanese auto companies are included in the $621 billion figure shown in the third column of row 2. Factor income also includes some labor income. For example, the wages of an American engineer who worked temporarily on a construction site in Dubai are counted in the $802 billion figure in the second column.

Row 3 shows *international transfers* for the U.S. in 2016—funds sent by American residents to residents of other countries and vice versa. The figure in the second column of row 3, $128 billion, includes payments sent home by skilled American workers who work abroad. The third column accounts for the major portion of international transfers. That figure, $289 billion, is composed mainly of remittances that immigrants who reside in the United States, such as the millions of Mexican-born workers employed in the United States, send to their families in their country of origin.

Row 4 of the table shows net payments accruing from sales and purchases of assets between American residents and foreigners in 2016. Such payments involve a wide variety of transactions, from Chinese companies purchasing U.S. firms to U.S. purchases of European stocks and bonds. The details of these transactions are complex, and if you add up all purchases the value is very large, which is why we focus only on the net value. Overall, according to official figures, and as you can see in the table, U.S. residents sold $406 billion more in assets than they purchased.

In laying out Table 18-2, we have separated rows 1, 2, and 3 into one group, to distinguish them from row 4, reflecting a fundamental difference in how these two groups of transactions affect the future. When a U.S. resident sells a good such as wheat to a foreigner, that's the end of the transaction. But a financial asset, such as a bond, is different: it is a promise to pay interest and principal in the future. So when a U.S. resident sells a bond to a foreigner, that sale creates a liability: the U.S. resident will have to pay interest and repay principal in the future. The balance of payments accounts distinguish between transactions that don't create liabilities and those that do.

A country's **balance of payments on current account,** or **current account,** is its balance of payments on goods and services plus net international transfer payments and factor income.

A country's **balance of payments on goods and services** is the difference between its exports and its imports during a given period.

The **merchandise trade balance,** or **trade balance,** is the difference between a country's exports and imports of goods.

A country's **balance of payments on financial account,** or simply its **financial account,** is the difference between its sales of assets to foreigners and its purchases of assets from foreigners for a given period.

Transactions that don't create liabilities are considered part of the **balance of payments on current account,** often referred to simply as the **current account:** the balance of payments on goods and services plus net international transfer payments and factor income. This corresponds to rows 1, 2, and 3 in Table 18-2. In practice, row 1 of the table, amounting to –$501 billion, corresponds to the most important part of the current account: the **balance of payments on goods and services,** the difference between the value of exports and the value of imports during a given period.

In economic news reports, you may see references to another measure, the **merchandise trade balance,** sometimes referred to as the trade balance for short. It is the difference between a country's exports and imports of goods alone—not including services. Economists sometimes focus on the merchandise trade balance, even though it's an incomplete measure, because data on international trade in services aren't as accurate as data on trade in physical goods, and they are also slower to arrive.

Transactions that involve the sale or purchase of assets, and therefore do create future liabilities, are considered part of the **balance of payments on financial account,** or the **financial account** for short, for a given period. This corresponds to row 4 in Table 18-2, which was $406 billion in 2016. (Until a few years ago, economists often referred to the financial account as the *capital account.* We'll use the modern term, but you may run across the older term.)

So how does it all add up? The rows shaded purple in Table 18-2 show the bottom lines: the overall U.S. current account and financial account for 2016. As you can see:

- The United States ran a *current account deficit:* the amount it paid to foreigners for goods, services, factors, and transfers was more than the amount it received.

- Simultaneously, it ran a *financial account surplus:* the value of the assets it sold to foreigners was more than the value of the assets it bought from foreigners.

- In the official data, the U.S. current account deficit and financial account surplus didn't offset each other: the financial account surplus in 2016 was $75 billion smaller than the current account deficit (shown in the final row of the table). But that was just a statistical error, reflecting the imperfection of official data. (The discrepancy may have reflected foreign purchases of U.S. assets that official data somehow missed.)

FOR INQUIRING MINDS   **GDP, GNP, and the Current Account**

When we discussed national income accounting in Chapter 7, we derived the basic equation relating GDP to the components of spending:

$$Y = C + I + G + X - IM$$

where X and IM are exports and imports, respectively, of goods and services. But as we've learned, the balance of payments on goods and services is only one component of the current account balance. Why doesn't the national income equation use the current account as a whole?

The answer is that gross domestic product, Y, is the value of goods and services produced domestically. So it doesn't include international factor income and international transfers, two sources of income that are included in the calculation of the current account balance. The profits of Ford Motors U.K. aren't included in the

U.S. GDP, and the funds Latin American immigrants send home to their families aren't subtracted from GDP.

Shouldn't we have a broader measure that does include these sources of income? Actually, gross *national* product—GNP—does include international factor income. Estimates of U.S. GNP differ slightly from estimates of GDP because GNP adds in items such as the earnings of U.S. companies abroad and subtracts items such as the interest payments on bonds owned by residents of China and Japan. There isn't, however, any regularly calculated measure that includes transfer payments.

Why do economists use GDP rather than a broader measure? Two reasons. First, the original purpose of the national accounts was to track production rather than income. Second, data on

international factor income and transfer payments are generally considered somewhat unreliable. So if you're trying to keep track of movements in the economy, it makes sense to focus on GDP, because it doesn't include these unreliable data.

mikeledray/Shutterstock

The funds Latin American immigrants send abroad are included in GDP because they were earned for services performed in the United States.

In fact, it's a basic rule of balance of payments accounting that the current account and the financial account must sum to zero:

(18-1) Current account (CA) + Financial account (FA) = 0

or

$$CA = -FA$$

Why must Equation 18-1 be true? We already saw the fundamental explanation in Table 18-1, which showed the accounts of the Costas family: in total, the sources of cash must equal the uses of cash. The same applies to balance of payments accounts. Figure 18-1, a variant on the circular-flow diagram we have found useful in discussing domestic macroeconomics, may help you visualize how this adding up works. Instead of showing the flow of money *within* a national economy, Figure 18-1 shows the flow of money *between* national economies.

Money flows into the United States from the rest of the world as payment for U.S. exports of goods and services, as payment for the use of U.S.-owned factors of production, and as transfer payments. These flows, indicated by the lower blue arrow, are the positive components of the U.S. current account. Money also flows into the United States from foreigners who purchase U.S. assets. They make up the positive component of the U.S. financial account and are shown by the lower green arrow.

At the same time, money flows from the United States to the rest of the world as payment for U.S. imports of goods and services, as payment for the use of foreign-owned factors of production, and as transfer payments. These flows, indicated by the upper blue arrow, are the negative components of the U.S. current account. Money also flows from the United States to purchase foreign assets. They make up the negative component of the U.S. financial account and are shown by the upper green arrow.

As in all circular-flow diagrams, the flow into a box and the flow out of a box are equal. This means that the sum of the blue and green arrows going into the United States (at the bottom of the diagram) is equal to the sum of the blue and green arrows going out of the United States (at the top of the diagram). That is,

(18-2) Positive current account entries + Positive financial account entries =
      (lower blue arrow)   (lower green arrow)

   Negative current account entries + Negative financial account entries
      (upper blue arrow)   (upper green arrow)

FIGURE 18-1 The Balance of Payments

The blue arrows represent payments that are counted in the current account. The green arrows represent payments that are counted in the financial account. Because the total flow into the United States must equal the total flow out of the United States, the sum of the current account plus the financial account is zero.

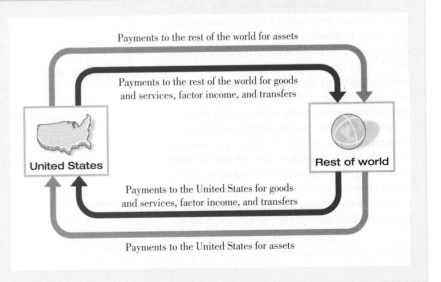

Equation 18-2 can be rearranged as follows:

(18-3) Positive current account entries – Negative current account entries +
Positive financial account entries – Negative financial account entries = 0

Equation 18-3 is equivalent to Equation 18-1: once we have summed up the positive and negative entries within each account, the current account plus the financial account is equal to zero.

But what determines the current account and the financial account?

Modeling the Financial Account

A country's financial account measures its net sales of assets to foreigners. There is, however, another way to think about the financial account: it's a measure of *capital inflows,* of foreign savings that are available to finance domestic investment spending.

What determines these capital inflows?

Part of the explanation will have to wait until later because some international capital flows are carried out by governments and central banks, which sometimes act very differently from private investors. But we can gain insight into the motivations for capital flows that are the result of private decisions by using the *loanable funds model* developed in Chapter 10 and, in particular, in Figures 10-7 and 10-8. In using this model to analyze the financial account, we make two important simplifications:

1. We assume that all international capital flows are in the form of loans. In reality, capital flows take many forms, including purchases of shares of stock in foreign companies and foreign real estate as well as *direct foreign investment,* in which companies build factories or acquire other productive assets abroad.

 GLOBAL COMPARISON **BIG SURPLUSES**

As we've seen, the United States generally runs a large deficit in its current account. In fact, America leads the world in its current account deficit; other countries run bigger deficits as a share of GDP, but they have much smaller economies, so the U.S. deficit is much bigger in absolute terms.

For the world as a whole, however, deficits on the part of some countries must be matched with surpluses on the part of other countries. So who are the surplus nations offsetting U.S. deficits, and what if anything do they have in common?

The accompanying figure shows the average current account surplus of the six countries that ran the largest surpluses over the period from 2007 to 2016. You may not be surprised to see China topping the list. For a time China had a deliberate policy of keeping its currency weak relative to other currencies. And Saudi Arabia, with its vast oil reserves, generates a current account surplus by exporting a lot of oil.

Germany, Japan, the Netherlands, and Switzerland run current account surpluses for more or less the same reasons: they are rich nations with high savings rates, giving them a lot of money to invest. They also have slow long-run growth, which reduces the opportunities for domestic investment. So much of their savings goes abroad, which means

that they run deficits on the financial account and surpluses on the current account.

The current account surpluses of Germany and the Netherlands have also grown thanks to the declining value of the euro. A lower euro has reduced the cost of their manufacturing goods on world markets, allowing them to export more.

Overall, the surplus countries are a diverse group. If your picture of the world is simply one of American deficits versus Chinese surpluses, you're missing a large part of the story.

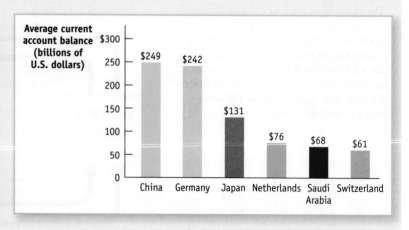

Data from: IMF World Economic Outlook, 2017.

2. We ignore the effects of expected changes in *exchange rates*, the relative values of different national currencies. We analyze the determination of exchange rates shortly.

Recall Figure 10-7 from our discussion of the global loanable funds market in Chapter 10. It shows a hypothetical world consisting of two countries, the United States and Britain, which would have different equilibrium interest rates—6% in the United States, 2% in Britain—in the absence of international capital flows. But this difference in interest rates will not persist if it is easy for British lenders to make their funds available to U.S. borrowers. In fact, if British lenders consider loans to Americans just as good as domestic loans, interest rates will fall in the United States and rise in Britain until they are the same in both countries, with the United States, in effect, importing loanable funds from Britain. This equalization of interest rates (at 4%) is shown in Figure 10-8.

However, given our two simplifying assumptions, the loanable funds the United States imports from Britain (which are Britain's excess savings or capital outflows), are precisely America's balance of payments on the financial account! So the financial account is determined by the supply and demand for loanable funds: capital moves from places where it would be cheap in the absence of international capital flows to places where it would be expensive in the absence of such flows.

Underlying Determinants of International Capital Flows

While the loanable funds model tells us the direction of capital flows—from countries in which capital is cheap to countries in which capital is expensive—it doesn't explain why. That is, why is capital cheap in one country but expensive in another?

International differences in investment opportunities generate international differences in the demand for capital. A country with a rapidly growing economy, other things equal, will offer more investment opportunities and a higher return to investors than a country with a slowly growing economy. So a country with a rapidly growing economy will typically have a higher demand for capital than the country with a slowly growing economy. As a result, capital tends to flow from slowly growing to rapidly growing economies.

International differences in the supply of funds reflect differences in savings across countries. These may be the result of differences in private savings rates, which vary among countries. They may also reflect differences in savings by governments. In particular, government budget deficits, which reduce overall national savings, can lead to capital inflows.

Now we can put together the demand for capital generated by investment opportunities within a country, with the supply for capital generated by savings within a country, to explain differences in interest rates across countries. Other things equal, countries with a high demand for capital and/or a low supply of capital will have higher interest rates. As a result, they will be the recipients of capital inflows.

Conversely, other things equal, countries with a low demand for funds and/or a high supply of funds will have lower interest rates. As a result, they will be the sources of capital outflows. The classic example of international capital flows—the flow of capital from Britain to the United States and other New World economies from 1870 to 1914—is described in the upcoming Economics in Action. During that era, the United States was rapidly industrializing and had a high demand for capital. But Britain, which already industrialized, had a slowly growing economy with a large amount of accumulated savings.

Two-Way Capital Flows

In fact, it is the direction of *net* capital flows—the excess of inflows into a country over outflows, or vice versa—that is explained by the loanable funds model. The direction of *net* flows, other things equal, is determined by differences in interest rates between countries. However, *gross* flows take place in both directions: for

Many American companies have opened plants in China to access the growing Chinese market and take advantage of low labor costs.

example, the United States both sells assets to foreigners and buys assets from foreigners. Why does capital move in both directions?

The answer to this question is that in the real world, as opposed to the simple model just described, there are other motives for international capital flows besides seeking a higher rate of interest.

Individual investors often seek to diversify against risk by buying stocks in several countries. Stocks in Europe may do well when stocks in the United States do badly, or vice versa, so investors in Europe try to reduce their risk by buying some U.S. stocks, as U.S. investors try to reduce their risk by buying some European stocks. The result is capital flows in both directions.

Meanwhile, corporations often engage in international investment as part of their business strategy—for example, auto companies may find that they can compete better in an overseas market if they assemble some of their cars in that location. Such business investments can also lead to two-way capital flows, as, say, European car makers build plants in the United States even as U.S. computer companies open facilities in Europe.

Finally, some countries, including the United States, are international banking centers: people from all over the world put money in U.S. financial institutions, which then invest many of those funds overseas.

The result of these two-way flows is that modern economies are typically both debtors (countries that owe money to the rest of the world) and creditors (countries to which the rest of the world owes money). Due to years of both capital inflows and outflows, at the end of 2016, the United States had accumulated foreign assets worth $23.9 trillion, and foreigners had accumulated assets in the United States worth $32.0 trillion.

ECONOMICS >> in Action
The Golden Age of Capital Flows

Technology, it's often said, shrinks the world. Jet planes have put most of the world's cities within a few hours of one another; while fiber-optic cables and satellites transmit information instantly around the globe. So you might think that international capital flows must now be larger than ever.

But if international capital flows are measured as a share of world savings and investment, that belief turns out not to be true. The golden age of capital flows actually preceded World War I—from 1870 to 1914.

These capital flows went mainly from European countries, especially Britain, to what were then known as *zones of recent settlement*, countries that were attracting large numbers of European immigrants. Among the big recipients of capital inflows were Australia, Argentina, Canada, and the United States.

The large capital flows reflected differences in investment opportunities. Britain, a mature industrial economy with limited natural resources and a slowly growing population, offered relatively limited opportunities for new investment. The zones of recent settlement, with rapidly growing populations and abundant natural resources, offered investors a higher return and attracted capital inflows. Estimates suggest that over this period Britain sent about 40% of its savings abroad, largely to finance railroads and other large projects. No country has matched that record in modern times.

Why can't we match the capital flows of our great-great-grandfathers? Economists aren't completely sure, but they have pointed to two causes: migration restrictions and political risks.

During the golden age of capital flows, capital movements were complementary to population movements: the big recipients of capital from Europe were also places to which large numbers of Europeans were moving. These large-scale population movements were possible before World War I because there were few legal restrictions on immigration. In today's world, by contrast, migration is limited by extensive legal barriers, as anyone considering a move to the United States or Europe can tell you. Although there are still important migration flows, such as the wave of refugees into Europe in recent years, overall they play a much smaller economic role than the flows of the late nineteenth and early twentieth century.

The other explanation for our inability to match the golden age of capital flows is political risk. Modern governments often limit foreign investment because they fear it will diminish their national autonomy. And due to political or security concerns, governments sometimes seize foreign property, a risk that deters investors from sending more than a relatively modest share of their wealth abroad. In the nineteenth century such actions were rare, partly because some major destinations of investment were still European colonies, partly because in those days governments had a habit of sending troops and gunboats to enforce the claims of their investors.

>> Check Your Understanding 18-1

Solutions appear at back of book.

1. Which of the balance of payments accounts do the following events affect?
   a. Boeing, a U.S.-based company, sells a newly built airplane to China.
   b. Chinese investors buy stock in Boeing from American residents.
   c. A Chinese company buys a used airplane from American Airlines and ships it to China.
   d. A Chinese investor who owns property in the United States buys a corporate jet, which he will keep in the United States so he can travel around America.
2. What effect do you think the collapse of the U.S. housing bubble in 2008, and the ensuing Great Recession, had on international capital flows into the United States?

>> Quick Review

- The **balance of payments accounts,** which track a country's international transactions, are composed of the **balance of payments on current account,** or the **current account,** plus the **balance of payments on financial account,** or the **financial account.** The most important component of the current account is the **balance of payments on goods and services,** which itself includes the **merchandise trade balance,** or the **trade balance.**

- Because the sources of payments must equal the uses of payments, the current account plus the financial account sum to zero.

- The direction of *net* capital flows—the excess of inflows over outflows, or vice versa—is determined by differences in interest rates. Interest rate differences across countries arise from the different types of investment opportunities available and variations in savings behavior.

- In the real world, countries experience two-way capital flows— *gross* flows of capital in and out— because factors other than interest rate differences affect investors' decisions.

The Role of the Exchange Rate

We've just seen how differences in the supply of loanable funds from savings and the demand for loanable funds for investment spending lead to international capital flows. We've also learned that a country's balance of payments on current account plus its balance of payments on financial account add to zero: a country that receives net capital inflows must run a matching current account deficit, and a country that generates net capital outflows must run a matching current account surplus.

The behavior of the financial account—reflecting inflows or outflows of capital—is best described by equilibrium in the global loanable funds market. At the same time, the balance of payments on goods and services, the main component of the current account, is determined by decisions in the international markets for goods and services.

So given that the financial account reflects the movement of capital and the current account reflects the movement of goods and services, what ensures that the balance of payments really does balance? That is, what ensures that the two accounts actually offset each other?

Not surprisingly, a price is what makes these two accounts balance. Specifically, that price is the *exchange rate,* which is determined in the *foreign exchange market.*

Currencies are traded in the **foreign exchange market.**

The prices at which currencies trade are known as **exchange rates.**

When a currency becomes more valuable in terms of other currencies, it **appreciates.**

When a currency becomes less valuable in terms of other currencies, it **depreciates.**

Understanding Exchange Rates

In general, goods, services, and assets produced in a country must be paid for in that country's currency. American products must be paid for in dollars; European products must be paid for in euros; Japanese products must be paid for in yen. Occasionally, sellers will accept payment in foreign currency, but they will then exchange that currency for domestic money.

International transactions, then, require a market—the **foreign exchange market**—in which currencies can be exchanged for each other. This market determines **exchange rates,** the prices at which currencies trade. (The foreign exchange market is, in fact, not located in any one geographic spot. Rather, it is a global electronic market that traders around the world use to buy and sell currencies.)

Table 18-3 shows exchange rates among the world's three most important currencies as of 3 P.M., EDT, on April 27, 2017. Each entry shows the price of the "row" currency in terms of the "column" currency. For example, at that time US$1 exchanged for €0.9198, so it took €0.9198 to buy US$1. Similarly, it took US$1.0872 to buy €1. These two numbers reflect the same rate of exchange between the euro and the U.S. dollar: 1/1.0872 = 0.9198.

There are two ways to write any given exchange rate. In this case, there were €0.9198 to US$1 and US$1.0872 to €1. Which is the correct way to write it? The answer is that there is no fixed rule. In most countries, people tend to express the exchange rate as the price of a dollar in domestic currency. However, this rule isn't universal, and the U.S. dollar–euro rate is commonly quoted both ways. The important thing is to be sure you know which one you are using, as explained in the accompanying Pitfalls.

When discussing movements in exchange rates, economists use specialized terms to avoid confusion. When a currency becomes more valuable in terms of other currencies, economists say that the currency **appreciates.** When a currency becomes less valuable in terms of other currencies, it **depreciates.** Suppose, for example, that the value of €1 went from $1 to $1.25, which means that the value of US$1 went from €1 to €0.80 (because 1/1.25 = 0.80). In this case, we would say that the euro appreciated and the U.S. dollar depreciated.

By the way, although *appreciate* and *depreciate* are the technical, more or less official terms for a rise or fall of a currency against other currencies, you will also often hear it said that an appreciating currency is getting "stronger," or a depreciating currency is getting "weaker." It's important to realize that these terms, while widely used, shouldn't be taken as value judgments: a strong dollar isn't necessarily a good thing and a weak dollar isn't necessarily a bad thing.

Movements in exchange rates, other things equal, affect the relative prices of goods, services, and assets in different countries. Suppose, for example, that the price of an American hotel room is US$100 and the price of a French hotel room is €100. If the exchange rate is €1 = US$1, these hotel rooms have the same price. If the exchange rate is €1.25 = US$1, the French hotel room is 20% cheaper than the American hotel room. If the exchange rate is €0.80 = US$1, the French hotel room is 25% more expensive than the American hotel room.

But what determines exchange rates? Supply and demand in the foreign exchange market.

TABLE 18-3 Exchange Rates, April 27, 2017, 3 P.M.

	U.S. dollars	Yen	Euros
One U.S. dollar exchanged for	1	111.26	0.9198
One yen exchanged for	0.0089	1	0.0082
One euro exchanged for	1.0872	120.99	1

PITFALLS

WHICH WAY IS UP?

You hear someone say, "The U.S. exchange rate is up." What does that person mean?

It isn't clear. Sometimes the exchange rate is measured as the price of a dollar in terms of foreign currency, sometimes as the price of foreign currency in terms of dollars. So the statement could mean either that the dollar appreciated or that it depreciated!

You have to be particularly careful when using published statistics. Most countries other than the United States state their exchange rates in terms of the price of a dollar in their domestic currency—for example, Mexican officials will say that the exchange rate is 10, meaning 10 pesos per dollar. But Britain, for historical reasons, usually states its exchange rate the other way. On April 27, 2017, US$1 was worth £0.7749, and £1 was worth US$1.2905. More often than not, this number is reported as an exchange rate of 1.2905. In fact, on occasion, professional economists and consultants embarrass themselves by getting the direction in which the pound is moving wrong!

By the way, Americans generally follow other countries' lead: we usually say that the exchange rate against Mexico is 10 pesos per dollar but that the exchange rate against Britain is 1.29 dollars per pound. But this rule isn't reliable; exchange rates against the euro are often stated both ways.

So it's always important to check before using exchange rate data: which way is the exchange rate being measured?

The Equilibrium Exchange Rate

Imagine, for the sake of simplicity, that there are only two currencies in the world: U.S. dollars and euros. Europeans wanting to purchase

American goods, services, and assets come to the foreign exchange market, wanting to exchange euros for U.S. dollars. That is, Europeans demand U.S. dollars from the foreign exchange market and, correspondingly, supply euros to that market. Americans wanting to buy European goods, services, and assets come to the foreign exchange market to exchange U.S. dollars for euros. That is, Americans supply U.S. dollars to the foreign exchange market and, correspondingly, demand euros from that market. (International transfers and payments of factor income also enter into the foreign exchange market, but to make things simple we'll ignore these.)

Figure 18-2 shows how the foreign exchange market works. The quantity of dollars demanded and supplied at any given euro–U.S. dollar exchange rate is shown on the horizontal axis, and the euro–U.S. dollar exchange rate is shown on the vertical axis. The exchange rate plays the same role as the price of a good or service in an ordinary supply and demand diagram.

The figure shows two curves, the demand curve for U.S. dollars and the supply curve for U.S. dollars. The key to understanding the slopes of these curves is that the level of the exchange rate affects exports and imports. When a country's currency appreciates (becomes more valuable), exports fall and imports rise. When a country's currency depreciates (becomes less valuable), exports rise and imports fall.

To understand why the demand curve for U.S. dollars slopes downward, recall that the exchange rate, other things equal, determines the prices of American goods, services, and assets relative to those of European goods, services, and assets.

If the U.S. dollar rises against the euro (the dollar appreciates), American products will become more expensive to Europeans relative to European products. So Europeans will buy less from the United States and will acquire fewer dollars in the foreign exchange market: the quantity of U.S. dollars demanded falls as the number of euros needed to buy a U.S. dollar rises.

If the U.S. dollar falls against the euro (the dollar depreciates), American products will become relatively cheaper for Europeans. Europeans will respond by buying more from the United States and acquiring more dollars in the foreign exchange market: the quantity of U.S. dollars demanded rises as the number of euros needed to buy a U.S. dollar falls.

A similar argument explains why the supply curve of U.S. dollars in Figure 18-2 slopes upward: the more euros required to buy a U.S. dollar, the more

---

FIGURE 18-2 The Foreign Exchange Market

The foreign exchange market matches up the demand for a currency from foreigners who want to buy domestic goods, services, and assets with the supply of a currency from domestic residents who want to buy foreign goods, services, and assets. Here the equilibrium in the market for dollars is at point *E*, corresponding to an equilibrium exchange rate of €0.80 per US$1.

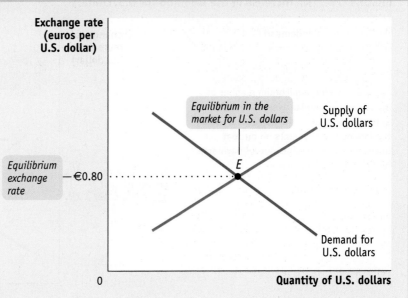

The **equilibrium exchange rate** is the exchange rate at which the quantity of a currency demanded in the foreign exchange market is equal to the quantity supplied.

dollars Americans will supply. Again, the reason is the effect of the exchange rate on relative prices. If the U.S. dollar rises against the euro, European products look cheaper to Americans—who will demand more of them. This will require Americans to convert more dollars into euros.

The **equilibrium exchange rate** is the exchange rate at which the quantity of U.S. dollars demanded in the foreign exchange market is equal to the quantity of U.S. dollars supplied. In Figure 18-2, the equilibrium is at point *E*, and the equilibrium exchange rate is 0.80. That is, at an exchange rate of €0.80 per US$1, the quantity of U.S. dollars supplied to the foreign exchange market is equal to the quantity of U.S. dollars demanded.

To understand the significance of the equilibrium exchange rate, it's helpful to consider a numerical example of what equilibrium in the foreign exchange market looks like. A hypothetical example is shown in Table 18-4. The first row shows European purchases of U.S. dollars, either to buy U.S. goods and services or to buy U.S. assets. The second row shows U.S. sales of U.S. dollars, either to buy European goods and services or to buy European assets. At the equilibrium exchange rate, the total quantity of U.S. dollars Europeans want to buy is equal to the total quantity of U.S. dollars Americans want to sell.

Remember that the balance of payments accounts divide international transactions into two types. Purchases and sales of goods and services are counted in the current account. (Again, we're leaving out transfers and factor income to keep things simple.) Purchases and sales of assets are counted in the financial account. At the equilibrium exchange rate, then, we have the situation shown in Table 18-4: the sum of the balance of payments on current account plus the balance of payments on financial account is zero.

Now let's briefly consider how a shift in the demand for U.S. dollars affects equilibrium in the foreign exchange market. Suppose that for some reason capital flows from Europe to the United States increase due to a change in the preferences of European investors. The effects are shown in Figure 18-3. The demand for U.S. dollars in the foreign exchange market increases as European investors

TABLE 18-4 A Hypothetical Equilibrium in the Foreign Exchange Market

	Current account	Financial account	Totals
European purchases of U.S. dollars (trillions of dollars)	To buy U.S. goods and services: 1.0	To buy U.S. assets: 1.0	2.0
U.S. sales of U.S. dollars (trillions of dollars)	To buy European goods and services: 1.5	To buy European assets: 0.5	2.0
U.S. balance of payments	−0.5	+0.5	

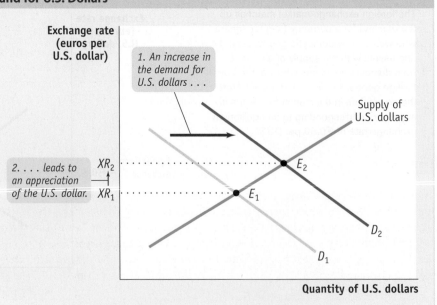

FIGURE 18-3 An Increase in the Demand for U.S. Dollars

An increase in the demand for U.S. dollars might result from a change in the preferences of European investors. The demand curve for U.S. dollars shifts from D_1 to D_2. So the equilibrium number of euros per U.S. dollar rises—the dollar appreciates against the euro. As a result, the balance of payments on current account falls as the balance of payments on financial account rises.

Exchange rate (euros per U.S. dollar)

1. An increase in the demand for U.S. dollars . . .

Supply of U.S. dollars

2. . . . leads to an appreciation of the U.S. dollar.

XR_2

XR_1

E_2

E_1

D_2

D_1

Quantity of U.S. dollars

convert euros into dollars to fund their new investments in the United States. This is shown by the shift of the demand curve from D_1 to D_2. As a result, the U.S. dollar appreciates against the euro: the number of euros per U.S. dollar at the equilibrium exchange rate rises from XR_1 to XR_2.

What are the consequences of this increased capital inflow for the balance of payments? The total quantity of U.S. dollars supplied to the foreign exchange market still must equal the total quantity of U.S. dollars demanded. So the increased capital inflow to the United States—an increase in the balance of payments on financial account—must be matched by a decline in the balance of payments on current account. What causes the balance of payments on current account to decline? The appreciation of the U.S. dollar. A rise in the number of euros per U.S. dollar leads Americans to buy more European goods and services and Europeans to buy fewer American goods and services.

Table 18-5 shows a hypothetical example of how this might work. Europeans are buying more U.S. assets, increasing the balance of payments on the financial account from 0.5 to 1.0. This is offset by a reduction in European purchases of U.S. goods and services and a rise in U.S. purchases of European goods and services, both the result of the dollar's appreciation.

So any change in the U.S. balance of payments on financial account generates an equal and opposite reaction in the balance of payments on current account. Movements in the exchange rate ensure that changes in the financial account and in the current account offset each other.

TABLE 18-5   A Hypothetical Example of Effects of Increased Capital Inflows

	Current account	Financial account	Totals
European purchases of U.S. dollars (trillions of dollars)	To buy U.S. goods and services: 0.75 (down 0.25)	To buy U.S. assets: 1.5 (up 0.5)	2.25
U.S. sales of U.S. dollars (trillions of dollars)	To buy European goods and services: 1.75 (up 0.25)	To buy European assets: 0.5 (no change)	2.25
U.S. balance of payments	–1.0 (down 0.5)	+1.0 (up 0.5)	

Let's briefly run this process in reverse. Suppose there is a reduction in capital flows from Europe to the United States—again due to a change in the preferences of European investors. The demand for U.S. dollars in the foreign exchange market falls, and the dollar depreciates: the number of euros per U.S. dollar at the equilibrium exchange rate falls. This leads Americans to buy fewer European products and Europeans to buy more American products. Ultimately, this generates an increase in the U.S. balance of payments on current account. So a fall in capital flows into the United States leads to a weaker dollar, which in turn generates an increase in U.S. net exports.

Inflation and Real Exchange Rates

In 1993 one U.S. dollar exchanged, on average, for 3.1 Mexican pesos. By 2017, the peso had fallen against the dollar by more than 80%, with an average exchange rate of more than 19 pesos per dollar. Did Mexican products also become drastically cheaper relative to U.S. products over that 24-year period? Did the price of Mexican products expressed in terms of U.S. dollars also fall by more than 80%? The answer to both questions is no, because Mexico had much higher inflation than the United States over that period. In fact, the relative price of U.S. and Mexican products fluctuated both up and down between 1993 and 2017, with no clear trend.

To take account of the effects of differences in inflation rates, economists calculate **real exchange rates,** exchange rates adjusted for international differences in aggregate price levels. Suppose that the exchange rate we are looking at is the number of Mexican pesos per U.S. dollar. Let P_{US} and P_{Mex} be indexes of the aggregate price levels in the United States and Mexico, respectively. Then the real exchange rate between the Mexican peso and the U.S. dollar is defined as:

(18-4) Real exchange rate = Mexican pesos per U.S. dollar $\times \dfrac{P_{US}}{P_{Mex}}$

Real exchange rates are exchange rates adjusted for international differences in aggregate price levels.

To distinguish it from the real exchange rate, the exchange rate unadjusted for aggregate price levels is sometimes called the *nominal* exchange rate.

To understand the significance of the difference between the real and nominal exchange rates, let's consider the following example. Suppose that the Mexican peso depreciates against the U.S. dollar, with the exchange rate going from 10 pesos per U.S. dollar to 15 pesos per U.S. dollar, a 50% change. But suppose that at the same time the price of everything in Mexico, measured in pesos, increases by 50%, so that the Mexican price index rises from 100 to 150. At the same time, suppose that there is no change in U.S. prices, so that the U.S. price index remains at 100. Then the initial real exchange rate is:

$$\text{Pesos per dollar before depreciation} \times \frac{P_{US}}{P_{Mex}} = 10 \times \frac{100}{100} = 10$$

After the peso depreciates and the Mexican price level increases, the real exchange rate is:

$$\text{Pesos per dollar after depreciation} \times \frac{P_{US}}{P_{Mex}} = 15 \times \frac{100}{150} = 10$$

In this example, the peso has depreciated substantially in terms of the U.S. dollar, but the *real* exchange rate between the peso and the U.S. dollar hasn't changed at all. And because the real peso–U.S. dollar exchange rate hasn't changed, the nominal depreciation of the peso against the U.S. dollar will have no effect either on the quantity of goods and services exported by Mexico to the United States or on the quantity of goods and services imported by Mexico from the United States.

It's the real exchange rate, not the nominal exchange rate, that counts in decisions about buying and selling abroad.

To see why, consider again the example of a hotel room. Suppose that this room initially costs 1,000 pesos per night, which is $100 at an exchange rate of 10 pesos per dollar. After both Mexican prices and the number of pesos per dollar rise by 50%, the hotel room costs 1,500 pesos per night—but 1,500 pesos divided by 15 pesos per dollar is $100, so the Mexican hotel room still costs $100. As a result, a U.S. tourist considering a trip to Mexico will have no reason to change plans.

The same is true for all goods and services that enter into trade: *the current account responds only to changes in the real exchange rate, not the nominal exchange rate.* A country's products become cheaper to foreigners only when that country's currency depreciates in real terms, and those products become more expensive to foreigners only when the currency appreciates in real terms. As a consequence, economists who analyze movements in exports and imports of goods and services focus on the real exchange rate, not the nominal exchange rate.

Figure 18-4 illustrates just how important it can be to distinguish between nominal and real exchange rates. The line labeled "Nominal exchange rate" shows the number of pesos it took to buy a U.S. dollar from 1993 to 2017. As you can see, the peso depreciated massively over that period. But the line labeled "Real exchange rate" shows the real exchange rate: it was calculated using Equation 18-4, with price indexes for both Mexico and the United States set so that 1993 = 100. In real terms, the peso depreciated between 1994 and 1995, but not by nearly as much as the nominal depreciation. By 2013, the real peso–U.S. dollar exchange rate was just about back where it started, although it rose again over the next two years.

FIGURE 18-4 Real versus Nominal Exchange Rates, 1993–2017

Between November 1993 and February 2017, the price of a dollar in Mexican pesos increased dramatically. But because Mexico had higher inflation than the United States, the real exchange rate, which measures the relative price of Mexican goods and services, ended up roughly where it started.

Data from: Federal Reserve Bank of St. Louis.

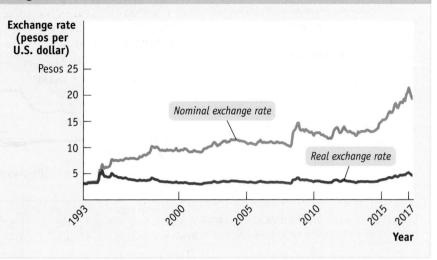

Purchasing Power Parity

A useful tool for analyzing exchange rates, closely connected to the concept of the real exchange rate, is known as *purchasing power parity*. The **purchasing power parity** between two countries' currencies is the nominal exchange rate at which a given basket of goods and services would cost the same amount in each country. Suppose, for example, that a basket of goods and services that costs $100 in the United States costs 1,000 pesos in Mexico. Then the purchasing power parity is 10 pesos per U.S. dollar: at that exchange rate, 1,000 pesos = $100, so the market basket costs the same amount in both countries.

The **purchasing power parity** between two countries' currencies is the nominal exchange rate at which a given basket of goods and services would cost the same amount in each country.

FOR INQUIRING MINDS   Burgernomics

The Economist magazine publishes an annual comparison of the cost in different countries of one particular consumption item that is found around the world—a McDonald's Big Mac. The magazine finds the price of a Big Mac in local currency, then computes two numbers: the price of a Big Mac in U.S. dollars using the prevailing exchange rate and the exchange rate at which the price of a Big Mac would equal the U.S. price.

If purchasing power parity held for Big Macs, the dollar price of a Big Mac would be the same everywhere. If purchasing power parity is a good theory for the long run, the exchange rate at which a Big Mac's price matches the U.S. price should offer some guidance about where the exchange rate will eventually end up.

Table 18-6 shows the *Economist* estimates for selected countries as of January 2017, ranked in increasing order of the dollar price of a Big Mac. The countries with the cheapest Big Macs, and therefore by this measure with the most undervalued

currencies, are Mexico, India, and China, all three developing countries. And topping the list, with a Big Mac some 25% more expensive than in the United States,

is Switzerland—the nation that, as we described in the opening story, has been taking extraordinary action in an effort to depreciate its currency.

TABLE 18-6 Purchasing Power Parity and the Price of a Big Mac

| Country | Big Mac price | | Local currency per dollar | |
	In local currency	In U.S. dollars	Implied PPP	Actual exchange rate
Mexico	Peso 49	2.23	9.68	21.95
India	Rupee 170	$2.49	33.60	68.33
China	Yuan 19.6	2.83	3.87	6.93
Japan	¥ 380	3.26	75.10	116.67
Britain	£ 3.09	3.73	0.61	0.83
Euro area	€ 3.88	4.06	0.77	0.96
United States	$5.06	5.06	1.00	1.00
Brazil	Real 16.5	5.12	3.26	3.22
Switzerland	SFr 6.50	6.35	1.28	1.02

Data from: The Economist.

FIGURE 18-5 Purchasing Power Parity versus the Nominal Exchange Rate, 1990–2016

The purchasing power parity between the United States and Canada—the exchange rate at which a basket of goods and services would have cost the same amount in both countries—changed very little over the period shown, staying near C$1.20 per US$1. But the nominal exchange rate fluctuated widely.

Data from: OECD.

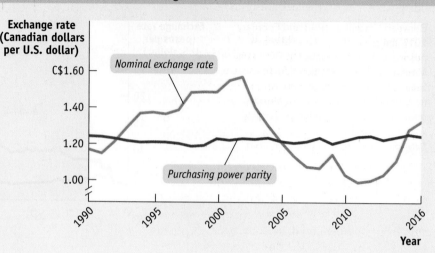

Calculations of purchasing power parities are usually made by estimating the cost of buying broad market baskets containing many goods and services—everything from cars and groceries to housing and internet service. But as the preceding For Inquiring Minds, "Burgernomics" illustrates, nominal exchange rates almost always differ from purchasing power parities. Some of these differences are systematic: in general, aggregate price levels are lower in poor countries than in rich countries because services tend to be cheaper in poor countries. But even among countries at roughly the same level of economic development, nominal exchange rates vary quite a lot from purchasing power parity.

Figure 18-5 shows the nominal exchange rate between the Canadian dollar and the U.S. dollar, measured as the number of Canadian dollars per U.S. dollar, from 1990 to 2016, together with an estimate of the purchasing power parity exchange rate between the United States and Canada over the same period. The purchasing power parity didn't change much over the whole period because the United States and Canada had about the same rate of inflation. For most of the 1990s through 2005, the nominal exchange rate was above the purchasing power parity, so a market basket was much cheaper in Canada than in the United States. But from 2005 to 2015, the Canadian dollar had appreciated, making a market basket more expensive in Canada.

Over the long run, however, purchasing power parities are pretty good at predicting actual changes in nominal exchange rates. In particular, nominal exchange rates between countries at similar levels of economic development tend to fluctuate around levels that lead to similar costs for a given market basket.

ECONOMICS >> *in Action*
Strong Dollar Woes

Does the exchange rate really matter for business? To answer this question, let's consider what happened to U.S. corporations from 2014 to 2015.

Over the course of these two years, the dollar strengthened sharply against many currencies, especially the euro and the Japanese yen. The dollar's rise largely reflected the weakness of other economies: troubles in Europe and Japan kept interest rates and investment demand low, and capital flowed to the United States, which was experiencing steady job growth and overall was doing a much better job recovering from the Great Recession.

While the strong dollar reflected (relatively) good news for the U.S. economy as a whole, it was bad news for U.S. companies that sell a lot to overseas markets—companies like Proctor and Gamble, which sells toothpaste and other toiletries around the world, or Johnson and Johnson, whose Huggies diapers protect many foreign babies' bottoms. Such companies reported large hits to their profits, and began either losing ground to foreign competitors or shifting some of their own production abroad.

Figure 18-6 illustrates the overall picture. It compares the *U.S. effective exchange rate,* a measure of the average value of the dollar against other currencies, with *real net exports,* exports minus imports, measured in 2009 dollars. From early 2014 to early 2016 the dollar rose about 15% on average, then stayed at that higher level into 2017, while real net exports moved considerably deeper into deficit.

In other words, the exchange rate does matter a lot for businesses that compete with foreign rivals. Earlier we noted that while it's common to describe an appreciating currency as "getting stronger," that doesn't mean it's a good thing. And the stronger dollar of 2014 to 2015 definitely wasn't a good thing for some U.S. companies.

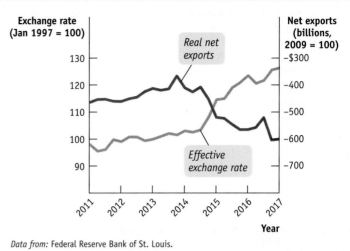

FIGURE 18-6 The Negative Impact of a Strong Dollar, 2011–2017

Data from: Federal Reserve Bank of St. Louis.

>> Check Your Understanding 18-2

Solutions appear at back of book.

1. Mexico discovers huge reserves of oil and starts exporting oil to the United States. Describe how this would affect the following.
   a. The nominal peso–U.S. dollar exchange rate
   b. Mexican exports to the United States of other goods and services
   c. Mexican imports from the United States of goods and services

2. A basket of goods and services that costs $100 in the United States costs 800 pesos in Mexico, and the current nominal exchange rate is 10 pesos per U.S. dollar. Over the next five years, the cost of that market basket rises to $120 in the United States and to 1,200 pesos in Mexico, although the nominal exchange rate remains at 10 pesos per U.S. dollar. Calculate the following.
   a. The real exchange rate now and five years from now, if today's price index in both countries is 100
   b. Purchasing power parity today and five years from now

Exchange Rate Policy

The nominal exchange rate, like other prices, is determined by supply and demand. Unlike the price of wheat or oil, however, the exchange rate is the price of a country's money (in terms of another country's money). Money isn't a good or service produced by the private sector; it's an asset whose quantity is determined by government policy. As a result, governments have much more power to influence nominal exchange rates than they have to influence ordinary prices.

The nominal exchange rate is a very important price for many countries because it determines the price of imports and the price of exports. In economies where exports and imports are large percentages of GDP, movements in

An **exchange rate regime** is a rule governing policy toward the exchange rate.

A country has a **fixed exchange rate** when the government keeps the exchange rate against some other currency at or near a particular target.

A country has a **floating exchange rate** when the government lets market forces determine the exchange rate.

the exchange rate can have major effects on aggregate output and the aggregate price level. What do governments do with their power to influence this important price?

The answer is, it depends. At different times and in different places, governments have adopted a variety of *exchange rate regimes*. Let's talk about these regimes, how they are enforced, and how governments choose a regime. (From now on, we'll adopt the convention that we mean the nominal exchange rate when we refer to the exchange rate.)

Exchange Rate Regimes

An **exchange rate regime** is a rule governing policy toward the exchange rate. There are two main kinds of exchange rate regimes. A country has a **fixed exchange rate** when the government keeps the exchange rate against some other currency at or near a particular target. For example, Hong Kong has an official policy of setting an exchange rate of HK$7.80 per US$1. In contrast, a country has a **floating exchange rate** when the government lets market forces determine the exchange rate. This is the policy followed by Britain, Canada, and the United States.

Fixed exchange rates and floating exchange rates aren't the only possibilities. At various times, countries have adopted compromise policies that lie somewhere between fixed and floating exchange rates. These include exchange rates that are fixed at any given time but are adjusted frequently, exchange rates that aren't fixed but are managed by the government to avoid wide swings, and exchange rates that float within a *target zone* but are prevented from leaving that zone. In this chapter, however, we'll focus on the two main exchange rate regimes.

Exchange rates play a very important role in the global economy.

The immediate puzzle posed by a fixed exchange rate is how a government can fix the exchange rate when the exchange rate is determined by supply and demand.

How Can an Exchange Rate Be Held Fixed?

To understand how it is possible for a country to fix its exchange rate, let's consider a hypothetical country, Genovia, which for some reason has decided to fix the value of its currency, the geno, at US$1.50.

The obvious problem is that $1.50 may not be the equilibrium exchange rate in the foreign exchange market: the equilibrium rate may be either higher or lower than the target exchange rate. Figure 18-7 shows the foreign exchange market for genos, with the quantities of genos supplied and demanded on the horizontal axis and the exchange rate of the geno, measured in U.S. dollars per geno, on the vertical axis. Panel (a) shows the case in which the equilibrium value of the geno is *below* the target exchange rate. Panel (b) shows the case in which the equilibrium value of the geno is *above* the target exchange rate.

Consider first the case in which the equilibrium value of the geno is below the target exchange rate. As panel (a) shows, at the target exchange rate of $1.50 per geno, there is a surplus of genos in the foreign exchange market, which would normally push the value of the geno down. How can the Genovian government support the value of the geno to keep the rate where it wants? There are three possible answers, all of which have been used by governments at some point.

One way the Genovian government can support the geno is to soak up the surplus of genos by buying its own currency in the foreign exchange market.

FIGURE 18-7 Exchange Market Intervention

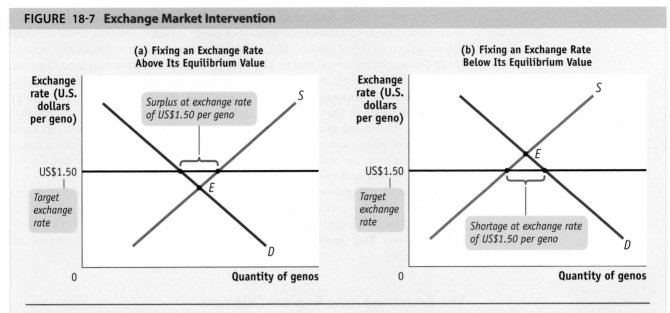

In both panels, the imaginary country of Genovia is trying to keep the exchange rate of the geno fixed at US$1.50 per geno. In panel (a), the equilibrium exchange rate is below $1.50, leading to a surplus of genos on the foreign exchange market. To keep the geno from falling below $1.50, the Genovian government can buy genos and sell U.S. dollars. In panel (b), the equilibrium exchange rate is above $1.50, leading to a shortage of genos on the foreign exchange market. To keep the geno from rising above $1.50, the Genovian government can sell genos and buy U.S. dollars.

A government purchase or sale of currency in the foreign exchange market is called an **exchange market intervention.** To buy genos in the foreign exchange market, of course, the Genovian government must have U.S. dollars to exchange for genos. In fact, most countries maintain **foreign exchange reserves,** stocks of foreign currency (usually U.S. dollars or euros) that they can use to buy their own currency to support its price.

We mentioned earlier in the chapter that an important part of international capital flows is the result of purchases and sales of foreign assets by governments and central banks. Now we can see why governments sell foreign assets: they are supporting their currency through exchange market intervention. As we'll see in a moment, governments that keep the value of their currency *down* through exchange market intervention must *buy* foreign assets. First, however, let's talk about the other ways governments fix exchange rates.

A second way for the Genovian government to support the geno is to try to shift the supply and demand curves for the geno in the foreign exchange market. Governments usually do this by changing monetary policy. For example, to support the geno the Genovian central bank can raise the Genovian interest rate. This will increase capital flows into Genovia, increasing the demand for genos, at the same time that it reduces capital flows out of Genovia, reducing the supply of genos. So, other things equal, an increase in a country's interest rate will increase the value of its currency.

Third, the Genovian government can support the geno by reducing the supply of genos to the foreign exchange market. It can do this by requiring domestic residents who want to buy foreign currency to get a license and giving these licenses only to people engaging in approved transactions (such as the purchase of imported goods the Genovian government thinks are essential). Licensing systems that limit the right of individuals to buy foreign currency are called **foreign exchange controls.** Other things equal, foreign exchange controls increase the value of a country's currency.

A government purchase or sale of currency in the foreign exchange market is an **exchange market intervention.**

Foreign exchange reserves are stocks of foreign currency that governments maintain to buy their own currency on the foreign exchange market.

Foreign exchange controls are licensing systems that limit the right of individuals to buy foreign currency.

So far we've been discussing a situation in which the government is trying to prevent a depreciation of the geno. Suppose, instead, that the situation is as shown in panel (b) of Figure 18-7, where the equilibrium value of the geno is *above* the target exchange rate of $1.50 per geno and there is a shortage of genos. To maintain the target exchange rate, the Genovian government can apply the same three basic options in the reverse direction. It can intervene in the foreign exchange market, in this case *selling* genos and acquiring U.S. dollars, which it can add to its foreign exchange reserves. It can *reduce* interest rates to increase the supply of genos and reduce the demand. Or it can impose foreign exchange controls that limit the ability of foreigners to buy genos. All of these actions, other things equal, will reduce the value of the geno.

As we said, all three techniques have been used to manage fixed exchange rates. But we haven't said whether fixing the exchange rate is a good idea. In fact, the choice of exchange rate regime poses a dilemma for policy makers, because fixed and floating exchange rates each have both advantages and disadvantages.

The Exchange Rate Regime Dilemma

Few questions in macroeconomics produce as many arguments as that of whether a country should adopt a fixed or a floating exchange rate. And there are so many arguments because both sides have a case.

To understand the case for a fixed exchange rate, consider for a moment how easy it is to conduct business across state lines in the United States. There are a number of things that make interstate commerce trouble-free, but one of them is the absence of any uncertainty about the value of money: a dollar is a dollar, in both New York City and Los Angeles.

By contrast, a dollar isn't a dollar in transactions between New York City and Toronto. The exchange rate between the Canadian dollar and the U.S. dollar fluctuates, sometimes widely. If a U.S. firm promises to pay a Canadian firm a given number of U.S. dollars a year from now, the value of that promise in Canadian currency can vary by 10% or more. This uncertainty has the effect of deterring trade between the two countries. So one benefit of a fixed exchange rate is certainty about the future value of a currency.

There is also, in some cases, an additional benefit to adopting a fixed exchange rate: by committing itself to a fixed rate, a country is also committing itself not to engage in inflationary policies. For example, in 1991 Argentina, which has a long history of irresponsible policies leading to severe inflation, adopted a fixed exchange rate of US$1 per Argentine peso in an attempt to commit itself to non-inflationary policies in the future. (Argentina's fixed exchange rate regime collapsed disastrously in late 2001. But that's another story.)

The point is that there is some economic value in having a stable exchange rate. Indeed, as the accompanying For Inquiring Minds explains, the presumed benefits of stable exchange rates motivated the international system of fixed exchange rates created after World War II. It was also a major reason for the creation of the euro.

However, there are also costs to fixing the exchange rate. To stabilize an exchange rate through intervention, a country must keep large quantities of foreign currency on hand—usually a low-return investment. Furthermore, even large reserves can be quickly exhausted when there are large capital flows out of a country. If a country chooses to stabilize an exchange rate by adjusting monetary policy rather than through intervention, it must divert monetary policy from other goals, notably stabilizing the economy and managing the inflation rate. Finally, foreign exchange controls, like import quotas and tariffs, distort incentives for importing and exporting goods and services. They can also create substantial costs in terms of red tape and corruption.

FOR INQUIRING MINDS **From Bretton Woods to the Euro**

In 1944, while World War II was still raging, representatives of Allied nations met in Bretton Woods, New Hampshire, to establish a postwar international monetary system of fixed exchange rates among major currencies. The system was highly successful at first, but it broke down in 1971. After a confusing interval during which policy makers tried unsuccessfully to establish a new fixed exchange rate system, by 1973 most economically advanced countries had moved to floating exchange rates.

In Europe, however, many policy makers were unhappy with floating exchange rates, which they believed created too much uncertainty for business. From the late 1970s onward they tried several times to create a system of more or less fixed exchange rates in Europe, culminating in an arrangement known as the Exchange Rate Mechanism. (The Exchange Rate Mechanism was, strictly speaking, a target zone system—European exchange rates were free to move within a narrow band, but not outside it.) And in 1991 they agreed to move to the ultimate in fixed exchange rates: a common European currency, the euro. To the surprise of many analysts, they pulled it off: today most of Europe has abandoned national currencies for the euro.

Figure 18-8 illustrates the history of European exchange rate arrangements. It shows the exchange rate between the French franc and the German mark, measured as francs per mark, from 1971 until their replacement by the euro.

The exchange rate fluctuated widely at first. The plateaus you can see in the data—eras when the exchange rate fluctuated only modestly—are periods when attempts to restore fixed exchange rates were in process. The Exchange Rate Mechanism, after a couple of false starts, became effective in 1987, stabilizing the exchange rate at about 3.4 francs per mark. (The wobbles in the early 1990s reflect two *currency crises*—episodes in which widespread expectations of imminent devaluations led to large but temporary capital flows.)

In 1999 the exchange rate was *locked*—no further fluctuations were allowed as the countries prepared to switch from francs and marks to the euro. At the end of 2001, the franc and the mark ceased to exist.

The transition to the euro has not been without costs. Countries that adopted the euro sacrificed some important policy tools: they could no longer tailor monetary policy to their specific economic circumstances, and they could no longer lower their costs relative to other European nations simply by letting their currencies depreciate.

FIGURE 18-8 The Road to the Euro

Data from: Federal Reserve Bank of St. Louis.

So there's a dilemma. Should a country let its currency float, which leaves monetary policy available for macroeconomic stabilization but creates uncertainty for business? Or should it fix the exchange rate, which eliminates the uncertainty but means giving up monetary policy, adopting exchange controls, or both?

Different countries reach different conclusions at different times. Most European countries, except for Britain, have long believed that exchange rates among major European economies, which do most of their international trade with each other, should be fixed. But Canada seems happy with a floating exchange rate with the United States, even though the United States accounts for most of Canada's trade.

Fortunately we don't have to resolve this dilemma. For the rest of the chapter, we'll take exchange rate regimes as given and ask how they affect macroeconomic policy.

ECONOMICS >> *in Action* 🌐
China Pegs the Yuan

In the early years of the twenty-first century, China provided a striking example of the lengths to which countries sometimes go to maintain a fixed exchange rate.

In the first act of this story, China acted to keep its currency down. The country's spectacular success as an exporter had produced a rising surplus on current account, and private investors became increasingly eager to shift funds into China, to invest in its growing domestic economy.

These capital flows were somewhat limited by foreign exchange controls—but kept coming in anyway. As a result of the current account surplus and private capital inflows, China found itself in the position described by panel (b) of Figure 18-7: at the target exchange rate, the demand for yuan exceeded the supply. Yet the Chinese government was determined to keep the exchange rate fixed at a value below its equilibrium level.

China provides a striking example of the lengths to which countries sometimes go to maintain a fixed exchange rate.

To keep the rate fixed, China had to engage in large-scale exchange market intervention, selling yuan, buying up other countries' currencies (mainly U.S. dollars) on the foreign exchange market, and adding them to its reserves. Indeed, between early 2009 and early 2014 China added $2 trillion to its foreign exchange reserves, which by mid-2014 had risen to a remarkable $4 trillion, roughly 40% of GDP. Not surprisingly, China's exchange rate policy led to some friction with its trading partners, who felt that it had the effect of subsidizing Chinese exports.

But then came the second act of the story. After 2012 China's current account surplus declined, partly reflecting rising wages and the rise of new competitors like Vietnam and Bangladesh. Also, China's economic growth, while still fast, slowed, and investors grew nervous about a possible financial or political crisis. So capital inflows turned into capital outflows: the 2015 outflow was estimated at an amazing $1 trillion, the great majority of it going to the United States.

In the absence of government intervention, this capital flight might well have caused a sharp decline in the yuan. But the Chinese government was as reluctant to see its currency fall as it had once been to see it rise. So China began using its reserves of foreign currency to buy large quantities of yuan. And by early 2017 reserves had fallen from $4 trillion to less than $3 trillion.

>> Quick Review

- Countries choose different **exchange rate regimes.** The two main regimes are **fixed exchange rates** and **floating exchange rates.**

- Exchange rates can be fixed through **exchange market intervention,** using **foreign exchange reserves.** Countries can also use domestic policies to shift supply and demand in the foreign exchange market (usually monetary policy), or they can impose **foreign exchange controls.**

- Choosing an exchange rate regime poses a dilemma. Stable exchange rates are good for business. But holding large foreign exchange reserves is costly, using domestic policy to fix the exchange rate makes it hard to pursue other objectives, and foreign exchange controls distort incentives.

>> Check Your Understanding 18-3
Solutions appear at back of book.

1. Draw a diagram, similar to Figure 18-7, representing the foreign exchange situation of China when it kept the exchange rate fixed. Express the exchange rate as U.S. dollars per yuan. Then show with a diagram how each of the following policy changes will eliminate the disequilibrium in the market.
   a. China no longer fixes its exchange rate and allows it to float freely.
   b. Placing restrictions on foreigners who want to invest in China
   c. Removing restrictions on Chinese who want to invest abroad
   d. Imposing taxes on Chinese exports, such as shipments of clothing, that are causing a political backlash in the importing countries

‖ Exchange Rates and Macroeconomic Policy

When the euro was created in 1999, there were celebrations across the nations of Europe where it was seen as a step toward a brighter future. But there were a few notable exceptions. You see, some countries chose not to adopt the new currency.

The most important of these was Britain, but other European countries, such as Sweden, also decided that the euro was not for them.

Why did Britain say no? Part of the answer was national pride: if Britain gave up the pound, it would also have to give up currency that bears the portrait of the queen. But there were also serious economic concerns about giving up the pound in favor of the euro. British economists who favored adoption of the euro argued that if Britain used the same currency as its neighbors, the country's international trade would expand and its economy would become more productive. But other economists pointed out that adopting the euro would take away Britain's ability to have an independent monetary policy and might lead to macroeconomic problems.

As this discussion suggests, the fact that modern economies are open to international trade and capital flows adds a new level of complication to our analysis of macroeconomic policy. Let's look at three policy issues raised by international aspects of macroeconomics:

1. Devaluation and revaluation of fixed exchange rates
2. Monetary policy under floating exchange rates
3. International business cycles

1. Devaluation and Revaluation of Fixed Exchange Rates

Historically, fixed exchange rates haven't been permanent commitments. Sometimes countries with a fixed exchange rate switch to a floating rate. In other cases, they retain a fixed rate but change the target exchange rate. Such adjustments in the target were common during the Bretton Woods era described in the preceding For Inquiring Minds. For example, in 1967 Britain changed the exchange rate of the pound against the U.S. dollar from US$2.80 per £1 to US$2.40 per £1. A modern example is Argentina, which maintained a fixed exchange rate against the dollar from 1991 to 2001 but switched to a floating exchange rate at the end of 2001.

A reduction in the value of a currency that is set under a fixed exchange rate regime is called a **devaluation.** As we've already learned, a *depreciation* is a downward move in a currency. A devaluation is a depreciation that is due to a revision in a fixed exchange rate target. An increase in the value of a currency that is set under a fixed exchange rate regime is called a **revaluation.**

A devaluation, like any depreciation, makes domestic goods cheaper in terms of foreign currency, which leads to higher exports. At the same time, it makes foreign goods more expensive in terms of domestic currency, which reduces imports. The effect is to increase the balance of payments on current account. Similarly, a revaluation makes domestic goods more expensive in terms of foreign currency, which reduces exports, and makes foreign goods cheaper in domestic currency, which increases imports. So a revaluation reduces the balance of payments on current account.

Devaluations and revaluations serve two purposes under fixed exchange rates. First, they can be used to eliminate shortages or surpluses in the foreign exchange market. For example, in 2010 some economists and politicians were urging China to revalue the yuan because they believed that China's exchange rate policy unfairly aided Chinese exports.

Second, devaluation and revaluation can be used as tools of macroeconomic policy. A devaluation, by increasing exports and reducing imports, increases aggregate demand. So a devaluation can be used to reduce or eliminate a recessionary gap. A revaluation has the opposite effect, reducing aggregate demand. So a revaluation can be used to reduce or eliminate an inflationary gap.

2. Monetary Policy Under Floating Exchange Rates

Under a floating exchange rate regime, a country's central bank retains its ability to pursue independent monetary policy: it can increase aggregate demand by

A **devaluation** is a reduction in the value of a currency that is set under a fixed exchange rate regime.

A **revaluation** is an increase in the value of a currency that is set under a fixed exchange rate regime.

cutting the interest rate or decrease aggregate demand by raising the interest rate. But the exchange rate adds another dimension to the effects of monetary policy. To see why, let's return to the hypothetical country of Genovia and ask what happens if the central bank cuts the interest rate.

Just as in an economy without international linkages, a lower interest rate leads to higher investment spending and higher consumer spending. But the decline in the interest rate also affects the foreign exchange market. Foreigners have less incentive to move funds into Genovia because they will receive a lower interest rate on their loans. As a result, they have less need to exchange U.S. dollars for genos, so the demand for genos falls. At the same time, Genovians have *more* incentive to move funds abroad because the interest rate on loans at home has fallen, making investments outside the country more attractive. As a result, they need to exchange more genos for U.S. dollars, so the supply of genos rises.

Figure 18-9 shows the effect of an interest rate reduction on the foreign exchange market. The demand curve for genos shifts leftward, from D_1 to D_2, and the supply curve shifts rightward, from S_1 to S_2. The equilibrium exchange rate, as measured in U.S. dollars per geno, falls from XR_1 to XR_2. That is, a reduction in the Genovian interest rate causes the geno to *depreciate*.

The depreciation of the geno, in turn, affects aggregate demand. We've already seen that a devaluation—a depreciation that is the result of a change in a fixed exchange rate—increases exports and reduces imports, thereby increasing aggregate demand. A depreciation that results from an interest rate cut has the same effect: it increases exports and reduces imports, increasing aggregate demand.

In other words, monetary policy under floating rates has effects beyond those we've described before. In the absence of international trade and capital flows, a reduction in the interest rate leads to a rise in aggregate demand because it leads to more investment spending and consumer spending. In an economy with a floating exchange rate, the interest rate reduction leads to increased investment spending and consumer spending, but it also increases aggregate demand in another way: it leads to a currency depreciation, which increases exports and reduces imports, and further increases aggregate demand.

FIGURE 18-9   Monetary Policy and the Exchange Rate

Here we show what happens in the foreign exchange market if Genovia cuts its interest rate. Residents of Genovia have a reduced incentive to keep their funds at home, so they invest more abroad. As a result, the supply of genos shifts rightward, from S_1 to S_2. Meanwhile, foreigners have less incentive to put funds into Genovia, so the demand for genos shifts leftward, from D_1 to D_2. The geno depreciates: the equilibrium exchange rate falls from XR_1 to XR_2.

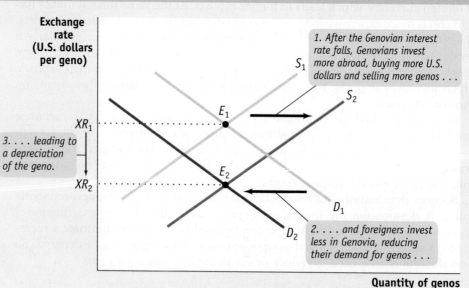

3. International Business Cycles

Up to this point, we have discussed macroeconomics as if all demand shocks originate from the domestic economy. In reality, however, economies sometimes face shocks coming from abroad. For example, recessions in the United States have historically led to recessions in Mexico.

The key point is that changes in aggregate demand affect the demand for goods and services produced abroad as well as at home: other things equal, a recession leads to a fall in imports and an expansion leads to a rise in imports. And one country's imports are another country's exports. This link between aggregate demand in different national economies is one reason business cycles in different countries sometimes—but not always—seem to be synchronized. The prime examples are the Great Depression of the 1930s and the Great Recession of 2008, both of which affected countries around the world.

The extent of this link depends, however, on the exchange rate regime. To see why, think about what happens if a recession abroad reduces the demand for Genovia's exports. A reduction in foreign demand for Genovian goods and services is also a reduction in demand for genos in the foreign exchange market. If Genovia has a fixed exchange rate, it responds to this decline with exchange market intervention. But if Genovia has a floating exchange rate, the geno depreciates. Because Genovian goods and services become cheaper to foreigners when the demand for exports falls, the quantity of goods and services exported doesn't fall by as much as it would under a fixed rate. At the same time, the fall in the geno makes imports more expensive to Genovians, leading to a fall in imports. Both effects limit the decline in Genovia's aggregate demand compared to what it would have been under a fixed exchange rate.

One of the virtues of a floating exchange rate, according to advocates of such exchange rates, is that they help insulate countries from recessions originating abroad. This theory looked pretty good in the early 2000s: Britain, with a floating exchange rate, managed to stay out of a recession that affected the rest of Europe, and Canada, which also has a floating rate, suffered a less severe recession than the United States.

In the Great Recession, however, a financial crisis that began in the United States led to a recession in virtually every country. In this case, it appears that the international linkages among financial markets were much stronger than any insulation from overseas disturbances provided by floating exchange rates.

ECONOMICS >> *in Action*
The Little Currency That Could

Iceland, with a population around 334,000, is a tiny country. And in 2008, it had a very big economic problem. Between 2003 and 2007 the country's main banks expanded very aggressively, mainly with money borrowed from banks in other countries, and the banking boom led in turn to a booming local economy. But then the boom went bust, as did the banks, and Iceland needed to go back to more mundane ways of making a living, like fishing and tourism. To do this it needed to reduce costs, mainly by cutting wages. It wasn't the only country in this position; other nations that had borrowed a lot of money, like Greece, also needed to make big adjustments.

But there was one big difference between Iceland and Greece (aside from the weather): Greece no longer had its own currency, because it had adopted the euro, whereas Iceland, tiny though it was, still had its own currency, the krona (plural kronur)—and Icelandic wages are set in kronur, not euros or dollars.

This made the process of cutting wages very different in Iceland than it was in euro-using countries. In Greece, employers actually had to tell workers that

FIGURE 18-10 Cutting Wages in Iceland and Greece, 2007–2015

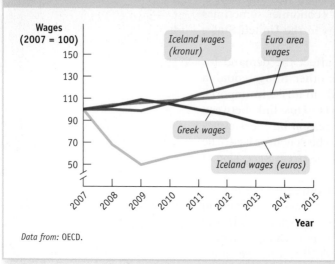

Data from: OECD.

they would be paid less—something companies are reluctant to do, because at best it creates bad feelings and at worst it leads to strikes. Iceland, however, could gain competitiveness without wage cuts, simply by letting the krona fall.

Figure 18-10 shows how the different options played out. The red line shows average wages in the euro area as a whole, with 2007 = 100, while the purple line shows Greek wages over the same period. As you can see, Greece did manage to cut wages gradually over time while wages in other European nations rose, so the Greek economy gradually became more competitive. It was, however, a slow and extremely painful process.

The other two lines show Iceland's story. The blue line shows wages in Iceland's own currency, kronurs. These continued to rise; there were no nominal wage cuts. The green line shows Icelandic wages in euros, which fell dramatically thanks to the depreciation of the krona.

It would be wrong to say that this process was painless—Icelandic workers saw the prices of imported goods rise, reducing their purchasing power. But it wasn't nearly as painful as Greece's adjustment. In Greece, unemployment rose year after year, peaking at 28% in late 2013 before it began inching down. In Iceland, by contrast, the jobs crisis only lasted about two years, and by late 2014 the unemployment rate was under 5%.

Overall, Iceland's experience was an object lesson in the advantages of having your own currency—even when your country is no bigger than a medium-sized American town.

>> Quick Review

• Countries can change fixed exchange rates. A **devaluation,** a reduction in the value of the currency, can help reduce surpluses in the foreign exchange market and can increase aggregate demand. A **revaluation,** an increase in the value of the currency, can help reduce shortages in the foreign exchange market and can reduce aggregate demand.

• In an open economy with a floating exchange rate, interest rates also affect the exchange rate, and so monetary policy affects aggregate demand through the effects of the exchange rate on imports and exports.

• Because one country's imports are another country's exports, business cycles are sometimes synchronized across countries. However, floating exchange rates may reduce this link.

>> Check Your Understanding 18-4

Solutions appear at back of book.

1. Look at the data in Figure 18-8. Where do you see devaluations and revaluations of the franc against the mark?

2. In the late 1980s Canadian economists argued that the high interest rate policies of the Bank of Canada weren't just causing high unemployment—they were also making it hard for Canadian manufacturers to compete with the United States. Explain this complaint, using our analysis of how monetary policy works under floating exchange rates.

A Yen for Japanese Cars

When Shinzo Abe became prime minister of Japan in 2012, he surprised most observers by seeking radical changes in Japan's economic policy that came to be known as *Abenomics*. With Japanese inflation running at a slightly negative rate, he oversaw a dramatic easing of monetary policy. The Bank of Japan greatly increased the monetary base and assured investors that it would do whatever it took to raise inflation to 2%. Over the next five years, one result of this policy was a much weaker yen. You can see this result in Figure 18-11. For most of 2012 the yen traded at around 80 per dollar, but in early 2017 the exchange rate was around 115 yen per dollar, a 44% depreciation.

The weaker yen, in turn, made some Japanese businesses happy—especially Japanese auto companies, who sell many of their vehicles in overseas markets. There were many headlines like these: "Weak yen fuels Japan

Inc." in the *Financial Times* (reporting on Toyota), or "Subaru profit soaring as weaker yen benefits exports." Abenomics had definitely helped Japan's car industry.

However, the benefits weren't equally spread: while Toyota was doing fairly well, Subaru was really taking off. Why? Well, over the years Toyota has moved the majority of its production out of Japan, operating numerous plants in the United States, Mexico, Canada, and various other countries. Subaru, which is a smaller company with a more limited product range, still mainly produces in Japan.

So while you can argue that what's good for Japan is good for Japanese auto companies—assuming, that is, that Abenomics actually works—it's better for some Japanese auto companies than others.

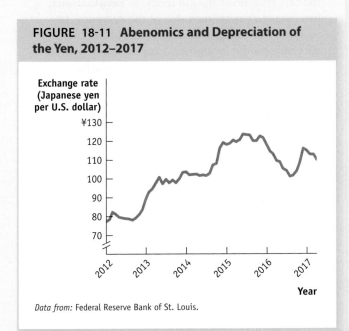

FIGURE 18-11 Abenomics and Depreciation of the Yen, 2012–2017

Exchange rate (Japanese yen per U.S. dollar)

Data from: Federal Reserve Bank of St. Louis.

QUESTIONS FOR THOUGHT

1. Why would Abenomics lead to a weaker yen?

2. Why is a weaker yen good for the profits of Japanese auto companies?

3. Why did Subaru gain more than Toyota?

SUMMARY

1. A country's **balance of payments accounts** summarize its transactions with the rest of the world. The **balance of payments on current account,** or **current account,** includes the **balance of payments on goods and services** together with balances on factor income and transfers. The **merchandise trade balance,** or **trade balance,** is a frequently cited component of the balance of payments on goods and services. The **balance of payments on financial account,** or **financial account,** measures capital flows. By definition, the balance of payments on current account plus the balance of payments on financial account is zero.

2. The loanable funds model shows that the direction of a net capital flows—the excess of inflows over outflows, or vice versa—across countries is determined by differences in interest rates that arise from differences in investment opportunities and savings behavior. Capital flows move to equalize interest rates across countries. In the real world, countries experience two-way capital flows—gross flows of capital in and out—because factors other than interest rate differences affect investors' decisions. Those factors are risk considerations, business strategy, and banking industry expertise.

3. Currencies are traded in the **foreign exchange market;** the prices at which they are traded are **exchange rates.** When a currency rises against another currency, it **appreciates;** when it falls, it **depreciates.** The **equilibrium exchange rate** matches the quantity of that currency supplied to the foreign exchange market to the quantity demanded.

4. To correct for international differences in inflation rates, economists calculate **real exchange rates,** which multiply the exchange rate between two countries' currencies by the ratio of the countries' price levels. The current account responds only to changes in the real exchange rate, not the nominal exchange rate. **Purchasing power parity** is the exchange rate that makes the cost of a basket of goods and services equal in two countries. While purchasing power parity and the nominal exchange rate almost always differ, purchasing power parity is a good predictor of actual changes in the nominal exchange rate.

5. Countries adopt different **exchange rate regimes,** rules governing exchange rate policy. The main types are **fixed exchange rates,** where the government takes action to keep the exchange rate at a target level, and **floating exchange rates,** where the exchange rate is free to fluctuate. Countries can fix exchange rates using **exchange market intervention,** which requires them to hold **foreign exchange reserves** that they use to buy any surplus of their currency. Alternatively, they can change domestic policies, especially monetary policy, to shift the demand and supply curves in the foreign exchange market. Finally, they can use **foreign exchange controls.**

6. Exchange rate policy poses a dilemma: there are economic payoffs to stable exchange rates, but the policies used to fix the exchange rate have costs. Exchange market intervention requires large reserves, and exchange controls distort incentives. If monetary policy is used to help fix the exchange rate, it isn't available to use for domestic policy.

7. Fixed exchange rates aren't always permanent commitments: countries with a fixed exchange rate sometimes engage in **devaluations,** reductions in the target value of the currency, or **revaluations,** increases in the target value of the currency. In addition to helping eliminate a surplus of domestic currency on the foreign exchange market, a devaluation increases aggregate demand. Similarly, a revaluation reduces shortages of domestic currency and reduces aggregate demand.

8. Under floating exchange rates, expansionary monetary policy works in part through the exchange rate: cutting domestic interest rates leads to a depreciation, and through that to higher exports and lower imports, which increases aggregate demand. Contractionary monetary policy has the reverse effect.

9. The fact that one country's imports are another country's exports creates a link between the business cycle in different countries. Floating exchange rates, however, may reduce the strength of that link.

KEY TERMS

PROBLEMS

interactive activity

1. How would the following transactions be categorized in the U.S. balance of payments accounts? Would they be entered in the current account (as a payment to or from a foreigner) or the financial account (as a sale of assets to or purchase of assets from a foreigner)? How will the balance of payments on the current and financial accounts change?

   a. A French importer buys a case of California wine for $500.

   b. An American who works for a French company deposits her paycheck, drawn on a Paris bank, into her San Francisco bank.

   c. An American buys a bond from a Japanese company for $10,000.

   d. An American charity sends $100,000 to Africa to help local residents buy food after a harvest shortfall.

2. The accompanying diagram shows foreign-owned assets in the United States and U.S.-owned assets abroad, both as a percentage of foreign GDP. As you can see from the diagram, both increased around five-fold from 1980 to 2016.

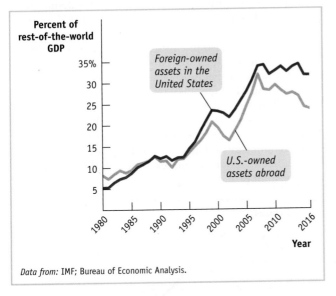

Percent of rest-of-the-world GDP

Data from: IMF; Bureau of Economic Analysis.

   a. As U.S.-owned assets abroad increased as a percentage of foreign GDP, does this mean that the United States, over the period, experienced net capital outflows?

   b. Does this diagram indicate that world economies were more tightly linked in 2016 than they were in 1980?

3. In the economy of Scottopia in 2016, exports equaled $400 billion of goods and $300 billion of services, imports equaled $500 billion of goods and $350 billion of services, and the rest of the world purchased

$250 billion of Scottopia's assets. What was the merchandise trade balance for Scottopia? What was the balance of payments on current account in Scottopia? What was the balance of payments on financial account? What was the value of Scottopia's purchases of assets from the rest of the world?

4. In the economy of Popania in 2016, total Popanian purchases of assets in the rest of the world equaled $300 billion, purchases of Popanian assets by the rest of the world equaled $400 billion, and Popania exported goods and services equal to $350 billion. What was Popania's balance of payments on financial account in 2016? What was its balance of payments on current account? What was the value of its imports?

5. Suppose that Northlandia and Southlandia are the only two trading countries in the world, that each nation runs a balance of payments on both current and financial accounts equal to zero, and that each nation sees the other's assets as identical to its own. Using the accompanying diagrams, explain how the demand and supply of loanable funds, the interest rate, and the balance of payments on current and financial accounts will change in each country if international capital flows are possible.

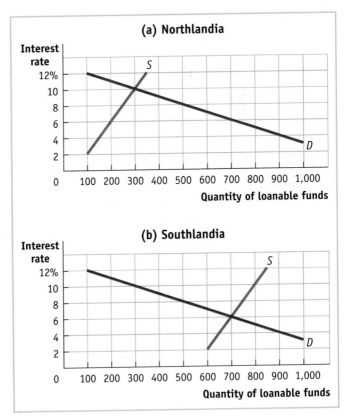

6. Based on the exchange rates for the trading days of 2016 and 2017 shown in the accompanying table, did the U.S. dollar appreciate or depreciate over the year? Did the movement in the value of the U.S. dollar make American goods and services more or less attractive to foreigners?

April 1, 2016	April 1, 2017
US$1.42 to buy 1 British pound sterling	US$1.25 to buy 1 British pound sterling
32.26 Taiwan dollars to buy US$1	30.40 Taiwan dollars to buy US$1
US$0.77 to buy 1 Canadian dollar	US$0.75 to buy 1 Canadian dollar
112.09 Japanese yen to buy US$1	111.39 Japanese yen to buy US$1
US$1.14 to buy 1 euro	US$1.07 to buy 1 euro
0.96 Swiss franc to buy US$1	1.00 Swiss franc to buy US$1

7. Go to http://fx.sauder.ubc.ca. Using the table labeled "The Most Recent Cross-Rates of Major Currencies," determine whether the British pound (GBP), the Canadian dollar (CAD), the Japanese yen (JPY), the euro (EUR), and the Swiss franc (CHF) have appreciated or depreciated against the U.S. dollar (USD) since April 1, 2017. The exchange rates on April 1, 2017 are listed in the table in Problem 6.

8. In January 2001, the U.S. federal funds rate was 6.5%, falling to 2% in November 2004. During the same period, the marginal lending rate at the European Central Bank fell from 5.75% to 3%.

a. Considering the change in interest rates over the period and using the loanable funds model, would you have expected funds to flow from the United States to Europe or from Europe to the United States over this period?

b. The accompanying diagram shows the exchange rate between the euro and the U.S. dollar from January 1, 2001, through September 2008. Is the movement of the exchange rate over the period January 2001 to November 2004 consistent with the movement in funds predicted in part a?

9. In each of the following scenarios, suppose that the two nations are the only trading nations in the world. Given inflation and the change in the nominal exchange rate, which nation's goods become more attractive?

a. Inflation is 10% in the United States and 5% in Japan; the U.S. dollar–Japanese yen exchange rate remains the same.

b. Inflation is 3% in the United States and 8% in Mexico; the price of the U.S. dollar falls from 12.50 to 10.25 Mexican pesos.

c. Inflation is 5% in the United States and 3% in the euro area; the price of the euro falls from $1.30 to $1.20.

d. Inflation is 8% in the United States and 4% in Canada; the price of the Canadian dollar rises from US$0.60 to US$0.75.

10. Starting from a position of equilibrium in the foreign exchange market under a fixed exchange rate regime, how must a government react to an increase in the demand for the nation's goods and services by the rest of the world to keep the exchange rate at its fixed value?

11. Suppose that Albernia's central bank has fixed the value of its currency, the bern, to the U.S. dollar (at a rate of US$1.50 to 1 bern) and is committed to that exchange rate. Initially, the foreign exchange market for the bern is also in equilibrium, as shown in the accompanying diagram. However, both Albernians and Americans begin to believe that there are big risks in holding Albernian assets; as a result, they become unwilling to hold Albernian assets unless they receive a higher rate of return on them than they do on U.S. assets. How would this affect the diagram? If the Albernian central bank tries to keep the exchange rate fixed using monetary policy, how will this affect the Albernian economy?

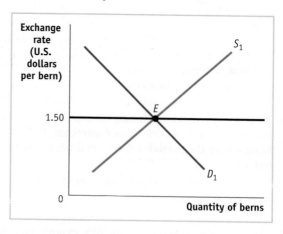

Data from: Federal Reserve Bank of St. Louis.

12. Access the Discovering Data exercise for Chapter 18 online to answer the following questions.

a. Using the most current data available, how has the exchange rate changed for Mexico, the United Kingdom, and Switzerland?

b. By how much did each of these three currencies appreciate and depreciate against the U.S. dollar?

c. How will the exchange rate change in each of the three countries affect their exports to the United States?

13. Your study partner asks you, "If central banks lose the ability to use discretionary monetary policy under fixed exchange rates, why would nations agree to a fixed exchange rate system?" How do you respond?

WORK IT OUT Interactive step-by-step help with solving this problem can be found online.

---

14. Suppose the United States and Japan are the only two trading countries in the world. What will happen to the value of the U.S. dollar if the following occur, other things equal?

a. Japan relaxes some of its import restrictions.

b. The United States imposes some import tariffs on Japanese goods.

c. Interest rates in the United States rise dramatically.

d. A report indicates that Japanese cars last much longer than previously thought, especially compared with American cars.

Macroeconomic Data Tables

TABLE 1
Macroeconomic Data for the United States 1929–2016[1]

	1929	1933	1939	1945	1950	1955	1960	1965
Nominal GDP and Its Components								
1. + Consumer spending (C)	77.4	45.9	67.2	120.0	192.2	258.7	331.6	443.6
2. + Investment spending (I)	17.2	2.3	10.2	12.4	56.5	73.8	86.5	129.6
3. + Government purchases of goods and services (G)	9.6	8.9	15.2	96.6	50.7	93.3	121.0	164.9
4. + Exports (X)	5.9	2.0	4.0	6.8	12.4	17.7	27.0	37.1
5. − Imports (IM)	5.6	1.9	3.1	7.5	11.6	17.2	22.8	31.5
6. = Gross Domestic Product (GDP)	**104.6**	**57.2**	**93.5**	**228.2**	**300.2**	**426.2**	**543.3**	**743.7**
7. + Income from abroad earned by Americans	1.1	0.4	0.7	0.8	2.2	3.5	4.9	7.9
8. − Income paid to foreigners	0.4	0.1	0.3	0.5	0.7	1.1	1.8	2.6
9. = Gross National Product (GNP)	**105.3**	**57.5**	**93.8**	**228.4**	**301.6**	**428.6**	**546.4**	**749.0**
10. National income	94.2	49.0	82.5	201.4	267.0	377.6	479.9	660.3
11. Government transfers	1.2	1.7	2.5	5.6	14.0	15.7	25.7	36.2
12. Taxes	1.7	0.8	1.5	19.4	18.9	32.9	46.1	57.7
13. Disposable income	83.5	46.4	72.1	156.3	215.0	291.7	376.5	513.2
14. Private savings	3.9	−0.4	3.9	35.2	20.0	28.2	37.8	58.3
Real GDP and Growth Measures								
15. Real GDP (billions of 2009 dollars)	1,056.6	778.3	1,163.6	2,217.8	2,184.0	2,739.0	3,108.7	3,976.7
16. Real GDP growth (percent change from previous year)	–	−1.3%	8.0%	−1.0%	8.7%	7.1%	2.6%	6.5%
17. Real GDP per capita (2009 dollars)	8,669	6,192	8,881	15,850	14,398	16,572	17,198	20,462
18. Real GDP per capita growth (percent change from previous year)	–	−1.8%	7.1%	−2.0%	6.9%	5.3%	0.5%	5.2%
Prices and Inflation								
19. Consumer Price Index (1982 − 1984 = 100)	17.2	12.9	13.9	18.0	24.1	26.8	29.6	31.5
20. CPI inflation rate	–	−5.2%	−1.3%	2.3%	1.1%	−0.3%	1.5%	1.6%
21. Producer Price Index (all commodities, 1982 = 100)	16.4	11.4	13.3	18.2	27.3	29.4	31.7	32.3
22. PPI inflation rate	–	1.8%	−2.2%	1.7%	3.8%	0.3%	0.0%	2.2%
23. GDP deflator (2009 = 100)	9.9	7.3	8.0	10.3	13.7	15.6	17.5	18.7
24. GDP deflator inflation rate	–	−2.8%	−0.9%	2.6%	1.2%	1.7%	1.4%	1.8%
Population and Employment								
25. Population (thousands)	121,878	125,690	131,028	139,928	151,684	165,275	180,760	194,347
26. Labor force (thousands)[2]	49,180	51,590	55,230	53,860	62,122	64,964	69,659	74,424
27. Unemployed (thousands)[2]	1,550	12,830	9,480	1,040	3,230	2,834	3,874	3,354
28. Unemployment rate	3.2%	24.9%	17.2%	1.9%	5.2%	4.4%	5.5%	4.5%
Government Finance and Money								
29. Federal budget balance	0.7	−2.6	−2.8	−47.6	−3.1	−3.0	0.3	−1.4
30. Budget balance (percent of GDP)	0.7%	−4.5%	−3.0%	−20.8%	−1.0%	−0.7%	0.1%	−0.2%
31. M1	–	–	–	–	–	–	140.3	163.4
32. M2	–	–	–	–	–	–	304.3	442.5
33. Federal funds (yearly average)	–	–	–	–	–	1.8%	3.2%	4.1%
International Trade								
34. Current account balance	–	–	–	–	−1.9	0.4	3.2	6.2

Data from: Bureau of Economic Analysis; Federal Bank of St. Louis; Office of Management and Budget.

1. Data in billions of current dollars unless otherwise stated. Only select dates shown for 1929 through 1965; annual data supplied for 1965 through 2016.
2. Until 1947, includes workers 14 years and older; 1948 and after, includes workers 16 years and older.

1966	1967	1968	1969	1970	1971	1972	1973	1974	1975	1976
480.6	507.4	557.4	604.5	647.7	701.0	769.4	851.1	932.0	1,032.8	1,150.2
144.2	142.7	156.9	173.6	170.1	196.8	228.1	266.9	274.5	257.3	323.2
186.4	208.1	226.8	240.4	254.2	269.3	288.2	306.4	343.1	382.9	405.8
40.9	43.5	47.9	51.9	59.7	63.0	70.8	95.3	126.7	138.7	149.5
37.1	39.9	46.6	50.5	55.8	62.3	74.2	91.2	127.5	122.7	151.1
815.0	**861.7**	**942.5**	**1,019.9**	**1,075.9**	**1,167.8**	**1,282.4**	**1,428.5**	**1,548.8**	**1,688.9**	**1,877.6**
8.1	8.7	10.1	11.8	12.8	14.0	16.3	23.5	29.8	28.0	32.4
3.0	3.3	4.0	5.7	6.4	6.4	7.7	10.9	14.3	15.0	15.5
820.1	**867.1**	**948.6**	**1,026.0**	**1,082.3**	**1,175.4**	**1,291.0**	**1,441.2**	**1,564.3**	**1,701.9**	**1,894.4**
719.7	760.2	832.1	899.5	940.1	1,017.0	1,123.0	1,257.0	1,350.8	1,451.1	1,614.8
39.6	48.0	56.1	62.3	74.7	88.1	97.9	112.6	133.3	170.0	184.3
66.4	73.0	87.0	104.5	103.1	101.7	123.6	132.4	151.0	147.6	172.7
554.2	592.8	643.8	695.8	761.5	830.4	899.9	1,006.1	1,098.3	1,219.3	1,325.8
61.4	72.2	72.1	75.0	96.1	110.1	109.2	131.8	141.7	159.0	147.3
4,238.9	4,355.2	4,569.0	4,712.5	4,722.0	4,877.6	5,134.3	5,424.1	5,396.0	5,385.4	5,675.4
6.6%	2.7%	4.9%	3.1%	0.2%	3.3%	5.3%	5.6%	−0.5%	−0.2%	5.4%
21,561	21,913	22,760	23,245	23,024	23,485	24,458	25,593	25,227	24,935	26,024
5.4%	1.6%	3.9%	2.1%	−0.9%	2.0%	4.1%	4.6%	−1.4%	−1.2%	4.4%
32.5	33.4	34.8	36.7	38.8	40.5	41.8	44.4	49.3	53.8	56.9
3.0%	2.8%	4.3%	5.5%	5.8%	4.3%	3.3%	6.2%	11.1%	9.1%	5.7%
33.3	33.4	34.2	35.6	36.9	38.1	39.8	45	53.5	58.4	61.1
3.1%	0.3%	2.4%	4.1%	3.7%	3.3%	4.5%	13.1%	18.9%	9.2%	4.6%
19.2	19.8	20.6	21.6	22.8	23.9	25.0	26.3	28.7	31.4	33.1
2.8%	2.9%	4.3%	4.9%	5.3%	5.1%	4.3%	5.4%	9.0%	9.3%	5.5%
196,599	198,752	200,745	202,736	205,089	207,692	209,924	211,939	213,898	215,981	218,086
75,745	77,348	78,710	80,705	82,796	84,376	87,011	89,411	91,976	93,770	96,151
2,867	2,972	2,797	2,830	4,127	5,022	4,876	4,359	5,173	7,940	7,398
3.8%	3.8%	3.6%	3.5%	5.0%	6.0%	5.6%	4.9%	5.6%	8.5%	7.7%
−3.7	−8.6	−25.2	3.2	−2.8	−23.0	−23.4	−14.9	−6.1	−53.2	−73.7
−0.5%	−1.0%	−2.7%	0.3%	−0.3%	−2.0%	−1.8%	−1.0%	−0.4%	−3.2%	−3.9%
171.0	177.7	190.1	201.4	209.1	223.1	239.0	256.3	269.1	281.3	297.2
471.4	503.6	545.3	578.7	601.5	674.4	758.2	831.8	880.6	963.5	1,086.5
5.1%	4.2%	5.7%	8.2%	7.2%	4.7%	4.4%	8.7%	10.5%	5.8%	5.1%
3.8	3.5	1.6	1.6	3.7	0.3	−4.1	8.9	6	19.9	7.1

(continued on next page)

Macroeconomic Data for the United States 1929–2016[1]

	1977	1978	1979	1980	1981	1982	1983	1984
Nominal GDP and Its Components								
1. + Consumer spending (*C*)	1,276.7	1,426.2	1,589.5	1,754.6	1,937.5	2,073.9	2,286.5	2,498.2
2. + Investment spending (*I*)	396.6	478.4	539.7	530.1	631.2	581.0	637.5	820.1
3. + Government purchases of goods and services (*G*)	435.8	477.4	525.5	590.8	654.7	710.0	765.7	825.2
4. + Exports (*X*)	159.4	186.9	230.1	280.8	305.2	283.2	277.0	302.4
5. − Imports (*IM*)	182.4	212.3	252.7	293.8	317.8	303.2	328.6	405.1
6. = Gross Domestic Product (GDP)	**2,086.0**	**2,356.6**	**2,632.1**	**2,862.5**	**3,211.0**	**3,345.0**	**3,638.1**	**4,040.7**
7. + Income from abroad earned by Americans	37.2	46.3	68.3	79.1	92.0	101.0	101.9	121.9
8. − Income paid to foreigners	16.9	24.7	36.4	44.9	59.1	64.5	64.8	85.6
9. = Gross National Product (GNP)	**2,106.2**	**2,378.2**	**2,664.1**	**2,896.7**	**3,243.9**	**3,381.5**	**3,675.2**	**4,077.0**
10. National income	1,798.7	2,029.9	2,248.2	2,426.8	2,722.1	2,840.4	3,060.5	3,444.0
11. Government transfers	194.6	209.9	235.6	280.1	319.0	355.5	384.3	400.6
12. Taxes	197.9	229.6	268.9	299.5	345.8	354.7	352.9	377.9
13. Disposable income	1,456.7	1,630.1	1,809.3	2,018.0	2,250.7	2,424.7	2,617.4	2,903.9
14. Private savings	148.2	166.6	177.5	213.2	252.5	277.7	247.0	312.1
Real GDP and Growth Measures								
15. Real GDP (billions of 2009 dollars)	5,937.0	6,267.2	6,466.2	6,450.4	6,617.7	6,491.3	6,792.0	7,285.0
16. Real GDP growth (percent change from previous year)	4.6%	5.6%	3.2%	−0.2%	2.6%	−1.9%	4.6%	7.3%
17. Real GDP per capita (2009 dollars)	26,951	28,151	28,725	28,325	28,772	27,953	28,984	30,817
18. Real GDP per capita growth (percent change from previous year)	3.6%	4.5%	2.0%	−1.4%	1.6%	−2.8%	3.7%	6.3%
Prices and Inflation								
19. Consumer Price Index (1982 – 1984 = 100)	60.6	65.2	72.6	82.4	90.9	96.5	99.6	103.9
20. CPI inflation rate	6.5%	7.6%	11.3%	13.5%	10.3%	6.1%	3.2%	4.3%
21. Producer Price Index (all commodities, 1982 = 100)	64.9	69.9	78.7	89.8	98	100	101.3	103.7
22. PPI inflation rate	6.2%	7.7%	12.6%	14.1%	9.1%	2.0%	1.3%	2.4%
23. GDP deflator (2009 = 100)	35.1	37.6	40.7	44.4	48.5	51.5	53.6	55.5
24. GDP deflator inflation rate	6.2%	7.0%	8.3%	9.0%	9.3%	6.2%	3.9%	3.5%
Population and Employment								
25. Population (thousands)	220,289	222,629	225,106	227,726	230,008	232,218	234,333	236,394
26. Labor force (thousands)[2]	98,984	102,233	104,961	106,974	108,676	110,244	111,515	113,532
27. Unemployed (thousands)[2]	6,967	6,187	6,135	7,671	8,276	10,715	10,694	8,529
28. Unemployment rate	7.1%	6.1%	5.9%	7.2%	7.6%	9.7%	9.6%	7.5%
Government Finance and Money								
29. Federal budget balance	−53.7	−59.2	−40.7	−73.8	−79.0	−128.0	−207.8	−185.4
30. Budget balance (percent of GDP)	−2.6%	−2.5%	−1.5%	−2.6%	−2.5%	−3.8%	−5.7%	−4.6%
31. M1	319.9	346.2	372.6	395.7	425.0	453.0	503.2	538.6
32. M2	1,221.2	1,322.2	1,425.7	1,540.2	1,679.3	1,831.1	2,054.8	2,219.3
33. Federal funds (yearly average)	5.5%	7.9%	11.2%	13.4%	16.4%	12.3%	9.1%	10.2%
International Trade								
34. Current account balance	−10.9	−12.7	−1.2	8.5	3.4	−3.3	−35.1	−90.1

Data from: Bureau of Economic Analysis; Federal Bank of St. Louis; Office of Management and Budget.

1. Data in billions of current dollars unless otherwise stated. Only select dates shown for 1929 through 1965; annual data supplied for 1965 through 2016.
2. Until 1947, includes workers 14 years and older; 1948 and after, includes workers 16 years and older.

1985	1986	1987	1988	1989	1990	1991	1992	1993	1994	1995
2,722.7	2,898.4	3,092.1	3,346.9	3,592.8	3,825.6	3,960.2	4,215.7	4,471.0	4,741.0	4,984.2
829.6	849.1	892.2	937.0	999.7	993.5	944.3	1,013.0	1,106.8	1,256.5	1,317.5
908.4	974.5	1,030.8	1,078.2	1,151.9	1,238.4	1,298.2	1,345.4	1,366.1	1,403.7	1,452.2
303.2	321.0	363.9	444.6	504.3	551.9	594.9	633.1	654.8	720.9	812.8
417.2	452.9	508.7	554.0	591.0	629.7	623.5	667.8	720.0	813.4	902.6
4,346.7	**4,590.2**	**4,870.2**	**5,252.6**	**5,657.7**	**5,979.6**	**6,174.0**	**6,539.3**	**6,878.7**	**7,308.8**	**7,664.1**
112.7	111.3	123.3	152.1	177.7	188.8	168.4	152.1	155.6	184.5	229.8
87.3	94.4	105.8	129.5	152.9	154.2	136.8	121.0	123.6	160.7	201.1
4,372.1	**4,607.1**	**4,887.7**	**5,275.3**	**5,682.5**	**6,014.3**	**6,205.6**	**6,570.4**	**6,910.7**	**7,332.6**	**7,692.8**
3,684.2	3,848.2	4,119.2	4,493.4	4,782.2	5,036.1	5,186.1	5,499.7	5,754.8	6,140.2	6,479.5
425.4	451.6	468.1	497.5	544.2	596.9	668.1	748.0	793.0	829.0	883.5
417.8	437.8	489.6	505.9	567.7	594.7	588.9	612.8	648.8	693.1	748.4
3,098.5	3,287.9	3,466.3	3,770.4	4,052.1	4,311.8	4,484.5	4,800.3	5,000.2	5,244.2	5,532.6
265.1	269.4	252.1	294.7	316.5	335.4	365.9	426.0	367.6	331.4	352.9
7,593.8	7,860.5	8,132.6	8,474.5	8,786.4	8,955.0	8,948.4	9,266.6	9,521.0	9,905.4	10,174.8
4.2%	3.5%	3.5%	4.2%	3.7%	1.9%	−0.1%	3.6%	2.7%	4.0%	2.7%
31,839	32,659	33,489	34,581	35,517	35,794	35,295	36,068	36,580	37,598	38,167
3.3%	2.6%	2.5%	3.3%	2.7%	0.8%	−1.4%	2.2%	1.4%	2.8%	1.5%
107.6	109.6	113.6	118.3	124.0	130.7	136.2	140.3	144.5	148.2	152.4
3.5%	1.9%	3.7%	4.1%	4.8%	5.4%	4.2%	3.0%	3.0%	2.6%	2.8%
103.2	100.2	102.8	106.9	112.2	116.3	116.5	117.2	118.9	120.5	124.8
−0.5%	−2.9%	2.6%	4.0%	5.0%	3.7%	0.2%	0.6%	1.5%	1.3%	3.6%
57.2	58.4	59.9	62.0	64.4	66.8	69.0	70.6	72.2	73.8	75.3
3.2%	2.0%	2.6%	3.5%	3.9%	3.7%	3.3%	2.3%	2.4%	2.1%	2.1%
238,506	240,683	242,843	245,061	247,387	250,181	253,530	256,922	260,282	263,455	266,588
115,467	117,846	119,853	121,671	123,851	125,857	126,352	128,099	129,185	131,047	132,315
8,313	8,245	7,414	6,697	6,524	7,061	8,640	9,611	8,927	7,976	7,407
7.2%	7.0%	6.2%	5.5%	5.3%	5.6%	6.9%	7.5%	6.9%	6.1%	5.6%
−212.3	−221.2	−149.7	−155.2	−152.6	−221.0	−269.2	−290.3	−255.1	−203.2	−164.0
−4.9%	−4.8%	−3.1%	−3.0%	−2.7%	−3.7%	−4.4%	−4.4%	−3.7%	−2.8%	−2.1%
587.0	666.3	743.6	774.8	782.2	810.6	859.0	965.9	1,078.4	1,145.2	1,143.0
2,416.9	2,613.6	2,783.9	2,933.5	3,056.3	3,223.6	3,342.0	3,403.4	3,437.8	3,482.2	3,553.0
8.1%	6.8%	6.7%	7.6%	9.2%	8.1%	5.7%	3.5%	3.0%	4.2%	5.8%
−114.3	−142.7	−154.1	−115.8	−92.4	−74.9	7.9	−45.6	−78.5	−114.7	−105.1

(continued on next page)

Macroeconomic Data for the United States 1929–2016[1]

	1996	1997	1998	1999	2000	2001	2002	2003
Nominal GDP and Its Components								
1. + Consumer spending (C)	5,268.1	5,560.7	5,903.0	6,307.0	6,792.4	7,103.1	7,384.1	7,765.5
2. + Investment spending (I)	1,432.1	1,595.6	1,735.3	1,884.2	2,033.8	1,928.6	1,925.0	2,027.9
3. + Government purchases of goods and services (G)	1,496.4	1,554.2	1,613.5	1,726.0	1,834.4	1,958.8	2,094.9	2,220.8
4. + Exports (X)	867.6	953.8	953.0	992.0	1,096.8	1,026.7	1,002.5	1,040.3
5. – Imports (IM)	964.0	1,055.8	1,115.7	1,248.6	1,472.6	1,395.4	1,429.0	1,543.9
6. = **Gross Domestic Product (GDP)**	**8,100.2**	**8,608.5**	**9,089.2**	**9,660.6**	**10,284.8**	**10,621.8**	**10,977.5**	**11,510.7**
7. + Income from abroad earned by Americans	246.4	280.1	286.8	321.4	382.7	325.3	315.8	356.1
8. – Income paid to foreigners	214.6	256.0	268.5	294.3	345.7	273.5	267.2	289.0
9. = **Gross National Product (GNP)**	**8,132.0**	**8,632.6**	**9,107.4**	**9,687.8**	**10,321.8**	**10,673.6**	**11,026.1**	**11,577.8**
10. National income	6,899.4	7,380.4	7,857.3	8,324.4	8,907.0	9,184.6	9,436.8	9,864.2
11. Government transfers	929.2	954.9	983.9	1,026.2	1,087.3	1,192.6	1,284.7	1,347.3
12. Taxes	837.1	931.8	1,032.4	1,112.1	1,236.6	1,239.3	1,054.7	1,005.3
13. Disposable income	5,829.9	6,148.9	6,561.3	6,876.3	7,400.5	7,752.3	8,099.2	8,485.8
14. Private savings	345.2	352.2	405.3	303.3	307.7	335.2	405.3	409.6
Real GDP and Growth Measures								
15. Real GDP (billions of 2009 dollars)	10,561.0	11,034.9	11,525.9	12,065.9	12,559.7	12,682.2	12,908.8	13,271.1
16. Real GDP growth (percent change from previous year)	3.8%	4.5%	4.4%	4.7%	4.1%	1.0%	1.8%	2.8%
17. Real GDP per capita (2009 dollars)	39,156	40,427	41,737	43,196	44,475	44,464	44,829	45,664
18. Real GDP per capita growth (percent change from previous year)	2.6%	3.2%	3.2%	3.5%	3.0%	0.0%	0.8%	1.9%
Prices and Inflation								
19. Consumer Price Index (1982 – 1984 = 100)	156.9	160.5	163.0	166.6	172.2	177.1	179.9	184.0
20. CPI inflation rate	2.9%	2.3%	1.6%	2.2%	3.4%	2.8%	1.6%	2.3%
21. Producer Price Index (all commodities, 1982 = 100)	127.7	127.6	124.4	125.5	132.7	134.2	131.1	138.1
22. PPI inflation rate	2.3%	−0.1%	−2.5%	0.9%	5.7%	1.1%	−2.3%	5.3%
23. GDP deflator (2009 = 100)	76.7	78.0	78.9	80.1	81.9	83.8	85.0	86.7
24. GDP deflator inflation rate	1.8%	1.7%	1.1%	1.5%	2.3%	2.3%	1.5%	2.0%
Population and Employment								
25. Population (thousands)	269,714	272,958	276,154	279,328	282,398	285,225	287,955	290,626
26. Labor force (thousands)[2]	133,951	136,301	137,680	139,380	142,586	143,769	144,856	146,500
27. Unemployed (thousands)[2]	7,231	6,729	6,204	5,879	5,685	6,830	8,375	8,770
28. Unemployment rate	5.4%	4.9%	4.5%	4.2%	4.0%	4.7%	5.8%	6.0%
Government Finance and Money								
29. Federal budget balance	−107.4	−21.9	69.3	125.6	236.2	128.2	−157.8	−377.6
30. Budget balance (percent of GDP)	−1.3%	−0.3%	0.8%	1.3%	2.3%	1.2%	−1.4%	−3.3%
31. M1	1,106.8	1,070.2	1,080.6	1,102.3	1,103.7	1,140.2	1,196.7	1,273.8
32. M2	3,723.5	3,910.4	4,189.5	4,497.2	4,769.2	5,178.9	5,561.8	5,949.9
33. Federal funds (yearly average)	5.3%	5.5%	5.4%	5.0%	6.2%	3.9%	1.7%	1.1%
International Trade								
34. Current account balance	−114.1	−129.3	−204.5	−286.6	−403.7	−388.8	−450.8	−515.7

Data from: Bureau of Economic Analysis; Federal Bank of St. Louis; Office of Management and Budget.

1. Data in billions of current dollars unless otherwise stated. Only select dates shown for 1929 through 1965; annual data supplied for 1965 through 2016.
2. Until 1947, includes workers 14 years and older; 1948 and after, includes workers 16 years and older.

2004	2005	2006	2007	2008	2009	2010	2011	2012	2013	2014
8,260.0	8,794.1	9,304.0	9,750.5	10,013.6	9,847.0	10,202.2	10,689.3	11,050.6	11,361.2	11,863.4
2,276.7	2,527.1	2,680.6	2,643.7	2,424.8	1,878.1	2,100.8	2,239.9	2,511.7	2,706.3	2,886.5
2,357.4	2,493.7	2,642.2	2,801.9	3,003.2	3,089.1	3,174.0	3,168.7	3,158.6	3,116.1	3,152.1
1,181.5	1,308.9	1,476.3	1,664.6	1,841.9	1,587.7	1,852.3	2,106.4	2,198.2	2,276.6	2,375.3
1,800.7	2,030.1	2,247.3	2,383.2	2,565.0	1,983.2	2,365.0	2,686.4	2,763.8	2,768.6	2,884.1
12,274.9	**13,093.7**	**13,855.9**	**14,477.6**	**14,718.6**	**14,418.7**	**14,964.4**	**15,517.9**	**16,155.3**	**16,691.5**	**17,393.1**
451.4	575.8	724.2	875.7	856.9	648.9	720.0	792.6	801.5	825.5	852.1
362.3	483.2	656.6	750.1	684.9	497.8	514.1	546.0	563.9	581.3	604.0
12,364.1	**13,186.3**	**13,923.5**	**14,603.2**	**14,890.6**	**14,569.8**	**15,170.3**	**15,764.6**	**16,392.8**	**16,935.8**	**17,641.2**
10,540.9	11,239.8	12,004.8	12,321.4	12,427.8	12,126.1	12,739.5	13,352.3	14,061.9	14,444.8	15,153.9
1,421.3	1,516.7	1,614.6	1,728.1	1,956.6	2,147.5	2,324.7	2,360.5	2,366.3	2,428.0	2,540.4
1,050.6	1,213.2	1,357.1	1,493.2	1,507.8	1,152.3	1,239.3	1,453.2	1,511.4	1,677.8	1,787.0
9,002.3	9,400.8	10,036.9	10,507.0	10,994.4	10,942.5	11,237.9	11,801.4	12,403.7	12,395.8	13,022.7
409.4	243.1	331.4	309.8	536.7	667.4	630	710.1	946.7	620.1	726.0
13,773.5	14,234.2	14,613.8	14,873.7	14,830.4	14,418.7	14,783.8	15,020.6	15,354.6	15,612.2	15,982.30
3.8%	3.3%	2.7%	1.8%	−0.3%	−2.8%	2.5%	1.6%	2.2%	1.7%	2.4%
46,967	48,090	48,905	49,300	48,697	46,930	47,720	48,125	48,841	49,317	50,119
2.9%	2.4%	1.7%	0.8%	−1.2%	−3.6%	1.7%	0.9%	1.6%	1.5%	1.5%
188.9	195.3	201.6	207.3	215.3	214.6	218.1	224.9	229.6	232.9	236.7
2.7%	3.4%	3.2%	2.9%	3.8%	−0.3%	1.6%	3.1%	2.1%	1.5%	1.6%
146.7	157.4	164.8	172.7	189.6	172.9	184.7	201.1	202.2	203.4	205.3
6.2%	7.3%	4.7%	4.8%	9.8%	−8.8%	6.8%	8.9%	0.5%	0.6%	0.9%
89.1	92.0	94.8	97.3	99.2	100.0	101.2	103.3	105.2	106.9	108.8
2.7%	3.2%	3.1%	2.7%	2.0%	0.8%	1.2%	2.1%	1.8%	1.7%	1.8%
293,262	295,993	298,818	301,696	304,543	307,240	309,801	312,114	314,377	316,569	318,887
147,380	149,289	151,409	153,123	154,322	154,189	153,885	153,624	154,974	155,395	155,906
8,140	7,579	6,991	7,073	8,948	14,295	14,808	13,739	12,499	11,457	9,598
5.5%	5.1%	4.6%	4.6%	5.8%	9.3%	9.6%	8.9%	8.1%	7.4%	6.2%
−412.7	−318.3	−248.2	−160.7	−458.6	−1,412.7	−1,294.4	−1,299.6	−1,087.0	−679.5	−484.6
−3.4%	−2.4%	−1.8%	−1.1%	−3.1%	−9.8%	−8.6%	−8.4%	−6.7%	−4.1%	−2.8%
1,344.3	1,371.8	1,374.8	1,372.6	1,434.3	1,637.6	1,741.9	2,009.6	2,311.4	2,548.3	2,811.9
6,236.3	6,505.6	6,848.0	7,269.9	7,766.2	8,392.3	8,601.2	9,229.4	10,019.2	10,694.2	11,355.1
1.4%	3.2%	5.0%	5.0%	1.9%	0.2%	0.2%	0.1%	0.1%	0.1%	0.1%
−627	−737.7	−802.2	−718.1	−691.6	−381.9	−445.9	−481.5	−468.2	−386.1	−401.7

(continued on next page)

Macroeconomic Data for the United States 1929–2016[1]

	2015	2016
Nominal GDP and Its Components		
1. + Consumer spending (*C*)	12,283.7	12,757.9
2. + Investment spending (*I*)	3,056.6	3,035.7
3. + Government purchases of goods and services (*G*)	3,218.3	3,276.7
4. + Exports (*X*)	2,264.3	2,232.4
5. – Imports (*IM*)	2,786.3	2,733.7
6. = Gross Domestic Product (GDP)	**18,036.6**	**18,569.1**
7. + Income from abroad earned by Americans	813.1	842.6
8. – Income paid to foreigners	607.4	635.8
9. = Gross National Product (GNP)	**18,242.4**	**18,776.0**
10. National income	15,665.3	16,130.4
11. Government transfers	2,678.6	2,775.4
12. Taxes	1,938.7	1,965.6
13. Disposable income	13,519.8	14,045.9
14. Private savings	783.6	818.8
Real GDP and Growth Measures		
15. Real GDP (billions of 2009 dollars)	16,397.20	16,662.10
16. Real GDP growth (percent change from previous year)	2.6%	1.6%
17. Real GDP per capita (2009 dollars)	51,054	51,523
18. Real GDP per capita growth (percent change from previous year)	1.5%	1.5%
Prices and Inflation		
19. Consumer Price Index (1982 – 1984 = 100)	237.0	240.0
20. CPI inflation rate	0.1%	1.3%
21. Producer Price Index (all commodities, 1982 = 100)	190.4	185.4
22. PPI inflation rate	−7.3%	−2.6%
23. GDP deflator (2009 = 100)	110.0	111.4
24. GDP deflator inflation rate	1.1%	1.3%
Population and Employment		
25. Population (thousands)	321,173	323,391
26. Labor force (thousands)[2]	157,128	159,186
27. Unemployed (thousands)[2]	8,288	7,750
28. Unemployment rate	5.3%	4.9%
Government Finance and Money		
29. Federal budget balance	−438.4	−587.4
30. Budget balance (percent of GDP)	−2.4%	−3.2%
31. M1	3,018.1	3,246.7
32. M2	12,013.7	12,832.6
33. Federal funds (yearly average)	0.1%	0.4%
International Trade		
34. Current account balance	−477.4	−467.5

Data from: Bureau of Economic Analysis; Federal Bank of St. Louis; Office of Management and Budget.

1. Data in billions of current dollars unless otherwise stated. Only select dates shown for 1929 through 1965; annual data supplied for 1965 through 2016.
2. Until 1947, includes workers 14 years and older; 1948 and after, includes workers 16 years and older.

TABLE 2
Macroeconomic Data for Select Countries
GDP (Billions of U.S. Dollars)

Country	1985	1986	1987	1988	1989	1990	1991	1992	1993
Argentina	95.59	114.95	117.85	138.04	88.57	153.21	205.52	247.99	256.37
Australia	174.56	181.66	213.31	271.40	308.28	323.92	324.60	318.15	309.64
Austria	68.47	97.16	121.50	133.29	132.97	166.49	174.05	195.07	189.96
Belgium	84.95	117.80	146.22	158.97	160.71	201.24	206.54	230.03	219.93
Brazil	236.80	274.69	298.99	334.01	458.53	475.12	416.60	399.08	447.83
Bulgaria	26.26	23.24	26.94	44.02	44.84	19.77	1.94	7.86	4.27
Canada	364.77	377.45	431.33	507.38	565.08	593.96	610.32	592.40	577.20
Chile	17.24	18.53	21.86	25.77	29.68	33.00	37.98	46.27	49.51
China	312.62	303.34	330.30	411.92	461.07	398.62	415.60	495.67	623.05
Colombia	48.88	48.94	50.95	54.93	55.38	56.41	58.31	69.00	78.20
Cyprus	2.61	3.32	3.98	4.59	4.90	6.00	6.20	7.42	7.10
Czech Republic	n/a	n/a	n/a	n/a	n/a	n/a	n/a	n/a	n/a
Denmark	62.68	88.10	109.43	115.57	112.44	138.26	139.27	152.96	143.21
Dominican Republic	6.94	8.43	8.87	8.13	9.18	8.54	10.57	12.33	13.88
Ecuador	18.83	13.82	12.91	12.28	12.05	12.24	13.73	15.01	17.54
Egypt	48.84	54.08	77.36	92.53	115.36	96.09	48.43	44.17	49.53
Estonia	n/a	n/a	n/a	n/a	n/a	n/a	n/a	n/a	1.74
Finland	56.23	73.66	91.78	108.81	119.24	141.81	128.28	113.10	89.32
France	559.85	776.12	939.45	1,025.68	1,031.31	1,278.67	1,280.30	1,412.10	1,331.66
Germany	658.78	940.83	1,170.62	1,262.02	1,252.92	1,592.71	1,869.10	2,128.56	2,069.77
Ghana	10.12	9.19	7.84	8.32	8.42	9.98	11.24	11.04	9.71
Greece	47.96	56.43	65.66	76.47	79.24	97.98	105.64	116.62	109.01
Guatemala	10.39	5.62	6.50	7.04	8.12	7.11	8.69	9.63	10.46
Hungary	21.38	24.62	27.06	29.62	30.23	34.26	34.65	38.62	40.01
Iceland	3.03	4.04	5.60	6.18	5.74	6.54	6.99	7.15	6.27
India	237.62	252.75	283.75	299.65	300.19	326.61	274.84	293.26	284.19
Ireland	21.01	28.35	33.60	36.79	37.98	48.03	48.64	54.76	50.75
Israel	26.54	32.68	39.03	48.35	49.19	58.05	65.84	73.58	73.95
Italy	458.98	650.04	815.84	903.85	939.88	1,173.06	1,239.53	1,314.81	1,057.44
Jamaica	1.99	2.37	2.67	3.18	3.69	4.66	4.29	4.33	5.52
Japan	1,401.01	2,075.62	2,514.97	3,051.17	3,052.90	3,140.67	3,582.80	3,898.14	4,467.12
Kenya	8.75	10.39	11.39	11.81	11.71	12.18	11.50	11.33	7.87
Korea	100.29	115.54	146.13	196.97	243.51	279.22	325.71	350.08	386.29
Latvia	n/a	n/a	n/a	n/a	n/a	n/a	n/a	1.69	2.73
Lithuania	n/a	n/a	n/a	n/a	n/a	n/a	n/a	n/a	n/a
Luxembourg	4.59	6.68	8.29	9.39	10.00	12.75	13.82	15.48	15.86
Malaysia	33.61	29.88	34.05	37.32	41.10	46.58	52.77	63.52	71.84
Mexico	223.10	154.47	169.40	207.24	252.55	298.04	357.29	414.35	504.02
Netherlands	141.52	197.22	241.53	258.31	254.54	314.02	323.51	358.00	348.10
New Zealand	22.52	27.40	36.93	45.44	44.06	45.77	43.58	41.60	44.80
Nigeria	n/a	n/a	n/a	n/a	n/a	62.17	60.13	52.28	56.81
Norway	65.44	78.71	94.24	101.91	102.65	119.80	121.90	130.89	120.27
Paraguay	4.21	5.03	4.22	5.58	4.05	4.90	6.98	7.16	7.25
Peru	16.82	25.24	41.67	32.97	40.69	28.32	33.99	35.38	34.33
Philippines	34.00	33.17	36.87	42.08	47.29	49.10	50.32	58.70	60.24
Poland	70.78	73.68	63.71	68.61	66.90	62.08	80.45	88.71	90.37
Portugal	27.23	37.87	47.39	55.44	59.81	79.45	89.91	108.13	95.15
Romania	48.60	52.63	58.85	60.93	54.58	38.76	29.26	19.91	26.80
Russia	n/a	n/a	n/a	n/a	n/a	n/a	n/a	91.94	197.43
Saudi Arabia	103.89	86.89	85.58	88.14	95.22	117.47	132.05	136.91	132.79
Singapore	18.56	18.76	21.61	26.52	31.39	38.90	45.47	52.13	60.64
South Africa	59.10	67.56	88.57	95.21	99.04	115.53	123.96	134.56	134.35
Spain	181.17	250.68	317.60	373.14	411.57	533.95	575.18	628.61	528.01
Sweden	111.57	147.32	179.09	202.62	213.08	255.95	268.68	279.57	209.98
Switzerland	107.58	154.15	192.95	208.80	201.67	257.54	260.54	271.05	263.45
Thailand	40.19	44.52	52.20	63.70	74.64	88.47	101.25	115.58	128.89
Turkey	92.76	102.90	118.69	124.84	147.55	207.12	208.39	218.93	248.30
Ukraine	n/a	n/a	n/a	n/a	n/a	n/a	n/a	22.19	35.03
United Arab Emirates	37.31	29.57	32.47	33.00	38.09	49.09	49.82	52.21	53.44
United Kingdom	534.24	651.40	807.38	982.79	999.36	1,183.00	1,235.09	1,273.73	1,139.20
United States	4,346.75	4,590.13	4,870.20	5,252.63	5,657.65	5,979.55	6,174.03	6,539.28	6,878.70
Vietnam	15.00	33.87	42.05	23.23	6.29	6.47	7.64	9.87	13.18

Data from: International Monetary Fund, World Economic Outlook Database, April 2017.

1994	1995	1996	1997	1998	1999	2000	2001	2002	2003	2004
279.15	280.08	295.12	317.55	324.24	307.67	308.49	291.74	108.73	138.15	164.92
353.22	379.77	425.59	426.67	381.09	411.83	399.30	376.91	424.52	540.43	657.44
203.51	240.75	236.83	212.61	217.99	217.01	197.00	197.12	213.73	261.22	300.26
239.93	289.90	281.47	255.17	260.97	260.54	238.60	238.05	259.78	319.61	371.39
558.37	786.48	850.80	883.53	864.02	599.44	655.45	559.98	509.80	558.23	669.29
7.50	12.56	9.49	10.02	13.23	13.50	13.15	14.08	16.28	20.98	25.96
578.14	604.03	628.57	652.83	631.85	676.01	742.32	736.43	757.98	892.50	1,023.17
57.11	73.60	78.03	84.92	81.59	75.12	77.83	70.97	69.73	75.64	99.24
566.47	736.87	867.22	965.32	1,032.58	1,097.13	1,214.91	1,344.10	1,477.48	1,671.07	1,966.22
98.26	111.24	116.84	128.27	118.44	103.76	99.88	98.20	97.95	94.65	117.09
8.00	9.94	10.02	9.55	10.26	10.50	9.99	10.40	11.42	14.55	17.33
n/a	59.52	66.80	61.60	66.35	64.72	61.47	67.38	81.68	99.32	118.97
156.18	185.04	187.64	173.56	177.01	177.96	164.19	164.82	178.65	218.14	251.37
15.50	17.54	19.40	20.95	22.65	23.21	25.67	26.64	28.30	22.59	23.41
21.15	22.97	24.04	27.01	27.47	19.74	18.32	24.47	28.55	32.43	36.59
54.55	63.26	71.11	79.77	89.19	95.04	104.75	102.27	90.26	85.16	82.86
2.44	3.80	4.75	5.07	5.62	5.74	5.71	6.26	7.35	9.85	12.07
103.76	134.35	132.16	127.01	134.11	135.40	125.91	129.36	140.05	171.40	197.04
1,404.48	1,611.20	1,614.71	1,462.61	1,512.96	1,502.25	1,372.45	1,383.41	1,505.65	1,851.66	2,127.00
2,211.02	2,594.37	2,504.67	2,221.74	2,246.45	2,202.85	1,955.67	1,952.33	2,086.50	2,510.53	2,823.07
8.87	10.52	11.30	11.20	12.16	12.58	8.11	8.65	10.03	12.42	14.45
116.54	136.97	145.88	143.34	144.65	149.04	132.20	136.31	154.38	202.31	240.85
11.86	13.31	14.22	16.10	17.49	16.49	17.19	18.70	20.78	21.92	23.97
43.02	46.30	46.54	47.18	48.66	49.08	47.21	53.70	67.56	85.05	103.70
6.44	7.17	7.52	7.60	8.47	8.93	8.95	8.14	9.20	11.30	13.71
333.01	366.60	399.79	423.19	428.77	466.84	476.64	493.93	523.77	618.37	721.59
55.71	69.18	75.82	82.78	90.11	98.75	99.83	109.10	127.97	164.29	193.95
84.41	100.28	109.95	114.71	115.95	117.20	132.33	130.64	120.94	126.68	135.37
1,090.60	1,171.51	1,309.32	1,240.58	1,268.03	1,250.20	1,145.11	1,163.32	1,270.99	1,572.65	1,800.76
5.53	6.54	7.05	8.08	8.46	8.50	8.70	8.84	9.33	8.99	9.74
4,907.58	5,450.81	4,834.02	4,415.72	4,034.45	4,546.05	4,887.30	4,304.76	4,115.20	4,447.38	4,815.77
9.42	11.94	13.57	13.74	15.74	14.35	14.14	14.54	14.76	16.80	18.06
455.65	556.45	598.06	557.55	374.14	485.26	561.60	533.19	609.02	680.58	764.89
4.53	5.41	5.97	6.53	7.18	7.53	7.95	8.35	9.55	11.75	14.38
n/a	6.70	8.39	10.12	11.24	10.97	11.54	12.25	14.28	18.80	22.65
17.65	20.77	20.66	18.60	19.45	21.29	21.44	21.07	23.39	29.26	34.39
79.99	95.40	108.30	107.57	77.51	85.00	100.72	99.64	108.30	118.34	133.97
527.32	343.81	397.40	480.56	502.03	579.45	683.65	724.69	741.56	713.28	770.27
373.92	446.93	445.85	412.72	433.09	442.56	414.02	426.94	467.02	572.96	651.42
52.87	62.21	69.07	68.89	56.78	58.85	54.14	53.11	62.05	82.47	101.58
80.13	132.23	172.69	187.87	209.68	57.48	67.82	73.13	93.98	102.94	130.35
127.09	152.05	163.52	161.37	154.18	162.32	171.33	174.02	195.42	227.62	264.20
7.87	9.06	9.79	9.97	9.03	8.39	8.20	7.66	6.33	6.59	8.03
43.79	52.14	54.09	56.91	54.60	49.38	51.01	51.61	54.45	59.05	66.71
71.00	82.12	91.79	91.23	72.21	83.00	81.02	76.26	81.36	83.91	91.37
103.68	139.09	156.68	157.18	172.05	167.80	171.28	190.43	198.68	217.51	253.71
99.70	118.22	122.66	117.25	124.17	127.63	118.71	121.65	134.70	165.28	189.44
30.57	36.07	35.92	35.87	42.82	36.18	37.47	40.72	46.17	59.87	76.22
297.49	336.82	420.97	435.11	291.23	210.49	279.03	329.41	371.21	462.33	635.00
135.00	143.15	158.45	165.74	146.78	161.72	189.52	184.14	189.61	215.81	258.74
73.78	87.89	96.40	100.17	85.72	86.29	95.84	89.29	91.94	97.00	114.18
139.80	155.46	147.70	152.61	137.69	136.55	136.45	121.60	115.75	175.25	228.93
529.82	612.41	638.50	587.97	616.96	634.38	597.15	626.51	707.64	908.59	1,071.01
226.11	264.09	288.13	264.51	266.83	270.74	259.84	239.96	263.94	331.11	381.74
291.88	341.96	329.76	286.67	294.75	289.60	271.85	278.82	301.32	352.36	393.04
146.68	169.28	183.04	150.18	113.68	126.67	126.39	120.30	134.30	152.28	172.90
179.20	233.29	250.27	261.80	276.02	256.48	273.09	200.31	238.34	311.94	404.86
38.01	38.28	46.08	51.87	43.32	32.66	32.33	39.31	43.96	52.01	67.23
57.45	63.64	70.99	76.17	73.39	82.87	103.89	103.31	109.82	124.35	147.82
1,220.82	1,320.62	1,394.48	1,537.56	1,623.79	1,652.54	1,638.70	1,613.59	1,760.45	2,030.63	2,390.27
7,308.70	7,664.05	8,100.18	8,608.53	9,089.15	9,660.63	10,284.75	10,621.83	10,977.53	11,510.68	12,274.93
16.31	20.80	24.69	26.89	27.23	28.70	31.18	32.52	35.10	39.56	49.52

(continued on next page)

Macroeconomic Data for Select Countries
GDP (Billions of U.S. Dollars)

Country	2005	2006	2007	2008	2009	2010	2011	2012	2013
Argentina	199.27	232.89	287.92	363.55	334.63	424.73	527.64	579.67	611.47
Australia	734.79	781.93	949.16	1,057.17	997.17	1,249.70	1,504.24	1,561.05	1,509.64
Austria	315.19	334.60	387.00	429.64	398.60	390.94	429.43	407.68	428.38
Belgium	388.03	410.17	472.48	521.08	485.78	484.45	527.49	498.16	520.25
Brazil	891.63	1,107.63	1,397.11	1,695.86	1,669.20	2,208.70	2,614.03	2,464.05	2,471.72
Bulgaria	29.64	34.13	44.41	54.41	51.89	50.61	57.42	53.90	55.76
Canada	1,169.47	1,315.52	1,464.98	1,549.07	1,371.15	1,613.46	1,788.65	1,824.29	1,842.63
Chile	122.96	154.78	173.47	179.51	172.51	218.27	252.07	267.03	278.34
China	2,308.79	2,774.31	3,571.45	4,604.29	5,121.68	6,066.35	7,522.10	8,570.35	9,635.03
Colombia	146.55	162.77	207.47	244.30	233.89	286.95	335.44	369.43	380.17
Cyprus	18.71	20.42	24.08	27.97	26.01	25.61	27.45	25.03	24.06
Czech Republic	135.99	155.21	188.61	235.51	205.85	207.02	227.95	207.38	209.40
Denmark	264.49	282.90	319.42	353.36	321.24	322.00	344.00	327.15	343.58
Dominican Republic	36.18	38.34	44.07	48.21	48.32	53.89	58.02	60.70	62.06
Ecuador	41.51	46.80	51.01	61.76	62.52	69.56	79.28	87.93	95.13
Egypt	94.13	112.90	137.06	170.80	198.32	230.02	247.73	278.77	288.01
Estonia	14.02	16.99	22.27	24.29	19.71	19.54	23.19	23.06	25.09
Finland	204.79	216.74	255.74	285.09	252.14	248.26	273.93	256.85	270.07
France	2,207.45	2,327.05	2,666.81	2,937.32	2,700.66	2,651.77	2,865.30	2,682.90	2,809.39
Germany	2,866.31	3,005.08	3,444.72	3,770.15	3,426.67	3,423.47	3,761.14	3,545.95	3,753.69
Ghana	17.46	20.40	24.76	28.53	25.59	32.17	39.57	41.94	47.81
Greece	248.21	273.56	318.94	356.14	330.84	299.92	288.06	245.81	239.94
Guatemala	27.21	30.23	34.11	39.14	37.73	41.34	47.66	50.39	53.85
Hungary	112.59	114.80	139.20	157.29	129.97	130.26	140.10	127.32	134.68
Iceland	16.69	17.04	21.30	17.64	12.89	13.26	14.68	14.22	15.48
India	834.22	949.12	1,238.70	1,224.10	1,365.37	1,708.46	1,822.99	1,828.12	1,857.24
Ireland	211.70	232.24	270.06	274.94	235.71	221.27	240.48	225.80	238.99
Israel	142.46	153.88	178.74	215.93	207.32	233.76	261.37	257.64	293.32
Italy	1,855.83	1,944.34	2,206.11	2,402.06	2,190.70	2,129.02	2,278.38	2,073.97	2,131.16
Jamaica	10.76	11.47	12.36	13.74	12.11	13.19	14.41	14.76	14.20
Japan	4,755.98	4,530.48	4,515.26	5,037.91	5,231.38	5,700.10	6,157.46	6,203.21	5,155.72
Kenya	21.00	25.83	31.96	35.90	37.02	40.00	41.67	50.42	55.13
Korea	898.14	1,012.04	1,122.68	1,002.22	901.94	1,094.50	1,202.46	1,222.81	1,305.61
Latvia	16.95	21.47	30.95	35.76	26.24	23.81	28.50	28.14	30.26
Lithuania	26.18	30.24	39.79	48.13	37.53	37.20	43.56	42.89	46.48
Luxembourg	37.04	41.95	50.39	55.41	50.52	53.01	59.63	56.44	61.56
Malaysia	148.25	168.08	199.96	238.65	208.91	255.02	297.96	314.44	323.28
Mexico	866.35	966.87	1,043.47	1,101.27	894.95	1,051.13	1,171.19	1,186.60	1,261.98
Netherlands	679.70	727.29	840.58	940.67	860.11	837.95	894.58	829.41	866.95
New Zealand	113.20	109.76	134.95	135.53	121.73	145.31	167.13	175.06	186.81
Nigeria	169.65	222.79	262.22	330.26	297.46	369.06	414.10	460.95	514.97
Norway	308.68	345.39	400.89	461.95	386.38	428.53	498.16	509.71	522.75
Paraguay	8.74	10.65	13.80	18.50	15.93	20.05	25.10	24.60	28.97
Peru	74.97	87.89	102.19	121.59	121.02	148.01	168.77	189.02	197.87
Philippines	103.07	122.21	149.36	173.60	168.49	199.59	224.14	250.09	271.84
Poland	304.43	343.27	429.17	530.17	436.82	479.16	528.57	500.84	524.38
Portugal	197.64	208.75	240.50	263.25	244.36	238.75	245.12	216.49	226.14
Romania	99.70	123.53	171.68	209.66	168.04	167.99	186.11	171.66	191.56
Russia	820.57	1,063.64	1,396.48	1,784.51	1,313.68	1,638.46	2,031.77	2,170.15	2,230.62
Saudi Arabia	328.21	376.40	415.69	519.80	429.10	526.81	671.24	735.98	746.65
Singapore	127.42	147.80	179.98	192.23	192.41	236.42	275.61	289.17	302.51
South Africa	257.67	271.81	299.03	287.10	297.22	375.30	416.88	396.35	367.77
Spain	1,159.26	1,265.66	1,481.39	1,642.74	1,502.88	1,434.26	1,489.38	1,336.69	1,362.20
Sweden	389.04	420.02	487.82	513.97	429.66	488.38	563.11	543.88	578.74
Switzerland	407.59	429.48	477.78	552.29	540.97	580.61	696.45	664.90	685.10
Thailand	189.32	221.76	262.94	291.38	281.71	341.11	370.82	397.56	420.53
Turkey	501.17	550.80	675.01	764.64	644.47	772.29	832.50	873.70	950.33
Ukraine	89.28	111.89	148.73	188.24	121.55	136.01	163.16	175.71	179.57
United Arab Emirates	180.62	222.12	257.92	315.48	253.55	286.19	348.53	373.43	388.60
United Kingdom	2,511.17	2,682.21	3,064.35	2,898.94	2,377.16	2,431.17	2,611.11	2,655.46	2,721.49
United States	13,093.70	13,855.90	14,477.63	14,718.58	14,418.73	14,964.40	15,517.93	16,155.25	16,691.50
Vietnam	57.65	66.39	77.52	98.27	101.63	112.77	134.58	155.48	170.44

Data from: International Monetary Fund, World Economic Outlook Database, April 2017.

2014	2015	2016
563.61	631.62	545.12
1,449.34	1,229.71	1,258.98
439.07	377.16	386.75
532.61	455.34	466.96
2,456.05	1,801.48	1,798.62
56.73	50.20	52.42
1,792.88	1,552.81	1,529.22
260.95	242.54	247.03
10,534.53	11,226.19	11,218.28
378.32	291.53	282.36
23.35	19.57	19.81
207.82	185.16	192.99
352.30	301.31	306.73
65.32	68.20	72.19
102.29	100.18	98.01
305.57	332.08	332.35
26.26	22.47	23.13
273.04	232.48	236.88
2,843.67	2,420.16	2,463.22
3,885.44	3,365.29	3,466.64
38.62	37.38	43.26
236.46	194.96	194.25
58.72	63.79	68.18
139.30	121.66	125.68
17.18	16.78	20.05
2,033.65	2,088.16	2,256.40
255.90	283.42	293.61
308.77	299.41	318.39
2,155.15	1,825.82	1,850.74
13.86	14.22	13.95
4,848.73	4,382.42	4,938.64
61.49	63.62	68.92
1,411.33	1,382.76	1,411.25
31.40	27.04	27.68
48.66	41.42	42.75
65.48	56.83	59.47
338.07	296.28	296.36
1,298.40	1,151.04	1,046.00
881.03	750.70	771.16
199.03	173.26	181.99
568.50	493.84	405.95
498.34	386.58	370.45
30.88	27.28	27.44
203.02	192.39	195.14
284.83	292.45	304.70
545.05	477.06	467.59
230.00	199.22	204.76
199.54	177.52	187.04
2,063.66	1,365.87	1,280.73
756.35	651.76	639.62
308.16	296.84	296.97
351.57	314.73	294.13
1,378.04	1,193.56	1,232.60
573.82	495.69	511.40
702.74	670.66	659.85
406.52	399.22	406.95
934.07	859.04	857.43
132.34	90.94	93.26
401.96	370.30	371.35
3,002.39	2,863.30	2,629.19
17,393.10	18,036.65	18,569.10
185.76	191.29	201.33

TABLE 3
Macroeconomic Data for Select Countries
GDP per Capita (Billions of U.S. Dollars)

Country	1985	1986	1987	1988	1989	1990	1991	1992	1993
Argentina	3,149.68	3,739.41	3,790.75	4,386.53	2,779.87	4,709.66	6,233.39	7,420.32	7,558.50
Australia	10,977.96	11,255.85	13,010.96	16,263.95	18,201.62	18,865.77	18,677.54	18,120.61	17,474.88
Austria	9,070.48	12,857.29	16,057.05	17,593.40	17,508.59	21,778.65	22,571.32	25,012.37	24,098.68
Belgium	8,617.62	11,948.55	14,821.92	16,096.82	16,187.81	20,229.10	20,680.41	22,952.52	21,843.98
Brazil	1,794.23	2,040.02	2,178.14	2,388.90	3,222.10	3,241.07	2,794.19	2,633.39	2,908.26
Bulgaria	2,930.41	2,599.52	3,025.77	4,973.36	5,101.20	2,267.40	224.19	919.07	504.08
Canada	14,131.19	14,479.54	16,339.73	18,966.34	20,763.52	21,495.15	21,807.26	20,915.03	20,145.56
Chile	1,424.39	1,504.46	1,743.91	2,021.08	2,289.49	2,503.91	2,829.79	3,386.04	3,559.40
China	295.34	282.16	302.20	371.02	409.09	348.65	358.83	423.03	525.71
Colombia	1,587.19	1,557.08	1,587.58	1,676.40	1,656.05	1,653.13	1,673.89	1,941.93	2,159.59
Cyprus	4,824.67	6,057.90	7,188.22	8,204.30	8,635.77	10,360.00	10,413.73	12,158.60	11,342.41
Czech Republic	n/a	n/a	n/a	n/a	n/a	n/a	n/a	n/a	n/a
Denmark	12,263.83	17,220.11	21,353.57	22,531.23	21,918.31	26,922.44	27,060.38	29,631.34	27,643.45
Dominican Republic	1,092.78	1,295.54	1,330.71	1,190.26	1,315.19	1,200.31	1,458.91	1,671.73	1,847.79
Ecuador	2,044.31	1,461.92	1,332.15	1,234.67	1,182.53	1,173.13	1,286.62	1,375.71	1,572.84
Egypt	1,049.33	1,132.46	1,585.22	1,858.03	2,266.44	1,870.85	923.84	825.45	906.80
Estonia	n/a	n/a	n/a	n/a	n/a	n/a	n/a	n/a	1,150.73
Finland	11,490.92	14,999.99	18,633.45	22,031.74	24,067.00	28,507.16	25,663.52	22,490.25	17,670.34
France	10,149.98	14,006.56	16,871.83	18,326.78	18,328.02	22,600.46	22,524.41	24,725.74	23,212.10
Germany	8,649.27	12,343.84	15,355.86	16,454.65	16,174.32	20,174.03	23,371.61	26,441.80	25,569.63
Ghana	802.72	710.80	591.41	611.47	603.89	697.57	765.98	733.93	629.47
Greece	4,835.33	5,672.32	6,575.76	7,634.36	7,878.32	9,680.90	10,283.81	11,249.33	10,450.67
Guatemala	1,319.91	695.84	785.76	829.95	933.46	797.52	952.65	1,031.16	1,094.99
Hungary	2,016.98	2,331.88	2,575.21	2,830.17	2,901.10	3,302.50	3,340.32	3,722.40	3,859.66
Iceland	12,501.60	16,536.77	22,598.47	24,537.97	22,598.45	25,577.21	26,923.81	27,260.73	23,657.07
India	311.40	324.25	356.25	368.34	361.45	385.41	318.01	332.54	315.42
Ireland	5,893.87	7,953.87	9,409.96	10,348.62	10,747.90	13,606.75	13,702.52	15,302.60	14,102.44
Israel	6,273.73	7,605.23	8,937.87	10,890.48	10,893.15	12,462.31	13,311.60	14,360.47	14,061.36
Italy	8,110.89	11,485.19	14,415.46	15,966.45	16,591.14	20,691.00	21,844.14	23,159.17	18,609.97
Jamaica	878.36	1,034.77	1,158.60	1,372.73	1,588.56	1,971.70	1,799.77	1,804.41	2,280.66
Japan	11,597.69	17,090.91	20,609.32	24,897.77	24,814.59	25,443.21	28,910.25	31,343.83	35,802.93
Kenya	467.40	536.79	569.04	570.52	546.95	552.68	506.80	484.70	326.99
Korea	2,457.69	2,803.37	3,510.95	4,686.32	5,736.47	6,513.16	7,522.98	8,002.15	8,740.71
Latvia	n/a	n/a	n/a	n/a	n/a	n/a	n/a	632.91	1,022.24
Lithuania	n/a	n/a	n/a	n/a	n/a	n/a	n/a	n/a	n/a
Luxembourg	12,514.20	18,134.87	22,360.54	25,112.03	26,477.91	33,378.59	35,688.49	39,438.95	39,859.78
Malaysia	2,124.29	1,837.93	2,041.02	2,182.86	2,347.18	2,549.61	2,844.90	3,331.39	3,664.87
Mexico	2,885.36	1,956.82	2,102.46	2,520.39	3,010.06	3,423.16	4,031.23	4,597.09	5,502.39
Netherlands	9,765.64	13,534.00	16,469.92	17,500.59	17,141.77	21,001.57	21,467.19	23,577.51	22,766.61
New Zealand	6,904.40	8,326.06	11,123.33	13,561.12	13,015.69	13,363.07	12,394.57	11,709.92	12,451.88
Nigeria	n/a	n/a	n/a	n/a	n/a	686.48	645.45	546.09	577.54
Norway	15,732.94	18,858.18	22,447.28	24,145.36	24,248.74	28,188.52	28,521.83	30,445.41	27,808.67
Paraguay	1,154.15	1,335.76	1,084.70	1,392.42	977.84	1,185.28	1,585.24	1,592.06	1,580.21
Peru	861.88	1,264.14	2,041.32	1,580.06	1,909.08	1,301.89	1,532.42	1,565.54	1,516.37
Philippines	627.54	597.84	648.26	723.48	794.10	805.63	806.94	919.70	922.19
Poland	1,896.08	1,961.68	1,687.80	1,815.82	1,768.61	1,625.84	2,101.35	2,311.09	2,347.12
Portugal	2,716.48	3,772.51	4,718.59	5,525.32	5,967.66	7,941.03	9,010.20	10,841.26	9,530.90
Romania	2,115.46	2,278.87	2,534.07	2,609.66	2,329.57	1,652.37	1,249.01	853.11	1,154.67
Russia	n/a	n/a	n/a	n/a	n/a	n/a	n/a	619.87	1,330.05
Saudi Arabia	8,732.74	6,955.05	6,524.16	6,398.84	6,583.29	7,734.98	8,280.18	8,077.77	7,686.01
Singapore	6,782.81	6,864.40	7,788.30	9,316.09	10,711.19	12,766.10	14,504.26	16,135.93	18,301.55
South Africa	1,792.07	2,003.02	2,570.27	2,705.51	2,754.28	3,140.35	3,289.06	3,481.42	3,390.85
Spain	4,683.16	6,461.29	8,167.06	9,574.95	10,540.02	13,649.99	14,665.33	15,974.76	13,376.49
Sweden	13,348.52	17,576.31	21,284.59	23,953.87	24,988.64	29,794.08	31,082.06	32,163.77	24,011.35
Switzerland	16,663.63	23,770.43	29,579.84	31,795.32	30,463.15	38,589.18	38,558.77	39,610.33	38,136.22
Thailand	775.78	840.48	969.08	1,159.09	1,349.93	1,571.26	1,777.47	1,999.97	2,218.56
Turkey	1,869.96	2,029.02	2,290.35	2,449.05	2,853.91	3,915.54	3,861.93	3,978.67	4,438.68
Ukraine	n/a	n/a	n/a	n/a	n/a	n/a	n/a	427.86	677.26
United Arab Emirates	27,036.00	20,533.02	21,644.07	18,435.20	20,478.53	26,621.51	25,847.41	25,960.97	25,654.37
United Kingdom	9,446.62	11,491.77	14,213.45	17,267.43	17,508.92	20,668.04	21,502.56	22,119.10	19,738.70
United States	18,231.83	19,078.41	20,062.55	21,442.13	22,878.98	23,913.66	24,365.53	25,466.73	26,441.65
Vietnam	251.20	556.02	674.88	365.89	97.16	98.03	113.65	144.15	189.26

Data from: International Monetary Fund, World Economic Outlook Database, April 2017.

1994	1995	1996	1997	1998	1999	2000	2001	2002	2003	2004
8,125.91	8,053.12	8,385.15	8,918.83	9,005.38	8,452.88	8,386.59	7,851.66	2,898.29	3,648.06	4,314.40
19,740.31	20,959.06	23,218.29	23,050.98	20,372.92	21,767.72	20,860.79	19,441.81	21,653.20	27,256.98	32,796.67
25,668.06	30,289.20	29,759.20	26,682.85	27,328.54	27,152.29	24,589.19	24,510.77	26,444.12	32,176.94	36,754.57
23,754.02	28,616.75	27,749.79	25,089.91	25,604.83	25,509.14	23,303.13	23,193.68	25,197.25	30,863.07	35,722.72
3,569.46	4,950.30	5,273.89	5,394.64	5,197.03	3,552.14	3,778.97	3,183.79	2,859.60	3,090.66	3,659.10
895.40	1,514.29	1,153.87	1,228.13	1,631.94	1,673.66	1,613.94	1,783.72	2,074.58	2,689.79	3,344.64
19,963.30	20,641.54	21,257.09	21,857.61	20,975.14	22,261.15	24,221.27	23,777.49	24,210.04	28,242.19	32,075.36
4,035.86	5,112.92	5,345.81	5,739.62	5,440.57	4,943.06	5,054.31	4,557.47	4,450.34	4,776.15	6,201.58
472.65	608.38	708.58	780.84	827.64	872.22	958.56	1,053.15	1,150.21	1,293.13	1,512.62
2,665.58	2,967.15	3,066.62	3,322.99	3,021.49	2,613.62	2,478.54	2,406.05	2,369.91	2,261.58	2,763.70
12,525.32	15,397.10	15,260.32	14,324.37	15,188.72	15,379.94	14,464.88	14,903.74	16,188.28	20,388.90	23,969.88
n/a	5,759.97	6,471.71	5,975.51	6,441.99	6,289.77	5,981.08	6,584.78	8,007.32	9,744.45	11,669.13
30,054.14	35,477.69	35,734.72	32,901.28	33,429.55	33,491.68	30,804.46	30,812.05	33,277.95	40,519.86	46,570.35
2,028.54	2,256.87	2,456.47	2,611.83	2,778.46	2,804.85	3,056.12	3,129.08	3,280.43	2,582.56	2,643.03
1,858.32	1,980.37	2,037.13	2,253.23	2,257.86	1,598.77	1,461.84	1,909.42	2,180.39	2,434.98	2,700.12
978.54	1,111.78	1,221.89	1,342.93	1,469.32	1,532.89	1,642.63	1,569.04	1,356.68	1,254.10	1,195.37
1,649.00	2,621.99	3,329.19	3,607.16	4,034.85	4,162.74	4,072.16	4,494.45	5,308.89	7,163.76	8,835.49
20,433.74	26,349.63	25,827.61	24,746.05	26,054.46	26,242.77	24,347.47	24,967.82	26,958.55	32,921.38	37,748.13
24,398.14	27,898.30	27,870.57	25,167.00	25,951.70	25,680.90	23,317.94	23,342.09	25,226.21	30,808.71	35,153.79
27,247.03	31,907.94	30,744.89	27,257.16	27,581.93	27,054.59	24,008.66	23,949.76	25,576.54	30,785.60	34,657.52
560.65	647.99	678.78	655.83	694.59	700.49	440.32	457.95	518.06	625.26	709.47
11,109.70	13,000.03	13,776.95	13,485.69	13,526.76	13,867.05	12,268.13	12,579.24	14,178.16	18,533.80	22,014.61
1,212.30	1,330.46	1,388.73	1,537.41	1,631.92	1,503.63	1,530.34	1,625.49	1,761.78	1,812.72	1,933.15
4,156.70	4,479.19	4,509.08	4,579.97	4,733.63	4,786.38	4,618.42	5,264.39	6,639.93	8,385.95	10,249.53
24,111.12	26,768.82	27,859.69	27,888.15	30,714.50	32,006.28	31,570.81	28,420.12	31,890.99	38,902.79	46,695.78
362.37	391.25	418.60	434.74	432.23	462.13	463.12	471.31	492.23	572.30	657.52
15,432.16	19,079.09	20,768.93	22,438.95	24,168.99	26,181.82	26,081.76	28,059.81	32,347.74	40,854.63	47,307.48
15,647.72	18,095.36	19,351.02	19,698.34	19,431.35	19,157.72	21,051.67	20,296.96	18,416.85	18,944.46	19,888.73
19,186.32	20,609.06	23,033.40	21,811.82	22,283.57	21,968.42	20,116.62	20,423.14	22,303.02	27,527.38	31,319.73
2,266.08	2,657.67	2,835.03	3,218.16	3,339.40	3,320.51	3,367.75	3,391.61	3,552.58	3,397.72	3,655.32
39,224.15	43,454.78	38,453.38	35,042.32	31,931.07	35,912.46	38,533.86	33,860.45	32,301.30	34,844.66	37,701.44
380.18	468.00	516.17	507.78	564.74	500.11	479.30	479.60	474.00	524.74	549.16
10,206.75	12,340.03	13,137.11	12,132.83	8,083.13	10,409.51	11,946.77	11,255.77	12,782.47	14,210.64	15,907.91
1,724.98	2,163.46	2,417.46	2,669.57	2,965.16	3,140.33	3,336.91	3,548.50	4,116.18	5,111.50	6,315.40
n/a	1,845.67	2,328.22	2,830.75	3,166.96	3,113.64	3,297.45	3,530.20	4,146.11	5,505.59	6,706.03
43,717.63	51,189.97	50,187.37	44,622.80	46,066.85	49,801.84	49,442.41	47,996.03	52,676.70	65,274.96	75,589.98
3,971.09	4,612.50	5,103.04	4,941.36	3,470.47	3,710.07	4,286.83	4,130.38	4,379.64	4,673.91	5,171.42
5,666.70	3,638.61	4,144.93	4,943.77	5,097.50	5,811.60	6,775.81	7,096.31	7,170.54	6,811.34	7,270.02
24,307.22	28,910.83	28,708.64	26,437.58	27,572.80	27,988.59	25,996.36	26,607.26	28,919.20	35,313.25	40,008.33
14,492.61	16,783.74	18,357.08	18,115.34	14,828.46	15,280.64	13,978.01	13,560.44	15,552.48	20,304.87	24,689.98
792.81	1,273.27	1,618.29	1,713.38	1,861.07	496.50	570.17	598.29	748.31	797.64	982.98
29,227.80	34,793.77	37,225.39	36,565.45	34,720.82	36,285.35	38,067.18	38,504.48	42,975.50	49,775.55	57,444.59
1,681.40	1,897.13	2,008.19	2,003.58	1,778.17	1,620.56	1,550.95	1,422.95	1,153.26	1,179.93	1,413.95
1,904.88	2,233.44	2,281.70	2,364.13	2,233.59	1,989.19	2,023.43	2,016.36	2,094.82	2,236.93	2,488.82
1,062.28	1,200.43	1,276.66	1,240.77	960.71	1,080.95	1,055.12	970.38	1,014.94	1,024.77	1,093.48
2,687.41	3,605.16	4,058.18	4,067.96	4,450.33	4,339.60	4,476.25	4,978.05	5,195.28	5,691.34	6,643.23
9,970.96	11,791.40	12,188.04	11,598.40	12,220.99	12,491.23	11,536.13	11,739.25	12,927.92	15,802.94	18,070.02
1,325.48	1,573.13	1,575.50	1,581.75	1,897.42	1,611.13	1,669.98	1,817.05	2,118.57	2,768.12	3,541.52
2,004.41	2,271.31	2,842.86	2,944.47	1,975.97	1,432.66	1,905.95	2,259.02	2,556.64	3,197.69	4,408.37
7,626.36	7,893.42	8,527.67	8,706.35	7,525.30	8,092.70	9,256.54	8,778.39	8,822.51	9,800.53	11,467.10
21,577.84	24,936.40	26,262.70	26,387.39	21,825.95	21,796.63	23,793.28	21,577.49	22,016.99	23,574.03	27,404.20
3,446.84	3,752.38	3,500.03	3,556.54	3,160.84	3,089.37	3,042.43	2,671.99	2,524.22	3,775.56	4,870.66
13,386.46	15,436.96	16,057.38	14,747.59	15,420.70	15,774.82	14,724.65	15,368.51	17,083.10	21,532.45	24,988.98
25,646.92	29,882.78	32,577.73	29,896.15	30,135.41	30,552.04	29,251.96	26,933.82	29,520.93	36,889.59	42,362.22
41,883.09	48,718.92	46,695.20	40,484.83	41,537.47	40,651.33	37,946.89	38,735.84	41,527.14	48,175.52	53,372.93
2,494.74	2,846.44	3,046.67	2,475.10	1,855.12	2,048.05	2,028.08	1,912.28	2,115.38	2,377.55	2,676.30
3,150.74	4,025.31	4,238.47	4,352.94	4,380.37	4,016.01	4,218.90	3,053.20	3,589.38	4,642.93	5,952.71
740.97	752.34	914.35	1,037.89	874.27	664.99	664.38	814.85	919.14	1,096.29	1,427.28
25,762.53	26,394.42	29,058.86	29,523.49	25,897.65	27,321.04	34,688.98	32,621.29	32,790.71	35,017.31	39,304.51
21,098.89	22,759.46	23,974.94	26,366.88	27,769.02	28,159.95	27,828.38	27,296.67	29,654.24	34,049.76	39,871.03
27,755.48	28,762.68	30,047.31	31,553.62	32,929.04	34,601.72	36,432.51	37,241.35	38,113.89	39,591.87	41,838.46
230.31	288.87	337.52	361.91	360.93	374.72	401.57	413.34	440.21	489.03	603.67

(continued on next page)

Macroeconomic Data for Select Countries
GDP per Capita (Billions of U.S. Dollars)

Country	2005	2006	2007	2008	2009	2010	2011	2012	2013
Argentina	5,163.55	5,976.08	7,315.73	9,146.79	8,337.81	10,412.95	12,787.81	13,889.79	14,488.83
Australia	36,175.80	37,907.27	45,163.63	49,226.57	45,604.43	56,362.84	66,794.67	68,106.35	64,831.04
Austria	38,319.39	40,469.86	46,652.91	51,629.65	47,785.56	46,757.13	51,192.57	48,381.44	50,533.29
Belgium	37,146.68	39,021.77	44,638.27	48,850.71	45,176.03	44,691.32	47,950.99	44,900.10	46,610.92
Brazil	4,815.71	5,912.55	7,374.08	8,854.16	8,624.42	11,297.84	13,242.49	12,367.14	12,295.09
Bulgaria	3,839.45	4,444.51	5,812.68	7,152.79	6,859.68	6,743.74	7,836.58	7,401.94	7,703.48
Canada	36,315.73	40,441.77	44,599.15	46,660.87	40,831.10	47,512.68	52,143.84	52,577.39	52,494.13
Chile	7,606.30	9,477.12	10,510.30	10,757.58	10,221.85	12,789.76	14,608.19	15,306.92	15,786.47
China	1,765.72	2,110.57	2,703.00	3,467.03	3,837.90	4,524.06	5,582.89	6,329.46	7,080.83
Colombia	3,416.90	3,749.84	4,722.94	5,495.98	5,200.05	6,305.29	7,284.99	7,930.75	8,067.94
Cyprus	25,526.70	27,448.82	31,774.79	36,030.55	32,635.92	31,262.53	32,692.53	29,032.12	27,791.66
Czech Republic	13,333.86	15,181.86	18,393.74	22,769.35	19,744.56	19,787.29	21,736.84	19,739.90	19,912.51
Denmark	48,876.18	52,122.98	58,641.19	64,531.12	58,286.54	58,177.16	61,864.09	58,623.41	61,325.58
Dominican Republic	4,034.63	4,226.12	4,803.47	5,194.80	5,151.17	5,685.77	6,056.59	6,270.30	6,342.71
Ecuador	3,025.01	3,351.48	3,588.31	4,267.47	4,241.94	4,633.25	5,192.88	5,664.89	6,030.50
Egypt	1,330.46	1,563.48	1,861.05	2,270.36	2,578.05	2,921.76	3,077.34	3,383.11	3,400.32
Estonia	10,320.60	12,576.70	16,579.40	18,144.14	14,757.47	14,654.28	17,441.45	17,398.38	19,004.34
Finland	39,106.58	41,240.45	48,463.31	53,785.14	47,337.94	46,391.71	50,960.18	47,553.40	49,766.13
France	36,209.52	37,900.03	43,155.50	47,273.32	43,234.25	42,249.06	45,430.28	42,333.09	44,104.92
Germany	35,239.90	37,020.35	42,531.38	46,681.07	42,576.34	42,641.68	46,853.22	44,089.69	46,545.09
Ghana	835.90	952.30	1,126.86	1,266.11	1,107.39	1,357.64	1,627.90	1,682.58	1,870.16
Greece	22,626.14	24,858.26	28,899.95	32,198.01	29,819.23	26,972.87	25,896.93	22,171.91	21,805.26
Guatemala	2,140.94	2,320.30	2,554.52	2,859.65	2,690.09	2,875.31	3,233.80	3,335.91	3,478.20
Hungary	11,149.64	11,392.40	13,828.55	15,658.63	12,956.37	13,007.56	14,029.50	12,819.29	13,591.73
Iceland	55,657.93	55,394.16	67,504.85	55,235.29	40,572.62	41,622.66	45,919.30	44,176.68	47,530.35
India	748.85	839.93	1,080.89	1,053.44	1,159.06	1,429.60	1,497.40	1,470.73	1,475.17
Ireland	50,405.87	53,749.16	60,756.36	60,881.50	51,837.70	48,439.10	52,504.31	49,133.29	51,853.26
Israel	20,566.61	21,821.41	24,907.71	29,552.87	27,708.89	30,673.39	33,668.77	32,582.94	36,409.71
Italy	32,066.38	33,486.01	37,890.20	40,953.86	37,130.15	35,969.19	38,379.31	34,918.74	35,706.62
Jamaica	4,011.91	4,253.27	4,563.62	5,054.54	4,435.33	4,812.07	5,230.73	5,330.88	5,101.92
Japan	37,228.23	35,464.64	35,342.48	39,453.50	41,014.19	44,673.61	48,168.81	48,632.91	40,490.16
Kenya	621.28	743.44	895.23	978.45	982.00	1,038.95	1,054.98	1,238.81	1,318.89
Korea	18,639.52	20,893.48	23,060.71	20,430.64	18,291.92	22,086.95	24,079.79	24,358.78	25,890.02
Latvia	7,533.79	9,635.17	14,010.23	16,316.83	12,131.33	11,228.13	13,735.61	13,762.17	14,951.83
Lithuania	7,880.30	9,246.51	12,313.17	15,047.25	11,866.63	12,010.68	14,386.61	14,354.25	15,714.78
Luxembourg	80,308.43	89,428.34	105,825.06	114,522.93	102,359.74	105,573.58	116,502.67	107,540.55	114,635.02
Malaysia	5,599.05	6,264.42	7,378.59	8,646.57	7,439.44	8,920.48	10,252.59	10,655.46	10,699.66
Mexico	8,085.29	8,918.71	9,504.48	9,894.73	7,930.26	9,199.80	10,124.10	10,137.24	10,659.08
Netherlands	41,647.99	44,493.25	51,311.40	57,197.22	52,033.16	50,433.31	53,589.91	49,501.99	51,591.95
New Zealand	27,206.07	26,077.68	31,784.36	31,662.47	28,100.34	33,221.93	37,988.81	39,553.92	41,737.76
Nigeria	1,245.07	1,591.33	1,822.79	2,234.36	1,958.58	2,365.01	2,582.57	2,797.86	3,042.05
Norway	66,643.39	73,930.33	84,904.37	96,499.70	79,786.85	87,309.30	100,171.70	101,169.35	102,573.67
Paraguay	1,511.25	1,811.41	2,308.91	3,047.44	2,582.97	3,199.48	3,944.46	3,806.71	4,416.19
Peru	2,754.34	3,179.68	3,621.00	4,242.94	4,158.56	5,008.68	5,669.17	6,280.35	6,491.04
Philippines	1,208.93	1,405.21	1,683.69	1,919.11	1,851.07	2,155.41	2,363.88	2,591.36	2,768.61
Poland	7,974.84	8,996.29	11,256.83	13,909.50	11,454.23	12,601.91	13,886.74	13,157.81	13,776.85
Portugal	18,817.16	19,838.81	22,811.56	24,933.17	23,122.54	22,580.68	23,217.36	20,588.89	21,625.48
Romania	4,662.67	5,811.44	8,124.69	10,160.35	8,220.82	8,277.34	9,213.94	8,542.09	9,568.36
Russia	5,713.36	7,420.48	9,753.26	12,468.38	9,178.45	11,445.13	14,187.19	15,145.38	15,558.80
Saudi Arabia	14,068.22	15,603.99	16,666.63	20,157.30	16,094.68	19,112.69	23,654.87	25,208.16	24,892.99
Singapore	29,870.33	33,579.42	39,223.54	39,722.15	38,577.17	46,569.40	53,167.70	54,432.20	56,028.80
South Africa	5,412.37	5,635.29	6,117.19	5,793.12	5,914.14	7,361.94	8,058.91	7,548.45	6,898.48
Spain	26,550.34	28,531.25	32,748.09	35,724.77	32,412.23	30,802.85	31,867.78	28,582.17	29,236.04
Sweden	42,998.84	46,088.54	53,122.33	55,525.76	45,998.35	51,869.16	59,381.87	56,915.73	60,005.20
Switzerland	54,968.52	57,578.38	63,628.14	72,736.31	70,237.12	74,570.66	88,493.84	83,582.89	85,222.51
Thailand	2,905.80	3,378.83	3,978.30	4,379.53	4,207.58	5,065.38	5,482.40	5,850.30	6,157.36
Turkey	7,278.23	7,899.13	9,562.92	10,691.71	8,881.72	10,475.61	11,140.96	11,552.71	12,395.36
Ukraine	1,909.80	2,407.90	3,219.88	4,095.44	2,654.99	2,982.81	3,589.63	3,872.53	3,968.80
United Arab Emirates	43,988.67	44,313.59	41,472.29	39,074.84	30,920.45	34,628.63	40,943.56	42,591.44	43,030.32
United Kingdom	41,566.63	44,095.77	49,973.92	46,890.22	38,180.57	38,737.56	41,259.50	41,683.67	42,452.95
United States	44,218.31	46,351.67	47,954.53	48,302.28	46,909.42	48,310.34	49,733.88	51,403.39	52,741.73
Vietnam	699.68	796.93	920.46	1,154.49	1,181.45	1,297.23	1,532.06	1,751.69	1,900.35

Data from: International Monetary Fund, World Economic Outlook Database, April 2017.

2014	2015	2016
13,208.83	14,643.92	12,502.82
61,357.79	51,363.90	51,850.27
51,390.00	43,749.55	44,498.37
47,635.67	40,520.10	41,283.27
12,112.57	8,810.50	8,726.90
7,877.09	7,017.11	7,368.52
50,509.59	43,349.62	42,210.13
14,644.66	13,469.47	13,576.00
7,701.69	8,166.76	8,113.26
7,937.63	6,047.97	5,792.18
27,208.11	23,105.40	23,351.87
19,768.84	17,569.89	18,286.33
62,605.70	53,237.28	53,743.97
6,609.19	6,833.24	7,159.50
6,382.31	6,153.80	5,929.69
3,524.42	3,731.18	3,684.57
19,953.51	17,111.30	17,632.70
50,087.85	42,487.05	43,169.22
44,413.12	37,612.91	38,127.65
47,978.61	41,197.41	41,902.28
1,472.99	1,390.11	1,569.04
21,639.94	17,955.19	17,900.73
3,700.31	3,921.87	4,088.95
14,102.92	12,344.16	12,778.29
52,199.83	50,472.94	59,629.05
1,594.32	1,615.79	1,723.30
55,371.58	60,896.18	62,562.27
37,599.21	35,743.46	37,262.40
35,456.70	30,032.11	30,507.18
4,953.12	5,052.68	4,930.54
38,143.11	34,513.36	38,917.29
1,430.09	1,439.46	1,516.33
27,811.37	27,105.08	27,538.81
15,689.52	13,614.47	14,060.40
16,594.61	14,259.60	14,890.07
119,116.12	100,950.49	103,198.82
11,009.10	9,500.52	9,360.47
10,845.95	9,512.27	8,554.62
52,240.30	44,322.83	45,282.63
43,698.17	37,281.09	38,345.40
3,268.39	2,763.20	2,210.64
96,643.94	74,264.43	70,391.57
4,638.74	4,038.42	4,003.28
6,589.66	6,176.68	6,198.61
2,844.06	2,862.90	2,924.29
14,336.78	12,552.29	12,315.65
22,112.53	19,225.67	19,831.61
10,000.58	8,934.01	9,465.42
14,388.00	9,521.08	8,928.70
24,580.47	21,013.58	20,150.13
56,338.30	53,628.76	52,960.73
6,492.89	5,721.15	5,260.90
29,663.94	25,717.56	26,608.87
58,869.07	50,319.11	51,164.51
86,331.16	81,410.02	79,242.28
5,921.09	5,799.39	5,899.42
12,022.14	10,909.69	10,742.70
3,095.05	2,135.18	2,194.36
43,213.26	38,649.91	37,677.91
46,478.84	43,976.42	40,095.95
54,559.86	56,174.94	57,436.41
2,047.43	2,086.53	2,173.27

Solutions to *Check Your Understanding* Questions

This section offers suggested answers to the *Check Your Understanding* questions found within chapters.

|| CHAPTER ONE

1-1 Check Your Understanding

1. **a.** This illustrates the concept of opportunity cost. Given that a person can only eat so much at one sitting, having a slice of chocolate cake requires that you forgo eating something else, such as a slice of coconut cream pie.

    b. This illustrates the concept that resources are scarce. Even if there were more resources in the world, the total amount of those resources would be limited. As a result, scarcity would still arise. For there to be no scarcity, there would have to be unlimited amounts of everything (including unlimited time in a human life), which is clearly impossible.

    c. This illustrates the concept that people usually exploit opportunities to make themselves better off. Students will seek to make themselves better off by signing up for the tutorials of teaching assistants with good reputations and avoiding those teaching assistants with poor reputations. It also illustrates the concept that resources are scarce. If there were unlimited spaces in tutorials with good teaching assistants, they would not fill up.

    d. This illustrates the concept of marginal analysis. Your decision about allocating your time is a "how much" decision: how much time spent exercising versus how much time spent studying. You make your decision by comparing the benefit of an additional hour of exercising to its cost, the effect on your grades of one fewer hour spent studying.

2. **a.** Yes. The increased time spent commuting is a cost you will incur if you accept the new job. That additional time spent commuting—or equivalently, the benefit you would get from spending that time doing something else—is an opportunity cost of the new job.

    b. Yes. One of the benefits of the new job is that you will be making $50,000. But if you take the new job, you will have to give up your current job; that is, you have to give up your current salary of $45,000. So $45,000 is one of the opportunity costs of taking the new job.

    c. No. A more spacious office is an additional benefit of your new job and does not involve forgoing something else. So it is not an opportunity cost.

1-2 Check Your Understanding

1. **a.** This illustrates the concept that markets usually lead to efficiency. Any seller who wants to sell a book for at least $30 does indeed sell to someone who is willing to buy a book for $30. As a result, there is no way to change how used textbooks are distributed among buyers and sellers in a way that would make one person better off without making someone else worse off.

    b. This illustrates the concept that there are gains from trade. Students trade tutoring services based on their different abilities in academic subjects.

    c. This illustrates the concept that when markets don't achieve efficiency, government intervention can improve society's welfare. In this case the market, left alone, will permit bars and nightclubs to impose costs on their neighbors in the form of loud music, costs that the bars and nightclubs have no incentive to take into account. This is an inefficient outcome because society as a whole can be made better off if bars and nightclubs are induced to reduce their noise.

    d. This illustrates the concept that resources should be used as efficiently as possible to achieve society's goals. By closing neighborhood clinics and shifting funds to the main hospital, better health care can be provided at a lower cost.

    e. This illustrates the concept that markets move toward equilibrium. Here, because books with the same amount of wear and tear sell for about the same price, no buyer or seller can be made better off by engaging in a different trade than he or she undertook. This means that the market for used textbooks has moved to an equilibrium.

2. **a.** This does not describe an equilibrium situation. Many students should want to change their behavior and switch to eating at the restaurants. Therefore, the situation described is not an equilibrium. An equilibrium will be established when students are equally as well off eating at the restaurants as eating at the dining hall—which would happen if, say, prices at the dining hall were higher than at the restaurants.

    b. This does describe an equilibrium situation. By changing your behavior and riding the bus, you would not be made better off. Therefore, you have no incentive to change your behavior.

1-3 Check Your Understanding

1. **a.** This illustrates the principle that government policies can change spending. The tax cut would increase people's after-tax incomes, leading to higher consumer spending.

    b. This illustrates the principle that one person's spending is another person's income. As oil companies decrease their spending on labor by laying off workers and pay remaining workers lower wages, those workers' incomes fall. In turn, those workers decrease their consumer spending, causing restaurants and other consumer businesses to lose income.

    c. This illustrates the principle that overall spending sometimes gets out of line with the economy's productive capacity. In this case, spending on housing was too high relative to the economy's capacity to create new housing. This first led to a rise in house prices, and then—as a result—to a rise in overall prices, or *inflation*.

‖ CHAPTER TWO

2-1 Check Your Understanding

1. **a.** False. An increase in the resources available to Boeing for use in producing Dreamliners and small jets changes the production possibility frontier by shifting it outward. This is because Boeing can now produce more small jets and Dreamliners than before. In the accompanying figure, the line labeled "Boeing's original *PPF*" represents Boeing's original production possibility frontier, and the line labeled "Boeing's new *PPF*" represents the new production possibility frontier that results from an increase in resources available to Boeing.

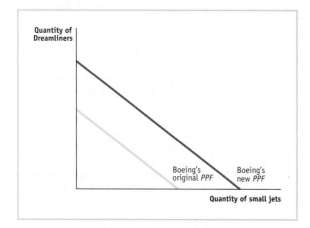

b. True. A technological change that allows Boeing to build more small jets for any amount of Dreamliners built results in a change in its production possibility frontier. This is illustrated in the accompanying figure: the new production possibility frontier is represented by the line labeled "Boeing's new *PPF*," and the original production frontier is represented by the line labeled "Boeing's original *PPF*." Since the maximum quantity of Dreamliners that Boeing can build is the same as before, the new production possibility frontier intersects the vertical axis at the same point as the original frontier. But since the maximum possible quantity of small jets is now greater than before, the new frontier intersects the horizontal axis to the right of the original frontier.

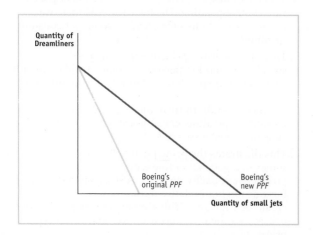

c. False. The production possibility frontier illustrates how much of one good an economy must give up to get more of another good only when resources are used efficiently in production. If an economy is producing inefficiently—that is, inside the frontier—then it does not have to give up a unit of one good in order to get another unit of the other good. Instead, by becoming more efficient in production, this economy can have more of both goods.

2. **a.** The United States has an absolute advantage in automobile production because it takes fewer Americans (6) to produce a car in one day than Italians (8). The United States also has an absolute advantage in washing machine production because it takes fewer Americans (2) to produce a washing machine in one day than Italians (3).

b. In Italy the opportunity cost of a washing machine in terms of an automobile is $3/8$: $3/8$ of a car can be produced with the same number of workers and in the same time it takes to produce 1 washing machine. In the United States the opportunity cost of a washing machine in terms of an automobile is $2/6 = 1/3$: $1/3$ of a car can be produced with the same number of workers and in the same time it takes to produce 1 washing machine. Since $1/3 < 3/8$, the United States has a comparative advantage in the production of washing machines: to produce a washing machine, only $1/3$ of a car must be given up in the United States but $3/8$ of a car must be given up in Italy. This means that Italy has a comparative advantage in automobiles. This can be checked as follows. The opportunity cost of an automobile in terms of a washing machine in Italy is $8/3$, equal to $2\,2/3$: $2\,2/3$ washing machines can be produced with the same number of workers and in the time it takes to produce 1 car in Italy. And the opportunity cost of an automobile in terms of a washing machine in the United States is $6/2$, equal to $3 : 3$ washing machines can be produced with the same number of workers and in the time it takes to produce 1 car in the United States. Since $2\,2/3 < 3$, Italy has a comparative advantage in producing automobiles.

c. The greatest gains are realized when each country specializes in producing the good for which it has a comparative advantage. Therefore, the United States should specialize in washing machines and Italy should specialize in automobiles.

3. At a trade of 10 U.S. large jets for 15 Brazilian small jets, Brazil gives up less for a large jet than it would if it were building large jets itself. Without trade, Brazil gives up 3 small jets for each large jet it produces. With trade, Brazil gives up only 1.5 small jets for each large jet from the United States. Likewise, the United States gives up less for a small jet than it would if it were producing small jets itself. Without trade, the United States gives up $3/4$ of a large jet for each small jet. With trade, the United States gives up only $2/3$ of a large jet for each small jet from Brazil.

4. An increase in the amount of money spent by households results in an increase in the flow of goods to households. This, in turn, generates an increase in demand for factors of production by firms. So, there is an increase in the number of jobs in the economy.

2-2 Check Your Understanding

1. a. This is a normative statement because it stipulates what should be done. In addition, it may have no "right" answer. That is, should people be prevented from all dangerous personal behavior if they enjoy that behavior—like skydiving? Your answer will depend on your point of view.

b. This is a positive statement because it is a description of fact.

2. a. True. Economists often have different value judgments about the desirability of a particular social goal. But despite those differences in value judgments, they will tend to agree that society, once it has decided to pursue a given social goal, should adopt the most efficient policy to achieve that goal. Therefore economists are likely to agree on adopting policy choice B.

b. False. Disagreements between economists are more likely to arise because they base their conclusions on different models or because they have different value judgments about the desirability of the policy.

CHAPTER THREE

3-1 Check Your Understanding

1. a. The quantity of umbrellas demanded is higher at any given price on a rainy day than on a dry day. This is a rightward *shift of* the demand curve, since at any given price the quantity demanded rises. This implies that any specific quantity can now be sold at a higher price.

b. The quantity of summer Caribbean cruises demanded rises in response to a price reduction. This is a *movement along* the demand curve for summer Caribbean cruises.

c. The demand for roses increases the week of Valentine's Day. This is a rightward *shift of* the demand curve.

d. The quantity of gasoline demanded falls in response to a rise in price. This is a *movement along* the demand curve.

3-2 Check Your Understanding

1. a. The quantity of houses supplied rises as a result of an increase in prices. This is a *movement along* the supply curve.

b. The quantity of strawberries supplied is higher at any given price. This is a rightward *shift of* the supply curve.

c. The quantity of labor supplied is lower at any given wage. This is a leftward *shift of* the supply curve compared to the supply curve during school vacation. So, in order to attract workers, fast-food chains have to offer higher wages.

d. The quantity of labor supplied rises in response to a rise in wages. This is a *movement along* the supply curve.

e. The quantity of cabins supplied is higher at any given price. This is a rightward *shift of* the supply curve.

3-3 Check Your Understanding

1. a. The supply curve shifts rightward. At the original equilibrium price of the year before, the quantity of grapes supplied exceeds the quantity demanded. This is a case of surplus. The price of grapes will fall.

b. The demand curve shifts leftward. At the original equilibrium price, the quantity of hotel rooms supplied exceeds the quantity demanded. This is a case of surplus. The rates for hotel rooms will fall.

c. The demand curve for second-hand snowblowers shifts rightward. At the original equilibrium price, the quantity of second-hand snowblowers demanded exceeds the quantity supplied. This is a case of shortage. The equilibrium price of second-hand snowblowers will rise.

3-4 Check Your Understanding

1. a. The market for large cars: this is a rightward shift in demand caused by a decrease in the price of a complement, gasoline. As a result of the shift, the equilibrium price of large cars will rise and the equilibrium quantity of large cars bought and sold will also rise.

b. The market for fresh paper made from recycled stock: this is a rightward shift in supply due to a technological innovation. As a result of this shift, the equilibrium price of fresh paper made from recycled stock will fall and the equilibrium quantity bought and sold will rise.

c. The market for movies at a local movie theater: this is a leftward shift in demand caused by a fall in the price of a substitute, on-demand films. As a result of this shift, the equilibrium price of movie tickets will fall and the equilibrium number of people who go to the movies will also fall.

2. Upon the announcement of the new chip, the demand curve for computers using the earlier chip shifts leftward, as demand decreases, and the supply curve for these computers shifts rightward, as supply increases.

a. If demand decreases relatively more than supply increases, then the equilibrium quantity falls, as shown here:

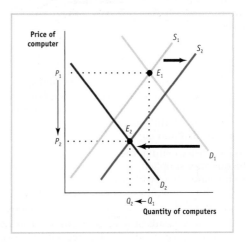

If supply increases relatively more than demand decreases, then the equilibrium quantity rises, as shown here:

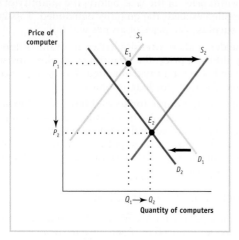

b. In both cases, the equilibrium price falls.

‖ CHAPTER FOUR

4-1 Check Your Understanding

1. a. Fewer homeowners are willing to rent out their driveways because the price ceiling has reduced the payment they receive. This is an example of a fall in price leading to a fall in the quantity supplied. It is shown in the accompanying diagram by the movement from point E to point A along the supply curve, a reduction in quantity of 400 parking spaces.

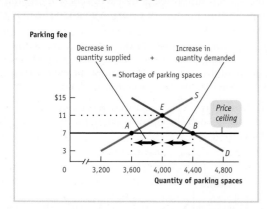

b. The quantity demanded increases by 400 spaces as the price decreases. At a lower price, more fans are willing to drive and rent a parking space. It is shown in the diagram by the movement from point E to point B along the demand curve.

c. Under a price ceiling, the quantity demanded exceeds the quantity supplied; as a result, shortages arise. In this case, there will be a shortage of 800 parking spaces. It is shown by the horizontal distance between points A and B.

d. Price ceilings result in wasted resources. The additional time fans spend to guarantee a parking space is wasted time.

e. Price ceilings lead to inefficient allocation of a good— here, the parking spaces—to consumers.

f. Price ceilings lead to black markets.

2. a. False. By lowering the price that producers receive, a price ceiling leads to a decrease in the quantity supplied.

b. True. A price ceiling leads to a lower quantity supplied than in an efficient, unregulated market. As a result, some people who would have been willing to pay the market price, and so would have gotten the good in an unregulated market, are unable to obtain it when a price ceiling is imposed.

c. True. Those producers who still sell the product now receive less for it and are therefore worse off. Other producers will no longer find it worthwhile to sell the product at all and so will also be made worse off.

4-2 Check Your Understanding

1. a. Some gas station owners will benefit from getting a higher price. Q_F indicates the sales made by these owners. But some will lose; there are those who make sales at the market equilibrium price of P_E but do not make sales at the regulated price of P_F. These missed sales are indicated on the graph by the fall in the quantity demanded along the demand curve, from point E to point A.

b. Those who buy gas at the higher price of P_F will probably receive better service; this is an example of *inefficiently high quality* caused by a price floor as gas station owners compete on quality rather than price. But opponents are correct to claim that consumers are generally worse off—those who buy at P_F would have been happy to buy at P_E, and many who were willing to buy at a price between P_E and P_F are now unwilling to buy. This is indicated on the graph by the fall in the quantity demanded along the demand curve, from point E to point A.

c. Proponents are wrong because consumers and some gas station owners are hurt by the price floor, which creates "missed opportunities"—desirable transactions between consumers and station owners that never take place. Moreover, the inefficiency of wasted resources arises as consumers spend time and money driving to other states. The price floor also tempts people to engage in black market activity. With the price floor, only Q_F units are sold. But at prices between P_E and P_F, there are drivers who cumulatively want to buy more than Q_F and owners who are willing to sell to them, a situation likely to lead to illegal activity.

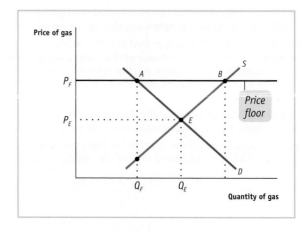

4-3 Check Your Understanding

1. **a.** The price of a ride is $7 since the quantity demanded at this price is 6 million: $7 is the *demand price* of 6 million rides. This is represented by point *A* in the accompanying figure.

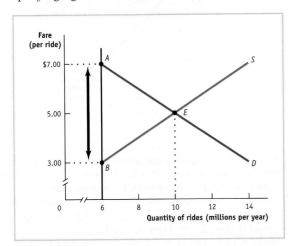

b. At 6 million rides, the supply price is $3 per ride, represented by point *B* in the figure. The wedge between the demand price of $7 per ride and the supply price of $3 per ride is the quota rent per ride, $4. This is represented in the figure above by the vertical distance between points *A* and *B*.

c. At 9 million rides, the demand price is $5.50 per ride, indicated by point *C* in the accompanying figure, and the supply price is $4.50 per ride, indicated by point *D*. The quota rent is the difference between the demand price and the supply price: $1.

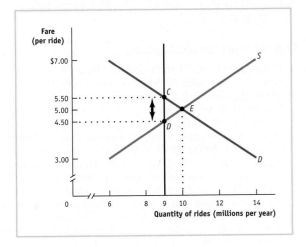

2. The accompanying figure shows a decrease in demand by 4 million rides, represented by a leftward shift of the demand curve from D_1 to D_2: at any given price, the quantity demanded falls by 4 million rides. (For example, at a price of $5, the quantity demanded falls from 10 million to 6 million rides per year.) This eliminates the effect of a quota limit of 8 million rides. At point E_2, the new market equilibrium, the equilibrium quantity is equal to the quota limit; as a result, the quota has no effect on the market.

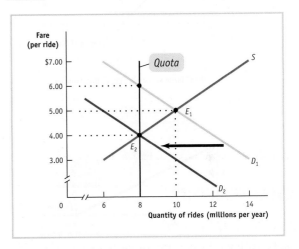

CHAPTER FIVE

5-1 Check Your Understanding

1. **a.** To determine comparative advantage, we must compare the two countries' opportunity costs for a given good. Take the opportunity cost of 1 ton of corn in terms of bicycles. In China, the opportunity cost of 1 bicycle is 0.01 ton of corn; so the opportunity cost of 1 ton of corn is 1/0.01 bicycles = 100 bicycles. The United States has the comparative advantage in corn since its opportunity cost in terms of bicycles is 50, a smaller number. Similarly, the opportunity cost in the United States of 1 bicycle in terms of corn is 1/50 ton of corn = 0.02 ton of corn. This is greater than 0.01, the Chinese opportunity cost of 1 bicycle in terms of corn, implying that China has a comparative advantage in bicycles.

b. Given that the United States can produce 200,000 bicycles if no corn is produced, it can produce 200,000 bicycles × 0.02 ton of corn/bicycle = 4,000 tons of corn when no bicycles are produced. Likewise, if China can produce 3,000 tons of corn if no bicycles are produced, it can produce 3,000 tons of corn × 100 bicycles/ton of corn = 300,000 bicycles if no corn is produced. These points determine the vertical and horizontal intercepts of the U.S. and Chinese production possibility frontiers, as shown in the accompanying diagram.

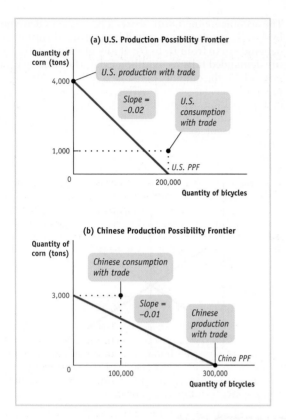

(a) U.S. Production Possibility Frontier

Quantity of corn (tons)

- U.S. production with trade
- 4,000
- Slope = −0.02
- U.S. consumption with trade
- 1,000
- U.S. PPF
- 0
- 200,000
- Quantity of bicycles

(b) Chinese Production Possibility Frontier

Quantity of corn (tons)

- Chinese consumption with trade
- 3,000
- Slope = −0.01
- Chinese production with trade
- China PPF
- 0
- 100,000
- 300,000
- Quantity of bicycles

c. The diagram shows the production and consumption points of the two countries. Each country is clearly better off with international trade because each now consumes a bundle of the two goods that lies outside its own production possibility frontier, indicating that these bundles were unattainable in autarky.

2. **a.** According to the Heckscher–Ohlin model, this pattern of trade occurs because the United States has a relatively larger endowment of factors of production, such as human capital and physical capital, that are suited to the production of movies, but France has a relatively larger endowment of factors of production suited to wine-making, such as vineyards and the human capital of vintners.

   b. According to the Heckscher–Ohlin model, this pattern of trade occurs because the United States has a relatively larger endowment of factors of production, such as human and physical capital, that are suited to making machinery, but Brazil has a relatively larger endowment of factors of production suited to shoe-making, such as unskilled labor and leather.

5-2 Check Your Understanding

1. In the accompanying diagram, P_A is the U.S. price of grapes in autarky and P_W is the world price of grapes under international trade. With trade, U.S. consumers pay a price of P_W for grapes and consume quantity Q_D, U.S. grape producers produce quantity Q_S, and the difference, $Q_D - Q_S$, represents imports of Mexican grapes. As a consequence of the strike by truckers, imports are halted, the price paid by American consumers rises to the autarky price, P_A, and U.S. consumption falls to the autarky quantity, Q_A.

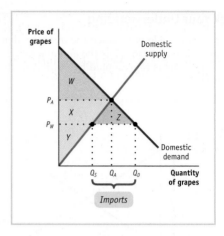

a. Before the strike, U.S. consumers enjoyed consumer surplus equal to areas $W + X + Z$. After the strike, their consumer surplus shrinks to W. So consumers are worse off, losing consumer surplus represented by $X + Z$.

b. Before the strike, U.S. producers had producer surplus equal to the area Y. After the strike, their producer surplus increases to $Y + X$. So U.S. producers are better off, gaining producer surplus represented by X.

c. U.S. total surplus falls as a result of the strike by an amount represented by area Z, the loss in consumer surplus that does not accrue to producers.

2. Mexican grape producers are worse off because they lose sales of exported grapes to the United States, and Mexican grape pickers are worse off because they lose the wages that were associated with the lost sales. The lower demand for Mexican grapes caused by the strike implies that the price Mexican consumers pay for grapes falls, making them better off. U.S. grape pickers are better off because their wages increase as a result of the increase of $Q_A - Q_S$ in U.S. sales.

5-3 Check Your Understanding

1. **a.** If the tariff is $0.50, the price paid by domestic consumers for a pound of imported butter is $0.50 + $0.50 = $1.00, the same price as a pound of domestic butter. Imported butter will no longer have a price advantage over domestic butter, imports will cease, and domestic producers will capture all the feasible sales to domestic consumers, selling amount Q_A in the accompanying figure. If the tariff is $0.25, the price paid by domestic consumers for a pound of imported butter is $0.50 + $0.25 = $0.75, $0.25 cheaper than a pound of domestic butter. American butter producers will gain sales in the amount of $Q_2 - Q_1$ as a result of the $0.25 tariff. But this is smaller than the amount they would have gained under the $0.50 tariff, the amount $Q_A - Q_1$.

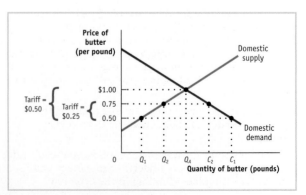

b. As long as the tariff is at least $0.50, increasing it more has no effect. At a tariff of $0.50, all imports are effectively blocked.

2. All imports are effectively blocked at a tariff of $0.50. So such a tariff corresponds to an import quota of 0.

5-4 Check Your Understanding

1. There are many fewer businesses that use steel as an input than there are consumers who buy sugar or clothing. So it will be easier for such businesses to communicate and coordinate among themselves to lobby against tariffs than it will be for consumers. In addition, each business will perceive that the cost of a steel tariff is quite costly to its profits, but an individual consumer is either unaware of or perceives little loss from tariffs on sugar or clothing.

2. Countries are often tempted to protect domestic industries by claiming that an import poses a quality, health, or environmental danger to domestic consumers. A WTO official should examine whether domestic producers are subject to the same stringency in the application of quality, health, or environmental regulations as foreign producers. If they are, then it is more likely that the regulations are for legitimate, non–trade protection purposes; if they are not, then it is more likely that the regulations are intended as trade protection measures.

CHAPTER SIX

6-1 Check Your Understanding

1. **a.** This is a microeconomic question because it addresses decisions made by consumers about a particular product.

   b. This is a macroeconomic question because it addresses consumer spending in the overall economy.

   c. This is a macroeconomic question because it addresses changes in the overall economy.

   d. This is a microeconomic question because it addresses changes in a particular market, in this case the market for economists.

   e. This is a microeconomic question because it addresses choices made by consumers and producers about which mode of transportation to use.

   f. This is a microeconomic question because it addresses changes in a particular market.

   g. This is a macroeconomic question because it addresses changes in a measure of the economy's overall price level.

2. **a.** When people can't get credit to finance their purchases, they will be unable to spend money. This will weaken the economy, and as others see the economy weaken, they will also cut back on their spending in order to save for future bad times. As a result, the credit shortfall will spark a compounding effect through the economy as people cut back their spending, making the economy worse, leading to more cutbacks in spending, and so on.

   b. If you believe the economy is self-regulating, then you would advocate doing nothing in response to the slump.

   c. If you believe in Keynesian economics, you would advocate that policy makers undertake monetary and fiscal policies to stimulate spending in the economy.

6-2 Check Your Understanding

1. We talk about business cycles for the economy as a whole because recessions and expansions are not confined to a few industries—they reflect downturns and upturns for the economy as a whole. In downturns, almost every sector of the economy reduces output and the number of people employed. Moreover, business cycles are an international phenomenon, sometimes moving in rough synchrony across countries.

2. A recession can hurt people throughout society. They cause large numbers of workers to lose their jobs and make it hard to find new jobs. Recessions hurt the standard of living of many families and are usually associated with a rise in the number of people living below the poverty line, an increase in the number of people who lose their houses because they can't afford their mortgage payments, and a fall in the percentage of Americans with health insurance. Recessions also hurt the profits of firms.

6-3 Check Your Understanding

1. Countries with high rates of population growth will have to maintain higher long-run growth rates of overall output than countries with low rates of population growth in order to achieve an increased standard of living per person because aggregate output will have to be divided among a larger number of people.

2. No, Argentina is not poorer than it was in the past. Both Argentina and Canada have experienced long-run growth. However, after World War II, Argentina did not make as much progress as Canada, perhaps because of political instability and bad macroeconomic policies. Also, Canada's economy grew much faster than Argentina's. Although Canada is now about three times as rich as Argentina, Argentina still experienced long-run growth.

6-4 Check Your Understanding

1. **a.** As some prices have risen but other prices have fallen, there may be overall inflation or deflation. The answer is ambiguous.

   b. As all prices have risen significantly, this sounds like inflation.

   c. As most prices have fallen and others have not changed, this sounds like deflation.

6-5 Check Your Understanding

1. **a.** This situation reflects comparative advantage. Canada's comparative advantage results from the development of oil—Canada now has an abundance of oil.

   b. This situation reflects comparative advantage. China's comparative advantage results from an abundance of labor; China is good at labor-intensive activities such as assembly.

   c. This situation reflects macroeconomic forces. Germany has been running a huge trade surplus because of underlying decisions regarding savings and investment spending with its savings in excess of its investment spending.

   d. This situation reflects macroeconomic forces. The United States was able to begin running a large trade deficit because the technology boom made the United States an attractive place to invest, with investment spending outstripping U.S. savings.

‖ CHAPTER SEVEN

7-1 Check Your Understanding

1. Let's start by considering the relationship between the total value added of all domestically produced final goods and services and aggregate spending on domestically produced final goods and services. These two quantities are equal because every final good and service produced in the economy is either purchased by someone or added to inventories. And additions to inventories are counted as spending by firms. Next, consider the relationship between aggregate spending on domestically produced final goods and services and total factor income. These two quantities are equal because all spending that is channeled to firms to pay for purchases of domestically produced final goods and services is revenue for firms. Those revenues must be paid out by firms to their factors of production in the form of wages, profit, interest, and rent. Taken together, this means that all three methods of calculating GDP are equivalent.

2. Firms make sales to other firms, households, the government, and the rest of the world. Households are linked to firms through the sale of factors of production to firms, through purchases from firms of final goods and services, and through lending funds to firms in the financial markets. Households are linked to the government through their payment of taxes, their receipt of transfers, and their lending of funds to the government via the financial markets. Finally, households are linked to the rest of the world through their purchases of imports and transactions with foreigners in financial markets.

3. You would be counting the value of the steel twice—once as it was sold by American Steel to American Motors and once as part of the car sold by American Motors.

7-2 Check Your Understanding

1. **a.** In 2015 nominal GDP was $(1,000,000 \times \$0.40) + (800,000 \times \$0.60) = \$400,000 + \$480,000 = \$880,000$. A 25% rise in the price of french fries from 2015 to 2016 means that the 2016 price of french fries was $1.25 \times \$0.40 = \$0.50$. A 10% fall in servings means that $1,000,000 \times 0.9 = 900,000$ servings were sold in 2016. As a result, the total value of sales of french fries in 2016 was $900,000 \times \$0.50 = \$450,000$. A 15% fall in the price of onion rings from 2015 to 2016 means that the 2016 price of onion rings was $0.85 \times \$0.60 = \$0.51$. A 5% rise in servings sold means that $800,000 \times 1.05 = 840,000$ servings were sold in 2016. As a result, the total value of sales of onion rings in 2016 was $840,000 \times \$0.51 = \$428,400$. Nominal GDP in 2016 was $\$450,000 + \$428,400 = \$878,400$. To find real GDP in 2016, we must calculate the value of sales in 2016 using 2015 prices: $(900,000 \text{ french fries} \times \$0.40) + (840,000 \text{ onion rings} \times \$0.60) = \$360,000 + \$504,000 = \$864,000$.

   b. The change in nominal GDP from 2015 to 2016 was $((\$878,400 - \$880,000)/\$880,000) \times 100 = -0.18\%$, a decline. But a comparison using real GDP shows a decline of $((\$864,000 - \$880,000)/\$880,000) \times 100 = -1.8\%$. That is, a calculation based on real GDP shows a drop 10 times larger (1.8%) than a calculation based on nominal GDP (0.18%). In this case, the calculation based on nominal GDP underestimates the true magnitude of the change.

2. A price index based on 2010 prices will contain a relatively high price of electronics and a relatively low price of housing compared to a price index based on 2015 prices. This means that a 2010 price index used to calculate real GDP in 2013 will magnify the value of electronics production in the economy, but a 2015 price index will magnify the value of housing production in the economy.

7-3 Check Your Understanding

1. This market basket costs, pre-frost, $(100 \times \$0.20) + (50 \times \$0.60) + (200 \times \$0.25) = \$20 + \$30 + \$50 = \$100$. The same market basket, post-frost, costs $(100 \times \$0.40) + (50 \times \$1.00) + (200 \times \$0.45) = \$40 + \$50 + \$90 = \$180$. So the price index is $(\$100/\$100) \times 100 = 100$ before the frost and $(\$180/\$100) \times 100 = 180$ after the frost, implying a rise in the price index of 80%. This increase in the price index is less than the 84.2% increase calculated in the text. The reason for this difference is that the new market basket of 100 oranges, 50 grapefruit, and 200 lemons contains proportionately more of the items that have experienced relatively lower price increases (the lemons, whose price has increased by 80%) and proportionately fewer of the items that have experienced relatively large price increases (the oranges, whose price has increased by 100%). This shows that the price index can be very sensitive to the composition of the market basket. If the market basket contains a large proportion of goods whose prices have risen faster than the prices of other goods, it will lead to a higher estimate of the increase in the price level. If it contains a large proportion of goods whose prices have risen more slowly than the prices of other goods, it will lead to a lower estimate of the increase in the price level.

2. **a.** A market basket determined 10 years ago will contain fewer cars than at present. Given that the average price of a car has grown faster than the average prices of other goods, this basket will underestimate the true increase in the cost of living because it contains relatively too few cars.

   b. A market basket determined 20 years ago will not contain broadband internet access. So it cannot track the fall in prices of internet access over the past few years. As a result, it will overestimate the true increase in the cost of living.

3. Using Equation 7-3, the inflation rate from 2015 to 2016 is $((242.821 - 237.846)/237.846) \times 100 = 2.09\%$.

‖ CHAPTER EIGHT

8-1 Check Your Understanding

1. Software improvements developed by employment websites that enable job-seekers to find jobs more quickly will reduce the unemployment rate over time. However, websites that induce discouraged workers to begin actively looking for work again will lead to an increase in the unemployment rate over time.

2. **a.** Rosa is not counted as unemployed because she is not actively looking for work, but she is counted in broader measures of labor underutilization as a discouraged worker.

   b. Anthony is not counted as unemployed; he is considered employed because he has a job.

c. Kanako is unemployed; she is not working and is actively looking for work.

d. Sergio is not unemployed, but underemployed; he is working part time for economic reasons. He is counted in broader measures of labor underutilization.

e. Natasha is not unemployed, but she is a marginally attached worker. She is counted in broader measures of labor underutilization.

3. Both parts a and b are consistent with the relationship, illustrated in Figure 8-5, between above-average or below-average growth in real GDP and changes in the unemployment rate: during years of above-average growth, the unemployment rate falls, and during years of below-average growth, the unemployment rate rises. However, part c is not consistent: it implies that a recession is associated with a fall in the unemployment rate, which is incorrect.

8-2 Check Your Understanding

1. **a.** When the pace of technological advance quickens, there will be higher rates of job creation and destruction as old industries disappear and new ones emerge. As a result, frictional unemployment will be higher as workers leave jobs in declining industries in search of jobs in expanding industries.

b. When the pace of technological advance quickens, there will be greater mismatch between the skills employees have and the skills employers are looking for, leading to higher structural unemployment.

c. When the unemployment rate is low, frictional unemployment will account for a larger share of total unemployment because other sources of unemployment will be diminished. So the share of total unemployment composed of the frictionally unemployed will rise.

2. A binding minimum wage represents a price floor below which wages cannot fall. As a result, actual wages cannot move toward equilibrium. So a minimum wage causes the quantity of labor supplied to exceed the quantity of labor demanded. Because this surplus of labor reflects unemployed workers, it affects the unemployment rate. Collective bargaining has a similar effect—unions are able to raise the wage above the equilibrium level to a level like W_U in the accompanying diagram. This will act like a minimum wage by causing the number of job-seekers to be larger than the number of workers firms are willing to hire. Collective bargaining causes the unemployment rate to be higher than it otherwise would be, as shown in the accompanying diagram.

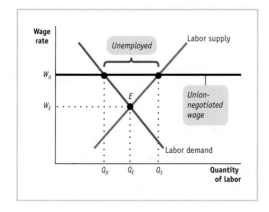

3. An increase in unemployment benefits at the peak of the business cycle reduces the cost to individuals of being unemployed, causing them to spend more time searching for new jobs. So the natural rate of unemployment would increase.

8-3 Check Your Understanding

1. Shoe-leather costs as a result of inflation will be lower because it is now less costly for individuals to manage their assets in order to economize on their money holdings. This reduction in the costs associated with converting other assets into money translates into lower shoe-leather costs.

2. If inflation came to an unexpected and complete stop over the next 15 or 20 years, the inflation rate would be zero, which of course is less than the expected inflation rate of 2% to 3%. Because the real interest rate is the nominal interest rate minus the inflation rate, the real interest rate on a loan would be higher than expected, and lenders would gain at the expense of borrowers. Borrowers would have to repay their loans with funds that have a higher real value than had been expected.

‖ CHAPTER NINE

9-1 Check Your Understanding

1. Economic progress raises the living standards of the average resident of a country. An increase in overall real GDP does not accurately reflect an increase in an average resident's living standard because it does not account for growth in the number of residents. If, for example, real GDP rises by 10% but population grows by 20%, the living standard of the average resident falls: after the change, the average resident has only $(110/120) \times 100 = 91.6\%$ as much real income as before the change. Similarly, an increase in nominal GDP per capita does not accurately reflect an increase in living standards because it does not account for any change in prices. For example, a 5% increase in nominal GDP per capita generated by a 5% increase in prices implies that there has been no change in living standards. Real GDP per capita is the only measure that accounts for both changes in the population and changes in prices.

2. Using the Rule of 70, the number of years it will take for China to double its real GDP per capita is $(70/7.9) = 8.86$, or approximately 9 years; India, $(70/4.1) = 17.07$, or approximately 17 years; Ireland, $(70/3.3) = 21.21$, or approximately 21 years; the United States, $(70/1.6) = 43.75$, or approximately 44 years; France, $(70/1.2) = 58.33$, or approximately 58 years; and Argentina, $(70/0.9) = 77.77$, or approximately 78 years. Since the Rule of 70 can only be applied to a positive growth rate, we cannot apply it to the case of Zimbabwe, which experienced negative growth. If India continues to have a higher growth rate of real GDP per capita than the United States, then India's real GDP per capita will eventually surpass that of the United States.

3. The United States began growing rapidly over a century ago, but China and India have begun growing rapidly only recently. As a result, the living standard of the typical Chinese or Indian household has not yet caught up with that of the typical American household.

9-2 Check Your Understanding

1. **a.** Significant technological progress will result in a positive growth rate of productivity even though physical capital per worker and human capital per worker are unchanged.

   b. The growth rate of productivity will fall but remain positive due to diminishing returns to physical capital.

2. **a.** If output has grown 3% per year and the labor force has grown 1% per year, then productivity—output per person—has grown at approximately 3% − 1% = 2% per year.

   b. If physical capital has grown 4% per year and the labor force has grown 1% per year, then physical capital per worker has grown at approximately 4% − 1% = 3% per year.

   c. According to estimates, each 1% rise in physical capital, other things equal, increases productivity by 0.3%. So, as physical capital per worker has increased by 3%, productivity growth that can be attributed to an increase in physical capital per worker is 0.3 × 3% = 0.9%. As a percentage of total productivity growth, this is 0.9%/2% × 100% = 45%.

   d. If the rest of productivity growth is due to technological progress, then technological progress has contributed 2% − 0.9% = 1.1% to productivity growth. As a percentage of total productivity growth, this is 1.1%/2% × 100% = 55%.

3. It will take a period of time for workers to learn how to use the new computer system and to adjust their routines. And because there are often setbacks in learning a new system, such as accidentally erasing your computer files, productivity at Multinomics may decrease for a period of time.

9-3 Check Your Understanding

1. A country that has high domestic savings is able to achieve a high rate of investment spending as a percent of GDP. This, in turn, allows the country to achieve a high growth rate.

2. It is likely that the United States will experience a greater pace of innovation and development of new drugs because closer links between private companies and academic research centers will lead to research and development more directly focused on producing new drugs rather than on pure research.

3. It is likely that these events resulted in a fall in the country's growth rate because the lack of property rights would have dissuaded people from making investments in a productive capacity.

9-4 Check Your Understanding

1. The conditional version of the convergence hypothesis says that countries grow faster, other things equal, when they start from relatively low GDP per capita. From this we can infer that they grow more slowly, other things equal, when their real GDP per capita is relatively higher. This points to lower future Asian growth. However, other things might not be equal: if Asian economies continue investing in human capital, if savings rates continue to be high, if governments invest in infrastructure, and so on, growth might continue at an accelerated pace.

2. The regions of East Asia, Western Europe, and the United States support the convergence hypothesis because a comparison among them shows that the growth rate of real GDP per capita falls as real GDP per capita rises. Eastern Europe, West Asia, Latin America, and Africa do not support the hypothesis because they all have much lower real GDP per capita than the United States but have either approximately the same growth rate (West Asia and Eastern Europe) or a lower growth rate (Africa and Latin America).

3. The evidence suggests that both sets of factors matter: better infrastructure is important for growth, but so is political and financial stability. Policies should try to address both areas.

9-5 Check Your Understanding

1. Economists are typically more concerned about environmental degradation than resource scarcity. The reason is that in modern economies the price response tends to alleviate the limits imposed by resource scarcity through conservation and the development of alternatives. However, because environmental degradation involves a cost imposed by individuals or firms on others without the requirement to pay compensation (known as a *negative externality*), effective government intervention is required to address it. As a result, economists are more concerned about the limits to growth imposed by environmental degradation because a market response would be inadequate.

2. Growth increases a country's greenhouse gas emissions. The current best estimates are that a large reduction in emissions will result in only a modest reduction in growth. The international burden sharing of greenhouse gas emissions reduction is contentious because rich countries are reluctant to pay the costs of reducing their emissions only to see newly emerging countries like China rapidly increase their emissions. Yet most of the current accumulation of gases is due to the past actions of rich countries. Poorer countries like China are equally reluctant to sacrifice their growth to pay for the past actions of rich countries.

CHAPTER TEN

10-1 Check Your Understanding

1. **a.** As there is a net capital inflow into the economy, the supply of loanable funds increases. This is illustrated by the shift of the supply curve from S_1 to S_2 in the accompanying diagram. As the equilibrium moves from E_1 to E_2, the equilibrium interest rate falls from r_1 to r_2, and the equilibrium quantity of loanable funds increases from Q_1 to Q_2.

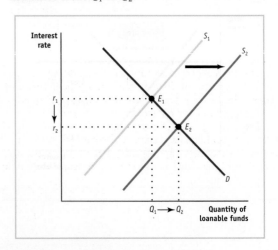

b. Savings fall due to the higher proportion of retired people, and the supply of loanable funds decreases. This is illustrated by the leftward shift of the supply curve from S_1 to S_2 in the accompanying diagram. The equilibrium moves from E_1 to E_2, the equilibrium interest rate rises from r_1 to r_2, and the equilibrium quantity of loanable funds falls from Q_1 to Q_2.

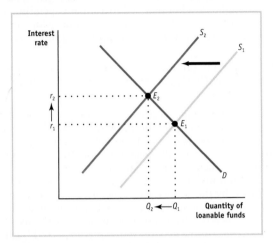

2. We know from the loanable funds market that as the interest rate rises, households want to save more and consume less. But at the same time, an increase in the interest rate lowers the number of investment spending projects with returns at least as high as the interest rate. The statement "households will want to save more money than businesses will want to invest" cannot represent an equilibrium in the loanable funds market because it says that the quantity of loanable funds offered exceeds the quantity of loanable funds demanded. If that were to occur, the interest rate must fall to make the quantity of loanable funds offered equal to the quantity of loanable funds demanded.

3. a. The real interest rate will not change. According to the Fisher effect, an increase in expected inflation drives up the nominal interest rate, leaving the real interest rate unchanged.

b. The nominal interest rate will rise by 3%. Each additional percentage point of expected inflation drives up the nominal interest rate by 1 percentage point.

c. As we saw in Figure 10-9, as long as inflation is expected, it does not affect the equilibrium quantity of loanable funds. Both the supply and demand curves for loanable funds are pushed upward, leaving the equilibrium quantity of loanable funds unchanged.

10-2 Check Your Understanding

1. The transaction costs for (a) a bank deposit and (b) a share of a mutual fund are approximately equal because each can typically be accomplished by making a phone call, going online, or visiting a branch office. Transaction costs are highest for (c) a share of a family business, since finding a buyer for the share consumes time and resources. The level of risk is lowest for (a) a bank deposit, since these deposits are insured by the Federal Deposit Insurance Corporation (FDIC) up to $250,000; somewhat higher for (b) a share of a mutual fund, since

despite diversification, there is still risk associated with holding mutual funds; and highest for (c) a share of a family business, since this investment is not diversified. The level of liquidity is highest for (a) a bank deposit, since withdrawals can usually be made immediately; somewhat lower for (b) a share of a mutual fund, since it may take a few days between selling your shares and the payment being processed; and lowest for (c) a share of a family business, since it can only be sold with the unanimous agreement of other members and it will take some time to find a buyer.

2. Economic development and growth are the result of, among other factors, investment spending on physical capital. Since investment spending is equal to savings, the greater the amount saved, the higher investment spending will be, and so the higher growth and economic development will be. So the existence of institutions that facilitate savings will help a country's growth and economic development. As a result, a country with a financial system that provides low transaction costs, opportunities for diversification of risk, and high liquidity to its savers will experience faster growth and economic development than a country that doesn't.

10-3 Check Your Understanding

1. a. Today's stock prices reflect the market's expectation of future stock prices, and according to the efficient markets hypothesis, stock prices always take account of all available information. The fact that this year's profits are low is not new information, so it is already built into the share price. However, when it becomes known that the company's profits will be high next year, the price of a share of its stock will rise today, reflecting this new information.

b. The expectations of investors about high profits were already built into the stock price. Since profits will be lower than expected, the market's expectations about the company's future stock price will be revised downward. This new information will lower the stock price.

c. When other companies in the same industry announce that sales are unexpectedly slow this year, investors are likely to conclude that sales will also be unexpectedly slow for this company. As a result, investors will revise downward their expectations of future profits and of the future stock price. This new information will result in a lower stock price today.

d. This announcement will either have no effect on the company's stock price or will increase it only slightly. It does not add any new information, beyond removing some uncertainty about whether the profit forecast was correct. It should therefore result in either no increase or only a small increase in the stock price.

2. The efficient markets hypothesis states that all available information is immediately taken into account in stock prices. So if investors consistently bought stocks the day after the Dow rose by 1%, a smart investor would *sell* on that day because demand—and so stock prices—would be high. If a profit can be made that way, eventually many investors would be selling, and it would no longer be true that investors always bought stocks the day after the Dow rose by 1%.

CHAPTER ELEVEN

11-1 Check Your Understanding

1. A decline in investment spending, like a rise in investment spending, has a multiplier effect on real GDP—the only difference in this case is that real GDP falls instead of rises. The fall in I leads to an initial fall in real GDP, which leads to a fall in disposable income, which leads to lower consumer spending, which leads to another fall in real GDP, and so on. So consumer spending falls as an indirect result of the fall in investment spending.

2. When the MPC is 0.5, the multiplier is equal to $1/(1 - 0.5) = 1/0.5 = 2$. When the MPC is 0.8, the multiplier is equal to $1/(1 - 0.8) = 1/0.2 = 5$.

3. The greater the share of GDP that is saved rather than spent, the lower the MPC. Disposable income that goes to savings is like a "leak" in the system, reducing the amount of spending that fuels a further expansion. So it is likely that Amerigo will have the larger multiplier.

11-2 Check Your Understanding

1. **a.** Angelina's autonomous consumer spending is $8,000. When her current disposable income rises by $10,000, her consumer spending rises by $12,000 – $8,000 = $4,000. So her MPC is $4,000/$10,000 = 0.4 and her consumption function is $c = \$8,000 + 0.4 \times yd$. Felicia's autonomous consumer spending is $6,500. When her current disposable income rises by $10,000, her consumer spending rises by $14,500 – $6,500 = $8,000. So her MPC is $8,000/$10,000 = 0.8 and her consumption function is $c = \$6,500 + 0.8 \times yd$. Marina's autonomous consumer spending is $7,250. When her current disposable income rises by $10,000, her consumer spending rises by $14,250 – $7,250 = $7,000. So her MPC is $7,000/$10,000 = 0.7 and her consumption function is $c = \$7,250 + 0.7 \times yd$.

   b. The aggregate autonomous consumer spending in this economy is $8,000 + $6,500 + $7,250 = $21,750. A $30,000 increase in disposable income (3 × $10,000) leads to a $4,000 + $8,000 + $7,000 = $19,000 increase in consumer spending. So the economy-wide MPC is $19,000/$30,000 = 0.63 and the aggregate consumption function is $C = \$21,750 + 0.63 \times YD$.

2. If you expect your future disposable income to fall, you would like to save some of today's disposable income to tide you over in the future. But you cannot do this if you cannot save. If you expect your future disposable income to rise, you would like to spend some of tomorrow's higher income today. But you cannot do this if you cannot borrow. If you cannot save or borrow, your expected future disposable income will have no effect on your consumer spending today. In fact, your MPC must always equal 1: you must consume all your current disposable income today, and you will be unable to smooth your consumption over time.

11-3 Check Your Understanding

1. **a.** An unexpected increase in consumer spending will result in a reduction in inventories as producers sell items from their inventories to satisfy this short-term increase in demand. This is negative unplanned inventory investment: it reduces the value of producers' inventories.

   b. A rise in the cost of borrowing is equivalent to a rise in the interest rate: fewer investment spending projects are now profitable to producers, whether they are financed through borrowing or retained earnings. As a result, producers will reduce the amount of planned investment spending.

   c. A sharp increase in the rate of real GDP growth leads to a higher level of planned investment spending by producers, according to the accelerator principle, as they increase production capacity to meet higher demand.

   d. As sales fall, producers sell less, and their inventories grow. This leads to positive unplanned inventory investment.

2. Since the marginal propensity to consume is less than 1—because consumers normally spend part but not all of an additional dollar of disposable income—consumer spending does not fully respond to fluctuations in current disposable income. This behavior diminishes the effect of fluctuations in the economy on consumer spending. In contrast, by the accelerator principle, investment spending is directly related to the expected future growth rate of GDP. As a result, investment spending will magnify fluctuations in the economy: a higher expected future growth rate of real GDP leads to higher planned investment spending; a lower expected future growth rate of real GDP leads to lower planned investment spending.

3. When consumer spending is sluggish, firms with excess production capacity will cut back on planned investment spending because they think their existing capacities are sufficient for expected future sales. Similarly, when consumer spending is sluggish and firms have a large amount of unplanned inventory investment, they are likely to cut back their production of output because they think their existing inventories are sufficient for expected future sales. So an inventory overhang is likely to depress current economic activity as firms cut back on their planned investment spending and on their output.

11-4 Check Your Understanding

1. A slump in planned investment spending will lead to a fall in real GDP in response to an unanticipated increase in inventories. The fall in real GDP will translate into a fall in households' disposable income, and households will respond by reducing consumer spending. The decrease in consumer spending leads producers to further decrease output, further lowering disposable income and leading to further reductions in consumer spending. So although the slump originated in investment spending, it will cause a reduction in consumer spending.

2. **a.** After an autonomous fall in planned aggregate spending, the economy is no longer in equilibrium: real GDP is greater than planned aggregate spending. The accompanying figure shows this autonomous fall in planned aggregate spending by the shift of the aggregate spending curve from AE_1 to AE_2. The difference between the two results in positive unplanned inventory investment: there is an unanticipated increase in inventories. Firms will respond by reducing production. This will eventually move the economy to a new equilibrium. In the accompanying figure, this is illustrated by the movement from the initial income–expenditure equilibrium at E_1 to the new income–expenditure equilibrium at E_2. As the economy moves to its new

equilibrium, real GDP falls from its initial income–expenditure equilibrium level at Y_1^* to its new lower level, Y_2^*.

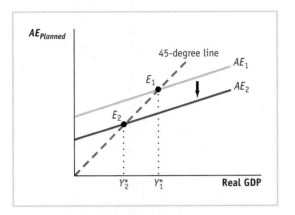

b. We know that the change in income–expenditure equilibrium GDP is given by Equation 11-17: $\Delta Y^* = $ Multiplier $\times \Delta AAE_{Planned}$. Here, the multiplier is equal to $1/(1 - 0.5) = 1/0.5 = 2$. So a $300 million autonomous reduction in planned aggregate spending will lead to a $2 \times \$300$ million $= \$600$ million ($0.6 billion) fall in income–expenditure equilibrium GDP. The new Y^* will be $500 billion – $0.6 billion = $499.4 billion.

‖ CHAPTER TWELVE

12-1 Check Your Understanding

1. **a.** This is a shift of the aggregate demand curve. A decrease in the quantity of money raises the interest rate, since people now want to borrow more and lend less. A higher interest rate reduces investment and consumer spending at any given aggregate price level. So the aggregate demand curve shifts to the left.

   b. This is a movement up along the aggregate demand curve. As the aggregate price level rises, the real value of money holdings falls. This is the interest rate effect of a change in the aggregate price level: as the value of money falls, people want to hold more money. They do so by borrowing more and lending less. This leads to a rise in the interest rate and a reduction in consumer and investment spending. So it is a movement along the aggregate demand curve.

   c. This is a shift of the aggregate demand curve. Expectations of a poor job market, and so lower average disposable incomes, will reduce people's consumer spending today at any given aggregate price level. So the aggregate demand curve shifts to the left.

   d. This is a shift of the aggregate demand curve. A fall in tax rates raises people's disposable income. At any given aggregate price level, consumer spending is now higher. So the aggregate demand curve shifts to the right.

   e. This is a movement down along the aggregate demand curve. As the aggregate price level falls, the real value of assets rises. This is the wealth effect of a change in the aggregate price level: as the value of assets rises, people will increase their consumption plans. This leads to higher consumer spending. So it is a movement along the aggregate demand curve.

   f. This is a shift of the aggregate demand curve. A rise in the real value of assets in the economy due to a surge in real estate values raises consumer spending at any given aggregate price level. So the aggregate demand curve shifts to the right.

12-2 Check Your Understanding

1. **a.** This represents a movement along the *SRAS* curve because the CPI—like the GDP deflator—is a measure of the aggregate price level, the overall price level of final goods and services in the economy.

   b. This represents a shift of the *SRAS* curve because oil is a commodity. The *SRAS* curve will shift to the right because production costs are now lower, leading to a higher quantity of aggregate output supplied at any given aggregate price level.

   c. This represents a shift of the *SRAS* curve because it involves a change in nominal wages. An increase in legally mandated benefits to workers is equivalent to an increase in nominal wages. As a result, the *SRAS* curve will shift leftward because production costs are now higher, leading to a lower quantity of aggregate output supplied at any given aggregate price level.

2. You would need to know what happened to the aggregate price level. If the increase in the quantity of aggregate output supplied was due to a movement along the *SRAS* curve, the aggregate price level would have increased at the same time as the quantity of aggregate output supplied increased. If the increase in the quantity of aggregate output supplied was due to a rightward shift of the *LRAS* curve, the aggregate price level might not rise. Alternatively, you could make the determination by observing what happened to aggregate output in the long run. If it fell back to its initial level in the long run, then the temporary increase in aggregate output was due to a movement along the *SRAS* curve. If it stayed at the higher level in the long run, the increase in aggregate output was due to a rightward shift of the *LRAS* curve.

12-3 Check Your Understanding

1. **a.** An increase in the minimum wage raises the nominal wage and, as a result, shifts the short-run aggregate supply curve to the left. As a result of this negative supply shock, the aggregate price level rises and aggregate output falls.

   b. Increased investment spending shifts the aggregate demand curve to the right. As a result of this positive demand shock, both the aggregate price level and aggregate output rise.

   c. An increase in taxes and a reduction in government spending both result in negative demand shocks, shifting the aggregate demand curve to the left. As a result, both the aggregate price level and aggregate output fall.

   d. This is a negative supply shock, shifting the short-run aggregate supply curve to the left. As a result, the aggregate price level rises and aggregate output falls.

2. As the rise in productivity increases potential output, the long-run aggregate supply curve shifts to the right. If, in the short run, there is now a recessionary gap (aggregate output is less than potential output), nominal wages will fall, shifting the short-run aggregate supply curve to the right. This results in a fall in the aggregate price level and a rise in aggregate output. As prices fall, we move

along the aggregate demand curve due to the wealth and interest rate effects of a change in the aggregate price level. Eventually, as long-run macroeconomic equilibrium is reestablished, aggregate output will rise to be equal to potential output.

12-4 Check Your Understanding

1. **a.** An economy is overstimulated when an inflationary gap is present. This will arise if an expansionary monetary or fiscal policy is implemented when the economy is currently in long-run macroeconomic equilibrium. This shifts the aggregate demand curve to the right, in the short run raising the aggregate price level and aggregate output and creating an inflationary gap. Eventually nominal wages will rise and shift the short-run aggregate supply curve to the left, and aggregate output will fall back to potential output. This is the scenario envisaged by the speaker.

    b. No, this is not a valid argument. When the economy is not currently in long-run macroeconomic equilibrium, an expansionary monetary or fiscal policy does not lead to the outcome described above. Suppose a negative demand shock has shifted the aggregate demand curve to the left, resulting in a recessionary gap. An expansionary monetary or fiscal policy can shift the aggregate demand curve back to its original position in long-run macroeconomic equilibrium. In this way, the short-run fall in aggregate output and deflation caused by the original negative demand shock can be avoided. So, if used in response to demand shocks, fiscal or monetary policy is an effective policy tool.

2. Those within the Fed who advocated lowering interest rates were focused on boosting aggregate demand in order to counteract the negative demand shock caused by the collapse of the housing bubble. Lowering interest rates will result in a rightward shift of the aggregate demand curve, increasing aggregate output but raising the aggregate price level. Those within the Fed who advocated holding interest rates steady were focused on the fact that fighting the slump in aggregate demand in the face of a negative supply shock could result in a rise in inflation. Holding interest rates steady relies on the ability of the economy to self-correct in the long run, with the aggregate price level and aggregate output only gradually returning to their levels before the negative supply shock.

‖ CHAPTER THIRTEEN

13-1 Check Your Understanding

1. **a.** This is a contractionary fiscal policy because it is a reduction in government purchases of goods and services.

    b. This is an expansionary fiscal policy because it is an increase in government transfers that will increase disposable income.

    c. This is a contractionary fiscal policy because it is an increase in taxes that will reduce disposable income.

2. Federal disaster relief that is quickly disbursed is more effective than legislated aid because there is very little time lag between the time of the disaster and the time it is received by victims. So it will stabilize the economy after a disaster. In contrast, legislated aid is likely to entail a time lag in its disbursement, potentially destabilizing the economy.

3. This statement implies that expansionary fiscal policy will result in crowding out of the private sector, and that the opposite, contractionary fiscal policy, will lead the private sector to grow. Whether this statement is true or not depends upon whether the economy is at full employment; it is only then that we should expect expansionary fiscal policy to lead to crowding out. If, instead, the economy has a recessionary gap, then we should expect instead that the private sector grows along with the fiscal expansion, and contracts along with a fiscal contraction.

13-2 Check Your Understanding

1. A \$500 million increase in government purchases of goods and services directly increases aggregate spending by \$500 million, which then starts the multiplier in motion. It will increase real GDP by \$500 million $\times$ $1/(1 - MPC)$. A \$500 million increase in government transfers increases aggregate spending only to the extent that it leads to an increase in consumer spending. Consumer spending rises by $MPC \times \$1$ for every \$1 increase in disposable income, where MPC is less than 1. So a \$500 million increase in government transfers will cause a rise in real GDP only MPC times as much as a \$500 million increase in government purchases of goods and services. It will increase real GDP by \$500 million $\times MPC/(1 - MPC)$.

2. This is the same issue as in Problem 1, but in reverse. If government purchases of goods and services fall by \$500 million, the initial fall in aggregate spending is \$500 million. If there is a \$500 million reduction in government transfers, the initial fall in aggregate spending is $MPC \times \$500$ million, which is less than \$500 million.

3. Boldovia will experience greater variation in its real GDP than Moldovia because Moldovia has automatic stabilizers while Boldovia does not. In Moldovia the effects of slumps will be lessened by unemployment insurance benefits that will support residents' incomes, while the effects of booms will be diminished because tax revenues will go up. In contrast, incomes will not be supported in Boldovia during slumps because there is no unemployment insurance. In addition, because Boldovia has lump-sum taxes, its booms will not be diminished by increases in tax revenue.

13-3 Check Your Understanding

1. The actual budget balance takes into account the effects of the business cycle on the budget deficit. During recessionary gaps, it incorporates the effect of lower tax revenues and higher transfers on the budget balance; during inflationary gaps, it incorporates the effect of higher tax revenues and reduced transfers. In contrast, the cyclically adjusted budget balance factors out the effects of the business cycle and assumes that real GDP is at potential output. Since, in the long run, real GDP tends to potential output, the cyclically adjusted budget balance is a better measure of the long-run sustainability of government policies.

2. In recessions, real GDP falls. This implies that consumers' incomes, consumer spending, and producers' profits also fall. So in recessions, states' tax revenue (which depends in large part on consumers' incomes, consumer spending, and producers' profits) falls. In order to balance the state budget, states have to cut spending or raise taxes. But that deepens the recession. Without a balanced-budget requirement, states could use expansionary fiscal policy during a recession to lessen the fall in real GDP.

13-4 Check Your Understanding

1. **a.** A higher growth rate of real GDP implies that tax revenue will increase. If government spending remains constant and the government runs a budget surplus, the size of the public debt will be less than it would otherwise have been.

   b. If retirees live longer, the average age of the population increases. As a result, the implicit liabilities of the government increase because spending on programs for older Americans, such as Social Security and Medicare, will rise.

   c. A decrease in tax revenue without offsetting reductions in government spending will cause the public debt to increase.

   d. Public debt will increase as a result of government borrowing to pay interest on its current public debt.

2. In order to stimulate the economy in the short run, the government can use fiscal policy to increase real GDP. This entails borrowing, increasing the size of the public debt further and leading to undesirable consequences: in extreme cases, governments can be forced to default on their debts. Even in less extreme cases, a large public debt is undesirable because government borrowing crowds out borrowing for private investment spending. This reduces the amount of investment spending, reducing the long-run growth of the economy.

3. A contractionary fiscal policy like austerity reduces government spending, which in turn reduces income and reduces tax revenue. With less tax revenue, the government is less able to pay its debts. Also, a failing economy causes lenders to have less confidence that a government is able to pay its debts and leads them to raise interest rates on the debt. Higher interest rates on the debt make it even less likely the government can repay.

CHAPTER FOURTEEN

14-1 Check Your Understanding

1. The defining characteristic of money is its liquidity: how easily it can be used to purchase goods and services. Although a gift card can easily be used to purchase a very defined set of goods or services (the goods or services available at the store issuing the gift card), it cannot be used to purchase any other goods or services. A gift card is therefore not money, since it cannot easily be used to purchase all goods and services.

2. Again, the important characteristic of money is its liquidity: how easily it can be used to purchase goods and services. M1, the narrowest definition of the money supply, contains only currency in circulation, checkable bank deposits, and traveler's checks. CDs aren't checkable—and they can't be made checkable without incurring a cost because there's a penalty for early withdrawal. This makes them less liquid than the assets counted in M1.

3. Commodity-backed money uses resources more efficiently than simple commodity money, like gold and silver coins, because commodity-backed money ties up fewer valuable resources. Although a bank must keep some of the commodity—generally gold and silver—on hand, it only has to keep enough to satisfy demand for redemptions. It can then lend out the remaining gold and silver, which allows society to use these resources for other purposes, with no loss in the ability to achieve gains from trade.

14-2 Check Your Understanding

1. Even though you know that the rumor about the bank is not true, you are concerned about other depositors pulling their money out of the bank. And you know that if enough other depositors pull their money out, the bank will fail. In that case, it is rational for you to pull your money out before the bank fails. All depositors will think like this, so even if they all know that the rumor is false, they may still rationally pull their money out, leading to a bank run. Deposit insurance leads depositors to worry less about the possibility of a bank run. Even if a bank fails, the FDIC will currently pay each depositor up to $250,000 per account. This will make you much less likely to pull your money out in response to a rumor. Since other depositors will think the same, there will be no bank run.

2. The aspects of modern bank regulation that would frustrate this scheme are *capital requirements* and *reserve requirements*. Capital requirements mean that a bank has to have a certain amount of capital—the difference between its assets (loans plus reserves) and its liabilities (deposits). So the con artist could not open a bank without putting any of his own wealth in because the bank needs a certain amount of capital—that is, it needs to hold more assets (loans plus reserves) than deposits. So the con artist would be at risk of losing his own wealth if his loans turn out badly.

14-3 Check Your Understanding

1. Since they only have to hold $100 in reserves, instead of $200, banks now lend out $100 of their reserves. Whoever borrows the $100 will deposit it in a bank, which will lend out $100 × (1 − rr) = $100 × 0.9 = $90. Whoever borrows the $90 will put it into a bank, which will lend out $90 × 0.9 = $81, and so on. Overall, deposits will increase by $100/0.1 = $1,000.

2. Silas puts $1,000 in the bank, of which the bank lends out $1,000 × (1 − rr) = $1,000 × 0.9 = $900. Whoever borrows the $900 will keep $450 in cash and deposit $450 in a bank. The bank will lend out $450 × 0.9 = $405. Whoever borrows the $405 will keep $202.50 in cash and deposit $202.50 in a bank. The bank will lend out $202.50 × 0.9 = $182.25, and so on. Overall, this leads to an increase in deposits of $1,000 + $450 + $202.50 + . . . But it decreases the amount of currency in circulation: the amount of cash is reduced by the $1,000 Silas puts into the bank. This is offset, but not fully, by the amount of cash held by each borrower. The amount of currency in circulation therefore changes by −$1,000 + $450 + $202.50 + . . . The money supply therefore increases by the sum of the increase in deposits and the change in currency in circulation, which is $1,000 − $1,000 + $450 + $450 + $202.50 + $202.50 + . . . and so on.

14-4 Check Your Understanding

1. An open-market purchase of $100 million by the Fed increases banks' reserves by $100 million as the Fed credits their accounts with additional reserves. In other words, this open-market purchase increases the monetary base (currency in circulation plus bank reserves) by $100 million. Banks lend out the additional $100 million. Whoever borrows the money puts it back into the banking system in the form of deposits. Of these deposits, banks lend out $100 million × (1 − rr) = $100 million × 0.9 = $90 million. Whoever borrows the money deposits it back into the banking system. And banks lend out $90 million × 0.9 = $81 million, and so on. As a result, bank deposits

increase by $100 million + $90 million + $81 million + ... = $100 million/$rr$ = $100 million/0.1 = $1,000 million = $1 billion. Since in this simplified example all money lent out is deposited back into the banking system, there is no increase of currency in circulation, so the increase in bank deposits is equal to the increase in the money supply. In other words, the money supply increases by $1 billion. This is greater than the increase in the monetary base by a factor of 10: in this simplified model in which deposits are the only component of the money supply and in which banks hold no excess reserves, the money multiplier is $1/rr$ = 10.

14-5 Check Your Understanding

1. The Panic of 1907, the S&L crisis, and the crisis of 2008 all involved losses by shadow bank–like financial institutions that were less regulated than traditional depository banks. In the crises of 1907 and 2008, there was a widespread loss of confidence in the financial sector and a collapse of credit markets. Like the crisis of 1907 and the S&L crisis, the crisis of 2008 exerted a powerful negative effect on the economy.

2. The creation of the Federal Reserve failed to prevent bank runs because it did not eradicate the fears of depositors that a bank collapse would cause them to lose their money. The bank runs eventually stopped after federal deposit insurance was instituted and the public came to understand that their deposits were now protected.

3. Extraordinary measures were needed to address the financial crisis of 2008 because the failure of unregulated shadow banks, like Lehman Brothers, led to increased panic in markets as asset prices tumbled and credit markets froze for households and businesses. The failure of shadow banks also put the entire financial system at risk of failure, both the financially sound traditional depository banks and nondepository financial institutions, that were eventually deemed too critical to the economy to fail.

‖ CHAPTER FIFTEEN

15-1 Check Your Understanding

1. **a.** By increasing the opportunity cost of holding money, a high interest rate reduces the quantity of money demanded. This is a movement up and to the left along the money demand curve.

   b. A 10% fall in prices reduces the quantity of money demanded at any given interest rate, shifting the money demand curve leftward.

   c. This technological change reduces the quantity of money demanded at any given interest rate. So it shifts the money demand curve leftward.

   d. This will increase the demand for money at any given interest rate. With more of the economy's assets in overseas bank accounts that are difficult to access, people will want to hold more cash to finance purchases. The money demand curve shifts to the right.

2. **a.** The 0.5% interest paid on cash balances will reduce the opportunity cost of holding cash for PayBuddy customers because they now forgo less by holding cash.

   b. An increase in the interest paid on six-month CDs raises the opportunity cost of holding cash because holding cash requires forgoing the higher interest paid.

c. One year of zero-interest financing on holiday purchases increases the opportunity cost of holding cash. A holiday shopper need not convert interest-paying assets into cash in order to avoid paying interest on credit card purchases. So what a shopper forgoes by paying for holiday purchases with cash instead of charging it on a credit card has increased.

15-2 Check Your Understanding

1. In the accompanying diagram, the increase in the demand for money is shown as a rightward shift of the money demand curve, from MD_1 to MD_2. This raises the equilibrium interest rate from r_1 to r_2.

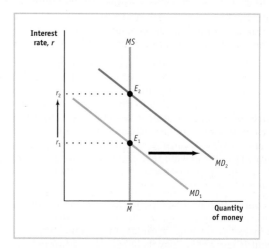

2. In order to prevent the interest rate from rising, the Federal Reserve must make an open-market purchase of Treasury bills, shifting the money supply curve rightward. This is shown in the accompanying diagram as the move from MS_1 to MS_2.

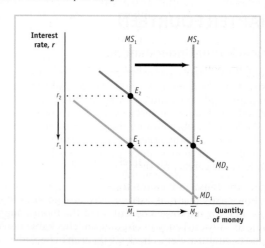

3. **a.** Malia is better off buying a one-year bond today and a one-year bond next year because this allows her to get the higher interest rate one year from now.

   b. Malia is better off buying a two-year bond today because it gives her a higher interest rate in the second year than if she bought two one-year bonds.

15-3 Check Your Understanding

1. **a.** The money supply curve shifts to the right.

   b. The equilibrium interest rate falls.

   c. Investment spending rises, due to the fall in the interest rate.

   d. Consumer spending rises, due to the multiplier process.

   e. Aggregate output rises because of the rightward shift of the aggregate demand curve.

2. The central bank that uses a Taylor rule is likely to respond more directly to a financial crisis than one that uses inflation targeting because with a Taylor rule the central bank does not have to set policy to meet a pre-specified inflation target. Additionally, under the Taylor rule, central banks will respond directly to a change in the unemployment rate because in a financial crisis unemployment is more likely to increase than inflation is to decrease.

15-4 Check Your Understanding

1. **a.** Aggregate output rises in the short run, then falls back to equal potential output in the long run.

   b. The aggregate price level rises in the short run, but by less than 25%. It rises further in the long run, for a total increase of 25%.

   c. The interest rate falls in the short run, then rises back to its original level in the long run.

2. In the short run, a change in the interest rate alters the economy because it affects investment spending, which in turn affects aggregate demand and real GDP through the multiplier process. However, in the long run, changes in consumer spending and investment spending will eventually result in changes in nominal wages and the nominal prices of other factors of production. For example, an expansionary monetary policy will eventually cause a rise in factor prices; a contractionary policy will eventually cause a fall in factor prices. In response, the short-run aggregate supply curve will shift to move the economy back to long-run equilibrium. So in the long run, monetary policy has no effect on the economy.

‖ CHAPTER SIXTEEN

16-1 Check Your Understanding

1. The inflation rate is more likely to quickly reflect changes in the money supply when the economy has had an extended period of high inflation. That's because an extended period of high inflation sensitizes workers and firms to raise nominal wages and prices of intermediate goods when the aggregate price level rises. As a result, there will be little or no increase in real output in the short run after an increase in the money supply, and the increase in the money supply will simply be reflected in an equal-sized percent increase in prices. In an economy where people are not sensitized to high inflation because of low inflation in the past, an increase in the money supply will lead to an increase in real output in the short run. This illustrates the fact that the classical model of the price level best applies to economies with *persistently* high inflation, not those with little or no history of high inflation even though they may currently have high inflation.

2. Yes, there can still be an inflation tax because the tax is levied on people who hold money. As long as people hold money, regardless of whether prices are indexed or not, the government is able to use seigniorage to capture real resources from the public.

16-2 Check Your Understanding

1. When real GDP equals potential output, cyclical unemployment is zero and the unemployment rate is equal to the natural rate. This is given by point E_1 in Figure 16-7. Assuming a 0% expected inflation rate, this also corresponds to a 6% unemployment rate on curve $SRPC_0$ in Figure 16-9. Any unemployment in excess of this 6% rate, or less than the 6% rate, represents cyclical unemployment. An increase in aggregate demand leads to a fall in the unemployment rate below the natural rate (negative cyclical unemployment) and an increase in the inflation rate. This is given by the movement from E_1 to E_2 in Figure 16-7 and traces a movement upward along the short-run Phillips curve. A reduction in aggregate demand leads to a rise in the unemployment rate above the natural rate (positive cyclical unemployment) and a fall in the inflation rate. This would be represented by a movement down along the short-run Phillips curve from point E_1. So for a given expected inflation rate, the short-run Phillips curve illustrates the relationship between cyclical unemployment and the actual inflation rate.

2. A fall in commodities prices leads to a positive supply shock, which lowers the aggregate price level and reduces inflation. As a result, any given level of unemployment can be sustained with a lower inflation rate now—meaning that the short-run Phillips curve has shifted downward. In contrast, a surge in commodities prices leads to a negative supply shock, which raises the aggregate price level and increases inflation. Any given level of unemployment can be sustained only with a higher inflation rate—meaning that the short-run Phillips curve has shifted upward.

16-3 Check Your Understanding

1. There is no long-run trade-off between unemployment and inflation because once expectations of inflation adjust, wages will also adjust, returning employment and the unemployment rate to their equilibrium (natural) levels. This implies that once expectations of inflation fully adjust to any change in actual inflation, the unemployment rate will return to the natural rate of unemployment, or NAIRU. This also implies that the long-run Phillips curve is vertical.

2. There are two possible explanations for this. First, negative supply shocks (for example, increases in the price of oil) will cause an increase in unemployment and an increase in inflation. Second, it is possible that British policy makers attempted to lower the unemployment rate below the natural rate of unemployment. Any attempt to lower the unemployment rate below the natural rate will result in an increase in inflation.

3. Disinflation is costly because to reduce the inflation rate, aggregate output in the short run must typically fall below potential output. This, in turn, results in an increase in the unemployment rate above the natural rate. In general, we would observe a reduction in real GDP. The costs of any disinflation will be lower if the central bank is credible and it announces in advance its policy to reduce inflation. In this situation, the adjustment to the

disinflationary policy will be more rapid, resulting in a smaller loss of aggregate output.

16-4 Check Your Understanding

1. If the nominal interest rate is negative, an individual is better off simply holding cash, which has a 0% nominal rate of return. If the options facing an individual are to lend and receive a negative nominal interest rate or to hold cash and receive a 0% nominal interest rate, the individual will hold cash. Such a scenario creates the possibility of a liquidity trap, in which monetary policy is ineffective because the nominal interest rate cannot fall more than a small amount below zero. Once the nominal interest rate falls to zero, further increases in the money supply will lead firms and individuals to simply hold the additional cash.

CHAPTER SEVENTEEN

17-1 Check Your Understanding

1. A classical economist would have said that although expansionary monetary policy would probably have some effect in the short run, the short run was unimportant. Instead, a classical economist would have stressed the long run, claiming expansionary monetary policy would result only in an increase in the aggregate price level without affecting aggregate output.

2. The statement would seem very familiar to a Keynesian economist. According to Keynes, business confidence (which he called "animal spirits") is mainly responsible for recessions. If business confidence is low, a Keynesian economist would think of this as a case for macroeconomic policy activism: that the government should use expansionary monetary and fiscal policy to help the economy recover.

17-2 Check Your Understanding

1. Fiscal policy is limited by time lags in recognizing economic problems, forming a response, passing legislation, and implementing the policies. Monetary policy is also limited by time lags, but these lags are not as severe as those for fiscal policy because the Federal Reserve tends to act more quickly than Congress. Attempts to reduce unemployment below the natural rate via both fiscal and monetary policy are limited by predictions of the natural rate hypothesis: that these attempts will result in accelerating inflation. Also, both fiscal and monetary policy are limited by concerns about the political business cycle: that they will be used to satisfy political ends and will end up destabilizing the economy.

2. a. Velocity is the ratio of nominal GDP to money supply. A soaring unemployment rate means that GDP is falling. An acceleration of the growth of M1 means that the money supply is growing more quickly. Both of these events will reduce velocity. Hence you can see in Figure 17-4 that velocity fell substantially starting in 2008. It's likely that Milton Friedman would have agreed with the Fed policy of accelerating the growth of M1, because we know that Friedman believed that the Fed should have undertaken a more expansionary monetary policy in the wake of the Great Depression.

b. The monetarist objections to fiscal policy are based on the problems of time lags in its implementation and crowding out. Monetarists also believe time lags undermine the effectiveness of monetary policy, but to a lesser extent than with fiscal policy. However, none of these objections applied during the Great Recession. Because it lasted so long, both fiscal policy and monetary policy were effective despite time lags. And because interest rates and investment spending plunged, crowding out by fiscal policy was not a problem.

17-3 Check Your Understanding

1. a. Rational expectations theorists would argue that only unexpected changes in the money supply would have any short-run effect on economic activity. They would also argue that expected changes in the money supply would affect only the aggregate price level, with no short-run effect on aggregate output. So such theorists would give credit to the Fed for limiting the severity of the Great Recession only if the Fed's monetary policy had been more aggressive than individuals expected during this period.

b. Real business cycle theorists would argue that the Fed's policy had no effect on ending the Great Recession because they believe that fluctuations in aggregate output are caused largely by changes in total factor productivity.

17-4 Check Your Understanding

1. The liquidity trap brought on by the Great Recession greatly diminished the Great Moderation consensus, which considered monetary policy to be the main policy tool, and monetary policy was now largely ineffective. The continuing disagreements over fiscal policy were now brought to the forefront. The dismal experience of European countries that had adopted fiscal austerity, when compared to the faster recovery of the United States which adopted fiscal expansionary policies, has led most economists to more or less agree with the Keynesian view about the effects of fiscal policy.

2. The Fed was criticized by inflation bears who thought it was doing too much and by secular stagnationists who thought it was doing too little. Inflation bears believed that the huge increase in the monetary base and quantitative easing would lead to high inflation. Secular stagnationists believed the economy was in a liquidity trap and in a state of secular stagnation. Therefore, the stagnationists advocated for a higher inflation target that would allow the Fed to push the real interest rate down while the nominal rate was near zero.

CHAPTER EIGHTEEN

18-1 Check Your Understanding

1. a. The sale of the new airplane to China represents an export of a good to China and so enters the current account.

b. The sale of Boeing stock to Chinese investors is a sale of a U.S. asset and so enters the financial account.

c. Even though the plane already exists, when it is shipped to China it is an export of a good from the United States. So the sale of the plane enters the current account.

d. Because the plane stays in the United States, the Chinese investor is buying a U.S. asset. So this is identical to the answer to part b: the sale of the jet enters the financial account.

2. The collapse of the U.S. housing bubble and the ensuing recession led to a dramatic fall in interest rates in the United States because of the deeply depressed economy. Consequently, capital inflows into the United States dried up.

18-2 Check Your Understanding

1. a. The increased purchase of Mexican oil will cause U.S. individuals (and firms) to increase their demand for the peso. To purchase pesos, individuals will increase their supply of U.S. dollars to the foreign exchange market, causing a rightward shift in the supply curve of U.S. dollars. This will cause the peso price of the dollar to fall (the amount of pesos per dollar will fall). The peso has appreciated and the U.S. dollar has depreciated as a result.

   b. This appreciation of the peso means it will take more U.S. dollars to obtain the same quantity of Mexican pesos. If we assume that the price level (measured in Mexican pesos) of other Mexican goods and services does not change, other Mexican goods and services become more expensive to U.S. households and firms. The dollar cost of other Mexican goods and services will rise as the peso appreciates. So Mexican exports to the United States of goods and services other than oil will fall.

   c. Assuming that the U.S. price level (measured in U.S. dollars) does not change, the appreciation of the peso will make U.S. goods and services cheaper in terms of pesos. So Mexican imports from the United States of goods and services will rise.

2. a. The real exchange rate equals

   $$\text{Pesos per U.S. dollar} \times \frac{\text{Aggregate price level in the U.S.}}{\text{Aggregate price level in Mexico}}$$

   Today, the aggregate price levels in both countries are both equal to 100. The real exchange rate today is 10 × (100/100) = 10. The aggregate price level in five years in the U.S. will be 100 × (120/100) = 120, and in Mexico it will be 100 × (1,200/800) = 150. The real exchange rate in five years, assuming the nominal exchange rate does not change, will be 10 × (120/150) = 8.

   b. Today, a basket of goods and services that costs $100 costs 800 pesos, so the purchasing power parity is 8 pesos per U.S. dollar. In five years, a basket that costs $120 will cost 1,200 pesos, so the purchasing power parity will be 10 pesos per U.S. dollar.

18-3 Check Your Understanding

1. The accompanying diagram shows the supply of and demand for the yuan, with the U.S. dollar price of the yuan on the vertical axis. In 2005, prior to the revaluation, the exchange rate was pegged at 8.28 yuan per U.S. dollar or, equivalently, 0.121 U.S. dollars per yuan ($0.121). At the target exchange rate of $0.121, the quantity of yuan demanded exceeded the quantity of yuan supplied, creating the shortage depicted in the diagram. Without any intervention by the Chinese government, the U.S. dollar price of the yuan would have been bid up, causing an appreciation of the yuan. The Chinese government, however, intervened to prevent this appreciation.

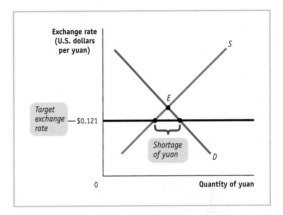

a. If the exchange rate is allowed to move freely, the U.S. dollar price of the exchange rate will move toward the equilibrium exchange rate (labeled XR^* in the accompanying diagram). This will occur as a result of the shortage, when buyers of the yuan will bid up its U.S. dollar price. As the exchange rate increases, the quantity of yuan demanded will fall and the quantity of yuan supplied will increase. If the exchange rate increases to XR^*, the disequilibrium will be entirely eliminated.

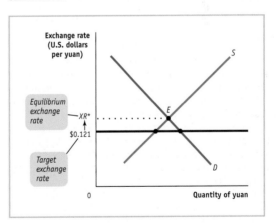

b. Placing restrictions on foreigners who want to invest in China will reduce the demand for the yuan, causing the demand curve to shift in the accompanying diagram from D_1 to a position like D_2. This will cause a reduction in the shortage of the yuan. If demand fell to D_3, the disequilibrium will be completely eliminated.

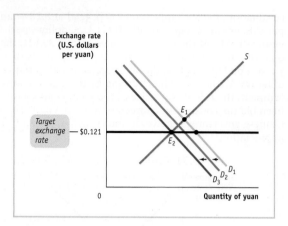

c. Removing restrictions on Chinese who wish to invest abroad will cause an increase in the supply of the yuan and a rightward shift in the supply curve. This increase in supply will also cause a reduction in the size of the shortage. If, for example, supply increased from S_1 to S_2, the disequilibrium will be eliminated completely in the accompanying diagram.

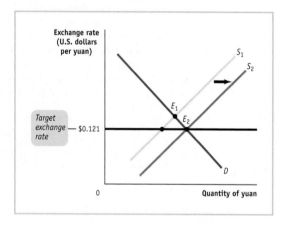

d. Imposing a tax on exports (Chinese goods sold to foreigners) will raise the price of these goods and decrease the amount of Chinese goods purchased. This will also decrease the demand for the yuan. The graphical analysis here is virtually identical to that found in the figure accompanying part b.

18-4 Check Your Understanding

1. The devaluations and revaluations most likely occurred in those periods when there was a sudden change in the franc–mark exchange rate: 1974, 1976, the early 1980s, 1986, and 1993–1994.

2. The high Canadian interest rates would likely have caused an increase in capital inflows to Canada. To obtain these assets (which yielded a relatively higher interest rate) in Canada, investors would first have had to obtain Canadian dollars. The increase in the demand for the Canadian dollar would have caused the Canadian dollar to appreciate. This appreciation of the Canadian currency would have raised the price of Canadian goods to foreigners (measured in terms of the foreign currency). This would have made it more difficult for Canadian firms to compete in other markets.

Glossary

A

absolute advantage the advantage conferred on an individual or country in an activity if the individual or country can do it better than others. A country with an absolute advantage can produce more output per worker than other countries.

absolute value the value of a number without regard to a plus or minus sign.

accelerator principle the proposition that a higher rate of growth in real GDP results in a higher level of planned investment spending, and a lower growth rate in real GDP leads to lower planned investment spending.

actual investment spending the sum of planned investment spending and unplanned inventory investment.

AD–AS model the basic model used to understand fluctuations in aggregate output and the aggregate price level. It uses the aggregate supply curve and the aggregate demand curve together to analyze the behavior of the economy in response to shocks or government policy.

aggregate consumption function the relationship for the economy as a whole between aggregate current disposable income and aggregate consumer spending.

aggregate demand curve a graphical representation that shows the relationship between the aggregate price level and the quantity of aggregate output demanded by households, firms, the government, and the rest of the world. The aggregate demand curve has a negative slope due to the wealth effect of a change in the aggregate price level and the interest rate effect of a change in the aggregate price level.

aggregate output the total quantity of final goods and services the economy produces for a given time period, usually a year. Real GDP is the numerical measure of aggregate output typically used by economists.

aggregate price level a single number that represents the overall price level for final goods and services in the economy.

aggregate production function a hypothetical function that shows how productivity (real GDP per worker) depends on the quantities of physical capital per worker and human capital per worker as well as the state of technology.

aggregate spending the total flow of funds into markets for domestically produced final goods and services; the sum of consumer spending, investment spending, government purchases of goods and services, and exports minus imports.

aggregate supply curve a graphical representation that shows the relationship between the aggregate price level and the total quantity of aggregate output supplied.

appreciation a rise in the value of one currency in terms of other currencies.

autarky a situation in which a country does not trade with other countries.

automatic stabilizers government spending and taxation rules that cause fiscal policy to be automatically expansionary when the economy contracts and automatically contractionary when the economy expands without requiring any deliberate actions by policy makers. Taxes that depend on disposable income are the most important example of automatic stabilizers.

autonomous change in aggregate spending an initial rise or fall in aggregate spending at a given level of real GDP.

B

balance of payments accounts a summary of a country's transactions with other countries for a given year, including two main elements: the balance of payments on current account and the balance of payments on financial account.

balance of payments on current account (current account) transactions that don't create liabilities; a country's balance of payments on goods and services plus net international transfer payments and factor income.

balance of payments on financial account (financial account) international transactions that involve the sale or purchase of assets, and therefore create future liabilities.

balance of payments on goods and services the difference between the value of exports and the value of imports during a given period.

bank a financial intermediary that provides liquid assets in the form of bank deposits to lenders and uses those funds to finance the illiquid investments or investment spending needs of borrowers.

bank deposit a claim on a bank that obliges the bank to give the depositor his or her cash when demanded.

bank reserves currency held by banks in their vaults plus their deposits at the Federal Reserve.

bank run a phenomenon in which many of a bank's depositors try to withdraw their funds because of fears of a bank failure.

bar graph a graph that uses bars of varying heights or lengths to show the comparative sizes of different observations of a variable.

barter the direct exchange of goods or services for other goods or services without the use of money.

black market a market in which goods or services are bought and sold illegally, either because it is illegal to sell them at all or because the prices charged are legally prohibited by a price ceiling.

bond a legal document based on borrowing in the form of an IOU that pays interest.

budget balance the difference between tax revenue and government spending. A positive budget balance is referred to as a budget surplus; a negative budget balance is referred to as a budget deficit.

budget deficit the difference between tax revenue and government spending when government spending exceeds tax revenue; dissaving by the government in the form of a budget deficit is a negative contribution to national savings.

budget surplus the difference between tax revenue and government spending when tax revenue exceeds government spending; saving by the government in the form of a budget surplus is a positive contribution to national savings.

business cycle the short-run alternation between economic downturns, known as recessions, and economic upturns, known as expansions.

business-cycle peak the point in time at which the economy shifts from expansion to recession.

business-cycle trough the point in time at which the economy shifts from recession to expansion.

C

causal relationship the relationship between two variables in which the value taken by one variable directly influences or determines the value taken by the other variable.

central bank an institution that oversees and regulates the banking system and controls the monetary base.

certificate of deposit (CD) a bank-issued asset in which customers deposit funds for a specified amount of time and earn a specified interest rate.

chained dollars method of calculating real GDP that splits the difference between growth rates calculated using early base years and the growth rate calculated using a late base year.

checkable bank deposits bank accounts that can be accessed by using checks, debit cards, and digital payments.

circular-flow diagram a diagram that represents the transactions in an economy by two kinds of flows around a circle: flows of physical things such as goods or labor in one direction and flows of money to pay for these physical things in the opposite direction.

classical model of the price level a simplified financial model of the price level in which the real quantity of money, M/P, is always at its long-run equilibrium level. This model ignores the distinction between the short run and the long run but is useful for analyzing the case of high inflation.

commercial bank a bank that accepts deposits and is covered by deposit insurance.

commodity money a medium of exchange that is a good, normally gold or silver, that has intrinsic value in other uses.

commodity-backed money a medium of exchange that has no intrinsic value whose ultimate value is guaranteed by a promise that it can be converted into valuable goods on demand.

comparative advantage the advantage conferred on an individual or country in producing a good or service if the opportunity cost of producing the good or service is lower for that individual or country than for other producers.

competitive market a market in which there are many buyers and sellers of the same good or service, none of whom can influence the price at which the good or service is sold.

complements pairs of goods for which a rise in the price of one good leads to a decrease in the demand for the other good.

consumer price index (CPI) a measure of prices; calculated by surveying market prices for a market basket intended to represent the consumption of a typical urban American family of four. The CPI is the most commonly used measure of prices in the United States.

consumer spending household spending on goods and services from domestic and foreign firms.

consumer surplus a term often used to refer both to individual consumer surplus and to total consumer surplus.

consumption function an equation showing how an individual household's consumer spending varies with the household's current disposable income.

contractionary fiscal policy fiscal policy that reduces aggregate demand by decreasing government purchases, increasing taxes, or decreasing transfers.

contractionary monetary policy monetary policy that, through the raising of the interest rate, reduces aggregate demand and therefore output.

convergence hypothesis a principle of economic growth that holds that international differences in real GDP per capita tend to narrow over time because countries that start with lower real GDP per capita tend to have higher growth rates.

cost (of seller) the lowest price at which a seller is willing to sell a good.

crowding out the negative effect of budget deficits on private investment, which occurs because government borrowing drives up interest rates.

currency in circulation actual cash held by the public.

current account (balance of payments on current account) transactions that don't create liabilities; a country's balance of payments on goods and services plus net international transfer payments and factor income.

curve a line on a graph, which may be curved or straight, that depicts a relationship between two variables.

cyclical unemployment the difference between the actual rate of unemployment and the natural rate of unemployment due to downturns in the business cycle.

cyclically adjusted budget balance an estimate of what the budget balance would be if real GDP were exactly equal to potential output.

D

debt deflation the reduction in aggregate demand arising from the increase in the real burden of outstanding debt caused by deflation; occurs because borrowers, whose real debt rises as a result of deflation, are likely to cut spending sharply, and lenders, whose real assets are now more valuable, are less likely to increase spending.

debt–GDP ratio government debt as a percentage of GDP, frequently used as a measure of a government's ability to pay its debts.

default the failure of a bond issuer to make payments as specified by the bond contract.

deflation a fall in the overall level of prices.

demand curve a graphical representation of the demand schedule, showing the relationship between quantity demanded and price.

demand price the price of a given quantity at which consumers will demand that quantity.

demand schedule a list or table showing how much of a good or service consumers will want to buy at different prices.

demand shock an event that shifts the aggregate demand curve. A positive demand shock is associated with higher demand for aggregate output at any price level and shifts the curve to the right. A negative demand shock is associated with lower demand for aggregate output at any price level and shifts the curve to the left.

dependent variable the determined variable in a causal relationship.

deposit insurance a guarantee that a bank's depositors will be paid even if the bank can't come up with the funds, up to a maximum amount per account.

depreciation a fall in the value of one currency in terms of other currencies.

devaluation a reduction in the value of a currency that is set under a fixed exchange rate regime.

diminishing returns to physical capital in an aggregate production function when the amount of human capital per worker and the state of technology are held fixed, each successive increase in the amount of physical capital per worker leads to a smaller increase in productivity.

discount rate the rate of interest the Federal Reserve charges on loans to banks that fall short of reserve requirements.

discount window a protection against bank runs in which the Federal Reserve stands ready to lend money to banks in trouble.

discouraged workers individuals who want to work but who have stated to government researchers that they aren't currently searching for a job because they see little prospect of finding one given the state of the job market.

discretionary fiscal policy fiscal policy that is the direct result of deliberate actions by policy makers rather than automatic adjustments or rules.

discretionary monetary policy policy actions, either changes in interest rates or changes in the money supply, undertaken by the central bank based on its assessment of the state of the economy.

disinflation the process of bringing down inflation that has become embedded in expectations.

diversification investment in several different assets with unrelated, or independent, risks, so that the possible losses are independent events.

domestic demand curve a demand curve that shows how the quantity of a good demanded by domestic consumers depends on the price of that good.

domestic supply curve a supply curve that shows how the quantity of a good supplied by domestic producers depends on the price of that good.

E

economic growth the growing ability of the economy to produce goods and services.

economics the social science that studies the production, distribution, and consumption of goods and services.

economy a system for coordinating society's productive activities.

efficiency wages wages that employers set above the equilibrium wage rate as an incentive for workers to deliver better performance.

efficient description of a market or economy that takes all opportunities to make some people better off without making other people worse off.

efficient markets hypothesis a principle of asset price determination that holds that asset prices embody all publicly available information. The hypothesis implies that stock prices should be unpredictable, or follow a random walk, since changes should occur only in response to new information about fundamentals.

employment the total number of people currently employed for pay in the economy, either full time or part time.

equilibrium an economic situation in which no individual would be better off doing something different.

equilibrium exchange rate the exchange rate at which the quantity of a currency demanded in the foreign exchange market is equal to the quantity supplied.

equilibrium interest rate a situation where the interest rate at which the quantity of loanable funds supplied equals the quantity of loanable funds demanded.

equilibrium price the price at which the market is in equilibrium, that is, the quantity of a good or service demanded equals the quantity of that good or service supplied; also referred to as the market-clearing price.

equilibrium quantity the quantity of a good or service bought and sold at the equilibrium (or market-clearing) price.

equity fairness; everyone gets his or her fair share. Since people can disagree about what's "fair," equity isn't as well defined a concept as efficiency.

European Union (EU) a customs union among 28 European nations.

excess reserves a bank's reserves over and above the reserves required by law or regulation.

exchange market intervention government purchases or sales of currency in the foreign exchange market.

exchange rate the price at which currencies trade, determined by the foreign exchange market.

exchange rate regime a rule governing policy toward the exchange rate.

expansion a period of economic upturn in which output and employment are rising; most economic numbers are following their normal upward trend; also referred to as a recovery.

expansionary fiscal policy fiscal policy that increases aggregate demand by increasing government purchases, decreasing taxes, or increasing transfers.

expansionary monetary policy monetary policy that, through the lowering of the interest rate, increases aggregate demand and therefore output.

expected rate of inflation the inflation rate that businesses and workers are expecting in the near future.

exporting industries industries that produce goods or services that are sold abroad.

exports goods and services sold to other countries.

F

factor intensity the difference in the ratio of factors used to produce a good in various industries. For example, oil refining is capital-intensive compared to auto seat production because oil refiners use a higher ratio of capital to labor than do producers of auto seats.

factor markets markets in which firms buy the resources they need to produce goods and services.

factors of production the resources used to produce goods and services. Labor and capital are examples of factors.

federal funds market a financial market that allows banks that fall short of reserve requirements to borrow funds from banks with excess reserves.

federal funds rate the interest rate at which funds are borrowed and lent in the federal funds market.

fiat money a medium of exchange whose value derives entirely from its official status as a means of payment.

final goods and services goods and services sold to the final, or end, user.

financial account (balance of payments on financial account) international transactions that involve the sale of purchase of assets, and therefore create future liabilities.

financial asset a paper claim that entitles the buyer to future income from the seller. Loans, stocks, bonds, and bank deposits are types of financial assets.

financial intermediary an institution, such as a mutual fund, pension fund, life insurance company, or bank, that transforms the funds it gathers from many individuals into financial assets.

financial markets the banking, stock, and bond markets, which channel private savings and foreign lending into investment spending, government borrowing, and foreign borrowing.

financial risk uncertainty about future outcomes that involve financial losses or gains.

financial system the collection of markets and institutions that facilitate the flow of funds from lenders to borrowers.

firm an organization that produces goods and services for sale.

fiscal policy changes in government spending and taxes designed to affect overall spending.

fiscal stimulus expansionary fiscal policy that takes the form of temporary spending measures and temporary tax cuts.

fiscal year the time period used for much of government accounting, running from October 1 to September 30 in the United States. Fiscal years are labeled by the calendar year in which they end.

Fisher effect the principle by which an increase in expected future inflation drives up the nominal interest rate, leaving the expected real interest rate unchanged.

fixed exchange rate an exchange rate regime in which the government keeps the exchange rate against some other currency at or near a particular target.

floating exchange rate an exchange rate regime in which the government lets market forces determine the exchange rate.

forecast a simple prediction of the future.

foreign exchange controls licensing systems that limit the right of individuals to buy foreign currency.

foreign exchange market the market in which currencies can be exchanged for each other.

foreign exchange reserves stocks of foreign currency that governments can use to buy their own currency on the foreign exchange market.

free trade trade that is unregulated by government tariffs or other artificial barriers; the levels of exports and imports occur naturally, as a result of supply and demand.

frictional unemployment unemployment due to time workers spend in job search.

G

gains from trade gains achieved by dividing tasks and trading; in this way people can get more of what they want through trade than they could if they tried to be self-sufficient.

GDP deflator a price measure for a given year that is equal to 100 times the ratio of nominal GDP to real GDP in that year.

GDP per capita GDP divided by the size of the population; equivalent to the average GDP per person.

globalization the phenomenon of growing economic linkages among countries.

global loanable funds market a situation in which international capital flows are so large that they equalize interest rates across countries.

government borrowing the total amount of funds borrowed by federal, state, and local governments in the financial markets.

government purchases of goods and services total purchases by federal, state, and local governments on goods and services.

Great Moderation the period from 1985 to 2007 when the U.S. economy experienced small fluctuations and low inflation.

Great Moderation consensus a belief in monetary policy as the main tool of stabilization combined with an independent central bank to avoid the political business cycle; fiscal policy reserved for exceptional circumstances such as a liquidity trap; and limitations on policy activism imposed by the natural rate of unemployment.

gross domestic product (GDP) the total value of all final goods and services produced in the economy during a given period, usually a year.

growth accounting accounting that estimates the contribution of each of the major factors (physical and human capital, labor, and technology) in the aggregate production function.

H

Heckscher–Ohlin model a model of international trade in which a country has a comparative advantage in a good whose production is intensive in the factors that are abundantly available in that country.

horizontal axis the horizontal number line of a graph along which values of the *x*-variable are measured; also referred to as the *x*-axis.

horizontal intercept the point at which a curve hits the horizontal axis; it indicates the value of the *x*-variable when the value of the *y*-variable is zero.

household a person or a group of people who share their income.

human capital the improvement in labor created by the education and knowledge embodied in the workforce.

hyperglobalization the phenomenon of extremely high levels of international trade.

I

illiquid describes an asset that cannot be quickly converted into cash with relatively little loss of value.

implicit liabilities spending promises made by governments that are effectively a debt despite the fact that they are not included in the usual debt statistics. In the United States, the largest implicit liabilities arise from Social Security and Medicare, which promise transfer payments to current and future retirees (Social Security) and to the elderly (Medicare).

import quota a legal limit on the quantity of a good that can be imported.

import-competing industries industries that produce goods or services that are also imported.

imports goods and services purchased from other countries.

incentive anything that offers rewards to people to change their behavior.

income distribution the way in which total income is divided among the owners of the various factors of production.

income–expenditure equilibrium a situation in which aggregate output, measured by real GDP, is equal to planned aggregate spending and firms have no incentive to change output.

income–expenditure equilibrium GDP the level of real GDP at which real GDP equals planned aggregate spending.

independent variable the determining variable in a causal relationship.

individual choice the decision by an individual of what to do, which necessarily involves a decision of what not to do.

individual consumer surplus the net gain to an individual buyer from the purchase of a good; equal to the difference between the buyer's willingness to pay and the price paid.

individual demand curve a graphical representation of the relationship between quantity demanded and price for an individual consumer.

individual producer surplus the net gain to an individual seller from selling a good; equal to the difference between the price received and the seller's cost.

individual supply curve a graphical representation of the relationship between quantity supplied and price for an individual producer.

inefficient allocation of sales among sellers a form of inefficiency in which sellers who would be willing to sell a good at the lowest price are not always those who actually manage to sell it; often the result of a price floor.

inefficient allocation to consumers a form of inefficiency in which people who want a good badly and are willing to pay a high price don't get it, and those who care relatively little about the good and are only willing to pay a low price do get it; often a result of a price ceiling.

inefficiently high quality a form of inefficiency in which sellers offer high-quality goods at a high price even though buyers would prefer a lower quality at a lower price; often the result of a price floor.

inefficiently low quality a form of inefficiency in which sellers offer low-quality goods at a low price even though buyers would prefer a higher quality at a higher price; often a result of a price ceiling.

inferior good a good for which a rise in income decreases the demand for the good.

inflation a rise in the overall level of prices.

inflation bear viewpoint a theory that expansionary monetary policy will cause inflation without raising output, even in a depressed economy.

inflation rate the annual percent change in a price index—typically the consumer price index. The inflation rate is positive when the aggregate price level is rising (inflation) and negative when the aggregate price level is falling (deflation).

inflation targeting an approach to monetary policy that requires that the central bank try to keep the inflation rate near a predetermined target rate.

inflation tax the reduction in the value of money held by the public as a result of inflation.

inflationary gap the gap that exists when aggregate output is above potential output.

infrastructure physical capital, such as roads, power lines, ports, information networks, and other parts of an economy, that provides the underpinnings, or foundation, for economic activity.

input a good or service used to produce another good or service.

interaction (of choices) my choices affect your choices, and vice versa; a feature of most economic situations. The results of this interaction are often quite different from what the individuals intend.

interest rate the price, calculated as a percentage of the amount borrowed, that a lender charges a borrower for the use of their savings for one year.

interest rate effect of a change in the aggregate price level the effect on consumer spending and investment spending caused by a change in the purchasing power of consumers' money holdings when the aggregate price level changes. A rise (fall) in the aggregate price level decreases (increases) the purchasing power of consumers' money holdings. In response, consumers try to increase (decrease) their money holdings, which drives up (down) interest rates, thereby decreasing (increasing) consumption and investment.

intermediate goods and services goods and services—bought from one firm by another firm—that are inputs for production of final goods and services.

international trade agreements treaties by which countries agree to lower trade protections against one another.

inventories stocks of goods and raw materials held to facilitate business operations.

inventory investment the value of the change in total inventories held in the economy during a given period. Unlike other types of investment spending, inventory investment can be negative, if inventories fall.

investment bank a bank that trades in financial assets and does not accept deposits, so it is not covered by deposit insurance.

investment spending spending on productive physical capital—such as machinery and construction of buildings—and on changes to inventories.

invisible hand a phrase used by Adam Smith to refer to the way in which an individual's pursuit of self-interest can lead, without the individual's intending it, to good results for society as a whole.

J

job search the time spent by workers in looking for employment.

jobless recovery a period in which real GDP growth rate is positive but the unemployment rate is still rising.

K

Keynesian cross a diagram that identifies income–expenditure equilibrium as the point where the planned aggregate spending line crosses the 45-degree line.

Keynesian economics a school of thought emerging out of the works of John Maynard Keynes; according to Keynesian economics, a depressed economy is the result of inadequate spending and government intervention can help a depressed economy through monetary policy and fiscal policy.

L

labor force the sum of employment and unemployment; that is, the number of people who are currently working plus the number of people who are currently looking for work.

labor force participation rate the percentage of the population age 16 or older that is in the labor force.

labor productivity output per worker; also referred to as simply productivity. Increases in labor productivity are the only source of long-run economic growth.

law of demand the principle that a higher price for a good or service, other things equal, leads people to demand a smaller quantity of that good or service.

liability a requirement to pay income in the future.

license the right, conferred by the government or an owner, to supply a good.

life insurance company a financial intermediary that sells policies guaranteeing a payment to a policyholder's beneficiaries when the policyholder dies.

linear relationship the relationship between two variables in which the slope is constant and therefore is depicted on a graph by a curve that is a straight line.

liquid describes an asset that can be quickly converted into cash with relatively little loss of value.

liquidity preference model of the interest rate a model of the market for money in which the interest rate is determined by the supply and demand for money.

liquidity trap the economy is in a liquidity trap when monetary policy is ineffective because nominal interest rates are up against the zero bound.

loan a lending agreement between an individual lender and an individual borrower. Loans are usually tailored to the individual borrower's needs and ability to pay but carry relatively high transaction costs.

loanable funds market a hypothetical market that brings together those who want to lend money (savers) and those who want to borrow (firms with investment spending projects).

loan-backed securities assets created by pooling individual loans and selling shares in that pool.

long-run aggregate supply curve a graphical representation that shows the relationship between the aggregate price level and the quantity of aggregate output supplied that would exist if all prices, including nominal wages, were fully flexible. The long-run aggregate supply curve is vertical because the aggregate price level has no effect on aggregate output in the long run; in the long run, aggregate output is determined by the economy's potential output.

long-run economic growth the sustained rise in the quantity of goods and services the economy produces.

long-run macroeconomic equilibrium the point at which the short-run macroeconomic equilibrium is on the long-run aggregate supply curve; so short-run equilibrium aggregate output is equal to potential output.

long-run Phillips curve a graphical representation of the relationship between unemployment and inflation in the long run after expectations of inflation have had time to adjust to experience.

long-term interest rate the interest rate on financial assets that mature a number of years into the future.

lump-sum tax a tax that is the same for everyone, regardless of any actions people take.

M

macroeconomic policy activism the use of monetary policy and fiscal policy to smooth out the business cycle.

macroeconomics the branch of economics that is concerned with the overall ups and downs in the economy.

marginal analysis the study of marginal decisions.

marginal decision a decision made at the "margin" of an activity to do a bit more or a bit less of that activity.

marginal propensity to consume (MPC) the increase in consumer spending when disposable income rises by $1. Because consumers normally spend part but not all of an additional dollar of disposable income, *MPC* is between 0 and 1.

marginal propensity to save (MPS) the fraction of an additional dollar of disposable income that is saved; *MPS* is equal to 1 − *MPC*.

marginally attached workers nonworking individuals who say they would like a job and have looked for work in the recent past but are not currently looking for work.

market basket a hypothetical consumption bundle of consumer purchases of goods and services, used to measure changes in overall price level.

market economy an economy in which decisions about production and consumption are made by individual producers and consumers.

market failure the point at which the individual pursuit of self-interest found in markets makes society worse off—that is, the market outcome is inefficient.

market-clearing price the price at which the market is in equilibrium, that is, the quantity of a good or service demanded equals the quantity of that good or service supplied; also referred to as the equilibrium price.

markets for goods and services markets in which firms sell goods and services that they produce to households.

maximum the highest point on a nonlinear curve, where the slope changes from positive to negative.

medium of exchange an asset that individuals acquire for the purpose of trading for goods and services rather than for their own consumption.

menu cost the real cost of changing a listed price.

merchandise trade balance (trade balance) the difference between a country's exports and imports of goods alone—not including services.

microeconomics the branch of economics that studies how people make decisions and how those decisions interact.

minimum the lowest point on a nonlinear curve, where the slope changes from negative to positive.

minimum wage a legal floor on the wage rate. The wage rate is the market price of labor.

model a simplified representation of a real situation that is used to better understand real-life situations.

monetarism a theory of business cycles, associated primarily with Milton Friedman, that asserts that GDP will grow steadily if the money supply grows steadily.

monetary aggregate an overall measure of the money supply. The most common monetary aggregates in the United States are M1, which includes currency in circulation, traveler's checks, and checkable bank deposits, and M2, which includes M1 as well as near-moneys.

monetary base the sum of currency in circulation and bank reserves.

monetary neutrality the concept that changes in the money supply have no real effects on the economy in the long run and only result in a proportional change in the price level.

monetary policy changes in the quantity of money in circulation designed to alter interest rates and affect the level of overall spending.

monetary policy rule a formula that determines the central bank's actions.

money any asset that can easily be used to purchase goods and services.

money demand curve a graphical representation of the relationship between the interest rate and the quantity of money demanded. The money demand curve slopes downward because, other things equal, a higher interest rate increases the opportunity cost of holding money.

money multiplier the ratio of the money supply to the monetary base.

money supply the total value of financial assets in the economy that are considered money.

money supply curve a graphical representation of the relationship between the quantity of money supplied by the Federal Reserve and the interest rate.

movement along the demand curve a change in the quantity demanded of a good that results from a change in the price of that good.

movement along the supply curve a change in the quantity supplied of a good that results from a change in the price of that good.

multiplier the ratio of total change in real GDP caused by an autonomous change in aggregate spending to the size of that autonomous change.

mutual fund a financial intermediary that creates a stock portfolio by buying and holding shares in companies and then selling shares of this portfolio to individual investors.

N

national income and product accounts (national accounts) method of calculating and keeping track of consumer spending, sales of producers, business investment spending, government purchases, and a variety of other flows of money between different sectors of the economy.

national savings the sum of private savings and the government's budget balance; the total amount of savings generated within the economy.

natural rate hypothesis the hypothesis that because inflation is eventually embedded into expectations, to avoid accelerating inflation over time the unemployment rate should be kept stable around the natural rate.

natural rate of unemployment the normal unemployment rate around which the actual unemployment rate fluctuates; the unemployment rate that arises from the effects of frictional and structural unemployment.

near-moneys financial assets that can't be directly used as a medium of exchange but can be readily converted into cash or checkable bank deposits.

negative relationship a relationship between two variables in which an increase in the value of one variable is associated with a decrease in the value of the other variable. It is illustrated by a curve that slopes downward from left to right.

net capital inflow the total inflow of funds into a country minus the total outflow of funds out of a country.

net exports the difference between the value of exports and the value of imports. A positive value for net exports indicates that a country is a net exporter of goods and services; a negative value indicates that a country is a net importer of goods and services.

new classical macroeconomics an approach to the business cycle that returns to the classical view that shifts in the aggregate demand curve affect only the aggregate price level, not aggregate output.

new Keynesian economics a theory that argues that market imperfections can lead to price stickiness for the economy as a whole.

nominal GDP the value of all final goods and services produced in the economy during a given year, calculated using the prices current in the year in which the output is produced.

nominal interest rate the interest rate in dollar terms.

nominal wage the dollar amount of any given wage paid.

nonaccelerating inflation rate of unemployment (NAIRU) the unemployment rate at which, other things equal, inflation does not change over time.

nonlinear curve a curve in which the slope is not the same between every pair of points.

nonlinear relationship the relationship between two variables in which the slope is not constant and therefore is depicted on a graph by a curve that is not a straight line.

normal good a good for which a rise in income increases the demand for that good—the "normal" case.

normative economics the branch of economic analysis that makes prescriptions about the way the economy should work.

North American Free Trade Agreement (NAFTA) a trade agreement among the United States, Canada, and Mexico.

o

offshore outsourcing the practice of businesses hiring people in another country to perform various tasks.

Okun's law the negative relationship between the output gap and the unemployment rate, whereby each additional percentage point of output gap reduces the unemployment rate by about ½ of a percentage point.

omitted variable an unobserved variable that, through its influence on other variables, creates the erroneous appearance of a direct causal relationship among those variables.

open economy an economy that trades goods and services with other countries.

open-market operation a purchase or sale of U.S. Treasury bills by the Federal Reserve, normally through a transaction with a commercial bank.

opportunity cost the real cost of an item: what you must give up in order to get it.

origin the point where the axes of a two-variable graph meet.

other things equal assumption in the development of a model, the assumption that all relevant factors except the one under study remain unchanged.

output gap the percentage difference between actual aggregate output and potential output.

P

Paris Agreement a commitment by 196 countries, signed in 2015, to reduce their greenhouse gas emissions in an effort to limit the rise in the earth's temperature to no more than 2 degrees centigrade.

pension fund a type of mutual fund that holds assets in order to provide retirement income to its members.

physical asset a claim on a tangible object that can be used to generate future income.

physical capital human-made resources such as buildings and machines.

pie chart a circular graph that shows how some total is divided among its components, usually expressed in percentages.

planned aggregate spending the total amount of planned spending in the economy; includes consumer spending and planned investment spending.

planned investment spending the investment spending that firms intend to undertake during a given period. Planned investment spending may differ from actual investment spending due to unplanned inventory investment.

political business cycle a business cycle that results from the use of macroeconomic policy to serve political ends.

positive economics the branch of economic analysis that describes the way the economy actually works.

positive relationship a relationship between two variables in which an increase in the value of one variable is associated with an increase in the value of the other variable. It is illustrated by a curve that slopes upward from left to right.

potential output the level of real GDP the economy would produce if all prices, including nominal wages, were fully flexible.

present value (of X) the amount of money needed today in order to receive X at a future date given the interest rate.

price ceiling the maximum price sellers are allowed to charge for a good or service; a form of price control.

price controls legal restrictions on how high or low a market price may go.

price floor the minimum price buyers are required to pay for a good or service; a form of price control.

price index a measure of the cost of purchasing a given market basket in a given year, where that cost is normalized so that it is equal to 100 in the selected base year; a measure of overall price level.

price stability a situation in which the overall cost of living is changing slowly or not at all.

producer price index (PPI) a measure of the cost of a typical basket of goods and services purchased by producers. Because these commodity prices respond quickly to changes in demand, the PPI is often regarded as a leading indicator of changes in the inflation rate.

producer surplus a term often used to refer to either individual producer surplus or total producer surplus.

production possibility frontier a model that illustrates the trade-offs facing an economy that produces only two goods. It shows the maximum quantity of one good that can be produced for any given quantity produced of the other.

productivity output per worker; a shortened form of the term *labor productivity*.

protection policies that limit imports; an alternative term for *trade protection*.

public debt government debt held by individuals and institutions outside the government.

purchasing power parity (between two countries' currencies) the nominal exchange rate at which a given basket of goods and services would cost the same amount in each country.

Q

quantity control an upper limit, set by the government, on the quantity of some good that can be bought or sold; also referred to as a quota.

quantity demanded the actual amount of a good or service consumers are willing to buy at some specific price.

quantity supplied the actual amount of a good or service producers are willing to sell at some specific price.

quota an upper limit, set by the government, on the quantity of some good that can be bought or sold; also referred to as a quantity control.

quota rent the difference between the demand price and the supply price at the quota limit; this difference, the earnings that accrue to the license holder, is equal to the market price of the license when the license is traded.

R

random walk the movement over time of an unpredictable variable.

rational expectations a theory of expectation formation that holds that individuals and firms make decisions optimally, using all available information.

rational expectations model a model of the economy in which expected changes in monetary policy have no effect on unemployment and output and only affect the price level.

real business cycle theory a theory of business cycles that asserts that fluctuations in the growth rate of total factor productivity cause the business cycle.

real exchange rate the exchange rate adjusted for international differences in aggregate price levels.

real GDP the total value of all final goods and services produced in the economy during a given year, calculated using the prices of a selected base year.

real income income divided by the price level.

real interest rate the nominal interest rate minus the inflation rate.

real wage the wage rate divided by the price level.

recession a downturn in the economy when output and employment are falling; also referred to as a contraction.

recessionary gap the gap that exists when aggregate output is below potential output.

research and development (R&D) spending to create new technologies and prepare them for practical use.

reserve ratio the fraction of bank deposits that a bank holds as reserves. In the United States, the minimum required reserve ratio is set by the Federal Reserve.

reserve requirements rules set by the Federal Reserve that set the minimum reserve ratio for banks. For checkable bank deposits in the United States, the minimum reserve ratio is set at 10%.

resource anything, such as land, labor, and capital, that can be used to produce something else; includes natural resources (from the physical environment) and human resources (labor, skill, intelligence).

revaluation an increase in the value of a currency that is set under a fixed exchange rate regime.

reverse causality the error committed when the true direction of causality between two variables is reversed, and the independent variable and the dependent variable are incorrectly identified.

Ricardian model of international trade a model that analyzes international trade under the assumption that opportunity costs are constant.

Rule of 70 a mathematical formula that states that the time it takes real GDP per capita, or any other variable that grows gradually over time, to double is approximately 70 divided by that variable's annual growth rate.

S

savings and loans (thrifts) deposit-taking banks, usually specialized in issuing home loans.

savings–investment spending identity an accounting fact that states that savings and investment spending are always equal for the economy as a whole.

scarce in short supply; a resource is scarce when there is not enough of the resource available to satisfy all the various ways a society wants to use it.

scatter diagram a graph that shows points that correspond to actual observations of the x- and y-variables; a curve is usually fitted to the scatter of points to indicate the trend in the data.

secular stagnation a state in which the interest rate that would be needed to achieve full employment is consistently below zero. Proponents of this view, known as *secular stagnationists*, advocate an active fiscal policy and unconventional monetary policy.

securitization the pooling of loans and mortgages made by a financial institution and the sale of shares in such a pool to other investors.

self-correcting describes an economy in which shocks to aggregate demand affect aggregate output in the short run but not in the long run.

self-regulating describes an economy in which problems such as unemployment are resolved without government intervention, through the working of the invisible hand, and in which government attempts to improve the economy's performance would be ineffective at best, and would probably make things worse.

shadow banking bank-like activities undertaken by nondepository financial firms such as investment banks and hedge funds, but without regulatory oversight and protection.

shift of the demand curve a change in the quantity demanded at any given price, represented graphically by the change of the original demand curve to a new position, denoted by a new demand curve.

shift of the supply curve a change in the quantity supplied of a good or service at any given price, represented graphically by the change of the original supply curve to a new position, denoted by a new supply curve.

shoe-leather costs (of inflation) the increased costs of transactions caused by inflation.

shortage the insufficiency of a good or service that occurs when the quantity demanded exceeds the quantity supplied; shortages occur when the price is below the equilibrium price.

short-run aggregate supply curve a graphical representation that shows the positive relationship between the aggregate price level and the quantity of aggregate output supplied that exists in the short run, the time period when many production costs, particularly nominal wages, can be taken as fixed. The short-run aggregate supply curve has a positive slope because a rise in the aggregate price level leads to a rise in profits, and therefore output, when production costs are fixed.

short-run equilibrium aggregate output the quantity of aggregate output produced in short-run macroeconomic equilibrium.

short-run equilibrium aggregate price level the aggregate price level in short-run macroeconomic equilibrium.

short-run macroeconomic equilibrium the point at which the quantity of aggregate output supplied is equal to the quantity demanded.

short-run Phillips curve a graphical representation of the negative short-run relationship between the unemployment rate and the inflation rate.

short-term interest rate the interest rate on financial assets that mature within less than a year.

slope a measure of how steep a line or curve is. The slope of a line is measured by "rise over run"—the change in the *y*-variable between two points on the line divided by the change in the *x*-variable between those same points.

social insurance government programs—like Social Security, Medicare, unemployment insurance, and food stamps—intended to protect families against economic hardship.

specialization the situation in which each person specializes in the task that he or she is good at performing.

stabilization policy the use of government policy to reduce the severity of recessions and to rein in excessively strong expansions. There are two main tools of stabilization policy: monetary policy and fiscal policy.

stagflation the combination of inflation and falling aggregate output.

sticky wages nominal wages that are slow to fall even in the face of high unemployment and slow to rise even in the face of labor shortages.

stock a share in the ownership of a company held by a shareholder.

store of value an asset that is a means of holding purchasing power over time.

structural unemployment unemployment that results when there are more people seeking jobs in a particular labor market than there are jobs available at the current wage rate, even when the economy is at the peak of the business cycle.

subprime lending lending to homebuyers who don't meet the usual criteria for qualifying for a loan.

substitutes pairs of goods for which a rise in the price of one of the goods leads to an increase in the demand for the other good.

supply and demand model a model of how a competitive market behaves.

supply curve a graphical representation of the supply schedule, showing the relationship between quantity supplied and price.

supply price the price of a given quantity at which producers will supply that quantity.

supply schedule a list or table showing how much of a good or service producers will supply at different prices.

supply shock an event that shifts the short-run aggregate supply curve. A negative supply shock raises production costs and reduces the quantity supplied at any aggregate price level, shifting the curve leftward. A positive supply shock decreases production costs and increases the quantity supplied at any aggregate price level, shifting the curve rightward.

surplus the excess of a good or service that occurs when the quantity supplied exceeds the quantity demanded; surpluses occur when the price is above the equilibrium price.

sustainable long-run economic growth long-run growth that can continue in the face of the limited supply of natural resources and with less negative impact on the environment.

T

T-account a simple tool that summarizes a business's financial position by showing, in a single table, the business's assets and liabilities, with assets on the left and liabilities on the right.

tangent line a straight line that just touches a nonlinear curve at a particular point; the slope of the tangent line is equal to the slope of the nonlinear curve at that point.

target federal funds rate the Federal Reserve's desired level for the federal funds rate. The Federal Reserve adjusts the money supply through the purchase and sale of Treasury bills until the actual rate equals the desired rate.

tariff a tax levied on imports.

Taylor rule for monetary policy a rule that sets the federal funds rate according to the level of the inflation rate and either the output gap or the unemployment rate.

technological progress an advance in the technical means of production of goods and services.

technology the technical means for producing goods and services.

theory of expansionary austerity a theory that fiscal austerity will lead to an increase in output and employment by raising private-sector confidence.

time-series graph a two-variable graph that has dates on the horizontal axis and values of a variable that occurred on those dates on the vertical axis.

total consumer surplus the sum of the individual consumer surpluses of all the buyers of a good in a market.

total factor productivity the amount of output that can be produced with a given amount of factor inputs.

total producer surplus the sum of the individual producer surpluses of all the sellers of a good in a market.

total surplus the total net gain to consumers and producers from trading in a market; the sum of the consumer surplus and the producer surplus.

trade the practice, in a market economy, in which individuals provide goods and services to others and receive goods and services in return.

trade balance (merchandise trade balance) the difference between a country's exports and imports of goods alone—not including services.

trade deficit the deficit that results when the value of the goods and services bought from foreigners is more than the value of the goods and services sold to consumers abroad.

trade protection policies that limit imports; also known simply as protection.

trade surplus the surplus that results when the value of goods and services bought from foreigners is less than the value of the goods and services sold to them.

trade-off a comparison of costs and benefits of doing something.

transaction costs the expenses of negotiating and executing a deal.

truncated cut; in a truncated axis, some of the range of values are omitted, usually to save space.

U

underemployment the number of people who work part time because they cannot find full-time jobs.

unemployment the total number of people who are actively looking for work but aren't currently employed.

unemployment rate the percentage of the total number of people in the labor force who are unemployed, calculated as unemployment/(unemployment + employment).

unit of account a measure used to set prices and make economic calculations.

unit-of-account costs (of inflation) costs arising from the way inflation makes money a less reliable unit of measurement.

unplanned inventory investment an unintended swing in inventory that occurs when actual sales are higher or lower than expected sales.

V

value added (of a producer) the value of a producer's sales minus the value of its purchases of intermediate goods and services.

variable a quantity that can take on more than one value.

velocity of money the ratio of nominal GDP to the money supply.

vertical axis the vertical number line of a graph along which values of the y-variable are measured; also referred to as the y-axis.

vertical intercept the point at which a curve hits the vertical axis; it shows the value of the y-variable when the value of the x-variable is zero.

W

wasted resources a form of inefficiency in which people expend money, effort, and time to cope with the shortages caused by a price ceiling.

wealth (of a household) the value of accumulated savings.

wealth effect of a change in the aggregate price level the effect on consumer spending caused by the change in the purchasing power of consumers' assets when the aggregate price level changes. A rise in the aggregate price level decreases the purchasing power of consumers' assets, so consumers decrease their consumption; a fall in the aggregate price level increases the purchasing power of consumers' assets, so consumers increase their consumption.

wedge the difference between the demand price of the quantity transacted and the supply price of the quantity transacted for a good when the supply of the good is legally restricted. Often created by a quantity control, or quota.

willingness to pay the maximum price a consumer is prepared to pay for a good.

world price the price at which a good can be bought or sold abroad.

World Trade Organization (WTO) an international organization of member countries that oversees international trade agreements and rules on disputes between countries over those agreements.

X

x-axis the horizontal number line of a graph along which values of the x-variable are measured; also referred to as the horizontal axis.

Y

y-axis the vertical number line of a graph along which values of the y-variable are measured; also referred to as the vertical axis.

Z

zero lower bound for interest rates statement of the fact that interest rates cannot fall below zero without causing significant problems.